3/98

WEST'S
ENCYCLOPEDIA
of
AMERICAN
LAW

WEST'S ENCYCLOPEDIA *of* AMERICAN LAW

Volume 10

WEST GROUP

This encyclopedia is the result of efforts by numerous individuals and entities from the Twin Cities and around the United States. West Group wishes to thank all who made this publication, its quality and content, a priority in their lives.

In addition to the individuals who worked on *West's Encyclopedia of American Law*, West Group recognizes Harold W. Chase (1922–1982) for his contributions to *The Guide to American Law: Everyone's Legal Encyclopedia*.

COPYRIGHT ©1998 By
  WEST GROUP
  610 Opperman Drive
  P.O. Box 64526
  St. Paul, MN 55164-0526
All rights reserved
Printed in the United States of America
05 04 03 02 01 00 99 98   8 7 6 5 4 3 2 1 0
Library of Congress Cataloging in
  Publication Data
ISBN: 0-314-20167-X (Hard)

West's encyclopedia of American law.
    p.   cm.
    Includes bibliographical references and
    indexes.
    ISBN 0-314-20167-X (hard :
    alk. paper)
    1. Law—United States—Encyclopedias.
    2. Law—United States—Popular works.
    I. West Publishing Company.
  KF154.W47 1997
  348.73'03—dc20
  [347.30803]   96-34350
                      CIP

PRODUCTION CREDITS
Cover, interior design, and page layout:
  David J. Farr, ImageSmythe
Composition: Carlisle Communications
Proofreading: Wiest International
Photo research: Elsa Peterson Ltd.
Art research: Nanette E. Bertaut
Editorial research: Pat Lewis
Artwork: Patricia Isaacs, Parrot Graphics
Indexing: Schroeder Indexing Services

This publication is designed to provide information on the subjects covered. It is sold with the understanding that the publisher is not engaged in rendering legal or other professional advice. If legal advice or other professional assistance is required, the services of a competent professional person should be sought.

WEST'S COMMITMENT TO THE ENVIRONMENT

In 1906, West Publishing Company began recycling materials left over from the production of books. This began a tradition of efficient and responsible use of resources. Today, 100 percent of our legal bound volumes are printed on acid-free, recycled paper consisting of 50 percent new paper pulp and 50 percent paper that has undergone a de-inking process. We also use vegetable-based inks to print all of our books. West recycles nearly 27,700,000 pounds of scrap paper annually—the equivalent of 229,300 trees. Since the 1960s, West has devised ways to capture and recycle waste inks, solvents, oils, and vapors created in the printing process. We also recycle plastics of all kinds, wood, glass, corrugated cardboard, and batteries, and have eliminated the use of polystyrene book packaging. We at West are proud of the longevity and the scope of our commitment to the environment.

West pocket parts and advance sheets are printed on recyclable paper and can be collected and recycled with newspapers. Staples do not have to be removed. Bound volumes can be recycled after removing the cover.

Production, printing, and binding by West Group.

PREFACE

The legal system of the United States is admired around the world for the freedoms it allows the individual and the fairness with which it attempts to treat all persons. On the surface, it may seem simple. Yet, those who have delved into it know that this system of federal and state constitutions, statutes, regulations, and common-law decisions is elaborate and complex. It derives from the English common law, but includes principles older than England, and from other lands. Many concepts are still phrased in Latin. The U.S. legal system, like many others, has a language all its own. Too often it is an unfamiliar language.

In 1983, West published *The Guide to American Law: Everyone's Legal Encyclopedia*, in response to a dearth of reference sources weaving the language of the law into the language of everyday life. *West's Encyclopedia of American Law (WEAL)*, developed with generous feedback from users of *The Guide*, replaces that set as an improved and updated legal encyclopedia. *WEAL* is a reference source devoted to the terms and concepts of U.S. law. It also covers a wide variety of persons, entities, and events that have shaped the U.S. legal system. *WEAL* contains thousands of entries, and a number of unique features and visual aids. It is the most complete reference source of its kind.

Main Features of This Set

Entries This encyclopedia contains over 4,000 entries devoted to terms, concepts, events, movements, cases, and persons significant to U.S. law. Entries on legal terms contain a definition of the term, followed by explanatory text if necessary. Entries are arranged alphabetically in standard encyclopedia format for ease of use. A wide variety of additional features, listed later in this preface, provide interesting background and supplemental information.

Definitions Every entry on a legal term is followed by a definition, which begins and ends with the symbol of an open book (📖). The appendix volume includes a glossary containing all the definitions from the *WEAL*.

Cross-References To facilitate research, *WEAL* provides two types of cross-references, within and following entries. Within the entries, terms are set in small capital letters—for example, LIEN—to indicate that they have their own entry in the encyclopedia. At the end of the entries, related entries the reader may wish to explore are listed alphabetically by title.

In Focus Pieces In Focus pieces accompany related entries and provide additional facts, details, and arguments on particularly interesting, important, or controversial issues raised by those entries. The subjects covered include hotly contested issues, such as abortion, capital punishment, and gay rights; detailed processes, such as the Food and Drug Administration's approval process for new drugs; and important historical or social issues, such as debates over the formation of the U.S. Constitution. In Focus pieces are marked by the symbol that appears in the margin.

Sidebars Sidebars provide brief highlights of some interesting facet of accompanying entries. They complement regular entries and In Focus pieces by adding informative details. Sidebar topics include the Million Man March, in Washington, D.C., and the branches of the

IN FOCUS

v

U.S. armed services. Sidebars appear at the top of a text page and are set in a blue box.

Biographies WEAL profiles a wide variety of interesting and influential people—including lawyers, judges, government and civic leaders, and historical and modern figures—who have played a part in creating or shaping U.S. law. Each biography includes a time line, which shows important moments in the subject's life as well as important historical events of the period. Biographies appear alphabetically by the subject's last name.

Additional Features of This Set

Milestones in the Law A special section, Milestones in the Law, appearing at the end of selected volumes, allows readers to take a close look at landmark cases in U.S. law. Readers can explore the reasoning of the judges and the arguments of the attorneys that produced major decisions on important legal and social issues. Included in the Milestones section are the opinions of the lower courts; the briefs presented by the parties to the U.S. Supreme Court; and the decision of the Supreme Court, including the majority opinion and all concurring and dissenting opinions for each case.

Enhancements Throughout WEAL, readers will find a broad array of photographs, charts, graphs, manuscripts, legal forms, and other visual aids enhancing the ideas presented in the text.

Tables and Indexes WEAL features several detailed tables and indexes at the back of each volume, as well as a cumulative index contained in a separate volume.

Appendixes An appendix volume included with WEAL contains hundreds of pages of documents, laws, manuscripts, and forms fundamental to and characteristic of U.S. law.

Citations Wherever possible, WEAL entries include citations for cases and statutes mentioned in the text. These allow readers wishing to do additional research to find the opinions and statutes cited. Two sample citations, with explanations of common citation terms, can be seen below and opposite.

Bibliography A bibliography is included at the end of each book and in the index volume.

Miranda v. Arizona, 384 U.S. 436, 86 S. Ct. 1602, 16 L. Ed. 2d 694 (1966)

1   2 3 4   5   6   7

1. *Case title.* The title of the case is set in italics and indicates the names of the parties. The suit in this sample citation was between Ernesto A. Miranda and the state of Arizona.
2. *Reporter volume number.* The number preceding the reporter name indicates the reporter volume containing the case. (The volume number appears on the spine of the reporter, along with the reporter name.)
3. *Reporter name.* The reporter name is abbreviated. The suit in the sample citation is from the reporter, or series of books, called *U.S. Reports,* which contains cases from the U.S. Supreme Court. (Numerous reporters publish cases from the federal and state courts.)

4. *Reporter page.* The number following the reporter name indicates the reporter page on which the case begins.
5. *Additional reporter citation.* Many cases may be found in more than one reporter. The suit in the sample citation also appears in volume 86 of the *Supreme Court Reporter,* beginning on page 1602.
6. *Additional reporter citation.* The suit in the sample citation is also reported in volume 16 of the *Lawyer's Edition,* second series, beginning on page 694.
7. *Year of decision.* The year the court issued its decision in the case appears in parentheses at the end of the cite.

Brady Handgun Violence Prevention Act, Pub. L. No. 103-159, 107 Stat. 1536 (18 U.S.C.A. §§ 921–925A)

    1   2   3   4   5   6   7   8

1. *Statute title.*
2. *Public law number.* In the sample citation, the number 103 indicates that this law was passed by the 103d Congress, and the number 159 indicates that it was the 159th law passed by that Congress.
3. *Reporter volume number.* The number preceding the reporter name indicates the reporter volume containing the statute.
4. *Reporter name.* The reporter name is abbreviated. The statute in the sample citation is from *Statutes at Large.*
5. *Reporter page.* The number following the reporter name indicates the reporter page on which the statute begins.
6. *Title number.* Federal laws are divided into major sections with specific titles. The number preceding a reference to the *U.S. Code Annotated* is the title number. Title 18 of the U.S. Code is Crimes and Criminal Procedure.
7. *Additional reporter.* The statute in the sample citation may also be found in the *U.S. Code Annotated.*
8. *Section numbers.* The section numbers following a reference to the *U.S. Code Annotated* indicate where the statute appears in that reporter.

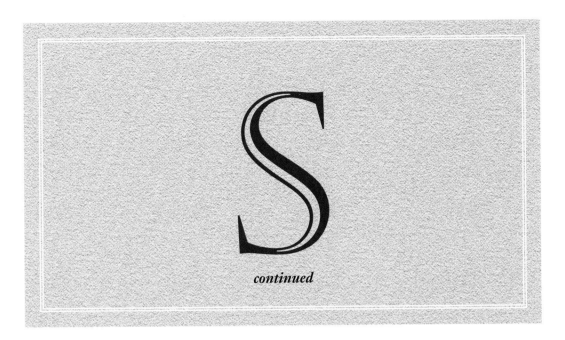

continued

SUBSTANTIAL 📖 Of real worth and importance; of considerable value; valuable. Belonging to substance; actually existing; real; not seeming or imaginary; not illusive; solid; true; veritable. 📖

The right to FREEDOM OF SPEECH, for example, is a substantial right.

SUBSTANTIATE 📖 To establish the existence or truth of a particular fact through the use of COMPETENT EVIDENCE; to verify. 📖

For example, an eyewitness might be called by a party to a lawsuit to substantiate that party's testimony.

SUBSTANTIVE DUE PROCESS 📖 The substantive limitations placed on the content or subject matter of state and federal laws by the Due Process Clauses of the Fifth and Fourteenth Amendments to the U.S. Constitution. 📖

In general, substantive due process prohibits the government from infringing on fundamental constitutional liberties. By contrast, procedural due process refers to the procedural limitations placed on the manner in which a law is administered, applied, or enforced. Thus, procedural due process prohibits the government from arbitrarily depriving individuals of legally protected interests without first giving them NOTICE and the opportunity to be heard.

The Due Process Clause provides that no person shall be "deprived of life, liberty, or property without due process of law." When courts face questions concerning procedural due process, the controlling word in this clause is *process*. Courts must determine how much process is due in a particular hearing to satisfy the fairness requirements of the Constitution. When courts face questions concerning substantive due process, the controlling issue is *liberty*. Courts must determine the nature and the scope of the LIBERTY protected by the Constitution before affording litigants a particular freedom.

Historical Development The concept of due process traces its roots to early English law. In 1215 MAGNA CHARTA provided that no freeman should be imprisoned, disseised, outlawed, exiled, or destroyed, unless by the "law of the land." As early as 1354 the words "due process of law" were used to explain the protections set forth in Magna Charta. By the end of the fourteenth century, "law of the land" and "due process of law" were considered virtually synonymous in England. According to the seventeenth-century English jurist SIR EDWARD COKE, "due process of law" and "law of the land" possessed both substantive and procedural qualities. Substantively, Coke believed that the liberty to pursue a livelihood, the right to purchase goods, and the right to be free from anti-competitive practices were all protected by the "law of the land" and "due process of law." Procedurally, Coke associated these terms with INDICTMENT by GRAND JURY and TRIAL by PETIT JURY.

When the Founding Fathers drafted the FIFTH AMENDMENT, it was unclear whether the Due Process Clause possessed any substantive qualities. Some prominent Americans, including ALEXANDER HAMILTON, understood the Due Process Clause to provide only procedural safeguards. Several states, however, followed the English practice of equating due process with the substantive protections offered by statutes and the COMMON LAW. This divergent understanding of due process continues today. During the first sixty years after the ratification of the Constitution, the Due Process Clause was confined to a procedural meaning. Over the last 140 years, however, DUE PROCESS OF LAW has taken on a pervasive substantive meaning.

The year 1856 marked the introduction of substantive due process into U.S. JURISPRUDENCE. In that year the U.S. Supreme Court faced a constitutional challenge to the MISSOURI COMPROMISE of 1820, a federal law that abolished SLAVERY in the territories. Under Missouri law, slaves who entered a free territory remained free for the rest of their lives. When a slave named Dred Scott returned to Missouri after visiting the free territory in what is now Minnesota, he sued for emancipation. Denying his claim, in *Dred Scott v. Sandford*, 60 U.S. (19 How.) 393, 15 L. Ed. 691 (1856), the Supreme Court ruled that the Due Process Clause protects the liberty of certain persons to own African American slaves. Because the Missouri Compromise deprived slave owners of this liberty in the territories, the Supreme Court declared it invalid.

After *Dred Scott* the doctrine of substantive due process lay dormant for nearly half a century. In *Lochner v. New York*, 198 U.S. 45, 25 S. Ct. 539, 49 L. Ed. 937 (1905), the Supreme Court reinvigorated the doctrine by invalidating a state law that regulated the number of hours employees could work each week in the baking industry. Maximum hour laws, the Court ruled, interfere with the liberty of contract guaranteed by the Due Process Clause. The Court said that the liberty of contract allows individuals to determine the terms and conditions of their employment, including the number of hours they work during a given period.

Over the next thirty-two years, the Supreme Court relied on *Lochner* in striking down several laws that interfered with the liberty of contract. Most of these laws were enacted pursuant to the inherent POLICE POWERS of state and federal governments. Police powers give lawmakers the authority to regulate health, safety, and welfare. For example, in *Adkins v. Children's Hospital*, 261 U.S. 525, 43 S. Ct. 394, 67 L. Ed. 785 (1923), the Supreme Court invalidated a MINIMUM WAGE law that had been enacted by the federal government pursuant to its police powers. Minimum wage laws, the Court said, violate the liberty of contract guaranteed to workers by the Due Process Clause.

By 1936 the doctrine of substantive due process had grown increasingly unpopular. The Court had invoked the doctrine to strike down a series of federal laws enacted as part of President FRANKLIN D. ROOSEVELT'S NEW DEAL, an economic stimulus program aimed at ame-

liorating the worst conditions of the Great Depression. On February 5, 1937, Roosevelt announced his court-packing plan, a proposal designed to enlarge the Supreme Court by enough justices to give the EXECUTIVE BRANCH control over the federal judiciary. One month later the Supreme Court released its decision in *West Coast Hotel Co. v. Parrish*, 300 U.S. 379, 57 S. Ct. 578, 81 L. Ed. 703 (1937).

In *West Coast Hotel* the Supreme Court upheld a Washington state minimum wage law over due process objections. Although the Court did not completely abandon the doctrine of substantive due process, it circumscribed its application. Because liberty of contract is not specifically mentioned in any provision of the federal Constitution, the Court said, this liberty must yield to competing government interests that are pursued through reasonable means. *West Coast Hotel* precipitated the onset of modern substantive due process analysis.

Modern Analysis Since 1937 the Court has employed a two-tiered analysis of substantive due process claims. Under the first tier, legislation concerning economic affairs, employment relations, and other business matters is subject to minimal judicial scrutiny, meaning that a particular law will be overturned only if it serves no rational government purpose. Under the second tier, legislation concerning fundamental liberties is subject to heightened judicial scrutiny, meaning that a law will be invalidated unless it is narrowly tailored to serve a significant government purpose.

The Supreme Court has identified two distinct categories of fundamental liberties. The first category includes most of the liberties expressly enumerated in the BILL OF RIGHTS. Through a process known as "selective incorporation," the Supreme Court has interpreted the Due Process Clause of the FOURTEENTH AMENDMENT to bar states from denying their residents the most important freedoms guaranteed in the first ten amendments to the federal Constitution. Only the SECOND AMENDMENT right to bear arms, the THIRD AMENDMENT right against involuntary quartering of soldiers, and the Fifth Amendment right to be indicted by a grand jury have not been made applicable to the states. Because these rights remain inapplicable to state governments, the Supreme Court is said to have "selectively incorporated" the Bill of Rights into the Due Process Clause of the Fourteenth Amendment.

The second category of fundamental liberties includes those liberties that are not expressly enumerated in the Bill of Rights, but which are nonetheless deemed essential to the concepts of freedom and equality in a democratic society. These unenumerated liberties are derived from Supreme Court PRECEDENTS, common law, moral philosophy, and deeply rooted traditions of U.S. legal history. The word *liberty* cannot be defined by a simple laundry list of rights, the Supreme Court has stressed. Instead, it must be viewed as a rational continuum of freedom through which every facet of human behavior is safeguarded from arbitrary impositions and purposeless restraints. In this light, the Supreme Court has observed, the Due Process Clause protects very abstract liberty interests, including the right to personal autonomy, bodily integrity, self-dignity, and SELF-DETERMINATION.

These interests often are grouped to form a general right to PRIVACY, which was first recognized in *Griswold v. Connecticut*, 381 U.S. 479, 85 S. Ct. 1678, 14 L. Ed. 2d 510 (1965), where the Supreme Court struck down a state statute forbidding married adults from using BIRTH CONTROL on the ground that the law violated the sanctity of the marital relationship. In *Griswold* the Supreme Court held that the First, Fourth, Fifth, and Ninth Amendments create a penumbra of privacy, which serves to insulate certain behavior from governmental coercion or intrusion. According to the Court, this PENUMBRA of privacy, though not expressly mentioned in the Bill of Rights, must be protected to establish a buffer zone of breathing space for those freedoms that are constitutionally enumerated.

Seven years later, in *Eisenstadt v. Baird*, 405 U.S. 438, 92 S. Ct. 1029, 31 L. Ed. 2d 349 (1972), the Supreme Court struck down a Massachusetts statute that made illegal the distribution of contraceptives to unmarried persons. In striking down this law, the Supreme Court enunciated a broader view of privacy, stating that all persons, married or single, enjoy the liberty to make certain intimate decisions free from government restraint, including the decision whether to bear or beget a child. *Eisenstadt* foreshadowed the decision in *Roe v. Wade*, 410 U.S. 113, 93 S. Ct. 705, 35 L. Ed. 2d 147 (1973), where the Supreme Court ruled that the Due Process Clause guarantees women the right to have an ABORTION during the first trimester of pregnancy without state interference. *Roe* subsequently was interpreted to prevent state and federal governments from passing laws that unduly burden a woman's right to terminate her pregnancy (*Webster v. Reproductive Health Services*, 492 U.S. 490, 109 S. Ct. 3040, 106 L. Ed. 2d 410 [1989]).

The liberty interest protected by the Due Process Clause places other substantive limitations on legislation regulating intimate decisions. For example, the Supreme Court has recognized a due process right of parents to raise their children as they see fit, including the right to educate their children in private schools (*Pierce v. Society of the Sisters*, 268 U.S. 510, 45 S. Ct. 571, 69 L. Ed. 1070 [1925]). Parents may not be compelled by the government to educate their children at public schools without violating principles of substantive due process. The Supreme Court also has ruled that members of extended families, such as grandparents and grandchildren, enjoy a due process right to live under the same roof, despite housing ORDINANCES that limit occupation of particular dwellings to immediate relatives (*Moore v. City of East Cleveland*, 431 U.S. 494, 97 S. Ct. 1932, 52 L. Ed. 2d 531 [1977]).

During the 1990s the Supreme Court was asked to recognize a general right to die under the doctrine of substantive due process. Although the Court stopped short of establishing such a far-reaching right, certain patients may exercise a constitutional liberty to hasten their deaths under a narrow set of circumstances. In *Cruzan v. Missouri Department of Health*, 497 U.S. 261, 110 S. Ct. 2841, 111 L. Ed. 2d 224 (1990), the Supreme Court ruled that the Due Process Clause guarantees the right of competent adults to make advanced directives for the withdrawal of life-sustaining measures should they become incapacitated by a disability that leaves them in a persistent vegetative state. Once it has been established by clear and convincing evidence that a mentally incompetent and persistently vegetative patient made such a prior directive, a spouse, parent, or other appropriate guardian may seek to terminate any form of artificial hydration or nutrition.

The U.S. Court of Appeals for the Ninth Circuit cited *Cruzan* in support of its decision establishing the right of competent, but terminally ill, patients to hasten their deaths by refusing medical treatment when the final stages of life are tortured by pain and indignity (*Compassion in Dying v. Washington*, 79 F.3d 790 [1996]). In *Washington v. Glucksberg*, __U.S. __, 117 S. Ct. 2258, 138 L. Ed. 2d 772 (1997), however, the Supreme Court reversed this decision, holding that there is no due process right to assisted SUICIDE.

The right to privacy does not protect all forms of behavior that are pursued behind closed doors. Adults have no constitutional right to engage in homosexual SODOMY, view child PORNOGRAPHY, or solicit prostitutes. The liberty interest recognized by the doctrine of substantive due process permits individuals to lead their lives free from unreasonable and arbitrary governmental impositions. Nevertheless, this liberty interest does not require the absence of all governmental restraint. Economic regulations will be upheld under the Due Process Clause so long as they serve a rational purpose, while noneconomic regulations normally will be sustained if they do not impinge on a fundamental liberty and otherwise are reasonable.

CROSS-REFERENCES

Compelling State Interest; Death and Dying; *Dred Scott v. Sandford*; *Griswold v. Connecticut*; Incorporation Doctrine; Labor Law; *Lochner v. New York*; *In re Quinlan*; Rational Basis Test; *Roe v. Wade*; Unenumerated Rights; *West Coast Hotel v. Parrish*.

SUBSTANTIVE LAW 📖 The part of the law that creates, defines, and regulates rights, including, for example, the law of CONTRACTS, TORTS, WILLS, and REAL PROPERTY; the essential substance of rights under law. 📖

Substantive law and PROCEDURAL LAW are the two main categories within the law. Substantive law refers to the body of rules that determine the rights and obligations of individuals and collective bodies. Procedural law is the body of legal rules that govern the process for determining the rights of parties.

Substantive law refers to all categories of public and PRIVATE LAW, including the law of contracts, real property, torts, and CRIMINAL LAW. For example, criminal law defines certain behavior as illegal and lists the elements the government must prove to convict a person of a crime. In contrast, the rights of an accused person that are guaranteed by the Fourth, Fifth, and Sixth Amendments to the U.S. Constitution are part of a body of criminal procedural law.

U.S. substantive law comes from the common law and from legislative statutes. Until the twentieth century, most substantive law was derived from principles found in judicial decisions. The COMMON-LAW tradition built upon prior decisions and applied legal PRECEDENTS to cases with similar fact situations. This tradition was essentially conservative, as the substance of law in a particular area changed little over time.

Substantive law has increased in volume and changed rapidly in the twentieth century as Congress and state legislatures have enacted statutes that displace many common-law principles. In addition, the National Conference of Commissioners on Uniform State Laws and the American Law Institute have proposed numerous model codes and laws for states to adopt. For example, these two groups drafted the UNIFORM COMMERCIAL CODE (UCC), which governs commercial transactions. The UCC has been adopted in whole or substantially by all states, replacing the common law and divergent state laws as the authoritative source of substantive commercial law.

See also MODEL ACTS; UNIFORM ACTS.

SUBSTITUTED SERVICE 📖 SERVICE OF PROCESS upon a defendant in any manner, authorized by statute or rule, other than PERSONAL SERVICE within the JURISDICTION; as by publication, by mailing a copy to his or her last known address, or by personal service in another state. 📖

SUCCESSION 📖 The transfer of TITLE to PROPERTY under the law of DESCENT AND DISTRIBUTION. The transfer of legal or official powers from an individual who formerly held them to another who undertakes current responsibilities to execute those powers. 📖

SUCCESSION OF STATES Succession occurs when one state ceases to exist or loses control over part of its territory, and another state comes into existence or assumes control over the territory lost by the first state. A central concern in this instance is whether the international obligations of the former state are taken over by the succeeding state. Changes in the form of government of one state, such as the replacement of a monarchy by a democratic form of government, do not modify or terminate the obligations incurred by the previous government.

When the state ceases to exist, however, the TREATIES it concluded generally are terminated and those of the successor state apply to the territory. These include political treaties like alliances, which depend on the existence of the state that concluded them. But certain obligations, such as agreements concerning BOUNDARIES or other matters of local significance, carry over to the successor state. More difficult to determine is the continuing legality of treaties granting concessions or contract rights. Scholarly opinion has diverged on this aspect of succession, and state practice has likewise divided. Consequently each case must be studied on its merits to determine whether the rights and duties under the contract or concession are such that the successor state is bound by the obligations of the previous state.

SUE 📖 To initiate a lawsuit or continue a legal proceeding for the recovery of a right; to PROSECUTE, assert a legal CLAIM, or bring ACTION against a particular party. 📖

SUFFER 📖 To admit, allow, or permit. 📖

The term *suffer* is used to convey the idea of acquiescence, passivity, indifference, or abstention from preventive action, as opposed to the taking of an affirmative step.

SUFFRAGE 📖 The right to vote at public ELECTIONS. 📖

SUICIDE 📖 The deliberate taking of one's own life. 📖

Under COMMON LAW, suicide, or the intentional taking of one's own life, was a FELONY that was punished by FORFEITURE of all the GOODS and CHATTELS of the offender. Under modern U.S. law, suicide is no longer a CRIME. Some states, however, classify attempted suicide as a criminal act, but prosecutions are rare, especially when the offender is terminally ill. Instead, some JURISDICTIONS require a person who attempts suicide to undergo temporary hospitalization and psychological observation. A person who causes the death of an innocent bystander or would-be rescuer while in the process of attempting suicide may be guilty of MURDER or MANSLAUGHTER.

More problematic is the situation in which someone helps another to commit suicide. Aiding or abetting a suicide or an attempted suicide is a crime in all states, but prosecutions are rare. Since the 1980s the question of whether physician-assisted suicide should be permitted for persons with terminal illnesses has been the subject of much debate, but as yet this issue has not been resolved.

The debate over physician-assisted suicide concerns persons with debilitating and painful terminal illnesses. Under current laws a doctor who assists a person's suicide could be charged with aiding and abetting suicide. Opponents of decriminalizing assisted suicide argue that decriminalization would lead to a "slippery slope" that would eventually result in doctors being allowed to assist persons who are not terminally ill to commit suicide.

The debate on physician-assisted suicide has intensified since 1990 when Dr. JACK KEVORKIAN, a retired Michigan pathologist, began to attend many suicides. Kevorkian has admitted to obtaining carbon monoxide and instructing persons who suffered from terminal or degenerative diseases on how to administer the gas so they would die. Despite the efforts of Michigan legislators and prosecutors to convict Kevorkian of murder, the pathologist, who was dubbed "Doctor Death," successfully fought the charges. Three murder charges were dismissed by Michigan courts and in 1994 Kevorkian was acquitted of violating Michigan's assisted suicide law (Mich. Comp. Laws § 752.1021 et seq.). Despite Kevorkian's acquittals other assisted suicide advocates believe his methods have actually hurt the cause. In 1997 the U.S. Supreme Court held that neither the Due Process Clause (*Washington v. Glucksberg*, __ U.S. __, 117 S. Ct. 2258, 138 L. Ed. 2d 772) nor the Equal Protection Clause (*Vacco v. Quill*, __ U.S. __, 117 S. Ct. 2293, 138 L. Ed. 2d 834) of the FOURTEENTH AMENDMENT includes a right to assisted suicide.

Since the 1970s, most large U.S. communities have established suicide prevention measures, including telephone hot lines where a person contemplating suicide can talk to a counselor.

CROSS-REFERENCES

Death and Dying; Patients' Rights; Physicians and Surgeons.

SUI GENERIS 📖 [*Latin, Of its own kind or class.*] That which is the only one of its kind. 📖

SUI JURIS 📖 [*Latin, Of his or her own right.*]

Possessing full social and CIVIL RIGHTS; not under any legal disability, or the power of another, or guardianship. Having the CAPACITY to manage one's own affairs; not under legal disability to act for one's self. 📖

SUIT 📖 A generic term, of comprehensive signification, referring to any proceeding by one person or persons against another or others in a court of law in which the plaintiff pursues the REMEDY that the law affords for the redress of an injury or the enforcement of a right, whether AT LAW or in EQUITY. 📖

SUMMARY 📖 As a noun, an abridgment; BRIEF; compendium; DIGEST; also a short application to a court or judge, without the formality of a full proceeding.

As an adjective, short; concise; immediate; peremptory; off-hand; without a jury; provisional; statutory. The term as used in connection with legal proceedings means a short, concise, and immediate proceeding. 📖

A summary JUDGMENT is a final decision in a CIVIL ACTION that does not involve lengthy presentations of EVIDENCE. It totally circumvents the need for trial because there is no genuine issue of fact concerning specified questions in the lawsuit that must be decided. In such an action, the party who believes that she is entitled to prevail as a MATTER OF LAW makes a MOTION for summary judgment. In deciding such a motion, the court considers the entire record of the case and, if the evidence warrants it, can even grant a summary judgment to the party who did not ask for it. Summary judgment is *governed* in FEDERAL COURTS by the Federal Rules of Civil Procedure and in state courts by state codes of CIVIL PROCEDURE.

SUMMARY JUDGMENT 📖 A procedural device used during civil litigation to promptly and expeditiously dispose of a case without a trial. It is used when there is no dispute as to the MATERIAL facts of the case and a party is entitled to JUDGMENT as a MATTER OF LAW. 📖

Any party may move for summary judgment; it is not uncommon for both parties to seek it. A judge may also determine on her own initiative that summary judgment is appropriate. Unlike with pretrial motions to dismiss, information such as AFFIDAVITS, INTERROGATORIES, DEPOSITIONS, and ADMISSIONS may be considered on a MOTION for summary judgment. Any EVIDENCE that would be ADMISSIBLE at trial under the rules of evidence may support a motion for summary judgment. Usually a court will hold oral arguments on a summary judgment motion, although it may decide the motion on the parties' BRIEFS and supporting documentation alone.

The purpose of summary judgment is to avoid unnecessary trials. It may also simplify a trial, as when partial summary judgment dispenses with certain issues or claims. For example, a court might grant partial summary judgment in a PERSONAL INJURY case on the issue of LIABILITY. A trial would still be necessary to determine the amount of DAMAGES.

Two criteria must be met before summary judgment may be properly granted: (1) there must be no genuine issues of material fact, and (2) the movant must be entitled to judgment as a matter of law. A genuine issue implies that certain facts are disputed. Usually a party opposing summary judgment must introduce evidence that contradicts the moving party's version of the facts. Moreover, the facts in dispute must be central to the case; irrelevant or minor factual disputes will not defeat a motion for summary judgment. Finally, the law as applied to the undisputed facts of the case must mandate judgment for the moving party. Summary judgment does not mean that a judge decides which side would prevail at trial, nor does a judge determine the credibility of WITNESSES. Rather, it is used when no factual questions exist for a judge or jury to decide.

The moving party has the initial burden to show that summary judgment is proper even if the moving party would not have the burden of proof at trial. The court generally examines the evidence presented with the motion in the light most favorable to the opposing party. Where the opposing party will bear the burden of proof at trial, the moving party may obtain summary judgment by showing that the opposing party has no evidence or that its evidence is insufficient to meet its burden at trial.

Jurisdictions vary in their requirements for opposing a summary judgment motion. Federal rule of civil procedure 56 governs the applicability of summary judgment in federal proceedings, and each state has its own rules. In some states it is sufficient if the party opposing the motion merely calls the court's attention to inconsistencies in the PLEADINGS and the movant's evidence without introducing further evidence. This approach rarely results in a court's granting summary judgment. On the other hand, other jurisdictions, including FEDERAL COURTS, do not permit a party opposing summary judgment to rest on the pleadings alone. Once the movant has met the initial burden of showing the absence of a genuine issue of material fact, the burden shifts to the opposing party to introduce evidence to contradict the movant's ALLEGATIONS.

SUMMARY PROCEEDINGS   An alternative form of litigation for the prompt disposition of legal ACTIONS.

LEGAL PROCEEDINGS are regarded as summary when they are shorter and simpler than the ordinary steps in a suit. Summary proceedings are ordinarily available for cases that require prompt action and generally involve a small number of clearcut issues.

SUMMARY PROCESS   A legal procedure used for enforcing a right that takes effect faster and more efficiently than ordinary methods. The legal papers—a court order, for example—used to achieve an expeditious resolution of the controversy.

Because summary process deprives a defendant of all the time and legal defenses usually available, a plaintiff may invoke it only when specifically permitted by law. For example, some states provide for a special procedure for evicting a tenant without the normal delays of a lawsuit, and some states allow summary process for resolving incidental issues that arise between the parties during the pendency of a lawsuit.

SUMMONS   The paper that tells a defendant that he or she is being sued and asserts the power of the court to hear and determine the case. A form of legal PROCESS that commands the defendant to appear before the court on a specific day and to answer the COMPLAINT made by the plaintiff.

The summons is the document that officially starts a lawsuit. It must be in a form prescribed by the law governing procedure in the court involved, and it must be properly served on, or delivered to, the defendant. If the prescribed formalities are not observed, the court lacks authority to hear the dispute.

In the federal district courts, the summons is prepared by the attorney for the plaintiff and given to the clerk of the court where the case will be heard. When the plaintiff's complaint, setting out his claim, is filed with the court, the clerk signs the summons and gives it and a copy

IN THE UNITED STATES DISTRICT COURT
FOR THE _____ DISTRICT
OF _____ , _____ DIVISION

United States of America
v.   } No. _____
John Doe
        Defendant.

To John Doe:
    You are hereby summoned to appear on the _____ day of _____ ,
19_____ , at _____ o'clock in the _____ noon, before _____ ,
United States Magistrate for the _____ District of _____ , at
_____ Street, _____ , to answer to a complaint which has been made to
me on oath by _____ on the _____ day of _____ , 19_____ ,
charging you with _____ in violation of Title _____ , United States
Code, Section _____ .

_____
United States Magistrate
_____ District of _____ .

A sample summons

of the complaint to a U.S. MARSHAL or to some-one else appointed to serve the papers. Once the summons and complaint are served on the defendant, she must respond to them within twenty days or whatever other time the court allows.

Some states follow this same procedure, but other states allow service of the summons and complaint by delivery directly to the defendant. In those states, the lawsuit is considered begun as soon as the defendant receives the papers, even though nothing has yet been filed with a court. Actions commenced in this way are sometimes called "hip pocket" suits.

See also SERVICE OF PROCESS.

SUMNER, CHARLES   Charles Sumner served as U.S. senator from Massachusetts for twenty-three years. He was born January 6, 1811, in Boston, Massachusetts. Sumner graduated from Harvard University with a bachelor of arts degree in 1830 and a bachelor of laws degree in 1833.

BIOGRAPHY

THE GRANGER COLLECTION, NEW YORK

Charles Sumner

After his admission to the bar in 1834, Sumner traveled through Europe from 1837 to 1840 to analyze foreign judicial systems. When he returned to the United States, he became interested in reform issues and emerged as a reform leader and an abolitionist. He was instrumental in the development of the Free-Soil party in 1848 and endorsed MARTIN VAN BUREN, the candidate of that party, in the presidential election of 1848.

In 1851 Sumner began a twenty-three year period of service as U.S. senator from Massachusetts. His career in the Senate was a turbulent one, marked by much controversy.

Sumner staunchly opposed SLAVERY and advocated the revocation of the FUGITIVE SLAVE ACT OF 1850 (9 Stat. 462). He vehemently attacked the Kansas-Nebraska Bill of 1854 (10 Stat. 277), which allowed residents of new territories to determine the slavery issue for their areas. In 1856, in a speech known as "The Crime Against Kansas," Sumner attacked

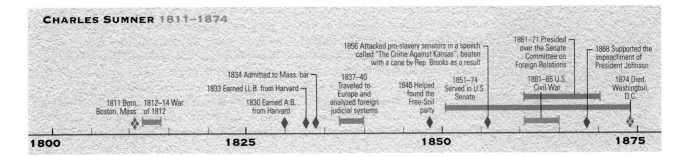

CHARLES SUMNER 1811–1874

1800 — 1825 — 1850 — 1875

1811 Born, Boston, Mass.

1812–14 War of 1812

1830 Earned A.B. from Harvard

1833 Earned LL.B. from Harvard

1834 Admitted to Mass. bar

1837–40 Traveled to Europe and analyzed foreign judicial systems

1848 Helped found the Free-Soil party

1851–74 Served in U.S. Senate

1856 Attacked pro-slavery senators in a speech called "The Crime Against Kansas"; beaten with a cane by Rep. Brooks as a result

1861–71 Presided over the Senate Committee on Foreign Relations

1861–65 U.S. Civil War

1868 Supported the impeachment of President Johnson

1874 Died, Washington, D.C.

STEPHEN A. DOUGLAS, the originator of the bill, and South Carolina senator Andrew Pickens Butler, who strongly supported slavery. After the scathing oration, Sumner was beaten with a cane by Representative Preston Smith Brooks, who was related to Senator Butler. The injuries Sumner sustained prevented him from actively participating in senatorial affairs for the next three years.

In 1861 Sumner became the presiding officer of the Senate Committee on Foreign Relations. He held that position until 1871, when his radical behavior resulted in his removal from that office.

During the Reconstruction period, Sumner was a member of the radical Republican faction. He opposed President ANDREW JOHNSON's conservative policy toward the South and advocated a policy that would allow freed men to own land that was previously a part of their owner's estates. Sumner also believed that the state legislatures should control the school system, and that all races should be allowed to attend public schools. Sumner and Johnson were often at odds over their conflicting policies, and Sumner supported the IMPEACHMENT of the president in 1868.

Sumner did not fare any better with the new administration of President ULYSSES S. GRANT. He opposed Grant's policy to annex Santo Domingo and demanded large REPARATIONS from Great Britain because that country had aided the Confederacy during the Civil War by supplying ships. Secretary of State Hamilton Fish spoke against Sumner's policy toward the British, saying that it interfered with current relations with that country. In 1871 Sumner was asked to leave his post as chairman of the Foreign Relations Committee, but he remained in the Senate until his death March 11, 1874, in Washington, D.C.

See also ABOLITION; KANSAS NEBRASKA ACT.

SUMPTUARY LAWS 📖 Rules made for the purpose of restraining luxury or extravagance. 📖

Sumptuary laws are designed to regulate habits, especially on moral or religious grounds. They are particularly directed against inordinate expenditures on apparel, drink, food, and luxury items.

These laws existed in Rome and were enacted in a variety of forms in England during the Middle Ages to regulate the ornateness of dress and to impose dietary restrictions. Sumptuary laws varied according to classes, with peasants being subjected to a different set of rules than the gentry. The primary purpose of the laws was to distinguish the different classes of people, and often, a person's social class could be determined by something as simple as the style or length of his or her coat.

Today sumptuary laws are ecclesiastical in nature and not part of the U.S. legal system.

SUNDAY CLOSING LAWS 📖 Laws that prohibit the conduct of business on Sundays. 📖

Also known as blue laws, Sabbath laws, and uniform day of rest laws, Sunday closing laws have a long and contentious history in the United States, although many of the laws either have been repealed or are routinely ignored. Although originally enacted for religious purposes, Sunday closing laws historically have had another purpose: to provide workers with a common day of rest while providing some protection to small shopkeepers from wealthy competitors able to pay workers on Sundays. The secular purpose of Sunday closing laws has taken on increasing significance in courtroom battles over their legality.

As early as the 1790s, ministers complained about travel, business, and dining out on Sundays. In the early nineteenth century, Sabbatarians, who favored a rigid observance of the Sabbath, vigorously promoted their views, but Sunday activities increased. Sunday newspapers, rarely seen before the Civil War, became the norm after the war in rapidly expanding cities. Restaurants, inns, and resorts were often open on Sundays, and commercial transportation was readily available. Moreover, exemptions for "necessary labor" commonly found their way into Sunday closing laws in the latter half of the nineteenth century. For example, drug stores typically were allowed to operate because they served the health and welfare of the general populace.

Prosecutions against retail businesses typically resulted in convictions, but a court decision from 1888, *Bucher v. Cheshire R.R. Co.*, 125 U.S. 555, 8 S. Ct. 974, 31 L. Ed. 795, illustrated how convoluted attitudes toward Sunday closing laws had become. A passenger sued a railroad for injuries sustained during a Sunday train wreck. The railroad was operating in violation of the Sabbath law. Instead of holding the railroad liable, the trial court barred the passenger from compensation, ruling that passengers traveling on Sunday in violation of the law did so at their own risk.

Often joined by unions, Sabbatarians embarked on a national campaign during the late 1880s and early 1890s to denominate Sunday as the common day of rest. Although unsuccessful, this alliance served to further secularize the rationale for Sunday closing laws. Ironically, businesses offering entertainment and leisure flourished because closing laws provided workers with more leisure time.

In the early twentieth century, some states, mainly in the West, followed California's example from 1883 and repealed their Sunday closing laws. Hard times in the late 1920s and 1930s spurred renewed support for closing laws as some retailers embraced the laws in an effort to thwart competitors. Although major courtroom battles still loomed, by the 1940s and 1950s, demands by U.S. consumers caused the number of Sunday closing laws to decline.

By the mid-twentieth century, Sunday closing laws were largely nonexistent in the far western United States but remained a hotly debated issue in the northeastern and mid-Atlantic states due to a combination of business competition and religious practices. As in the past, the laws and their exemptions caused inconsistent results. New York's law, for example, made it illegal to sell uncooked meat on Sunday, although a restaurant could sell cooked meat.

A quartet of Sunday closing law cases from 1961 established the legality, albeit not the popularity, of Sunday closing laws. In the mid-1950s, *Gallagher v. Crown Kosher Super Market of Massachusetts*, 366 U.S. 617, 81 S. Ct. 1122, 6 L. Ed. 2d 536, a Massachusetts case, began its slow march to the Supreme Court. A market that closed for its owner's Jewish Sabbath on Saturday reopened on Sunday in violation of the law. The market generated about one-third of its gross weekly sales on Sunday. Pennsylvania's *Two Guys from Harrison-Allentown, Inc. v. McGinley*, 366 U.S. 582, 81 S. Ct. 1135, 6 L. Ed. 2d 551, began when a discount chain opened a new store with the intention of operating on Sundays, knowing that local authorities had not enforced the Sunday closing law for years. Although the store violated the law for business reasons, it eventually argued that the Sunday closing laws established one RELIGION in preference over others. These two cases, along with *McGowan v. Maryland*, 366 U.S. 420, 81 S. Ct. 1101, 6 L. Ed. 2d 393, and *Braunfeld v. Brown*, 366 U.S. 599, 81 S. Ct. 1144, 6 L. Ed. 2d 563, resulted in similar and complementary rulings that the Sunday closing laws were valid. The Supreme Court recognized the religious origins of the laws but determined that the present purpose of the laws was not religious and that the laws were not invalid because they worked an economic disadvantage to some religious sects.

The Supreme Court has adhered to its view that Sunday closing laws are secular in nature. In *Thornton v. Caldor, Inc.*, 472 U.S. 703, 105 S. Ct. 2914, 86 L. Ed. 2d 557 (1985), the Court agreed with the Connecticut Supreme Court that a statute granting employees the absolute right not to work on their chosen Sabbath violated the FIRST AMENDMENT Establishment Clause. Because the challenged statute expressly referred to a "Sabbath," it failed to show a secular purpose. Moreover, only those workers who observed a Sabbath could avail themselves of the law.

Sunday closing laws still exist in some states and localities, but numerous exemptions and little interest in enforcement means that the general public is rarely inconvenienced. Nevertheless, challenges to the laws still occur. The methods used to challenge the laws vary as much as the outcome of these cases. Because arguments based on establishment of religion or free exercise grounds are usually unsuccessful, modern litigants have turned to arguments focusing on EQUAL PROTECTION claims or arguments that the laws are arbitrary or VAGUE, violate the COMMERCE CLAUSE of the Constitution, or create an unlawful MONOPOLY.

SUNSET PROVISION A statutory provision providing that a particular agency, benefit, or law will expire on a particular date, unless it is reauthorized by the legislature.

Federal and state governments grew dramatically in the 1950s and 1960s. Many EXECUTIVE BRANCH administrative agencies were established to oversee government programs. The escalation of government budgets and the perception that government BUREAUCRACY was not accountable led Congress and many state legislatures in the 1970s to enact "sunset" laws.

Sunset laws state that a given agency will cease to exist after a fixed period of time unless the legislature reenacts its statutory charter. Sunset provisions differ greatly in their details, but they share the common belief that it is useful to compel the Congress or a state legislature to periodically reexamine its delegations of authority and to assess the utility of those delegations in the light of experience.

There are two types of sunset provisions. In some instances the statute creating a particular ADMINISTRATIVE AGENCY contains a sunset provision applicable only to that agency. In other instances a state may enact a general sunset law that may eliminate any agency that is unable to demonstrate its effectiveness.

Sunset provisions have had a checkered history. Although they were popular at the state level in the 1970s and early 1980s, sunset laws have produced mixed results, and many states have repealed ineffective sunset legislation. Few agencies have been terminated under sunset provisions, in part because agencies develop constituents who do not want the service to end. In addition, the cost of disbanding agencies and reassigning work can be expensive.

Attempts to pass a federal sunset law in the 1990s, which would have required formal reauthorization of federal programs every ten years, were unsuccessful. Advocates of accountability have abandoned the idea of "sunsetting" agencies and have sought to strengthen agency reauthorization requirements by incorporating rigorous performance measurements and enforcing appropriate discipline in government.

In addition to their application to government agencies, sunset provisions have been applied to laws themselves and to benefits, such as immigration benefits. Without reauthorization by the legislature, the law or benefit ceases on a particular date.

SUNSHINE LAWS 📖 Statutes that mandate that meetings of governmental agencies and departments be open to the public at large. 📖

Through sunshine laws, administrative agencies are required to do their work in public, and as a result, the process is sometimes called "government in the sunshine." A law that requires open meetings ordinarily specifies the only instances when a meeting can be closed to the public and mandates that certain procedures be followed before a particular meeting is closed. The FREEDOM OF INFORMATION ACT (5 U.S.C.A. § 552) requires agencies to share information they have obtained with the public. Exceptions are permitted, in general, in the interest of national security or to safeguard the privacy of businesses.

See also ADMINISTRATIVE AGENCY; ADMINISTRATIVE LAW AND PROCEDURE.

SUPERIOR 📖 One who has a right to give orders; belonging to a higher grade. 📖

A superior is someone or something entitled to command, influence, or control. In the judicial system, a superior court has general or extensive jurisdiction, as opposed to an INFERIOR COURT. A superior court bears a different meaning in different states. In some states, it is a tribunal of intermediate JURISDICTION between the trial courts and the chief APPELLATE court; in other states, however, it is the name given to trial courts.

In the law of NEGLIGENCE, a superior force is an uncontrollable and irresistible force that produces results that could not be avoided.

In REAL PROPERTY, a holder of a superior ESTATE has an EASEMENT, or a nonpossessory interest in land, in an inferior estate.

SUPERSEDE 📖 To obliterate, replace, make void, or useless. 📖

Supersede means to take the place of, as by reason of superior worth or right. A recently enacted statute that repeals an older law is said to supersede the prior legislation.

A *superseding cause* is an act of a third person or some intervening force that prevents a TORTFEASOR from being held liable for harm to another. A supervening act is one that insulates an actor from responsibility for negligently causing a dangerous condition that results in an injury to the plaintiff.

SUPERSEDEAS 📖 The name given to a WRIT, a court order, from a higher court commanding a lower court to suspend a particular proceeding. 📖

A supersedeas is a writ that suspends the authority of a trial court to issue an execution on a JUDGMENT that has been appealed. It is a process designed to stop enforcement of a trial court judgment brought up for review. The term is often used interchangeably with a stay of proceeding.

SUPERVENING 📖 Unforeseen, intervening, an additional event or cause. 📖

A *supervening cause* is an event that operates independently of anything else and becomes the PROXIMATE CAUSE of an accident.

For an event to fall within the doctrine of supervening NEGLIGENCE, also known as LAST CLEAR CHANCE, four conditions must be satisfied. These conditions are that the injured party has already come into a perilous position; the TORTFEASOR in the exercise of ordinary prudence becomes or ought to have become aware that the party in peril cannot safely avoid injury; the tortfeasor has the opportunity to save the other person from harm; and he or she fails to exercise such care.

SUPPLEMENTARY PROCEEDINGS 📖 A proceeding in which a JUDGMENT DEBTOR is summoned into court for questioning by a JUDGMENT CREDITOR who has not received payment. 📖

A supplementary proceeding provides the creditor with a chance to discover whether the debtor has any money or property that can be used to satisfy the JUDGMENT. If the debtor is found to have money or property, the court can order the debtor to use it to satisfy the judgment.

SUPPORT 📖 As a verb, furnishing funds or means for maintenance; to maintain; to provide for; to enable to continue; to carry on. To provide a means of livelihood. To vindicate, to maintain, to defend, to uphold with aid or countenance.

As a noun, that which furnishes a livelihood; a source or means of living; subsistence, sustenance, maintenance, or living. 📖

Support includes all sources of living that enable a person to live in a degree of comfort suitable and befitting her station in life. Support encompasses housing, food, clothing, health, nursing, and medical needs, along with adequate recreation expenses. Most states impose a legal duty on an individual to support his or her spouse and children. See also CHILD SUPPORT.

SUPPRESS 📖 To stop something or someone; to prevent, prohibit, or subdue. 📖

To suppress EVIDENCE is to keep it from being admitted at trial by showing either that it was illegally obtained or that it is irrelevant.

SUPRA 📖 [*Latin, Above; beyond.*] A term used in legal research to indicate that the matter under current consideration has appeared in the preceding pages of the text in which the reference is made. 📖

SUPREMACY CLAUSE 📖 The clause of Article VI of the U.S. Constitution that declares that all laws and treaties made by the federal government shall be the "supreme law of the land." 📖

Article VI, Section 2, of the U.S. Constitution is known as the Supremacy Clause because it provides that the "Constitution, and the Laws of the United States . . . shall be the supreme Law of the Land." It means that the federal government, in exercising any of the powers enumerated in the Constitution, must prevail over any conflicting or inconsistent state exercise of power.

The concept of federal supremacy was developed by Chief Justice JOHN MARSHALL, who led the Supreme Court from 1801 to 1835. In *McCulloch v. Maryland*, 17 U.S. (4 Wheat.) 316, 4 L. Ed. 579 (1819), the Court invalidated a Maryland law that taxed all banks in the state, including a branch of the national bank located at Baltimore. Marshall held that although none of the enumerated powers of Congress explicitly authorized the incorporation of the national bank, the Necessary and Proper Clause provided the basis for Congress's action. Having established that the exercise of authority was proper, Marshall concluded that "the government of the Union, though limited in its power, is supreme within its sphere of action."

After the Civil War, the Supreme Court was more supportive of STATES' RIGHTS and used the TENTH AMENDMENT, which provides that the powers not delegated to the federal government are reserved to the states or to the people, to justify its position. It was not until the 1930s that the Court shifted its position and invoked the Supremacy Clause to give the federal government broad national power. The federal government cannot involuntarily be subjected to the laws of any state.

The Supremacy Clause also requires state legislatures to take into account policies adopted by the federal government. Two issues arise when state action is in apparent conflict with federal law. The first is whether the congressional action falls within the powers granted to Congress. If Congress exceeded its authority, the congressional act is invalid and, despite the Supremacy Clause, has no priority over state action. The second issue is whether Congress intended its policy to supersede state policy. Congress often acts without intent to preempt state policy making or with an intent to preempt state policy on a limited set of issues. Congress may intend state and federal policies to coexist.

However, some federal legislation preempts state law, usually because Congress believes its law should be supreme for reasons of national uniformity. For example, the NATIONAL LABOR RELATIONS ACT of 1935 (Wagner Act) (29 U.S.C.A. § 151 et seq.) preempts most state law dealing with LABOR UNIONS and labor-management relations.

In *Pennsylvania v. Nelson*, 350 U.S. 497, 76 S. Ct. 477, 100 L. Ed. 640 (1956), the Supreme Court developed criteria for assessing whether federal law preempts state action when Congress has not specifically stated its intent. These criteria include whether the scheme of federal regulations is "so pervasive as to make the inference that Congress left no room for the States to supplement it," whether the federal interest "is so dominant that the federal system [must] be assumed to preclude enforcement of state laws on the same subject," or whether the enforcement of a state law "presents a serious danger of conflict with the administration of the federal program."

CROSS-REFERENCES

Federalism; *McCulloch v. Maryland*; Preemption.

SUPREME COURT 📖 An APPELLATE tribunal with high powers and broad authority within its JURISDICTION. 📖

The U.S. government and each state government has a supreme court, though some states have given their highest court a different name. A supreme court is the highest court in its jurisdiction. It decides the most important issues of constitutional and statutory law and is intended to provide legal clarity and consistency for the lower appellate and trial COURTS. Because it is the court of last resort, a supreme court's decisions also produce finality. In addition, a supreme court oversees the administration of the jurisdiction's judicial system.

A supreme court is established by a provision in the state or federal constitution. The legislative bodies of the jurisdiction enact statutes that create a court system and provide funding for it. A supreme court usually consists of five, seven, or nine judges, who are called justices. In the FEDERAL COURTS, the justices are appointed for life, whereas the states have a variety of selection methods. Typically the state governor will appoint a state supreme court justice, and then he will stand for election within two years to serve a full term, which may be from six to twelve years. A judicial election may involve a contest between the justice and another candidate, or it may be a retention election, where the voters must decide whether the judge should be retained for another term.

A supreme court consists of the justices, their administrative support staff, law clerks, and staff attorneys. As an APPELLATE COURT, it is limited to reviewing trial proceedings and, if applicable, intermediate appellate court decisions. No new TESTIMONY is taken, and the arguments before the court by the parties are confined to points of SUBSTANTIVE LAW and procedure. A supreme court holds public proceedings, called oral arguments, in which the attorneys for the parties are given a short amount of time to advocate their positions and answer questions from members of the court. The justices, who have been briefed on the case prior to the oral arguments, conduct a conference on the case following the oral arguments.

At this meeting the justices express their opinions and vote on the case. The CHIEF JUSTICE typically assigns a member of the court to write the majority opinion. Once a justice circulates an opinion to the court, the other justices are free to comment, criticize, and offer suggestions on how the opinion can be improved. The author of the opinion generally tries to accommodate the other justices' ideas. However, if a fundamental difference arises during the circulation process, justices may shift sides and change the outcome of the decision. At that point, a justice in the new majority will be assigned to write the opinion. A justice is always permitted to file a dissenting opinion if she disagrees with the outcome.

Once the court releases an opinion, it is published in an official report. The decision of the court is generally final, absent special circumstances. If the court's decision is based on an interpretation of a constitutional provision, it is final unless the constitution is amended or the court reverses itself at some later time. This is rarely done. For example, the U.S. Supreme Court decision in *Roe v. Wade*, 410 U.S. 113, 93 S. Ct. 705, 35 L. Ed. 2d 147 (1973), legalized ABORTION based on a constitutional right of PRIVACY. Those opposed to abortion have sought to have Congress pass a CONSTITUTIONAL AMEND-MENT to overturn the decision or to convince the Court to reverse its decision, but without success.

If a supreme court's decision is based on statutory interpretation, its reading of legislative intent or purpose may be overridden by the legislature. A law can be enacted that "corrects" the court and directs it to honor specific intentions of the legislature.

Every supreme court has a procedure to limit the number of cases it hears. The U.S. Supreme Court uses a WRIT of CERTIORARI, which is a legal PLEADING that requests the Court to hear the case. State supreme courts have similar pleadings, sometimes called petitions for review, which also allow the court discretion in choosing cases to consider. Typically cases are chosen to resolve conflicts in the lower courts or to decide new legal issues.

Apart from discretionary review, supreme courts permit direct APPEAL, or appeal by right, on a limited set of cases. At the state level, appeals of first-degree murder and death penalty cases are heard by supreme courts, bypassing the intermediate court of appeals. The U.S. Supreme Court hears direct appeals of cases involving federal reapportionment, disputes between states, and a few other issues.

Supreme courts also administer their judicial systems, overseeing the trial and intermediate appellate courts. In addition, supreme courts enact the rules of procedure that govern the workings of their court systems. Examples include rules of civil, criminal, and appellate procedure, as well as rules of EVIDENCE. Most state supreme courts also oversee the admission of attorneys to the bar and discipline attorneys for ethical violations.

See also COURT OPINION; STATE COURTS.

SUPREME COURT OF THE UNITED STATES

The Supreme Court of the United States is the highest federal court. Although it was explicitly recognized in Article III of the Constitution, it was not formally established until passage of the JUDICIARY ACT OF 1789 (1 Stat. 73) and was not organized until 1790. Though its size and JURISDICTION have changed over time, the Supreme Court has fulfilled its two main functions: acting as the final interpreter of state and federal law and establishing procedural rules for the FEDERAL COURTS.

Composition The Supreme Court, sometimes called the High Court, is comprised of a CHIEF JUSTICE and eight ASSOCIATE JUSTICES. Article III provides that the justices of the Court are to be appointed by the president with the advice and consent of the Senate. Once appointed, a justice may not be removed from office except by congressional IMPEACHMENT. Because of this provision, many justices have remained on the bench into their eighties.

In 1789 the Court was initially comprised of six members, but membership was increased to seven in 1807. In 1837 an eighth and ninth justice were added, and in 1863 the number rose to ten. Congress lowered the number to eight to prevent President ANDREW JOHNSON from appointing anyone, and since 1869 the Court has been comprised of nine justices.

The only modern attempt to alter the size of the Court occurred in 1937, when President FRANKLIN D. ROOSEVELT attempted to "pack" the Court by trying to add justices more sympathetic to his political ideals. Between 1935 and 1937, the Supreme Court struck down as unconstitutional numerous pieces of Roosevelt's NEW DEAL program that attempted to regulate the national economy. Most of the conservative judges who voted against the New Deal statutes were over the age of seventy. Roosevelt proposed that justices be allowed to retire at age seventy with full pay. Any judge who declined this offer would be forced to have an assistant with full voting rights. This plan was met with hostility by Democrats and Republicans and ultimately rejected as an act of political interference.

When the office of chief justice is vacant, the president may choose the new chief justice from among the associate justices but does not need to do so. Whenever the chief justice is unable to perform his or her duties or the office is vacant, the associate justice who has been on the Court the longest performs the duties. The Court can take official action with as few as six members joining in deliberation. However, extremely important cases will sometimes be postponed until all nine justices can participate.

Court Term The Court sits in Washington, D.C., and begins its term on the first Monday in October of each year. It may also hold adjourned terms or special terms whenever required. These special calendars are reserved for emergency matters that usually occur when the Court is in recess between July and October. Between October and June 30 of the following year, the Court hears oral arguments for each case in its courtroom, confers and votes on the case, and then assigns a justice to write the majority opinion. An opinion must be released on every case by the end of the Court's term. However, if the Court cannot agree on how to resolve a case, it may hold the case over until the next term and schedule further oral arguments.

Administration of the Court The law provides for the appointment of a clerk of the Supreme Court, a deputy clerk, a marshal, a

court reporter, a librarian, judicial law clerks, secretaries to the justices, and an administrative assistant to help with court management. The law also provides for the printing of Supreme Court decisions to ensure that they will be available to the public. The Court also disseminates its opinions electronically.

Jurisdiction The Judiciary Act of 1789 gave the Supreme Court authority to hear certain APPEALS brought from the lower federal courts and the STATE COURTS. The Court was also given power to issue various kinds of orders, or WRITS, to enforce its decisions.

Article III of the Constitution declares that the Supreme Court shall have ORIGINAL JURISDICTION "[i]n all Cases affecting Ambassadors, other public Ministers and Consuls, and those in which a state shall be a party. . . ." Original jurisdiction is the authority to hear a case from the outset. Nevertheless, Congress has enacted legislation giving the district courts CONCURRENT JURISDICTION in cases dealing with ambassadors and foreign consul as well as in cases between the U.S. government and one or more state governments. The Supreme Court retains exclusive jurisdiction only in suits between state governments, which often involve boundary disputes. These cases arise infrequently and are usually placed before special masters who hear the evidence, make findings, and recommend a decision that is acceptable to the Court.

Article III states that the Supreme Court's APPELLATE jurisdiction extends to all federal cases "with such Exceptions, and under such Regulations as the Congress shall make." Appellate cases coming to the Court from the lower federal courts usually come from the thirteen courts of appeals, although they may come from the Court of Military Appeals or, under special circumstances, directly from the DISTRICT COURTS. Appellate cases may also come from the state courts of last resort, usually the state's SUPREME COURT.

Until 1891 losing parties in the lower federal courts and state courts of last resort had the right to appeal their cases to the Supreme Court. The Court's DOCKET was crowded with appeals, many of which raised routine or frivolous claims. In 1891 Congress created nine courts of appeals to correct errors in routine cases. (28 U.S.C.A. ch. 3). This reduced the Supreme Court's caseload, but parties often retained statutory rights to have their cases reviewed by the Court.

In 1925 Congress reformed, at the Court's insistence, the Supreme Court's appellate jurisdiction by restricting the categories of cases in which litigants were afforded an appeal by right to the Supreme Court. In addition, the Judiciary Act of 1925, 43 Stat. 936, gave the Court the power to issue writs of CERTIORARI to review all cases, federal or state, posing "federal questions of substance." The writ of certiorari gives the Court discretionary review, allowing it to address some issues and ignore others. Because of these reforms, the courts of appeals are the final decision-making courts in 98 percent of federal cases.

In 1988 Congress passed the Act to Improve the Administration of Justice, 102 Stat. 663. This law eliminated most appeals by right to the Supreme Court, requiring the Court to hear appeals only in cases involving federal CIVIL RIGHTS laws, legislative reapportionment, federal antitrust actions, and a few other matters. As a result of this growth in discretionary jurisdiction, the Supreme Court has the ability to set its own agenda.

A party who seeks review of a decision petitions the Court for a writ of certiorari, an ancient PLEADING form that grants the right for review. The justices deliberate in private to decide whether the issues presented by the case are significant enough to merit review. They operate under an informal rule of four, which means that certiorari will be granted if any four justices favor it. If certiorari is granted, the justices can decide the case on the papers submitted or schedule a full argument before the Court. If certiorari is denied, the matter ends there. With discretionary review, the justices have complete freedom in deciding whether to hear the case, and no one may question or appeal their decision.

The Supreme Court also has special jurisdiction to answer certified questions sent to it from a federal COURT OF APPEALS or from the U.S. Claims Court. The Supreme Court can either give instructions that the lower court is bound to follow or require the court to provide the record so that the Supreme Court can decide the entire lawsuit. Certification is rarely used.

Decisions The decisions of the Supreme Court, whether by a denial of certiorari or by an opinion issued following oral argument, are final and cannot be appealed. A Supreme Court decision based on an interpretation of the Constitution may be changed by CONSTITUTIONAL AMENDMENT. Congress may modify a decision that is based on the interpretation of an act of Congress by passing a law that directs the Court as to congressional intent and purpose. Finally, the Court may overrule itself, although it rarely does so.

Rule Making Congress has conferred upon the Supreme Court the power to prescribe rules of procedure that the Court and the lower federal courts must follow. The Court has promulgated rules that govern civil and criminal cases in the district courts, BANKRUPTCY proceedings, admiralty cases, COPYRIGHTS cases, and appellate proceedings.

See also JUDICIAL REVIEW.

SURCHARGE   An overcharge or additional cost.

A surcharge is an added liability imposed on something that is already due, such as a tax on tax. It also refers to the penalty a court can impose on a FIDUCIARY for breaching a duty.

In EQUITY, surcharging means to show that a particular item, in favor of the party surcharging, should be included in an account that is alleged to be settled or complete.

SURETY   An individual who undertakes an obligation to pay a sum of money or to perform some duty or promise for another in the event that person fails to act.

SURGEON GENERAL   The U.S. Surgeon General is charged with the protection and advancement of health in the United States. Since the 1960s the surgeon general has become a highly visible federal public health official, speaking out against known health risks such as TOBACCO use, and promoting disease prevention measures such as exercise and community water fluoridation.

The U.S. Surgeon General's Office is a unit of the Office of Public Health and Science, which is a major component of the Department of Health and Human Services (HHS). The surgeon general is appointed by the president and serves as a highly recognized symbol of the federal government's commitment to protecting and improving public health.

The surgeon general performs four major functions: promoting disease prevention and health in the United States through special health initiatives, advising the president and the secretary of the HHS on public health issues, encouraging the enhancement of public health practice in the professional disciplines, and administering the Public Health Service Commission Corps in ongoing and emergency response activities. The corps is comprised of approximately 6,000 doctors, nurses, pharmacists, and scientists.

The surgeon general oversees research on public health matters and writes reports that inform the medical profession and the public about ways of preventing disease. These reports have dealt with topics such as tobacco use, HIV and AIDS prevention, drug abuse, and the need for physical exercise.

The 1964 report of surgeon general Dr. Luther L. Terry on tobacco, entitled *Smoking*

A SMOKE-FREE FUTURE

Today, smokers risk more than their health. Bans and restrictions on smoking have swept through nearly every walk of public life, driving smokers out of offices, restaurants, and public buildings. Some firms even limit hiring to nonsmokers. In the short three decades from the mid-1960s to the mid-1990s, the antismoking movement won major victories in changing social attitudes and laws that govern this age-old habit. Leading this change were numerous studies warning that exposure to secondhand smoke kills thousands of U.S. citizens each year. Increasingly provoked by the antismoking clampdown, smokers' rights groups and the U.S. tobacco industry protest what they see as discriminatory treatment.

IN FOCUS

Laws against smoking date back to the late nineteenth century, when fourteen states prohibited cigarettes. Contemporary antismoking efforts began with a U.S. surgeon general's report in 1964 endorsing medical findings that smoking causes cancer. Congress required warning labels on tobacco products in 1965. In 1967 the Federal Communications Commission (FCC) mandated that broadcasters carry antismoking messages in proportion to tobacco advertisements. This ruling led to the disappearance of tobacco ads from television and radio.

In the 1970s, public concern shifted. A long-standing awareness of smokers' personal health risks was surmounted by growing fears about hazards to the public in general. Increased attention to secondhand smoke, or environmental tobacco smoke (ETS), fueled this significant change. A 1972 report by the U.S. Surgeon General's Office, containing a chapter on ETS, gave antismoking activists a powerful new weapon (The Health Consequences of Smoking—A Report of the Surgeon General). Restrictions on public smoking began to appear. In 1973 the Civil Aeronautics Board required airlines to provide separate smoking and nonsmoking sections. States passed clean indoor

air acts to protect the health of nonsmokers, beginning with Arizona in 1973 (Ariz. Rev. Stat. Ann. § 36-601.01). The U.S. tobacco industry lobbied strongly against such measures and defeated a 1977 California bill, but momentum was with the antismoking movement. By the early 1990s, all but five states had enacted some form of state antismoking law.

The next victory for nonsmokers came in a landmark 1976 court case that upheld a worker's right to a smoke-free work environment (*Shimp v. New Jersey Bell Telephone*, 145 N.J. Super. 516, 368 A. 2d 408 [N.J. 1976]). Donna Shimp, an office worker, successfully sued her employer after complaining that an allergy to smoke caused her physical suffering. Her employer installed an exhaust fan, but when this proved ineffective, Shimp was asked to move to a different work site; the move amounted to a demotion and pay cut. In *Shimp*, the court ruled that workers who are especially sensitive to smoke must not be subjected to it in the course of performing their job. The court's opinion cited clear and overwhelming evidence that cigarette smoke poses general health hazards by contaminating the air.

A turning point came in 1986 when Surgeon General C. Everett Koop issued a report titled *The Health Effects of Involuntary Smoking*. The report concluded that ETS causes lung cancer and other diseases in nonsmokers. It carried a dramatic warning: separating smokers and nonsmokers within the same airspace might reduce—but could not eliminate—the hazards of breathing ETS. Koop's report coincided with a study by the National Academy of Sciences that reached similar conclusions. Although the tobacco industry disputed these findings, the reports galvanized the antismoking movement.

The first effect on federal legislation was seen in December 1987, when Congress enacted an amendment to the Federal Aviation Act of 1958

(§ 404[d][1][A]) that placed a two-year ban on smoking on all domestic airline flights of less than two hours' duration.

Debate over the amendment was fierce. Supporters of the ban included flight attendants and a coalition of health groups, including the American Cancer Society. Their argument centered on the perils of ETS. The airline industry noted that smoking on airplanes created many problems, ranging from damage to aircraft interiors to the difficulty of purifying recirculated cabin air. Opponents, particularly members from tobacco-producing states, argued that the ban would depress tobacco prices. They also said it would be difficult to enforce. But enforcement proved effective because Congress granted the FAA the power to fine violators without resort to judicial intervention. After the two-year ban expired, Congress passed a law permanently banning smoking on all domestic airline flights under six hours' duration (103 Stat. 1098 [49 U.S.C.A. § 1374(d) app.]), which went into effect February 25, 1990.

Surgeon General Koop's report also sparked a surge of state legislation. In June 1989, New Jersey became the third state in the nation, after Kansas and Utah, to ban smoking in buildings owned by boards of education. The New Jersey law, New Jersey Statutes Annotated, section 26.3D-17(b) (West 1990 Supp.), was aimed at preventing teenagers from picking up the smoking habit. Many other states passed antismoking laws as well, including Virginia, a tobacco industry stronghold. Virginia's law, Code of Virginia Annotated, section 15.1-291.2 (West 1990 Supp.), restricted smoking in public places such as common areas of schools, government buildings, and restaurants. A more comprehensive New York law, New York Public Health Law I, sections 1399-n to 1399-x (McKinney 1990), took effect January 1, 1990, and targeted most public areas and workplaces. The law permitted smoking at work in limited areas as long as all present agree to allow it.

(continued on next page)

A SMOKE-FREE FUTURE
(CONTINUED)

Federal policy making followed this trend. In 1987 the General Services Administration (GSA) banned smoking in its sixty-nine hundred federal buildings, and Amtrak, the federal passenger rail line, imposed new limits on smoking in its trains, effective April 1, 1990. Also in 1990, the Interstate Commerce Commission banned smoking on interstate buses.

Private bans on smoking also increased. Some companies, such as Turner Broadcasting, in Atlanta, and Northern Life Insurance, in Seattle, refused to hire smokers.

Many smokers view laws dictating when and where they may smoke as an infringement of their personal rights. However, a federal appeals court in 1987 rejected the argument that the U.S. Constitution protects the right to smoke. In *Grusendorf v. City of Oklahoma*, 816 F.2d 539 (10th Cir. 1987), the court upheld a city fire department's dismissal of a trainee for smoking during a lunch break in violation of a policy prohibiting smoking both on and off the job. The ruling said this limit on individual liberty was justified by a rational purpose: namely, to protect the health of employees in an industry that demands that its workers be in good physical condition.

Supported by civil libertarians and tobacco industry lobbying, smokers have had some success seeking laws designed to protect them from being fired or passed over for job promotions. By 1992, thirteen states had passed smokers' rights legislation. Not everywhere have such laws been successful, however. In New Jersey, Governor James J. Florio vetoed smokers' rights legislation in January 1991. The New Jersey bill would have protected smokers in much the same way civil rights laws now protect people against job discrimination on the basis of race, religion, and sex. Florio refused to put smoking into that category.

On January 7, 1993, the Environmental Protection Agency (EPA) handed antismoking forces further ammunition in a report on secondhand smoke (Respiratory Health Effects of Passive Smoking: Lung Cancer and Other Disorders [EPA Report EPA/600/6-90/006F]). Based on several years of research, the report designated ETS as a potent carcinogen that kills about three thousand U.S. citizens annually and causes hundreds of thousands of respiratory illnesses in children. Strikingly, the agency placed ETS in the same risk category as radon and asbestos.

Reaction to the EPA risk assessment was swift and dramatic. In the six months that followed, approximately 145 local governments banned smoking in public buildings. Los Angeles passed far-reaching legislation that banned smoking in most restaurants. Effective August 2, 1993, the law applied to some seven thousand indoor restaurants, permitting smoking only in outdoor seating areas. Violators face citations of up to $250, and restaurant owners who permit indoor smoking face jail sentences of up to six months and $1,000 fines. An effort to repeal the controversial law was soon underway.

Antismoking laws are likely to continue to proliferate. The U.S. Surgeon General's Office has called for a smoke-free United States by the year 2000, and activists envision even greater prohibitions on tobacco use. Tobacco firms remain resolutely opposed to further controls, arguing that these would endanger a legitimate $37 billion industry. But the trends since the mid-1960s suggest that smokers will find fewer and fewer places to light up legally.

and Health, is perhaps the most famous example of how the surgeon general draws public attention to public health concerns. In 1964, 46 percent of all U.S. citizens smoked, and smoking was accepted in offices, airplanes, and elevators. Television programs were sponsored by cigarette brands. Terry's report concluded that smoking causes cancer. This conclusion became the foundation for later efforts to ban tobacco advertising from television, to restrict smoking in public places, and to place warning labels on cigarette packages. Since the 1964 report, smoking rates have declined from 46 percent to 25 percent.

Other surgeons general have sparked public controversy as well. In the 1980s Dr. C. Everett Koop's advocacy of the use of condoms to reduce the spread of HIV and AIDS angered religious groups and others. Dr. M. Joycelyn Elders, who was sworn in as surgeon general in September 1993, was forced to resign in December 1994 for promoting masturbation for young people as a way to avoid teenage pregnancy and sexually transmitted diseases.

See also ACQUIRED IMMUNE DEFICIENCY SYNDROME; HEALTH CARE LAW.

SURPLUSAGE 📖 Extraneous matter; impertinent, superfluous, or unnecessary. 📖

In PLEADINGS, surplusage refers to ALLEGATIONS that are not relevant to the CAUSE OF ACTION. Under the Federal Rules of CIVIL PROCEDURE, upon a MOTION, a court can strike from the pleadings any surplusage, such as an insufficient defense or an immaterial matter.

SURPRISE 📖 An unexpected action, sudden confusion, or an unanticipated event. 📖

As a ground for a new trial, surprise means the condition in which a party to a lawsuit is unexpectedly placed and that is detrimental to that party's case. The situation must be one that the party could not reasonably have anticipated and that could not be guarded against or prevented.

When a party is taken by surprise by the TESTIMONY of his or her own WITNESS, the party may be permitted to discredit the witness by showing that the witness made prior contradictory or inconsistent statements.

SURREBUTTER 📖 In COMMON-LAW PLEADING, the plaintiff's factual reply to the defendant's REBUTTER or ANSWER. 📖

Surrebutter is governed by the same rules as REPLICATION and is no longer required under modern practice and pleading.

SURREJOINDER 📖 In the second stage of COMMON-LAW PLEADING, the plaintiff's answer to the defendant's REJOINDER. 📖

SURRENDER 📖 To give up, return, or yield. 📖

The word *surrender* presupposes the POSSESSION or ownership of the thing that is to be returned or given up. It indicates a transfer of TITLE as well as possession, but it does not express or in any way suggest the transaction of a sale and DELIVERY. Instead, it involves yielding or delivering in response to a demand. A surrender may be compelled or it may be voluntary.

In landlord-tenant law, surrender occurs when a TENANT agrees to return the leased premises to the LANDLORD before the expiration of the LEASE and the landlord agrees to accept the return of the premises.

In this respect a surrender differs from ABANDONMENT, which is simply a unilateral act on the part of the tenant. In contrast, a surrender arises through a mutual agreement between the LESSOR and LESSEE.

Surrender is used in many areas of SUBSTANTIVE LAW. For example, in criminal law it refers to a suspect's giving up to the police. In INSURANCE law the "cash surrender" value is the amount of money a person will receive when he elects to end a policy and take the proceeds allocated under the insurance contract.

SURROGATE COURT 📖 A tribunal in some states with SUBJECT MATTER JURISDICTION over actions and proceedings involving, among other things, the PROBATE of WILLS, affairs of DECEDENTS, and the guardianship of the property of INFANTS. 📖

SURROGATE MOTHERHOOD 📖 A relationship in which one woman bears and gives birth to a child for a person or a couple who then adopts or takes legal custody of the child; also called mothering by proxy. 📖

In surrogate motherhood, one woman acts as a surrogate, or replacement, mother for another woman, sometimes called the intended mother, who either cannot produce fertile eggs or cannot carry a pregnancy through to birth, or term.

Surrogate mothering can be accomplished in a number of ways. Most often, the husband's sperm is implanted in the surrogate by a procedure called ARTIFICIAL INSEMINATION. In this case, the surrogate mother is both the genetic mother and the birth, or gestational mother, of the child. This method of surrogacy is sometimes called traditional surrogacy.

Less often, when the intended mother can produce fertile eggs but cannot carry a child to birth, the intended mother's egg is removed, combined with the husband's or another man's sperm in a process called in vitro fertilization (first performed in the late 1970s), and implanted in the surrogate mother. This method is called gestational surrogacy.

Surrogacy arrangements are categorized as either commercial or altruistic. In commercial surrogacy, the surrogate is paid a fee plus any expenses incurred in her pregnancy. In altruistic surrogacy, the surrogate is paid only for expenses incurred or is not paid at all.

The first recognized surrogate mother arrangement was made in 1976. Between 1976 and 1988, roughly six hundred children were born in the United States to surrogate mothers. Since the late 1980s, surrogacy has been more common: between 1987 and 1992, an estimated five thousand surrogate births occurred in the United States.

The issue of surrogate motherhood came to national attention during the 1980s, with the *Baby M* case. In 1984 a New Jersey couple, William Stern and Elizabeth Stern, contracted to pay Mary Beth Whitehead $10,000 to be artificially inseminated with William Stern's sperm and carry the resulting child to term. Whitehead decided to keep the child after it was born, refused to receive the $10,000 payment, and fled to Florida. In July 1985, the police arrested Whitehead and returned the child to the Sterns.

In 1987 the New Jersey Superior Court upheld the Stern-Whitehead contract (*In re Baby M.*, 217 N.J. Super. 313, 525 A.2d 1128). The court took all parental and visitation rights away from Whitehead and permitted the Sterns to legally adopt the baby, whom they named Melissa Stern. A year later, the New Jersey Supreme Court reversed much of this decision (*In re Baby M.*, 109 N.J. 396, 537 A.2d 1227). That court declared the contract unenforceable but allowed the Sterns to retain physical custody of the child. The court also restored some of Whitehead's parental rights, including visita-

DOES SURROGACY INVOLVE MAKING FAMILIES OR SELLING BABIES?

Medical science continues to devise new procedures and treatments that test the boundaries of law and ethics. One such result is modern surrogate motherhood, which has been made possible by artificial insemination and in vitro fertilization.

Surrogate motherhood has both advocates and detractors, each with strong arguments in their favor. A number of important questions lie at the heart of the debate over the ethics and legality of surrogacy: Does surrogacy necessarily involve the exploitation of the woman serving as the surrogate mother, or turn her into a commodity? What rights does the surrogate mother have? Is surrogacy equivalent to baby selling? Should brokers or third parties be allowed to make a profit from surrogacy arrangements?

The Case against Surrogacy

Nearly all opponents of surrogacy find it to be a morally repugnant practice, particularly when it involves a commercial transaction. Many base their opposition on religious grounds, whereas others judge it using philosophical, legal, or political criteria.

The Roman Catholic Church is just one of many religious institutions that oppose surrogacy. It is against all forms of surrogacy, even altruistic surrogacy, which does not involve the payment of a fee to the surrogate. It holds that surrogacy violates the sanctity of marriage and the spiritual connection between mother, father, and child. It finds commercial surrogacy to be especially offensive. Commercial surrogacy turns the

IN FOCUS

miracle of human birth into a financial transaction, the church maintains, reducing the child and the woman bearing it to objects of negotiation and purchase. It turns women into reproductive machines and exploiters of children. The church argues that surrogacy also leads to a confused parent-child relationship that ultimately damages the institution of the family.

Some feminists oppose surrogacy because of its political and economic context. They disagree with the notion that women freely choose to become surrogates. They argue that coercion at the societal level, rather than the personal level, causes poor women to become surrogate mothers for rich women. If surrogacy contracts are legalized, they maintain, the reproductive abilities of a whole class of women will be turned into a brokered commodity. Some feminists have gone so far as to call surrogacy reproductive prostitution.

Other critics join with Catholics and feminists to decry surrogacy as baby selling and a vehicle for the exploitation of poor women.

The Case for Surrogacy

Advocates for surrogate motherhood propose it as a humane solution to the problem of infertility. They note that infertility is common, affecting almost one out of six couples, and that surrogacy may represent the only option for some couples who wish to have children to whom they are genetically related. Advocates also point out that infertility is likely to increase as more women enter the workforce and defer childbirth

to a later age, when fertility problems are more common.

Advocates of surrogacy also argue that adoption does not adequately meet the needs of infertile couples who wish to have a baby. They point out that there are many times more couples than available infants. Moreover, couples must wait three to seven years on average to adopt an infant. Here, too, social trends have contributed to a greater call for alternative reproductive options. Most important, an increased use of contraceptives and abortion and a greater acceptance of unwed mothers have led to a shortage of adoptable babies.

Those who favor commercial surrogacy object to characterizations of the practice as baby selling. A surrogacy contract, they assert, is a contract to bear a child, not to sell a child. Advocates of surrogacy see payment to a surrogate as a fee for gestational services, just like the fees paid to lawyers and doctors for their services. Some advocates even argue that the prohibition of commercial surrogacy infringes on a woman's constitutional right to contract.

Surrogacy is also supported by those who believe that society is served best when the liberty of individuals is maximized. They claim that women and society as a whole benefit from the increased opportunity of choice offered by surrogacy.

Advocates also maintain that in a successful surrogacy arrangement, all parties benefit. The intended parents take home a cherished child, and the surrogate receives a monetary reward and the satisfaction of knowing that she has helped someone realize a special goal.

tion rights, and voided the adoption by the Sterns. Most important, the decision voided all surrogacy CONTRACTS on the ground that they conflict with state PUBLIC POLICY. However, the court still permitted voluntary surrogacy arrangements.

The *Baby M.* decision inspired state legislatures around the United States to pass laws

regarding surrogate motherhood. Most of those laws prohibit or strictly limit surrogacy arrangements. Michigan responded first, making it a FELONY to arrange surrogate mother contracts for money and imposing a $50,000 fine and five years' imprisonment as punishment for the offense (37 Mich. Comp. Laws § 722.859). Florida, Louisiana, Nebraska, and Kentucky enacted similar legislation, and Arkansas and Nevada passed laws permitting surrogacy contracts under judicial regulation.

In 1989 the AMERICAN BAR ASSOCIATION (ABA) drafted two alternative model laws involving surrogate motherhood. These laws are not binding but are intended to guide states as they formulate their own laws. One legalizes the practice of surrogate motherhood and makes surrogacy contracts enforceable in court; the other bars the enforcement of contracts in which a surrogate mother is paid to have a child and then give up any claim to the child.

Under either ABA model, states legalizing surrogate contracts limit them to agreements between a surrogate mother and a married couple. A genetic link must be established between the couple and the child, by the husband's supplying sperm or the wife's contributing an egg, or both. To be valid, the contract must be approved by a judge before conception takes place, and it must be accompanied by proof that the wife is unable to bear a child. The surrogate mother has the right to repudiate the contract up to 180 days after conception, in which case she may keep the child. If she does not repudiate the contract during that time, the couple becomes the child's legal parents 180 days after conception.

In 1993 the California Supreme Court issued a landmark ruling declaring surrogacy contracts legal in California. The case, *Johnson v. Calvert*, 5 Cal. 4th 84, 19 Cal. Rptr. 2d 494, 851 P.2d 776, involved a surrogacy contract between a married couple, Mark Calvert and Crispina Calvert, and Anna L. Johnson. Crispina Calvert was unable to bear children. In 1990 the Calverts and Johnson signed a surrogacy contract in which the Calverts agreed to pay Johnson $10,000 to carry an embryo created from the Calverts' ovum and sperm. Disagreements ensued, and later that year, Johnson became the first surrogate mother to seek custody of a child to whom she was not genetically related.

After the child's birth, the Calverts were awarded custody. Johnson appealed the decision. The state supreme court finally upheld the legality of surrogacy contracts under both the state and federal constitutions. The court held such contracts valid whether or not the surrogate mother provides the egg. The U.S. Supreme Court declined to hear Johnson's APPEAL.

In many states, surrogacy contracts are considered unenforceable because of existing adoption laws designed to discourage "baby selling." These laws may, for example, forbid any consent to adoption given prior to the birth of the child. They may also make it illegal for a birth mother to receive payment for consenting to give up a child or for an intermediary or BROKER to receive a fee for arranging an adoption. In states with these laws, a surrogate mother who wishes to keep the child rather than give it up for adoption may successfully challenge an already established surrogacy contract.

Laws concerning artificial insemination can also conflict with surrogacy agreements. Some states have laws maintaining that semen donors are not legally the fathers of children created with their sperm. These laws were originally designed to facilitate the development of sperm banks. In a surrogacy arrangement, they conflict with an attempt to adopt the surrogate child. Increasingly, states are drafting laws that clarify the legal status of surrogacy arrangements, including who is the rightful parent of a child born through surrogate mothering.

By 1995 nineteen states had adopted laws regarding surrogate motherhood. Most of these are designed to prevent or discourage surrogacy. Arizona, the District of Columbia, Kentucky, and Utah all have complete bans on surrogacy. Thirteen states bar the enforcement of paid surrogacy contracts. Ten JURISDICTIONS prohibit a third party, such as a lawyer or physician, from collecting compensation for arranging surrogacy agreements.

State laws differ in the way they handle disputes over custody. Surrogacy laws in Michigan and Washington make custody determinations on a case-by-case basis, attempting to reach the decision that best serves the interests of the child. In New Hampshire and Virginia, such laws presume that the contracting couple are the legal parents, but give the surrogate a period of time to change her mind. In North Dakota and Arizona, the surrogate and her husband are the legal parents of the child.

Arkansas, Florida, and Nevada are the only states that allow surrogacy contracts. These states permit the intended parents named in the contract to be the legal parents. In Florida and Nevada, the surrogacy laws apply only to gestational surrogacy, where the egg used is not the surrogate's.

CROSS-REFERENCES

Adoption; Child Custody; Family Law; Parent and Child.

SURTAX An additional charge on an item that is already taxed.

A surtax is a tax on a tax. For example, if a person pays one hundred dollars of tax on one thousand dollars of income, a 5 percent surtax would amount to an additional five dollars.

SURVEILLANCE   See ELECTRONIC SURVEILLANCE; WIRETAPPING.

SURVIVORSHIP   See RIGHT OF SURVIVORSHIP.

SUSPECT CLASSIFICATION   A presumptively unconstitutional distinction made between individuals on the basis of race, national origin, alienage, or religious affiliation, in a statute, ORDINANCE, regulation, or policy.

The U.S. Supreme Court has held that certain kinds of government discrimination are inherently suspect and must be subjected to strict judicial scrutiny. The suspect classification doctrine has its constitutional basis in the FIFTH AMENDMENT and the Equal Protection Clause of the FOURTEENTH AMENDMENT, and it applies to actions taken by federal and state governments. When a suspect classification is at issue, the government has the burden of proving that the challenged policy is constitutional.

The concept of suspect classifications was first discussed by the Supreme Court in *Korematsu v. United States*, 323 U.S. 214, 65 S. Ct. 193, 89 L. Ed. 194 (1944). The Court upheld the "relocation" of Japanese Americans living on the West Coast during World War II, yet Justice HUGO L. BLACK, in his majority opinion, stated that

> all legal restrictions which curtail the civil rights of a single group are immediately suspect. That is not to say that all such restrictions are unconstitutional. It is to say that courts must subject them to the most rigid scrutiny. Pressing public necessity may sometimes justify the existence of such restrictions; racial antagonism never can.

Though it is now widely recognized that no compelling justification existed for the relocation order and that racial prejudice rather than national security led to the forced removal of Japanese Americans, *Korematsu* did signal the Court's willingness to apply the Equal Protection Clause to suspect classifications.

STRICT SCRUTINY of a suspect classification reverses the ordinary presumption of constitutionality, with the government carrying the burden of proving that its challenged policy is constitutional. To withstand strict scrutiny, the government must show that its policy is necessary to achieve a COMPELLING STATE INTEREST. If this is proved, the state must then demonstrate that the legislation is narrowly tailored to achieve the intended result. Although strict scrutiny is not a precise test, it is far more stringent than the traditional RATIONAL BASIS TEST, which only requires the government to offer a REASONABLE ground for the legislation.

Race is the clearest example of a suspect classification. For example, the Supreme Court in *Loving v. Virginia*, 388 U.S. 1, 87 S. Ct. 1817, 198 L. Ed. 2d 1010 (1967), scrutinized a Virginia statute that prohibited interracial marriages. The Court noted that race was the basis for the classification and that it was, therefore, suspect. The Court struck down the law because Virginia failed to prove a compelling state interest in preventing interracial marriages. Legislation discriminating on the basis of religion or ethnicity, as well as those statutes that affect fundamental rights, also are inherently suspect. The Supreme Court has not recognized age and gender as suspect classifications, though some lower courts treat gender as a suspect or quasi-suspect classification.

CROSS-REFERENCES

Equal Protection; Japanese American Evacuation Cases; *Korematsu v. United States*.

SUSPENDED SENTENCE   A sentence given after the formal conviction of a crime that the convicted person is not required to serve.

In criminal cases a trial judge has the ability to suspend the sentence of a convicted person. The judge must first pronounce a penalty of a FINE or IMPRISONMENT, or both, and then suspend the implementation of the sentence.

There are two types of suspended sentences. A judge may unconditionally discharge the defendant of all obligations and restraints. An unconditionally suspended sentence ends the court system's involvement in the matter, and the defendant has no penalty to pay. However, the defendant's criminal conviction will remain part of the public record. A judge may also issue a conditionally suspended sentence. This type of sentence withholds execution of the penalty as long as the defendant exhibits GOOD BEHAVIOR. For example, if a person was convicted of shoplifting for the first time, the judge could impose thirty days of INCARCERATION as a penalty and then suspend the imprisonment on the condition that the defendant not commit any crimes during the next year. Once the year passes without incident, the penalty is discharged. If, however, the defendant does commit another crime, the judge is entitled to revoke the suspension and have the defendant serve the thirty days in jail.

Whether a conditionally suspended sentence is considered equivalent or complementary to a PROBATION order or is considered an entirely distinct legal action depends on the JURISDICTION. Under a probation order, the convicted person is not incarcerated but is placed under the supervision of a probation officer for a specified length of time. A person who violates probation will likely have his probation revoked and will have to serve the original sentence.

In some jurisdictions a postponement of SENTENCING is also considered to be a suspended sentence. A postponement of a criminal sentence means that the judge does not pronounce a penalty immediately after a conviction. Courts use postponement and conditionally suspended sentences to encourage convicted persons to stay out of trouble. In most cases courts will impose these types of conditional sentences for less serious crimes and for persons who do not have a criminal record. Where there is overcrowding in jails, suspended sentences for petty crimes may be used to prevent further congestion.

SUSPICION 📖 The apprehension of something without proof to verify the belief. 📖

Suspicion implies a belief or opinion based upon facts or circumstances that do not constitute proof.

SUSTAIN 📖 To carry on; to maintain. To affirm, uphold or approve, as when an APPELLATE COURT sustains the decision of a lower court. To grant, as when a judge sustains an OBJECTION to TESTIMONY or EVIDENCE, he or she agrees with the objection and gives it effect. 📖

SUTHERLAND, GEORGE George Sutherland served as associate justice of the U.S. Supreme Court from 1922 to 1938. A conservative jurist, Sutherland opposed the efforts of Congress and state legislatures to regulate business and working conditions. During the 1930s he was part of a conservative bloc that ruled unconstitutional major parts of President FRANKLIN D. ROOSEVELT'S NEW DEAL program.

Sutherland was born on March 25, 1862, in Buckinghamshire, England. When Sutherland was a young child, his parents emigrated to the United States, settling in Provo, Utah. Sutherland graduated from Brigham Young University in 1881 and attended the University of Michigan Law School in 1882 and 1883. He was admitted to the Michigan bar in 1883 but

"[THE] SADDEST EPITAPH WHICH CAN BE CARVED IN MEMORY [FOR] A VANISHED LIBERTY IS THAT IT WAS LOST BECAUSE ITS POSSESSORS FAILED TO STRETCH FORTH A SAVING HAND WHILE YET THERE WAS TIME."

BIOGRAPHY

PORTRAIT BY NICHOLAS RICHARD BREWER, COLLECTION OF THE SUPREME COURT OF THE UNITED STATES.

George Sutherland

returned that same year to Utah, where he established a law practice in Salt Lake City.

Sutherland took an interest in politics and served in the territorial legislature. In 1896, after Utah had become a state, Sutherland was elected to the first Utah Senate as a Republican party member. In 1901 he was elected to the U.S. House of Representatives, and in 1905 he became a U.S. senator from Utah.

Despite Sutherland's reputation as a political conservative in Congress, he did support President THEODORE ROOSEVELT'S reform programs. He also supported WORKERS' COMPENSATION legislation for railroad workers and the NINETEENTH AMENDMENT to the U.S. Constitution, which provided for women's suffrage. Nevertheless, he believed that individual rights were paramount and that government should not intrude on most economic activities.

After being defeated in the 1916 Senate election, Sutherland became involved in national Republican politics and served as an adviser to President WARREN G. HARDING, who was elected in 1920. Sutherland's name had been mentioned for several years as a possible Supreme Court appointee, and in September 1922 Harding nominated Sutherland to the Court.

Sutherland joined a Supreme Court dominated by conservatives. Like the conservative majority, Sutherland believed in the doctrine of substantive DUE PROCESS, which held that the Due Process Clauses of the Fifth and Fourteenth Amendments to the U.S. Constitution could be invoked to impose limits on the substance of government regulations and other activities by which government affects "life, liberty, and property." Since the 1880s the Supreme Court had invoked substantive due process to strike down a variety of state and federal laws that regulated working conditions, wages, and business activities.

Sutherland also adhered to the concept of liberty of contract, which held that the government should not interfere with the right of individuals to contract with their employers

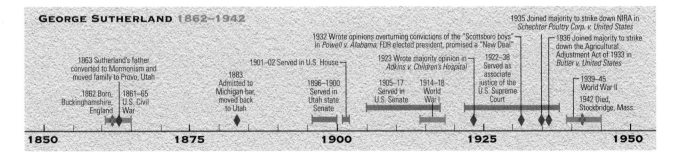

GEORGE SUTHERLAND 1862–1942

1863 Sutherland's father converted to Mormonism and moved family to Provo, Utah

1862 Born; Buckinghamshire, England

1861–65 U.S. Civil War

1883 Admitted to Michigan bar, moved back to Utah

1901–02 Served in U.S. House

1896–1900 Served in Utah state Senate

1932 Wrote opinions overturning convictions of the "Scottsboro boys" in *Powell v. Alabama*; FDR elected president, promised a "New Deal"

1923 Wrote majority opinion in *Adkins v. Children's Hospital*

1905–17 Served in U.S. Senate

1914–18 World War I

1922–38 Served as associate justice of the U.S. Supreme Court

1935 Joined majority to strike down NIRA in *Schechter Poultry Corp. v. United States*

1936 Joined majority to strike down the Agricultural Adjustment Act of 1933 in *Butler v. United States*

1939–45 World War II

1942 Died, Stockbridge, Mass.

1850   1875   1900   1925   1950

concerning wages, hours, and working conditions. Sutherland wrote the majority opinion in *Adkins v. Children's Hospital,* 261 U.S. 525, 43 S. Ct. 394, 67 L. Ed. 785 (1923), in which the Court struck down a federal MINIMUM WAGE law for women workers in the District of Columbia. Sutherland concluded that employer and employee had the constitutional right to negotiate whatever terms they pleased concerning wages. Sutherland rejected the idea that Congress had the authority to correct social and economic disparities that hurt society in general.

With the stock market crash of 1929 and the Great Depression of the 1930s, the conservative majority on the Court came under intense public and political scrutiny. Franklin D. Roosevelt's election in 1932 signaled a change in philosophy concerning the role of the federal government. Roosevelt's New Deal was premised on national economic planning and the creation of administrative agencies to regulate business and labor. This was anathema to Sutherland and his conservative brethren.

From 1933 to 1937 the Court struck down numerous New Deal measures. Sutherland, along with Justices JAMES C. MCREYNOLDS, WILLIS VAN DEVANTER, and PIERCE BUTLER, formed the core of opposition to federal efforts to revitalize the economy and create a social safety net. The so-called Four Horsemen helped strike down as unconstitutional the NATIONAL INDUSTRIAL RECOVERY ACT of 1933 in *Schechter Poultry Corporation v. United States,* 295 U.S. 495, 55 S. Ct. 837, 79 L. Ed. 1570 (1935), and the Agricultural Adjustment Act of 1933 in *United States v. Butler,* 297 U.S. 1, 56 S. Ct. 312, 80 L. Ed. 477 (1936).

Roosevelt responded by proposing a court-packing plan that would have added an additional justice to the Court for each member over the age of seventy. This plan targeted the Four Horsemen and, if implemented, would have canceled out their votes. Although Roosevelt's plan was rejected by Congress, the national debate over the role of the federal government and the recalcitrance of the Supreme Court led more moderate members of

the Court to change their positions and vote in favor of New Deal proposals. With the tide turning, Sutherland retired in 1938.

Despite his conservative views on government and business, Sutherland defended liberty rights as well as property rights. In *Powell v. Alabama,* 287 U.S. 45, 53 S. Ct. 55, 77 L. Ed. 158 (1932), Sutherland overturned the convictions of the "Scottsboro boys," a group of young African Americans sentenced to death for an alleged sexual assault on two white women. Sutherland ruled that the Sixth Amendment guarantees adequate legal counsel in state criminal proceedings.

Sutherland died on July 18, 1942, in Stockbridge, Massachusetts.

See also POWELL V. ALABAMA; SCHECHTER POULTRY CORPORATION V. UNITED STATES.

PORTRAIT BY CASIMIR GREGORY STAPKO COLLECTION OF THE SUPREME COURT OF THE UNITED STATES

Noah Haynes Swayne

SWAYNE, NOAH HAYNES   Noah Haynes Swayne served as associate justice of the U.S. Supreme Court from 1862 to 1881. A prominent Ohio attorney for almost forty years before becoming a judge, Swayne was President ABRAHAM LINCOLN's first Supreme Court appointment. His tenure on the Court was relatively undistinguished.

Swayne was born on December 7, 1804, in Frederick County, Virginia. He studied law with two Virginia attorneys and was admitted to the Virginia bar in 1823. His antislavery views proved troublesome, however, and he moved his law practice to Coshocton, Ohio. Appointed county attorney in 1826, Swayne soon became involved in Democratic party politics. An ardent supporter of President ANDREW JACKSON, Swayne was elected to the Ohio state legislature in 1829. In 1830 Jackson named him U.S. district attorney, a position he held for almost ten years. He moved to Columbus, Ohio, to administer his office.

By 1840 Swayne had returned to private practice, but he served on many public commissions in Ohio, including a commission to arbitrate a boundary dispute between Ohio and Michigan. He left the Democratic party in 1856 because he disagreed with the party's support of

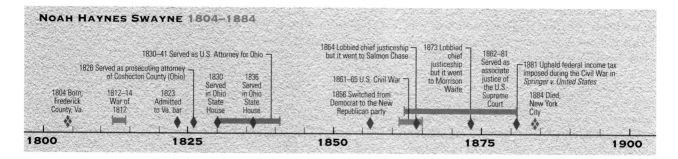

NOAH HAYNES SWAYNE 1804–1884

1804 Born, Frederick County, Va.

1812–14 War of 1812

1823 Admitted to Va. bar

1826 Served as prosecuting attorney of Coshocton County (Ohio)

1830–41 Served as U.S. Attorney for Ohio

1830 Served in Ohio State House

1836 Served in Ohio State House

1856 Switched from Democrat to the New Republican party

1861–65 U.S. Civil War

1864 Lobbied chief justiceship but it went to Salmon Chase

1862–81 Served as associate justice of the U.S. Supreme Court

1873 Lobbied chief justiceship but it went to Morrison Waite

1881 Upheld federal income tax imposed during the Civil War in *Springer v. United States*

1884 Died, New York City

1800   1825   1850   1875   1900

SLAVERY and joined the newly formed Republican party. As a lawyer, he represented several runaway slaves in legal proceedings in which slaveholders sought to reclaim their property.

In 1862 Justice JOHN MCLEAN, an Ohio native and friend of Swayne, died suddenly. Swayne used his Ohio political connections to lobby for an appointment to the Supreme Court. President Lincoln nominated Swayne in January 1862. He was confirmed two days later.

Though Swayne spent almost twenty years on the Supreme Court, he left no mark on the institution. An inveterate politician, he lobbied for the position of chief justice in 1864 and 1873. During the Civil War, he was a consistent supporter of Lincoln's emergency war measures, including the imposition of MARTIAL LAW and the issuance of paper money called "greenbacks," which were not redeemable for gold or silver. In addition, he upheld the constitutionality of a federal INCOME TAX imposed during the Civil War (*Springer v. United States*, 102 U.S. (12 Otto) 586, 26 L. Ed. 253 [1881]).

Swayne retired from the Court in 1881. He died on June 8, 1884, in New York City.

SWIFT v. TYSON   For almost one hundred years, the U.S. Supreme Court's decision in *Swift v. Tyson*, 41 U.S. (16 Pet.) 1, 10 L. Ed. 865 (1842), allowed the FEDERAL COURTS to create their own body of civil COMMON LAW in cases in which the parties were from different states. In exercising its diversity JURISDICTION, a federal court was free to ignore the pertinent common law of the state in which it sat and apply federal common law. Though it was intended to encourage the development of a uniform set of commercial law principles, the *Swift* decision was sharply criticized as an unwarranted intrusion into areas reserved to state courts.

Swift involved a legal dispute over the law of negotiable instruments. A NEGOTIABLE INSTRUMENT is a document by which one party promises to pay either money or goods to another party, called the BEARER. For example, a CHECK written on a person's bank account is a negotiable instrument. Negotiable instruments used by business are called COMMERCIAL PAPER and played an important role in the U.S. economy in the early nineteenth century. An unresolved issue was whether the bearer could ASSIGN a BILL OF EXCHANGE to a third party, who could then collect on the obligation.

The question of ASSIGNMENTS was at the heart of *Swift*. A third-party assignee of a bill of exchange drawn in New York presented it for payment and was refused. The third party, who was not a New York resident, sued in New York federal district court. The New York common law held that a bill of exchange could not be assigned, and the federal judge ruled accordingly. Because New York was the leading commercial center in the United States, this ruling had serious implications for the national economy.

On appeal, the Supreme Court overturned the decision by reinterpreting the federal RULES OF DECISION ACT, originally section 34 of the JUDICIARY ACT OF 1789 (1 Stat. 73). In its original form, the act provided that "the laws of the several states . . . shall be regarded as rules of decision in trials at common law in the courts of the United States in cases where they apply." The main issue before the Court concerned the meaning of the word *laws*. Was the word limited to legislatively enacted statutes or did it include state common-law decisions as well?

Justice JOSEPH STORY, writing for a unanimous Court, concluded that the term *laws* did not include common-law decisions. Such decisions were "at most, only evidence of what the laws are, and are not, of themselves, laws." Except for decisions of a "local" nature, such as those dealing with real estate, a federal judge was not required to apply a "general" state common-law rule involving commerce to a diversity-based case. Under the act a federal judge could apply only state statutes to a legal dispute.

Story, who was the leading U.S. authority on commercial law and commercial paper, believed it was imperative for the growth of the U.S. economy that the United States develop a uniform national law of commerce for the federal courts to apply. Therefore, he declared that federal common law permitted the assignment of commercial paper. Economic and legal historians have concluded that *Swift* did contribute to the growth of multistate transactions and the national economy. Businesses were able to assign commercial paper without fear that a state would invalidate the assignment.

Nevertheless, the decision angered many who believed a federal common law interfered with the right of states to develop their own principles of commercial law. The *Swift* doctrine also led to situations in which the substantive law applied to litigants might be determined simply by the fortuity of their residences. Two cases might have different legal results depending only on whether the plaintiff and the defendant were from the same state or from different states. This led to significant unfairness and FORUM shopping. For example, in *Black & White Taxicab & Transfer Co. v. Brown & Yellow Taxicab and Transfer Co.*, 276 U.S. 518, 48

S. Ct. 404, 72 L. Ed. 681 (1928), a Kentucky corporation dissolved and reincorporated in Tennessee to obtain the benefit of substantive federal common law against another Kentucky corporation.

Faced with mounting criticism of *Swift*, in 1938 the Supreme Court overturned the decision in *Erie Railroad Co. v. Tompkins*, 304 U.S. 64, 58 S. Ct. 817, 82 L. Ed. 1188. Federal courts were again required to apply state law, whether statutory or common, in diversity jurisdiction cases. In a radical shift from *Swift*, federal district courts periodically refer questions to state supreme courts, asking for a ruling on what the state law is on a specific issue.

See also ERIE RAILROAD CO. v. TOMPKINS.

SYLLABUS 📖 A HEADNOTE; a short note preceding the text of a reported case that briefly summarizes the rulings of the court on the points decided in the case. 📖

The syllabus appears before the text of the opinion. The syllabus generally is not part of the opinion of the court but is prepared by a legal editor employed by a private law book company that publishes court decisions to serve as a quick reference for a researcher. Some courts prepare the syllabus for their own decisions, but in many states the syllabus has no legal effect. Ohio is one exception, however, where the court-prepared syllabus is part of the decision and is considered a statement of the law. In most states, only the opinion of the court containing the original statement of the grounds for the opinion may be used in legal papers in a lawsuit to convince a court or jury of a particular point of law.

See also COURT OPINION.

SYMBOLIC DELIVERY 📖 The constructive CONVEYANCE of the subject matter of a GIFT or SALE, when it is either inaccessible or cumbersome, through the offering of some substitute article that indicates the donative intent of the donor or seller and is accepted as the representative of the original item. 📖

For example, when one individual wishes to make a gift of a car to another individual, he or she might do so by handing over the keys and all documents indicating ownership thereof. In the law of REAL PROPERTY, the transfer of a twig or clod of dirt from the grantor of land to the grantee was LIVERY OF SEISIN that constituted symbolic delivery of the right of legal possession or ownership of land pursuant to a FREEHOLD estate. Today the transfer of a DEED from the seller to a buyer demonstrates the change in ownership of property.

SYMBOLIC SPEECH 📖 Nonverbal gestures and actions that are meant to communicate a message. 📖

The term *symbolic speech* is applied to a wide range of nonverbal communication. Many political activities, including marching, wearing armbands, and displaying or mutilating the U.S. FLAG, are considered forms of symbolic expression. The U.S. Supreme Court has held that this form of communicative behavior is entitled to the protection of the FIRST AMENDMENT to the U.S. Constitution, but the scope and nature of that protection have varied.

The Supreme Court first gave symbolic speech First Amendment protection in *Stromberg v. California*, 283 U.S. 359, 51 S. Ct. 532, 75 L. Ed. 1117 (1931). The Court overturned a California statute that prohibited the display of a red flag as a "sign, symbol or emblem of opposition to organized government." But not until the VIETNAM WAR era did the Court articulate the rules to be followed in determining whether symbolic expression is entitled to the protection of the First Amendment.

In *United States v. O'Brien*, 391 U.S. 367, 88 S. Ct. 1673, 20 L. Ed. 2d 672 (1968), the Court reviewed the conviction of David Paul O'Brien for violating a 1965 amendment to the Selective Service Act (50 U.S.C.A. App. § 451 et seq.) that prohibited any draft registrant from knowingly destroying or mutilating his draft card. O'Brien had burned his Selective Service card on the steps of the South Boston Courthouse at a rally protesting the Vietnam War. He claimed that his act of burning his card was symbolic speech protected by the First Amendment. The government argued that it could prohibit this conduct because it had a legitimate interest in requiring registrants to have draft cards always in their possession as a means of ensuring the proper functioning of the military draft.

The Supreme Court sided with the government, with Chief Justice EARL WARREN rejecting "the view that an apparently limitless variety of conduct can be labeled speech whenever the person engaging in the conduct intends thereby to express his idea." When "speech" and "nonspeech" elements are combined in the same course of conduct, a lesser burden will be placed on the government to justify its restrictions. Accordingly, the Court announced the appropriate constitutional standard:

[A] government regulation is sufficiently justified if it is within the constitutional power of the Government; if it furthers an important or substantial government inter-

FLAG BURNING: DESECRATION OR FREE EXPRESSION?

The Supreme Court's decision in *Texas v. Johnson*, 491 U.S. 397, 109 S. Ct. 2533, 105 L. Ed. 2d 342 (1989), striking down a Texas law that made burning the U.S. flag a crime, was endorsed by the American Civil Liberties Union (ACLU) and other groups that seek to preserve freedom of expression under the First Amendment. Other groups and individuals, however, were dismayed that the Court would strike down a law that protected the symbol of the United States. Congress responded by passing the federal Flag Protection Act of 1989, 103 Stat. 777, which made flag burning a federal crime. When the Supreme Court struck down the federal law in *United States v. Eichman*, 496 U.S. 310, 110 S. Ct. 2404, 110 L. Ed. 2d 287 (1990), opponents of flag burning began to campaign for a constitutional amendment that would make such a law constitutional.

IN FOCUS

The proponents of a flag protection amendment have been led by the Citizens Flag Alliance (CFA), a nonpartisan, nonprofit national coalition that includes more than one hundred organizations and is funded, in large part, by the American Legion. The proposed amendment states that "Congress shall have power to prohibit the physical desecration of the flag of the United States." The House of Representatives overwhelmingly passed the amendment in June 1995, but the Senate defeated the amendment by three votes in December 1995.

Despite this defeat, the CFA has continued to campaign for the amendment, noting that opinion polls consistently show that 80 percent of U.S. citizens support the amendment. In addition, forty-nine state legislatures have passed resolutions asking Congress to pass a flag protection amendment—eleven more states than are needed to ratify an amendment. The amendment was reintroduced in Congress in 1997. The House passed the measure by a vote of 310–114, but a vote in the Senate was delayed.

Proponents of the amendment contend that it does not restrict freedom of expression or limit the First Amendment. They note that there have always been limits on free speech and that the Supreme Court has never regarded the guarantees of the First Amendment as absolute. Proponents point to Chief Justice William H. Rehnquist's dissent in *Johnson*, in which he characterized flag burning as "the equivalent of an inarticulate grunt or roar" and the flag as a national symbol deserving of protection.

In addition, supporters of the amendment deny that flag burning is symbolic speech. They argue that the act of flag desecration is conduct rather than speech and is thus outside the First Amendment's protection. The Supreme Court's decisions have regarded flag burning as protected symbolic speech, however, so this argument can only prevail if the Court's interpretation is overridden by an amendment to the Constitution.

Supporters of the amendment contend that the flag has a special place in U.S. society and culture and serves as a unifying symbol for a heterogeneous nation. Because of its unique status, the flag must be honored and respected. They argue that the freedom to desecrate the flag is not a fundamental freedom deeply rooted in the First Amendment. Therefore, they conclude, it is reasonable for a balance to be struck between the rights of the individual and her responsibility to society. In this instance societal values should prevail over individual interests.

Proponents of the amendment strenuously object to the charge that they are restricting freedom of speech. The amendment does not prevent a person from criticizing, in speech or writing, the government, government officials, or even the flag itself. The amendment simply gives Congress the authority to pass legislation that prohibits the desecration of the U.S. flag.

Opponents of the amendment, led by the ACLU, insist that the passage of the flag amendment would limit freedom of expression and restrict the First Amendment. They point out that the word *desecration* is a religious concept that means to profane or violate the sanctity of something. According to opponents, the flag amendment would implicitly constitutionalize the flag as the sacred or divine object of the United States. Such an action would run counter to the Bill of Rights.

Opponents of the amendment contend that flag burning is a rare event that does not merit the amending of the Constitution. No more than five or six persons were prosecuted annually for flag burning before the *Johnson* decision. Opponents worry that once a flag desecration amendment is passed, it will open the door to the revocation of other individual freedoms. The Constitution and the Bill of Rights were designed to prevent the tyranny of the majority. Just because a flag desecration amendment has broad support does not make it right. Once flag burning is banned, legislators and pressure groups will seek to restrict other freedoms.

Those opposed to the amendment also argue that the Supreme Court's decision in *Johnson* contained the best reason for rejecting it. As Justice William J. Brennan, Jr., stated, "We do not consecrate the flag by punishing its desecration, for in doing so we dilute the freedom that this cherished emblem represents." Opponents see the toleration of actions such as flag burning as a sign and source of national strength. In their view the flag stands for the freedoms each U.S. citizen enjoys, including the right to burn that very symbol.

est; if the governmental interest is unrelated to the suppression of free expression; and if the incidental restriction on First Amendment freedoms is no greater than is essential to the furtherance of that interest.

Applying this test to the statute involved in *O'Brien*, the Court found the law constitutional.

A less defiant form of symbolic speech was extended constitutional protection during the Vietnam War. In *Tinker v. Des Moines Independent Community School District*, 393 U.S. 503, 89 S. Ct. 733, 21 L. Ed. 2d 731 (1969), high school officials in Des Moines, Iowa, had suspended students for wearing black armbands to school to protest U.S. involvement in the Vietnam War. Justice ABE FORTAS, in his majority opinion, rejected the idea that the school's response was "reasonable" because it was based on the fear that the wearing of the armbands would create a disturbance. Fortas ruled that the wearing of the armbands was "closely akin to 'pure speech' which . . . is entitled to comprehensive protection under the First Amendment. . . ." Public school officials could not ban expression out of the "mere desire to avoid discomfort and unpleasantness that always accompany an unpopular viewpoint."

Political protesters have often used the U.S. flag as a vehicle to express opposition to government policies. During the Vietnam War era, the mutilation or burning of the flag became commonplace. Such actions angered many people, and legislation was passed at the state level to prohibit this conduct. In *Street v. New York*, 394 U.S. 576, 89 S. Ct. 1354, 22 L. Ed. 2d 572 (1969), the Supreme Court had the opportunity to address the question of whether flag burning is entitled to constitutional protection as symbolic speech. However, the Court focused on the element of verbal expression also presented in this case and effectively avoided the symbolic speech issue. In a 1974 case, the Court did strike down a Washington state law that prohibited the display of the U.S. flag with "extraneous material" attached to it (*Spence v. Washington*, 418 U.S. 405, 94 S. Ct. 2727, 41 L. Ed. 2d 842).

The *Street* decision left open the question of whether flag burning per se was a form of symbolic speech protected by the First Amendment. In 1989, in the highly publicized case of *Texas v. Johnson*, 491 U.S. 397, 109 S. Ct. 2533, 105 L. Ed. 2d 342, the Court surprised many observers by ruling that flag burning was protected. After publicly burning the U.S. flag outside the 1984 Republican National Conven-

tion in Dallas, Texas, Gregory Lee Johnson was charged with violating a Texas law prohibiting flag desecration. Johnson was convicted at trial, but his conviction was reversed by the Texas Court of Criminal Appeals, which held that the law violated the First Amendment. On a 5–4 vote, the U.S. Supreme Court agreed.

Writing for the majority, Justice WILLIAM J. BRENNAN, JR., noted that "[t]he expressive, overtly political nature of [Johnson's] conduct was both intentional and overwhelmingly apparent." It was clear that "Johnson was convicted for engaging in expressive conduct." Rejecting the assertion by Texas that the law prevented BREACHES OF THE PEACE, the Court concluded that "Johnson's conduct did not threaten to disturb the peace. Nor does the State's interest in preserving the flag as a symbol of nationhood and national unity justify his criminal conviction for engaging in political expression."

Chief Justice WILLIAM H. REHNQUIST, in a dissenting opinion, dismissed the idea that flag burning was a form of symbolic speech. On the contrary, he stated, "flag burning is the equivalent of an inarticulate grunt or roar that . . . is most likely to be indulged in not to express any particular idea, but to antagonize others. . . ." Rehnquist argued that the flag "as the symbol of our Nation, [has] a uniqueness that justifies a governmental prohibition against flag burning . . . ."

The *Johnson* decision angered conservatives, who called for a CONSTITUTIONAL AMENDMENT to place flag burning beyond the First Amendment's protection. When the amendment proposal failed to gain support, Congress passed the federal Flag Protection Act of 1989, 103 Stat. 777, which made flag burning a federal crime. In *United States v. Eichman*, 496 U.S. 310, 110 S. Ct. 2404, 110 L. Ed. 2d 287 (1990), the Court struck down the Flag Protection Act as applied to flag burning as a means of political protest.

Many commentators have criticized the way the Supreme Court has treated the symbolic speech area. In particular, observers have noted that the line between "speech" and nonverbal "conduct" is impossible to draw and that the real emphasis should be placed on the motive behind the government regulation. This approach would determine whether the regulation was intended to censor certain ideas or whether it was directed at the noncommunicative impact of the behavior.

CROSS-REFERENCES

Censorship; Freedom of Speech; *Texas v. Johnson*.

SYNDICATE 📖 An association of individuals formed for the purpose of conducting a particular business; a JOINT VENTURE. 📖

A syndicate is a general term describing any group that is formed to conduct some type of business. For example, a syndicate may be formed by a group of investment bankers who underwrite and distribute new issues of SECURITIES or blocks of outstanding issues. Syndicates can be organized as CORPORATIONS or PARTNERSHIPS.

Newspaper or press syndicates came into existence after the Civil War. A press syndicate sells the exclusive rights to entertainment features, such as gossip and advice columns, comic strips, and serialized books, to a subscribing newspaper in each territory. These "syndicated" features, which appear simultaneously around the United States, can generate large sums for the creators of the features and for the syndicate that sells them. Similarly, when television programs are syndicated, one station in each television market is allowed to broadcast a popular game show or rebroadcast a popular network series. A syndicated show may be televised at different times depending on the schedule of the local station. In contrast, on network television, a program is televised nationally at one scheduled time.

The term *syndicate* is also associated with ORGANIZED CRIME. In the 1930s, the term *crime syndicate* was often used to describe a loose association of racketeers in control of organized crime throughout the United States. For example, the infamous "Murder, Inc." of the 1930s, which was part of a national crime syndicate, was founded to threaten, assault, or murder designated victims for a price. A member of the crime syndicate anywhere in the United States could contract with Murder, Inc., to hire a "hit man" to kill a person.

SYNDICATED CRIME See ORGANIZED CRIME.

SYNOPSIS 📖 A summary; a brief statement, less than the whole. 📖

A synopsis is a condensation of something— for example, a synopsis of a trial record.

TABLE OF CASES 📖 An alphabetized list of the judicial decisions that are cited, referred to, or explained in a book with references to the sections, pages, or paragraphs where they are cited. 📖

A table of cases is commonly found in either the prefix or appendix of the book.

TACIT 📖 Implied, inferred, understood without being expressly stated. 📖

Tacit refers to something done or made in silence, as in a *tacit agreement*. A *tacit understanding* is manifested by the fact that no contradiction or objection is made and is thus inferred from the situation and the circumstances.

TACKING 📖 The process whereby an individual who is in ADVERSE POSSESSION of REAL PROPERTY adds his or her period of POSSESSION to that of a prior adverse possessor. 📖

In order for TITLE to property to VEST in an adverse possessor, occupancy must be continuous, regular, and uninterrupted for the full statutory period. If PRIVITY exists between the parties, such that one possessor gives possession of the land to the next, the time periods that the successive occupants have had possession of the property may be added or tacked together to meet the continuity requirement.

Tacking is allowed only when no time lapses between the end of one occupant's possession and the beginning of another's occupancy. In addition, possession by the prior occupant must have been adverse or under COLOR OF TITLE.

TAFT, ALPHONSO Alphonso Taft served as attorney general of the United States from 1876 to 1877, under President ULYSSES S. GRANT.

Taft was born November 5, 1810, in Townsend, Vermont, to pioneers Peter Rawson Taft and Sylvia Howard Taft. He was well aware of his family's long history and tradition of public service in the American colonies. His father was a descendant of Edward Rawson, a 1636 settler who had served as secretary of the Massachusetts Province. Other Taft family members held positions of responsibility and influence in communities all along the eastern seaboard.

Although Taft's parents were of modest financial means, they had a strong commitment to education, and Taft was well schooled. Taft left Vermont to attend Yale University in 1829, where he received a bachelor of arts degree in 1833 and his law degree in 1836.

Like many young men of his day, Taft saw his future in the West. In 1839 Taft moved to

BIOGRAPHY

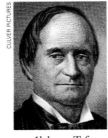

CULVER PICTURES

Alphonso Taft

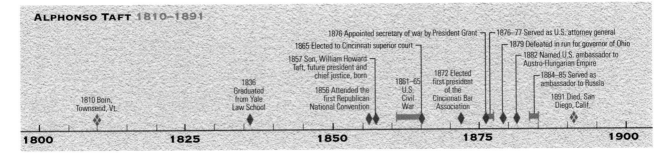

ALPHONSO TAFT 1810–1891

1810 Born, Townsend, Vt.

1836 Graduated from Yale Law School

1856 Attended the first Republican National Convention

1857 Son, William Howard Taft, future president and chief justice, born

1861–65 U.S. Civil War

1865 Elected to Cincinnati superior court

1872 Elected first president of the Cincinnati Bar Association

1876 Appointed secretary of war by President Grant

1876–77 Served as U.S. attorney general

1879 Defeated in run for governor of Ohio

1882 Named U.S. ambassador to Austro-Hungarian Empire

1884–85 Served as ambassador to Russia

1891 Died, San Diego, Calif.

1800　1825　1850　1875　1900

Cincinnati, Ohio, and opened his law practice. On August 29, 1841, he married Fanny Phelps, the daughter of family friends Charles Phelps and Eliza Houghton Phelps. Fanny died in 1852. Taft remarried in 1853, to Louise Maria Torret. They had three sons and one daughter, including WILLIAM HOWARD TAFT, who became the twenty-seventh president of the United States and the tenth Chief Justice of the U.S. Supreme Court.

Taft played an important role in organizing his influential friends to support the national Republican effort, and he is personally credited with the birth of the REPUBLICAN PARTY in Cincinnati. He was chosen to represent Hamilton County at the first Republican National Convention, in 1856. He later sought to represent Ohio's first district in the Thirty-fifth Congress. He ran as a Republican candidate, but was defeated. He remained active in Republican party politics for most of his life.

In 1865 Taft was appointed to fill the remaining term of a Cincinnati superior court judge. Later that year, he was elected in his own right, and he served as a judge of the Superior Court of Cincinnati from 1865 to 1872.

In 1872 Taft left the bench to practice law with his grown sons. He took an active role in the establishment and organization of the Cincinnati Bar Association, and he was elected the first president of the new organization in March 1872. Taft's political, judicial, and legal activities during the late 1860s and early 1870s elevated him to national attention, so few were surprised when President Grant appointed him secretary of war in March 1876. (It was a position his son William Howard Taft would also hold thirty years later, under President THEODORE ROOSEVELT.) Only two months later, Grant named Taft to be attorney general.

Taft served as attorney general from May 1876 to January 1877. In November 1876, the government's policy of suspending pay to sailors who were jailed or removed from duty was challenged. Taft rendered an opinion finding "nothing in the law of the naval service which justifies the view that confinement or suspen-

"THE GOVERNMENT IS NEUTRAL, AND, WHILE PROTECTING ALL, IT PREFERS NONE AND DISPARAGES NONE."

BIOGRAPHY

William Howard Taft

sion from duty under sentence of court-martial is attended by forfeiture or loss of pay" (15 Op. Att'y Gen. 175, 176).

Following his term as attorney general, Taft made several unsuccessful bids for elected office. He was defeated in his run for a U.S. Senate seat in 1878. And he was defeated in two attempts at the Ohio governor's seat, in 1877 and 1879.

In April 1882, he was named U.S. ambassador to the Austro-Hungarian Empire. In 1884 Taft was offered the ambassadorship to Russia. He accepted, and served until August 1885.

At the close of his foreign service, Taft settled in California. In retirement, he devoted his time to a number of educational institutions, including Yale University, where he was a fellow of the college, and the University of Cincinnati, where he was a charter trustee. After his death on May 21, 1891, in San Diego, the University of Cincinnati's Alphonso Taft School of Law was named in his honor.

TAFT, WILLIAM HOWARD William Howard Taft is the only person to serve as both president and chief justice of the United States. A gifted judge and administrator, Taft helped modernize the way the U.S. Supreme Court conducted its business and was the driving force behind the construction of the Supreme Court Building in Washington, D.C.

Taft was born on September 15, 1857, in Cincinnati, Ohio. His father, ALPHONSO TAFT, served as secretary of war and attorney general in President ULYSSES S. GRANT's administration. Taft graduated from Yale University in 1878 and earned a law degree from Cincinnati Law College (now University of Cincinnati College of Law) in 1880. He established a law practice in Cincinnati and served as prosecutor for Hamilton County, Ohio, from 1881 to 1882. Taft was assistant county solicitor from 1885 to 1887 and a superior court judge from 1887 to 1890.

Though only thirty-three years old, Taft lobbied President BENJAMIN HARRISON for a seat on the U.S. Supreme Court in 1890. Although Harrison demurred, he did make Taft U.S. solicitor general, the person who argues on

WILLIAM HOWARD TAFT 1857–1930

1857 Born, Cincinnati, Ohio

1861–65 U.S. Civil War

1878 Graduated from Yale University

1881–82 Served as prosecutor for Hamilton County, Ohio

1887–90 Served as superior court judge for Hamilton County, Ohio

1890 Appointed U.S. solicitor general

1892–1900 Served on U.S. Court of Appeals for the Sixth Circuit

1898 Spanish-American War

1901–04 Served as first civilian governor of the Philippines

1904–08 Served as secretary of war under President Roosevelt

1909–13 Served as U.S. president

1914–18 World War I

1925 Developed the Judiciary Act of 1925, which gave the Court greater discretion over its docket

1921–30 Served as chief justice of the Supreme Court

1928–35 Design and construction of U.S. Supreme Court Building

1930 Died, Washington, D.C.

1939–45 World War II

1850   1875   1900   1925   1950

behalf of the federal government before the Supreme Court. Taft won sixteen of the eighteen cases he argued before 1892, when Harrison appointed him to the U.S. Court of Appeals for the Sixth Circuit.

The JURISDICTION of the Sixth Circuit included Chicago and other industrialized cities of the Midwest, which were the scenes of conflict between LABOR UNIONS and large manufacturing companies. Taft, like most conservative judges of his time, upheld the use of the labor INJUNCTION to prevent labor strikes and violence. The use of the injunction removed an important bargaining tool and seriously weakened labor unions. Taft, however, did believe workers had a right to organize and could legally strike, if the STRIKE was peaceful.

Taft left the court in 1900 at the request of President WILLIAM MCKINLEY. In the aftermath of the SPANISH-AMERICAN WAR (1898), the United States had taken possession of the Philippine Islands. Taft was chosen to lead a commission that would help establish a civil government in the islands and end military rule. In 1901 he became the first civilian governor of the Philippines and drew praise from the Philippine people for his administration. Taft reluctantly returned to Washington in 1904 at the request of President THEODORE ROOSEVELT to become secretary of war. As secretary, Taft supervised the construction of the Panama Canal, established the U.S. Canal Zone, and helped negotiate a treaty that ended the Russo-Japanese War in 1905.

When Roosevelt declined to run for another term in 1908, Taft was nominated as the Republican candidate. He easily defeated the Democratic candidate, WILLIAM JENNINGS BRYAN, in the general election and assumed office in 1909 as Roosevelt's political heir. Taft's administration proved to be lackluster at best, however. Though he was an able administrator, he lacked the political skills necessary to succeed in Washington. He alienated Roosevelt and other liberal Republicans by appeasing conservative Republicans, splitting the party in the process.

Taft did carry on Roosevelt's "trust-busting" initiatives, attacking business trusts under the SHERMAN ANTI-TRUST ACT (15 U.S.C.A. § 1 et seq.) and supporting the Mann-Elkins Act of 1910 (49 U.S.C.A. § 1 et seq.), which gave more power to the INTERSTATE COMMERCE COMMISSION. He also established the Department of Labor. In foreign affairs Taft adopted a policy of "dollar diplomacy" as an economic substitute for military aid to underdeveloped countries.

Taft's political downfall began in 1910 with his support of Speaker of the House of Repre-

"THE ORDINARY RESULT OF HUMAN PUNISHMENT IS THAT THOSE NEAR TO THE CRIMINAL, OR DEPENDENT UPON HIM, SUFFER IN MANY CASES MORE THAN HE DOES."

sentatives Joseph Cannon, a conservative Republican who ran the House with an iron fist. Liberals had counted on Taft to help them break Cannon's power, but he refused. When Taft approved the development of Alaskan coal resources, he drew public criticism from Gifford A. Pinchot of the Forestry Service, a promoter of conservation and Roosevelt's close ally.

In 1912 Roosevelt ran against Taft for the Republican presidential nomination. When Taft won the endorsement, Roosevelt formed the Progressive party, effectively guaranteeing that Democrat WOODROW WILSON would be elected president. Taft carried only Utah and Vermont and split the Republican vote with Roosevelt, allowing Wilson to win handily.

After leaving the presidency, Taft became a law professor at Yale University. During World War I he served on the National War Labor Board and advocated the establishment of the LEAGUE OF NATIONS and U.S. participation in that world organization.

In 1921 President WARREN G. HARDING appointed Taft chief justice of the United States. On a Court dominated by conservatives, Taft usually went along with his brethren in striking down laws that sought to regulate business and labor practices.

Taft distinguished himself more as an administrator than as a judge. He developed and lobbied for the Judiciary Act of 1925, 43 Stat. 936, which gave the Court almost complete discretion over its DOCKET. Under Taft the Court developed the writ of CERTIORARI process, whereby a party files a PETITION seeking review by the Court. Because only a small fraction of these petitions are granted, the process has dramatically reduced the work of the Court. Taft also lobbied Congress for funds to construct a separate building for the Court. Although he did not live to see its completion, the Supreme Court Building, which was designed by CASS GILBERT, proved to be a lasting monument to Taft's administrative talents.

Taft's health began to fail in 1928, and he was forced to resign from the Court in February 1930. He died on March 8, 1930, in Washington, D.C.

TAFT-HARTLEY ACT ◪ The amendments to the National Labor Relations Act, also known as the WAGNER ACT of 1935 (29 U.S.C.A. § 151 et seq.), which were enacted to counteract the advantage labor unions had gained under the original legislation by imposing corresponding duties on unions. ◪

Over President HARRY S TRUMAN's veto, the Taft-Hartley Act—which is also called the Labor-Management Relations Act (29 U.S.C.A.

SLOBODAN DIMITROV/IMPACT VISUALS

§ 141 et seq.)—was passed in 1947 to establish remedies for UNFAIR LABOR PRACTICES committed by unions. Prior to the amendments, the National Labor Relations Act had proscribed the unfair labor practices committed by management.

The principal changes imposed by the act encompass the following: prohibiting secondary BOYCOTTS; abolishing the CLOSED SHOP but allowing the UNION SHOP to exist under conditions specified in the act; exempting supervisors from coverage under the act; requiring the National Labor Relations Board (NLRB) to accord equal treatment to both independent and affiliated unions; permitting the employer to file a representation petition even though only one union seeks to represent the employees; granting employees the right not only to organize and bargain collectively but also to refrain from such activities; allowing employees to file decertification petitions for elections to determine whether employees want to revoke the designation of a union as their BARGAINING AGENT; declaring certain union activities to constitute unfair labor practices; affording to employers, employees, and unions new guarantees of the right of free speech; proscribing strikes to compel an employer to discharge an employee due to his or her union affiliation, or lack of it; and

Union employees, such as these electrical workers, may strike to bargain for improved working conditions. The Taft-Hartley Act, passed in 1947, ended certain union practices, including closed shops and secondary boycotts.

BIOGRAPHY

providing for settlement by the NLRB of certain jurisdictional disputes.

The act also makes COLLECTIVE BARGAINING AGREEMENTS enforceable in federal district court, and it provides a civil remedy for DAMAGES to private parties injured by secondary boycotts. The statute thereby marks a shift away from a federal policy encouraging unionization, which has been embodied in the Wagner Act, to a more neutral stance, which, however, maintained the right of employees to be free from employer coercion.

See also LABOR LAW; LABOR UNION.

TAIL 🕮 Limited, abridged, reduced, or curtailed. 🕮

An *estate in tail* is a legally recognizable interest of INHERITANCE that goes to the HEIRS of the donee's body instead of descending to the donee's heirs generally. The heirs of the donee's body are his or her lawful issue (children, grandchildren, great-grandchildren, and so on, in a direct line for as long as the descendants endure in a regular order and course of DESCENT). Upon the death of the first owner to die without issue, the ESTATE tail ends.

See also ENTAIL.

TAKEOVER 🕮 To assume control or management of a CORPORATION without necessarily obtaining actual TITLE to it. 🕮

A *takeover bid* or TENDER OFFER is a proposal made by one company to purchase shares of stock of another company, in order to acquire control thereof.

See also MERGERS AND ACQUISITIONS.

TALESMAN 🕮 An individual called to act as a juror from among the bystanders in a court. 🕮

A talesman refers to a person who is summoned as an additional juror to make up for a deficiency in a JURY panel.

TAMM, EDWARD ALLEN   Edward Allen Tamm served the federal bench with distinction for almost forty years, as a district and appellate court judge. For much of his life, he was a guiding force in the field of judicial ethics. His committee work for the U.S. Judicial Conference helped to set the standards for judicial conduct throughout the nation and to instill

EDWARD ALLEN TAMM 1906–1985

1969–78 Served as chairman of the Judicial Conference Ethics Review Committee

1965–85 Served on the U.S. Court of Appeals for the District of Columbia

1972–79 Served as cochairman of the Joint Committee on the Code of Judicial Conduct

1940–48 Worked as special assistant to J. Edgar Hoover

1948–65 Served on the U.S. District Court for the District of Columbia

1961–73 Vietnam War

1977 Ruled against FCC censorship in the *Seven Dirty Words* case—*Pacifica Foundation v. FCC*

1939–45 World War II

1950–53 Korean War

1906 Born, St. Paul, Minn.

1914–18 World War I

1934 Became assistant director of FBI

1978–85 Served as chairman of Judicial Ethics Committee

1985 Died, Washington, D.C.

1900   1925   1950   1975   2000

public confidence in the fair administration of justice. (The Judicial Conference is the principal machinery through which the federal court system operates. This group establishes the standards and shapes the policies governing the federal judiciary.)

Tamm was born April 21, 1906, in St. Paul, Minnesota. Shortly afterward, his family moved to Washington State. Tamm attended Mount Saint Charles College, in Helena, Montana, and the University of Montana. In 1928 he moved to Washington, D.C., and he earned his doctor of jurisprudence degree from Georgetown University Law School in 1930.

After graduating from law school, Tamm joined the Federal Bureau of Investigation (FBI). There, he advanced quickly, achieving a promotion to assistant director in 1934. From 1940 to 1948, he worked closely with Director J. EDGAR HOOVER as a special assistant and, as such, traveled around the world. In 1945, Tamm served as special adviser to the U.S. delegation to the U.N. Conference on International Organizations. During the World War II years, Tamm also served his country in the Navy Reserve, attaining the rank of lieutenant commander.

In 1948 Tamm was appointed U.S. district judge for the District of Columbia by President HARRY S TRUMAN. Because of Tamm's background with the FBI and his lack of trial experience, the appointment was met with mixed reaction. Eventually confirmed, Tamm served the district court for the next seventeen years. At the time of his appointment, the district court not only handled federal cases but also was a court of GENERAL JURISDICTION for the District of Columbia. This meant that Tamm handled local cases, including traffic and small claims issues, as well as federal issues. Therefore, Tamm had ample opportunity to develop his skills as a trial judge. He heard a wide variety of cases that normally would have been tried before state courts.

As a district judge, Tamm cultivated an interest in JUDICIAL ADMINISTRATION. He established a reputation for knowing how to move cases through the court. In the late 1950s, Tamm chaired a district courts committee to explore the use of electronic equipment for court reporting. He also pioneered the use of six-member juries for civil cases. His vision was a long time coming, but in the mid-1990s, electronic court reporting methods were widely used, and six-member jury panels for civil matters were the rule in most of the nation's FEDERAL COURTS.

"TO THE OLD ADAGE THAT DEATH AND TAXES SHARE A CERTAIN INEVITABLE CHARACTER, FEDERAL JUDGES MAY BE EXCUSED FOR ADDING ATTORNEY'S FEES CASES."

Tamm was elevated to the U.S. Court of Appeals for the District of Columbia Circuit in 1965, by President LYNDON B. JOHNSON. Tamm's work on the trial bench deeply influenced his opinion writing as an APPELLATE judge. His opinions were usually short and to the point; they were written to provide trial courts with a clear guide to the proper application of the law—and not to impress the reader with the judge's literary skill.

The case for which Tamm is best known is often called the *Seven Dirty Words* case—*Pacifica Foundation v. FCC*, 556 F.2d 9, 181 U.S. App. D.C. 132 (D.C. Cir. Mar. 16, 1977). In it, Tamm set aside a FEDERAL COMMUNICATIONS COMMISSION (FCC) ruling that a recording containing seven specific words (referring to such things as sexual acts and portions of human anatomy) could not be aired on the radio. He wrote that the FCC order banning air play of the explicit excerpts from George Carlin's *Occupation Foole* album carried the agency into the "forbidden realm of censorship." Tamm's decision was ultimately overturned by the U.S. Supreme Court, in a 5–4 ruling concluding that neither the FIRST AMENDMENT guarantee of free speech nor federal law against broadcast CENSORSHIP barred the FCC from revoking the license of any station that aired explicit material during the daytime or early evening hours (*Pacifica Foundation*, 438 U.S. 726, 98 S. Ct. 3026, 57 L. Ed. 2d 1073 [1978]).

As an appellate judge, Tamm continued his commitment to improving the administration of justice and increased his participation on Judicial Conference committees. During these years, Tamm also took up the cause of monitoring judicial ethics. He served as chairman of the Judicial Conference Ethics Review Committee (1969–78), chairman of the Judicial Ethics Committee (1978–85), member of the Judicial Conference Committee on Court Administration (1970–85), cochairman of the Joint Committee on the Code of Judicial Conduct (1972–79), and member of the Advisory Committee on Federal Rules of Appellate Procedure (1979–85). As chairman of the committee responsible for administering both self-imposed Judicial Conference ethical standards and, later, congressionally mandated financial reporting, Tamm personally examined or reviewed the thousands of financial statements submitted by federal judges and employees each year.

Tamm died on September 22, 1985, at his home in Washington, D.C. He was survived by his wife of fifty years, Grace Monica Sullivan Tamm.

In the spring of 1986, Tamm was posthumously awarded the Devitt Distinguished Service to Justice Award, which is administered by the American Judicature Society. This award is named for Edward J. Devitt, a former chief U.S. district judge for Minnesota. It acknowledges the dedication and contributions to justice made by all federal judges, by recognizing the specific achievements of one judge who has contributed significantly to the profession. Tamm was acknowledged for administrative innovations that improved the performance of the courts and for his work in promoting and monitoring judicial ethics.

See also JUDICIAL CONFERENCE OF THE UNITED STATES.

TAMMANY HALL Political machines have traditionally wielded influence in U.S. society, and one of the most notorious was Tammany Hall in New York. Controlled by the DEMOCRATIC PARTY, the power of Tammany Hall grew to such an extent that its members dominated New York government for nearly two centuries.

Founded by William Mooney in 1789, Tammany Hall was originally a fraternal and patriotic organization first called the Society of St. Tammany, or the Columbian Order. The name *Tammany* evolved from Tamanend, a legendary Delaware Indian chief, and the members of Tammany Hall used many Indian words to designate their various titles. Each trustee was a sachem, and the presiding officer was a grand sachem; the only person to receive the honor of great grand sachem was a president of the United States. The member who served as secretary was known as a scribe, and the building that housed the Tammany meetings was called a wigwam.

The members of Tammany Hall had a corrupt stronghold on New York City politics from the early 1800s until the 1930s.

CORBIS-BETTMANN

From these innocent beginnings, Tammany Hall grew into a political force. Affiliates of the organization actively participated in politics in the early nineteenth century. In 1812 the association moved into the first Tammany Hall with a membership of approximately fifteen hundred members. By 1821 the association was receiving widespread support in New York City. Unfortunately Tammany Hall was also gaining a reputation for corruption, control, and subterfuge.

In 1854 Tammany Hall member Fernando Wood was elected mayor of New York City. From then until 1933, City Hall was dominated almost exclusively by Tammany Hall.

The most corrupt and infamous member of Tammany Hall was William Marcy Tweed, called "Boss" Tweed. He served as a state senator in 1868 and, with his followers, known as the Tweed Ring, dominated state government and defrauded New York City of millions of dollars.

The corruption continued under subsequent Tammany Hall leaders, such as "Honest John" Kelly, Richard F. Croker, and Charles F. Murphy. By 1930, however, Samuel Seabury had begun to direct revealing inquiries against the city magistrates' courts. These investigations led to the downfall of Tammany Hall and the resignation of incumbent mayor James J. Walker in 1932. Fiorello LaGuardia was elected mayor in 1933, and an anti-Tammany Hall era began. The once-powerful Tammany Hall machine was resurrected briefly in the 1950s by politician Carmine DeSapio but never regained the stronghold in New York politics that it once enjoyed.

TAMPER 📖 To meddle, alter, or improperly interfere with something; to make changes or corrupt, as in tampering with the EVIDENCE. 📖

TANEY, ROGER BROOKE Roger Brooke Taney served as chief justice of the U.S. Supreme Court from 1836 to 1864. During his almost thirty years on the bench, Taney sought to encourage economic growth and competition by rendering decisions that reshaped the traditional law concerning PROPERTY RIGHTS and commerce. Although he served with great distinction on the Court, he is best known as the author of the infamous decision in Dred Scott's case, *Dred Scott v. Sandford*, 60 U.S. (19 How.) 393, 15 L. Ed. 691 (1857). This decision fueled sectional hostility and moved the nation closer to civil war.

Taney was born on March 17, 1777, in Calvert County, Maryland. A descendant of an aristocratic tobacco-growing family, Taney graduated from Dickinson College in 1795, studied law, and was admitted to the Maryland bar in 1799. That same year he was elected to a

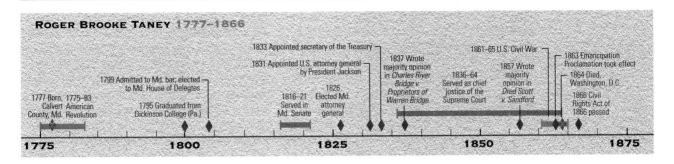

ROGER BROOKE TANEY 1777–1866

1833 Appointed secretary of the Treasury

1831 Appointed U.S. attorney general by President Jackson

1837 Wrote majority opinion in *Charles River Bridge v. Proprietors of Warren Bridge*

1861–65 U.S. Civil War

1863 Emancipation Proclamation took effect

1799 Admitted to Md. bar; elected to Md. House of Delegtes.

1826 Elected Md. attorney general

1836–64 Served as chief justice of the Supreme Court

1857 Wrote majority opinion in *Dred Scott v. Sandford*

1864 Died, Washington, D.C.

1777 Born, 1775–83 Calvert American County, Md. Revolution

1795 Graduated from Dickinson College (Pa.)

1816–21 Served in Md. Senate

1866 Civil Rights Act of 1866 passed

1775   1800   1825   1850   1875

one-year term in the Maryland House of Delegates. Taney practiced briefly in Annapolis before settling in Frederick, where he soon was recognized as a distinguished attorney.

Taney was elected to the Maryland Senate in 1816 as a member of the Federalist party. Despite the party's belief in a strong national government, Taney endorsed STATES' RIGHTS. By the time he left the Senate in 1821, the Federalist party was on the verge of extinction. Taney switched his allegiance to the Democratic party and soon became an influential figure in the Maryland state party leadership. He was elected Maryland attorney general in 1826 and served until 1831.

President ANDREW JACKSON appointed Taney U.S. attorney general in 1831. Taney supported the president's opposition to rechartering the Second BANK OF THE UNITED STATES and helped him write the VETO message. Jackson and the Democrats saw the bank as a dangerous institution that would enhance the power of the national government. Having vetoed the rechartering, in 1833 Jackson ordered Secretary of the Treasury William J. Duane to withdraw the deposits of the federal government from the bank, but Duane resigned instead. Jackson then appointed Taney secretary of the treasury so that he could carry out the order. Confirmation of Taney's appointment as treasury secretary was frustrated by members of the Whig party in the U.S. Senate, but by that time Taney had succeeded in distributing the federal funds among several state banks.

Taney returned to private practice, but President Jackson wanted him on the U.S. Supreme Court. In 1835 he nominated Taney as an associate justice, but the Senate, still disgruntled about the bank deposit issue, refused to confirm the appointment. The composition of the Senate soon changed, however, and upon the death of JOHN MARSHALL in 1836, Taney was nominated and confirmed as chief justice.

In his first major opinion as chief justice, in the case of *Charles River Bridge v. Proprietors of Warren Bridge*, 36 U.S. (11 Pet.) 420, 9 L. Ed. 773 (1837), Taney wrote for the majority of a

BIOGRAPHY

Roger Brooke Taney

divided Court. Taney decided that a FRANCHISE to operate a toll bridge that had been granted by the state of Massachusetts in the late eighteenth century, in the absence of explicit provisions, could not be construed as granting a MONOPOLY to the toll bridge operator. Therefore, when the Massachusetts state legislature later granted another franchise to operate a competing toll bridge nearby, the legislature did not violate Article I, Section 10, of the U.S. Constitution, which forbids states from impairing the obligation of CONTRACTS. The opinion demonstrated Taney's belief that economic development could best be promoted and the public good most expeditiously furthered by fostering competition.

Until *Dred Scott* Taney had demonstrated a reluctance to make the Supreme Court the arbiter of national political issues. By the mid-1850s, however, the national debate over SLAVERY had almost reached the boiling point. Taney believed a decision by the Court would have a tempering effect on the country. He was clearly wrong.

Dred Scott was a slave owned by an army surgeon, John Emerson, who resided in Missouri. In 1836 Emerson took Scott to Fort Snelling, in what is now Minnesota, but was then a territory in which slavery had been expressly forbidden by the MISSOURI COMPROMISE of 1820. In 1846 Scott sued for his freedom in a Missouri state court, arguing that his residence in a free territory released him from slavery. The Missouri Supreme Court rejected his argument, and Scott appealed to the U.S. Supreme Court.

The Court heard arguments in *Dred Scott* in 1855 and 1856. The Court could have properly disposed of the case on narrow procedural grounds, but Taney decided that the Court needed to address the status of slavery in the territories. He wrote a tortuous opinion, arguing that because of the prevailing attitudes toward slavery and African Americans in 1787–1789, when the Constitution was drafted and ratified, a slave was not and never could become a federal citizen. In addition, Taney ruled that the free descendants of slaves were not federal CITIZENS and that property in slaves was entitled to such protection that Congress could not constitutionally forbid slavery in the territories.

The immediate effect of the *Dred Scott* decision was to convince abolitionists that the South and the Supreme Court planned to impose slavery throughout the Union. Taney was attacked as a former slave owner (though he had freed his slaves, whom he had inherited) and was called wicked, cowardly, and hypocritical. With the outbreak of the Civil War in 1861, it became clear that Taney's decision had failed to achieve its essential purpose.

Taney remained loyal to the Union during the Civil War, yet his effectiveness and that of the Court had been seriously compromised by *Dred Scott.* Taney sought to protect constitutional rights during the Civil War, ruling that even in wartime the EXECUTIVE BRANCH and the military had no power to suspend constitutional protections (*Ex Parte Merryman*, 17 Fed. Cas. 144 [1861]). Though Taney saw the Court as a restraining influence on the exercise of arbitrary power by other branches of government, his efforts were ineffective. The Radical Republican–controlled Congress and President ABRAHAM LINCOLN ignored the pronouncements of the Court. From Lincoln's EMANCIPATION PROCLAMATION and the CIVIL RIGHTS ACT OF 1866 (14 Stat. 27) through the passage of the Thirteenth, Fourteenth, and Fifteenth Amendments to the Constitution, the Republicans repeatedly repudiated *Dred Scott.* Nevertheless, Taney continued to hold the office of chief justice until his death on October 12, 1864, in Washington, D.C.

CROSS-REFERENCES
Charles River Bridge v. Warren Bridge; Dred Scott v. Sandford.

TANGIBLE 📖 Possessing a physical form that can be touched or felt. 📖

Tangible refers to that which can be seen, weighed, measured, or apprehended by the senses. A tangible object is something that is real and substantial. An automobile is an example of tangible PERSONAL PROPERTY.

TARIFF 📖 The list of items upon which a duty is imposed when they are imported into the United States, together with the rates at which such articles are taxed. 📖

The term *tariff* is also used in reference to the actual custom or duty payable on such items.

See also CUSTOMS DUTIES; IMPORT QUOTAS.

TAXABLE INCOME 📖 Under the federal tax law, GROSS INCOME reduced by adjustments and allowable DEDUCTIONS. It is the income

against which tax rates are applied to compute an individual or entity's tax liability. The essence of taxable income is the accrual of some gain, profit, or benefit to a taxpayer. 📖

See also INCOME TAX.

TAXABLE SITUS 📖 The location where charges may be levied upon PERSONAL PROPERTY by a government, pursuant to provisions of its tax laws. 📖

The situs of property for tax purposes is determined on the basis of whether the state imposing the tax has adequate contact with the property it is seeking to tax so that the particular tax is justified in fairness. Ordinarily personal property has its taxable situs in the place where its owner is domiciled or in the state where the owner has a true, fixed, and permanent home.

TAXATION 📖 The process whereby charges are imposed on individuals or property by the legislative branch of the federal government and by many state governments to raise funds for public purposes. 📖

The theory that underlies taxation is that charges are imposed to support the government in exchange for the general advantages and protection afforded by the government to the taxpayer and his or her property. The existence of government is a necessity that cannot continue without financial means to pay its expenses; therefore, the government has the right to compel all citizens and property within its limits to share its costs. The state and federal governments both have the power to impose taxes upon their citizens.

Kinds of Taxes The two basic kinds of taxes are *excise taxes* and *property taxes.*

Excise Tax An excise tax is directly imposed by the law-making body of a government on merchandise, products, or certain types of transactions, including carrying on a profession or business, obtaining a LICENSE, or transferring property. It is a fixed and absolute charge that does not depend upon the taxpayer's financial status or the value that the taxed property has to the taxpayer.

An estate tax is a tax that is placed on, and paid by, the ESTATE of a DECEDENT prior to the distribution of the property among the HEIRS in exchange for the privilege of transferring the property. Individuals who inherit property may be required to pay an inheritance tax on the value of the particular property received. Gift taxes are incurred by an individual who gives another a valuable gift.

Another type of excise tax is a SALES TAX, which is placed on certain goods and services. Precisely what goods and services are taxed is

> "WE MUST LOOK AT THE INSTITUTION OF SLAVERY AS PUBLICISTS, AND NOT AS CASUISTS. IT IS A QUESTION OF LAW, AND NOT A CASE OF CONSCIENCE."

Federal, State and Local Tax Revenues

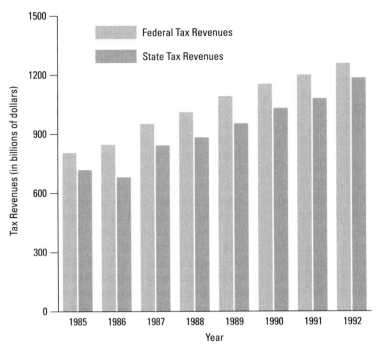

Source: U.S. Bureau of the Census, Government Finances, series No. 5, annual.

determined by the individual state legislatures. In some instances, a sales tax placed upon expensive items that are considered luxuries is known as a *luxury tax*.

A *corporate tax* is an excise tax imposed upon the privilege of conducting business in the corporate capacity, which provides certain advantages to individuals, such as limited liability. It is measured by the income of the CORPORATION involved.

Other common examples of excise taxes are those imposed upon the processing of meat, tobacco, cheese, and sugar.

Property Tax A property tax takes the taxpayer's wealth into account, as represented by the taxpayer's income or the property he or she owns. INCOME TAX, for example, is a property tax that is assessed and levied upon the taxpayer's income; *property taxes* are imposed mainly on REAL PROPERTY.

Direct and Indirect Taxes Taxes are also classified as direct and indirect. A DIRECT TAX is one that is assessed upon the property, business, or income of the individual who is to pay the tax. Conversely *indirect taxes* are taxes that are levied upon commodities before they reach the consumer who ultimately pay the taxes as part of the market price of the commodity. A common example of an indirect tax is a *value-added tax*, which is paid on the value added to the product at each stage of production, distribution, and sales.

Federal Tax The Constitution and laws passed by Congress have given the U.S. government authorization to collect various taxes. For example, duties are taxes imposed upon imports and can be either AD VALOREM (a percentage of the value of the property) or specific (a fixed amount). An IMPOST is another name for an import tax. Congress may not, however, tax exports.

The SIXTEENTH AMENDMENT to the Constitution gives Congress the power to impose a federal income tax. Congress has also enacted laws that allow the federal government to tax estates remaining after people die and gifts made while people are alive.

State Tax States possess the inherent power to levy both property and excise taxes. The TENTH AMENDMENT to the Constitution, which reserves to the states powers that have neither been granted to the United States nor proscribed to the states by the Constitution, implicitly acknowledges this fundamental right. A state may raise funds by taxation in aid of its own welfare, provided the tax does not constitute unjust discrimination among those who are to share the tax burden. Property taxes, for example, may properly be imposed on landowners within the JURISDICTION. In addition, the state may levy income, gift, estate, and inheritance taxes upon its residents.

Equality Equality is a fundamental principle of taxation. The taxing power of the legislature must always be exercised in such a way that the burdens imposed by taxation are laid as equally as possible on all classes. The PROGRESSIVE TAX, which imposes a higher rate of taxation upon individuals with large incomes than on those with small incomes, is an attempt to achieve this objective.

Equality in taxation is achieved when no higher rate in proportion to value is imposed on one individual or his or her property than on other people or property in similar circumstances. Equality does not mandate that the benefits that arise from taxation should be enjoyed by all the people in equal degree or that each individual should share in each particular benefit. For example, the fact that a husband and wife have no children or choose to send their children to private school does not signify that they are permitted to stop paying their share of school tax.

Uniformity The principle of uniformity of taxation bears a close relation to the concept of equality because similar items are taxed equally only if the mode of ASSESSMENT is the same or uniform.

A tax that is levied upon property must be in proportion or according to its value, ordinarily determined as its fair cash or FAIR MARKET VALUE. This requirement protects equality and uniformity of taxation by preventing arbitrary or inconsistent methods of determining how much tax is due. This requirement applies only to property taxes, not to excise taxes.

CROSS-REFERENCES

Customs Duties; Estate and Gift Taxes; Internal Revenue Service; Taxpayer Bill of Rights; Tax Rate.

TAX AVOIDANCE 📖 The process whereby an individual plans his or her finances so as to apply all exemptions and deductions provided by tax laws to reduce TAXABLE INCOME. 📖

Through tax avoidance, an individual takes advantage of all legal opportunities to minimize his or her state or federal INCOME TAX, gift tax, or estate tax. An individual may, for example, avoid federal income tax by investing a large sum of money in municipal BONDS, since the interest on such bonds is not considered taxable income on which federal tax is due. Interest on the same amount of money placed in a savings account must be included as taxable income.

Tax avoidance must be distinguished from TAX EVASION, which is the employment of unlawful methods to circumvent the payment of taxes. Tax evasion is a crime; tax avoidance is not.

TAX COURT 📖 A specialized federal or state court that decides cases involving tax-related controversies. 📖

All state governments and the federal government provide a means of adjudicating cases dealing with TAXATION. Tax courts deal solely with tax disputes, which may involve the valuation of REAL PROPERTY, the amount of tax the state or federal revenue agency seeks to collect, or the tax status of a pension plan or a charitable organization.

The U.S. Tax Court is organized under Article I of the U.S. Constitution (26 U.S.C.A. § 7441). Currently an independent judicial body in the legislative branch, the court was originally created as the U.S. Board of Tax Appeals, an independent agency in the executive branch, by the Revenue Act of 1924 (43 Stat. 336) and continued by the Revenue Act of 1926 (44 Stat. 105) and the INTERNAL REVENUE CODES of 1939, 1954, and 1986. The court's name was changed to the Tax Court of the United States by the Revenue Act of 1942 (56 Stat. 957), and the Article I status and change in name to U.S. Tax Court were effected by the Tax Reform Act of 1969 (83 Stat. 730).

The court is composed of nineteen judges. Its strength is augmented by senior judges who may be recalled by the chief judge to perform further judicial duties and by fourteen special trial judges who are appointed by the chief judge and serve at the pleasure of the court. The chief judge is elected biennially from among the nineteen judges of the court.

The Tax Court tries and adjudicates controversies involving deficiencies or overpayments in income, estate, gift, and generation-skipping transfer taxes in cases where deficiencies have been determined by the commissioner of Internal Revenue. It also hears cases started by transferees and fiduciaries who have been issued notices of liability by the commissioner.

The Tax Court has JURISDICTION to redetermine excise taxes and penalties imposed on private foundations. It also has jurisdiction over excise taxes with regard to public CHARITIES, qualified PENSION plans, and real estate investment trusts.

At the option of the individual taxpayer, simplified procedures may be used for the trial of small tax cases. In a case conducted under these procedures, the decision of the court is final and is not subject to review by any court. The jurisdictional maximum for such cases is $10,000 for any disputed year.

In disputes relating to public inspection of written determinations by the INTERNAL REVENUE SERVICE (IRS), the Tax Court has jurisdiction to restrain disclosure or to obtain additional disclosure of written determinations or background files.

The Tax Court also has jurisdiction to make DECLARATORY JUDGMENTS relating to the qualification of retirement plans, including pension, profit sharing, STOCK bonus, ANNUITY, and BOND purchase plans; the tax-exempt status of a charitable organization, qualified charitable donee, private foundation, or private operating foundation; and the status of interest on certain government obligations. Under the Technical and Miscellaneous Revenue Act of 1988 (102 Stat. 3342), the Tax Court also has injunctive authority over certain assessment procedures, authority to review certain assessments and levies, and authority to hear and decide appeals by taxpayers concerning the denial of administrative costs by the IRS.

All decisions, other than those in small tax cases, are subject to review by the U.S. courts of appeals and thereafter by the U.S. Supreme Court upon the granting of a writ of CERTIORARI.

The office of the court and all of its judges are located in Washington, D.C., with the exception of a field office located in Los Angeles, California. The court conducts trial sessions at various locations in the United States as convenient to taxpayers as is practicable. Each trial session is conducted by a single judge or a special trial judge. All proceedings are public and are conducted judicially in accordance with the court's rules of practice and the rules of EVIDENCE applicable in trials without a jury in the U.S. District Court for the District of Columbia. A fee of $60 is required for filing a PETITION. Practice before the court is limited to practitioners admitted under the court's rules.

State tax courts are generally part of the EXECUTIVE BRANCH of government. These courts handle cases from taxpayers that are primarily concerned with the valuation of real and personal property.

TAX DEED 📖 A written instrument that provides proof of ownership of REAL PROPERTY purchased from the government at a TAX SALE, conducted after the property has been taken from its owner by the government and sold for delinquent taxes. 📖

TAX EVASION 📖 The process whereby a person, through commission of FRAUD, unlawfully pays less tax than the law mandates. 📖

Tax evasion is a criminal offense under federal and state statutes. A person who is convicted is subject to a prison sentence, a fine, or both. The failure to file a federal TAX RETURN is a MISDEMEANOR, but a consistent pattern of failure to file for several years will constitute EVIDENCE that these failures were part of a scheme to avoid the payment of taxes. If this pattern is established, the violator may be charged with a FELONY under section 7201 of the Internal Revenue Code.

The U.S. Supreme Court, in *Spies v. United States*, 317 U.S. 492, 63 S. Ct. 364, 87 L. Ed. 418 (1943), ruled that an OVERT act is necessary to give rise to the crime of income tax evasion. Therefore, the government must show that the taxpayer attempted to evade the tax rather than passively neglected to file a return, which could be prosecuted under section 7203 as a misdemeanor. A person who has evaded taxes over the course of several years may be charged with multiple counts for each year taxes were allegedly evaded.

According to the Supreme Court in *Sansone v. United States*, 380 U.S. 343, 85 S. Ct. 1004, 13 L. Ed. 2d 882 (1965), a conviction under section 7201 requires proof BEYOND A REASONABLE DOUBT as to each of three elements: the existence of a tax deficiency, willfulness in an attempted evasion of tax, and an affirmative act constituting an evasion or attempted evasion of the tax.

An affirmative act is anything done to mislead the government or conceal funds to avoid payment of an admitted and accurate deficiency. Affirmative behavior can take two forms: the evasion of assessment and the evasion of payment. Affirmative acts of evasion include evading taxes by placing ASSETS in another's name, dealing in cash, and having receipts or DEBTS paid through and in the name of another person. Merely failing to pay assessed tax, without more, does not constitute tax evasion.

The keeping of a double set of books or the making of false invoices or documents can be proof of tax evasion. In some cases the mailing of a false return may constitute the overt act required under section 7201.

See also TAXATION; TAX AVOIDANCE.

TAXING COSTS 📖 The designation given to the process of determining and charging to the losing party in a legal ACTION the expenses involved in initiating or defending the action, to which the successful side is lawfully entitled. 📖

See also COSTS.

TAXPAYER BILL OF RIGHTS 📖 A federal or state law that gives taxpayers procedural and substantive protection when dealing with a revenue department concerning a tax collection dispute. 📖

Perceived abuses by the federal INTERNAL REVENUE SERVICE (IRS) during tax AUDITS led to the enactment of the "Omnibus Taxpayer Bill of Rights" in 1988 (Pub. L. No. 100-647). A second set of provisions was enacted in 1996 (Pub. L. No. 104-168) to give taxpayers increased leverage in dealings with the IRS. The 1988 act also spurred many states to enact similar taxpayer bill of rights laws.

Although the rights given to taxpayers under these federal acts do not reduce the chance of being audited or diminish IRS authority to penalize taxpayers for inaccuracies or cheating on their returns, the provisions correct many of the perceived abuses in IRS auditing and collection procedures. The bill of rights seeks to relieve taxpayers from the unfettered discretion of IRS agents. Congress stated that the aim of the 1988 act was "to inject reason and protection for individual rights into the tax collection process."

The bill of rights requires the IRS to explain the audit and collection process to the taxpayer before any initial audit or collection interviews and to include on all tax notices a description of the basis for taxes, interest, or penalties due. The bill also requires the IRS to inform taxpayers of their rights, including the right to be represented by an attorney or tax accountant, whenever an audit notice is sent. The bill allows the taxpayer to make an audio recording of the interview with the IRS agent, provided prior notice is given. An actual audit interview can be stopped, without prejudice, so that the taxpayer

Taxpayers enjoy certain rights in their dealings with government tax collectors. In 1997 Carol Ward received $325,000 in damages for wrongful behavior by IRS officials in a 1993 audit of the clothing store for which Ward was the bookkeeper.

can consult with an attorney or accountant. Another key provision prohibits the IRS from imposing quotas or goals on agents with respect to the number of returns they audit and the amount of taxes and fines collected.

The 1988 act created the Office of Taxpayer Ombudsman, which served as the primary advocate for taxpayers within the IRS. The 1996 act shifted this role to the newly established Office of the Taxpayer Advocate. This office helps taxpayers resolve problems with the IRS, identifies areas in which taxpayers have problems in dealings with the IRS, proposes changes in the administrative practices of the IRS, and suggests potential legislative changes that may reduce these problems. To ensure independence from the IRS, the Taxpayer Advocate reports directly to Congress twice a year.

The Taxpayer Advocate also has broad authority to issue Taxpayer Assistance Orders. These orders can release property or require the IRS to cease any action, or refrain from taking any action, that will cause significant hardship as a result of the administration of the internal revenue laws.

Under the bill of rights, before the IRS can put a LIEN on or seize taxpayer property, it must give the taxpayer thirty days' notice instead of the previous ten days' notice. Taxpayers are permitted to sue the IRS for DAMAGES suffered as a result of tax or property collection actions or refusals to release a lien; they can be awarded court costs and legal and administrative fees if they win an administrative or court action against the IRS.

Under the bill of rights, the IRS is authorized to make INSTALLMENT agreements with taxpayers to alleviate the burden on a taxpayer who would experience financial hardship if forced to make a lump-sum payment. The IRS

must give thirty days' notice before altering, modifying, or terminating a previously agreed upon installment agreement, unless the change is caused by a determination that the collection of tax is in jeopardy.

Another provision of the law states that if the IRS believes additional taxes are owed, the agency must send the taxpayer a written notice that explains and identifies all amounts due. The IRS must also describe the procedures that it will use to collect any amounts due. Previously, the IRS generally explained the basis for a tax deficiency but was not required to explain penalties or how they would be collected. Instead, the IRS simply sued the taxpayer.

The bill of rights gives the IRS authority to abate interest for delays or unreasonable errors caused by nondiscretionary procedural acts of the IRS or by IRS managerial acts such as loss of records by the IRS or transfers, extended illnesses, leave, or professional training of IRS personnel.

See also INCOME TAX; TAXATION.

TAXPAYER'S SUIT An action brought by an individual whose income is subjected to charges imposed by the state or federal government, for the benefit of that individual and others in order to prevent the unlawful diversion of public funds.

For example, because every taxpayer of a TOWN has an interest in the preservation of an orderly government, many state laws grant individual taxpayers the right to sue town officers, boards, or commissions to recover money that has been wrongfully spent.

TAX RATE The amount of charges imposed by the government upon personal or corporate income, capital gains, gifts, estates, and sales that are within its statutory authority to regulate.

Tax rate schedules are utilized by taxpayers whose TAXABLE INCOMES exceed certain designated amounts. Separate schedules are provided for married individuals who file jointly, unmarried people who maintain a household, single people, estates, trusts, and married couples who file separate returns.

See also INCOME TAX; TAXATION.

TAX REFORM ACT OF 1986 The Tax Reform Act of 1986 (100 Stat. 2085, 26 U.S.C.A. §§ 47, 1042) made major changes in how income was taxed. The act either altered or eliminated many deductions, changed the tax rates, and eliminated several special calculations that had been permitted on the basis of marriage or fluctuating income. Though the act was the most massive overhaul of the tax system in decades, some of its key provisions were

changed in the Revenue Reconciliation Act of 1993 (107 Stat. 416).

The 1986 act reduced the number of INCOME TAX rates to two rates of 15 percent and 28 percent for most taxpayers, although a third rate of 33 percent was imposed on income within a certain upper-middle income bracket. Congress and the administration of President RONALD REAGAN believed a policy of low rates on a broad tax base would stimulate the economy and end an era of complex tax laws and regulations that mainly benefited those who knew how to manipulate the system.

The 1986 act also sought to eliminate special incentives that made tax shelters attractive and the tax law more complicated. Income derived from REAL ESTATE became distinguishable on the basis of whether it was "active" or "passive." Passive income is income derived from a situation in which the taxpayer does not have an active management role, but it does not include capital gains on STOCKS, interest income on BONDS, or interest on money market accounts. Before 1986 wealthy individuals could use passive income losses from a real estate tax shelter to offset active income. The 1986 act limited the deduction of passive losses to the amount of passive income but allowed taxpayers to carry forward any excess passive losses to the next year.

The act also eliminated the deductibility of nonmortgage consumer interest payments such as interest on credit card balances, automobile loans, and life insurance loans. It also established the floor for miscellaneous expenses at two percent of ADJUSTED GROSS INCOME for taxpayers who itemized DEDUCTIONS.

INDIVIDUAL RETIREMENT ACCOUNTS (IRAs) once allowed a taxpayer to invest before-tax dollars and enjoy tax-free compounding of in-

Calling the bill a victory for fairness, President Ronald Reagan signed the 1986 tax reform act into law on the south lawn of the White House.

terest. The 1986 statute ended full deductibility of IRAs for single employees covered by qualified retirement plans and earning more than $35,000 annually. For married employees the cutoff for full deductibility was set at $50,000. In addition, the law imposed a penalty on withdrawals of IRA contributions before the age of fifty-nine and a half years.

Another retirement plan, the KEOGH PLAN, permitted under section 401(k), once allowed a taxpayer to invest up to $30,000 a year without paying taxes on this income. The ceiling dropped to $7,000 in 1987.

The act also eliminated a provision that had enabled two-income married couples to reduce their taxes. A couple can no longer take a deduction based on the lower salary of the two; the deduction had allowed them to pay the same tax on the lower salary as a single person would pay on that amount. The act also abolished "income averaging." Formerly, individuals whose incomes varied considerably from year to year could average their income over several years, a calculation that resulted in lower taxes owed in the years of highest income.

The ballooning FEDERAL BUDGET deficits of the late 1980s and early 1990s led Congress to make changes in the 1986 act. The 1993 Revenue Reconciliation Act revamped the rate structure, imposing rates of 15, 28, 31, 36, and 39.6 percent. The act also limited itemized deductions for upper-income taxpayers and removed the limit on earned income subject to MEDICARE tax. The 1993 act also established tax incentives for selected groups and reduced the amount that can be deducted for moving expenses and meals and entertainment.

See also TAXATION.

TAX RETURN ◻ The form that the government requires a taxpayer to file with the appropriate official by a designated date to disclose and detail income subject to TAXATION and eligibility for DEDUCTIONS and exemptions, along with a remittance of the tax due or a claim for a refund of taxes that were overpaid. ◻

The federal and state governments specify the deadlines for filing tax returns without incurring any additional interest or penalties for lateness. For most income taxpayers, the deadline of April 15 of the year following the close of the tax year for which the report is filed applies to both federal and many state returns. For persons who have made taxable gifts, the federal gift tax return is due annually on or before April 15 of the year following the tax year (as opposed to the former requirement of quarterly filing). For executors or administrators of estates that owe estate tax, a federal estate tax return must be filed within nine months of the date of death of the decedent. States may have comparable deadlines for gift and estate tax returns.

See also ESTATE AND GIFT TAXES; INCOME TAX.

TAX SALE 📖 A transfer of REAL PROPERTY in exchange for money to satisfy charges imposed thereupon by the government that have remained unpaid after the legal period for their payment has expired. 📖

Tax sales are authorized by state statutes to collect taxes that are long overdue to the state government from negligent or unwilling individuals.

Requirements Any sale of real property for delinquent taxes must be conducted in compliance with legally imposed requirements, or it is not valid. Ordinarily the tax collector is required to make and publish a list of property on which taxes have not been paid. Such a list must contain an adequate description of each parcel of land to be sold, the owner's name, the amount due, and the period of time for which the taxes are due. The interest permitted by law on the delinquent taxes, penalties for DEFAULT in payment, and the costs incurred for the sale may be included in the amount due. Certain states mandate that this delinquency list must be filed or recorded in the office of the county clerk, and statutes may indicate specifically the newspapers in which the list is to be published.

Notice The purpose of a notice of a tax sale is to warn the owner of the property that it will be sold and to furnish information to prospective buyers. Failure to provide notice to the owner renders any subsequent sale of the property invalid. This rule is consistent with DUE PROCESS requirements that any individual must be given notice and opportunity to defend himself or herself before being deprived of his or her property. The notice given to the owner must adequately describe the property, the amount of tax owed, and for what years it is due.

Manner State statutes regulate the manner in which tax sales may be conducted. Ordinarily the sale is open to the public in order to ascertain that a fair price for the property will be obtained in the open market. A private sale is valid, however, when authorized by statute.

Price The general rule is that land offered at a tax sale must bring at least the total amount of taxes due on it, plus legal COSTS and charges. In some JURISDICTIONS, a sale for a smaller amount is invalid.

In the event that the land is sold at the tax sale for a price that exceeds the amount owed, the sale might be valid, depending upon the state; however, the excess must be given to the delinquent taxpayer.

Buyer Any individual who is not disqualified by statute may purchase land at a tax sale provided he or she is the highest bidder. Upon payment of the amount bid, the buyer will be given a TAX DEED that serves as proof of his or her ownership of the property. Certain states mandate that a tax sale be confirmed in a court proceeding before the purchaser actually takes TITLE or ownership to the property.

A state, county, municipal corporation, or other governmental unit may buy land sold at a tax sale only if authorized by statute.

Redemption The owner of property that is the subject of a tax sale is given a statutory right of REDEMPTION—that is, if, within a certain period, the owner pays the back taxes plus any other legal charges due, he or she will regain complete ownership of the property free of the prior tax debt. The PUBLIC POLICY behind such a statute is to provide the taxpayer with every reasonable opportunity to redeem property since FORFEITURE of land has always been regarded as a drastic remedy. Generally any individual interested in the property sold for taxes is entitled to redeem it if his or her interest in the property will be affected by the purchaser taking complete ownership of the land, such as in the case of an individual who has a LIFE ESTATE in the property.

Redemption must occur within the time and in the manner specified by the statute.

Sale Prohibited Courts can proscribe a tax sale in cases where (1) a sale would be unlawful, so that the buyer's ownership of the land would be open to question; (2) the taxes have been paid; (3) the LEVY or ASSESSMENT was unlawful or fraudulent; or (4) the valuation was grossly excessive.

The government has the power to seize and sell property to pay delinquent taxes, as was done with this property in Massachusetts.

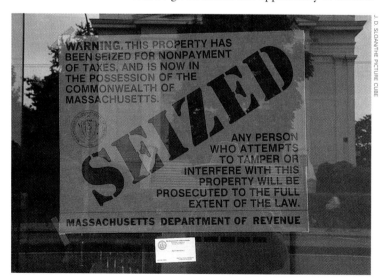

J. D. SLOAN/THE PICTURE CUBE

WARNING: THIS PROPERTY HAS BEEN SEIZED FOR NONPAYMENT OF TAXES, AND IS NOW IN THE POSSESSION OF THE COMMONWEALTH OF MASSACHUSETTS.

SEIZED

ANY PERSON WHO ATTEMPTS TO TAMPER OR INTERFERE WITH THIS PROPERTY WILL BE PROSECUTED TO THE FULL EXTENT OF THE LAW.

MASSACHUSETTS DEPARTMENT OF REVENUE

Where errors or irregularities exist in the assessment that could have been rectified if promptly brought to the attention of the proper authorities, the tax sale will not be enjoined if such errors have no effect upon the substantial justice of the tax or the liability of the property for its satisfaction.

TAYLOR, ZACHARY Zachary Taylor served as the twelfth president of the United States from 1849 until his death in 1850. A famous military general, Taylor was an apolitical leader who accomplished little during his sixteen months in office.

Taylor was born on November 24, 1784, in Orange County, Virginia, but moved as a child to Kentucky. He enlisted in the U.S. Army in 1808 and was commissioned as a first lieutenant in the infantry that same year. Taylor quickly emerged as a military hero during the War of 1812 while serving under General WILLIAM HENRY HARRISON. He distinguished himself during the Black Hawk War in 1832 and the Second Seminole War in Florida between 1835 and 1842. He was promoted to brigadier general in 1837 after his victory at the Battle of Lake Okeechobee.

In 1845, soon after the annexation of Texas, President JAMES K. POLK ordered Taylor and an army of four thousand men to the Rio Grande. Border hostilities with Mexico over the boundary between the two countries escalated into full battles in May of 1845. Taylor's troops defeated an invading Mexican army at the Battles of Palo Alto and Resaca de la Palma. That same month the United States declared war on Mexico.

Taylor and his army invaded Mexico and advanced to Monterrey, capturing the city in late September. His military career was put in doubt, however, when a letter became public in which Taylor criticized President Polk and his secretary of war, William L. Marcy. An angry Polk could not relieve the popular war hero of his command, but he stripped Taylor of his best troops and ordered him to adopt a defensive posture. Taylor, who was nicknamed "Old Rough and Ready," disobeyed Polk's orders and

BIOGRAPHY

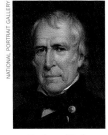

Zachary Taylor

"LET US INVOKE A CONTINUANCE OF THE SAME PROTECTING CARE WHICH HAS LED US FROM SMALL BEGINNINGS TO THE EMINENCE WE THIS DAY OCCUPY . . . WHICH SHALL ACKNOWLEDGE NO LIMITS BUT THOSE OF OUR OWN WIDE-SPREAD REPUBLIC."

defeated a Mexican army that outnumbered his troops by four to one at the Battle of Buena Vista in February 1847. This stunning victory guaranteed Taylor the status of national hero.

The Whig party nominated Taylor as its presidential candidate in 1848, even though Taylor had no interest in politics (he had never voted in an election) and was a slave owner. Taylor defeated the Democratic candidate, Lewis Cass, in the November general election.

Taylor's brief service as president was unremarkable. Having no political background, Taylor was unprepared for the give-and-take of Washington politics. The biggest issue facing him was statehood for California and New Mexico, which had been acquired from Mexico as a result of the war. Although he owned slaves, Taylor was opposed to the expansion of SLAVERY into the new territories, a position that alienated Southern Whigs and Democrats in Congress. When California voted to prohibit slavery, the South opposed its admission to the Union. Attempts by Senator HENRY CLAY of Kentucky to negotiate a compromise were rebuffed by Taylor.

As this political conflict unfolded in the summer of 1850, Taylor contracted cholera. He died on July 9, 1850, in Washington, D.C.

Taylor was succeeded by Vice President MILLARD FILLMORE, who quickly agreed to resolve the Mexican territories issue with the COMPROMISE OF 1850. This act admitted California into the Union as a free state, gave the territories of Utah and New Mexico the right to determine the slavery issue for themselves at the time of their admission to the Union, outlawed the slave trade in the District of Columbia, and gave the federal government the right to return fugitive slaves in the FUGITIVE SLAVE ACT (9 Stat. 462).

TEAPOT DOME The presidential administration of WARREN G. HARDING from 1921 to 1923 was characterized by scandal and corruption, the most controversial of which was the Teapot Dome oil scandal.

Conservation was a popular cause throughout the first quarter of the twentieth century and was encouraged by various presidents. As a

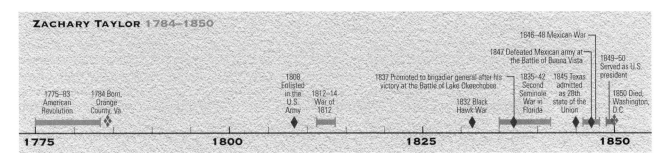

ZACHARY TAYLOR 1784–1850

1775–83 American Revolution

1784 Born, Orange County, Va.

1808 Enlisted in the U.S. Army

1812–14 War of 1812

1832 Black Hawk War

1835–42 Second Seminole War in Florida

1837 Promoted to brigadier general after his victory at the Battle of Lake Okeechobee

1845 Texas admitted as 28th state of the Union

1846–48 Mexican War

1847 Defeated Mexican army at the Battle of Buena Vista

1849–50 Served as U.S. president

1850 Died, Washington, D.C.

1775   1800   1825   1850

result, several oil reserves for the exclusive use of the U.S. Navy were established in Wyoming and California. The oil was kept in storage places called domes, one of which, located near Casper, Wyoming, was christened Teapot Dome due to a rock formation in the area that resembled a teapot.

Although many politicians favored the establishment of the oil reserves, others believed they were superfluous. One opponent of the oil policy was Senator Albert B. Fall of New Mexico, who sought to make the reserves accessible to private industry.

In 1921, Senator Fall was selected as secretary of the interior in the Harding cabinet. Authority over the oil fields was transferred from the Department of the Navy to the Department of the Interior, with the consent of Edwin Denby, Secretary of the Navy. Fall was in a position to lease the oil reserves, without public bidding, to private parties. In 1922, Harry F. Sinclair, president of the Mammoth Oil Company, received rights to Teapot Dome, and Edward L. Doheny, a friend of Fall and prominent in the Pan-American Petroleum and Transport Company, leased the Elk Hills fields in California. Fall received approximately four hundred thousand dollars in kickbacks in exchange for his favoritism.

Senator Thomas J. Walsh of Montana initiated a Senate investigation of the oil reserve lands at the recommendation of Senator ROBERT M. LaFOLLETTE of Wisconsin. Eventually the U.S. Supreme Court declared the leases inoperative, and the oil fields at Teapot Dome and Elk Hills were returned to the U.S. government. Sinclair served nine months in prison for contempt of court, but both he and Doheny were found not guilty of BRIBERY. Fall, who had left the cabinet in 1923, was found guilty in 1929 of accepting bribes; his penalty was one year in jail and a fine of $100,000. President Harding died in office in 1923, never aware of the notoriety of his administration.

TELECOMMUNICATIONS 📖 The transmission of words, sounds, images, or data in the form of electronic or electromagnetic signals or impulses. 📖

From the introduction of the telegraph in the United States in the 1840s to the present-day Internet computer network, telecommunication has been a central part of American culture and society. With each new telecommunication technology, more and higher-quality types of information have been transmitted into and out of businesses, government, and homes. Telephone, radio, broadcast television, cable television, satellite television, facsimile (fax machines), cellular telephones, and computer networks have become integral parts of modern life. Federal and state governments have regulated the pricing of telecommunication systems and the content of transmitted material. However, the federal Telecommunications Act of 1996 (Pub. L. No. 104-104) deregulated much of the telecommunication business, allowing competition in markets previously reserved for government-regulated monopolies.

Telegraph The first telegraph system in the United States was completed in 1844. Originally used as a way of managing railroad traffic, the telegraph soon became an essential means of transmitting news around the United States. The Associated Press was formed in 1848 to pool telegraph expenses, and other "wire services" soon followed.

Many telegraph companies were formed in the early years of the business, but by 1856 Western Union Telegraph Company had become the first dominant national telegraph system. In 1861 it completed the first transcontinental line, connecting San Francisco first to the Midwest and then on to the East Coast. As worldwide interest increased in applications of the telegraph, the International Telegraph Union was formed in 1865 to establish standards for use in international communication. In 1866 the first transatlantic cables were completed.

The telegraph era came to an end after World War II, with the advent of high-speed transmission technologies that did not use telegraph and telephone wires. By 1988 Western Union was reorganized to handle money transfers and related services.

Telephone Systems The invention of the telephone in the late nineteenth century led to the creation of the American Telephone and Telegraph Company (AT&T). The company owned virtually all telephones, equipment, and long-distance and local wires for personal and business service in the national telephone system. Smaller companies seeking a part of the long-distance telephone market challenged AT&T's MONOPOLY in the 1970s.

In 1982 the U.S. Department of Justice allowed AT&T to settle a lawsuit alleging antitrust violations because of its monopolistic holdings. AT&T agreed to divest itself of its local operating companies by January 1, 1984, while retaining control of its long-distance, research, and manufacturing activities. Seven regional telephone companies (known as the Baby Bells) were given responsibility for local telephone service. Other companies now compete with AT&T to provide long-distance service to telephone customers.

However, the Telecommunications Act of 1996, in an effort to spur competition, allowed the seven regional phone companies to compete in the long-distance telephone market. The act also permitted AT&T and other long-distance carriers, as well as cable companies, to sell local telephone service.

Local telephone rates are regulated by state commissions, which also work to see that the regional telephone companies provide good maintenance and services. In addition, the use of a telephone for an unlawful purpose is a crime under state and federal laws, as is the WIRETAPPING of telephone conversations.

Radio In the early twentieth century, radio was regarded primarily as a device to make maritime operations safer and a potential advancement of military technology. However, during World War I entrepreneurs began to recognize the commercial possibilities of radio. By the mid-1920s, commercial radio stations were operating in many parts of the United States, as owners began selling air time for advertisements. The Federal Radio Commission was created in 1927 to assign applicants designated frequencies under specific engineering rules and to create and enforce standards for the broadcasters' privilege of using the public's airwaves.

The commission later became the FEDERAL COMMUNICATIONS COMMISSION (FCC), which was established by the Communications Act of 1934 (47 U.S.C.A. § 151 et seq.). The FCC issues LICENSES to radio and television stations, which permit the stations to use specific frequencies to transmit programming. Licenses are issued only on a showing that public convenience, interest, and necessity will be served and that an applicant satisfies certain requirements, such as citizenship, good character, financial capability, and technical expertise.

Before 1996 the FCC restricted persons or entities from acquiring excessive power through ownership of a number of radio and television facilities. The rule was based on the assumption that if one person or company owned most or all of the media outlets in an area, the diversity of information and programming on these stations would be restricted.

The Telecommunications Act of 1996 eliminated the limit on the number of radio stations that one entity may own nationally. The FCC was also directed to reduce the restrictions on locally owned radio stations. Congress determined that less regulation was in the PUBLIC INTEREST.

The FCC has sought to prohibit the broadcast of OBSCENE and indecent material. The Supreme Court has upheld regulations banning obscene material, because OBSCENITY is not protected by the FIRST AMENDMENT. It has also permitted the FCC to prohibit material that is "patently offensive," and either "sexual" or "excretory," from being broadcast during times when children are presumed to be in the audience (*FCC v. Pacifica Foundation*, 438 U.S. 726, 98 S. Ct. 3026, 57 L. Ed. 2d 1073 [1978]).

Television The commercial exploitation of TELEVISION did not begin in the United States until the late 1940s. The FCC followed its example from radio and established licensing procedures for stations seeking permission to transmit television signals. It became the oversight body for the U.S. television industry.

The FCC has applied to television a prohibition similar to that imposed on radio against the broadcast of obscene and indecent material. For purposes of parental control, the Telecommunications Act of 1996 also mandated the establishment of an advisory committee to rate video programming that contains indecent material. The act also stated that by 1998 new television sets had to be equipped with a so-called V-chip to allow parents to block programs with a predesignated rating for sex and violence.

CABLE TELEVISION became a viable commercial form of telecommunication in the 1980s. Both the FCC and local governments had an interest in regulating cable systems, with municipalities awarding a cable system FRANCHISE to one vendor. Cable operators negotiated system requirements and pricing with local governments, but federal law imposed some restrictions on rates to consumers. Concerns about rate regulation led Congress to enact the Cable Television Consumer Protection and Competition Act of 1992 (Pub. L. No. 102-385). The act gave the

Microsoft chief Bill Gates communicates with a group of journalists via telecommunications satellite.

THE GAMMA LIAISON NETWORK

FCC greater control of the cable television industry and set rate structures to control the price of cable subscriptions. However, the Telecommunications Act of 1996 reversed the 1992 act by ending all rate regulation. The act also allowed the seven regional telephone companies to compete in the cable television market to end the monopoly that cable systems had enjoyed under the previous regulatory scheme.

The transmission of television signals by satellite has been a practical solution for customers who cannot obtain cable television because they live in remote or rural areas. Since their introduction in the 1990s, direct broadcast satellite systems have competed with cable television systems, offering higher-quality video and audio signals.

Transmission of Digital Data   In the 1980s and 1990s, the use of digital data transmission revolutionized the communication of words, images, sounds, and data. Computer-driven means of telecommunication have made possible electronic mail (E-MAIL), the sharing of computer files, and, most importantly, the Internet.

The INTERNET is a network of computers linking the United States with the rest of the world. Originally developed as a way for U.S. research scientists to communicate with each other, by the mid-1990s the Internet had become a popular form of telecommunication for personal computer users. Written text represents a significant portion of the Net's content, in the form of both E-mail and articles posted to electronic discussion forums known as Usenet news groups. In the mid-1990s, the appearance of the World Wide Web made the Internet even more popular. The Web is a multimedia interface that allows for the transmission of what are known as Web pages, which resemble pages in a magazine. In addition to combining text and pictures or graphics, the multimedia interface makes it possible to add audio and video components. Together these various elements have made the Internet a medium for communication and for the retrieval of information on virtually any topic.

The federal government has sought to regulate this form of telecommunication. Congress passed the Electronic Communications Privacy Act of 1986 (ECPA) (18 U.S.C.A. § 2701 et seq. [1994]), also known as the Wiretap Act, which made it illegal to read private E-mail. The ECPA extended to electronic mail most of the protection already granted to conventional mail. However, this protection has not been extended to all E-mail that is transmitted in the workplace.

A controversial issue in the workplace is whether an employer should be able to monitor the E-mail messages of its employees. An employer has a strong legal and financial motive to prohibit unauthorized and inappropriate use of its E-mail system. Under the Wiretap Act, a company is not restricted in its ability to review messages stored on its own internal E-mail system. In addition, interception of electronic communications is permitted when it is done in the ordinary course of business or to protect the employer's rights or property. This exception would apply when, for example, an employer has reasons to suspect that an employee is using the E-mail system to disclose information to a competitor or to send harassing messages to a coworker. Finally, the prohibitions of the Wiretap Act do not apply if the employee whose messages are monitored has explicitly or implicitly consented to such monitoring.

Congress sought to curb the transmission of indecent content on the Internet and other computer network telecommunications systems by enacting the Communications Decency Act (CDA) (47 U.S.C.A. § 223(a)–(h)) as part of the Telecommunications Act of 1996. The CDA made it a federal crime to use telecommunications to transmit "any comment, request, suggestion, proposal, image, or other communication which is obscene or indecent, knowing that the recipient of the communication is under 18 years of age, regardless of whether the maker of such communication placed the call or initiated the communication." It includes penalties for violations of up to five years imprisonment and fines of up to $250,000.

In *Reno v. American Civil Liberties Union,* ___ U.S. ___, 117 S. Ct. 2329, 138 L. Ed. 2d 874 (1997), the Supreme Court struck down the "indecent" provision as a violation of the First Amendment right of free speech.

Standards in Telecommunication   Certain telecommunication methods have become standards in the telecommunication industry because devices with different standards cannot communicate with each other. Standards are developed either through the widespread use of a particular method or by a standard-setting organization. The International Telecommunication Union, a United Nations agency, which sits in Geneva, Switzerland, and one of its operational bodies, the International Telegraph and Telephone Consultative Committee, play a key role in standardizing telecommunication methods. For example, the committee's standards for the fax machine that were adopted in the 1980s facilitated the dramatic increase in use of this form of telecommunication.

CROSS-REFERENCES

Broadcasting; Electronic Surveillance; Employment Law; Entertainment Law; Fairness Doctrine; Privacy; Pornography.

TELEVISION Television is the most powerful medium of mass communication seen regularly by most persons in the United States. Television signals may be delivered by using antennas (broadcast), communication satellites, or cable systems. Because of television's societal impact, the federal government regulates companies that operate television systems.

Experimental television systems were developed in the 1930s, but commercial exploitation did not occur in the United States until the late 1940s. Initially, television signals were broadcast from antennas and received by a television set in a person's home or business. Improved technology led to the replacement of black-and-white images with color signals in the 1960s.

The FEDERAL COMMUNICATIONS COMMISSION (FCC), which was established by the Communications Act of 1934 (47 U.S.C.A. § 151 et seq.), originally was charged with the regulation of radio. With the introduction of television and the need for television stations to obtain FCC licenses to use broadcast frequencies, the FCC assumed sole JURISDICTION over the television industry.

Television broadcasts may be regulated for content. Typically, this regulation has focused on broadcasts of allegedly OBSCENE or indecent material. The U.S. Supreme Court has upheld regulations banning obscene material, as OBSCENITY is not protected by the FIRST AMENDMENT to the U.S. Constitution. It has also permitted the FCC to prohibit material that is "patently offensive" and either "sexual" or "excretory" from being broadcast during times when children are presumed to be in the audience (*FCC v. Pacifica Foundation*, 438 U.S. 726, 98 S. Ct. 3026, 57 L. Ed. 2d 1073 [1978]).

The Telecommunications Act of 1996 (Pub. L. No. 104-104) mandates the establishment of an advisory committee for the rating of video programming that contains indecent materials for purposes of parental control. The act also requires that by 1998 all manufactured televisions with screens thirteen inches or larger must be equipped with a so-called V chip to allow parents to block programs having a predesignated rating for sex and violence.

Individualized live interactive television is a service offered by ACTV Inc., whose president, David W. Reese, demonstrated the product at a cable TV convention in Texas.

CABLE TELEVISION has grown tremendously since the 1980s. Cable television originally served communities in mountainous regions that had difficulty receiving broadcast transmissions. Many communities solved this problem by erecting tall receiving towers to capture broadcast signals and retransmit them over wires running from the tower to homes that subscribed to this service.

During the 1970s and 1980s, large corporations installed cable systems in every large metropolitan area in the United States, as well as in many rural areas. Independent programming was transmitted on cable systems by companies such as Home Box Office (HBO) and Cable News Network (CNN).

Although cable television could not be categorized as broadcasting in the traditional sense, the FCC adopted the first general federal regulation of cable systems. Local government also became involved, as each municipality had to award a cable system FRANCHISE to one vendor. Cable operators negotiated system requirements and pricing with local governments, but federal law imposed some restrictions on rates to consumers.

The Telecommunications Act of 1996 deregulated cable television rates, in part because of increased interest by telephone companies in entering the cable market by sending programming through existing phone lines. The act permits phone companies to provide video programming directly to subscribers in their service areas.

The transmission of television signals by satellite has been a practical solution for customers who cannot obtain cable television programming because they live in remote or rural areas. In the 1990s direct broadcast satellite

(DBS) systems began to compete with cable television systems. The DBS systems offer higher-quality video and audio signals.

The development of digital high-definition television (HDTV) was the broadcast television industry's top priority in the 1990s. HDTV, which has a significantly finer picture resolution than an ordinary television screen, requires additional broadcast frequencies, which the FCC must license to broadcasters. Broadcast television, which saw its viewership steadily drop as cable and DBS became popular, sees HDTV as a way to reclaim its market share.

CROSS-REFERENCES

Broadcasting; Fairness Doctrine; Mass Communications Law; Telecommunications.

TEMPERANCE MOVEMENT 📖 A movement in the United States to moderate or eliminate the consumption of alcoholic beverages. 📖

The temperance movement in the United States first became a national crusade in the early nineteenth century. An initial source of the movement was a groundswell of popular religion that focused on abstention from ALCOHOL. Evangelical preachers of various Christian denominations denounced drinking alcohol as a sin. People who drank, they claimed, lost their faith in God and ceased to observe the teachings of Christ.

Other supporters of the first temperance movement objected to alcohol's destructive effects on individuals, communities, and the nation as a whole. According to these activists, the consumption of alcohol was responsible for many personal and societal problems, including unemployment, absenteeism in the workplace, and physical violence. Scores of short stories and books published in the mid-nineteenth century described in dramatic detail the abuse suffered by the families of alcoholics. Alcoholics were characterized as dangerous to themselves, their families, and even their nation's security. In the words of temperance advocate Lyman Beecher, a drunk electorate would "dig the grave of our liberties and entomb our glory."

The temperance movement was marked by an undercurrent of ethnic and religious hostility. Some of the first advocates were people of Anglo-Saxon heritage who associated alcohol with the growing number of Catholic immigrants from Ireland and the European continent. Supposedly, the Catholics were loud and boisterous as a result of too much drinking.

Most of the first temperance advocates were sincerely concerned for the welfare of others, however, and were not motivated by such faulty perceptions. The public's rate of alcohol consumption was, in fact, increasing steadily during the nineteenth century, and the reformers saw the banishment of alcohol not as a punishment but as necessary to an orderly, safe, and prosperous society. Despite its good intentions, the first movement splintered. The largest rift occurred between a minority of abolitionists, who favored the promotion of total abstinence from alcohol, and the majority of reformers, who favored only abstinence from hard liquor.

Although it lacked cohesion, the first temperance movement yielded some legislative reforms. In 1846 Maine became the first state to enact a law prohibiting liquor consumption. Twelve other states followed suit, but the laws were difficult to enforce, and public support for the laws quickly waned. By 1868 Maine was the only state left with a liquor prohibition law, and the temperance movement appeared to have come and gone.

Groups such as the Women's Christian Temperance Union (WCTU) and the Anti-Saloon League were at the forefront of the onslaught on alcohol. Members of these groups spoke publicly in favor of PROHIBITION and lobbied elected officials for laws banning the consumption of alcohol. Some of the more active members disrupted business at saloons and liquor stores. One of the most visible prohibitionists, Carry Nation, used a hatchet to smash liquor bottles and break furniture in saloons.

In the 1870s some prohibitionists began to form political parties and nominate candidates for public office. Leaders in the so-called Progressive movement were instrumental in the resurgence of the temperance movement. The Progressives called for sweeping governmental controls in response to perceived social crises, and they began to promote the abolition of alcohol as part of a plan to clean up cities and eliminate poverty. By the time World War I began in 1914, an increasing number of politicians were advocating a ban on alcohol, and the conservation efforts for the war gave the temperance movement additional momentum.

Congress enacted the Lever Act of 1917 (40 Stat. 276) to outlaw the use of grain in the manufacture of alcoholic beverages, and many state and local governments passed laws prohibiting the distribution and consumption of alcohol. Two years later, the states ratified the EIGHTEENTH AMENDMENT to the U.S. Constitution, which prohibited the manufacture, transportation, and sale of alcoholic beverages in the United States. The complete ban on alcohol was put into effect by the VOLSTEAD ACT (41 Stat. 305). President WOODROW WILSON vetoed the act, but Congress overrode the VETO and the United States became officially dry in January 1920.

The effect of Prohibition was to drive drinking underground. Saloons were replaced by speakeasies, hidden drinking places that, in some areas, were tolerated by local police. The more enterprising individuals set up homemade stills to produce alcohol for their own consumption. Others turned to bootlegging, or the illegal sale of alcohol. Prices on the black market were markedly higher than they had been prior to Prohibition, and gangsters used violence to acquire and maintain control over the highly profitable bootlegging business. Bootlegging was so profitable because so many people wanted to drink alcohol. Federal, state, and local law enforcement officials found themselves at war not only with gangsters, but with the general public as well.

Popular support for Prohibition quickly waned after the Eighteenth Amendment was passed, but it took thirteen years to end it. HERBERT HOOVER, who served as president from 1929 to 1933, supported Prohibition, calling it "an experiment noble in purpose." Hoover was defeated in his bid for reelection, however, and in 1933 President FRANKLIN D. ROOSEVELT called for an amendment to the Volstead Act that would legalize light wine and beer consumption. The bill passed quickly and received widespread public support, and Congress set about the task of repealing Prohibition. On December 5, 1933, the TWENTY-FIRST AMENDMENT to the U.S. Constitution was ratified, and the "noble experiment" was dismantled.

See also CAPONE, ALPHONSE; ORGANIZED CRIME.

TEMPORARY RESTRAINING ORDER

📖 A court ORDER that lasts only until the court can hear further EVIDENCE. 📖

A temporary restraining order (TRO) is a court order of limited duration. A TRO commands the parties in the case to maintain a certain status until the court can hear further evidence and decide whether to issue a PRELIMINARY INJUNCTION.

Under federal and state rules of CIVIL PROCEDURE, a person may obtain a TRO by visiting a judge or MAGISTRATE without NOTICE to, or the presence of, the adverse party. A TRO may be issued by a court only if (1) it appears from specific facts shown in a signed, sworn AFFIDAVIT or COMPLAINT that immediate IRREPARABLE INJURY, loss, or damage will result to the applicant before the adverse party or the adverse party's attorney can be heard in opposition; and (2) the applicant's attorney describes to the court in writing the efforts, if any, that have been made to give notice to the adverse party and gives reasons to support the claim that notice should not be required.

Temporary restraining orders are extraordinary measures because they are court orders issued against a party without notice to that party and without giving the party an opportunity to argue against the order. A TRO usually lasts only two or three days, until the court can hear both sides of the issue and decide whether to issue a preliminary injunction. A court generally hears arguments on the preliminary injunction as soon as possible after the TRO is issued. On the federal level, rule 65 of the Federal Rules of Civil Procedure mandates that a TRO should not last longer than ten days, and that a TRO may be renewed only for an additional ten days. State courts have similar provisions in their rules of civil procedure.

The immediate potential for irreparable harm is the GRAVAMEN of the TRO. If an applicant is unable to prove that the harm suffered will be irreparable or that the irreparable harm is IMMINENT, a court will not approve a TRO. Assume that a person purchases a car with financing from the dealership. The buyer then becomes embroiled in a dispute with the dealership over the car and stops making payments; the dealership responds by threatening to repossess the car. If the buyer applies for a TRO preventing the dealership from taking the car, a court would likely refuse the request, because the loss of the car is not imminent. Moreover, the loss of a car is not an irreparable injury; a court would likely expect the buyer to carry on with other modes of transportation.

Now assume that the purchased vehicle is a large utility van that the buyer has customized to use in her catering business. The loss of the van for a few days would be disastrous to the business and could eventually lead to BANKRUPTCY, so the buyer would likely be able to obtain a TRO, provided the harm was sufficiently imminent.

The adverse party cannot APPEAL the issuance of a TRO to a higher court. The best remedy for an adverse party is to obtain a court HEARING as soon as possible on the issuance of a preliminary injunction. Preliminary injunctions may be appealed to higher courts.

TROs are commonly issued in situations involving STALKING and harassment or damage to property. Other common TRO situations include UNFAIR COMPETITION and TRADEMARK, COPYRIGHT, or PATENT infringement, all of which involve potentially irreparable damage to a party's economic livelihood.

TENANCY

📖 A situation that arises when one individual conveys REAL PROPERTY to another individual by way of a LEASE. The relation of an individual to the land he or she holds that designates the extent of that person's ESTATE in real property. ▥

A *tenancy* is the occupancy or possession of land or premises by lease. The occupant, known as the TENANT, must acquire control and possession of the property for the duration of the lawful occupancy. A tenancy can be created by any words that indicate the owner's intent to convey a property interest on another individual.

See also LANDLORD AND TENANT.

TENANCY BY THE ENTIRETY ▥ A type

of CONCURRENT ESTATE in REAL PROPERTY held by a HUSBAND AND WIFE whereby each owns the undivided whole of the property, coupled with the RIGHT OF SURVIVORSHIP, so that upon the death of one, the survivor is entitled to the decedent's share. ▥

A tenancy by the entirety allows spouses to own property together as a single legal entity. Under a tenancy by the entirety, CREDITORS of an individual spouse may not attach and sell the interest of a DEBTOR spouse: only creditors of the couple may attach and sell the interest in the property owned by tenancy by the entirety.

There are three types of concurrent ownership, or ownership of property by two or more persons: tenancy by the entirety, JOINT TENANCY, and TENANCY IN COMMON. A tenancy by the entirety can be created only by married persons. A married couple may choose to create a joint tenancy or a tenancy in common. In most states a married couple is presumed to take TITLE to property as tenants by the entirety, unless the DEED or conveyancing document states otherwise.

The most important difference between a tenancy by the entirety and a joint tenancy or tenancy in common is that a tenant by the entirety may not sell or give away his interest in the property without the consent of the other tenant. Upon the death of one of the spouses, the deceased spouse's interest in the property devolves to the surviving spouse, and not to other HEIRS of the deceased spouse. This is called the right of survivorship.

Tenants in common do not have a right of survivorship. In a tenancy in common, persons may sell or give away their ownership interest. Joint tenants do have a right of survivorship, but a joint tenant may sell or give away her interest in the property. If a joint tenant sells her interest in a joint tenancy, the tenancy becomes a tenancy in common, and no tenant has a right of survivorship. A tenancy by the entirety cannot be reduced to a joint tenancy or

tenancy in common by a CONVEYANCE of property. Generally, the couple must DIVORCE, obtain an ANNULMENT, or agree to amend the title to the property to extinguish a tenancy by the entirety.

TENANCY IN COMMON ▥ A form of con-

current ownership of REAL PROPERTY in which two or more persons possess the property simultaneously; it can be created by DEED, WILL, or OPERATION OF LAW. ▥

Tenancy in common is a specific type of concurrent, or simultaneous, ownership of real property by two or more parties. Generally, concurrent ownership can take three forms: JOINT TENANCY, TENANCY BY THE ENTIRETY, and tenancy in common. These forms of concurrent ownership give individuals a choice in the way that co-ownership of property will be carried out. Each type of tenancy is distinguishable from the others by the rights of the co-owners.

Usually, the term *tenant* is understood to describe a person who rents or leases a piece of property. In the context of CONCURRENT ESTATES, however, a TENANT is a co-owner of real property.

All tenants in common hold an individual, undivided ownership interest in the property. This means that each party has the right to ALIENATE, or transfer the ownership of, her ownership interest. This can be done by deed, will, or other CONVEYANCE. In a tenancy by the entirety (a concurrent estate between married persons), neither tenant has the right of alienation without the consent of the other. When a tenant by the entirety dies, the surviving spouse receives the deceased spouse's interest, thus acquiring full ownership of the property. This is called a RIGHT OF SURVIVORSHIP. Joint tenants also have a right of survivorship. A joint tenant may alienate his property, but if that occurs, the tenancy is changed to a tenancy in common and no tenant has a right of survivorship.

Another difference between tenants in common and joint tenants or tenants by the entirety is that tenants in common may hold unequal interests. By contrast, joint tenants and tenants by the entirety own equal shares of the property. Furthermore, tenants in common may acquire their interests from different instruments: joint tenants and tenants by the entirety must obtain their interests at the same time and in the same document.

TENANCY IN COPARCENARY ▥ A type

of CONCURRENT ESTATE in REAL PROPERTY by which property rights were acquired only through INTESTACY by the female HEIRS when there were no surviving male heirs. ▥

This type of estate, which has only historical value today, occurred when an ancestor left no son who could take property by PRIMOGENITURE.

TENANT 📖 An individual who occupies or possesses land or premises by way of a grant of an ESTATE of some type, such as in fee, for life, for years, or at will. A person who has the right to temporary use and possession of particular REAL PROPERTY, which has been conveyed to that person by a LANDLORD. 📖

See also LANDLORD AND TENANT.

TENDER 📖 An offer of money; the act by which one individual offers someone who is holding a claim or demand against him or her the amount of money that the offeror regards and admits is due, in order to satisfy the claim or demand, in the absence of any contingency or stipulation attached to the offer. 📖

The two essential characteristics of tender are an unconditional offer to perform, together with manifested ability to do so, and the production of the subject matter of tender. The term is generally used in reference to an offer to pay money; however, it may properly be used in reference to an offer of other kinds of property.

See also TENDER OFFER.

TENDER OFFER 📖 A proposal to buy shares of stock from the stockholders of a CORPORATION, made by a group or company that desires to obtain control of the corporation. 📖

A tender offer to purchase may be for cash or some type of corporate security of the acquiring company—for example, stock, warrants, or DEBENTURES. Such an offer is sometimes subject to either a minimum or maximum that the offeror will accept and is communicated to the stockholders through newspaper advertisements or a general mailing to the complete list of stockholders. Tender offers are subject to regulations by state and federal securities laws, such as the WILLIAMS ACT (15 U.S.C.A. § 78a et seq.).

See also MERGERS AND ACQUISITIONS; STOCK WARRANT.

TENDER YEARS DOCTRINE 📖 A doctrine rarely employed in CHILD CUSTODY disputes that provides that, when all other factors are equal, custody of a child of tender years—generally under the age of thirteen years—should be awarded to the mother. 📖

The tender years doctrine is a judicial PRESUMPTION that operates in DIVORCE cases to give custody of a young child to the mother. Most states have eliminated this presumption, and some courts have held that the tender years doctrine violates the EQUAL PROTECTION Clause of the FOURTEENTH AMENDMENT to the U.S. Constitution because it discriminates on the basis of sex.

Early English COMMON LAW originally gave custody of the children of divorcing parents to the father. Women had few individual rights until the nineteenth century; most of their rights were derived through their fathers and husbands. Under these conditions women had no right to raise their children after a divorce.

In the early nineteenth century, Mrs. Caroline Norton, a prominent London hostess, author, and journalist, began to campaign for the right of women to have custody of their children. Norton, who had undergone a divorce and been deprived of her children, was able to convince the British Parliament to enact legislation to protect mothers' rights. The result was the Custody of Infants Act of 1839, which gave some discretion to the judge in a child custody case and established a presumption of maternal custody for children under the age of seven years. In 1873 Parliament extended the presumption of maternal custody until a child reached sixteen years of age. Courts made exceptions in cases in which the father established that the mother had committed ADULTERY.

Many courts and legislatures in the United States adopted the tender years presumption. To grant custody of a child to a father was "to hold nature in contempt, and snatch helpless, puling infancy from the bosom of an affectionate mother, and place it in the coarse hands of the father." The mother was "the softest and safest nurse of infancy" (*Ex parte Devine*, 398 So. 2d 686 [Ala. 1981], quoting *Helms v. Franciscus*, 2 Bland Ch. [Md.] 544 [1830]).

The tender years presumption in child custody cases persisted for more than one hundred years, with the majority of states recognizing the presumption. In the latter half of the twentieth century, courts and legislatures began to reverse decisions and repeal laws that recognized the tender years presumption in favor of gender-neutral considerations. In most states the best interests of the child are now the primary consideration in child custody cases, and the primary caretaker is presumed to be the best parent to handle primary custody of a small child. Some state courts have gone so far as to hold that the tender years doctrine violates the Equal Protection Clause of the state constitution. (See, e.g., *King v. Vancil*, 34 Ill. App. 3d 831, 341 N.E.2d 65 [Ill. 1975].)

A small number of states still recognize the tender years presumption, but only in certain cases. In *Pennington v. Pennington*, 711 P.2d 254 (Utah 1985), the Supreme Court of Utah stated that it had "long expressed a preference for placing very young children in the mother's custody." The court noted, however, that "the preference operates only when all other things are equal." The *Pennington* court held that the best interests of the child were to be given primary consideration, and it went on to affirm the award of child custody to the father in the case.

In other areas of the law, the term *tender years* may refer to a law that creates special rules for small children. For example, some states enact special laws governing HEARSAY evidence in child sex abuse cases. These tender years laws create exceptions to evidentiary rules by allowing the introduction of hearsay statements and video-taped TESTIMONY of children under a certain age.

CROSS-REFERENCES

Child Abuse; Children's Rights; Family Law; Sexual Abuse.

TENEMENT 📖 A comprehensive legal term

for any type of PROPERTY of a permanent nature—including land, houses, and other buildings as well as rights attaching thereto, such as the right to collect rent. 📖

In the law of easements, a dominant tenement or ESTATE is that for which the advantage or benefit of an EASEMENT exists; a servient tenement or estate is a tenement that is subject to the burden of an easement.

The term *tenement* is also used in reference to a building with rooms or apartments that are leased for residential purposes. It is frequently defined by statute, and its meaning therefore varies from one JURISDICTION to another.

TENNESSEE VALLEY AUTHORITY   In

1933, U.S. President FRANKLIN DELANO ROOSEVELT approved the passage of the TENNESSEE VALLEY AUTHORITY ACT (16 U.S.C.A. § 831 et seq.). The act provided for a source of hydroelectric power, control of a troublesome flood situation, revitalization of forest areas, and navigation and economic benefits for the region. These goals, announced during a devastating nationwide depression, made the Tennessee Valley Authority (TVA) an ambitious project of the era.

The idea for the project was originally developed in 1918, when two nitrate facilities and a dam were constructed at Muscle Shoals, Alabama, on the Tennessee River. Previously the area had been prone to severe floods, and water travel was impeded by sandbanks. The area had abundant natural resources, but the surrounding basin was depleted, and the region had experienced a depressed economy even before the hard times suffered throughout the nation in the Depression of the 1930s.

Politicians and developers of the project envisioned a growth of industry and water power in the Tennessee Valley, as well as the manufacture of low-priced fertilizer and public control of the valuable resources. Debates over whether the project area should be rented to private parties or be controlled by the government continued throughout the 1920s. Senator GEORGE W. NORRIS of Nebraska was instrumental in the passage of measures by Congress advocating government control, but these bills did not receive presidential approval until 1933, when Roosevelt based his Tennessee Valley plan on the Norris proposals.

Roosevelt's Tennessee Valley Act authorized the establishment of a corporation owned by the federal government and directed by Arthur

The Norris Dam, near Norris, Tennessee, was one of the first major projects of the Tennessee Valley Authority.

CULVER PICTURES

E. Morgan, the chairman, and Harcourt A. Morgan, and David Lilienthal. The early years of TVA were fraught with adversity, particularly when its constitutionality was questioned. Disputes between the directors and an investigation conducted by Congress hampered its initial achievements, but the TVA continued its work despite these difficulties.

The TVA succeeded in its projected goals. Since the development of its dams and reservoirs, the region has not been subjected to serious floods. The electrical system developed by the TVA afforded the region power at a low cost, and throughout the decades, power development has been extended to include coal and nuclear systems. The TVA also benefited agrarian interests by encouraging conservation, replenishment of forests, and agricultural and fertilizer research. Although the power program of the TVA is financially self-supporting today, other programs conducted by the authority are financed primarily by appropriations from Congress.

TENNESSEE VALLEY AUTHORITY ACT

Legislation passed by Congress in 1933 that established the TENNESSEE VALLEY AUTHORITY (TVA), an autonomous federal corporate agency responsible for the integrated development of the Tennessee River basin.

The concept of the TVA Act (16 U.S.C.A. § 831 et seq.) initially appeared in the early 1920s, when Senator GEORGE W. NORRIS introduced a plan to have the government assume the operation of the Wilson Dam and other installations the government had constructed at Muscle Shoals, Alabama, for national security reasons during World War I. However, President CALVIN COOLIDGE and President HERBERT HOOVER, in 1928 and 1931, respectively, vetoed the legislation. In 1933, President FRANKLIN DELANO ROOSEVELT reworked the legislation, and Congress passed the TVA Act. This version significantly expanded the scope of the previous legislation in that it propelled the federal government into a comprehensive scheme of regional planning and development. This marked the first time one agency was directed to coordinate the entire resource development of a major region, and the endeavor served as the prototype for similar river projects.

The TVA was responsible for resolving the problems arising from serious floods, substantially eroded land, a lackluster economy, and continual emigration from the region. It has revitalized the economy of the Tennessee River basin, particularly by the construction of reservoirs and multipurpose dams. Other noteworthy projects of the TVA, executed in conjunction with local authorities, have included malaria control; tree planting; the development of mineral, fish, and wildlife resources; land conservation; educational and social programs; and the construction of recreational facilities adjacent to reservoir banks.

TENOR

An exact replica of a legal document in words and figures.

For example, the tenor of a CHECK would be the exact amount payable, as indicated on its face.

TENTH AMENDMENT

The Tenth Amendment to the U.S. Constitution reads:

> The powers not delegated to the United States by the Constitution, nor prohibited by it to the States, are reserved to the States, respectively, or to the people.

Ratified in 1791, the Tenth Amendment to the Constitution embodies the general principles of FEDERALISM in a republican form of government. The Constitution specifies the parameters of authority that may be exercised by the three branches of the federal government: executive, legislative, and judicial. The Tenth Amendment reserves to the states all powers that are not granted to the federal government by the Constitution, except for those powers that states are constitutionally forbidden from exercising.

For example, nowhere in the federal Constitution is Congress given authority to regulate local matters concerning the health, safety, and morality of state residents. Known as POLICE POWERS, such authority is reserved to the states under the Tenth Amendment. Conversely, no state may enter into a TREATY with a foreign government because such agreements are prohibited by the plain language of Article I to the Constitution.

At the time the states adopted the Tenth Amendment, two primary conceptions of government were under consideration. Many federalists supported a centralized national authority, with power concentrated in a single entity. This type of government was exemplified by the English constitutional system, which vested absolute authority in the monarchy during the seventeenth century and in Parliament during the eighteenth century.

On the other hand, many anti-federalists supported a more republican form of government consisting of a loose CONFEDERATION of sovereign states that would form an alliance only for the purpose of mutual defense. The ARTICLES OF CONFEDERATION, which governed the thirteen states in national matters until 1787, when the Constitution was ratified, epito-

In this draft of the Bill of Rights, the Tenth Amendment to the Constitution appears as Article the Twelfth, reserving to the states or to the people powers not delegated to the federal government.

mized this form of government. Under the Articles of Confederation, the national government was unable to levy and collect taxes on its own behalf.

Many federalists, such as JAMES MADISON, argued that the Tenth Amendment was unnecessary because the powers of the federal government are carefully enumerated and limited in the Constitution. Because the Constitution does not give Congress, the president, or the federal judiciary the prerogative to regulate wholly local matters, Madison concluded that no such power existed and no such power would ever be exercised. However, British oppression had made the Founding Fathers fearful of unchecked centralized power. The Tenth Amendment was enacted to limit federal power. Although it appears clear on its face, the Tenth Amendment has not been consistently applied.

Before the Civil War, nearly every state urged a broad reading of the Tenth Amendment. Although no state wanted a federal government that was impotent against internal enemies or foreign aggressors, many state politicians challenged the authority of the federal government to regulate any matter that could otherwise be handled by local authorities. For example, immediately after the U.S. Revolution, all thirteen states resisted federal efforts to force local governments to return the property of British loyalists taken during the war. During the first half of the nineteenth century,

southern states objected to federal legislation that attempted to limit SLAVERY. State SOVEREIGNTY reached its height when eleven states seceded from the Union to form the Confederacy.

Following the Civil War, the Tenth Amendment was virtually suspended. For a number of years during the Reconstruction era, the federal government occupied the former Confederate states with military troops and required each occupied state to ratify the Civil War Amendments, which outlawed slavery, gave blacks the right vote, and declared the equality of all races. To a large extent the federal government ran local matters in southern states during this period.

In 1883 the Tenth Amendment regained some of its force. In that year the Supreme Court invalidated the federal CIVIL RIGHTS ACT of 1875 (18 Stat. 335), which criminalized racial discrimination in public accommodations, such as hotels and restaurants, because it violated state sovereignty under the Tenth Amendment (*Civil Rights Cases*, 109 U.S. 3, 3 S. Ct. 18, 27 L. Ed. 835 [1883]). In 1909 the Supreme Court struck down the White Slave Traffic Act (34 Stat. 898), which Congress had passed to prohibit the harboring of alien women for the purposes of PROSTITUTION, because it violated the Tenth Amendment (*Keller v. United States*, 213 U.S. 138, 29 S. Ct. 470, 53 L. Ed. 737 [1909]).

Nine years later the Court struck down another congressional law prohibiting the interstate shipment of products that had been manufactured by certain businesses that employed children under the age of fourteen (*Hammer v. Dagenhart*, 247 U.S. 251, 38 S. Ct. 529, 62 L. Ed. 1101 [1918]). "In interpreting the Constitution," the Court said in *Hammer*, "it must never be forgotten that the nation is made up of states to which are entrusted the powers of local government. And to them the powers not expressly delegated to the national government are reserved."

During the depth of the Great Depression, the Tenth Amendment returned to a dormant condition. President FRANKLIN ROOSEVELT worked with Congress to pass the New Deal, a series of programs designed to stimulate the troubled economy. After the Supreme Court upheld a provision of the National Labor Relations Act (mandatory COLLECTIVE BARGAINING) in *N.L.R.B. v. Jones & Laughlin Steel Corp.*, 301 U.S. 1, 57 S. Ct. 615, 81 L. Ed. 893 (1937), Congress began exercising unprecedented lawmaking power over state and local matters. For the next forty years, the Supreme Court upheld congressional authority to regulate a variety of matters that had been traditionally addressed by state legislatures. For example, in one case the

Supreme Court upheld the Agricultural Adjustment Act of 1938 (7 U.S.C.A. § 1281 et seq.) over objections that it allowed Congress to regulate individuals who produced and consumed their own foodstuffs entirely within the confines of a family farm (*Wickard v. Filburn*, 317 U.S. 111, 63 S. Ct. 82, 87 L. Ed. 122 [1942]).

The Tenth Amendment enjoyed a brief resurgence in 1976 when the Supreme Court held that the application of the FAIR LABOR STANDARDS ACT of 1938 (29 U.S.C.A. § 201 et seq.) to state and local governments was unconstitutional. In *National League of Cities v. Usery*, 426 U.S. 833, 96 S. Ct. 2465, 49 L. Ed. 2d 245 (1976), the Court said that the MINIMUM WAGE and maximum hour provisions of this act significantly altered and displaced the states' abilities to structure employment relationships in such areas as fire prevention, police protection, sanitation, public health, and parks and recreation. These services, the Court emphasized, are historically reserved to state and local governments. If Congress may withdraw from the states the authority to make such fundamental employment decisions, the Court concluded, "there would be little left of the states' separate and independent existence," or of the Tenth Amendment.

National League of Cities proved to be an unworkable constitutional precedent. It cast doubt on congressional authority to regulate many aspects of local affairs that most of society had come to rely upon. It was unclear, for example, whether the Occupational Safety and Health Administration, a federal agency established by Congress to regulate workplace safety, retained any constitutional authority after the Supreme Court announced its decision in *National League of Cities*.

The Supreme Court eliminated these concerns by overturning *National League of Cities* in *Garcia v. San Antonio Metropolitan Transit Authority*, 469 U.S. 528, 105 S. Ct. 1005, 83 L. Ed. 2d 1016 (1985). In *Garcia* the Court upheld the minimum wage and maximum hour provisions of the Fair Labor Standards Act as it applied to a city-owned public transportation system. In reaching this decision, the Court said that if certain states are worried about the extent of federal authority over a particular local matter, the residents of such states should contact their senators and representatives who are constitutionally authorized to narrow federal regulatory power through appropriate legislation. JUDICIAL REVIEW of federal regulations under the Tenth Amendment, the Supreme Court suggested, is not the proper vehicle to achieve this end.

The ebb and flow of Tenth Amendment JURISPRUDENCE reflects the delicate constitutional balance created by the Founding Fathers. The states ratified the Constitution because the Articles of Confederation created a national government that was too weak to defend itself and could not raise or collect revenue. Although the federal Constitution created a much stronger centralized government, the Founders did not want the states to lose all of their power to the federal government, as the colonies had lost their powers to Parliament. The Tenth Amendment continues to be defined as courts and legislatures address the balance of federal and state power.

CROSS-REFERENCES
Civil Rights Cases; Constitution of the United States; *Federalist Papers*; Labor Union; *NLRB v. Jones and Laughlin Steel Corp.*; States' Rights.

TENURE A right, term, or mode of holding or occupying something of value for a period of time.

In feudal law, the principal mode or system by which a person held land from a superior in exchange for the rendition of service and loyalty to the grantor. See also FEUDALISM.

The status given to an educator who has satisfactorily completed teaching for a trial period and is, therefore, protected against summary dismissal by the employer.

A length of time during which an individual has a right to occupy a public or private office.

In a general sense, the term *tenure* describes the length of time that a person holds a job, position, or something of value. In the context of academic employment, tenure refers to a faculty appointment for an indefinite period of time. When an academic institution gives tenure to an educator, it gives up the right to terminate that person without GOOD CAUSE.

In medieval England, tenure referred to the prevailing system of land ownership and land possession. Under the tenure system, a landholder, called a TENANT, held land at the will of a lord, who gave the tenant possession of the land in exchange for a good or service provided by the tenant. The various types of arrangements between the tenant and lord were called tenures. The most common tenures provided for military service, agricultural work, economic tribute, or religious duties in exchange for land.

TENURE OF OFFICE ACT The ASSASSINATION of President ABRAHAM LINCOLN on April 14, 1865, left the post–Civil War United States in the hands of his ineffectual and unpopular successor, ANDREW JOHNSON. It became Johnson's responsibility to determine a reconstruction policy, and he incurred the anger of the Radical

Republicans in Congress when he chose a moderate treatment of the rebellious South.

Congress sought to diminish Johnson's authority to select or remove officials from office, and the Radical Republicans particularly wanted to protect Lincoln's secretary of war, EDWIN M. STANTON. Stanton, a valuable member of the existing cabinet, supported the Radicals' Reconstruction policies and openly opposed Johnson. On March 2, 1867, Congress enacted the Tenure of Office Act (14 Stat. 430), which stated that a U.S. president could not remove any official originally appointed with senatorial consent without again obtaining the approval of the Senate.

Andrew Johnson vetoed the measure and challenged its effectiveness when he removed the dissident Stanton from office. Stanton refused to leave, and the House of Representatives invoked the new act to initiate IMPEACHMENT proceedings against Johnson in 1868. The president was acquitted, however, when the Senate failed by one vote to convict him. Stanton subsequently relinquished his office, and the Tenure of Office Act, never a popular measure, was repealed in 1887.

TERM 📖 An expression, word, or phrase that has a fixed and known meaning in a particular art, science, or profession. A specified period of time. 📖

The term of a court is the legally prescribed period for which it may be in SESSION. Although the session of the court is the time that it actually sits, the words *term* and *session* are frequently used interchangeably.

In reference to a LEASE, a term is the period granted during which the LESSEE is entitled to occupy the rented premises. It does not include the period of time between the creation of the lease and the entry of the TENANT. Similarly when used in reference to estates, the term is the period of time for which an ESTATE is granted. An estate for five years, for example, is one with a five-year term.

A term of office is the time during which an official who has been appointed or elected may hold the office, perform its functions, and partake of its EMOLUMENTS and privileges.

TERMINATION 📖 Cessation; conclusion; end in time or existence. 📖

When used in connection with litigation, the term signifies the final determination of the ACTION.

The termination or cancellation of a CONTRACT signifies the process whereby an end is put to whatever remains to be performed thereunder. It differs from RESCISSION, which refers to the restoration of the parties to the positions they occupied prior to the contract.

The termination of a LEASE refers to the severance of the LANDLORD AND TENANT relationship before the LEASEHOLD term expires through the ordinary passage of time.

TERM LIMITS See ELECTIONS.

TERM OF ART 📖 A word or phrase that has special meaning in a particular context. 📖

A term of art is a word or phrase that has a particular meaning. Terms of art abound in the law. For example, the phrase *double jeopardy* can be used in common parlance to describe any situation that poses two risks. In the law, DOUBLE JEOPARDY refers specifically to an impermissible second trial of a defendant for the same offense that gave rise to the first trial.

The classification of a word or phrase as a term of art can have legal consequences. In *Molzof v. United States*, 502 U.S. 301, 112 S. Ct. 711, 116 L. Ed. 2d 731 (1992), Shirley M. Molzof brought suit against the federal government after her husband, Robert E. Molzof, suffered irreversible brain damage while under the care of government hospital workers. The federal government conceded LIABILITY, and the parties tried the issue of DAMAGES before the U.S. District Court for the Western District of Wisconsin. Molzof had brought the claim as executor of her husband's estate under the Federal Tort Claims Act (FTCA) (28 U.S.C.A. §§ 1346(b), 2671–2680 [1988]), which prohibits the assessment of PUNITIVE DAMAGES against the federal government. The court granted recovery to Molzof for her husband's injuries that resulted from the NEGLIGENCE of federal employees, but it denied recovery for future medical expenses and for loss of ENJOYMENT of life. According to the court, such damages were punitive damages, which could not be recovered against the federal government.

The U.S. Court of Appeals for the Seventh Circuit agreed with the trial court, but the U.S. Supreme Court disagreed. According to the Court, punitive damages is a legal term of art that has a widely accepted COMMON-LAW meaning under state law. Congress was aware of this meaning at the time it passed the FTCA. Under traditional common-law principles, punitive damages are designed to punish a party. Since damages for future medical expenses and for loss of enjoyment of life were meant to compensate Molzof rather than punish the government, the Court reversed the decision and remanded the case to the Seventh Circuit.

TERRELL, MARY ELIZA CHURCH Mary Eliza Church Terrell was an influential African American writer, lecturer, and social activist, whose work began when the SEPARATE-BUT-EQUAL doctrine of racial segregation was adopted by the U.S. legal system and ended as

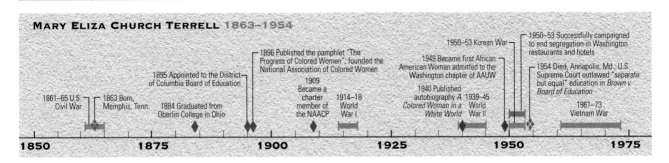

MARY ELIZA CHURCH TERRELL 1863–1954

1861–65 U.S. Civil War

1863 Born, Memphis, Tenn.

1884 Graduated from Oberlin College in Ohio

1895 Appointed to the District of Columbia Board of Education

1896 Published the pamphlet "The Progress of Colored Women"; founded the National Association of Colored Women

1909 Became a charter member of the NAACP

1914–18 World War I

1940 Published autobiography *A Colored Woman in a White World*

1939–45 World War II

1949 Became first African American Woman admitted to the Washington chapter of AAUW

1950–53 Korean War

1950–53 Successfully campaigned to end segregation in Washington restaurants and hotels

1954 Died, Annapolis, Md.; U.S. Supreme Court outlawed "separate but equal" education in *Brown v. Board of Education*

1961–73 Vietnam War

1850   1875   1900   1925   1950   1975

the U.S. Supreme Court, in *Brown v. Board of Education of Topeka, Kansas*, 347 U.S. 483, 74 S. Ct. 686, 98 L. Ed. 873 (1954), rejected the doctrine of state-sponsored segregation. Terrell was also an advocate of WOMEN'S RIGHTS, including the right to vote.

Mary Church was born on September 23, 1863, in Memphis, Tennessee. She was raised in a middle-class family and attended Oberlin College in Ohio, graduating in 1884. She taught at Wilberforce University in Xenia, Ohio, in 1885 and at a secondary school in Washington, D.C., in 1886 before taking a two-year tour of Europe. In 1888 she obtained a master's degree from Oberlin and married Robert Heberton Terrell, an attorney who would become the first African American municipal judge in Washington, D.C.

Terrell became an active member of the National American Suffrage Association and focused her attention on the special concerns of African American women. In her 1896 pamphlet, "The Progress of Colored Women," Terrell noted the "almost insurmountable obstacles" that had confronted African American women. Not only were "colored women with ambition and aspiration handicapped on account of their sex, but they are everywhere baffled and mocked on account of their race."

In 1896 Terrell founded the National Association of Colored Women and established its headquarters in Washington, D.C. As the first president, Terrell used the association as a means of achieving educational and social reform and bringing an end to racial and sex discrimination. She was appointed to the District of Columbia Board of Education in 1895, the first African American woman to hold such a position.

Terrell became a charter member of the NATIONAL ASSOCIATION FOR THE ADVANCEMENT OF COLORED PEOPLE (NAACP) in 1909 and continued her CIVIL RIGHTS crusade through the 1950s. She worked for the end of racial segregation and other barriers that affected the rights of African Americans. In 1949 Terrell was admitted to the Washington chapter of the American Association of University Women, ending the

BIOGRAPHY

THE GRANGER COLLECTION, NEW YORK

Mary Eliza Church Terrell

"IF WE FIGHT, WE GET OUR RIGHTS. WE'RE SECOND-CLASS CITIZENS BECAUSE WE SIT IDLY BY."

association's all-white membership policy. In 1950, at age eighty-seven, Terrell began a campaign to end segregation in restaurants and hotels in Washington, D.C. Three years later she achieved her goal.

Terrell published her autobiography, *A Colored Woman in a White World*, in 1940. She died on July 24, 1954, in Annapolis, Maryland.

TERRITORIAL COURTS 📖 Federal tribunals that serve as both federal and state courts in possessions of the United States—such as Guam and the Virgin Islands—that are not within the limits of any state but are organized with separate legislatures and executive and judicial officers appointed by the president. 📖

Territorial courts are LEGISLATIVE COURTS created by Congress pursuant to its constitutional power under Article I, Section 8, Clause 9, to create tribunals inferior to the Supreme Court. They are not constitutional courts created by Article III of the Constitution. Congress vests territorial courts with JURISDICTION comparable to that exercised by federal DISTRICT COURTS. Congress can, however, impose restrictions and duties on territorial courts that cannot be imposed on federal district courts, such as limiting the tenure of the members of the bench. Once a TERRITORY is admitted to the Union as a state, the jurisdiction of its territorial court is extinguished. Pending cases are transferred to the appropriate tribunals according to the nature of the particular ACTION.

The Supreme Court reviews decisions rendered by territorial courts if they satisfy certain requirements.

TERRITORIALITY 📖 A term that signifies a connection or limitation with reference to a particular geographic area or country. 📖

TERRITORIAL WATERS 📖 The part of the ocean adjacent to the coast of a state that is considered to be part of the territory of that state and subject to its SOVEREIGNTY. 📖

In INTERNATIONAL LAW the term *territorial waters* refers to that part of the ocean immediately adjacent to the shores of a state and subject to its territorial jurisdiction. The state possesses both the jurisdictional right to regulate, police, and adjudicate the territorial waters and the proprietary right to control and exploit natural resources in those waters and exclude others from them. Territorial waters differ from the high seas, which are common to all nations and are governed by the principle of freedom of the seas. The high seas are not subject to appropriation by persons or states but are available to everyone for navigation, exploitation of resources, and other lawful uses. The legal status of territorial waters also extends to the seabed and subsoil under them and to the airspace above them.

From the eighteenth to the middle of the twentieth century, international law set the width of territorial waters at one league (three nautical miles), although the practice was never wholly uniform. The United States established a three-mile territorial limit in 1793. International law also established the principle that foreign ships are entitled to innocent passage through territorial waters.

By the 1970s, however, more than forty countries had asserted a twelve-mile limit for their territorial waters. In 1988 President RONALD REAGAN issued Executive Proclamation 5928, which officially increased the outer limit of U.S. territorial waters from three to twelve miles (54 Fed. Reg. 777). This limit also applies to Puerto Rico, Guam, American Samoa, the U.S. Virgin Islands, and the Northern Mariana Islands. The Reagan administration claimed the extension of the limit was primarily motivated by national security concerns, specifically to hinder the operations of spy vessels from the Soviet Union that plied the U.S. coastline. Another reason for the extension was the recognition that most countries had moved to a twelve-mile limit. In 1982, at the Third United Nations Conference on the Law of the Sea, 130 member countries ratified the Convention on the Law of the Sea, which included a recognition of the twelve-mile limit as a provision of customary international law. Although the United States voted against the convention, 104 countries had officially claimed a twelve-mile territorial sea by 1988.

See also LAW OF THE SEA; NAVIGABLE WATERS.

TERRITORIES OF THE UNITED STATES

◫ Portions of the United States that are not within the limits of any state and have not been admitted as states. ◫

The United States holds three territories: American Samoa and Guam in the Pacific Ocean and the U.S. Virgin Islands in the Caribbean Sea. Although they are governed by the United States, the territories do not have statehood status, and this lesser legal and political status sets them apart from the rest of the United States.

The three U.S. territories are not the only U.S. government land holdings without statehood status. These various lands fall under the broad description of insular political communities affiliated with the United States. Puerto Rico in the Caribbean and the Northern Mariana Islands in the Pacific Ocean belong to the United States and have the status of commonwealth, a legal and political status that is above a TERRITORY but still below a state.

The United States also has a number of islands in the Pacific Ocean that are called variously territories and possessions. U.S. possessions have the lowest legal and political status because these islands do not have permanent populations and do not seek self-determination and autonomy. U.S. possessions include Baker, Howland, Kingman Reef, Jarvis, Johnston, Midway, Palmyra, and Wake Islands.

Finally, land used as a military base is considered a form of territory. These areas are inhabited almost exclusively by military personnel. They are governed largely by military laws, and not by the political structures in place for commonwealths and territories. The United States has military bases at various locations around the world, including Okinawa, Japan, and Guantánamo Bay, Cuba.

A precise definition of territories and territorial law in the United States is difficult to fashion. The U.S. government has long been in the habit of determining policy as it goes along. The United States was established through a defensive effort against British forces and then through alternately defensive and offensive battles against Native Americans. From this chaotic beginning, the United States has struggled to fashion a coherent policy on the acquisition and possession of land.

The U.S. Constitution does not state exactly how the United States may acquire land. Instead, the Constitution essentially delegates the power to decide the matter to Congress. Article IV, Section 3, Clause 1, of the Constitution provides that "New States may be admitted by the Congress into this Union; but no new State shall be formed . . . by the Junction of two or more States, or Parts of States, without the Consent of the Legislatures of the States concerned as well as of the Congress." The same section of the Constitution gives Congress the "Power to dispose of and make all needful Rules and Regulations respecting the Territory or other Property belonging to the United States."

Under INTERNATIONAL LAW the United States and other nation-states may acquire additional territory in several ways, including OCCUPATION of territory that is not already a part of a state;

U.S. Territories and Their Admission as States

Name of the Territory	Date of Act Organizing the Territory	Date Admitted as a State	Years as a Territory
Northwest Territory[1]	July 13, 1787	March 1, 1803[2]	16
Territory southwest of the Ohio River	May 26, 1790	June 1, 1796[3]	6
Mississippi	April 7, 1798	December 10, 1817	19
Indiana	May 7, 1800	December 11, 1816	16
Orleans	March 26, 1804	April 30, 1812[4]	7
Michigan	January 11, 1805	January 26, 1837	31
Louisiana-Missouri[5]	March 3, 1805	August 10, 1821	16
Illinois	February 3, 1809	December 3, 1818	9
Alabama	March 3, 1817	December 14, 1819	2
Arkansas	March 2, 1819	June 15, 1836	17
Florida	March 30, 1822	March 3, 1845	23
Wisconsin	April 20, 1836	May 29, 1848	12
Iowa	June 12, 1838	December 28, 1846	7
Oregon	August 14, 1848	February 14, 1859	10
Minnesota	March 3, 1849	May 11, 1858	9
New Mexico	September 9, 1850	January 6, 1912	61
Utah	September 9, 1850	January 4, 1896	44
Washington	March 2, 1853	November 11, 1889	36
Nebraska	May 30, 1854	March 1, 1867	12
Kansas	May 30, 1854	January 29, 1861	6
Colorado	February 28, 1861	August 1, 1876	15
Nevada	March 2, 1861	October 31, 1864	3
Dakota	March 2, 1861	November 2, 1889	28
Arizona	February 24, 1863	February 14, 1912	49
Idaho	March 3, 1863	July 3, 1890	27
Montana	May 26, 1864	November 8, 1889	25
Wyoming	July 25, 1868	July 10, 1890	22
Alaska[6]	May 17, 1884	January 3, 1959	75
Oklahoma	May 2, 1890	November 16, 1907	17
Hawaii	April 30, 1900	August 21, 1959	59

[1]The Northwest Territory included what are now the states of Ohio, Indiana, Illinois, Michigan, and Wisconsin and eastern Minnesota.
[2]Only the state of Ohio was admitted to the Union in 1803; the remainder of the Northwest Territory was organized as several territories, which entered the Union later in the nineteenth century.
[3]The territory entered the Union as the state of Tennessee.
[4]The territory entered the Union as the state of Louisiana.
[5]A separate act organizing the Missouri Territory was enacted on June 4, 1812.
[6]Alaska was actually organized as a district on May 17, 1884, but it was unofficially administered as a territory. A statute of August 24, 1912, formally organized Alaska as a territory.

conquest, where allowed by the international community; cession of land by another nation in a treaty; and accretion, or the growth of new land within a nation's existing boundaries.

Through various statutes and court opinions, Congress and the U.S. Supreme Court have devised a system that gives Congress and the president control over U.S. territories. Congress delegates some of its policy-making and administrative duties to the Office of Insular Affairs within the Department of the Interior. The president of the United States appoints judges and executive officers to offices in the territories. Congress devises court systems for the territories, and the Supreme Court may review decisions made by territorial courts.

Congress may pass laws governing a territory with due deference to the customs and sensibilities of the native people. Congress may not pass territorial laws that violate a fundamental constitutional right. Such rights have not been defined concretely by the Supreme Court in the context of territorial law, but they

Most states, other than the original thirteen, entered the Union after having been territories for a number of years

can include the right to be free from unreasonable SEARCHES AND SEIZURES, the right to free speech, and the rights to EQUAL PROTECTION and DUE PROCESS (*Torres v. Commonwealth of Puerto Rico,* 442 U.S. 465, 99 S. Ct. 2425, 61 L. Ed. 2d 1 [1979]).

Persons living in U.S. territories do not have the right to vote for members of Congress. They may elect their own legislature, but the laws passed by the territorial legislature may be nullified by Congress. Each territory may elect a delegate who attends congressional sessions, hearings, and conferences in Washington, D.C. These delegates may propose legislation and vote on legislation in committees, but they may not participate in final votes.

U.S. territories have less political power than do U.S. commonwealths. Commonwealths are afforded a higher degree of internal political autonomy than are territories. Congress and the commonwealth work together to fashion a political system that is acceptable to both parties. By contrast, Congress tends to impose its will on territories. Commonwealth status once inevitably led to statehood, but such a progression is no longer automatic.

See also LOUISIANA PURCHASE; TERRITORIAL COURTS.

TERRITORY ◫ A part of a country separated from the rest and subject to a particular jurisdiction. ◫

The term *territory* has various meanings in different contexts. Generally, the term refers to a particular or indeterminate geographical area. In a legal context, territory usually denotes a geographical area that has been acquired by a particular country but has not been recognized as a full participant in that country's affairs. In the United States, Guam is one example of a territory. Though it is considered a part of the United States and is governed by the U.S. Congress, Guam does not have full rights of statehood, such as full representation in Congress or full coverage under the U.S. Constitution.

The term *territory* is also used in the law to describe an assigned area of responsibility. A salesperson, for example, may work in a certain area. A salesperson's territory may be legally significant in a contract case. Assume that Sally has agreed to sell widgets on commission in a specific territory on the condition that no other seller from the widget supplier will do business in that territory. If the supplier arranges for another seller to encroach on Sally's territory, Sally may take legal action against the supplier.

See also TERRITORIES OF THE UNITED STATES.

TERRORISM 📖 The unlawful use of force or violence against persons or property in order to coerce or intimidate a government or the civilian population in furtherance of political or social objectives. 📖

Terrorism is the systematic use of terror or violence to achieve political goals. The targets of terrorism include government officials, identified individuals or groups, and innocent bystanders. In most cases terrorists seek to overthrow or destabilize an existing political regime, but totalitarian and dictatorial governments use terror to maintain their power. In the United States, a series of terrorist actions in the 1990s led to the enactment of the Antiterrorism and Effective Death Penalty Act of 1996 (Pub. L. No. 104-132). This act sought to combat and prevent terrorism through the development of antiterrorism programs and the strengthening of procedures and penalties.

Terrorism has been used throughout human history and in every part of the world. Roman emperors practiced terror to maintain their regimes, the Spanish Inquisition used it to root out religious heretics, the French Revolution went through a period called the Reign of Terror, and in the post–Civil War southern United States, the KU KLUX KLAN used illegal threats and violence to intimidate supporters of Reconstruction.

In the late twentieth century, terrorism became a tool of political groups in Europe, the Middle East, and Asia. The growth of international terrorism led to KIDNAPPINGS, HIJACKING of airplanes, bombing of airplanes and buildings, and armed attacks on government and public facilities. In the 1980s several countries including Libya, Iran, and Iraq were identified as supporting international terrorism by providing training, weapons, and safe havens.

In February 1993 the bombing of the World Trade Center in New York City, New York, killed six people and injured more than a thousand others. The bomb left a crater 200 by 100 feet wide and five stories deep. The FEDERAL BUREAU OF INVESTIGATION (FBI) and the Joint Terrorist Task Force identified and helped bring to trial twenty-two Islamic fundamentalist conspirators. The trial revealed extensive plans for terrorist acts in the United States, including attacks on government facilities.

In the 1990s the United States also became more concerned about domestic terrorist activities carried out by U.S. citizens without any foreign involvement. Beginning in 1978, a person who came to be known as the Unabomber targeted university scientists, airline employees, and other persons he associated with a dehumanized, technology driven society. The suspect killed three people and injured twenty-three others with package bombs. At his insistence major newspapers published his 35,000-word manifesto describing his antitechnology philosophy. In April 1996 a suspect, Theodore Kaczynski, was arrested for crimes associated with the Unabomber.

More than the Unabomber, however, the bombing of the Alfred P. Murrah Federal

International Terrorist Incidents, 1977 to 1996

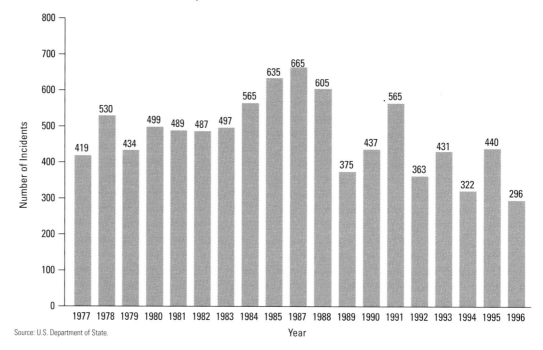

Source: U.S. Department of State.

The Oklahoma City Bombing

In June 1997 the murder and conspiracy trial of Timothy J. McVeigh ended in the death sentence. The twenty-nine-year-old former Army sergeant was convicted of bombing the Alfred P. Murrah Federal Building in Oklahoma City on April 19, 1995. The blast, which claimed 168 lives, was the worst terrorist act ever committed on U.S. soil. McVeigh pleaded innocent, but the elaborate case mounted by federal prosecutors led to a swift jury verdict of guilty on all eleven counts.

After a nationwide manhunt, investigators from the Federal Bureau of Investigation (FBI) had linked McVeigh to the blast using remnants of a Ryder rental truck believed to have carried the bomb. At trial, prosecutors established further ties: telephone records and testimony by the owner of the rental office suggested McVeigh had rented the truck under an alias in Junction City, Kansas, two days before the bombing. Residue from explosives had also been found on McVeigh's clothing.

Prosecutors portrayed McVeigh as an antigovernment extremist. The defendant's sister, Jennifer McVeigh, told the court that he was angry over the government's destruction of the Branch Davidian compound in Waco, Texas, in April 1993, and that he had hinted at taking action. Personal correspondence was introduced as evidence in an effort to round out the portrait of McVeigh as a follower of far-right politics, who was disillusioned and willing to commit acts of terror. Key testimony came from Michael J. Fortier, an Army friend and co-conspirator who had surveyed the Federal Building with McVeigh, and his wife, Lori Fortier. The Fortiers said that McVeigh wanted the bombing to start a civil war.

Led by Oklahoma attorney Stephen Jones, the defense team was critical of every phase of the prosecution. Defense attorneys attacked the methodology of the FBI in preparing physical evidence as well as the government's witnesses. In particular, they charged that the Fortiers were liars who hoped to escape prison time and to profit financially from their testimony. Maintaining that McVeigh was railroaded, the defense pointed to the existence of a human leg found in the ruins of the building to suggest that the actual Oklahoma City bomber had died in the explosion.

After the jurors returned a guilty verdict on June 2, the trial moved into an unusual penalty phase. The defense, seeking leniency, made a lengthy presentation about the Waco siege, at which McVeigh had been present, in what seemed to observers an odd effort to explain his motives in Oklahoma City. It also called to the stand William McVeigh, who made an emotionally charged appeal for his son's life. But the statements of survivors who had lost family and friends in the Oklahoma massacre apparently swayed the jurors, who decided on execution.

Building in Oklahoma City, Oklahoma, on April 19, 1995, galvanized concerns about domestic terrorism. The bombing killed 168 people and injured more than 500 others. The FBI arrested Timothy J. McVeigh and Terry Nichols, who were charged with murder and conspiracy. McVeigh and Nichols have been connected to the right-wing MILITIA movement, which opposes the powers held by the federal government and believes that its members' right to bear arms is threatened. In June 1997 McVeigh was found guilty of MURDER and CONSPIRACY and sentenced to death.

In the aftermath of the Oklahoma City bombing, President BILL CLINTON and members of Congress proposed measures to address terrorism. The Antiterrorism Act was signed into law in April 1996. The law allocated $1 billion to fund federal programs to combat terrorism. The act also established a federal death penalty for terrorist murders and strengthened penalties for crimes committed against federal employees while performing their official duties.

In addition, the act increased the penalties for conspiracies involving explosives and for the possession of nuclear materials, criminalized the use of chemical weapons, and required plastic explosives to contain "tagging" elements in the explosive materials for detection and identification purposes.

Under the law, the U.S. secretary of state can designate groups as terrorist organizations and prohibit fund-raising on behalf of these groups in the United States. The secretary of the treasury is authorized to freeze ASSETS of these terrorist organizations and forbid U.S. citizens from conducting financial transactions with known terrorist states. In addition, any person who is a representative or member of a designated terrorist organization can be denied entry to the United States, and the U.S. attorney general can deny asylum to suspected terrorists.

See also SECOND AMENDMENT.

TERRY v. OHIO In *Terry v. Ohio*, 392 U.S. 1, 88 S. Ct. 1868, 20 L. Ed. 2d 889 (1968), the U.S. Supreme Court ruled that the FOURTH

AMENDMENT to the U.S. Constitution permits a law enforcement officer to stop, detain, and frisk persons who are suspected of criminal activity without first obtaining their consent, even though the officer may lack a WARRANT to conduct a search or PROBABLE CAUSE to make an arrest. Now known as a *Terry* stop, this type of police encounter is constitutionally permissible only when an officer can articulate a particularized, objective, and REASONABLE basis for believing that criminal activity may be afoot or that a given suspect may be armed and dangerous.

The case stems from an incident in Cleveland, Ohio, in 1963. Police officer Martin McFadden observed three men engaging in suspicious behavior near the corner of Euclid Avenue and Huron Road. One of the suspects was the defendant, John Terry. Along with codefendant Richard Chilton and a third man, known only as Katz, Terry was seen pacing in front of a downtown store. Occasionally, the men would pause to confer with each other. More often, McFadden witnessed the men peering into the store's front window. Over a period of ten to twelve minutes, the three men looked into the same store window approximately twenty-four times.

Based on his training as an officer and thirty-nine years of experience on the police force, including thirty-five as a detective, McFadden believed that the suspects were "casing" the store for a stickup. Attempting to forestall a possible ROBBERY, McFadden approached the three men and identified himself as a police officer. Not being familiar with any of the suspects, McFadden asked for their names. When the men mumbled unintelligibly in response, McFadden grabbed Terry, quickly patted down his overcoat, and discovered a .38-caliber revolver. After removing the pistol from Terry's coat pocket, McFadden patted down the other two suspects, finding another revolver in Chilton's overcoat. Katz was not armed.

Terry and Chilton were charged with carrying concealed weapons. Prior to trial the two defendants brought a motion to suppress the incriminating EVIDENCE seized by McFadden. The defendants argued that the weapons were INADMISSIBLE because McFadden had discovered them during an unlawful search. McFadden, the defendants pointed out, possessed neither a valid SEARCH WARRANT authorizing the pat down nor probable cause to detain them. Denying their MOTION to suppress, the court scheduled the matter for trial where both defendants were found guilty. The Supreme Court of Ohio affirmed the convictions, and the defendants appealed to the nation's highest court. The U.S. Supreme Court divided its opinion into three parts.

First, the Supreme Court ruled that the defendants enjoyed qualified protection from temporary police detention under the Fourth Amendment. Before a court will examine the propriety of police activity under the Fourth Amendment, it must first determine whether the interests asserted by a defendant are constitutionally protected. The Fourth Amendment governs areas where individuals maintain a reasonable expectation of PRIVACY, including a zone of personal freedom in which every individual is secure from unnecessary and unreasonable governmental intrusion. Walking down the streets of Cleveland, the Court said, Terry and Chilton held a reasonable expectation that their personal liberty would not be unlawfully restrained by law enforcement.

Second, the Court ruled that the defendants' freedom was effectively impeded by their encounter with McFadden. Any time a police officer accosts an individual to detain him for questioning, the Court emphasized, the officer has "seized" that person within the meaning of the Fourth Amendment. It would be nothing less than "torture of the English language," the Court added, to suggest that McFadden's pat down of the suspects' clothing was anything other than a "search" as that term is defined in the Constitution.

Third, the Court ruled that McFadden acted reasonably during his encounter with the defendants. Acknowledging that the Constitution generally requires probable cause to effect an arrest and a lawfully executed warrant to conduct a search, the Court identified a third area of police activity that is permissible under the Fourth Amendment, though it may amount to neither a full-blown search nor a technical arrest. The central inquiry under the Fourth Amendment, the Court wrote, is whether the police have acted reasonably under the circumstances. The express language of the Fourth Amendment does not prohibit all warrantless searches performed without probable cause, but only those that are unreasonable.

In dealing with rapidly unfolding and increasingly dangerous situations, the Court said, police may find it impractical or impossible to obtain a search warrant before choosing to intervene. In other situations, injury or harm may result to bystanders if law enforcement is made to wait until it has probable cause before acting. The Court indicated that the Fourth Amendment gives law enforcement flexibility to investigate, detect, and prevent criminal activity. According to *Terry*, this flexibility includes the right of police officers to stop persons suspected of criminal activity and detain them for questioning. If during questioning police are led to believe that a suspect is armed and dangerous, an officer may frisk the suspect without violating the Fourth Amendment.

In this case the Court noted that McFadden personally witnessed the two defendants engaging in what appeared to be preparations for a robbery. It would have been negligent, the Court thought, for McFadden to have turned a blind eye to such behavior. Having chosen to investigate further, the Court said it was reasonable for McFadden to assure himself that none of the suspects were armed, especially after they failed to respond intelligibly to his request for identification. In patting down and frisking the defendants, McFadden chose a prudent course to stave off threats to his security and the security of others.

The Court reached its holding by balancing the legitimate needs of law enforcement against the privacy interests of individuals. Forcible detention of individuals for questioning is far from a petty indignity. Even a limited search of outer clothing, the Court stressed, constitutes a "serious intrusion upon the sanctity of the person, which may inflict great indignity and arouse strong resentment, and it is not to be undertaken lightly." At the same time, law enforcement must not be hamstrung from doing its job in a proficient manner. The Fourth Amendment does not restrict police from intervening until after a crime has been committed. Crime prevention is a bona fide goal of law enforcement, the Court said, and the Fourth Amendment places only reasonable restrictions upon pursuit of that goal.

Outlining these restrictions, the Court said that no police officer may lawfully stop and detain a person for questioning unless the officer first observes unusual conduct that arouses a reasonable suspicion of criminal activity. A stop may be no longer than necessary to confirm or dispel an officer's suspicion and must not be unnecessarily restrictive or intrusive. During the period of detention, no searches may be performed unless the officer has an objective and particularized basis for believing the suspect is armed and dangerous. Any search must be limited to the suspect's outer clothing and may be performed only for the purpose of discovering concealed weapons. Evidence obtained during searches that comport with these restrictions, the Court said, is ADMISSIBLE under the Fourth Amendment. Evidence obtained in violation of the limitations set forth in *Terry*

may be suppressed under the EXCLUSIONARY RULE.

See also SEARCH AND SEIZURE; STOP AND FRISK.

TESTACY The condition or state of leaving a valid WILL at one's death to direct the distribution of one's ESTATE.

TESTAMENT Another name for a WILL.

TESTAMENTARY Relating to WILLS.

An individual is said to have testamentary CAPACITY to make a will when that person has sufficient mental ability to comprehend what he or she is doing, the nature and extent of his or her property, the natural objects (which means appropriate persons or recipients) of his or her bounty, and the interrelationships among these three concepts.

TESTATE One who dies leaving a valid WILL, or the description of this status.

TESTATOR One who makes or has made a WILL; one who dies leaving a will.

A testator is a person who makes a valid will. A will is the document through which a deceased person disposes of his property. A person who dies without having made a will is said to have died INTESTATE.

A testator must be of sound mind when making a will. In part to ensure that a testator is of sound mind, states require that the signing of a will be witnessed by multiple persons. A testator also should be making the will without DURESS and free of COERCION from other persons. If the testator is not acting of her own free will in consenting to the terms of the will, a court may later void all or part of it.

TEST CASE A suit brought specifically for the establishment of an important legal right or principle.

The term *test case* describes a case that tests the validity of a particular law. Test cases are useful because they establish legal rights or principles and thereby serve as PRECEDENT for future similar cases. Test cases save the judicial system the time and expense of conducting proceedings for each and every case that involves the same issue or issues.

To illustrate, assume that Congress passes a law that makes using a cellular phone while driving a MISDEMEANOR punishable by up to one year in jail and a fine of $10,000. Such a law would likely be challenged by a large number of cell phone owners, all of whom are in essentially identical circumstances and all of whom have the same arguments against the law. In such a situation, attorneys representing the plaintiffs might look for a case with a sympathetic set of facts with which to challenge the law. For example, they might select a case involving a driver who was charged with violating the law when she used her cell phone to request medical assistance for a family member. Other observant law firms would postpone or otherwise delay their own similar cases to wait for the outcome of the test case.

A test case need not concern a new law. Suppose, for example, an attorney or client is dissatisfied with the current state of a particular law and has strong arguments in favor of changing it. If the facts of the case give the attorney or client a good chance of prevailing, the case may be called a test case because the outcome would change the law for future persons in similar circumstances.

In some cases, a person may choose to violate an existing law to provoke a lawsuit, prosecution, or penalty. The person may then challenge the lawsuit, prosecution, or penalty and use the case to try and change the law through a judicial opinion. In *Druker v. Commissioner of Internal Revenue*, 697 F.2d 46 (2d Cir. 1982), *cert. den.*, 461 U.S. 957, 103 S. Ct. 2429, 77 L. Ed. 2d 1316 (1983), for example, James O. and Joan Druker, a married couple, intentionally used the lower tax rates for unmarried individuals in computing their 1975 and 1976 INCOME TAX because they believed the federal tax scheme was unconstitutional under the Equal Protection Clause of the FOURTEENTH AMENDMENT. Before the INTERNAL REVENUE SERVICE (IRS) could take action against the Drukers, the Drukers filed suit against the commissioner of the IRS. The Drukers were unsuccessful, but had they received a favorable disposition, they would have succeeded in changing the law on federal taxation of married couples.

See also CASE LAW; STARE DECISIS.

TESTIFY ▩ To provide EVIDENCE as a WITNESS, subject to an OATH or AFFIRMATION, in order to establish a particular fact or set of facts. ▩

Court rules require witnesses to testify about the facts they know that are relevant to the determination of the outcome of the case. Under the law a person may not testify until he is sworn in. This requirement is usually met by a witness swearing to speak the truth. A person who does not believe in appealing to God may affirm to the court that the TESTIMONY about to be given is the truth.

A witness may testify as to facts directly observed, which is called DIRECT EVIDENCE; facts learned indirectly, which is called CIRCUMSTANTIAL EVIDENCE; or, in the case of an expert, an opinion the expert has formed based on facts embodied in a hypothetical question. The parties to the court proceeding are free to question a witness as to the truthfulness of the testimony or the competence of the witness.

The FIFTH AMENDMENT to the U.S. Constitu-

AP/WIDE WORLD PHOTOS

Beverage makers frequently call on Oscar Freyer, physics professor emeritus at Drury College in Missouri, to testify in trials involving broken bottles. Freyer is an expert on the dynamics of breaking glass.

tion gives the defendant in a criminal trial the right not to testify, so as to avoid SELF-INCRIMINATION. In addition, the rule that a person must testify when called as a witness has several exceptions based on the existence of a special relationship between the defendant and the potential witness. Among the most important of these exceptions are CONFIDENTIAL COMMUNICATIONS between a HUSBAND AND A WIFE, an attorney and a client, a doctor and a patient, and a priest and penitent.

The rules of evidence govern what a person may testify about at a court proceeding. Though there are numerous exceptions, generally a witness may not testify about what she heard another say if that testimony is offered to prove the truth of the matter asserted. Such testimony is known as HEARSAY. For example, if the witness testifies that he heard that John Doe was married and this statement is offered to prove that John Doe was married, it is hearsay and the court will strike the testimony from the record.

CROSS-REFERENCES

Attorney-Client Privilege; Marital Communication Privilege; Physician-Patient Privilege; Privileged Communication.

TESTIMONY ▩ Oral EVIDENCE offered by a competent WITNESS under oath, which is used to establish some fact or set of facts. ▩

Testimony is distinguishable from evidence that is acquired through the use of written sources, such as documents.

TEXAS v. JOHNSON In *Texas v. Johnson*, 491 U.S. 397, 109 S. Ct. 2533, 105 L. Ed. 2d 342 (1989), the U.S. Supreme Court was asked to review the constitutionality of a Texas statute prohibiting the desecration of certain venerated objects, including state and national flags. The defendant was convicted under the statute for burning the U.S. FLAG during a political demonstration. In striking down the statute, the Supreme Court ruled that flag burning is symbolic expression protected by the Free Speech Clause of the FIRST AMENDMENT to the U.S. Constitution. The case splintered the nine justices sitting on the Court, much as the issue of flag burning splintered the rest of the nation.

The case stemmed from an incident during the 1984 Republican National Convention in Dallas, Texas. Outside the convention center a group of demonstrators marched through the streets to protest the policies of President RONALD REAGAN. Several demonstrators distributed literature, shouted slogans, and made speeches. One demonstrator, Gregory Lee Johnson, unfurled a U.S. flag, doused it with kerosene, and set it on fire. While the flag burned, several protestors chanted: "America, the red, white, and blue, we spit on you." Several bystanders were offended by the flag burning, and one took the flag's remains home to his backyard where he buried them. No violence or altercations took place at any time during the demonstration, however.

Johnson was convicted of desecrating a venerated object in violation of Texas Penal Code section 42.09(a)(3) (1989). He was sentenced to one year in prison and fined $2,000. His conviction was affirmed by the Fifth District Court of Appeals in Dallas. Johnson's case was then reviewed by the Texas Court of Criminal Appeals, which reversed his conviction, holding that the state could not punish Johnson for burning the U.S. flag under these circumstances (*Johnson v. State*, 755 S.W.2d 92 [Tex. Crim. App. 1988]). The Free Speech Clause, the court ruled, forbids the government from establishing an orthodox symbol of national unity that is insulated from public criticism, symbolic or otherwise.

In a 5–4 decision the U.S. Supreme Court affirmed the holding of the Texas Court of Criminal Appeals. Joined by Justices THURGOOD MARSHALL, HARRY A. BLACKMUN, ANTONIN SCALIA, and ANTHONY KENNEDY, Justice WILLIAM J. BRENNAN, JR., wrote the majority opinion for the Court. Chief Justice WILLIAM H. REHNQUIST, joined by Justices SANDRA DAY O'CONNOR, BYRON WHITE, and JOHN PAUL STEVENS, wrote the dissenting opinion. The majority opinion was divided into two parts.

First, the Court ruled that flag burning is expressive conduct for First Amendment purposes. The Court noted that the defendant's method of protest was not confined to the written or spoken word, which traditionally receives the most constitutional protection from governmental restraint. Nevertheless, the Court said, flag burning could not be fairly characterized as mere conduct devoid of any communicative qualities, which traditionally receives little or no protection under the Free Speech Clause. Instead, the Court observed, the defendant burned the flag as the symbolic culmination of an ardent political demonstration. "The expressive, overtly political nature of the conduct," the Court wrote, "was both intentional and overwhelmingly apparent."

Symbolic expression has long been associated with the U.S. flag under the federal Constitution. In *West Virginia State Board of Education v. Barnette*, 319 U.S. 624, 63 S. Ct. 1178, 87 L. Ed. 1628 (1943), the Supreme Court ruled that public school children cannot be compelled to salute the flag when doing so would violate their religious beliefs, which are protected by the First Amendment. In *Spence v. Washington*, 418 U.S. 405, 94 S. Ct. 2727, 41 L. Ed. 2d 842 (1974), the Court ruled that the Free Speech Clause guarantees the right of individuals to attach a peace symbol to the flag in protest of U.S. foreign policy. Finally, in *Smith v. Goguen*, 415 U.S. 566, 94 S. Ct. 1242, 39 L. Ed. 2d 605 (1974), the Court ruled that individuals enjoy a First Amendment right to express themselves by affixing the flag to articles of clothing, even if that means allowing certain individuals to display the flag on the seat of their pants. Each of these cases was cited by the Court in *Texas v. Johnson* to illustrate that the defendant's method of protest was just another manifestation of symbolic expression involving the U.S. flag.

Second, the Supreme Court ruled that the interests asserted by the government were insufficient to overcome the defendant's right to engage in symbolic expression. The government had argued that the Texas statute represented a legislative attempt to prevent societal disorder, which presumably would result if flag burning were permitted. But the Court determined that the defendant's actions neither resulted in disorder, nor created a substantial likelihood that disorder would ensue. Although several onlookers were seriously offended by the defendant's symbolic protest, the Court said that the First Amendment is designed to protect even the most disagreeable speech unless it is likely to produce imminent lawlessness, such as a BREACH OF THE PEACE. Had disorder resulted on this particular occasion, the Court pointed out, the defendant could have been prosecuted under the relevant provisions of the Texas Penal Code prohibiting breach of the peace. Because no arrests were made for breaching the peace, the Court held, the government's interest in preventing disorder was not implicated in this case.

The government also argued that the Texas flag desecration statute was a justifiable means of promoting national unity. The national flag, the government contended, is the country's most visceral image of nationhood, reflecting the solidarity of the fifty states for the common good. Flag burning, by contrast, tends to cast doubt on the strength of this image, the government asserted, causing Americans to question whether the United States is really united at all. The Supreme Court agreed with the government in part, acknowledging that the flag has come to symbolize two hundred years of nationhood no less than the combination of letters found in the word "America."

At the same time, the Court cautioned, the flag does not mean the same thing to everyone. For some Americans the flag stands for an imperialistic foreign policy and a legacy of CIVIL RIGHTS violations. The defendant no doubt had his own list of things symbolized by the flag. In prohibiting flag burning and other forms of desecration, the Court continued, the state of Texas was attempting to prescribe a single patriotic meaning for this national political symbol. The Court noted, however, that the government has no constitutional authority to restrict the content of political expression, whether it be written, spoken, or symbolic, without offering a compelling reason for doing so.

In this case, no compelling reasons were offered. If the flag were protected from desecration under the First Amendment, the Court reasoned, the government might seek to protect other national symbols from destruction as well, including copies of the federal Constitution and the Declaration of Independence. The Court was unwilling to allow the government to embark on this path for fear of where it might lead. The only proper remedy for the state of Texas, the Court emphasized, was to publicly encourage proper respect for the flag by honoring it through state-sponsored ceremonies such as Flag Day. In the marketplace of ideas, the Court opined, the only way to combat pernicious speech is through persuasive countervailing speech. The First Amendment requires individuals to persuade each other with sound arguments, not silence each other through governmental suppression.

In his dissenting opinion, Chief Justice Rehnquist wrote that "No other American symbol has been as universally honored as the flag." The chief justice paid tribute to the men and women of the armed forces who have sacrificed their lives to preserve the freedom symbolized by the flag. According to the chief justice, flag burning evinces a distinct lack of respect for the memory of those who have fought and died for the cause of liberty in the United States. While burning the flag might be considered expressive conduct, Rehnquist argued, the state of Texas, as well as every other state in the Union, has a compelling interest in preserving it from destruction and desecration.

Justice Brennan tried to address some of the concerns raised by Rehnquist in a brief paragraph included in the Court's majority opinion. "We are tempted to say . . .," Brennan wrote, "that the flag's deservedly cherished place in our community will be strengthened, not weakened, by our holding today." The Court's decision, Brennan stressed, underscores the "principles of freedom and inclusiveness that the flag best reflects" and reaffirms "the conviction that our toleration of criticism such as Johnson's is a sign and source of our strength." Brennan reiterated many of these points a year later in *United States v. Eichman*, 496 U.S. 310, 110 S. Ct. 2404, 110 L. Ed. 2d 287 (1990), when the Supreme Court struck down the Flag Protection Act, Pub. L. 101-131, 103 Stat. 777, which Congress enacted in 1989 to offer federal protection against flag desecration. Congress—no more than a state legislature—the Court said in *Eichman*, may not enact a law curtailing an individual's right to symbolic political expression.

See also FREEDOM OF SPEECH; SYMBOLIC SPEECH.

TEXAS v. WHITE In the aftermath of the Civil War, several questions about the legal status of the Southern states that had seceded from the Union remained unanswered. These questions included whether these states had, in fact, left the Union, whether the acts of the secessionist governments had legal effect after the war, and whether the imposition of military rule by the president and Congress on these states during the postwar Reconstruction meant that the states were not fully restored to the Union.

The Supreme Court addressed these issues in *Texas v. White*, 74 U.S. (7 Wall.) 700, 19 L. Ed. 227 (1869), which involved a dispute over the payment of U.S. BONDS. In 1850 Texas had received $10 million in bonds from the United States in settlement of boundary claims. The bonds were payable to the state and redeemable after December 31, 1864. Texas law required the governor to endorse the bonds before they could be redeemed or transferred. When Texas seceded from the Union in 1862, however, the Confederate legislature repealed the gubernatorial endorsement requirement and established a military board to sell the bonds to finance the war effort.

In 1865 George White and John Chiles, among others, purchased the bonds in exchange for cotton and medicine. None of the bonds were endorsed by the governor. After the war the people of Texas convened and established a constitution under which they elected a governor in 1866. The convention also authorized the governor to seek recovery of the bonds. In 1867 Congress enacted the Reconstruction Acts, which created five military districts in Texas, each with a military commander. The military rule was imposed to ensure the restoration of civil peace in the Southern states and to protect the rights of the newly freed slaves.

Texas filed suit in the U.S. Supreme Court seeking recovery of the bonds sold to White and Chiles and subsequently resold to citizens of many states. The state also asked that the United States be enjoined from paying the bonds because they had not been endorsed by the governor and were past due when presented for payment. White argued that Texas had no right to bring the suit and that the Supreme Court had no JURISDICTION to hear the case because Texas's status as a state had changed due to its SECESSION during the Civil War. Thus, federal law was not applicable at the time the bonds were transferred.

The Supreme Court rejected the bondholders' arguments. Chief Justice SALMON P. CHASE, in his majority opinion, held that the Constitution "in all its provisions, looks to an indestructible Union, composed of indestructible States." Once a TERRITORY gained admission to the Union as a state, its relationship to the Union was perpetual and indissoluble unless terminated by REVOLUTION or consent of the states. Therefore, the secession of the insurgent government from the Union was VOID. Texas remained a state during the Civil War, and its citizens were still citizens of the United States.

The defeat of the secessionist Texas regime left Texas without a lawful government, and its rights as a member of the Union were suspended. The Court ruled that under the Guarantee Clause of the U.S. Constitution the U.S. government had the right to provide Texas with a republican form of government. Hence, the president was authorized to establish a provisional government. This action, which had been ratified by Congress in the Reconstruction Acts, buttressed the federal government's right to oversee the post–Civil War South.

Based on these principles, the Court easily disposed of the substantive issues. The Court held that the state had retained TITLE to the bonds. The contract made by the illegal secessionist government with White and other bondholders was void, as this government had no legal authority to make the contract. The bonds themselves were not negotiable because they were not endorsed by the governor. The repealing statute enacted by the Confederate government was void because of its illegal purpose. The bondholders who had purchased the bonds from White and Chiles could be denied payment because they had assumed a risk of bad title, as the bonds were already past due and were sold at a price substantially lower than FACE VALUE.

THEATERS AND SHOWS 📖 Comprehensive terms for places where all types of entertainment events can be viewed, including films, plays, and exhibitions. 📖

Since these types of entertainment affect the PUBLIC INTEREST, they may properly be subjected to government regulation. The power to regulate must, however, be exercised reasonably since it restrains the free speech rights of performers, filmmakers, and distributors. A city is not permitted to prohibit all theaters or shows,

The famous Apollo Theater in Harlem advanced the careers of dozens of famous black entertainers. Beginning in the 1930s it became a premier performance venue in New York City.

PHOTO RESEARCHERS

for example, but it can properly set forth regulations governing fire safety and crowd control. In addition, MINORS, unaccompanied by a parent or GUARDIAN, can be forbidden to attend shows or performances after dark or deemed "adult entertainment." Public séances for money-making purposes are sometimes unlawful because they can be used to cheat certain individuals. Temporary shows likely to attract large crowds over a short period of time, such as outdoor rock music concerts, must be approved in advance by authorities who must supervise plans to protect the health and safety of both the people attending the show and those who reside in the area. Local regulations may require that theater buildings be constructed with flameproof materials for floors, walls, seats, curtains, and carpeting; that, in general, a certain amount of light be on even during performances; and that exits large enough to handle crowds be placed at different sides of the building and clearly marked. Theaters are ordinarily required to have ushers on duty to maintain order by supervising the movement of crowds.

Ticket Sales To protect the public, a number of communities have enacted statutes regulating the resale of tickets for any kind of theater or show in order to discourage speculation, which weakens the market for the tickets. Such measures also prevent scalping (the process whereby large numbers of tickets purchased at the normal price in order to create a shortage are then sold at extremely inflated prices). A state or local government may make it a criminal offense to sell a ticket for more than the price stamped on it.

Frequently the statutory scheme that proscribes resale of tickets for more than the printed price includes special provisions for ticket BROKERS, who are in the business of selling tickets for a number of theaters to members of the public. Brokers are strictly regulated to protect the public from FRAUD, EXTORTION, and exorbitant rates. A dishonest broker could possibly sell tickets for performances not scheduled, sell seats already sold, or scalp the tickets. For the public protection, a state or city may require anyone reselling tickets to be licensed and may revoke the LICENSE of any broker who abuses the privilege.

Obscenity Communities have a proper interest in placing limitations upon OBSCENITY in theaters. It is deemed appropriate to protect unsuspecting or unwilling adults from assaults of indecency and to protect children from graphic displays of PORNOGRAPHY. The U.S. Supreme Court has interpreted the Constitution to permit individuals to view OBSCENE materials in the PRIVACY of their own homes; however, since theaters are public places, the law may regulate indecent exhibitions, even where everyone present expected to view pornography and willingly entered. Some states, however, decline to prosecute the spectators under such circumstances. Exhibitors of lewd films in coin-operated booths in amusement arcades cannot claim any right of privacy even though patrons view the films alone in the booths.

CENSORSHIP of obscene shows is lawful; however, it is sometimes difficult to determine what is obscene. The U.S. Supreme Court has decided that works that describe or depict sexual conduct can be regulated if, when taken as a whole, they appeal to a prurient interest, portray sexual conduct in a patently offensive way, and lack serious literary, artistic, political, or scientific value. In addition, the Supreme Court has said that communities may apply their own local standards in judging shows, which has led to conflicting decisions in various courts.

A state can regulate theaters and shows in order to control pornography in a number of ways. For example, a state might require distributors or exhibitors who handle films commercially to be licensed, and may revoke the license of anyone who traffics in obscene films. Certain states and municipalities have set up a board of censors who are authorized to view films prior to their exhibition to the public. The concept of censorship by PRIOR RESTRAINT is in direct conflict with notions of free speech.

CROSS-REFERENCES

Entertainment Law; First Amendment; Freedom of Speech; Movie Rating; X Rating.

THEFT 📖 A criminal act in which PROPERTY belonging to another is taken without that person's consent. 📖

The term *theft* is sometimes used synonymously with LARCENY. *Theft*, however, is actually a broader term, encompassing many forms of deceitful taking of property, including swindling, EMBEZZLEMENT, and FALSE PRETENSES. Some states categorize all these offenses under a single statutory crime of theft.

See also BURGLARY; ROBBERY.

THEODOSIAN CODE 📖 The legal code of the Roman Empire promulgated in A.D. 438 by the emperor Theodosius II of the East and accepted by the emperor Valentinian III of the West. 📖

The Theodosian Code was designed to eliminate superfluous material and to organize the complex body of imperial constitutions that had been in effect since the time of the emperor Constantine I (306–337). It was derived primarily from two private collections: the Gregorian Code, or Codex Gregorianus, a collection of constitutions from the emperor Hadrian (117–138) down to Constantine compiled by the Roman jurist Gregorius in the fifth century; and the Hermogenian Code, or Codex Hermogenianus, a collection of the constitutions of the emperors Diocletian (284–305) and Maximian (285–305) prepared by the fifth-century jurist Hermogenes to supplement the Gregorian Code. The Theodosian Code was one of the sources of the CIVIL LAW, the system of Roman jurisprudence compiled and codified in the CORPUS JURIS CIVILIS in A.D. 528–534 under the direction of the Byzantine emperor JUSTINIAN. Until the twelfth century, when the Corpus Juris Civilis became known in the West, the Theodosian Code was the only authentic body of civil law in widespread use in Western Europe.

See also ROMAN LAW.

THIRD AMENDMENT   The Third Amendment to the U.S. Constitution reads:

> No Soldier shall, in time of peace be quartered in any house, without the consent of the Owner, nor in time of war, but in a manner to be prescribed by law.

Ratified in 1791, the Third Amendment to the U.S. Constitution sets forth two basic requirements. During times of peace, the military may not house its troops in private residences without the consent of the owners. During times of war, the military may not house its troops in private residences except in accordance with established legal procedure. By placing these limitations on the private quartering of combatants, the Third Amendment subordinates military authority to civilian control and safeguards against abuses that can be perpetrated by standing armies and professional soldiers.

The Third Amendment traces its roots to English law. In 1689 the English Bill of Rights prohibited the maintenance of a standing army in time of peace without the consent of Parliament. Less than a century later Parliament passed the Quartering Acts of 1765 and 1774, which authorized British troops to take shelter in colonial homes by military fiat. During the American Revolution, British Red Coats frequently relied on this authorization, making themselves unwelcome guests at private residences throughout the colonies. By 1776 the DECLARATION OF INDEPENDENCE was assailing the king of England for quartering "large bodies of troops among us" and keeping "standing armies without the consent of our legislature."

Against this backdrop, a number of colonies enacted laws prohibiting the nonconsensual quartering of soldiers. The Delaware Declaration of Rights of 1776, for example, provided that "no soldier ought to be quartered in any house in time of peace without the consent of the owner, and in time of war in such a manner only as the legislature shall direct." Similar expressions also appeared in the Maryland Declaration of Rights of 1776, the Massachusetts Declaration of Rights of 1780, and the New Hampshire Bill of Rights of 1784. Originally drafted by JAMES MADISON in 1789, the Third Amendment embodies the spirit and intent of its colonial antecedents.

Primarily because the United States has not been regularly confronted by standing armies during its history, the Third Amendment has produced little litigation. The Supreme Court has never had occasion to decide a case based solely on the Third Amendment, though the Court has cited its protections against the quartering of soldiers as a basis for the constitutional right to PRIVACY (see *Griswold v. Connecticut*, 381 U.S. 479, 85 S. Ct. 1678, 14 L. Ed. 2d 510 [1965]). In lower federal courts, Third Amendment claims typically have been rejected without much discussion.

However, in 1982 the U.S. Court of Appeals for the Second Circuit issued the seminal interpretation of the Third Amendment in *Engblom v. Carey*, 677 F.2d 957 (1982). *Engblom* raised the issue of whether the state of New York had violated the Third Amendment by housing members of the NATIONAL GUARD at the residences of two correctional officers who were living in a dormitory on the grounds of a state penitentiary. The governor had activated the guard to quell disorder at the penitentiary during a protracted labor strike. Although the Second Circuit court did not decide whether the Third Amendment had been violated, it made three other important rulings. First, the court ruled that under the Due Process Clause of the FOURTEENTH AMENDMENT, the Third Amendment applies to action taken by the state governments no less than it applies to actions by the federal government. Second, the court ruled that the two correctional officers were "owners" of their residences for the purposes of the Third Amendment, even though they were renting their dormitory room from the state of New York. Any person who lawfully possesses or controls a particular dwelling, the court said, enjoys a reasonable expectation of privacy in that dwelling that precludes the nonconsensual quartering of soldiers. Third, the court ruled that members of the National Guard are "soldiers" governed by the strictures of the Third Amendment. No federal court has had the opportunity to reexamine these Third Amendment issues since *Engblom*.

See also BILL OF RIGHTS; INCORPORATION DOCTRINE.

THIRD DEGREE 📖 A colloquial term used to describe unlawful methods of coercing an individual to confess to a criminal offense by overcoming his or her free will through the use of psychological or physical violence.

The least serious grade of a specific crime—the grades being classified by the law according to the circumstances under which the crime is committed—for which the least punishment specified by statute will be imposed. 📖

THIRD PARTY 📖 A generic legal term for any individual who does not have a direct connection with a legal transaction but who might be affected by it. 📖

A *third-party beneficiary* is an individual for whose benefit a CONTRACT is created even though that person is a stranger to both the agreement and the CONSIDERATION. Such an individual can usually bring suit to enforce the contract or promise made for his or her benefit.

A *third-party action* is another name for the procedural device of IMPLEADER, which is used in a CIVIL ACTION by a defendant who wants to bring a third party into a lawsuit because that party will ultimately be liable for all, or part of, the DAMAGES that may be awarded to the plaintiff.

THIRTEENTH AMENDMENT The Thirteenth Amendment to the U.S. Constitution reads:

> *Section 1.* Neither slavery nor involuntary servitude, except as a punishment for crime whereof the party shall have been duly convicted, shall exist within the United States, or any place subject to their jurisdiction.
>
> *Section 2.* Congress shall have power to enforce this article by appropriate legislation.

The Thirteenth, Fourteenth, and Fifteenth Amendments to the U.S. Constitution were approved by Congress and ratified by the states after the Civil War. Known collectively as the Civil War Amendments, they were designed to protect individual rights. The Thirteenth Amendment forbids INVOLUNTARY SERVITUDE or SLAVERY, except where the condition is imposed on an individual as punishment for a crime.

For many decades, however, the goals of the Civil War Amendments were frustrated. Due perhaps to the waning public support for postwar Reconstruction and the nation's lack of sensitivity to individual rights, the U.S. Supreme Court severely curtailed the application of the amendments. The Supreme Court thwarted the amendments in two ways: by re-strictively interpreting the substantive provisions of the amendments and by rigidly confining Congress's enforcement power.

Congress enacted a number of statutes to enforce the provisions of the Civil War Amendments, but by the end of the nineteenth century, most of those statutes had been overturned by the courts, repealed, or nullified by subsequent legislation. For example, Congress enacted the CIVIL RIGHTS ACT of 1875 (18 Stat. 336), which provided that all persons should have full and equal enjoyment of public inns, parks, theaters, and other places of amusement, regardless of race or color. Although some federal courts upheld the constitutionality of the act, many courts struck it down. These decisions were then appealed together to the U.S. Supreme Court and became known as the *Civil Rights* cases, 109 U.S. 3, 3 S. Ct. 18, 27 L. Ed. 835 (1883). The cases involved theaters in New York and California that would not seat blacks, a hotel in Missouri and a restaurant in Kansas that would not serve blacks, and a train in Tennessee that would not allow a black woman in the "ladies" car. The Supreme Court struck down the Civil Rights Act of 1875 by an 8–1 vote, holding that Congress had exceeded its authority to enforce the Thirteenth and Fourteenth Amendments. The Court held that private DISCRIMINATION against blacks did not violate the Thirteenth Amendment's ban on slavery. Following this decision, several northern and western states began enacting their own bans on discrimination in public places. But many other states did the opposite: they began codifying racial segregation and discrimination in laws that became known as the JIM CROW LAWS.

In 1896 the U.S. Supreme Court decided the case of *Plessy v. Ferguson*, 163 U.S. 537, 16 S. Ct. 1138, 41 L. Ed. 256, in which it upheld segregation on railroad cars. Desegregationists had hoped that the Supreme Court would acknowledge that the federal government's power to regulate interstate commerce allowed it to ban segregation on public transportation. But the Court avoided this issue, holding that this particular railway was a purely local line. In addition, the Court found that the segregation rules did not violate the Thirteenth Amendment because they did not establish a state of involuntary servitude, although they did distinguish between races. In a lone dissent, Justice JOHN MARSHALL HARLAN argued that the "arbitrary separation of citizens, on the basis of race, while they are on a public highway, is a badge of servitude wholly inconsistent with the civil freedom and the equality before the law established by the constitution."

During the next six decades, the U.S. Supreme Court continued to uphold segregation of the races in schools, public accommodations, public transportation, and various other aspects of public life, so long as the treatment of the races was equal. The Court refused to hear cases arguing that the Thirteenth Amendment was violated by private COVENANTS between whites who agreed not to sell or lease their homes to African Americans. Thus, the covenants were allowed to stand. Gradually, though, the Supreme Court's narrow view of the Civil War Amendments expanded, resulting in significant changes in civil and criminal law. This expansion began in 1954, when the Court overturned its decision in *Plessy v. Ferguson* and outlawed the SEPARATE-BUT-EQUAL doctrine (*Brown v. Board of Education of Topeka, Kansas*, 347 U.S. 483, 74 S. Ct. 686, 98 L. Ed. 873 [1954]).

Although the Supreme Court had declared invalid the Civil Rights Act of 1875, it had not invalidated an earlier act, the Civil Rights Act of 1866 (42 U.S.C.A. § 1982). The Civil Rights Act of 1866 was specifically enacted to enforce the Thirteenth Amendment's ban on slavery. By 1968 the U.S. Supreme Court was relying on the Civil Rights Act of 1866 to prohibit individuals from discriminating against racial minorities in the sale or LEASE of housing (*Jones v. Alfred H. Mayer Co.*, 392 U.S. 409, 88 S. Ct. 2186, 20 L. Ed. 2d 1189 [1968]). This decision was issued just weeks after Congress enacted the first federal fair housing laws. In reaching the decision in *Jones*, the Supreme Court first had to decide whether Congress had the power to enact the Civil Rights Act of 1866. Justice POTTER STEWART, writing for the majority, turned to the Thirteenth Amendment and observed that it was adopted to remove the "badges of slavery" and that it gave Congress power to effect that removal. Stewart wrote:

> Congress has the power under the Thirteenth Amendment rationally to determine what are the badges and the incidents of slavery, and the authority to translate that determination into effective legislation. . . . [W]hen racial discrimination herds men into ghettos and makes their ability to buy property turn on the color of their skin, then it too is a relic of slavery.

The Supreme Court continues to address issues that arise under the Thirteenth Amendment. In the 1988 case of *United States v. Kozminski*, 487 U.S. 931, 108 S. Ct. 2751, 100 L. Ed. 2d 788, the Court explored the meaning of the term *involuntary servitude*. This case addressed the Thirteenth Amendment as well as a federal criminal statute (18 U.S.C.A. § 1584) that forbids involuntary servitude. At issue in the case were two mentally retarded men in poor health who had been kept laboring on a farm. The men worked seven days a week, seventeen hours a day, initially for $15 per week and then for no pay at all. Their employers used various forms of physical and psychological threats and force to keep the men on the farm. The Court held that "involuntary servitude" requires more than mere psychological coercion; it also requires physical or legal coercion. But, the Court noted, the Thirteenth Amendment was designed not only to abolish slavery of African Americans, but also to prevent other forms of compulsory labor akin to that slavery.

Observing that the definition of slavery has shifted since the Civil War, courts have held that involuntary servitude does not necessarily require a black slave and a white master (*Steirer v. Bethlehem Area School District*, 789 F. Supp. 1337 [E.D. Pa. 1992]). The courts have found that religious sects may be guilty of subjecting an individual to involuntary servitude if the sect knowingly and willfully holds an individual against her will (*United States v. Lewis*, 644 F. Supp. 1391 [W.D. Mich. 1986], *aff'd*, 840 F.2d 1276 (6th Cir.), *cert. denied*, 488 U.S. 894, 109 S. Ct. 234, 102 L. Ed. 2d 224 [1988]). In addition, forcing a mental patient to perform nontherapeutic labor may be a form of involuntary servitude (*Weidenfeller v. Kidulis*, 380 F. Supp. 445 [E.D. Wis. 1974]). However, laws that prohibit landlords from evicting long-term tenants have been held by the courts not to constitute involuntary servitude (*Dawson v. Higgins*, 610 N.Y.S.2d 200 [App. Div. 1994]).

The Thirteenth Amendment does not prohibit the government from compelling citizens to perform certain civic duties, such as serving on a jury (see *Hurtado v. United States*, 410 U.S. 578, 93 S. Ct. 1157, 35 L. Ed. 2d 508 [1973]) or participating in the military draft (*Selective Draft Law* cases, 245 U.S. 366, 38 S. Ct. 159, 62 L. Ed. 349 [1918]).

A related statute is the Anti-Peonage Act (42 U.S.C.A. § 1994). PEONAGE is defined as compulsory service based upon the indebtedness of the peon to the master. The courts have held that neither the Thirteenth Amendment nor the Anti-Peonage Act prevents a convicted person from being required to work on public streets as part of his sentence (*Loeb v. Jennings*, 67 S.E. 101 (Ga. 1910), *aff'd*, 219 U.S. 582, 31 S. Ct. 469, 55 L. Ed. 345 [1911]). In addition, neither of these laws prevents the government from garnishing wages or using the court's

CONTEMPT power to collect overdue taxes or CHILD SUPPORT (*Beltran v. Cohen*, 303 F. Supp. 889 [N.D. Cal. 1969]; *Knight v. Knight*, 996 F.2d 1225 [9th Cir. 1993]).

The courts have also held that state workfare programs that require or encourage citizens to obtain gainful employment in order to participate in the state's public assistance programs do not constitute involuntary servitude or peonage (*Brogan v. San Mateo County*, 901 F.2d 762 [9th Cir. 1990]). In another interesting application of these laws, a federal court held that a high school program that required all students to complete sixty hours of community service in order to graduate did not constitute involuntary servitude or peonage (*Steirer v. Bethlehem Area School District*, 789 F. Supp. 1337 [E.D. Pa. 1992]).

CROSS-REFERENCES

Brown v. Board of Education of Topeka, Kansas; Civil Rights; Fifteenth Amendment; Fourteenth Amendment; *Plessy v. Ferguson*.

THOMAS, CLARENCE Associate Justice Clarence Thomas survived tense, nationally televised Senate confirmation hearings in 1991 to become the second African American in U.S. history to reach the High Court.

Thomas was born June 23, 1948, in Pin Point, Georgia, a small town near Savannah. He attended Savannah's Saint Benedict the Moor, Saint Pius X High School, and Saint John Vianney Minor Seminary. When he graduated from Saint John in 1967, he was the only African American in his class. After just one year as a seminarian at Missouri's Immaculate Conception Seminary, Thomas abandoned his plans to become a priest. Instead, he enrolled in Massachusetts's Holy Cross College. After graduating in 1971, he attended Connecticut's Yale University Law School, and earned a doctor of jurisprudence degree in 1974.

Thomas married Kathy Grace Ambush in 1971. The couple had a son, Jamal Thomas, in 1973, and divorced in 1984. In 1986, he married Virginia Lamp, a political activist and a lawyer for the U.S. Department of Labor.

Thomas's first job out of law school was as assistant to Missouri's Republican attorney general John C. Danforth. Thomas specialized in

BIOGRAPHY

Clarence Thomas

"WE DO NOT START FROM THE PREMISE THAT [STATUTORY] LANGUAGE IS IMPRECISE. INSTEAD, WE ASSUME THAT IN DRAFTING . . . LEGISLATION, CONGRESS SAID WHAT IT MEANT."

tax and environmental issues. In 1977 he accepted a position in the law department of Monsanto Chemical Corporation. Thomas returned to public service in 1979, when Danforth was elected to the U.S. Senate. Danforth invited Thomas to work for him as a legislative aide in Washington, D.C.

Thomas's star rose quickly during the Republican administration of President RONALD REAGAN. In 1981 he was appointed assistant secretary in the CIVIL RIGHTS division of the U.S. Department of Education. It was here that his path crossed that of Anita Hill, a recent Yale University Law School graduate. In 1982, when Thomas became chair of the Equal Employment Opportunity Commission (EEOC), Hill also moved to the federal agency.

In 1990 Thomas became a federal judge for the Court of Appeals for the District of Columbia. In 1991 President GEORGE BUSH nominated Thomas to the U.S. Supreme Court. During the confirmation process, Hill accused Thomas of sexually harassing her while she worked for him at the EEOC. After tense hearings before the U.S. Senate, Thomas was confirmed by a vote of 52–48. On October 18, 1991, he was sworn in as the 106th justice of the U.S. Supreme Court.

Thomas is known as a conservative justice, voting to uphold states' rights and limit the powers of the federal government. He frequently votes with Justice ANTONIN SCALIA and Chief Justice WILLIAM REHNQUIST.

CROSS-REFERENCES

Hill, Anita Faye; Sexual Harassment *In Focus*: Clarence Thomas and Anita Hill Hearings.

THOMPSON, SMITH Smith Thompson served as associate justice of the U.S. Supreme Court from 1824 until his death in 1843. A prominent member of the New York bar and chief justice of the New York Supreme Court, Thompson also served as secretary of the navy during President JAMES MONROE's administration.

Thompson was born on January 17, 1768, in New York City, New York. After graduating from Princeton University in 1788, he studied law with Gilbert Livingston, a member of a politically powerful family, and JAMES KENT, a

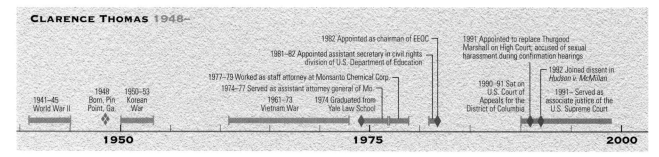

CLARENCE THOMAS 1948–

1941–45 World War II

1948 Born, Pin Point, Ga.

1950–53 Korean War

1961–73 Vietnam War

1974 Graduated from Yale Law School

1974–77 Served as assistant attorney general of Mo.

1977–79 Worked as staff attorney at Monsanto Chemical Corp.

1981–82 Appointed assistant secretary in civil rights division of U.S. Department of Education

1982 Appointed as chairman of EEOC

1990–91 Sat on U.S. Court of Appeals for the District of Columbia

1991 Appointed to replace Thurgood Marshall on High Court; accused of sexual harassment during confirmation hearings

1991– Served as associate justice of the U.S. Supreme Court

1992 Joined dissent in *Hudson v. McMillan*

1950   1975   2000

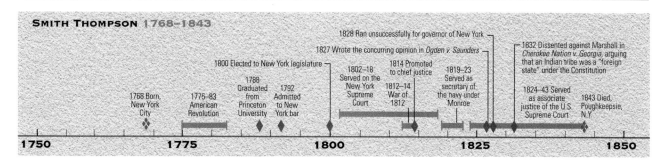

SMITH THOMPSON 1768–1843

1828 Ran unsuccessfully for governor of New York

1827 Wrote the concurring opinion in *Ogden v. Saunders*

1832 Dissented against Marshall in *Cherokee Nation v. Georgia*, arguing that an Indian tribe was a "foreign state" under the Constitution

1800 Elected to New York legislature

1814 Promoted to chief justice

1802–18 Served on the New York Supreme Court

1819–23 Served as secretary of the navy under Monroe

1788 Graduated from Princeton University

1792 Admitted to New York bar

1812–14 War of 1812

1824–43 Served as associate justice of the U.S. Supreme Court

1768 Born, New York City

1775–83 American Revolution

1843 Died, Poughkeepsie, N.Y.

1750   1775   1800   1825   1850

towering figure in U.S. jurisprudence. Thompson was admitted to the New York bar in 1792. When Kent left the law firm in 1795, Thompson became Livingston's partner and eventually married Livingston's daughter Sarah.

Thompson was elected to the New York legislature in 1800 and then used Livingston's political connections to obtain an appointment to the state supreme court in 1802. He was promoted to chief justice in 1814, in which position he presided until 1818.

President Monroe appointed Thompson secretary of the navy in 1819. As head of the department, Thompson earned Monroe's trust and respect. Although he had presidential ambitions, Thompson agreed to accept Monroe's offer of a seat on the U.S. Supreme Court, joining the Court in 1824. In 1828, however, he returned to politics, running unsuccessfully for the governorship of New York even though he did not resign from the bench.

As a justice, Thompson believed that the states should be allowed to regulate commerce unless their laws directly conflicted with federal law. This position put him in conflict with Chief Justice JOHN MARSHALL and Justice JOSEPH STORY, who interpreted the Constitution's COMMERCE CLAUSE as giving the federal government the exclusive right to regulate interstate commerce. Thompson wrote the concurring opinion in the landmark case of *Ogden v. Saunders*, 25 U.S. (12 Wheat.) 213, 6 L. Ed. 606 (1827), which held that any law passed after the execution of a contract, in this case a New York insolvency statute, was part of the contract. In another important case, *Kendall v. United States ex rel. Stokes*, 37 U.S. (12 Pet.) 524, 9 L. Ed.

BIOGRAPHY

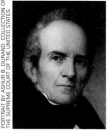

Smith Thompson

1181 (1838), Thompson supported the right of federal courts to issue a writ of MANDAMUS to compel a cabinet officer to perform nondiscretionary, ministerial obligations.

Thompson died on December 18, 1843, in Poughkeepsie, New York.

THOREAU, HENRY DAVID   Henry David Thoreau was a nineteenth-century philosopher and writer who denounced materialistic modes of living and encouraged people to act according to their own beliefs of right and wrong, even if doing so required breaking the law. His writings, especially his call for nonviolent resistance to government injustice, have inspired many later reformers.

Thoreau was born on July 12, 1817, in Concord, Massachusetts. He graduated from Harvard College in 1837. During his college years, he was greatly influenced by Ralph Waldo Emerson, the leader of the transcendental movement. Thoreau became a personal friend of the eminent author and spent several years as Emerson's houseguest. Their long friendship was a significant influence on Thoreau's writing and philosophy.

Through Emerson, Thoreau met many other brilliant thinkers and writers of the time, including Margaret Fuller, Nathaniel Hawthorne, and Amos Bronson Alcott. This group of transcendentalists supported a plain and simple lifestyle spent searching for the truth beyond one's taught beliefs. Unlike some of the other transcendentalists, Thoreau lived out many of their beliefs. Thoreau's first work, *A Week on the Concord and Merrimack Rivers*, was published in 1849 and is considered the definitive statement of his transcendalist beliefs.

BIOGRAPHY

Henry David Thoreau

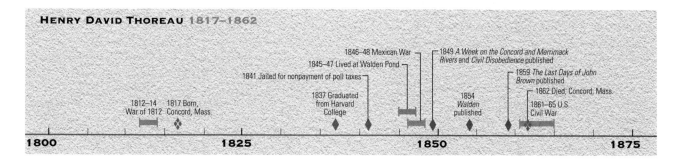

HENRY DAVID THOREAU 1817–1862

1846–48 Mexican War

1849 *A Week on the Concord and Merrimack Rivers* and *Civil Disobedience* published

1845–47 Lived at Walden Pond

1859 *The Last Days of John Brown* published

1841 Jailed for nonpayment of poll taxes

1862 Died, Concord, Mass.

1837 Graduated from Harvard College

1854 *Walden* published

1812–14 War of 1812

1817 Born, Concord, Mass.

1861–65 U.S. Civil War

1800   1825   1850   1875

For several years in the 1830s and 1840s, Thoreau refused to pay poll taxes to the government as a way of protesting SLAVERY, which the government permitted. The POLL TAX was levied on all men over the age of twenty. Thoreau was finally jailed overnight for this refusal in 1841 but was bailed out by his relatives who paid his back taxes for him.

From July 4, 1845, to September 6, 1847, Thoreau lived alone at Walden Pond, Massachusetts, on a plot of land owned by Emerson. There Thoreau devoted his time to studying nature and writing. While at Walden Pond, he wrote *Walden*, a collection of essays about nature and human nature that was published in 1854.

Later Thoreau became outraged by the Mexican War, which he believed was caused by greed for Mexican land, and by the FUGITIVE SLAVE ACT, which helped slave owners recover escaped slaves. As a result of this outrage, Thoreau wrote an essay that was published in 1849 under the title *Civil Disobedience* (Thoreau's original title was *Resistance to Civil Government*). The essay contended that each person owes a greater duty to his own conscience and belief system than is owed to the government. Thus, Thoreau encouraged people to refuse to obey laws that they believe are unjust.

Civil Disobedience also supported theories of anarchy based upon Thoreau's insistence that people misuse government. He argued that the Mexican War was started by just a few people who used the U.S. government as a tool. Thoreau maintained that because the U.S. system of government was slow to correct itself through the will of the majority, people should immediately withdraw their support from government and act according to their beliefs of what is right.

Thoreau did not approve of violent resistance to government, however. He advocated peaceful or passive resistance. In 1859, when John Brown staged a violent revolt against slavery, Thoreau believed that Brown was right in acting according to his beliefs even though his actions were against the law. Although Thoreau did not admire the violent method that Brown used in trying to stop slavery, Thoreau did admire Brown's commitment to doing what he believed was right. In 1859 Thoreau published *The Last Days of John Brown*, an essay describing how Brown's actions convinced many Northerners that slavery must be totally abolished.

Thoreau's writings and philosophy greatly influenced many important world figures. For example, the reformer Leo Tolstoy of Russia, Mohandas Gandhi of India, MARTIN LUTHER KING, JR., and other leaders of the U.S. CIVIL RIGHTS MOVEMENT were inspired by Thoreau's ideas. Thoreau died of tuberculosis on May 6, 1862, in Concord, Massachusetts.

See also ANARCHISM.

"I WISH TO LIVE DELIBERATELY, TO FRONT ONLY THE ESSENTIAL FACTS OF LIFE, AND SEE IF I COULD LEARN WHAT IT HAD TO TEACH."

BIOGRAPHY

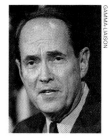

GAMMA-LIAISON

Richard Lewis Thornburgh

THORNBURGH, RICHARD LEWIS Richard Lewis Thornburgh served as U.S. attorney general from 1988 to 1991, working for the Reagan and Bush administrations. A former governor of Pennsylvania, Thornburgh put a strong emphasis on criminal enforcement during his tenure and moved away from the ideological social issues favored by his predecessor, EDWIN MEESE III.

Thornburgh was born on July 16, 1932, in Carnegie, Pennsylvania. He graduated from Yale University with an engineering degree in 1954 and earned a law degree from the University of Pittsburgh in 1957. After his admission to the Pennsylvania bar in 1958, he joined the Pittsburgh law firm of Kirkpatrick, Lockhart, Johnson, and Hutchinson.

In 1969 President RICHARD M. NIXON appointed Thornburgh U.S. attorney for western Pennsylvania. He served as U.S. attorney until 1975, when he joined the Department of Justice as an assistant attorney general. As head of the department's criminal division, Thornburgh was instrumental in setting up the public integrity section that investigated alleged improprieties by department personnel.

After leaving office in 1977, Thornburgh returned to the Kirkpatrick law firm in Pittsburgh, but he was intent on beginning a political career. In 1978 he was elected governor of

RICHARD LEWIS THORNBURGH 1925–

1932 Born, Carnegie, Pa.

1939–45 World War II

1950–53 Korean War

1958 Admitted to Pa. bar and joined firm of Kirkpatrick, Lockhart, Johnson, and Hutchinson

1961–73 Vietnam War

1969–75 Served as U.S. attorney for western Pennsylvania

1975–77 Served as assistant U.S. attorney general in charge of the Justice Department's criminal division

1978–87 Served as governor of Pa.

1979 Three Mile Island nuclear accident occurred

1988–91 Served as U.S. attorney general under Reagan and Bush

1989 Initiated the Sentencing Reform Act

1991 Ran unsuccessfully for U.S. Senate

1992–93 Served as undersecretary general of the United Nations

1993 Rejoined Kirkpatrick & Lockhart in their Washington office

1925   1950   1975   2000

Pennsylvania, an office he held until 1987. In his early days as governor, Thornburgh was thrust into the national limelight. The nuclear accident at the Three Mile Island nuclear power plant in the spring of 1979 set off a wave of panic in Pennsylvania. Thornburgh was credited with bringing calm to the state.

In July 1988 President RONALD REAGAN appointed Thornburgh U.S. attorney general, succeeding Edwin Meese. Meese had become a controversial figure in the Reagan administration. He had stressed social issues such as ABORTION and PORNOGRAPHY and had pushed for an end to AFFIRMATIVE ACTION. Meese also had come under scrutiny for possible criminal conflict-of-interest charges. He resigned only after an independent counsel declined to file criminal charges.

Taking office under these circumstances, Thornburgh sought to restore integrity and credibility to the department. During the last months of the Reagan administration, he moved to revitalize management of the department, refocus its energies on prosecuting crimes involving guns or drugs, and aggressively pursue white-collar criminals.

His early months in office convinced President GEORGE BUSH to reappoint Thornburgh attorney general. His tenure in the Bush administration drew criticism from some conservative groups for his prosecution of environmental crimes and for his strong enforcement of CIVIL RIGHTS protection for disabled persons. Within the department, his management style provoked criticism. Career department officials called him aloof and alleged that he employed political partisanship in the administration of justice.

Thornburgh resigned as attorney general in July 1991 to run for the U.S. Senate from Pennsylvania in a special election. Harris Wofford, his Democratic opponent, had been appointed senator to fill the seat until the special election. At the beginning of the campaign, Thornburgh enjoyed a forty-point lead in the opinion polls. Wofford, however, argued that the country needed a national HEALTH INSURANCE system and reminded voters of the economy, which was in recession. Thornburgh's lead crumbled. Wofford easily defeated him, earning 55 percent of the vote to Thornburgh's 45 percent.

In 1992 President Bush appointed Thornburgh undersecretary general of the United Nations, a position he held until 1993. Thornburgh rejoined the Kirkpatrick law firm's Washington, D.C., office and served as a legal commentator on several television network news and talk shows.

"THIS COLLECTIVE AMNESIA THAT SEEMS TO AFFECT THE WHITE HOUSE STAFF WOULD CONCERN ME IF I WERE THE PRESIDENT."

THREATS Spoken or written words tending to intimidate or menace others.

Statutes in a number of JURISDICTIONS prohibit the use of threats and unlawful communications by any person. Some of the more common types of threats forbidden by law are those made with an intent to obtain a pecuniary advantage or to compel a person to act against his or her will. In all states, it is an offense to threaten to (1) use a deadly weapon on another person; (2) injure another's person or property; or (3) injure another's reputation.

It is a federal offense to threaten to harm the president or to use the mail to transmit threatening communications. These laws must be balanced against FIRST AMENDMENT rights.

Unlawful communications include, among other things, the use of threats to prevent another from engaging in a lawful occupation and writing LIBELOUS letters or letters that tend to provoke a BREACH OF THE PEACE. The use of intimidation for purposes of collecting an unpaid debt has been held to constitute an unlawful communication but might be prosecuted as EXTORTION.

A mere threat that does not cause any harm is generally not ACTIONABLE. When combined with apparently imminent bodily harm, however, a threat is an ASSAULT for which the offender might be subject to civil or criminal liability. In most jurisdictions, a plaintiff can recover DAMAGES for the intentional infliction of severe mental or emotional suffering caused by threats or unlawful communications.

In those jurisdictions that have statutes prohibiting unlawful communications, such as letters that tend to provoke a breach of the peace, a violation of the statute gives rise to a CIVIL ACTION for damages.

THURMOND, JAMES STROM   James Strom Thurmond began serving as U.S. senator from South Carolina in 1954. An outspoken opponent of federal CIVIL RIGHTS legislation for most of his career, Thurmond softened his views in the 1970s. Originally a member of the Democratic party, Thurmond joined the Republican party in 1964.

Thurmond was born on December 5, 1902, in Edgefield, South Carolina. Thurmond's father, John William Thurmond, was an attorney who served as county prosecutor and later as U.S. district attorney. He was also a powerful political leader in Edgefield County. Strom, as he preferred to be called, graduated from Clemson University in 1923. He was a teacher and athletic coach in several South Carolina school districts before becoming superintendent of education for Edgefield County in 1929.

BIOGRAPHY

UPI/CORBIS-BETTMANN

James Strom Thurmond

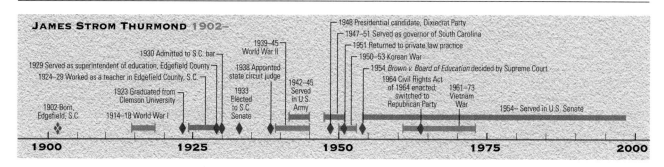

1948 Presidential candidate, Dixiecrat Party
1947–51 Served as governor of South Carolina
1951 Returned to private law practice
1950–53 Korean War
1954 *Brown v. Board of Education* decided by Supreme Court
1964 Civil Rights Act of 1964 enacted; switched to Republican Party
1961–73 Vietnam War
1954– Served in U.S. Senate

1939–45 World War II
1938 Appointed state circuit judge
1942–45 Served in U.S. Army

1930 Admitted to S.C. bar
1929 Served as superintendent of education, Edgefield County
1924–29 Worked as a teacher in Edgefield County, S.C.
1933 Elected to S.C. Senate

1923 Graduated from Clemson University

1902 Born, Edgefield, S.C.
1914–18 World War I

1900 1925 1950 1975 2000

While serving as superintendent, Thurmond studied the law under his father, who had become a state judge. In 1930 Thurmond was admitted to the South Carolina bar. He became a full-time attorney in 1933 and soon became county attorney. It was then that Thurmond decided to pursue a political career. He was elected as a state senator in 1933, serving until 1938, when he gave up his office to accept an appointment as a state circuit judge. He took a leave of absence in 1942 to serve with the Eighty-second Airborne Division during World War II.

On his return to South Carolina, Thurmond resumed his political career. He was elected governor in 1947, serving until 1951. Thurmond believed, as most southern Democrats did, that state-enforced racial segregation was legitimate public policy and that the federal government had no authority to end it. At the 1948 national Democratic party convention, southern Democrats on the platform committee removed President HARRY S. TRUMAN'S proposals for civil rights legislation. When the convention, under the leadership of HUBERT H. HUMPHREY, restored Truman's proposals, many southern Democrats, including Thurmond, walked out of the convention and started a splinter party, the States' Rights Democratic party. It was popularly known as the Dixiecrat party.

The Dixiecrats nominated Thurmond to run for president in the 1948 election. President Truman won the election, winning twenty-eight states. Republican nominee THOMAS E. DEWEY won sixteen states, and Thurmond won four southern states, the third largest independent electoral vote in U.S. history. Thurmond left the governorship in 1951 and resumed the practice of law in Aiken, South Carolina. In 1954 he was elected to the U.S. Senate as a write-in candidate, the first person ever to be elected to the Senate or any other major office by this method. He took the unusual step of resigning in April 1956 to fulfill a 1954 campaign promise that he would allow a REFEREN-

"I DON'T KNOW HOW I GOT SUCH A REPUTATION AS A SEGREGATIONIST . . . I GUESS IT WAS BECAUSE WHEN I WAS THE GOVERNOR OF SOUTH CAROLINA IT WAS MY DUTY TO UPHOLD THE LAW AND THE LAW REQUIRED SEGREGATION, SO I WAS JUST DOING MY DUTY."

DUM on his service in two years. He was re-elected in November 1956 and again in 1960, 1966, 1972, 1978, 1984, 1990, and 1996.

During the 1950s and 1960s, Thurmond was a leading opponent of federal civil rights legislation and social welfare programs. His opposition to the CIVIL RIGHTS ACT of 1964 (42 U.S.C.A. § 2000a et seq.) and President LYNDON B. JOHNSON'S policies led Thurmond in 1964 to switch to the Republican party. Changing political parties is always unusual for political leaders, but it was especially so for Thurmond. The Democratic party dominated the southern states, making them virtually one-party states. Thurmond's defection to the Republican party was a significant act, signaling a major shift in political power in the South that would accelerate in the 1970s and 1980s.

For much of his Senate career, Thurmond served on the Armed Services Committee, the Judiciary Committee, and the Veterans' Affairs Committee. From 1981 to 1987 he was chair of the Judiciary Committee, where he helped President RONALD REAGAN secure Senate confirmation of his judicial appointments. During this period he was also president pro tempore of the Senate. The president pro tempore presides over the Senate when the vice president is absent. From 1988 to 1996 Thurmond chaired the Armed Services Committee.

Thurmond served as adjunct professor of political science at Clemson and distinguished lecturer at its Strom Thurmond Institute. His name has been attached to many public buildings, highways, and other public works in South Carolina.

See also STATES' RIGHTS.

TILDEN, SAMUEL JONES Samuel Jones Tilden was a New York lawyer, political reformer, governor, and Democratic candidate for president in the famous disputed election of 1876. Tilden's acceptance of his defeat in the election may have prevented civil unrest.

Tilden was born on February 9, 1814, in New Lebanon, New York. He attended Yale University and studied law at New York Uni-

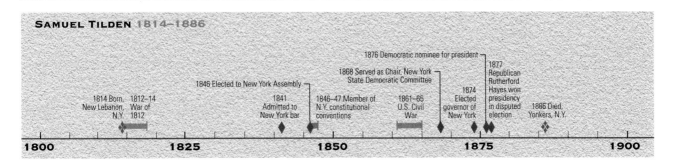

SAMUEL TILDEN 1814–1886

1876 Democratic nominee for president

1868 Served as Chair, New York
State Democratic Committee

1846 Elected to New York Assembly

1877 Republican Rutherford Hayes won presidency in disputed election

1814 Born, New Lebanon, N.Y.

1812–14 War of 1812

1841 Admitted to New York bar

1846–47 Member of N.Y. constitutional conventions

1861–65 U.S. Civil War

1874 Elected governor of New York

1886 Died, Yonkers, N.Y.

1800   1825   1850   1875   1900

versity before being admitted to the New York bar in 1841. Although Tilden suffered frequent illnesses during his life, he soon became a successful corporate attorney, representing powerful RAILROAD and business entities.

In the 1840s Tilden became active in New York Democratic party politics. He served in the New York Assembly in 1846 and was a member of the state constitutional conventions in 1846 and 1847. Opposed to SLAVERY, he actively supported the Union during the Civil War.

In 1868 Tilden began his rise to political prominence. He presided over the New York State Democratic Committee and led a reform movement that collected evidence and prosecuted the notorious Tweed Ring, the corrupt Democratic political machine that controlled and defrauded New York City. Tilden's reforms led to his election as governor of New York in 1874. He continued to enhance his reputation as reformer when he exposed the Canal Ring, a CONSPIRACY of politicians and contractors who had defrauded the state of money intended to pay for the construction of canals.

In 1876, as a result of his accomplishments in New York, Tilden won the Democratic nomination for president and ran against the Republican candidate RUTHERFORD B. HAYES. The campaign was close and heated. Tilden won a majority of the popular votes, and preliminary returns showed that he had 184 of the 185 electoral votes needed to win. Hayes had 165 electoral votes. However, the electoral votes for Florida, Louisiana, and South Carolina were in dispute, and the status of one of Oregon's three electors also was in question. Republicans quickly calculated that if Hayes received every one of the disputed votes, he would win the presidency by a vote of 185 to 184.

Congress was charged under the Constitution with resolving the electoral claims. It created an electoral commission, composed of five members from the House of Representatives, four from the Senate, and five justices from the Supreme Court. The legislative membership

BIOGRAPHY

Samuel Jones Tilden

"NEW YORK [CANNOT] REMAIN THE CENTER OF COMMERCE AND CAPITAL FOR THIS CONTINENT, UNLESS IT HAS AN INDEPENDENT BAR AND AN HONEST JUDICIARY."

was evenly divided between Democratic and Republican members. The commission voted to award all the disputed votes to Hayes. Tilden, who had shown no leadership during this crisis and had made no effort to marshal support, acquiesced, fearing that any further efforts to fight the result would lead to violence. Southern Democrats also went along with the commission's result in exchange for the withdrawal of federal troops from the South and the end of Reconstruction. Hayes removed the troops by the end of April 1877.

After his defeat, Tilden retained influence in the Democratic party. He was considered for the party's presidential nomination in 1880 and 1884, but he declined the opportunity on both occasions.

Tilden died on August 4, 1886, in Yonkers, New York. A wealthy man, Tilden left the bulk of his estate in trust for the establishment of a free public library for New York City. This bequest eventually was used to help build the New York City Library in Manhattan.

TIME   It is legally recognized that time is divided into years, months, weeks, days, hours, minutes, and seconds. The time kept by a municipality is known as civic time. A local government may not use a system of time different from that adopted by its state legislature. During daylight saving time, the customary time system is advanced one hour to take advantage of the longer periods of daylight during the summer months.

Time Zones   In the past, the states followed various standards of time until the railroads of the nation cooperated in establishing a standard time zone system, which was then adopted by federal statutes. Under the standard time zone system, the continental United States is divided into four different zones. The time in each zone is based upon the mean solar time at a specified degree of longitude west from Greenwich, England. Eastern standard time is based on the mean solar time at 75° longitude west; Central standard time, on 90° longitude west; Mountain time, on 105° longitude west; and Pacific time on 120° longitude west.

Calculations A year is the period during which the earth revolves around the sun. A calendar year is 365 days, except for every fourth year, which is 366 days. The year is divided into twelve months. A week ordinarily means seven consecutive days, either beginning with no particular day, or from a Sunday through the following Saturday. A day is twenty-four hours, extending from midnight to midnight. When distinguished from night, however, a day refers to the period from sunrise to sunset.

In calculating a specified number of days, it is customary to exclude the first and include the last. As a consequence, when a LEASE provides that it shall continue for a specified period from a particular day, that day is excluded in computing the term. This rule is applied in calculating the time for matters of practice and procedure. The rule governs, for example, the period in which a lawsuit may be commenced, so that the day the CAUSE OF ACTION accrues is excluded for STATUTE OF LIMITATIONS purposes.

The general rule is that when the last day of a period within which an act is to be performed falls on a Sunday or a holiday, that day is excluded from the computation. The act may rightfully be done on the following business day. This rule has been applied in figuring the deadline for conducting a meeting of corporate shareholders; for filing a claim against a dead person's ESTATE; for filing a statement proposing a new ORDINANCE for a MUNICIPAL CORPORATION; for recording a MORTGAGE; and for redeeming property from a sale foreclosing a mortgage.

TIME DRAFT 📖 A written order to pay a certain sum in money that is payable at a particular future date. 📖

Time drafts, sometimes called time bills or time loans, are frequently used by merchants to finance the transportation of goods.

See also COMMERCIAL PAPER.

TIME IS OF THE ESSENCE 📖 A phrase in a CONTRACT that means that performance by one PARTY at or within the period specified in the contract is necessary to enable that party to require PERFORMANCE by the other party. 📖

Failure to act within the time required constitutes a breach of the contract. The general rule is that time is not of the essence unless the contract expressly so provides. As a result, with respect to REAL ESTATE transactions, the modern view is that time is not of the essence unless the parties have manifested such an intent. The same is generally true in construction contracts and in contracts relating to the manufacture of GOODS. When time is not of the essence, courts generally permit parties to perform their obligations within a reasonable time.

TIMELY 📖 Existing or taking place within the designated period; seasonable. 📖

A legal ACTION is timely filed, for example, when it is brought within the time period set by the STATUTE OF LIMITATIONS.

The meaning of the term *timely* must, in a number of situations, be determined on the basis of the facts and circumstances of each individual case. Courts have extensive discretion in determining whether a particular party has acted in a timely manner in filing papers, serving notices, or bringing MOTIONS in a legal action.

TIME, PLACE, AND MANNER RE-STRICTIONS 📖 Limits that government can impose on the occasion, location, and type of individual expression in some circumstances. 📖

The FIRST AMENDMENT to the U.S. Constitution guarantees FREEDOM OF SPEECH. This guarantee generally safeguards the right of individuals to express themselves without governmental restraint. Nevertheless, the Free Speech Clause of the First Amendment is not absolute. It has never been interpreted to guarantee all forms of speech without any restraint whatsoever. Instead, the U.S. Supreme Court has repeatedly ruled that state and federal governments may

A sample time draft

$ _____   [*City, State*] _____, 19__

_____ after date pay to the order of _____ [*or* to bearer] the sum of _____ dollars. Value received and charge to the account of _____ [*or* to my account].

To _____   [*Signature of Drawer*]

FREDERICK CHARLES/THE GAMMA LIAISON NETWORK

place reasonable restrictions on the time, place, and manner of individual expression. Time, place, and manner (TPM) restrictions accommodate public convenience and promote order by regulating traffic flow, preserving property interests, conserving the environment, and protecting the administration of justice.

The Supreme Court has developed a four-part analysis to evaluate the constitutionality of TPM restrictions. To pass muster under the First Amendment, TPM restrictions must be content-neutral, be narrowly drawn, serve a significant government interest, and leave open alternative channels of communication. Application of this analysis varies in accordance with the circumstances of each case.

The rationale supporting a particular TPM restriction may receive less rigorous scrutiny when the government seeks to regulate speech of lower value such as OBSCENITY and fighting words. OBSCENE speech includes most hard-core PORNOGRAPHY, while fighting words include offensive speech that would incite a REASONABLE person to violence. Conversely, the government must offer "compelling" reasons for regulating highly valued forms of expression, such as political speech. Some speech, such as commercial advertisements, is valued less than political speech but more than obscenity or fighting words. The government may impose reasonable TPM restrictions on this intermediate category of speech only if it can advance a "significant" or "important" reason for doing so.

Time restrictions regulate when individuals may express themselves. At certain times of the day, the government may curtail or prohibit speech to address legitimate societal concerns, such as traffic congestion and crowd control. For example, political protesters may seek to

Laws prohibiting the posting of bills have been challenged in court on First Amendment grounds. Cities defend such laws as reasonable time, place, and manner restrictions.

demonstrate in densely populated cities to draw maximum attention to their cause. The First Amendment permits protesters to take such action, but not whenever they choose. The Supreme Court has held on more than one occasion that no one may "insist upon a street meeting in the middle of Times Square at the rush hour as a form of freedom of speech" (*Cox v. Louisiana*, 379 U.S. 536, 85 S. Ct. 453, 13 L. Ed. 2d 471 [1965]). In most instances a commuter's interest in getting to and from work outweighs an individual's right to tie up traffic through political expression.

Place restrictions regulate where individuals may express themselves. The Supreme Court has recognized three FORUMS of public expression: traditional PUBLIC FORUMS, limited public forums, and nonpublic forums. Traditional public forums are those places historically reserved for the dissemination of information and the communication of ideas. Consisting of parks, sidewalks, and streets, traditional public forums are an especially important medium for the least powerful members of society who lack access to other channels of expression, such as radio and television. Under the First Amendment, the government may not close traditional public forums but may place reasonable restrictions on their use.

The reasonableness of any such restriction will be evaluated in light of specific guidelines that have been established by the Supreme Court. First, a restriction must be content-neutral, which means the government may not prohibit entire classes of expression, such as speech concerning poverty, drug abuse, or race relations. Second, a restriction must be viewpoint-neutral, which means that it must apply uniformly to all speech; that is, it may not silence only those speakers whom the government opposes or sanction only those whom the government supports. Third, a restriction must burden speech no more than is necessary to serve an important government interest. Restrictions that are carefully aimed at controlling the harmful consequences of speech, such as litter, unrest, and disorder, will normally satisfy these guidelines.

Limited public forums are those places held out by the government for civic discussion. Capitol grounds, courthouses, state fairs, and public universities have all qualified as limited public forums for First Amendment purposes. Although the government may designate such places as sites for public speech under certain circumstances, the Supreme Court has recognized that individual expression is not the sole objective served by limited public forums. For example, courthouses are primarily designed to administer justice, though important social discourse often takes place on the courthouse steps. Consequently, the First Amendment gives the government greater latitude in regulating limited public forums than traditional public forums.

The government is allowed to regulate nonpublic forums with even greater latitude. Nonpublic forums include privately owned property and publicly owned property devoted almost exclusively to purposes other than individual expression. Airports, jailhouses, military bases, and private residential property have all been deemed to be nonpublic forums under the First Amendment. Public sidewalks and streets that abut private property normally retain their status as traditional public forums, however (*Frisby v. Schultz*, 487 U.S. 474, 108 S. Ct. 2495, 101 L. Ed. 2d 420 [1988]).

In nonpublic forums the government may impose speech restrictions that are reasonably related to the forum's function, including restrictions that discriminate against particular viewpoints. For example, in *Perry Educ. Ass'n v. Perry Local Educators' Ass'n*, 460 U.S. 37, 103 S. Ct. 948, 74 L. Ed. 2d 794 (1983), the Supreme Court ruled that a rival teachers' union could be denied access to public school mailboxes, even though the elected union representative had been given access by the educational association. This restriction was reasonable, the Court said, in light of the elected representative's responsibilities to negotiate labor agreements on behalf of the union.

Manner restrictions regulate the mode of individual expression. Not every form of expression requires use of the written or spoken word. Some of the most visceral impressions are made by SYMBOLIC SPEECH. Symbolic speech can include something as complicated as an algebraic equation or as simple as the nod of a head. Under the First Amendment, symbolic expression often takes the form of political protest. FLAG burning is a recent example of symbolic speech that the Supreme Court found to be protected by the Free Speech Clause (*Texas v. Johnson*, 491 U.S. 397, 109 S. Ct. 2533, 105 L. Ed. 2d 342 [1989]).

When the government attempts to regulate symbolic expression, courts balance the competing interests asserted by the litigants. Regulations that are targeted at suppressing a symbolic message will be closely scrutinized by the judiciary, while regulations that serve compelling government interests unrelated to the expression of ideas will be subject to less exacting judicial scrutiny. For example, in *Clark v. Community for Creative Non-Violence*, 468 U.S. 288, 104 S. Ct. 3065, 82 L. Ed. 2d 221 (1984), the Supreme Court upheld a federal regulation that prohibited sleeping in certain national parks, despite the objections of protesters who had camped out in a national park to symbolize the plight of the homeless. The Court said that the regulation was not aimed at suppressing symbolic expression, because it applied to all persons, and not just the protesters involved in the case. The Court also noted that the regulation was reasonably designed to preserve national parks by minimizing the wear and tear that can be caused by campers. Finally, the Court emphasized that the protesters were free to carry out their vigil at other venues across the country.

All TPM restrictions must provide speakers with alternative channels for communicating ideas or disseminating information. Unlike millionaire moguls and corporate giants, the average person on the street does not commonly communicate through the mass media. Most people do not hold press conferences, and if they did, few members of the media would attend. Instead, the great bulk of communication takes place through the circulation of leaflets, handbills, and pamphlets, which most people can distribute and read in a cheap and efficient manner. As a result, courts are generally sensitive to protecting these modes of communication, and TPM restrictions limiting their distribution usually founder.

See also COMPELLING STATE INTEREST; TEXAS V. JOHNSON.

TIME-PRICE DIFFERENTIAL 📖 A method whereby a seller charges one amount for the immediate cash payment of merchandise and another amount for the same item or items when payment is rendered at a future date or in INSTALLMENTS. 📖

The immediate payment price is called the *cash-price*; the later price is known as the *time-price* or *credit-price*. The *time-price differential* is the difference between the two prices.

TIMESHARE 📖 A form of shared PROPERTY ownership, commonly in vacation or recreation condominium property, in which rights VEST in several owners to use property for a specified period each year. 📖

Timeshare ownership of vacation or recreation condominium property is a popular choice for persons who wish to secure a long-term commitment to a particular location. Timesharing is common in Hawaii, Florida, Arizona, Colorado, and Mexico, as well as in certain other popular vacation spots in the

United States. When a person signs a contract to purchase a "timeshare," she is agreeing to pay the owner of the property a sum of money for the exclusive right to use or occupy the property for a specified time during the year. One or two weeks is the typical period that may be purchased. Usually, the timeshare agreement is made for improved property, such as a vacation home or a particular unit in a condominium complex.

The form of a timeshare agreement varies. Usually, the person has the right of exclusive use of the unit during the same time each year or other specified period. Each timeshare unit is considered an ESTATE or interest in real property, separate and distinct from all other timeshare estates in the same unit or any other unit. Therefore, estates may be separately conveyed and encumbered.

The cost of purchasing a timeshare depends on the time of year selected; premium prices are charged for the most popular times of the year. The annual maintenance fee for the condominium unit and the annual property taxes are divided proportionally among the timeshare owners. A person who does not plan to use the property during the specified period may rent the timeshare to a third party, but the company managing the property may require that it BROKER such transactions and receive a fee for the rentals.

Timeshare agreements are affected by various federal and state statutes. States generally require developers of timeshares to file detailed statements that demonstrate compliance with all applicable statutory requirements. For example, states typically require the developer to fully disclose how the project is to be financed and to give examples of all CONTRACTS, DEEDS, fact sheets, and other instruments that will be used in marketing, financing, and conveying timeshare interests. Some states also require information from the developer concerning the management of the project, including a copy of the management agreement, disclosure of any relationship between the developer and the management company, and a statement as to whether the management agent will be bonded or insured.

See also CONDOMINIUMS AND COOPERATIVES.

TITHING 📖 In Western ecclesiastical law, the act of paying a percentage of one's income to further religious purposes. One of the political subdivisions of England that was composed of ten families who held FREEHOLD estates. 📖

Residents of a tithing were joined in a society and bound to the king to maintain peaceful relations with each other. The person responsible for the administration of the tithing was called the tithing-man; he was a forerunner of the CONSTABLE.

TITLE 📖 In PROPERTY LAW, a comprehensive term referring to the legal basis of the ownership of property, encompassing real and personal property and INTANGIBLE and TANGIBLE interests therein; also a document serving as EVIDENCE of ownership of property, such as the certificate of title to a motor vehicle.

In regard to legislation, the heading or preliminary part of a particular STATUTE that designates the name by which that act is known.

In the law of TRADEMARKS, the name of an item that may be used exclusively by an individual for identification purposes to indicate the quality and origin of the item. 📖

In the law of property, title in its broadest sense refers to all rights that can be secured and enjoyed under the law. It is frequently synonymous with absolute ownership. Title to property ordinarily signifies an ESTATE in FEE SIMPLE, which means that the holder has full and absolute ownership. The term does not necessarily imply absolute ownership, however; it can also mean mere POSSESSION or the right thereof.

The title of a statute is ordinarily prefixed to the text of a statute in the form of a concise summary of its contents, such as "An act for the prevention of the abuse of narcotics." Other statutes are given titles that briefly describe the subject matter, such as the "Americans with Disabilities Act." State constitutions commonly provide that every BILL introduced in the state legislature must have a single subject expressed by the bill's title. Congress is under no such restriction under the U.S. Constitution, but House and Senate rules do have some guidelines for federal bills and statutes. Many, though not all, federal statutes have titles.

Under trademark law, if a publisher adopts a name, or title, for a magazine and uses it extensively in compliance with the law, the publisher may acquire a right to be protected in the exclusive use of that title. A trademark of the title can only be acquired through actual use of the title in connection with the goods, in this example, the magazine. Merely planning to use the title does not give rise to legally enforceable trademark rights.

See also TITLE INSURANCE; TITLE SEARCH.

TITLE INSURANCE 📖 A contractual arrangement entered into to INDEMNIFY loss or damage resulting from defects or problems relating to the ownership of REAL PROPERTY, or from the enforcement of LIENS that exist against it. 📖

A sample title
insurance policy

TITLE INSURANCE POLICY
_____ TITLE GUARANTY & MORTGAGE COMPANY

IN CONSIDERATION of the payment of its charges for the examination of title and its premium for insurance, insures the within named insured against all loss or damage not exceeding the amount of insurance stated herein and in addition the costs and expenses of defending the title, estate or interest insured, which the insured shall sustain by reason of any defect or defects of title affecting the premises described in Schedule A or affecting the interest of the insured herein set forth, or by reason of the unmarketability of the title of the insured to or in the premises, or by reason of liens or incumbrances affecting title at the date hereof, or by reason of any statutory lien for labor or material furnished prior to the date hereof which has now gained or may hereafter gain priority over the interest secured hereby, or by reason of a lack of access to and from the premises, excepting all loss and damage by reason of the estates, interests, defects, objections, liens, incumbrances, and other matters set forth in Schedule B, or by the conditions of this policy hereby incorporated into this contract, the loss and the amount to be ascertained in the manner provided in said conditions and to be payable upon compliance by the insured with the stipulations of said conditions, and not otherwise.

IN WITNESS WHEREOF, _____ TITLE GUARANTY & MORTGAGE COMPANY has caused this policy to be signed and sealed on its date of issue set forth herein.

President: _____

[_Seal_]   Attest:

_____

Validating Officer   Secretary

Name of Insured: [Purchasers' names]

Policy No. _S-000000_   Amount of Insurance: _$90,000._

Date of Issue: _August 8, 1980_

The estate or interest insured by this policy is fee simple absolute, vested in the insured by means of deed from [Sellers' names], _dated August 8, 1980 and recorded in the Office of the_ _____ _County Clerk on August 11, 1980 in L. 5000 Cp. 500._

SCHEDULE A

The premises in which the insured has the estate or interest covered by this policy are described as follows:

[_Description_]

SCHEDULE B

The following estates, interests, defects, objections to title, liens, and incumbrances, and other matters are excepted from the coverage of this policy.

1. Defects and incumbrances arising or becoming a lien after the date of this policy, except as herein provided.

2. Consequences of the exercise and enforcement or attempted enforcement of any governmental, war or police powers over the premises.

3. Any laws, regulations or ordinances (including, but not limited to zoning, building, and environmental protection) as to the use, occupancy, subdivision or improvement of the premises adopted or imposed by any governmental body, or the effect of any noncompliance with or any violation thereof.

4. Judgments against the insured or estates, interests, defects, objections, liens or incumbrances created, suffered, assumed or agreed to by or with the privity of the insured.

5. Title to any property beyond the lines of the premises, or title to areas within or rights or easements in any abutting streets, roads, avenues, lanes, ways or waterways, or the right to maintain therein vaults, tunnels, ramps or any other structure or improvement, unless this policy specifically provides that such titles, rights, or easements are insured. Not-

withstanding any provisions in this paragraph to the contrary, this policy, unless otherwise excepted, insures the ordinary rights of access and egress belonging to abutting owners.

6. Title to any personal property, whether the same be attached to or used in connection with said premises or otherwise.

7. Zoning restrictions or ordinances imposed by any governmental body.

8. *Mortgage in the amount of $56,622.87 and interest thereon, held by the _____ Savings Bank of _____.*

9. *Covenants and restrictions recorded in L. 1000 Cp. 10, L. 1100 Cp. 110 and L. 3000 Cp. 300.*

10. *Any state of facts an inspection of the premises would disclose.*

11. *Rights of present tenants, or persons, if any, in possession of the premises.*

12. *Survey made by _____ , dated July 15, 1980 shows two story frame dwelling; no encroachments or variations.*

CONDITIONS OF THIS POLICY

Section One. Definitions.

(a) Wherever the term "insured" is used in this policy it includes those who succeed to the interest or the insured by operation of law including, without limitation, heirs, distributees, devisees, survivors, personal representatives, next of kin or corporate successors, as the case may be, and those to whom the insured has assigned this policy where such assignment is permitted by the terms hereof, and wherever the term "insured" is used in the conditions of this policy it also includes the attorneys and agents of the "insured."

(b) Wherever the term "this company" is used in this policy it means _____ Title Guaranty and Mortgage Company.

(c) Wherever the term "final determination" or "finally determined" is used in this policy, it means the final determination of a court of competent jurisdiction after disposition of all appeals or after the time to appeal has expired.

(d) Wherever the term "the premises" is used in this policy, it means the property insured herein as described in Schedule A of this policy including such buildings and improvements thereon which by law constitute real property.

(e) Wherever the term "recorded" is used in this policy it means, unless otherwise indicated, recorded in the office of the recording officer of the county in which property insured herein lies.

Section Two. Defense and Prosecution of Suits.

(a) This company will, at its own cost, defend the insured in all actions or proceedings founded on a claim of title or incumbrances not excepted in this policy.

(b) This company shall have the right and may, at its own cost, maintain or defend any action or proceeding relating to the title or interest hereby insured, or upon or under any covenant or contract relating thereto which it considers desirable to prevent or reduce loss hereunder.

(c) In all cases where this policy requires or permits this company to prosecute or defend, the insured shall secure to it the right and opportunity to maintain or defend the action or proceeding, and all appeals from any determination therein, and give it all reasonable aid therein, and hereby permits it to use therein, at its option, its own name or the name of the insured.

(d) The provisions of this section shall survive payment by this company of any specific loss or payment of the entire amount of this policy to the extent that this company shall deem it necessary in recovering the loss from those who may be liable therefore to the insured or to this company.

Section Three. Cases Where Liability Arises.

No claim for damages shall arise or be maintainable under this policy except in the following cases:

(a) Where there has been a final determination under which the insured may be dispossessed, evicted or ejected from the premises or from some part or undivided share or interest therein.

(b) Where there has been a final determination adverse to the title, upon a lien or incumbrance not excepted in this policy.

(c) Where the insured shall have contracted in good faith in writing to sell the insured estate or interest, or where the insured estate has been sold for the benefit of the insured pursuant to the judgment or order of a court and the title has been rejected because of a defect or incumbrance not excepted in this policy and there has been a final determination sustaining the objection to the title.

(d) Where the insurance is upon the interest of a mortgagee and the mortgage has been adjudged by a final determination to be invalid or ineffectual to charge the insured's estate or interest in the premises, or subject to a prior lien or incumbrance not excepted in this policy; or where a recording officer has refused to accept from the insured a satisfaction of the insured mortgage and there has been a final determination sustaining the refusal because of a defect in the title to the said mortgage.

(e) Where the insured shall have negotiated a loan to be made on the security of a mortgage on the insured's estate or interest in the premises and the title shall have been rejected by the proposed lender and it shall have been finally determined that the rejection of the title was justified because of a defect or incumbrance not excepted in this policy.

(f) Where the insured shall have transferred the title insured by an instrument containing covenants in regard to title or warranty thereof and there shall have been a final determination on any of such covenants or warranty, against the insured, because of a defect or incumbrance not excepted in this policy.

(g) Where the insured estate or interest or a part thereof has been taken by condemnation and it has been finally determined that the insured is not entitled to a full award for the estate or interest taken because of a defect or incumbrance not excepted in this policy.

No claim for damages shall arise or be maintainable under this policy (1) if this company, after having received notice of an alleged defect or incumbrance, removes such defect or incumbrance within thirty days after receipt of such notice; or (2) for liability voluntarily assumed by the insured in settling any claim or suit without the written consent of this company.

Section Four. Notice of Claim.

In a case a purchaser or proposed mortgage lender raises any question as to the sufficiency of the title hereby insured, or in case actual knowledge shall come to the insured of any claim adverse to the title insured hereby, or in case of the service on or receipt by the insured of any paper, or of any notice, summons process or pleading in any action or proceeding, the object or effect of which shall or may be to impugn, attack or call in question the validity of the title hereby insured, the insured shall promptly notify this company thereof in writing at its main office and forward to this company such paper or such notice, summons, process or pleading. Delay in giving this notice and delay in forwarding such paper or such notice, summons, process or pleading shall not affect this company's liability if such failure has not prejudiced and cannot in the future prejudice this company.

Section Five. Payment of Loss.

(a) This company will pay, in addition to the loss, all statutory costs and allowances imposed on the insured in litigation carried on by this company for the insured under the terms of this policy. This company shall not be liable for and will not pay the fees of any council or attorney employed by the insured.

(b) In every case where claim is made for loss or damage this company (1) reserves the right to settle, at its own cost, any claim or suit which may involve liability under this policy; or (2) may terminate its liability hereunder by paying or tendering the full amount of this policy; or (3) may, without conceding liability, demand a valuation of the insured estate or interest, to be made, by three arbitrators or any two of them, one to be chosen by the insured and one by the company, and the two thus chosen selecting an umpire. Such valuation, less the amount of any incumbrances on said insured estate and interest not hereby insured against, shall be the extent of this company's liability for such claim and no right of action shall accrue hereunder for the recovery thereof until thirty days after notice of such valuation shall have been served upon this company, and the insured shall have tendered a conveyance or assignment of the insured estate or interest to this company or its designee at such valuation, diminished as aforesaid. The foregoing option to fix a valuation by arbitration shall not apply to a policy insuring a mortgage or leasehold interest.

(c) Liability to any collateral holder of this policy shall not exceed the amount of the pecuniary interest of such collateral holder in the premises.

A sample title
insurance policy
(continued)

(d) All payments made by this company under this policy shall reduce the amount hereof pro tanto except (1) payments made for counsel fees and disbursements in defending or prosecuting actions or proceedings in behalf of the insured and for statutory costs and allowances imposed on the insured in such actions and proceedings, and (2) if the insured is a mortgagee, payments made to satisfy or subordinate prior liens or incumbrances not set forth in Schedule B.

(e) When liability has been definitely fixed in accordance with the conditions of this policy, the loss or damage shall be payable within thirty days thereafter.

[Balance omitted for purpose of illustration.]

Title insurance is ordinarily taken out by a purchaser of the property, or by an individual lending money on the MORTGAGE, in an amount equivalent to the purchase price of the property. To be entitled to coverage, the purchaser typically pays one lump sum PREMIUM, usually at the day of the CLOSING. Title insurance companies are specially organized for this purpose. They retain complete sets of ABSTRACTS OF TITLE or duplicates of the record, hire expert title examiners, and prepare all types of CONVEYANCES and transfers. Following a TITLE SEARCH, such companies furnish a *certificate of title*, indicating the findings of the title examiner with respect to the state of the title to the property involved. Title insurance companies are liable only for a lack of care, skill, or diligence on the part of their examiner when a title certificate is issued up to the face amount of the policy. An *insurance of title*, however, warrants the validity of the title in any and all events.

See also RECORDING OF LAND TITLES; REGISTRATION OF LAND TITLES.

TITLE SEARCH 📖 The process of examining official county records to determine whether an owner's rights in REAL PROPERTY are good. 📖

A title search is conducted to discover whether there are any defects in the ownership of a particular tract of land. An ABSTRACT OF TITLE, prepared by the examiner subsequent to such an investigation, is a condensed history of the title to the land.

See also RECORDING OF LAND TITLES; REGISTRATION OF LAND TITLES.

TOBACCO For centuries the leaves of the tobacco plant have been used for making smoking tobacco and chewing tobacco. Tobacco contains small amounts of nicotine, a stimulant that acts on the heart and other organs and the nervous system when tobacco is inhaled, ingested, or absorbed. Nicotine's effect on the nervous system causes people to become addicted to it, and the stimulating effects make smoking and chewing tobacco pleasurable. Concentrated amounts of nicotine are poisonous, however. Although the use of tobacco was condemned on occasion in the past, not until the latter half of the twentieth century have concerted efforts been made to curb tobacco use in the United States.

History Before the arrival of Europeans in America, Native Americans were growing and harvesting tobacco to be smoked in pipes. Europeans exploring America learned of this practice and took tobacco seeds back to Europe where tobacco was grown and used as a medicine to help people relax. European physicians believed that tobacco should be used only for medicinal purposes. Commercial production of tobacco began in the colony of Virginia in the early seventeenth century where it soon became an important crop. The expansion of tobacco farming, especially in the southern colonies, contributed to the demand for and practice of slavery in America. Most tobacco grown in the American colonies was shipped to Europe until the Revolutionary War, when manufacturers began using their crops to produce chewing and smoking tobacco.

The use of tobacco for other than medicinal purposes was controversial, however: the Puritans in America believed that tobacco was a dangerous narcotic. Nevertheless, chewing and smoking tobacco became increasingly popular. Cigars were first manufactured in the United States in the early nineteenth century. Hand-rolled cigarettes became popular in the mid-nineteenth century, and by the 1880s, a cigarette-making machine had been invented. In the twentieth century tobacco use, especially cigarette smoking, continued to expand in the United States.

By the 1960s, however, scientists had confirmed that smoking could cause lung cancer, heart disease, and other illnesses. Some cigarette manufacturers reacted to these findings by reducing the levels of nicotine and tar in their cigarettes, but the medical community established that these measures did not eliminate the

Cipollone v. Liggett Group, Inc.

Cipollone v. Liggett Group, Inc., 693 F. Supp. 208 (D.N.J. 1988), aff'd in part, rev'd in part, 893 F.2d 541 (3d Cir. [N.J.] 1990), cert. granted, 499 U.S. 935, 111 S. Ct. 1386, 113 L. Ed. 2d 443 (1991), aff'd in part, rev'd in part, 505 U.S. 504, 112 S. Ct. 2608, 120 L. Ed. 2d 407 (1992), was the first case in which a former smoker recovered monetary damages against the U.S. tobacco industry. It is also considered a landmark tobacco case because of the legal precedent it established.

Rose Cipollone smoked cigarettes manufactured by defendant Lorillard for forty years. She started smoking at an early age because she thought it was the cool and grown-up thing to do and soon found that she could not stop the habit. Cipollone developed lung cancer, requiring the removal of her right lung. She died before her case went to trial, but her husband pursued her claims on her behalf.

Cipollone brought fourteen claims against Liggett Group, Inc., Philip Morris, Inc., and Lorillard, including strict liability, negligence, breach of warranty, intentional tort, and conspiracy. The intentional tort claims included the allegation that the tobacco companies had fraudulently misrepresented that smoking was safe through their advertising and conspired to keep the public from learning about the scientific evidence that clearly demonstrated the health hazards of smoking.

The tobacco companies argued that Rose Cipollone knowingly chose to smoke and therefore accepted all of the dangers and health consequences associated with it. On the other hand, the tobacco companies vehemently maintained that there is no medical or scientific basis to show that smoking is linked to cancer or other diseases.

The Cipollone case lasted ten years and included the filing of one hundred motions, four interlocutory appeals, four months of trial, an appeal from the jury verdict, two petitions of certiorari to the U.S. Supreme Court, and argument and then reargument before the Court. Although the jury in the first trial awarded the plaintiff $400,000 in damages, the verdict was ultimately overturned on appeal due to technical mistakes, and a retrial was ordered. By that time, the three legal firms representing the plaintiff had spent collectively more than $6.2 million on the case and could not afford to continue. In contrast, the defendants spent $40 million and never had to pay one cent to the Cipollones.

This case made history at the pretrial stage because the court ordered the tobacco industry to release thousands of pages of confidential internal documents that the plaintiff needed to prove that the tobacco industry conspired to prevent the public from being informed of the health hazards of smoking (649 F. Supp. 664). The court also held that, because of the enormous public interest in these documents, they could be released to third parties and used in other related cases (113 F.R.D. 86 [D.N.J. 1986]; 822 F.2d 335 [3d Cir. 1987], cert. denied, 479 U.S. 1043, 107 S. Ct. 907, 93 L. Ed. 2d 857 [1987]). However, the defendants were still able to protect the most damaging documents by asserting the attorney-client privilege and the work product doctrine (140 F.R.D. 684). Without those damaging documents, the jury rejected the plaintiff's theories of conspiracy or misrepresentation, but did find in her favor on the claim of breach of the express warranty that cigarettes were safe.

Cipollone is also the definitive case regarding the preemption of state tort claims by the Federal Cigarette Labeling and Advertising Act (FCLAA) (79 Stat. 282). The Supreme Court held that the FCLAA preempts state law damage claims that are based on a cigarette manufacturer's failure to warn of the health risks of smoking and its neutralization of the federally mandated warnings through advertising techniques, to the extent that those claims rely on omissions or inclusions in the manufacturer's advertisements or promotions (505 U.S. 504, 112 S. Ct. 2608, 120 L. Ed. 2d 407 [1992]). However, the Supreme Court also held that the FCLAA does not preempt claims that are based on strict liability, negligent design, express warranty, intentional fraud and misrepresentation, or conspiracy.

health risks of smoking. Subsequently, extensive research linked cigarette smoking and tobacco chewing to many serious illnesses.

In 1990 an estimated 419,000 deaths in the United States were directly attributable to smoking. The American Cancer Society estimated that smoking caused nearly one-third of all cancer deaths in 1995. Tobacco is responsible for more deaths in the United States than car accidents, ACQUIRED IMMUNE DEFICIENCY SYNDROME (AIDS), ALCOHOL, illegal drugs, HOMICIDES, SUICIDES, and fires combined.

Medical research has not only proved that smoking is injurious to the health of the smoker, but it has also established that nonsmokers can be harmed by inhaling the cigarette smoke of others. This type of smoke is called secondhand smoke, passive smoke, involuntary smoke, or environmental tobacco smoke (ETS). In 1993 the ENVIRONMENTAL

PROTECTION AGENCY (EPA) classified ETS as a known human (Group A) carcinogen because it causes lung cancer in adult nonsmokers and impairs the respiratory and cardiovascular health of nonsmoking children. ETS, which is the third leading preventable cause of death in the United States, contains the same carcinogenic compounds as are found in the smoke inhaled by smokers.

As these research findings have appeared, concern over tobacco's effect on health has played an important role in encouraging government regulation of tobacco. At the same time, however, the popularity of tobacco use has resulted in considerable political and financial strength for the tobacco industry. By the 1990s tobacco had become the seventh largest cash crop in the United States, and tobacco growers and manufacturers were realizing $47 billion annually. With such revenues available, the tobacco industry has been able to exert significant influence over tobacco regulation. In 1995 the tobacco industry gave more than $1 million directly to politicians and nearly $3 million in "soft money" (unrestricted donations to political party organizations). Because the industry is also central to the economies of many tobacco-producing states, members of Congress from those states have opposed restrictions on tobacco companies.

Despite the tobacco companies' efforts, the industry is subject to extensive federal and state regulation. Among the federal agencies with minor regulatory interests in tobacco and tobacco products are the Bureau of Alcohol, Tobacco and Firearms, the Department of Health and Human Services, the Department of Agriculture, and the INTERNAL REVENUE SERVICE. Federal agencies with broader power to regulate tobacco include the Federal Trade Commission (FTC), the FEDERAL COMMUNICATIONS COMMISSION (FCC), and, the most recent to assert JURISDICTION, the FOOD AND DRUG ADMINISTRATION (FDA).

Federal Regulation of Tobacco Advertising and Labeling   In the 1950s the federal government began to regulate the sale and production of chewing and smoking tobacco because of the growing concern over its adverse effects on the health of consumers. Traditionally, the FTC was the federal agency primarily responsible for the regulation of tobacco products, especially with regard to labeling and advertising. In 1955 the FTC promulgated guidelines that prohibited cigarette advertisements from carrying therapeutic health claims. In 1964 the commission issued a Trade Regulation Rule on Cigarette Labeling and Advertising that strictly controlled the advertising and labeling of tobacco products. The FTC claimed that the failure to warn consumers of the dangers of smoking constituted an unfair and deceptive trade practice under the Federal Trade Commission Act (15 U.S.C.A. § 41 [1994]).

Shortly after the FTC issued its trade regulation rule, Congress intervened by enacting the Federal Cigarette Labeling and Advertising Act (FCLAA) (15 U.S.C.A. § 1331 et seq. [1965]), which was more moderate than the FTC regulation and preempted agency action. The FCLAA required that a health warning be conspicuously displayed on all packages and cartons of cigarettes. As originally enacted, the FCLAA required only the warning, "Caution: Cigarette Smoking May Be Hazardous to Your Health." Subsequently, however, this act was amended to require more explicit warnings. Under amendments added in 1984, cigarette manufacturers must use one of the following labels to satisfy the health warning requirement:

> SURGEON GENERAL'S WARNING: Smoking Causes Lung Cancer, Heart Disease, Emphysema, and May Complicate Pregnancy.
> SURGEON GENERAL'S WARNING: Quitting Smoking Now Greatly Reduces Serious Risks to Your Health.
> SURGEON GENERAL'S WARNING: Smoking by Pregnant Women May Result in Fetal Injury, Premature Birth, and Low Birth Weight.
> SURGEON GENERAL'S WARNING: Cigarette Smoke Contains Carbon Monoxide.

The warning labels must also appear on all cigarette advertising, including magazine advertisements and billboards.

In 1986 Congress enacted the Comprehensive Smokeless Tobacco Health Education Act (CSTHEA) (15 U.S.C.A. § 4401 et seq.), which requires smokeless tobacco products to carry one of the following warning labels:

> "WARNING: THIS PRODUCT MAY CAUSE MOUTH CANCER"
> "WARNING: THIS PRODUCT MAY CAUSE GUM DISEASE AND TOOTH LOSS"
> "WARNING: THIS PRODUCT IS NOT A SAFE ALTERNATIVE TO CIGARETTES"

The CSTHEA also requires all manufacturers, packagers, and importers of smokeless tobacco to provide the secretary of the Depart-

AP/WIDE WORLD PHOTOS

Ohio's attorney general, Betty Montgomery, announced in April 1997 that she would sue the tobacco companies to recover costs incurred by the state in treating illnesses related to smoking.

ment of Health and Human Services with a list of all ingredients used in the manufacture of the product, as well as the quantity of nicotine contained in the product. The act further requires the secretary to report biennially to Congress with a summary of research on the health effects of smokeless tobacco, information about whether its ingredients pose a health risk, and recommendations for legislative or administrative action. Finally, the act requires the FTC to report biennially to Congress about the state of smokeless tobacco sales, advertising, and marketing practices and also to make recommendations for legislative or administrative action. Amendments to the FC-LAA require similar reports on smoking tobacco products.

In 1967 the FCC decided to act upon citizen complaints it had received regarding broadcast cigarette advertising. The FCC implemented a rule requiring any station that broadcast cigarette advertising to also air public service announcements prepared by various health organizations in an effort to inform listeners and viewers of the dangers of smoking. This FCC regulation was challenged in the courts but upheld under the FAIRNESS DOCTRINE, which requires broadcasters to provide a balanced representation and fair coverage of controversial issues of public importance (*Banzhaf v. FCC*, 405 F.2d 1082 [D.C. Cir. 1968]).

A few years later, Congress also intervened on the issue of broadcast advertising, electing to ban all television and radio advertising of cigarettes. Congress enacted the Public Health Cigarette Smoking Act of 1969 (Pub. L. No. 91-222, § 6, 84 Stat. 87, 89), which was codified as an amendment to the earlier FCLAA. The new regulations took effect in 1971 and prohibited all advertising of cigarettes and small cigars

via electronic communication, subject to the jurisdiction of the FCC (15 U.S.C.A. § 1335). The tobacco companies challenged the constitutionality of the Public Health Cigarette Smoking Act, but it was upheld by the courts (*Capital Broadcasting Co. v. Mitchell*, 333 F. Supp. 582 [D.D.C. 1971], *aff'd mem.*, 405 U.S. 1000, 92 S. Ct. 1289, 321 L. Ed. 2d 472 [1982]). Beginning in 1986, Congress also made it illegal to advertise smokeless tobacco on any medium of electronic communication that is subject to the jurisdiction of the FCC (15 U.S.C.A. § 4402(f)).

The FCLAA, as amended by the Public Health Cigarette Smoking Act of 1969, did not work wholly to the detriment of the tobacco industry. In fact, some legal commentators argue that it actually benefited the tobacco companies. The warning labels that were required to help inform consumers of the health risks associated with tobacco worked to provide the manufacturers with a shield against tort LIABILITY. In fact, before the matter was taken up by the U.S. Supreme Court in 1992, several circuit courts held that the FCLAA had preempted state claims against the tobacco companies based on a failure-to-warn legal theory (see *Pennington v. Vistron Corp.*, 876 F.2d 414 [5th Cir. 1989]; *Roysdon v. R. J. Reynolds Tobacco Co.*, 849 F.2d 230 [6th Cir. 1988]; *Palmer v. Liggett Group*, 825 F.2d 620 [1st Cir. 1987]; *Stephen v. American Brands*, 825 F.2d 312 [11th Cir. 1987]). In *Cipollone v. Liggett Group*, 505 U.S. 504, 112 S. Ct. 2608, 120 L. Ed. 2d 407 [1992], the U.S. Supreme Court held that the FCLAA had preempted state law damage claims based on a failure to warn and the neutralization of federally mandated warnings to the extent that those claims relied on omissions or inclusions in the manufacturers' advertisements or promotions. The Supreme Court also held, however, that the FCLAA did not preempt claims based on STRICT LIABILITY, negligent design, express WARRANTY, intentional FRAUD and MISREPRESENTATION, or CONSPIRACY.

The tobacco industry also benefited indirectly from the FCLAA's ban on advertising because when television advertising ceased, so did the antismoking public service messages that broadcasters were previously required to air. In fact, Judge Skelly Wright, the author of the dissenting opinion in *Capital Broadcasting Co.*, noted that the Public Health Cigarette Smoking Act of 1969 was a legislative coup on the part of the tobacco industry. Wright accurately predicted that the loss of the broadcast antismoking messages would result in a rise in cigarette consumption.

NATIONAL CLEAN AIR DEBATE

On April 5, 1994, the Occupational Safety and Health Administration (OSHA) published proposed nationwide indoor air quality regulations that would prevent smoking in all indoor workplaces, including office buildings, government buildings, restaurants, stores, and bars, except in designated smoking areas with separate ventilation systems (59 Fed. Reg. 15,968–16,039). OSHA provided a public comment period followed by public hearings, which were extended a number of times, and finally closed the hearings in January 1996. OSHA also sought post-hearing comments, but by the end of 1997 the administration had not announced when, or whether, it would issue its final rules addressing this controversial topic. The dispute over the OSHA regulations frames the larger debate between advocates and opponents of smoking regulations.

Proponents of the indoor air quality regulations argue that if people are freely allowed to smoke in the workplace, they contaminate the air that nonsmokers breathe, subjecting everyone around them to severe health consequences. Proponents cite decades of scientific and medical studies that demonstrate the health effects of environmental tobacco smoke (ETS). They refer to studies that show that ETS causes lung cancer and heart disease in adults and various respiratory disorders in children.

Various government agencies support OSHA's proposed regulations. The U.S. surgeon general has published numerous reports warning of the dangers of ETS. The Department of Labor reported to OSHA that 83 percent of all worker health complaints related to indoor air quality are linked to ETS. Since 1992, the U.S. Environmental Protection Agency has classified ETS as a known Group A human carcinogen. Various other medical and research organizations support the proposed regulations as well. The National Academy of Sciences has warned of the dangers

of ETS. A 1995 study published in the *Journal of the American Medical Association* found that nicotine levels in the air at work sites with no restrictions on smoking were triple the amount considered hazardous by U.S. regulatory standards.

Proponents of the regulations are concerned for the health of the nonsmokers, but they also cite many economic reasons for instituting the indoor air quality regulations nationwide. For example, employers must pay more for health insurance for their employees when their employees smoke or are exposed to ETS. Employers also suffer productivity losses when their employees are sick or disabled due to smoking-related illnesses. Smoking also causes premature deaths in employees, which results in a productivity loss to the employer. When smoking is allowed in the workplace, there is more trash, such as cigarette butts, to clean up. Proponents of the smoking regulations also argue that computer equipment, carpets, furniture, and other furnishings need more maintenance and must be replaced more frequently when smoking is permitted in the workplace. Finally, employers who are forced to choose between the rights of smoking workers and the rights of nonsmoking workers fear that they will be liable for nonsmoker injuries. For example, under the Americans with Disabilities Act, 104 Stat. 327, if ETS prevents a worker from being able to perform her job, the employer may be responsible for allowing the ETS in the workplace.

Opponents of the indoor air quality regulations include restaurant, bar, and hotel owners, trade associations, cigarette manufacturers, smokers, and those who seek to protect individual freedoms from government regulation. Activist organizations that promote smokers' rights include the National Smokers Alliance, the United Smokers Association, and the American Puffer Alliance. These groups point out that their numbers are large; in fact, there are ap-

IN FOCUS

proximately fifty-two million Americans who do not support the crusade to stop smoking. Further, many of these groups stand for principles of tolerance, fairness, and inclusion and seek to promote accommodation of the wishes of smokers as well as nonsmokers.

Opponents of the regulations argue that exposure to ETS really is not as dangerous to nonsmokers as many anti-smoker groups contend. In fact, the opponents have scientific research to support their theories. In addition, they attack contrary studies as being statistically flawed and claim that any conclusions showing an association between ETS and disease are really due to confounding variables in the studies. Other opponents, particularly restaurant, bar, and hotel owners, reject the proposed workplace smoking ban as overly restrictive and likely to lead to a serious financial loss to business owners. Some opponents of the regulations focus on the fact that their freedom to smoke is a liberty interest and a privacy right that is being impinged.

A large opponent of the proposed indoor air quality regulations is the Center for Indoor Air Research (CIAR), a nonprofit, independent research organization founded in 1988 by three large tobacco companies. CIAR has been instrumental in providing research results to refute those that suggest that ETS is harmful. A 1992 study conducted by CIAR concluded that moderate amounts of smoking indoors will not interfere with acceptable air quality. CIAR also conducted a study to determine the quantities of ETS that people are actually exposed to in the workplace. Finding that most people are exposed to very little ETS on the job, CIAR concluded that the federal government does not need to regulate smoking in the workplace. Another CIAR study that examined workplace smoking policies, ventilation, and indoor air quality concluded that the role ETS plays in contributing to poor indoor air quality is very minor, if it plays any role at all. The findings from this study show that OSHA's proposal to

NATIONAL CLEAN AIR DEBATE
(CONTINUED)

require separate ventilation systems for smoking areas is unnecessarily restrictive. Another CIAR study concerning indoor air quality, published in 1992, and criticized by a congressional subcommittee in 1994 as being flawed due to falsified or fabricated data, concluded that the levels of ETS in "light smoking" rooms were very similar to the levels of ETS in "nonsmoking" rooms within hundreds of different office buildings.

In addition to quoting studies conducted by CIAR and other tobacco-industry-funded organizations, opponents of the OSHA regulations cite to studies that were not funded by the tobacco industry and thus do not convey the appearance of bias. For example, a 1995 study by the Congressional Research Service (CRS), the research arm of the Library of Congress, found no statistically significant correlation between ETS and lung cancer.

Restaurant and bar owners nationwide fear that the regulations will cause a decline in their business and result in serious financial consequences for them.

In fact, these groups can already demonstrate the validity of their fears: studies of restaurants in cities and states that already have smoking bans have shown that these businesses have suffered an average decline of 24 percent in sales.

Others argue that banning smoking in the workplace is an infringement of personal rights. Specifically, they argue that workplace smoking bans violate the right to privacy and liberty interests protected by the Constitution. Opponents of the proposed nationwide ban can cite to judicial decisions that hold that federal regulations imposed on smoking employees must have a rational basis related to on-the-job performance. (In *Grusendorf v. Oklahoma City*, 816 F.2d 539 [10th Cir. 1987], a one-year smoking ban for firefighter trainees was upheld.) Other courts have held that employers cannot prohibit all smoking on their property if a ban violates a collective bargaining agreement (*Johns-Manville Sales Corp. v. International Ass'n of Machinists*, 621 F.2d 756 [5th Cir. 1980]). In addition, several states have

enacted "smokers' rights laws" that stop employers from regulating off-duty smoking habits of employees and from discriminating against employees or job applicants based on their smoking habits outside the workplace. Opponents of OSHA's proposed indoor air quality regulations argue that employers likewise have no right to impinge upon their employees' freedom to smoke while at work.

Smokers also argue that their decision to smoke and the risks involved are no different from other personal lifestyle choices. If smoking is banned in the workplace, then there is no limit as to what other risky, but legal, behaviors may be banned in the workplace. For example, employers could prohibit the consumption of fatty foods. The crux of the issue, argue opponents, is that smoking is a legal activity and smokers should be left alone in deciding which risks they want to take in their lives.

See also Air Pollution; Employment Law; Environmental Law; Privacy.

Federal and State Regulation of Tobacco through Taxation In 1994 the tobacco industry spent an estimated $4 billion on tobacco advertising. Even though cigarettes cannot be advertised on radio or television, they are the most heavily advertised product in the United States.

In the early 1990s, in an attempt to raise revenue for the federal government, bills were introduced in Congress to restrict the amount of advertising expenses that tobacco manufacturers could deduct from their gross income. In 1993 tobacco companies deducted an estimated $1 billion from their gross income for advertising expenses. The proposed bills would have used the extra revenue to fund education programs to stop underage smokers and to reduce the federal deficit. The bills did not become law, however.

States have long collected excise taxes on sales of cigarettes. As of 1995, Washington State imposed the highest excise tax, at 85 cents per pack, and Missouri had one of the lowest, at

17 cents per pack. Excise taxes were also imposed on chewing tobacco products. Studies completed in the 1980s demonstrated that as the price of chewing and smoking tobacco increases, consumption of those products decreases.

Federal Regulation of Tobacco as a Drug In 1988 the SURGEON GENERAL of the United States issued a report detailing the addictive effects of nicotine. Later scientific studies confirmed this finding. Despite this research the tobacco companies continued to deny that any relation existed between smoking and disease or that smoking was addictive. In an April 1994 congressional hearing on nicotine manipulation, the chief executive officers of seven tobacco companies testified under OATH that they believed nicotine is not addictive and that smoking has not been shown to cause cancer. Later, however, some former tobacco company officials publicly confessed that cigarette manufacturers had long known about the health hazards of smoking and had deliberately concealed that information from the public. The first and perhaps best known of these officials was Jeffrey Wigand, the former head of research at Brown and Williamson, one of the large tobacco companies. Voluminous internal records showing that cigarette manufacturers were aware of the dangers of smoking, including the addictive properties of nicotine, were also leaked to the public. One paralegal at Brown and Williamson copied more than four thousand documents and provided them to tobacco opponents. An annotated compilation of those documents was published in 1996 under the title *The Cigarette Papers.* As a direct result of this growing body of information demonstrating that the manufacturers knew that nicotine in smoking and chewing tobacco can lead to addiction, the FDA in 1994 began examining whether nicotine qualified as a drug under the Food, Drug and Cosmetic Act (21 U.S.C.A. § 301 et seq.), and thus could be regulated as such by the FDA.

The FDA had formerly asserted jurisdiction over tobacco products only to the extent that they carried therapeutic claims. By 1996, however, the FDA had determined that cigarettes and other tobacco products are intended by their manufacturers to be delivery devices for nicotine, a drug resulting in significant pharmacological effects on the body, including addiction. Based on the Food, Drug and Cosmetic Act definition of a drug as an article "intended to affect the structure or any function of the body" and on the FDA's determination that the cigarette and smokeless tobacco manufacturers "intend" these effects, the FDA declared in August 1996 that it had jurisdiction to regulate tobacco products.

The FDA then announced that it would begin by regulating the sale and distribution of cigarettes and smokeless tobacco products to children and adolescents. The issue of children smoking has aroused widespread concern. Studies in the late 1980s and early 1990s demonstrated that despite state laws prohibiting the use of tobacco before the age of eighteen, children had easy access to tobacco products and many had become regular smokers before their eighteenth birthday. In 1996 the FDA estimated that 4.5 million children and adolescents in the United States smoke and that another 1 million children use smokeless tobacco. Accordingly, the FDA promulgated a proposed rule to reduce children's access to tobacco and limit its appeal to them. The proposed rule was published in August 1995, and the FDA invited public comment. The FDA received more than 700,000 pieces of mail on the proposed regulation, the most that any proposed regulation had ever received. After reviewing and analyzing the comments, the FDA published its final rule in August 1996 (21 CFR § 897).

The final FDA rule treated nicotine addiction as a pediatric disease because the use of tobacco products and the resulting nicotine addiction begin predominantly in children and adolescents. The FDA concluded that children do not fully understand the risks associated with consuming tobacco and that they are vulnerable to the sophisticated marketing techniques used by the tobacco industry.

Under the FDA rule, selling cigarettes or smokeless tobacco products to anyone under the age of eighteen is a federal violation. The rule also forbids the distribution of free samples of tobacco products and limits most retail sales to face-to-face situations by excluding most sales via vending machines and self-service displays. In addition, the rule limits tobacco advertising to black-and-white, text-only formats. Billboards and other forms of outdoor advertising are not allowed within a thousand feet of schools and public playgrounds. Sponsorship by tobacco companies of sporting and other events is limited to the corporate name only; the use of logos or mascots such as Joe Camel is forbidden. The rule also forbids the sale and distribution of nontobacco items that carry cigarette logos, such as T-shirts and hats.

The tobacco companies immediately challenged the FDA rule on several grounds, including whether the FDA has jurisdiction to regulate cigarettes as a "device" under the Food, Drug and Cosmetic Act and whether the rule violates advertisers' FREEDOM OF SPEECH. In at least one case, a federal court restricted the scope of the FDA's jurisdiction. In *Coyne Beahm v. FDA*, 966 F. Supp. 1374 (M.D. N.C. 1997), tobacco companies and advertising agencies challenged the FDA's regulation of tobacco products. In April 1997 the district court ruled on the plaintiffs' motion for SUMMARY JUDGMENT, holding that the FDA could regulate the sale, distribution, and use of smoking and chewing tobacco, but not the advertising or promotion of tobacco products. Both parties planned to appeal the ruling.

State Regulation of Tobacco State and local governments may also regulate tobacco and tobacco products to the extent that their regulations are not preempted (already addressed) by federal laws. By 1997 every state had some form of regulation of chewing and smoking tobacco products. State governments typically restrict the use of tobacco by MINORS, require LICENSES for those who sell tobacco products, and restrict vending machine and individual cigarette sales.

In the Alcohol, Drug Abuse, and Mental Health Amendments Reorganization Act of 1992 (Pub. L. No. 102-321, 106 Stat. 323), Congress declared that it was the responsibility of the states, with help from federal agencies, to restrict minors' access to tobacco products. By 1996 when the FDA called for a minimum age of eighteen for the use of tobacco products, all fifty states already had laws in place establishing eighteen as the minimum age for tobacco use.

The scope of state and local regulation is limited because it may not extend to areas already being regulated by the federal government. For example, because the FCLAA already regulates advertising based on smoking and health considerations, states and localities can restrict advertising only for other reasons, such as to protect citizens' aesthetic sensibilities, to control the location or types of cigarette displays, or to protect children from promotions blatantly aimed at them as consumers.

Whether the FCLAA preempts state regulation of promotions aimed at children is in dispute in the courts. In *Penn Advertising v. City of Baltimore*, 862 F. Supp. 1402 (D. Md. 1994), *aff'd*, 63 F.3d 1318 (4th Cir. 1995), *cert. granted and judgment vacated*, *Penn Advertising v. Schmoke*, __U.S. __, 116 S. Ct. 2575, 135 L. Ed. 2d 1090, *aff'd on remand*, 101 F.3d 322 (4th Cir. 1996), the court held that the FCLAA did not PREEMPT a local ORDINANCE that barred cigarette advertising in certain locations where children were likely to be found, such as near schools. But in *Chiglo v. City of Preston*, 909 F. Supp. 675 (D. Minn. 1995), the court overturned a city ordinance that restricted from certain areas cigarette advertising that contained logos, cartoon characters, or any distinctive brand advertising. The court in *Chiglo* held that the ordinance regulated the content of the advertising and hence was preempted by the FCLAA.

Local laws can also be preempted by state laws if the state law addresses the same issue. Well aware of this limitation, the tobacco industry began a campaign in the 1980s to encourage the adoption of weak, industry-friendly tobacco control legislation at the state level to preempt local governments from imposing stricter controls on the sale and use of tobacco.

Clean Indoor Air Acts Armed with information showing the effects of ETS, the federal, state, and local governments began considering statutes to prohibit smoking in nonresidential buildings. Federal laws were passed to restrict smoking in transportation systems (49 C.F.R. § 1061.1 [1991]), in government buildings (41 C.F.R. § 101-20.105-3 [1991]), and aboard domestic AIRLINE flights (14 C.F.R. § 129.29). Federal regulation of private-sector workplaces has yet to take effect. Federal legislation was proposed, but the tobacco industry was able to muster great resistance to it. As of mid-1997, the proposed legislation was not yet finalized.

States and localities have responded to the concern over ETS by regulating smoking in various public areas. In 1997 more than forty states and the District of Columbia had some form of regulation in place. A minority of states have enacted indoor air quality acts, similar to the rules proposed by the Occupational Safety and Health Administration (OSHA). Some local governments have passed laws restricting smoking in places of entertainment, restaurants, and workplaces and on public transportation. Most of the state and local smoking regulations do not ban smoking in the workplace entirely, but limit smoking to designated areas or private offices.

Many private employers have voluntarily restricted smoking in the workplace. A 1985 survey found that more than 33 percent of employers were already regulating smoking in the workplace, and by 1991 that number had grown to 85 percent. By 1997 many private businesses had established policies that made it nearly impossible for employees to work and smoke. For example, some businesses would not allow anyone who had smoked within a certain time period to enter the building. Other businesses began charging smoking employees more for HEALTH INSURANCE benefits. Indeed, businesses are motivated to regulate smoking in part because of the higher absenteeism and increased health care costs of smoking employees.

Tobacco Litigation Tobacco litigation can be divided into three distinct time frames based on the types of claims pursued and the legal theories on which those claims were based. The first wave of tobacco litigation (1954–1973) involved cases based mainly on the theories of DECEIT, breach of express and implied warranties, and NEGLIGENCE. Cases filed during the second wave of tobacco litigation (1983–1992) were based on the legal theories of failure to warn and strict liability. Neither of the first two waves of litigation proved to be successful for the plaintiffs.

The first wave of litigation was characterized by the tobacco industry's adamant claims that smoking and chewing tobacco products were not harmful to consumers. Plaintiffs during that time did not have the extensive medical studies demonstrating serious health consequences that are available today to support their claims. Thus, plaintiffs had a difficult time establishing the essential element of PROXIMATE CAUSE (causal connection to the injury) in their tort cases. By the time of the second wave of tobacco litigation, the connection between smoking and illness had been firmly established, but the tobacco industry was still able to argue with great success that smokers assumed the risks of smoking by freely deciding to smoke. The FCLAA's requirement that a warning label be placed on all cigarette packaging and advertising supported the tobacco companies' defenses of contributory negligence and assumption of the risk.

During the first two waves of litigation, the tobacco companies were also successful in using their size and financial strength to make litigation as difficult as possible for the plaintiffs. The tobacco industry filed and argued every conceivable MOTION, took countless DEPOSITIONS, and sent out extensive INTERROGATORIES. As a result, it was extremely burdensome and expensive for plaintiffs and their attorneys to pursue their cases.

The third wave of tobacco litigation began in the early 1990s and consists of CLASS ACTION suits brought by those injured by tobacco products and medical cost reimbursement suits brought by states and INSURANCE companies. Legal scholars expect the third wave of litigation to produce more favorable results for plaintiffs and to regulate the sale and use of tobacco more effectively than conventional legislative and administrative regulation has been able to do. The strong-arm tactics used by tobacco companies to successfully fend off plaintiffs in the earlier litigation are not likely to work in the third wave because the class of plaintiffs and their respective attorneys have organized and are working together to their mutual benefit. Plaintiffs also now have new EVIDENCE obtained from internal tobacco company documents and former tobacco industry researchers that will significantly bolster their cases.

By the mid-1990s, the tobacco industry faced an enormous amount of exposure to liability. It has been estimated that cigarette-related illnesses and losses in productivity cost more than two dollars per pack of cigarettes in 1985 dollars. Further, studies have demonstrated a direct correlation between an increase in the cost of cigarettes and a reduction in consumption, especially by underage smokers. A reduction in smoking also clearly correlates with fewer adverse health effects and lower health care costs.

For these reasons, in 1996 the Board of Trustees of the American Medical Association endorsed litigation against the tobacco companies. Legal experts have theorized that the long-term effects of plaintiff victories in the third wave of tobacco litigation could devastate and ultimately destroy the industry, much as plaintiff victories did in the recent asbestos litigation.

The claims in the third wave of tobacco litigation are based on some new legal theories. First, plaintiffs can demonstrate that tobacco companies knew that nicotine is pharmacologically active and highly addictive but hid that knowledge and, in fact, denied it under oath. Second, plaintiffs can show that tobacco companies manipulated nicotine levels in their products in an attempt to foster addiction in their consumers. Common legal theories used in the third wave of litigation include fraud, intentional and negligent misrepresentation, emotional distress, violation of CONSUMER PROTECTION statutes, breach of express and implied warranties, strict liability, conspiracy, ANTITRUST, negligent performance of a voluntary undertaking, UNJUST ENRICHMENT or INDEMNITY, civil claims under the Federal RACKETEER INFLUENCED AND CORRUPT ORGANIZATIONS (RICO) ACT (18 U.S.C.A. § 1961 et seq. [1970]), and various criminal theories.

The third wave of litigation began with the certification of two class action suits (*Broin v. Philip Morris*, 641 So. 2d 888 [Fla. App. 3d Dist. 1994], *review denied, Philip Morris Inc. v. Broin*, 654 So. 2d 919 [Fla. 1995], and *Castano v. American Tobacco*, 84 F.3d 734 [5th Cir. 1996]). The class members in *Broin* were nonsmoking flight attendants who claimed that they suffered from various illnesses caused by their exposure to ETS from air travelers' cigarettes. *Castano* was based on plaintiffs' claims that the tobacco

Flight attendant Patty Young, left, was one of 60,000 flight attendants who sued the tobacco industry in a class action to recover for injuries they claim were sustained from breathing second-hand smoke.

AP/WIDE WORLD PHOTOS

companies intentionally manipulated nicotine levels, even though the companies knew that nicotine was a hazardous and addictive substance. The *Castano* class consisted of all nicotine-dependent persons or their ESTATES, HEIRS, family members, or "significant others" in the United States and its territories and possessions, who have bought and smoked cigarettes manufactured by the defendants. Because of the breadth of the class, the U.S. Court of Appeals for the Fifth Circuit ruled that the plaintiffs in *Castano* should not have been certified as a class; had the court allowed the case to proceed, it would likely have become the largest class action in U.S. history. After the decertification of the *Castano* class, plaintiffs' lawyers decided to pursue statewide class action suits in state courts around the nation.

Lawsuits since *Castano* have sought to eliminate the problem of certifying a large class. For example, *Engle v. R. J. Reynolds*, 672 So. 2d 39 [Ct. App. Fla. 3d Dist. 1996], *review denied*, 682 So. 2d 1100 (Fla. 1996), involves essentially the same claims as *Castano*, but the class is much smaller. The class certified in *Engle* consists of Florida citizens and residents, and their survivors, who have suffered, presently suffer, or have died from diseases and other medical conditions caused by their addiction to cigarettes. The *Engle* class action has been allowed to proceed. Several class action suits modeled on *Engle* have since been brought, and still more are anticipated.

The wave of state reimbursement suits was initiated in May 1994, when the state of Mississippi filed an unprecedented lawsuit on behalf of the state's taxpayers against the tobacco industry to recoup the state's share of MEDICAID costs incurred as a result of tobacco-related illnesses (*Moore v. American Tobacco*, No. 94-1429 [Miss. Chan. Ct. 1994]). The state of Mississippi proceeded on legal theories of unjust enrichment and RESTITUTION, based on the fact that the state's taxpayers had been directly injured by the actions of the tobacco industry because they were forced to pay Medicaid costs associated with tobacco-related illnesses. By the middle of 1997, thirty-seven states had filed medical cost reimbursement suits based on legal theories similar to those pursued by Mississippi. In addition, some of the other states brought claims never before considered in this wave of litigation.

In 1994, when the state of Minnesota filed a medical cost reimbursement suit, the insurance company Blue Cross–Blue Shield of Minnesota joined as co-plaintiff, seeking reimbursement for its share of tobacco-related health care costs in Minnesota (*Minnesota v. Philip Morris*, No. 94-8565 [D.Minn. 1994]). When West Virginia filed its medical reimbursement lawsuit, it named as defendants not only tobacco companies, but also the Kimberly-Clarke Corporation, developer of the tobacco reconstitution process that enables tobacco companies to manipulate nicotine levels. In 1995 the state of Florida filed a lawsuit against the tobacco industry under Florida's Medicaid Third-Party Liability Act, effectively preventing tobacco industry defendants from prevailing under defenses of ASSUMPTION OF RISK and contributory negligence. Texas filed suit in 1996 and brought claims based in part on the RICO Act and on theories of mail and wire fraud, antitrust violations, and public NUISANCE. The state of Washington additionally has sued the law firms that have represented the tobacco companies for many years, arguing that they unlawfully helped their clients keep certain documents confidential. Some of the states have asked that in addition to awarding monetary DAMAGES, the courts order the tobacco industry to publish all previous research on the link between smoking and health, establish funds for public education campaigns designed to discourage smoking, disclose the amounts of nicotine in their tobacco products, and order the dissolution of the tobacco industry's nonprofit organizations, the Council for Tobacco Research and the Tobacco Institute.

The most recent tobacco litigation has resulted in a historic SETTLEMENT agreement. On March 15, 1996, the states of West Virginia, Florida, Mississippi, Massachusetts, and Louisiana entered into an agreement with Brooke Group and Liggett Group to settle those companies' portion of the states' medical cost reimbursement actions. This settlement was noteworthy because it represented the end of the tobacco industry's efforts to present a unified front and to refuse to willingly pay out monetary damages.

By March 1997 the Brooke Group/Liggett settlement agreement had been amended to include twenty-two states. In addition, in conjunction with the settlement agreement, Liggett Group, one of the five largest U.S. tobacco companies, publicly admitted that cigarettes and cigarette smoking cause lung cancer, heart disease, and emphysema. Liggett admitted that nicotine is addictive and that the tobacco industry actively and illegally markets to young people under the age of eighteen. As part of the amended settlement, Liggett agreed to cooperate fully with the twenty-two states by waiving ATTORNEY-CLIENT PRIVILEGE and turning over privileged documents. Liggett also agreed to substantially comply with the new FDA regulations and to put warning labels on its cigarettes stating "Warning: Smoking Is Addictive." Liggett further promised to pay 25 percent of its pre-tax profits for the next twenty-five years to settle these actions.

Following several successful lawsuits, the Brooke Group/Liggett settlement agreement, and the FDA's promulgation of its rule regulating tobacco, discussion began regarding a possible global legislative settlement of all tobacco litigation. U.S. Senate Majority Leader Trent Lott agreed to broker an agreement that would allow the tobacco industry to avoid FDA regulation and receive IMMUNITY from PRODUCT LIABILITY suits for fifteen years. Talks regarding this proposed global settlement began in March 1997.

Preliminary reports indicate that the proposed settlement calls for the tobacco industry to pay billions of dollars in increasing amounts over fifteen years. The money would be administered by an administrator appointed by the president and would be paid out in grants to all fifty states. The plan also calls for the industry to drop the lawsuits it has brought against industry defectors and whistle-blowers in exchange for immunity from virtually all liability suits for the next fifteen years. By late 1997, the global settlement talks had not produced a final agreement but were proceeding. The parties reported that they were hopeful that an agreement would be reached in the near future.

Criminal Charges   In the 1990s federal criminal investigators began to prepare a case against the tobacco companies and their executives and scientists, four trade associations and industry-funded groups, a scientific consulting group, a public relations consulting firm, two companies that serve as suppliers to the tobacco companies, and a company-funded research group. The alleged crimes include federal PERJURY, MAIL FRAUD, wire fraud, FALSE ADVERTISING, criminal conspiracy, criminal racketeering, and the deception of the public, federal agencies, and Congress. One criminal investigation is looking at possible perjury on the part of the

industry's chief executive officers while testifying before Congress in April 1994 regarding the addictive qualities of nicotine. Another criminal probe is considering whether the industry misled its shareholders by misrepresenting industry knowledge of the physiological effects of tobacco products. Another investigation is focusing on ALLEGATIONS that an indoor air quality testing company accepted money from tobacco companies to distort test results. Still another probe is investigating the industry's Council for Tobacco Research, including the validity of its nonprofit status and whether it hid research results regarding smoking and health from the government. Finally, a probe is investigating allegations that tobacco companies smuggled cigarettes into Canada to avoid paying Canada's high cigarette taxes. The results of these criminal investigations remain to be seen.

See also TORT LAW.

TODD, THOMAS   Thomas Todd served as associate justice of the U.S. Supreme Court from 1807 to 1826. Trained as a land surveyor as well as a lawyer, Todd's handful of opinions on the Court mostly concerned land claims.

Todd was born in King and Queen County, Virginia, on January 23, 1765. As a teenager he served briefly in the Revolutionary War before attending Liberty Hall, now called Washington and Lee University. Todd studied surveying before moving to Kentucky in 1783 when his first cousin, Harry Innes, was appointed to the Kentucky district of the Virginia Supreme Court. Todd was admitted to the Kentucky bar in 1786, but he gained positions of influence by becoming a recorder.

Todd was the clerk for the ten conventions called between 1784 and 1792 to arrange Kentucky's separation from Virginia. He served as clerk to the federal district court in Kentucky (1787–1792), clerk of the Kentucky House of Representatives (1792), and clerk of the Kentucky Court of Appeals (1792–1801) before being appointed a judge of the appellate court in 1801.

Todd proved adept at resolving the land disputes created by the complicated law that

BIOGRAPHY

PORTRAIT BY MATTHEW HARRIS JOUETT, COLLECTION OF THE SUPREME COURT OF THE UNITED STATES.

Thomas Todd

THOMAS TODD 1765–1826

1787–92 Served as clerk to federal district court in Ky.

1783 Graduated from Liberty Hall (now Washington and Lee University)

1765 Born, King and Queen County, Va.

1775–83 American Revolution

1786 Admitted to Ky. bar

1792–1801 Served as clerk of the Ky. Court of Appeals

1801–07 Held judgeship on the Ky. Court of Appeals

1806 Became chief justice of the court

1812 Wrote opinion in *M'Kim v. Voorhies,* which held that a state court could not enjoin the judgment of a federal circuit court

1812–14 War of 1812

1807–26 Served as associate justice of the U.S. Supreme Court

1826 Died, Frankfort, Ky.

1750   1775   1800   1825   1850

Kentucky had inherited from Virginia. In 1806 he was named chief judge of the appeals court but served only briefly in that position.

In 1807 the U.S. Supreme Court was expanded to seven members. The western states (Kentucky, Tennessee, and Ohio) urged President THOMAS JEFFERSON to nominate Todd to the new seat, as the new justice would be responsible for presiding as circuit judge in the newly established Seventh Circuit. Jefferson agreed and nominated Todd in early 1807. Todd took his seat in 1808.

During his time on the Court, Todd served under Chief Justice JOHN MARSHALL. Although they had different political beliefs, Todd adopted Marshall's views on constitutional construction. Todd's knowledge of land laws made him a valuable member of the Court, even though he wrote very few opinions. His absence from the Court for six terms because of illness, family matters, and the difficulty of traveling to Washington also diminished his effectiveness. Todd died on February 7, 1826, in Frankfort, Kentucky.

TOKYO TRIAL After WORLD WAR II eleven of the Allied Powers (Australia, Canada, China, France, India, the Netherlands, New Zealand, the Philippines, the Soviet Union, the United Kingdom, and the United States) prosecuted twenty-eight of Japan's top military, political, and diplomatic leaders for an assortment of WAR CRIMES committed in Southeast Asia between 1928 and 1945. Known as the Tokyo trial for the city in which it took place, this legal proceeding stands along side the NUREMBERG TRIALS for its contribution to INTERNATIONAL LAW and the RULES OF WAR.

American involvement in World War II formally began on December 8, 1941, when the United States declared war on Japan, and formally ended on September 2, 1945, when the Japanese surrendered in Tokyo Bay aboard the USS *Missouri*. For more than a decade before the war, the Japanese military had been expanding its foothold on the Asiatic mainland. During the war itself, Japan invaded or attacked Burma, China, Indochina, the Philippines, Malaysia, Manchuria, Wake Island, Hong Kong, Singapore, and the Aleutians, committing an array of atrocities. The Tokyo trial was the Allies' effort to hold Japan responsible for its crimes during this period of military aggression.

The International Military Tribunal for the Far East (IMT) was established on January 19, 1946, by order of General Douglas MacArthur, the supreme commander of Allied Forces in the South Pacific. MacArthur appointed eleven judges to preside, one from each of the Allied countries participating in the proceeding. All decisions made by the IMT were by majority vote, with MacArthur retaining plenary power over appeals. Because the vanquished government of Japan consented to the JURISDICTION of the IMT, the tribunal sidestepped some of the murkier legal issues confronting the judges at Nuremberg who had faced repeated challenges to their authority under international law.

Each of the participating Allied Powers was represented by a chief prosecutor and a support staff comprised of assistant prosecutors, investigators, and miscellaneous other personnel. The defendants were represented by over one hundred attorneys, three-quarters Japanese and one-quarter American, plus a support staff of their own. The prosecution began opening statements on May 3, 1946, and took 192 days to present its case. The defense opened its case on January 27, 1947, and finished its presentation 225 days later. The IMT delivered its JUDGMENT over a period of 4 days, concluding the trial on November 12, 1948. During 818 public sessions held by the IMT, 230 translators were employed, 419 WITNESSES gave TESTIMONY, 4,336 exhibits were introduced, and more than 53,000 pages of transcript were printed.

Although the IMT heard evidence regarding fifty-five counts of war crimes, most of the transgressions fell into one of three categories: crimes against peace, crimes against humanity, and conventional war crimes. Crimes against peace included the planning, initiating, and waging of "aggressive war," which was broadly defined as any hostile military act that violated the territorial boundaries or political independence of a sovereign nation. Crimes against humanity included the murder, persecution, and enslavement of civilian populations. Conventional war crimes included violations of the international rules and customs of warfare that have been recognized by civilized societies and govern hostilities between combatants, the behavior of occupying powers, and the treatment of prisoners of war (POWs).

The prosecution offered compelling evidence that the defendants had violated more than a hundred international treaties and committed countless war crimes over the previous twenty years. In particular, the evidence showed that when Japan invaded Nanking, China, in 1937 at least 20,000 women were raped by Japanese soldiers, and at least 100,000 civilians were slaughtered. Thousands of Chinese civilians were captured during the massacre and deported to Japanese labor camps where they were forced to work at gunpoint. Other evidence revealed that the Japanese army had brutally marched 50,000 U.S. POWs across the Bataan peninsula in 1942. Many of these prisoners were underfed, dehydrated, and malnourished, while some were tortured, shot, and buried alive in what became known as the "Bataan Death March." Additionally, prosecution witnesses gave testimony that U.S., Soviet, Filipino, and Chinese POWs had been used as subjects in barbaric scientific experiments performed at Japanese concentration camps throughout the war.

The IMT spent six months reaching judgment and drafting its 1,781-page opinion. Nine judges were persuaded by the prosecution's evidence, and two were not. The judges from France and India wrote separate dissenting opinions. Twenty-five defendants were found guilty of committing war crimes; seven of them were sentenced to death by hanging, sixteen to life imprisonment, one to a term of twenty years, and one to a term of seven years. Two defendants died before the proceedings ended, and one was declared incompetent to stand trial by reason of insanity.

The highest ranking official prosecuted by the Allies was Hideki Tojo, the prime minister of Japan during the attack on Pearl Harbor in Hawaii in 1941. He was found guilty of waging aggressive war and sentenced to death. Tojo's predecessor, Kuki Hirota, was prime minister during Japan's invasion of China in 1937. He was convicted of crimes against humanity and sentenced to death for negligently failing to stop the massacre at Nanking after learning about the terror and carnage in its early stages. HIROHITO, the Japanese emperor during World War II, was spared from prosecution as a condition of Japan's surrender in 1945.

TOLL 📖 A sum of money paid for the right to use a road, HIGHWAY, or bridge. To postpone or suspend. For example, to toll a STATUTE OF LIMITATIONS means to postpone the running of the time period it specifies. 📖

TONKIN GULF RESOLUTION In August 1964 Congress passed the Tonkin Gulf Resolution (78 Stat. 384), approving and supporting President LYNDON B. JOHNSON's determination to repel any armed attack against U.S. forces in Southeast Asia. Johnson subsequently relied on the measure as his chief authorization for the escalation of the VIETNAM WAR.

The resolution was prompted by Johnson's report to Congress that the North Vietnamese had fired upon two U.S. destroyers in international waters in the Gulf of Tonkin, off the coast of North Vietnam. Johnson requested that Congress grant him wide PRESIDENTIAL POWERS to respond to the attacks of the North Vietnamese. Both houses of Congress voted overwhelmingly in favor of the resolution; only two senators opposed it and no representatives. The resolution gave the president power to "take all necessary measures to repel any armed attack against the forces of the United States and to prevent further aggression." According to the resolution, its purpose was to promote international peace and security and support the defense of U.S. naval vessels lawfully present in international waters from deliberate and repeated attacks by naval units of the Communist regime in Vietnam.

It was later revealed that the federal government had drafted the Tonkin Gulf Resolution fully six months before the attacks on the U.S. vessels occurred. It was also revealed that the United States provoked the attack by assisting the South Vietnamese in mounting clandestine military attacks against the North Vietnamese. Although the two U.S. vessels attacked were actually on intelligence-gathering missions, the North Vietnamese could not distinguish them from the South Vietnamese raiding ships. Johnson had also exaggerated the gravity of the attack itself, which did not harm either of the ships.

Although no formal declaration of war was ever issued for the Vietnam War, the Department of Justice and the State Department relied on the Tonkin Gulf Resolution as the functional equivalent. Thus, Johnson was able to send U.S. troops to Vietnam without an official war declaration. In early 1965 the Viet Cong raided a U.S. air base in South Vietnam, killing seven Americans. In response to that action, and in accordance with the Tonkin Gulf Resolution, Johnson began a large-scale escalation of U.S. involvement in the Vietnam War. The number of U.S. soldiers in South Vietnam grew from 25,000 in early 1965 to 184,000 by the end of that year. The escalation continued, and by 1968 543,000 U.S. soldiers were in South Vietnam.

Although the war initially had widespread support, by 1968 growing numbers of Americans had begun to protest and question Johnson's decisions to escalate U.S. involvement. For a number of reasons, the public felt the president had deceived them. In the 1964 presidential elections, Johnson had campaigned on a promise to keep U.S. troops out of the fighting in Vietnam. In addition, the public learned through the release of the Pentagon Papers that the Tonkin Gulf incident was actually instigated by the United States and was not as damaging as the government had suggested. Some constitutional law authorities argued that it was irrelevant whether Congress was deceived by the executive in passing the Tonkin Gulf Resolution because the resolution provided that Congress could repeal it at any time. In addition, the scholars argued that Congress had the power to stop appropriating money to support the war effort.

In January 1971 Congress repealed the Tonkin Gulf Resolution. President RICHARD M. NIXON continued the war effort, however, by relying on the commander in chief provisions of the U.S. Constitution. Congress continued to appropriate money to support the war effort. The Vietnam War was the longest, costliest, and most controversial war in U.S. history, and the Tonkin Gulf Resolution was the focal point of much of the controversy.

See also WAR; WAR POWERS RESOLUTION.

TONTINE ⚏ An organization of individuals who enter into an agreement to pool sums of money or something of value other than money, permitting the last survivor of the group to take everything. ⚏

The holders of tontine life INSURANCE contracts enter into an agreement to pay PREMIUMS for a certain amount of time before they gain the right to acquire DIVIDENDS. In the event that a policyholder dies during the tontine policy, his or her BENEFICIARY will be entitled to benefits, but no dividends. The earnings that ordinarily would be used to pay dividends are accumulated during the tontine period and subsequently given only to policyholders who are still alive at the end of the term. This type of policy is known as a dividend-deferred policy. A number of states proscribe such policies.

TORRENS TITLE SYSTEM ⚏ A system for recording land titles under which a court may direct the issuance of a certificate of TITLE upon application by the landowner. ⚏

The Torrens title system is a method of registering titles to REAL ESTATE. Real estate that is recorded using this method is also called *registered property* or *Torrens property*. The system is used in the British Commonwealth countries, including Canada, and in Europe but has not been widely adopted in the United States. The first U.S. Torrens system was enacted by Illinois in 1897.

The system is named after Sir Robert R. Torrens, who introduced it in South Australia in 1858 and later lobbied for its adoption in other parts of the country. He wrote several books on the subject, arguing that his system simplified the transfer of REAL PROPERTY and eliminated the need for repeated examinations of land titles.

Under the traditional system of transferring, or conveying, land, the history of the PROPERTY in question must be examined to ensure that the seller can convey good title to the purchaser. When property is sold, a DEED is filed and recorded with the county land office; the deed contains the names of the seller and the buyer; the ownership relationship of the sellers and buyers, if more than one seller or one buyer is involved (for example, joint tenants or tenants in common); and the legal description of the property being transferred. This information is abstracted from each deed and recorded in a document called an ABSTRACT OF TITLE. An attorney or a real estate title examiner inspects each entry to determine that good title has been passed with each transaction. If any problems exist with the title, they must be remedied before the purchaser may obtain good title.

A Torrens system does away with this process. A court or bureau of registration operates the system, with an examiner of titles and a registrar as the key officers. The owner of a piece of land files a petition with the registrar to have the land registered. The examiner of titles reviews the legal history of the land to determine if good title exists. If good title does exist, the registrar issues a certificate of title to the owner. This certificate is ordinarily conclusive as to the person's rights in the property and cannot be challenged or overcome by a court of law. If a mistake is made by the examiner of titles, an insurance fund pays the person who holds a claim against the land. The fees charged to examine and register property pay for the insurance fund and the operation of the registration office.

When the owner sells the property, the certificate alone is EVIDENCE of good title, eliminating the need for a new examination of title. The purchaser presents the deed and the certificate of title to the registrar, who records the purchaser's name on the title.

The one drawback to a Torrens system is the initial cost of registering the property. The system is most effective when unimproved land is subdivided for the first time because it reduces the number of deed entries an examiner must review.

CROSS-REFERENCES

Recording of Land Titles; Registration of Land Titles; Title Search.

TORTFEASOR ⚏ A wrongdoer; an individual who commits a wrongful act that injures another and for which the law provides a legal right to seek relief; a defendant in a civil tort ACTION. ⚏

See also TORT LAW.

TORTIOUS ⚏ Wrongful; conduct of such character as to subject the actor to civil LIABILITY under tort law. ⚏

In order to establish that a particular act was tortious, a plaintiff must prove that an ACTIONABLE wrong existed and that DAMAGES ensued from that wrong.

See also TORT LAW.

TORT LAW 📖 A body of rights, obligations, and remedies that is applied by courts in civil proceedings to provide RELIEF for persons who have suffered harm from the wrongful acts of others. The person who sustains INJURY or suffers pecuniary damage as the result of tortious conduct is known as the PLAINTIFF, and the person who is responsible for inflicting the injury and incurs LIABILITY for the damage is known as the DEFENDANT or TORTFEASOR. 📖

Three elements must be established in every tort ACTION. First, the plaintiff must establish that the defendant was under a legal DUTY to act in a particular fashion. Second, the plaintiff must demonstrate that the defendant breached this duty by failing to conform her behavior accordingly. Third, the plaintiff must prove that he suffered injury or loss as a direct result of the defendant's breach.

The law of torts is derived from a combination of common-law principles and legislative enactments. Unlike actions for breach of CONTRACT, tort actions are not dependent upon an AGREEMENT between the parties to a lawsuit. Unlike criminal prosecutions, which are brought by the government, tort actions are brought by private citizens. Remedies for tortious acts include money DAMAGES and INJUNCTIONS (court orders compelling or forbidding particular conduct). Tortfeasors are subject to neither FINE nor INCARCERATION in civil court.

The word *tort* comes from the Latin term *torquere*, which means "twisted or wrong." The English COMMON LAW recognized no separate legal action in tort. Instead, the British legal system afforded litigants two central avenues of redress: TRESPASS for direct injuries, and actions "on the case" for indirect injuries. Gradually, the common law recognized other CIVIL ACTIONS, including DEFAMATION, LIBEL, and SLANDER. Most of the American colonies adopted the English common law in the eighteenth century. During the nineteenth century, the first U.S. legal treatises were published in which a portion of the common law was synthesized under the heading of torts.

Over the last century, tort law has touched on nearly every aspect of life in the United States. In economic affairs, tort law provides remedies for businesses that are harmed by the unfair and deceptive trade practices of a competitor. In the workplace, tort law protects employees from the intentional or negligent infliction of emotional distress. Tort law also helps regulate the environment, providing remedies against both individuals and businesses that pollute the air, land, and water to such an extent that it amounts to a NUISANCE.

Sometimes tort law governs life's most intimate relations, as when individuals are held liable for knowingly transmitting communicable diseases to their sexual partners. When a loved one is killed by a tortious act, surviving family members may bring a WRONGFUL DEATH action to recover pecuniary loss. Tort law also governs a wide array of behavior in less intimate settings, including the operation of motor vehicles on public roadways.

The law of torts serves four objectives. First, it seeks to compensate victims for injuries suffered by the culpable action or inaction of others. Second, it seeks to shift the cost of such injuries to the person or persons who are legally

Tort Cases

Types of Tort Cases

Product liability
3%

Toxic substances
2%

Other
13%

Auto
accidents
60%

Premises
liability
17%

Medical
malpractice
5%

Injuries of Damages Alleged in Cases

Property
damage
5%

Financial loss or
injury to reputation
3%

Personal
injury
92%

Case Processing Time

More than
two years
26%

Less than
one year
44%

One to
two years
30%

Source: "Tort Cases in Large Counties," by Steven K. Smith, Carol J. DeFrances and Patrick A. Langan, *Bureau of Justice Statistics Bulletin*, 1997.

CAMERIQUE/THE PICTURE CUBE

Skydivers rely on their instructor and their equipment to bring them to the ground softly. Any failure of equipment or negligence in instruction could be grounds for a tort suit.

responsible for inflicting them. Third, it seeks to discourage injurious, careless, and risky behavior in the future. Fourth, it seeks to vindicate legal rights and interests that have been compromised, diminished, or emasculated. In theory these objectives are served when tort LIABILITY is imposed on tortfeasors for intentional wrongdoing, negligence, and ultrahazardous activities.

Intentional Torts An intentional tort is any deliberate interference with a legally recognized interest, such as the rights to bodily integrity, emotional tranquility, dominion over property, seclusion from public scrutiny, and freedom from confinement or deception. These interests are violated by the intentional torts of ASSAULT, BATTERY, trespass, FALSE IMPRISONMENT, invasion of PRIVACY, CONVERSION, MISREPRESENTATION, and FRAUD. The intent element of these torts is satisfied when the tortfeasor acts with the desire to bring about harmful consequences and is substantially certain that such consequences will follow. Mere reckless behavior, sometimes called WILLFUL and wanton behavior, does not rise to the level of an intentional tort.

Under certain circumstances the law permits individuals to intentionally pursue a course of conduct that will necessarily result in harm to others. The harm that results from such conduct is said to be outweighed by more important interests. Self-preservation is one such interest and is embodied in the right of self-defense. Individuals may exert sufficient force in SELF-DEFENSE to repel an IMMINENT threat of bodily harm. DEADLY FORCE may only be used by persons who reasonably believe that their lives

are endangered and for whom there are no REASONABLE means of escape. Reasonable force, but not deadly force, may be employed in defense of property.

CONSENT is a defense to virtually every intentional tort. The law will not compensate persons who knowingly allow someone to injure them. However, consent must be given freely and voluntarily to be effective. Consent induced by COERCION, DURESS, UNDUE INFLUENCE, or chicanery is not legally effective. Nor is consent legally effective when given by an incompetent person. Consent to intentional torts involving grievous bodily harm is also deemed ineffective in a number of JURISDICTIONS.

Negligence Most injuries that result from tortious behavior are the product of NEGLIGENCE, not intentional wrongdoing. Negligence is the term used by tort law to characterize behavior that creates unreasonable risks of harm to persons and property. A person acts negligently when her behavior departs from the conduct ordinarily expected of a reasonably prudent person under the circumstances. In general, the law requires jurors to use their common sense and life experience in determining the proper degree of care and vigilance with which people must lead their lives to avoid imperiling the safety of others.

Not every ACCIDENT producing injury gives rise to liability for negligence. Some accidents cannot be avoided even with the exercise of reasonable care. An accident that results from a defendant's sudden and unexpected physical ailment, such as a seizure or a blackout, generally relieves the defendant of liability for harm caused during his period of unconsciousness. However, defendants who have reason to know of such medical problems are expected to take reasonable precautions against the risks the problems create. In some jurisdictions unavoidable accidents are called ACTS OF GOD.

ASSUMPTION OF RISK is another defense to negligence actions. This defense prevents plaintiffs from recovering for injuries sustained as a result of a relationship or transaction they entered with full knowledge and acceptance of the risks commonly associated with such undertakings. Assumed risks include most of those encountered by spectators attending sporting events. However, the law will not assume that individuals accept the RISK of intentionally inflicted harm or damage, such as injuries resulting from ASSAULT AND BATTERY.

Strict Liability In some cases tort law imposes liability on defendants who are neither negligent nor guilty of intentional wrongdoing.

Known as strict liability, or liability without fault, this branch of torts seeks to regulate those activities that are useful and necessary but that create abnormally dangerous risks to society. These activities include blasting, transporting hazardous materials, storing dangerous substances, and keeping certain wild animals in captivity.

A distinction is sometimes drawn between moral FAULT and legal fault. Persons who negligently or intentionally cause injury to others are often considered morally blameworthy for having failed to live up to a minimal threshold of human conduct. On the other hand, legal fault is more of an artificial standard of conduct that is created by government for the protection of society.

Persons who engage in ultrahazardous activities may be morally blameless because no amount of care or diligence can make their activities safe for society. However, such persons will nonetheless be held legally responsible for harm that results from their activities as a means of shifting the costs of injury from potential victims to tortfeasors. As a matter of social policy, then, individuals and entities that engage in abnormally dangerous activities for profit must be willing to ensure the safety of others as a price of doing business.

Consumers who have been injured by defectively manufactured products also rely on strict liability. Under the doctrine of strict product liability, a manufacturer must guarantee that its goods are suitable for their intended use when they are placed on the market for public consumption. The law of torts will hold manufacturers strictly liable for any injuries that result from placing unreasonably dangerous products into the stream of commerce, without regard to the amount of care exercised in preparing the product for sale and distribution and without regard to whether the consumer purchased the product from, or entered into a contractual relationship with, the manufacturer.

Causation Causation is an element common to all three branches of torts: strict liability, negligence, and intentional wrongs. Causation has two prongs. First, a tort must be the cause in fact of a particular injury, which means that a specific act must actually have resulted in injury to another. In its simplest form, cause in fact is established by evidence that shows that a tortfeasor's act or omission was a necessary antecedent to the plaintiff's injury. Courts analyze this issue by determining whether the plaintiff's injury would have occurred "but for" the defendant's conduct. If an injury would

have occurred independent of the defendant's conduct, cause in fact has not been established, and no tort has been committed. When multiple factors have led to a particular injury, the plaintiff must demonstrate that the tortfeasor's action played a substantial role in causing the injury.

Second, plaintiffs must establish that a particular tort was the PROXIMATE CAUSE of an injury before liability will be imposed. The term *proximate cause* is somewhat misleading because it has little to do with proximity or causation. Proximate cause limits the scope of liability to those injuries that bear some reasonable relationship to the risk created by the defendant. Proximate cause is evaluated in terms of foreseeability. If the defendant should have foreseen the tortious injury, he or she will be held liable for the resulting loss. If a given risk could not have been reasonably anticipated, proximate cause has not been established, and liability will not be imposed.

When duty, breach, and proximate cause have been established in a tort action, the plaintiff may recover damages for the pecuniary losses sustained. The measure of damages is determined by the nature of the tort committed and the type of injury suffered. Damages for tortious acts generally fall into one of four categories: damages for injury to person, damages for injury to PERSONAL PROPERTY, damages for injury to REAL PROPERTY, and PUNITIVE DAMAGES.

Damages PERSONAL INJURY tort victims must normally recover all their damages—past, present, and future—during a single lawsuit. Damages may be recovered for physical, psychological, and emotional injury. Specifically, these injuries may include permanent disability, pain and suffering, disfigurement, humiliation, embarrassment, distress, impairment of earning capacity, lost wages or profits, medical costs, and out-of-pocket expenses. Courts typically rely on expert testimony to translate such losses into dollar figures.

Plaintiffs suffering damage to personal property must elect between two methods of recovery. First, plaintiffs may elect to recover the difference between the value of the property before the tort and the value of the property after it. Second, plaintiffs may elect to recover the reasonable costs of repair for damaged personal property. However, if the property is destroyed, irreparable, or economically infeasible to repair, damages are measured by the replacement value of the property. Persons who are temporarily deprived of personalty may sue to recover the rental value of the property for the period of deprivation.

Damages for injury to real property may be measured by the difference in the realty's value before and after the tort. Alternatively, plaintiffs may elect to recover the reasonable costs of restoring the property to its original condition. In either case plaintiffs may also recover the rental value of their property if its use and enjoyment has been interrupted by tortious behavior. Mental, emotional, and physical harm that is sustained in the process of a tortious injury to real property is compensable as well.

Punitive damages, called exemplary damages in some jurisdictions, are recoverable against tortfeasors whose injurious conduct is sufficiently egregious. Although punitive damages are typically awarded for injuries suffered from intentional torts, they can also be awarded against tortfeasors who act with reckless indifference to the safety of others. Because one purpose of punitive damages is to punish the defendant, plaintiffs may introduce EVIDENCE regarding a tortfeasor's wealth to allow the jury to better assess the amount of damages necessary for punishment. Such evidence is normally deemed irrelevant or prejudicial in almost every other type of damage claim.

In addition to damages for past tortious conduct, plaintiffs may seek injunctive relief to prevent future harm. Manufacturing plants that billow smoke that pollutes the air, companies that discharge chemicals that poison the water, and factories that store chemicals that migrate through the soil create risks of injury that are likely to recur over time. In tort law, operations that produce recurring injuries like these are called nuisances. If the harmfulness of such operations outweighs their usefulness, plaintiffs may successfully obtain a court order enjoining or restraining them.

Immunity Certain individuals and entities are granted IMMUNITY from both damage awards and assessments of liability in tort. An immunity is a defense to a legal action where PUBLIC POLICY demands special protection for an entity or a class of persons participating in a particular field or activity. Historically, immunity from tort litigation has been granted to government units, public officials, CHARITIES, educational institutions, spouses, parents, and children.

Government immunity, also known as sovereign immunity, insulates federal, state, and local governments from liability for torts that an employee commits within the scope of her or his official duties. Public policy, as reflected by legislation, common-law precedent, and popular opinion, has required courts to protect the government from unnecessary disruptions that invariably result from civil litigation. Similarly, educational institutions generally have been immunized from tort actions to protect students and faculty from distraction.

In a number of states, tortfeasors have been given immunity from liability if they are related to the victim as husband or wife, or parent or child. These states concluded that family harmony should not be traumatized by the adversarial nature of tort litigation. Charities and other philanthropic organizations have been given qualified immunity from tort liability as well. This immunity is based on the fear that donors would stop giving money to charities if the funds were used to pay tort claims.

Over the last quarter century, nearly every jurisdiction has curtailed tort immunity in some fashion. Several jurisdictions have abolished tort immunity for entire groups and entities. The movement to restrict tort immunity has been based in part on the rule of law, which requires all persons, organizations, and government officials to be treated equally under the law. Despite the efforts of this movement, tort immunity persists in various forms at the federal, state, and local levels.

CROSS-REFERENCES

"But For" Rule; Consumer Protection; Environmental Law; Federal Tort Claims Act; Feres Doctrine; *MacPherson v. Buick Motor Co.*; Product Liability; *Rylands v. Fletcher*.

TOTTEN TRUST 📖 An arrangement created by a person depositing his or her own money in his or her own name in a bank account for the benefit of another. 📖

A Totten trust is a tentative trust, revocable at will, until the depositor dies or completes the gift in his or her lifetime by some unequivocal act or declaration, such as delivery of the passbook or notice to the BENEFICIARY. If the depositor dies before the beneficiary without revocation or some resolute act or declaration of disaffirmance, the PRESUMPTION arises that an absolute trust was created as to the balance on hand at the death of the depositor.

The beneficiary need not know about the arrangement, and the depositor is entitled to deposit and withdraw funds from the account as he or she deems fit. The depositor can even close out or revoke the account without obtaining the beneficiary's permission. When the depositor dies, any funds in the account automatically become the property of the beneficiary,

A sample Totten trust

I hereby establish with _____ [*Name of Bank*] Savings Account Number _____ . All deposits made at any time therein are for the benefit of _____ to whom or to whose legal

(Name of Beneficiary)   (Residence)

representative these deposits, or the balance then remaining, together with interest thereon, shall be payable upon my death.

This instrument constitutes a Declaration of Trust immediately effective, subject to my right to revoke the trust now created, in whole or in part, by making withdrawals from this account. Any such revocation will be effective to the extent of such withdrawals. No revocation of the trust, in whole or in part, express or implied, shall be effective unless accompanied by actual withdrawal during my life; however, the death of the beneficiary prior to my death will revoke this trust.

The beneficiary named herein is declared hereby to have a present interest hereunder. Such interest, however, is limited by the terms hereof and shall not, during my life, be assignable or anticipated in any way by the beneficiary. This interest of the beneficiary shall not be subject in any way to the claims of the beneficiary's creditors.

Dated _____ , 19___ .   _____ , Trustee

Identification of Beneficiary

Date of Birth: _____ .   _____

(Relationship to Trustee)

[Reverse side]

I hereby agree that this trust Account is governed by the Bylaws, Rules and Regulations of _____ [*Name of Bank*] relating to Savings Deposits and that it is subject to the conditions of the Declaration of Trust on the reverse side of this card.

Signature: _____ , Trustee

For: _____ (Beneficiary)

Identification of Trustee

Address: _____

Where Born: _____   Date of Birth: _____

Occupation: _____   Mother's Maiden Name: _____

Employer: _____   Telephone: _____

Date Opened: _____   Opened by: _____   Initial Deposit: _____

but they might be subject to the claims of the decedent's CREDITORS. Totten trusts are usually established to avoid the inconvenience of making a will and the expense and delay of PROBATE and ADMINISTRATION. Such an arrangement is known as a testamentary substitute, since a will is thereby obviated. Frequently such TRUSTS are established because the depositor wants to conceal his or her financial situation from others.

BIOGRAPHY

TOUCEY, ISAAC Isaac Toucey served as U.S. attorney general from 1848 to 1849. A leading Connecticut politician before his appointment by President JAMES POLK, Toucey went on to serve as secretary of the navy in the administration of JAMES BUCHANAN.

Toucey was born on November 5, 1796, in Newton, Massachusetts. He studied law as a young man and was admitted to the Connecti-

ISAAC TOUCEY 1796–1869

1775–83 American Revolution

1796 Born, Newton, Mass.

1812–14 War of 1812

1818 Admitted to Conn. bar; began law practice in Hartford

1822–35 Served as Connecticut's state's attorney

1835–39 Served in U.S. House

1842 Reappointed state's attorney

1846–48 Served as governor of Connecticut

1848–49 Served as U.S. attorney general under Polk

1850 Elected to Conn. state senate

1852–57 Served in U.S. Senate

1857–61 Served as secretary of the navy under Buchanan

1861–65 U.S. Civil War

1869 Died, Hartford, Conn.

1775   1800   1825   1850   1875

cut bar in 1818. After practicing law in Hartford, Connecticut, for several years, Toucey was appointed state's attorney in 1822. He held that office until 1835.

In 1835 Toucey was elected to the U.S. House of Representatives as a member of the Democratic party. He left Congress in 1839 and returned to Connecticut. Though he was reappointed state's attorney in 1842, his political ambitions remained paramount. He became governor of Connecticut in 1846.

President Polk took office in 1845. His first attorney general was JOHN Y. MASON, who left the position after a year to become secretary of the navy. Mason's successor, NATHAN CLIFFORD, remained until 1848, when Polk sent him to Mexico to negotiate the treaty that ended the Mexican War and ceded California to the United States. In June 1848, with less than a year left in his administration, Polk appointed Toucey attorney general. Toucey's brief tenure, which ended in March 1849, was unremarkable.

Nevertheless, Toucey capitalized on the national stature he attained as attorney general. He was elected a Connecticut state senator in 1850 and a U.S. senator in 1852. In March 1857 Toucey resigned from the Senate to become secretary of the navy for President Buchanan. He remained as secretary for the entire presidential term, which ended in March 1861.

Retiring from politics and government service, Toucey returned to Connecticut and resumed the practice of law. He died on July 30, 1869, in Hartford.

TOWAGE SERVICE 📖 An act by which one vessel, known as the tug, supplies power in order to draw another vessel, called the tow. 📖

Towing involves dragging a vessel forward in the water through the use of a rope or cable attached to another vessel. Various state laws require that bright lights be placed upon vessels that are towing or being towed.

TO WIT 📖 That is to say; namely. 📖

TOWN 📖 A civil and political subdivision of a state, which varies in size and significance according to location but is ordinarily a division of a COUNTY. 📖

A town, which is a type of MUNICIPAL CORPORATION, can be formed by a state legislature when a large number of dwellings have concentrated in a particular location. A town is a creation of the state, designed and authorized to perform certain governmental functions on the local level. Its main purpose is to exercise the power of the state to promote greater prosperity, safety, convenience, health, and the common good of the general community.

The terms *township* and *town* are frequently used interchangeably in certain geographic locations, although in some parts of the United States the term TOWNSHIP denotes a group of several towns.

Since towns can be formed only from contiguous territory, tracts of land that are entirely separate cannot be included in a town. Subject to constitutional restrictions, ordinarily, the state legislature has full power to create, enlarge, diminish, consolidate, and otherwise alter the BOUNDARIES of towns without the consent of those affected.

Powers In general, towns have only the powers conferred upon them by the state legislature. However, the capacity of a town to acquire and hold REAL PROPERTY has long been recognized under English COMMON LAW. Towns are, therefore, generally given the power to construct their own public buildings and usually have the power to LEASE their property.

Towns are ordinarily granted the power to enact ORDINANCES concerning local matters, provided the ordinances are reasonable and protect the GENERAL WELFARE of the public to an appreciable degree. For example, a town might enact ZONING ordinances to restrict the use of land in certain designated areas to safeguard the public health and safety.

Ordinances enacted by a town are subject to JUDICIAL REVIEW, especially concerning their reasonableness.

Meetings Town meetings or boards are the primary vehicles by which a town governs itself since in many states a town exercises its powers by vote of a town meeting or a town council. Town meetings serve both legislative and executive functions; qualified residents meet to discuss and vote, if necessary, on matters dealing with their self-government. In most states, a person who pays town taxes is eligible

Tug boats provide towage service for vessels that are too large to negotiate certain channels safely.

SANDRA BAKER/LIAISON INTERNATIONAL

Citizens raise their hands to participate in a town meeting in Henniker, New Hampshire.

to vote at the town meeting. State statutes regulate all kinds of town meetings as well as the business to be transacted and the conduct that is acceptable.

Boards or Councils Town boards or councils are created by the legislative power of the state for the supervision of town affairs. All of their duties are either legislative or administrative in character. Their powers include selecting police officers and town attorneys, effecting public improvements, and providing for the audit and payment of claims against the town.

The selectmen of a town are officers elected by the towns to the boards to execute general business and to exercise various executive powers. Generally a board can function only when a majority of selectmen are present at a meeting. A SELECTMAN is ineligible to vote on propositions in which he or she has a financial interest in cases where his or her vote may be decisive. Town boards speak by their records, which are maintained by the town CLERK in a record book. In general, other duties of the town clerk include the issuance of calls for town meetings and the performance of the general secretarial duties.

Taxation A town is permitted to raise revenue through TAXATION only if the state legislature has granted it the power to do so. Township boards or the electors at a town meeting can decide the amount of taxes needed for township purposes, or the normal operating expenses of the town, such as for maintenance of the HIGHWAYS. A small part of the tax may be set aside for miscellaneous or emergency expenses. In addition, a town may properly impose taxes for special purposes, such as the erection of a town hall. All property not legally exempt within the limits of a town or a township is subject to ASSESSMENT and taxation by it.

Upon the LEVY of a town tax, inhabitants must pay the tax to the appropriate officer, ordinarily the town tax collector. Failure to do so, or failure to pay taxes on property correctly assessed, will entitle the town to a LIEN on the property, which means that the property cannot be sold until the taxes have been paid. After a number of years prescribed by statute, the town can have the taxpayer's property sold at a TAX SALE to pay the overdue taxes plus any accrued interests and COSTS. Any excess funds will be given to the taxpayer.

Taxpayer's Suit Since every taxpayer of a town has a vital interest in, and a right to, the preservation of an orderly and lawful government, a number of statutes give the individual taxpayer the right to bring an ACTION against officers, boards, or commissions of a town to recover money that has been wrongfully spent. This type of legal action is commonly known as a TAXPAYER'S SUIT.

Claims To protect their funds, towns or townships generally establish a regular and orderly procedure for the allowance and payment of claims against them, which must be followed before any CLAIM will be satisfied. The courts may review the decision of boards permitting or disallowing claims against towns or townships.

Claims against the town may be settled or submitted to ARBITRATION at the direction of town supervisors or following a vote at a town meeting.

TOWNSHEND ACTS The Revolutionary War in America was the result of a series of acts levied against the colonists by the English Parliament. One of these measures, the Townshend Acts, not only contributed to the American Revolution but precipitated the Boston Massacre as well.

In 1767 Parliament decided to reduce the property tax in England. To compensate for the deficit, Charles Townshend, chancellor of the exchequer, proposed legislation that would raise revenue from various taxes directed at the colonists. These laws, called the Townshend Acts, imposed duties on the importation of such articles as lead, glass, paint, tea, and paper into the colonies. The money collected from the colonists was to be applied to the payment of wages of English officials assigned to the colonies.

In addition to the taxes, the acts also provided for the maintenance of the American Board of Customs Commissioners in Boston. A third aspect of the legislation involved the disbanding of the New York legislature. This assembly had staunchly opposed and refused to accept the Quartering Act of 1765, and all its

Five colonists were killed in the "Boston Massacre" when British troops fired into a crowd protesting the taxes imposed by the Townshend Acts.

meetings were suspended until it complied with the unpopular act.

Antagonism between the colonists and English officials over the Townshend Acts increased, and English troops were sent to quell disturbances. Agitation continued, and on March 5, 1770, the Boston Massacre occurred when English soldiers fired into a crowd of hostile colonists, killing five men.

The colonists drafted nonimportation agreements and boycotted English goods. English merchants felt the loss of revenue, and in 1770 the Townshend Acts were repealed with the exception of a tax on tea. This tax, retained to reaffirm the right of Parliament to levy taxes on the colonists, led to the Boston Tea Party.

See also BOSTON MASSACRE SOLDIERS; STAMP ACT.

TOWNSHIP ▢ In a government survey, a square tract of land six miles on each side, constituting thirty-six square miles. In some states, the name given to the political subdivision of a COUNTY. ▢

See also TOWN.

TRADE DRESS ▢ A product's physical appearance, including its size, shape, color, design, and texture. ▢

In addition to a product's physical appearance, trade dress may also refer to the manner in which a product is packaged, wrapped, labeled, presented, promoted, or advertised, including the use of distinctive graphics, configurations, and marketing strategies. In INTELLECTUAL PROPERTY law, a CAUSE OF ACTION for trade dress INFRINGEMENT may arise when the trade dress of two businesses is sufficiently similar to cause confusion among consumers. In such situations the business with the more established or recognizable trade dress will ordinarily prevail. Two remedies are available for trade dress infringement: injunctive relief (a court ORDER restraining one party from infringing on another's trade dress) and money DAMAGES (compensation for any losses suffered by an injured business).

Like TRADEMARKS, trade dress is regulated by the law of UNFAIR COMPETITION. At the federal level, trade dress infringement is governed primarily by the Lanham Trademark Act (15 U.S.C.A. § 1051 et seq.); at the state level, it is governed by similar intellectual property statutes and various COMMON-LAW doctrines. Both state and federal laws prohibit businesses from duplicating, imitating, or appropriating a competitor's trade dress in order to pass off their merchandise to unwary consumers.

To establish a claim for trade dress infringement, a company must demonstrate the distinctiveness of its product's appearance. Trade dress will not receive protection from infringement unless it is unique, unusual, or widely recognized by the public. Courts have found a variety of trade dress to be distinctive, including magazine cover formats, greeting card arrangements, waitress uniform stitching, luggage designs, linen patterns, cereal configurations, and the interior and exterior features of commercial establishments. In certain contexts courts may find that distinctive color combinations are protected from infringement, as when a federal court found the silver, blue, and white foiled wrapping in which Klondike ice cream bars are packaged to be part of an identifiable trade dress (*AmBrit v. Kraft*, 812 F.2d 1531 [11th Cir. 1986]).

Goods that are packaged or promoted in an ordinary, unremarkable, or generic fashion normally receive no legal protection under the law of trade dress. For example, containers shaped like rockets and bombs are considered hackneyed devices for marketing fireworks and will not be insulated from trade dress infringement. At the same time, something as simple as a grille on the front end of an automobile may be considered sufficiently original if the manufacturer takes deliberate and tangible steps to promote that aspect of the vehicle over a long period of time.

The law of trade dress serves four purposes. First, the law seeks to protect the economic, intellectual, and creative investments made by businesses in distinguishing their products. Second, the law seeks to preserve the GOOD WILL and reputation that are often associated with the trade dress of a particular business and its merchandise. Third, the law seeks to promote clarity and stability in the marketplace by encouraging consumers to rely on a business's trade dress when evaluating the quality of a product. Fourth, the law seeks to increase competition by requiring businesses to associate their own trade dress with the value and quality of the goods they sell.

Trade dress is different from a trademark, SERVICE MARK, or TRADE NAME. Trademarks are words, symbols, phrases, mottos, logos, emblems, and other devices that are affixed to goods to demonstrate their authenticity to consumers. Levi's jeans, Nabisco cookies, Bic pens, Ford trucks, Rolex watches, and Heinz ketchup are just a few examples of well-known trademarks. Service marks identify services rather than goods. Roto-Rooter, for example, is the service mark of a familiar plumbing company. Trade names distinguish entire businesses from each other, as opposed to their individual goods and services. Coca-cola, for example, uses its trade name to distinguish itself from other soft drink manufacturers. Under state and federal law, it is advantageous for businesses to register their trademarks, service marks, and trade names with the government. Conversely, trade dress has no formal registration requirements and receives legal protection simply by being distinctive and recognizable.

TRADEMARKS Distinctive symbols of authenticity through which the products of particular manufacturers or the salable commodities of particular merchants can be distinguished from those of others.

A trademark is a device, word or combination of words, or symbol that indicates the source or ownership of a product or service. A trademark can be a name, such as Adidas, or a symbol, such as McDonald's golden arches, or it can be a combination of the two, such as when the NIKE name is written with the "swoosh" symbol beneath it. In very limited cases, a shape or even a distinctive color can become a trademark.

People rely on trademarks to make informed decisions about the products they buy. A trademark acts as a guarantee of the quality and origin of a particular good. A competing manufacturer may not use another company's trademark. The owner of a trademark may challenge any use of the mark that infringes upon the owner's rights.

The presence of trademark protection for the name or logo of a company or product is often indicated by the small symbol of an *R* in a circle placed near the trademark. The *R* means that the mark is a registered trademark and is a warning that the law prevents unauthorized use of it. A party may indicate that it is claiming rights to a particular mark by displaying a *TM*

rather than an *R* symbol. Marks bearing the *TM* symbol are not registered, but the presence of the symbol shows an intent to register.

Origins and Development of Trademark Law Trademark law in the United States is governed by the Trademark Act of 1946, also known as the LANHAM ACT (15 U.S.C.A. § 1051 et seq). The Lanham Act defines trademarks as including words, names, symbols, or combinations thereof that a person uses or intends to use in commerce to distinguish his or her goods from those made or sold by another. Potential trademarks are categorized by the functions they perform. Within trademark law are several specialized terms used to categorize marks that may be subject to protection. The categories are form, mode of use, and, most commonly, strength. The four subcategories of strength are generic, descriptive, suggestive, and arbitrary or fanciful.

A generic name is the common name for a product and will never be considered a trademark. *Shoe*, *ball*, *hat*, and *lightbulb* are all generic product names. Some marks that do not begin as generic may later become generic if the public adopts the mark as the general name for that product. Examples of marks that were not originally generic but later became so are *cellophane* and *aspirin*. Generic marks are not "strong" because they are not distinctive. To give trademark status to the generic or common name of a product would prevent all other manufacturers of the product from identifying it. To prevent that from occurring, granting trademark status to the generic name of a product is prohibited.

A descriptive term tells the consumer something about the product and may only become a trademark after it has acquired secondary meaning. This occurs after a period of time

Trademarks, such as this Nike symbol, assist consumers by identifying the producer of a particular product. Many consumers look for particular trademarks when shopping.

In the King's Name

Although Elvis Presley died in 1977, his name and likeness have been trademarked by Elvis Presley Enterprises (EPE). EPE earns millions of dollars each year through a licensing program that grants licensees the right to manufacture and sell Elvis Presley merchandise worldwide. EPE also operates two restaurants and an ice cream parlor at Graceland, the Elvis Presley home in Memphis, Tennessee, which Presley fans consider to be a shrine to the king of rock and roll.

In 1995 EPE filed suit in federal court, alleging that a Houston, Texas, nightclub operating under the name "The Velvet Elvis" infringed on EPE's trademarks (*Elvis Presley Enterprises, Inc. v. Capece*, 950 F. Supp. 783 [S.D. Texas 1996]). The name of the nightclub comes from a black velvet painting of Presley that hangs in the back lounge of the bar. Newspaper advertisements for the club depicted images and likenesses of Presley and made explicit references to the singer, including "The King Lives," "Viva la Elvis," and "Elvis has *not* left the building."

The court ruled that the name "The Velvet Elvis" did not create the likelihood of confusion as to the "Elvis" trademarks held by EPE. The court agreed with the club owner that the bar was meant to parody 1960s popular culture. Replete with lava lamps, beaded curtains, vinyl furniture, and black velvet nude paintings, the bar was a humorous jab at the culture that created the Presley myth. Even if EPE operated its own "Elvis" nightclub, the Houston bar would not create confusion as to the EPE trademarks. The court noted that the typical customers of The Velvet Elvis were young professionals ranging in age from their early twenties to their late thirties. The majority of Presley fans were middle-aged white women.

The court also ruled, however, that the use of Presley's name and likeness in advertisements infringed on the EPE trademarks. The advertisements did not indicate that the nightclub was a parody of 1960s popular culture, and therefore they created the likelihood of confusion as to the sponsorship of the nightclub.

The court ordered the owner of The Velvet Elvis not to display in his advertisements the image of Elvis or make direct references to his identity as a celebrity or to emphasize the word *Elvis* in the name The Velvet Elvis. Apart from this remedy, the court dismissed all other relief sought by EPE. The nightclub could continue, in the words found on its menu, as "The King of Dive Bars."

---

during which the term's association with that product is exclusive. This acquisition of secondary meaning is sufficient to make a mark distinct, meaning that in the eyes of consumers it has come to represent that products bearing the mark come from a particular source. The mark "Brooklyn Dodgers" is an example of a descriptive mark that is exclusively associated with a professional baseball team formerly from New York.

A suggestive term, rather than describing the product, merely makes a subtle suggestion about the type of product and its qualities. It requires consumers to use their imaginations to make the intellectual jump between the suggestion and the actual product. For those reasons, it can be a trademark immediately upon use. Examples of suggestive marks are Orange Crush (orange-flavored soft drink), Playboy (sexually oriented magazine for men), and Ivory (white soap).

When distinguishing between descriptive and generic terms, courts try to determine the viewpoint of the prospective consumer. Courts look for the meaning that the buyer of a product assigns to the contested word. Courts may also look at the term as used by dictionaries, third parties, trademark owners, texts, patents, newspapers, literature, and surveys. Use of a term as a common name indicates that the word may be the generic name of a product.

The strongest marks are arbitrary and fanciful marks, which need not acquire secondary meaning. They are strong because they bear little or no relationship to the products with which they are affiliated, and thus their use is not unfair to others trying to compete in the marketplace with similar products. Arbitrary marks are common words used in an uncommon way and are used in connection with the goods in a way that does not describe the goods or suggest anything about them. Examples include Camels in reference to cigarettes and Dial as the name of a brand of soap. Fanciful words, on the other hand, are invented and (at least at the time they are first applied to the goods) have no dictionary meaning. Examples of fanciful marks are Kodak, Exxon, and Rolex.

These considerations force a producer to select or create a symbol or name for its prod-

TRADEMARK/SERVICE MARK APPLICATION, PRINCIPAL REGISTER, WITH DECLARATION	MARK (Word(s) and/or Design)	CLASS NO. (If known)

TO THE ASSISTANT COMMISSIONER FOR TRADEMARKS:

APPLICANT'S NAME:

APPLICANT'S MAILING ADDRESS:

(Display address exactly as it should appear on registration)

_____

_____

_____

_____

APPLICANT'S ENTITY TYPE: (**Check one** and supply requested information)

[ ]	Individual - Citizen of (Country):
[ ]	Partnership - State where organized (Country, if appropriate): _____ Names and Citizenship (Country) of General Partners: _____
[ ]	Corporation - State (Country, if appropriate) of Incorporation:
[ ]	Other (Specify Nature of Entity and Domicile):

GOODS AND/OR SERVICES:

Applicant requests registration of the trademark/service mark shown in the accompanying drawing in the United States Patent and Trademark Office on the Principal Register established by the Act of July 5, 1946 (15 U.S.C. 1051 et seq., as amended) for the following goods/services (SPECIFIC GOODS AND/OR SERVICES MUST BE INSERTED HERE):

_____

_____

_____

_____

_____

BASIS FOR APPLICATION: (Check boxes which apply, **but never both the first AND second boxes,** and supply requested information related to each box checked.)

[ ]	Applicant is using the mark in commerce on or in connection with the above identified goods/services. (15 U.S.C. 1051(a), as amended.) Three specimens showing the mark as used in commerce are submitted with this application. •Date of first use of the mark in commerce which the U.S. Congress may regulate (for example, interstate or between the U.S. and a foreign country): _____ • Specify the type of commerce: _____ (for example, interstate or between the U.S. and a specified foreign country) • Date of first use anywhere (the same as or before use in commerce date): _____ • Specify intended manner or mode of use of mark on or in connection with the goods/services: _____ (for example, trademark is applied to labels, service mark is used in advertisements)
[ ]	Applicant has a bona fide intention to use the mark in commerce on or in connection with the above identified goods/services. (15 U.S.C. 1051(b), as amended.) •Specify manner or mode of use of mark on or in connection with the goods/services: _____ (for example, trademark will be applied to labels, service mark will be used in advertisements)
[ ]	Applicant has a bona fide intention to use the mark in commerce on or in connection with the above identified goods/services, and asserts a claim of priority based upon a foreign application in accordance with 15 U.S.C. 1126(d), as amended. • Country of foreign filing: _____ •Date of foreign filing: _____
[ ]	Applicant has a bona fide intention to use the mark in commerce on or in connection with the above identified goods/services and, accompanying this application, submits a certification or certified copy of a foreign registration in accordance with 15 U.S.C 1126(e), as amended. • Country of registration: _____ • Registration number: _____

NOTE: Declaration, on Reverse Side, MUST be Signed

DECLARATION

The undersigned being hereby warned that willful false statements and the like so made are punishable by fine or imprisonment, or both, under 18 U.S.C. 1001, and that such willful false statements may jeopardize the validity of the application or any resulting registration, declares that he/she is properly authorized to execute this application on behalf of the applicant; he/she believes the applicant to be the owner of the trademark/service mark sought to be registered, or if the application is being filed under 15 U.S.C. 1051(b), he/she believes the applicant to be entitled to use such mark in commerce; to the best of his/her knowledge and belief no other person, firm, corporation, or association has the right to use the above identified mark in commerce, either in the identical form thereof or in such near resemblance thereto as to be likely, when used on or in connection with the goods/services of such other person, to cause confusion, or to cause mistake, or to deceive; and that all statements made of his/her own knowledge are true and that all statements made on information and belief are believed to be true.

_____   _____
DATE   SIGNATURE

_____   _____
TELEPHONE NUMBER   PRINT OR TYPE NAME AND POSITION

INSTRUCTIONS AND INFORMATION FOR APPLICANT

TO RECEIVE A FILING DATE, THE APPLICATION <u>MUST</u> BE COMPLETED AND SIGNED BY THE APPLICANT AND SUBMITTED ALONG WITH:

1. The prescribed **FEE ($245.00)** for each class of goods/services listed in the application;
2. A **DRAWING PAGE** displaying the mark in conformance with 37 CFR 2.52;
3. If the application is based on use of the mark in commerce, **THREE (3) SPECIMENS** (evidence) of the mark as used in commerce for each class of goods/services listed in the application. All three specimens may be the same. Examples of good specimens include: (a) labels showing the mark which are placed on the goods; (b) photographs of the mark as it appears on the goods, (c) brochures or advertisements showing the mark as used in connection with the services.
4. An **APPLICATION WITH DECLARATION** (this form) - The application must be signed in order for the application to receive a filing date. Only the following persons may sign the declaration, depending on the applicant's legal entity: (a) the individual applicant; (b) an officer of the corporate applicant; (c) one general partner of a partnership applicant; (d) all joint applicants.

SEND APPLICATION FORM, DRAWING PAGE, FEE, AND SPECIMENS (IF APPROPRIATE) TO:

**Assistant Commissioner for Trademarks
Box New App/Fee
2900 Crystal Drive
Arlington, VA 22202-3513**

Additional information concerning the requirements for filing an application is available in a booklet entitled **Basic Facts About Registering a Trademark,** which may be obtained by writing to the above address or by calling: (703) 308-HELP.

This form is estimated to take an average of 1 hour to complete, including time required for reading and understanding instructions, gathering necessary information, recordkeeping, and actually providing the information. Any comments on this form, including the amount of time required to complete this form, should be sent to the Office of Management and Organization, U.S. Patent and Trademark Office, U.S. Department of Commerce, Washington, D.C. 20231. Do NOT send completed forms to this address.

The Mark

Indicate the mark (for example, "THEORYTEC" or "PINSTRIPES and DESIGN"). This should agree with the mark shown on the mark drawing page.

Classification

It is not necessary to fill in this box. The PTO will determine the proper International Classification based upon the identification of the goods and services in the application. However if the applicant knows the International Class number(s) for the goods and services, the applicant may place the number(s) in this box. The International Classes are listed inside of the back cover of this booklet. If the PTO determines that the goods and services listed are in more than one class, the PTO will notify the applicant during examination of the application, and the applicant will have the opportunity to pay the fees for any additional classes or to limit the goods and services to one or more classes.

Owner of the Mark

The name of the owner of the mark must be entered in this box. The application must be filed in the name of the owner of the mark or the application will be void, and the applicant will forfeit the filing fee. Thus it is very important to determine who owns the mark before applying. The owner of the mark is the party who controls the nature and quality of the goods sold, or services rendered, under the mark. The owner may be an individual, a partnership, a corporation, or an association or similar firm. If the applicant is a corporation, the applicant's name is the name under which it is incorporated. If the applicant is a partnership, the applicant's name is the name under which it is organized.

The Owner's Address

Enter the applicant's business address. If the applicant is an individual, enter either the applicant's business or home address.

Entity Type and Citizenship/Domicile

The applicant must check the box which indicates the type of entity that is being applied for. In addition, in the blank following the box, the applicant must specify the following information:

> Space 3(a) -- for an **individual**, the applicant's national citizenship;
> Space 3(b) -- for a **partnership**, the names and national citizenship of the general partners and the state where the
> partnership is organized (if a U.S. partnership) or country (if a foreign partnership);
> Space 3 (c) -- for a **corporation**, the state of incorporation (if a U.S. corporation) , or country (if a foreign corporation); or
> Space 3(d) -- for another type of entity, specify the nature of the entity and the state where it is organized (if in the U.S.) or
> country where it is organized (if a foreign entity).

Identification of Goods and/or Services

Applicant requests registration of the trademark/service mark shown in the accompanying drawing in the U.S. Patent and Trademark Office on the Principal Register established by the Act of July 1946 (15 U.S.C. 1051 et seq., as amended) for the goods/services in this blank.

In this blank the applicant must state the goods and services for which registration is sought and with which the applicant has actually used the mark in commerce, or in the case of an "intent to use" application, has a bona fide intention to use the mark in commerce. Use clear and concise terms specifying the actual goods and services by their common commercial names. A mark can only be registered for specific goods and services. The goods and services listed will establish the scope of the applicant's rights in the relevant mark. The goods and services listed must be the applicant's actual "goods in trade" or the actual services the applicant renders for the benefit of others. Use language readily understandable to the general public. For example, if the applicant uses or intends to use the mark to identify "candy,"" word processors," "baseballs and baseball bats," the identification should clearly and concisely list each such item. If the applicant uses indefinite terms such as "accessories," "components," "devices," "equipment," "food," "parts" or like, then those words must be followed by the word "namely" and the goods or services listed by their common name(s).

The applicant must be very careful when identifying the goods and services. Because the filing of an application establishes certain presumptions of rights as of the filing date, the application may not be amended later to add product or services not within scope of the identification. For example, the identification of "clothing" could be amended to "shirts and jackets," which narrows the scope, but could not be amended to "retail clothing store services," which would change the scope. Similarly, "physical therapy services" could not be changed to "medical services" because this would broaden the scope of the identification.

The **identification of goods and services** must not describe **the mode** of use of the mark, such as on labels, sign, menus, stationary, containers or in advertising.

If nothing appears in this blank, or if the identification does not identify any recognizable goods or services, the applicant will be denied a filing date and the application will be returned to applicant.

Basis for Filing

The applicant must check at least one of the four boxes to specify a basis for filing the application. The applicant should also fill in blanks which follow the checked box(es). Usually an application is based upon either (1) prior use of the mark in commerce (the first box), or (2) a bona fide intention to use the mark in commerce (the second box). **You may *not* check the first and second box. If both the first and second boxes are checked, the PTO will *not* accept the application and will return it to the applicant without processing.** If an applicant wishes to apply to register a mark for certain goods and services for which use in commerce has begun and other goods and services based on future use, separate applications must be filed to separate the relevant goods and services from each other.

uct that is suitable for trademark protection. A producer labors to create a good name for a product, and a protected trademark prevents competitors from unfairly capitalizing on the reputation of that name. When trying to decide what mark is appropriate, the potential trademark owner should keep in mind a fundamental rule of trademark selection: in most situations, one will not be allowed to use a trademark that another entity already uses. Before an entity incorporates under a certain name, or attempts to sell a service or product bearing a particular name, it should conduct a search or hire an attorney to investigate prior or existing use of the name. Those companies that fail to conduct this kind of a search or blatantly ignore existing use of a trademark are likely to face a lawsuit by any existing owner of the mark. Such a lawsuit may lead to a court order to stop any infringing use and an award of damages to the holder of the mark.

Uniqueness is a major consideration to the potential trademark owner, regardless of whether the mark is descriptive, suggestive, and arbitrary or fanciful. The fewer unique characteristics a mark possesses, the less legal protection it receives. The potential trademark owner must consider whether others need to use a particular mark in conjunction with a product in order to compete. A unique mark that bears little relationship to the product is preferred over a mark that is more generic.

A company has a better chance of procuring protection for a mark when, by using the mark, it is the first to cause consumers to see an association between the mark and the product.

The Lanham Act distinguishes trademarks from trade names and service marks and also addresses certification marks and collective marks. A service mark is used to identify and distinguish the services of one company from another, such as Sears for retail stores, and American Express for credit cards. A trade name or commercial name distinguishes and identifies a business. The same name or portion of a name may also serve as a trademark, trade name, or service mark. An example is the name Ford Motor Company, which is the trade name of a company that builds and sells cars and trucks that bear the trademark "Ford." In short, trademarks apply to products, service marks to services, and trade names to businesses. Certification marks endorse products and certify approval of their origin, quality, or authenticity. A certification mark is not the property of the maker of the products upon which the mark will be affixed. Examples are the Union Label in garments and various seals of approval.

When the provider of goods or services belongs to an association, it often advertises or attaches a collective mark to announce that relationship. The mark is used on products or services not provided by the owner of the mark, typically as a symbol guaranteeing quality and taking advantage of the supposed benefits to the consumer that stem from the product's association with the owner of the mark.

Trademark Registration Traditionally, trademark rights had depended on prior use, but since 1988 a party with a genuine intent to use a mark may apply for trademark registration. The applicant must intend to use the mark in commerce and must intend to do so in order to sell a product, not merely to reserve rights for future use.

Registration begins with application to the commissioner of patents and trademarks in the PATENT AND TRADEMARK OFFICE. Registration of a mark means that others will be presumed to know that the mark is owned and protected. By itself, registration is considered evidence that the registrant has ownership and that the registration is valid.

Registration benefits the trademark owner because it suggests that the registrant did everything necessary to protect its mark. While trademark rights actually stem from use, a party may have difficulty convincing a court that it had good reasons to not register a mark for which it now claims a protected right. This is particularly so when a claimed symbol's status as a trademark is uncertain, such as in a dispute over the design of a product as a trademark.

One may apply with either the principal register or supplemental register of the Patent and Trademark Office. The principal register is for arbitrary, fanciful, suggestive, or descriptive marks that have acquired secondary meaning or distinctiveness. The supplemental register is for descriptive terms capable of acquiring secondary meaning. Once a mark establishes secondary meaning, it can be transferred to the principal register.

Registration with the principal register is preferable to supplemental registration for many reasons. Principal registration is proof that the mark is valid, registered, and the INTELLECTUAL PROPERTY of the registrant, which has exclusive rights to use the mark in commerce. Further, a registered mark is presumed to have been in continuous use since the application filing date. After five years of continuous use, a registered mark may not be contested. Registration with the principal register means that a potential infringer will be considered to know about the registrant's claim of trademark ownership. The owner of a mark registered with the principal register has the right to bring suit in federal court. Those who counterfeit registered marks face criminal and civil penalties. The owner of a trademark that registers with the principal register and deposits the registration with the U.S. Customs Service can prevent goods bearing infringing marks from being imported.

A mark on the supplemental register may become a trademark, but its status as such has not yet been determined. For this reason, the presumption created by registration with the principal register, that the registrant can be the only valid owner, does not apply to supplemental registration.

The owners of registered trademarks can lose their rights in a number of ways. When a trade or the general public adopts a trademark as the name for a type of goods, the mark is no longer distinctive and the rights to it are lost. The owner of trademark rights must be vigilant to ensure that this does not occur. For instance, the Rollerblade company introduced a new product of roller skates where the wheels are arranged in a single line (offering performance similar to the blade on an ice skate) rather than side by side. Initially Rollerblade was the only company selling this type of skates, and the name Rollerblade became widely known. When competing producers of this new skate emerged on the marketplace, the consuming public often used the word *rollerblade* to describe the type of skates, no matter what company was making and selling them. Further, the public often called the activity of using such skates, no matter the manufacturer, rollerblading. The Rollerblade company spent millions of dollars in advertising and lawsuits to ensure that the trademark Rollerblade was not used to describe a product whose proper generic name is in-line skates. To protect its rights to the trademark, the Rollerblade company must actively oppose any use by competitors or consumers of the words *rollerblade* or *rollerblading* to describe generic in-line skates and the activity of in-line skating.

Registrants forfeit rights to their marks if they use them deceptively, use them in FRAUDULENT trades, or abandon them. Registrants abandon their marks by failing to renew within ten years or by deliberately transferring rights with consent.

Trademark Infringement Once they have established their trademarks, owners have the duty to guard against INFRINGEMENT and to be vigilant to preserve and protect their rights. The Lanham Act aids owners in protecting their rights and protects consumers from being tricked or confused by misleading marks.

The six most common CAUSES OF ACTION in infringement lawsuits charge that a defendant has infringed on a plaintiff's registered trademark; undermined a plaintiff's unregistered mark in a manner that affects commerce; violated COMMON-LAW trademark infringement standards and unfair competition principles; violated state deceptive trade practice laws; diluted a plaintiff's trademark; and misappropriated a plaintiff's mark.

Trademark infringement claims generally involve the issues of likelihood of confusion, COUNTERFEIT marks, and dilution of marks. Likelihood of confusion occurs in situations where consumers are likely to be confused or misled about marks being used by two parties. To constitute infringement, this confusion must be probable, not merely possible. The complaining party must show that because of the similar marks, many consumers are likely to be confused or misled about the source of the products that bear these marks.

In a likelihood of confusion cause of action, the defendant can defend on the basis that confusion is not likely or that although confusion may be likely, the plaintiff has behaved improperly regarding the mark or the mark is somehow defective.

The Lanham Act defines a counterfeit mark as being "identical with, or substantially indistinguishable from, a registered mark." All counterfeits are infringements. The product or service bearing the counterfeit mark must be of the same type of product or service bearing the protected mark. The defendant must have knowingly produced or trafficked a counterfeit mark.

Dilution is lessening the individuality or impact of a mark. The usefulness of a trademark depends on its recognizability and individuality. In cases of dilution, the challenged mark does not necessarily have to be used on products in direct competition with the products of the complaining party, nor is it necessary that the mark is causing confusion. The complaining party only needs to show that the strength and impact of the registered mark is somehow lessened by the presence of similar marks. A trademark owner uses its mark as a means of recognition and as a symbol representing its GOODWILL, and when similar marks flood the marketplace, this message is considered to be diluted. The product or service thus becomes psychologically less identifiable and less distinguishable. Trademark law prohibits this dilution and prevents the infringing party from unfairly profiting from an association with an established name.

To establish an infringement cause of action based on dilution, the plaintiff must initially show that its trademark is genuinely unique. Similar to the standard for confusion, dilution because of defendant's conduct must be likely or probable, rather than merely possible.

The defendant in an infringement case can invoke any of several affirmative defenses. An affirmative defense is a response that attacks the plaintiff's legal right to bring an action, as opposed to attacking the truth of the claim. The defendant can argue that the plaintiff abandoned the trademark or that the mark is generic. Defendants may claim that they made "fair use" of the mark, in that their purpose for using the mark did not unfairly compete with the plaintiff. Another affirmative defense is that the plaintiff has "unclean hands" from acting in an unfair or deceptive manner. The defendant can charge that the plaintiff engaged in trademark misuse and used the mark in a manner that went against the PUBLIC POLICY that allowed the trademark to be granted in the first place. The defendant may charge the plaintiff with fraudulent use of a trademark. The defendant can argue that the plaintiff violated ANTITRUST LAWS, which are designed to protect commerce and trade against unlawful restraints, PRICE FIXING, and MONOPOLIES. Finally, the defendant can offer the affirmative defense of LACHES, which provides that the party that unreasonably delays in asserting legal rights forfeits them.

See also COPYRIGHT; PATENTS.

TRADE NAME ▨ Names or designations used by companies to identify themselves and distinguish their businesses from others in the same field. ▨

Trade names are used by profit and nonprofit entities, political and religious organizations, industry and agriculture, manufacturers and producers, wholesalers and retailers, SOLE PROPRIETORSHIPS and JOINT VENTURES, PARTNERSHIPS and CORPORATIONS, and a host of other business associations. A trade name may be the actual name of a given business or an assumed name under which a business operates and holds itself out to the public.

Trade name regulation derives from the COMMON LAW of UNFAIR COMPETITION. The common law distinguishes between TRADEMARKS and trade names. Trademarks consist of symbols, logos, and other devices that are affixed to goods to signify their authenticity to the public. The common law of trade names encompasses a broader class of INTELLECTUAL PROPERTY interests, including TRADE DRESS and SERVICE MARKS.

Trade dress is used by competitors to distinguish their products by visual appearance, including size, shape, and color, while service marks are used by competitors to distinguish their services from each other. Gradually, the law of trade dress and service marks has evolved into separate causes of action, independent from the law of trade name INFRINGEMENT.

To maintain a CAUSE OF ACTION for trade name infringement, a plaintiff must establish that it owned the right to operate its business under a certain name and that the defendant violated this right by use of a deceptively similar name. The right to use a particular trade name ordinarily is established by priority of adoption. In states that require registration of trade names, a business may acquire the rights to a trade name by being the first to file for protection with the appropriate governmental office, usually the secretary of state. In states that do not require registration, a business may acquire the rights to a trade name through public use, which means that the law will afford protection only if it can be demonstrated that a business and its trade name have become inseparable in the public's mind. Under federal law businesses may acquire the rights to a trade name only through regular and continued public use of an individual name. Federal law will not protect trade names that are used sporadically or irregularly.

Once a business has established the right to use a particular trade name, it must then prove that the defendant fraudulently attempted to pass itself off as the plaintiff through use of a deceptively similar name. Not every trade name that resembles an existing one will give rise to LIABILITY for infringement. The law will not forbid two unrelated businesses from using the same trade name so long as their coexistence creates no substantial risk of confusion among the public. For instance, two businesses may call themselves "Triple Play" if one business is a video store and the other is a sports bar and grill. By the same token, the law permits businesses in different geographic markets to use identical trade names, unless the GOOD WILL and reputation of an existing business extend into the market where a new business has opened.

A greater degree of protection is afforded to fanciful trade names than to names in common use. Generic words that are widely used to describe any number of businesses in the same field may not be appropriated by a single competitor. For example, a professional partnership of attorneys would receive no trade name protection for emblazoning the name "law office" across its front doors. Such a name would be considered generic in nature, telling consumers nothing unique or unusual about that particular business. The same partnership would receive full protection for a name that identifies the firm by the individual names of each partner in the office.

Trade name regulation serves four purposes. First, the law seeks to protect the economic, intellectual, and creative investments made by businesses in distinguishing their trades. Second, the law seeks to preserve the good will and reputation that are often associated with a particular trade name. Third, the law seeks to promote clarity and stability in the marketplace by encouraging consumers to rely on a merchant's trade name when evaluating the quality of its merchandise. Fourth, the law seeks to increase competition by requiring businesses to associate their own trade names with the value and quality of their goods and services.

Both state and federal laws provide protection against trade name infringement. At the federal level, trade names are regulated by the Lanham Trademark Act (15 U.S.C. § 1051 et seq.). At the state level, trade names are regulated by analogous intellectual property statutes and various common-law doctrines. In general, the law of trade name infringement attempts to protect consumers from deceptive trade practices. The law does not treat consumers as unwitting dupes and may require them to make reasonable distinctions between competitors under appropriate circumstances. When consumers have been deceived by use of a deceptively similar trade name, an injured business may avail itself of two remedies for infringement: injunctive relief (a court order restraining one party from infringing on another's trade name) and money DAMAGES (compensation for any losses suffered by the injured business).

See also LANHAM ACT.

TRADE SECRET 📖 Any valuable commercial information that provides a business with an advantage over competitors who do not have that information. 📖

In general terms trade secrets include inventions, ideas, or compilations of data that are used by a business to make itself more successful. Specifically, trade secrets include any useful formula, plan, pattern, process, program, tool, technique, mechanism, compound, or device that is not generally known or readily ascertainable by the public. Whatever type of information is represented by a trade secret, a business must take reasonable steps to safeguard it from disclosure.

Absolute secrecy is not required, however. Commercial PRIVACY need only be protected from ESPIONAGE that can be reasonably anticipated and prevented. Trade secrets may be revealed to AGENTS, employees, and others ordinarily entrusted with such information, so long as it is understood that the information is confidential and disclosure is forbidden. At the same time, keeping information strictly confidential does not make it a trade secret unless the information is useful or valuable. Information that is common knowledge will never receive protection as a trade secret. Information must rise to a sufficient level of originality, novelty, or utility before a court will recognize it as a COMMODITY.

Similarly, merely because something has been classified as a trade secret does not make every public disclosure of it the THEFT of a trade secret. For LIABILITY to attach for trade secret theft, the owner of valuable commercial information must demonstrate that it was appropriated through a breach of CONTRACT, a violation of a confidence, the use of surreptitious surveillance, or other improper means. For example, most employees who work in a commercially sensitive field are required to sign a contract prohibiting them from disclosing their employer's trade secrets to a competitor or the general public. These contracts normally bind employees even after their employment relationship has ended.

In the absence of a contractual obligation, employees and others may still be held liable for disclosing a trade secret if a court finds they had reason to know that the information was valuable and were expected to keep it confidential. For example, engineers and scientists who consult on a commercial project are ordinarily bound by a duty of strict confidentiality that precludes them from later sharing any information they acquire or using it to facilitate their own research. Although many businesses require consultants to sign a nondisclosure agreement before beginning work on a sensitive project, this duty of confidentiality arises from the circumstances surrounding a particular venture, independent of any formal agreement reached between the parties.

Imposition of liability for theft of a trade secret is not contingent upon a relationship between the owner of commercial information and the individual or entity that appropriated it. Liability may be premised solely on the means used to acquire confidential commercial information. Industrial espionage, which includes both aerial and ELECTRONIC SURVEILLANCE, is an indefensible means of acquiring a trade secret. TRESPASS, BRIBERY, FRAUD, and MISREPRESENTATION are similarly illegal. However, the law permits businesses to purchase a competitor's products and subject them to laboratory analysis for the purpose of unlocking hidden secrets of the trade. Called "reverse engineering," this process is considered by some courts to be the only proper means of obtaining valuable commercial information without the owner's consent.

The owner of a trade secret has the exclusive right to its use and enjoyment. Like any other property right, a trade secret may be sold, assigned, licensed, or otherwise used for pecuniary gain. If the owner of a trade secret knowingly permits it to enter the PUBLIC DOMAIN, however, he has waived the right to its exclusive use and enjoyment. An owner who has been injured by the wrongful disclosure or appropriation of a trade secret may pursue two remedies: injunctive relief and damages. An INJUNCTION (a court order restraining or compelling certain action) is the proper remedy when the owner of a trade secret desires to prevent its ongoing use by the individual or entity who wrongfully appropriated it. Money DAMAGES are the appropriate remedy when theft of a trade secret has resulted in a measurable pecuniary loss to its owner.

TRADE UNION 📖 An organization of workers in the same skilled occupation or related skilled occupations who act together to secure for all members favorable wages, hours, and other working conditions. 📖

Trade unions in the United States were first organized in the early nineteenth century. The main purpose of a trade union is to collectively bargain with employers for wages, hours, and working conditions. Until the 1930s trade unions were at a severe disadvantage with management, mainly because few laws recognized the right of workers to organize. With the passage of the NATIONAL LABOR RELATIONS ACT (WAGNER ACT) of 1935 (29 U.S.C.A. § 151 et seq.), the right of employees to form, join, or aid LABOR UNIONS was recognized by the federal government.

Trade unions are entitled to conduct a STRIKE against employers. A strike is usually the last resort of a trade union, but when negotiations have reached an impasse, a strike may be the only bargaining tool left for employees.

There are two principal types of trade unions: CRAFT UNIONS and INDUSTRIAL UNIONS. Craft unions are composed of workers performing a specific trade, such as electricians, carpenters, plumbers, or printers. Industrial union workers include all workers in a specific industry, no matter what their trade, such as automobile or steel workers. In the United States, craft and industrial unions were represented by different national labor organizations until 1955. The craft unions that dominated the American Federation of Labor (AFL) opposed organizing industrial workers.

During the 1930s several AFL unions seeking a national organization of industrial workers formed the Committee for Industrial Organization (CIO). The CIO aggressively organized millions of industrial workers who labored in automobile, steel, and rubber plants. In 1938 the AFL expelled the unions that had formed the CIO. The CIO then formed its own organization and changed its name to Congress of Industrial Organizations. In 1955 the AFL and CIO merged into a single organization, the AFL-CIO.

Membership in U.S. trade unions has fallen since the 1950s, as the number of workers in the manufacturing sector of the U.S. economy has steadily declined. Union membership in 1995 comprised just 14.9 percent of the workforce, compared with a high of 34.7 percent in 1954.

See also COLLECTIVE BARGAINING; LABOR LAW.

TRADE USAGE 📖 Any system, custom, or practice of doing business used so commonly in a vocation, field, or place that an expectation

Major Collective Bargaining Agreements—Average Percent Wage Rate Changes Under All Agreements, 1970 to 1994

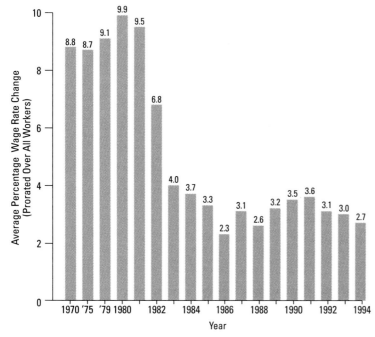

Data represent all wage rate changes implemented under the terms of private nonfarm industry agreements affecting 1,000 workers of more. Series covers production and related workers in manufacturing and nonsupervisory workers in nonmanufacturing industries.

Source: U.S. Bureau of Labor Statistics.

arises that it will be observed in a particular transaction. 📖

The concept of trade usage recognizes that words and practices take on specialized meanings in different areas of business. Though these common understandings may not be set out explicitly in a written sales or service AGREEMENT, the courts will generally employ them when construing a commercial CONTRACT. In the United States, the UNIFORM COMMERCIAL CODE (UCC), which has been adopted in some form in all fifty states, permits trade usage to be used in the interpretation of sales agreements.

Trade usage supplements, qualifies, and imparts particular meanings to the terms of an agreement for the purpose of the agreement's interpretation. Contractual language cannot be interpreted out of the context of the agreement of the parties.

The enforcement of contractual promises protects the justified expectations of the promisee, the person to whom the promises were made. Trade usage emphasizes such expectations. If a particular trade follows a practice so regularly that the promisee is justified in expecting that the promisor considered that practice when making the PROMISE, the practice becomes a part of the agreement between the parties. Sometimes usage becomes so common in an industry that written trade codes are compiled to provide specific language on contract interpretation.

Section 1-2.05 of the UCC adopts the principle of trade usage. In a contractual dispute, the party who asserts a trade usage must prove the "existence and scope of such usage." If the trade usage is proved, a court may use it to "supplement or qualify terms of an agreement." The express terms of an agreement and trade usage must be construed "wherever reasonable as consistent with each other." If the construction is unreasonable, however, the court will ignore trade usage and apply the EXPRESS terms of the agreement.

In the absence of EVIDENCE to the contrary, courts assume that when persons in business employ trade terms, they intend the terms to have their commercial significance. To counter this assumption, the parties must expressly state within the contract their intention to render the terms devoid of their trade significance and reduce them to their ordinary meaning. The failure to do so indicates the parties' intention to use the trade terms according to their commercial meaning.

The contract language does not have to be ambiguous before a court may consider trade usage. To protect against unfair surprise, however, evidence of trade usage is inadmissible unless sufficient NOTICE has been provided to the other party.

See also SALES LAW.

TRADING STAMPS AND COUPONS

📖 A comprehensive term for any type of tickets, CERTIFICATES, or order blanks that can be offered in exchange for money or something of value, or for a reduction in price when a particular item is purchased. 📖

U.S. businesses attempt to attract customers by using advertising, promising low prices, and claiming to offer high-quality goods and services. Another way of attracting business is by offering potential customers incentives, such as trading stamps, COUPONS, and price REBATES. Though trading stamps have declined in popularity since the 1960s, the idea of awarding some type of credit for purchasing goods and services has survived. When commercial AIRLINES award "frequent-flier miles" to their passengers, they are offering a variation on the trading stamp concept.

Trading stamps became popular during the Great Depression of the 1930s. They are printed stamps that can be saved and pasted into booklets until the individual collecting them has a sufficient number to exchange them for a particular item of merchandise. A trading stamp company negotiates agreements that allow retail merchants to give stamps to customers in proportion to how much they spend at the merchant's store. When the books are filled, they can be offered in exchange for merchandise provided by the trading stamp company through a catalog or at a redemption center. In effect, the customer receives an additional benefit for the price she pays for merchandise.

The merchant receives the benefit of the advertising done by the trading stamp company. The merchant also expects to attract more customers than a merchant who charges the same price for goods but does not offer stamps. The trading stamp company earns money by selling the stamps to the retailer.

In the heyday of trading stamp collection, various trading stamp companies competed for this lucrative market, which drew much of its business from grocery stores. The largest and most famous was the Sperry and Hutchinson (S&H) Company, which offered S&H Green Stamps. S&H filed lawsuits in the 1960s to prevent its stamps from being brokered by persons and companies other than licensed retailers. Though the lawsuits were unsuccessful, the downfall of trading stamps came from retail merchandisers who offered consumers price discounts large enough to lure them from merchants who offered stamps. In addition, in the burgeoning consumer economy of the 1960s and 1970s, merchandise was easily affordable, and consumers were no longer willing to defer their purchases while they patiently collected stamps.

Though trading stamps have virtually disappeared, the concept is still used. For example, airline frequent-flier miles allow the customer who flies commercial airlines to accumulate miles toward free tickets. The airlines believe that a person will prefer to "earn" miles by flying with one company. Computer technology has also spurred experiments with recording points electronically when a person makes a retail purchase.

Whether the points are measured in stamps or miles, the law recognizes them as tokens of legal obligations. The points are not merchandise in and of themselves, but they do represent a promise by the company offering the incentive to redeem them for something of value. Ownership of the stamps, miles, or points remains with the offering company. This gives the company the ability to control the manner in which the rights represented by the incentives can be transferred.

Merchandise coupons are a popular way to attract business to a particular store or to a particular product. Coupons can be printed and distributed in advertising circulars, newspapers, and magazines or be enclosed with packaging for a product. A coupon gives rise to legal OBLIGATIONS based upon its terms. In general, the coupon constitutes proof of a PROMISE by a manufacturer to give something of value to an individual who purchases the product of the manufacturer and presents the coupon for redemption. The coupon may be in the form of a rebate to be mailed to the purchaser from the manufacturer. To obtain a cash rebate, the purchaser must usually send in the rebate coupon and a sales slip as proof of purchase of the product, but individual companies may impose different requirements.

A number of coupons offer a discount that is granted at the time of purchase. The coupon informs the merchant that it may be returned to the manufacturer for the FACE VALUE of the coupon plus a small service charge for each coupon returned. The merchant is required to submit proof that a sufficient amount of stock was purchased to have made the sales claimed.

The promise of the manufacturer on the coupon constitutes a UNILATERAL CONTRACT that is enforceable as soon as a retail merchant accepts the offer of the manufacturer. The manufacturer has the right to require proof of purchase as a condition to performing the contract.

The obligations that are created by advertising coupons may be enforceable by criminal penalties as well as by contract law. In many JURISDICTIONS misuse of coupons is a form of business FRAUD. For example, a merchant who returns thousands of coupons to a manufacturer and claims a refund without ever having sold the product may be guilty of a criminal offense in some jurisdictions.

TRANSCRIPT 📖 A generic term for any kind of copy, particularly an official or certified representation of the record of what took place in a court during a trial or other legal proceeding. 📖

A *transcript of record* is the printed record of the proceedings and PLEADINGS of a case, required by the APPELLATE COURT for a review of the history of the case.

TRANSFER 📖 To remove or convey from one place or person to another. The removal of a case from one court to another court within the same system where it might have been instituted. An act of the parties, or of the law, by which the TITLE to PROPERTY is conveyed from one person to another. 📖

Transfer encompasses the SALE and every other method, direct or indirect, of (1) disposing of property or an interest therein or possession thereof; or (2) fixing a LIEN (a charge against property to secure a DEBT) absolutely or conditionally, voluntarily or involuntarily, with or without judicial proceedings, in the form of a CONVEYANCE, sale, payment, PLEDGE, lien, MORTGAGE, GIFT, or otherwise. The term *transfer* has a general meaning and can include the act of giving property by WILL.

Transfer is the comprehensive term used by the UNIFORM COMMERCIAL CODE (UCC)—a body of law adopted by the states that governs MERCANTILE transactions—to describe the act that passes an interest in an INSTRUMENT (a written legal document) from one person to another.

TRANSFER OF ASSETS 📖 The CONVEYANCE of something of value from one person, place, or situation to another. 📖

The law recognizes that persons are generally entitled to TRANSFER their ASSETS to whomever they wish and for whatever reason. The most common means of transfer are wills, trusts, and GIFTS. Increasingly, however, persons are transferring property and money in order to qualify for government-funded nursing care or to avoid paying CREDITORS or the INTERNAL REVENUE SERVICE. State and federal laws prohibit transfers that defraud creditors, however. If a creditor can show that a transfer was made in BAD FAITH and for the purpose of avoiding a lawful DEBT, the transfer will be voided.

A WILL is a common way of transferring assets. The TESTATOR, the person writing and signing the will, states in writing how the assets of his ESTATE shall be divided and transferred upon his death. The estate of the testator is subject to inheritance taxes, but the remainder is transferred to the HEIRS and BENEFICIARIES in the will. If a person dies INTESTATE, without writing a will, state statutes direct how the assets shall be divided and transferred among family members.

For persons who have substantial assets, the transfer may be accomplished by using a TRUST. There are many types of trusts, some of which are part of a will and go into effect upon the death of the testator. Instead of being transferred directly to persons, the assets are transferred to a TRUSTEE, who distributes funds based on the terms in the trust documents. The use of a trust generally reduces inheritance taxes. A person may also transfer assets to a trust while living to reduce her INCOME TAX burden. Income earned by the trust will be taxed to the trust, which usually is in a lower tax bracket than the person transferring the assets. The trust must benefit others, however, not just the person transferring the assets.

Living persons may also make gifts to others. An INTER VIVOS gift, which takes effect during the lifetime of the donor and the donee, is irrevocable when made. Federal tax law permits a person to give up to $10,000 yearly to each recipient without having to pay any gift tax or file a gift tax return. All gifts in excess of the annual exclusions are taxable.

Other types of transfers of assets have also become popular in the United States. Some middle-class older persons, faced with the high cost of nursing home care and wanting to leave their property to their children, transfer all their assets to their children. By doing so, the older person can meet income and net asset guidelines to qualify for government-subsidized nursing home care. State and federal governments have sought to prevent this practice because it takes funds away from those who are truly indigent.

A growing trend is transferring assets to avoid paying court judgments. Companies offer "asset-protection plans" that seek to insulate, for example, a doctor from the possibility of paying a large MALPRACTICE damages award. By transferring assets to a foreign country, the plan makes it difficult to ascertain the amount of the doctor's assets. Also, collecting on a JUDGMENT in a foreign court is often impossible.

A more radical device is transferring assets outside the United States to a foreign trust, which manages the assets and distributes funds to the beneficiaries. The foreign trustee controls the assets and is not subject to a lawsuit seeking collection of a judgment against the transferee. Critics charge that besides allowing a person to avoid paying a debt, foreign trusts encourage income TAX EVASION. Defenders of asset protection contend that the purpose of foreign trusts is to avoid lawsuits, not taxes.

TRANSFER TAX The charge levied by the government on the sale of shares of STOCK. A charge imposed by the federal and state governments upon the passing of TITLE to REAL PROPERTY or a valuable interest in such property, or on the transfer of a decedent's ESTATE by INHERITANCE, DEVISE, or BEQUEST.

The states also impose transfer tax on DEEDS used to convey real property.

TRANSITORY ACTION A lawsuit that can be commenced in any place where personal SERVICE OF PROCESS can be made on the defendant.

Common examples of transitory actions are lawsuits brought to recover DAMAGES in breach of CONTRACT or TORT actions. Transitory actions are distinguishable from local actions, which can be brought only where the subject matter of the controversy exists. For example, the classic type of LOCAL ACTION is one in which TITLE to REAL PROPERTY will be directly affected by the judgment of the court. Such actions generally must be tried in the COUNTY where the particular property is located.

TRANSNATIONAL CORPORATION Any corporation that is registered and operates in more than one country at a time; also called a multinational corporation.

A transnational, or multinational, corporation has its headquarters in one country and operates wholly or partially owned SUBSIDIARIES in one or more other countries. The subsidiaries report to the central headquarters. The growth in the number and size of transnational CORPORATIONS since the 1950s has generated controversy because of their economic and political power and the mobility and complexity of their operations. Some critics argue that transnational corporations exhibit no loyalty to the countries in which they are incorporated but act solely in their own best interests.

U.S. corporations have various motives for establishing a corporate presence in other countries. One possible motive is a desire for growth. A corporation may have reached a plateau meeting domestic demands and anticipate little additional growth. A new foreign market might provide opportunities for new growth.

Other corporations desire to escape the protectionist policies of an importing country. Through direct foreign investment, a corporation can bypass high TARIFFS that prevent its goods from being competitively priced. For example, when the European Common Market (the predecessor of the European Union) placed tariffs on goods produced by outsiders, U.S. corporations responded by setting up European subsidiaries.

Two other motives are more controversial. One is preventing competition. The most certain method of preventing actual or potential competition from foreign businesses is to acquire those businesses. Another motive for establishing subsidiaries in other nations is to reduce costs, mainly through the use of cheap foreign labor in developing countries. A transnational corporation can hold down costs by shifting some or all of its production facilities abroad.

Transnational corporations with headquarters in the United States have played an increasingly dominant role in the world economy. This dominance is most pronounced in the developing countries that rely primarily on a narrow range of exports, usually primary goods. A transnational corporation has the ability to disrupt traditional economies, impose monopolistic practices, and assert a political and economic agenda on a country.

Another concern with transnational corporations is their ability to use foreign subsidiaries to minimize their tax liability. The INTERNAL REVENUE SERVICE (IRS) must analyze the movement of goods and services between a transnational company's domestic and foreign operations and then assess whether the transfer price that was assigned on paper to each transaction was fair. IRS studies indicate that U.S. transnational corporations have an incentive to set their transfer prices so as to shift income away from the United States and its higher corporate tax rates and to shift deductible expenses into the United States. Foreign-owned corporations doing business in the United States have a similar incentive. Critics argue that these tax incentives also motivate U.S. transnational corporations to move plants and jobs overseas.

TRANSNATIONAL LAW 📖 All the law—national, international, or mixed—that applies to all persons, businesses, and governments that perform or have influence across state lines. 📖

Transnational law applies to transactions that cross national boundaries, such as the shipment of these automobiles overseas.

Transnational law regulates actions or events that transcend national frontiers. It involves individuals, CORPORATIONS, states, or other groups—not just the official relations between governments of states.

An almost infinite variety of transnational situations might arise, but there are rules or law bearing upon each. Since applicable legal rules might conflict with each other, "choice of law" is determined by rules of conflict of laws or PRIVATE INTERNATIONAL LAW. The choice, usually between rules of different national laws, is made by a national court.

In other types of situations, the choice might be between a rule of national law and a rule of "public international law," in which case the choice is made by an international tribunal or some nonjudicial decision-maker, such as an appointed body.

See also INTERNATIONAL LAW.

TRANSPORTATION DEPARTMENT The U.S. Department of Transportation (DOT) establishes overall transportation policy for the United States. Under the DOT's umbrella are ten administrations whose jurisdictions include HIGHWAY planning, development, and construction; urban mass transit; RAILROADS; aviation; and the safety of waterways, ports, highways, and oil and GAS pipelines. Decisions made by the department in conjunction with appropriate state and local officials can significantly affect other programs such as land planning, energy conservation, scarce resource utilization, and technological change.

The DOT was established by Congress in 1966 (49 U.S.C.A. § 102) "to assure the coordinated, effective administration of the transportation programs of the Federal Government" and to develop "national transportation policies and programs conducive to the provision of

Transportation Department

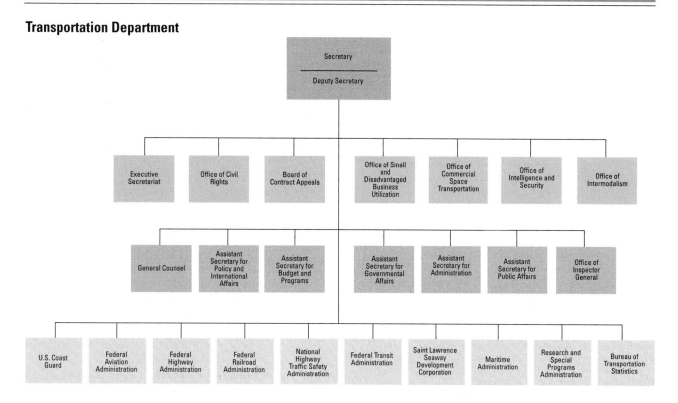

fast, safe, efficient, and convenient transportation at the lowest cost consistent therewith." The department became operational in April 1967 with elements transferred from eight other major departments and agencies. It currently consists of the office of the secretary and ten operating administrations whose heads report directly to the secretary and have highly decentralized authority.

Office of the Secretary of Transportation The DOT is administered by the secretary of transportation, who is the principal adviser to the president in all matters relating to federal transportation programs. The secretary administers the department with the assistance of a deputy secretary of transportation, an associate deputy secretary, the assistant secretaries, a general counsel, the inspector general, and several directors and chairpersons.

U.S. Coast Guard The Coast Guard, which was established by Congress in 1915 (14 U.S.C.A. § 1), became a component of the DOT on April 1, 1967. The Coast Guard is a branch of the armed forces of the United States at all times and is a service within the DOT except when operating as part of the Navy in time of war or when the president directs.

The predecessor of the Coast Guard, the Revenue Marine, was established in 1790 as a federal maritime law enforcement agency. Many other major responsibilities have since been added.

The Coast Guard maintains a system of rescue vessels, aircraft, and communications facilities to carry out its function of saving life and property in and over the high seas and the NAVIGABLE WATERS of the United States. Its duties include providing flood relief and removing hazards to navigation.

The Coast Guard is the primary maritime law enforcement agency for the United States. It enforces or assists in the enforcement of applicable federal laws and treaties and other international agreements to which the United States is a party, regarding the high seas and waters subject to the JURISDICTION of the United States. The Coast Guard may conduct investigations into suspected violations of such laws and international agreements. It works with other federal agencies to enforce the laws pertaining to the protection of living and nonliving resources and the suppression of SMUGGLING and illicit drug trafficking.

In addition, the Coast Guard is charged with formulating, administering, and enforcing various safety standards for the design, construction, equipment, and maintenance of commercial vessels of the United States and offshore structures on the outer continental shelf. The program includes enforcement of safety standards on foreign vessels subject to U.S. jurisdiction. The Coast Guard administers a system for evaluating and licensing U.S. merchant marine personnel. This program develops safety standards for personnel aboard commercial vessels. The Coast Guard also maintains oversight and approval authority for the numerous mariner training programs.

The Coast Guard is also responsible for enforcing the Federal Water Pollution Control Act (33 U.S.C.A. § 1251) and various other laws aimed at protecting the marine environment. Program objectives include ensuring that public health and welfare and the environment are protected when spills occur. Under these laws, U.S. and foreign vessels are prohibited from using U.S. waters unless they have INSURANCE or other guarantees that potential liability for cleanup of POLLUTION and damages will be met. The Coast Guard is authorized to enforce rules and regulations governing the safety and security of ports and anchorages and the movement of vessels and prevention of pollution in U.S. waters. Port safety and security functions include supervising cargo transfer operations; conducting harbor patrols and waterfront facility inspections; establishing security zones as required; and controlling movement of vessels.

The Coast Guard plays a significant role in the safe and orderly passage of cargo, people, and vessels on U.S. waterways. It has established vessel traffic services in six major ports to provide for the safe movement of vessels at all times, but particularly during hazardous conditions, restricted visibility, or bad weather. The program's goal is to ensure the safe, efficient flow of commerce. The Coast Guard also regulates the installation of equipment necessary for vessel safety.

The Coast Guard develops and directs a national boating safety program aimed at making the operation of small craft in U.S. waters both pleasurable and safe. This program establishes uniform safety standards for recreational boats and associated equipment, encourages state efforts through a grant-in-aid and liaison program, coordinates public education and information programs, administers the Coast Guard Auxiliary, and enforces compliance with federal laws and regulations relating to the safe use of small boats and safety equipment requirements for them.

The Coast Guard Auxiliary is a nonmilitary volunteer organization of private citizens who own small boats, aircraft, or radio stations. Auxiliary members assist the Coast Guard by conducting boating education programs, patrolling marine regattas, participating in search and rescue operations, and conducting examinations of boaters' knowledge of the rules of marine courtesy.

As required by law, the Coast Guard maintains a state of readiness to function as a spe-

The transportation industry, which serves millions of people each year, is subject to broad regulation to ensure passenger safety. Despite the publicity that plane crashes receive, flying remains one of the safest means of travel.

cialized service in the Navy in time of war or as directed by the president. Coastal and harbor defense, including port security, is the most important military task assigned to the Coast Guard in times of national crisis.

Federal Aviation Administration The FEDERAL AVIATION ADMINISTRATION (FAA), formerly the Federal Aviation Agency, was established by the Federal Aviation Act of 1958 (49 U.S.C.A. § 106) and became a component of the DOT in 1967. The FAA is charged with regulating air commerce in ways that best promote its development and safety and fulfill the requirements of national defense; controlling the use of the navigable airspace of the United States by regulating both civil and military operations in that airspace in the interest of safety and efficiency; promoting, encouraging, and developing civil aeronautics; and consolidating research and development with respect to air navigation facilities.

The FAA is responsible for installing and operating air navigation facilities; developing and operating a common system of air traffic control and navigation for both civil and military aircraft; and developing and implementing programs and regulations to control aircraft noise, sonic booms, and other environmental effects of civil aviation.

In addition, the FAA operates a network of airport traffic control towers, air route traffic control centers, and flight service stations. It develops air traffic rules and regulations and allocates the use of the airspace. It also provides for the security control of air traffic to meet national defense requirements.

The FAA is also responsible for the location, construction or installation, maintenance, operation, and quality assurance of federal visual and electronic aids to air navigation. The agency operates and maintains voice/data communications equipment, radar facilities, computer systems, and visual display equipment at flight service stations, airport traffic control towers, and air route traffic control centers.

The agency maintains a national plan of airport requirements, administers a grant program for the development of public use airports to assure and improve safety and to meet current and future airport capacity needs, evaluates the environmental impacts of airport development, and administers an airport noise compatibility program with the goal of reducing noncompatible uses around airports. It also develops standards and technical guidance on airport planning, design, safety, and operations and provides grants to assist public agencies in airport system and master planning and airport development and improvement.

The FAA provides a system for registering aircraft and recording documents that affect title or interest in the aircraft, aircraft engines, propellers, appliances, and spare parts.

Under the Federal Aviation Act of 1958 and the International Aviation Facilities Act (49 U.S.C.A. § 1151), the agency promotes aviation safety and civil aviation abroad by exchanging aeronautical information with foreign aviation authorities; certifying foreign repair stations, air personnel, and mechanics; negotiating bilateral airworthiness agreements to facilitate the import and export of aircraft and components; and providing technical assistance and training in all areas of the agency's expertise.

One of the FAA's most important functions is the regulation and promotion of the U.S. commercial space transportation industry. It licenses the private-sector launching of space payloads on expendable launch vehicles and commercial space launch facilities. The FAA also sets insurance requirements for the protection of persons and property and ensures that space transportation activities comply with U.S. domestic and foreign policy. See also AIRLINES.

Federal Highway Administration

The Federal Highway Administration became a component of the DOT in 1967. It administers the highway transportation programs of the DOT under title 23 U.S.C.A., and other pertinent legislation. The administration oversees highway transportation in its broadest scope, seeking to coordinate highways with other modes of transportation to achieve the most effective balance of transportation systems and facilities.

The administration administers the federal aid highway program, which provides funding to the states to assist in constructing highways and making highway and traffic operations more efficient. This program provides for the improvement of approximately 159,000 miles of the National Highway System, which includes the 43,000-mile Dwight D. Eisenhower system of interstate and defense highways and other public roads. The federal government generally provides 90 percent of the funding for the construction and preservation of the interstate system, and the relevant states provide 10 percent. For projects not on the interstate system and most projects on other roads, 80 percent of the funding comes from the federal government and 20 percent from the states.

The administration is also responsible for the Highway Bridge Replacement and Rehabilitation Program, which assists in the inspection, analysis, and rehabilitation or replacement of bridges on public roads. In addition, it administers an emergency program to assist in the repair or reconstruction of federal aid highways and certain federal roads that have suffered serious damage over a wide area from natural disasters or catastrophic failures.

The Congestion Mitigation and Air Quality Improvement (CMAQ) Program provides funding to reduce AIR POLLUTION. Transportation improvement projects and programs that reduce transportation-related emissions are eligible for funding. Funds can be used for highway, transit, and other transportation purposes.

The administration is responsible for several highway-related safety programs, including a state and community safety program jointly administered with the National Highway Traffic Safety Administration and a highway safety construction program to eliminate road hazards and improve rail-highway crossing safety. These safety construction programs fund activities that remove, relocate, or shield roadside obstacles; identify and correct hazardous locations; eliminate or reduce hazards at railroad crossings; and improve signs, pavement markings, and signals.

Under the provisions of the Surface Transportation Assistance Act of 1982 (23 U.S.C.A. § 101), the administration is authorized to establish and maintain a national network for trucks, review state programs regulating truck size and weight, and assist in obtaining uniformity among the states in commercial motor carrier registration and taxation reporting. The administration works cooperatively with states and private industry to achieve uniform safety regulations, inspections and fines, licensing, registration and taxation, and accident data for motor carriers.

The agency also exercises federal regulatory jurisdiction over the safety performance of all commercial motor CARRIERS engaged in interstate or foreign commerce. It deals with more than 330,000 carriers and approximately 36,000 shippers of hazardous materials. The administration conducts reviews at the carrier's facilities to determine the safety of the carrier's over-the-road operations. These reviews may lead to prosecution or other sanctions against violators of the federal motor carrier safety regulations or the hazardous materials transportation regulations.

The Commercial Motor Vehicle Safety Act of 1986 (49 U.S.C.A. § 2701) authorizes the administration to establish national standards for a single commercial vehicle driver's LICENSE for state issuance, a national information system clearinghouse for commercial driver's license information, knowledge and skills tests for licensing commercial vehicle drivers, and disqualification of drivers for serious traffic offenses, including ALCOHOL and drug abuse. The agency administers the Motor Carrier Safety Assistance Program, a partnership between the federal government and the states, under the provisions of sections 401–404 of the Surface Transportation Assistance Act of 1982 (49 U.S.C.A. §§ 2301–2304).

Federal Railroad Administration The purpose of the Federal Railroad Administration is to promulgate and enforce rail safety regulations, administer railroad financial assistance programs, conduct research and development in support of improved railroad safety and national rail transportation policy, provide for

Although train travel remains popular in Europe, cars and planes have largely displaced the train as a form of transportation in the U.S.

DAVID WELLS/THE IMAGE WORKS

the rehabilitation of Northeast Corridor rail passenger service, and consolidate government support of rail transportation activities.

The administration administers and enforces the federal laws and related regulations designed to promote safety on railroads and exercises jurisdiction over all areas of rail safety, such as track maintenance, inspection standards, equipment standards, and operating practices. It also administers and enforces regulations enacted pursuant to railroad safety legislation for locomotives, signals, safety appliances, power brakes, hours of service, transportation of explosives and other dangerous articles, and the reporting and investigation of railroad accidents. Railroad and related industry equipment, facilities, and records are inspected and required reports reviewed. In addition, the administration educates the public about safety at highway-rail grade crossings and the danger of trespassing on rail property.

National Highway Traffic Safety Administration The National Highway Traffic Safety Administration (NHTSA) was established by the Highway Safety Act of 1970 (23 U.S.C.A. § 401). The NHTSA carries out programs concerning the safety performance of motor vehicles and related equipment and the safety of motor vehicle drivers, occupants, and pedestrians. The administration conducts general motor vehicle programs aimed at reducing the damage that motor vehicles sustain as a result of crashes. It also administers the federal odometer law, issues theft prevention standards, and promulgates average fuel economy standards for passenger and nonpassenger motor vehicles.

Under the NHTSA's program, Federal Motor Vehicle Safety Standards are issued that prescribe safety features and levels of safety-related performance for vehicles and motor vehicle equipment. Damage susceptibility, crashworthiness, and theft prevention are studied and reported to Congress and the public.

The Energy Policy and Conservation Act, as amended (42 U.S.C.A. § 6201), sets automotive fuel economy standards for passenger cars for model years 1985 and thereafter. The NHTSA has the option of altering the standards for the post-1985 period. The NHTSA develops and promulgates mandatory fuel economy standards for light trucks for each model year and administers the fuel economy regulatory program. The administration also establishes rules for collecting and reporting information concerning manufacturers' ability to meet fuel economy standards. This information is used to evaluate technological alternatives and manufacturers' economic ability to meet fuel economy standards.

The NHTSA maintains a national register of information on individuals who have had their licenses to operate a motor vehicle revoked, suspended, canceled, or denied, or who have been convicted of certain traffic-related violations, such as driving while impaired by alcohol or other drugs. The information obtained from the register assists state licensing officials in determining whether or not to issue a driver's license.

The Highway Safety Act provides federal matching funds to states and local communities to assist them with their highway safety programs. Areas of primary emphasis include impaired driving, occupant protection, motorcycle safety, police traffic services, pedestrian and bicycle safety, emergency medical services, speed control, and traffic records. The NHTSA provides guidance and technical assistance in all of these areas. The Highway Safety Act also provides incentive funds to encourage states to implement effective impaired-driving programs and to encourage the use of safety belts and motorcycle helmets. See also AUTOMOBILES.

Federal Transit Administration The Federal Transit Administration (FTA) was established as a component of the DOT in 1968. The FTA works with public and private mass transportation companies to develop improved mass transportation facilities, equipment, techniques, and methods. The administration encourages the planning and establishment of areawide urban mass transportation systems, helps state and local governments finance such systems, and provides financial assistance to state and local governments to increase mobility for older, disabled, and economically disadvantaged persons.

Maritime Administration The Maritime Administration was transferred to the DOT in 1981. The Maritime Administration administers programs to aid in the development, promotion, and operation of the U.S. merchant marine. It is also charged with organizing and directing emergency merchant ship operations.

Through the Maritime Subsidy Board, the Maritime Administration administers subsidy programs under which the federal government, subject to statutory limitations, pays the difference between certain costs of operating ships under the U.S. flag and foreign competitive flags. The government also subsidizes the difference between the costs of constructing ships in U.S. and foreign shipyards. The Maritime Administration provides financing guarantees

for the construction, reconstruction, and reconditioning of ships and enters into capital construction fund agreements that grant tax deferrals on moneys to be used for the acquisition, construction, or reconstruction of ships.

The administration constructs or supervises the construction of merchant-type ships for the federal government. It helps industry generate increased business for U.S. ships and conducts programs to promote domestic shipping and to develop ports, facilities, and intermodal transport.

Under emergency conditions the Maritime Administration charters government-owned ships to U.S. operators, requisitions or procures ships owned by U.S. citizens, and allocates them to meet defense needs. It maintains a National Defense Reserve Fleet of government-owned ships that it operates through ship managers and general agents when required for the national defense. An element of this activity is the Ready Reserve Force, consisting of a number of ships that can be activated for quick response.

The administration regulates sales to ALIENS and transfers to foreign registry of ships that are fully or partially owned by U.S. citizens. It also disposes of government-owned ships found nonessential for national defense.

The administration operates the U.S. Merchant Marine Academy in Kings Point, New York, where young people are trained to become merchant marine officers, and conducts training in shipboard firefighting in Earle, New Jersey, and Toledo, Ohio. It also administers a federal assistance program for the maritime academies operated by California, Maine, Massachusetts, Michigan, New York, and Texas.

Saint Lawrence Seaway Development Corporation The Saint Lawrence Seaway Development Corporation was established by Congress in 1954 (33 U.S.C.A. §§ 981–990) as an operating administration of the DOT. The corporation, a wholly government-owned enterprise, is responsible for the development, operation, and maintenance of the part of the Saint Lawrence Seaway that is between the port of Montreal and Lake Erie and within the territorial limits of the United States. It is the function of the Seaway Corporation to provide a safe, efficient, and effective water artery for maritime commerce, both in peacetime and in time of national emergency.

The corporation coordinates its activities with its Canadian counterpart, particularly with respect to overall operations, traffic control, navigation aids, safety, navigation dates, and related programs designed to fully develop the seaway system. The corporation encourages the development of traffic through the Great Lakes/Saint Lawrence Seaway system in order to contribute to the economic and environmental development of the entire region.

Research and Special Programs Administration The Research and Special Programs Administration was established in 1977. It is responsible for hazardous materials transportation and pipeline safety, transportation emergency preparedness, safety training, and transportation research and development activities.

TRASK, MILILANI Mililani Trask, a native Hawaiian attorney, is the leader of a Hawaiian SOVEREIGNTY movement that seeks the establishment of a separate nation for native Hawaiians and the return of the state-managed lands to which native Hawaiians are legally entitled.

Trask was born into a politically active family. Her grandfather, David Trask, Sr., was a territorial senator, and her uncle, David Trask, Jr., became a prominent labor leader who organized a powerful union for state government employees. Trask graduated from the Kamehameha Schools, an educational institution set up by Princess Bernice Pauahi Bishop, of Hawaii, for native Hawaiian children. She attended Johnston College, University of Redlands in California, but left school before graduating to work with labor organizer CESAR CHAVEZ's fieldworkers and the Black Panther Childcare Project. Trask received a bachelor of arts degree in political science from San Jose State University in 1974, and graduated from the University of Santa Clara School of Law in 1978, at the age of twenty-seven.

Trask returned to Hawaii and joined the growing native struggle over land control and development. She began community organizing on sovereignty issues, setting up conferences and workshops and doing extensive legal research into native land claims.

In 1987, Trask and others founded the group Ka Lahui Hawai'i (the Hawaiian People). Ka Lahui is a self-proclaimed sovereign Hawaiian nation with over ten thousand members; a democratic constitution with a bill of rights;

BIOGRAPHY

"ALL THE TALK NOW IS ABOUT MODELS OF SOVEREIGNTY. A MODEL IS JUST A PROTOTYPE. IT'S NOT REAL. WE'RE NOT A MODEL. A MODEL DOESN'T HAVE 25,000 PEOPLE."

and four branches of government—including an elected legislature (the Pakaukau), representing thirty-three districts, and a judiciary system made up of elected judges and an elders council. Voting is restricted to those with Hawaiian blood. (Native Hawaiians are the 220,000 people of Hawaiian ancestry in the state, of whom about 10,000 are pure-blooded.) Trask has twice been elected *kia'aina* of the group, the equivalent of governor or prime minister.

Trask hopes the nation will eventually be rooted in the nearly two hundred thousand acres of Hawaiian homelands and the 1.4 million acres of original Hawaiian lands ceded to the state by the federal government. In Ka Lahui Hawai'i, according to Trask, native Hawaiians would have a relationship similar to that existing between the United States and federally recognized Native American tribes and native Alaskans. The tribes, whose members have dual status as citizens of the United States and as "citizens" of the tribe, can impose taxes, make laws, and control their lands.

See also NATIVE AMERICAN RIGHTS.

TRAVERSE In COMMON-LAW PLEADING, a denial of the plaintiff's assertions.

For example, a plaintiff could bring a lawsuit in order to collect money that he claimed the defendant owed him. If the defendant answered the plaintiff's CLAIM by stating in ANSWER that she did not fail to pay the money owed on the date it was due, this is a denial of a fact essential to the plaintiff's case. The defendant can be said to traverse the plaintiff's declaration of an outstanding debt, and her PLEA itself could be called a traverse.

The system of common-law pleading has been replaced throughout the United States by CODE PLEADING and by rules patterned on the system of pleading in Federal civil procedure, but lawyers still use the word *traverse* for a denial. In some instances, it has taken on specialized meanings for different purposes. For example, in criminal practice, a traverse is a denial of the charges in an INDICTMENT that usually has the effect of delaying a trial on the indictment until a later term of the court. A

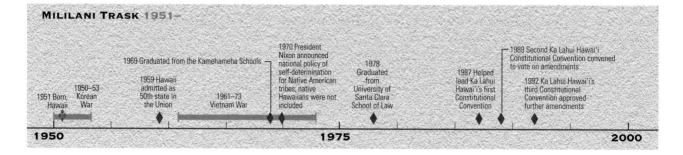

MILILANI TRASK 1951–

1951 Born, Hawaii

1950–53 Korean War

1959 Hawaii admitted as 50th state in the Union

1969 Graduated from the Kamehameha Schools

1961–73 Vietnam War

1970 President Nixon announced national policy of self-determination for Native American tribes; native Hawaiians were not included

1978 Graduated from University of Santa Clara School of Law

1987 Helped lead Ka Lahui Hawai'i's first Constitutional Convention

1989 Second Ka Lahui Hawai'i Constitutional Convention convened to vote on amendments

1992 Ka Lahui Hawai'i's third Constitutional Convention approved further amendments

1950   1975   2000

traverse jury is one that hears the claims of the plaintiff and denials of the defendant—a trial JURY or PETIT JURY. A traverse hearing may be a pretrial hearing to determine whether the court has authority to hear the case—as when the defendant denies having been properly served with the plaintiff's SUMMONS and COMPLAINT.

TRAYNOR, ROGER JOHN

Among the most influential and highly esteemed jurists of the twentieth century, Roger J. Traynor was a professor, author, and justice of the California Supreme Court from 1940 to 1970. During Traynor's six years as that court's chief justice, it was regarded as the preeminent state court in the nation. Readily open to reform and to novel legal ideas, Traynor made long-lasting contributions to various areas of the law including taxes, NEGLIGENCE, and FOURTH AMENDMENT jurisprudence. In addition to hundreds of judicial opinions, Traynor also wrote prodigiously as a legal scholar and contributed to a number of legal reform efforts.

Born on February 12, 1900, Traynor was the son of a miner. In the 1920s he studied law and political science at the University of California at Berkeley, where he simultaneously earned a J.D. and Ph.D. while editing the *California Law Review*. In 1928 he joined the law school's staff. Over the next twelve years, he served as a consultant to various state and national agencies, including the U.S. Treasury Department. In California his advisory work led to major reforms of sales and use taxes (1933 Cal. Stat. 2599 and 1935 Cal. Stat. 1297), personal income taxes (1943 Cal. Stat. 2354), and bank and corporation franchise taxes (1929 Cal. Stat. 19).

In 1940 Governor Culbert Olson appointed Traynor to the California Supreme Court, making him the first law school professor to be appointed directly to the court. Although he had little experience in private practice, Traynor had earned renown as one of the nation's leading tax scholars. Over the next three decades, he not only wrote more than 950 opinions but also continued his scholarly work, writing more than seventy-five law review articles on a wide variety of topics.

BIOGRAPHY

Roger John Traynor

"UNABLE LIKE SOLOMON TO CARVE THE CHILD, [A COURT] MAY CARVE OUT OF THE SUM OF CUSTODIAL RIGHTS, CERTAIN RIGHTS TO BE EXERCISED BY EACH PARENT."

Traynor had a reformist philosophy, viewing the law as a fluid, changing force that was necessarily responsive to the needs of society. He believed that a judge can and should change the law. Among his most influential opinions was his concurrence in *Escola v. Coca Cola Bottling Co.*, 24 Cal. 2d 453, 150 P.2d 436 (1944), which would dramatically change PRODUCT LIABILITY LAW. Traynor's idea that consumers should be entitled to sue the manufacturers of defective products was novel at the time. Yet, two decades later, the idea was embraced by the full California Supreme Court (*Greenman v. Yuba Power Products, Inc.*, 59 Cal. 2d 57, 27 Cal. Rptr. 697, 377 P.2d 897 [1963]) and soon became the law of the land.

Traynor's jurisprudence amounted to a historic reform of long-standing common-law doctrines, and his ideas influenced courts nationwide. His precedent-setting opinions included *People v. Cahan*, 44 Cal. 2d 434, 282 P.2d 905 (1955), which restricted the admissibility of illegally secured evidence, and *Muskopf v. Corning Hospital District*, 55 Cal. 2d 211, 359 P.2d 457, 11 Cal. Rptr. 89 (1961), which eliminated the defense of SOVEREIGN IMMUNITY—the doctrine that precludes bringing suit against the government without its consent—in tort cases.

In 1964 Governor Edmund G. Brown, Sr., elevated Traynor to the position of chief justice. Over the next six years, the California Supreme Court became the most prestigious state court in the nation. Among the innovations Traynor introduced was the use of LAW REVIEW citations in the court's opinions, thus ensuring that legal scholarship would inform legal opinion. Upon his retirement from the court at the age of seventy, he was praised for his work in transforming and modernizing the COMMON LAW. His accomplishments were compared to the reform efforts of BENJAMIN CARDOZO, the legendary New York appellate justice.

After his retirement from the court, Traynor chaired the American Bar Association's Special Committee on Standards of Judicial Conduct, which produced, in 1972, modern standards for the governance of judges. Traynor taught at

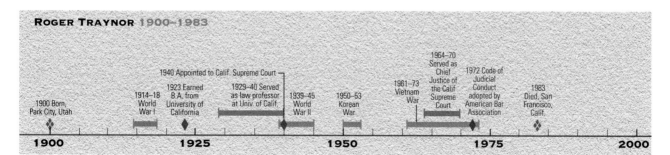

ROGER TRAYNOR 1900–1983

1900 Born, Park City, Utah

1914–18 World War I

1923 Earned B.A. from University of California

1929–40 Served as law professor at Univ. of Calif.

1940 Appointed to Calif. Supreme Court

1939–45 World War II

1950–53 Korean War

1961–73 Vietnam War

1964–70 Served as Chief Justice of the Calif. Supreme Court

1972 Code of Judicial Conduct adopted by American Bar Association

1983 Died, San Francisco, Calif.

1900   1925   1950   1975   2000

Hastings College of the Law, the Universities of Virginia and Utah, and as a visiting professor at Cambridge University in England. He also served as chair of the National Press Council. Traynor died in Berkeley, California, on May 13, 1983.

TREASON 📖 The betrayal of one's own country by waging WAR against it or by consciously or purposely acting to aid its enemies. 📖

Article III, Section 3, of the federal Constitution sets forth the definition of treason in the United States. Any person who levies war against the United States or adheres to its enemies by giving them AID AND COMFORT has committed treason within the meaning of the Constitution. The term *aid and comfort* refers to any act that manifests a betrayal of allegiance to the United States, such as furnishing enemies with arms, troops, transportation, shelter, or classified information. If a subversive act has any tendency to weaken the power of the United States to attack or resist its enemies, aid and comfort has been given.

The Treason Clause applies only to disloyal acts committed during times of war. Acts of disloyalty during peacetime are not considered treasonous under the Constitution. Nor do acts of ESPIONAGE committed on behalf of an ally constitute treason. For example, JULIUS AND ETHEL ROSENBERG were convicted of espionage in 1951 for helping the Soviet Union steal atomic secrets from the United States during World War II. The Rosenbergs were not tried for treason because the United States and the Soviet Union were allies during World War II.

Under Article III a person can levy war against the United States without the use of arms, weapons, or military equipment. Persons who play only a peripheral role in a CONSPIRACY to levy war are still considered traitors under the Constitution if an armed rebellion against the United States results. After the Civil War, for example, all Confederate soldiers were vulnerable to charges of treason, regardless of their role in the SECESSION or INSURRECTION of the Southern states. No treason charges were filed against these soldiers, however, because President ANDREW JOHNSON issued a universal AMNESTY.

The crime of treason requires a traitorous INTENT. If a person unwittingly or unintentionally gives aid and comfort to an enemy of the United States during wartime, treason has not occurred. Similarly, a person who pursues a course of action that is intended to benefit the United States but mistakenly helps an enemy is not guilty of treason. Inadvertent disloyalty is never punishable as treason, no matter how much damage the United States suffers.

As in any other criminal trial in the United States, a defendant charged with treason is presumed innocent until proved guilty BEYOND A REASONABLE DOUBT. Treason may be proved by a voluntary CONFESSION in open court or by EVIDENCE that the defendant committed an OVERT act of treason. Each overt act must be witnessed by at least two people, or a conviction for treason will not stand. By requiring this type of DIRECT EVIDENCE, the Constitution minimizes the danger of convicting an innocent person and forestalls the possibility of partisan witch-hunts waged by a single adversary.

Unexpressed seditious thoughts do not constitute treason, even if those thoughts contemplate a bloody REVOLUTION or coup. Nor does the public expression of subversive opinions, including vehement criticism of the government and its policies, constitute treason. The FIRST AMENDMENT to the U.S. Constitution guarantees the right of all Americans to advocate the violent overthrow of their government unless such advocacy is directed toward inciting imminent lawless action and is likely to produce it (*Brandenburg v. Ohio*, 395 U.S. 444, 89 S. Ct. 1827, 23 L. Ed. 2d 430 [1969]). On the other hand, the U.S. Supreme Court ruled that the distribution of leaflets protesting the draft during World War I was not constitutionally protected speech (*Schenck v. United States*, 249 U.S. 47, 39 S. Ct. 247, 63 L. Ed. 470 [1919]).

Because treason involves the betrayal of allegiance to the United States, a person need not be a U.S. citizen to commit treason under the Constitution. Persons who owe temporary allegiance to the United States can commit treason. ALIENS who are domiciliaries of the United States, for example, can commit traitorous acts during the period of their domicile. A subversive act does not need to occur on U.S. soil to be punishable as treason. For example, Mildred Gillars, a U.S. citizen who became known as Axis Sally, was convicted of treason for broadcasting demoralizing propaganda to Allied forces in Europe from a Nazi radio station in Germany during World War II.

Treason is punishable by death. If a death sentence is not imposed, defendants face a minimum penalty of five years in prison and a $10,000 fine (18 U.S.C.A. § 2381). A person who is convicted of treason may not hold federal office at any time thereafter.

The English COMMON LAW required defendants to forfeit all of their property, real and personal, upon conviction for treason. In some cases, the British Crown confiscated the property of immediate family members as well. The common law also precluded convicted traitors from bequeathing their property through a WILL. Relatives were presumed to be tainted by the blood of the traitor and were not permitted to inherit from him. Article III of the U.S. Constitution outlaws such "corruption of the blood" and limits the penalty of FORFEITURE to "the life of the person attainted." Under this provision relatives cannot be made to forfeit their property or inheritance for crimes committed by traitorous family members.

The Treason Clause traces its roots back to an English statute enacted during the reign of Edward III (1327–1377). This statute prohibited levying war against the king, adhering to his enemies, or contemplating his death. Although this law defined treason to include disloyal and subversive thoughts, it effectively circumscribed the crime as it existed under the common law. During the thirteenth century, the crime of treason encompassed virtually every act contrary to the king's will and became a political tool of the Crown. Building on the tradition begun by Edward III, the Founding Fathers carefully delineated the crime of treason in Article III of the U.S. Constitution, narrowly defining its elements and setting forth stringent evidentiary requirements.

See also SCHENCK V. UNITED STATES.

TREASURY DEPARTMENT The U.S. Department of the Treasury performs four basic functions: formulating and recommending economic, financial, tax, and fiscal policies; serving as financial agent for the U.S. government; enforcing the law; and manufacturing coins and currency. The Treasury Department was created by an act of September 2, 1789 (31 U.S.C.A. § 301). Many subsequent acts have affected the development of the department and created its numerous bureaus and divisions.

Secretary As a major policy adviser to the president, the secretary of the treasury has primary responsibility for formulating and recommending domestic and international financial, economic, and tax policy, participating in the formulation of broad fiscal policies that have general significance for the economy, and managing the public debt. The secretary also oversees the activities of the department in carrying out its major law enforcement responsibility, serving as the financial agent for the U.S. government, and manufacturing coins, currency, and other products for customer agencies.

In addition, the secretary has many responsibilities as chief financial officer of the government. The secretary serves as chair pro tempore of the Economic Policy Council and as U.S. governor of the INTERNATIONAL MONETARY FUND, the International Bank for Reconstruction and Development, the Inter-American Development Bank, and the African Development Bank. The Office of the Secretary includes the offices of deputy secretary, general counsel, inspector general, the under secretaries, the assistant secretaries, and treasurer.

Bureau of Alcohol, Tobacco and Firearms The Bureau of Alcohol, Tobacco and Firearms was established by Treasury Department Order No. 221, effective July 1, 1972. The order transferred the functions, powers, and duties arising under laws relating to ALCOHOL, TOBACCO, firearms, and explosives from the Internal Revenue Service to the bureau. On December 5, 1978, Treasury Department Order No. 120-1 assigned to the bureau responsibility for enforcing chapter 114 of title 18 of the United States Code (18 U.S.C.A. § 2341 et seq.) relating to interstate trafficking in contraband cigarettes. The Anti-Arson Act of 1982, 96 Stat. 1319, gave the bureau the additional responsibility of addressing commercial ARSON nationwide.

The bureau is responsible for enforcing and administering firearms and EXPLOSIVES laws, as well as laws covering the production, taxation, and distribution of alcohol and tobacco products. The bureau performs two basic functions: criminal enforcement and regulatory enforcement.

The criminal enforcement branch of the bureau seeks to stop illegal trafficking, possession, and use of firearms, destructive devices, and explosives and also tries to suppress trafficking in illicit distilled spirits and contraband cigarettes. The objectives of the regulatory enforcement branch of the bureau include determining and ensuring the full collection of revenue due from legal alcohol, tobacco, firearms, and ammunition manufacturing industries; fulfilling the bureau's responsibility to ensure product integrity and provide health warning statements; and preventing commercial BRIBERY, consumer deception, and other improper trade practices in the alcohol beverage industry. See also ALCOHOL, TOBACCO, AND FIREARMS, BUREAU OF.

Office of the Comptroller of the Currency The Office of the Comptroller of the Currency (OCC) was created on February 25, 1863 (12 Stat. 665), as a bureau of the Treasury Department. Its primary mission is to regulate national banks. The OCC is headed by the comptroller, who is appointed for a five-year term by the president with the advice and consent of the Senate. By statute, the comptroller also serves a concurrent term as director of the FEDERAL DEPOSIT INSURANCE CORPORATION.

Treasury Department

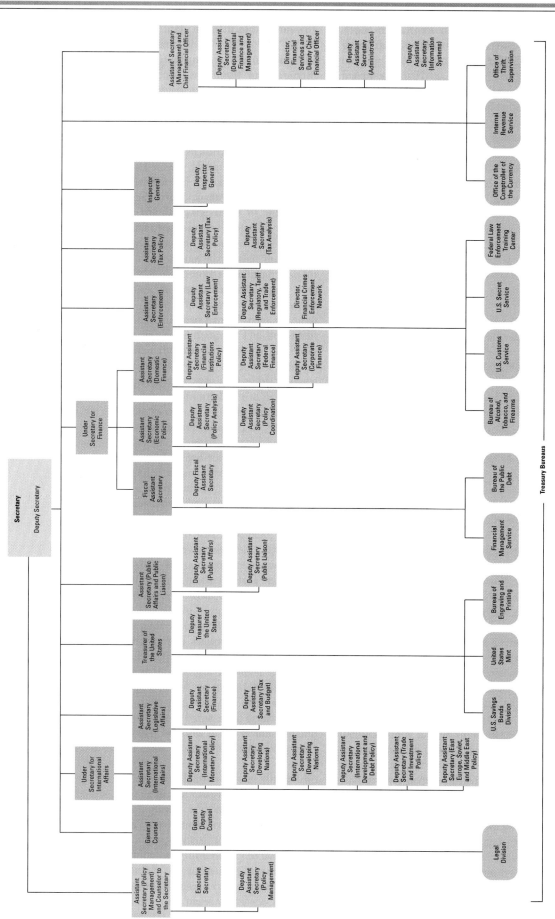

[1]Assistant Secretary (Management) is the Chief Financial Officer (CFO).

The OCC supervises approximately 3,300 national banks, including their trust activities and overseas operations. The OCC has the power to examine banks; approve or deny applications for new bank charters, branches, or mergers; take enforcement action—such as bank closures—against banks that are not in compliance with laws and regulations; and issue rules, regulations, and interpretations related to banking practices. Each bank is examined annually through a nationwide staff of approximately 2,400 bank examiners supervised by six district offices. The OCC is independently funded through assessments on the assets of national banks. See also BANKS AND BANKING.

U.S. Customs Service The fifth act of the first Congress, passed on July 31, 1789 (1 Stat. 29), established customs districts and authorized customs officers to collect duties on goods, wares, and merchandise. The Bureau of Customs was established as a separate agency under the Treasury Department on March 3, 1927 (19 U.S.C.A. § 2071), and, effective August 1, 1973, was redesignated the U.S. Customs Service by Treasury Department Order No. 165-23 of April 4, 1973.

The Customs Service enforces customs and related laws and collects revenue from imports. The service also administers the Tariff Act of 1930, as amended (19 U.S.C.A. § 1654), and other customs laws. The Customs Service is specifically charged with interdicting and seizing CONTRABAND, including narcotics and illegal drugs; assessing and collecting CUSTOMS DUTIES, excise taxes, fees, and penalties due on imported merchandise; processing persons, carriers, cargo, and mail into and out of the United States; administering certain navigation laws; and detecting and apprehending persons engaged in FRAUDULENT practices designed to circumvent customs duties and related laws.

Because the Customs Service is the principal border enforcement agency, its mission has been extended over the years. Currently, the service assists in the administration and enforcement of some four hundred provisions of law on behalf of more than forty government agencies. In addition to enforcing the Tariff Act of 1930 and other customs statutes, the Customs Service cooperates with other federal agencies and foreign governments in suppressing the traffic of illegal narcotics and PORNOGRAPHY, enforces export control laws, and intercepts illegal high-technology and weapons exports.

The Customs Service is involved extensively with outside commercial and policy organizations, trade associations, international organizations, and foreign customs services. The service

is a member of the multinational World Customs Organization, the Cabinet Committee to Combat Terrorism, and the International Narcotics Control Program. In addition, the Customs Service participates in and supports the activities and programs of various international organizations and agreements, including the World Trade Organization, the International Civil Aviation Organization, and the Organization of American States. See also DRUGS AND NARCOTICS; SMUGGLING; TARIFF.

Bureau of Engraving and Printing The Bureau of Engraving and Printing operates on basic authorities conferred by an act of July 11, 1862 (31 U.S.C.A. § 303), and additional authorities contained in past appropriations made to the bureau that are still in force. A working capital fund was established in accordance with the provisions of section 2 of the act of August 4, 1950, as amended (31 U.S.C.A. § 5142), which placed the bureau on a completely reimbursable basis. The bureau is headed by a director, who is appointed by the secretary of the treasury and reports to the treasurer of the United States.

At the Bureau of Engraving and Printing, the artistry of the engraver is combined with the most technologically advanced printing equipment to produce U.S. securities. The bureau designs, prints, and finishes all U.S. paper currency (Federal Reserve notes), as well as U.S. postage stamps, treasury SECURITIES, certificates, and other security products, including White House invitations and military identification cards. It is also responsible for advising and assisting federal agencies in the design and production of other government documents that, because of their innate value or for other reasons, require security or counterfeit-deterrence characteristics.

Officers of the U.S. Customs Service inspect boxes of fruit brought into the United States. The Customs Service is part of the Treasury Department.

The bureau has its headquarters in Washington, D.C., and operates a second currency manufacturing plant in Fort Worth, Texas.

Federal Law Enforcement Training Center The Federal Law Enforcement Training Center was established by Treasury Department Order No. 217, effective March 2, 1970, and reaffirmed by Treasury Department Order No. 140-01 of September 20, 1994. The Federal Law Enforcement Training Center is headed by a director, who is appointed by the secretary of the treasury. The center conducts operations at its training facility in Glynco, Georgia.

The center is an interagency training facility serving more than seventy-two federal law enforcement organizations. The training focuses on teaching common areas of law enforcement skills to police and investigative personnel. The center also conducts advanced programs in areas of common need, such as white-collar crime, the use of microcomputers as an investigative tool, advanced law enforcement photography, international banking/MONEY LAUNDERING, marine law enforcement, and instructor training. In addition to the basic and common advanced programs, the center provides facilities and support services for participating organizations to conduct advanced training for their own law enforcement personnel.

The center offers selective, highly specialized training programs to state and local officers as an aid in deterring crime. These programs include a variety of areas such as FRAUD and financial investigations, marine law enforcement, arson for profit, international banking/money laundering, and criminal intelligence analyst training.

Financial Management Service The mission of the Financial Management Service (FMS) is to improve the quality of government financial management. The service is committed to helping its government customers achieve success. The FMS serves taxpayers, the Treasury Department, federal program agencies, and government policymakers by linking program and financial management objectives and by providing financial services, information, and advice to its customers.

The FMS is responsible for programs to improve cash management, CREDIT management, DEBT collection, and financial management systems throughout the government. For cash management, the service issues guidelines and regulations and assists other agencies in managing financial transactions to maximize investment earnings and reduce the interest costs of borrowed funds. For credit manage-

ment, the service issues guidelines and regulations and helps program agencies manage credit activities, including loan programs, so as to improve all parts of the credit cycle, such as credit extension, loan servicing, debt collection, and write-off procedures. The service works with other agencies to take advantage of new automation technology and improve financial management systems and government handling of payments, collections, and receivables.

The service issues approximately 426 million treasury CHECKS and close to 407 million electronic fund transfer payments annually for federal salaries and wages, payments to suppliers of goods and services to the federal government, income tax refunds, and payments under major government programs such as Social Security and veterans' benefits. The FMS also supervises the collection of government receipts and operates and maintains the systems for collecting these receipts. The service works with all federal agencies to improve the availability of collected funds and the reporting of collection information to the treasury.

Internal Revenue Service The Office of the Commissioner of Internal Revenue was established by an act of July 1, 1862 (26 U.S.C.A. § 7802). The INTERNAL REVENUE SERVICE (IRS) is responsible for administering and enforcing the internal revenue laws and related statutes, except those relating to alcohol, tobacco, firearms, and explosives. Its mission is to collect the proper amount of tax revenue at the least cost to the public and in a manner that warrants the highest degree of public confidence in the service's integrity, efficiency, and fairness.

To achieve that purpose, the IRS seeks to achieve the highest possible degree of voluntary compliance with the tax laws and regulations. It advises the members of the public of their rights and responsibilities, determines the extent of compliance and the causes of noncompliance, administers and enforces the tax laws, and seeks more efficient ways of accomplishing its mission.

The IRS determines, assesses, and collects internal revenue taxes, determines PENSION plan qualifications and exempt organization status, and prepares and issues rulings and regulations to supplement the provisions of the Internal Revenue Code.

The source of most revenues collected is the individual INCOME TAX and the social insurance and retirement taxes. Other major sources include the corporation income, excise, estate, and gift taxes. See also ESTATE AND GIFT TAXES; TAXATION.

U.S. Mint   The establishment of a mint was authorized by an act of April 2, 1792 (1 Stat. 246). The Bureau of the Mint was established by an act of February 12, 1873 (17 Stat. 424), and recodified on September 13, 1982 (31 U.S.C.A. §§ 304, 5131). The name was changed to the U.S. Mint by secretarial order dated January 9, 1984.

The primary mission of the mint is to produce an adequate volume of circulating coinage for the United States to conduct its trade and commerce. The mint also produces and sells numismatic coins, American eagle gold and silver bullion coins, and national medals. In addition, the Fort Knox Bullion Depository is the primary storage facility for the nation's gold bullion.

Bureau of the Public Debt   The Bureau of the Public Debt was established on June 30, 1940, pursuant to the Reorganization Act of 1939 (31 U.S.C.A. § 306). Its mission is to borrow the money needed to operate the federal government, account for the resulting public debt, and issue treasury securities to refund maturing debt and raise new money.

The bureau fulfills its mission through six programs: commercial book-entry securities, direct access securities, savings securities, government securities, market regulation, and public debt accounting. The bureau issues and auctions treasury bills, notes, and bonds and manages the U.S. Savings Bond Program.

In addition, the bureau implements the regulations for the government securities market. These regulations provide for investor protection while maintaining a fair and liquid market for government securities.

See also FEDERAL BUDGET.

U.S. Secret Service   Pursuant to certain sections of titles 3 and 18 of the United States Code, the mission of the Secret Service includes the authority and responsibility to protect the president, the vice president, the president-elect, the vice president elect, and members of their immediate families, major presidential and vice presidential candidates, former presidents and their spouses, minor children of a former president until the age of sixteen, visiting heads of foreign states or governments, other distinguished foreign visitors to the United States, and official representatives of the United States performing special missions abroad, as directed by the president.

The service provides security at the White House complex and other presidential offices, the temporary official residence of the vice president in the District of Columbia, and foreign diplomatic missions in the Washington,

D.C., metropolitan area and throughout the United States.

The Secret Service is also charged with detecting and arresting any person committing any offense against the laws of the United States relating to currency, coins, obligations, and securities of the United States or foreign governments. The service works to suppress FORGERY and fraudulent negotiation or redemption with respect to federal government checks, BONDS, and other obligations or securities of the United States.

Office of Thrift Supervision   The Office of Thrift Supervision (OTS) was established as a bureau of the Treasury Department in August 1989 and became operational in October 1989 as part of a major reorganization of the thrift regulatory structure mandated by the Financial Institutions Reform, Recovery and Enforcement Act (103 Stat. 183). In that act, Congress gave the OTS authority to charter federal thrift institutions and serve as the primary regulator of approximately 1,700 federal and state-chartered thrifts belonging to the Savings Association Insurance Fund.

The office's mission is to regulate savings associations in order to maintain the safety, soundness, and viability of the industry and to support the industry's efforts to meet housing and other financial services needs. The OTS carries out this responsibility through risk-focused supervision that includes adopting regulations governing the savings and loan industry, examining and supervising thrift institutions and their affiliates, and enforcing compliance with federal laws and regulations. In addition to overseeing thrift institutions, the OTS also regulates, examines, and supervises HOLDING COMPANIES that own thrifts and controls the acquisition of thrifts by such holding companies.

The office is headed by a director appointed by the president and confirmed by the Senate to serve a five-year term. The director also serves on the boards of the Federal Deposit Insurance Corporation and the Neighborhood Reinvestment Corporation. See also SAVINGS AND LOAN ASSOCIATION.

TREASURY STOCK   Corporate STOCK that is issued, completely paid for, and reacquired by the CORPORATION at a later point in time.

Treasury stock or shares may be purchased by the corporation, or reacquired through donation, forfeiture, or some other method. It is then regarded as the PERSONAL PROPERTY of the corporation and part of its ASSETS. The corporation can sell the stock for cash or credit, for PAR value or market value, or upon any terms that it could be sold by a stockholder. Shares that the corporation has not issued in spite of its authority to do so are ordinarily not regarded as treasury shares but are merely unissued shares.

TREATIES IN FORCE 📖 A publication compiled by the Treaty Affairs Staff, Office of the Legal Adviser, Department of State, which lists treaties and other international agreements of the United States that are on record with the Department of State. 📖

Treaties in Force lists those treaties and other agreements that had not expired on the date of publication, had not been repudiated by the parties, had not been replaced by other agreements, or had not otherwise been terminated. It employs the term *treaties* in its broad, generic sense as alluding to all international agreements of the United States. In its narrower sense, in the United States, the word *treaties* denotes international agreements executed by the president with the advice and consent of two-thirds of the Senate.

This publication also includes agreements in force between the United States and foreign nations that the president has made pursuant to, or in accordance with, existing legislation or a TREATY, subject to congressional approval or effectuation, or under and in accordance with the president's power under the Constitution.

TREATISE 📖 A scholarly legal publication containing all the law relating to a particular area, such as criminal law or land-use control. 📖

Lawyers commonly use treatises in order to review the law and update their knowledge of pertinent case decisions and statutes.

TREATY 📖 A compact made between two or more independent nations with a view to the public welfare. 📖

A treaty is an AGREEMENT in written form between nation-states (or international agencies, such as the UNITED NATIONS, that have been given treaty-making capacity by the states that created them) that is intended to establish a relationship governed by INTERNATIONAL LAW. It may be contained in a single instrument or in two or more related instruments such as an exchange of diplomatic notes. Various terms have been used for such an agreement, including treaty, convention, PROTOCOL, declaration, CHARTER, COVENANT, pact, act, STATUTE, exchange of notes, agreement, *modus vivendi* ("manner of living" or practical compromise), and understanding. The particular designation does not affect the agreement's legal character.

Though a treaty may take many forms, an international agreement customarily includes four or five basic elements. The first is the PREAMBLE, which gives the names of the parties, a statement of the general aims of the treaty, and a statement naming the plenipotentiaries (the persons invested with the power to negotiate) who negotiated the agreement and verifying that they have the power to make the treaty. The substance of the treaty is contained in articles that describe what the parties have agreed upon; these articles are followed by an article providing for RATIFICATION and the time and place for the exchange of ratifications. At the end of the document are a clause that states "in witness whereof the respective plenipotentiaries have affixed their names and seals" and a place for signatures and dates. Sometimes additional articles are appended to the treaty and signed by the plenipotentiaries along with a declaration stating that the articles have the same force as those contained in the body of the agreement.

Article II, Section 2, Clause 2, of the U.S. Constitution gives the PRESIDENT the power to negotiate and ratify treaties, but he must obtain the advice and consent of the SENATE (in practice solicited only after negotiation); two-thirds of the senators present must concur. Article I, Section 10, of the Constitution forbids the states to enter into a "treaty, alliance, or confederation," although they may enter into an "agreement or compact" with other states, domestic or foreign, but only with the consent of Congress.

The U.S. Supreme Court, in *Missouri v. Holland*, 252 U.S. 416, 40 S. Ct. 382, 64 L. Ed. 641 (1920), established that U.S. treaties are superior to state law. Acts of Congress, however, are equivalent to a treaty. Thus, if a treaty and a law of Congress are inconsistent, the one later in time prevails. The Court has never found a treaty to be unconstitutional, and few treaties have been challenged. In general, the Court views a dispute over a treaty as a political question outside its JURISDICTION.

Traditionally, international law required treaties to be ratified in the same form by all parties. Consequently, reservations or amendments proposed by one party had to be accepted by all. Because of the large number of participating states, this unanimity rule has proved difficult to enforce in modern multilateral treaties sponsored by international agencies for the purpose of creating legal regimes or codifying rules of international law. Where agreement exists on the essential elements of a treaty, international law increasingly is allowing reservations as to minor points not unanimously accepted. Treaties for which ratification is specified come into effect upon the exchange of ratifications between the parties or upon deposit of the ratifications with a designated party or international agency, such as the Secretariat of the United Nations.

A treaty may be terminated in accordance with specifications in the treaty or by consent of the parties. War between the parties does not invariably terminate treaties, as some treaties are made to regulate the conduct of hostilities and treatment of prisoners. Other treaties may be suspended for the duration of the hostilities and then resumed. An unjustified, unilateral abrogation of a treaty may give rise to possible international claims for any injury suffered by the other parties.

Treaties are usually interpreted according to the ordinary sense of their words in context and the apparent purposes to be achieved. If the meaning of the language is unclear or there is doubt that it expresses the intention of the parties, the work product of the negotiation process may be consulted as well as other EX-TRINSIC EVIDENCE.

TREATY OF PARIS The Treaty of Paris of 1783 ended the U.S. Revolutionary War and granted the thirteen colonies political independence. A preliminary treaty between Great Britain and the United States was signed in 1782, but the final agreement was not signed until September 3, 1783.

The surrender of the British army at Yorktown, Virginia, on October 19, 1781, ended the major military hostilities of the Revolutionary War, but sporadic fighting, mostly in the south and west, continued for more than a year. The defeat led to the resignation of the British prime minister, Lord North. The coalition cabinet formed after North's resignation decided to begin peace negotiations with the colonial revolutionaries.

The negotiations began in Paris, France, in April 1782. The U.S. delegation included BEN-JAMIN FRANKLIN, JOHN ADAMS, JOHN JAY, and Henry Laurens, while the British were represented by Richard Oswald and Henry Strachey. The negotiators concluded the preliminary treaty on November 30, 1782, but the agreement did not take effect until Great Britain concluded treaties with France and Spain concerning other British colonies.

The United States ratified the preliminary treaty on April 15, 1783. In the final agreement that was signed in September 1783, the British recognized the independence of the United States. The treaty established generous boundaries for the United States: U.S. territory would extend from the Atlantic Ocean to the Mississippi River in the west, and from the Great Lakes and Canada in the north to the thirty-

John Jay, John Adams, Benjamin Franklin, and Henry Laurens at the signing of the Treaty of Paris.

first parallel in the south. The U.S. fishing fleet was guaranteed access to the fisheries off the coast of Newfoundland.

Under the treaty navigation of the Mississippi River was to be open to both the United States and Great Britain. Creditors of both countries were not to be impeded from collecting their debts, and Congress was to recommend to the states that loyalists to the British cause during the war be treated fairly and have their rights and confiscated property restored.

See also WAR OF INDEPENDENCE.

TREATY OF VERSAILLES The Treaty of Versailles was the agreement negotiated during the Paris Peace Conference of 1919 that ended WORLD WAR I and imposed disarmament, reparations, and territorial changes on the defeated Germany. The treaty also established the LEAGUE OF NATIONS, an international organization dedicated to resolving world conflicts peacefully. The treaty has been criticized for its harsh treatment of Germany, which many historians believe contributed to the rise of Nazism and ADOLF HITLER in the 1930s.

President WOODROW WILSON played an important role in ending the hostilities and convening a peace conference. When the United States entered the war in January 1917, Wilson intended to use U.S. influence to end the long cycle of peace and war in Europe and create an international peace organization. On January 8, 1918, he delivered an address to Congress that named Fourteen Points to be used as the guide for a peace settlement. Nine of the points covered new territorial consignments, while the other five were of a general nature. In October 1918 Germany asked Wilson to arrange both a

THE GRANGER COLLECTION, NEW YORK

The signers of the Treaty of Versailles, which ended World War I, gathered in the Hotel Crillon in Paris. From left to right are Vittorio Orlando of Italy, David Lloyd George of Great Britain, Georges Clemenceau of France, and Woodrow Wilson of the U.S.

general ARMISTICE based on the Fourteen Points and a conference to begin peace negotiations. On November 11 the armistice was concluded.

The Paris Peace Conference began in January 1919. The conference was dominated by David Lloyd George of Great Britain, Georges Clemenceau of France, and Wilson of the United States, with Vittorio Orlando of Italy playing a lesser role. These leaders agreed that Germany and its allies would have no role in negotiating the treaty.

The first of Wilson's Fourteen Points stated that it was essential for a postwar settlement to have "open covenants of peace, openly arrived at, after which there shall be no private international understandings of any kind but diplomacy shall proceed always frankly and in the public view." Wilson's lofty vision, however, was undercut in Paris by secret treaties that Great Britain, France, and Italy had made during the war with Greece, Romania, and each other.

In addition, the European Allies demanded compensation from Germany for the damage their civilian populations had suffered and for German aggression in general. Wilson's loftier ideas gave way to the stern demands of the Allies.

The Treaty of Versailles was signed on June 28, 1919, in the Hall of Mirrors of the Palace of Versailles. The terms dictated to Germany included a war guilt clause, in which Germany accepted responsibility as the aggressor in the war. Based on this clause, the Allies imposed REPARATIONS for war damage. Though the treaty did not specify an exact amount, a commission established in 1921 assessed $33 billion of reparations.

The boundaries of Germany and other parts of Europe were changed. Germany was re-

quired to return the territories of Alsace and Lorraine to France and to place the Saarland under the supervision of the League of Nations until 1935. Several territories were given to Belgium and Holland, and the nation of Poland was created from portions of German Silesia and Prussia. The Austro-Hungarian Empire was dismantled, and the countries of Austria, Hungary, Czechoslovakia, Bulgaria, and Romania were recognized. All German overseas colonies in China, the Pacific, and Africa were taken over by Great Britain, France, Japan, and other Allied nations.

France, which had been invaded by Germany in 1871 and 1914, was adamant about disarming Germany. The treaty reduced the German army to 100,000 troops, eliminated the general staff, and prohibited Germany from manufacturing armored cars, tanks, submarines, airplanes, and poison gas. In addition, all German territory west of the Rhine River (Rhineland), was established as a demilitarized zone.

The Treaty of Versailles also created the League of Nations, which was to enforce the treaty and encourage the peaceful resolution of international conflicts. Many Americans were opposed to joining the League of Nations, however, and despite Wilson's efforts, the U.S. Senate failed to ratify the treaty. Hence, instead of signing the Treaty of Versailles, the United States signed a separate peace treaty with Germany, the Treaty of Berlin, on July 2, 1921. This treaty conformed to the Versailles agreement except for the omission of the League of Nations provisions.

The Treaty of Versailles has been criticized as a vindictive agreement that violated the spirit of Wilson's Fourteen Points. The harsh terms hurt the German economy in the 1920s and contributed to the popularity of leaders such as Hitler who argued for the restoration of German honor through remilitarization.

TREBLE DAMAGES A recovery of three times the amount of actual financial losses suffered which is provided by statute for certain kinds of cases.

The statute authorizing treble damages directs the judge to multiply by three the amount of monetary DAMAGES awarded by the jury in those cases and to give JUDGMENT to the plaintiff in that tripled amount. The CLAYTON ACT (15 U.S.C.A. § 12 et seq.), for example, directs that treble damages be awarded for violations of ANTITRUST LAWS.

TRENT AFFAIR The *Trent* affair, which occurred during the early years of the Civil War, challenged the traditional concepts of freedom of the seas and the rights of neutrals and almost

Early in the Civil War, the Union warship San Jacinto *intercepted the British ship* Trent. *Two Confederate emissaries bound for England were captured and brought aboard the* San Jacinto.

precipitated a war between the United States and Great Britain.

In 1861, the newly established Confederacy appointed two emissaries to represent its government overseas. James Murray Mason was assigned to London, England, and John Slidell was sent to Paris, France. The two envoys successfully made their way to Havana, Cuba, where they boarded an English ship, the *Trent*, which set sail on November 7. The next day, the *San Jacinto*, a Union warship under the command of Captain Charles Wilkes, an officer in the U.S. Navy, intercepted the *Trent*. Wilkes acted upon his own authority and detained the English ship. He ordered a search of the *Trent*, and when the two Confederates were discovered, he ordered them to be transferred to the *San Jacinto* and transported to Fort Warren in Boston. The *Trent* was allowed to continue without further interference.

Although Wilkes was praised by Northerners and several members of the cabinet of President ABRAHAM LINCOLN for his action against the Confederacy, his disregard for their rights as a neutral power angered the English. Wilkes had made the error of conducting the operation by himself rather than ordering the ship to port to undergo legal proceedings to determine if England had violated the rules of neutrality. Since Wilkes had not followed established legal procedure, he had no right to remove any cargo, human or otherwise, from another vessel.

English tempers flared and threats of war were issued. The English demands included a public apology and the release of the two Confederates. The English representative to the United States awaited orders to return to England if these demands were not met.

In England, however, news of the impending death of Prince Albert diverted attention from the *Trent* affair. When the English demands were received in the United States, Charles Francis Adams, U.S. diplomat to England, was ordered to explain to the English that Wilkes had acted of his own accord, without instructions from the government. In the meantime, Secretary of State William H. Seward studied the matter carefully; he knew that Wilkes's conduct had not been correct. Seward was also aware that he had two choices: war with England or release of the incarcerated Confederates. In a communiqué to England, Seward admitted the mistake of Wilkes, reported the release of Mason and Slidell, and upheld the sanctity of freedom of the seas. War with England was averted, and navigation rights were maintained.

See also ADMIRALTY AND MARITIME LAW.

TRESPASS An unlawful intrusion that interferes with one's person or PROPERTY.

TORT LAW originated in England with the ACTION of trespass. In modern law trespass is an unauthorized entry upon land, but initially trespass was any wrongful conduct directly causing injury or loss. A trespass gives the aggrieved party the right to bring a civil lawsuit and collect DAMAGES as compensation for the interference and for any harm suffered. Trespass is an intentional tort and in some circumstances can be punished as a crime.

Common-Law Form of Action Trespass is one of the ancient FORMS OF ACTION that arose under the COMMON LAW of England as early as the thirteenth century. It was considered a breach of the king's peace for which the wrongdoer might be summoned before the king's court to respond in a civil proceeding for the harm caused. Because the king's courts were primarily interested in land ownership disputes, the more personal action of trespass developed slowly at first.

Around the middle of the fourteenth century, the clerks of the king's courts began routinely giving out WRITS that permitted a plaintiff to begin a trespass action. Before that time criminal remedies for trespass were more common. The courts were primarily concerned with punishing the trespasser rather than compensating the landowner. From the beginning a defendant convicted of trespass was fined; a defendant who could not pay the fine was imprisoned. The fine in this criminal proceeding developed into an award of damages to the plaintiff. This change marked the beginning of tort action under the common law.

As trespass developed into a means of compelling the defendant to compensate the plaintiff for injury to his property interests, it took two forms: an action for trespass on REAL PROPERTY and an action for injury to PERSONAL PROPERTY.

In an action for trespass on land, the plaintiff could recover damages for the defendant's forcible interference with the plaintiff's possession of his land. Even the slightest entry onto the land without the plaintiff's permission gave the plaintiff the right to damages in a nominal sum.

An action for trespass to CHATTELS was available to seek damages from anyone who had intentionally or forcibly injured personal property. The injury could include carrying off the plaintiff's property or harming it, destroying it, or keeping the plaintiff from holding or using it as she had a right to do.

Later, an additional CAUSE OF ACTION was recognized for injuries that were not forcible or direct. This action was called *trespass on the case* or *action on the case* because its purpose was to protect the plaintiff's legal rights, rather than her person or land, from intentional force.

Over the years the courts recognized other forms of actions that permitted recovery for injuries that did not exactly fit the forms of trespass or trespass on the case. Eventually, writs were also issued for these various types of actions. For example, a *continuing trespass* was a permanent invasion of someone's rights, as when a building overhung a neighbor's land. A *trespass for mesne profits* was a form of action against a tenant who wrongfully took profits, such as a CROP, from the property while he occupied it. A *trespass to try title* was a form of action to recover possession of real property from someone who was not entitled to it. This action "tried title" so that the court could order POSSESSION for the person who turned out to be the rightful owner.

These common-law forms of action had serious shortcomings. A plaintiff who could not fit her COMPLAINT exactly into one of the forms could not proceed in court, even if she obviously had been wronged. Modern law has remedied this situation by enacting rules of CIVIL PROCEDURE that replace the common-law forms with more flexible ways of wording a civil complaint. The various trespass actions are still important, however, because modern PROPERTY LAWS are largely based on them. The rights protected remain in force, and frequently even the old names are still used.

Trespass to Land   In modern law the word *trespass* is used most commonly to describe the intentional and wrongful invasion of another's real property. An action for trespass can be maintained by the owner or anyone else who has a lawful right to occupy the real property, such as the owner of an apartment building, a TENANT, or a member of the tenant's family. The action can be maintained against anyone who interferes with the right of ownership or possession, whether the invasion is by a person or by something that a person has set in motion. For example, a hunter who enters fields where hunting is forbidden is a trespasser, and so is a company that throws rocks onto neighboring land when it is blasting.

Every unlawful entry onto another's property is trespass, even if no harm is done to the property. A person who has a right to come onto the land may become a trespasser by committing wrongful acts after entry. For example, a mail carrier has a privilege to walk up the sidewalk at a private home but is not entitled to go through the front door. A person who enters property with permission but stays after he has been told to leave also commits a trespass. Moreover, an intruder cannot defend himself in a trespass action by showing that the plaintiff did not have a completely valid legal right to the property. The reason for all of these rules is that the action of trespass exists to prevent BREACHES OF THE PEACE by protecting the quiet possession of real property.

In a trespass action, the plaintiff does not have to show that the defendant intended to trespass but only that she intended to do whatever caused the trespass. It is no excuse that the trespasser mistakenly believed that she was not doing wrong or that she did not understand the wrong. A child can be a trespasser, as can a person who thought that she was on her own land.

Injury to the property is not necessary for the defendant to be guilty of trespass, although the amount of damages awarded will generally reflect the extent of the harm done to the property. For example, a person could sue bird-watchers who intruded onto his land but would probably receive only NOMINAL DAMAGES. A farmer who discovers several persons cutting down valuable hardwood trees for firewood could recover a more substantial amount in damages.

Trespassers are responsible for nearly all the consequences of their unlawful entry, including those that could not have been anticipated or are the result of nothing more wrongful than the trespass itself. For example, if a trespasser carefully lights a fire in the stove of a lake cabin and a fault in the stove causes the cabin to burn down, the trespasser can be held liable for the fire damage.

Courts have had to consider how far above and below the ground the right to possession of land extends. In *United States v. Causby*, 328 U.S. 256, 66 S. Ct. 1062, 90 L. Ed. 1206 (1946), the U.S. Supreme Court held the federal government liable for harm caused to a poultry business by low-altitude military flights. The Court concluded that because the airspace above land is like a public highway, ordinary airplane flights cannot commit trespass. In this case, however, the planes were flying below levels approved by federal law and regulations, so the government was held responsible. Its activity was a "taking" of private property, for which the FIFTH AMENDMENT to the U.S. Constitution requires JUST COMPENSATION. See also EMINENT DOMAIN.

It may be a trespass to tunnel or mine under another person's property, to force water or soil under the property, or to build a foundation that crosses under the BOUNDARY line. Underground encroachments are usually an exception to the rule that no harm needs to be shown in order to prove a trespass. Generally, trespass actions are permitted only where there is some damage to the surface or some interference with the owner's rights to use her property.

Trespass by One Entitled to Possession In nearly all states, a person who forcibly enters onto land is guilty of a crime, even if that person is entitled to possession of the land. To discourage self-help that is likely to lead to violence, the states provide legal procedures for the rightful owner to use to recover his land. For example, a LANDLORD who personally tries to eject a tenant creates a potentially explosive situation. The real property will not disappear, so the public is entitled to insist that the true owner or rightful possessor pursue his remedies in court and endure the temporary inconvenience of legal procedures. Many states do not let the illegal occupant sue the rightful owner in trespass for his forcible entry, but the occupant can sue for ASSAULT AND BATTERY or damage to her personal property.

Continuing Trespass A trespass is continuing when the offending object remains on the property of the person entitled to possession. A building or fence that encroaches on a neighbor's property creates a continuing trespass, as does a tree that has fallen across a boundary line. Some courts have allowed a series of lawsuits where there is a continuing trespass, but the prevailing view is that the dispute should be settled in its entirety in one action.

The remedies can be tailored to the particular kind of harm done. A defendant might have to pay damages to repair the plaintiff's property or compensate the plaintiff for the diminished value of her property. Where a structure or object is on the plaintiff's property, the defendant may be ordered to remove it.

Defenses In some cases a defendant is not liable for trespass even though she has intruded onto another's property. Public officials, for example, do not have any special right to trespass, but a housing inspector with a SEARCH WARRANT can enter someone's building whether the owner consents or not. A police officer can pursue a criminal across private property without liability for trespass. The police officer's defense to a claim of trespass is her lawful authority to enter.

A hotel employee who enters a guest's room to perform housekeeping services is not a trespasser because it is customary to assume that guests want such services. If charged with trespass by the guest, the hotel would claim the guest consented to the employee's entry.

A landlord does not have the right to enter a tenant's apartment whenever the landlord wants. However, the landlord usually has the right to enter to make repairs. The landlord must arrange a reasonable time for the repairs, but the tenant's consent to this arrangement is either contained in the LEASE or is implied from the landlord's assumption of responsibility for making repairs inside the apartment. See also LANDLORD AND TENANT.

A person is not guilty of trespass if he goes onto another's land to protect life or property during an emergency. For example, a passerby who sees someone pointing a gun at another person may cross onto the property and subdue the person with the gun. Someone at the scene of a traffic accident may go onto private property to pull a victim from one of the vehicles.

Permission to enter someone else's property can be given either by CONSENT or by LICENSE. Consent simply means giving permission or allowing another onto the land. For example, a person who lets neighborhood children play in her yard has given consent. Consent may be implied from all the circumstances. A homeowner who calls a house painter and asks for an estimate cannot later complain that the painter trespassed by coming into her yard.

Sometimes consent to enter another's land is called a license, or legal permission. This license is not necessarily a CERTIFICATE and may be in the form of a written agreement. For example, an electric company might have a license to enter private property to maintain electrical lines or to read the electric meter. The employees cannot act unreasonably when they make repairs, and they and the company are liable for any damage they cause to the property.

Duty to Trespassers   A homeowner is limited in what he can do to protect his family and property from trespassers. The homeowner cannot shoot children who keep cutting across the lawn or set traps or deadly spring-operated guns to kill anyone who trespasses on the property. DEADLY FORCE in any manner is generally not justifiable except in SELF-DEFENSE while preventing a violent FELONY. Mere trespass is not a felony.

The owner or person in possession of real property can be held liable if guests are injured on the property because of the owner's NEGLIGENCE. A property owner generally does not have the same duty to make the premises safe for a trespasser, however. A trespasser assumes the risk of being injured by an unguarded excavation, a fence accidentally electrified by a falling wire, or a broken stair. The occupant of real property has a duty only to refrain from intentionally injuring a trespasser on the premises.

These general rules have several exceptions, however. A property owner who knows that people frequently trespass at a particular place on his land must act affirmatively to keep them out or exercise care to prevent their injury. If the trespasser is a child, most states require an occupant of land to be more careful because a child cannot always be expected to understand and appreciate dangers. Therefore, if the property owner has a swimming pool, the law would classify this as an *attractive nuisance* that could be expected to cause harm to a child. The property owner must take reasonable precautions to prevent a trespassing child from harm. In this case the erection of a fence around the swimming pool would likely shield the property owner from LIABILITY if a child trespassed and drowned in the pool.

Criminal Trespass   At common law a trespass was not criminal unless it was accomplished by violence or breached the peace.

Some modern statutes make any unlawful entry onto another's property a crime. When the trespass involves violence or injury to a person or property, it is always considered criminal, and penalties may be increased for more serious or malicious acts. Criminal intent may have to be proved to convict under some statutes, but in some states trespass is a criminal offense regardless of the defendant's intent.

Some statutes consider a trespass criminal only if the defendant has an unlawful purpose in entering or remaining in the place where he has no right to be. The unlawful purpose may be an attempt to disrupt a government office, THEFT, or ARSON. Statutes in some states specify that a trespass is not criminal until after a warning, either spoken or by posted signs, has been given to the trespasser. Criminal trespass is punishable by fine or imprisonment or both.

TRESPASS TO TRY TITLE 📖 Another name for an EJECTMENT action to recover possession of land wrongfully occupied by a defendant. 📖

TRIAL 📖 A judicial examination and determination of facts and legal issues arising between parties to a civil or criminal ACTION. 📖

In the United States, the trial is the principal method for resolving legal disputes that parties cannot settle by themselves or through less formal methods. The chief purpose of a trial is to secure fair and impartial administration of justice between the parties to the action. A trial seeks to ascertain the truth of the matters in issue between the parties and to apply the law to those matters. Also, a trial provides a final legal determination of the dispute between the parties.

The two main types of trials are civil trials and criminal trials. Civil trials resolve CIVIL ACTIONS, which are brought to enforce, redress, or protect private rights. In general, all types of actions other than criminal actions are civil actions. In a criminal trial, a person charged with a crime is found guilty or not guilty and sentenced. The government brings a criminal action on behalf of the citizens to punish an infraction of the criminal laws.

The cornerstone of the legal system in the United States is the JURY trial. Many of the opinions of the U.S. Supreme Court, which set forth the law of the land, are based on the issues and disputes raised in jury trials. The jury trial method of resolving disputes is premised on the belief that justice is best achieved by pitting the parties against each other as adversaries, with each PARTY advocating its own version of the truth. Under the ADVERSARY SYSTEM, the jury, a group of citizens from the community, decides which facts in dispute are true. A judge presides at the trial and determines and applies the law. At the end of the trial, the judge will enter a JUDGMENT that constitutes the decision of the court. The parties must adhere to the judgment of the court.

Not all trials are jury trials. A case may also be tried before a judge. This is known as a court trial or a BENCH TRIAL. A court trial is basically identical to a jury trial, except the judge decides both the facts and the law applicable to the action. A criminal defendant is always entitled to a trial by jury. Also, COMMON-LAW civil claims usually are tried by jury. Often, however, actions created by statute may be tried only before the court. In some court trials, the court will have an advisory jury. The advisory jury observes the proceedings just as an ordinary jury would, but the judge need not accept the advisory jury's VERDICT.

Historical Background   The first settlers from England brought the jury trial to the United States because King James declared that certain crimes in the colonies were to be tried before juries. Jury trials were introduced in the Massachusetts Bay Colony in 1628. In early civil trials, the parties could choose, by mutual consent, a jury or court trial. Criminal defendants could also choose a jury or court trial. By the late 1600s, several states were holding jury trials, but jury trials were unavailable to many citizens.

During the revolutionary period, many documents noted the importance of jury trials. The colonists feared that they could not get a fair trial before a judge who usually was appointed by the king or his representatives. The First CONTINENTAL CONGRESS declared in 1774 that the colonists were entitled to the "great and inestimable privilege of being tried by their peers of the vicinage." The 1775 Declaration of Causes and Necessities and Taking Up Arms specifically noted the deprivation of jury trials as a justification for forcibly resisting English rule. The DECLARATION OF INDEPENDENCE noted that many colonists were not permitted jury trials.

The constitution of Virginia, which is considered the first written constitution of modern republican government, contained a bill of rights providing for a jury of twelve and a unanimous verdict in criminal cases, and trial by jury in civil cases. After several other states adopted similar provisions in their constitutions, the U.S. Constitution was drafted to require trial by jury in criminal cases. Although the Constitution did not provide for jury trials in civil cases, the first Congress incorporated

trial by jury in civil cases into the BILL OF RIGHTS. Since that time, the trial by jury has become universal in the courts of the United States, although juries are not used in all cases.

Pretrial Matters   Technically, a trial begins after the preliminary matters in the action have been resolved and the jury or court is ready to begin the examination of the facts. The trial ends when the examination is completed and a judgment can be entered. The trial of a jury case ends on the formal acceptance and recording of a verdict decisive of the entire action. Before the trial may begin, however, certain preliminary matters must be resolved.

Venue   VENUE refers to the particular county or city in which a court with JURISDICTION may conduct a trial. The proper venue for most trials is the city or county in which the injury in dispute allegedly occurred or where the parties reside. Venue may, however, be changed to a different jurisdiction. Sometimes the proper venue for a trial is difficult to determine, such as in cases involving multinational corporations, or CLASS ACTIONS involving plaintiffs from many different states. The venue for a criminal trial can change if a defendant persuades the trial court that he cannot obtain a fair trial in that venue. Venue is sometimes changed because of extensive PRETRIAL PUBLICITY about the defendant that prejudices the public to the extent that the defendant cannot expect a fair and impartial jury in that venue.

Pretrial Motions and Conference   MOTIONS may be made by the parties at any time prior to trial and may have a significant impact on the case. For example, in a criminal case, the trial judge might rule that the primary piece of incriminating EVIDENCE is not ADMISSIBLE in court. In a civil case, the judge might grant SUMMARY JUDGMENT, which means that no significant facts are in dispute and judgment may be entered without the need for a trial. Before the trial begins, the court holds a PRETRIAL CONFERENCE with the parties' attorneys. At the pretrial conference, the parties narrow the issues to be tried and decide on a wide variety of other matters necessary to the disposition of the case.

Public vs. Closed Trials   Although most trials are presumptively open to the public, sometimes a court may decide to close a trial. Generally a trial may be closed to the public only to ensure order and dignity in the courtroom or to keep secret sensitive information that will come to light during the trial. Thus, a trial might be closed to the public to protect classified documents, protect TRADE SECRETS, avoid intimidation of WITNESSES, guard the safety of undercover police officers, or protect the identity of a juvenile. Although trials are usually open to the public, most jurisdictions do not permit television cameras or other recording devices in the courtroom. A growing minority of states permits cameras in the courtroom, although the judge still has the discretion to exclude the cameras if she feels that their presence will interfere with the trial.

Trial Participants

Judge The JUDGE presides over the court and is the central figure in a trial. It is the presiding judge's responsibility to conduct an orderly trial and to assure the proper administration of justice in his court. The judge decides all legal questions that arise during the trial, controls the presentation of evidence by the parties, instructs the jury, and generally directs every aspect of the trial. The judge must be impartial, and any matter that lends even the appearance of impartiality to the trial may disqualify the judge. Because of his importance, the presiding judge must be present in court from the opening of the trial until its close and must be easily accessible during jury trials while the jury is deliberating on its verdict.

The judge holds a place of honor in the courtroom. The judge sits above the attorneys, the parties, the jury, and the witness stand. Everyone in the courtroom must stand when the judge enters or exits the courtroom. The judge is addressed as "your Honor" or "the Court." In the United States, judges usually wear black robes during trials, which signify the judges' importance. The judge will conduct the trial with dignity. If the judge feels that a person is detracting from the dignity of the proceedings or otherwise disrupting the courtroom, she may have the person removed.

A trial judge has broad powers in his courtroom. In general, the presiding judge has discretion on all matters relating to the orderly conduct of a trial, except those matters regulated by rule or statute. The judge controls routine matters such as the time when court convenes and adjourns and the length of a recess. When the parties offer evidence, the judge rules on any legal objections. The judge also instructs the jury on the law after all of the evidence has been submitted.

Although the judge has broad discretion during the trial, her rulings must not be arbitrary or unfair. Also, the judge must not prejudice the jury against any of the parties. Unless special circumstances are present, however, a party can do little during the trial if it disagrees with a ruling by the judge. The judge's decision is usually final for the duration of the trial, and the party's only recourse is to appeal the judge's decision after the trial has ended.

Parties In a trial, the term *party* refers to an individual, organization, or government that participates in the trial and has an interest in the trial's outcome. The main parties to a lawsuit are the PLAINTIFF and the DEFENDANT. In a civil trial, the plaintiff initiates the lawsuit and seeks a REMEDY from the court for private civil wrongs allegedly committed by the defendant or defendants. There may be more than one plaintiff in a civil trial if they ALLEGE similar wrongs against a common defendant. In a criminal trial, the plaintiff is the government, and the defendant is an individual accused of a crime.

A party in a civil trial may be represented by counsel or may represent himself. Each party has a fundamental right to be present at every critical stage of the proceedings, although this right is not absolute. A party may, however, choose not to attend the trial and be represented in court solely by an attorney. The absence of a party does not deprive the court of jurisdiction. The court must afford the parties the opportunity to be present, but if the opportunity is given, a party's absence does not affect the court's right to proceed with the civil trial.

In a criminal trial, the government is represented by an attorney, known as the PROSECUTOR, who seeks to prove the guilt of the defendant. Although a criminal defendant may represent herself during trial, she is entitled to representation by counsel. If a defendant cannot afford an attorney, the court will appoint one for her. A criminal defendant has a constitutional right in most jurisdictions to be present at every critical stage of the trial, from jury selection to SENTENCING. Also, many court decisions have held that the trial of an accused without her presence at every critical stage of the trial violates her constitutional right to due process. A defendant may waive this right and choose not to attend the trial or portions of the trial.

Jury The jury is a group of citizens who are charged with finding facts and reaching a verdict based on the evidence presented during the trial. The jury renders a verdict decisive of the action by applying the facts to the law, which is explained to the jury by the judge. The jury is chosen from the men and women in the community where the trial is held. The number of jurors required for the trial is set by statute or court rule. Criminal trials usually require twelve jurors, whereas civil trials commonly use six-person juries. Also, alternate jurors are selected in the event that a regular juror becomes unable to serve during the trial. Longer trials require more alternate jurors. The jurors sit in the jury box and observe all of the evidence offered during the trial. After the evidence is offered, the judge instructs the jury on the law, and the jury then begins deliberations, after which it will render a verdict based on the evidence and the judge's instructions on the law. In civil trials, the jury determines whether the defendant is liable for the injuries claimed by the plaintiff. In criminal trials, the jury determines the guilt of the accused.

Attorneys Every party in a trial has the right to be represented by an ATTORNEY or attorneys, although a party is free to conduct the trial himself. If a party elects to be represented by an attorney, the court must hear the attorney's arguments; to refuse to hear the attorney would deny the party DUE PROCESS OF LAW. In a criminal trial, the defendant has a right to be represented by an attorney, or attorneys, of his choosing. If the defendant cannot afford an attorney, and the crime is more serious than a petty offense, the court will appoint one for him. An indigent party in a civil lawsuit is generally not entitled to a court-appointed attorney, although a court may appoint an attorney to represent an indigent prisoner in a CIVIL RIGHTS case. See also RIGHT TO COUNSEL.

The attorneys are present in a trial to represent the parties, but they also have a duty to see that the trial is fair and impartial. The trial judge may dismiss an attorney or impose other sanctions for improper conduct. Thus, attorneys must at all times conform their conduct to the law. Attorneys must avoid any conduct that might tend to improperly influence the jury. Also, attorneys' conduct is governed by various ethical rules. Within these bounds, however, the attorney may zealously represent her client and conduct the trial as she sees fit.

Witnesses A witness is a person who testifies at trial to what he has seen, heard, or otherwise observed. WITNESSES provide the chief means by which evidence is offered in a trial. Through witnesses, a party will attempt to establish the facts that make up the elements of his case. A witness may TESTIFY on virtually any matter if the matter is relevant to the issues in the trial and the witness observed or has knowledge of the events to which he is testifying. Witnesses are also used to provide the foundation for documents and other physical evidence. For example, if the state wishes to introduce the defendant's FINGERPRINTS from a crime scene in a criminal trial, it must call as a witness the police officer who identified the fingerprints in order for the fingerprints to be admitted as evidence. The police officer would testify that he found the fingerprints at the crime scene and that he determined that the fingerprints matched the defendant's fingerprints.

A witness must testify truthfully. Before giving TESTIMONY in a trial, a witness takes an OATH or AFFIRMATION to tell the truth; a witness who refuses the oath or affirmation will not be permitted to testify. A typical oath states, "I swear to tell the truth, the whole truth and nothing but the truth, so help me God." The exact wording of the oath is not important, however. As long as the judge is satisfied that the witness will tell the truth, the witness may take the witness stand.

A witness who testifies falsely commits the crime of PERJURY. Nonparty witnesses are sometimes not permitted to observe the testimony of other witnesses in order to eliminate the danger of a witness's changing her testimony to make it consistent with the testimony of other witnesses.

Virtually anyone may be a witness in a trial. Generally, a person is COMPETENT to be a witness in a trial if he is able to perceive, remember, and communicate the events to which he is to testify and understands his obligation to tell the truth. Thus, even a young child may be a witness, as long as the judge is satisfied that the child is able to relate the events to which he will testify and understands that he must tell the truth. Similarly, people with mental disabilities may testify at a trial if they meet the above criteria.

One special type of witness is an expert witness. Normally, a witness may only testify as to what she saw, heard, or otherwise observed. An expert witness, if properly qualified, may offer her opinion on the subject of her expertise. Expert witnesses are used when the subject matter of the witness's testimony is outside the jury's common knowledge or experience. Expert witness testimony is often extremely important in lawsuits. For example, in a criminal trial where the defendant pleads the INSANITY DEFENSE, the experts' opinions on whether the defendant was insane at the time of the crime will most likely decide the outcome of the trial.

Support Personnel A number of people may assist the trial judge in conducting the trial. The court REPORTER, also known as the stenographer, records every word stated during the trial, except where the judge holds a conference off the record. The court reporter prepares an official TRANSCRIPT of the trial if a party requests it. The BAILIFF is an officer of the court who keeps order in the courtroom, has custody of the jury, and has custody of prisoners who appear in the courtroom. In federal court, U.S. MARSHALS have custody of prisoners who appear in court. A language interpreter is present in a courtroom when a party or witness is unable to speak English. Finally, most judges have a law clerk who assists the judge in conducting research and drafting legal opinions.

Trial Process

Jury Selection Although a trial does not technically begin until after the jury is seated, jury selection, or VOIR DIRE, is commonly referred to as the first stage of a trial. At the beginning of a trial, the jury is chosen from the jury pool, a group of citizens who have been randomly selected from the community for jury duty. The judge and the attorneys representing the parties question each of the prospective jurors. If a prospective juror is for any reason not able to judge the evidence fairly, he will not be allowed to sit on the jury. This is known as a challenge for cause. A prospective juror may be challenged for conviction of a serious crime, a financial interest in the outcome of the controversy, involvement in another proceeding concerning one of the parties, a business, professional, personal, or family relationship with a party, or any other reason that might indicate bias. In addition to challenges for cause, the parties' attorneys may issue a certain number of PEREMPTORY CHALLENGES against prospective jurors. An attorney may use a peremptory challenge to keep any prospective juror off the jury even if he has no reason to believe that the prospective juror would judge the trial unfairly. A peremptory challenge may not be based on race, however.

Once the jurors and alternate jurors are seated, the judge usually gives the jury preliminary INSTRUCTIONS on the law. The purpose of the preliminary instructions is to orient the jurors and explain their duties. Typically, the judge will summarize the jurors' duties, instruct them on how to conduct themselves during recesses, and describe how trials are conducted. The judge may summarize the nature of the CAUSE OF ACTION and the applicable law. The preliminary instructions usually last only a few minutes.

Opening Statements After the judge gives the preliminary instructions, the attorneys for the parties give their OPENING STATEMENTS to the jury. During opening statements, the lawyers outline the issues in the case and tell the jury what they expect the evidence will prove during the trial. The purpose of the opening statement is to give a general picture of the facts and issues to help the jury better understand the evidence. The opening statements usually last ten to thirty minutes, although sometimes they are much longer. The judge can limit the time for opening statements.

Usually an attorney will present her opening statement as a story, giving a chronological overview of what happened from the party's viewpoint. Although the attorneys will present the case in the best possible light for their clients, the opening statements should be factual, not argumentative. The opening statements are not evidence, and the attorneys should not offer their opinion of the evidence. Attorneys are not permitted to make statements that cannot be supported by the evidence they expect to present during the trial.

Cases in Chief After the opening statements, the plaintiff, who has the burden of proving his ALLEGATIONS, begins his case in chief, in which he attempts to prove each element of each legal CLAIM alleged in the COMPLAINT (civil) or INDICTMENT (criminal). After the plaintiff has concluded his case in chief (and assuming the judge does not dismiss the plaintiff's claim for lack of PROOF), the defendant presents his case in chief. The defendant presents evidence to refute the plaintiff's proof and establish any affirmative defenses. The defendant may also present evidence to support claims he has against the plaintiff (COUNTERCLAIMS) or third parties (CROSS-CLAIMS).

During the case in chief, a party may offer evidence of any type in any order it wishes. Before the evidence may be presented to the jury, however, it must be admitted into evidence by the judge. If a party objects to the admission of any evidence, the judge must rule on the OBJECTION. The admission of evidence is governed by the rules of evidence. Each jurisdiction has its own rules of evidence, but the rules in most jurisdictions are patterned after the Federal Rules of Evidence. The rules of evidence are extensive and require hours of study by trial attorneys. If the judge determines that evidence offered by a party is admissible under the rules, she will admit the evidence.

During their cases in chief, the parties have four possible sources of proof: witnesses, exhibits, stipulations, and judicial notice. The parties elicit proof from a witness through an examination. The party who calls the witness conducts the initial examination, known as the DIRECT EXAMINATION. The party's attorney asks the witness questions designed to elicit testimony helpful to his case. After the direct examination is completed, the opposing party may cross-examine the witness. During CROSS-EXAMINATION, a party will often attempt to discredit the witness's testimony by questioning the truthfulness of the witness or raising inconsistencies or weaknesses in the witness's testimony. In most jurisdictions a party may only cross-examine the witness about the subjects discussed in the testimony given during the direct examination. The party who originally called the witness may continue to question the witness following the cross-examination. This is known as redirect examination and is usually used to clarify or rebut issues raised during the cross-examination. The other party could then recross-examine the witness concerning the testimony offered during the redirect examination. In some jurisdictions the judge may ask the witness questions, and a few jurisdictions permit the jury to ask the witness questions, usually written questions read by the judge.

Witnesses can offer proof in a variety of ways. Most commonly, a witness will simply describe what she saw, heard, or observed to establish events making up elements of a party's claim. For example, in an ASSAULT AND BATTERY trial, the plaintiff might call a witness to testify that she saw the defendant strike the victim. A witness might be used to establish the foundation for the admission of other evidence, such as business records. Many jurisdictions allow character witnesses. Usually used in criminal cases, character witnesses can offer evidence of specific character traits or evidence of truthfulness or untruthfulness. Also, as noted earlier, expert witnesses may offer opinions on matters outside the common experience of ordinary jurors.

Rules of evidence govern the testimony of witnesses. Although the rules are far too extensive to discuss in depth, several rules are important in every trial. Rule 402 states the basic tenet of evidence law: evidence that is relevant to a fact in issue in the trial is admissible, and evidence that is not relevant is not admissible (subject to various exceptions stated in the rules). Virtually any evidence may be excluded from a trial under this rule if the trial judge believes that it will not help prove a fact at issue in the trial. Rule 802 is the "hearsay rule," which prohibits a witness from testifying about statements made out of court, unless special circumstances apply. Such statements are known as HEARSAY statements and are thought to be unreliable evidence. Thus, generally, witnesses may only testify about their own knowledge and observations. The hearsay rule contains many complicated exceptions, however, and is often criticized as being too rigid and overly complicated.

Although the rules of evidence apply to both criminal and civil trials, certain rules have heightened importance in criminal trials. Rule 609 generally prohibits the admission of evidence that a witness has been previously convicted of a crime when the evidence is used to attack the witness's CREDIBILITY. Evidence of prior convictions *is* admissible to attack the credibility of a witness when the prior crime was serious or involved dishonesty or false statement. The judge can still exclude such evidence if a long period of time has passed since the conviction or if the evidence would unduly prejudice the jury. This rule is often important when a criminal defendant with a criminal record is considering whether to testify in his defense. Also, Rule 608 generally prohibits evidence attacking the character of a witness. However, the rule does allow evidence concerning the veracity of the witness. A party may not offer evidence of the truthfulness of a witness, however, unless the other party has questioned the witness's credibility. Finally, although not a rule of evidence, the FIFTH AMENDMENT of the U.S. Constitution provides that a witness cannot be compelled to testify if the testimony could lead to the witness's SELF-INCRIMINATION.

Besides witnesses, EXHIBITS are the other principal form of evidence in a trial. The four principal types of exhibits are real objects (guns, blood, machinery), items used for demonstration (diagrams, models, maps), writings (CONTRACTS, PROMISSORY NOTES, CHECKS, letters), and records (private business and public records). Before an exhibit may be admitted as evidence in a trial, a foundation for its admissibility must be laid. To provide foundation, the party offering the exhibit need only establish that the item is what it purports to be. The foundation for the evidence may come from witness testimony or other methods. As with witness testimony, the admissibility of exhibits is governed by rules of evidence and is within the discretion of the trial judge.

The third type of evidence that the parties may offer during their case in chief is the STIPULATION. A stipulation is an agreement between the parties that certain facts exist and are not in dispute. Stipulations are shown or read to the jury. The purpose of a stipulation is to make the presentation of undisputed evidence more efficient. For example, the parties might stipulate that an expert witness is an expert in her field so that time is not wasted establishing the witness's credentials.

JUDICIAL NOTICE is the fourth method of offering evidence to the jury. If the judge takes judicial notice of a fact, the fact is assumed true and admitted as evidence. Judges take judicial notice of facts that are commonly known in the jurisdiction where the trial is held (the Empire State Building is in Manhattan) and facts that are easily determined and verified from a reliable source (it rained in Manhattan on May 28, 1997). As with stipulations, the primary purpose of judicial notice is to speed the presentation of evidence that is relevant but not in dispute. When a party finishes offering evidence to the jury, he rests his case.

Rebuttals After the defendant rests her case in chief, and any motions are decided, the plaintiff may introduce evidence that REBUTS the defendant's evidence. Rebuttal evidence is usually offered to prove a DEFENSE to the defendant's counterclaims or to refute specific evidence introduced by the defendant. Finally, the defendant may rebut evidence offered during the plaintiff's rebuttal case. This is known as the defendant's surrebuttal case.

Motions Although motions might be made on a variety of issues at any moment in a trial, certain important motions are made during virtually every trial. After the plaintiff rests his case in chief, the defendant usually moves for a DIRECTED VERDICT. (This motion has different names in different jurisdictions. In criminal cases, this type of motion is often called a motion for judgment of ACQUITTAL. The substance of the motion is the same in virtually every jurisdiction.) A motion for directed verdict asserts that the plaintiff failed to establish a critical element of his claim during his case in chief. If the plaintiff has failed to offer any evidence to support an element of his claim, the judge will enter judgment for the defendant. The defendant need not offer any evidence; the trial is over. For purposes of the motion, the judge will consider all of the plaintiff's evidence in the light most favorable to the plaintiff. For example, the judge will consider all of the testimony offered by the plaintiff's witnesses to be true. Although motions for directed verdict are made in virtually every trial, they seldom are granted.

After the defendant's case in chief, the plaintiff may move for a directed verdict on any of the defendant's affirmative defenses and counterclaims. The motion is identical to a defendant's motion for a directed verdict, except that the judge will consider the defendant's evidence in the light most favorable to the defendant. If the defendant has offered evidence to support all of the elements of her affirmative defense or counterclaim, the plaintiff's motion for directed verdict is denied. Finally, either party may make a motion for directed verdict after the close of all evidence. Again the judge considers the evidence in the light least favorable to the party making the motion and decides whether PROBATIVE evidence supports the nonmoving party's claims.

Closing Arguments After both sides have rested, the attorneys give their CLOSING ARGUMENTS. During closing arguments, the attorneys attempt to persuade the jury to render a verdict in their clients' favor. Typically, the attorneys tell the jury what the evidence has proved, how it ties into the jury instructions (which the attorneys and judge agreed upon in a conference held before closing arguments), and why the evidence and the law require a verdict in their favor. Because closing arguments provide the attorneys with their last chance to persuade the jury, the closing arguments often provide the most dramatic moments of a trial. Closing arguments typically last thirty to sixty minutes, although they can take much longer. In most jurisdictions, the plaintiff argues first and last. That is, the plaintiff argues first, then the defendant argues, and then the plaintiff makes a rebuttal argument. Actually, the party with the burden of proof usually argues first and last. This is almost always the plaintiff, but sometimes the only issues remaining for the jury to decide are affirmative defenses or counterclaims raised by the defendant. Also, a few jurisdictions allow only one argument per side, and in a few of these, the defendant argues first, plaintiff last.

Jury Instructions After the attorneys have completed their closing arguments, the judge instructs the jury on the law applicable to the case. In most jurisdictions the judge will both read the instructions and provide written instructions to the jury. A few jurisdictions only read the instructions. The jury will also be given verdict forms. On the verdict form, the jury will indicate how it finds on each of the claims presented during the trial. Sometimes the jury may be given a special verdict form asking how the jury finds on a specific issue of fact or law. The jury instructions normally last ten or fifteen minutes, although they may take much longer in complex cases.

Jury Deliberations and Verdict After the judge has finished instructing the jury, the jury retires to the jury room to begin deliberations. At this time the alternate jurors are dismissed, although some jurisdictions allow the alternate jurors to participate in deliberations. The court bailiff brings the exhibits and written instructions to the jury room and safeguards the jury's privacy during deliberations.

It is largely up to the jury to decide how to organize itself and conduct the deliberations. The judge usually only instructs the jurors to select a foreperson to preside over the deliberations and to sign the verdict forms that reflect their decisions. Jurors sometimes have questions during their deliberations. Usually, they write their questions and give them to the bailiff, who takes them to the judge. The judge confers with the attorneys and sends a written response to the jury. A jury might deliberate anywhere from a few minutes to several days.

Usually the jury must reach a unanimous verdict, although majority verdicts are sometimes allowed in civil cases. If the jury tells the judge it cannot reach a verdict, the judge usually gives the jury some further instructions and returns it to the jury room for further deliberations. If the jury still cannot reach a verdict, however, the jury is deadlocked, and a MISTRIAL is declared. The case must then be retried. Usually, however, the jury reaches a verdict. When the jury reaches a verdict and signs the verdict forms, it notifies the judge that it has reached a decision. The attorneys, if they are not in the courtroom, are called, and everyone returns to the courtroom. The judge asks the foreperson if the jury has reached a verdict. The foreperson responds "yes," and the verdict forms are read aloud, usually by the court clerk. In most jurisdictions the parties may POLL THE JURY by asking each individual juror if he or she agrees with the verdict. Obviously, in a court trial without an advisory jury, there is no jury deliberation or verdict. The judge simply enters a judgment based on the applicable law and his own view of the facts.

Posttrial Motions and Appeal Although a jury trial technically ends when the verdict is read, the attorneys normally file posttrial motions. The losing party often will file a motion for judgment notwithstanding the verdict. This motion asks the judge to set aside the jury's verdict as manifestly against the weight of the evidence presented at the trial and to enter judgment for the moving party instead. This motion is not applicable to a court trial. Also, the losing party will often move for a new trial, claiming that errors made during the trial by the judge require the case to be retried. Usually the judge will conduct a hearing on posttrial motions.

After the judge decides the posttrial motions, she enters judgment in accordance with the jury verdict and the posttrial motions. Once the judge enters the judgment, the court loses jurisdiction, and the case ends in the trial court. If the losing party still believes that errors in the trial caused an incorrect judgment, it may AP-PEAL to an appellate court. The appellate court may agree and order a new trial, in which case the trial process begins anew.

See also CIVIL PROCEDURE; CRIMINAL PROCEDURE.

TRIBUNAL A general term for a court, or the seat of a judge.

In ROMAN LAW, the term applied to an elevated seat occupied by the chief judicial magistrate when he heard causes.

TRIMBLE, ROBERT Robert Trimble served as associate justice of the U.S. Supreme Court from 1826 until his death in 1828. A prominent Kentucky attorney and judge, Trimble was a strong nationalist who supported the views of Chief Justice JOHN MARSHALL.

Trimble was born on November 17, 1776, in Augusta County, Virginia. His family moved to central Kentucky when Trimble was a young boy. He was educated at the Kentucky Academy in Woodford County, Kentucky, before reading the law with two prominent attorneys in the area. He was admitted to the Kentucky bar in 1800 and established a lucrative law practice in Paris, Kentucky.

In 1802 Trimble was elected to the Kentucky legislature. In 1807 he was appointed to the Kentucky Court of Appeals. He resigned in 1809 to return to his law practice. In 1813 Trimble was appointed U.S. district attorney and then returned to the bench when President JAMES MADISON named him a U.S. district judge in 1817. In 1820 Trimble also served on a boundary commission that settled a dispute between Kentucky and Tennessee.

President JOHN QUINCY ADAMS appointed Trimble to the U.S. Supreme Court in 1826, making him the first U.S. district judge to serve on the Court. Trimble's nomination did not go smoothly, however, as he encountered opposition from the Kentucky congressional delegation. The opposition was based on Trimble's nationalist views, which ran counter to the STATES' RIGHTS position of the Kentucky legislators. Despite the opposition Trimble was confirmed.

Trimble joined the Court at a time when Chief Justice Marshall's nationalist philosophy

BIOGRAPHY

Robert Trimble

"THE ILLUSTRIOUS FRAMERS OF THE CONSTITUTION COULD NOT BE IGNORANT THAT THERE WERE, OR MIGHT BE, MANY CONTRACTS WITHOUT OBLIGATION, AND MANY OBLIGATIONS WITHOUT CONTRACTS."

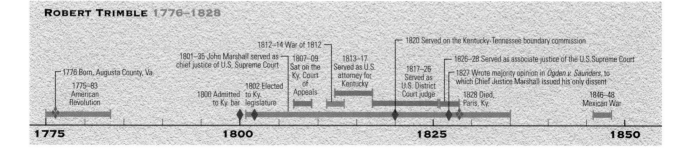

ROBERT TRIMBLE 1776–1828

- 1775–83 American Revolution
- 1776 Born, Augusta County, Va.
- 1800 Admitted to Ky. bar
- 1801–35 John Marshall served as chief justice of U.S. Supreme Court
- 1802 Elected to Ky. legislature
- 1807–09 Sat on the Ky. Court of Appeals
- 1812–14 War of 1812
- 1813–17 Served as U.S. attorney for Kentucky
- 1817–26 Served as U.S. District Court judge
- 1820 Served on the Kentucky-Tennessee boundary commission
- 1826–28 Served as associate justice of the U.S. Supreme Court
- 1827 Wrote majority opinion in *Ogden v. Saunders*, to which Chief Justice Marshall issued his only dissent
- 1828 Died, Paris, Ky.
- 1846–48 Mexican War

1775 ◆ 1800 ◆ 1825 ◆ 1850

was dominant. The Court's preference for construing federal powers broadly aroused concerns that the federal government would become too powerful and upset the balance of power between it and the states. During his brief time on the Court, Trimble adhered to the nationalist philosophy, emphasizing the supremacy of federal laws over state laws. He did, however, differ from Marshall in *Ogden v. Saunders*, 25 U.S. (12 Wheat.) 213, 6 L. Ed. 606 (1827). Trimble ruled that a state BANKRUPTCY law that applied to debts incurred after the passage of the statute did not violate the Contract Clause in Article I of the U.S. Constitution. Marshall disagreed and issued his only judicial dissent.

Trimble died on August 25, 1828, in Paris, Kentucky.

TROVER 📖 One of the old common-law FORMS OF ACTION; a legal remedy for CONVERSION, or the wrongful appropriation of the plaintiff's PERSONAL PROPERTY. 📖

Early in its history, the English COMMON LAW recognized the rights of a person whose property was wrongfully held (or detained). Such a person could bring an ACTION of DETINUE to recover the goods or, later, could bring an action on the case to recover the value of the goods. In the course of the sixteenth century, the action of trover developed as a specialized form of action on the case.

The action of trover originally served the plaintiff who had lost property and was trying to recover it from a defendant who had found it. Soon the lost and found portions of the plaintiff's claim came to be considered a LEGAL FICTION. The plaintiff still included them in the COMPLAINT, but they did not have to be proved, and the defendant had no right to disprove them. This brought the dispute immediately to the issue of whether the plaintiff had a right to property that the defendant would not give over to him or her. For some cases, it still was necessary for the plaintiff to demand a return of the property and be refused before he or she could sue in trover. It was reasonable to expect an owner to ask for his or her watch, for

example, before the repairperson holding it could be sued for DAMAGES. The measure of damages in trover was the full value of the property at the time the conversion took place, and this was the amount of money the plaintiff recovered if he or she won the lawsuit.

Trover proved to be more convenient for many plaintiffs than the older action of detinue because a defendant could defeat a plaintiff in detinue by WAGER OF LAW. This meant that the defendant could win the case by testifying under oath in court and having eleven neighbors swear that they believed him or her. In addition, the plaintiff in trover was not obligated to settle for a return of the property, regardless of its current condition, and did not have to prove that he or she had made a demand for the property if the defendant had stolen it. Since it was the plaintiff who selected the form of the action, he or she was more likely to choose trover over detinue.

Today the ancient forms of action have been abolished, but the word *trover* is still used sometimes for an action to recover possession of personal property, and its history has contributed to developments in this area of the law.

TRUE BILL 📖 A term endorsed on an INDICTMENT to indicate that a majority of GRAND JURY members found that the EVIDENCE presented to them was adequate to justify a prosecution. 📖

TRUMAN, HARRY S. Harry S. Truman served as the thirty-third president of the United States from 1945 to 1953. Truman, who became president upon the death of President FRANKLIN D. ROOSEVELT on April 12, 1945, made some of the most momentous decisions in U.S. history, including the dropping of atomic bombs on Hiroshima and Nagasaki, Japan, the rebuilding of Europe under the MARSHALL PLAN, and the fighting of the KOREAN WAR. A defender of Roosevelt's NEW DEAL domestic programs, in 1948 Truman fought unsuccessfully for a federal CIVIL RIGHTS law that would have outlawed racial discrimination in employment. Though Truman was unpopular when he left office, by the 1960s his reputation had rebounded dra-

BIOGRAPHY

Harry S. Truman

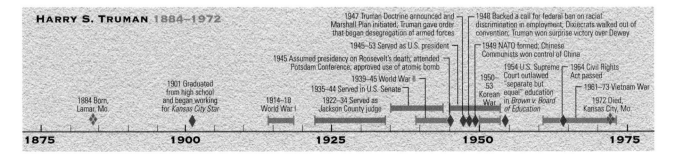

HARRY S. TRUMAN 1884–1972

1884 Born, Lamar, Mo.

1901 Graduated from high school and began working for *Kansas City Star*

1914–18 World War I

1922–34 Served as Jackson County judge

1935–44 Served in U.S. Senate

1939–45 World War II

1945 Assumed presidency on Roosevelt's death; attended Potsdam Conference; approved use of atomic bomb

1945–53 Served as U.S. president

1947 Truman Doctrine announced and Marshall Plan initiated; Truman gave order that began desegregation of armed forces

1948 Backed a call for federal ban on racial discrimination in employment; Dixiecrats walked out of convention; Truman won surprise victory over Dewey

1949 NATO formed; Chinese Communists won control of China

1950–53 Korean War

1954 U.S. Supreme Court outlawed "separate but equal" education in *Brown v. Board of Education*

1964 Civil Rights Act passed

1961–73 Vietnam War

1972 Died, Kansas City, Mo.

1875   1900   1925   1950   1975

matically. Many political historians consider him one of the greatest U.S. presidents.

Truman was born on May 8, 1884, in Lamar, Missouri, the son of a farmer and mule trader. After graduation from high school in Independence, Missouri, in 1910, Truman held a succession of jobs. During World War I, he entered the U.S. Army and distinguished himself as a captain of a gunnery unit during fighting in France. After the war Truman's career choices did not improve. He became a partner in a men's clothing store but lost his savings when the business went bankrupt in the postwar economic depression.

At that point Truman entered politics, developing an association with Thomas J. Pendergast, the Democratic leader who ran Kansas City and Jackson County, Missouri. With Pendergast's backing, Truman became a county judge in 1922, at a time when a law degree was not required to be a judge. Truman proved an able judge and administrator, but anti-Pendergast forces defeated him in 1924. He was reelected to the judgeship in 1926, however, and served until 1934. During this period Truman studied law at the Kansas City School of Law.

In 1934 Pendergast had difficulty finding a U.S. senatorial candidate. He selected Truman, his fourth choice, and in November 1934 Truman was elected amid rumors that Pendergast had rigged the votes in Jackson County to ensure the victory.

As a U.S. senator, Truman was viewed at first as a Pendergast stooge, but he soon convinced his colleagues of his independence and intelligence. An ardent defender of Roosevelt's New Deal programs, Truman entered the national limelight during WORLD WAR II as the head of a Senate committee that investigated defense spending. Truman drew praise for uncovering GRAFT, mismanagement, and inefficiency in the U.S. war production industries.

In 1944 Roosevelt, who was running for an unprecedented fourth term, replaced Vice President Henry A. Wallace with Truman. After his reelection Roosevelt had little to do with his new vice president; before his death on April 12, 1945, he met only twice with Truman.

When he assumed office, Truman faced grave decisions in both domestic and foreign policy as World War II drew to a close. The fighting in Europe ended with Germany's surrender on May 7, 1945. Truman attended the Potsdam Conference in July to discuss the postwar future of Europe, but little was decided besides the division of Germany into zones to be governed by the Allies. U.S. relations with

the Soviet Union began to chill as it became apparent that the Soviets would maintain control over Eastern Europe.

In August 1945 Truman approved the use of atomic bombs against Japan. On August 6 a bomb was dropped on Hiroshima, and three days later Nagasaki was also devastated by nuclear attack. Japan opened peace negotiations on August 10 and surrendered on September 2. Truman justified his actions based on the belief that without the use of the atomic bombs, U.S. troops would have had to invade the Japanese mainland at great loss of military and civilian life.

By 1946 it was clear that an official "cold war" existed between the United States and the Soviet Union. Truman maintained a strong stand against the Soviets and the danger of Communist intervention in Europe. In 1947 he announced the Truman Doctrine, which promised U.S. aid to countries that resisted Communist aggression. Based on this doctrine, Truman provided military and financial assistance to Greece and Turkey to help them to remain independent.

Truman followed up this initiative with the Marshall Plan of 1947. This plan aided the restoration of Western Europe by providing massive amounts of financial aid to rebuild the European infrastructure. In 1949 Truman encouraged the acceptance of the NORTH ATLANTIC TREATY ORGANIZATION (NATO), by which the United States and European nations not under Communist rule pledged mutual protection against aggression.

On the domestic front, Truman faced a difficult situation. In 1946 the Republican party won control of both the U.S. House of Representatives and the Senate for the first time in a generation. Truman fought unsuccessfully to prevent the passage of the TAFT-HARTLEY ACT, also known as the Labor Management Relations Act (29 U.S.C.A. § 141 et seq.), which restricted some of the powers that LABOR UNIONS had acquired in the 1930s. By 1948 it appeared that Truman would not win election to a full term.

At the Democratic National Convention in Philadelphia, Pennsylvania, Truman backed a platform plank that called for a federal civil rights bill that would ban racial discrimination in employment. Many southern Democrats walked out of the convention, formed the segregationist Dixiecrat party, and nominated South Carolina governor STROM THURMOND for president. A left-wing offshoot, the Progressive party, nominated Henry Wallace, Roosevelt's vice president before Truman, for president.

"DEMOCRACY IS BASED ON THE CONVICTION THAT MAN HAS THE MORAL AND INTELLECTUAL CAPACITY, AS WELL AS THE INALIENABLE RIGHT, TO GOVERN HIMSELF WITH REASON AND JUSTICE."

The Republican party nominated New York governor THOMAS E. DEWEY, who in the early weeks of the campaign appeared to have an insurmountable lead.

Truman demonstrated his political acumen by calling the Republican Congress back into session after the political conventions to consider his legislative proposals. When the Republicans turned these aside, he labeled them the "do nothing Congress" and began a cross-country campaign during which he delighted crowds with his "give 'em hell" speeches. To the surprise of most commentators, Truman beat Dewey by 114 electoral votes.

Truman made little progress on his domestic agenda, which he called the Fair Deal. His second term was beset with foreign problems. The Chinese Communists won control of their country, and in 1950 North Korea invaded South Korea. Truman authorized the sending of U.S. troops to Korea under the sponsorship of the United Nations to prevent the fall of South Korea to the Communist North Koreans. After General Douglas MacArthur led U.S. troops deep into North Korea, the Communist Chinese joined the fighting and pushed the U.S. forces back. Soon the war was a stalemate.

Truman's popularity declined after he removed MacArthur from his command for insubordination—the general had stated publicly that the United States should bomb China. Domestically, Truman took the controversial step of seizing the steel industry in 1952 to prohibit a strike that would have crippled the national defense. In *Youngstown Sheet & Tube Co. v. Sawyer*, 343 U.S. 579, 72 S. Ct. 863, 96 L. Ed. 1153 (1952), popularly known as the *Steel Seizure* case, the U.S. Supreme Court refused to allow the government to seize and operate the steel mills and rejected Truman's argument that he had inherent executive power to issue the seizure order.

In 1952 Truman decided not to run for a second term. He retired to Independence, Missouri, to oversee the Truman presidential library but remained a prominent Democratic leader for the remainder of his life. He died on December 26, 1972, in Kansas City, Missouri.

See also COLD WAR; YOUNGSTOWN SHEET AND TUBE CO. V. SAWYER.

TRUST 📖 A relationship created at the direction of an individual, in which one or more persons hold the individual's PROPERTY subject to certain duties to use and protect it for the benefit of others. 📖

Individuals may control the distribution of their property during their lives or after their deaths through the use of a trust. There are many types of trusts and many purposes for their creation. A trust may be created for the financial benefit of the person creating the trust, a surviving spouse or minor children, or a charitable purpose. Though a variety of trusts are permitted by law, trust arrangements that are attempts to evade CREDITORS or lawful responsibilities will be declared void by the courts.

The law of trusts is voluminous and often complicated, but generally it is concerned with whether a trust has been created, whether it is a public or private trust, whether it is legal, and whether the trustee has lawfully managed the trust and trust property.

Basic Concepts The person who creates the trust is the SETTLOR. The person who holds the property for another's benefit is the TRUSTEE. The person who is benefited by the trust is the BENEFICIARY, or *cestui que trust*. The property that comprises the trust is the trust RES, CORPUS, PRINCIPAL, or subject matter. For example, a parent signs over certain stock to a bank to manage for a child, with instructions to give the DIVIDEND checks to him each year until he becomes twenty-one years of age, at which time he is to receive all the stock. The parent is the settlor, the bank is the trustee, the stock is the trust res, and the child is the beneficiary.

A FIDUCIARY relationship exists in the law of trusts whenever the settlor relies on the trustee and places special confidence in her. The trustee must act in GOOD FAITH with strict honesty and due regard to protect and serve the interests of the beneficiaries. The trustee also has a fiduciary relationship with the beneficiaries of the trust.

A trustee takes LEGAL TITLE to the trust res, which means that the trustee's interest in the property appears to be one of complete ownership and POSSESSION, but the trustee does not have the right to receive any benefits from the property. The right to benefit from the property, known as equitable title, belongs to the beneficiary.

The terms of the trust are the duties and powers of the trustee and the rights of the beneficiary conferred by the settlor when he created the trust.

State statutes and court decisions govern the law of trusts. The validity of a trust of REAL PROPERTY is determined by the law of the state where the property is located. The law of the state of the permanent RESIDENCE (domicile) of the settlor frequently governs a trust of PERSONAL PROPERTY, but courts also consider a number of factors—such as the intention of the settlor, the state where the settlor lives, the state where the trustee lives, and the location of the trust property—when deciding which state has the greatest interest in regulating the trust property.

As a general rule, personal property can be held in a trust created orally. EXPRESS trusts of real property, however, must be in writing to be enforced. When a person creates a trust in his WILL, the resulting TESTAMENTARY trust will be valid only if the will itself conforms to the requirements of state law for wills. Some states have adopted all or part of the Uniform Probate Code, which governs both wills and testamentary trusts.

Private Trusts An express trust is created when the settlor expresses an intention either orally or in writing to establish the trust and complies with the required formalities. An express trust is what people usually mean when they refer to a trust.

Every private trust consists of four distinct elements: an intention of the settlor to create the trust, a res or subject matter, a trustee, and a beneficiary. Unless these elements are present, a court cannot enforce an arrangement as a trust.

Intention The settlor must intend to impose enforceable duties on a trustee to deal with the property for the benefit of another. INTENT can be demonstrated by words, conduct, or both. It is immaterial whether the word *trust* is used in the trust document. Sometimes, however, the words used by the settlor are equivocal and there is doubt whether the settlor intended to create a trust. If the settlor uses words that express merely the desire to do something, such as the terms *desire, wish,* or *hope,* these precatory words (words expressing a wish) may create a moral obligation, but they do not create a legal one. In this situation a court will consider the entire document and the circumstances of the person who attempted to create the trust to determine whether a trust should be established.

The settlor must intend to create a present trust. Demonstrating an intent to create a trust in the future is legally ineffective. When a settlor does not immediately designate the beneficiary, the trustee, or the trust property, a trust is not created until the designations are made.

Res or Subject Matter An essential element of every trust is the trust property or res. Property must exist and be definite or definitely ascertainable at the time the trust is created and throughout its existence. Although stocks, BONDS, and DEEDS are the most common types of trust property, any property interest that can be freely transferred by the settlor can be held in trust, including PATENTS, COPYRIGHTS, and TRADEMARKS. A mere EXPECTANCY—the anticipation of receiving a GIFT by will, for example—cannot be held in trust for another because no property interest exists at that time.

If the subject matter of a trust is totally destroyed, the trust ends. The beneficiary might have a CLAIM against the trustee for breach of trust, however, if the trustee was negligent in failing to insure the trust property. If INSURANCE proceeds are paid as a result of the destruction, the trust should be administered from them.

Trustee Any person who has the legal capacity to take, hold, and administer property for her own use can take, hold, and administer property in trust. Nonresidents of the state in which the trust is to be administered can be trustees. State law determines whether an alien can act as a trustee.

A CORPORATION can act as a trustee. For example, a TRUST COMPANY is a bank that has been named by a settlor to act as trustee in managing a trust. A PARTNERSHIP can serve as a trustee if state law permits. An unincorporated association, such as a LABOR UNION or social club, usually cannot serve as a trustee.

The United States, a state, or a MUNICIPAL CORPORATION can take and hold property as trustee. This arrangement usually occurs when a settlor creates a trust for the benefit of a military academy or a state college, or when the settlor sets aside property as a park for the community.

The failure of a settlor to name a trustee does not VOID a trust. The court appoints a trustee to administer the trust and orders the person having legal title to the property to convey it to the appointed trustee.

If two or more trustees are appointed, they always hold the TITLE to trust property in JOINT TENANCY with the RIGHT OF SURVIVORSHIP. If one joint tenant dies, the surviving joint tenant inherits the entire interest, not just her proportionate share.

A trustee cannot resign without the permission of the court unless the trust instrument so provides or unless all of the beneficiaries who are legally capable to do so consent to the resignation. The court usually permits the trustee to resign if continuing to serve will be an unreasonable burden for the trustee and the resignation will not be greatly detrimental to the trust.

The removal of a trustee is within the discretion of the court. A trustee can be removed for habitual drunkenness, dishonesty, incompetency in handling trust property, or the dissipa-

A sample living
trust

Agreement made the _____ day of _____ , 19____ , between _____ , residing at _____ , as Donor, and _____ Trust Company, _____ , as Trustee.

1. **True Estate.** For the good and valuable consideration the Donor hereby conveys, assigns, and delivers to the Trustee the property described in "Schedule A" annexed hereto (the
receipt of which property is hereby acknowledged by the Trustee), to be held in trust, upon
the terms herein set forth.

2. **Additional Property.** The Trustee is authorized to receive property added to the trust
fund, provided such property is acceptable to the Trustee.

3. **Dispositive Provisions.** The Trustee shall collect all income, and, after deducting the
commissions on income of the Trustee and such expenses as are properly payable from income, shall pay the net income in quarterly installments to _____ .

(Provision should be made for payment of income and for distribution of principal of trust fund.)

4. **Powers of Trustee.** The Trustee shall have the following powers and discretions, in
addition to any conferred by law:

(a) *Retention.* To retain the property described in Schedule A and any property added to
the trust fund, without liability for any decrease in value.

(b) *Investments.* To sell or exchange any property comprising the trust fund and without
being restricted to property authorized by the laws of the State of _____ or of any
other jurisdiction for trust investment, to invest in any kind of property whatsoever, real or
personal, whether or not productive of income, and without regard to the proportion that
such property, or property of a similar character held, may bear to the entire trust fund.

(c) *Real Estate.* To sell, exchange, lease, mortgage, partition or improve any real estate
comprising the trust fund, upon such terms as it may deem proper, and to execute and deliver deeds, leases, mortgages or other instruments relating thereto. Any lease may be made
for such period of time as it may deem proper without regard to the duration of the trust or
any statutory restrictions on leasing and without the approval of any Court.

(d) *Proxies.* To vote in person or by proxy upon securities held by it, and in such connection to delegate its discretionary powers.

(e) *Rights.* To exercise options, conversion privileges or rights to subscribe for additional
securities and to make payments therefor.

(f) *Reorganizations.* To consent to or participate in dissolutions, reorganizations, consolida-
tions, mergers, sales, leases, mortgages, transfers or other changes affecting securities held by
it and in such connection to delegate its discretionary powers and to pay assessments, subscriptions and other charges.

(g) *Mortgages.* To extend or modify the terms of any bond and mortgage; to foreclose any
mortgage or take title by deed in lieu of foreclosure or otherwise; to protect or redeem any
property from forfeiture for nonpayment of taxes or other liens; and generally to exercise as
to such bond and mortgage or such property all powers that an absolute owner might exercise.

(h) *Retention.* To retain any property acquired in connection with the foregoing provisions
whether or not such property shall be authorized by the laws of the State of _____ or
of any other jurisdiction for trust investment.

(i) *Nominee Registration.* To register any property in the name of its nominee or in its own
name or to hold it unregistered or in such other form that title shall pass by delivery, but
without thereby increasing or decreasing its liability as Trustee.

(j) *Distribution in Cash or Property.* To make any division or distribution required by this
agreement in cash or in other property, real or personal, or undivided interests therein, or
partly in cash and partly in property.

(k) *In Solido.* To hold separate parts or shares of the trust fund wholly or partially *in solido*
for convenience of investment and administration.

(l) *Invested Income.* The provisions of this Article shall also apply to any income which the
Trustee may be authorized or required to accumulate and to property constituting investments of accumulated income.

5. **Third Persons.** No person or corporation dealing with the Trustee shall be required
to investigate the Trustee's authority for entering into any transaction or to see the application of the proceeds of any transaction.

6. **Amortization.** If securities are purchased or received at a premium or at a price in
excess of the call or redemption price or the amount payable at maturity or on liquidation

the Trustee may in its discretion, but shall not be required to, use any part of the income from such securities to amortize or restore to principal such premium or excess.

7. **Dividends.** (a) *Allocation.* Dividends received by the Trustee shall be treated as follows:

(i) Regular or ordinary dividends payable in cash, stock, bonds, or other property (including those of so-called wasting asset corporations) shall be income regardless of whether or not such dividends represent either wholly or in part assets of the declaring corporation other than earnings.

(ii) Extraordinary dividends payable in the stock of the corporation declaring the dividend shall be principal.

(iii) All other extraordinary dividends payable in cash, bonds or other property of the declaring corporation (or in stock, bonds or other property of a nondeclaring corporation) to the extent that they represent or are charged against earnings of the declaring corporation, regardless of when earned, shall be income.

(b) *Discretion.* The Trustees shall have discretion to resolve any doubts concerning the application of the above paragraph, or the allocation of any property between principal and income for which no express provision is made in this agreement, and its decision shall be binding upon all interested parties.

(c) *Primary Benefit.* The primary concern of the Donor in creating this trust is for the income beneficiary and the Donor requests the Trustee in exercising the foregoing discretions to take such fact into consideration.

(d) *Dividends Declared Prior to Receipt of Stock.* With respect to the property described in Schedule A and any property added to the trust fund pursuant to paragraph 2 hereof: all dividends declared but unpaid having a record date prior to the receipt of such property by the Trustee shall belong to the Donor or the transferor, whereas all other dividends declared but unpaid and all interest accrued but unpaid at the time of the receipt of such property by the Trustee shall belong to the trust and shall be income, except as otherwise provided in Article Fifth.

8. **Compensation.** _____ Trust Company shall receive, without judicial authorization, the commissions allowed on principal and income by the laws of the State of

_____ to a sole testamentary trustee computed in the manner and at the rates in effect at the time such compensation shall be payable.

9. **Agents.** The Trustee may employ counsel and agents and pay them reasonable compensation, and it shall be entitled to reimbursement therefor and for other expenses and charges out of principal or income as the Trustee shall determine.

10. **Removal or Resignation.** The Trustee may resign by written notice to the Donor during his lifetime or after his death to _____. The Trustee may be removed at any time by the Donor or after the Donor's death by _____ by written notice to the Trustee. Until the accounts of the Trustee are settled and the Trustee discharged it shall continue to have all the powers and discretions granted to it hereunder or conferred by law.

In case of resignation or removal of the Trustee, the Donor, or after his death

_____ may by instrument signed and acknowledged appoint a successor Trustee and such successor Trustee upon executing an acknowledged acceptance of the Trusteeship, and upon the settlement of the accounts and discharge of the prior Trustee, shall be vested without further act on the part of anyone, with all the estate, title, powers, duties, immunities and discretions granted to its predecessor. The prior Trustee shall however execute and deliver such assignments or other instruments as may be deemed advisable. If a successor Trustee is not appointed within thirty days after the giving of notice of resignation or removal, the Trustee may apply to a court of competent jurisdiction for the appointment of a successor.

The Trustee shall be entitled to reimbursement from the trust fund for all expenses incurred by it in connection with the settlement of its accounts and the transfer and delivery of the trust assets to its successor. If the Trustee is removed it shall be entitled to full commissions as if the trust had terminated while it was still acting. If the Trustee resigns it shall be entitled to retain the commissions theretofore taken and to take any commissions then accrued but unpaid.

11. **Revocation.** The Donor may from time to time by instrument signed, acknowledged and delivered to the Trustee, modify or revoke in whole or in part this agreement or the

[*continued on page 154*]

trust hereby created. No modification shall diminish the compensation of the Trustee or increase its obligations without its consent in writing.

[*Alternate Clause Making Trust Irrevocable*] The Donor hereby declares that this agreement and the trust hereby created shall be irrevocable and not subject to modification.

12. **Powers upon Termination.** The title, powers, duties, immunities and discretions herein conferred upon the Trustee shall continue, after the termination of the trust, until final distribution.

13. **Situs.** This trust has been accepted by the Trustee in the State of _____ , and all questions pertaining to its validity, construction and administration shall be determined in accordance with the laws of that State.

14. **Successors Bound.** This agreement shall be binding upon the executors, administrators, successors and assigns of the parties hereto.

In Witness Whereof, the Donor has hereunto set his hand and seal and the Trustee has caused this agreement to be signed and its corporate seal to be affixed by its authorized officers as of the date first above written.

_____ [*Seal*]
Donor

Attest:

_____   _____ Trust Company
                                          By _____

[*Acknowledgments*]

tion of the trustee ESTATE. Mere friction or incompatibility between the trustee and the beneficiary is insufficient, however, to justify removal unless it endangers the trust property or makes the accomplishment of the trust impossible.

Beneficiary Every private trust must have a designated beneficiary or one so described that his identity can be learned when the trust is created or within the time limit of the RULE AGAINST PERPETUITIES, which is usually measured by the life of a person alive or conceived at the time the trust is created plus twenty-one years. This rule of law, which varies from state to state, is designed to prevent a person from tying up property in a trust for an unlimited number of years.

A person or corporation legally capable of taking and holding legal title to property can be a beneficiary of a trust. Partnerships and unincorporated associations can also be beneficiaries. Unless restricted by law, ALIENS can also be beneficiaries.

A class of persons can be named the beneficiary of a trust as long as the class is definite or definitely ascertainable. If property is left in trust for "my children," the class is definite and the trust is valid. When a trust is designated "for my family," the validity of the trust depends on whether the court construes the term to mean immediate family—in which case the class is definite—or all relations. If the latter is meant, the trust will fail because the class is indefinite.

When an ascertainable class exists, a settlor may grant the trustee the right to select beneficiaries from that class. However, a trust created for the benefit of any person selected by the trustee is not enforceable.

If the settlor's designation of an individual beneficiary or a class of beneficiaries is so vague or indefinite that the individual or group cannot be determined with reasonable clarity, the trust will fail.

The beneficiaries of a trust hold their equitable interest as tenants in common unless the trust instrument provides that they shall hold as joint tenants. For example, three beneficiaries each own an undivided one-third of the equitable title in the trust property. If they take as tenants in common, upon their deaths their HEIRS will inherit their proportionate shares. If, however, the settlor specified in the trust document that they are to take as joint tenants, then upon the death of one, the two beneficiaries will divide his share. Upon the death of one of the remaining two, the lone survivor will enjoy the complete benefits of the trust.

Creation of Express Trusts To create an express trust, the settlor must own or have POWER OF ATTORNEY over the property that is to become the trust property or must have the power to create such property. The settlor must be legally competent to create a trust.

A trust cannot be created for an illegal purpose, such as to DEFRAUD creditors or to deprive a spouse of her rightful ELECTIVE SHARE. The purpose of a trust is considered illegal when it is aimed at accomplishing objectives contrary to PUBLIC POLICY. For example, a trust provision that encourages DIVORCE, prevents a MARRIAGE, or violates the rule against perpetuities generally will not be enforced.

If the illegal provision pertains to the whole trust, the trust fails in its entirety. If, however, it does not affect the entire trust, only the illegal provision is stricken, and the trust is given effect without it.

Methods of Creation A trust may be created by an express declaration of trust, a transfer in trust made either during a settlor's lifetime or under her will, an exercise of the power of appointment, a contractual arrangement, or statute. The method used for creating the trust depends on the relationship of the settlor to the property interest that is to constitute the trust property.

Declaration of Trust A trust is created by a DECLARATION OF TRUST when the owner of property announces that she holds it as a trustee for the benefit of another. There is no need for a transfer because the trustee already has legal title. An oral declaration is usually sufficient to transfer equitable title to personal property, but a written declaration is usually required with respect to real property.

Trust Transfers A trust is created when property is transferred in trust to a trustee for the benefit of another or even for the benefit of the settlor. Legal title passes to the trustee, and the beneficiary receives equitable title in the property. The settlor has no remaining interest in the property. A transfer in trust can be executed by a deed or some other arrangement during the settlor's lifetime. This is known as an inter vivos trust or LIVING TRUST.

Powers of Appointment A power of appointment is the right that one person, called the donor, gives in a deed or a will to another, the donee, to "APPOINT" or select individuals, the appointees, who should benefit from the donor's will, deed, or trust. A person holding a general power of appointment can create a trust according to the donor's direction by appointing a person as trustee to hold the trust property for anyone, including herself or her estate. If that person holds a special power of appointment, she can appoint only among particular persons and cannot appoint herself.

Contracts Trusts can be created by various types of contractual arrangements. For example, a person can take out a life insurance policy on his own life and pay the PREMIUMS on the policy. The INSURER, in return, promises to pay the proceeds of the policy to an individual who is to act as a trustee for an individual named by the INSURED. The trustee is given the duty to support the beneficiary of this trust from the proceeds during the beneficiary's life. The insured as settlor creates a trust by entering into a contract with the insurance company in favor of a trustee. The trust, called an insurance trust, is created when the insurance company issues its policy.

Statute Statutes provide for the creation of trusts in various instances. In the case of WRONGFUL DEATH, statutes often provide that a RIGHT OF ACTION exists in the surviving spouse or executor or administrator of the DECEDENT with any recovery held in trust for the designated beneficiaries.

Protection of Beneficiary's Interest from Creditors Various trust devices have been developed to protect a beneficiary's interest from creditors. The most common are spendthrift trusts, discretionary trusts, and support trusts. Such devices safeguard the trust property while the trustee retains it. Once funds have been paid to the beneficiary, however, any attempt at imposing restraint on the transferability of his interest is invalid.

Spendthrift Trusts A SPENDTHRIFT TRUST is one in which, because of either a direction of the settlor or statute, the beneficiary is unable to transfer his right to future payments of income or capital, and creditors are unable to obtain the beneficiary's interest in future distributions from the trust for the payment of DEBTS. Such trusts are ordinarily created with the aim of providing a fund for the maintenance of another, known as the spendthrift, while at the same time protecting the trust against the beneficiary's shortsightedness, extravagance, and inability to manage his financial affairs. Such trusts do not restrict creditors' rights to the property after the beneficiary receives it, but the creditors cannot compel the trustee to pay them directly.

The majority of states authorize spendthrift trusts. Those that do not will void such provisions so that the beneficiary can transfer his rights and creditors can reach the right to future income.

Discretionary Trusts A DISCRETIONARY TRUST authorizes the trustee to pay to the beneficiary only as much of the income or capital of the trust as the trustee sees fit to use for that purpose, with the remaining income or capital reserved for another purpose. This discretion allows the trustee to give the beneficiary some benefits under the trust or to give her nothing. The beneficiary cannot force the trustee to use any of the trust property for the beneficiary's benefit. Such a trust gives the beneficiary no interest that can be transferred or reached by creditors until the trustee has decided to pay or apply some of the trust property for the beneficiary.

Support Trusts A trust that directs that the trustee shall pay or apply only so much of the income and principal as is necessary for the education and support of a beneficiary is a support trust. The interest of the beneficiary cannot be transferred. Paying money to an assignee of the beneficiary or to creditors would defeat the objectives of the trust. Support trusts are used, for the most part, in JURISDICTIONS that prohibit spendthrift trusts.

Charitable Trusts The purpose of a CHARITABLE TRUST is to accomplish a substantial social benefit for some portion of the public. The law favors charitable trusts by according them certain privileges, such as an advantageous tax status. Before a court will enforce a charitable trust, however, it must examine the alleged CHARITY and evaluate its social benefits. The court cannot rely on the settlor's view that the trust is charitable.

To be valid, a charitable trust must meet certain requirements. The settlor must have the intent to create a charitable trust, there must be a trustee to administer the trust, which consists of some trust property, and the charitable purpose must be expressly designated. The beneficiary must be a definite segment of the community composed of indefinite persons. Selected persons within the class must actually receive the benefit. The requirements of intention, trustee, and res in a charitable trust are the same as those in a private trust.

Charitable Purpose A charitable purpose is one that benefits, improves, or uplifts humankind mentally, morally, or physically. The relief of poverty, the improvement of government, and the advancement of religion, education, or health are some examples of charitable purposes.

Beneficiaries The class to be benefited in a charitable trust must be a definite segment of the public. It must be large enough so that the community in general is affected and has an interest in the enforcement of the trust, yet it must not include the entire human race. Within the class, however, the specific persons to benefit must be indefinite. A trust "for the benefit of orphans of veterans of the 1991 Gulf War" is charitable because the class or category of beneficiaries is definite. The indefinite persons within the class are the individuals ultimately selected by the trustee to receive the provided benefit.

A trust for designated persons or a trust for profit cannot be a charitable trust. A trust to "erect and maintain a hospital" might be charitable even though the hospital charges the patients who are served, provided that any profits are used solely to continue the charitable services of the hospital.

As a general rule, a charitable trust may last forever, unlike a private trust. In a private trust, the designated beneficiary is the proper person to enforce the trust. In a charitable trust, the state attorney general, who represents the public interest, is the proper person to enforce the trust.

Cy Pres Doctrine The doctrine of CY PRES, taken from the phrase *cy pres comme possible* (French for "as near as possible"), refers to the power of a court to change administrative provisions in a charitable trust when the settlor's directions hinder the trustee in accomplishing the trust purpose. A court also has the power under the cy pres doctrine to order the trust funds to be applied to a charitable purpose other than the one named by the settlor. This will occur if it has become impossible, impractical, or inexpedient to accomplish the settlor's charitable purpose. Because a charitable trust can last forever, many purposes become obsolete because of changing economic, social, political, or other conditions. For example, a trust created in 1930 to combat smallpox would be of little practical value today because medical advances have virtually eliminated the disease. When the cy pres doctrine is applied, the court reasons that the settlor would have wanted her general charitable purposes implemented despite the changing conditions.

The cy pres doctrine can be applied only by a court, never by the trustees of the trust, who must execute the terms of the trust. Trustees can apply to the court, however, for cy pres instructions when they believe that the trust arrangements warrant it.

Management The terms of a trust instrument, when a writing is required, or the statements of a settlor, when she creates a trust, set specific powers or duties that the trustee has in administering the trust property. These express powers, which are unequivocal and directly granted to the trustee, frequently consist of the power to sell the original trust property, invest the proceeds of any property sold, and collect the income of the trust property and pay it to the beneficiaries. The trustee also has IMPLIED powers that the settlor is deemed to have intended because they are necessary to fulfill the purposes of the trust.

A settlor can order the trustee to perform a certain act during the administration of the trust, such as selling trust realty as soon as possible and investing the proceeds in bonds. This power to sell is a mandatory or an imperative power. If the trustee fails to execute this power, he has committed a breach of trust. The beneficiary can obtain a court ORDER compelling the trustee to perform the act, or the court can order the trustee to pay DAMAGES for delaying or failing to use the power. The court can also remove the trustee and appoint one who will exercise the power.

Courts usually will not set aside the decision of a trustee as long as the trustee made the decision in good faith after considering the settlor's intended purpose of the trust and the circumstances of the beneficiaries. A court will not tell a trustee how to exercise his discretionary powers. It will only direct the trustee to use his own judgment. If, however, the trustee refuses to do so or does so in BAD FAITH or arbitrarily, a beneficiary can seek court intervention.

A trustee, as a fiduciary, must administer the trust with the skill and prudence that any REASONABLE and careful person would use in conducting her own financial affairs. The trustee's actions must conform to the trust purposes. Failure to act in this manner will render a trustee liable for breach of trust, regardless of whether she acted in good faith.

A trustee must be loyal to the beneficiaries, administering the trust solely for their benefit and to the exclusion of any considerations of personal profit or advantage. A trustee would violate her fiduciary duty and demonstrate a CONFLICT OF INTEREST if, for example, she sold trust property to herself.

A trustee has the duty to defend the trust and the interests of the beneficiaries against baseless claims that the trust is invalid. If the claim is valid, however, and it would be useless to defend against such a challenge, the trustee should accede to the claim to avoid any unnecessary waste of property.

Trust property must be designated as such and segregated from a trustee's individual property and from property the trustee might hold in trust for others. This requirement enables a trustee to properly maintain the property and allows the beneficiary to easily trace it in the event of the trustee's death or INSOLVENCY.

Generally, a trustee is directed to collect and distribute income and has the duty to invest the trust property in income-producing ASSETS as soon as is reasonable. This duty of INVESTMENT is controlled by the settlor's directions in the trust document, court orders, the consent of the beneficiaries, or statute. Some states have statutes that list various types of investments that a trustee may or must make. Such laws are known as LEGAL LIST STATUTES.

One of the principal duties of a trustee is to make payments of income and distribute the trust principal according to the terms of the trust, unless otherwise directed by a court. Unless a settlor expressly reserves such power when creating the trust, she cannot modify its payment provisions. In addition, the trustee cannot alter the terms of payment without obtaining approval of all the beneficiaries. Courts are empowered to permit the trustee to deviate from the trust terms with respect to the time and the form of payment, but the relative size of the beneficiaries' interests cannot be changed. If a beneficiary is in dire need of funds, courts will accelerate the payment. This is called "hastening the enjoyment."

Revocation or Modification The creation of a trust is actually a CONVEYANCE of the settlor's property, usually as a gift. A trust cannot be cancelled or set aside at the option of the settlor should the settlor change his mind or become dissatisfied with the trust, unless the trust instrument so provides. If the settlor reserves the power to REVOKE or modify only in a particular manner, he can do so only in that manner. Otherwise, the REVOCATION or modification can be accomplished in any manner that sufficiently demonstrates the settlor's intention to revoke or modify.

Termination The period of time for which a trust is to operate is usually expressly prescribed in the trust instrument. A settlor can state that the trust shall last until the beneficiary reaches a particular age or until the beneficiary marries. When this period expires, the trust ends.

When the duration of a trust is not expressly fixed, the basic rule is that a trust will last no longer than necessary for the accomplishment of its purpose. A trust to educate a person's grandchildren would terminate when their education is completed. A trust also concludes when its purposes become impossible or illegal.

When all the beneficiaries and the settlor join in applying to the court to have the trust terminated, it will be ended even though the purposes that the settlor originally contemplated have not been accomplished. If the settlor does not join in the action, and if one or more of the purposes of the trust can still be attained by continuing the trust, the majority of

U.S. courts refuse to grant a decree of termination. Testamentary trusts cannot be terminated.

See also HONORARY TRUST; RESULTING TRUST; VIDAL V. GIRARD'S EXECUTORS.

TRUST COMPANY 📖 A corporation formed for the purpose of managing property set aside to be used for the benefit of individuals or organizations. 📖

The SETTLOR (the individual who creates the TRUST) names the trust company in order to ascertain that the property will be handled in accordance with his or her wishes as delineated in the terms of the trust.

Trust companies sometimes act as fiscal agents for CORPORATIONS by attending to the registration and transfer of their STOCKS and BONDS, serving as a TRUSTEE for their bond and mortgage creditors, and transacting general banking and loan business.

TRUST DEED 📖 A legal document that evidences an agreement of a borrower to transfer legal TITLE to REAL PROPERTY to an impartial third party, a TRUSTEE, for the benefit of a lender, as security for the borrower's DEBT. 📖

A trust deed, also called a DEED OF TRUST or a Potomac mortgage, is used in some states in place of a MORTGAGE.

TRUSTEE 📖 An individual or CORPORATION named by an individual, who sets aside property to be used for the benefit of another person, to manage the property as provided by the terms of the document that created the arrangement. 📖

A trustee manages property that is held in TRUST. A trust is an arrangement in which one person holds the property of another for the benefit of a third party, called the BENEFICIARY. The beneficiary is usually the owner of the property or a person designated as the beneficiary by the owner of the property. A trustee may be either an individual or a corporation.

Trusts are useful for investment purposes, and they offer various tax advantages. Another purpose of trusts is to keep the trust property, usually money, out of the hands of the owner. This may be desirable if the beneficiary of the trust is incompetent, immature, or a SPENDTHRIFT.

Trustees have certain obligations to the beneficiary of the trust. State statutes may address the duties of a trustee, but much of the law covering such obligations is often found in a state's CASE LAW, or court opinions.

A trustee is a FIDUCIARY of the trust beneficiary. A fiduciary is legally bound to act, within the confines of the law, in the best interests of the beneficiary. A trustee is in a special position of confidence in relation to the beneficiary because the trustee has control of property that is essentially owned by the beneficiary.

Most trustees possess special knowledge about trusts and investments. By contrast, many beneficiaries are ignorant of such matters. This special knowledge is another feature of the trustee-beneficiary relationship that makes a trustee a fiduciary. A trustee must submit honest reports to the beneficiary and keep the beneficiary informed of all matters relevant to the trust.

Trustees must fulfill the terms of the trust, which address such matters as when and how the trust property will be given to the beneficiary and the kinds of transactions the trustee may conduct with the trust property. Unless the terms of the trust state otherwise, a trustee may invest trust property but must use reasonable skill and judgment in making the investments. In some states a trustee is required by statute to make certain investments under certain conditions, but most states let trustees decide on their own whether to invest the trust property. However, a trustee may not invest property if it is prohibited by the terms of the trust.

In BANKRUPTCY cases a court may appoint a trustee to manage the funds of the insolvent party. Trustees who are appointed by bankruptcy courts are paid for their services from public funds. Trustees who manage trusts for private parties also are paid for their services, but their compensation comes from the creator of the trust or from the trust's funds.

TRUSTEES OF DARTMOUTH COLLEGE v. WOODWARD The legal structure of the modern U.S. business corporation had its genesis in *Trustees of Dartmouth College v. Woodward*, 17 U.S. (4 Wheat.) 518, 4 L. Ed. 629 (1819), which held that private corporate CHARTERS are protected from state interference by the Contracts Clause of the U.S. Constitution (art. I, § 10).

Dartmouth College was founded in 1769 by Reverend Eleazer Wheelock as a school for missionaries and Native Americans. During the 1750s, Wheelock had financed the school with his own money. He launched an extensive fundraising effort in England and Scotland in the 1760s and received generous contributions. However, his benefactors wanted assurances that the money they were sending overseas would be properly spent. To allay their concerns, Wheelock instituted a management structure by which an English board controlled the school's finances and a colonial board managed the everyday affairs of the school and its missions. In 1769, Wheelock obtained a corporate charter from the royal governor of New Hampshire. The charter outlined the governing structure of the school, including the English and colonial boards of trustees.

Dartmouth College in New Hampshire was the subject of a famous lawsuit argued on behalf of the college by 1801 graduate Daniel Webster. Webster won the case before the Supreme Court.

After Wheelock's death in 1779, his son, John Wheelock, assumed the presidency of Dartmouth College. During the ensuing years, various circumstances, including the American Revolution, brought severe hardships to the college. Funding was scarce, land TITLES were uncertain, and the value of the college's ASSETS diminished. Disputes arose between Wheelock and the colonial—now U.S.—board of trustees over the administration of the college, and in August 1815, a group of dissatisfied board members prepared resolutions to remove Wheelock from office. A struggle for control followed, and the dissident faction, composed of Republicans who wanted the state of New Hampshire to control the school, enlisted the support of the legislature. In December 1816, the legislature passed a law that renamed the college Dartmouth University and made it a public school controlled by a state-appointed governing board.

The controlling faction on the old board, most of whom were Federalists who supported Wheelock, wanted to maintain Dartmouth College's private, sectarian character. They maintained that the school's charter was a CONTRACT between King George III and the trustees. Because Article I, Section 10, of the U.S. Constitution prohibits states from passing any law that impairs contractual obligations, they argued that the legislature could not alter the governing method prescribed in the charter. The Republicans maintained that because the charter was handed down by the English monarchy before the American Revolution, it had no legal effect in a U.S. court. Furthermore,

they contended that even if the charter was valid, it was not a contract within the meaning of Article I, Section 10, but rather an amendable legislative act.

In February 1817, the trustees filed a lawsuit against William H. Woodward, a former secretary of the old board who had transferred his allegiance and become the secretary-treasurer of the new state-appointed board. The suit claimed that the legislature's actions violated the old board's constitutional freedom of contract, and petitioned the court to compel Woodward to return the college's records, books, and seal, and to pay $50,000 in damages. The New Hampshire Supreme Court ruled against the plaintiffs, holding that Dartmouth College's charter was not a contract entitled to constitutional protection (*Dartmouth College*, 1 N.H. 111 [1817]).

The trustees appealed to the U.S. Supreme Court and enlisted the brilliant lawyer and orator DANIEL WEBSTER to argue their cause. An 1801 graduate of Dartmouth, Webster made an impassioned plea to the Court to uphold the original charter and maintain the school's private character. He argued that the school was created out of the bounty of its founder, and that the founder conferred on the trustees certain rights. Although the institution may have some public characteristics, Webster contended that it was still a private enterprise whose trustees could not be deprived of their property, immunities, or privileges without DUE PROCESS OF LAW. He further argued that a charter constitutes a contract in the fullest sense of the law, because it includes all the elements of a contract: COMPETENT parties, subject matter, mutual CONSIDERATION, agreement of the parties, and mutual obligations. Webster reminded the justices of the dangers of unchecked legislative power. He argued that no less than the future of all private colleges hung in the balance of the Court's decision, and that if the New Hampshire statute were upheld, all colleges would be subject to the vagaries of politics. He concluded his arguments by addressing Chief Justice JOHN MARSHALL: "It is, sir, as I have said, a small college. And yet there are those who love it." Webster's eloquence reportedly moved some observers, including Marshall, to tears.

The parties completed their arguments near the end of the Court's 1818 term. At the close of the term, Justice Marshall announced that the Court was undecided and would continue its consideration of the case to the 1819 term. On February 2, 1819, Marshall read the Court's opinion, which he had written: "The opinion of the court . . . is, that [the charter] is a contract, the obligation of which cannot be impaired without violating the constitution." The Court held that Wheelock and the college's trustees had received the charter in return for their agreement to operate the school under the terms of the charter. This mutual obligation was the basis of the Court's finding that a contract existed and that the contract fell within the Contracts Clause's protection.

Marshall's opinion defined a corporation as "an artificial being, invisible, intangible, and existing only in contemplation of law." According to the Court, a corporation possesses only the properties and powers conferred upon it by law. Dartmouth College was a corporation and, as a party to the contract created by the charter, could enforce its constitutional right to be free from impairment of its obligation.

The *Dartmouth College* case had far-reaching implications. By establishing that private corporate charters are contracts protected by the Constitution, it enabled business corporations to operate under whatever terms are dictated in their charters, without fear of interference by the state. This freedom was an important agent in the enormous growth of corporations in the nineteenth and early twentieth centuries, a necessary adjunct to the development of the U.S. economy. In addition, the case was the first to recognize that a corporation is a "person" for legal purposes, able to sue and be sued. It also established the principle that vested PROPERTY RIGHTS, such as those granted in a corporate charter, fall within the purview of the Contracts Clause. By so doing, the case established that the Contracts Clause protects the right to acquire and dispose of property. This protection, in turn, encouraged economic venture and development.

Although the *Dartmouth College* case is most often cited for its effect on the law of business corporations, it also significantly influenced the development of higher education in the United States. By confirming the autonomy of Dartmouth College as a private institution, the Court ensured that other private colleges would operate free of state interference. The decision probably influenced the growth of public colleges, as the only schools states could legally control were those founded by the states. Finally, by prohibiting the legislature from interfering with Dartmouth's trustees, faculty, and students, the Court, perhaps inadvertently, bolstered the concepts of ACADEMIC FREEDOM and tenure for academic faculty. Webster, in his arguments before the justices, implored them to protect the Dartmouth faculty's "sacred" property rights, to which they were entitled by virtue of their forgoing "the advantages of professional and public employments, . . . to devote themselves to science and literature, and the instruction of youth."

The *Dartmouth College* case was criticized by some as awarding free rein to corporations and usurping state regulatory power. However, the case was interpreted not to prevent states from regulating businesses, but rather to restrict states from interfering with a corporation's charter provisions. In fact, states have always regulated business corporations to benefit the PUBLIC INTEREST. The Court made it clear through subsequent decisions that *Dartmouth College* was not to be interpreted as corporate carte blanche. For example, in *Providence Bank v. Billings*, 29 U.S. (4 Pet.) 514, 7 L. Ed. 939 (1830), the plaintiff argued that its charter implied an exemption from TAXATION, and that a general tax on banks would be a burden on its freedom of contract. The Court held that the *Dartmouth College* doctrine did not prohibit states from taxing banks. Corporations have the legal characteristics of any individual, and all individuals are obligated to share in the public burden of taxation. A further refinement of the doctrine came in *West River Bridge v. Dix*, 47 U.S. (6 How.) 507, 12 L. Ed. 535 (1848), in which the Court held that all contracts are subject to the superseding power of EMINENT DOMAIN and "the preexisting and higher authority of the laws of nature, of nations, or of the community." That higher authority gives states the right to tax and regulate corporations.

See also COLLEGES AND UNIVERSITIES; CORPORATIONS.

TRUSTIES 📖 PRISON inmates who through their good conduct earn a certain measure of freedom in and around the prison in exchange for assuming certain responsibilities. 📖

A prison trusty might, for example, be charged with the responsibility of maintaining order among fellow inmates.

TRUST RECEIPT 📖 A document by which one individual lends money to purchase something and the borrower promises to hold the item for the benefit of the lender until such time as the DEBT is paid. 📖

A trust receipt was a device used before the adoption of the UNIFORM COMMERCIAL CODE (UCC); it is now governed by Article 9 of the UCC, which concerns secured transactions. A trust receipt stated that the buyer had possession of the goods for the benefit of the financier. Currently there ordinarily must be a security agreement, together with the filing of a financing statement, to protect a lender's interest in goods purchased on CREDIT by a buyer.

TRUTH, SOJOURNER Sojourner Truth was a nineteenth-century African American evangelist who embraced abolitionism and women's rights. A charismatic speaker, she became one of the best-known abolitionists of her day.

Born a slave around 1797 in Ulster County, New York, Isabella Baumfree, as she was originally named, lived with several masters. She bore at least five children to a fellow slave named Thomas and took the name of her last master, Isaac Van Wagener, in 1827. She was freed in 1828 when a New York law abolished SLAVERY within the state, and with the help of Quaker friends, she recovered a young son who had been illegally sold into slavery in the South.

In 1829 she moved to New York City and worked as a domestic servant. Since childhood she had experienced visions and heard voices, which she attributed to God. Her mystic bent led her to become associated with Elijah Person, a New York religious missionary. She worked and preached with Person in the streets of the city, and in 1843 she had a religious experience in which she believed that God commanded her to travel beyond New York to

"THERE IS A GREAT STIR ABOUT COLORED MEN GETTING THEIR RIGHTS, BUT NOT A WORD ABOUT COLORED WOMEN; IF COLORED MEN GET THEIR RIGHTS AND NOT COLORED WOMEN THEIRS, YOU SEE THE COLORED MEN WILL BE MASTERS OVER THE WOMEN, AND IT WILL BE JUST AS HARD AS IT WAS BEFORE."

BIOGRAPHY

THE BETTMANN ARCHIVE

Sojourner Truth

spread the Christian gospel. She took the name Sojourner Truth and traveled throughout the eastern states as an evangelist.

Truth soon became acquainted with the abolitionist movement and its leaders. She adopted their message, speaking out against slavery. Her speaking tours expanded as abolitionists realized her effectiveness as a lecturer. In 1850 she toured the Midwest and drew large, enthusiastic crowds. Because she was illiterate, she dictated her life story, *The Narrative of Sojourner Truth*, and sold the book at her lectures as a means of supporting herself.

In the early 1850s, she met leaders of the emerging WOMEN'S RIGHTS movement, most notably Lucretia Mott. Truth recognized the connection between the inferior legal status of African Americans and women in general. Soon she was speaking before women's rights groups, advocating the right to vote. Her most famous speech was entitled *Ain't I a Woman?*

During the 1850s, Truth settled in Battle Creek, Michigan, but went to Washington, D.C., in 1864 to meet with President ABRAHAM LINCOLN. She remained in Washington to help the war effort, collecting supplies for black volunteer regiments serving in the Union army and helping escaped slaves find jobs and homes.

After the war she joined the National Freedmen's Relief Association, working with former slaves to prepare them for a different type of life. Truth believed that former slaves should be given free land in the West, but her "Negro State" proposal failed to interest Congress. Nevertheless, during the 1870s she encouraged African Americans to resettle in Kansas and Missouri.

Truth remained on the public speaking circuit until 1875, when she retired to Battle Creek. She died there on November 26, 1883.

TRUTH-IN-LENDING ACT 📖 Legislation contained in Title I of the CONSUMER CREDIT PROTECTION ACT (15 U.S.C.A. § 1601 et seq.), which is designed to assure that every customer who needs CONSUMER CREDIT is given meaningful information concerning the cost of such credit. 📖

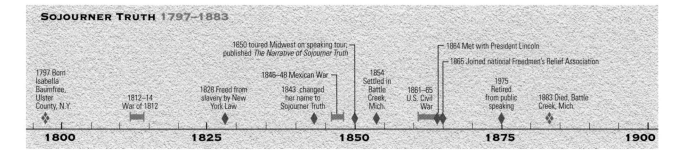

SOJOURNER TRUTH 1797–1883

1797 Born Isabella Baumfree, Ulster County, N.Y.

1812–14 War of 1812

1828 Freed from slavery by New York Law

1843 changed her name to Sojourner Truth

1846–48 Mexican War

1850 toured Midwest on speaking tour; published *The Narrative of Sojourner Truth*

1854 Settled in Battle Creek, Mich.

1861–65 U.S. Civil War

1864 Met with President Lincoln

1865 Joined national Freedmen's Relief Association

1975 Retired from public speaking

1883 Died, Battle Creek, Mich.

1800   1825   1850   1875   1900

The Truth-in-Lending Act requires that the terms in transactions involving consumer credit be fully explained to the prospective DEBTORS. This act sets forth three basic rules: (1) a CREDITOR cannot advertise a deal that ordinarily is not available to anyone except a preferred borrower; (2) advertisements must contain either all of the terms of a CREDIT transaction or none of them; and (3) if the credit is to be repaid in more than four payments, the agreement must indicate, in clear and conspicuous print, that "the cost of credit is included in the price quoted for the goods and services."

This law does not impose regulations upon the advertising media, only upon the prospective creditor.

See also CONSUMER PROTECTION.

TRY To litigate a legal controversy; to argue a lawsuit in court as an attorney; to sit in the role of a judge or jury to investigate and decide upon questions of law and fact presented in such an ACTION.

TUCKER ACT Legislation enacted by Congress in 1887 to remedy inadequacies in the original statutory measures that created the former COURT OF CLAIMS in 1855.

The Tucker Act (28 U.S.C.A. § 1346 [1887]) extended the JURISDICTION of the Court of Claims (now the United States Claims Court) to claims founded upon the Constitution, acts of Congress, or regulations of executive departments. The court was also empowered to entertain claims for liquidated and unliquidated DAMAGES in nontort actions. It retained jurisdiction to hear CONTRACT cases, which it was given under the 1855 measure that created it.

TURPITUDE Conduct that is unjust, depraved, or shameful; that which is contrary to justice, modesty, or good morals.

MORAL TURPITUDE is a term that frequently appears in statutes, especially those providing that if a WITNESS has been convicted of a crime involving moral turpitude, that conviction can be used to IMPEACH his or her CREDIBILITY. Similar statutes authorize revocation of a professional LICENSE for conduct involving moral turpitude.

AP/WIDE WORLD PHOTOS

Elbert Parr Tuttle

"LIKE LOVE, TALENT IS ONLY USEFUL IN ITS EXPENDITURE, AND IT IS NEVER EXHAUSTED."

TUTTLE, ELBERT PARR Elbert Parr Tuttle will be remembered as an influential jurist of the CIVIL RIGHTS era. As judge, and later chief judge, of the old Fifth Circuit Court of Appeals, he ruled on cases from six southern states (Alabama, Florida, Georgia, Louisiana, Mississippi, and Texas) through the storm of civil rights litigation following *Brown v. Board of Education*, 347 U.S. 483, 74 S. Ct. 686, 98 L. Ed. 873 (1954)—the landmark 1954 Supreme Court decision that held racial segregation in public education to be against the law.

Because racial segregation was law throughout most of the South, the Fifth Circuit became the United States' proving ground for civil rights in the late 1950s and 1960s. Tuttle and fellow judges John R. Brown, of Houston, Texas, Richard T. Rives, of Montgomery, Alabama, and JOHN MINOR WISDOM, of New Orleans—known derisively as the Four—faced delaying tactics, political pressures, and all manner of threats as they worked to make the Supreme Court's landmark ruling a reality in key states of the old Confederacy.

The judges of the Fifth Circuit changed the South, and therefore the nation. Under their gavels, JIM CROW LAWS were declared unconstitutional, African Americans were granted VOTING RIGHTS, racial discrimination in JURY selection was curbed, state universities and colleges were desegregated, and equal opportunity in education became a reality.

Tuttle probably reflected on his own schooling when championing equal education for all. He was born July 17, 1897, in Pasadena, California. In 1906, Tuttle's father, Guy Harmon Tuttle, moved his family to Hawaii so that he could accept a position as bookkeeper on a sugar plantation. Young Tuttle, and his older brother Malcolm, were enrolled at the Punahou Academy, in Honolulu, where *they* were the minority students among classmates of native Hawaiian, Chinese, Japanese, and Portuguese descent.

Tuttle returned to the mainland in 1914 to enter college. He received his bachelor of arts degree in 1918 and bachelor of law degree in 1923 from Cornell University.

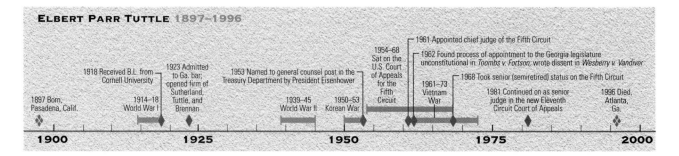

ELBERT PARR TUTTLE 1897–1996

1897 Born, Pasadena, Calif.

1914–18 World War I

1918 Received B.L. from Cornell University

1923 Admitted to Ga. bar; opened firm of Sutherland, Tuttle, and Brennan

1939–45 World War II

1950–53 Korean War

1953 Named to general counsel post in the Treasury Department by President Eisenhower

1954–68 Sat on the U.S. Court of Appeals for the Fifth Circuit

1961–73 Vietnam War

1961 Appointed chief judge of the Fifth Circuit

1962 Found process of appointment to the Georgia legislature unconstitutional in *Toombs v. Fortson;* wrote dissent in *Wesberry v. Vandiver*

1968 Took senior (semiretired) status on the Fifth Circuit

1981 Continued on as senior judge in the new Eleventh Circuit Court of Appeals

1996 Died, Atlanta, Ga.

1900   1925   1950   1975   2000

Following law school, Tuttle and his brother-in-law, William Sutherland, started to look for a promising location to establish a law practice. After investigating several locations in the South, they settled on Atlanta. Also in 1923, after being admitted to the Georgia bar, they opened the firm of Sutherland, Tuttle, and Brennan.

Though Tuttle specialized in tax litigation, he also tried several civil rights cases, including a battle to win a new trial for a black man convicted of raping a white woman, and a challenge to a Georgia statute under which a black man had been sentenced to twenty years on a chain gang for distributing Communist party literature. At a time when pro bono work (work donated for the public good) was unusual, Tuttle frequently represented people who could not afford an attorney.

Tuttle began organizing support for Republican party candidates in Georgia and was acknowledged as a state Republican leader by the late 1940s. He said he allied himself with the Republican party because he was appalled at the whites-only policies of Georgia's Democratic party.

In 1953 President DWIGHT D. EISENHOWER named Tuttle to a general counsel post in the Treasury Department. In 1954 just three months after school desegregation was struck down by the Supreme Court's *Brown* decision, the president asked Tuttle to sit on the U.S. Court of Appeals for the Fifth Circuit.

It was not easy for Tuttle to decide whether to accept the president's offer. Nevertheless, mindful of the social and legal upheaval that would follow the Supreme Court's decision, he chose to take on the challenge. Though he received threats and hate mail for following the *Brown* decision, Tuttle faced frustrated segregationists head on—and in the process helped to change the course of a nation.

Two of Tuttle's early opinions on the Fifth Circuit helped to shape the political history of the state of Georgia. In *Toombs v. Fortson*, 205 F. Supp. 248 (1962), Tuttle found the process of appointment to the Georgia legislature to be unconstitutional and ordered it changed. In *Wesberry v. Vandiver*, 206 F. Supp. 276 (1962), Tuttle wrote a dissenting opinion concerning congressional district reapportionment; on appeal, the U.S. Supreme Court agreed with his dissent. Although Tuttle was in favor of correcting the malapportionment that diminished the power of black votes, he believed that such action should arise from the states, not the courts.

By 1961 Tuttle had become the Fifth Circuit's chief judge. During his tenure, he decided many landmark cases involving Jim Crow laws, voting rights, jury discrimination, employment discrimination, reapportionment, and SCHOOL DESEGREGATION—including the order to admit JAMES MEREDITH, an African American, to the then all-white University of Mississippi in 1962. Tuttle stepped down as chief judge in 1968, taking senior (or semiretired) status. He died June 23, 1996, in Atlanta, Georgia.

CROSS-REFERENCES

Apportionment; *Brown v. Board of Education of Topeka, Kansas*; Integration.

TWELFTH AMENDMENT The Twelfth Amendment to the U.S. Constitution reads:

> The Electors shall meet in their respective states and vote by ballot for President and Vice-President, one of whom, at least, shall not be an inhabitant of the same state with themselves; they shall name in their ballots the person voted for as President, and in distinct ballots the person voted for as Vice-President, and they shall make distinct lists of all persons voted for as President, and of all persons voted for as Vice-President, and of the number of votes for each, which lists they shall sign and certify, and transmit sealed to the seat of the government of the United States, directed to the President of the Senate;—The President of the Senate shall, in the presence of the Senate and House of Representatives, open all the certificates and the votes shall then be counted;—The person having the greatest number of votes for President, shall be the President, if such number be a majority of the whole number of Electors appointed; and if no person have such majority, then from the persons having the highest numbers not exceeding three on the list of those voted for as President, the House of Representatives shall choose immediately, by ballot, the President. But in choosing the President, the votes shall be taken by states, the representation from each state having one vote; a quorum for this purpose shall consist of a member or members from two-thirds of the states, and a majority of all the states shall be necessary to a choice. And if the House of Representatives shall not choose a President whenever the right of choice shall devolve upon them, before the fourth day of March next following, then the Vice-President shall act as President, as in the case of the death or other constitutional disability of the President.—The person having the greatest number of votes as Vice-President,

shall be the Vice-President, if such number be a majority of the whole number of Electors appointed, and if no person have a majority, then from the two highest numbers on the list, the Senate shall choose the Vice-President; a quorum for the purpose shall consist of two-thirds of the whole number of Senators, and a majority of the whole number shall be necessary to a choice. But no person constitutionally ineligible to the office of President shall be eligible to that of Vice-President of the United States.

The Twelfth Amendment was proposed on December 9, 1803, and ratified on July 27, 1804. It superseded Article 2, Section 2, Clause 3, and changed the method used to select the PRESIDENT and VICE PRESIDENT in the ELECTORAL COLLEGE. The amendment resulted from the emergence of the two-party system and the presidential election of 1800.

The Framers of the U.S. Constitution provided for an indirect method of presidential selection. Under this arrangement each state was authorized to appoint as many electors as it had senators and representatives in Congress. This electoral college, as it came to be called, was empowered to choose the president, and the person receiving the second highest number of votes served as vice president. Each elector voted for two individuals without specifying which he wanted for president. It was assumed that the electors would act independently of the people in making their selections.

In the 1790s, however, the two-party system developed, and the Federalist party and the Democratic-Republican party became bitter rivals. The two parties selected their slates of electors, which reduced the independent role of the electors. In 1796 JOHN ADAMS, a Federalist, defeated THOMAS JEFFERSON, a Democratic-Republican, for president, but Jefferson served as Adams's vice president because he had the second highest vote total.

The presidential election of 1800 precipitated the Twelfth Amendment. The two Democratic-Republican candidates—Thomas Jefferson, the presidential candidate, and AARON BURR, the vice presidential candidate—received the same number of votes. The tie threw the election into the House of Representatives. After thirty-five ballots the House chose Jefferson as president, but the divisive battle took so long that it aroused fears that there would be no president to take office on inauguration day.

The amendment was quickly and overwhelmingly ratified. Of the sixteen states then admitted to the Union, only Delaware and Connecticut rejected the amendment.

TWENTIETH AMENDMENT The Twentieth Amendment to the U.S. Constitution reads:

Section 1. The terms of the President and Vice President shall end at noon on the 20th day of January, and the terms of Senators and Representatives at noon on the 3d day of January, of the years in which such terms would have ended if this article had not been ratified; and the terms of their successors shall then begin.

Section 2. The Congress shall assemble at least once in every year, and such meeting shall begin at noon on the 3d day of January, unless they shall by law appoint a different day.

Section 3. If, at the time fixed for the beginning of the term of the President, the President elect shall have died, the Vice President elect shall become President. If a President shall not have been chosen before the time fixed for the beginning of his term, or if the President elect shall have failed to qualify, then the Vice President elect shall act as President until a President shall have qualified; and the Congress may by law provide for the case wherein neither a President elect nor a Vice President elect shall have qualified, declaring who shall then act as President, or the manner in which one who is to act shall be selected, and such person shall act accordingly until a President or Vice President shall have qualified.

Section 4. The Congress may by law provide for the case of the death of any of the persons from whom the House of Representatives may choose a President whenever the right of choice shall have devolved upon them, and for the case of the death of any of the persons from whom the Senate may choose a Vice President whenever the right of choice shall have devolved upon them.

Section 5. Sections 1 and 2 shall take effect on the 15th day of October following the ratification of this article.

Section 6. This article shall be inoperative unless it shall have been ratified as an amendment to the Constitution by the legislatures of three-fourths of the several States within seven years from the date of its submission.

The Twentieth Amendment was proposed on March 2, 1932, and ratified on January 23, 1933. The amendment moved the date on which new presidential and vice presidential terms begin as well as the date for beginning new congressional terms, ended the abbreviated congressional session that had formerly convened in even-numbered years, and fixed procedures for presidential succession if the president-elect dies before inauguration day.

Senator GEORGE W. NORRIS of Nebraska was the primary sponsor of the Twentieth Amendment. He was concerned about the gap between the holding of federal ELECTIONS on the first Tuesday in November and the installation of the newly elected officials in March of the following year. The Constitution specified that the presidential and vice presidential terms should begin on March 4 and the congressional terms on March 3. As a result, senators and representatives who were defeated in November could remain in office and vote on measures for four months, thereby earning the name "lame ducks."

The Constitution also required Congress to hold an abbreviated session in even-numbered years from early December until the next Congress convened in March. These "lame duck" sessions were generally unproductive, as the members engaged in virtually no legislative activity. At the same time, however, these sessions provided the opportunity for defeated members to vote on measures without any accountability to the voters.

Under the Twentieth Amendment, the presidential and vice presidential terms begin on January 20, and congressional terms begin on January 3. The lame duck session requirement was also abolished.

Another section of the amendment deals with presidential succession should the president-elect die before taking office. The amendment provides that the VICE PRESIDENT elect shall become the president-elect and take office on January 20; the amendment also authorizes Congress to legislate on other matters of presidential succession.

TWENTY-FIFTH AMENDMENT The Twenty-fifth Amendment to the U.S. Constitution reads:

Section 1. In case of the removal of the President from office or of his death or resignation, the Vice President shall become President.

Section 2. Whenever there is a vacancy in the office of the Vice President, the President shall nominate a Vice President who shall take office upon confirmation by a majority vote of both Houses of Congress.

Section 3. Whenever the President transmits to the President pro tempore of the

Senate and the Speaker of the House of Representatives his written declaration that he is unable to discharge the powers and duties of his office, and until he transmits to them a written declaration to the contrary, such powers and duties shall be discharged by the Vice President as Acting President.

Section 4. Whenever the Vice President and a majority of either the principal officers of the executive departments or of such other body as Congress may by law provide, transmit to the President pro tempore of the Senate and the Speaker of the House of Representatives their written declaration that the President is unable to discharge the powers and duties of his office, the Vice President shall immediately assume the powers and duties of the office as Acting President.

Thereafter, when the President transmits to the President pro tempore of the Senate and the Speaker of the House of Representatives his written declaration that no inability exists, he shall resume the powers and duties of his office unless the Vice President and a majority of either the principal officers of the executive department or of such other body as Congress may by law provide, transmit within four days to the President pro tempore of the Senate and the Speaker of the House of Representatives their written declaration that the President is unable to discharge the powers and duties of his office. Thereupon Congress shall decide the issue, assembling within forty-eight hours for that purpose if not in session. If the Congress, within twenty-one days after receipt of the latter written declaration, or, if Congress is not in session, within twenty-one days after Congress is required to assemble, determines by two-thirds vote of both Houses that the President is unable to discharge the powers and duties of his office, the Vice President shall continue to discharge the same as Acting President; otherwise, the President shall resume the powers and duties of his office.

The Twenty-fifth Amendment was proposed on July 6, 1965, and ratified on February 10, 1967. The amendment establishes the procedure for replacing the PRESIDENT or VICE PRESIDENT when either office is vacant. The amendment, which was proposed in the aftermath of the ASSASSINATION of President JOHN F. KENNEDY in 1963, has been used during the presidential terms of RICHARD M. NIXON, GERALD R. FORD, and RONALD REAGAN.

Section 1 of the amendment states that in the event of "the removal of the President from office or of his death or resignation, the Vice President shall become President." This section reaffirmed a precedent set by Vice President JOHN TYLER in 1841 when President WILLIAM HENRY HARRISON died after only one month in office. Tyler rejected the concept of serving as acting president during the remaining forty-seven months of Harrison's term. Instead, he announced that he would assume the full duties and powers of the office and become president.

Section 2 of the amendment established a new procedure for selecting a vice president if a vacancy occurs. This section was enacted in reaction to the situation after the Kennedy assassination. When Vice President LYNDON B. JOHNSON assumed the presidency on November 22, 1963, the Constitution left the office of vice president unfilled. Under the Constitution, if Johnson had died or been removed from office, his successor would have been the Speaker of the House of Representatives, who at the time was John McCormick, then in his eighties. Section 2 permits the president to choose a vice president, subject to confirmation by a majority vote of both houses of Congress.

Section 2 was used twice in the 1970s in the wake of political scandals in the Nixon administration. In 1973 Gerald R. Ford became the first person chosen as vice president using this method. Nixon appointed Ford to replace Vice President Spiro T. Agnew, who resigned in the face of criminal BRIBERY charges. When Nixon resigned in August 1974 because of the WATERGATE scandal, Ford became president. Ford then appointed Nelson A. Rockefeller as vice president under the authority of Section 2.

Sections 3 and 4 of the amendment deal with presidential disability. Several presidents have been temporarily disabled during their terms of office, but until the amendment, the Constitution contained no provision for the temporary replacement of a disabled president and provided no guidance as to who should have actual decision-making authority when the president is disabled. President WOODROW WILSON, for example, was seriously disabled by a stroke in 1919 and was totally incapacitated for a number of weeks. His wife, Edith, took on much of the responsibility of the office, an arrangement that aroused sharp criticism.

Section 3 deals with a situation in which the president communicates in writing to Congress that he is "unable to discharge the powers and duties" of the office. The vice president then assumes the role of acting president. The vice president continues in this role unless and until the president is able to transmit a declaration to the contrary.

Section 4 deals with the more difficult situation of a president who is unable or unwilling to acknowledge the inability to perform the duties of the office. The section authorizes the vice president and a majority of the presidential cabinet members to determine whether the president is unable to discharge the powers and duties of the office. If they agree that the president is incapacitated, the vice president immediately becomes acting president. The president may transmit to Congress a statement declaring that no inability exists and resume the duties of president. The vice president and the majority of the cabinet, however, may send a declaration to Congress within four days disputing the assertion of the president that he is able to discharge the duties of the office. If this happens, Congress must vote by a two-thirds majority in both houses that the president is unable to serve. Otherwise, the president will reassume office.

The disability procedures were used for seven hours on July 13, 1985, when President Reagan underwent surgery for cancer. Vice President GEORGE BUSH temporarily assumed the powers and duties of the office as acting president.

TWENTY-FIRST AMENDMENT   The Twenty-first Amendment to the U.S. Constitution reads:

> *Section 1.* The eighteenth article of amendment to the Constitution of the United States is hereby repealed.
>
> *Section 2.* The transportation or importation into any State, Territory, or possession of the United States for delivery or use therein of intoxicating liquors, in violation of the laws thereof, is hereby prohibited.
>
> *Section 3.* This article shall be inoperative unless it shall have been ratified as an amendment to the Constitution by conventions in the several States, as provided in the Constitution, within seven years from the date of the submission hereof to the States by the Congress.

The Twenty-first Amendment was proposed on February 20, 1933, and ratified on December 5, 1933. It is the only amendment to repeal another amendment, the Eighteenth, and the only one to be ratified by state conventions rather than by state legislatures.

Repeal of the EIGHTEENTH AMENDMENT ended fourteen years of PROHIBITION, a failed national experiment that sought to eliminate the consumption of intoxicating liquors. Though consumption was reduced, federal and state law enforcement officials could not prevent the illegal manufacture and sale of "bootleg" alcohol. ORGANIZED CRIME profited from the ban on ALCOHOL, which enabled criminals such as Chicago gangster AL CAPONE to become multimillionaires. Critics of Prohibition argued that the increase in crime and lawlessness offset any gains from reducing the consumption of liquor.

Prohibition was supported most strongly in rural areas. In urban areas enforcement was difficult. Cities had large populations of immigrants who did not see anything morally wrong with consuming alcohol. In the early 1930s, as production and sales of illegal liquor continued to rise, the onset of the Great Depression led to calls for repeal of the Eighteenth Amendment. A legalized liquor industry would provide more jobs at a time when millions were out of work.

At its national convention in 1932, the Democratic party adopted a platform plank calling for repeal. The landslide Democratic victory of 1932 signaled the end of Prohibition. In February 1933 a resolution proposing the Twenty-first Amendment was introduced in Congress; it contained a provision requiring RATIFICATION by state conventions rather than by state legislatures. Though Article V of the Constitution authorizes this ratification method, it had never been used. Supporters of repeal did not want the state legislatures, which generally were dominated by rural legislators supportive of Prohibition, to vote against ratification.

During 1933 thirty-eight states elected delegates to state conventions to consider the amendment. Almost three-quarters of the voters supported repeal in these elections. Therefore, it was not surprising that the ratification conventions certified the results and ratified the Twenty-first Amendment on December 5, 1933.

Section 2 of the amendment gives states the right to prohibit the transportation or importation of intoxicating liquors. Many states enacted their own prohibition laws in the 1930s, but all had been repealed by 1966. The regulation of liquor is now primarily a local issue.

TWENTY-FOURTH AMENDMENT The Twenty-fourth Amendment to the U.S. Constitution reads:

> *Section 1.* The right of citizens of the United States to vote in any primary or other election for President or Vice President, for electors for President or Vice President, or for Senator or Representative in Congress, shall not be denied or abridged by the United States or any State by reason of failure to pay any poll tax or other tax.
>
> *Section 2.* The Congress shall have power to enforce this article by appropriate legislation.

The Twenty-fourth Amendment was proposed on August 27, 1962, and ratified on January 23, 1964. It prohibits the federal government or the states from making voters pay a POLL TAX before they can vote in a national ELECTION. A poll tax, also called a head tax, is a tax collected equally from all voters. The amendment was proposed as a CIVIL RIGHTS measure because southern states had used the poll tax to keep African Americans from VOTING.

Poll taxes were commonly imposed in the United States at the time the Constitution was adopted but had fallen into disuse by the mid-nineteenth century. After the ratification of the FIFTEENTH AMENDMENT in 1870, the poll tax was revived in the South as a way to prevent African Americans, who were mostly poor, from voting. The poll tax also denied poor whites the right to vote. Typically, the unpaid fees would accumulate from election to election, making it more difficult for poor persons to find the economic resources to qualify for voting.

In *Breedlove v. Suttles*, 302 U.S. 277, 58 S. Ct. 205, 82 L. Ed. 252 (1937), the U.S. Supreme Court ruled that poll taxes, by themselves, did not violate the Fourteenth or Fifteenth Amendments. *Breedlove* led to the introduction of the first poll tax constitutional amendment in 1939 and to efforts to abolish the poll tax through state action. By 1960 only five southern states still had poll taxes.

The abolition of the poll tax was not a controversial issue, even at a time of fierce southern resistance to racial desegregation. The amendment was limited to federal elections, however, leaving state elections outside its scope. Following the ratification of the Twenty-fourth Amendment, the Supreme Court abandoned the *Breedlove* precedent. In *Harper v. Virginia State Board of Elections*, 383 U.S. 663, 86 S. Ct. 1079, 16 L. Ed. 2d 169 (1966), the Court struck down poll taxes in state and local elections, ruling that such taxes violated the FOURTEENTH AMENDMENT's Equal Protection Clause.

TWENTY-SECOND AMENDMENT The Twenty-second Amendment to the U.S. Constitution reads:

> *Section 1.* No person shall be elected to the office of the President more than twice, and no person who has held the office of

President, or acted as President, for more than two years of a term to which some other person was elected President shall be elected to the office of the President more than once. But this Article shall not apply to any person holding the office of President when this Article was proposed by the Congress, and shall not prevent any person who may be holding the office of President, or acting as President, during the term within which this Article becomes operative from holding the office of President or acting as President during the remainder of such term.

Section 2. This article shall be inoperative unless it shall have been ratified as an amendment to the Constitution by the legislatures of three-fourths of the several States within seven years from the date of its submission to the States by the Congress.

The Twenty-second Amendment was proposed on March 24, 1947, and ratified on February 27, 1951. The amendment imposed term limits on the office of PRESIDENT OF THE UNITED STATES.

The Framers of the Constitution vested power in a single executive, elected for a term of four years. Participants at the Constitutional Convention discussed the wisdom of limiting presidential terms, but in the end the convention refused to limit the number of terms. The Framers believed a four-year term and an independent ELECTORAL COLLEGE would prevent a president from seeking more than two terms.

President GEORGE WASHINGTON declined the offer of a third term, as did THOMAS JEFFERSON. Once the tradition of serving no more than two terms had been established in the early 1800s, it became a canon of U.S. politics. President FRANKLIN D. ROOSEVELT ignored the tradition in 1940, however, when he chose to run for a third term. He did so in the belief that U.S. involvement in World War II was imminent. In making his bid for a third term, Roosevelt ignored the advice of some members of the Democratic party. In 1944, with the war raging, Roosevelt was elected to an unprecedented fourth term. In declining health when elected, he died in 1945.

After the 1946 election, which produced Republican majorities in both houses of Congress, the Republicans sought to prevent a repetition of Roosevelt's actions. The Twenty-second Amendment was introduced in 1947 and adopted in 1951. The amendment prohibits a person from serving more than two four-year terms. A person who serves more than two years of a term to which some other person was

elected president may be elected only for one full term. For example, if a president dies in the first year of the term, the VICE PRESIDENT who becomes president may be elected to only one four-year term. If, however, the president dies in the third year of the term, the vice president would be eligible to serve a maximum of ten years.

TWENTY-SEVENTH AMENDMENT The Twenty-seventh Amendment to the U.S. Constitution reads:

> No law, varying the compensation for the services of Senators and Representatives, shall take effect, until an election of Representatives shall have intervened.

The long history of the Twenty-seventh Amendment is curious and unprecedented. The amendment was first drafted by JAMES MADISON in 1789 and proposed by the First Congress in 1789 as part of the original BILL OF RIGHTS. The proposed amendment did not fare well, as only six states ratified it during the period in which the first ten amendments were ratified by the requisite three-fourths of the states. The amendment was largely neglected for the next two centuries; Ohio was the only state to approve the amendment in that period, ratifying it in 1873.

In 1982 Gregory Watson, a twenty-year-old student at the University of Texas, wrote a term paper arguing for RATIFICATION of the amendment. Watson received a 'C' grade for the paper and then embarked on a one-man campaign for the amendment's ratification. From his home in Austin, Texas, Watson wrote letters to state legislators across the country on an electric typewriter. During the 1980s, as state legislatures passed pay raises, public debate over the raises reached a fever pitch and state legislatures began to pass the measure, mostly as a symbolic gesture to appease voters. Few observers believed that the amendment would ever be ratified by the required thirty-eight states, but the tally of ratifying states began to mount. On May 7, 1992, Michigan became the thirty-eighth state to ratify the amendment, causing it to become part of the U.S. Constitution.

The effect of the Twenty-seventh Amendment is to prevent salary increases for federal legislators from taking effect until after an intervening election of members of the HOUSE OF REPRESENTATIVES. The amendment is an expression of the concern that members of Congress, if left to their own devices, may choose to act in their own interests rather than the public interest. Because the amendment postpones salary increases until after an election, members of

Congress may not immediately raise their own salaries. All Representatives must endure an election before a pay raise takes effect because Representatives are elected once every two years; Senators need not necessarily succeed in an election before a pay raise takes effect unless the pay raise is approved within two years of the Senator's next re-election effort.

The ratification process of the Twenty-seventh Amendment was by far the longest-running amendment effort in the history of the United States. Before the Twenty-seventh Amendment was ratified, the longest it had taken to ratify an amendment was four years. That measure, the TWENTY-SECOND AMENDMENT limiting the president to two terms in office, was ratified in 1951. The proposed EQUAL RIGHTS AMENDMENT, which would have become the Twenty-seventh Amendment had it passed, failed to win ratification by the required thirty-eight states during the ten-year period Congress had allowed for its consideration by the states.

The gradual manner in which the Twenty-seventh Amendment was passed has raised questions about its validity, with concerns centering on the wisdom of allowing changes to the Constitution without reference to the passage of time. In *Dillon v. Gloss*, 256 U.S. 368, 41 S. Ct. 510, 65 L. Ed. 994 (1921), the U.S. Supreme Court stated a requirement that ratification of amendments be contemporaneous with their proposal, but in *Coleman v. Miller*, 307 U.S. 433, 59 S. Ct. 972, 83 L. Ed. 1385 (1939), the High Court left it for Congress to decide whether a ratification was contemporaneous with its proposal. In *Boehner v. Anderson*, 809 F.Supp. 138 (D.D.C. 1992), aff'd, 30 F.3d 156, 308 U.S.App.D.C. 94 (1994), the District Court for the District of Columbia rejected a challenge to the constitutionality of pay raises in the Ethics Reform Act of 1989, Pub. L. 101-194, 103 Stat 1716 (1989). The court observed that the pay raises complied with the Twenty-seventh Amendment because they took effect after an election had intervened.

TWENTY-SIXTH AMENDMENT The Twenty-sixth Amendment to the U.S. Constitution reads:

> *Section 1.* The right of citizens of the United States, who are eighteen years of age or older, to vote shall not be denied or abridged by the United States or by any State on account of age.
> *Section 2.* The Congress shall have the power to enforce this article by appropriate legislation.

The Twenty-sixth Amendment was proposed on March 23, 1971, and ratified on July 1, 1971. The ratification period of 107 days was the shortest in U.S. history. The amendment, which lowered the VOTING age from twenty-one to eighteen, was passed quickly to avert potential problems in the 1972 ELECTIONS.

The drive for lowering the voting age began with young people who had been drawn into the political arena by the VIETNAM WAR. Proponents argued that if eighteen-year-olds were old enough to be drafted into military service and sent into combat, they were also old enough to vote. This line of argument was not new. It had persuaded Georgia and Kentucky to lower the minimum voting age to eighteen during World War II. The one flaw in the argument was that women were not drafted and were not allowed to serve in combat units if they enlisted in the armed forces.

Nevertheless, the drive for lowering the voting age gained momentum. In 1970 Congress passed a measure that lowered the voting age from twenty-one to eighteen in both federal and state elections (84 Stat. 314).

The U.S. Supreme Court, however, declared part of this measure unconstitutional in *Oregon v. Mitchell*, 400 U.S. 112, 91 S. Ct. 260, 27 L. Ed. 2d 272 (1970). The decision was closely divided. Four justices believed Congress had the constitutional authority to lower the voting age in all elections, four justices believed the opposite, and one justice, HUGO L. BLACK, concluded that Congress could lower the voting age by statute only in federal elections, not in state elections.

The Court's decision allowed eighteen-year-olds to vote in the 1972 presidential and congressional elections but left the states to decide if they wished to lower the voting age in their state elections. The potential for chaos was clear. Congress responded by proposing the Twenty-sixth Amendment, which required the states as well as the federal government to lower the voting age to eighteen.

TWENTY-THIRD AMENDMENT The Twenty-third Amendment to the U.S. Constitution reads:

> *Section 1.* The District constituting the seat of Government of the United States shall appoint in such manner as the Congress may direct:
> A number of electors of President and Vice President equal to the whole number of Senators and Representatives in Congress to which the District would be entitled if it were a State, but in no event

more than the least populous State; they shall be in addition to those appointed by the States, but they shall be considered, for the purposes of the election of President and Vice President, to be electors appointed by a State; and they shall meet in the District and perform such duties as provided by the twelfth article of amendment.

Section 2. The Congress shall have power to enforce this article by appropriate legislation.

The Twenty-third Amendment was proposed on June 16, 1960, and ratified on March 29, 1961. The amendment rectified an omission in the Constitution that prevented residents of the DISTRICT OF COLUMBIA from voting in presidential ELECTIONS.

Article I of the Constitution gives Congress the authority to accept land from the states and administer it as the seat of national government. The District of Columbia was organized under this provision from land given to the federal government by Virginia and Maryland.

The government of the city of Washington and the District of Columbia has been dominated by Congress for most of the district's history. Congress is empowered by Article I to exercise exclusive authority over the seat of government. In the 1820s Congress allowed citizens of the district to vote for a mayor and city council. In 1871 Congress created a territorial form of government for the district. All the officials, including a legislative assembly, were appointed by the president. This system was abandoned in 1874, when Congress reestablished direct control over the city government.

From the 1870s until 1961, residents of the district were denied all rights to vote. Though residents paid federal and local taxes and were drafted into the military services, they could not vote. The Twenty-third Amendment gave district residents the right to vote for president. Under the amendment the number of the district's electors cannot exceed that of the state with the smallest population. In practice, this means that the district elects three presidential electors.

The amendment did not address the issue of representation in Congress. Later, a constitutional amendment that would have given residents the right to vote for congressional representatives was proposed, but it failed to win ratification. In 1970 Congress created the position of nonvoting delegate to the House of Representatives, to be elected by the district's residents.

TYING ARRANGEMENT

An agreement in which a VENDOR conditions the sale of a particular product on a VENDEE'S promise to purchase an additional, unrelated product.

In a tying arrangement, the product that the vendee actually wants to purchase is known as the "tying product," while the additional product that the vendee must purchase to consummate the sale is known as the "tied product." Typically, the tying product is a desirable good that is in considerable demand by vendees in a given market. The tied product is normally less desirable, of poorer quality, or otherwise difficult to sell. For example, motion picture distributors frequently tie the sale of popular video-cassettes to the purchase of second-rate films that are piling up in their warehouses for lack of demand.

Tying arrangements are governed by the law of UNFAIR COMPETITION. Such arrangements tend to restrain competition by requiring buyers to purchase inferior goods that they do not want or more expensive goods that they could purchase elsewhere for less. In addition, competitors may reduce their prices to below market level to attract purchasers away from prospective tying arrangements. Competitors who sell their products at below-market prices for an extended period can suffer enormous losses or go out of business.

Not every tying arrangement is illegal under the law of unfair competition. Four elements

If the owner of this hardware store required customers who purchased a snow blower to also purchase a shovel, this requirement would be called a tying arrangement. Some tying arrangements are illegal.

must be proved to establish that a particular tying arrangement is illegal. First, the tying arrangement must involve two different products. Manufactured products and their component parts, such as an automobile and its engine, are not considered different products and may be tied together without violating the law. However, the law does not permit a shoe manufacturer to tie the purchase of promotional T-shirts to the sale of athletic footwear because these items are considered unrelated.

Second, the purchase of one product must be conditioned on the purchase of another product. A buyer need not actually purchase a tied product in order to bring a claim. If a vendor refuses to sell a tying product unless a tied product is purchased, or agrees to sell a tying product separately only at an unreasonably high price, a court will declare the tying arrangement illegal. If a buyer can purchase a tying product separately on nondiscriminatory terms, however, there is no tie.

Third, a seller must have sufficient market power in a tying product to restrain competition in a tied product. Market power is measured by the number of buyers the seller has enticed to enter a particular tying arrangement. Sellers expand their market power by enticing additional buyers to purchase a tied product. However, sellers are prohibited from dominating a given market by locking up an unreasonably large share of prospective buyers in tying arrangements.

Fourth, a tying arrangement must be shown to appreciably restrain commerce. Evidence of anticompetitive effects includes unreasonably high prices for tied products and unreasonably low prices for competing products in a tied market. A plaintiff need not establish that a business has actually controlled prices through a tying arrangement, as is required to establish certain monopolistic practices, but only that prices and other market conditions have been significantly influenced.

Tying arrangements are regulated at both the state and the federal level. At the federal level, tying arrangements are regulated by the

SHERMAN ANTITRUST ACT (15 U.S.C.A. § 1) and the CLAYTON ACT (15 U.S.C.A. § 14). At the state level, tying arrangements are regulated by analogous statutes and various COMMON-LAW doctrines. At either level both purchasers and businesses that are injured by illegal tying arrangements have two remedies available: money DAMAGES (compensation for pecuniary losses) and injunctive relief (a court ORDER restraining a business from tying its products).

See also ANTITRUST LAW.

BIOGRAPHY

John Tyler

TYLER, JOHN John Tyler served as the tenth president of the United States from 1841 to 1845. A political maverick and a proponent of states' rights, Tyler was the first VICE PRESIDENT to succeed to the office because of the death of a president. Rejecting the concept of an acting president, Tyler established the right of the vice president to assume the powers and duties of president.

Tyler was born into a politically active family on March 29, 1790, in Greenway, Virginia. He graduated from the College of William and Mary in 1807 and was admitted to the Virginia bar in 1809. He began his political career in 1811 when he was elected as a member of the Democratic party to the Virginia legislature. In 1817 he was elected to the U.S. House of Representatives, where he remained until 1821. During his years in the House, he was a consistent supporter of states' rights, believing that the role of the federal government should be limited. Tyler, who owned slaves, objected to the MISSOURI COMPROMISE of 1820, which placed restrictions on the expansion of SLAVERY to new states.

In 1823 Tyler returned to the Virginia legislature, where he served two years. In 1825 he was elected governor of Virginia, and in 1827 he was elected to the U.S. Senate.

During his nine years in the Senate, Tyler opposed several of President ANDREW JACKSON'S policies though he and Jackson were both Democrats. In 1832 South Carolina issued its nullification policy, declaring its right as a state to reject federal TARIFF regulations. Jackson, in retaliation, initiated the Force Act of 1833 (4

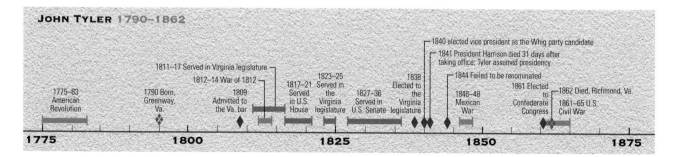

JOHN TYLER 1790–1862

1775–83 American Revolution

1790 Born, Greenway, Va.

1809 Admitted to the Va. bar

1811–17 Served in Virginia legislature

1812–14 War of 1812

1817–21 Served in U.S. House

1823–25 Served in the Virginia legislature

1827–36 Served in U.S. Senate

1838 Elected to the Virginia legislature

1840 elected vice president as the Whig party candidate

1841 President Harrison died 31 days after taking office; Tyler assumed presidency

1844 Failed to be renominated

1846–48 Mexican War

1861 Elected to Confederate Congress

1861–65 U.S. Civil War

1862 Died, Richmond, Va.

1775   1800   1825   1850   1875

Stat. 633), which permitted the president to use the military, if necessary, to collect tariff revenues. Tyler did not agree with South Carolina's actions, but he vehemently opposed Jackson's use of federal power to bring the state to heel.

Tyler lost the support of Virginia Democrats when he refused to reverse his 1834 vote of censure against Jackson for removing deposits from the BANK OF THE UNITED STATES. In 1836, when the Virginia legislature gave him a direct order to change his vote, Tyler resigned from the Senate rather than obey. He returned to Virginia, where he was elected again to the Virginia legislature in 1838.

In the presidential election of 1840, the Whig party sought to broaden its northern political base by selecting a vice presidential candidate who could attract southern voters. Accordingly, Tyler was chosen to be the vice presidential candidate to run with WILLIAM HENRY HARRISON, known as "Tippecanoe" from the battle where he had defeated Chief Tecumseh of the Shawnee tribe. In a campaign devoid of political ideas, the political slogan "Tippecanoe and Tyler too" popularized the two Whig candidates, who won the election.

The elderly Harrison died thirty-one days after becoming president, and Tyler assumed the presidency on April 4, 1841. As the first vice president to become president because of the death of the chief executive, Tyler rejected the idea that he serve as acting president. Though

"THE GREAT PRIMARY AND CONTROLLING INTEREST OF THE AMERICAN PEOPLE IS UNION—UNION NOT ONLY IN THE MERE FORMS OF GOVERNMENT . . . BUT UNION FOUNDED IN AN ATTACHMENT OF . . . INDIVIDUALS FOR EACH OTHER."

the U.S. Constitution was silent on the matter of succession, Tyler announced that he would assume the full powers and duties of the office, setting a precedent that would be followed by other vice presidents. (Procedures for presidential succession were added to the Constitution by the TWENTY-FIFTH AMENDMENT in 1967.)

Tyler's maverick streak, which had once stung the Democrats, soon offended the Whigs. Still a staunch supporter of STATES' RIGHTS, Tyler twice vetoed a Whig-sponsored act establishing a national bank. As a result, his entire CABINET resigned, with the exception of the secretary of state, DANIEL WEBSTER. For the remainder of his term, Tyler was a chief executive without a political party. Consequently, his accomplishments were few. He did approve the annexation of Texas and he signed the Preemption Act of 1841 (5 Stat. 453), which gave squatters on government land the right to buy 160 acres of land at the minimum auction price without competitive bidding.

After leaving office in 1845, Tyler continued to defend states' rights. In 1861, before the outbreak of the Civil War, Tyler directed the Washington conference, which was convened in a final attempt to avert war. When that meeting failed, Tyler favored SECESSION and was elected as a member of the Confederate Congress. He died on January 18, 1862, in Richmond, Virginia, however, before he could take his seat in the secessionist Congress.

UCC 📖 An abbreviation for the UNIFORM COMMERCIAL CODE. 📖

UCCC 📖 An abbreviation for the UNIFORM CONSUMER CREDIT CODE. 📖

UCMJ 📖 An abbreviation for the UNIFORM CODE OF MILITARY JUSTICE (10 U.S.C.A. § 801 et seq.). 📖

ULTIMATE FACTS 📖 Information essential to a plaintiff's right of ACTION or a defendant's assertion of a DEFENSE. 📖

The concept of ultimate facts used to be an essential part of preparing a PLEADING in a CIVIL ACTION. Until the late 1930s, the rules of CIVIL PROCEDURE in federal and state courts required parties to plead on the basis of a statement of facts constituting the CAUSE OF ACTION or defense. These ultimate facts alleged the substance of the cause of action and were distinguished from evidentiary facts, which concerned the particular events of the case, and conclusions of law. The highly technical distinctions among ultimate facts, evidentiary facts, and CONCLUSIONS OF LAW created great confusion and often led to the dismissal of cases based on a pleading mistake.

The development of these distinctions can be traced to the 1848 New York Code of Civil Procedure, which was largely drafted by DAVID DUDLEY FIELD. During the next few decades, most of the states, except those on the East Coast, adopted what came to be known as the Field Code. The Field Code was a significant improvement over COMMON-LAW systems of procedure. However, the code required that the COMPLAINT contain "a plain and concise statement of the facts constituting plaintiff's cause of action," and used the pleading as a way of narrowing and defining the dispute rather than as a general means of initiating a civil action.

Over time, however, CODE PLEADING became very technical and required the pleader to set forth the facts underlying and demonstrating the existence of the cause of action. The pleading of ultimate facts was necessary, while the inclusion of evidentiary facts and conclusions of law was improper. Judges and attorneys found it difficult, if not impossible, to draw meaningful and consistent distinctions among these three terms. With no clear dividing line between a fact that demonstrated a cause of action and one that introduced specific EVIDENCE, courts made formal and often arbitrary decisions that were unrelated to the MERITS of the case. Courts demanded a high degree of specificity and bound the parties to prove the ultimate facts alleged or lose the lawsuit. This requirement was particularly harsh because it forced a party to ALLEGE detailed facts early in the case when there was still uncertainty over what facts had occurred.

By the 1930s legal commentators agreed that the need to plead ultimate facts was hindering the cause of justice. The Federal Rules of Civil Procedure, which were adopted in 1938, eliminated the ultimate fact requirement and changed the philosophy behind the plaintiff's complaint and the defendant's ANSWER. In place of ultimate facts, rule 8(a) provides that the complaint shall contain "a short and plain statement of the claim showing that the pleader is entitled to relief." Likewise, the defendant "shall state in short and plain terms" the defenses to the plaintiff's complaint. The rules do not require that only facts be alleged. Most states have adopted the federal rules in whole or in part, and the need to state ultimate facts in a pleading is no longer of great importance.

ULTRA VIRES 📖 [*Latin, Beyond the powers.*] The doctrine in the law of CORPORATIONS that holds that if a corporation enters into a CONTRACT that is beyond the scope of its corporate powers, the contract is illegal. 📖

The doctrine of ultra vires played an important role in the development of corporate powers. Though largely obsolete in modern private corporation law, the doctrine remains in full force for government entities. An ultra vires act is one beyond the purposes or powers of a corporation. The earliest legal view was that such acts were VOID. Under this approach a corporation was formed only for limited purposes and could do only what it was authorized to do in its corporate CHARTER.

This early view proved unworkable and unfair. It permitted a corporation to accept the benefits of a contract and then refuse to perform its obligations on the ground that the contract was ultra vires. The doctrine also impaired the security of TITLE to property in fully executed transactions in which a corporation participated. Therefore, the courts adopted the view that such acts were VOIDABLE rather than void and that the facts should dictate whether a corporate act should have effect.

Over time a body of principles developed that prevented the application of the ultra vires doctrine. These principles included the ability of shareholders to ratify an ultra vires transaction; the application of the doctrine of ESTOPPEL, which prevented the defense of ultra vires when the transaction was fully performed by one party; and the prohibition against asserting ultra vires when both parties had fully performed the contract. The law also held that if an AGENT of a corporation committed a TORT within the scope of the agent's employment, the corporation could not defend on the ground that the act was ultra vires. See also SCOPE OF EMPLOYMENT.

Despite these principles the ultra vires doctrine was applied inconsistently and erratically. Accordingly, modern corporation law has sought to remove the possibility that ultra vires acts may occur. Most importantly, multiple purposes clauses and general clauses that permit corporations to engage in any lawful business are now included in the ARTICLES OF INCORPORATION. In addition, purposes clauses can now be easily amended if the corporation seeks to do business in new areas. For example, under traditional ultra vires doctrine, a corporation that had as its purpose the manufacturing of shoes could not, under its charter, manufacture motorcycles. Under modern corporate law, the purposes clause would either be so general as to allow the corporation to go into the motorcycle business, or the corporation would amend its purposes clause to reflect the new venture.

State laws in almost every JURISDICTION have also sharply reduced the importance of the ultra vires doctrine. For example, section 3.04(a) of the Revised Model Business Corporation Act, drafted in 1984, states that "the validity of corporate action may not be challenged on the ground that the corporation lacks or lacked power to act." There are three exceptions to this prohibition: it may be asserted by the corporation or its shareholders against the present or former officers or directors of the corporation for exceeding their authority, by the attorney general of the state in a proceeding to dissolve the corporation or to enjoin it from the transaction of unauthorized business, or by shareholders against the corporation to enjoin the commission of an ultra vires act or the ultra vires transfer of real or personal property.

Government entities created by a state are public corporations governed by municipal charters and other statutorily imposed grants of power. These grants of authority are analogous to a private corporation's articles of incorporation. Historically, the ultra vires concept has been used to construe the powers of a government entity narrowly. Failure to observe the statutory limits has been characterized as ultra vires.

In the case of a private business entity, the act of an employee who is not authorized to act on the entity's behalf may, nevertheless, bind the entity contractually if such an employee would normally be expected to have that authority. With a government entity, however, to prevent a contract from being voided as ultra vires, it is normally necessary to prove that the employee actually had authority to act. Where a government employee exceeds her authority, the government entity may seek to RESCIND the contract based on an ultra vires claim.

UMPIRE 📖 A person chosen to decide a question in a controversy that has been submitted to ARBITRATION but has not been resolved because the arbitrators cannot reach agreement, or one who has been chosen to be a permanent arbitrator for the duration of a COLLECTIVE BARGAINING AGREEMENT. 📖

Arbitration is the submission of a dispute to an unbiased third person designated by the parties to the controversy, who agree in advance to comply with the decision. Arbitration is quicker, less expensive, and more informal than a court proceeding. Commercial arbitration and labor arbitration are commonplace in the United States. Persons who hear these types of dispute resolution cases are called arbitrators and umpires. Umpires are used either to break an impasse in arbitration or to serve as specialized, long-term decision makers.

An arbitrator is a person selected by the parties to hear the dispute. An arbitrator must be mutually agreed upon by the parties and may be named, for example, in a labor-management collective bargaining agreement or may be chosen after the dispute has arisen. In labor arbitration a single arbitrator may hear a case, but frequently a three-member arbitration panel hears the dispute. The three members consist of an arbitrator selected by management, another chosen by labor, and a chairperson selected either by the parties or by the two arbitrators appointed by the parties. The arbitrators selected by the parties act like advocates, but the chairperson is expected to be neutral.

If the three-person panel cannot agree on a decision, the arbitrators may name an umpire to decide the controversy. The umpire acts independently and is vested with the sole authority to decide the issues that have been presented.

An umpire is also sometimes used in labor-management grievance proceedings. In this situation a single, permanent umpire is appointed to resolve disputes for the term of the collective bargaining agreement. The umpire becomes familiar with the economic, financial, and day-to-day working conditions of an industry and may rely on precedents developed by previous umpires. This form of umpire system began in the anthracite coal mining industry in the early 1900s and has been used in other industries, including clothing manufacturing and newspaper printing.

CROSS-REFERENCES

Alternative Dispute Resolution; Grievance Procedure; Labor Law; Labor Union.

UNAUTHORIZED PRACTICE 📖 The performance of professional services, such as the rendering of medical treatment or legal assistance, by a person who is not licensed by the state to do so. 📖

The unauthorized practice of a profession is prohibited by state laws. Violators of these laws are generally subject to criminal sanctions, but what constitutes unauthorized practice is con-

Some legal matters may be handled by non-attorneys, which benefits clients with little money. The unauthorized practice of law occurs when someone without an attorney's license handles a matter for which professional training is required.

stantly changing and is the subject of dispute. For example, persons opposed to laws that ban the unauthorized practice of law argue that the legal profession uses these statutes to maintain a MONOPOLY over legal services, many of which can be performed by nonlawyers.

The professions have sought the enactment of unauthorized practice statutes in part to protect the public from persons who are not trained to give professional assistance and who may give substandard treatment. The elements of a profession include a rigorous course of training, the certification of competency by a professional society or state agency, state licensure, and an obligation to follow a code of ETHICS. Based on these elements, the professions and most state legislatures believe that the PUBLIC INTEREST is best served by restricting the performance of medical, legal, and other services to the members of their respective professions.

The unauthorized practice of law has become a matter of public debate. Nonlawyers can read laws, interpret laws, draft documents, and proceed in legal matters on their own behalf, but in most states they cannot draft documents for others, give specific legal advice, or appear in court for another person. Nevertheless, most states allow nonlawyers to sell legal forms and general instructions and offer typing services for completing legal documents.

Those critical of lawyers contend that nonlawyers should be permitted to draft simple legal documents because they can provide their services at a considerably lower price than an ATTORNEY.

The existence of statutes prohibiting the unauthorized practice of law does not guarantee that those statutes will be enforced, an issue that is a concern to the legal profession. Enforcement is difficult both because proof of the unauthorized practice of law is difficult to obtain and because many prosecutors place a low priority on pursuing these violations.

A person who has been harmed by relying on the advice of someone not authorized to practice a profession may sue that person in a TORT action for DAMAGES sustained.

See also LICENSE.

UNCONSCIONABLE 📖 Unusually harsh and shocking to the conscience; that which is so grossly unfair that a court will proscribe it. 📖

When a court uses the word *unconscionable* to describe conduct, it means that the conduct does not conform to the dictates of conscience. In addition, when something is judged unconscionable, a court will refuse to allow the perpetrator of the conduct to benefit.

In CONTRACT law an unconscionable contract is one that is unjust or extremely one-sided in favor of the person who has the superior bargaining power. An unconscionable contract is one that no person who is mentally competent would enter into and that no fair and honest person would accept. Courts find that unconscionable contracts usually result from the exploitation of consumers who are often poorly educated, impoverished, and unable to find the best price available in the competitive marketplace.

Contractual provisions that indicate gross one-sidedness in favor of the seller include provisions that limit DAMAGES against the seller, limit the rights of the purchaser to seek court relief against the seller, or disclaim a WARRANTY. State and federal CONSUMER PROTECTION and CONSUMER CREDIT laws were enacted to prevent many of these unconscionable contract provisions from being included in sales contracts.

Unconscionability is determined by examining the circumstances of the parties when the contract was made; these circumstances include, for example, the bargaining power, age, and mental capacity of the parties. The doctrine is applied only where it would be an affront to the integrity of the judicial system to enforce such contracts.

Unconscionable conduct is also found in acts of FRAUD and DECEIT, where the deliberate MISREPRESENTATION of fact deprives someone of a valuable possession. Whenever someone takes unconscionable advantage of another person, the action may be treated as criminal fraud or the CIVIL ACTION of deceit.

No standardized criteria exist for measuring whether an action is unconscionable. A court of law applies its conscience, or moral sense, to the facts before it and makes a subjective judgment. The U.S. Supreme Court's "SHOCK THE CONSCIENCE TEST" in *Rochin v. California*, 342 U.S. 165, 72 S. Ct. 205, 96 L. Ed. 183 (1952), demonstrates this approach. The Court ruled that pumping the stomach of a criminal suspect in search of drugs offends "those canons of decency and fairness which express the notions of justice of English-speaking peoples." The Court relied on these general historical and moral traditions as the basis for ruling unconstitutional an unconscionable act.

See also ROCHIN V. CALIFORNIA.

UNDERINCLUSIVENESS 📖 A characteristic of a statute or administrative rule dealing with FIRST AMENDMENT rights and other fundamental LIBERTY interests, whereby the statute prohibits some conduct but fails to prohibit other, similar conduct. 📖

An underinclusive law is not necessarily unconstitutional or invalid. The U.S. Supreme Court has recognized that all laws are underinclusive and selective to some extent. If a law is substantially underinclusive, however, it may be unconstitutional.

The case of *Church of Lukumi Babalu Aye, Inc. v. City of Hialeah*, 508 U.S. 520, 113 S. Ct. 2217, 124 L. Ed. 2d 472 (1993), illustrates unconstitutional underinclusiveness. The Church of Lukumi Babalu Aye is a religious sect that practices Santeria, which involves the ritual killing of animals. Shortly after officials of the city of Hialeah, Florida, learned that the church had purchased property in that city, the city passed certain ORDINANCES for the stated purpose of promoting public health and preventing cruelty to animals. Because the ordinances prohibited the ritual killing of animals, the church's practice of animal sacrifice was made illegal.

According to the Supreme Court, the ordinances infringed on the freedom of the church to practice its RELIGION. Furthermore, the ordinances were so underinclusive in their attempt to promote public health and prevent animal cruelty that they violated the First Amendment to the U.S. Constitution. The ordinances failed to punish other, nonreligious conduct that endangered the city's interest in animal welfare, such as fishing or hunting for sport. The ordinances also failed to cover other, nonreligious animal killing that threatened the city's interest in public health. The ordinances did not, for example, prevent hunters from bringing animal carcasses to their homes. Ultimately, the Court concluded, the ordinances had "every appearance of a prohibition that society is prepared to impose upon Santeria worshippers but not upon itself."

If a law infringes on constitutionally protected free speech, press, or associational rights, it may be unconstitutionally underinclusive if it is based on the content of the speech or somehow regulates ideas. In *R.A.V. v. City of St. Paul*, 505 U.S. 377, 112 S. Ct. 2538, 120 L. Ed. 2d 305 (1992), the Supreme Court struck down a hate speech ordinance that prohibited "the display of a symbol which one knows or has reason to know 'arouses anger, alarm or resentment in others on the basis of race, color, creed, religion or gender.'" A youth in St. Paul, Minnesota, had been prosecuted under the ordinance for burning a cross in the yard of an African American family. The Court held that the law was unconstitutionally underinclusive under the First Amendment because it punished only certain speech addressing particular topics; the law addressed the content, rather than the manner, of the speech.

A law is not necessarily invalid just because it is underinclusive. For example, a statute that prohibited the use of loudspeaker systems near a hospital might be underinclusive for failing to prohibit shouting or the use of car horns in the same area. This type of underinclusiveness concerns only the manner of delivering speech, however, and is therefore more likely to pass constitutional scrutiny than a statute that prohibits speech on particular subjects.

See also HATE CRIME; TIME, PLACE, AND MANNER RESTRICTIONS.

UNDERSTANDING 📖 A general term referring to an AGREEMENT, either EXPRESS or IMPLIED, written or oral. 📖

The term *understanding* is an ambiguous one; in order to determine whether a particular understanding would constitute a CONTRACT that is legally binding on the parties involved, the circumstances must be examined to discover whether a meeting of the minds and an intent to be bound occurred.

See also MEETING OF MINDS.

UNDERTAKING 📖 A written PROMISE offered as SECURITY for the performance of a particular act required in a legal ACTION. 📖

In a criminal case, an undertaking of BAIL is security for the appearance of the defendant. In the event the defendant fails to appear, the amount posted as bail is forfeited.

An undertaking with adequate security is a BOND. The term is used in a general sense to refer to any type of promise or STIPULATION.

UNDERWRITE 📖 To insure; to sell an issue of STOCKS and BONDS or to guarantee the purchase of unsold stocks and bonds after a public issue. 📖

The word *underwrite* has two meanings. To issue an INSURANCE policy on the life of a person or on property of another is to underwrite that person or property; hence insurance companies are also referred to as underwriters.

The other meaning refers to the issuing of stocks or bonds by a CORPORATION or a government agency to raise capital. The underwriter is a company, often an investment bank, that agrees to sell the SECURITIES. Under its contract with the corporation, the underwriter agrees to pay for any unsold shares.

An underwriter operates by purchasing all of the new issue of stocks or bonds from the corporation at one price and selling the issue in smaller lots to public investors at a price high enough to cover the expenses associated with the sale and to provide a profit. When making a PUBLIC OFFERING of securities, an underwriter is responsible for setting the offering price. It uses its knowledge of the STOCK MARKET and current interest rates and yields to determine the likely demand for the issue.

Typically, an underwriter does not underwrite and distribute a security issue alone but instead organizes a SYNDICATE for the venture. Syndicates are often used when the amount of capital sought by a corporation is much larger than a single underwriter cares to risk. By dividing the underwriting of the securities issue, the risk is spread among the various members of the syndicate. The firm that originates the issue acts as manager of the syndicate.

If an underwriter cannot organize a syndicate large enough to cover the entire issue, it usually will arrange with stock brokerage firms to purchase shares at a reduced price, called a concession. This price reduction provides the brokerage firms with a margin to cover expenses and a small profit upon resale.

A corporation selects an underwriter either through private negotiation of a CONTRACT or through competitive bidding. In a bidding process, the corporation sets the terms of the issue and then invites potential underwriters to submit bids. The issue is then sold to the highest bidder.

UNDUE INFLUENCE 📖 A judicially created DEFENSE to transactions that have been imposed upon weak and vulnerable persons that allows the transactions to be set aside. 📖

Virtually any act of persuasion that overcomes the free will and judgment of another, including exhortations, importunings, insinuations, flattery, trickery, and deception, may amount to undue influence. Undue influence differs from DURESS, which consists of the intentional use of force, or threat of force, to coerce another into a grossly unfair transaction. BLACKMAIL, EXTORTION, BAD FAITH threats of criminal prosecution, and oppressive ABUSE OF PROCESS are classic examples of duress.

Four elements must be shown to establish undue influence. First, it must be demonstrated that the victim was susceptible to OVERREACHING. Such conditions as mental, psychological, or physical disability or dependency may be used to show susceptibility. Second, there must be an opportunity for exercising undue influence. Typically, this opportunity arises through a confidential relationship. Courts have found opportunity for undue influence in confidential relationships between HUSBAND AND WIFE, fiancé and fiancée, PARENT AND CHILD, TRUSTEE and BENEFICIARY, ADMINISTRATOR and LEGATEE, GUARDIAN and WARD, ATTORNEY and CLIENT, doctor and patient, and pastor and parishioner. Third, there must be evidence that the defendant was inclined to exercise undue influence over the victim. Defendants who aggressively initiate a transaction, insulate a relationship from outside supervision, or discourage a weaker party from seeking independent advice may be attempting to exercise undue influence. Fourth, the record must reveal an unnatural or suspicious transaction. Courts are wary, for example, of TESTATORS who make abrupt changes in their last WILL and testament after being diagnosed with a terminal illness or being declared incompetent, especially if the changes are made at the behest of a beneficiary who stands to benefit from the new or revised testamentary disposition.

Nevertheless, courts will examine the facts closely before finding that a transaction has been tainted by undue influence. Mere suspicion, surmise, or conjecture of overreaching is insufficient. The law permits loved ones and confidants to advise and comfort those in need of their support without fear of litigation. Courts are also aware that the doctrine of undue influence can be used as a sword by the vindictive and avaricious who seek to invalidate a perfectly legal transaction for personal gain. When undue influence is found to have altered a transaction, however, courts will make every effort to return the parties to the same position they would have occupied had the overreaching not occurred.

UNEMPLOYMENT COMPENSATION

📖 INSURANCE benefits paid by the state or federal government to individuals who are involuntarily out of work in order to provide them with necessities, such as food, clothing, and shelter. 📖

Unemployment compensation for U.S. workers was established by the federal SOCIAL SECURITY ACT of 1935 (42 U.S.C.A. § 301 et seq.). Unemployment insurance provides workers who have lost their job through no fault of their own with monetary payments for a given period of time or until they find a new job. This compensation is designed to give an unemployed worker time to find a new job equivalent to the one lost without major financial distress. Unemployment compensation is also justified as a way to provide the U.S. economy with consumer spending during an economic downturn.

The mass unemployment during the Great Depression of the 1930s led to the enactment of the federal unemployment compensation law. States had resisted establishing their own unemployment compensation plans because the first states to tax employers to fund such a plan would lose business and jobs to other states. Therefore, a federal program was needed. Much of the federal plan was implemented under the Federal Unemployment Tax Act of 1935 (26 U.S.C.A. § 3301 et seq.). A combination of federal and state taxes is levied on employers to fund state-administered programs that meet minimum federal standards. Federal funds are also used for administrative costs and to set up employment offices that attempt to match workers with new jobs.

In general, a tax on employers provides the funds to pay unemployment compensation. An employer who has more than a specified minimum number of employees is ordinarily required to file regular reports that disclose the number of employees and the amount of their wages, including tips. A standard or basic rate is charged against the employer based on the amount of wages paid. If the employer does not lay off employees, the employer will be entitled to a credit. An employer's record is unaffected if an employee quits or is discharged for GOOD CAUSE. An employer of eight or more persons is permitted to subtract what she pays to the state unemployment compensation fund from her federal unemployment tax.

Each state establishes which employers are obligated to pay state unemployment taxes. Ordinarily a state will require payment of the tax from every individual, partnership, or corporation that pays wages to a specified minimum number of people to do work. Certain types of employment are excluded from mandated coverage, including some agricultural labor, some charitable or nonprofit work, and some government work. In addition, individuals who are self-employed are not entitled to unemployment compensation.

Reasons for Unemployment, August 1997

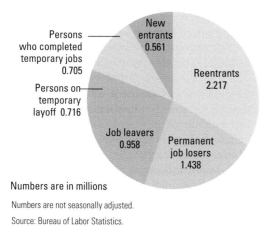

Persons who completed temporary jobs 0.705

Persons on temporary layoff 0.716

New entrants 0.561

Reentrants 2.217

Job leavers 0.958

Permanent job losers 1.438

Numbers are in millions

Numbers are not seasonally adjusted.

Source: Bureau of Labor Statistics.

Duration of Unemployment, August 1997

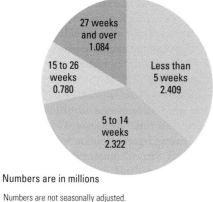

27 weeks and over 1.084

15 to 26 weeks 0.780

Less than 5 weeks 2.409

5 to 14 weeks 2.322

Numbers are in millions

Numbers are not seasonally adjusted.

Source: Bureau of Labor Statistics.

Any individual who qualifies under the terms of the state unemployment compensation law is entitled to collect benefits. To be eligible, an individual must have worked for a certain minimum number of weeks and earned wages in at least the amount set by state law. Certain states will pay reduced benefits where part-time work provides only a small amount of money.

Unemployment compensation is paid for a certain number of weeks. However, during economic recessions the federal government has provided emergency assistance to allow states to extend the time during which individuals can receive benefits. The states are allowed to use money they have deposited in special accounts of the federal Unemployment Trust Fund. For a state to use this emergency benefit system, the unemployment rate usually must reach a designated percentage within the state or the country.

An unemployed worker is not required to submit proof that he needs money or that he has no other means of support. Anyone who qualifies has a right to collect benefits because payments are designed to replace part of the wages lost during temporary periods of unemployment. Severance pay does not necessarily preclude payment of benefits, but some state laws treat it as earnings for the amount of time such payments cover and do not allow payment of unemployment compensation until that time has expired. Accumulated vacation time, vacation pay, or a leave of absence also serve to postpone or prevent the payment of benefits.

Ordinarily, state unemployment compensation statutes provide benefits for those who are unemployed because of their employer's inability to provide work for them. An employee who is discharged may receive benefits unless he was discharged for good cause. Good cause for discharge usually is related to recent misconduct on the job. Misconduct in private life or during off-duty hours may constitute good cause for firing an employee if it affects the person's work. Carelessness, disregard for the employer's interest, intoxication, the use of illegal drugs, illegal work slowdowns, use of abusive language, absenteeism, and habitual lateness can be reasons for a discharge and denial of unemployment benefits. A person denied benefits may appeal this determination, first to a state administrative office and then to a court of law.

An unemployed worker is required to be available for work. This means that the person must actively seek a new job while collecting benefits. In cases where it appears that the person is not willing and able to work, she has no right to receive unemployment compensation. Workers who leave a job to find a better job or to attend school are not eligible for benefits. An individual who is too ill to work, who has no means of transportation, or who refuses to accept more than a small amount of work to avoid forfeiting retirement benefits is not regarded as being available for work. Employees who are on STRIKE generally cannot collect unemployment compensation. However, a few states do provide some benefits. Individuals in such circumstances may qualify for other types of government aid, but they are not eligible for unemployment benefits.

A state may not discriminate because of gender or religious beliefs in the awarding of unemployment compensation. In *Wimberly v. Labor and Industrial Relations Commission*, 479 U.S. 511, 107 S. Ct. 821, 93 L. Ed. 2d 909 (1987), the U.S. Supreme Court ruled that no person may be denied compensation solely on the basis of pregnancy or the termination of pregnancy. The Court, in *Hobbie v. Unemployment Appeals Commission*, 480 U.S. 136, 107 S.

Ct. 1046, 94 L. Ed. 2d 190 (1987), held that a state may not deny unemployment benefits to a worker who is discharged for refusing to work because of religious beliefs that he or she adopted after becoming employed.

A state cannot assume that a parent who is responsible for the care of small children is unavailable for work. When a person applies for unemployment compensation, the decision to grant or deny the claim must be based on whether the applicant is actually willing and able to work but is involuntarily unemployed.

An individual who is out of work is given no guarantee that she will find an attractive and convenient job. If jobs are available, even outside the person's local area, she is required to find one. An individual is not, however, disqualified from receiving unemployment compensation merely because she has recently moved, except in cases where no employment is available in the new locality. An unemployed worker cannot decline to accept a new job because he does not like the wages or hours. A person who refuses to accept a job is no longer entitled to receive unemployment compensation if the job is reasonable and suited to his skills.

Federal law (42 U.S.C.A. § 351 et seq.) provides unemployment compensation for railroad workers who lose their jobs.

CROSS-REFERENCES

Employment Law; Labor Law; New Deal; Old-Age, Survivors, and Disability Insurance; Religion; Worker's Compensation.

UNENUMERATED RIGHTS 📖 Rights that are not expressly mentioned in the written text of a CONSTITUTION but instead are inferred from the language, history, and structure of the constitution, or cases interpreting it. 📖

Typically, the term *unenumerated rights* describes certain fundamental rights that have been recognized by the U.S. Supreme Court under the U.S. Constitution. In addition, state courts have recognized unenumerated rights emanating from the principles enunciated by their own state constitutions. No comprehensive list of unenumerated rights has ever been compiled nor could such a list be readily produced precisely because these rights are unenumerated.

Nevertheless, a partial list of unenumerated rights might include those specifically recognized by the Supreme Court, such as the right to travel, the right to PRIVACY, the right to autonomy, the right to dignity, and the right to an ABORTION, which is based on the right to privacy. Other rights could easily be added to this list, and no doubt will be in the future. In *Washington v. Glucksberg*, 117 S. Ct. 2258 (1997), the Supreme Court ruled that there is

no unenumerated constitutional right to die.

Unenumerated rights commonly are derived through a reasoned elaboration of express constitutional provisions. The FIRST AMENDMENT, for example, guarantees FREEDOM OF SPEECH but says nothing about the nature of the speech protected. Through the process of interpretation, the Supreme Court has held that the Free Speech Clause protects both verbal and nonverbal expression, as well as communicative conduct. The right to engage in offensive symbolic expression, such as FLAG burning, forms an essential part of the freedoms contemplated by the First Amendment, freedoms that are integral to maintaining an open and democratic society (*Texas v. Johnson*, 491 U.S. 397, 109 S. Ct. 2533, 105 L. Ed. 2d 342 [1989]). Judicial protection of such unenumerated rights, the Court has reasoned, helps establish a PENUMBRA or buffer that insulates expressly enumerated liberties from governmental encroachment.

Courts are ordinarily reluctant to recognize new unenumerated rights. Most judges are sensitive to accusations of "inventing" new liberties out of whole cloth. Critics charge that judges who recognize new unenumerated rights are imposing their personal values on the law, rather than faithfully interpreting the text of the Constitution. The role of judges, these critics contend, is solely to apply the law, while only legislators are empowered to make new law through the exercise of value-laden judgments.

The Supreme Court attempts to deflect such criticism by relying on history as justification for its decisions recognizing certain unenumerated rights. For example, the Fifth and Fourteenth Amendments to the U.S. Constitution prohibit the government from depriving any person of life, liberty, or property without "due process of law." Yet the amendments do not define "due process," nor do they address issues such as how much process is due during a given legal proceeding. Although the Supreme Court has interpreted this provision to require procedural fairness in civil and criminal litigation, each procedural right the Court has recognized is technically unenumerated because the Due Process Clause offers no hints as to what legal procedures it contemplates.

In criminal cases the Supreme Court has held that the Due Process Clause guarantees every defendant the right to be presumed innocent by the trier of fact, either a judge or a jury, until proved guilty BEYOND A REASONABLE DOUBT by the government (*In re Winship*, 397 U.S. 358, 90 S. Ct. 1068, 25 L. Ed. 2d 368 [1970]). In reaching this decision, the Supreme Court stated that the reasonable doubt and PRESUMPTION OF INNOCENCE standards have been associated with the concept of due process since early colonial times. By citing history and tradition as the basis for many of its controversial decisions, the Supreme Court provides an answer to its critics who claim that unenumerated rights have no basis other than personal predilections of the judges who recognize them.

CROSS-REFERENCES

Bill of Rights; Due Process of Law; Fourteenth Amendment; Judicial Review.

UNETHICAL CONDUCT ◫ Behavior that falls below or violates the professional standards in a particular field, such as law or medicine. ◫

The standards for conduct to be observed by attorneys can be found in the CODE OF PROFESSIONAL RESPONSIBILITY; members of the judiciary adhere to those found in the CANONS OF JUDICIAL ETHICS.

See also ATTORNEY MISCONDUCT; ETHICS.

UNFAIR COMPETITION ◫ Any FRAUDULENT, deceptive, or dishonest trade practice that is prohibited by statute, regulation, or the COMMON LAW. ◫

Unfair competition consists of a body of related doctrines that give rise to several different CAUSES OF ACTION, including actions for the INFRINGEMENT of PATENTS, TRADEMARKS, and COPYRIGHTS; actions for the wrongful appropriation of TRADE DRESS, TRADE NAMES, TRADE SECRETS, and SERVICE MARKS; and actions for the publication of defamatory, false, and misleading REPRESENTATIONS.

The law of unfair competition serves five purposes. First, the law seeks to protect the economic, intellectual, and creative investments made by businesses in distinguishing themselves and their products. Second, the law seeks to preserve the GOOD WILL that businesses have established with consumers. Third, the law seeks to deter businesses from appropriating the good will of their competitors. Fourth, the law seeks to promote clarity and stability by encouraging consumers to rely on a merchant's good will and reputation when evaluating the quality of rival products. Fifth, the law seeks to increase competition by providing businesses with incentives to offer better goods and services than others in the same field.

Although the law of unfair competition helps protect consumers from injuries caused by deceptive trade practices, the remedies provided to redress such injuries are available only to business entities and proprietors. Consumers who are injured by deceptive trade practices must avail themselves of the remedies provided by state and federal CONSUMER PROTECTION laws. In general, businesses and proprietors injured by unfair competition have two remedies: injunctive relief (a court order restraining a competitor from engaging in a particular fraudulent or deceptive practice) and money DAMAGES (compensation for any losses suffered by an injured business).

General Principles The freedom to pursue a livelihood, operate a business, and otherwise compete in the marketplace is essential to any free enterprise system. Competition creates incentives for businesses to earn customer loyalty by offering quality goods at REASONABLE prices. At the same time, competition can also inflict harm. The freedom to compete gives businesses the right to lure customers away from each other. When one business entices enough customers away from competitors, those rival businesses may be forced to shut down or move.

The law of unfair competition will not penalize a business merely for being successful in the marketplace. Nor will the law impose LIABILITY simply because a business is aggressively marketing its product. The law assumes, however, that for every dollar earned by one business, a dollar will be lost by a competitor. Accordingly, the law prohibits a business from *unfairly* profiting at a competitor's expense. What constitutes unfair competition varies according to the cause of action asserted in each case.

Interference with Business Relations No business can compete effectively without establishing good relationships with its employees and customers. In some instances parties execute a formal written CONTRACT to memorialize the terms of their relationship. In other instances business relations are based on an oral agreement. Most often, however, business relations are conducted informally with no contract or agreement at all. Grocery shoppers, for example, typically have no contractual relationship with the supermarkets they patronize. The law of unfair competition prohibits competitors from unreasonably interfering with all three types of relationships.

Business relations are often formalized by written contracts. Merchant and patron, employer and employee, labor and management, wholesaler and retailer, and manufacturer and distributor all frequently reduce their relationships to contractual terms. These contractual relationships create an expectation of mutual performance (that each party will perform its part under the contract's terms) upon which each party relies. Protection of these relationships from outside interference facilitates performance and helps stabilize commercial undertakings. Interference with contractual relations upsets expectations, destabilizes commercial affairs, and increases the costs of doing business by involving competitors in petty squabbles or litigation.

Virtually any contract, whether written or oral, qualifies for protection from unreasonable interference. Noncompetition contracts are a recurrent source of litigation in this area of law. These contracts commonly arise in professional employment settings where an employer requires a skilled employee to sign an agreement promising not to go to work for a competitor in the same geographic market. Such agreements are generally enforceable unless they operate to deprive an employee of the right to meaningfully pursue a livelihood. An employee who chooses to violate a noncompetition contract is guilty of breach of contract, and the business that lured the employee away may be held liable for interfering with an existing contractual relationship in violation of the law of unfair competition. See also NONCOMPETE AGREEMENT.

Informal trade relations that have not been reduced to contractual terms are also protected from outside interference. The law of unfair competition prohibits businesses from intentionally inflicting injury upon a competitor's informal business relations through improper means or for an improper purpose. Improper means include the use of violence, UNDUE INFLUENCE, and COERCION to threaten competitors or intimidate customers. For example, it is illegal for a business to blockade the entryway to a competitor's shop or impede the delivery of supplies with a show of force. The mere refusal to deal with a competitor, however, is not considered an improper means of competition, even if the refusal is motivated by spite.

Any MALICIOUS or monopolistic practice aimed at injuring a competitor may constitute an improper purpose of competition. Monopolistic behavior includes any agreement between two or more people that has as its purpose the exclusion or reduction of competition in a given market. The SHERMAN ANTI-TRUST ACT of 1890 (15 U.S.C.A. § 1 et seq.) makes such behavior illegal by forbidding the formation of contracts, combinations, and conspiracies in RESTRAINT OF TRADE. Corporate MERGERS AND ACQUISITIONS that suppress competition are prohibited by the CLAYTON ACT of 1914, as amended by the ROBINSON-PATMAN ACT of 1936 (15 U.S.C.A. § 12 et seq.). See also COMBINATION IN RESTRAINT OF TRADE.

The Clayton Act also regulates the use of predatory pricing, tying agreements, and exclusive dealing agreements. Predatory pricing is the use of below-market prices to inflict pecuniary injury on competitors. A tying agreement is an agreement in which a vendor agrees to sell a particular good on the condition that the vendee buy an additional or "tied" product. Exclusive dealing agreements require vendees to satisfy all of their needs for a particular good exclusively through a designated vendor. Although none of these practices is considered inherently illegal, any of them may be deemed improper if it manifests a tendency to appreciably restrain competition, substantially increase prices, or significantly reduce output. See also TYING ARRANGEMENTS.

Trade Name, Trademark, Service Mark, and Trade Dress Infringement

Before a business can establish commercial relations with its customers, it must create an identity for itself, as well as for its goods and services. Economic competition is based on the premise that consumers can distinguish between products offered in the marketplace. Competition is made difficult when rival products become indistinguishable or interchangeable. Part of a business's identity is the good will it has established with consumers, while part of a product's identity is the reputation it has earned for quality and value. As a result, businesses spend tremendous amounts of resources to identify their goods, distinguish their services, and cultivate good will.

The four principal devices businesses use to distinguish themselves are trade names, trademarks, service marks, and trade dress. Trade names are used to identify CORPORATIONS, PARTNERSHIPS, SOLE PROPRIETORSHIPS, and other business entities. A trade name may be the actual name of a business that is registered with the government, or it may be an assumed name under which a business operates and holds itself out to the public. For example, a husband and wife might register their business under the name "Sam and Betty's Bar and Grill," while doing business as "The Corner Tavern." Both names are considered trade names under the law of unfair competition.

Trademarks consist of words, symbols, emblems, and other devices that are affixed to goods for the purpose of signifying their authenticity to the public. The circular emblem attached to the rear end of vehicles manufactured by Bavarian Motor Works (BMW) is a familiar example of a trademark designed to signify meticulous craftsmanship. Whereas trademarks are attached to goods through tags and labels, service marks are generally displayed through advertising. As their name suggests, service marks identify services rather than goods. Orkin pest control is a well-known example of a service mark.

Trade dress refers to a product's physical appearance, including its size, shape, texture, and design. Trade dress can also include the manner in which a product is packaged, wrapped, presented, or promoted. In certain circumstances particular color combinations may serve as a company's trade dress. For example, the trade dress of Chevron Chemical Company includes the red and yellow color scheme found on many of its agricultural products (*Chevron Chemical Co. v. Voluntary Purchasing Groups, Inc.*, 659 F.2d 695 [5th Cir. 1981]).

To receive protection from infringement, trade names, trademarks, service marks, and trade dress must be distinctive. Generic language that is used to describe a business or its goods and services rarely qualifies for protection. For example, the law would not allow a certified public accountant to acquire the exclusive rights to market his business under the name "Accounting Services." Such a name does nothing to distinguish the services offered by one accountant from those offered by others in the same field. A court would be more inclined to confer protection upon a unique or unusual name like "Accurate Accounting and Actuarial Acumen."

When competitors share deceptively similar trade names, trademarks, service marks, or trade dress, a cause of action for infringement may exist. The law of unfair competition forbids competitors from confusing consumers through the use of identifying trade devices that are indistinguishable or difficult to distinguish. Actual confusion need not be demonstrated to establish a claim for infringement, so long as there is a likelihood that consumers will be confused by similar identifying trade devices. Greater latitude is given to businesses that share similar identifying trade devices in unrelated fields or in different geographic markets. For example, a court would be more likely to allow two businesses to share the name "Hot Handguns," where one business sells firearms downtown, and the other business runs a country western theater in the suburbs.

Claims for infringement are cognizable under both state and federal law. At the federal level, infringement claims may be brought under the Lanham Trademark Act (15 U.S.C.A. § 1051 et seq.). At the state level, claims for infringement may be brought under analogous INTELLECTUAL PROPERTY statutes and miscellaneous common-law doctrines. Claims for infringement can be strengthened through registration. The first business to register a trademark or a service mark with the federal government is normally protected against any subsequent appropriation by a competitor. Although trade names may not be registered with the federal government, most states require businesses to register their trade names, usually with the secretary of state, and provide protection for the first trade name registered. Trade dress typically receives legal protection by being distinctive and recognizable without any formal registration requirements at the state or federal level.

Theft of Trade Secrets and Infringement of Copyrights and Patents The intangible assets of a business include not only its trade name and other identifying devices but also its inventions, creative works, and artistic efforts. Broadly defined as trade secrets, this body of commercial information may consist of any formula, pattern, process, program, tool, technique, mechanism or compound that provides a business with the opportunity to gain advantage over competitors. Although a trade secret is not patented or copyrighted, it is entrusted only to a select group of people. The law of unfair competition awards individuals and businesses a PROPERTY RIGHT in any valuable trade information they discover and attempt to keep secret through reasonable steps.

The owner of a trade secret is entitled to its exclusive use and enjoyment. A trade secret is valuable not only because it enables a company to gain advantage over a competitor but also because it may be sold or licensed like any other property right. In contrast, commercial information that is revealed to the public, or at least to a competitor, retains limited commercial value. Consequently, courts vigilantly protect trade secrets from disclosure, appropriation, and theft. Businesses or opportunistic members of the general public may be held liable for any economic injuries that result from their theft of a trade secret. Employees may be held liable for disclosing their employer's trade secrets, even if the disclosure occurs after the employment relationship has ended.

Valuable business information that is disclosed to the public may still be protected from infringement by copyright and patent law. Copyright law gives individuals and businesses the exclusive rights to any original works they create, including movies, books, musical scores, sound recordings, dramatic creations, and pantomimes. Patent law gives individuals and businesses the right to exclude all others from making, using, and selling specific types of inventions, such as mechanical devices, manufacturing processes, chemical formulas, and electrical equipment. Federal law grants these exclusive rights in exchange for full public disclosure of an original work or invention. The inventor or author receives complete legal protection for her intellectual efforts, while the public obtains valuable information that can be used to make life easier, healthier, or more pleasant.

Like the law of trade secrets, patent and copyright law offers protection to individuals and businesses that have invested considerable resources in creating something useful or valuable and wish to exploit that investment commercially. Unlike trade secrets, which may be protected indefinitely, patents and copyrights are protected only for a finite period of time. Applications for copyrights are governed by the Copyrights Act (17 U.S.C.A. § 401), and patent applications are governed by the Patent Act (35 U.S.C.A. § 1).

False Advertising, Trade Defamation, and Misappropriation of a Name or Likeness A business that successfully protects its creative works from theft or infringement may still be harmed by FALSE ADVERTISING. Advertising need not be entirely false to be actionable under the law of unfair competition, so long as it is sufficiently inaccurate to mislead or deceive consumers in a manner that inflicts injury on a competitor. In general, businesses are prohibited from placing ads that either unfairly disparage the goods or services of a competitor or unfairly inflate the value of their own goods and services. False advertising deprives consumers of the opportunity to make intelligent comparisons between rival products. It also drives up costs for consumers who must spend additional resources in examining and sampling products.

Both federal and state laws regulate deceptive advertising. The Lanham Trademark Act regulates false advertising at the federal level. Many states have adopted the Uniform Deceptive Trade Practices Act, which prohibits three specific types of representations: (1) false representations that goods or services have certain characteristics, ingredients, uses, benefits, or quantities; (2) false representations that goods or services are new or original; and (3) false representations that goods or services are of a particular grade, standard, or quality. Advertisements that are only partially accurate may give rise to LIABILITY if they are likely to confuse prospective consumers. Ambiguous representations may require clarification to prevent the imposition of liability. For example, a business that accuses a competitor of being "untrustworthy" may be required to clarify that description with additional information if consumer confusion is likely to result.

Trade DEFAMATION is a close relative of false advertising. The law of false advertising regulates inaccurate representations that tend to mislead or deceive the public. The law of trade defamation regulates communications that tend to lower the reputation of a business in the eyes

of the community. Trade defamation is divided into two categories: LIBEL AND SLANDER.

Trade libel generally refers to written communications that tend to bring a business into disrepute, whereas trade slander refers to defamatory oral communications. Before a business may be held liable under either category of trade defamation, the FIRST AMENDMENT requires proof that a defamatory statement was published with "actual malice," which the Supreme Court defines as any representation that is made with knowledge of its falsity or in reckless disregard of its truth (*New York Times v. Sullivan*, 376 U.S. 254, 84 S. Ct. 710, 11 L. Ed. 2d 686 [1964]). The actual malice standard places some burden on businesses to verify, prior to publication, the veracity of any attacks they level against competitors in the print or electronic media.

It is also considered tortious for a business to use the name or likeness of a famous individual for commercial advantage. All individuals are vested with an exclusive property right in their identity. No person, business, or other entity may appropriate an individual's name or likeness without permission. Despite the existence of this common-law tort, businesses occasionally associate their products with popular celebrities without first obtaining consent. A business that falsely suggests that a celebrity has sponsored or endorsed one of its products will be held liable for money damages equal to the economic gain derived from the wrongful appropriation of the celebrity's likeness.

A Simpler Definition The law of unfair competition includes several related doctrines. Nevertheless, some courts have attempted to simplify the law by defining unfair competition as any trade practice whose harm outweighs its benefits. The U.S. legal system is a cornerstone of the free enterprise system. But the freedom to compete does not imply the right to engage in predatory, monopolistic, fraudulent, deceptive, misleading, or unfair competition. On balance, competition becomes unfair when its effects on trade, consumers, and society as a whole are more detrimental than beneficial. Each cause of action for unfair competition embodies this principle to a large extent.

CROSS-REFERENCES

Antitrust Law; Lanham Act; Monopoly; *New York Times v. Sullivan*.

UNFAIR LABOR PRACTICE 🔖 Conduct prohibited by federal law regulating relations between employers, employees, and labor organizations. 🔖

Before 1935 U.S. LABOR UNIONS received little protection from the law. Employers used many

BANNING THE PERMANENT REPLACEMENT OF ECONOMIC STRIKERS: FAIR OR UNFAIR?

The National Labor Relations Act (NLRA) of 1935, also known as the Wagner Act (29 U.S.C.A. § 151 et seq.), affirms the right of employees to strike in order to force an employer to provide better wages or working conditions. Workers who strike for economic gain may be permanently replaced by the employer, however, as long as the replacement workers do not receive better terms than those offered to the strikers. The NLRA prohibits the replacement of workers who strike to protest an unfair labor practice.

Unions have long sought to amend the NLRA to prohibit the permanent replacement of striking workers in all strikes, not just unfair labor practice strikes. They see the use of permanent replacement workers as the ultimate unfair labor practice and argue that it gives the employer disproportionate bargaining power in labor-management negotiations over wages and working conditions. Meanwhile employers contend that banning permanent replacement workers would give unions too much power and would cripple U.S. business.

Legislation that would ban permanent replacement workers has been defeated repeatedly in Congress. After the last congressional defeat of such legislation, President Bill Clinton issued Executive Order No. 12,954 on March 8, 1995 (60 FR 13023). This order barred businesses that permanently replace striking workers from receiving federal contracts. The president concluded that the hiring of permanent replacements escalated labor disputes and led to longer strikes, both of which are contrary to sound labor policy.

A coalition of business groups immediately challenged the order. In *Chamber of Commerce of the United States v. Reich*, 74 F.3d 1322 (D.C. Cir. 1996), a three-judge federal appeals panel struck down the executive order, ruling that federal labor law preempted executive action. Efforts by some state legislatures to ban permanent replacement workers

have also been struck down on the basis that the NLRA preempts state action.

Union leaders continue to seek modification of the NLRA. The leaders of big industrial unions blame the loss of some strikes on the hiring of permanent replacements. Though employers have had the right to hire permanent replacements for decades, the unions

IN FOCUS

contend that employers have only used this type of hardball tactic on a consistent basis since the 1980s. According to the unions, the loss of strikes because of this tactic has demoralized their members and put unions on the defensive in wage and working condition negotiations.

Unions argue that it is unfair for U.S. workers to lose their jobs when they exercise the fundamental right to strike. The hiring of permanent replacements is a strikebreaking tactic that undermines the collective bargaining process set out by the NLRA by ultimately giving employers the upper hand in negotiations. An employer's express or implied threat to hire permanent replacements also threatens union solidarity, as members question the wisdom of going on strike.

In addition, unions are concerned that the hiring of permanent replacements can result in the demise of the union at the company that has been struck. Replacement workers, who are subjected to the threats and taunts of strikers, are unlikely to join the union at some future time. Thus, the employer not only prevails in a labor strike but also secures a nonunion workforce.

Apart from the effect on union-management relations and bargaining power, supporters of a ban on permanent replacements contend that consumers are hurt by such hiring. They argue that permanent replacements threaten the reliability and quality of products because those workers are less experienced and cannot perform as well as those with longtime service to a company.

U.S. businesses, however, believe strongly in the right to hire permanent replacement workers. They reject the idea that hiring temporary replacement workers during a strike is a viable option. Temporary replacements must be fired after an economic strike has been settled because union workers are entitled to reclaim their jobs. Employers point out that temporary workers require a substantial investment in training and that it is difficult to promote morale and loyalty among workers whose jobs will end with the resolution of the strike. Employers argue that it is more efficient to hire permanent replacements and provide them with sufficient training to ensure that the quality and reliability of a company's products will not suffer.

Defenders of replacement workers also believe that the right to hire during a strike is essential to the balance that exists between labor and business. The right of labor to strike for better wages and working conditions is matched by the right of business to hire permanent replacements. If permanent replacements were banned, employers would be forced to capitulate to overreaching union economic demands or face more frequent and crippling strikes.

In addition, nonunion employers fear that a ban on replacement workers would give unions more leverage in organizing workers. A union could promise that workers who joined the union would be able to resume their jobs after a strike for economic demands, no matter how excessive.

Business leaders also contend that a ban on permanent replacement workers would drive up labor costs, which would be bad for the national economy. A ban would give unions too much power and encourage them to strike. Businesses assert that permitting the hiring of permanent replacements deters unions from striking and leads to more reasonable and productive collective bargaining.

tactics to prevent employees from joining unions and to disrupt union activities in the workplace. The passage of the NATIONAL LABOR RELATIONS ACT (NLRA) of 1935, also known as the WAGNER ACT (29 U.S.C.A. § 151 et seq.), marked the beginning of affirmative federal government support of unionization and COLLECTIVE BARGAINING. The NLRA prohibits employers from taking certain actions against their employees and the unions that represent them. A prohibited action is called an unfair labor practice.

Section 158 of the NLRA lists employer actions that constitute unfair labor practices. Section 158(a)(1) prohibits employers from interfering with the rights of employees to establish, belong to, or aid labor organizations; to conduct collective bargaining through the employees' chosen representatives; and to participate in concerted activities, such as STRIKES, for the purpose of collective bargaining or other mutual aid or protection.

Section 158(a)(3) outlaws employer-formed or -dominated "company unions." Section 158(a)(3) forbids employers to discriminate in hiring, firing, and other aspects of employment on the basis of union activity. Section 158(a)(4) prohibits firing or discriminating against any employee because he has filed charges or testified before the agency charged with enforcing the statute. Section 158(a)(5) requires employers to engage in collective bargaining with employee representatives.

The NLRA proved to be an effective tool for labor unions. Union membership and economic power grew so rapidly between 1935 and 1945 that the business community complained that unions were abusing their new strength. As a result, in 1947 Congress passed the TAFT-HARTLEY ACT, also known as the Labor-Management Relations Act (29 U.S.C.A. § 141 et seq.), which amended the NLRA by prohibiting certain union activities as unfair labor practices. These activities include SECONDARY BOYCOTTS (boycotts against the employer's customers or suppliers), jurisdictional strikes over work assignments, and strikes to force an employer to discharge an employee on account of her union affiliation or lack of it.

The NLRA also established the National Labor Relations Board (NLRB) as an ADMINISTRATIVE AGENCY to administer and interpret the unfair labor practice provisions. The NLRB hears allegations of unfair labor practices and makes rulings, which may be appealed in the federal courts.

See also LABOR LAW.

UNIFORM ACTS 📖 Laws that are designed to be adopted generally by all the states so that the law in one JURISDICTION is the same as in another jurisdiction. 📖

Uniform acts or laws are prepared and sponsored by the National Conference of Commissioners on Uniform State Laws, whose members are experienced lawyers, judges, and professors of law generally appointed to the commission by state governors. Uniform acts or laws are adopted, in whole or substantially, by individual states at their option. Uniform laws are intended to promote fairness through the equal operation of standards upon the citizens of all states without distinction or discrimination. One uniform law, the Uniform Controlled Substances Act, is a comprehensive law that governs the use, sale, and distribution of DRUGS AND NARCOTICS in most states.

See also MODEL ACTS.

UNIFORM CODE OF MILITARY JUSTICE The Uniform Code of Military Justice (UCMJ) was enacted by Congress in 1950 (10 U.S.C.A. § 801 et seq.) to establish a standard set of procedural and substantive criminal laws for all the U.S. military services. The UCMJ applies to all members of the military, including those on active duty, students at military academies, prisoners of war, and, in some cases, retired or reserve personnel. The UCMJ changed MILITARY LAW in several ways, especially by providing substantial procedural safeguards for an accused, such as the right to be represented by counsel, to be informed of the nature of the accusation, to remain silent, and to be told of these rights.

Military law exists separately from civilian law. The rights of individuals serving in the ARMED SERVICES are not as extensive as civilians' rights because the military is regulated by the overriding demands of discipline and duty. Recognizing this need for a separate body of regulations to govern the military, Article I, Section 8, Clause 14, of the Constitution empowers Congress "to make Rules for the Government and Regulation of the land and naval Forces."

Until the enactment of the UCMJ, the Army and Navy each had its own system of military justice, known as the Articles of War in the Army and the Articles for the Government of the Navy. The UCMJ ensures that any accused member of the armed services will be subject to the same substantive charges and procedural rules and will be guaranteed identical procedural safeguards.

Some provisions of the UCMJ deal with COMMON-LAW crimes, such as MURDER, RAPE, LAR-

CENY, and ARSON. The elements of these offenses do not differ from those in state codes and statutes. Other provisions deal with offenses that are unique to the military, including absence offenses, duties and orders offenses, superior-subordinate relationship offenses, and combat-related offenses.

Absence offenses include absence without leave (art. 86, 10 U.S.C.A. § 886) and desertion (art. 85, 10 U.S.C.A. § 885). These are the most prevalent crimes in the military. Approximately 75 percent of all courts-martial involve charges of being absent without leave under article 86.

Duties and orders offenses include failure to obey an order or regulation (art. 92, 10 U.S.C.A. § 892) and being drunk on duty (art. 112, 10 U.S.C.A. § 912). Superior-subordinate relationship offenses include violations such as CONTEMPT for officials (art. 88, 10 U.S.C.A. § 888) and MUTINY (art. 94, 10 U.S.C.A. § 894). Combat-related offenses include misbehavior before the enemy (art. 99, 10 U.S.C.A. § 899) and misconduct as a prisoner (art. 105, 10 U.S.C.A. § 905).

The UCMJ also includes the so-called General Articles (arts. 133 and 134, 10 U.S.C.A. §§ 933, 934), which proscribe certain conduct in nonspecific terms. Article 133 makes unlawful any conduct by an officer that is "unbecoming to an officer and a gentleman." Article 134 proscribes "all disorders and neglects to the prejudice of a good order and discipline . . ., [and] all conduct of a nature to bring discredit upon the armed forces." The constitutionality of these articles was upheld in the face of a FIRST AMENDMENT challenge in *Parker v. Levy*, 417 U.S. 733, 94 S. Ct. 2547, 41 L. Ed. 2d 439 (1974).

Article 15 (10 U.S.C.A. § 815) of the UCMJ provides for nonjudicial punishment. Most minor violations of the UCMJ are processed under this article. The accused appears before his commanding officer, who passes judgment and imposes the sentence, if any. The military favors nonjudicial punishment because it gives the commanding officer a direct method of discipline, the process is quick and efficient, and the accused's record is not marred by a COURT-MARTIAL conviction.

Procedurally, the UCMJ provides for a three-level system of courts that is similar to the structure of civilian courts. Criminal matters are handled by courts-martial, which are analogous to civilian trial courts. There are three types of court-martial: the general court-martial, the special court-martial, and the summary court-martial. A general court-martial is used for serious offenses. The court has five or more members, but a defendant also has the right to have a military judge hear the case. The prosecutor, defense counsel, and military judge in a general court-martial must be lawyers. The military judge advises the court on matters of law and makes rulings as to the introduction of EVIDENCE. A general court-martial may impose any penalty that is authorized by the UCMJ as punishment for the offense.

A special court-martial deals with intermediate-level offenses. The court has three or more members, but the defendant may elect to be tried by a military judge. The maximum sentence that may be imposed by a special court-martial is six months of confinement, forfeiture of pay, reduction in rank, and a bad conduct discharge.

A summary court-martial may be used only to prosecute enlisted personnel for minor offenses. Only one officer hears the case, and the maximum penalty is confinement for one month, forfeiture of two-thirds of a month's pay, and reduction in rank.

Under the UCMJ all cases in which the sentence involves death, a punitive discharge, or imprisonment for a term of one year or more must be reviewed by a Court of Criminal Appeals (CCA). A CCA must also affirm any sentence imposed by a court-martial before the sentence can be executed. Each branch of the armed services has its own CCA. Generally, a three-judge panel reviews court-martial convictions and sentences. CCA judges may be commissioned officers or civilians, but all must be lawyers.

The U.S. Court of Appeals for the Armed Forces (USCAAF), formerly known as the Court of Military Appeals, is the highest civilian court responsible for reviewing the decisions of military courts. It is an APPELLATE COURT and consists of three civilian judges appointed by the president to serve fifteen-year terms. The USCAAF hears all cases where the death penalty is imposed, all cases forwarded by the judge advocate general of each service for review after CCA review, and certain discretionary APPEALS. Its decisions are appealable to the U.S. Supreme Court.

The UCMJ has been attacked by critics who believe it severely and unnecessarily restricts First Amendment and other constitutional rights of military personnel. Article 15's nonjudicial punishment has been criticized as susceptible to abuse, bias, and CONFLICTS OF INTEREST. Because the military courts are necessarily different from civilian courts, the Supreme Court has limited the JURISDICTION of the UCMJ. Discharged soldiers cannot be court-martialed for offenses committed while in the military. Civilian employees of the armed forces overseas and civilian dependents of military personnel accompanying them overseas are also not subject to the UCMJ. In addition, a crime committed by a member of the armed services must be related to military service for the UCMJ to apply.

UNIFORM COMMERCIAL CODE 📖 A general and inclusive group of laws adopted, at least partially, by all the states to further uniformity and fair dealing in business and commercial transactions. 📖

The Uniform Commercial Code (UCC) is a set of suggested laws relating to commercial transactions. The UCC was one of many uniform codes that grew out of a late nineteenth-century movement toward uniformity among state laws. In 1890 the AMERICAN BAR ASSOCIATION, an association of lawyers, proposed that states identify areas of law that could be made uniform throughout the nation, prepare lists of such areas, and suggest appropriate legislative changes. In 1892 the National Conference of Commissioners on Uniform State Laws (NCCUSL) met for the first time in Saratoga, New York. Only seven states sent representatives to the meeting.

In 1986 the NCCUSL offered up its first act, the Uniform Negotiable Instruments Act. The NCCUSL drafted a variety of other uniform acts. Some of these dealt with commerce, including the Uniform Conditional Sales Act and the Uniform Trust Receipts Act. The uniform acts on commercial issues were fragmented by the 1930s and in 1940, the NCCUSL proposed revising the commerce-oriented uniform codes and combining them into one uniform set of model laws. In 1941 the American Law Institute (ALI) joined the discussion, and over the next several years lawyers, judges, and professors in the ALI and NCCUSL prepared a number of drafts of the Uniform Commercial Code.

In September 1951 a final draft of the UCC was completed and approved by the American Law Institute (ALI) and the NCCUSL, and then by the House of Delegates of the American Bar Association. After some additional amendments and changes, the official edition, with explanatory comments, was published in 1952. Pennsylvania was the first state to adopt the UCC, followed by Massachusetts. By 1967 the District of Columbia and all the states, with the exception of Louisiana, had adopted the UCC in whole or in part. Louisiana eventually adopted all the articles in the UCC except articles 2 and 2A.

The UCC is divided into nine articles, each containing provisions that relate to a specific area of commercial law. Article 1, General Provisions, provides definitions and general principles that apply to the entire code. Article 2 covers the sale of goods. Article 3, Commercial Paper, addresses NEGOTIABLE INSTRUMENTS, such as PROMISSORY NOTES and CHECKS. Article 4 deals with banks and their handling of checks and other financial documents. Article 5 provides model laws on LETTERS OF CREDIT, which are promises by a bank or some other party to pay the purchases of a buyer without delay and without reference to the buyer's financial solvency. Article 6, on BULK TRANSFERS, imposes an obligation on buyers who order the major part of the INVENTORY for certain types of businesses. Most notably, article 6 provisions require that such buyers notify creditors of the seller of the inventory so that creditors can take steps to see that the seller pays her debts when she receives payments from the buyer. Article 7 offers rules on the relationships between buyers and sellers and any transporters of goods, called CARRIERS. These rules primarily cover the issuance and transfer of WAREHOUSE RECEIPTS and bills of lading. A BILL OF LADING is a document showing that the carrier has delivered an item to a buyer. Article 8 contains rules on the issuance and transfer of STOCKS, BONDS, and other INVESTMENT securities. Article 9, Secured Transactions, covers security interests in REAL PROPERTY. A security interest is a partial or total claim to a piece of property to secure the performance of some obligation, usually the payment of a DEBT. This article identifies when and how a secured interest may be created and the rights of the CREDITOR to foreclose on the property if the debtor defaults on his obligation. The article also establishes which creditors can collect first from a defaulting debtor.

The ALI and the NCCUSL periodically review and revise the UCC. Since the code was originally devised, the House of Delegates of the American Bar Association has approved two additional articles: article 2A on personal property LEASES, and article 4A on fund transfers. Article 2A establishes model rules for the leasing or renting of PERSONAL PROPERTY (as opposed to real property, such as houses and apartments). Article 4A covers transfers of funds from one party to another party through a bank. This article is intended to address the issues that arise with the use of new technologies for handling money.

Most states have adopted at least some of the provisions in the UCC. The least popular article has been article 6 on bulk transfers. These provisions require the reporting of payments made, which many legislators consider an unnecessary intrusion on commercial relationships.

CROSS-REFERENCES

Commissioners on Uniform Laws; Contracts; Llewellyn, Karl N; Model Acts; Sales Law.

UNIFORM CONSUMER CREDIT CODE

The Uniform Consumer Credit Code (UCCC) is a model statute that provides standards for credit transactions entered into by individuals who purchase, use, maintain, and dispose of products and services. The UCCC was originally approved by the National Conference of Commissioners on Uniform State Laws in 1968. It was revised in 1974 following criticism from consumer groups and has been adopted in nine states: Colorado, Idaho, Indiana, Iowa, Kansas, Maine, Oklahoma, Utah and Wyoming. South Carolina and Wisconsin have enacted CONSUMER PROTECTION codes that are substantially similar to the UCCC, and many states have included particular provisions from it in their CONSUMER CREDIT laws.

The UCCC is designed to provide protection to consumers who buy goods and services on CREDIT. It attempts to simplify, clarify, and update legislation governing consumer credit and USURY, which is the illegal charging of high interest rates. The UCCC also sets ceilings on the rates consumers can be charged for credit.

Other provisions protect consumers against unfair practices by certain consumer credit suppliers by limiting the ability of CREDITORS to use state court systems to execute on a consumer DEBTOR's assets or to garnish a consumer debtor's wages. In addition, CONFESSION OF JUDGMENT clauses are barred from consumer credit contracts. Such clauses require a person who borrows money or buys on credit to agree in advance to allow the attorney for the lender to get a court JUDGMENT against the borrower in the event of DEFAULT without even telling the borrower.

The UCCC also seeks to comply with the disclosure regulations in consumer credit transactions in accordance with the federal CONSUMER CREDIT PROTECTION ACT of 1968 (16 U.S.C.A. § 1601 et seq.), which mandates that consumers purchasing on credit be given complete information on the interest rate, its calculation, the total amount of interest over the life of the contract, payment due dates, late penalties, and collection costs.

The UCCC was also proposed as a means of making the law of consumer credit, including administrative rules, more uniform throughout the fifty states. Because it has only been adopted in whole in nine states, the UCCC has not completely met this objective. Nevertheless, the

many analogous provisions in state and federal consumer credit laws suggest a common purpose.

UNIFORM PROBATE CODE The Uniform Probate Code (UPC) is a comprehensive statute that unifies, clarifies, and modernizes the laws governing the affairs of DECEDENTS and their ESTATES, certain transfers accomplished other than by a WILL, and TRUSTS and their administration. The UPC was originally approved by the National Conference of Commissioners on Uniform State Laws and the House of Delegates of the AMERICAN BAR ASSOCIATION in 1969. The purpose of the UPC is to modernize PROBATE law and probate administration and to encourage uniformity through the adoption of the code by all fifty states. The UPC, which has been amended numerous times, has been adopted in its entirety by sixteen states: Alaska, Arizona, Colorado, Florida, Hawaii, Idaho, Maine, Michigan, Minnesota, Montana, Nebraska, New Mexico, North Dakota, South Carolina, South Dakota, and Utah. The other thirty-four states have adopted parts of the UPC, but in general the UPC has not succeeded in providing a uniform body of substantive and procedural probate law.

The UPC contains seven substantive articles. Article I contains general provisions, definitions, and jurisdictional topics. Article II governs wills and INTESTATE SUCCESSION, which occurs when a person dies without leaving a will. Article III deals with the probate of wills and the administration of estates, article IV concerns the probating of estates in states other than the domicile of the decedent, article V extends protection to persons under disability and their property, and article VI governs nonprobate transfers of property. Article VII contains comprehensive provisions on trust administration.

U.S. shoppers rely on credit cards for a substantial portion of their purchases. The Uniform Consumer Credit Code is a model code designed to protect consumers who shop by credit.

The prime objective of the UPC is to simplify the probate process. For example, article III provides for supervised and unsupervised administration of probate. For estates with few ASSETS and no disputes among the BENEFICIARIES, the UPC allows unsupervised administration. In this case the executor of the will, who is called a PERSONAL REPRESENTATIVE in the UPC, handles the probating of the estate without direct supervision by the probate court. The personal representative handles every step of the probate process by filing a series of simple forms with the probate court. Unsupervised administration reduces the cost of probate and speeds up the process. Probate courts are freed from dealing with routine matters and may concentrate their efforts on estates with substantial assets or contested matters, where supervised administration is necessary.

The adoption of the UPC by state legislatures has been fought both by attorneys, who are opposed to unsupervised administration and to the overturning of current state laws governing probate, and by bonding companies, which stand to lose business because unsupervised probate does not require the posting of a BOND. In light of this opposition, the Commissioners on Uniform State Laws have developed freestanding acts from similar provisions integrated into the UPC. This technique permits provisions, such as those involving POWERS OF ATTORNEY and guardianship, to become law without disturbing other parts of a state's probate code.

See also DESCENT AND DISTRIBUTION; EXECUTORS AND ADMINISTRATORS.

UNILATERAL CONTRACT 📖 A CONTRACT in which only one party makes an express PROMISE, or undertakes a PERFORMANCE without first securing a reciprocal agreement from the other party. 📖

In a unilateral, or one-sided, contract, one party, known as the offeror, makes a promise in exchange for an act (or abstention from acting) by another party, known as the offeree. If the offeree acts on the offeror's promise, the offeror is legally obligated to fulfill the contract, but an offeree cannot be forced to act (or not act), because no return promise has been made to the offeror. After an offeree has performed, only one enforceable promise exists, that of the offeror.

A unilateral contract differs from a BILATERAL CONTRACT, in which the parties exchange mutual promises. Bilateral contracts are commonly used in business transactions; a sale of goods is a type of bilateral contract.

REWARD offers are usually unilateral contracts. The offeror (the party offering the reward) cannot impel anyone to fulfill the reward offer. An offeree can sue for breach of contract, however, if the offeror does not provide the reward after the offeree has fulfilled the contract's requirements.

UNION SHOP 📖 A type of business in which an employer is allowed to hire a nonunion worker, who, however, must subsequently join the union in order to be permitted to continue work. 📖

A union shop is different from a CLOSED SHOP; in the latter situation, the employee must be a union member before being hired.

See also LABOR LAW; LABOR UNION.

UNITED NATIONS The United Nations (U.N.) is an organization of 185 states that strives to attain international peace and security, promotes fundamental HUMAN RIGHTS and equal rights for men and women, and encourages social progress. The successor to the LEAGUE OF NATIONS, the United Nations stems from the 1941 Inter-Allied Declaration signed by representatives of fourteen countries (not including the United States) and the Atlantic Charter signed by President FRANKLIN D. ROOSEVELT and Prime Minister Winston Churchill of the United Kingdom. In 1942 twenty-six countries met in Washington, D.C., and signed the Declaration by United Nations in a cooperative effort to triumph over German dictator ADOLF HITLER during WORLD WAR II. In addition, wartime conferences in Moscow, Tehran, Yalta, and Washington, D.C. (at the Dumbarton Oaks estate in Georgetown), laid the foundation of the future organization. On June 25, 1945, delegates from fifty nations met in San Francisco and unanimously adopted the Charter of the United Nations. By October 24, 1945, China, France, the United States, the Soviet Union, the United Kingdom, and a majority of the charter's other signatories had ratified it, and the United Nations was officially established. Shortly thereafter the U.S. Congress unanimously invited the United Nations to set up headquarters in the United States, and the organization chose New York City as its permanent home.

The United Nations is open to all "peace-loving" states, a requirement construed liberally over the years. The United Nations comprises six major organs: the General Assembly, the Security Council, the Economic and Social Council, the Secretariat, the INTERNATIONAL COURT OF JUSTICE (WORLD COURT), and the Trusteeship Council. The Trusteeship Council, which was established to encourage governments to prepare trust territories for self-government or independence, has largely com-

SANDRA BAKER/LIAISON INTERNATIONAL

pleted its original task of supervising eleven non-self-governing territories. In 1994 the Security Council terminated the Trusteeship Agreement of Belau, a trust territory in the western Pacific that had been administered by the United States. As all other trust territories had previously obtained independence or self-government, the Trusteeship Council amended its rules and now meets only as situations requiring action arise.

The main deliberative body of the United Nations, the General Assembly, somewhat resembles a parliament; each nation has one vote. The General Assembly has no power to compel any action by a member state, however: it only has the right to discuss and make recommendations on matters within the scope of the U.N. Charter. Headed by a president elected at each session, the assembly ordinarily meets from mid-September to mid-December; other sessions are held as necessary. Ordinary matters require only a majority vote, but important matters, such as recommendations on peace and security, election of members to the Security Council or the Economic and Social Council, or admission of member states, require a two-thirds majority. The assembly also approves the U.N. budget (including peacekeeping operations), sets policies, determines programs for the U.N. Secretariat, and, in conjunction with the Security Council's recommendation, appoints the U.N. secretary-general, the chief administrative officer of the United Nations.

The Security Council has the primary responsibility for maintaining peace and security. Five permanent members—the United States, China, France, the Russian Federation (replacing the Soviet Union), and the United Kingdom—join ten other members elected by the General Assembly for two-year terms. A

Although the United Nations has been unsuccessful in preventing war between nations, it remains an important forum for nations to air grievances and foster international cooperation.

representative of each member of the Security Council must always be present at U.N. headquarters so that the council can convene any time peace is threatened. Unlike the other U.N. organs, member states are obligated under the charter to carry out economic and diplomatic decisions by the council. All decisions require nine votes, but on all questions except procedural matters, the permanent members must vote unanimously or abstain. This veto power has been exercised many times and can seriously undermine the Security Council's ability to take bold steps in tenuous situations.

The Security Council usually seeks peaceful means such as mediation or settlement when international peace is threatened. Peacekeepers may be sent to prevent the outbreak of a conflict, or the council may issue a cease-fire directive once fighting has begun. The Security Council may impose economic sanctions and order collective military action.

The United Nations has been involved in approximately forty peacekeeping operations since 1948; more than two dozen operations have occurred since 1988. Military personnel are drawn from member states; more than 750,000 persons have served. More than 1,400 peacekeepers have lost their lives. In early 1996 seventeen U.N. operations deployed approximately 26,300 personnel, including troops, civilian police, and military observers, from seventy countries.

The reality of U.N. peacekeeping efforts often falls short of the organization's ideals. For example, in the early 1990s U.N. troops attempted to restore order and provide humanitarian relief during the civil war in Somalia. Warring Somali factions greatly impeded the troops' efforts, however, and in 1995 the U.N. forces withdrew without succeeding in their mission. In addition, U.N. members sometimes pledge support for a mission but fail to deliver tangible evidence of that support. In 1994 the secretary-general determined that 35,000 troops would be needed to deter attacks on so-called safe areas in Bosnia and Herzegovina. Member states authorized fewer than 8,000 troops and took a year to provide them. Nevertheless, the United Nations has had some successes: its operations in Kashmir, Cyprus, Lebanon, Suez, Cambodia, and Mozambique have been highly praised. Other strife-torn areas receiving assistance in recent years include Angola, Afghanistan, Iran, Iraq, the former Yugoslavia, and a number of Central American countries. The United Nations also monitored or observed elections in El Salvador, Nicaragua, Haiti, and South Africa.

The Economic and Social Council, which has fifty-four members, coordinates the economic and social work of the United Nations and its specialized agencies and institutions. Among other tasks, the council recommends and directs activities to promote economic growth in developing countries, promotes the observance of human rights, and attempts to foster cooperation in creating housing, controlling population growth, and preventing crime.

Fourteen specialized agencies are separate, autonomous organizations connected to the United Nations by specific agreements, mainly through the Economic and Social Council. Specialized agencies include the World Health Organization (WHO), the World Bank, the INTERNATIONAL MONETARY FUND (IMF), and the U.N. Educational, Scientific, and Cultural Organization (UNESCO).

UNICEF, the United Nations Children's Fund (originally the United Nations International Children's Emergency Fund), is a semiautonomous organization reporting to the General Assembly and the Economic and Social Council. UNICEF has programs in 144 countries addressing children's needs, including immunization, nutrition, primary health care, and education. A joint UNICEF-WHO program claims to have immunized 80 percent of the world's children against polio, tetanus, measles, whooping cough, diphtheria, and tuberculosis.

The United Nations also provides humanitarian aid for countries stricken by war, natural disaster, or famine through UNICEF, the World Food Programme, and other U.N. programs. In addition, the Office of the U.N. High Commissioner for Refugees, part of the Secretariat, helps assist and protect many millions displaced by strife.

With a staff numbering in the thousands, the Secretariat carries out the United Nations' day-to-day functions in New York and throughout the world. Headed by the secretary-general, the Secretariat's staff represents nearly every member country. The Security Council recommends a candidate for secretary-general to the General Assembly, which appoints the secretary-general for a five-year term. In addition to administrative duties, the secretary-general plays an active role in worldwide peacemaking through diplomacy, by employing mediators, or by sending representatives to negotiate settlements or otherwise assist in resolving conflicts.

The International Court of Justice, also known as the World Court, is the judicial branch of the United Nations and meets in The Hague, Netherlands. Its fifteen judges are elected by the General Assembly and the Security Council for nine-year terms. Jurisdiction applies only to countries, not individuals. Unless required by a treaty, a country is not obligated to submit to the court's JURISDICTION. However, a country agreeing to have a matter determined by the World Court is obligated to comply with the court's decision.

Competing needs, shifting alliances, problems of managing a huge worldwide bureaucracy, and the inevitable politics of the organization make it difficult for the United Nations to attain the goals set forth in its charter. Financial difficulties present further challenges. The United Nations is funded by dues from member states and is prohibited from borrowing from financial institutions. By 1997 members were more than $3 billion in arrears; the United States was responsible for more than half that amount. Despite these obstacles, however, the United Nations has had some success in resolving conflicts and bettering the lives of the world's citizens.

See also INTERNATIONAL LAW.

UNITED STATES–CANADA FREE TRADE AGREEMENT See NORTH AMERICAN FREE TRADE AGREEMENT.

UNITED STATES GOVERNMENT MANUAL A comprehensive directory, published annually, that contains general information about the federal government with emphasis on the EXECUTIVE BRANCH and regulatory agencies, and also information about Congress and the judicial branch of government.

In the *United States Government Manual*, the description of each executive department and ADMINISTRATIVE AGENCY is described according to (1) relevant statutes that created and affect the agency or its institutional antecedents; (2) an explanation of the functions and authority of the agency; (3) facts concerning subsidiary units, bureaus, and agencies; (4) the names and functions of the major officials of the agency; (5) organizational charts; and (6) sources of information provided by the agency.

UNITED STATES v. CAROLENE PRODUCTS CO. See FOOTNOTE FOUR.

UNITED STATES v. NIXON In *United States v. Nixon*, 418 U.S. 683, 94 S. Ct. 3090, 41 L. Ed. 2d 1039 (1974), the U.S. Supreme Court recognized the doctrine of EXECUTIVE PRIVILEGE but held that it could not prevent the disclosure of materials needed for a criminal prosecution. The case arose during the WATERGATE political scandal, which involved President RICHARD M. NIXON and numerous members of his administration. The Court had to consider whether Nixon was required to turn over secret White House tape recordings to government prosecu-

President Nixon argued that executive privilege allowed him to withhold from Watergate investigators thousands of hours of tape recordings he had made at the White House.

tors. Nixon claimed that the doctrine of executive privilege allowed him to refuse to release the tapes, while prosecutors argued that they had a right to obtain EVIDENCE of possible crimes, even if that evidence was held by the president of the United States.

The Watergate scandal began during the presidential campaign of 1972, in which Nixon defeated his Democratic opponent, Senator George McGovern of South Dakota, by a wide margin. Several months before the election, on June 17, a group of burglars broke into the Democratic party campaign headquarters in the Watergate building complex in Washington, D.C. Aggressive investigative reporting by the *Washington Post* uncovered connections to officials in the Nixon administration. Though the administration denied any wrongdoing, it soon became clear that members of the administration had tried to cover up the BURGLARY and connections to it that might include the president.

Under congressional and public pressure, Nixon appointed a SPECIAL PROSECUTOR. When it was revealed that the president had secretly taped conversations in the Oval Office in the White House, the prosecutor, ARCHIBALD COX, filed a SUBPOENA to secure tapes that he believed were relevant to the criminal investigation. When Cox refused to withdraw his request, Nixon had him fired. The resulting public

outrage forced Nixon to appoint LEON JAWORSKI as a new special prosecutor.

In March 1974 a federal GRAND JURY indicted seven Nixon associates for CONSPIRACY to obstruct justice and for other offenses related to the Watergate burglary. Nixon himself was named as an unindicted co-conspirator. Upon Jaworski's motion the U.S. district court issued a new subpoena to the president, requiring him to produce certain tapes and documents pertaining to precisely identified meetings between the president and others. Although Nixon released edited transcripts of some of the subpoenaed conversations, his attorney moved to QUASH, or VOID, the subpoena on the grounds of executive privilege. When the district court denied the MOTION, the president appealed, and the case was quickly brought to the U.S. Supreme Court.

Nixon refused to release the tapes, contending that the doctrine of executive privilege gave him the right to withhold documents from Congress and the courts. Executive privilege, though not mentioned in the U.S. Constitution, was first asserted by GEORGE WASHINGTON. Presidents have argued that the privilege is inherent in executive power and is necessary to maintain the secrecy of information related to national security and to protect the confidentiality of their deliberations. Executive privilege did not become a major point of contention until the Nixon presidency, however. Nixon routinely used it during his first term to thwart congressional inquiries.

The Supreme Court, in a unanimous decision (Justice WILLIAM H. REHNQUIST recused himself because he had served in the Nixon administration), recognized for the first time the general legitimacy of executive privilege. Nevertheless, Chief Justice WARREN E. BURGER, writing for the Court, rejected Nixon's claim of "an absolute, unqualified Presidential privilege of immunity from judicial process under all circumstances." Burger found that [a]bsent a claim of need to protect military, diplomatic, or sensitive national security secrets," the need for protecting the confidentiality of presidential communications must give way to a legitimate request by the courts for information vital to a criminal prosecution. Burger noted that the judge would review the subpoenaed tapes in private to determine what portions should be released to the prosecutors. This confidential review would prevent sensitive but irrelevant information from being disclosed.

Nixon obeyed the order and turned the tapes over to the district court. When relevant portions were released, they revealed that the president had been intimately involved with the attempt to cover up White House involvement in the Watergate burglary. Less than three weeks after the Court announced its decision, Nixon resigned the presidency, thereby avoiding IMPEACHMENT by Congress.

UNITED STATES v. VIRGINIA In *United States v. Virginia*, __U.S. __ , 116 S. Ct. 2264, 135 L. Ed. 2d 735 (1996), the U.S. Supreme Court issued a landmark decision on sex-based discrimination when it ruled that Virginia Military Institute (VMI), a publicly funded military college, must give up its all-male enrollment policy and admit women. The decision, which also affected The Citadel, South Carolina's state-run, all-male, military school, was a decisive blow to state-sponsored discrimination. In so ruling, the Court rejected a proposal by Virginia that it establish a separate military program for women at a private college.

The case began in 1990 when a female high school student complained to the U.S. Justice Department about VMI's male-only admission policy. Her application had been rejected without regard to her qualifications. The Justice Department sued the Commonwealth of Virginia and VMI, arguing that DISCRIMINATION on the basis of sex violated the Equal Protection Clause of the FOURTEENTH AMENDMENT.

The district court ruled in VMI's favor, grounding the decision on the need to preserve the "VMI experience," a physically and emotionally demanding military regimen that has remained unchanged since the early nineteenth century (*United States v. Virginia*, 766 F. Supp. 1407 [W.D. Va. 1991]). The court concluded that this "adversative" method of education could not work in a coeducational environment. The critical component of this method was the subjection of first-year students to the "rat line." First-year students are called "rats" because, as one expert testified, the rat is "probably the lowest animal on earth." During the first seven months of college, the rats are treated miserably.

Features of the rat line include "indoctrination, egalitarian treatment, rituals, minute regulation of individual behaviors, frequent punishment, and the use of privileges to support desired behaviors." Rats have no privacy. The tradition of constant supervision of cadets has led to stark, unaccommodating barracks without curtains, door locks, or other physical barriers that promote privacy.

The judge concluded that coeducation would prevent both men and women from undergoing the "VMI experience." The presence of women would "distract male students from their studies," while tending to "impair the *esprit de corps* and egalitarian atmosphere." The barracks would have to be modified to provide privacy, and the physical education requirements would have to be altered for women. If women were admitted, VMI would eventually drop the adversative model. Therefore, the judge ruled that VMI was "fully justified" in prohibiting women. The same-sex admission policy promoted diversity of educational opportunities because out of fifteen state-funded colleges and universities in Virginia, VMI alone had this policy. This diversity was a legitimate state objective that rebutted the claim of unequal protection of the law.

The Justice Department appealed the decision. The Fourth Circuit Court of Appeals vacated the decision and sent the case back to the district court (*United States v. Virginia*, 976 F.2d 890 [4th Cir. 1992]). In his majority opinion, Judge Paul Niemeyer accepted the district court's factual determinations that VMI's adversative model justified a single-sex admission policy and that critical elements of the model would be substantially changed if women were admitted. The appeals court also pointed out that all the parties acknowledged "the positive and unique aspects of the program."

The appeals court concluded, however, that the Commonwealth of Virginia had failed to "articulate an important objective which supports the provision of this unique educational opportunity to men only." Judge Niemeyer stated that the "decisive question" was why the state offered this educational opportunity only to men. The state was required to articulate an objective because of the type of constitutional review in this case. In lawsuits challenging sex discrimination by the government, the government must show that the sex-based classification is "substantially related to an important government objective."

The "unique benefit" offered by VMI did not answer the question of whether women could be denied admission under a policy of diversity. Judge Niemeyer found nothing in the record that explained why the Commonwealth of Virginia offered this unique benefit only to men. Though VMI had "adequately defended" its system, it had failed to identify or establish the existence of a government objective that justified its single-sex admission policy on the basis of educational diversity.

The appeals court remanded the case to the district court. Virginia then advanced a proposal to create a parallel program for women, called the Virginia Women's Institute for Leadership (VWIL). VWIL would be located at

Mary Baldwin College, a private liberal arts college for women. VMI would remain all-male. The district court accepted the plan (*United States v. Virginia*, 852 F. Supp. 471 [W.D. Va. 1994]). The Justice Department appealed again to the Fourth Circuit, but this time the appeals court upheld the remedial plan. The court concluded that Virginia's plan for single-gender options was a legitimate objective. It also found that VMI and VWIL would provide "substantively comparable" benefits (*United States v. Virginia*, 44 F.3d 1229 [4th Cir. 1995]).

The U.S. Supreme Court found no merit in the lower courts' justifications for maintaining VMI's male-only admission policy. Justice RUTH BADER GINSBURG, in her majority opinion, essentially agreed with the first decision of the court of appeals, which found no basis for the male-only policy. In her view, "[n]either the goal of producing citizen-soldiers nor VMI's implementing methodology is inherently unsuitable to women."

Ginsburg rejected Virginia's contention that single-sex education yields educational benefits important enough to justify the exclusion of women from VMI. The generalizations about the differences between men and women that were offered to justify the exclusion of women were suspect. According to Ginsburg, the generalizations were too broad and stereotypical, and the predictions that VMI's stature would suffer if women were admitted were no more than self-fulfilling prophecies. The categorical exclusion of women from VMI denied EQUAL PROTECTION to women.

The categorical exclusion was unnecessary because the VMI adversative method of training could be modified without destroying the program. In Ginsburg's view, "neither the goal of producing citizen-soldiers, VMI's *raison d'être*, nor VMI's implementing methodology is inherently unsuitable to women."

The Court was also unimpressed with the creation of the VWIL as a remedy for the constitutional violation of equal protection. Justice Ginsburg noted numerous deficiencies, pointing out that VWIL afforded women no opportunity to "experience the rigorous military training for which VMI is famed." VWIL did not propose to use the adversative method, nor would the student body, faculty, course offerings, or facilities match VMI's. Ginsburg called the VWIL a "pale shadow" of VMI that would lack substantial equality with the all-male college.

Finally, the Court rejected the appeals court's "substantive comparability" test as plain error. The appellate court's "deferential analysis" did not accord with the "heightened scrutiny" test required when allegations of sex-based discrimination are made. Calling the VWIL remedy "substantially different and significantly unequal," Ginsburg noted that the court of appeals should have inquired as to whether the proposed remedy placed women who were denied the VMI advantage in the position they would have occupied in the absence of discrimination. The answer to this inquiry was clearly negative, thus invalidating the VWIL remedy. Ginsburg stated that "[w]omen seeking and fit for a VMI-quality education cannot be offered anything less under the state's obligation to afford them genuinely equal protection."

See also SEX DISCRIMINATION; WOMEN'S RIGHTS.

UNITED STEELWORKERS v. WEBER In

United Steelworkers Union v. Weber, 443 U.S. 193, 99 S. Ct. 2721, 61 L. Ed. 2d 480 (1979), the U.S. Supreme Court held that an employer could grant preferential treatment to racial minorities under a private, voluntary AFFIRMATIVE ACTION program. Affirmative action is a concerted effort by an employer to rectify past DISCRIMINATION against specific classes of individuals by giving temporary preferential treatment to individuals from these classes when hiring and promoting until true equal opportunity is achieved. The use of affirmative action to correct past racial discrimination in employment resulted from the passage of title VII of the CIVIL RIGHTS ACT of 1964 (42 U.S.C.A. § 2000e et seq.). Affirmative action has proved controversial; many white people claim that it is in fact "reverse discrimination."

Brian Weber, a white production worker at a Kaiser Aluminum plant in Gramercy, Louisi-

Brian Weber sued the United Steelworkers Union, arguing that its policy providing specialized training to black employees with less seniority than interested white employees constituted reverse discrimination.

APWIDE WORLD PHOTOS

ana, claimed that the company's efforts to increase the number of African Americans in historically segregated categories of employment unfairly prejudiced white workers like himself. In 1974 Kaiser and the United Steelworkers signed a COLLECTIVE BARGAINING AGREEMENT that contained an affirmative action plan designed to eliminate the substantial racial imbalance in Kaiser's craft workforce. Craft trainees were to be selected on the basis of seniority, with the provision that 50 percent of the openings would be reserved for African American workers until the percentage of African American craftworkers in a plant equaled the percentage of African Americans in the local workforce. During the first year the plan was in operation, seven African American and six white workers were selected for craft training. Several of the successful African American applicants had less seniority than Weber.

Weber filed suit, claiming that the minority admissions quota violated the ban in title VII on racial discrimination in employment. The district court and the court of appeals agreed with him, but the Supreme Court, on a 5–2 vote, with two members not participating, reversed the lower courts and held that the Kaiser plan was valid.

Justice WILLIAM J. BRENNAN, JR., in his majority opinion, agreed that Weber's literal interpretation of the act had some justification but noted that the whole purpose of title VII was to "better the plight of the Negro in our economy." African Americans had been excluded from craft positions such as carpenter, electrician, plumber, and painter throughout U.S. history. To adopt Weber's position would prevent employers from voluntarily seeking ways of correcting past discrimination. Brennan wrote that "[i]t would be ironic indeed if a law triggered by a Nation's concern over centuries of racial injustice [constituted] the first legislative prohibition of all voluntary, private, race-conscious efforts to abolish traditional patterns of racial segregation and hierarchy."

The Court held that an affirmative action program was legal if it did not "unnecessarily trammel" the interests of white employees, lead to their discharge, or permanently prevent their promotion. The Kaiser plan was not permanent but ended when the percentage of skilled African Americans in the plant matched the percentage of African Americans in the local workforce. Therefore, the Court concluded that the affirmative action program was designed to correct a manifest racial imbalance rather than maintain racial balance.

Justice WILLIAM H. REHNQUIST, in a dissenting opinion, contended that the language of title VII made it unlawful to discriminate on the basis of race. He argued that Congress made a commitment to equality in hiring, not to "preferential treatment of minorities." The Kaiser plan, even though temporary, imposed a "racial quota."

CROSS-REFERENCES

Civil Rights; Employment Law; Equal Protection; Equal Employment Opportunity Commission; *Wygant v. Jackson Board of Education.*

UNITIES 📖 In REAL PROPERTY law, the four characteristics that are peculiar to property owned by several individuals as joint tenants. 📖

The four unities are unity of time, unity of title, unity of interest, and unity of possession.

Unity of time is a characteristic because each joint tenant receives his or her interest at the same time—that is, upon DELIVERY of the DEED to the property. Unity of title exists because each tenant receives his or her TITLE from the same GRANTOR, and unity of interest because each tenant owns an undivided interest in the property. Unity of possession exists because each tenant has the right of possession of every part of the whole property.

See also ESTATE; JOINT TENANCY.

UNITRUST 📖 A right of property, real or personal, held by one person, the TRUSTEE, for the benefit of another, the BENEFICIARY, from which a fixed percentage of the net FAIR MARKET VALUE of the ASSETS, valued annually, is paid each year to the beneficiary. 📖

A unitrust, also known as a charitable remainder trust, is a legal device defined by federal tax laws that is frequently used by wealthy individuals who wish to make a substantial contribution to a school or charitable organization. To establish a unitrust, a donor transfers property to a TRUST, while retaining the right to receive payments from the trust for a term chosen by the donor. The payments may continue for the lifetime of the trust's named beneficiaries, a fixed term of not more than twenty years, or a combination of the two. Usually, the term is for the donor's life and the life of the donor's spouse. When the term has ended, the trust ESTATE is paid to a public charity designated by the donor.

The unitrust donor irrevocably transfers assets, usually cash, SECURITIES, or REAL ESTATE, to a trustee of the donor's choice. The trustee could be the charitable organization that will ultimately receive the assets or a bank trust department. During the unitrust's term, the trustee invests the unitrust's assets and pays a fixed percentage of the unitrust's current value, as determined annually, to the income beneficiaries. If the unitrust's value goes up from one year to the next, its payout increases proportionately. Likewise, if the unitrust's value goes down, the amount it distributes also declines. Payments must be at least five percent of the trust's annual value and are made out of trust income, or trust PRINCIPAL if income is not adequate. Payments may be made annually, semiannually, or quarterly. When the unitrust term ends, the unitrust's principal passes to the designated charitable organization to be used for the purposes the donor has designated.

A unitrust can be financially attractive to a donor because he is allowed a charitable deduction on his income tax return equal to the present value of the charitable organization's REMAINDER interest in the unitrust, as determined by reference to U.S. Treasury Regulations. The deduction is based on the fair market value of the asset transferred, the payout rate chosen, and either the age and number of beneficiaries or the term of years.

See also CHARITABLE TRUST; CHARITIES.

UNIVERSAL DECLARATION OF HUMAN RIGHTS, 1948 See HUMAN RIGHTS.

UNJUST ENRICHMENT 📖 A general equitable principle that no person should be allowed to profit at another's expense without making RESTITUTION for the reasonable value of any property, services, or other benefits that have been unfairly received and retained. 📖

Although the unjust enrichment doctrine is sometimes referred to as a quasi-contractual remedy, unjust enrichment is not based on an EXPRESS contract. Instead, litigants normally resort to the remedy of unjust enrichment when they have no written or verbal CONTRACT to support their claim for relief. In such instances litigants ask a court to find a contractual relationship that is IMPLIED in law, a fictitious relationship created by courts to do justice in a particular case.

Unjust enrichment has three elements. First, the plaintiff must have provided the defendant with something of value while expecting compensation in return. Second, the defendant must have acknowledged, accepted, and benefited from whatever the plaintiff provided. Third, the plaintiff must show that it would be inequitable or UNCONSCIONABLE for the defendant to enjoy the benefit of the plaintiff's actions without paying for it. A court will closely examine the facts of each case before awarding this remedy and will deny claims for unjust enrichment that frustrate PUBLIC POLICY or violate the law.

In some circumstances unjust enrichment is the appropriate remedy when a formally executed agreement has been ruled unenforceable due to INCAPACITY, MISTAKE, IMPOSSIBILITY of PERFORMANCE, or the STATUTE OF FRAUDS. In certain states, for example, contracts with MINORS are VOIDABLE at the minor's discretion because persons under the AGE OF MAJORITY are deemed legally incapable of entering into contracts. But if the minor has received a benefit from the other party's performance before nullifying the contract, the law of unjust enrichment will require the minor to pay for the FAIR MARKET VALUE of the benefit received. If the adult used DURESS or UNDUE INFLUENCE to induce the minor to enter the contract, however, the court will deny recovery in unjust enrichment because the adult lacked "clean hands."

In other circumstances unjust enrichment is the appropriate remedy for parties who have entered a legally enforceable contract, but where performance by one party exceeds the precise requirements of the agreement. For example, suppose a homeowner and a builder have entered into a legally binding contract under which the builder is to construct a two-car garage. One day the owner returns to her residence and discovers that in addition to constructing a two-car garage, the builder has paved the driveway. The owner says nothing about the driveway but later refuses to compensate the builder for the paving job. The builder has a claim for unjust enrichment in an amount representing the reasonable value of the labor and materials used in paving the driveway.

Suppose, instead, that after completing half the job, the builder tells the owner that he cannot finish the garage as originally agreed, but that he wants to be paid for the work he has done. The owner balks at this demand, arguing that the builder has breached his contractual obligations and is entitled to nothing. A minority of JURISDICTIONS would allow the builder to recover the reasonable value of his services, minus any damages suffered by the owner as a result of the breach. A majority of jurisdictions, however, adhere to the rule that a party who fails to perform contractual obligations has no remedy regardless of the amount of hardship he might endure.

The doctrine of unjust enrichment also governs many situations where the litigants have no contractual relationship. For example, the law finds an implied PROMISE to pay for emergency medical treatment that is neither requested nor consented to by a patient. In some jurisdictions the law finds an implied promise to pay for lifesaving medical treatment even when a patient objects to receiving it. The law also requires parents to reimburse a person who voluntarily supplies NECESSARIES such as food, shelter, and clothing to their children. As these examples demonstrate, unjust enrichment is a flexible remedy that allows courts great latitude in shifting the gains and losses between the parties as EQUITY, fairness, and justice dictate.

See also QUASI CONTRACT.

UNLAWFUL 📖 Contrary to or unauthorized by law; illegal. 📖

When applied to promises, agreements, or CONTRACTS, the term denotes that such agreements have no legal effect. The law disapproves of such conduct because it is immoral or contrary to PUBLIC POLICY. *Unlawful* does not necessarily imply criminality, although the term is sufficiently broad to include it.

UNLAWFUL ASSEMBLY 📖 A meeting of three or more individuals to commit a crime or carry out a lawful or unlawful purpose in a manner likely to imperil the peace and tranquillity of the neighborhood. 📖

The FIRST AMENDMENT to the U.S. Constitution guarantees individuals the right of freedom of assembly. Under the COMMON LAW and modern statutes, however, the meeting of three or more persons may constitute an unlawful assembly if the persons have an illegal purpose or if their meeting will breach the public peace of the community. If they actually execute their purpose, they have committed the criminal offense of RIOT.

Under the common law, when three or more individuals assembled for an illegal purpose, the offense of unlawful assembly was complete without the commission of any additional overt act. Some modern state statutes require both assembly and the commission of one of the acts proscribed by the statutes, even if the purpose of the assembly is not completed. Generally, an unlawful assembly is a MISDEMEANOR under both common law and statutes.

The basis of the offense of unlawful assembly is the intent with which the individuals assemble. The members of the assembled group must have in mind a fixed purpose to perform an illegal act. The time when the INTENT is formed is immaterial, and it does not matter whether the purpose of the group is lawful or unlawful if they intend to carry out that purpose in a way that is likely to precipitate a BREACH OF THE PEACE.

An assembly of individuals to carry on their ordinary business is not unlawful. Conversely, when three or more persons assemble and act jointly in committing a criminal offense, such as ASSAULT AND BATTERY, the assembly is unlawful. All those who participate in unlawful assemblies incur criminal responsibility for the acts of their associates performed in furtherance of their common objective. The mere presence of an individual in an unlawful assembly is enough to charge that person with participation in the illegal gathering.

Political gatherings and demonstrations raise the most troublesome issues involving unlawful assembly. The line between protecting freedom of assembly and protecting the peace and tranquillity of the community is often difficult for courts to draw. In the 1960s, in a series of decisions involving organized public protests against racial segregation in southern and border states, the U.S. Supreme Court threw out breach-of-the-peace convictions involving African Americans who had participated in peaceful public demonstrations. For example, in *Edwards v. South Carolina*, 372 U.S. 229, 83 S. Ct. 680, 9 L. Ed. 2d 697 (1963), the Court held that the conviction of 187 African American students for demonstrating on the grounds of the state capitol in Columbia, South Carolina, had infringed on their "constitutionally protected rights of free speech, free assembly, and freedom to petition for redress of their grievances."

In *Adderley v. Florida*, 385 U.S. 39, 87 S. Ct. 242, 17 L. Ed. 2d 149 (1966), however, the Court also made clear that assemblies are not lawful merely because they involve a political issue. In this case Harriet L. Adderly and other college students had protested the arrest of CIVIL RIGHTS protesters by blocking a jail driveway. When the students ignored requests to leave the area, they were arrested and charged with TRESPASS. The Court held that "[t]he State, no less than a private owner of property, has power to preserve the property under its control for the use to which it is lawfully dedicated."

In general, a unit of government may reasonably regulate parades, processions, and large public gatherings by requiring a LICENSE. Licenses cannot, however, be denied based on the

Peaceful protests, such as this one by anti-nuclear demonstrators, are protected by the First Amendment. However, when individuals gather to commit a crime or disturb the peace, their actions may constitute unlawful assembly.

political message of the group. Persons who refuse to obtain a license and hold their march or gathering may be charged with unlawful assembly.

See also FREEDOM OF SPEECH; TIME; PLACE, AND MANNER RESTRICTIONS.

UNLAWFUL COMMUNICATIONS

▨ Spoken or written words tending to intimidate, menace, or harm others. ▨

The guarantee of FREEDOM OF SPEECH in the FIRST AMENDMENT to the U.S. Constitution is not absolute. Many state and federal criminal laws prohibit persons from making THREATS and other unlawful communications. In addition, a person who makes unlawful communications may be sued in a civil TORT action for DAMAGES resulting from the threats or communications.

It is unlawful to threaten a person with the intent to obtain a pecuniary advantage or to compel the person to act against her will. This type of threat constitutes the crime of EXTORTION. For example, Colorado law states that any person "who communicates threats to another person with the intention thereby to obtain anything of value or any acquittance, advantage, or immunity is guilty of extortion" (C.S.S. § 28-3.1-543).

Nineteen states have laws against terrorizing or making terroristic threats. Terrorizing usually means threatening to commit a crime of violence or unlawfully causing the evacuation of a building or facility. Terroristic threat is generally defined as threatening to kill another with the intent of putting that person in fear of IMMINENT death and under circumstances that would reasonably cause the victim to believe that the threat will be carried out.

Many states have also enacted antistalking laws, which deal with unwanted communications. STALKING is a criminal activity consisting of a series of actions that are designed to threaten but, taken individually, might constitute legal behavior. For example, sending flowers, writing love notes, and waiting for someone outside her place of work are actions that, on their own, are not criminal. When these actions are coupled with an INTENT to injure or instill fear, however, they may constitute a pattern of behavior that is illegal. A stalking victim may ask a court to issue a protection or RESTRAINING ORDER that directs the defendant not to communicate or come within the vicinity of the victim. If the defendant persists in communicating with the victim, a court may hold the defendant in CONTEMPT, impose fines, or incarcerate the defendant, depending on state law.

Other specialized criminal offenses also deal with unlawful communications. For example, threatening to harm the president of the United States and using the U.S. mail to transmit threatening communications are federal offenses.

Under the civil tort actions of LIBEL AND SLANDER, a person who defames the good name and reputation of another may be sued for damages. The ACTION of libel is based on a written defamatory communication, and a slander action is based on oral DEFAMATION. In addition, a plaintiff can recover damages for the intentional infliction of severe mental or emotional suffering or for the unreasonable intrusion upon his PRIVACY caused by threats or unlawful communications.

UNLAWFUL DETAINER ▨ The act of retaining POSSESSION of property without legal right. ▨

The term *unlawful detainer* ordinarily refers to the conduct of a TENANT who is in possession of an apartment or leased property and refuses to leave the premises upon the expiration or termination of the LEASE. Typically, the LANDLORD wishes to evict the tenant for not paying the rent or for endangering the safety of the other tenants or the landlord's property.

Under COMMON LAW a landlord was personally permitted to enter and remove a tenant by force for nonpayment or violation of the lease. U.S. state laws, however, require a landlord to file what is called an unlawful detainer ACTION in a court of law. To satisfy the DUE PROCESS rights guaranteed to the tenant by the FIFTH AMENDMENT to the U.S. Constitution, the landlord must strictly follow the statutory procedures, or the tenant can challenge the unlawful detainer proceedings on technicalities and force the landlord to start over again.

Each state has its own type of unlawful detainer proceeding. In Minnesota, for example, the landlord must show cause (have a legitimate reason) to bring such an action. According to Minnesota law, legitimate reasons include the tenant's nonpayment of rent, other breach of the lease, or refusal to leave after notice to vacate has been properly served and the tenancy's last day has passed (Minn. Stat. § 566.03 [1992]).

Both landlords and tenants must take a number of steps in an unlawful detainer action. In Minnesota, for example, the landlord must file a COMPLAINT against the tenant in district court. The landlord must then serve the tenant with a SUMMONS (at least seven days before the court date) ordering the tenant to appear in court (Minn. Stat. § 566.05). Within seven to fourteen days after the summons is issued, a court hearing takes place, and both the tenant and the landlord are asked to give their sides of the story (Minn. Stat. § 566.05). The judge then delivers a decision. If the judge decides that the tenant has no legal reason for refusing to leave or pay the rent, the judge orders the tenant to vacate and, if necessary, orders the SHERIFF to force the tenant out.

If the tenant can show that immediate EVICTION will cause substantial hardship, however, the court may give the tenant up to one week in which to move. A delay based on hardship is not available if the tenant is causing a nuisance or seriously endangering the safety of other residents, their property, or the landlord's property (Minn. Stat. § 566.09, subd. 1).

If a tenant has paid the landlord or the court the amount of rent owed, but is unable to pay the interest, costs, and attorney's fees, the court may issue a WRIT of restitution that permits the tenant to pay these amounts during the period the court delays issuing an eviction order (Minn. Stat. § 504.02, subd. 1). If the unlawful detainer action was brought because the tenant had not paid the rent, and the landlord prevails, the tenant may pay the back rent plus costs and still remain in possession of the unit, provided payment is made before possession of the rental unit is delivered to the landlord. If the action was brought because the tenant withheld the rent due to disrepair, and the tenant prevails, the judge may order that the rent be abated (reduced) in part or completely.

Only a sheriff or sheriff's deputy can physically evict a tenant. The tenant must be given notice that an eviction order has been issued. Most states give the tenant at least twenty-four hours' notice before the sheriff arrives to perform the actual eviction.

See also LANDLORD AND TENANT.

UNLIQUIDATED 📖 Unassessed or settled; not ascertained in amount. 📖

An unliquidated DEBT, for example, is one for which the precise amount owed cannot be determined from the terms of the contractual agreement or another standard.

UNWRITTEN LAW 📖 Unwritten rules, principles, and norms that have the effect and force of law though they have not been formally enacted by the government. 📖

Most laws in America are written. The U.S. Code, the Code of Federal Regulations, and the Federal Rules of Civil Procedure are three examples of written laws that are frequently cited in federal court. Each state has a similar body of written laws. By contrast, unwritten law consists of those customs, traditions, practices, USAGES, and other MAXIMS of human conduct that

the government has recognized and enforced.

Unwritten law is most commonly found in primitive societies where illiteracy is prevalent. Because many residents in such societies cannot read or write, there is little point in publishing written laws to govern their conduct. Instead, societal disputes in primitive societies are resolved informally, through appeal to unwritten maxims of fairness or popularly accepted modes of behavior. Litigants present their claims orally in most primitive societies, and judges announce their decisions in the same fashion. The governing body in primitive societies typically enforces the useful traditions that are widely practiced in the community, while those practices that are novel or harmful fall into disuse or are discouraged.

Much of INTERNATIONAL LAW is a form of primitive unwritten law. For centuries the rules of war governing hostilities between belligerents consisted of a body of unwritten law. While some of these rules have been codified by international bodies such as the UNITED NATIONS, many have not. For example, retaliatory reprisals against acts of TERRORISM by a foreign government are still governed by unwritten customs in the international community. Each nation also retains discretion in formulating a response to the aggressive acts of a neighboring state.

In the United States, unwritten law takes on a variety of forms. In constitutional law the Supreme Court has ruled that the Due Process Clause of the Fifth and Fourteenth Amendments to the U.S. Constitution protects the right to PRIVACY even though the word *privacy* is not mentioned in the written text of the Constitution. In commercial law the UNIFORM COMMERCIAL CODE permits merchants to resolve legal disputes by introducing evidence of unwritten customs, practices, and usages that others in the same trade generally follow. The entire body of COMMON LAW, comprising cases decided by judges on matters relating to torts and contracts, among other things, is said to reflect unwritten standards that have evolved over time. In each case, however, once a court, legislature, or other government body formally adopts a standard, principle, or maxim in writing, it ceases to be an unwritten law.

See also CASE LAW; TRADE USAGE.

UPSET PRICE 📖 The dollar amount below which property, either real or personal, that is scheduled for sale at an AUCTION is not to be sold. 📖

An upset price is intended as a minimum price. In a decree for a JUDICIAL SALE, it constitutes a direction to the officer conducting the sale not to accept any bid that falls below the fixed price. In a final decree in a FORECLOSURE sale, an upset price should be sufficient to cover costs and allowances made by the court, the certificates and interest of the RECEIVER, and any LIENS in existence.

USAGE A REASONABLE and legal practice in a particular location, or among persons in a specific business or trade, that is either known to the individuals involved or is well established, general, and uniform to such an extent that a PRESUMPTION may properly be made that the parties acted with reference to it in their transactions.

The term *usage* refers to a uniform practice or course of conduct followed in certain lines of business or professions that is relied upon by the parties to a contractual transaction. A court will apply the usage of a business when it determines that doing so is necessary to resolve a contractual dispute. Ignoring usage may result in the misreading of a document and the intent of the parties who signed it.

The law has developed different forms of usage. *Local usage* refers to a practice or method of dealing regularly observed in a particular place. Under certain circumstances it may be considered by a court when interpreting a document. *General usage* is a practice that prevails generally throughout the country, or is followed generally by a given profession or trade, and is not local in its nature or observance.

A *trade usage* is the prevailing and accepted custom within a particular trade or industry and is not tied to a geographic location. The law assumes that merchants are aware of the usage of their trade. TRADE USAGE supplements, qualifies, and imparts particular meaning to the terms of an agreement for the purpose of their interpretation.

The term *custom and usage* is commonly used in commercial law, but "custom" and "usage" can be distinguished. A *usage* is a repetition of acts whereas *custom* is the law or general rule that arises from such repetition. A usage may exist without a custom, but a custom cannot arise without a usage accompanying it or preceding it. Usage derives its authority from the assent of the parties to a transaction and is applicable only to consensual arrangements. Custom derives its authority from its adoption into the law and is binding regardless of any acts of assent by the parties. In modern law, however, the two principles are often merged into one by the courts.

USC An abbreviation for U.S. CODE.

USCA® An abbreviation for U.S. CODE ANNOTATED.

USCCAN® An abbreviation for *United States Code Congressional and Administrative News*, a source of new federal PUBLIC laws that is published by West Group every two weeks when Congress is in session and once a month when Congress is not in session.

USCCAN first appears in an ADVANCE SHEET edition, which contains the full text of all public laws as well as some LEGISLATIVE HISTORY in the form of committee reports on the more significant enactments. In addition, it carries selected administrative regulations, executive documents, and various tables and indexes helpful in conducting research involving such legislation. At the end of each session of Congress, the pamphlet is bound to provide a permanent record of congressional laws.

U.S. CIVIL WAR The U.S. Civil War, also called the War between the States, was waged from April 1861 until April 1865. The war was precipitated by the SECESSION of eleven Southern states during 1860 and 1861 and their formation of the Confederate States of America under President Jefferson Davis. The Southern states had feared that the new president, ABRAHAM LINCOLN, who had been elected in 1860, and Northern politicians would block the expansion of SLAVERY and endanger the existing slaveholding system. Though Lincoln did free Southern slaves during the war by issuing the EMANCIPATION PROCLAMATION, he fought primarily to restore the Union.

The war began on April 12, 1861, when Confederate artillery fired on Fort Sumter in Charleston, South Carolina. In the ten weeks between the fall of Fort Sumter and the convening of Congress in July 1861, Lincoln began drafting men for military service, approved a naval blockade of Southern ports, and suspended the WRIT of HABEAS CORPUS. The U.S. Supreme Court upheld Lincoln's authority to take these actions in the *Prize* cases, 67 U.S. (2 Black) 635, 17 L. Ed. 459; 70 U.S. (3 Wall.) 451, 18 L. Ed. 197; 70 U.S. (3 Wall.) 514, 18 L. Ed. 200; 70 U.S. 559, 18 L. Ed. 220 (1863). The Court concluded that the president had the authority to resist force without the need for special legislative action.

On July 21, 30,000 Union troops marched on Richmond, Virginia, the capital of the Confederacy. They were routed at the Battle of Bull Run and forced to retreat to Washington, D.C. The defeat shocked Lincoln and Union leaders, who called for 500,000 new troops for the Union Army of the Potomac.

General ULYSSES S. GRANT brought the Union its first victory in February 1862, when his troops captured Forts Henry and Donelson

Civil War battles were often fought at close range. In this drawing, Confederate troops capture a supply train near Jasper, Tennessee.

in Tennessee. Grant fought in the Battles of Shiloh and Corinth, Tennessee, before forcing the surrender of Vicksburg, Mississippi, on July 4, 1862.

The Army of the Potomac, however, did not have such success. A Union summer offensive against Confederate forces led by General Robert E. Lee fared badly. Union forces were defeated at the Seven Days Battle and later that summer at the Second Battle of Bull Run. Lee then invaded Maryland but was checked at Antietam on September 17, 1862.

Lincoln despaired at the poor leadership demonstrated by the commanders of the Army of the Potomac. He replaced General George B. McClellan with General A. E. (Ambrose Everett) Burnside, but when Burnside faltered, Lincoln appointed General Joseph Hooker commander. Hooker proved no better. His attempt to outmaneuver Lee's forces at Chancellorsville, Virginia, in May 1863 led to defeat, retreat, and Hooker's dismissal as commander. Lee then invaded Pennsylvania, where a chance encounter of small units led to the Battle of Gettysburg on July 1. The new Union commander, General George G. Meade, directed a successful defense at Gettysburg, forcing Lee to return to Virginia.

In March 1864 Lincoln gave Grant command of the Union armies. Grant planned a campaign of attrition that would rely on the Union's overwhelming superiority in numbers and supplies. Though Union forces would suffer enormous casualties as a result of this strategy, he concluded that the devastation experi-

enced by the Confederate troops would be even greater.

In the late summer of 1864, Grant sent General William T. Sherman and his troops into Georgia. Sherman captured and burned the city of Atlanta in September and then set out on his march through Georgia, destroying everything in his path. He reached Savannah on December 10 and soon captured the city.

In the spring of 1864, Grant commanded the Army of the Potomac against Lee's forces in the Wilderness Campaign, a series of violent battles that took place in Virginia. Battles at Spotsylvania and Cold Harbor extracted heavy Union casualties, but Lee's smaller army was, as Grant had hoped, devastated. Grant laid siege to Petersburg for ten months, pinning down Lee's troops and slowly destroying their morale.

By March 1865 Lee's army had suffered numerous casualties and desertions. Grant began the final advance on April 1 and captured Richmond on April 3. On April 9, 1865, at Appomattox Court House, Lee surrendered his Confederate forces, signaling an end to the Civil War.

The casualties had been enormous for both sides. More than 359,000 Union soldiers had died, while the Confederate dead numbered 258,000.

The war ended slavery. On September 22, 1862, Lincoln had announced the abolition of slavery in areas occupied by the Confederacy effective January 1, 1863. The wording of the Emancipation Proclamation on that date had made clear that slavery was still to be tolerated in the border states and areas occupied by Union troops so as not to jeopardize the war effort. Lincoln was uncertain that the Supreme Court would uphold the constitutionality of his action, so he lobbied Congress to adopt the THIRTEENTH AMENDMENT to the U.S. Constitution, which abolished slavery.

Lincoln's wartime suspension of the writ of habeas corpus meant that military commanders could arrest persons suspected of being sympathetic to the Confederacy and have them imprisoned indefinitely. After the war the Supreme Court, in *Ex parte Milligan*, 71 U.S. 2, 18 L. Ed. 281 (1866), condemned Lincoln's directive establishing military jurisdiction over civilians outside the immediate war zone. The Court strongly affirmed the fundamental right of a civilian to be tried in a regular court of law with all the required procedural safeguards.

CROSS-REFERENCES

Johnson, Andrew; Military Government; *Milligan, Ex parte; Texas v. White.*

U.S. CODE ▣ A multivolume publication of the text of statutes enacted by Congress. ▣

Until 1926, the POSITIVE LAW for federal legislation was published in one volume of the REVISED STATUTES of 1875, and then in each subsequent volume of the STATUTES AT LARGE. In 1925, Congress authorized the preparation of the U.S. Code and appointed a revisor of statutes to extract all the sections of the Revised Statutes of 1875 that had not been repealed and all of the PUBLIC LAWS that were still in effect from the Statutes at Large since 1873. These laws were rearranged into fifty titles and published in four volumes as the U.S. Code, 1926 edition. Thereafter, an annual cumulative supplement containing all the laws passed since 1926 was published. In 1932, a new edition of the code was published, which incorporated the cumulative supplements to the 1926 edition. This became the U.S. Code, 1932 edition. Every six years, a new edition of the code is published, incorporating the annual cumulative supplements prepared since the previous edition.

U.S. CODE ANNOTATED® ▣ A multivolume work published by West Group that contains the complete text of federal laws enacted by Congress that are included in the U.S. CODE, together with case notes (known as ANNOTATIONS) of state and federal decisions that interpret and apply specific sections of federal statutes, plus the text of presidential proclamations and EXECUTIVE ORDERS. ▣

The U.S. Code Annotated, popularly referred to by its abbreviation U.S.C.A., also includes editorially prepared research aids, such as cross-references to related statutory sections, historical notes, and library references, that facilitate research. U.S.C.A. is also available on-line and in CD-ROM format.

U.S. COMMISSIONERS ▣ The former designation for U.S. MAGISTRATES. ▣

U.S. CONSTITUTION See CONSTITUTION OF THE UNITED STATES.

U.S. COURT OF VETERANS APPEALS

After nearly four decades of debate on the subject, Congress exercised its power under Article I of the Constitution and passed the Veterans Judicial Review Act of 1988 (VJRA) (102 Stat. 4105 [38 U.S.C.A. § 4051] [recodified at 38 U.S.C.A. § 7252 [1991]]). The U.S. Court of Veterans Appeals came into existence on November 18, 1988, the day President GEORGE BUSH signed the VJRA.

One of several specialized federal courts established by Congress under Article I—including the U.S. Court of Military Appeals, the U.S. Court of Federal Claims, and the U.S. Tax Court—the U.S. Court of Veterans Appeals exercises exclusive jurisdiction over the decisions of the Board of Veterans Appeals (BVA). People seeking veterans' benefits who are turned down by the BVA may appeal their case to the U.S. Court of Veterans Appeals. Claimants may further avail themselves of the judiciary by appealing unfavorable U.S. Court of Veterans Appeals decisions to the limited review of the U.S. Court of Appeals for the Federal Circuit and ultimately to the Supreme Court of the United States.

In the mid-1980s, 75 million U.S. citizens—one-third of the population of the United States of America—were eligible for some form of veterans' benefits. Then, as now, war veterans and their dependents and survivors could apply to one of the fifty-eight regional offices of the VETERANS ADMINISTRATION (VA) for disability, loan eligibility, education, and other benefits. In an average year in the 1980s, nearly eight hundred thousand disability claims were filed, about half of which were granted by the regional offices. Before the U.S. Court of Veterans Appeals was created, people whose claims were turned down had limited recourse, which did not include review by a court of law. If a regional office of the VA denied a claim, the claimant could appeal that decision within the VA to the BVA. If the BVA denied the appeal—which it did in about 75 percent of cases—the claimant had just one remaining option: to reopen the claim on the basis of new and material evidence and begin the process over again.

Comprising one chief judge and two to six associate judges—all appointed to a term of fifteen years by the president with the advice and consent of the Senate—the U.S. Court of Veterans Appeals has the "power to affirm, modify, or reverse a decision of the [BVA] or to remand the matter, as appropriate" (38 U.S.C.A. § 4051(a) [recodified at 38 U.S.C.A. § 7252(a) [1991]]). (When a court REMANDS a case, it sends the case back to the lower court or, in the instance of the BVA, ruling body.) The Veterans Appeals Court's primary mission, according to Associate Judge John J. Farley, is to review cases for errors of law. As an APPELLATE COURT, the U.S. Court of Veterans Appeals cannot hear new TESTIMONY or allow new EVIDENCE to be introduced in a case. Cases are heard by judges sitting alone, in panels of three, or EN BANC (all together).

The U.S. Court of Veterans Appeals heard its first case—*Erspamer v. Derwinski*, 1 Vet. App. 3, 58 U.S.L.W. 2556—in February 1990. Jean A. Erspamer, the widow of Ernest Erspamer, a Minnesota veteran exposed to radiation during atomic bomb tests in the Pacific in 1946, asked the court to compel the VA to take action on her claims for disability compensation and death benefits. Erspamer's husband had in June 1979 filed with the VA a claim for service-connected disability payments. After he died of leukemia in 1980, Erspamer continued to seek VA benefits and was eventually successful in her quest—after the Court of Veterans Appeals heard her case.

Between February 1990 and June 30, 1992, the court reviewed 1,931 cases and terminated 1,897. As of September 1, 1991, more than 64 percent of all cases brought before the court were filed by claimants appearing without benefit of representation. In June 1993, the Eleventh Annual Judicial Conference of the U.S. Court of Appeals for the Federal Circuit noted, "Filings from the Court of Veterans Appeals have increased but still remain few in absolute numbers" compared with filings from other federal courts (153 F.R.D. 177 [1993]).

Based in Washington, D.C., but able to convene anywhere in the country, the U.S. Court of Veterans Appeals can only decide cases or controversies presented to it. The court is not a policy-making body and thus may not conduct policy actions, such as reviewing the VA's schedule of disability ratings.

U.S. COURTS OF APPEALS The U.S. Courts of Appeals are intermediate federal APPELLATE COURTS. Created in 1891 pursuant to Article III of the U.S. Constitution, the courts

relieve the U.S. Supreme Court from the burden of handling all APPEALS from cases decided by federal trial (district) courts. These appellate courts have JURISDICTION to review all FINAL DECISIONS and some INTERLOCUTORY decisions of federal DISTRICT COURTS. In addition, the courts review and enforce orders of numerous federal administrative bodies.

A typical appeal from a district court decision consists of the trial court record, oral arguments, and supporting briefs. A three-judge panel usually considers each appeal. However, a court may sit EN BANC, that is, with all judges of the circuit present. A decision by a court of appeals is final, unless the U.S. Supreme Court accepts the case for review.

Each state is assigned on the basis of its geographical location to one of eleven judicial CIRCUITS. The District of Columbia has its own circuit; U.S. territories are assigned to the first, third, and ninth circuits. The more than 175 circuit judges are appointed by the president, subject to the advice and consent of the Senate.

In addition to the twelve circuits, Congress created the U.S. Court of Appeals for the Federal Circuit in 1982. This court is the successor to the former U.S. Court of Customs and Patent Appeals and the U.S. Court of Claims. The court has nationwide jurisdiction and hears appeals from federal district courts in patent cases, contract cases, and certain other CIVIL ACTIONS in which the United States is a defendant. It also hears appeals from the U.S. Court of International Trade, the U.S. Court of Federal Claims, and the U.S. Court of Veterans Appeals. The court also reviews certain admin-

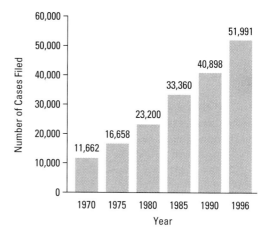

U.S. Courts of Appeals Case Filings, 1970–1996

Source: Administrative Office of the U.S. Courts.

U.S. Courts of Appeals

1 First Circuit also includes Puerto Rico
2 Third Circuit also includes U.S. Virgin Islands
3 Ninth Circuit also includes Guam and Northern Mariana Islands

istrative rulings, rule making by the Department of Veterans Affairs, and certain decisions by the U.S. Senate Select Committee on Ethics, in addition to other matters.

See also FEDERAL COURTS.

USDC An abbreviation for U.S. DISTRICT COURT.

USE The fact of being habitually employed in a certain manner. In REAL PROPERTY law, a right held by an individual (called a *cestui que use*) to take the profits arising from a particular parcel of land that was owned and possessed by another individual.

For example, a seller of goods might make an IMPLIED WARRANTY of fitness for a particular use, which signifies that an item or a product is fit to be used for a specific purpose, such as a tire meant for use in the snow. See also PRODUCT LIABILITY; SALES.

The *cestui que use* received the benefits from the property even though TITLE to such land was in another individual. This theory is no longer part of the U.S. legal system; however, the modern law of TRUSTS evolved from the law relating to uses.

USE AND OCCUPATION A kind of action brought by a LANDLORD against an individual who had OCCUPANCY of the landlord's land or premises under an express or implied agreement requiring payment, but not under a LEASEHOLD contract that would allow the landlord to initiate an action for rent.

For example, property might be occupied under a LEASE that is rendered VOID because it does not comply with the STATUTE OF FRAUDS. In such a situation, the landlord could bring a use and occupation action for the value of the use of the property.

See also LANDLORD AND TENANT.

USE TAX A charge imposed on the use or possession of PERSONAL PROPERTY.

Governments employ use taxes to accomplish two purposes. A use tax may be imposed to prevent someone from evading a SALES TAX by buying goods in a nontaxing state and shipping them into the state that imposes the sales tax. Use taxes are also used to help defray the cost of public services associated with particular types of personal property.

States and municipalities impose use taxes on purchases or rentals that are made outside the taxing JURISDICTION but would have been taxable had they taken place within it. Such transactions escape the normal sales tax collection because retailers outside the state or municipality are not required to collect the sales tax. The use tax protects retailers located in the state or municipality because it removes the incentive for consumers to shop outside that locality in order to avoid paying the sales tax. For example, suppose a person buys a car from a dealer in a nearby state that does not impose a sales tax. The buyer must pay use tax on the purchase price when he returns to his state or city.

In addition, persons who order catalog merchandise from out-of-state companies that do not charge sales tax are obligated to pay the use tax themselves. Collecting the tax in this situation is difficult, however, because the government has no effective way of monitoring these sales.

The other purpose of a use tax is to help recoup the cost of public services directly related to the use of certain types of personal property. The most common use taxes are assessed on motor vehicle and boat LICENSES. User fees are also charged for docking privileges in airports or harbors.

The use tax on motor vehicles is generally allocated to the maintenance of roads and bridges and to the regulation and administration of motor vehicles. The federal government collected a use tax on motor vehicles during World War II, but the tax was shifted to the states after the war. The use tax on vehicles and boats also serves as a method for identifying all vehicles and boats in the jurisdiction.

U.S. INFORMATION AGENCY The U.S. Information Agency (USIA) is the public diplomacy arm of the U.S. government. The USIA exists "to further the national interest by improving United States relations with other countries and peoples through the broadest possible sharing of ideas, information, and educational and cultural activities" (22 U.S.C.A. § 1461 [1988]). Generally, this means that the USIA is responsible for sharing information about the United States with the citizens of other countries.

The roots of the USIA can be found in information efforts made during World War I

and World War II. During World War I, the Committee on Public Information was created to inform the world of U.S. aims in the war. In 1938 the federal government began to promote cultural relations with Latin America through the State Department's Division of Cultural Cooperation. In 1940 the government sent its first international radio broadcasts into Latin America.

During World War II, the Office of War Information conducted information and propaganda campaigns aimed at enemy countries and occupied territories. To assist in the campaign, the government expanded its radio broadcasts. In 1942, during a broadcast in the German language, an announcer first used the term "voice of America" to describe the broadcast. The name stuck, and the international news and information broadcast has been called the Voice of America ever since.

In 1948 Congress passed the United States Information and Educational Exchange Act (ch. 36, 62 Stat. 6, [codified as amended at 22 U.S.C.A. § 1431 et seq. (1988 & Supp. V 1993)]). This act, known as the Smith-Mundt Act, created the U.S. International Communication Agency (USICA). According to the Smith-Mundt Act, the USICA was created to distribute information to other countries about the "United States, its people, and [its] policies" (Pub. L. No. 80-402, § 501 1948 U.S.C.C.A.N. [79 Stat.] 6, 9 [1948] [codified at 22 U.S.C.A. § 1431 et seq., as amended]).

The USICA gained status as an independent federal agency under President DWIGHT D. EISENHOWER's Reorganization Plan No. 8 of 1953 (18 Fed. Reg. 4562 [1953], reprinted in 22 U.S.C.A. § 1461 app. at 763 [West 1990]). The USICA was redesignated the U.S. Information Agency in 1982, but the function of the agency remained the same.

The USIA uses a variety of methods to disseminate information. These include the Voice of America radio broadcast system, radio and television broadcast service to Cuba, the Worldnet Satellite television service, educational and cultural exchanges, and magazines, films, and information centers in foreign countries.

Until 1994, when Congress modified this rule, the USIA was prohibited from disseminating its program materials within the United States (22 U.S.C.A. § 1461-1a [1988]). The primary reason for this restriction was the desire to avoid creating a powerful propaganda agency to guide public opinion, such as the information ministries in Nazi Germany and the Soviet Union. Congress also wanted to

U.S. Information Agency

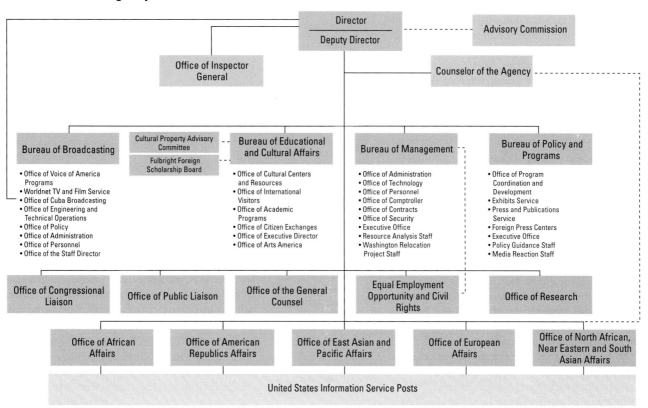

isolate government-sponsored programming from competition with domestic commercial media outlets.

The fall of Communism and technological advances prompted a reorganization of the USIA's structure and activities. In 1992 the USIA stopped publishing *Problems of Communism*, an anti-Communist magazine. *Problems of Communism* was the only USIA material ever disseminated within the United States. In 1994 Congress created the Broadcasting Board of Governors to oversee a new USIA International Broadcasting Bureau. Under the International Broadcasting Act (Foreign Relations Authorization Act, Fiscal Years 1994 and 1995, Pub. L. No. 103-236 [1994]), the bureau was charged with oversight of the property and programming of government broadcasting, including the Voice of America and its commercial counterparts, Radio Free Europe and Radio Liberty. The bureau was also put in charge of a newly created Radio Free Asia.

Congress has also modified the ban on dissemination of USIA materials within the United States. In a 1994 amendment to the Smith-Mundt Act, Congress provided that the ban "shall not prohibit the [USIA] from responding to inquiries from members of the public about its operations, policies, or pro-

grams" (22 U.S.C.A. § 1461-1a). The wording of this amendment does not require the USIA to distribute its materials within the United States. Rather, it requires only that the USIA respond to inquiries about its materials.

Also in 1994, the USIA began publishing its English-language news stories on the INTERNET computer system. Though the stories include a disclaimer stating that the information is intended for international audiences only, the USIA has no way to enforce this restriction. Furthermore, Worldnet, the federal government television service, is transmitted by satellite, and anyone who has a satellite dish may receive the broadcast. Thus, technology has circumvented the prohibition on domestic dissemination of USIA programs. Because the USIA is a creation of Congress, and because technological advances show no sign of slowing, the structure and mission of the USIA will continue to change.

U.S. MAGISTRATES See MAGISTRATE.

U.S. MARSHALS SERVICE The U.S. Marshals Service, a division of the Department of Justice, is the oldest federal law enforcement agency, having served as a link between the executive and judicial branches of the government since 1789. The president appoints U.S. marshals for terms of four years. The Senate must confirm the appointments, but the president has the power to remove marshals before the expiration of their terms.

The U.S. marshals are the chief law officers of the FEDERAL COURTS. A MARSHAL is appointed for each of the ninety-four federal judicial districts in the United States. The U.S. attorney general designates where the marshal's office will be located in each district. The marshals and their support staff of approximately 3,700 deputy marshals and administrative personnel operate from 427 office locations throughout the United States.

The service is responsible for providing support and protection for the federal courts, including security for more than seven hundred judicial facilities and nearly two thousand judges and MAGISTRATES, as well as trial participants such as jurors and attorneys. The service also operates the Federal Witness Security Program, ensuring the safety of endangered government WITNESSES.

U.S. marshals maintain custody of and transport thousands of federal prisoners annually, execute court orders and arrest WARRANTS, and apprehend most federal fugitives. They seize, manage, and sell property forfeited to the government by drug traffickers and other criminals and assist the Justice Department's Asset Forfeiture Program.

The service's Special Operations Group responds to emergencies such as civil disturbances and terrorist incidents and restores order during RIOTS and mob violence. The service also operates the U.S. Marshals Service Training Academy.

The director of the U.S. Marshals Service, who is appointed by the president, supervises the operations of the service throughout the United States and its territories. The director is assisted by a deputy director, three associate directors, and four assistant directors.

U.S. POSTAL SERVICE   The U.S. Postal Service processes and delivers mail to individuals and businesses within the United States. The service seeks to improve its performance through the development of efficient mail-handling systems and operates its own planning and engineering programs. The service is also responsible for protecting the mails from loss or THEFT and apprehending those who violate postal laws.

The postal service was created as an independent establishment of the EXECUTIVE BRANCH by the Postal Reorganization Act (39 U.S.C.A. § 101 et seq.), which was approved August 12, 1970. The U.S. Postal Service began operations on July 1, 1971, replacing the Post Office

The winter holidays are the busiest time of the year for the post office. This worker in New York sorts through large and perishable items during the Christmas rush.

Department, which after years of financial neglect and fragmented control had proved unable to process the mail efficiently. Despite the availability of new technology, as well as skyrocketing mail volume, the department handled mail the same way it did in the 1870s.

The postal service has approximately 753,000 employees and handles about 181 billion pieces of mail annually. The chief executive officer of the postal service, the postmaster general, is appointed by the nine governors of the postal service, who are appointed by the president, with the advice and consent of the Senate, for overlapping nine-year terms. The governors and the postmaster general appoint the deputy postmaster general, and these eleven people constitute the board of governors.

In addition to its national headquarters, the postal service has area and district offices, which supervise approximately 39,000 post offices, branches, stations, and community post offices throughout the United States.

In order to expand and improve service to the public, the postal service is engaged in customer cooperation activities, including the development of programs for both the general public and major customers. The consumer advocate, a postal ombudsman, represents the interests of the individual mail customer in matters involving the postal service by bringing complaints and suggestions to the attention of top postal management and solving the problems of individual customers. To provide postal services that are responsive to public needs, the postal service operates its own planning, research, engineering, real estate, and procurement programs, which are specially adapted to postal requirements. The service also maintains close ties with international postal organizations.

The postal service is the only federal agency whose employment policies are governed by COLLECTIVE BARGAINING. Labor contract negotiations affecting all bargaining unit personnel are conducted by the Labor Relations or Human Resources divisions. These divisions also handle personnel matters involving employees not covered by COLLECTIVE BARGAINING AGREEMENTS.

The U.S. Postal Inspection Service is the federal law enforcement agency with JURISDICTION over criminal matters affecting the integrity and security of the mail. It operates as the inspector general for the postal service. Postal inspectors enforce more than one hundred federal statutes involving MAIL FRAUD, mail bombs, child PORNOGRAPHY, illegal drugs, mail theft, and other postal crimes. The inspectors are also responsible for the protection of all postal employees. In addition, inspectors audit postal contracts and financial accounts.

Most postal regulations are contained in postal service manuals covering domestic mail, international mail, postal operations, administrative support, employee and labor relations, financial management, and procurement.

U.S. SUPREME COURT See SUPREME COURT OF THE UNITED STATES.

U.S. TAXPAYERS PARTY 📖 A political party with offices and candidates throughout the United States that takes an ultraconservative stance on fiscal and moral issues. 📖

The U.S. Taxpayers party was formed in 1992 by Howard Phillips, a former colleague of PATRICK J. BUCHANAN, a speechwriter in the administration of President RICHARD M. NIXON. Phillips, a graduate of Harvard University, has been an active political conservative since 1964, when he organized a movement to draft Arizona Governor BARRY M. GOLDWATER onto the Republican party presidential ticket. In 1986 Phillips, a devout anti-Communist, broke away from the Republican party after Republican President RONALD REAGAN began talks with the Soviet Union.

Phillips founded the U.S. Taxpayers party as an alternative for conservatives disenchanted with the Republican party and as a political vehicle for Buchanan. Since the party's inception, Phillips has courted Buchanan, a media commentator and part-time politician since his stint in the Nixon White House, to abandon the Republican party and become the presidential candidate for the U.S. Taxpayers party. As of 1996, however, Buchanan had not converted. Phillips was the party's presidential candidate in the 1992 and 1996 elections, appearing on twenty-one ballots in 1992 and forty in 1996.

The U.S. Taxpayers party platform addresses a combination of fiscal matters and moral issues. The party supports the abolition of public WELFARE assistance, the INTERNAL REVENUE SERVICE, and the Federal Reserve System, which weds the federal government to private banking institutions. The party is opposed to unchecked free trade: party candidates argue that agreements such as the GENERAL AGREEMENT ON TARIFFS and TRADE (GATT) and the NORTH AMERICAN FREE TRADE AGREEMENT (NAFTA) only serve to ship U.S. jobs to other countries. The party supports increased use of the death penalty, and it opposes legal ABORTION, GAY AND LESBIAN RIGHTS, and GUN CONTROL laws.

See also INDEPENDENT PARTIES.

U.S. TRADE REPRESENTATIVE, OFFICE OF The Office of the U.S. Trade Representative was created by Congress in the Trade Expansion Act of 1962 (19 U.S.C.A. § 1801) and implemented by President JOHN F. KENNEDY in Executive Order No. 11,075 on January 15, 1963 (27 FR 473). Initially named the Office of the Special Trade Representative, this agency was authorized to negotiate all trade agreements under the Tariff Act of 1930 (19 U.S.C.A. § 1351) and the Trade Expansion Act of 1962. As part of the Trade Act of 1974 (19 U.S.C.A. § 2171), Congress established the office as a cabinet-level agency within the Executive Office of the President and gave it other powers and responsibilities for coordinating trade policy.

In 1980 the office was renamed the Office of the U.S. Trade Representative (USTR). USTR refers both to the agency and to the agency's head, the U.S. trade representative. President JIMMY CARTER's Executive Order No. 12,188 of January 4, 1980 (45 FR 989), authorized the USTR to set and administer overall trade policy. The USTR was also designated as the nation's chief trade negotiator and as the representative of the United States in major international trade organizations.

The U.S. trade representative is a cabinet-level official with the rank of ambassador who is directly responsible to the president and the Congress. The USTR is responsible for developing and coordinating U.S. international trade, commodity, and direct investment policy and for leading or directing negotiations with other countries on such matters. Through an interagency structure, the USTR coordinates trade policy, resolves agency disagreements, and frames issues for presidential decision. The agency has offices in Washington, D.C., and Geneva, Switzerland.

The agency provides trade policy leadership and negotiating expertise in its major areas of responsibility. Among these areas are the following: all matters within the World Trade Organization (WTO), formerly the GENERAL AGREEMENT ON TARIFFS AND TRADE (GATT); trade, commodity, and direct investment matters dealt with by international institutions such as the Organization for Economic Cooperation and Development (OECD) and the United Nations Conference on Trade and Development (UNCTAD); export expansion policy; industrial and services trade policy; international commodity agreements and policy; bilateral and multilateral trade and investment issues; trade-related INTELLECTUAL PROPERTY protection issues; and import policy.

Interagency coordination is accomplished by the USTR through the Trade Policy Review Group (TPRG) and the Trade Policy Staff Committee (TPSC). These groups, which are administered and chaired by the USTR, are composed of seventeen federal agencies and offices. They develop and coordinate U.S. government positions on international trade and trade-related investment issues. The final tier of the interagency trade policy mechanism is the National Economic Council (NEC), chaired by the president. The NEC deputies committee considers decision memoranda from the TPRG, as well as particularly important or controversial trade-related issues.

The USTR also serves as vice chairperson of the Overseas Private Investment Corporation (OPIC), is a nonvoting member of the EXPORT-IMPORT BANK, and serves on the National Advisory Committee on International Monetary and Financial Policies. The USTR does not handle several significant trade and related policy areas however. These include export financing, export controls, multilateral development bank lending, international fisheries, aviation, and maritime policies.

The private sector plays a continuing role in trade negotiations through the mechanism of advisory committees. This advisory process was extremely helpful during the creation of the NORTH AMERICAN FREE TRADE AGREEMENT (NAFTA) and other trade initiatives. The committees' role has been expanded to include advice on the development and implementation of overall U.S. trade policy and on priorities for actions to implement such policy.

In the Trade Act of 1974, Congress broadened and codified the trade representative's policy-making and negotiating functions and established close congressional consultative, advisory, and oversight relationships with the agency. Five members from each House are formally appointed as official congressional advisers on trade policy, and additional members may be appointed as advisers on particular issues or negotiations.

USUFRUCT 📖 A CIVIL LAW term referring to the right of one individual to use and enjoy the PROPERTY of another, provided its substance is neither impaired nor altered. 📖

For example, a *usufructuary right* would be the right to use water from a stream in order to generate electrical power. Such a right is distinguishable from a claim of legal ownership of the water itself.

USURIOUS 📖 Characterized by an UNCONSCIONABLE or exorbitant rate of INTEREST. 📖

A usurious CONTRACT is one where the interest due is in excess of the maximum rate prescribed by statute.

See also USURY.

USURPATION 📖 The illegal ENCROACHMENT or assumption of the use of authority, power, or property properly belonging to another; the interruption or disturbance of an individual in his or her right or possession. 📖

The term *usurpation* is also used in reference to the unlawful assumption or seizure of sovereign power, in derogation of the constitution and rights of the proper ruler.

USURY 📖 The crime of charging higher INTEREST on a loan than the law permits. 📖

State laws set the maximum amount of interest that can be charged for a loan of money. A lender that charges higher than the maximum amount of interest is guilty of the crime of usury. In addition, courts may modify CONTRACTS that contain usurious rates of interest by reducing the interest to the legal maximum.

The charging of excessive interest in exchange for a monetary loan has been considered reprehensible from the earliest times. Chinese and Hindu law prohibited it, while the Athenians scorned persons who charged more than a moderate rate of interest for a loan. The Romans at one time abolished the practice of charging interest. Although they later revived it, the rates were strictly regulated.

During the Middle Ages in western Europe, the Catholic Church censured usurers, and when they died, the Crown confiscated their lands and property. In England, until the thirteenth century charging any interest was defined as usury. As commerce and trade increased, however, the demand for CREDIT grew, and usury was redefined to mean exorbitant interest rates. In 1545 the English Parliament set a legal maximum interest rate. Charging higher interest constituted usury.

The United States followed the English practice, as states passed laws that set maximum

RENT-TO-OWN CONTRACTS: SHOULD THEY BE SUBJECT TO USURY LAWS?

For more than thirty years, the legal status of rent-to-own (RTO) contracts has been the subject of debate. Consumer advocates decry the high cost of these contracts, which typically involve furniture, appliances, televisions, and other electronic goods. The RTO industry argues that it has been unfairly accused of consumer exploitation, when in fact it provides a needed service to individuals who either have poor credit or prefer to rent certain consumer goods. In most states RTO businesses must follow disclosure requirements when making RTO contracts, yet these businesses are allowed to charge rates that, if characterized as credit, would violate state usury laws.

IN FOCUS

The RTO industry, which serves close to 3 million customers a year and generates almost $4 billion in revenues annually, is composed of dealers who rent consumer goods with an option to buy. An RTO contract normally allows a customer to rent something for one week or one month at a time. At the end of the week or month, the customer can either terminate the agreement without any cost or obligation or renew the contract by making another advance rental payment. If the contract is renewed a prescribed number of times—typically, a period of eighteen months—and the customer meets the terms of the rental agreement, the store conveys ownership of the item to the customer.

Critics of RTO contracts contend that the cost of an eighteen-month contract greatly exceeds the value of the item purchased. If the contract was considered a credit sale rather than a lease, it would violate state usury laws. Usury laws are designed to prohibit excessive finance charges and to prevent creditors from gouging consumers, who are typically in a weaker bargaining position. Consumer advocates contend that RTO customers are mostly poor and uneducated and have poor credit histories. These customers spend a larger percentage of their disposable income on

RTO contracts than more affluent consumers do using traditional credit arrangements. Consequently, these critics believe states should reclassify RTO contracts as installment sales rather than as leases.

Consumer advocates note that if RTO contracts were recognized as credit sales, the federal Consumer Credit Protection Act, also known as the Truth in Lending Act (15 U.S.C.A. § 1601 et seq. [1968]), would apply. The act requires strict disclosures in consumer credit sales, as do state retail installment sales (RIS) laws. An RTO dealer would have to disclose the contract price of the consumer good, the total RTO price, the associated finance charges, and the applicable interest rate. In theory, such disclosures would allow a consumer to shop around for the best RTO deal.

More than forty states have adopted some type of RTO legislation. For example, Minnesota's Rental Purchase Agreement Act (RPAA) (Minn. Stat. § 325F.84 et seq. [1990]), provides a number of protections to consumers. It requires specific disclosures in the RTO contract, in advertising, and on in-store merchandise tags. The RPAA also provides restrictions and protections in the event of the customer's default, gives the consumer reinstatement rights, and limits delivery charges, security deposits, and collection fees.

The RTO industry rejects the idea that consumers are subjected to usurious interest rates when they enter into a contract. The industry says that an overwhelming majority of customers do not pursue the ownership option. Dealers point out that 75 percent of customers return the rented item within the first four months and that fewer than 25 percent rent long enough to own the item.

RTO supporters also challenge the stereotype of the typical RTO customer. A 1994 survey, sponsored by the Association of Progressive Rental Organizations (APRO), a national industry

group, found that almost 60 percent of RTO customers earned between $24,000 and $75,000 annually. In addition, a 1996 APRO survey found that 45 percent of RTO customers had a high school education and almost 30 percent had some college education. The industry's customer base includes students, business executives on temporary assignment, military personnel, and families in transit. The RTO business contends that it provides products to consumers who have immediate needs for consumer household goods but who either do not want or cannot accept long-term obligations, as well as to customers who do not have access to traditional credit arrangements.

The RTO industry challenges the claim that it wishes to keep customers in the dark about the cost of RTO contracts. The industry, which sees potential for continued growth, is taking steps to protect customers and ensure that RTO dealers are ethical. The APRO notes that it has participated in the debate and drafting of RTO disclosure laws in forty-four states. The industry agrees that contracts should disclose basic information, including the cash price of the product, the amount of each rental payment, the number of payments necessary to acquire ownership, and the total cost of the product acquired. The RTO industry believes that once this information is disclosed, customers should have the freedom to make an RTO contract.

The industry does not agree that state usury laws should be applied to RTO agreements. RTO operators note that no one is compelled to enter into an agreement. In addition, the costs of doing business in the RTO market dictate the rental rates charged to customers. RTO businesses must provide full service, including repairs, loaners, and pickup and delivery. Finally, RTO dealers do not agree that an RTO agreement is a credit sales agreement. Instead, they see it as a no-obligation, no-debt agreement that gives the customer the option of ending the agreement at the end of the rental cycle.

Product Breakdown of Rental Items

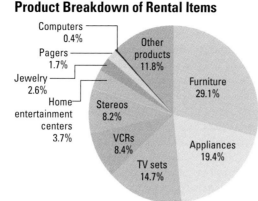

Computers
0.4%

Pagers
1.7%

Jewelry
2.6%

Home
entertainment
centers
3.7%

Other
products
11.8%

Furniture
29.1%

Stereos
8.2%

VCRs
8.4%

TV sets
14.7%

Appliances
19.4%

Source: Association of Progressive Rental Organizations.

legal interest rates. Rate restrictions vary from state to state, and different limits are set for different kinds of loans. For example, higher interest rates are usually allowed on consumer loans than on home MORTGAGES. Some states do not restrict the interest rates that CORPORATIONS can be charged under the assumption that corporations have sufficient bargaining power and business sense to negotiate a fair rate independently.

Restrictions on legal interest rates apply to banks, consumer loan companies, and other businesses that extend credit. Loan agreements between private individuals are also governed by state usury laws. For example, if a person agrees to lend a friend $5,000, the interest rate cannot exceed the maximum set by the state usury statute. Persons who charge excess interest and then threaten extortion are known as *loan sharks*. They may be prosecuted for usury and, if convicted, fined and possibly imprisoned. The persons who typically borrow from a LOAN SHARK are those who cannot qualify for a loan from a commercial lender. ORGANIZED CRIME has traditionally relied on loan sharking as a source of income.

The penalty for usury is ordinarily a FINE, FORFEITURE of the interest, or both. In some cases involving CONSUMER CREDIT, courts may modify usurious contracts and allow the borrower to pay only the PRINCIPAL sum and legal interest. Courts have often concluded, for example, that the high interest rates charged by "rent-to-own" businesses for the rental of consumer goods, such as furniture and televisions, are usurious and force the consumer to pay an exorbitant price for the goods.

The UNIFORM CONSUMER CREDIT CODE (UCCC) was drafted to address many of these consumer credit problems. Though only nine states have adopted the code in its entirety,

most states have included selected provisions from it in their consumer credit laws. The UCCC is designed to provide protection to consumers who buy goods and services on credit. It attempts to simplify, clarify, and update legislation governing consumer credit and usury. The UCCC also sets interest rate ceilings to ensure that consumers are not overcharged for credit. The UCCC works in concert with the federal CONSUMER CREDIT PROTECTION ACT of 1968 (16 U.S.C.A. § 1601 et seq.), which mandates that consumers purchasing on credit be provided with full disclosure on the cost of the loan.

See also CONSUMER PROTECTION.

UTILITARIANISM Utilitarianism is a philosophy of JURISPRUDENCE whose adherents believe that law must be made to conform to its most socially useful purpose. Although utilitarians differ as to the meaning of the word *useful*, most agree that a law's usefulness, or utility, may be defined in terms of its ability to increase happiness, wealth, or justice in society. Alternatively, some utilitarians measure a law's utility by its ability to decrease unhappiness, poverty, or injustice.

The utilitarianism movement originated in Great Britain during the eighteenth and nineteenth centuries when philosophers JEREMY BENTHAM, JOHN AUSTIN, JOHN STUART MILL, and Henry Sidgwick began criticizing various aspects of the COMMON LAW. Bentham, the progenitor of the movement, criticized the law for being written in dense and unintelligible prose. He sought to cut through the thicket of legal verbiage by reducing law to what he thought were its most basic elements—pain and pleasure.

Bentham believed that all human behavior is motivated by a desire to maximize pleasure and avoid pain. Yet he observed that law is often written in vague terms of rights and obligations. For example, a law might say that a person has a RIGHT to take action under one set of circumstances but an OBLIGATION to refrain from action under different circumstances. Bentham thought that law could be simplified by translating the language of rights and obligations into a pain-pleasure calculus.

Utilitarians have tried to apply Bentham's hedonistic calculus to CRIMINAL LAW. They assert that punishment is a form of government-imposed pain. At the same time, utilitarians believe that criminals break the law only because they do not fully comprehend the confusing language of rights and obligations. Accordingly, utilitarians conclude that law must be stripped of such confusing terms and redrafted in language that equates socially undesirable conduct with pain and socially desirable conduct with pleasure.

Utilitarians measure the desirability of human conduct by the amount of happiness it generates in society. They maintain that the ultimate aim of any law should be to promote the greatest happiness for the greatest number of people. Utilitarians would permit conduct that produces more happiness in society than unhappiness and would proscribe conduct that results in more unhappiness than happiness. Some utilitarians envision a democratic society where the happiness and unhappiness produced by a particular measure would be determined precisely by giving everyone the right to vote on the issue. Thus, those in power would know exactly how the citizenry felt about every issue.

Although the application of utilitarian principles may strengthen majority rule, unfettered democracy can lead to tyranny. Utilitarians are frequently criticized for sacrificing the interests of minorities to achieve majoritarian satisfaction. In a pure utilitarian form of government, a voting majority could pass laws to enslave minority groups so long as the institution of SLAVERY continued to satisfy a preponderance of the population. Concepts such as EQUAL PROTECTION, human dignity, and individual LIBERTY would be recognized only to the extent that a majority of the population valued them.

Modern utilitarians have attempted to soften the harshness of their philosophy by expanding the definition of social utility. Law and economics is a school of modern utilitarianism that has achieved prominence in legal circles. Proponents of law and economics believe that all law should be based on a cost-benefit analysis in which judges and lawmakers seek to maximize societal wealth in the most efficient fashion. Here the term *wealth* possesses both pecuniary and nonpecuniary qualities. The nonpecuniary qualities of wealth may include the right to self-determination and other fundamental freedoms that society deems important, including FREEDOM OF SPEECH and RELIGION. Under such an analysis, institutions like slavery that deny basic individual liberties would be declared illegal because they decrease society's overall nonpecuniary wealth.

Economic analysis of law has more practical applications as well. RICHARD A. POSNER, chief judge for the Seventh Circuit Court of Appeals, is a pioneer in the law and economics movement. He advocates applying economic analysis of law to most legal disputes. For example, in NEGLIGENCE actions Posner believes that LIABILITY should be imposed only after a court weighs three factors: the pecuniary injury suffered by the plaintiff, the cost to the defendant in taking precautions against injurious behavior, and the probability that a particular injury could have been avoided by the defendant. This cost-benefit analysis is widely accepted and is applied in negligence actions by both state and federal courts. Thus, through economic analysis of law, utilitarianism and its permutations continue to influence legal thinking in the United States.

See also CHICAGO SCHOOL.

UTI POSSIDETIS A term used in INTERNATIONAL LAW to indicate that the parties to a particular TREATY are to retain possession of that which they forcibly seized during a war.

A treaty ending a war may adopt the principle of *uti possidetis*, the principle of *status quo ante bellum* (Latin for "the state of things before the war"), or a combination of the two. Upon a default of any treaty stipulation, the doctrine of *uti possidetis* prevails.

UTTER To publish or offer; to send into circulation.

The term *utter* is frequently used in reference to COMMERCIAL PAPER. To utter and publish an instrument is to declare, either directly or indirectly through words or action, that it is good. It constitutes a CRIME, for example, to utter a forged CHECK.

UXOR [*Latin, Wife.*] A woman who is legally married.

The term *et uxor* (Latin for "and his wife"), frequently abbreviated to *et ux.*, is used in indexing CONVEYANCES, particularly in cases where a HUSBAND AND WIFE are joint GRANTORS or GRANTEES.

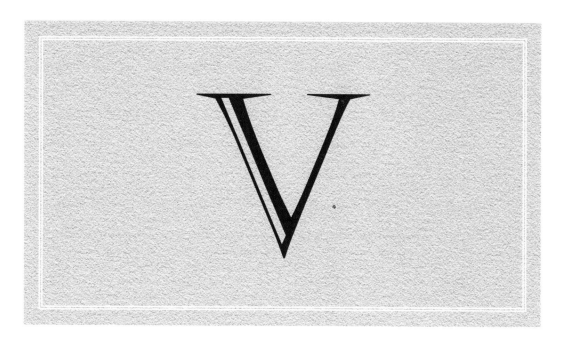

VACATE 📖 To annul, set aside, or render VOID; to surrender POSSESSION or OCCUPANCY. 📖

The term *vacate* has two common usages in the law. With respect to REAL PROPERTY, to vacate the premises means to give up possession of the property and leave the area totally devoid of contents. To vacate a court ORDER or JUDGMENT means to cancel it or render it null and void.

A person may vacate property voluntarily or involuntarily through the issuance of an EVICTION order by a court. Rental and LEASE agreements usually contain a provision concerning when and how the tenant is to vacate the premises at the end of the lease period. Many landlords require renters to make damage deposits, which are refunded after the tenant vacates the property if the landlord determines that no serious damage has been done and that the renter has not left behind PERSONAL PROPERTY that must be disposed of by the landlord. Otherwise, the landlord may keep all or a portion of the deposit. See also LANDLORD AND TENANT.

The other common legal usage of *vacate* refers to the canceling or rescinding of court judgments and orders. State and federal rules of CIVIL PROCEDURE give courts the authority to modify prior judgments. A judgment is the definitive act in a lawsuit that puts an end to the litigation by specifically granting or denying the RELIEF requested by the parties. Once a judgment granting relief has been entered, the plaintiff may legally collect the DAMAGES awarded by the court.

A MOTION to vacate a judgment must be based on a substantial issue. Rule 60(b) of the Federal Rules of Civil Procedure permits a FEDERAL COURT to relieve a party from an adverse judgment on various grounds including FRAUD, MISTAKE, newly discovered EVIDENCE, and SATISFACTION of the judgment.

Another common ground for seeking a motion to vacate is the failure to provide the person against whom the judgment is entered with sufficient NOTICE of the ACTION. If, for example, the plaintiff claims that after making a GOOD FAITH effort, he cannot locate the defendant to serve notice of the pending action, the court may permit service by publication in a newspaper. On the day of the hearing, if the defendant does not appear, the court may enter a DEFAULT JUDGMENT in favor of the plaintiff. However, if the defendant discovers the judgment has been filed, she can make a motion to vacate. The defendant might argue that the plaintiff could have easily served the papers personally and given the defendant the opportunity to appear in court and argue the MERITS of the case.

Courts are generally reluctant to grant a motion to vacate a judgment, especially on the ground of newly discovered evidence. A court will not grant a motion to vacate where the complaining litigant failed to exercise due diligence in securing the evidence in sufficient time to offer it in the original lawsuit. Some JURISDICTIONS do not allow any judgments to be vacated due to newly discovered evidence.

VAGRANCY 📖 The condition of an individual who is idle, has no visible means of support, and travels from place to place without working. 📖

At COMMON LAW the term *vagrant* referred to a person who was idle, refused to work although capable of doing so, and lived on the charity of others. Until the 1970s state vagrancy statutes

Most vagrancy laws have been struck down as unconstitutionally vague, and the term vagrant *has been replaced by the term* homeless person.

were used by police to charge persons who were suspected of criminal activity, but whose actions had not gone far enough to constitute a criminal attempt. Court decisions, however, have struck down vagrancy laws as unconstitutionally VAGUE. In addition, the term *vagrant* has been replaced by *homeless person* as a way of describing a person who is without means or a permanent home.

Traditionally, communities tended to regard vagrants with suspicion and view them either as beggars or as persons likely to commit crimes. In England vagrants were whipped, branded, conscripted into military service, or exiled to penal colonies. In colonial America vagrancy statutes were common. A person who wandered into a town and did not find work was told to leave the community or face criminal prosecution.

After the Civil War, the defeated Southern states enacted *Black Codes*, sets of laws that sought to maintain white control over the newly freed African American slaves. The concern that African Americans would leave their communities and deplete the labor supply led to the inclusion of vagrancy laws in these codes. Unemployed African Americans who had no permanent residence could be arrested and fined. Typically, the person could not pay the fine and was therefore either sent for a term of labor with the county or hired out to a private employer.

The abuse of vagrancy laws by the police throughout the United States was common. Such laws were vague and undefined, allowing police to arrest persons merely on the suspicion they were about to do something illegal. In 1972 the U.S. Supreme Court addressed this problem in *Papachristou v. Jacksonville*, 405 U.S. 156, 92 S. Ct. 839, 31 L. Ed. 2d 110. The Court

ruled that a Florida vagrancy statute was unconstitutional because it was too vague to be understood. The Court emphasized that members of the public cannot avoid engaging in criminal conduct, if prior to engaging in it, they cannot determine that the conduct is forbidden by law. The Court also concluded that the vagrancy law's vagueness lent itself to arbitrary enforcement: police, prosecutors, and juries could enforce the law more stringently against one person than against another, even though the two individuals' conduct was similar.

After *Papachristou* the validity of vagrancy statutes was put in doubt. Prosecutions for vagrancy must now be tied to observable acts, such as public begging. Prosecutions are rare, however, because local governments do not want to spend their financial resources incarcerating persons for such offenses.

See also HOMELESS PERSON; VOID FOR VAGUENESS.

VAGUE 📖 Imprecise; uncertain; indefinite. 📖

The term *vague* is frequently used in reference to a statute written in language that is so indefinite or lacking in precision that an individual of ordinary intelligence is forced to guess at its meaning. Statutes that are vague are ordinarily void on that ground.

See also VOID FOR VAGUENESS.

VALID 📖 Binding; possessing legal force or strength; legally sufficient. 📖

A valid CONTRACT, for example, is one that has been executed in compliance with all the requisite legal formalities and is binding upon, and enforceable by, the individuals who executed it.

VALUABLE CONSIDERATION 📖 In the formation of a valid and binding CONTRACT, something of worth or VALUE that is either a DETRIMENT incurred by the person making the PROMISE or a benefit received by the other person. 📖

In contract law CONSIDERATION is required as an inducement to enter into a contract that is enforceable in the courts. It is an essential element for the formation of a contract. What constitutes sufficient consideration, however, has been the subject of continuing legal debate. Contracts and courts generally use the term *valuable consideration* to signify consideration sufficient to sustain an enforceable AGREEMENT.

In general, consideration consists of a promise to perform a desired act or a promise to refrain from doing an act that one is legally entitled to do. Thus, a person who seeks to enforce a promise must have paid or obligated herself to pay money, delivered goods, expended time and labor, or forgone some other profitable activity or legal right. For example, in a contract for the sale of goods the money paid is the valuable consideration for the vendor, and the property sold is the consideration for the purchaser.

In early COMMON LAW nominal consideration was sufficient to establish a contract. The consideration could be as small as a peppercorn or a cent as long as it demonstrated that the parties intended to enter into an agreement. Eventually, the courts developed the requirement of valuable consideration, but what constitutes it has varied over time. Valuable consideration does not necessarily have to be equal in value to what is received, and it need not be translatable into dollars and cents. It is sufficient for the consideration to consist of a PERFORMANCE or a promise to perform that the promisor (the person making the promise) regards as having value. It is not essential that the person to whom the consideration moves should be benefited, provided the person from whom it moves is, in a legal sense, injured. The injury can consist of refusing to sue on a disputed claim or to exercise a legal right. The alteration in position is regarded as a detriment that forms consideration independent of the actual value of the right relinquished.

VALUE 📖 The estimated or appraised worth of any object or property, calculated in money. 📖

The word *value* has many meanings and may be used in different senses. Because value is usually a relative term, its true meaning must be determined by the context in which it appears.

Value sometimes expresses the inherent usefulness of an object and sometimes the power of purchasing other goods with it. The first is called *value in use*, the latter *value in exchange*. Value in use is the utility of an object in satisfying, directly or indirectly, the needs or desires of human beings. Value in exchange is the amount of commodities, commonly represented by money, for which a thing can be exchanged in an open market. This concept is usually referred to as MARKET VALUE.

Courts have frequently used the word *value* without any clear indication of whether it re-

ferred to value in use or market value. Generally, however, the courts and parties in CIVIL ACTIONS are concerned with market value. Though courts may refer to salable value, actual value, fair value, reasonable value, and cash value, these terms are synonymous with market value.

Value is also employed in various phrases in business and commercial usage. The phrase ACTUAL CASH VALUE is used in INSURANCE to signify the cost of purchasing new replacement property less normal DEPRECIATION, though it may also be determined by the current market value of similar property or by the cost of replacing or repairing the property. CASH SURRENDER VALUE is used in life insurance to refer to the amount that the insurer will pay the policyholder if the policy is canceled before the death of the insured.

BOOK VALUE is the value at which the ASSETS of a business are carried on the company's books. The book value of a FIXED ASSET is arrived at by subtracting accumulated depreciation from the cost of the asset. Book value may also refer to the NET WORTH of a business, which is calculated by subtracting liabilities from assets. *Liquidation value* is the value of a business or an asset when it is sold other than in the ordinary course of business, as in the LIQUIDATION of a business.

In the stock market, *par value* is the nominal value of STOCK; it is calculated by dividing the total stated CAPITAL STOCK by the number of shares authorized. *Stated value* is the value of no par stock established by the CORPORATION as constituting the capital of the corporation.

See also FAIR MARKET VALUE.

VAN BUREN, MARTIN Prominent political leader, U.S. senator, secretary of state, vice president, and eighth president of the United States, Martin Van Buren led the nation during its first major economic crisis. The New York native built a career based on machine politics—the control of local political power by a well-disciplined organization. Van Buren held top positions in his home state before entering national politics, where his instinct for party building helped create the Democratic party in

BIOGRAPHY

LIBRARY OF CONGRESS

Martin Van Buren

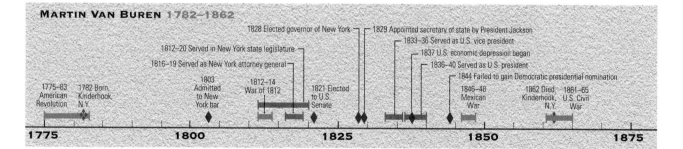

MARTIN VAN BUREN 1782–1862

1775–83 American Revolution

1782 Born, Kinderhook, N.Y.

1803 Admitted to New York bar

1812–20 Served in New York state legislature

1816–19 Served as New York attorney general

1812–14 War of 1812

1821 Elected to U.S. Senate

1828 Elected governor of New York

1829 Appointed secretary of state by President Jackson

1833–36 Served as U.S. vice president

1837 U.S. economic depression began

1836–40 Served as U.S. president

1844 Failed to gain Democratic presidential nomination

1846–48 Mexican War

1862 Died, Kinderhook, N.Y.

1861–65 U.S. Civil War

1775   1800   1825   1850   1875

the 1820s. Elected vice president in 1832 and president in 1836, he sought to protect federal monetary reserves during the depression that began shortly after he took office.

Born in Kinderhook, New York, on December 5, 1782, Van Buren was the third of five children born to Dutch working-class parents. He began to study law at the early age of fourteen and gained admission to the New York bar four years later in 1803. He was elected to the New York legislature in 1812 and continued to be reelected until 1820. From 1816 until 1819, he also served as the state attorney general.

Van Buren's political views came directly from Jeffersonian Republicanism. Like THOMAS JEFFERSON, he believed in states' rights and opposed a strong federal government. During the early years of his career in New York, Van Buren controlled the so-called Albany Regency, a political machine that was very influential in state politics. Later, in the 1820s, he joined forces with ANDREW JACKSON and helped to forge the political alliances that would lead to the formation of the Democratic party.

As in state politics, Van Buren enjoyed steady success at the national level. He won election to the U.S. Senate in 1821 and retained his senatorial seat until 1828 when he became governor of New York. He resigned the office a mere twelve weeks later, however, to become secretary of state under President Jackson. His support of Jackson through the president's turbulent first administration paid off: in 1832 Jackson chose Van Buren as his vice presidential running mate over the incumbent JOHN C. CALHOUN, and the two were elected.

Van Buren's own election as president in 1836 was precipitated by crisis. Under the Jackson administration, land speculation had run rampant nationwide. When Congress failed to intervene, banks issued great numbers of loans without backing them up with security. The speculation continued until Jackson ordered the government to accept only gold or silver as payment on land. The result was the so-called Panic of 1837, a devastating financial crash that led to the first large-scale economic depression in U.S. history. By 1840 Van Buren had convinced Congress to pass the Independent Treasury Bill. It provided for federally controlled vaults to store all federal monies; transactions were to be conducted in hard currency. The independent treasury protected federal deposits until 1841, when it was abolished. President JAMES K. POLK brought it back in 1846.

Van Buren sought reelection in 1840, running as the only presidential candidate without a vice presidential candidate in history. De-

feated by WILLIAM HENRY HARRISON, he attempted to gain the Democratic nomination again in 1844 but was unsuccessful. His popularity had deteriorated both because of the depression and because of his positions on other domestic issues. He opposed the annexation of Texas, which he feared would precipitate a war with Mexico, and an expensive war against Seminole Indians in Florida. He tried once more to win the Democratic presidential nomination in 1848 but was defeated again. He died on July 24, 1862, in Kinderhook, New York.

VANDALISM ◫ The intentional and MALICIOUS destruction of or damage to the property of another. ◫

The intentional destruction of property is popularly referred to as vandalism. It includes behavior such as breaking windows, slashing tires, spray painting a wall with graffiti, and destroying a computer system through the use of a computer virus. Vandalism is a malicious act and may reflect personal ill will, although the perpetrators need not know their victim to commit vandalism. The RECKLESSNESS of the act imputes both INTENT and MALICE.

Because the destruction of public and private property poses a threat to society, modern statutes make vandalism a crime. The penalties upon conviction may be a fine, a jail sentence, an order to pay for repairs or replacement, or all three. In addition, a person who commits vandalism may be sued in a civil TORT ACTION for damages so that the damaged property can be repaired or replaced.

Vandalism is a general term that may not actually appear in criminal statutes. Frequently, these statutes employ the terms *criminal mischief*, *malicious mischief*, or *malicious trespass* as opposed to vandalism. A group of individuals can be convicted of conspiring or acting concertedly to commit vandalism. Generally, the attempt to commit vandalism is an offense as well, but the penalties for attempted vandalism are not as severe as the penalties for a completed act. Penalties also depend on the value of the property destroyed or the cost of repairing it.

To obtain a conviction the prosecution must ordinarily prove that the accused damaged or destroyed some property, that the property did not belong to the accused, and that the accused acted willfully and with malice. In the absence of proof of damage, the defendant may be guilty of TRESPASS, but not vandalism. If there is no proof that the defendant intentionally damaged the property, the defendant cannot be convicted of the crime but can be held liable for monetary damages in a CIVIL ACTION.

Vandalism

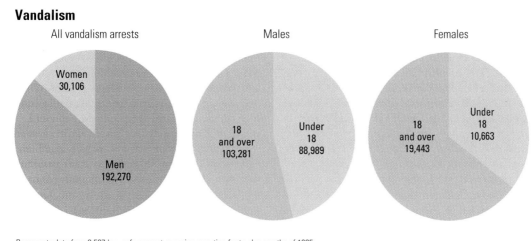

All vandalism arrests

Women
30,106

Men
192,270

Males

18
and over
103,281

Under
18
88,989

Females

18
and over
19,443

Under
18
10,663

Represents data from 8,587 law enforcement agencies reporting for twelve months of 1995.

Source: U.S. Department of Justice, Federal Bureau of Investigation, *Crime in the United States, 1995.*

Some state statutes impose more stringent penalties for the destruction of certain types of property. Such statutes might cover the desecration of a church or synagogue, the destruction of jail or prison property by inmates, and the intentional destruction of property belonging to a PUBLIC UTILITY.

Destructive acts will not be excused merely because the defendants acted out of what they thought was a noble purpose. Political demonstrators may exercise their FIRST AMENDMENT rights of FREEDOM OF SPEECH and assembly, but if they deface, for example, government property with spray-painted slogans, they can be convicted of vandalism.

The peak period for committing relatively minor property crimes is between the ages of fifteen and twenty-one. In the United States adolescent vandalism, including the wanton destruction of schools, causes millions of dollars of damage each year. Apprehending vandals is often difficult, and the costs of repairing the damage are passed on to taxpayers, private property owners, and insurance companies. Some states hold parents financially responsible for vandalism committed by their MINOR children, up to specified limits. These statutes are designed to encourage parental supervision and

to shift part of the cost of vandalism from the public to the individuals who are best able to supervise the children who destroyed the property.

See also JUVENILE LAW; MALICIOUS MISCHIEF.

VAN DEVANTER, WILLIS As an associate justice of the U.S. Supreme Court from 1910 to 1937, Willis Van Devanter was considered the leading conservative justice of the era. Van Devanter's background in education, politics, and the law brought him to the bench, first as chief justice of the Wyoming Supreme Court and then as a U.S. circuit judge. In his twenty-six years on the U.S. Supreme Court, he consistently opposed the expansion of government power. His opposition was fiercest during the administration of President FRANKLIN D. ROOSEVELT, when he joined three other conservative justices of the Supreme Court in fighting Roosevelt's legislative program, the NEW DEAL. Their like-minded opinions, which earned them the nickname the "Four Horsemen," led to a sharp confrontation with the president.

Born on April 17, 1859, in Marion, Indiana, Van Devanter was the first of eight children born to Violetta Spencer and Isaac Van Devanter, a lawyer and abolitionist. He excelled in academics, graduating in 1878 from Indiana

BIOGRAPHY

PORTRAIT BY THOMAS E. STEPHENS, COLLECTION OF THE SUPREME COURT OF THE UNITED STATES.

Willis Van Devanter

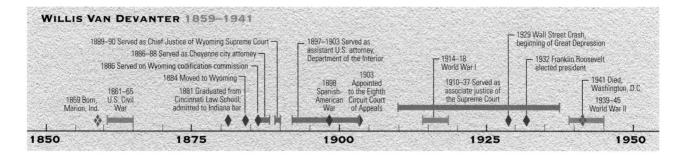

WILLIS VAN DEVANTER 1859–1941

1889–90 Served as Chief Justice of Wyoming Supreme Court
1886–88 Served as Cheyenne city attorney
1886 Served on Wyoming codification commission
1884 Moved to Wyoming
1897–1903 Served as assistant U.S. attorney, Department of the Interior
1929 Wall Street Crash, beginning of Great Depression
1932 Franklin Roosevelt elected president

1861–65 U.S. Civil War
1881 Graduated from Cincinnati Law School; admitted to Indiana bar
1898 Spanish-American War
1903 Appointed to the Eighth Circuit Court of Appeals
1914–18 World War I
1910–37 Served as associate justice of the Supreme Court
1941 Died, Washington, D.C.
1939–45 World War II

1859 Born, Marion, Ind.

1850   1875   1900   1925   1950

Asbury University (now DePauw University) with a near perfect record in history, math, Greek, and Latin. In 1881 he earned a bachelor of laws degree from the Cincinnati Law School and established a law practice in Indiana. He soon moved to Wyoming where he represented railroads, helped to amend the state's statutes in 1886, and served as city attorney for two years. In 1888 he was a representative at the territorial legislature and chaired the Judiciary Committee. Van Devanter also found time for hunting grizzly bears with the legendary Buffalo Bill (William F. Cody).

For the next two decades, Van Devanter's energies were divided among the judiciary, education, and Republican party politics. He presided as chief justice of the Wyoming Supreme Court from 1889 to 1890. From 1896 to 1900, he was an assistant U.S. attorney general to the Department of the Interior, concurrently serving as a delegate to the Republican National Committee. He also taught law at Columbian College, now George Washington University. In 1903 President THEODORE ROOSEVELT appointed him to the Eighth Circuit Court of Appeals, and in 1910 President WILLIAM HOWARD TAFT nominated him to the Supreme Court.

On the Court, Van Devanter wrote few noteworthy opinions. His contributions came mainly in obscure legal areas that he had mastered while on the circuit court: land claims, WATER RIGHTS, and jurisdictional issues. Rather than writing opinions, Van Devanter preferred to assert his influence in discussions among the justices. He often voiced his belief that government power should be limited. He took an especially narrow view of the powers that could be asserted under the U.S. Constitution's Commerce, Tax, and Due Process Clauses. From 1918 to 1923, he joined majority opinions that found federal CHILD LABOR LAWS and state MINIMUM WAGE legislation unconstitutional.

Ironically, Van Devanter's most significant opinion marked a rare departure from his ideology. In *McGrain v. Daugherty*, 273 U.S. 135, 47 S. Ct. 319, 71 L. Ed. 580 (1927), he asserted that Congress had broad powers to subpoena and conduct investigations. The opinion's impact was felt dramatically two decades later during congressional investigations of labor corruption and COMMUNISM.

In the 1930s Van Devanter's desire to restrain government kept him on the Court. He had apparently decided to retire in 1932 but changed his mind because of what he regarded as the excesses of President Franklin Roosevelt. The president had embarked on the ambitious

❦

"WE ARE OF THE OPINION THAT THE POWER OF INQUIRY—WITH PROCESS TO ENFORCE IT—IS AN ESSENTIAL AND APPROPRIATE AUXILIARY TO THE LEGISLATIVE FUNCTION."

The Parental and Cultural Fun Group of Crookston, Minnesota, had to get a variance from the city to paint this mural on the side of the town's Grand Theater.

New Deal, a broad legislative response to the economic hardships of the Great Depression.

Sharing Van Devanter's opposition to these programs were three other conservative justices: JAMES C. MCREYNOLDS, GEORGE SUTHERLAND, and PIERCE BUTLER. Critics dubbed them the "Four Horsemen," after the four horsemen of the Apocalypse. In a string of decisions, they voted as a bloc to strike down key New Deal laws. Among these decisions was *Schecter Poultry Corp. v. United States*, 295 U.S. 495, 55 S. Ct. 837, 79 L. Ed. 1570 (1935), which voided a key part of Roosevelt's plan for economic recovery and provoked the president into seeking a means to ensure that his legislation survived. Two years later, Roosevelt responded with an extraordinary attempt to expand the number of justices on the Court—his so-called court-packing plan. In the face of this challenge, the Court backed down and began upholding New Deal legislation.

Van Devanter resigned at the end of 1936. Although branded a reactionary during his tenure, in retirement he received accolades from his fellow justices, conservative and liberal alike. He died on February 8, 1941, in Washington, D.C.

VARIANCE 📖 The discrepancy between what a party to a lawsuit alleges will be proved in PLEADINGS and what the party actually proves at trial.

In ZONING law, an official permit to use property in a manner that departs from the way in which other property in the same locality can be used. 📖

The term *variance* is used both in litigation and in zoning law. In both instances it has the general meaning of a difference or divergence.

A party to a civil lawsuit or a prosecutor in a criminal trial must prove the ALLEGATIONS set

forth in a COMPLAINT, INDICTMENT, or INFORMA-TION. If there is a substantial difference or discrepancy between the allegations and the proof offered in support, a *variance* exists. For example, if the crime of ROBBERY is alleged and the crime of BURGLARY is proved instead, the failure of proof on the robbery charge constitutes a variance that will lead to the dismissal of the case.

Most U.S. communities have zoning laws that control and direct the development of property within their borders according to its present and potential uses. Typically, a community is divided into zoning districts based on the type of use permitted: residential, commercial, and industrial. Additional restrictions may limit population density and building height within these districts. A *variance* is an exception to one or more of the zoning restrictions on a piece of property.

A variance is different from a NONCONFORM-ING USE, which permits existing structures and uses to continue when zoning is first instituted. Once a zoning plan has been established, a property owner who wishes to diverge from it must seek a variance from the municipal government. The variance will be granted when "unnecessary hardship" would result to the landowner if it were denied. Although other forms of administrative relief from zoning restrictions are available, such as rezoning the area, variances are most frequently used.

There are two types of variances: area variances and use variances. An area variance is usually not controversial because it is generally granted due to some odd configuration of the lot or some peculiar natural condition that prevents normal construction in compliance with zoning restrictions. For example, if the odd shape of a lot prevents a house from being set back the minimum number of feet from the street, the municipality will usually relax the requirement.

Use variances are more controversial because they attempt a change in the permitted use. For example, if a lot is zoned single-family residential, a person who wishes to build a multifamily dwelling must obtain a variance. Residents of an area will generally object to applications for variances that seek to change the character of their neighborhood. Although the municipality may heed these objections, it will likely grant the variance if it believes unnecessary hardship would result without the variance. If, however, the owner seeking a variance for a multifamily dwelling bought the property with notice of the current zoning restrictions, the variance will probably be denied. Applicants for a variance cannot argue hardship based on actions they commit that result in self-induced hardship.

If many use variances are sought in a particular area on the basis of unique or peculiar circumstances, it may be a sign that the entire neighborhood needs to be rezoned rather than forcing property owners to seek variances in a piecemeal fashion. Properly used, variances provide a remedy for hardships affecting a single lot or a relatively small area.

See also LAND-USE CONTROL; SETBACK.

BIOGRAPHY

VAUGHN, GEORGE L. George L. Vaughn was an African American lawyer and civic leader who became a prominent member of the Democratic party. Vaughn, who practiced in St. Louis, Missouri, is best remembered for representing J. D. Shelley in the landmark CIVIL RIGHTS case of *Shelley v. Kraemer*, 334 U.S. 1, 68 S. Ct. 836, 92 L. Ed. 1161 (1948), which struck down racially discriminatory REAL ESTATE covenants.

Vaughn was born in Kentucky in 1885, the son of former slaves. He attended Lane College in Jackson, Tennessee, and went to law school at Walden University in Nashville, Tennessee. He served in the artillery as a first lieutenant in World War I. After the war he moved to St. Louis, where he practiced law. In 1936 Vaughn was appointed a St. Louis justice of the peace, and in 1941 he ran unsuccessfully for city alderman as a Democrat.

Vaughn became nationally known for his representation of J. D. Shelley. Shelley, an African American, was employed at a government-owned munitions factory and had saved enough money to make a down payment on a house. Using an African American real estate broker,

GEORGE L. VAUGHN 1885–1950

1885 Born, Ky.

1907 Graduated from Lane College (Tennessee)

1910 Graduated from Walden University Law School

1914–18 World War I

1919 Helped found the Citizen Liberty League in St. Louis, which sought election of more blacks to public office and serving on party committees

1936 Appointed justice of the peace in St. Louis

1941 Ran unsuccessfully for city alderman as a Democrat

1939–45 World War II

1945 J.D. Shelley and his family purchased and moved into St. Louis house governed by a restrictive covenant barring blacks

1948 Supreme Court ruled restrictive land covenants unconstitutional in *Shelley v. Kraemer*; Vaughn played a prominent role in the Democratic National Convention

1950 Died, St. Louis, Mo.

1875   1900   1925   1950

he purchased a house in St. Louis and moved his family to the property in October 1945. An association of white homeowners was outraged at the sale of the house to an African American and served an EVICTION order on Shelley. An association of African American real estate brokers assisted Shelley by hiring Vaughn to fight the order.

The homeowners justified the eviction on the basis of a RESTRICTIVE COVENANT contained in the DEED, which stated that the property could not be "occupied by any person not of the Caucasian race." Vaughn opposed the eviction and won at the trial court. However, the Missouri Supreme Court upheld the validity of the restrictive covenant and the eviction (*Kraemer v. Shelley*, 355 Mo. 814, 198 S.W.2d 679, 681 [1946]).

With the support of the African American real estate brokers, Vaughn successfully petitioned the U.S. Supreme Court to hear an appeal. At oral argument he called racially restrictive covenants "the Achilles heel" of U.S. democracy. The Supreme Court agreed in its 1948 decision, ruling that such covenants could not be enforced in state courts because they violated the FOURTEENTH AMENDMENT by infringing upon the right of a citizen to purchase and dispose of property.

That same year Vaughn played a prominent role in the Democratic National Convention in Philadelphia. As a Missouri delegate, Vaughn proposed a resolution that would bar the seating of the Mississippi delegation because of the white supremacy provisions contained in the Mississippi state constitution. His resolution fell just 115 votes short of prevailing.

Vaughn died in St. Louis in 1950.

VEL NON   [*Latin, Or not.*] A term used by the courts in reference to the existence or nonexistence of an issue for determination; for example: "We come to the merits vel non of this appeal," means "we come to the merits, or not, of this appeal," and refers to the possibility that the appeal backs merit.

VENDEE   Buyer or purchaser; an individual to whom anything is transferred by a sale.

The term *vendee* is ordinarily used in reference to a buyer of REAL PROPERTY.

VENDOR   Seller; an individual who transfers property for sale; merchant; retail dealer; supplier.

The term *vendor* is frequently used in reference to an individual who sells REAL PROPERTY.

VENDOR AND PURCHASER   The legal relationship between the buyer and the seller of land during the interim period between the EXECUTION of the CONTRACT and the date of its consummation.

The sale of REAL PROPERTY is treated differently by the law than the sale of PERSONAL PROPERTY. The relationship between the seller and the buyer has traditionally been labeled that of vendor and purchaser. A contract to sell real property (for example, a house, a building, farmland, or a vacant lot) does not automatically mean the sale will be consummated. The vendor will be required to prove that she can convey a MARKETABLE TITLE to the land.

A contract for the sale of real property is executed when the vendor and the purchaser sign an AGREEMENT in which the vendor promises to convey ownership of the property to the purchaser, who promises to pay an agreed sum. The contract is consummated when the vendor delivers a DEED to the purchaser and the purchaser pays the vendor her price. Consummation of the contract is variously referred to as the closing of ESCROW, the date of closing, or simply the CLOSING.

The vendor-purchaser relationship is based on the unique nature of land. TITLE to any particular parcel has always involved more complications than arise with the ownership of personal property. The status of the vendor's title is a matter of great concern to any prospective purchaser, but that title is often subject to deficiencies.

Most purchasers offer to buy land before they have made an investigation of the seller's title to it. To protect the purchaser in this situation, the law permits him to demand a marketable title from the vendor and to withdraw from a sales contract if the title turns out to be unmarketable. Therefore, every contract for the sale of land includes the implied requirement that the vendor's title be marketable, unless the contract specifically provides otherwise.

A marketable title is a title that the vendor does in fact have and that is not subject to ENCUMBRANCES, which are interests in the property held by someone other than the vendor or purchaser. Unless an agreement indicates otherwise, the purchaser is entitled to receive an absolutely undivided interest in all the property he has contracted to buy. For example, if the vendor promises to convey forty acres in the sales agreement and the next day the purchaser discovers that the vendor has title to only twenty-five acres, the purchaser is not obligated to honor the contract because the vendor lacks marketable title to the land she agreed to convey.

If the vendor's title is subject to an outstanding MORTGAGE, the title may be unmarketable. The mere existence of an encumbrance does not necessarily cause the title to be unmarket-

DAVID ULMER/STOCK BOSTON

able, however, if the parties have provided for it in their contract. For example, in the sale of a vendor's house that has an outstanding mortgage, the purchaser's money will first be applied to paying off the vendor's mortgage before the vendor receives any proceeds.

To avoid confusion and frustration of the parties' intentions, contracts of sale usually require an insurable title to the property as evidenced by a TITLE INSURANCE policy. The purchaser must accept the vendor's title, provided an insurance company indicates its willingness to insure the title without making exceptions to the coverage.

Because land has always been regarded as a unique ASSET, a prospective purchaser can usually enforce a sales agreement whether the vendor wants to proceed or not. This power has the effect of giving the purchaser an interest in the land itself, as well as personal contract rights against the vendor. By executing the sales contract, the purchaser becomes the equitable owner of the land. The vendor retains LEGAL TITLE, but she holds the title only as SECURITY for payment. This legal fiction is known as the doctrine of equitable conversion.

In some states the doctrine of equitable conversion shifts any loss or damage to the property to the purchaser before the closing. As the true owner of the property, the purchaser is required to bear the RISK of loss during the contract period and cannot withdraw from the agreement. Thus, if a fire caused by neither party destroys the premises two weeks before the closing, the purchaser will still be obligated to complete the contract and pay the vendor's price.

Some courts reject this application of equitable conversion, holding that the contract fails if the vendor cannot deliver the premises in the original condition on the day of closing. This view treats the continued existence of undam-

The vendor and purchaser of real property, such as one of these Illinois homes, have specific rights that protect their interests during the course of a sale.

aged property as an implied condition of the sales agreement. The purchaser is entitled to withdraw from the contract if the property is damaged prior to closing.

Several states have adopted the Uniform Vendor and Purchaser Risk Act, under which innocent losses occurring during the contract period are allocated to the vendor, unless the purchaser has taken POSSESSION prior to closing. The risk of loss is on the person in possession because that person is in the best position to take care of the property.

See also SALES LAW; TITLE SEARCH.

VENIRE FACIAS 📖 [*Latin, Cause to come.*] A judicial order or WRIT addressed to the SHERIFF of a COUNTY where a legal action is to take place, commanding the sheriff to assemble a JURY. 📖

A *venireman* is a member of a jury summoned by a writ of *venire facias.*

VENIREMAN 📖 A member of a JURY which has been summoned by a WRIT of VENIRE FACIAS. 📖

VENUE 📖 A place, such as the territory from which residents are selected to serve as jurors.

A proper place, such as the correct COURT to hear a case because it has authority over events that have occurred within a certain geographical area. 📖

A basic principle of U.S. law is that a civil or criminal ACTION will be decided by a court in the locality where the dispute or criminal offense occurred. This principle is expressed in the concept of *venue*. In accordance with this principle a CIVIL ACTION must be started where either the plaintiff or the defendant resides, where the CAUSE OF ACTION arose, or, if REAL PROPERTY is at issue, where the real property is situated. In criminal cases proper venue is in the locality where the crime was committed or where a dead body was discovered.

State and federal venue statutes govern where a case will be tried. State venue statutes list a variety of factors that determine in which county and in which court a lawsuit should be brought, including where the defendant resides, where the defendant does business, where the plaintiff does business, or where the seat of government is located.

A plaintiff may bring his action in any of the places permitted by state law. Most commonly, states allow a lawsuit to be brought in the county where the defendant resides. Choosing the wrong place is not fatal to the plaintiff's action, however. Statutes usually provide that a JUDGMENT rendered by a STATE COURT is valid even if venue is improper. If a defendant believes the suit is being tried in the wrong venue, she usually must object at the outset of the case, or she will be presumed to have waived the right to object.

Venue and the Oklahoma City Bombing Case

Trial judges are generally reluctant to grant a defendant's request for a change of venue in a criminal trial. A change of venue is inconvenient to the trial participants and is often financially costly. Nevertheless, when a judge believes that a defendant cannot receive a fair trial in the place where the crime was committed, he can order that the trial be moved to another location.

The attorneys for Timothy J. McVeigh and Terry L. Nichols, who were charged in federal court with the April 19, 1995 bombing of the federal office building in Oklahoma City, Oklahoma, that resulted in the deaths of 168 people, sought a change of venue from Oklahoma City. The defense attorneys argued that there was substantial prejudice against McVeigh and Nichols in Oklahoma City and the state of Oklahoma, making it impossible for them to receive a fair and impartial trial.

In an order issued on February 20, 1996, Judge Richard P. Matsch agreed. The news coverage of the events surrounding the bombing, its aftermath, and the arrest of McVeigh and Nichols had been extensive in Oklahoma. Matsch noted that the Oklahoma news media had "demonized" the defendants and run news stories suggesting that they had been associated with right-wing militia groups. Because the defendants had been charged with capital crimes, Matsch was concerned that Oklahoma jurors would not be able to set aside their prejudices and emotions to determine first whether the defendants were guilty or innocent and then, if found guilty, whether they deserved to be executed.

Therefore, Matsch ordered a change of venue to Denver, Colorado. Though he acknowledged that the victims of the bombing wished to attend the trials and that a change of venue would cause them hardship, Matsch concluded that the "interests of the victims in being able to attend this trial in Oklahoma are outweighed by the court's obligation to assure that the trial be conducted with fundamental fairness and with due regard for all constitutional requirements."

In June 1997 McVeigh was found guilty of bombing the federal building and was sentenced to death. Nichols' trial began in October 1997.

In criminal cases the defendant must be tried in the venue where the crime was committed or where the body of a victim was discovered. In extraordinary circumstances, however, a court may grant a change of venue. The request for a change of venue is usually made by the defendant, but it can be made by the prosecutor. The court itself may also initiate the transfer of venue.

Changes of venue are governed by statute, but the court has great discretion in applying the statutory grounds. In Alaska, for example, the law gives the court the ability to move a case from one place to another place within the judicial district or to a place in another judicial district. Reasons for a change of venue in Alaska include the belief that an impartial trial cannot be held or that the convenience of WITNESSES and the ends of justice would be promoted by the change (Alaska Stat. § 22.10.040). The most common reason for a change of venue in criminal cases is PRETRIAL PUBLICITY that makes it unlikely that an impartial JURY could be selected in the community where the crime occurred.

Different rules regulate venue in the FEDERAL COURTS. The federal court system is divided into judicial districts, which can cover an entire state or, in the case of populous states, only a portion of the state. The federal venue statute (28 U.S.C.A. § 1391) refers to these districts in the way state venue statutes refer to counties. Except when a special law applies to a particular type of case, proper venue is determined by the factor that allows the case to be brought in federal court.

If the court derives its authority because the plaintiffs and defendants are residents of different states (known as diversity jurisdiction), then the proper venue is the judicial district where all the plaintiffs or all the defendants reside or the district where the claim arose. In lawsuits where the federal court has JURISDICTION because a question of federal law is involved (known as FEDERAL QUESTION jurisdiction), venue lies only in the district where all the defendants reside or where the claim arose.

Special statutes set different rules for admiralty, PATENT, and INTERPLEADER lawsuits and lawsuits in which the United States is a party. An ALIEN can be sued in any district in the United States, but if the alien is a defendant along with citizens, venue lies where all the citizens reside. A case transferred by removal from a state court to a federal court goes to the federal court in the district where the state action was started.

VERBA [*Latin, Words.*] A term used in many legal MAXIMS, including *verba sunt indices animi*, which means "words are the indicators of the mind or thought"; and *verba accipienda ut sortiantur effectum*, or "words are to be taken so that they may have some effect."

VERDICT The formal decision or finding made by a JURY concerning the questions submitted to it during a TRIAL. The jury reports the verdict to the COURT, which generally accepts it.

The decision of a jury is called a verdict. A jury is charged with hearing the EVIDENCE presented by both sides in a trial, determining the FACTS of the case, applying the relevant law to the facts, and voting on a final verdict. There are different types of verdicts, and the votes required to render a verdict differ depending on whether the jury hears a criminal or civil case. Though most verdicts are upheld by the judge presiding at the trial, the judge has the discretion to set aside a verdict in certain circumstances.

A GENERAL VERDICT is the most common form of verdict. It is a comprehensive decision on an issue. In civil cases the jury makes a decision in favor of the plaintiff or the defendant, determining LIABILITY and the amount of money DAMAGES. In criminal cases the jury decides "guilty" or "not guilty" on the charge or charges against the defendant. In cases involving a major crime the verdict must be unanimous. In minor criminal cases, however, some states allow either a majority vote or a vote of 10 to 2. In civil cases many states have moved away from the unanimity requirement and now allow votes of 10 to 2.

A *special verdict* is sometimes used in civil cases where complex and technical questions of fact are involved and the parties seek to assert greater control over the decision-making process. The judge gives the jury a series of specific, written, factual questions. Based upon the jury's answers, or findings of fact, the judge will determine the verdict. Special verdicts are used only infrequently because parties often have a difficult time agreeing on the precise set of questions.

U.S. law does not permit chance verdicts. A CHANCE VERDICT is one that has been determined not by deliberation but by a form of chance, such as the flip of a coin or the drawing of lots. Although such verdicts were once acceptable, they are now unlawful.

A *directed verdict* is not made by a jury. It is a verdict ordered by the court after the evidence has been presented and the court finds it insufficient for a jury to return a verdict for the side

APWIDE WORLD PHOTOS

with the burden of proof. A court may enter a directed verdict before the jury renders its verdict. If the court allows the jury to make a verdict but then disagrees with the jury's evaluation of the evidence, the court can decide the case by issuing an ORDER. For example, under rule 29 of the Federal Rules of Criminal Procedure, a court can grant a JUDGMENT of ACQUITTAL to a defendant. In civil cases the court can issue a JUDGMENT NOTWITHSTANDING THE VERDICT.

VERIFY To make certain, to substantiate, or to confirm by formal OATH, AFFIRMATION, or AFFIDAVIT.

The U.S. legal system relies on its participants to tell the truth. Before WITNESSES can give TESTIMONY at a trial or some other proceeding, they must swear or affirm that the testimony about to be given will be truthful. Apart from witnesses, when a particular PLEADING, statement, or other document is submitted to the court, the court requires that the person offering it *verify* its correctness, truth, or authenticity.

The verification takes the form of a written certification that is generally attached to the document in question. The most common form of certification is an *affidavit*. An affidavit is a written statement sworn to or affirmed before an officer authorized to administer an oath or affirmation, usually a NOTARY PUBLIC. The affidavit names the place of execution and certifies that the person making the affidavit states particular facts and that he appeared before the officer on a certain date and swore to and signed the statement.

A common verification is called an *affidavit of service*. The person swears or affirms that the attached legal document has been served (delivered) personally or by mail to the persons listed in the affidavit on a certain date. The affidavit

The jury's verdict is the tense finale to a criminal trial. Here, New York City police officer Frank Speringo reacts as the jury finds him guilty of second-degree manslaughter in the shooting death of a woman during a drunken brawl.

of SERVICE verifies to the court that the document has, in fact, been sent to all parties who should receive it. Though this type of verification is a routine matter, it is essential to fairness and the DUE PROCESS OF LAW.

The need for verification is illustrated in criminal law. Law enforcement officers and others use affidavits to provide information to a MAGISTRATE to establish PROBABLE CAUSE for the issuance of an ARREST WARRANT or a SEARCH WARRANT. The officer making the affidavit must set forth sufficient facts to satisfy the magistrate that an offense has been committed and that the person accused is the guilty party. If the officer falsely swears to the truthfulness of the affidavit's contents, a court may dismiss the charges. The officer, like anyone else who falsely verifies the truthfulness of a statement, may be charged with the crime of PERJURY.

The rules of EVIDENCE recognize the legitimacy of a *verified copy*, which is a copy of a document that is shown by independent evidence to be true. A verified copy will be allowed into evidence if successive witnesses trace the original into the hands of a witness who made or compared the copy.

VERSUS 📖 [*Latin, Against.*] A designation used in the CAPTION of a lawsuit to indicate the opposite positions taken by the parties. 📖

In the title of a lawsuit, the plaintiff's name appears first; the word *versus* follows; then the defendant's name appears, as in "A versus B." *Versus* is commonly abbreviated *vs.* or *v.*

VERTICAL MERGER 📖 A merger between two business firms that have a buyer-seller relationship. 📖

Business mergers can take two forms: horizontal and vertical. In a *horizontal merger,* one firm acquires another firm that produces and sells an identical or similar product in the same geographic area. This type of merger eliminates competition between the two firms. In a *vertical merger,* one firm acquires either a customer or a supplier. Because horizontal mergers pose a direct threat to competition, they have been regulated more aggressively by the federal government than vertical mergers. Nevertheless, vertical mergers may, in some circumstances, be anticompetitive and violate federal ANTITRUST LAWS.

Firms vertically integrate for many reasons. Some of the most common are to reduce uncertainty over the availability or quality of supplies or the demand for output, to take advantage of available economies of integration, to protect against monopolistic practices of either suppliers or buyers with which the firm must otherwise deal, and to reduce transactions costs such as sales taxes and marketing expenses. Through a vertical merger, the acquiring firm may lower its cost of production and distribution and make more productive use of its resources.

Vertical mergers are subject to the provisions of the CLAYTON ACT (15 U.S.C.A. § 12 et seq.) governing transactions that come within the ambit of antitrust acts. Vertical integration by merger does not reduce the total number of economic entities operating at one level of the market, but it may change patterns of industry behavior. Suppliers may lose a market for their goods, retail outlets may be deprived of supplies, and competitors may find that both supplies and outlets are blocked. Vertical mergers may also be anticompetitive because their entrenched market power may discourage new businesses from entering the market.

The U.S. Supreme Court has decided only three vertical merger cases under section 7 of the Clayton Act since 1950. In the first case, *United States v. E. I. du Pont de Nemours & Co.,* 353 U.S. 586, 77 S. Ct. 872, 1 L. Ed. 2d 1057 (1957), the Court upset the general assumption that section 7 did not apply to vertical mergers. After finding that du Pont's acquisition of 23 percent of General Motors (GM) stock foreclosed sales to GM by other suppliers of automotive paints and fabric, the Court held that the vertical merger had an illegal anticompetitive effect.

The next vertical merger case to come before the Court, *Brown Shoe Co. v. United States,* 370 U.S. 294, 82 S. Ct. 1502, 8 L. Ed. 2d 510 (1962), remains the leading decision in this area of antitrust law. The Court stated that the "primary vice of a vertical merger" is the foreclosure of competitors, which acts as a "clog on competition" and "deprive[s] . . . rivals of a fair opportunity to compete." The Court noted that market share would be an important, but seldom decisive consideration. The Court identified other "economic and historical factors" that would determine the legality of the merger. The first and "most important such factor" was the nature and purpose of the arrangement. Another was the trend toward concentration in the industry.

In the only other vertical merger case decided by the Supreme Court, *Ford Motor Co. v. United States,* 405 U.S. 562, 92 S. Ct. 1142, 31 L. Ed. 2d 492 (1972), the Court condemned Ford's attempted acquisition of Autolite, a spark plug manufacturer, and emphasized the heightened barriers that the merger would pose to other companies that attempted to enter the market. The Court also emphasized that Ford's argument that the acquisition had made Autolite a more effective competitor was irrelevant.

CROSS-REFERENCES

Mergers and Acquisitions; Monopoly; Restraint of Trade; Unfair Competition.

VEST To give an immediate, fixed right of present or future enjoyment.

The term *vest* is significant in the law, because it means that a person has an absolute right to some present or future interest in something of value. When a right has *vested*, the person is legally entitled to what has been promised and may seek relief in court if the benefit is not given.

In U.S. property law a *vested remainder* is a future interest held by an identifiable person (the remainderman), which, upon the happening of a certain event, will become the remainderman's. When property is given to one person for life and, at the person's death, the property is to go to another living person, this second person has a vested remainder in the property.

A *vested legacy* is an inheritance given in such terms that there is a fixed, irrevocable right to its payment. For example, a LEGACY contained in a will that states that the inheritance shall not be paid until the person reaches the age of twenty-one is a vested legacy, because it is given unconditionally and absolutely and therefore vests an immediate interest in the person receiving the legacy. Only the enjoyment of the legacy is deferred or postponed.

In contemporary U.S. law the term *vesting* refers to the right that an employee acquires to various employer-contributed benefits, such as a PENSION, after having been employed for a requisite number of years. The federal EMPLOYEE RETIREMENT INCOME SECURITY ACT (ERISA) of 1974 (29 U.S.C.A. § 1001 et seq.) governs the funding, vesting, administration, and termination of employee benefit plans. ERISA was enacted as a result of congressional dissatisfaction with private pension plans. Under some plans an employee's pension benefits did not vest before retirement or vested only after such a long period of time (as long as thirty years) that few employees ever became entitled to them. ERISA ensures that all pension benefits will vest within a reasonable time. Once pension benefits are vested, an employee has the right to them even if the employment relationship terminates before the employee retires.

In constitutional law *vested rights* are those that are so completely and definitely settled in a person that they are not subject to defeat or cancellation by the act of any other private person. Once a person can prove to a court the validity of the vested rights, the court will recognize and protect these rights so as to prevent injustice.

VETERANS AFFAIRS DEPARTMENT

The Department of Veterans Affairs (VA) operates programs to benefit veterans and members of their families. Benefits include compensation payments for disabilities or death related to military service, pensions, education, and rehabilitation. The VA also guarantees home loans, provides burial services for veterans, and operates a medical care program that includes nursing homes, clinics, and medical centers.

The Department of Veterans Affairs was established in 1988 as an executive department by the Department of Veterans Affairs Act (38 U.S.C.A. § 201 note). Its establishment came after more than twenty-four years of effort by members of Congress to elevate the department's predecessor, the Veterans Administration, to CABINET status. Proponents argued that promotion to cabinet level would increase the political accountability of the VA and improve the quality of its services. The Veterans Administration was established as an independent agency under the president by Executive Order No. 5398 of July 21, 1930, in accordance with the act of July 3, 1930 (46 Stat. 1016). This act authorized the president to consolidate and coordinate the U.S. Veterans Bureau, the Bureau of Pensions, and the National Home for Volunteer Soldiers.

The Department of Veterans Affairs comprises three organizations that administer veterans' programs: the Veterans Health Administration, the Veterans Benefits Administration, and the National Cemetery System. Each organization has field facilities and a central office. Each central office also includes separate offices that provide support to the organization's operations as well as to VA executives. Central office managers, including the inspector general and general counsel, report to the highest level of department management, which consists of the secretary of veterans affairs and the deputy secretary.

Board of Veterans' Appeals The Board of Veterans' Appeals (BVA) is responsible, on behalf of the secretary of veterans affairs, for entering the final appellate decisions in claims of entitlement to veterans' benefits. The board is also responsible for deciding matters concerning fees charged by attorneys and agents for representation of veterans before the VA. The mission of the board (contained in 38 U.S.C.A. §§ 7101–7109) is to conduct hearings, consider and dispose of appeals properly before the board in a timely manner, and issue quality decisions in compliance with the law. The board is headed by a chairperson who is appointed by the president and confirmed by the Senate. The chairperson is directly responsible to the secretary of veterans affairs. Members of the board are appointed by the secretary with the approval of the president and are

Veterans Affairs Department

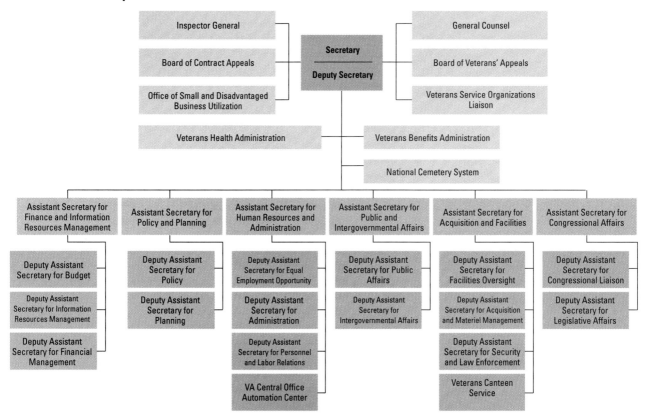

under the administrative control and supervision of the chairperson. Each BVA decision is signed by a board member acting as an agent of the secretary. Final BVA decisions are appealable to the U.S. Court of Veterans Appeals.

Board of Contract Appeals The Board of Contract Appeals was established on March 1, 1979, pursuant to the Contract Disputes Act of 1978 (41 U.S.C.A. §§ 601–613). The board is a statutory, quasi-judicial tribunal that hears and decides appeals from decisions of contracting officers on claims relating to CONTRACTS awarded by the VA or by any other agency when such agency or the administrator for federal procurement policy has designated the board to decide the appeal.

In August 1985 the board's JURISDICTION was expanded to include applications for attorneys' fees and expenses under the Equal Access to Justice Act, as amended (5 U.S.C.A. § 504 note). Board decisions are final within the VA but may be appealed, either by the government or by the contractor, to the U.S. Court of Appeals for the Federal Circuit.

Additionally, the chairperson of the board is the senior official within the department responsible for promoting ALTERNATIVE DISPUTE RESOLUTION pursuant to the Administrative Dispute Resolution Act (5 U.S.C.A. § 581 note).

Finally, the board is charged with resolving disputes between drug manufacturers and the secretary with regard to provisions of the Veterans Health Care Act of 1992 (38 U.S.C.A. § 101 note) dealing with pharmaceutical pricing agreements.

Health Services The Veterans Health Administration (formerly the Veterans Health Services and Research Administration) provides hospital, nursing home, and domiciliary care and outpatient medical and dental care to eligible veterans of military service in the armed forces. It operates 173 medical centers, 39 domiciliaries, 376 outpatient clinics, 131 nursing home care units, and 205 Vietnam Veteran Outreach Centers in the United States, the Commonwealth of Puerto Rico, and the Republic of the Philippines. The administration also provides for similar care under VA auspices in non-VA hospitals and community nursing homes and for visits by veterans to non-VA physicians and dentists for outpatient treatment. It also supports veterans under care in hospitals, nursing homes, and domiciliaries operated by thirty-five states. Under the Civilian Health and Medical Program, dependents of certain veterans are provided with medical care supplied by non-VA institutions and physicians.

The administration conducts both individual medical and health care delivery research projects and multihospital research programs. It assists in the education of physicians and dentists and with the training of many other health care professionals through affiliations with educational institutions and organizations. These programs are all conducted as prescribed by the secretary of veterans affairs pursuant to 38 U.S.C.A. §§ 4101–4115 and other statutory authority and regulations.

Veterans Benefits The Veterans Benefits Administration (VBA), formerly the Department of Veterans Benefits, conducts an integrated program of veterans' benefits. It provides information, advice, and assistance to veterans, their dependents, beneficiaries, and representatives, and others applying for VA benefits. It also cooperates with the Department of Labor and other federal, state, and local agencies in developing employment opportunities for veterans and referrals for assistance in resolving socioeconomic, housing, and other related problems. In addition, the VBA provides information regarding veterans' benefits to various branches of the armed forces.

Programs are provided through VA regional offices, medical centers, visits to communities, and a special toll-free telephone service. The programs are available in all fifty states, the District of Columbia, and Puerto Rico.

Compensation and Pension The Compensation and Pension Service has responsibility for claims for disability compensation and pensions, automobile allowances and special adaptive equipment, claims for specially adapted housing, special clothing allowances, emergency officers' retirement pay, and eligibility determinations based on military service for

other VA benefits and services or those of other government agencies. The service also processes survivors' claims for death compensation, dependency and INDEMNITY compensation, death pensions, burial and plot allowance claims, claims for accrued benefits, claims for adjusted compensation in death cases, and claims for reimbursement for headstones or markers.

Education The Education Service has responsibility for the Montgomery GI Bill—Active Duty and Selected Reserve, the Post Vietnam Era Veterans' Educational Assistance Program, the Survivors' and Dependents' Educational Assistance Program, and school approvals, compliance surveys, and work study. See also GI BILL.

Vocational Rehabilitation The Vocational Rehabilitation Service has responsibility for providing outreach, motivation, evaluation, counseling, training, employment, and other rehabilitation services to disabled veterans. The service also provides evaluation, counseling, and miscellaneous services to veterans and service persons and other VA education programs, as well as to sons, daughters, and spouses of totally and permanently disabled veterans and to surviving orphans, widows, or widowers of certain deceased veterans. Rehabilitation services are provided to certain disabled dependents.

Loan Guaranty The department has played a major part in the financing of homes since the end of World War II. Loan guaranty operations include appraising properties to establish their value, supervising the construction of new residential properties, establishing the eligibility of veterans for the program, assessing the ability of a veteran to repay a loan and the associated credit risk, servicing and liquidating defaulted loans, and disposing of real estate acquired as the consequence of defaulted loans.

Insurance Life INSURANCE operations are conducted for the benefit of service members and veterans and their beneficiaries. The day-to-day processing of all matters related to individual insurance accounts is handled by a regional office and insurance centers in Philadelphia, Pennsylvania, and St. Paul, Minnesota. These two centers provide the full range of functional activities necessary for a national life insurance program. Activities include the complete maintenance of individual accounts, underwriting functions, and life and death insurance claims awards, as well as other insurance-related transactions.

The agency is also responsible for the administration of the Veterans Mortgage Life Insurance Program for those disabled veterans who receive a VA grant for specially adapted

Federal Expenditures on Veterans' Benefits, 1940–1995

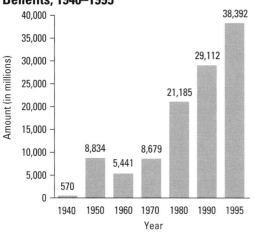

Source: U.S. Office of Management and Budget.

housing. In addition, the agency is responsible for supervising the Servicemen's Group Life Insurance (SGLI) and Veterans Group Life Insurance (VGLI) Programs.

Veterans Assistance The Veterans Assistance Service provides information, advice, and assistance to veterans, their dependents, beneficiaries, representatives, and others applying for benefits administered by the Department of Veterans Affairs. In addition, the Veterans Assistance Service cooperates with the Department of Labor and other federal, state, and local agencies in developing employment opportunities for veterans and referrals for assistance in resolving socioeconomic, housing, and other related problems. The service is responsible for maintaining a benefits protection program (FIDUCIARY activities) for minors and incompetent adult beneficiaries. It also provides field investigative services for other VA components.

The service ensures that schools and training institutions comply with VA directives. It also ensures compliance with title VI of the CIVIL RIGHTS ACT of 1964 (42 U.S.C.A. § 2000d), title IX of the Education Amendments of 1972 (20 U.S.C.A. § 1681), section 504 of the Rehabilitation Act of 1973 (29 U.S.C.A. § 794), and the Age Discrimination Act of 1975, as amended (42 U.S.C.A. § 6101).

The service's programs are provided through VA regional offices, VA medical centers, itinerant visits to communities, and a special toll-free telephone service available in all fifty states, the District of Columbia, and Puerto Rico.

The Veterans Assistance Service also provides information on veterans' benefits to the various branches of the armed forces in the United States and abroad and to veterans residing in foreign countries through U.S. embassies and consular offices. The service also coordinates veterans' activities with foreign governments.

National Cemetery System The National Cemetery System (NCS) provides services to veterans, active duty personnel, reservists, and National Guard members with twenty years' qualifying service and their families by operating national cemeteries and furnishing headstones and markers for graves. The NCS provides presidential memorial certificates to the loved ones of honorably discharged, deceased service members and veterans. The NCS also awards grants to aid states in developing, improving, and expanding veterans' cemeteries.

The National Cemetery area offices (located in Atlanta, Georgia, Philadelphia, Pennsylvania, and Denver, Colorado) provide direct support to the 114 national cemeteries located throughout the United States and Puerto Rico.

VETO ◫ The refusal of an executive officer to assent to a BILL that has been created and approved by the LEGISLATURE, thereby depriving the bill of any legally binding effect. ◫

Congressional Bills Vetoed, 1961 to 1996

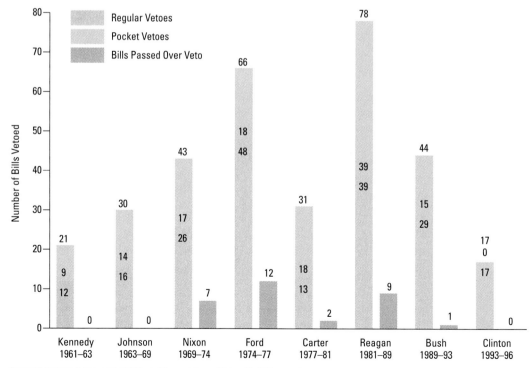

Source: U.S. Congress, *Calendars of the U.S. House of Representatives and History of Legislation,* annual.

SHOULD THE PRESIDENT HAVE THE LINE-ITEM VETO?

The passage of the Line Item Veto Act of 1996 (2 U.S.C.A. §§ 691–692) was a momentous legislative event. Since 1876, when President Ulysses S. Grant first proposed a line-item veto for the president, many bills and constitutional amendments had been introduced in Congress, only to be rejected more than two hundred times. The 1996 act grants the president a limited line-item veto with respect to appropriations, new direct spending, and limited tax benefits.

IN FOCUS

Congress's historical resistance to giving the president the authority to veto selected provisions of bills was rooted in the belief that the line-item veto was unconstitutional, because it would violate the separation of powers and the Framers' carefully designed plan of checks and balances. Though forty-three states have amended their constitutions to give the governor the line-item veto, opponents of the presidential veto have argued that the situation is different at the national level.

Members of Congress who voted against the 1996 act immediately challenged its constitutionality. In *Raines v. Byrd*, __ U.S. __ , 117 S. Ct. 2312, __ L. Ed. 2d __ (1997), the U.S. Supreme Court refused to address the merits of the case, dismissing the action because the legislators failed to show they had suffered a personal injury because of the legislation. The Court left open a future appeal by someone who suffers a "judicially cognizable injury as a result of the Act."

Proponents of the presidential line-item veto contend that it can be a valuable tool for eliminating congressional "pork"—appropriations or programs included by a legislator as a political gift to constituents—and other frivolous expenditures. They argue that the act will dramatically change the way appropriations bills are written. Senators and representatives have become adept at including "riders"—provisions that, although unrelated to the principal purpose of the rest of the legislation, are attached to appropriations bills—that drive up the costs of government. Supporters of the act also believe the line-item veto will deter members of Congress from even attaching frivolous expenditures to appropriations bills for fear that the president will veto the spending and publicly target the member for seeking to supply political pork.

Those who favor the line-item veto point out that it has been used successfully at the state level. They contend that governors rarely use the line-item veto for legislative arm twisting and deal making. In addition, they note that the line-item veto has helped balance state budgets and provide a means of accountability for state officials. Thus, they argue, the line-item veto can be a legitimate tool for reducing the federal budget deficit.

Opponents of the 1996 act argue that the law violates the Constitution, specifically the Presentment Clause in Article I, Section 7. This clause requires that any bill making or changing federal law must first be passed by both houses of Congress and then presented to the president, who acts upon it in its entirety, either making it or allowing it to become law or returning it to Congress for reconsideration.

Opponents of the line-item veto argue that the president's primary duty under the Presentment Clause is to approve or disapprove. If the president approves of the bill in total, signing it is a ministerial formality. If the president does not approve of the total bill, the president has the duty to return the bill, with his "objections," to the house in which it originated. The line-item veto act, however, authorizes the president to sign the bill while disapproving of it, or parts of it, in violation of the Presentment Clause. The effect of the act is to produce laws that have not passed either house of Congress in the form originally enacted.

Opponents note that under the act the president is given the partial veto power only after the bill has been enacted. The president has five days to cancel provisions of a law she has signed. Unlike acts of Congress that give the president the right not to spend appropriated funds (the impoundment power), the president now has the power to radically change the shape of an appropriations bill. Thus, the line-item veto constitutes a significant transfer of power from the legislative to the executive, a transfer that is not sanctioned by the Constitution's separation of powers among the legislative, executive, and judicial branches.

Opponents believe that Congress does not have the authority to give the president the permanent power to rescind an appropriation or tax benefit that has become the law of the United States. That power is held by Congress alone and may not be delegated. The only constitutional means of giving the president this authority, they contend, would be by constitutional amendment.

Apart from constitutional concerns, opponents fear that the shift of power from the legislative to the executive branch will distort the traditional checks and balances between the branches. They argue that the president will use the line-item veto power to impose his legislative agenda rather than merely cutting pork. The president now has, they contend, a tool to manipulate legislators. The president can threaten to veto certain parts of bills unless items he favors are included in the legislation.

Some opponents of the line-item veto also question how effective it will be in reducing the federal budget. They note that most governors exercise the line-item veto in a limited fashion, in large part because they fear the wrath of legislators who will continue to review executive branch legislative proposals in the months and years ahead.

Article I, Section 7, of the U.S. Constitution states that "every bill" and "every order, resolution or vote to which the concurrence of the Senate and the House of Representatives may be necessary" must be presented to the president for approval. If the president disapproves of the LEGISLATION and declines to sign the bill, he issues a *veto*, returning the bill unsigned to Congress. Similar provisions in state constitutions give governors the same veto power, and municipal charters often give the mayor the right to veto legislation from the city council.

The veto power gives the executive a central role in the legislative process. By threatening a veto before legislation is passed, the executive can force the legislature to compromise and pass amendments it would otherwise find unacceptable. Though there is great power in the veto, most executives use it cautiously, as overuse can antagonize the legislature and create political risk for the executive.

Under the Constitution the president has ten days (not counting Sundays) in which to consider legislation presented for approval. The president has three options: sign the bill, making it law; veto the bill; or take no action on the bill during the ten-day period. A veto can be overridden by a two-thirds majority of both houses of Congress. If the president takes no action, the bill automatically becomes law after ten days. If Congress adjourns before the ten days have expired and the president has not signed the bill, however, the bill is said to have been subjected to a *pocket veto*. A pocket veto deprives Congress of the chance to override a formal veto. State governors have similar veto and pocket veto powers, and state legislatures usually are required to override vetoes by a two-thirds majority of both houses.

In forty-three states the governor also has the authority to select particular items from an appropriations bill and veto them individually. This authority, called the line-item veto, is popular because it allows the executive to cancel specific appropriations items from bills that are hundreds of pages long.

In the 1980s and early 1990s Presidents RONALD REAGAN and GEORGE BUSH called for a CONSTITUTIONAL AMENDMENT that would provide the president with a line-item veto. After years of debate, Congress rejected the idea of enacting such an amendment and instead approved federal line-item veto authority in a 1996 statute (2 U.S.C.A. §§ 691–692), giving the president the ability to impose cuts in the FEDERAL BUDGET. A line-item veto, like a regular veto, can be overridden at the state and federal level by a two-thirds majority vote.

A widely used means of congressional oversight has been the *legislative veto*. A legislative veto is a statutory device that subjects proposals and decisions of EXECUTIVE BRANCH administrative agencies to additional legislative consideration. The legislature may disapprove agency action by a committee, one-house, or concurrent resolution.

Since it was first used in the 1930s, the legislative veto has been the subject of controversy. The legislative veto circumvents traditional bill-passing procedures in that the legislative action is not presented to the executive for approval. This veto has been defended on the ground that it is not a legislative act. In *Immigration and Naturalization Service v. Chadha*, 462 U.S. 919, 103 S. Ct. 2764, 77 L. Ed. 2d 317 (1983), the U.S. Supreme Court invalidated legislative veto provisions involving immigration and naturalization on the ground that these provisions violated the SEPARATION OF POWERS between the legislative and executive branches. Despite *Chadha*, Congress has not systematically removed legislative veto provisions from federal statutes, and some states continue to use the legislative veto.

See also CONGRESS OF THE UNITED STATES; PRESIDENTIAL POWERS.

VEXATIOUS LITIGATION 📖 A legal ACTION or proceeding initiated maliciously and without PROBABLE CAUSE by an individual who is not acting in GOOD FAITH for the purpose of annoying or embarrassing an opponent. 📖

The U.S. legal system permits persons to file civil lawsuits to seek redress for injuries committed by a defendant. However, a legal action that is not likely to lead to any practical result is classified as *vexatious litigation*. Such litigation is regarded as FRIVOLOUS and will result in the dismissal of the action by the court. A person who has been subjected to vexatious litigation may sue the plaintiff for MALICIOUS PROSECUTION, seeking DAMAGES for any costs and injuries associated with the original lawsuit.

Litigation is typically classified as vexatious when an attorney or a PRO SE litigant (a person representing himself without an attorney) repeatedly files groundless lawsuits and repeatedly loses. Under the common law, the frequent incitement of lawsuits by an attorney constituted the crime of BARRATRY. In modern law, however, barratry is viewed as an archaic crime and is rarely enforced. Attorneys who encourage vexatious litigation are subject to discipline for violating rules of professional conduct and may be suspended from the practice of law or disbarred.

Sometimes pro se litigants who have lost their initial lawsuits file new actions based on the dispute contained in the original suit. Because the JUDGMENT of the original case is dispositive, a court will ultimately dismiss these new actions. To avoid the expenditure of court resources, as well as the costs associated with the defendant's defense of repeated frivolous claims, a court may issue an order forbidding the pro se litigant to file any new actions without permission of the court.

Vexatious litigation is a type of malicious prosecution that enables the defendant to file a TORT action against the plaintiff. A plaintiff in a malicious prosecution must prove that a legal proceeding (or multiple proceedings) was instituted by the defendant, that the original proceeding was terminated in favor of the plaintiff, that there was no probable cause for the original proceeding, and that MALICE, or a primary purpose other than that of bringing the original action, motivated the defendant. A plaintiff in such an action may recover, for example, the expenses incurred in defending the original suit or suits, as well as resulting financial loss or injury. A plaintiff may also recover damages for mental suffering of a kind that would normally be expected to follow from the original action.

VICARIOUS LIABILITY ▥ The tort doctrine that imposes responsibility upon one person for the failure of another, with whom the person has a special relationship (such as parent and child, employer and employee, or owner of vehicle and driver), to exercise such care as a reasonably prudent person would use under similar circumstances. ▥

Vicarious liability is a legal doctrine that assigns LIABILITY for an INJURY to a person who did not cause the injury but who has a particular legal relationship to the person who did act negligently. It is also referred to as IMPUTED negligence. Legal relationships that can lead to imputed negligence include the relationship between PARENT AND CHILD, HUSBAND AND WIFE, owner of a vehicle and driver, and employer and employee. Ordinarily the independent negligence of one person is not imputable to another person.

Other theories of liability that are premised on imputed negligence include the RESPONDEAT SUPERIOR doctrine and the FAMILY CAR DOCTRINE.

The doctrine of respondeat superior (Latin for "let the master answer") is based on the employer-employee relationship. The doctrine makes the employer responsible for a lack of care on the part of an employee in relation to those to whom the employer owes a duty of care. For respondeat superior to apply, the employee's NEGLIGENCE must occur within the scope of her employment.

The employer is charged with legal responsibility for the negligence of the employee because the employee is held to be an AGENT of the employer. If a negligent act is committed by an employee acting within the general scope of her or his employment, the employer will be held liable for DAMAGES. For example, if the driver of a gasoline delivery truck runs a red light on the way to a gas station and strikes another car, causing injury, the gasoline delivery company will be responsible for the damages if the driver is found to be negligent. Because the company will automatically be found liable if the driver is negligent, respondeat superior is a form of STRICT LIABILITY.

Another common example of imputed negligence is attributing liability to the owner of a car, where the driver of the car committed a negligent act. This type of relationship has been labeled the family car doctrine. The doctrine is based on the assumption that the head of the household provides a car for the family's use and, therefore, the operator of the car acts as an agent of the owner. When, for example, a child drives a car, registered to a parent, for a family purpose, the parent is responsible for the negligent acts of the child at the wheel.

Liability can also be imputed to an owner of a car who lends it to a friend. Again, the driver of the car is acting as the agent of the owner. If the owner is injured by the driver's negligence and sues the driver, the owner can lose the lawsuit because the negligence of the driver can be imputed to the owner, thereby rendering him contributorily negligent. This concept is known as imputed contributory negligence.

See also SCOPE OF EMPLOYMENT; TORT LAW.

VICE ▥ A fault, flaw, defect, or imperfection. Immoral conduct, practice, or habit. ▥

In CIVIL LAW, redhibitory vices are defects or flaws in the subject matter of a sale that entitle the buyer to return the item and recover the purchase price.

A VICE CRIME is any type of immoral and illegal activity, such as PROSTITUTION, the sale of DRUGS AND NARCOTICS, and gambling.

VICE CRIMES ▥ A generic legal term for offenses involving immorality, including PROSTITUTION, LEWDNESS, LASCIVIOUSNESS, and OBSCENITY. ▥

VICE PRESIDENT The vice president of the United States occupies a high position in government, yet is given little responsibility under the U.S. Constitution. A person elected vice president presides over the Senate, but apart from that duty, he must rely upon the president to assign additional responsibilities. Eight times in U.S. history, however, a vice president has become president because of the death of the president, and Vice President GERALD R. FORD became president in 1974 when President RICHARD M. NIXON resigned in the face of IMPEACHMENT charges.

Under the Constitution, a vice president of the United States must be a native-born citizen, thirty-five years of age or older, who has resided in the United States for at least fourteen years. The ELECTORAL COLLEGE chooses the vice president, who holds office for a term of four years.

Until 1804, under Article II, Section 2, Clause 3, of the Constitution, each member of the electoral college was permitted to vote for two persons. The person receiving the highest total became president, and the person receiving the second highest total became vice president. The ratification of the TWELFTH AMENDMENT to the Constitution in 1804 changed this procedure by requiring each elector to vote for president and vice president on separate ballots instead of voting for two persons on a single ballot as before.

During the early years of the Republic, the vice president was limited to the only function set forth in the Constitution, that of president of the Senate. The vice president occupies a largely ceremonial role, having no vote unless the senators are equally divided on a particular issue.

In 1841 Vice President JOHN TYLER became the first vice president to become president because of the death of the chief executive, in this case President WILLIAM HENRY HARRISON.

Presidents have differed in the amount of responsibility they have given to their vice presidents. Al Gore, President Bill Clinton's vice president, has enjoyed a fairly high profile.

DIANA WALKER/THE GAMMA LIAISON NETWORK

Article II of the Constitution was silent on the matter of succession, and some political leaders suggested that Tyler serve as acting president. Tyler rejected this idea, however, and announced that he would assume the full powers and duties of the office, setting a precedent that would be followed by other vice presidents.

Vice presidential succession was clarified by the Twentieth and Twenty-fifth Amendments to the Constitution. Under the TWENTIETH AMENDMENT, if a president-elect dies before assuming office, the vice president elect becomes president. Under the TWENTY-FIFTH AMENDMENT, if the president is removed from office, dies, or resigns during her term of office, the vice president becomes president of the United States.

The Twenty-fifth Amendment also provides a method for the vice president to become acting president. If the president transmits a message to both houses of Congress that states that he cannot discharge the powers and duties of the office, the vice president becomes acting president. Until the president subsequently transmits a written declaration to the contrary, the vice president remains acting president.

The amendment also deals with the situation in which the president is unwilling to declare that she is unable to govern. In that case the vice president and a majority of the CABINET may transmit to both houses of Congress a declaration that the president is unable to discharge the powers and duties of the office. If this occurs, the vice president must immediately assume the powers and duties of the office as acting president.

The president may resume his duties by notifying the president pro tempore of the Senate and the Speaker of the House of Representatives that the disability no longer exists. However, the vice president and the majority of the cabinet may send a declaration to Congress within four days disputing the assertion of the president that he is able to discharge the duties of the office. If this happens, Congress must vote by a two-thirds majority in both houses that the president is unable to serve. Otherwise, the president will reassume office.

If a vice president dies in office or resigns, the Twenty-fifth Amendment authorizes the president to choose a new vice president, subject to confirmation by a majority vote of both houses of Congress. This situation occurred twice during the Nixon and Ford administrations. In 1973 President Nixon appointed Gerald R. Ford to replace Vice President Spiro T. Agnew, who resigned in the face of criminal bribery charges. When Nixon resigned in August 1974 because of the WATERGATE scandal, Ford became president. Ford then appointed Nelson A. Rockefeller vice president.

The executive functions of the vice president include participation in all cabinet meetings and, by statute, membership in the NATIONAL SECURITY COUNCIL, the Domestic Council, and the board of regents of the Smithsonian Institution.

VICTIMS OF CRIME Until the 1970s victims of crimes were often forgotten by the criminal justice system. As a result, victims sometimes came to believe that they had fewer rights than the criminals who had injured them. In addition, some victims became so alienated from the criminal justice process that PROSECUTORS had difficulty persuading them to TESTIFY at trial. This environment began to change in the 1970s with the establishment of victim compensation funds. Not until the 1980s, however, did a national movement for "victims' rights" spark wholesale changes in the criminal justice system.

Right to Sue Victims have always had the right to sue for money DAMAGES a person who injures them during a criminal act. For most crime victims, however, this solution has generally not proved practical because victims frequently do not know who committed the crime against them and the criminals are not always apprehended. Even when a criminal is available to be sued, the victim may not have adequate funds to pay for a lawsuit, or the criminal may have no money to pay damages if the victim is successful.

Victim Compensation Laws During the 1970s many states enacted victim compensation statutes, which authorize payment of money from the public treasury to crime victims so that they are not forced to bear the full burden of the crime. Although compensation can be provided for lost earnings, medical expenses, and the replacement of missing property, the majority of plans do not replace every dollar lost.

Most compensation plans provide benefits only to victims who have low income or few resources, although some plans allow anyone who is an innocent victim or did not contribute to the cause of her injuries to receive benefits. Some plans pay benefits only to victims who are physically injured or to the families of victims who are killed.

An individual who wishes to apply for crime victim compensation must do so promptly after the injury. Ordinarily, this is done by filling out a form provided by the state official or victim compensation board responsible for administering the program. States generally will not consider applications filed later than a specified period after the crime.

As part of a victim compensation plan, a state may take any profit a criminal makes from the crime and hold it in TRUST to pay victims who successfully sue the criminal. This feature is designed to encourage victims who would ordinarily not sue because they are aware that most criminals cannot pay judgments. Under such a plan, any money paid to a convicted criminal for a book, story, or dramatization of the crime must be turned over to the state and the funds deposited into a special ESCROW account and held available to pay any victim who successfully sues the criminal. Forty-one states have adopted such laws, and the federal government established a similar process in the Victims of Crime Act of 1984 (18 U.S.C.A. §§ 3681–3682).

These statutes are known as "SON OF SAM" LAWS after David Berkowitz, a New York serial killer who left a note signed "Son of Sam" at the scene of one of his crimes and was thereafter nicknamed Son of Sam by the New York press. The first Son of Sam law (N.Y. Exec. Law § 632-a [McKinney 1990]) was enacted by the New York state legislature in 1977 after it learned that Berkowitz was planning to sell his story of serial killing.

The U.S. Supreme Court struck down the New York law in *Simon and Schuster v. New York Victims Crime Board*, 502 U.S. 105, 112 S. Ct. 501, 116 L. Ed. 2d 476 (1991). The Court held that the law was based on the content of a publication and therefore violated the FIRST AMENDMENT. New York quickly amended its law to apply to any economic benefit the criminal derived from the crime, not just the proceeds from the sale of the offender's story. This redefinition was intended to eliminate the unconstitutional regulation of expressive activity and reconceptualize the law as a regulation of economic proceeds from crime. Other states have modified their laws as well, but it remains to be seen if they will be found constitutional.

Victims' Rights Laws In the early 1980s, groups such as Mothers Against Drunk Driving (MADD), the National Coalition against Domestic Violence, and Parents of Murdered Children began calling for legislative recognition of victims' rights. Partly as a result of their efforts, in 1982 Congress enacted the Victim and Witness Protection Act (VWPA) (18 U.S.C.A. §§ 1512–1515, 3663–3664), which provides penalties for interfering with witnesses, victims, or informants and allows for RESTITUTION to victims of federal crimes. The

An Automated Victim Notification System

Crime victims commonly worry about the day when an inmate convicted in their case is released from custody. Women who have been stalked and victimized by boyfriends and former spouses fear that they will return again. Only rarely is the victim promptly notified of an inmate's release. In 1997 the state of Kentucky addressed this problem by introducing the first completely automated victim notification system.

The Kentucky system, called Victim Information and Notification Everyday (VINE), is a statewide system that seeks to help crime victims, especially those who have been subjected to domestic violence. The VINE system keeps tabs on inmates in Kentucky's seventeen state prisons and eighty-three county jails.

To obtain information, a person dials a toll-free number and supplies the prisoner's name or prison identification number. A computer then provides information as to where the prisoner is incarcerated, the telephone number and address of the jail or prison, the date of the inmate's next parole hearing, and the date the sentence expires.

In addition, a person may confidentially register with the automated system and request to be notified when an inmate is released. Registered persons automatically receive a telephone call within ten minutes of an inmate's transfer or release, giving them time to take precautions.

VWPA has served as a model for many state victim protection laws, especially those providing for restitution to crime victims. The 1984 Victims of Crime Act also provided $150 million to support compensation and victim assistance programs.

Most states have adopted provisions in support of victims' rights. The majority have been enacted through legislation, but several take the form of state constitutional amendments. These laws require victims to be treated with dignity and fairness, and many require that the victim be kept informed of the status of the case and be notified when the criminal is released from prison. A key part of these initiatives deals with "victim impact statements." A victim impact statement is made by the victim or a member of the victim's family at the time of SENTENCING or during a PAROLE hearing. The speaker describes the impact the crime has had upon the victim and her family.

In *Booth v. Maryland*, 482 U.S. 496, 107 S. Ct. 2529, 96 L. Ed. 2d 440 (1987), the U.S. Supreme Court forbade the use of victim impact statements in death penalty cases. The Court reasoned that the imposition of CAPITAL PUNISHMENT could be based on subjective feelings for the victim rather than objective criteria indicating the defendant's guilt. In *Payne v. Tennessee*, 501 U.S. 808, 111 S. Ct. 2597, 115 L. Ed. 2d 720 (1991), however, the Court reversed itself and held that the EIGHTH AMENDMENT does not bar the jury from considering victim impact statements.

Victim Advocates In response to the growing support for victims' rights, the criminal justice system has created the position of victim advocate. Victim advocates first gained prominence during the women's and victims' rights movements of the 1970s and 1980s. RAPE and domestic abuse counselors saw the need for advocates to support and guide victims through the ordeal of trial.

Victim advocates counsel victims and their families, keep them informed about the progress of an investigation, prepare them for trial, refer them to needed services, explain court proceedings, and act as a liaison with state and local agencies. By providing support to people who have been devastated by a crime, they free police officers and prosecutors from the task of dealing with distraught families and friends.

See also SHIELD LAWS; STALKING.

VIDAL v. GIRARD'S EXECUTORS *Vidal v. Girard's Executors* was an 1844 decision by the Supreme Court, 43 U.S. (2 How.) 127, 11 L.Ed. 205, that held that the city of Philadelphia, Pennsylvania, had power, pursuant to its CHARTER, to accept and administer a CHARITABLE TRUST.

Stephen Girard was a native of France who emigrated to the American colonies shortly before the Declaration of Independence. Prior to 1783, he became a resident of the city of Philadelphia, where he died, a childless widower, in December 1831. In addition to some minor real estate holdings near Bordeaux, France, Girard owned REAL PROPERTY in the United States that had cost him $1,700,000 and PERSONAL PROPERTY worth approximately $5,000,000. On December 25, 1830, he executed a WILL making various BEQUESTS to his relatives and friends, to the city of New Orleans, and to specified CHARITIES. His will and two CODICILS were admitted to PROBATE on December 31, 1831. His closest relatives were a brother and a niece, who sought to have a portion of his will set aside, and three other nieces, who were named defendants in the action. The lower court ruled in favor of the defendants, and the plaintiffs appealed to the Supreme Court.

The controversial clauses of Girard's will established a college for impoverished white male orphans between the ages of six and ten years. In addition to specifying the subject matter to be taught, the will barred clergymen of any denomination from holding any post within the college and from visiting the premises. Girard also bequeathed $500,000 to be invested and the income therefrom applied to the construction, lighting, and paving of a street in eastern Philadelphia, fronting the Delaware River, to be called "Delaware Avenue." He also gave $300,000 to the commonwealth of Pennsylvania to improve canal navigation. To implement these provisions, Girard bequeathed the residue and REMAINDER of his real and personal property to the mayor, aldermen, and citizens of Philadelphia in TRUST.

The HEIRS of Girard instituted an ACTION to have the DEVISE of the residue of the real property to the mayor, aldermen, and citizens of Philadelphia in trust be declared VOID, on the theory that the recipients lacked the CAPACITY to take lands by devise; or if they were deemed capable of taking by devise for their own benefit, they lacked capacity to take the lands in trust. The plaintiffs also asserted that because the beneficiaries of the charity for which the lands were devised in trust were ambiguous, indefinite, and vague, the will had not created a trust that could be executed or recognized at law or in EQUITY. The COMPLAINT sought the establishment of a RESULTING TRUST for the heirs, an ACCOUNTING, and other relief.

This case contained three principal issues. The initial question focused on whether the CORPORATION of the city of Philadelphia had the capacity to take the real and personal property for the construction and maintenance of a college pursuant to the trust established by the will. The second issue centered on whether the charitable purposes were valid and capable of being effectuated in accordance with the laws of Pennsylvania. The third issue involved the effect of the invalidation of the trust upon a finding that it violated Pennsylvania law, in terms of whether the property would fall into the residue of the estate and belong to the

corporation of the city through the RESIDUARY CLAUSE of the will or belong, as a resulting trust, to the heirs of Girard.

With respect to the first issue, the Court held that where a corporation has the legal capacity to take real or personal property, it can accept it and administer it in trust to the same extent and in the same manner as a private person might execute a trust. The act of March 11, 1789, that incorporated the city of Philadelphia expressly conferred upon it the power to own and otherwise benefit from real and personal property. The Court noted that if the trust were inconsistent with the purposes for which the corporation was established, the trust itself would not be void, assuming that it was otherwise valid. Rather, a court, in the exercise of its equity jurisdiction, would simply order the substitution of a new TRUSTEE to execute the trust.

The Pennsylvania legislature passed the acts of March 24 and April 4, 1832, to implement particular improvements and execute certain trusts, pursuant to Girard's will. The Court acknowledged that this legislation was not a judicial decision, and entitled to the full force and effect of such, but indicated that it was a legislative ratification of the competency of the corporation to take the property and implement the trusts. If the trusts were otherwise valid, the legislature could not challenge the competency of the corporation in this regard. In addition, neither the heirs nor any other private persons could contest the right of the corporation to take the property or to administer the trusts. This right was reserved solely for the state in its sovereign capacity.

The second issue involved a challenge of the trusts on the theory that because the Statute of Charitable Uses was not in effect in Pennsylvania, no charitable trust could be created. The Statute of Charitable Uses validated charitable trusts and that such trusts did not have an independent existence apart from that statute and its successors. As a result, if the statute had been expressly repealed or had been declared not a part of the COMMON LAW of a particular state, no charitable trust could be established in that state. The Court, however, rejected this theory and stated that charitable uses were known and upheld prior to the Statute of Charitable Uses; the statute merely acknowledged the existence of such uses and provided for their enforcement. The Court cited the then recent report of the Commissioners of Public Records in England, which contained a collection of early CHANCERY cases involving charitable trusts, to support this finding and to dispose of the plaintiffs' contention that the trust was void because the beneficiaries were too uncertain and indefinite for the bequest to have any legal effect. These early cases showed that charitable uses were valid at the common law and enforceable in Chancery pursuant to the general jurisdiction of the court. The Court of Chancery exercised such jurisdiction both prior to and subsequent to the enactment of the Statute of Charitable Uses. The cases also established that the Court of Chancery enforced charitable trusts created for the benefit of general and indefinite charities, as well as for specific charities. Chancery had also upheld trusts in cases where either no trustees were appointed or the trustees were not COMPETENT to execute the trust.

In terms of the second issue, the heirs also asserted that the trust that established the college for orphans was void because its terms violated the constitution, the common law, and the PUBLIC POLICY of Pennsylvania. The purported violations consisted of (1) excluding all religious personnel of any sect from positions within the college or from visiting the premises and (2) limiting instruction to purely moral concepts of goodness, truth, and honor, thereby implicitly excluding all instruction in the Christian religion.

The Court ruled that Girard had adopted a position of neutrality with respect to the exclusion of all religious influence from the administration of the college. He had not explicitly impugned Christianity, which, in a qualified sense, was a part of the common law of Pennsylvania, or any other religion. Rather, he had merely wanted the students to remain free from sectarian controversy and wished them to study a curriculum that did not place inordinate emphasis on religious subjects. He did not proscribe members of the laity from teaching the general principles of Christianity or analyzing the Bible from a historical perspective. The Court concluded that Girard's provisions did not contravene the laws, the constitution, or the public policy of Pennsylvania.

The Court affirmed the ruling of the lower court upholding the trust and thereby deemed it unnecessary to examine the third issue in this case, which involved the question of to whom the property would belong if the trust were declared void.

VIETNAM WAR The Vietnam War was a twenty-year conflict in Southeast Asia (1955–1975) between the government of South Vietnam and the Communist government of North Vietnam. The North Vietnamese sought the reunification of the two countries under its form of rule. The United States, determined to prevent Communist aggression, supported the government of South Vietnam and became increasingly involved militarily in the conflict in the early 1960s. By 1965 U.S. involvement had escalated, and U.S. armed forces had been introduced. Opposition to the war in the United States grew steadily, resulting in one of the most divisive periods in U.S. history. The United States ultimately withdrew its forces in 1973. Within two years the North Vietnamese defeated the South Vietnamese armed forces and took control of the country.

The War in Vietnam During World War II, the Viet Minh, a nationalist party seeking an end to French colonial rule of Vietnam, was organized. After the defeat of the Japanese and their withdrawal from what was then known as French Indochina, the Viet Minh, under the leadership of Ho Chi Minh, formally declared independence. France refused to recognize Vietnamese independence, and war broke out between the French and the Viet Minh. In 1954 the French withdrew after suffering a devastating defeat at the Battle of Dien Bien Phu.

After the French withdrawal, participants at an international conference in Geneva, Switzerland, divided Vietnam at the 17th parallel. The Viet Minh were given control of the north, which became known as North Vietnam, while the non-Communist southern half became South Vietnam. The South Vietnamese government was headed by Prime Minister Ngo Dinh Diem, who refused to allow free elections on reunification in 1956 as agreed by the Geneva Accords. Diem rightly feared that Ho Chi Minh and the Communists would win the election. The United States supported Diem's defiance, which led the North Vietnamese to seek unification through military force.

The Diem regime, which soon proved to be corrupt and ineffective, had difficulty fighting

American soldiers in the Vietnam War carry large caliber ammunition past an Army helicopter. Americans fought and died in Vietnam even though the United States never issued a formal declaration of war.

the Viet Cong, a South Vietnamese army of guerrilla soldiers who were trained and armed by the North Vietnamese. The Viet Cong became part of the National Liberation Front (NLF), a Communist-backed insurgent organization. In 1961 President JOHN F. KENNEDY began to send more U.S. military advisers to South Vietnam, and by the end of 1962, their number had risen from 900 to 11,000. Kennedy, however, was dissatisfied with the Diem regime and allowed a military coup to occur on November 1, 1963. Diem was assassinated during the coup, but none of the lackluster military leaders who followed him was able to stop the Communists from gaining more ground.

Direct U.S. military involvement in Vietnam began in 1964. On August 2, 1964, President LYNDON B. JOHNSON announced that North Vietnamese ships had attacked U.S. naval vessels in the Gulf of Tonkin. Johnson asked Congress for the authority to employ any necessary course of action to safeguard U.S. troops. Based on what turned out to be inaccurate information supplied by the Johnson administration, Congress gave the president this authority in the TONKIN GULF RESOLUTION (78 Stat. 384).

Johnson used this resolution to justify military escalation in the absence of a congressional declaration of war. Following attacks on U.S. forces in February 1965, he authorized the bombing of North Vietnam. To continue the protection of the South Vietnamese government, Johnson increased the number of U.S. soldiers fighting in South Vietnam from 20,000 to 500,000 during the next three years.

U.S. military leaders had difficulty fighting a guerrilla army, yet repeatedly claimed that Viet Cong and North Vietnamese forces were losing the war. On January 30, 1968, the Viet Cong and the North Vietnamese made a surprise attack on thirty-six major cities and towns during the Tet (lunar new year) festival. Though U.S. troops repelled these attacks, the Tet offensive undermined the credibility of U.S. military leaders and of Johnson himself, who had claimed the war was close to being won. Antiwar sentiment in the United States grew after Tet as the public became skeptical about whether the war could be won and, if it could, how many years it would take to achieve victory.

The 1968 presidential campaign of Minnesota antiwar Senator EUGENE MCCARTHY gained popularity after Tet. On March 31, 1968, Johnson announced that the United States would stop bombing North Vietnam above the 20th parallel and that he would not seek reelection to the presidency. Johnson ordered a total

bombing halt in October, when North Vietnam agreed to begin preliminary peace talks in Paris. These discussions dragged on during the fall election campaign, which saw Republican RICHARD M. NIXON elected president.

Nixon sought to preserve the South Vietnamese government while withdrawing U.S. troops. He began a policy of "Vietnamization," which promised to gradually transfer all military operations to the South Vietnamese. During this process the United States would provide massive amounts of military aid. In 1969, when the number of U.S. military personnel in South Vietnam had reached a high of 540,000, Nixon announced a modest troop withdrawal. During 1969 the Paris peace talks continued with the NLF, North Vietnamese, and South Vietnamese, but little progress was made.

In the spring of 1970, Nixon expanded the war as U.S. and South Vietnamese forces invaded Cambodia to destroy North Vietnamese military sanctuaries there. The Cambodian action created a firestorm on U.S. college and university campuses, where antiwar protests led to the closing of many institutions for the remainder of the spring. Nevertheless, Nixon persevered with his policies. He authorized the bombing of Cambodia and Laos by B-52 bombers, destabilizing the Cambodian government and destroying large sections of both countries. By late 1970 the number of U.S. military personnel in South Vietnam had declined to 335,000. A year later the number had dropped to 160,000 military personnel.

In March 1972 the North Vietnamese invaded the northern section of South Vietnam and the central highlands. Nixon responded by ordering the mining of Haiphong and other North Vietnamese ports and large-scale bombing of North Vietnam. In the fall of 1972, a peace treaty appeared likely, but the talks broke off in mid-December. Nixon then ordered intense bombing of Hanoi and other North Vietnamese cities. The "Christmas bombing" lasted eleven days.

The peace talks then resumed, and on January 27, 1973, the parties agreed to a cease-fire the following day, the withdrawal of all U.S. forces, the release of all prisoners of war, and the creation of an international force to keep the peace. The South Vietnamese were to have the right to determine their own future, but North Vietnamese troops stationed in the south could remain. By the end of 1973, almost all U.S. military personnel had left South Vietnam.

The conflict in the south continued in 1974. The United States cut military aid to South Vietnam in August 1974, resulting in the demoralization of the South Vietnamese army.

Vietnam War Timeline

1954	French Indochina War ends with French defeat at Dien Bien Phu.
1955	United States agrees to help train South Vietnamese army
1956	President Eisenhower announces first U.S. advisers sent to Vietnam.
1957	North Vietnamese guerrilla (Vietcong) activity directed against South Vietnam begins.
1959	First U.S. military advisers killed in Vietcong attack.
1961	President Kennedy agrees to increase 685-member military advisory group and to arm and supply 20,000 South Vietnamese troops (June 16); first U.S. aircraft carrier arrives off Vietnam with armed helicopters to aid the South Vietnamese army.
1962	President Kennedy states that U.S. military advisers in Vietnam will return fire if fired upon. U.S. noncombat troops number 12,000 by year's end.
1963	South Vietnam president Ngo Dinh Diem assassinated (Nov. 2).
1964	North Vietnamese patrol boats attack U.S. destroyers in the Gulf of Tonkin. U.S. Congress passes resolution (Aug. 7) that President Johnson uses as basis for later U.S. troop buildup in Vietnam. United States announces massive aid increase to counter Hanoi's support of Vietcong (December 11).
1965	First U.S. air attacks in North Vietnam begin (Feb. 24); first major deployment of U.S. ground troops (March 7–9). U.S. troops number 184,300 at year's end.
1966	Bombing of Hanoi begins (June 29). U.S. troops number 389,000 at year's end.
1967	U.S. troops number 480,000 at year's end.
1968	"Tet" offensive by North Vietnamese (Jan. 30 to Feb. 29); My Lai massacre by U.S. troops (March 16). Start of Paris peace talks.
1969	U.S. troop deployment reaches highest point of the war in April: 543,000. Nixon begins U.S. troop withdrawal on May 14.
1970	U.S. and South Vietnamese forces cross Cambodian border to get at enemy bases (April 30).
1971	U.S. bombers strike massively in North Vietnam for alleged violations of 1968 bombing halt agreement (Dec. 26 to 30). U.S. troops number 140,000 at year's end.
1972	North Vietnamese launch bombing offensive across demilitarized zone (March 30); U.S. resumes bombing of Hanoi (April 15); U.S. announces mining of North Vietnam ports. Last U.S. combat troops leave (Aug. 11).
1973	Cease-fire accord signed (Jan. 27); last non-combat U.S. troops withdraw from Vietnam (March 29); last U.S. prisoners of war released (April 1). Some U.S. civilians remain.
1975	President Thieu's government of South Vietnam surrenders to Communists April 30; United States abandons Embassy. All U.S. civilians leave Vietnam. 140,000 South Vietnamese refugees flown to United States.
1976	Vietnam reunified; large-scale resettlement and reeducation programs started.

SOURCES: R. Ernest Dupuy and Trevor N. Dupuy, *The Harper Encyclopedia of Military History*; New York Public Library's *Book of Chronologies*.

The North Vietnamese, sensing that the end was near, attacked a provincial capital sixty miles north of Saigon in December 1974. After the city of Phuoc Binh fell in early January 1975, the North Vietnamese launched a full-scale offensive in the central highlands in March. The South Vietnamese army fell apart and a general panic ensued. On April 30 the South Vietnamese government surrendered. On July 2, 1976, the country was officially united as the Socialist Republic of Vietnam.

More than 47,000 U.S. military personnel were killed in action during the war, and nearly 11,000 died of other causes. Approximately 200,000 South Vietnamese military personnel were killed, and 900,000 North Vietnamese and Viet Cong soldiers lost their lives. The civilian population was devastated by the war. An estimated one million North and South Vietnamese civilians were killed during the war. Large

parts of the countryside were destroyed through bombing and the spraying of chemical defoliants.

The War and U.S. Law The war provoked many legal and constitutional controversies in the United States. Though the U.S. Supreme Court refused to decide whether the war was constitutional, it did rule on several war-related issues. In *United States v. O'Brien*, 391 U.S. 367, 88 S. Ct. 1673, 20 L. Ed. 2d 672 (1968), the Court upheld the conviction of David Paul O'Brien for violating a 1965 amendment to the Selective Service Act (50 U.S.C.A. App. § 451 et seq.) prohibiting any draft registrant from knowingly destroying or mutilating his draft card. The Court rejected O'Brien's contention that his burning of his draft card was SYMBOLIC SPEECH protected by the FIRST AMENDMENT. In *Tinker v. Des Moines Independent Community School District*, 393 U.S. 503, 89 S. Ct. 733, 21 L. Ed. 2d 731 (1969), however, the Court ruled that high school students had the First Amendment right to wear black armbands to school to protest U.S. involvement in Vietnam.

In *Welsh v. United States*, 398 U.S. 333, 90 S. Ct. 1792, 26 L. Ed. 2d 308 (1970), the Court held that a person could be exempted from compulsory military service based on purely moral or ethical beliefs against war.

One of the most significant Court decisions of the Vietnam War period involved the publication of the Pentagon Papers, a highly classified government report on the history of U.S. involvement in Vietnam. The Nixon administration sought to prevent the *New York Times* and the *Washington Post* from publishing excerpts from the study on the ground that publication would hurt national security interests. In *New York Times v. United States*, 403 U.S. 713, 91 S. Ct. 2140, 29 L. Ed. 2d 822, the Supreme Court, by a 6–3 vote, held that the government's efforts to block publication amounted to an unconstitutional PRIOR RESTRAINT.

CROSS-REFERENCES

Cold War; Communism; Conscientious Objector; Kissinger, Henry; *New York Times v. United States*.

VILL 📖 In old English law, a division of a HUNDRED or WAPENTAKE; a town or a city. 📖

VINSON, FREDERICK MOORE As the thirteenth chief justice, Frederick Moore Vinson led the U.S. Supreme Court from 1946 to 1953. Vinson rose to the Court after a long career as a lawyer, district attorney, member of Congress, federal appellate judge, and secretary of the treasury. His nomination to the Supreme Court by President HARRY S. TRUMAN followed a dramatic controversy over filling the position,

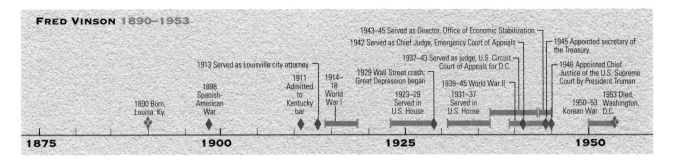

FRED VINSON 1890–1953

1943–45 Served as Director, Office of Economic Stabilization
1942 Served as Chief Judge, Emergency Court of Appeals
1945 Appointed secretary of the Treasury.
1913 Served as Louisville city attorney
1937–43 Served as judge, U.S. Circuit Court of Appeals for D.C.
1946 Appointed Chief Justice of the U.S. Supreme Court by President Truman
1911 Admitted to Kentucky bar
1914–18 World War I
1929 Wall Street crash; Great Depression began
1898 Spanish-American War
1939–45 World War II
1890 Born, Louisa, Ky.
1923–29 Served in U.S. House
1931–37 Served in U.S. House
1950–53 Korean War
1953 Died, Washington, D.C.

1875   1900   1925   1950

and Vinson inherited a sharply divided Court. His effectiveness as an administrator helped hold the justices together. Because he was generally disinterested in writing opinions, however, critics have judged his tenure harshly. Despite his liberal attitudes during his political career, he emerged as a predominantly conservative justice except for his support of CIVIL RIGHTS.

Born on January 22, 1890, in Louisa, Kentucky, Vinson was the son of a jailer. He graduated from Kentucky Normal College in 1908. In 1909 and 1911, he earned bachelor of arts and laws degrees from Center College in Danville, Kentucky, with the highest marks ever recorded at that school. Establishing his law practice in his hometown, he practiced law for two years before serving as city attorney in 1913 and as district attorney from 1921 to 1924.

In the mid-1920s, Vinson's visibility as a prosecutor led him into national politics. He represented Kentucky in the U.S. House of Representatives from 1923 to 1929 and again from 1931 to 1937. In his last four terms in Congress, he was a strong backer of President FRANKLIN D. ROOSEVELT's liberal economic recovery program, known popularly as the NEW DEAL.

The support engendered a long relationship between the two men. In 1937 Roosevelt appointed Vinson to the federal bench, and he served from 1937 to 1943 on the U.S. Court of Appeals for the District of Columbia. He became chief justice of the U.S. Emergency Court of Appeals in 1942 and the following year joined the Roosevelt administration as head of the Office of Economic Stabilization. A series of administrative positions culminated with Vinson's appointment as secretary of the treasury under President Truman in 1945.

In 1946 the death of Chief Justice HARLAN F. STONE set off a controversy over his successor. The question for Truman was whether he should elevate an associate justice or select an outsider. Two associate justices—ROBERT H. JACKSON and HUGO L. BLACK—were known to want the job, and each threatened to resign if the other were nominated. To settle the conflict, Truman turned to Vinson, who had both the requisite experience and a calm temperament. Vinson's

BIOGRAPHY

Frederick Moore Vinson

"FREEDOM FROM DISCRIMINATION BY THE STATES IN THE ENJOYMENT OF PROPERTY RIGHTS WAS AMONG THE BASIC OBJECTIVES SOUGHT TO BE EFFECTUATED BY THE FRAMERS OF THE FOURTEENTH AMENDMENT."

record of support for a strong federal government was also important to Truman.

During his seven years on the Court, Vinson more or less lived up to these hopes. His steady administration appears to have been effective during a tempestuous era on the Court. As a justice, however, he was less impressive. Vinson was rumored to have given the bulk of his opinion writing to his clerks. Moreover, his pragmatism showed no great philosophic appreciation of constitutional law. He generally voted conservatively except when supporting decisions that upheld the discrimination claims of African Americans; this valuable support for civil rights would be taken further by his successor, EARL WARREN. At the same time, Vinson's anti-Communism fanned the flames of the COLD WAR. In *Dennis v. United States*, 341 U.S. 494, 71 S. Ct. 857, 95 L. Ed. 1137 (1951), he upheld the convictions of American Communist party leaders.

Vinson's eagerness to bolster federal power can be seen in his most famous opinion, a dissent in *Youngstown Sheet and Tube Co. v. Sawyer*, 343 U.S. 579, 72 S. Ct. 863, 96 L. Ed. 1153 (1952). During the Korean War, Truman temporarily seized control of most of the nation's steel mills in order to supply the military. The White House asserted that the seizure was necessary to prevent a national catastrophe, but the steel industry argued that the seizure was tantamount to lawmaking—a power held only by Congress. Although the majority in *Youngstown Sheet* held that the executive decision was unconstitutional, Vinson stated that Truman had acted "in full conformity with his duties under the Constitution."

Vinson died on September 8, 1953, while still serving on the Court. In retrospect, some critics have regarded his tenure as a failure: his lack of vision and his apparent disinterest in writing his own opinions have provoked charges that he was among the few outright failures in Supreme Court history. On balance, his administrative skills seem to have outstripped his judicial ability; he managed a deeply divided Court with tact and diplomacy.

See also DENNIS V. UNITED STATES; YOUNGSTOWN SHEET AND TUBE CO. V. SAWYER.

VIRGINIA AND KENTUCKY RESOLVES

Resolutions passed by the Virginia and Kentucky legislatures in 1798 and 1799 protesting the federal Alien and Sedition Acts of 1798.

The Virginia and Kentucky Resolves were expressions of opposition by the Jeffersonian Republicans against the Federalist-sponsored Alien and Sedition Acts of 1798. Besides opposing these particular measures, the legislative resolutions proposed a "compact" theory of the U.S. Constitution that contended that state legislatures possessed all powers not specifically granted to the federal government and gave the states the right to rule upon the constitutionality of federal legislation. The resolutions became the basis for nineteenth-century STATES' RIGHTS doctrines, which were employed by Southern states to defend the institution of SLAVERY.

The Alien and Sedition Acts were passed as internal security laws, restricting ALIENS and limiting FREEDOM OF THE PRESS, based on the assumption in 1798 that the United States might soon be at war with France. Though the acts were widely popular, THOMAS JEFFERSON (then vice president in the administration of JOHN ADAMS) and JAMES MADISON (one of the primary architects of the U.S. Constitution) opposed the measures. They expressed their opposition through the Virginia and Kentucky Resolves. Madison drafted the Virginia Resolves (December 21, 1798), and Jefferson wrote the Kentucky Resolves (November 10, 1798, and November 14, 1799), though their roles were not disclosed to the public for twenty-five years.

The resolves expressed the Republicans' theory of the limited nature of the grant of power to the federal government under the U.S. Constitution. This theory was buttressed by the TENTH AMENDMENT, which stipulates that "powers not delegated to the United States by the Constitution, nor prohibited by it to the States, are reserved to the States respectively, or to the people." Because the Constitution did not give Congress the express power to provide for the expulsion of aliens who had committed no crimes and whose countries were not at war with the United States, the Republicans reasoned that the provisions of the Alien and Sedition Acts that provided for such DEPORTATION proceedings were unconstitutional. Likewise, Congress had not been given the express power to impose punishments for seditious libel, leading Republicans to conclude that these provisions were unconstitutional.

Jefferson and Madison asserted in the resolves that state legislatures had the right to determine whether the federal government was complying with the mandate of the Constitution. Under their compact theory of the Constitution, they argued that the grant of power to the federal government was in the nature of an authorization to act as an agent for the individual state legislatures. The resolves maintained that the individual state legislatures retained the ultimate SOVEREIGNTY of the people. Therefore, state legislatures, as equal parties to the Constitution, had the right to determine whether the federal government was complying with the original agency directives, and they had the right to declare noncompliance. Jefferson and Madison also argued that the states had the right to be released from the compact (the Constitution) if compliance was not forthcoming, thereby suggesting that SECESSION from the Union was legitimate.

Jefferson, in the second of the Kentucky Resolves, contended that the "sovereign and independent states" had the right to "interpose" themselves between their citizens and improper national legislative actions and to "nullify" acts of Congress they deemed unconstitutional. The Federalists strenuously objected to this theory, fearing that the federal government would be seriously weakened. The Federalists argued that only the FEDERAL COURTS could rule on the constitutionality of the Alien and Sedition Acts, which they said represented valid exercises of implied powers in time of national crisis. The acts, they argued, were authorized by Article I, Section 8, Clause 18, of the Constitution, which directs Congress "to make all Laws which shall be necessary and proper for carrying into Execution" the powers vested by the Constitution in the government of the United States. Because the federal government was vested with the power of conducting the national defense, the Federalists asserted, exercises of reasonable security measures, such as the Alien and Sedition Acts, were permissible.

No other state legislatures passed resolves in support of those of Virginia and Kentucky, including the legislatures of Republican-controlled states, in large part because of opposition to France, based on the XYZ Affair, in which the French refused to recognize U.S. diplomats and demanded bribes before any such recognition would be forthcoming. In this political climate, state legislatures supported the Alien and Sedition Acts.

The acts expired or were repealed between 1800 and 1802, after Jefferson became president. Nevertheless, the theories of limited federal government and nullification remained popular during the early nineteenth century. New England states asserted nullification during the War of 1812, and South Carolina asserted it in opposition to federal TARIFF legislation in 1832. South Carolina statesman and political theorist JOHN C. CALHOUN further developed Jefferson's theory, giving the states the right to dissolve their contractual relationship with the federal government rather than submit to policies they saw as destructive to their local self-interests. These ideas ultimately became the legal justification for the secession of Southern states from the Union in 1861.

See also KENTUCKY RESOLUTIONS; XYZ AFFAIR.

VIRGINIA CONVENTIONS

The Virginia Conventions were a series of five meetings that were held after the Boston Tea Party in which representatives from the colonies gathered to decide the future relations between the colonies and England.

The first convention, which opened August 1, 1774, in Williamsburg, Virginia, was the result of a serious conflict with England that had occurred three months earlier. On May 26, the Virginia legislature, the House of Burgesses, had declared a day of prayer and fasting to acknowledge the plight of Bostonians after the English had closed the port of Boston as punishment for the Boston Tea Party. The royal governor of Virginia, Lord Dunmore, ordered the House of Burgesses to be closed to discourage any display of sympathy for the rebellious Bostonians. Angered by Lord Dunmore's actions, the Virginia burgesses issued a plan for a meeting of representatives from all the colonies.

In August, the colonists met in Williamsburg and chose Peyton Randolph as their presiding officer. The convention adopted several resolutions including one on the nonimportation of English merchandise and another that said that the colonists should refuse to export colonial goods to England unless the English agreed to come to terms with them. THOMAS JEFFERSON'S work *A Summary View of the Rights of British America*, which was introduced at this convention, was used as a guideline at future meetings.

The second convention met in Richmond, Virginia, for a one-week period in 1775, from March 20 to March 27. At this convention, PATRICK HENRY initiated a program for defensive action and presented his celebrated "Give me liberty or give me death" speech, which inspired the colonists to follow the cause.

The third meeting was held in Richmond on July 17, 1775. There the representatives denounced the actions that the royal governor had taken against Virginia, including disbanding the assembly and mobilizing troops. When the governor fled to the sanctuary of an English ship, the convention became the governing force of Virginia. The delegates enacted legislation and established a Committee of Safety to direct military activities.

Williamsburg was the site of the fourth convention, which was held in December 1775. With Edmund Pendleton as president, the delegates empowered the Committee of Safety to be the source of governmental authority in Virginia.

By May 6, 1776, the date of the final convention, the colonists were moving determinedly toward complete independence from England. In Williamsburg, the delegates declared their desire for freedom in a statement issued to their congressional representatives. Virginia initiated the action, and on June 12, the convention ratified the Virginia Bill of Rights. This BILL OF RIGHTS served as a model for similar documents in the other colonies. Virginia was the first state to have a new constitution, and Patrick Henry served as the first governor under the new government.

VIRGINIA DECLARATION OF RIGHTS

Statement of rights adopted by the colony of Virginia in 1776, which served as the model for the U.S. Constitution's BILL OF RIGHTS.

The Virginia Declaration of Rights is an important document in U.S. constitutional history. Adopted by the Virginia Constitutional Convention on June 12, 1776, its sixteen sections enumerated specific civil liberties that government could not legitimately take away. The declaration was adopted during the last months of British colonial rule. THOMAS JEFFERSON used parts of it in the DECLARATION OF INDEPENDENCE, and it later served as a model for the Bill of Rights that was added to the U.S. Constitution.

In the spring of 1776 the Virginia Convention of Delegates convened in the colonial capitol of Williamsburg to decide the form of government Virginia should have and the rights its citizens should enjoy. The convention took place at a time when British attempts to tax and regulate the thirteen colonies had generated colonial resistance and a growing desire for political independence.

The Virginia Declaration of Rights was largely the product of GEORGE MASON, a plantation owner, real estate speculator, and neighbor of GEORGE WASHINGTON. A strong believer in human liberty and limited government, Mason crafted a document that guaranteed the citizens of Virginia, upon achieving independence from Great Britain, all the civil liberties they had lost under British rule.

In its opening sentence the declaration states that "all men are by nature equally free and independent, and have certain inherent rights" which they cannot surrender, "namely, the enjoyment of life, and liberty, with the means of acquiring and possessing property, and pursuing and obtaining happiness and safety." Jefferson's famous phrase "life, liberty, and the pursuit of happiness" in the Declaration of Independence was influenced by Mason and JOHN LOCKE, the English philosopher who first broached the idea of natural and inherent rights in the 17th century.

The declaration of rights enumerates specific civil liberties, including FREEDOM OF THE PRESS, the free exercise of RELIGION, and the injunction that "no man be deprived of his liberty, except by the law of the land or the judgement of his peers." Other provisions include a prohibition against excessive BAIL or CRUEL AND UNUSUAL PUNISHMENTS, the requirements of evidence and good cause before obtaining a SEARCH WARRANT to enter a place, the right to trial by JURY, and the need for a "well regulated militia" to be "under strict subordination" to the civilian government.

Many of these provisions were incorporated into the Bill of Rights. The Virginia Declaration of Rights was widely read and won an international reputation as an inspirational document.

VIS 📖 [*Latin, Force or violence.*] A term employed in many legal phrases and maxims, such as *vis injuriosa*, "wrongful force." 📖

VISA 📖 An official endorsement on a PASSPORT or other document required to secure an alien's admission to a country. 📖

Under U.S. immigration law, an alien is any person who is not a CITIZEN or national of the United States. Two types of visas exist: nonimmigrant and immigrant. The immigration laws delineate specific categories of persons who may be eligible for an immigrant visa, which generally allows a person to live in the United States permanently and perhaps eventually seek citizenship. Persons visiting the United States on a temporary basis to engage in an activity delineated under the nonimmigrant classifications of the federal immigration laws must generally possess a nonimmigrant visa. A visit under a nonimmigrant visa may be of very short duration or may validly last for years, depending on the classification of nonimmigrant visa used.

Immigrant visa classifications include family-sponsored immigrants, employment-based immigrants, diversity immigrants, and immediate relatives of U.S. citizens (8 U.S.C.A. § 1101(a)(15) et seq.). Immediate relatives are the children, spouse, and parents of a U.S. citizen. Only a specified number of visas may be issued in each of the first three categories each year. Demand often exceeds supply for these visas, creating a backlog. The immediate relative classification, along with certain other categories, is not subject to numerical limitation (8 U.S.C.A. § 1151).

A variety of nonimmigrant visa categories exist, including visitors coming to the United States for business or pleasure; ambassadors and certain diplomatic officers; a crew member on board a vessel or aircraft; certain kinds of workers; the fiancée or fiancé of a U.S. citizen; persons with "extraordinary ability in the sciences, arts, education, business, or athletics"; artists and entertainers; participants in approved international cultural exchange programs; and religious workers. Some nonimmigrant visa classifications permit family members or servants to accompany the principal alien.

Most immigrant visa categories require a U.S. citizen or entity to first file a visa petition on behalf of the alien. Once the visa petition is approved, the alien typically submits a visa application to the appropriate U.S. consulate. Immigrant visa applications may include a questionnaire, fingerprints, an oath and signature before the consular officer, photographs, and results of a medical examination. A visa applicant might also be required to provide police or prison records, military records, and a birth certificate. The alien has the burden to establish eligibility to receive the visa.

Documentation and other information needed for nonimmigrant visas vary with the type of visa sought but are generally less extensive than those required for an immigrant visa. A few categories require an approved visa petition; certain classifications require a medical exam. A nonimmigrant visa specifies the nonimmigrant classification, such as B-2 for a visitor for pleasure, and the length of time the visa is valid. Typically a nonimmigrant visa is evidenced by documentation placed in an alien's passport. On the other hand, an arriving immigrant usually surrenders the visa to the immigration officer at the port of entry, who notes the date, port of entry, identity of vessel or other means of transportation, and any other information that is required under federal regulations.

Possession of a valid visa does not ensure admission to the United States; an alien must still be admissible under all immigration laws at the time of arrival.

VISIBLE MEANS OF SUPPORT 📖 A term employed in VAGRANCY statutes to test whether an individual has any apparent ability to provide for himself or herself financially. 📖

A person who has no visible means of support and loiters in a public place might be arrested and prosecuted for vagrancy.

VITIATE 📖 To impair or make VOID; to destroy or annul, either completely or partially, the force and effect of an act or instrument. 📖

MUTUAL MISTAKE or FRAUD, for example, might vitiate a contract.

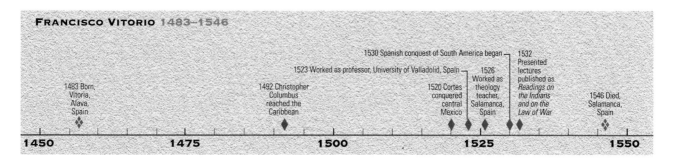

FRANCISCO VITORIO 1483–1546

1530 Spanish conquest of South America began
1523 Worked as professor, University of Valladolid, Spain
1483 Born, Vitoria, Alava, Spain
1492 Christopher Columbus reached the Caribbean
1520 Cortes conquered central Mexico
1526 Worked as theology teacher, Salamanca, Spain
1532 Presented lectures published as *Readings on the Indians and on the Law of War*
1546 Died, Salamanca, Spain

1450   1475   1500   1525   1550

VITORIA, FRANCISCO DE

Francisco de Vitoria was a Spanish theologian, teacher, and defender of the rights of the Native Americans who inhabited the newly discovered continents of North and South America.

Vitoria was born circa 1483 in Vitoria, Álava, Spain. He taught at the University of Valladolid from 1523 until 1526. In that year, he moved to Salamanca, Spain, where he taught theology for the next twenty years.

Vitoria's campaign for the rights of native peoples started in 1532, when he began a series of lectures on that subject. He incorporated the substance of these lectures into a TREATISE entitled *De Indis et de iure belli relectiones* [*Readings on the Indians and on the Law of War*]. The work not only advocated the case for the Native Americans but also presented basic precepts on the LAW OF NATIONS.

In his fight for freedom for Native Americans, Vitoria asserted that they owned the territories they inhabited and opposed their compulsory conversion to Christianity. He believed that the Spanish government should establish a ruling system that would benefit, not injure, the native people.

Vitoria believed that an ideal government would receive its authority from the people and would rely on the tenets of NATURAL LAW and reason to enact laws beneficial to all.

See also NATIVE AMERICAN RIGHTS.

VIVA VOCE 📖 [*Latin, With the living voice; by word of mouth.*] Verbally; orally. 📖

When applied to the examination of WITNESSES, the term *viva voce* means oral TESTIMONY as opposed to testimony contained in DEPOSITIONS or AFFIDAVITS.

Viva voce voting is voting by speech, as distinguished from voting by a written or printed ballot.

VIZ. 📖 [*Latin, A contraction of the term* videlicet, *to wit, namely, or that is to say.*] A term used to highlight or make more specific something previously indicated only in general terms. 📖

VOID 📖 That which is NULL and completely without legal force or binding effect. 📖

The term *void* has a precise meaning that has sometimes been confused with the more liberal

BIOGRAPHY

"[JUS GENTIUM] IS WHAT NATURAL REASON HAS ESTABLISHED AMONG NATIONS."

term *voidable*. Something that is VOIDABLE may be avoided or declared void by one or more of the parties, but such an agreement is not void per se.

A void CONTRACT is not a contract at all because the parties are not, and cannot be, bound by its terms. Therefore, no action can be maintained for breach of a void contract, and it cannot be made valid by ratification. Because it is nugatory, a void contract need not be rescinded or otherwise declared invalid in a court of law.

A void MARRIAGE is one that is invalid from its inception. In contrast to a voidable marriage, the parties to a void marriage may not ratify the union by living together as HUSBAND AND WIFE. No DIVORCE or ANNULMENT is required. Nevertheless, parties frequently do seek, and are permitted to seek, such a decree in order to remove any doubt about the validity of the marriage. Unlike a voidable marriage, a void marriage can be challenged even after the death of one or both parties.

In most JURISDICTIONS a bigamous marriage, one involving a person who has a living spouse from an undissolved prior marriage, is void from the outset. In addition, statutes typically prohibit marriage between an ancestor and descendant; between a brother and a sister (whether related by whole blood, half blood, or ADOPTION); and between an uncle and niece or aunt and nephew. See also BIGAMY; CONSANGUINITY.

A JUDGMENT entered by a court is void if a court lacks jurisdiction over the parties or subject matter of a lawsuit. A void judgment may be entirely disregarded without a judicial declaration that the judgment is void and differs from an erroneous, irregular, or voidable judgment. In practice, however, an attack on a void judgment is commonly used to make the judgment's flaw a matter of public record.

A law is considered void on its FACE if its meaning is so VAGUE that persons of ordinary intelligence must guess at its meaning and may differ as to the statute's application (*Connally v. General Construction Co.*, 269 U.S. 385, 46 S. Ct. 126, 70 L. Ed. 2d 322 [1926]). DUE PROCESS requires that citizens receive fair notice of what sort of conduct to avoid. For example, a Cincinnati, Ohio, city ordinance made it a criminal offense for three or more persons to assemble on a sidewalk and conduct themselves in a manner that was annoying to passersby. A conviction carried the possibility of a $50 fine and between one and thirty days imprisonment. The U.S. Supreme Court reversed the convictions of several persons found guilty of violating the ordinance after a demonstration and picketing (*Coates v. Cincinnati*, 402 U.S. 611, 91 S. Ct. 1686, 29 L. Ed. 2d 214 [1971]). The Court ruled that the ordinance was unconstitutionally vague because it subjected citizens to an unascertainable standard. Stating that "conduct that annoys some people does not annoy others," the Court said that the ordinance left citizens to guess at the proper conduct required. The Court noted that the city could lawfully prohibit persons from blocking the sidewalks, littering, obstructing traffic, committing assaults, or engaging in other types of undesirable behavior through "ordinances directed with reasonable specificity toward the conduct to be prohibited."

See also VOID FOR VAGUENESS DOCTRINE.

VOIDABLE 📖 That which is not absolutely VOID, but may be avoided. 📖

In CONTRACTS, *voidable* is a term typically used with respect to a contract that is valid and binding unless avoided or declared void by a party to the contract who is legitimately exercising a power to avoid the contractual obligations.

A contract may be voidable on the grounds of FRAUD, MISTAKE, MISREPRESENTATION, lack of CAPACITY, DURESS, UNDUE INFLUENCE, or abuse of a FIDUCIARY relationship. A contract that is based on one of these grounds is not automatically void but is voidable at the option of the party entitled to avoid it. For example, a person who was induced by fraud to enter into a contract may disclaim the contract by taking some positive action to disaffirm the contract. Or the victim of the fraud may ratify the contract by his or her conduct or by an express affirmation after acquiring full knowledge of the facts. Likewise, a contract between a MINOR and another party is generally viewed as voidable by the minor. The minor may legally decide to ratify the contract or disaffirm the contract.

A voidable MARRIAGE is a marriage that is valid when entered into and remains completely valid until a party obtains a court order nullifying the relationship. The parties may ratify a voidable marriage upon removal of the impediment preventing a lawful marriage, thus making the union valid. Living together as HUSBAND AND WIFE following the removal of the impediment typically constitutes a ratification. A voidable marriage can only be attacked by a direct action brought by one of the parties against the other and therefore cannot be attacked after the death of a spouse. It differs from a void marriage where no valid marital relationship ever existed.

Most JURISDICTIONS hold that the marriage of a person under the statutory AGE OF CONSENT but over the age of seven is voidable rather than void. Such a marriage may be subject to attack through an ANNULMENT or may be ratified when the underage party reaches the age of consent. Some jurisdictions have determined that a marriage involving an incompetent party is void, but others hold that such a marriage is only voidable. A voidable marriage involving an incompetent party may be ratified during periods when the party is lucid or after she or he regains competency. Generally, a marriage procured or induced by certain types of fraud is viewed as voidable; voluntary COHABITATION following a disclosure of all pertinent facts ratifies the marriage. A marriage made without the voluntary consent of one of the parties is generally considered voidable. Moreover, a person who is so intoxicated at the time of marriage as to be incapable of understanding the nature of the marital contract lacks the capacity to consent, and such a marriage is voidable.

VOID FOR VAGUENESS DOCTRINE
📖 A doctrine derived from the Due Process Clauses of the Fifth and Fourteenth Amendments to the U.S. Constitution that requires criminal laws to be drafted in language that is clear enough for the average person to comprehend. 📖

If a person of ordinary intelligence cannot determine what persons are regulated, what conduct is prohibited, or what punishment may be imposed under a particular law, then the law will be deemed unconstitutionally VAGUE. The U.S. Supreme Court has said that no one may be required at peril of life, liberty, or property to speculate as to the meaning of a penal law. Everyone is entitled to know what the government commands or forbids.

The void for vagueness doctrine advances four underlying policies. First, the doctrine encourages the government to clearly distinguish conduct that is lawful from that which is unlawful. Under the Due Process Clauses, individuals must be given adequate notice of their legal obligations so they can govern their behavior accordingly. When individuals are left uncertain by the wording of an imprecise statute, the law becomes a standardless trap for the unwary.

For example, VAGRANCY is a crime that is frequently regulated by lawmakers despite difficulties that have been encountered in defining it. Vagrancy laws are often drafted in such a way as to encompass ordinarily innocent activity. In one case the Supreme Court struck down an ordinance that prohibited "loafing," "strolling," or "wandering around from place to place" because such activity comprises an innocuous part of nearly everyone's life (*Papachristou v. City of Jacksonville*, 405 U.S. 156, 92 S. Ct. 839, 31 L. Ed. 2d 110 [1972]). The Court concluded that the ordinance did not provide society with adequate warning as to what type of conduct might be subject to prosecution.

Second, the void for vagueness doctrine curbs the arbitrary and discriminatory enforcement of criminal statutes. Penal laws must be understood not only by those persons who are required to obey them but by those persons who are charged with the duty of enforcing them. Statutes that do not carefully outline detailed procedures by which police officers may perform an investigation, conduct a search, or make an arrest confer wide discretion upon each officer to act as he or she sees fit. Precisely worded statutes are intended to confine an officer's activities to the letter of the law.

Third, the void for vagueness doctrine discourages judges from attempting to apply sloppily worded laws. Like the rest of society, judges often labor without success when interpreting poorly worded legislation. In particular cases, courts may attempt to narrowly construe a vague statute so that it applies only to a finite set of circumstances. For example, some courts will permit prosecution under a vague law if the government can demonstrate that the defendant acted with a SPECIFIC INTENT to commit an offense, which means that the defendant must have acted wilfully, knowingly, or deliberately. By reading a specific intent requirement into a vaguely worded law, courts attempt to insulate innocent behavior from criminal sanction.

However, such judicial constructions are not always possible. Ultimately, a confusing law that cannot be cured by a narrow judicial interpretation will not be submitted to a jury for consideration but will be struck down as an unconstitutional violation of the Due Process Clauses.

A fourth reason for the void for vagueness doctrine is to avoid encroachment on FIRST AMENDMENT freedoms, such as FREEDOM OF SPEECH and RELIGION. Because vague laws cause uncertainty in the minds of average citizens, some citizens will inevitably decline to take risky behavior that might land them in jail. When the vague provisions of a state or federal statute deter citizens from engaging in certain political or religious discourse, courts will apply heightened scrutiny to ensure that protected expression is not suppressed. For example, a law

that prohibits "sacrilegious" speech would simultaneously chill the freedoms of expression and religion in violation of the void for vagueness doctrine (*Joseph Burstyn, Inc. v. Wilson*, 343 U.S. 495, 72 S. Ct. 777, 96 L. Ed. 1098 [1952]).

Although courts scrutinize a vague law that touches on a fundamental freedom, in all other cases the void for vagueness doctrine does not typically require mathematical precision on the part of legislators. Laws that regulate the economy are scrutinized less closely than laws that regulate individual behavior, and laws that impose civil or administrative penalties may be drafted with less clarity than laws imposing criminal sanctions.

CROSS-REFERENCES

Chilling Effect Doctrine; Due Process of Law; Fifth Amendment; Fourteenth Amendment.

VOIR DIRE [*Old French, To speak the truth.*] The preliminary examination of prospective jurors to determine their qualifications and suitability to serve on a JURY, in order to ensure the selection of fair and impartial jury.

Voir dire consists of oral questions asked of prospective jurors by the judge, the parties, or the attorneys, or some combination thereof. This oral questioning, often supplemented by a prior written questionnaire, is used to determine whether a potential juror is biased, knows any of the parties, counsel, or WITNESSES, or should otherwise be excluded from jury duty. Voir dire is a tool used to achieve the constitutional right to an impartial jury, but it is not a constitutional right in itself.

Typically, a number of prospective jurors are called to the jury box, given an OATH, and then questioned as a group by counsel or the court. Local federal rules generally provide for questioning by the judge. Individual or sequestered voir dire is used in rare cases where extensive publicity may potentially damage a defendant's

Voir dire is the process through which the attorneys for the opposing parties in a trial select jury members. The jury should be representative of the community in which the trial is being held.

AP/WIDE WORLD PHOTOS

case; some JURISDICTIONS mandate it in death penalty cases. A prospective juror must answer questions fully and truthfully but cannot be faulted for failing to disclose information that was not sought.

The purpose of voir dire is not to educate jurors but to enable the parties to select an impartial panel. Therefore, voir dire questions should test the capacity and competency of the jurors without intentionally or unintentionally planting prejudicial matter in their minds. Trial judges have wide latitude in setting the parameters of questioning, including the abilities to determine the materiality and propriety of the questions and to set the time allowed for voir dire.

A party may move for dismissal for cause to remove any potential juror shown to be connected to or biased in the case. A court may sustain counsel's request to strike a juror for cause, in which case the juror steps aside and another is called. Or a judge may overrule a challenge for cause if a suitable reason has not been sufficiently established. Challenges for cause are not limited in number.

Each side also exercises PEREMPTORY CHALLENGES to further shape the composition of the jury. Peremptory challenges are used to dismiss a prospective juror without the need to provide a reason for dismissal. Statutes or court rules typically set the number of peremptory challenges afforded to a party.

Voir dire also describes a court's preliminary examination of a prospective witness whose competency or qualifications have been challenged.

VOLENTI NON FIT INJURIA 📖 [*Latin, To the consenting, no injury is done.*] In the law of NEGLIGENCE, the precept that denotes that a person who knows and comprehends the peril and voluntarily exposes himself or herself to it, although not negligent in doing so, is regarded as engaging in an assumption of the risk and is precluded from a recovery for an injury ensuing therefrom. 📖

See also ASSUMPTION OF RISK.

VOLSTEAD, ANDREW JOHN Andrew John Volstead was a midwestern lawyer and ten-term U.S. representative from Minnesota who gained national prominence as the originator of the VOLSTEAD Act, officially the National Prohibition ACT (41 Stat. 305). The Volstead Act was a comprehensive statute enacted to enforce the EIGHTEENTH AMENDMENT to the U.S. Constitution. It prohibited the manufacture, sale, or transportation of intoxicating liquor. The Volstead Act was later rendered inoperative by the passage of the TWENTY-FIRST AMENDMENT, which repealed PROHIBITION.

BIOGRAPHY

Andrew John Volstead

Volstead, a reluctant national symbol of Prohibition, was the product of modest, rural beginnings. His parents had been Norwegian farmers who earned their living by selling surplus produce in Oslo street markets until they immigrated to the United States in 1854, where they eventually settled on a farm near the town of Kenyon, in Goodhue County, Minnesota.

Volstead was born October 31, 1860. After attending local public schools, he went on to Saint Olaf College, in Northfield, Minnesota, and the Decorah Institute, in Decorah, Iowa. He graduated from Decorah in 1881. After graduation, he taught school in Iowa, and studied law with two Decorah attorneys. Volstead was admitted to the Iowa bar in 1883 and to the Minnesota bar one year later. He practiced law in Granite Falls, Minnesota.

In 1887, one year after his arrival, Volstead was named Yellow Medicine County attorney—a post he held for fourteen years. He was a member and president of the Granite Falls Board of Education, a Granite Falls city attorney, and a Granite Falls mayor. Volstead married Helen ("Nellie") Mary Osler Gilruth on August 6, 1894.

From his platform as mayor of Granite Falls, Volstead launched his first major political campaign in 1902. Running as a Republican, he sought to represent Minnesota's seventh congressional district in the U.S. House of Representatives. He was elected, and was returned to office nine times, serving for a total of almost twenty years.

Volstead sought to protect the interests of the small farmer in general—and western Minnesota wheat farmers in particular. He opposed legislation that favored big cities, big business, and big labor. He believed in competition, he hated monopolies, and he supported early legislative attempts to regulate the RAILROAD industry. Though he had supported President WOODROW WILSON's World War I policies, Volstead opposed many of the administration's domestic programs. He believed the Underwood Tariff Act of 1913 (19 U.S.C.A. §§ 128, 130, 131 [1982]) discriminated against the farmer, the Federal Reserve Act of 1913 (12 U.S.C.A. § 321 [1989]) benefited large city banks, and the Clayton Anti-Trust Act of 1914 (15 U.S.C.A. § 12 [1994]) exempted labor from federal laws.

In spite of, or perhaps because of, his opposition to Wilson's domestic agenda, Volstead was admired and supported by his conservative rural constituents. He was also respected by his Washington, D.C., colleagues. Over the years, he earned a reputation as a hardworking public

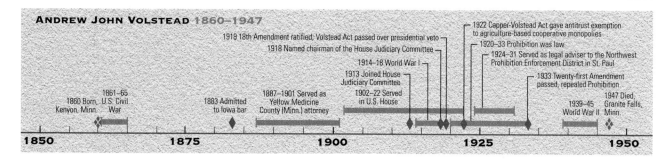

1919 18th Amendment ratified; Volstead Act passed over presidential veto

1918 Named chairman of the House Judiciary Committee

1922 Capper-Volstead Act gave antitrust exemption to agriculture-based cooperative monopolies

1920–33 Prohibition was law

1924–31 Served as legal adviser to the Northwest Prohibition Enforcement District in St. Paul

1914–18 World War I

1913 Joined House Judiciary Committee

1933 Twenty-first Amendment passed, repealed Prohibition

1861–65 U.S. Civil War

1860 Born, Kenyon, Minn.

1883 Admitted to Iowa bar

1887–1901 Served as Yellow Medicine County (Minn.) attorney

1902–22 Served in U.S. House

1947 Died, Granite Falls, Minn.

1939–45 World War II

1850   1875   1900   1925   1950

servant with a fine legal mind. Volstead joined the House Judiciary Committee in 1913. As a committee member, he frequently demonstrated his ability to frame successful bills and to move them through the legislative process.

Volstead's professional skills were put to the test in 1918. Shortly after the passage of the Eighteenth Amendment, he was named chairman of the House Judiciary Committee. In this capacity, he was called upon to draft a new law to enforce Prohibition. Volstead's bill permitted the sale of ALCOHOL for industrial, medicinal, and sacramental purposes. It outlawed any beverage containing more than one-half of one percent of alcohol; provided concurrent state and federal power to allow for the enforcement of stricter state laws; included a SEARCH AND SEIZURE clause; and provided for INJUNCTIONS against, and the padlocking of, establishments selling alcoholic beverages. The bill was passed in 1919 over President Wilson's VETO.

Although Volstead's bill was less drastic than an earlier measure drafted by Wayne B. Wheeler, of the Anti-Saloon League, and less strict than existing laws in Ohio and New York, it was not well received by those against Prohibition. Passage of the National Prohibition Act forced the quiet Minnesota congressman into the national spotlight, and made him a central figure in the country's ongoing debate between wet and dry factions.

It is somewhat ironic that Volstead became so closely associated with the Prohibition debate. He *was* a nondrinker who supported Prohibition, but he had never made a speech on the issue before his bill was passed. And, though he was proud of the act that came to carry his name, he expressed disappointment in later years that the Volstead Act got more attention than other legislative contributions that he deemed equally or more important.

In spite of his outstanding record of support for Minnesota farmers, Volstead's notoriety following the passage of the Volstead Act made him vulnerable in reelection bids. A coalition of Prohibition opponents was unable to defeat him in 1920, but two years later, Ole J. Kvale, a

"EVERY LAWYER IS FAMILIAR WITH THE . . . LARGE CORPORATE INTERESTS . . . THAT APPEAL TO OUR COURTS TO SET ASIDE THE WILL OF THE PEOPLE AS EXPRESSED BY OUR STATE LEGISLATURES. [T]HOSE WHO SEEK TO THWART THE WILL OF THE PEOPLE SHOULD NOT HAVE [THAT] ADVANTAGE."

Lutheran minister, was elected to replace the ten-term congressman.

Volstead refused to profit from the Prohibition debate, and he turned down lucrative speaking engagements with some regularity. He did, however, continue to support the cause that had cost him reelection. From 1924 to 1931, he lived in St. Paul and served as the legal adviser to the Northwest Prohibition Enforcement District. The Volstead Act was repealed by the Twenty-first Amendment in 1933.

He died in Granite Falls at age eighty-seven, on January 20, 1947.

VOLSTEAD ACT A popular name for the National Prohibition Act (41 Stat. 305), a comprehensive statute that was enacted to enforce the EIGHTEENTH AMENDMENT to the U.S. Constitution and to prohibit the manufacture and sale of intoxicating liquors.

The Volstead Act was later rendered inoperative by passage of the TWENTY-FIRST AMENDMENT, which repealed PROHIBITION.

See also ALCOHOL.

VOLUNTARY ACT A crime that is the product of conscious choice and independent will.

No crime can be committed by bad thoughts alone. One basic premise of U.S. law is that every crime requires the commission of some act before a person may be held accountable to the justice system. A criminal act may take the form of affirmative conduct, such as the crime of murder, or it may take the form of an omission to act, such as the crime of withholding information from the police. However, in order for an act to be considered criminal, it must be voluntary.

To constitute a voluntary act for which a person may be held criminally liable, the act must result from the person's conscious choice. The choice need not be the product of thorough deliberation but may stem from an impulse, as long as the person is physically and mentally capable of exercising restraint and discretion consistent with the requirements of the law. A person who suddenly slips on a mountain trail and reaches out to grab the arm of a bystander to avoid falling has acted voluntarily because his mind has quickly grasped the situation and dictated a response.

Acts over which a person has no physical or mental control are not voluntary. A muscle reflex driven by the autonomic nervous system, such as a knee jerk, is not considered voluntary under the law. Acts committed during seizures, convulsions, hypnosis, or unconscious mental states also lack sufficient volition and judgment needed to impose criminal LIABILITY. For the same reasons, acts committed during episodes of sleepwalking are not considered voluntary.

On the other hand, acts that are not fully the result of independent will but are committed with extreme indifference to human life are usually treated as voluntary. A conscious person who points a loaded gun at another, for example, will typically be held liable for any harm that results from its accidental discharge because the act of brandishing a loaded gun is treated as a voluntary choice manifesting a RECKLESSNESS toward the safety of others. Similarly, an intoxicated person who passes out behind the wheel of a car cannot escape liability for any criminal acts that ensue, because they followed from the voluntary acts of drinking and driving. Persons who have a history of seizures, fainting spells, or blackouts may be held responsible for criminal acts that result during such episodes if a court finds that reasonable precautions could have been taken to avoid the dangers created by these physical and mental conditions.

In the majority of criminal cases, the voluntary nature of a defendant's act is not at issue. Until something in EVIDENCE indicates to the contrary, a court may presume that a defendant has acted with the INTENT to carry out the bodily movements for which she is being prosecuted. The law expects every person to take responsibility for her own actions and anticipate the natural consequences that might reasonably follow from particular behavior. Medical testimony is commonly required to place a defendant's mental state into question and raise the defense of voluntariness before a judge or jury.

Involuntary criminal acts should be distinguished from acts that are the product of DURESS. Duress includes the use of force, or threat of force, to coerce another to commit a criminal act. Crimes committed under duress are considered voluntary because an individual's decision to succumb is normally based on a cost-benefit analysis in which he weighs the consequences of acting and refusing to act. Nonetheless, the law protects individuals who succumb to COERCION by allowing them to assert the defense of duress. The defense of duress is based on the idea that the deterrent and retributive value of criminal law is not served by punishing individuals for behavior that is not the product of free and independent will.

See also INSANITY DEFENSE.

VOTING The right to vote is a fundamental element of the United States' system of representative democracy. In this form of government, policy decisions are made by representatives chosen in periodic ELECTIONS based on the principle of universal SUFFRAGE, which requires that all CITIZENS (or at least all COMPETENT adults not guilty of serious crimes) be eligible to vote in elections. Democratic governments are premised on political equality. Although individuals are inherently unequal with respect to their talents and virtues, they are deemed equal in their essential worth and dignity as human beings. Each individual has an equal right to participate in politics under the law.

Though these principles of representative democracy and universal suffrage have been idealized throughout U.S. history, citizens often have needed to struggle to make these principles a reality. The Framers of the U.S. Constitution did not explicitly define qualifications for voting but delegated to the states the right to set voting requirements. At the time the Constitution was ratified, property qualifications for voting still existed, and the franchise was granted originally only to white men.

The Growth of Enfranchisement
The movement toward universal suffrage can be traced to the advent of Jacksonian democracy in the 1830s. Property qualifications rapidly diminished for white voters by the beginning of the Civil War. The end of SLAVERY led in 1870 to the adoption of the FIFTEENTH AMENDMENT, which theoretically granted the right to vote to African Americans. It was not until the 1960s that this right became a reality.

The NINETEENTH AMENDMENT, ratified in 1920, removed gender as a qualification for voting. The SEVENTEENTH AMENDMENT, ratified in 1913, provided for the direct election of U.S. senators. They had previously been elected by state legislatures. The TWENTY-FOURTH AMENDMENT, ratified in 1964, abolished poll taxes as prerequisites for voting in federal elections. Finally, the TWENTY-SIXTH AMENDMENT, ratified in 1971, lowered the voting age to eighteen. These constitutional amendments reveal the slow movement toward universal suffrage, but it would take court decisions as well as federal legislation to ensure that citizens were not denied their constitutional right to vote.

Attempts at Disenfranchisement
For a hundred years the legislatures of southern and border states used a succession of different

types of legislation to disenfranchise African Americans and the members of other minority groups. These laws were challenged in court, leading to a steady stream of decisions that restricted the ability of legislatures to limit voting rights. Beginning in the 1960s, the federal government became actively involved in ending discriminatory voting practices. Federal legislation triggered a new set of issues involving minority representation. In addition, the federal government set new procedures for voter registration, which made it easier to register and vote.

Despite the passage of the Fifteenth Amendment in 1870, African Americans had difficulty exercising their right to vote. In some states, public officials ignored the Fifteenth Amendment, and in other areas, groups such as the Ku Klux Klan used terrorism to prevent African Americans from voting. The U.S. Supreme Court struck down congressional attempts to enforce the Fifteenth Amendment in *United States v. Reese*, 92 U.S. (2 Otto) 214, 23 L. Ed. 563 (1875). The Court reversed itself in *Ex Parte Yarbrough*, 110 U.S. 651, 4 S. Ct. 152, 28 L. Ed. 274 (1884), yet in the 1880s Congress showed little interest in securing African American voting rights.

Southern and border states realized, however, that the federal government had the power to ensure the enfranchisement of African Americans. Therefore, these states sought ways of excluding African Americans from the political process; these methods appeared neutral but were employed solely against persons of color.

Grandfather Clause The most blatant official means of preventing African Americans from voting was the GRANDFATHER CLAUSE. First enacted by Mississippi in 1890, this method soon spread throughout the southern and border states. Typically these clauses required literacy tests for all voters whose ancestors had not been entitled to vote prior to 1866. This meant that African Americans were subject to literacy tests arbitrarily administered by white officials, whereas illiterate whites were exempted from this requirement because their ancestors could vote in 1866. In 1915 the Supreme Court struck down Oklahoma's grandfather clause in *Guinn v. United States*, 238 U.S. 347, 35 S. Ct. 926, 59 L. Ed. 1340.

White Primary After the grandfather clause was ruled unconstitutional, southern states adopted the white primary as a way of excluding African Americans from voting in a meaningful way. The Democratic party in many states adopted a rule excluding African Americans from party membership. The state legislatures worked in concert with the party, closing

National Voter Turnout in Presidential Elections, 1960–1996

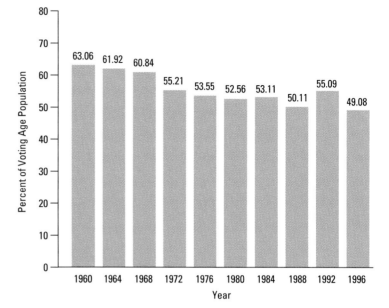

Source: Congressional Research Service.

the party primaries to everyone except party members. Because nomination by the Democratic party was tantamount to election in these essentially one-party states, African Americans were effectively disenfranchised. The Supreme Court, in *Smith v. Allwright*, 321 U.S. 649, 64 S. Ct. 757, 88 L. Ed. 987 (1944), struck down the white primary as a violation of the Fifteenth Amendment's prohibition against voting discrimination based on race.

Literacy Tests The end of grandfather clauses and white primaries led to the use of other exclusionary tactics. Many states relied on literacy tests that, despite superficial neutrality, were administered in a racially discriminatory manner. White people rarely had to take the test, even if their literacy was questionable. However, because the Constitution had left the determination of voting qualifications to the states and the literacy tests were on their face racially neutral, the Supreme Court refused to strike them down. Ultimately, Congress abolished literacy tests through the Voting Rights Act of 1965 (42 U.S.C.A. § 1973 et seq.).

Poll Tax Another less common means of preventing African Americans from voting was the POLL TAX. At the time the Constitution was adopted, poll taxes were used as a legitimate means of raising revenue. By the 1850s poll taxes had disappeared, but they were revived in the early twentieth century by states seeking to exclude African Americans from the political process. The tax generally amounted to $2 per election, an amount large enough to deter most persons of color, as well as poor whites, from voting. On its face, the poll tax was racially neutral. The Supreme Court initially upheld the tax in *Breedlove v. Suttles*, 302 U.S. 277, 58 S. Ct. 205, 82 L. Ed. 252 (1937), but over time it became clear that it was being used in a racially discriminatory manner. The Twenty-fourth Amendment, ratified in 1963, abolished the use of the poll tax in federal elections. In 1966 the Supreme Court, in *Harper v. Virginia State Board of Elections*, 383 U.S. 663, 86 S. Ct. 1079, 16 L. Ed. 2d 169, struck down the use of poll taxes in state and local elections, ruling that such taxes violated the Fourteenth Amendment's Equal Protection Clause.

Voting Reforms

Voting Rights Act of 1965 The passage of the Voting Rights Act of 1965 was a watershed event in U.S. history. For the first time the federal government undertook voting reforms that had traditionally been left to the states. The act prohibits the states and their political subdivisions from imposing voting qualifications or prerequisites to voting, or standards, practices, or procedures that deny or curtail the right of a U.S. citizen to vote because of race, color, or membership in a language minority group. The act was extended in 1970 and again in 1982, when its provisions were renewed for an additional twenty-five years.

Southern states challenged the legislation as a dangerous attack on States' rights, but the Supreme Court, in *South Carolina v. Katzenbach*, 383 U.S. 301, 86 S. Ct. 803, 15 L. Ed. 2d 769 (1966), upheld the constitutionality of the act, despite the fact that the law was, in the words of Chief Justice Earl Warren, "inventive."

The initial act covered the seven states in the South that had used poll taxes, literacy tests, and other devices to obstruct registration by African Americans. Under the law, a federal court can appoint federal examiners, who are authorized to place qualified persons on the list of eligible voters. The act waived accumulated poll taxes and abolished literacy tests and similar devices in those areas to which the statute applied.

In addition, the act required the seven states to obtain "preclearance" from the Department of Justice or the U.S. District Court for the District of Columbia before making changes in the electoral system. The 1982 extension of the act revised this provision, extending it to all states. This means that a voter may challenge a voting practice or procedure on the ground that it is racially discriminatory either by intent or by effect.

Motor Voter Laws A state has the right to require bona fide residency as a prerequisite to the exercise of the right to vote in its elections. The courts have also upheld durational residency requirements (how long a person must have resided in the state) for voting. Beginning in the mid-1970s, however, many states began to abandon durational requirements, making it possible for a new resident to register to vote when he applies for a state driver's license. This "motor voter" statute was first enacted in Minnesota (Minn. Stat. Ann. § 201.161 [1992]), and by 1992 twenty-seven states had some form of motor voter law. Congress eliminated durational residency requirements for voting with the passage of the National Voter Registration Act of 1993 (42 U.S.C.A. § 1973gg et seq.). The act allows anyone over the age of eighteen to register to vote while obtaining a driver's license.

Apportionment Guaranteeing an individual the right to vote does not necessarily mean that the voters in a particular district have the same voting strength as voters in another district. Since the 1960s, however, the implementation of the concept of One Person, One Vote has meant that unreasonable disparities in voting strength have been eliminated. Nevertheless, racially discriminatory dilutions of voting strength have led the federal courts to become intimately involved in the drawing of election districts.

One Person, One Vote The Supreme Court, in *Reynolds v. Sims*, 377 U.S. 533, 84 S. Ct. 1362, 12 L. Ed. 2d 506 (1964), established the principle of "one person, one vote" based on the Equal Protection Clause of the Fourteenth Amendment. The decision resulted in almost every state's redrawing its legislative districts and in the shifting of power from rural to urban areas. All subsequent constitutional law on Apportionment has relied on the principles established in *Reynolds*.

Until the *Reynolds* decision, most state legislatures gave more seats to sparsely populated rural areas than to heavily populated urban areas. Because rural legislators controlled the legislature and had a vested interest in perpetuating this apportionment scheme, legislative change had proved impossible. In *Reynolds* the Supreme Court concluded that to permit the minority to have power over the majority would be a violation of the Equal Protection Clause. The dilution of the weight of a person's vote because of where that person lives qualified as invidious discrimination, just as if the decision had been based on that person's race or financial status. Therefore, the Court required that "each citizen have an equally effective voice in the election of members of his state legislature."

Rock the Vote and Motor Voter

The campaign to pass the National Voter Registration Act (NVRA) of 1993 (42 U.S.C.A. § 1973gg et seq.), popularly known as the "motor-voter" law, was led by the Motor Voter Coalition, an umbrella organization of nonpartisan groups. Some of the organizations that participated, such as the League of Women Voters and the National Association for the Advancement of Colored People (NAACP), had a long history of promoting voting rights. Many secretaries of state, the state officials who administer elections, also supported the NVRA.

The most publicity, however, was attracted by the Rock the Vote organization. Rock the Vote is a nonpartisan group based in Los Angeles, California, that is funded primarily by contributions from the popular music industry. Rock the Vote was established in 1990 to fight music censorship and promote the First Amendment through the registration of voters between the ages of eighteen and twenty-four. Soon, however, Rock the Vote became a vocal supporter of the motor-voter bill, which simplifies voter registration and relaxes residency requirements.

Rock the Vote enlisted the help of many famous popular singers, rock bands, and rap artists to encourage the passage of the motor-voter bill. The rock group R.E.M. even included a postcard with one of its recordings that could be sent by a listener to Congress in support of the bill. President Bill Clinton, who benefited from Rock the Vote's 1992 drive to register young voters, acknowledged the organization's efforts at the bill-signing ceremony on May 20, 1993.

Racially Discriminatory Apportionment The Voting Rights Act of 1965 gave the courts the right to review racially discriminatory election districts. The federal courts have struck down at-large elections, in which a number of officials are chosen to represent the district, as opposed to an arrangement under which each of the officials represents one smaller district or ward. Southern cities where whites were in the majority used the at-large election system to perpetuate all-white rule. Courts have required the creation of smaller wards or districts that give African Americans and other protected groups a reasonable opportunity to elect a person of color to city council.

Racial Gerrymandering The courts have also tackled the issue of racial gerrymandering, which is the intentional manipulation of legislative districts for political purposes. In these cases districts have been drawn in bizarre shapes to include or exclude voters of a particular race.

In the first cases white politicians gerrymandered districts to prevent African Americans from having enough voting strength to elect a person of color. In the 1990s the debate moved to the legitimacy of creating, under the authority of the Voting Rights Act of 1965, unusually shaped congressional districts that contained a majority of minority voters to elect a person of color. The Supreme Court, in *Shaw v. Hunt,* __U.S.__, 116 S. Ct. 1894, 135 L. Ed. 2d 207 (1996), ruled that the redrawing of a North Carolina congressional district into a "bizarre-looking" shape so as to include a majority of African Americans could not be justified by the Voting Rights Act of 1965, because it violated the Equal Protection Clause of the Fourteenth Amendment. Justice Sandra Day O'Connor found it "unsettling how closely the North Carolina plan resembles the most egregious racial gerrymandering of the past." O'Connor agreed that prior cases had never made race-conscious redistricting "impermissible in all circumstances," yet agreed with the white plaintiffs that the redistricting was "so extremely irregular on its face that it rationally can be viewed only as an effort to segregate races for purposes of voting, without regard for traditional districting principles and without sufficiently compelling justification."

Voting Procedures The passage of the federal motor voter law eliminated restrictive voter registration requirements. A person may now register when applying for a state driver's license. In addition, a person may register at the polling place in her voting district by showing a state driver's license and having two witnesses vouch for her. Persons who will not be able to vote at a polling place on election day may apply for an absentee ballot and vote ahead of time. These ballots are not opened until after the polls close on election day.

Since 1884 the United States has used the secret ballot. Originally paper ballots were used, but in many areas of the United States mechanical voting machines are employed. Voting systems are also in place in which a machine optically scans a paper ballot and tabulates the votes for each office. Enhanced technology has allowed quicker reporting of results and fewer arithmetical errors. Nevertheless, candidates may ask for a recount of the ballots, and in circumstances where the vote is very close or where FRAUD is alleged, each ballot is examined for accuracy and compliance with the law.

Generally the results of each election race are reported to a local board, which certifies the result to the state's secretary of state. The secretary, in turn, reviews the results and issues an official certificate of election to the successful candidate.

CROSS REFERENCES

Baker v. Carr; Civil Rights; Democratic Party; Equal Protection; Gerrymander; Independent Parties; Republican Party; *Reynolds v. Sims*; Women's Rights.

VOTING RIGHTS ACT OF 1965 ▨ An enactment by Congress in 1965 (42 U.S.C.A. § 1973 et seq.) that prohibits the states and their political subdivisions from imposing VOTING qualifications or prerequisites to voting, or standards, practices, or procedures that deny or curtail the right of a U.S. citizen to vote because of race, color, or membership in a language minority group. ▨

The Voting Rights Act of 1965 is a sweeping federal law that seeks to prevent voting discrimination based on race, color, or membership in a language minority group. A product of the CIVIL RIGHTS MOVEMENT of the 1960s, the Voting Rights Act has proven to be an effective, but controversial, piece of legislation. The act was extended in 1970 and again in 1982, when its provisions were renewed for an additional twenty-five years.

In the early 1960s very few African Americans in the South were allowed to vote. Southern states used literacy tests and physical and economic coercion to prevent African Americans from registering to vote. The state legal system supported these practices, leaving African Americans and other minority groups with few options to challenge voting discrimination. CIVIL RIGHTS leaders organized public protests and voter registration drives, but met intense resistance from local authorities.

A 1965 march to Selma, Alabama, by Dr. MARTIN LUTHER KING, JR., and other civil rights supporters to demand voting rights led to police violence and the murder of several marchers. The Selma violence galvanized voting rights supporters in Congress. President LYNDON B. JOHNSON responded by introducing the Voting Rights Act, the toughest civil rights law in one hundred years. Congress enacted the measure five months later.

Congress based its authority to regulate voting practices on the FIFTEENTH AMENDMENT to the U.S. Constitution, which gives all citizens the right to vote regardless of race, color, or previous condition of servitude. The passage of the act ended the traditional practice of allowing states to handle all matters concerning voting and ELECTIONS. The Voting Rights Act is premised on the active participation of the U.S. Department of Justice and the FEDERAL COURTS. Southern states challenged the legislation as a dangerous attack on STATES' RIGHTS, but the U.S. Supreme Court, in *South Carolina v. Katzenbach*, 383 U.S. 301, 86 S. Ct. 803, 15 L. Ed. 2d 769 (1966), upheld the constitutionality of the act, despite the fact that the law was, in the words of Chief Justice EARL WARREN, "inventive."

The original act was directed at seven southern states—Alabama, Georgia, Louisiana, Mississippi, North Carolina, South Carolina, and Virginia—which had used POLL TAXES, literacy tests, and other devices to obstruct registration by African Americans.

Under the law, a federal court can appoint federal examiners, who are authorized to place qualified persons on the list of eligible voters. The act waived accumulated poll taxes and abolished literacy tests and similar devices in those areas to which the statute applied. It required that bilingual election materials be made available in areas where more than five percent of the citizens are members of a single-language minority.

The act also required the seven states to obtain "preclearance" from the Department of Justice or the U.S. District Court for the District of Columbia before making changes in the electoral system. The state has the burden of proving that the proposed changes do not have the purpose or effect of "denying or abridging the right to vote on account of race or color." The Supreme Court has liberally construed this provision to require approval of even inconsequential alterations. As a result, relocation of polling sites, changes in ballot forms, reapportionment of election districts, municipal annexations, and revision of rules pertaining to the qualifications of candidates and the appointive or elective nature of the office fall within the ambit of federal supervision. If a modification of the election law, such as redistricting, has the purpose or effect of denying or curtailing the right to vote on the basis of race, it may be held to violate the Voting Rights Act. The 1982 extension of the act revised this provision, extending it to all states. This means that a voter may challenge a voting practice or procedure

A sample voting
trust agreement

VOTING TRUST AGREEMENT
With Respect to
COMMON SHARES,
Par Value $_____ per share
of

_____
CORPORATION

_____
Dated _____ , 19____ .

VOTING TRUST AGREEMENT

THIS AGREEMENT, dated _____ , 19____ , by and between _____ , _____ ,
and _____ , and their successors as Voting Trustees hereunder (hereinafter called the
Voting Trustees); certain holders of Common Shares of _____ Corporation, a New
York corporation (hereinafter sometimes called the Corporation), listed on Schedule A at-
tached hereto, and the successive holders of Voting Trust Certificates issued hereunder; and
_____ Corporation;

WHEREAS the Corporation has entered into an agreement with _____ as the
attorney-in-fact under powers of attorney for himself and all other holders of record of all
the outstanding Common Shares of _____ , Inc., a New York corporation (hereinafter
called _____ , Inc.,) providing for the sale by such holders to the Corporation of the
shares of Common Shares of _____ , Inc., held by them in exchange for shares of
Common Shares, par value _____ ($_____) Dollars per share (hereinafter called
Common Shares) of the Corporation; and

WHEREAS the former shareholders of shares listed in Schedule A attached hereto (hereinafter sometimes for convenience called Depositing Shareholders), now following the consummation of such sale, own at least the number of shares of Common Shares set forth opposite their respective names on Schedule A; and

WHEREAS it is deemed for the best interests of the Corporation and its shareholders that
the voting power of the Common Shares to be held by the Depositing Shareholders be
vested in the Voting Trustees to the extent and upon the terms and conditions stated herein;

NOW, THEREFORE, the parties hereto agree as follows:

I. [Certain Definitions.] The term "Common Shares" shall mean the Common Shares
of _____ Corporation as of the date of this Agreement and any other shares of
_____ Corporation or any successor corporation at any time outstanding having general
voting power.

II. [Agreements by Depositing Shareholders.] Each Depositing Shareholder simultaneously with the execution of this Agreement will deliver to the Voting Trustees certificates
representing the number of shares of Common Shares of the Corporation set forth opposite
his name on Schedule A, duly endorsed by him or on his behalf in blank for transfer to the
Voting Trustees or accompanied by proper instruments duly executed by him or on his behalf in blank for transfer thereof to the Voting Trustees, and shall do all things necessary for
the transfer of their respective shares to the trustees on the books of the said company, and
accepts in exchange therefor Voting Trust Certificates substantially in the form attached as
Exhibit I hereto.

Each Depositing Shareholder represents to the Corporation and to the Voting Trustees
that the Voting Trust Certificates issued to him hereunder are being acquired by him for the
purpose of investment and not with a view to or in connection with any distribution thereof.

[Portions omitted for purpose of illustration.]

[continued on page 256]

on the ground that it is racially discriminatory
either by intent or by effect.

The most controversial issue for the courts
has been whether voting districts can be re-
drawn to facilitate the election of racial minorities. The lower federal courts had approved
such reapportionment plans, but the Supreme
Court dealt a severe blow to these attempts in
Shaw v. Hunt, __U.S.__, 116 S. Ct. 1894, 135
L. Ed. 2d 207 (1996). In *Shaw* the Court ruled
that the redrawing of a North Carolina congressional district into a "bizarre-looking"

A sample voting trust agreement (continued)

IN WITNESS WHEREOF, _____ , _____ , and _____ have executed this Agreement as Voting Trustees; and the holders of Common Shares of _____ Corporation listed on Schedule A have signed the same personally or by their attorney-in-fact, and _____ Corporation has caused this Agreement to be signed by its President or one of its Vice-Presidents and its corporate seal to be affixed hereto and the same to be attested by the signature of its Secretary or an Assistant Secretary, all as of the day and year first above written.

_____

_____

_____
As Voting Trustees
The Depositing Shareholders Listed on Schedule A Attached Hereto
by _____

_____ Corporation
By _____ President

[*Corporate Seal*]
Attest:

_____
Secretary

shape so as to include a majority of African Americans could not be justified by the Voting Rights Act, because it violated the Equal Protection Clause of the FOURTEENTH AMENDMENT.

The Voting Rights Act has proven effective in breaking down discriminatory barriers to voting. Enforcement of the act in the South resulted in substantially higher levels of voter registration among African Americans. Many politicians who formerly made overt appeals to white supremacy tempered their racist rhetoric to draw support from new black voters. In addition, many African Americans have been elected to public office in areas where whites had ruled exclusively.

See also EQUAL PROTECTION; GERRYMANDER.

VOTING TRUST A type of agreement by which two or more individuals who own corporate STOCK that carries voting rights transfer their shares to another party for voting purposes, so as to control corporate affairs.

A voting trust is created by an agreement between a group of stockholders and the TRUSTEE to whom they transfer their voting rights or by a group of identical agreements between individual shareholders and a common trustee. Such agreements ordinarily provide that control of stock is given to the trustee for a term of years, for a time period contingent upon a certain event, or until the termination of the agreement. Voting trust agreements may provide that the stockholders can direct how the stock is to be voted.

VOUCHEE Under a procedure in COMMON LAW, a person from whom a defendant will seek INDEMNITY if a plaintiff is successful in his or her ACTION against the defendant.

VOUCHER A receipt or release which provides EVIDENCE of payment or other DISCHARGE of a DEBT, often for purposes of reimbursement, or attests to the accuracy of the accounts.

Government or corporate employees usually submit vouchers to their employers to recover living expenses they have paid while on business trips.

VOUCHING-IN A procedural device used in COMMON LAW by which a defendant notifies another, not presently a party to a lawsuit, that if a plaintiff is successful, the defendant will seek INDEMNITY from that individual.

The notice that an individual, the vouchee, receives as a result of vouching-in constitutes an OFFER for him or her to defend in the ACTION against the defendant. If the vouchee refuses to do so, he or she will be bound in any later actions between the plaintiff and the defendant involving factual determinations necessary to the original judgment.

Although vouching-in has been largely replaced by third-party practice, called impleader, under Rule 14 of the Federal Rules of Civil Procedure, it has not been abolished.

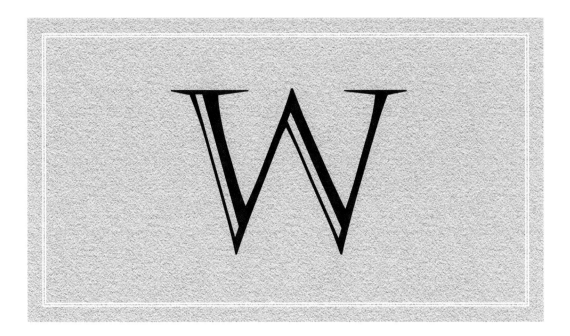

WADSET 📖 In Scotland, the ancient term for a MORTGAGE. 📖

A wadset is a right by which lands or other property are pledged by their owner to a CREDITOR in SECURITY for a DEBT. It is usually in the form of a mutual contract, in which one party sells the land and the other grants the right of REVERSION.

WAGE ASSIGNMENT 📖 The voluntary transfer in advance of a debtor's pay, generally in connection with a particular DEBT or JUDGMENT. 📖

A DEBTOR may negotiate with a CREDITOR a wage assignment plan in which a portion of the debtor's paycheck is transferred to the creditor by the employer. This voluntary agreement is in contrast to *garnishment*, in which a creditor obtains an order from the court to collect part of a debtor's wages from the employer. Both wage assignments and GARNISHMENT are governed by statutes in most states.

A wage assignment is similar to an ASSIGNMENT FOR BENEFIT OF CREDITORS, in which the debtor assigns PERSONAL PROPERTY to a TRUSTEE. Typically, the trustee sells the property and applies the proceeds to the debt. Any amount in excess of the debt is returned to the debtor.

Since the 1980s wage assignments have become an important method of making CHILD SUPPORT payments in the United States. In 1984 the federal government required all states to implement child support guidelines for WELFARE recipients. As time passed, those guidelines were implemented across the board in all cases involving child support. While a wage assignment has typically been viewed as a voluntary act by the assignee, courts now issue wage assignment orders directing employers to withhold child support payments and send the funds to a designated recipient such as a custodial parent, the court, or a state agency.

Although the paying parent may be a responsible individual who would never miss a payment, and the recipient parent may honestly report all payments received, the wage assignment eliminates potential conflict by using a neutral third party to implement the paying and reporting of payments. Employers generally do not impute bad character to an employee paying child support through a wage assignment, and the courts routinely issue orders without finding fault. Wage assignment orders are appropriate for salaried employees but do not work effectively for self-employed individuals or people in cash businesses.

A wage assignment may also be used when an employee obtains a loan from his employer and wants to repay the loan by having the employer withhold money from future paychecks. An employer who lends an employee a sum of money cannot take it out of the employee's next paycheck without a proper, written, notarized assignment from the employee. State statutes require that legal formalities be followed, or the withholding of money can be considered an unlawful assignment of wages.

WAGE EARNER'S PLAN 📖 A form of BANKRUPTCY under a former federal law whereby an individual retained her property and paid off a DEBT over a period of time, as determined by a court and subject to supervision by the court. 📖

Under Chapter Thirteen of the federal bankruptcy statutes (11 U.S.C.A. § 1301 et seq.), individuals who are unable to repay their debts when due may develop a plan for full or partial repayment. This procedure was formerly called a wage earner's plan because it was available only to persons who earned a regular wage. Changes in the statute now permit the owners of unincorporated small businesses to participate in this procedure, which is now known as either a Chapter Thirteen proceeding or a rehabilitation. A REHABILITATION process enables the debtor to regain good credit and financial standing.

To qualify, an individual must have unsecured debts (those not backed by COLLATERAL to guarantee their repayment) of less than $100,000 and secured debts (backed by collateral) of less than $350,000. A debtor files a Chapter Thirteen petition listing all of his debts. Upon the filing, the debtor's CREDITORS must suspend their efforts to collect or enforce their claims, pending the outcome of the proceeding.

The debtor has the exclusive right to propose a plan for repayment to the bankruptcy court. No matter how many creditors may exist, they cannot force a plan upon the debtor. A Chapter Thirteen petition might include a repayment plan that lasts five years and lists wage earnings and the sale of a portion of the debtor's property as sources for the repayment. The plan, which is overseen by a bankruptcy TRUSTEE, must treat all creditors who have comparable claims equally. The repayment plan may cntail paying off only a portion of each debt, which is called a composition; receiving extra time to pay the debts, called an extension; or both. See also COMPOSITION WITH CREDITORS.

The debtor's plan can be approved only by the court, unlike a Chapter Eleven reorganization plan, which requires both acceptance by the creditors and confirmation by the court. After the debtor has completed payments pursuant to the plan, she is discharged from LIABILITY. A Chapter Thirteen plan does not, however, relieve a debtor from liability for ALIMONY and CHILD SUPPORT, federal student loans, and taxes.

WAGER OF BATTEL 📖 A type of trial by combat between accuser and accused that was introduced into England by William the Conqueror (King William I) and his Norman followers after the Norman Conquest of 1066. 📖

Wager of battel was founded on the belief that God would give victory to the party who was in the right. The kings maintained control over the practice, and it came to be reserved for cases affecting royal interests, such as serious criminal cases or disputes over land.

King William and his successors had distributed much land to their loyal supporters, but a century after the conquest it was impossible to produce witnesses who had seen the symbolic delivery of a clod of dirt or a twig representing title to the land. A party could, therefore, hire someone, a champion, to swear that the champion's father had told him on his deathbed that the party was the true owner of the land. The other party also produced a champion who swore just the opposite. The defendant's champion came forward and threw down his glove as a pledge. The plaintiff's champion accepted the challenge by picking up the glove, and the two waged battle or set a time to do so. The winner was held to have good TITLE to the land. It was said that many monasteries, which owned vast tracts of land, had virtual stables of champions in waiting to settle disputes that might arise.

In the early twelfth century King Henry I specifically recognized the right to defend by BATTEL, but the party accused might elect wager of battel or trial by JURY. If he chose the wager of battel, he answered the charge before the court by saying that he would be tried by God; if he chose a trial by jury, his plea was that he would be tried by the country. The last demand for wager of battel occurred in 1818. The practice was abolished by statute during the reign of George III (1760-1820).

See also FEUDALISM.

WAGER OF LAW 📖 A procedure for defending oneself that could be used in a trial before one of the ancient courts of England. 📖

A defendant who elected to "make his law" was permitted to make a statement before the tribunal, swear an OATH that it was true, and present one or more individuals who swore that they believed he had told the truth under oath. This was the predominant form of defense in the feudal courts, and it persisted for a time in the COMMON-LAW COURTS.

It had originated in Anglo-Saxon England in the ties of kinship that bound people together in the period before the year 1000, a time when each man was responsible for the acts of his blood relatives. Later, kinship gave way to a more tribal affiliation and a loyalty to the place of one's birth. When disputes more often than not led to violence, it seemed natural that neighbors would band together. They aligned themselves with a neighbor who was accused in court and swore that in good conscience they believed he was telling the truth. The number of oath-helpers required depended on the defendant's rank and the character of the lawsuit. Eventually it became standard practice to bring eleven neighbors into court to swear for the defendant. The oathhelpers were called COMPURGATORS, and the wager of law was called *compurgation*.

As the kings consolidated their power, suppressing violence and increasing the authority of the courts, the wager of law lost some of its ancient power and became a nuisance to litigants, who suspected that it frequently opened the door to false swearing. Different FORMS OF ACTION developed that did not permit the wager of law as a defense, and plaintiffs used them as much as possible. The procedure of wager of law had long since been obsolete when it was abolished during the reign of Henry IV (1399-1413).

See also FEUDALISM; HENRY II OF ENGLAND.

WAGNER, ROBERT FERDINAND

Robert Ferdinand Wagner served as a U.S. senator from New York from 1927 to 1949. Wagner was a strong believer in the social welfare state and sponsored many federal laws that have shaped U.S. law and society. In the 1930s he worked closely with President FRANKLIN D. ROOSEVELT and helped to implement much of Roosevelt's NEW DEAL agenda.

Wagner was born on June 8, 1877, in Nastätten, Germany. With his family he immigrated to the United States in 1885, settling in a New York City tenement neighborhood. He graduated from City College in New York in 1898 and studied law at New York Law School, where he earned his degree in 1900.

Wagner was admitted to the New York bar in 1900 and practiced law on his own for a short time. He then abandoned his law practice to enter Democratic party politics. Wagner worked his way up the party ladder and won a seat in the state legislature in 1904. In 1908 he was elected to the New York Senate, where he soon established himself as a socially progressive leader, investigating industrial working conditions and introducing legislation that sought to use the power of government to improve the lives of blue-collar workers and the poor.

Wagner became a judge of the New York Supreme Court in 1919 but resigned in 1926 to run as the Democratic party candidate for the U.S. Senate. He won the election and took office in 1927 during the heyday of the "Roar-

BIOGRAPHY

LIBRARY OF CONGRESS

Robert Ferdinand Wagner

"IT IS SIMPLY ABSURD TO SAY THAT AN INDIVIDUAL, ONE OF 10,000 WORKERS, IS ON AN EQUALITY WITH HIS EMPLOYER IN BARGAINING FOR HIS WAGES."

ing Twenties." The U.S. economy was at its postwar zenith, and the Republican party controlled Congress. Wagner introduced legislation to help organized labor and the unemployed, but his proposals were unsuccessful.

Wagner's political fortunes changed dramatically with the Great Depression of the 1930s and the election of President Roosevelt in 1932. Like Wagner, Roosevelt believed that the federal government needed to play a larger role in the activities of the national economy and in the lives of U.S. citizens. Wagner helped draft and sponsor the NATIONAL INDUSTRIAL RECOVERY ACT (NIRA) of 1933 (48 Stat. 195), which established the NATIONAL RECOVERY ADMINISTRATION to administer codes of fair practice within each industry. Under these codes, labor and management negotiated MINIMUM WAGES, maximum hours, and fair trade practices for each industry. The Roosevelt administration sought to use these codes to stabilize production, raise prices, and protect labor and consumers. In *Schecter Poultry Corp. v. United States*, 295 U.S. 495, 55 S. Ct. 837, 79 L. Ed. 1570 (1935), however, the U.S. Supreme Court invalidated the NIRA.

Wagner also sponsored the SOCIAL SECURITY ACT (42 U.S.C.A. § 301 et seq.), the bedrock of U.S. social welfare law. He is best remembered for the WAGNER ACT, also known as the National Labor Relations Act of 1935 (29 U.S.C.A. § 151 et seq.). The Wagner Act recognized for the first time the right of workers to organize unions and to collectively bargain with employers. The statute also established the National Labor Relations Board to enforce labor-management relations in the United States.

Wagner sponsored numerous New Deal programs, including the Civilian Conservation Corps, the Federal Emergency Relief Administration, and the U.S. Housing Authority, which provided loans for low-cost public housing. When World War II began, the country's attention shifted to international issues, and Wagner's social welfare agenda fell out of favor. He lobbied unsuccessfully for a national health care system and for antilynching legislation.

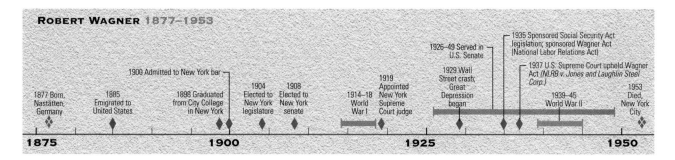

ROBERT WAGNER 1877–1953

1877 Born, Nastätten, Germany

1885 Emigrated to United States

1898 Graduated from City College in New York

1900 Admitted to New York bar

1904 Elected to New York legislature

1908 Elected to New York senate

1914–18 World War I

1919 Appointed New York Supreme Court judge

1926–49 Served in U.S. Senate

1929 Wall Street crash; Great Depression began

1935 Sponsored Social Security Act legislation; sponsored Wagner Act (National Labor Relations Act)

1937 U.S. Supreme Court upheld Wagner Act (NLRB v. Jones and Laughlin Steel Corp.)

1939–45 World War II

1953 Died, New York City

1875   1900   1925   1950

Wagner resigned from the Senate for health reasons in 1949. He died on May 5, 1953, in New York City. In 1954 his son, Robert F. Wagner, Jr., was elected mayor of New York City and served until 1965.

WAGNER ACT The Wagner Act, also known as the NATIONAL LABOR RELATIONS ACT of 1935 (29 U.S.C.A. § 151 et seq.), is the most important piece of labor legislation enacted in U.S. history. It made the federal government the arbiter of employer-employee relations through the creation of the National Labor Relations Board (NLRB) and recognized for the first time the right of workers to organize and bargain collectively with their employers. The act overturned decades of court decisions that asserted that LABOR UNIONS violated an employee's liberty of contract.

Senator ROBERT F. WAGNER, a Democrat from New York, introduced the legislation in 1935, when the United States was in the midst of the Great Depression. President FRANKLIN D. ROOSEVELT initially opposed the legislation out of fear that labor organizing might interfere with economic recovery, but gave his support when passage became inevitable.

Congress based its right to pass national labor-management legislation on the U.S. Constitution's COMMERCE CLAUSE. The act states that unequal bargaining power between employees and employers leads to economic instability, whereas the refusal of employers to recognize the right to bargain collectively leads to strikes. Because these disturbances impede the flow of interstate commerce, Congress may take steps to continue the free flow of commerce by encouraging COLLECTIVE BARGAINING and unionizing.

The Wagner Act established the rights of employees to organize, join, or aid labor unions and to participate in collective bargaining through their representatives. The act also authorized unions to take "concerted action" for these purposes. This meant that workers could lawfully STRIKE and take other peaceful action as a way of placing pressure on an employer. This provision was coupled with another that prohibited employers from engaging in UNFAIR LABOR PRACTICES that interfere with the union rights of employees. Unfair labor practices include prohibiting employees from joining unions, firing employees because of their union membership, or establishing a company-dominated union. In addition to requiring employers to bargain collectively with the union duly selected by the employees, the act set up procedures for establishing appropriate bargaining units (homogeneous groups of employees) where employees can elect a BARGAINING AGENT (a representative for labor negotiations) by a secret ballot.

The act also created the NLRB, a federal ADMINISTRATIVE AGENCY, to administer and enforce its unfair labor practice and representation provisions. The NLRB hears cases involving unfair labor practices and makes decisions that the federal courts of appeals may review.

At the time of its enactment, some observers doubted that the Wagner Act would be found constitutional by the U.S. Supreme Court. The Court had struck down numerous New Deal statutes on the basis that business and labor laws were matters that should be left to the marketplace or to state legislatures. In *NLRB v. Jones & Laughlin Steel Corp.*, 301 U.S. 1, 57 S. Ct. 615, 81 L. Ed. 893 (1937), however, the Court reversed course and held that the Wagner Act was constitutional.

The Wagner Act was one of the most dramatic legislative measures of the New Deal. Not only did the legislation indicate that the federal government was prepared to move against employers to enforce the rights of labor to unionize and to bargain collectively, but it imposed no reciprocal obligations on unions.

The law was amended by the TAFT-HARTLEY ACT of 1947, also known as the Labor Management Relations Act (29 U.S.C.A. § 141 et seq.), which balanced some of the advantages given to unions under the Wagner Act by imposing corresponding duties upon unions to deal fairly with management. The act was further modified by the LANDRUM-GRIFFIN ACT of 1959 (29 U.S.C.A. § 401 et seq.), which sought to end abuses of power by union officials in handling union funds and internal affairs. See also LABOR LAW.

WAIT-AND-SEE DOCTRINE 📖 A rule that permits consideration of events occurring subsequent to the inception of an instrument that pertains to the vesting of a future interest. If the specified contingency on which the creation of the interest depends actually occurs within the period of the RULE AGAINST PERPETUITIES, the interest is legally enforceable. 📖

Under the COMMON LAW, the Rule Against Perpetuities provides that no interest in property is valid unless it becomes fixed, if at all, not later than twenty-one years, plus the period of gestation, after some life or lives in being at the time of the creation of the interest. The period of gestation is included to cover cases of posthumous birth. A property interest vests when it is given to a person in being, and when the interest is not subject to a condition precedent. The courts developed the Rule Against Perpetuities during the seventeenth century in order to restrict a person's power to control the ownership and possession of his or her property after his or her death, and to ensure the transferability of property.

In order to mitigate the harshness of the Rule Against Perpetuities, some states have embodied the wait-and-see doctrine in statutes. The general concept of wait-and-see is that a perpetuity violation should occur only if an interest actually fails to VEST within the perpetuity period. In contrast to the traditional view, which prescribes that the situation is examined as it exists when the interests are created, thereby invalidating the interests if a possibility exists that they will fail to vest in due time, one must wait and see whether, in fact, the possibility turns out to be an actuality.

The wait-and-see doctrine is also deemed to be an extension of the SECOND LOOK DOCTRINE.

See also ESTATE.

WAITE, MORRISON REMICK

Morrison Remick Waite served as chief justice of the United States from 1874 to 1888. Waite's rise to national prominence came unexpectedly. Although a distinguished lawyer in Ohio, he had never argued before the Supreme Court. Nevertheless, in 1871 he was asked to represent the United States in post–Civil War claims against Great Britain, and his success brought him widespread acclaim. On the strength of this reputation, President ULYSSES S. GRANT nominated Waite to lead the U.S. Supreme Court. His performance there, however, never won him the same praise. Waite's business decisions provoked the ire of powerful interests, and twentieth-century critics have condemned his limited view of CIVIL RIGHTS.

Born on November 29, 1816, in Lyme, Connecticut, Waite was the son of a successful attorney and jurist who was the state court's chief justice. Educated at Yale University, Waite graduated in 1837, studied law under his father, and then was admitted to the Ohio bar in 1839. Over the next decade, he split his time between legal practice and politics. He was elected to the Ohio legislature in 1849 as a member of the Whig party, and later helped to form the state's branch of the Republican party.

By the late 1800s, Waite was quite successful.

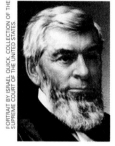

Morrison Remick Waite

"FOR PROTECTION AGAINST ABUSERS BY LEGISLATURES THE PEOPLE MUST RESORT TO THE POLLS, NOT TO THE COURTS."

He had built two law firms and enjoyed prominence within Ohio. Yet because he had no significant national reputation, he was surprised when, in 1871, he was chosen for a task of national importance: representing the United States in its post–Civil War arbitration with Great Britain, better known as the *Alabama* claims. The United States charged that Great Britain had aided the Confederacy by supplying warships during the Civil War, and it sought to recover damages at the 1871 Geneva Arbitration Council. Waite and his two colleagues succeeded spectacularly, winning a $15 million settlement. At home, they were showered with acclaim. Two years later, Waite added to his growing reputation by serving as president of the Ohio Constitutional Convention.

Upon the sudden death of Chief Justice SALMON P. CHASE, President Grant looked unsuccessfully for a replacement before turning to Waite. Grant's administration had not fared well; choosing one of the heroes of the Geneva victory appeared fortuitous. Although Waite had no experience before the Supreme Court, he accepted the appointment and overcame long odds against success. His status as an outsider and the presence of a strong-minded group of associate justices did not deter him from administering the Court effectively.

In outlook, Waite was a supporter of STATES' RIGHTS. He usually favored state power to regulate business and determine civil rights. Yet both in his time and afterward, his decisions have drawn condemnation. In *Munn v. Illinois*, 94 U.S. 113, 24 L. Ed. 77 (1876), he upheld an Illinois law that imposed charges on the owners of grain elevators, asserting that such regulation was proper in areas "affected with a public interest." This position provoked fierce criticism from powerful business interests. Waite's reputation also suffered posthumously in the wake of the twentieth century's embrace of civil rights. His decision in *Minor v. Happersett*, 88 U.S. (21 Wall.) 162, 22 L. Ed. 627 (1874), allowed states to deny women the right to vote. Waite held that voting privileges were a right of U.S. citizenship and stated that the FOURTEENTH AMENDMENT to the U.S. Constitution did not confer additional

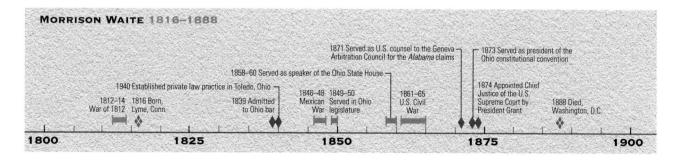

MORRISON WAITE 1816–1888

1871 Served as U.S. counsel to the Geneva Arbitration Council for the *Alabama* claims

1873 Served as president of the Ohio constitutional convention

1858–60 Served as speaker of the Ohio State House

1940 Established private law practice in Toledo, Ohio

1874 Appointed Chief Justice of the U.S. Supreme Court by President Grant

1812–14 War of 1812

1816 Born, Lyme, Conn.

1839 Admitted to Ohio bar

1846–48 Mexican War

1849–50 Served in Ohio legislature

1861–65 U.S. Civil War

1888 Died, Washington, D.C.

1800   1825   1850   1875   1900

PRIVILEGES AND IMMUNITIES upon citizens.

In *United States v. Cruikshank*, 92 U.S. 542, 23 L. Ed. 588 (1875), Waite set aside the convictions of white men who had taken part in the killing of more than one hundred black men in the 1873 Colfax Massacre, which followed a disputed election. Always concerned about the encroachment of federal power, Waite ruled that their INDICTMENT under federal law was faulty; such cases, he said, belonged in state courts. But state courts in the post–Civil War South were unlikely to prosecute such cases, and rather than leading to prosecutions, the decision only encouraged more bloodshed while dealing a blow to Congress's plan for Reconstruction in the South.

In appraising Waite's jurisprudence, twentieth-century critics have been harsh. They have criticized his narrow interpretation of the Fourteenth Amendment as a repudiation of the intent of the amendment's framers. In defense, some observers have noted his valuation of state power to regulate the economy. He died on March 23, 1888, in Washington, D.C.

WAIVE 📖 To intentionally or voluntarily relinquish a known right or engage in conduct warranting an inference that a right has been surrendered. 📖

For example, an individual is said to waive the right to bring a TORT action when he or she renounces the REMEDY provided by law for such a wrong.

WAIVER 📖 The voluntary surrender of a known right; conduct supporting an inference that a particular right has been relinquished. 📖

The term *waiver* is used in many legal contexts. A waiver is essentially a unilateral act of one person that results in the surrender of a legal right. The legal right may be constitutional, statutory, or contractual, but the key issue for a court reviewing a claim of waiver is whether the person voluntarily gave up the right. If voluntarily surrendered, it is considered an EXPRESS waiver.

In CRIMINAL LAW the PRIVILEGE AGAINST SELF-INCRIMINATION is guaranteed by the FIFTH AMENDMENT to the U.S. Constitution. The Supreme Court, in *Miranda v. Arizona*, 384 U.S. 436, 86 S. Ct. 1602, 16 L. Ed. 2d 694 (1966), held that the police must inform arrested persons that they need not answer questions and that they may have an attorney present during questioning. These requirements are known as the *Miranda* warning. A criminal defendant may waive the right to remain silent and make a CONFESSION, but the law enforcement officials must demonstrate to the court that the waiver was the product of a free and deliberate choice rather than a decision based on intimidation,

COERCION, or deception. They must also convince the court that the defendant was fully aware of the rights being abandoned and the consequences that would result from the abandonment. Based on the totality of these circumstances, a court may conclude that the defendant waived his *Miranda* rights. See also CUSTODIAL INTERROGATION; MIRANDA V. ARIZONA.

A waiver may be shown by a person's actions. For example, a criminal defendant waives the privilege against self-incrimination merely by going on the WITNESS stand. Such an action is called an IMPLIED waiver.

In INSURANCE law waiver is used in numerous contexts. For example, under the doctrine of waiver, if the insurer has knowledge of facts that would bar its primary LIABILITY for a policy it has written but proceeds to treat the policy as being in force, it will not be allowed to plead such facts in court to avoid its primary liability.

A waiver of PREMIUM clause is a provision in an insurance policy that permits the waiver of premium payments upon the disability of the insured. Commonly such waivers take effect only after a certain time of disability.

Various waiver provisions are inserted into CONTRACTS. The parties may agree to surrender a substantive right granted by statute, such as a limitation on the amount of property that may be exempted from debt collection, or a procedural right that requires a certain number of days notice before an action can be taken.

WAIVING TIME 📖 The process whereby an individual permits a court to take longer than usual in trying him or her on a criminal charge. 📖

WALLACE, GEORGE CORLEY As the governor of Alabama and a presidential aspirant, George Corley Wallace did battle with the CIVIL RIGHTS MOVEMENT and defied federal efforts to desegregate schools in his state. His fight against school integration pitted him against federal courts, troops, and the administration of President JOHN F. KENNEDY in a showdown over federal authority. Only the pressure of the Alabama National Guard, which Kennedy took command of in June 1963, managed to remove Wallace from the door of the University of Alabama, where he stood blocking the admission of two African American students. His schoolhouse stand, as it came to be known, lionized Wallace in the hearts and minds of southerners and helped launch an increasingly successful national political career. While scoring victories in the 1972 Democratic presidential primaries, he was left partially paralyzed by gunshots from a would-be assassin—an incident that precipitated a political metamorphosis in Wallace. Though he failed to gain the presi-

BIOGRAPHY

MICHAEL ABRAMSON/LIAISON

George Corley Wallace

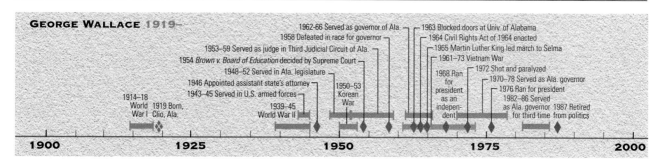

1962-66 Served as governor of Ala.
1958 Defeated in race for governor
1953–59 Served as judge in Third Judicial Circuit of Ala.
1954 *Brown v. Board of Education* decided by Supreme Court
1948–52 Served in Ala. legislature
1946 Appointed assistant state's attorney
1943–45 Served in U.S. armed forces

1963 Blocked doors at Univ. of Alabama
1964 Civil Rights Act of 1964 enacted
1965 Martin Luther King led march to Selma
1961–73 Vietnam War
1972 Shot and paralyzed
1968 Ran for president as an independent
1970–78 Served as Ala. governor
1976 Ran for president
1982–86 Served as Ala. governor
1987 Retired for third time from politics

1914–18 World War I
1919 Born, Clio, Ala.
1939–45 World War II
1950–53 Korean War

1900   1925   1950   1975   2000

dency, he continued to serve the state of Alabama until 1987, when poor health forced him to leave the office after four terms and seventeen-and-a-half years.

Wallace was born August 25, 1919, the first of four children of George Wallace, Sr., and Mozelle Smith Wallace. Only a few hundred people lived in his birthplace, the small town of Clio, Alabama. His father weathered the Depression by leasing land to sharecroppers, although the family never had much money. Wallace was encouraged by his father in two areas: politics and boxing. At the age of fifteen, he became a page in the Alabama state legislature. A good student, athletic and popular, he finished high school as his senior class president. His punch served him well, too, and in 1936 and 1937, he won the Alabama Golden Gloves Championship.

In 1937 Wallace entered the University of Alabama, with only two shirts and the desire to have a career in politics. He took four jobs, finished his degree, and remained at the university to study law. He earned his law degree in 1942, and enlisted in the Army Air Corps for pilot training. Soon after, a near-fatal case of spinal meningitis ended his dreams of being a pilot, but in World War II, he went to the Pacific as a flight engineer on a B-29 bomber called *The Sentimental Education.*

After the war, his political career quickly took off. His first appointment was as state assistant attorney general. Then, in 1946, at the age of twenty-seven, Wallace won election to the Alabama House of Representatives. He soon established a high profile, twice being voted an outstanding member of the house. Wallace sponsored a number of liberal bills. He supported legislation that provided social security for county and municipal employees, created junior colleges and trade schools, and offered free tuition to the widows and children of men who had died at war.

Drawing on his name recognition as a legislator, he ran for a judgeship in 1952, winning election to Alabama's Third Circuit Court.

In 1958 he launched his first gubernatorial campaign. This election would be a turning

"IF ANY DEMONSTRATOR EVER LAYS DOWN IN FRONT OF MY CAR, IT'LL BE THE LAST CAR HE'LL EVER LAY DOWN IN FRONT OF."

point in Wallace's politics. Wallace's chief opponent in the Democratic primary was state attorney general John Patterson. Both candidates favored segregation, but Patterson's campaign had an edge: it was backed by the KU KLUX KLAN. When Wallace lost the election by nearly sixty-five thousand votes, he vowed publicly never again to be "out-segged." After spending four years in private law practice with his brother Gerald, Wallace returned to politics in 1962 to run for governor again. This time, his opponent was former governor James Folsom. Wallace won the election and took office just as the civil rights movement was gaining momentum.

Wallace and other segregationists were determined to keep the civil rights movement out of Alabama. When MARTIN LUTHER KING, JR., and his fellow activists set out to integrate the city of Birmingham in 1963, violence met them repeatedly. Birmingham police officers unleashed water hoses, dogs, and clubs on the demonstrators and then Wallace dispatched the state troopers. Wearing steel helmets painted with Confederate flags, this force entered Birmingham with shotguns to crush the demonstration. Throughout the summer, while Ku Klux Klan members visited the governor's mansion to offer their services, there were bombings and shootings in Wallace's Alabama.

In the same year a federal judge ordered the University of Alabama to allow two black students to enroll. When Wallace vowed to prevent them from entering the university, U.S. attorney general ROBERT F. KENNEDY traveled to Alabama to warn him that the Kennedy administration would enforce the court's decree.

On June 11, 1963, Wallace, having advised citizens of Alabama to stay away from the university, stood at a podium before the school door. Attorney General Kennedy telephoned once more, only to be told that the governor was unavailable. As reporters, photographers, and police officers watched, Wallace held up his hand to prevent Vivian Malone and James Hood from entering. Then he holed himself up inside the school for four hours. Meanwhile, President Kennedy federalized the Alabama

National Guard, which then moved in and forced Wallace to admit the students.

In 1964 Wallace sought the Republican party's presidential nomination. He did well in two early primaries, but the endorsement went to Senator BARRY M. GOLDWATER, of Arizona. Wallace ran again as an independent in 1968, with moderate success, and sought the Democratic nomination four years later. In this race, he swept aside challengers such as George S. McGovern, HUBERT H. HUMPHREY, and John V. Lindsay in the Florida primary. But he would not complete the race.

On May 15, 1972, moments after giving a speech at a Laurel, Maryland, shopping center, Wallace was shot five times. His would-be assassin, Arthur Bremer, was caught, convicted, and sentenced to fifty-three years in prison. The shooting left the governor paralyzed from the waist down. It also began a provocative transformation of identity.

Reelected as governor in 1974, and serving consecutive terms until his retirement in 1986, Wallace gradually retreated from his segregationist views.

When poor health forced Wallace to forego running for a fifth term as governor in 1986, he left a legacy far different from the one suggested by his first term in office. In contrast to the obstinate figure blocking the door to the University of Alabama, he had become a leader recognized for lasting contributions to both blacks and whites. He had appointed several African Americans to important state posts. A statewide junior college system, increased state aid to black universities, support for inner cities, and improved industrial development were all credited to him.

See also INTEGRATION; SCHOOL DESEGREGATION.

WALLACE, JOHN WILLIAM John William Wallace served as REPORTER of decisions for the U.S. Supreme Court from 1863 to 1875. Wallace is noted for being the last reporter to privately publish decisions of the Court and for having his name on the spine of each volume. For example, the citation 87 U.S. (20 Wall.) 590 indicates that the decision is to be found on

"I WAITED IN VAIN TO HEAR THE COMMERCIAL LAW OF MY OWN, FREE, GREAT, COMMERCIAL COUNTRY . . . BECAUSE NO MAN CAN SAY THAT SUCH A SYSTEM EXISTS."

BIOGRAPHY

page 590 of volume 87 of *United States Reports* (the cumulative number of volumes, regardless of the reporter), which is volume 20 of those reports published by Wallace.

Wallace was born on February 17, 1815, in Philadelphia, Pennsylvania. The son of a distinguished Philadelphia lawyer, Wallace graduated from the University of Pennsylvania in 1833. He studied law in his father's office but decided to devote himself to being a law librarian. In 1841 Wallace became the librarian of the Law Association of Philadelphia. He assumed his first reporting task in 1849, when he published the first of three volumes of the opinions of the U.S. Court of Appeals for the Third Circuit.

During the 1840s and early 1850s Wallace concentrated on the scholarly examination of English law reports and reporters. In 1844 he published *The Reporters, Chronologically Arranged: with Occasional Remarks upon their Reporting Merits.* The work was warmly received for its scholarship and commentary and was republished frequently in the nineteenth century. Wallace also provided notes on U.S. cases included in a series of volumes known as the *British Crown Cases Reserved (1839–1853).*

In 1863 Wallace became the seventh reporter of decisions for the Supreme Court, replacing JEREMIAH S. BLACK. Between 1863 and 1875 Wallace published twenty-three volumes of reports, which form volumes 68–90 of *United States Reports.* His volumes were praised for their accuracy and quality of editing.

Wallace resigned in 1875 after Congress appropriated $25,000 to be used for publishing Court decisions. After leaving his position, Wallace wrote many scholarly articles and became president of the Historical Society of Pennsylvania.

Wallace died on January 12, 1884, in Philadelphia.

WANT ◫ The absence or deficiency of what is needed or desired. ◫

Want of jurisdiction, for example, is a lack of authority to exercise in a particular manner a power possessed by a tribunal or board.

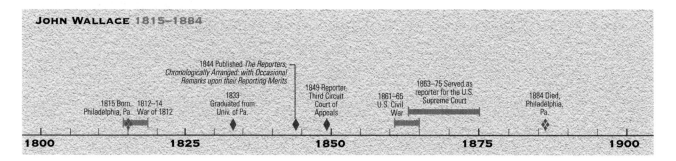

JOHN WALLACE 1815–1884

1844 Published *The Reporters, Chronologically Arranged: with Occasional Remarks upon their Reporting Merits*

1863–75 Served as reporter for the U.S. Supreme Court

1815 Born, Philadelphia, Pa.

1812–14 War of 1812

1833 Graduated from Univ. of Pa.

1849 Reporter, Third Circuit Court of Appeals

1861–65 U.S. Civil War

1884 Died, Philadelphia, Pa.

1800   1825   1850   1875   1900

WANT OF CONSIDERATION 📖 A comprehensive term for all transactions or situations where no inducement to a CONTRACT was intended to pass between the parties thereto and, therefore, no legally enforceable contract is created. 📖

Want of consideration differs from FAILURE OF CONSIDERATION, which refers to a situation wherein CONSIDERATION was originally existing and valid but has since become valueless or ceased to exist.

WANTON 📖 Grossly careless or negligent; reckless; MALICIOUS. 📖

The term *wanton* implies a reckless disregard for the consequences of one's behavior. A *wanton act* is one done in heedless disregard for the life, limbs, health, safety, reputation, or PROPERTY rights of another individual. Such an act is more than NEGLIGENCE or GROSS NEGLIGENCE; it is equivalent in its results to an act of WILLFUL misconduct. A *wanton injury* is one precipitated by a conscious and intentional wrongful act or by an omission of a known obligation with reckless indifference to potential harmful consequences.

WAPENTAKE 📖 A local division of a shire or county in old English law; the term used north of the Trent River for the territory called a HUNDRED in other parts of England. 📖

The name *wapentake* is said to come from *weapon* and *take*, an indication that it referred to an area organized for military purposes.

WAR 📖 Conflicts arising between the armed forces of two or more nations and the methods employed to guard and protect such nations, under the authority of their respective governments. 📖

Under the U.S. Constitution, only the federal government possesses the power to make war. When the United States has gone to war, the courts have allowed the federal government to take extraordinary measures to further the war effort. The great deference shown by the courts during war has led, however, to the suppression of political dissent and other actions that would have been unconstitutional during peacetime.

Declaration and Commencement Only Congress has the power to declare war. The president of the United States, as commander in chief of the U.S. armed forces, does have the power to repel invasions in the absence of any declaration of war by Congress. Subject to this power, the president can order the hostilities to be carried into the invader's own land.

The president's power is illustrated by President ABRAHAM LINCOLN's actions at the beginning of the Civil War. In the ten weeks between

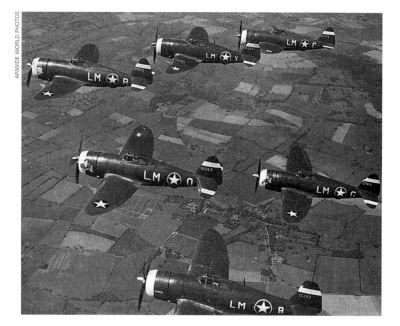

the fall of Fort Sumter and the convening of Congress in July 1861, Lincoln made war preparations based on his authority as commander in chief. He initiated the drafting of men for military service, approved of a Southern naval BLOCKADE, and suspended the WRIT of HABEAS CORPUS. Congress later ratified most of Lincoln's actions.

In the twentieth century several U.S. presidents have committed U.S. armed forces without a declaration of war. President HARRY S. TRUMAN ordered troops to Korea in 1951 as part of a UNITED NATIONS "police action." Presidents LYNDON B. JOHNSON and RICHARD M. NIXON prosecuted the VIETNAM WAR without a congressional declaration. In response Congress passed the WAR POWERS RESOLUTION of 1973 (50 U.S.C.A. § 1541 et seq.), which restricts the president's power to mobilize the military during undeclared war. It requires the president to make a full report to Congress when sending troops into foreign areas, limits the duration of troop commitment without congressional authorization, and provides a veto mechanism that allows Congress to force a recall of troops at any time.

Status and Rights of Citizens During a time of war, the U.S. government may properly compel the services of all its citizens and subjects. It can recall nationals who are abroad and subject them to penalty if they do not obey. The government can take steps it deems necessary for national security against enemy ALIENS. Enemy aliens residing in the United States at the outbreak of a declared war or who enter the United States during a war are properly subject to arrest, detention, internment, or DEPORTATION.

The conduct of war brings dramatic changes to warring countries. This squadron of American Thunderbolt fighter planes executes maneuvers over the English countryside in WWII.

Enemy Intercourse The general rule is that, during a declared war, all intercourse, correspondence, and traffic between U.S. citizens and subjects of enemy states that might be advantageous or provide comfort to the enemy are prohibited. For example, it is illegal to transmit money across enemy lines. In addition, a U.S. citizen cannot lawfully make a contract with a citizen of an enemy state while war exists, and any such contract is, therefore, void. The laws of war proscribe all trading with the enemy and all other commercial relations while a state of war exists.

Requisition of Private Property In times of war, Congress and the president, as commander in chief, have the power to REQUISITION private property necessary for the war effort.

A military commander can seize or requisition a citizen's property for public use or to prevent it from falling into enemy hands. The commander can do this, however, only in situations involving imminent and impending danger or necessity. The services and production of a business organization, such as a shipping company, can properly be requisitioned.

An individual whose private property is requisitioned is entitled to fair compensation. However, the compensation does not have to be paid in advance or at the time the property is seized. When compensation is made, the owner is entitled to receive the reasonable value of the property. The MARKET VALUE of the requisitioned property is generally used as the measure of fair compensation.

Martial Rule Martial rule exists when military authorities exercise varying degrees of control over civilians in territory where, due to war or public commotion, the civil government is not able to maintain order and enforce the law.

War Powers of the U.S. Government The power of the federal government to conduct war extends to every matter and activity that has an effect on its conduct and progress. The war powers embrace every phase of national defense, including the mobilization and use of all resources of the nation and the protection of war materials. Most of these powers have not been used since World War II, because the United States did not fight under a declaration of war while engaged in conflicts in Korea, Vietnam, and the Persian Gulf.

Congress has the authority to stimulate the production of the war equipment and supplies by all proper methods, including the payment of subsidies or the imposition of limits on profits.

Congress can control the food supply during war to ensure that military and civilian needs are met. Other materials may be rationed as well, including gasoline. Congress also can regulate and control prices as a wartime emergency measure to prevent inflation. Price controls are designated to stabilize economic conditions, prevent speculative and abnormal increases in prices, increase production, and ensure a sufficient supply of goods at fair prices. The federal government can also impose rent control on housing.

Civil liberties can also be curtailed during wartime. The government can censor news that affects national security, such as reports of troop movements. It is within the power of Congress to enact SEDITION laws that prohibit political speech that disrupts the war effort or gives aid and comfort to the enemy.

During the early months of U.S. involvement in World War II, President FRANKLIN D. ROOSEVELT ordered the removal of people of Japanese ancestry from the West Coast. At the time the action was justified on national security grounds, because military commanders believed that California was vulnerable to Japanese spies and saboteurs. The U.S. Supreme Court, in *Korematsu v. United States*, 323 U.S. 214, 65 S. Ct. 193, 89 L. Ed. 194 (1944), upheld the removal. Thousands of Japanese Americans lost their property and businesses and were "relocated" to concentration camps for the duration of the war.

CROSS-REFERENCES

Armed Services; Arms Control and Disarmament; Japanese American Evacuation Cases; Korean War; *Korematsu v. United States*; Martial Law; Military Government; Military Law; Military Occupation; Militia; *Milligan, Ex Parte*; Rules of War; Tonkin Gulf Resolution; World War I; World War II.

WAR CRIMES 📖 Those acts that violate the international laws, treaties, customs, and practices governing military conflict between belligerent states or parties. 📖

War crimes may be committed by a country's regular armed forces, such as its army, navy, or air force, or by irregular armed forces, such as guerrillas and insurgents. Soldiers may be punished for war crimes, as may military and political leaders, members of the judiciary, industrialists, and civilians who are enlisted by a belligerent to contravene the RULES OF WAR.

However, isolated instances of TERRORISM and single acts of rebellion are rarely, if ever, treated as war crimes punishable under the international rules of warfare. Instead, they are ordinarily treated as criminal violations punishable under the domestic laws of the country in which they occur.

Most war crimes fall into one of three categories: crimes against peace, crimes against humanity, and traditional war crimes. Crimes against peace include the planning, commencement, and waging of aggressive WAR, or war in violation of international agreements. Aggressive war is broadly defined to include any hostile military act that disregards the territorial boundaries of another country, disrespects the political independence of another regime, or otherwise interferes with the sovereignty of an internationally recognized state. Wars fought in self-defense are not aggressive wars.

Following WORLD WAR II, for example, the Allies prosecuted a number of leading Nazi officials at the NUREMBERG TRIALS for crimes against peace. During the war, the Nazis had invaded and occupied a series of sovereign states, including France, Czechoslovakia, Poland, and Austria. Because those invasions were made in an effort to accumulate wealth, power, and territory for the Third Reich, Nazi officials could not claim to be acting in self-defense. Thus, those officials who participated in the planning, initiation, or execution of those invasions were guilty of crimes against peace.

Hermann Göring, chief of the Luftwaffe (the German Air Force), was one Nazi official who was convicted of crimes against peace at the Nuremberg trials. The international military tribunal presiding at Nuremberg, comprised of judges selected from the four Allied powers (France, Great Britain, the Soviet Union, and the United States), found that Göring had helped plan and carry out the invasions of Poland and Austria and had ordered the destruction of Rotterdam, Holland, after the city had effectively surrendered.

Crimes against humanity include the deportation, enslavement, persecution, and extermination of certain peoples based on their race, religion, ethnic origin, or some other identifiable characteristic. This category of war crimes was created almost entirely from the catalog of atrocities committed by the Nazi regime in World War II. Although other regimes have since committed horrors of their own, the Nazis established the standard by which the wartime misconduct of all subsequent regimes is now measured.

As part of the Nazi blitzkrieg, the Germans constructed concentration camps around Europe where they gassed, tortured, and incinerated millions of Jews and other persons they deemed impure or subversive to the Aryan race. Millions of others who escaped this fate were deported to Nazi labor camps in occupied countries where they were compelled at gunpoint to work on behalf of the Third Reich. The Nazi leaders who were responsible for implementing this totalitarian system of terror were guilty of crimes against humanity.

Many Nazi leaders were prosecuted for crimes against humanity during the Nuremberg trials. For example, Ernst Kaltenbrunner, head of the Nazi security organization in charge of the gestapo (the German secret police), was convicted and sentenced to death based on evidence that he had authorized the extermination of Jews at concentration camps and ordered the conscription and deportation of civilians to foreign labor camps.

Traditional war crimes consist of those acts that violate the accepted customs, practices, and laws of warfare that have been followed by civilized nations for centuries. These rules of war prescribe the rights and obligations of belligerent states, prisoners of war, and occupying powers, as well as those of combatants and civilians. They also set restrictions on the types of weapons that belligerents may employ during combat. Soldiers, officers, and members of the high command can all be held responsible for violating the accepted customs and practices of war, regardless of whether they issue an order commanding an illegal act or simply follow such an order.

Soldiers, officers, and the high command can also be held responsible for failing to prevent war crimes. Military personnel in a position of authority have an obligation to instruct their subordinates on the customs and practices of war and a duty to supervise and oversee their conduct on the battlefield. A military commander who neglects this duty can be punished for any war crimes committed by his troops. Following World War II, for example, Japanese General Tomoyuki Yamashita was prosecuted and sentenced to death by a U.S. military tribunal in the South Pacific for dereliction of duty in "failing to provide effective control" of his troops who had massacred, raped, and pillaged innocent noncombatant civilians and mistreated U.S. prisoners of war in the Philippines (Christenson 1991, 491).

For more than five centuries, the rules of war have been applied to military conflicts between countries. Until the last decade, many observers contended that the rules of war do not govern hostilities between combatants in CIVIL WARS that take place wholly within the territorial boundaries of a single state. However, during the 1990s the UNITED NATIONS established two international military tribunals to investigate and prosecute war crimes that allegedly took place in the civil wars fought within Bosnia-Herzegovina and Rwanda.

The two tribunals indicted soldiers and other combatants in both countries for committing a litany of war crimes, including the torture of political and military enemies, the programmatic raping of women, and GENOCIDE. Although the litigants questioned the JURISDICTION and authority of each tribunal, trials proceeded against certain defendants who had been captured. Thus, the theater in which war crimes can be committed and punished has expanded from international military conflicts to intranational civil wars.

See also HITLER, ADOLF; TOKYO TRIAL.

WARD 📖 A person, especially an INFANT or incompetent, placed by the court in the care of a guardian. 📖 See also GUARDIAN AND WARD.

WARD, NATHANIEL Nathaniel Ward was a Puritan minister, attorney, and writer who compiled a code of statutes for colonial Massachusetts entitled *The Body of Liberties*, which was adopted by the colony in 1641. This code, which combined English common law with Mosaic law (laws derived from the Old Testament of the Bible), was the first comprehensive set of laws enacted in New England.

Ward was born around 1578 in Haverhill, Suffolk, England. He graduated from Cambridge University in 1599 and then studied law at Lincoln's Inn in London. He practiced law for ten years and then decided to enter the ministry. Attracted to Puritan religious doctrine, Ward was dismissed from his ministry in 1633 and forced to leave England to avoid religious persecution. He arrived in Massachusetts in 1634 and became co-pastor of a church in Agawam. In 1636, however, he left the ministry and returned to the field of law.

Ward served on a committee charged with writing a code of laws for the Massachusetts Colony. In 1636 John Cotton, a Puritan minister, prepared a draft of a code, entitled *Moses His Judicials*. This code was a major departure from English common law, as it relied heavily upon Scripture. Cotton's code was not enacted

BIOGRAPHY

into law, however, and another committee was formed in 1638 to prepare a second code.

In November 1639 Ward submitted his draft of a code to the General Court of the colony. His code, which became known as *The Body of Liberties*, was comprised of one hundred sections and used much of Cotton's earlier draft. The General Court enacted Ward's code in 1641. The code underwent several revisions, resulting in the production of the *Laws and Liberties Concerning the Inhabitants of Massachusetts* (1648), which served as the basis for civil and criminal law in the colony until the eighteenth century.

Ward's code was based on the Bible. Section 65 of the code states that "No custome or prescription shall ever prevaile amongst us . . . that can be proved to bee morrallie sinfull by the word of God." At the same time, *The Body of Liberties* enumerated civil rights and liberties and incorporated many of the principles of English COMMON LAW. Other provisions guaranteed equal justice under law to every person within the jurisdiction and assured freedom from arbitrary arrest and imprisonment, DOUBLE JEOPARDY, cruel punishments, impressment, and torture. In a major departure from English common law, however, the code limited capital crimes to twelve specific offenses found in the Bible. At the time English law recognized more than fifty capital crimes.

In 1647 Ward returned to his ministry in England, where he remained until his death. He published several books, including *The Simple Cobbler of Aggawam* (1647), which defended the status quo and attacked religious tolerance and modes of fashion. Ward died in October 1652 in Shenfield, Essex, England.

WAREHOUSEMAN 📖 An individual who is regularly engaged in the business of receiving and storing GOODS of others in exchange for compensation or profit. 📖

The business of warehousemen can be either public or private in nature because they may store either goods belonging to the general public or those goods of certain individuals. Article 7 of the UNIFORM COMMERCIAL CODE sets forth the rights and liabilities of warehousemen.

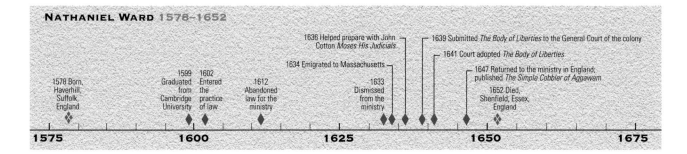

NATHANIEL WARD 1578–1652

1578 Born, Haverhill, Suffolk, England

1599 Graduated from Cambridge University

1602 Entered the practice of law

1612 Abandoned law for the ministry

1633 Dismissed from the ministry

1634 Emigrated to Massachusetts

1636 Helped prepare with John Cotton *Moses His Judicials*

1639 Submitted *The Body of Liberties* to the General Court of the colony

1641 Court adopted *The Body of Liberties*

1647 Returned to the ministry in England; published *The Simple Cobbler of Aggawam*

1652 Died, Shenfield, Essex, England

1575   1600   1625   1650   1675

WAREHOUSE RECEIPT ⬛ A written document given by a WAREHOUSEMAN for items received for storage in his or her warehouse, which serves as EVIDENCE of TITLE to the stored GOODS. ⬛

A number of warehouse receipts are NEGOTIABLE INSTRUMENTS, and the law governing such receipts is embodied in Article 7 of the UNIFORM COMMERCIAL CODE (UCC).

The general rule is that warehouse receipts need not be in any particular form. They must, however, contain the following information: the location of the warehouse and the place where the goods are stored; the date when the receipt was issued; the consecutive number of the receipts; terms indicating whether the goods are to be delivered to the bearer of the receipt, to a particular individual, or to a particular individual on his or her order; the storage rate or handling charges; a statement describing the goods or the manner in which they are packed; the signature of the warehouseman or his or her agent; the amount of advance payment made, if any; and any other terms that do not impair the warehouseman's duty.

In situations where a warehouse receipt does not contain these provisions, the warehouseman can be held liable in DAMAGES to anyone who sustains financial injury because of the omission.

WAR OF 1812 The War of 1812 between the United States and Great Britain was a conflict fought over the right of neutral countries to participate in foreign trade without the interference of other nations and the desire of many in the United States to end British occupation of Canada. The war, which lasted from 1812 to 1815, proved inconclusive, with both countries agreeing to revert to their prewar status as much as possible.

The U.S. declaration of war against Great Britain that President JAMES MADISON signed on June 18, 1812, culminated nearly a decade of antagonism between the nations. The British, who from 1802 to 1815 were involved in the Napoleonic Wars with France, sought to prevent the United States, a neutral, from trading

A sample warehouse delivery order and receipt

_____ WAREHOUSE COMPANY
[*Address*]

Carrier

Date

For Account of:

HANDLING TIME THIS ORDER
No. of Workers _____
Starting Time _____
Finish Time _____
Total Time _____

Consigned to   Street
Destination   State of
                 Delivering
Route   Carrier   Car Initial   Car No.

No. Pkgs.		Lot No.	Location	Weight	

Del. by

Remarks:

Received in Good order from _____
WAREHOUSE COMPANY (Except as Noted)

Sign
Firm Name _____
                    Truck No. _____
By _____

The defeat and capture of HMS Macedonian *by USS* United States *in 1812. The War of 1812 was fought between the United States and Britain over the right of the United States to trade with France, which was at war with Britain. The war was inconclusive, and at the end of the Napoleonic Wars tensions eased.*

with France. Britain imposed a BLOCKADE on France and required that U.S. ships stop at British ports and pay duties on goods bound for France. In addition, outrage grew in the United States over the British practice of boarding U.S. ships on the high seas and impressing seamen (seizing them and forcing them to serve Great Britain) who the British claimed had deserted the Royal Navy. More than ten thousand U.S. seamen were impressed between 1802 and 1812.

In 1807 President THOMAS JEFFERSON succeeded in convincing Congress to pass the EMBARGO ACT, which prevented virtually all U.S. ships from sailing overseas. The economic consequences of this law were disastrous to the U.S. economy, forcing the act's repeal in 1809. In its place, Congress enacted the Non-Intercourse Act, which forbade trade only with Great Britain and France. A third law, passed in 1810, allowed trade with both nations but stipulated the revival of nonintercourse against whichever nation did not remove its trade restrictions. When France announced an end to its trade decrees, the United States banned trade with Great Britain.

Anger against Britain was also fueled by a group of expansionist congressmen, nicknamed the War Hawks, who wanted more land for settlement and military action against the British in Canada. British support of the American Indians on the frontier had led to Indian wars against U.S. settlers.

The war itself provided limited success for the United States. Though a U.S. naval squadron under the command of Oliver Hazard Perry captured the British fleet on Lake Erie in 1813, battles in northern New York and Ontario, Canada, proved inconclusive. After U.S. forces burned the city of York (now Toronto),

Ontario, the British attacked Washington, D.C., on September 13 and 14, 1814. The British burned the U.S. Capitol and the White House.

Both sides realized the futility of the struggle and began treaty negotiations in 1813. Because of the military stalemate, neither side could extract concessions from the other. The United States and Great Britain agreed, in the Treaty of Ghent, to return to the prewar status quo. The treaty, which was signed on December 24, 1814, in Ghent, Belgium, was ratified by the U.S. Senate on February 16, 1815. However, the Battle of New Orleans was fought on January 8, 1815, before news of the treaty reached the two armies. General ANDREW JACKSON led his troops to a decisive victory over the British forces, providing the U.S. public with the illusion that the United States had won the war. The battle also enhanced Jackson's national reputation and helped pave the way for his presidency.

The frictions that had precipitated the war disappeared. The end of the Napoleonic Wars ended both the need for a British naval blockade and the impressing of U.S. seamen. Although the United States did not acquire Canada, American Indian opposition to expansion was weakened, and U.S. nationalism increased.

WAR OF INDEPENDENCE The War of Independence, also known as the American Revolution and the Revolutionary War, was fought from 1775 to 1783 between Great Britain and the thirteen British colonies in North America. The 1783 TREATY OF PARIS, which ended the war, gave the thirteen colonies political independence and led to the formation of the United States of America.

The war had its roots in the growing economic power of the colonies and the limited political freedom granted by Great Britain to the colonists to manage their affairs. Acts of British Parliament in the 1760s that imposed taxes and import duties on the colonies increased these tensions.

The British victory in the French and Indian War, also known as the Seven Years' War (1756–63), removed France as a power in North America, yet the costs of the war were staggering for Great Britain. Faced with a large national debt, Parliament passed the Molasses Act and the Sugar Act in 1764, which imposed a duty on molasses and sugar imported by the colonies. The STAMP ACT of 1765 taxed papers such as legal documents, newspapers, and almanacs. The Quartering Act indirectly taxed the colonists by requiring them to house, feed, and supply British troops.

American colonists reacted angrily to these tax measures, believing that it was unfair of Great Britain to subject them to taxation without representation. British leaders repealed the Stamp Act in 1766, but the following year Parliament passed the TOWNSHEND ACT, which imposed a series of new taxes on goods arriving at American ports. The new taxes were designed to pay the salaries of royal governors and other colonial appointees of Britain's King George III. The Townshend Act also restructured the customs service in the colonies, placing its headquarters in Boston.

The Townshend Act evoked more protests from the colonists. Groups such as the Sons of Liberty and the Daughters of Liberty organized protests against customs officials and BOYCOTTS of taxed goods. Merchants agreed not to sell imported goods.

British customs agents in Boston extorted money and seized American ships with little justification, leading to a riot in March 1770. The British troops, popularly known as redcoats because of their red uniforms, fired on the crowd, killing five people. The episode became known as the Boston Massacre.

Great Britain again reacted to economic pressure by removing most of the Townshend Act taxes. A notable exception was the tax on tea, which remained a symbol of Parliament's authority to tax colonists. In 1773 Britain tried to save the financially troubled British East India Company by passing the Tea Act, which lowered the tax on tea shipped by the company to the colonies, giving the company an edge over tea smugglers. The colonists responded by refusing to buy English tea or even allow it to be unloaded from British ships. In Boston protesters dressed as American Indians dumped the crates of tea into the water, and the event came to be known as the Boston Tea Party.

Parliament retaliated in 1774 by passing the Coercive Acts, which were labeled the "Intolerable Acts" by the colonists. These laws closed the port of Boston until the East India Company was repaid for the dumped tea, restricted the powers of the Massachusetts colonial legislature, and permitted British soldiers and officials accused of capital crimes to be tried in England rather than in the hostile colony. In addition, Parliament appointed General Thomas Gage, commander of the British Army in North America, as the governor of Massachusetts. Gage was to enforce the Coercive Acts.

Representatives of twelve colonies and Canada met in September 1774 to consider what action to take against Parliament. The delegates to the First CONTINENTAL CONGRESS

THE GRANGER COLLECTION, NEW YORK

agreed that the colonies, and not Parliament, had the right to tax and make laws for the colonies. They called for a complete trade boycott against Britain until the Coercive Acts were repealed, but they acknowledged Parliament's right to regulate trade. The Congress did not call for independence from Great Britain.

The war began in 1775 when General Gage tried to break up a Massachusetts militia group and seize its ammunition and supplies. On the evening of April 18, 1775, Gage ordered his troops to seize munitions at Concord. Militia messengers, including silversmith Paul Revere, rode the eighteen miles from Boston to Concord on horseback to warn the MILITIA. Militia forces met the redcoats in Lexington, and they exchanged fire. The British killed eight men and proceeded to Concord, where they again encountered militia companies. The British retreated to Boston after 273 redcoats were killed in the battle. The militia followed, laying siege to the city for almost one year.

In early May 1775 colonial delegates met in Philadelphia for the Second Continental Congress. The New England militia was renamed the Continental Army, and GEORGE WASHINGTON, a Virginia plantation owner who had served in the French and Indian War, was named commander. The delegates also made the Congress the central government for "The United Colonies of America."

King George III replaced Gage with General William Howe. The king had become concerned over mounting British casualties that accompanied battles in Massachusetts, including the Battle of Bunker Hill. On August 23, 1775, the king declared the colonies to be in rebellion and subjected colonial ships to seizure.

American troops invaded Canada in August 1775, capturing Montreal in November. How-

The Battle of Lexington in April of 1775 broke out when British troops were sent to collect arms gathered by the patriot militia outside of Boston, Massachusetts.

ever, their efforts to take the city of Quebec failed, and the troops were forced to withdraw. During the winter of 1775–76, Washington positioned artillery around Boston. In March 1776 a massive artillery attack on the city led British troops and more than one thousand Loyalists (colonists who supported the British) to flee on ships to Nova Scotia, Canada.

In June 1776, as the British assembled reinforcements for an invasion, the Continental Congress debated a declaration of the colonies' independence from Britain. THOMAS JEFFERSON borrowed from the recently completed VIRGINIA DECLARATION OF RIGHTS in drafting the DECLARATION OF INDEPENDENCE. The Virginia declaration, written by GEORGE MASON, stated that government derived from the people, that individuals were created equally free and independent, and that they had inalienable rights that the government could not legitimately deny them. On July 4, 1776, the Congress declared that the colonies were free and independent states, and it adopted the Declaration of Independence.

On June 29, 1776, Howe led an invasion force of thirty-two thousand troops, including eight thousand German mercenaries (Hessian troops), that landed off Sandy Hook, New Jersey. The British attacked Washington's forces in New York on August 22, and by the end of the year Washington had abandoned New York City and had moved his troops into Pennsylvania. He made a successful surprise attack on Trenton, New Jersey, on December 25, 1776. On January 3, 1777, Washington's troops defeated the British at Princeton, New Jersey. The two victories were critical to maintaining colonial morale, and by the spring of 1777 more than eight thousand new soldiers had joined the Continental Army.

The British implemented a plan in 1777 that sought to end the war that year by separating New England from the colonies in the south. General John Burgoyne led British forces from Montreal toward Albany, New York. After securing a victory at Fort Ticonderoga on July 5, Burgoyne became overconfident. The Continental Army and local militia counterattacked, forcing Burgoyne to surrender his army after a battle at Saratoga, New York, on October 17.

To the south, Washington vainly tried to stop the British from taking Philadelphia, the home of the Continental Congress. His troops lost at the battle of Brandywine Creek, and Philadelphia fell to the British on September 26. The Congress moved to Baltimore, Maryland.

Despite the loss of Philadelphia and some discontent with Washington's leadership during the winter of 1777–78, American fortunes brightened in 1778. In February France signed a formal treaty of commerce and alliance with the American states. France sent a naval fleet along with military advisers and financial aid.

In June 1778 Washington attacked the British at Monmouth, New Jersey, but again was defeated. He then shifted his military strategy, keeping his troops encamped around British forces in Connecticut, New York, and New Jersey. Although American forces led by George Rogers Clark regained control of the Ohio River Valley, British troops had success in South Carolina in 1779. However, in 1780 American troops prevailed in the Battle of Kings Mountain and again in the Battle of Cowpens in 1781. The British attempt to control the southern colonies ended in a stalemate.

In 1781 Washington's troops, with the assistance of the French Navy, cut off British forces led by General Charles Cornwallis at Yorktown, Virginia. The Battle of Yorktown, in which British troops were outnumbered two to one, ended in a British surrender on October 19, 1781. This marked the end of major military actions in the War of Independence.

The defeat at Yorktown led to the resignation of the British prime minister and a desire by the new cabinet to begin peace negotiations, which commenced in Paris, France, in April 1782. The U.S. delegation included BENJAMIN FRANKLIN, JOHN ADAMS, and JOHN JAY. The negotiators concluded a preliminary treaty on November 30, 1782, and a final agreement was signed in September 1783 and ratified by the Continental Congress on January 14, 1784.

In the Treaty of Paris the British recognized the independence of the United States. The treaty established generous boundaries for the

General George Washington and his troops spent the winter of 1777–1778 in Valley Forge, preparing themselves for battle in the spring. Many soldiers died during the harsh winter.

THE GRANGER COLLECTION, NEW YORK

United States, with U.S. territory extending from the Atlantic Ocean to the Mississippi River in the west, and from the Great Lakes and Canada in the north to the thirty-first parallel in the south. The U.S. fishing fleet was guaranteed access to the fisheries off the coast of Newfoundland, Canada. Navigation of the Mississippi River was to be open to both the United States and Great Britain.

During the War of Independence, the Continental Congress struggled to formulate a constitution for the entity known as the United States of America. Colonists were not interested in establishing a central government with broad powers, because they feared replacing undemocratic British authority with a local version. Therefore, the ARTICLES OF CONFEDERATION that were drafted in 1777, but not ratified until 1781 by all the states, created only a national congress of limited authority. By the end of the war, Congress found itself receiving less cooperation from the individual states. The failure of the Articles of Confederation became apparent after the Treaty of Paris was ratified, leading to the Constitutional Convention in Philadelphia in 1787 where the Founding Fathers would write the U.S. Constitution.

See also BOSTON MASSACRE SOLDIERS; PAINE, THOMAS.

WAR POWERS RESOLUTION See PRESIDENTIAL POWERS.

WARRANT 📖 A written order issued by a judicial officer or other authorized person commanding a law enforcement officer to perform some act incident to the administration of justice. 📖

Warrants are recognized in many different forms and for a variety of purposes in the law. Most commonly, police use warrants as the basis to arrest a suspect and to conduct a search of property for EVIDENCE of a crime. Warrants are also used to bring persons to court who have ignored a SUBPOENA or a court appearance. In another context, warrants may be issued to collect taxes or to pay out money.

The FOURTH AMENDMENT to the U.S. Constitution states that "no Warrants shall issue, but upon probable cause, supported by Oath or affirmation, and particularly describing the place to be searched, and the persons or things to be seized." There are three principal types of criminal warrants: arrest warrants, search warrants, and bench warrants.

An ARREST WARRANT is a written order issued by a judge or other proper judicial officer, upon PROBABLE CAUSE, directing a law enforcement officer to arrest a particular person. An arrest warrant is issued on the basis of a sworn COM-PLAINT charging that the accused person has committed a crime. The arrest warrant must identify the person to be arrested by name or other unique characteristics and must describe the crime. When a warrant for arrest does not identify a person by name, it is sometimes called a "John Doe warrant" or a "no name warrant."

A SEARCH WARRANT is an order in writing, issued by a judge or judicial officer, commanding a law enforcement officer to search a specified person or premises for specified property and to bring it before the judicial authority named in the warrant. Before issuing the search warrant, the judicial officer must determine whether there is probable cause to search based on the information supplied in an AFFIDAVIT by a law enforcement officer or other person. Generally the types of property for which a search warrant may be issued, as specified in statutes or rules of court, are weapons, CONTRABAND, fruits of crimes, instrumentalities of crimes (for example, a mask used in a robbery), and other evidence of crime.

A BENCH WARRANT is initiated by and issued from the bench or court directing a law enforcement officer to bring a specified person before the court. A bench warrant is used, among other purposes, when a person has failed to appear in response to a subpoena, SUMMONS, or CITATION. It is also used when an accused person needs to be transferred from jail to court for trial, and when a person's failure to obey a court order puts her or him in CONTEMPT of court. A bench warrant is sometimes called a "CAPIAS" or an "alias warrant."

Warrants may be used for financial transactions. For example, a private individual may draw up a warrant authorizing another person to pay out or deliver a sum of money or something else of value.

Police officers, such as Washington state trooper John Sager, frequently run warrant searches on drivers they stop for traffic violations.

APWIDE WORLD PHOTOS

A warrant may be issued to a collector of taxes, empowering him or her to collect taxes as itemized on the ASSESSMENT role and to enforce the assessments by tax sales where necessary.

WARRANT OF ATTORNEY 📖 A written authorization that allows an ATTORNEY named in it to appear in court and admit the LIABILITY of the person giving the warrant in an ACTION to collect a DEBT. 📖

This writing is usually given to help ensure that the person signing it will pay the amount that he or she would be obliged to pay if a JUDGMENT were entered against him or her. It usually contains an agreement that no action will be started against the signer if the obligation described in the paper is satisfied. Essentially the warrant of attorney is a COGNOVIT NOTE that permits a CONFESSION OF JUDGMENT (a shortcut to obtaining a judgment against a debtor that is now illegal in most states).

WARRANTY 📖 An assurance, PROMISE, or GUARANTY by one party that a particular statement of fact is true and may be relied upon by the other party. 📖

Warranties are used in a variety of commercial situations. In many instances a business may voluntarily make a warranty. In other situations the law implies a warranty where no EXPRESS warranty was made. Most warranties are made with respect to real estate, insurance, and sales and leases of goods and services.

A car buyer and salesman shake hands over the purchase of a new car. The dealer or manufacturer typically provides a warranty against a variety of potential problems.

JOSE CARRILLO/STOCK BOSTON

Real Estate When land, houses, apartments, and other forms of REAL ESTATE are sold or leased, the real estate usually comes with at least one warranty. In a sale of realty, the seller usually includes a warranty regarding the TITLE to the property. In some cases the title may have a cloud on it. This means that some party other than the seller has a CLAIM to the property. Such claims may be made by a bank, a JUDGMENT DEBTOR, a construction company, or any other party that has obtained a LIEN against the property. If the seller thinks that the title is clouded, the seller may offer a QUITCLAIM DEED. This type of DEED contains no promises as to the title and releases the seller from any LIABILITY to the buyer if a lien holder later makes a claim to the property. See also CLOUD ON TITLE.

In other real estate transactions, the seller may warrant that the title is clear. In this situation the seller gives the buyer a GENERAL WARRANTY DEED. This kind of deed warrants that the title is clear and that the seller will be liable for any defects in the title that existed at the time of the sale.

Other types of warranties related to real estate titles include special warranty deeds and covenants of further assurances. A special warranty deed warrants only that no party made a claim to the property during the seller's ownership. Under a special warranty deed, the seller is not liable for any defects in the title attributable to her predecessors. A seller may add to a deed a COVENANT of further assurances, which promises that the seller will take any steps necessary to satisfy any claims to the property.

Sellers and buyers of real estate may negotiate warranties regarding the title to the property. They also may negotiate additional warranties regarding the property, such as warranties on plumbing or electricity or any other matter of special concern.

If the seller of real estate is the same party who constructed a building on the property, a warranty of HABITABILITY may be automatically included in a sale of the property. A warranty of habitability in the context of a sale of REAL PROPERTY is a promise that the dwelling complies with local building codes, was built in a professional manner, and is suitable for human habitation.

Warranties also accompany LEASES of real property. All states, through either statutes or court decisions, require landlords to observe the warranty of habitability in leases of residential property. In this context the warranty of habitability is a promise that the premises comply with all relevant building codes and that they will be properly maintained and will be fit for habitation throughout the period of the tenancy. Specifically, the LANDLORD promises to make necessary repairs in a prompt and reasonable fashion and to provide such basic services as water, heat, and electricity. If a landlord breaches the implied warranty of habitability, the TENANT may withhold rent and sue for any financial losses resulting from the breach.

Insurance A warranty in an INSURANCE policy is a promise by the INSURED party that statements affecting the validity of the contract are true. Most insurance CONTRACTS require the insured to make certain warranties. For example, to obtain a HEALTH INSURANCE policy, an insured may have to warrant that he does not suffer from a terminal disease. If a warranty made by an insured turns out to be untrue, the INSURER may cancel the POLICY and refuse to cover claims by the insured.

Not all misstatements made by an insured give the insurer the right to cancel a policy or refuse a claim. Only MISREPRESENTATIONS on conditions and warranties in the contract give an insurer such rights. To qualify as a condition or warranty, the statement must be expressly included in the contract, and the provision must clearly show that the parties intended that the rights of the insured and insurer would depend on the truth of the statement.

Warranties in insurance contracts can be divided into two types: affirmative or promissory. An affirmative warranty is a statement regarding a fact at the time the contract was made. A promissory warranty is a statement about future facts or about facts that will continue to be true throughout the term of the policy. An untruthful affirmative warranty makes an insurance contract VOID at its inception. If a promissory warranty becomes true, the insurer may cancel coverage at such time as the warranty becomes untrue. For example, if an insured warrants that property to be covered by a fire insurance policy will never be used for the mixing of explosives, the insurer may cancel the policy if the insured decides to start mixing explosives on the property. Warranty provisions should contain language indicating whether they are affirmative or promissory.

Many states have created laws that protect insureds from cancellations due to misrepresented warranties. Courts tend to favor insureds by classifying indefinite warranties as affirmative. Many state legislatures have created laws providing that no misrepresented warranty should cancel an insurance contract if the misrepresentation was not FRAUDULENT and did not increase the risks covered by the policy.

Sales and Leases of Goods Every contract for the sale or lease of GOODS contains a warranty that the seller or lessor actually owns the property. Courts hold that this warranty is implied if it is not included in the contract, and a seller or lessor cannot disclaim it.

The two basic types of sales warranties are EXPRESS warranties and implied warranties. Express warranties are specific promises made by the seller and include oral representations, written representations, descriptions of the goods or services, representations in samples and models, and prior quality of the goods or services. PUFFING, or the seller's exaggerated opinion of quality, does not constitute a warranty. For example, if a car salesperson says, "This car will last you a lifetime," a court would likely consider such a statement puffing and not an express warranty.

Implied warranties are warranties that courts assume are implied in sales made by merchants. A merchant is a person who is in the business of selling the good or service being sold in the contract. All sales contracts made by merchants contain an IMPLIED WARRANTY of merchantability. This is a promise that the goods, as they are described in the contract, pass without objection in the merchant's trade, are fit for the ordinary purpose for which they are normally used, are adequately contained, packaged, and labeled, and conform to any promises or affirmations of fact made on the container or label. If the goods are FUNGIBLE, or easily replaced or substituted, such as grain or oil, the replacement goods must be of fair and average quality, fit for their ordinary purposes, and similar to previous goods delivered in the same contract or previous similar contracts.

In some situations a sales contract may include an implied warranty of fitness for a particular purpose. This kind of warranty is a promise that the goods are useful for a special function. Courts infer this warranty is implied when the seller has reason to know of a particular purpose for which the goods are required and also knows that the buyer is relying on the seller's skill and knowledge in choosing the goods. The buyer does not need to specifically inform the seller that the goods are for a particular purpose; it is enough that a REASONABLE seller would be aware of the purpose.

For example, assume that a farmer, intending to plant no-till soybeans, approaches a seller to buy herbicide. Assume further that the buyer requests a particular herbicide mix but the seller suggests a less expensive mix. If the chemicals fail to kill crabgrass and the farmer has a low yield of soybeans, the farmer could sue the seller for breach of the warranty of fitness for a particular purpose because the seller knew what the farmer required.

In some cases an implied warranty may be lost or waived. If a seller issues a DISCLAIMER— for example, states that the goods are AS IS— and the buyer examines or refuses to examine the goods, the buyer may lose any implied warranties. One important caveat is that courts will not find that an implied warranty has been waived if, under the circumstances of the sale, it is unreasonable to expect that the buyer would have understood that there were no warranties under the circumstances of the transaction.

A seller may disclaim the warranty of merchantability either orally or in writing, but a seller cannot orally disclaim a warranty of fitness for a particular purpose. A disclaimer of the warranty of fitness for a particular purpose must be in writing, and the disclaimer must be conspicuous to the buyer. Express warranties made by a seller may not be disclaimed. However, if a disclaimer and an express warranty can be construed as consistent, a court may uphold the disclaimer.

CROSS-REFERENCES

Consumer Protection; Landlord and Tenant; Merchantable; Product Liability; Sales Law.

WARRANTY DEED 📖 An instrument that transfers REAL PROPERTY from one person to another and in which the GRANTOR promises that TITLE is good and clear of any CLAIMS. 📖

A DEED is a written instrument that transfers the title of property from one person to another. Although many types of deeds exist, title is usually transferred by a warranty deed. A warranty deed provides the greatest protection to the purchaser because the grantor (seller) pledges or warrants that she legally owns the property and that there are no outstanding LIENS, MORTGAGES, or other ENCUMBRANCES against it. A warranty deed is also a guarantee of title, which means that the seller may be held liable for DAMAGES if the GRANTEE (buyer) discovers the title is defective.

There are two types of warranty deeds: general and special. A GENERAL WARRANTY DEED not only conveys to the grantee all of the grantor's interest in and title to the property but also guarantees that if the title is defective or has a "cloud" on it, such as a mortgage claim, tax lien, title claim, JUDGMENT, or MECHANIC'S LIEN, the grantee may hold the grantor liable.

A SPECIAL WARRANTY DEED conveys the grantor's title to the grantee and promises to protect the grantee against title defects or claims asserted by the grantor and any persons whose right to assert a claim against the title arose during the period in which the grantor held title to the property. In a special warranty deed, the grantor guarantees to the grantee that the grantor has done nothing during the time he held title to the property that might in the future impair the grantee's title.

A warranty deed should contain an accurate description of the property being conveyed, be signed and witnessed according to the laws of the state where the property is located, and be delivered to the purchaser at closing. The deed should be recorded by the buyers of the property at the public records office, which is usually located in the county courthouse. Recording a deed gives "notice to the world" that a particular piece of property has been sold. Though the grantor guarantees good title in a warranty deed, the deed is no substitute for TITLE INSURANCE because a warranty from a grantor who later dies or goes bankrupt may have little value.

CROSS-REFERENCES

Cloud on Title; Property Law; Recording of Land Titles; Registration of Land Titles; Title Search.

BIOGRAPHY

Earl Warren

PORTRAIT BY C. J. FOX, COLLECTION OF THE SUPREME COURT OF THE UNITED STATES

WARREN, EARL Earl Warren served as the fourteenth chief justice of the U.S. Supreme Court from 1953 to 1969. A former prosecutor, state attorney general, and governor of California, Warren previously had not served as a judge. In spite of his lack of judicial experience, Warren led a constitutional revolution that reshaped U.S. law and society and granted the lower federal courts wide latitude in enforcing individual constitutional rights. Although criticized by conservatives for his judicial activism, Warren has also been hailed as one of the greatest chief justices in U.S. history.

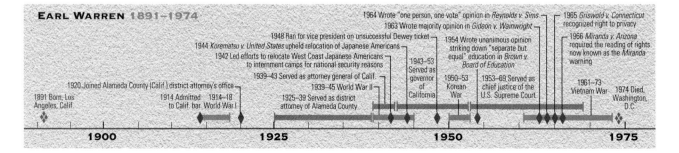

EARL WARREN 1891–1974

1891 Born, Los Angeles, Calif.

1914 Admitted to Calif. bar   1914–18 World War I

1920 Joined Alameda County (Calif.) district attorney's office

1925–39 Served as district attorney of Alameda County

1939–43 Served as attorney general of Calif.

1939–45 World War II

1942 Led efforts to relocate West Coast Japanese Americans to internment camps for national security reasons

1943–53 Served as governor of California

1944 *Korematsu v. United States* upheld relocation of Japanese Americans

1948 Ran for vice president on unsuccessful Dewey ticket

1950–53 Korean War

1953–69 Served as chief justice of the U.S. Supreme Court

1954 Wrote unanimous opinion striking down "separate but equal" education in *Brown v. Board of Education*

1961–73 Vietnam War

1963 Wrote majority opinion in *Gideon v. Wainwright*

1964 Wrote "one person, one vote" opinion in *Reynolds v. Sims*

1965 *Griswold v. Connecticut* recognized right to privacy

1966 *Miranda v. Arizona* required the reading of rights now known as the *Miranda* warning

1974 Died, Washington, D.C.

1900   1925   1950   1975

Warren was born on March 19, 1891, in Los Angeles, California, but moved with his family to Bakersfield, California, as a young boy. The son of a railroad worker, Warren worked summers on railroad crews as a young man to earn money to attend college. He earned a bachelor's degree and a law degree from the University of California at Berkeley and was admitted to the California bar in 1914. After a brief period of service in the Army during World War I, Warren returned to northern California where he practiced law for a short time in San Francisco.

Warren joined the Alameda County district attorney's office in 1920 and in 1925 was elected district attorney. Reelected two times, Warren established a reputation as a tough but fair prosecutor. A liberal Republican, he was elected California attorney general in 1938. Though he helped modernize the office during his term as attorney general, Warren's record was tarnished by his actions during the early months of U.S. involvement in World War II.

In 1942 Warren was a key leader in demanding the removal of people of Japanese ancestry from the West Coast. At the time, Warren and others justified the removal of Japanese Americans on national security grounds, believing that California was vulnerable to Japanese spies and saboteurs. The U.S. Supreme Court, in *Korematsu v. United States*, 323 U.S. 214, 65 S. Ct. 193, 89 L. Ed. 194 (1944), upheld the removal. Thousands of Japanese Americans lost their property and businesses and were "relocated" to concentration camps for the duration of the war. Warren defended his actions throughout his public career, but in retirement he admitted the relocation was a mistake based on hysteria and unsubstantiated fears.

Warren was elected governor of California in 1942 and proved a popular political leader. He was reelected with Republican and Democratic party support in 1946 and 1950. Warren's only political defeat came in 1948, when he was the Republican vice-presidential candidate on the ticket headed by THOMAS E. DEWEY that lost to President HARRY S. TRUMAN. In 1952 he played a key role in securing the Republican presidential nomination for DWIGHT D. EISENHOWER, who in return promised Warren an appointment to the Supreme Court when a vacancy occurred.

When Chief Justice FRED M. VINSON died unexpectedly in September 1953, Eisenhower appointed Warren as his successor. In his first term as chief justice, Warren confronted the issue of state-mandated racial segregation in public schools. The case, which the Court had

"IN CIVILIZED LIFE, LAW FLOATS IN A SEA OF ETHICS. EACH IS INDISPENSABLE TO CIVILIZATION. WITHOUT LAW, WE SHOULD BE AT THE MERCY OF THE LEAST SCRUPULOUS; WITHOUT ETHICS, LAW COULD NOT EXIST."

heard the previous year but was unable to decide, came back for reargument. In May 1954 Warren wrote the opinion for a unanimous Court in *Brown v. Board of Education*, 347 U.S. 483, 74 S. Ct. 686, 98 L. Ed. 873 (1954). *Brown* overruled the 1896 Supreme Court decision of *Plessy v. Ferguson*, 163 U.S. 537, 16 S. Ct. 1138, 41 L. Ed. 256, which had allowed racially segregated facilities on trains and by implication in public schools. Writing that "separate educational facilities are inherently unequal," Warren held that racial segregation in Kansas denied African Americans EQUAL PROTECTION of the laws.

Brown unleashed a torrent of controversy and protest in the South and immediately established Warren's image as a liberal. Throughout the South, billboards appeared that read "Impeach Earl Warren." Nevertheless, in 1955 the Court ordered Kansas and other states with segregated schools to move with "all deliberate speed" to dismantle their dual school systems. The modern CIVIL RIGHTS MOVEMENT was founded in this decision, which radically altered the traditional legal position on racial discrimination. When comprehensive federal CIVIL RIGHTS legislation was enacted in the 1960s, the Warren Court easily upheld the CIVIL RIGHTS ACT of 1964 (42 U.S.C.A. § 2000a et seq.) and the VOTING RIGHTS ACT OF 1965 (42 U.S.C.A. § 1973 et seq.).

The Warren Court was marked by its strict scrutiny of legislation that directly abridged the exercise of fundamental rights or narrowed the number of people who might exercise them, and of legislation that discriminated against various suspect classes. The STRICT SCRUTINY standard of review shifted to the government the burden of proving a COMPELLING STATE INTEREST that could justify discriminatory legislation. On most occasions the government could not meet this burden. In addition, the Court "read into" the FOURTEENTH AMENDMENT, applicable to the states, most of the provisions of the BILL OF RIGHTS, which until then had been applicable only to the federal government.

Warren himself believed that his most important contribution to the law came in the area of legislative reapportionment. Most state legislatures had not apportioned their seats since the early 1900s. The allocation of seats was based on geographic areas and favored rural districts with small populations over growing urban and suburban areas. Political change was almost impossible because rural-dominated legislatures prevented reapportionment. Until the 1960s the Supreme Court had refused to intervene, concluding that cases challenging APPOR-

TIONMENT were POLITICAL QUESTIONS beyond the Court's JURISDICTION.

In *Baker v. Carr*, 369 U.S. 186, 82 S. Ct. 691, 7 L. Ed. 2d 663 (1962), the Court held that itdid have jurisdiction, and two years later, in *Reynolds v. Sims*, 377 U.S. 533, 84 S. Ct. 1362, 12 L. Ed. 2d 506 (1964), Warren wrote the opinion that has come to be known as the ONE PERSON, ONE VOTE decision. *Reynolds* and a series of cases that followed forced state legislatures to be apportioned equally on the basis of population rather than geographic areas. Warren noted that "citizens, not history or economic interests cast votes," and that "legislators represent people, not acres or trees." Reapportionment based on population resulted in a shift of political power away from sparsely populated rural areas to metropolitan areas.

Warren also reshaped U.S. CRIMINAL PROCEDURE, in the process drawing protest from law enforcement officials and those citizens who believed the Court was tipping the balance in favor of criminals. Many cases of this era limited police SEARCHES AND SEIZURES and the use of confessions and extended the RIGHT TO COUNSEL to poor persons accused of felonies.

In *Gideon v. Wainwright*, 372 U.S. 335, 83 S. Ct. 792, 9 L. Ed. 2d 799 (1963), the Court held that the SIXTH AMENDMENT right to legal counsel encompassed state as well as federal criminal proceedings. Therefore, the state was required to appoint an attorney to represent an indigent person charged with a crime. In *Miranda v. Arizona*, 384 U.S. 436, 86 S. Ct. 1602, 16 L. Ed. 2d 694 (1966), the Court required what has come to be known as the *Miranda* warning: the police must inform arrested persons that they need not answer questions and that they may have an attorney present during questioning. Warren sought to ensure that suspects who are not sophisticated in law or who are not able to afford ready counsel are not disadvantaged. Nevertheless, rising crime convinced many citizens that the Court gave away too much of the government's authority in *Miranda*.

The Warren Court also recognized the constitutional right of PRIVACY in *Griswold v. Connecticut*, 381 U.S. 479, 85 S. Ct. 1678, 14 L. Ed. 2d 510 (1965). *Griswold* struck down a Connecticut statute that prohibited the dissemination of BIRTH CONTROL information. In declaring the right of privacy, the Court laid the groundwork for the post–Warren Court decision in *Roe v. Wade*, 410 U.S. 113, 93 S. Ct. 705, 35 L. Ed. 2d 147 (1973), which gave women the right to have an ABORTION.

In 1963 President LYNDON B. JOHNSON persuaded Warren to head a commission investigating the ASSASSINATION of President JOHN F. KENNEDY. Warren reluctantly agreed to the request but was uncomfortable participating in this extrajudicial activity. The 1964 WARREN COMMISSION report has remained controversial. Critics have attacked its conclusions that Lee Harvey Oswald was the lone assassin and that there was no conspiracy to kill the president.

Warren informed President Johnson in June 1968 of his intent to retire but left the date of his resignation open. When Republicans blocked Johnson's nomination of Justice ABE FORTAS in the fall of 1968, Warren agreed to serve until the next president took office in 1969, leaving the bench in July 1969. President RICHARD M. NIXON appointed WARREN E. BURGER as Warren's successor.

Many commentators have praised Warren's tenure as chief justice, but critics have charged that his judicial activism was outside the proper role of the Court and that many of the decisions were based on his personal values rather than the Constitution or other legal sources. Both Chief Justice Burger and his successor, Chief Justice WILLIAM H. REHNQUIST, have eschewed Warren's approach, applying more conservative principles.

Warren died on July 9, 1974, in Washington, D.C.

CROSS-REFERENCES

Baker v. Carr; *Brown v. Board of Education of Topeka, Kansas*; *Gideon v. Wainwright*; *Griswold v. Connecticut*; Japanese American Evacuation Cases; Judicial Review; *Korematsu v. United States*; *Miranda v. Arizona*; *Reynolds v. Sims*; School Desegregation; Warren Court.

WARREN COMMISSION The ASSASSINATION of President JOHN F. KENNEDY in Dallas, Texas, on November 22, 1963, was a shocking event that immediately raised questions about the circumstances surrounding the death of the president. Those questions increased when the alleged assassin, Lee Harvey Oswald, was murdered while in the custody of Dallas police on November 25 by JACK RUBY, a Dallas nightclub owner.

President LYNDON B. JOHNSON moved quickly to reassure the nation that a thorough inquiry would take place by creating a commission of distinguished public servants to investigate the evidence. On November 29, 1963, Johnson appointed EARL WARREN, chief justice of the U.S. Supreme Court, to head the commission, which became known as the Warren Commission. Its 1964 report, which sought to put to rest many issues, proved controversial, provoking charges of a whitewash. The facts surrounding the Kennedy assassination remain the subject of debate.

Chief Justice Warren, fearing that his service disrupted the traditional SEPARATION OF POWERS, reluctantly agreed to serve as director of the commission. The other members of the commission were Senators Richard B. Russell of Georgia and John Sherman Cooper of Kentucky; two members of the House of Representatives, Hale Boggs of Louisiana and GERALD R. FORD of Michigan; Allen W. Dulles, former head of the Central Intelligence Agency; John J. McCloy, former head of the World Bank; and James Lee Rankin, former U.S. solicitor general, who was appointed general counsel for the commission.

The Warren Commission began its investigations on December 3, 1963. The commission used accounts and statements provided by the Dallas police force, the Secret Service, the FEDERAL BUREAU OF INVESTIGATION, the military, and government and congressional commissions. Over the course of ten months, the commission took testimony from 552 witnesses.

The commission published its conclusions, popularly known as the *Warren Report*, in September 1964. According to the commission, Oswald acted alone in the assassination. The commission characterized Oswald as a resentful, belligerent man who hated authority. The commission endorsed the "single bullet theory," which concluded that only one bullet, rather than two, struck President Kennedy and Texas governor John Connally, who was sitting directly in front of the president in the open convertible. This was important because it appeared unlikely that Oswald could have fired his rifle twice in succession quickly enough to strike the two men. It found no connection between Oswald's Communist affiliation, his time living in the Soviet Union, and the murder, nor between Oswald and his murderer, Jack Ruby. The commission also found no evidence that Ruby was part of a CONSPIRACY. It criticized the security measures taken to protect Kennedy and recommended that more effective measures be taken in the future.

Although the conclusions of the commission were well received at first, public skepticism soon grew about the findings. In 1966 two influential books were published that challenged the methods and conclusions of the commission. Both *Inquest* by Edward Jay Epstein and *Rush to Judgment* by Mark Lane declared that the commission had not investigated deeply enough to produce conclusive results. In that same year, Jim Garrison, a New Orleans district attorney, stunned the public with his revelations of a conspiracy and his accusations against prominent businessman Clay Shaw. Shaw was tried on conspiracy charges but was acquitted in 1969.

Since the release of the Warren Commission report, thousands of articles and books have been published promoting various theories sur-

rounding the assassination. A 1979 special committee of the House of Representatives reexamined the evidence and concluded that Kennedy "was probably assassinated as a result of a conspiracy."

Allegations that federal agencies withheld assassination evidence led Congress to enact the President John F. Kennedy Assassination Records Collection Act of 1992 (44 U.S.C.A. § 2107). The act created the Assassination Records Review Board, an independent federal agency that oversees the identification and release of records related to the assassination of President Kennedy. The act granted the review board the mandate and the authority to identify, secure, and make available, through the National Archives and Records Administration, records related to Kennedy's assassination. Creation of the review board has allowed the release of thousands of previously secret government documents and files.

WARREN COURT From 1953 to 1969, EARL WARREN presided as chief justice of the U.S. Supreme Court. Under Warren's leadership, the Court actively used JUDICIAL REVIEW to strictly scrutinize and overturn state and federal statutes, to apply many provisions of the BILL OF RIGHTS to the states, and to provide opportunities for those groups in society that had been excluded from the political process. During Warren's tenure, the Court became increasingly liberal and activist, drawing the fire of political and judicial conservatives who believed that the Warren Court had overstepped its constitutional role and had become a legislative body. The Warren Court itself became a catalyst for change, initiating reforms rather than responding to pressures applied by other branches of government.

The Warren Court was committed to the promotion of a libertarian and egalitarian soci-

Three members of the Warren Commission stand in front of the Texas school book depository, from which the shots that killed President Kennedy were fired.

ety. The Court used the STRICT SCRUTINY test of constitutional review to strike down legislation that directly abridged the exercise of fundamental rights or narrowed the number of people who might exercise them, and to invalidate legislation that discriminated on the basis of race, religion, and other SUSPECT CLASSIFICATIONS. Under strict scrutiny, the government has the burden of proving that a COMPELLING STATE INTEREST exists for the legislation and that the law was narrowly tailored to minimize the restriction on the fundamental right. This burden proved difficult to meet during the Warren Court years, turning the FEDERAL COURTS into institutions that protected the interests of politically unpopular individuals and members of relatively powerless minority groups who had been victimized by pervasive historical, political, economic, and social DISCRIMINATION.

Racial Discrimination The first major decision of the Warren Court is arguably its most important. In *Brown v. Board of Education*, 347 U.S. 483, 74 S. Ct. 686, 98 L. Ed. 873 (1954), the Court overruled the 1896 Supreme Court decision of *Plessy v. Ferguson*, 163 U.S. 537, 16 S. Ct. 1138, 41 L. Ed. 256, which had allowed racially segregated facilities on trains and by implication in public schools. The Court made clear that state-sponsored racial segregation of public schools was inherently unequal and that it violated the Equal Protection Clause of the FOURTEENTH AMENDMENT.

The *Brown* decision helped trigger the modern CIVIL RIGHTS MOVEMENT. During the 1960s the Warren Court upheld federal CIVIL RIGHTS legislation, including the CIVIL RIGHTS ACT of 1964 (42 U.S.C.A. § 2000a et seq.) and the VOTING RIGHTS ACT OF 1965 (42 U.S.C.A. § 1973 et seq.). The Court struck down state laws that were racially discriminatory, including statutes that forbade racially mixed marriages. The Court applied the THIRTEENTH AMENDMENT, which abolished SLAVERY, to outlaw all discrimination in the sale and rental of property and in the making of contracts.

Voting and Reapportionment Apart from upholding the Voting Rights Act of 1965, the Warren Court removed impediments to VOTING by striking down state POLL TAX and property qualifications, unreasonable RESIDENCY requirements, and obstacles to putting third political parties on the ballot.

The Court also changed the makeup of state legislatures by reversing PRECEDENT and agreeing to hear legislative reapportionment cases. In *Reynolds v. Sims*, 377 U.S. 533, 84 S. Ct. 1362, 12 L. Ed. 2d 506 (1964), Warren wrote the opinion that has come to be known as the "ONE PERSON, ONE VOTE" decision. *Reynolds* and a series

of cases that followed forced state legislatures to be apportioned equally on the basis of population rather than geographic areas. Reapportionment based on population resulted in a shift of political power away from sparsely populated rural areas to metropolitan areas.

Criminal Procedure The Warren Court aroused bitter controversy with its decisions in CRIMINAL PROCEDURE. The Court sought to provide equal justice by providing criminal defendants with an attorney in FELONY cases if they could not afford one (*Gideon v. Wainwright*, 372 U.S. 335, 83 S. Ct. 792, 9 L. Ed. 2d 799 [1963]). It also ruled that indigent defendants could not be denied the opportunity to APPEAL their cases or to participate fully in post-conviction proceedings because of a lack of funds to obtain the necessary transcripts or to hire counsel.

The decision in *Miranda v. Arizona*, 384 U.S. 436, 86 S. Ct. 1602, 16 L. Ed. 2d 694 (1966), proved to be the Warren Court's most controversial criminal procedure case. The Court required what has come to be known as the *Miranda* warning: police must inform arrested persons that they need not answer questions and that they may have an attorney present during questioning.

In addition, the Court used the Fourteenth Amendment to incorporate federal constitutional rights, thus making them applicable to the states. Using this process, the Court applied the EXCLUSIONARY RULE to the states. This meant that evidence seized in violation of the FOURTH AMENDMENT could not be used in a criminal prosecution. The Warren Court also applied to the states the federal constitutional right against CRUEL AND UNUSUAL PUNISHMENT in the EIGHTH AMENDMENT, the RIGHT TO COUNSEL in the SIXTH AMENDMENT, the right against compelled SELF-INCRIMINATION in the Fifth Amendment, and the rights to confront witnesses and to a JURY trial in all criminal cases, which are guaranteed by the Sixth Amendment. These decisions radically changed the criminal justice system and generated criticism that the Court had gone too far in protecting the accused.

First Amendment The Warren Court sought to protect FIRST AMENDMENT rights. It invalidated the Georgia House of Representatives' exclusion of one of its members because of his antiwar and antidraft statements. The Court also attacked vagueness and overbreadth in compulsory LOYALTY OATHS and ruled against the compulsory disclosure of organization memberships. It moved to invalidate attempts in southern states to inhibit the functioning of the NATIONAL ASSOCIATION FOR THE ADVANCEMENT OF COLORED PEOPLE, to make public the identities of the organization's members, and to deny its members opportunities for public employment.

During the 1960s, the Court upheld the legitimacy of demonstrations at state capitols and in the streets and sit-ins at segregated lunch counters. It also upheld the right of individuals to picket in a privately owned shopping center and the right of high school students to express their opposition to the Vietnam War by wearing black armbands to school.

The Warren Court also changed state slander and libel laws that stifled open discussion of controversial issues. It held that persons who are public officials or PUBLIC FIGURES cannot recover DAMAGES in a DEFAMATION action unless they prove that a false statement was made with "actual malice" (with knowledge that it was false or with reckless disregard of whether it was false).

The Court also reviewed many freedom of RELIGION cases, provoking controversy over its interpretation of the Establishment Clause of the First Amendment. The Warren Court struck down Bible reading and the reciting of state-written prayers in public schools, even those religious acts done on a voluntary basis. The Court did, however, uphold, with qualifications, state aid to children attending religious schools. As to the First Amendment's Free Exercise Clause, the Court sought to protect the rights of religious dissenters and nonconformists when it struck down a Maryland constitutional provision requiring the declaration of a belief in God as a prerequisite to holding public office. It also held that an individual need not believe in a supreme being to be eligible for CONSCIENTIOUS OBJECTOR status.

Right to Privacy One of the most significant rulings of the Warren Court was its recognition of the constitutional right of PRIVACY. In *Griswold v. Connecticut*, 381 U.S. 479, 85 S. Ct. 1678, 14 L. Ed. 2d 510 (1965), the Court struck down a Connecticut statute that prohibited the dissemination of BIRTH CONTROL information. In declaring the right of privacy, the Court laid the groundwork for the post–Warren Court decision in *Roe v. Wade*, 410 U.S. 113, 93 S. Ct. 705,

BIOGRAPHY

PORTRAIT BY ADRIAN LAMB, AFTER CHESTER HARDING. COLLECTION OF THE SUPREME COURT OF THE UNITED STATES.

Bushrod Washington

"IT IS BUT A DECENT RESPECT DUE TO THE WISDOM, THE INTEGRITY, AND THE PATRIOTISM OF THE LEGISLATIVE BODY, BY WHICH ANY LAW IS PASSED, TO PRESUME IN FAVOR OF ITS VALIDITY, UNTIL ITS VIOLATION OF THE CONSTITUTION IS PROVED BEYOND ALL REASONABLE DOUBT."

35 L. Ed. 2d 147 (1973), which gave women the right to have an ABORTION.

CROSS-REFERENCES

Apportionment; *Baker v. Carr*; *Brown v. Board of Education of Topeka, Kansas*; Custodial Interrogation; Equal Protection; *Gideon v. Wainwright*; Incorporation Doctrine; Libel and Slander; *Mapp v. Ohio*; *Miranda v. Arizona*; *New York Times v. Sullivan*; Overbreadth Doctrine; *Plessy v. Ferguson*; *Reynolds v. Sims*; School Desegregation; Symbolic Speech; Void for Vagueness.

WASHINGTON, BUSHROD

Bushrod Washington served on the U.S. Supreme Court as an associate justice from 1798 to 1829. A strong Federalist and able jurist, Washington was tolerant and well-liked by other members of the bar. His reputation, though respectable, might shine more brightly today if it was not overshadowed by that of his contemporary and friend, Chief Justice JOHN MARSHALL. Washington concurred with Marshall's opinions so often that jokes were made about them being one justice. Although he wrote a handful of significant opinions on contract law, Washington is remembered primarily as a stalwart supporter of the chief justice.

Born on June 5, 1762, in Westmoreland County, Virginia, Washington enjoyed the benefits of an aristocratic life. He was a nephew of George Washington, the nation's first president, and the two were close. He inherited the president's estate at Mount Vernon. Tutored at home in his childhood, Washington later attended the College of William and Mary, graduating in 1778. He studied law privately until 1781 and then served in the Revolutionary War. In 1784 he was admitted to the Virginia bar.

Washington first practiced law in Alexandria, Virginia, where he also became involved in politics. In these early years of the young lawyer's life, he specialized in chancery cases—typical lawsuits under the now-antiquated system of EQUITY law. Yet he had an eager mind and kept expanding the range of his experience. He became a keen supporter of FEDERALISM, embracing its belief in strong federal government, and in 1787 won election to the Virginia House of Delegates. In 1788, as the nation was preparing to ratify the Constitution, he served as a

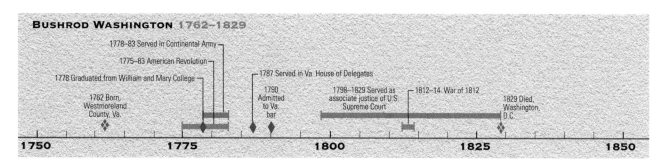

BUSHROD WASHINGTON 1762–1829

1778–83 Served in Continental Army
1775–83 American Revolution
1778 Graduated from William and Mary College
1762 Born, Westmoreland County, Va.
1787 Served in Va. House of Delegates
1790 Admitted to Va. bar
1798–1829 Served as associate justice of U.S. Supreme Court
1812–14 War of 1812
1829 Died, Washington, D.C.

1750   1775   1800   1825   1850

delegate to Virginia's ratifying convention. By the late 1790s, Washington had established his own practice in Richmond, trained numerous lawyers, and written two enormous volumes of reports on cases as a recorder for the state's court of appeals. His legal and political experience prompted President JOHN ADAMS to appoint him to the Supreme Court in 1798.

On the Court, Washington almost always followed the lead of Chief Justice Marshall. The two had been friends since their student days and shared political sympathies. Marshall, widely viewed as the greatest leader of the Court in history, was also an ardent judicial Federalist. Only three times did Washington vote differently from Marshall, and only once did he attach a concurring opinion to the chief justice's opinion. This was in *Dartmouth College v. Woodward*, 17 U.S. (4 Wheat.) 518, 4 L. Ed. 629 (1819), a landmark case that upheld the inviolability of CONTRACTS. Washington's cautious concurrence sought to limit the implications of the decision.

If the two men differed philosophically, it was only by degree. Washington wished to avoid conflicts with STATES' RIGHTS whenever possible. He dissented only twice during thirty-one years on the Court. In fact, as a trusted supporter of the chief justice during the early tumultuous years of Marshall's tenure, he even went so far as to discourage his colleagues from writing dissents when ordinary issues were involved.

Washington also made independent contributions to the Court. He wrote the first part of the decision in *Ogden v. Saunders*, 25 U.S. (12 Wheat.) 213, 6 L. Ed. 606 (1827), which stated that any law passed before the execution of a contract is a valid part of that contract. He was noted for his fairness while "circuit riding"—traveling and performing the duties of a circuit judge, a routine though difficult task for Supreme Court justices in the early nineteenth century.

Washington died in Philadelphia on November 26, 1829.

THE GRANGER COLLECTION, NEW YORK

George Washington

WASHINGTON, GEORGE George Washington was a U.S. military leader, statesperson, and the first president of the United States from 1789 to 1797. A leader of mythic proportion in U.S. history, Washington's leadership from the American Revolution to the end of his presidential administrations proved crucial to winning independence from Great Britain and establishing a national union of states based on the U.S. Constitution.

Washington was born on February 22, 1732, in Westmoreland County, Virginia. Born into the colonial aristocracy, Washington attended local schools and supplemented his formal education by reading widely. As a young man he became a surveyor, and in 1749 he was appointed county surveyor for Culpeper County, Virginia. In 1752, at the age of twenty, Washington inherited the family estate at Mount Vernon and embarked on a military career.

During the French and Indian War, Washington gained his first military experience. The war was fought to determine whether France or Great Britain would rule North America. In 1753 Washington requested and received the assignment of delivering an ultimatum to the French, ordering them to retreat from the Ohio Valley. The French refused, and Washington led troops against them. Although Washington won an initial victory in 1754, the French counterattacked in force and Washington had to surrender his camp at Fort Necessity, Pennsylvania. He resigned his commission, but in May 1755 Washington became an unpaid volunteer, serving as aide-de-camp to the British general Edward Braddock. Braddock was ambushed and killed later that year near Fort Duquesne, and Washington himself narrowly escaped. In August 1755 Washington was promoted to colonel and given command of the Virginia MILITIA, which defended the western frontier of the colony. During the remainder of the war, Washington successfully protected the frontier.

In 1759 Washington returned to Mount Vernon, where he married Martha Custes, a young

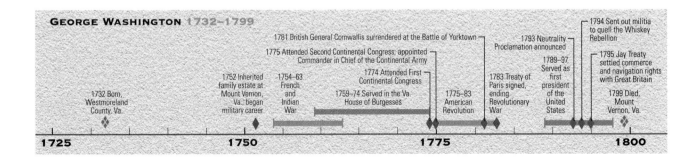

GEORGE WASHINGTON 1732–1799

1794 Sent out militia to quell the Whiskey Rebellion

1781 British General Cornwallis surrendered at the Battle of Yorktown

1775 Attended Second Continental Congress; appointed Commander in Chief of the Continental Army

1793 Neutrality Proclamation announced

1795 Jay Treaty settled commerce and navigation rights with Great Britain

1774 Attended First Continental Congress

1789–97 Served as first president of the United States

1752 Inherited family estate at Mount Vernon, Va.; began military career

1754–63 French and Indian War

1783 Treaty of Paris signed, ending Revolutionary War

1799 Died, Mount Vernon, Va.

1732 Born, Westmoreland County, Va.

1759–74 Served in the Va. House of Burgesses

1775–83 American Revolution

1725   1750   1775   1800

widow with a large estate. The marriage made Washington one of the wealthiest men in Virginia. He was elected to the Virginia House of Burgesses in 1759, serving until 1774. During this period, colonial anger at British taxation and control began to steadily build. Great Britain believed that the taxes were justified to help repay the war debt and recognize British efforts to successfully remove France from North America. Washington, like many other colonial leaders, joined the protest against British interference and in 1774 endorsed the Fairfax Resolves, which called for a stringent BOYCOTT of British imports. In 1774 and 1775 he attended the First and Second CONTINENTAL CONGRESSES as a delegate from Virginia.

In 1775, as the Revolutionary War was imminent, the Congress appointed Washington commander in chief of the American forces, which were known as the Continental Army. It was hoped that Washington's appointment would promote unity between Virginia and New England.

Washington's years as commander in chief were a mix of defeats and victories. In March 1776 he successfully forced the British out of Boston, but in August the British defeated his forces at New York City. Washington then sought safety in New Jersey and emerged victorious again with his surprise attack on Trenton on December 25, 1776. On January 3, 1777, Washington's troops defeated the British at Princeton, New Jersey. The two victories were critical to maintaining colonial morale, and by the spring of 1777, more than eight thousand new soldiers had joined the Continental Army.

The tide turned, however, in September 1777, when Washington unsuccessfully tried to stop British forces from advancing on Philadelphia at the battle of Brandywine Creek. After the British occupied Philadelphia, Washington made a futile attack at nearby Germantown. During the winter of 1777 and 1778, Washington's troops stayed at Valley Forge, west of Philadelphia. The conditions were adverse, requiring all of Washington's leadership skills to hold his army together. During the winter his actions aroused dissent in Congress, and his critics sought to have General Horatio Gates replace Washington as commander in chief. Several congressmen and military officers backed Gates, but the public rallied behind Washington.

In June 1778 Washington attacked the British at Monmouth, New Jersey, but again was defeated. He then shifted his military strategy, keeping his troops encamped around British forces in Connecticut, New York, and New Jersey. In 1781 Washington defeated General

"LIBERTY, WHEN IT BEGINS TO TAKE ROOT, IS A PLANT OF RAPID GROWTH."

Charles Cornwallis at the Battle of Yorktown in Virginia. The surrender of Cornwallis marked the end of major military actions in the Revolutionary War. The signing of the TREATY OF PARIS in 1783 officially ended the conflict, with Great Britain recognizing the independence of the thirteen colonies and the geographic boundaries of the new nation.

After the war Washington returned to Mount Vernon, but he was soon drawn back into politics. The ARTICLES OF CONFEDERATION proved ineffective for governing the national affairs of the thirteen states. SHAYS'S REBELLION, named after its leader Daniel Shays, was an armed insurrection in Massachusetts in 1787 and 1788 that convinced U.S. political leaders that a strong national government was needed. Washington agreed and consented to serve as president at the Constitutional Convention of 1787 in Philadelphia. Though he played no part in the drafting of the Constitution and did not participate in behind-the-scenes political discussions, Washington's presence lent legitimacy to the effort to craft a new government.

As the leading national figure, Washington was the logical choice to become the first president of the United States. His election in 1788 helped shape the EXECUTIVE BRANCH of federal government. Washington decided to surround himself with a group of national leaders as his advisors and administrators. Though the presidential CABINET is not discussed in the Constitution, Washington's use of it made it a traditional part of a president's administration.

The first cabinet included THOMAS JEFFERSON as secretary of state and ALEXANDER HAMILTON as secretary of the treasury. Washington was sympathetic to Hamilton's belief that a strong national government was needed, including the establishment of a national bank. In contrast, Jefferson believed that the states should continue to be dominant, with the national government confined to the enumerated powers contained in the Constitution. The conflict between Hamilton and Jefferson dominated Washington's administration.

Jefferson supported the French Revolution, whereas Hamilton favored British efforts to organize a coalition to topple the new regime through warfare. As events unfolded, Washington announced in the Neutrality Proclamation of 1793 that the United States favored neutrality in the war between France and the British coalition. U.S. neutrality clearly favored the British. When the French emissary Edmond-Charles Genet tried to recruit U.S. soldiers to serve as volunteers for the French cause, Washington had Genet recalled and repudiated the

1778 treaty with France. Jefferson opposed Washington's actions and resigned as secretary of state, causing a rift in the Republican party and precipitating the formation of the Federalist party, with Hamilton as its leader.

Reelected in 1792, Washington faced domestic problems in 1794 with the WHISKEY REBELLION in Pennsylvania. Organized as a protest against a federal liquor tax, the Pennsylvania uprising was quelled when Washington ordered the militia to maintain peace.

In 1795 Washington faced opposition to the Jay Treaty with Great Britain, which JOHN JAY had negotiated to settle commerce and navigation rights. One section of the treaty permitted the British to search U.S. ships. The treaty was adopted because of Washington's popularity, but both the president and the treaty were severely criticized.

Washington did not seek reelection in 1796. In his celebrated *Farewell Address,* he advised against "entangling alliances" with European nations. He returned to Mount Vernon, where he spent the rest of his years managing his estate.

Washington died on December 14, 1799, at Mount Vernon.

WASHINGTON v. GLUCKSBERG   In *Washington v. Glucksberg,* __U.S. __ , 117 S. Ct. 2258, 138 L. Ed. 2d 772 (1997), the U.S. Supreme Court was asked to review the constitutionality of a Washington state statute prohibiting physician-assisted SUICIDE. By upholding the statute and denying mentally competent, terminally ill patients a constitutional right to hasten their death through lethal doses of self-administered, doctor-prescribed medication, the Supreme Court returned this controversial issue to the states where it continues to be debated among residents, legislators, and judges. In handing down its decision, the Court was careful to point out that it was not foreclosing reconsideration of the issue at some later time.

The case arose in January 1994 when four Washington physicians, three gravely ill patients, and a nonprofit organization that counsels people considering doctor-assisted suicide filed a lawsuit in the U.S. District Court for the Western District of Washington. The lawsuit challenged the constitutionality of Washington Revised Code section 9A.36.060, which makes it a crime to knowingly assist, aid, or cause the suicide of another person. The district court ruled the statute unconstitutional on the ground that it violated the LIBERTY interest protected by the Due Process Clause of the Fifth and Fourteenth Amendments to the U.S. Constitution (*Compassion in Dying v. Washington,* 850 F. Supp. 1454).

The case was then appealed to the U.S. Court of Appeals for the Ninth Circuit, where a panel of judges reversed the district court's ruling and reinstated the Washington statute. In a 2–1 decision, the court of appeals emphasized that no right to assisted suicide has ever been recognized by a court of final JURISDICTION anywhere in the United States (*Compassion in Dying v. Washington,* 49 F.3d 586 (1995). Agreeing to rehear the case en banc (before eleven judges on the ninth circuit), the court of appeals reversed the panel's decision and affirmed the district court's ruling, which had invalidated the Washington statute (*Compassion in Dying v. Washington,* 79 F.3d 790 (1996). In an 8–3 decision, the APPELLATE COURT said that "the Constitution encompasses a due process liberty interest in controlling the time and manner of one's death," including the liberty interest of certain patients to hasten their deaths by taking deadly amounts of medication prescribed by their physicians.

When the case reached the Supreme Court, Chief Justice WILLIAM H. REHNQUIST cast the issue in a slightly different light. In an opinion joined by Justices SANDRA DAY O'CONNOR, ANTONIN SCALIA, ANTHONY M. KENNEDY, and CLARENCE THOMAS, Rehnquist said that the case turned on whether the Due Process Clause protects the right to commit suicide with another's assistance. According to the Court, three reasons supported its decision to reject such a constitutional claim.

First, the Court observed that suicide and assisted suicide have been disapproved by Anglo-Saxon law for more than seven hundred years. From thirteenth-century England through nineteenth-century America, the Court said, the COMMON LAW has consistently authorized the punishment of those who have attempted to kill themselves or assisted others in doing so. Second, the Court pointed to the overwhelming majority of states that currently prohibit physician-assisted suicide. Only Oregon expressly allows doctors to help their patients hasten their demise through lethal doses of prescribed medication, and the law that allows this practice is presently being challenged in court. Third, the Court found that the history of the Due Process Clause does not support the asserted right to assisted suicide.

Although the Due Process Clause protects certain fundamental rights, the Court wrote, the asserted right to physician-assisted suicide does not rise to this level of importance. Before a right may be deemed fundamental in nature, it must be deeply rooted in the nation's legal history. Because the Court found the asserted right to physician-assisted suicide to be contrary to U.S. history, tradition, and practice, it concluded that it was not a fundamental right. This conclusion meant that the Court would not apply the STRICT SCRUTINY standard of judicial review that is required when a piece of legislation affects a highly valued liberty or freedom.

Instead, the Court applied a minimal standard of judicial scrutiny. Known as the rational relationship test, this standard of judicial scrutiny requires courts to uphold laws that are reasonably related to some legitimate government interest. In this case the Court said that the state of Washington had a legitimate interest in preserving life, preventing suicide, protecting the integrity and ethics of the medical profession, and safeguarding vulnerable members of society, such as the poor, elderly, and disabled, from friends and relatives who see physician-assisted suicide as a way to end the heartache and burden that often accompany the protracted illness of a loved one.

On the same day that the Court released its decision in *Glucksberg*, it announced its decision in a companion case, *Vacco v. Quill*, __U.S. __ , 117 S. Ct. 2293, 138 L. Ed. 2d 834 (1997). *Vacco* differed from *Glucksberg* in that the plaintiffs in *Vacco* (three doctors and three terminally ill patients) challenged a New York law prohibiting physician-assisted suicide on the ground that it violated the Equal Protection Clause of the FOURTEENTH AMENDMENT to the U.S. Constitution. New York Penal Law section 125.15 makes it a crime to intentionally help another person commit suicide. However, pursuant to the Supreme Court's decision in *Cruzan v. Director, Missouri Department of Health*, 497 U.S. 261, 110 S. Ct. 2841, 111 L. Ed. 2d 224 (1990), New York permits competent adult patients to terminate life-sustaining treatment, such as artificial hydration, nutrition, and respiration.

The Equal Protection Clause requires the government to provide equal treatment to all similarly situated people. The Fourteenth Amendment prohibits the government from denying legal rights to one group of persons when those same rights are afforded to another group confronted by indistinguishable circumstances. The plaintiffs argued that the withdrawal of life-sustaining treatment is tantamount to suicide, because by definition its withdrawal typically ends life by ceasing to sustain it. The plaintiffs in *Vacco* contended that, in allowing some patients to hasten their death by terminating life-sustaining measures but not allowing other patients to hasten their deaths by taking lethal doses of prescribed medication,

New York had denied patients EQUAL PROTECTION of the laws.

The Supreme Court disagreed. A fundamental distinction exists between letting a patient die and killing her, Chief Justice Rehnquist wrote in the majority opinion that was again joined by Justices O'Connor, Scalia, Kennedy, and Thomas. In one instance, the patient is allowed to die by natural causes when life-sustaining treatment is withdrawn. The patient's cause of death in that instance, the Court said, is the underlying illness. In the other instance, the Court continued, death is intentionally inflicted by the joint effort of doctor and patient. The cause of death in that instance, the Court emphasized, is not the underlying illness, but human action.

The Court also pointed out that the *Cruzan* decision was based on the ancient common-law tradition of protecting patients from unwanted medical treatment. Under the common law, it is considered a BATTERY (an intentional TORT that makes any unwanted touching actionable) for a physician to force a COMPETENT adult to undergo life-sustaining treatment over a clearly voiced objection. Based in part on this common-law tradition, the Court in *Cruzan* recognized a limited constitutional right of a competent, adult patient to disconnect hydration, nutrition, and respiration equipment, even if exercising this right would necessarily result in the patient's death. However, the Court in *Vacco* noted that a right to physician-assisted suicide has never been approved by the common law but has been historically discouraged by both common-law and statutory schemes throughout the United States. Thus, the Court concluded that physician-assisted suicide is not substantially similar to refusing medical treatment and that the legal systems of New York and other states may treat each practice differently without running afoul of the Equal Protection Clause.

Although the decisions in *Glucksberg* and *Vacco* were both unanimous, a number of justices wrote concurring opinions that were applicable to both cases. In a concurring opinion by Justice O'Connor, which was joined by Justice RUTH BADER GINSBURG, O'Connor stressed that the states remain free to establish a right to physician-assisted suicide or to otherwise strike a proper balance between the interests of terminally ill patients and the interests of society. State legislatures, O'Connor suggested, are a more appropriate forum for making such difficult decisions because their members are accountable to the electorate at the ballot box. By contrast, the federal judiciary is often insulated from public opinion because their members are appointed to the bench for life. Relying on several studies undertaken by the states to evaluate the problem of physician-assisted suicide, O'Connor said that the right to die must first be grappled with at the local level before entangling FEDERAL COURTS in the controversy.

Justice JOHN PAUL STEVENS's concurring opinion also underscored the need for further national debate on the propriety of physician-assisted suicide, but in a different vein. Although the states' interests may have been adequately served in *Glucksberg* and *Vacco*, Stevens cautioned, the Court's holding in these two cases does not foreclose the possibility that other circumstances might arise in which such statutes would infringe on a constitutionally protected area. There will be times, Stevens wrote, when a patient's interests in hastening his death will outweigh the state's countervailing interests in preserving his life. Although Stevens did not speculate about the circumstances in which a patient might successfully assert a right-to-die claim, Justice STEPHEN BREYER took the opportunity to do so in his concurring opinion.

Breyer suggested that the right to die should be renamed "the right-to-die with dignity." Once recognized by the Court, Breyer said, the right to die with dignity would include a competent patient's right to control the manner of her death, the quality and degree of professional care and intervention, and the amount of physical pain and suffering. According to Breyer, a statute that would prevent patients from obtaining access to certain palliative care aimed at reducing pain and suffering might infringe on the right to die with dignity. Competent, terminally ill adult patients, Breyer intimated, may enjoy a constitutional right to prescription medication that will minimize the agony that often tortures the final days of their existence.

Justice DAVID H. SOUTER articulated a different method of analysis for evaluating right-to-die cases. Souter argued that the so-called right to die is a species of SUBSTANTIVE DUE PROCESS. Substantive due process, Souter reminded the Court, is a doctrine under which a judge evaluates the substantive merits of a statute, as opposed to the procedure by which it is implemented or administered. Under the rubric of substantive due process, the Court has recognized an individual's interest in dignity, autonomy, and PRIVACY, among other things, over the course of the last century. The right to refuse unwanted medical treatment recognized by the Court in *Cruzan*, for example, was designed in part to serve these three interests.

Souter contended that the doctrine of substantive due process protects individuals from "arbitrary impositions" and "purposeless restraints" created by the government. Souter advocated viewing substantive due process claims on a continuum of liberty in which the level of judicial scrutiny would increase in direct proportion to the level of government restraint or imposition. First enunciated by Justice JOHN MARSHALL HARLAN in his dissenting opinion in *Poe v. Ullman*, 367 U.S. 497, 81 S. Ct. 1752, 6 L. Ed. 2d 989 (1961), this approach to substantive due process would require courts to carefully balance the competing interests presented by the litigants in each right-to-die case.

Souter contrasted this simpler approach with the more complicated analysis presently employed by the Court, an analysis that involves multiple tiers of judicial scrutiny, ranging from strict to minimal scrutiny, different categories of constitutional rights, ranging from fundamental to non-fundamental rights, and different classes of protected status into which a plaintiff may fall, ranging from suspect to non-suspect classes. A BALANCING approach like the one articulated in *Poe*, Souter maintained, would allow for the gradual evolution of a constitutional right to die, instead of the complicated all-or-nothing approach that the Court has effectively adopted.

CROSS-REFERENCES

Death and Dying; Living Will; *In re Quinlan.*

WASH SALE 📖 The buying and selling of the same or a similar ASSET within a short period of time.

A fictitious type of arrangement whereby a BROKER, upon receiving an order from one individual to purchase and an order from another individual to sell a certain amount of a particular STOCK or COMMODITY, transfers it from one principal to the other and retains the difference in value. 📖

For the purposes of INCOME TAX, losses on a wash sale of stock may not be recognized as capital losses if stock of equal value is obtained within thirty days prior or subsequent to the date of sale.

Various stock exchanges disallow this practice because the orders to buy and sell should be executed separately to the advantage of each of the broker's clients.

WASTE 📖 Harmful or destructive use of REAL PROPERTY by one in rightful POSSESSION of the property. 📖

Waste is an unreasonable or improper use of land by an individual in rightful possession of the land. A party with an interest in a parcel of land may file a CIVIL ACTION based on waste committed by an individual who also has an interest in the land. Such disputes may arise between life tenants and remainderpersons and LANDLORDS and TENANTS. The lawsuit may seek an INJUNCTION to stop the waste, DAMAGES for the waste, or both. ACTIONS based on waste ordinarily arise when an owner of land takes exception to the manner in which the possessor or tenant is using the land.

The four common types of waste are voluntary, permissive, ameliorating, and equitable waste. Voluntary waste is the willful destruction or carrying away of something attached to the property. In an action for voluntary waste, the plaintiff must show that the waste was caused by an affirmative act of the tenant. Such waste might occur if a life tenant (a person who possesses the land for his lifetime, after which a remainderperson takes possession) chops down all the trees on the occupied land and sells them as lumber.

Voluntary waste will also occur, for example, if the tenant of an apartment removes kitchen appliances that are attached to the apartment floors and walls. More commonly, the tenant breaks a window, damages walls or woodwork, or otherwise damages the apartment. Landlords typically protect against this type of voluntary waste by requiring a damage or security deposit from the tenant at the commencement of the lease. When the tenant vacates the apartment, the landlord inspects for waste. If the apartment has been damaged, the landlord will use part or all of the deposit for repairs. If the damage exceeds the deposit, however, the landlord may file an action seeking damages for the repairs not covered by the deposit.

Permissive waste is an INJURY caused by an omission, rather than an affirmative act, on the part of the tenant. This type of waste might occur, for example, if a tenant permits a house to fall into disrepair by not making reasonable maintenance repairs.

Ameliorating waste is an alteration in the physical characteristics of the premises by an unauthorized act of the tenant that increases the value of the property. For example, a tenant might make improvements that increase the value of the property, such as remodeling a bathroom. Generally, a tenant is not held liable if she commits this type of waste.

Equitable waste is a harm to the reversionary interest in land that is inconsistent with fruitful use. This CAUSE OF ACTION is recognized only by courts of EQUITY and is not regarded as legal waste in courts of law. For example, if the life tenant begins to cut down immature trees, the remainderperson, who will someday take possession of the property, may file an action in equity seeking an injunction to stop the cutting. The remainderperson would argue that the cutting imperils the productive use of the land in the future, because the value of the land after the immature trees have been cut would be decreased.

In an action for waste, a plaintiff commonly will seek damages for acts that have already occurred and request an injunction against future acts. A court will order an injunction if it finds that irreparable harm will occur and that the legal remedy would be inadequate, unless otherwise provided by statute. Certain laws provide for temporary relief if acts of waste are either threatened or committed.

The ordinary measure of damages for waste is the diminution in value of the property to the nonpossessor as a result of the acts of the possessor. This is frequently difficult to measure, particularly in situations where a significant period of time will elapse before the plaintiff is entitled to actual possession.

See also LANDLORD AND TENANT; LIFE ESTATE.

WATERGATE Watergate is the name given to the scandals involving President RICHARD M. NIXON, members of his administration, and operatives working for Nixon's 1972 reelection organization. The name comes from the Watergate apartment and hotel complex in Washington, D.C., which in 1972 was the location of the Democratic National Committee (DNC). On June 17, 1972, several burglars were caught breaking in to DNC headquarters. The break-in and the subsequent cover-up by Nixon and his aides culminated two years later in the president's resignation. Nixon's departure on August 9, 1974, prevented his IMPEACHMENT by the Senate. President GERALD R. FORD'S PARDON of Nixon one month later prevented any criminal charges from being filed against the former president.

It has never been disclosed what the burglars who broke into DNC headquarters were seeking, but they were acting on orders from Nixon's first attorney general, JOHN N. MITCHELL, who was heading Nixon's reelection campaign, and several other high officials in the campaign staff and the White House. Though Nixon may not have known in advance about the break-in, by June 23, 1972, six days later, he had begun to participate in the cover-up. On that date he ordered the CENTRAL INTELLIGENCE AGENCY (CIA) to direct the FEDERAL BUREAU OF INVESTIGATION (FBI) to stop investigating the BURGLARY, on the pretense that an investigation would endanger national security. This particular plan failed, but

The Watergate scandal involved a series of prosecutors, including, from left, Elliot Richardson, Archibald Cox, Leon Jaworski, and Henry Ruth.

Nixon and his aides contained the damage during the fall presidential campaign. Nixon won a landslide victory over Democratic Senator George S. McGovern of South Dakota in November 1972.

During the first two months of 1973, Watergate receded from the public eye. However, on March 23, 1973, Judge John J. Sirica of the U.S. District Court for the District of Columbia imposed harsh sentences on the Watergate burglars. Sirica, who had presided at the trial, was convinced that the burglars were acting at the direction of others not yet revealed. He told the burglars that he would reduce their sentences if they cooperated with the investigation then being conducted by the U.S. Senate. He also released a letter from convicted burglar James W. McCord, Jr., who said that pressure had been applied to convince the burglars not to reveal all that they knew, that administration officials had committed PERJURY, and that higher-ups were involved.

A federal GRAND JURY soon began to receive information from campaign insiders about campaign and White House involvement in the cover-up. In addition, the continuing investigative work of *Washington Post* reporters Carl Bernstein and Bob Woodward provided more details about the inner workings of Nixon's 1972 campaign and its connections with the White House. Finally, the Senate investigating committee headed by Senator SAM J. ERVIN, JR., began to call Nixon aides to testify before it.

Nixon, who initially called the break-in "a third rate burglary," sought to have his chief aides, John D. Ehrlichman and H. R. ("Bob") Haldeman, "stonewall" prosecutors. The three men attempted to make John Mitchell the scapegoat, but public pressure forced Nixon to accept the resignations of Ehrlichman, Haldeman, White House counsel John W. Dean III,

and Attorney General RICHARD G. KLEINDIENST on April 30, 1973.

Nixon appointed ELLIOT L. RICHARDSON attorney general to succeed Kleindienst, who had been accused of political improprieties. Richardson appointed Harvard law professor ARCHIBALD COX as special Watergate prosecutor to investigate whether federal laws had been broken in connection with the break-in and the attempted cover-up. Richardson assured Cox, who was a personal friend, that he would have complete independence in his work.

At the Senate hearings, Dean and others disclosed the "dirty tricks" used by Nixon's political operatives and the cover-up activities after the break-in. However, in July 1973 the Watergate investigation changed course when Alexander Butterfield, a Haldeman aide, disclosed that Nixon had secretly taped all conversations in the Oval Office. Cox immediately subpoenaed the tapes of the conversations. When Nixon refused to honor the SUBPOENA, Judge Sirica ordered Nixon to turn over the tapes. After the federal court of appeals upheld the order, Nixon offered to provide Cox with written summaries of the conversations in return for an agreement that Cox would not seek the release of any more presidential documents.

Cox refused the proposal. On Saturday, October 20, Nixon ordered Richardson to fire Cox. Richardson and his deputy attorney general, William D. Ruckelshaus, resigned rather than carry out the order. Cox was fired that night by solicitor general ROBERT H. BORK. The two resignations and the firing of Cox became known as the Saturday Night Massacre. The national outrage at Nixon's actions forced him to appoint a new prosecutor, LEON JAWORSKI. Jaworski immediately renewed the request for the tapes.

Although Nixon released edited transcripts of some of the subpoenaed conversations, he refused to turn over the unedited tapes on the grounds of EXECUTIVE PRIVILEGE. When the district court denied Nixon's motion to QUASH the subpoena, he appealed, and the case was quickly brought to the Supreme Court.

Nixon contended that the doctrine of executive privilege gave him the right to withhold documents from Congress and the courts. In *United States v. Nixon*, 418 U.S. 683, 94 S. Ct. 3090, 41 L. Ed. 2d 1039 (1974), the Supreme Court recognized the legitimacy of the doctrine of executive privilege, but held that it could not prevent the disclosure of materials needed for a criminal prosecution. The Court ordered the judge to review the subpoenaed tapes in private to determine which portions should be released to prosecutors. This confidential review would prevent sensitive but irrelevant information from being disclosed. Nonetheless, the Court directed Nixon to turn over the tapes.

The decision was handed down on July 24, 1974, at the same time the House Judiciary Committee was nearing completion of its impeachment hearings. Despite more than a year of damaging disclosures, many congressional Republicans remained loyal to the president, arguing that he had committed no criminal offenses that would make him liable for impeachment. Nevertheless, the committee voted three ARTICLES OF IMPEACHMENT against Nixon: for obstructing justice in the Watergate investigation, for exceeding PRESIDENTIAL POWER in waging a secret war in Cambodia without congressional approval, and for failing to cooperate with Congress in its attempt to gather EVIDENCE against him.

Nixon complied with the Supreme Court decision and turned over the tapes. When prosecutors discovered the June 23, 1972, conversation in which Nixon directed the CIA to halt the FBI investigation, they knew they had the "smoking gun" that tied Nixon to the cover-up. On August 6, 1974, Republican congressional leaders were informed about the contents of this tape. Nixon's political support vanished.

Faced with an impeachment trial, Nixon announced his resignation on August 8, 1974, and left office the next day. Though President Ford pardoned Nixon, most of the other participants in Watergate were convicted for their crimes. Mitchell, Haldeman, and Ehrlichman, among others, spent time in prison.

See also SPECIAL PROSECUTOR; UNITED STATES v. NIXON.

WATER POLLUTION Without healthy water for drinking, cooking, fishing, and farming, the human race would perish. Clean water is also necessary for recreational interests such as swimming, boating, and water skiing. Yet, when Congress began assessing national water quality during the early 1970s, it found that much of the country's groundwater and surface water was contaminated or severely compromised. Studies revealed that the nation's three primary sources of water pollution—industry, agriculture, and municipalities—had been regularly discharging harmful materials into water supplies throughout the country over a number of years.

These harmful materials included organic wastes, sediments, minerals, nutrients, thermal pollutants, toxic chemicals, and other hazardous substances. Organic wastes are produced by animals and humans, and include such things as fecal matter, crop debris, yard clippings, food wastes, rubber, plastic, wood, and disposable diapers. Such wastes require oxygen to decompose. When they are dumped into streams and lakes and begin to break down, they can deprive aquatic life of the oxygen it needs to survive.

Sediments may be deposited into lakes and streams through soil erosion caused by the clearing, excavating, grading, transporting, and filling of land. Minerals, such as iron, copper, chromium, platinum, nickel, zinc, and tin, can be discharged into streams and lakes as a result of various mining activities. Excessive levels of sediments and minerals in water can inhibit the penetration of sunlight, which reduces the production of photosynthetic organisms.

Nutrients, like phosphorus and nitrogen, support the growth of algae and other plants forming the lower levels of the food chain. However, excessive levels of nutrients from sources such as fertilizer can cause eutrophication, which is the overgrowth of aquatic vegetation. This overgrowth clouds the water and smothers some plants. Over time, excessive nutrient levels can

Stricter laws on water pollution have been motivated in part by scenes like this accumulation of garbage and chemicals in the port of Houston, Texas.

PAUL S. HOWELL/LIAISON INTERNATIONAL

accelerate the natural process by which bodies of water evolve into dry land.

Thermal pollution results from the release of heated water into lakes and streams. Most thermal pollution is generated by power plant cooling systems. Power plants use water to cool their reactors and turbines, and discharge it into lakes and tributaries after it has become heated. Higher water temperatures accelerate biological and chemical processes in rivers and streams, reducing the water's ability to retain dissolved oxygen. This can hasten the growth of algae and disrupt the reproduction of fish.

Toxic chemicals and other hazardous materials present the most imminent threat to water quality. The ENVIRONMENTAL PROTECTION AGENCY (EPA) has identified 403 highly toxic chemicals, which are produced by 577 U.S. companies, manufactured in twelve thousand plants, and stored in four-hundred thousand locations across the country. Some chemical plants incinerate toxic wastes, which produces dangerous by-products like furans and chlorinated dioxins, two of the most deadly carcinogens known to the human race. Other hazardous materials are produced or stored by households (motor oil, antifreeze, paints, and pesticides), dry cleaners (chlorinated solvents), farms (insecticides, fungicides, rodenticides, and herbicides), and gas stations and airports (fuel).

Water pollution regulation consists of a labyrinth of state and federal statutes, administrative rules, and COMMON-LAW principles.

Statutory Law Federal statutory regulation of water pollution has been governed primarily by three pieces of legislation: the Refuse Act, the Federal Water Pollution Control Act, and the Clean Water Act. The Rivers and Harbors Appropriations Act of 1899, 33 U.S.C.A. § 401 et seq., commonly known as the Refuse Act, was the first major piece of federal legislation regulating water pollution. The Refuse Act set effluent standards for the discharge of pollutants into bodies of water. An effluent standard limits the amount of pollutant that can be released from a specific point or source, such as a smokestack or sewage pipe. The Refuse Act flatly prohibited pollution discharged from ship and shore installations.

The Refuse Act was followed by the Federal Water Pollution Control Act of 1948 (FW-PCA), 33 U.S.C.A. § 1251 et seq. Instead of focusing on sources of pollution through effluent standards, the FWPCA created water quality standards, which prescribed the levels of pollutants permitted in a given body of water. Where the Refuse Act concentrated on determining specific types of polluters, the FWPCA concentrated on reducing specific types of pollution.

Since 1972, federal regulation of water pollution has been primarily governed by the Clean Water Act (CWA), which overhauled FWCPA. The CWA forbids any person to discharge pollutants into U.S. waters unless the discharge conforms with certain provisions of the act. Among those provisions are several that call upon the EPA to promulgate effluent standards for particular categories of water polluters.

To implement these standards, the CWA requires each polluter to obtain a discharge permit issued by the EPA through the National Pollutant Discharge Elimination System (NPDES). Although the EPA closely monitors water pollution dischargers through the NPDES, primary responsibility for enforcement of the CWA rests with the states. Most states have also drafted permit systems similar to the NPDES. These systems are designed to protect local supplies of groundwater, surface water, and drinking water. Persons who violate either the federal or state permit system face civil fines, criminal penalties, and suspension of their discharge privileges.

The CWA also relies on modern technology to curb water pollution. It requires many polluters to implement the best practicable control technology, the best available technology economically achievable, or the best practicable waste treatment technology. The development of such technology for nontoxic polluters is based on a cost-benefit analysis in which the feasibility and expense of the technology is balanced against the expected benefits to the environment.

The CWA was amended in 1977 to address the nation's increasing concern about toxic pollutants. Pursuant to the 1977 amendments, the EPA increased the number of pollutants it deemed toxic from nine to sixty-five, and set effluent limitations for the twenty-one industries that discharge them. These limitations are based on measures of the danger these pollutants pose to the public health rather than on cost-benefit analyses.

Many states have enacted their own water pollution legislation regulating the discharge of toxic and other pollutants into their streams and lakes.

The mining industry presents persistent water pollution problems for state and federal governments. It has polluted over a thousand miles of streams in Appalachia with acid drainage. In response, the affected state governments now require strip miners to obtain LICENSES before commencing activity. Many states also require miners to post BONDS in an amount sufficient to repair potential damage to surrounding lakes and streams. Similarly, the federal government, under the Mineral Leasing Act, 30 U.S.C.A. § 201 et seq., requires each mining applicant to "submit a plan of construction, operation and rehabilitation" for the affected area, that takes into account the need for "restoration, revegetation and curtailment of erosion."

The commercial timber industry also presents persistent water pollution problems. Tree harvesting, yarding (the collection of felled trees), and road building can all deposit soil sediments into watercourses, thereby reducing the water quality for aquatic life. State governments have offered similar responses to these problems. For instance, clear-cutting (the removal of substantially all the trees from a given area) has been prohibited by most states. Other states have created buffer zones around particularly vulnerable watercourses, and banned unusually harmful activities in certain areas. Enforcement of these water pollution measures has been frustrated by vaguely worded legislation and a scarcity of inspectors in several states.

Common Law State and federal water pollution statutes provide one avenue of legal recourse for those harmed by water pollution. The common-law doctrines of NUISANCE, TRESPASS, NEGLIGENCE, strict liability, and riparian ownership provide alternative remedies.

Nuisances can be public or private. Private nuisances interfere with the rights and interests of private citizens, whereas public nuisances interfere with the common rights and interests of the people at large. Both types of nuisance must result from the "unreasonable" activities of a polluter, and inflict "substantial" harm on neighboring landowners. An injury that is minor or inconsequential will not result in LIABILITY under common-law nuisance. For example, dumping trace amounts of fertilizer into a stream abutting neighboring property will not amount to a public or private nuisance.

The oil and agricultural industries are frequently involved in state nuisance actions. Oil companies often run afoul of nuisance principles for improperly storing, transporting, and disposing of hazardous materials. Farmers represent a unique class of persons who fall prey to water pollution nuisances almost as often as they create them. Their abundant use of fungicides, herbicides, insecticides, and rodenticides makes them frequent creators of nuisances, and their use of streams, rivers, and groundwater for irrigation systems makes them frequent victims.

Nuisance actions deal primarily with continuing or repetitive injuries. Trespass actions provide relief even when an injury results from a single event. A polluter who spills oil, dumps chemicals, or otherwise contaminates a neighboring water supply on one occasion might avoid liability under nuisance law but not under the law of trespass. Trespass does not require proof of a substantial injury. However, only NOMINAL DAMAGES will be awarded to a landowner whose water supply suffers little harm from the trespass of a polluter.

Trespass requires proof that a polluter intentionally or knowingly contaminated a particular course of water. Yet, water contamination often results from unintentional behavior, such as industrial accidents. In such instances, the polluter may be liable under common-law principles of negligence. Negligence occurs when a polluter fails to exercise the degree of care that would be reasonable under the circumstances. Thus, a landowner whose water supply was inadvertently contaminated might bring a successful lawsuit against the polluter for common-law negligence where a lawsuit for nuisance or trespass would fail.

Even when a polluter exercises the utmost diligence to prevent water contamination, an injured landowner may still have recourse under the doctrine of strict liability. Under this doctrine, polluters who engage in "abnormally dangerous" activities are held responsible for any water contamination that results. Courts consider six factors when determining whether a particular activity is abnormally dangerous: the probability that the activity will cause harm to another, the likelihood that the harm will be great, the ability to eliminate the risk by exercising reasonable care, the extent to which the activity is uncommon or unusual, the activity's appropriateness for a particular location, and the activity's value or danger to the community.

The doctrine of strict liability arose out of a national conflict between competing values during the industrial revolution. This conflict pitted those who believed it was necessary to create an environment that promoted commerce against those who believed it was necessary to preserve a healthy and clean environment. For many years, courts were reluctant to impose strict liability on U.S. businesses, out of concern over retarding industrial growth.

Since the early 1970s, courts have placed greater emphasis on preserving a healthy and clean environment. In *Cities Service Co. v. State*, 312 So. 2d 799 (Fla. App. 1975), the court explained that "though many hazardous activities . . . are socially desirable, it now seems reasonable that they pay their own way." *Cities Service* involved a situation in which a dam burst during a phosphate mining operation, releasing a billion gallons of phosphate slime into adjacent waterways, where fish and other aquatic life were killed. The court concluded that this mining activity was abnormally dangerous.

Some activities inherently create abnormally dangerous risks to abutting waterways. In such cases, courts do not employ a BALANCING test to determine whether an activity is abnormally dangerous. Instead, they consider these activities to be dangerous in and of themselves. The transportation and storage of high explosives and the operation of oil and gas wells are activities courts have held to create inherent risks of abnormally dangerous proportions.

The doctrine of riparian ownership forms the final prong of common-law recovery. A riparian proprietor is the owner of land abutting a stream of water, and has the right to divert the water for any useful purpose. Some courts define the term *useful purpose* broadly to include almost any purpose whatsoever, whereas other courts define it more narrowly to include only purposes that are reasonable or profitable.

In any event, downstream riparian proprietors are often placed at a disadvantage because the law protects upstream owners' initial use of the water. For example, an upstream proprietor may construct a dam to appropriate a reasonable amount of water without compensating a downstream proprietor. However, cases involving thermal pollution provide an exception to this rule. For example, downstream owners who use river water to make ice can seek injunctive relief to prevent upstream owners from engaging in any activities that raise the water temperature by even one degree Fahrenheit.

CROSS-REFERENCES

Environmental Law; Fish and Fishing; Law of the Sea; Mine and Mineral Law; Pollution; Riparian Rights; Solid Wastes, Hazardous Substances, and Toxic Pollutants; Tort Law; Water Rights.

WATER RIGHTS A group of rights designed to protect the use and enjoyment of water that travels in streams, rivers, lakes, and ponds, gathers on the surface of the earth, or collects underground.

Water rights generally emerge from a person's ownership of the land bordering the banks of a watercourse or from a person's actual use of a watercourse. Water rights are conferred and regulated by judge-made COMMON LAW, state and federal legislative bodies, and other government

departments. Water rights can also be created by CONTRACT, as when one person transfers his water rights to another.

In the eighteenth century, regulation of water was primarily governed by custom and practice. As the U.S. population expanded over the next two centuries, however, and the use of water for agrarian and domestic purposes increased, water became viewed as a finite and frequently scarce resource. As a result, laws were passed to establish guidelines for the fair distribution of this resource. Courts began developing common-law doctrines to accommodate landowners who asserted competing claims over a body of water. These doctrines govern three areas: RIPARIAN RIGHTS, surface water rights, and underground water rights.

An owner or possessor of land that abuts a natural stream, RIVER, pond, or lake is called a riparian owner or proprietor. The law gives riparian owners certain rights to water that are incident to possession of the adjacent land. Depending on the JURISDICTION in which a watercourse is located, riparian rights generally fall into one of three categories.

First, riparian owners may be entitled to the "natural flow" of a watercourse. Under the natural flow doctrine, riparian owners have a right to enjoy the natural condition of a watercourse, undiminished in quantity or quality by other riparian owners. Every riparian owner enjoys this right to the same extent and degree, and each such owner maintains a qualified right to use the water for domestic purposes, such as drinking and bathing.

However, this qualified right does not entitle riparian owners to transport water away from the land abutting the watercourse. Nor does it permit riparian owners to use the water for most irrigation projects or commercial enterprises. Sprinkling gardens and watering animals are normally considered permissible uses under the natural flow doctrine of riparian rights.

Second, riparian owners may be entitled to the "reasonable use" of a watercourse. States that recognize the reasonable use doctrine found the natural flow doctrine too restrictive. During the industrial revolution of the nineteenth century, some U.S. courts applied the natural flow doctrine to prohibit riparian owners from detaining or diverting a watercourse for commercial development, such as manufacturing and milling, because such development impermissibly altered the water's original condition.

In replacing the natural flow doctrine, a majority of jurisdictions in the United States now permit riparian owners to make any reasonable use of water that does not unduly interfere with the competing rights and interests of other riparian owners. Unlike the natural flow doctrine, which seeks to preserve water in its original condition, the reasonable use doctrine facilitates domestic and commercial endeavors that are carried out in a productive and reasonable manner.

When two riparian owners assert competing claims over the exercise of certain water rights, courts applying the reasonable use doctrine generally attempt to measure the economic value of the water rights to each owner. Courts also try to evaluate the prospective value to society that would result from a riparian owner's proposed use, as well as its probable costs. No single factor is decisive in a court's analysis.

Third, riparian owners may be entitled to the "prior appropriation" of a watercourse. Where the reasonable use doctrine requires courts to balance the competing interests of riparian owners, the doctrine of prior appropriation initially grants a superior legal right to the first riparian owner who makes a beneficial use of a watercourse. The prior appropriation doctrine is applied in most arid western states, including Arizona, Colorado, Idaho, Montana, Nevada, New Mexico, Utah, and Wyoming and requires the riparian owner to demonstrate that she is using the water in an economically efficient manner. Consequently, the rights of a riparian owner under the prior appropriation doctrine are always subject to the rights of other riparian owners who can demonstrate a more economically efficient use.

Under any of the three doctrines, the interests of riparian owners are limited by the constitutional authority of the state and federal governments. The COMMERCE CLAUSE of the U.S. Constitution gives Congress the power to regulate NAVIGABLE WATERS, a power that Congress has exercised in a variety of ways, including the construction of dams. In those instances where Congress does not exercise its power under the Commerce Clause, states retain authority under their own constitutions to regulate waterways for the public good.

However, the EMINENT DOMAIN Clause of the FIFTH AMENDMENT to the U.S. Constitution limits the power of state and federal governments to impinge on the riparian rights of landowners by prohibiting the enactment of any laws or regulations that amount to a "taking" of private property. Laws and regulations that completely deprive a riparian owner of legally cognizable water rights constitute an illegal governmental taking of private property for Fifth Amendment purposes. The Fifth Amendment requires the government to pay the victims of takings an amount equal to the FAIR MARKET VALUE of the water rights.

Some litigation arises not from the manner in which neighboring owners appropriate water but from the manner in which they get rid of it. The disposal of surface waters, which consist of drainage from rain, springs, and melting snow, is typically the source of such litigation. This type of water gathers on the surface of the earth but never joins a stream, lake, or other well-defined body of water.

Litigation arises when one owner drains excess surface water onto neighboring property. Individuals who own elevated property may precipitate a dispute by accelerating the force or quantity of surface water running downhill, and individuals who own property on a lower level may rankle their neighbors by backing up surface water through damming and filling. Courts are split on how to resolve such disputes.

Some courts apply the common-law rule that allows landowners to use any method of surface water removal they choose without LIABILITY for flooding that may result to nearby property. Application of this rule generally rewards assertive and clever landowners and does not discourage neighbors from engaging in petty or vindictive squabbles over surface water removal.

Other courts apply the CIVIL-LAW rule, which stems from Louisiana, a civil-law jurisdiction. This rule imposes STRICT LIABILITY for any damage caused by a landowner who interrupts or alters the natural flow of water. The civil-law rule encourages neighbors to let nature take its course and live with the consequences that may follow from excessive accumulation of standing surface water.

Over the last quarter century many courts have begun applying the reasonable use rule to surface water disputes. This rule enables landowners to make reasonable alterations to their land for drainage purposes as long as the alteration does not unduly interfere with a neighbor's right to do the same. In applying this rule, courts balance the neighbors' competing needs, the feasibility of more appropriate methods of drainage, and the comparative severity of injuries.

Surface water that seeps underground can also create conditions ripe for litigation. Sand, sod, gravel, and even rock are permeable substances in which natural springs may form and moisture can collect. Underground reservoirs can be tapped by artificial wells that are used in conjunction by commercial, municipal, and private parties. When an underground water supply is appreciably depleted by one party, other parties with an interest in the well may sue for damages.

As with surface water and riparian rights, three theories of underground water rights have evolved. The first theory, known as the absolute ownership theory, derives from English law and affords landowners the right to withdraw as much underground water as they wish, for whatever purpose, requiring their neighbors to fend for themselves. Under the second theory, known as the American rule, landowners may withdraw as much underground water as they like as long as it is not done for a MALICIOUS purpose or in a wasteful manner. This theory is now applied in a majority of jurisdictions in the United States.

California has developed a third theory of underground water rights, known as the correlative theory. The correlative theory provides each landowner with an equal right to use underground water for a beneficial purpose. But landowners are not given the prerogative to seriously deplete a neighbor's water supply. In the event of water shortage, courts may apportion an underground supply among landowners. Many states facing acute or chronic shortages have adopted the correlative theory of underground water rights.

Water rights can also be affected by the natural AVULSION or ACCRETION of lands underlying or bordering a watercourse. Avulsions are marked by a sudden and violent change to the bed or course of a stream or river, causing a measurable loss or addition to land. Accretions are marked by the natural erosion of soil on one side of a watercourse and the gradual addition of soil to the other side. The extended shoreline made by sedimentary deposits is called an ALLUVION. Water rights are not altered by avulsions. However, any accretions of soil enure to the benefit of the landowner whose holdings have increased by the alluvion addition.

Although water covers more than two-thirds of the earth's surface, U.S. law treats water as a limited resource that is in great demand. The manner in which this demand is satisfied varies according to the jurisdiction in which a water

supply is located. In some jurisdictions the most productive use is rewarded, whereas in other jurisdictions the first use is protected. Several jurisdictions are dissatisfied with both approaches and allow a water supply to be reasonably appropriated by all interested parties. Each approach has its weaknesses, and jurisdictions will continue experimenting with established legal doctrines to better accommodate the supply and demand of water rights.

CROSS-REFERENCES

Environmental Law; Land-Use Control; Law of the Sea; Pollution; Solid Wastes, Hazardous Substances, and Toxic Pollutants; Water Pollution.

BIOGRAPHY

"WE'RE NOT SAYING ABORTION IS RIGHT OR WRONG OR PREACHING A MORAL CAUSE, BECAUSE THAT IS A VERY PERSONAL DECISION. WHAT WE ARE SAYING IS THAT THE GOVERNMENT HAS NO RIGHT TELLING WOMEN WHAT TO DO WITH THEIR LIVES."

WATTLETON, ALYCE FAYE From 1978 to 1992, Alyce Faye Wattleton held the stage as an articulate and telegenic defender of reproductive rights for U.S. women. As president of the Planned Parenthood Federation of America, Wattleton was a national spokesperson for reproductive freedom and a lightning rod in the highly charged debate over ABORTION. Wattleton was the first woman and the first African American to head Planned Parenthood, the oldest voluntary family planning organization in the United States. During her fourteen-year tenure, she took an unequivocal stand on abortion rights and fought for improved reproductive health care for women with low incomes. Wattleton was known for her tremendous poise during confrontations with abortion foes and for her intelligent television interviews. As U.S. courts and lawmakers chipped away at abortion rights, Wattleton held fast to her conviction that women, not governments, had the right to control their reproductive destiny.

Born in St. Louis on July 8, 1943, Wattleton was the only child of George Wattleton, a factory employee, and Ozie Garret Wattleton, a seamstress and a Fundamentalist minister in the Church of God. Wattleton credits her parents for developing in her a strong social conscience and a will to succeed. She excelled in school and was only sixteen years old when she enrolled in Ohio State University. After graduating from Ohio State in 1964 with a nursing degree,

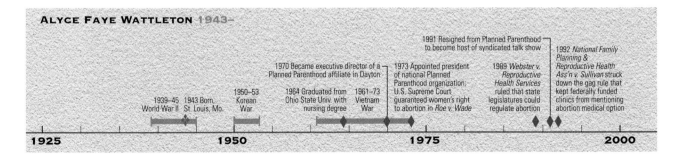

ALYCE FAYE WATTLETON 1943–

1939–45 World War II

1943 Born, St. Louis, Mo.

1950–53 Korean War

1964 Graduated from Ohio State Univ. with nursing degree

1961–73 Vietnam War

1970 Became executive director of a Planned Parenthood affiliate in Dayton

1973 Appointed president of national Planned Parenthood organization; U.S. Supreme Court guaranteed women's right to abortion in *Roe v. Wade*

1989 *Webster v. Reproductive Health Services* ruled that state legislatures could regulate abortion

1991 Resigned from Planned Parenthood to become host of syndicated talk show

1992 *National Family Planning & Reproductive Health Ass'n v. Sullivan* struck down the gag rule that kept federally funded clinics from mentioning abortion medical option

1925   1950   1975   2000

Wattleton taught at Miami Valley Hospital School, in Dayton. She left that position in 1966 to begin work on a master's degree in maternal and infant health care, at New York's Columbia University.

While at Columbia on a full scholarship, Wattleton trained as a midwife in New York City's Harlem Hospital. In the 1960s, abortion was prohibited by law in most states. At Harlem Hospital, Wattleton saw firsthand the appalling medical consequences of illegal abortions. She witnessed the blood poisoning, torn uteruses, and painful deaths of desperate women who tried to induce abortions with chemicals or sharp instruments. These grim cases influenced Wattleton's decision to join Planned Parenthood and to support reproductive freedom. To Wattleton, the issue was one of self-determination and basic human rights for women.

After earning her master's degree in 1967, Wattleton became assistant director of the Montgomery County Combined Public Health District, in Dayton. As a public health nurse, she helped increase the prenatal health care services in the area. In 1970, Wattleton became executive director of a Planned Parenthood affiliate in Dayton. She married social worker and musician Franklin Gordon in 1971, and had a daughter, Felicia Gordon, in 1976. Wattleton and Gordon were divorced in 1981.

Wattleton's work ethic and her successful outreach and fund-raising efforts in Dayton led to her appointment in 1973 as president of the national Planned Parenthood organization. At age thirty-four, Wattleton became the youngest person ever to head the huge family planning enterprise. (By the time Wattleton resigned in the early 1990s, Planned Parenthood would have nine-hundred U.S. affiliates and an annual budget of $380 million.) Wattleton assumed leadership at a time when donating funds to Planned Parenthood was neither controversial nor a political act. Once Wattleton began to lobby for abortion rights, Planned Parenthood's reputation and perceived mission changed dramatically.

Although Planned Parenthood became synonymous with abortion, Wattleton pointed out that only a relatively small part of its operation was involved in terminating pregnancies. Only one-third of its U.S. clinics even performed abortions. BIRTH CONTROL, gynecologic exams, and prenatal care were the services most commonly provided. Whereas 130,000 abortions were performed at Planned Parenthood clinics in 1990 (when 1.5 million abortions were performed nationwide), 3 million women received pregnancy tests, contraceptives, and prenatal exams from Planned Parenthood during the same year.

Wattleton placed Planned Parenthood squarely in the pro-choice camp because she was concerned about the erosion of *Roe v. Wade*, 410 U.S. 113, 93 S. Ct. 705, 35 L. Ed. 2d 147 (1973), a landmark U.S. Supreme Court case guaranteeing a woman's right to choose an abortion. When President RONALD REAGAN took office in 1982, he aligned his administration with the antiabortion faction. During his two terms in office, federal funds for family planning clinics under title X of the Public Health Service Act (42 U.S.C.A. § 300–300a-41 [1970]) were cut significantly. Also, the Justice Department attempted to prevent federally funded clinics from even mentioning abortion as a medical option (42 C.F.R. 59.8). Its so-called gag rule was denounced by Wattleton as a violation of free speech and an unfair restriction on poor women. The controversial regulation was enjoined by federal courts and ultimately struck down by a U.S. district court in 1992 (*National Family Planning & Reproductive Health Ass'n v. Sullivan*, 979 F.2d 227 [1992]).

Perhaps the most discouraging blow to Wattleton and the pro-choice movement was the U.S. Supreme Court's decision in *Webster v. Reproductive Health Services*, 492 U.S. 490, 109 S. Ct. 3040, 106 L. Ed. 2d 410 (1989). In *Webster* the High Court ruled that individual state legislatures had the power to regulate abortion. As a result, an increase in state laws limiting access to abortion was likely.

Wattleton supported the introduction into the United States of RU486, an abortion-inducing drug not yet approved by the federal government. She also backed a reproductive rights amendment to the U.S. Constitution. Although Wattleton was a staunch abortion rights advocate, she was equally emphatic about the need to prevent unwanted pregnancies in the first place. She campaigned for the establishment of comprehensive health education programs in the schools and the community.

Because of her high profile and pro-choice position, Wattleton received several death threats while head of Planned Parenthood. During her term, several U.S. affiliates were bombed, picketed, and besieged by anti-choice groups.

In 1991 Wattleton resigned from Planned Parenthood to become host of a syndicated talk show in Chicago. She left behind a strengthened organization with a defined course of action, and a powerful example of living one's life according to principles.

See also REPRODUCTION; ROE V. WADE.

WAYNE, JAMES MOORE   As an associate justice, James Moore Wayne served on the U.S. Supreme Court from 1835 to 1867. Wayne rose to prominence in his native Georgia in the early 1800s, establishing himself as a local politician with cosmopolitan views. Nominated to the Court by President ANDREW JACKSON, he shared the president's strong federalist views, and Wayne often took an expansive view of federal power in his opinions. His FEDERALISM was put to the test, however, because of his support of SLAVERY. Loyal in his support for the Union during the Civil War, he paid a dear price in the south for choosing to remain on the Court even as other southern judges quit the federal bench.

Born in Savannah, Georgia, in 1790, Wayne was the son of aristocratic parents. In his teens, he chose to leave Georgia in order to attend Princeton University. He graduated in 1808, and two years later returned home to establish a law practice. After brief service as a captain in the War of 1812, he set out on an intermittent political career. From 1815 to 1816, he served in the Georgia House of Representatives and was then elected mayor of Savannah. His local political career soon gave way to a judicial one. In 1819 he was elected judge of the Savannah Court of Common Pleas, and in 1822 he became a judge of the superior court.

In 1828, Wayne's interest in national affairs took him to Washington. Winning election to the U.S. House of Representatives, he became a strong supporter of Andrew Jackson over the course of three terms in office. In 1834, when President Jackson needed a southerner to fill the vacancy left by the death of Associate Justice WILLIAM JOHNSON, Jackson nominated Wayne.

On the Court Wayne's federalism expressed itself repeatedly. His specialty was admiralty law—the law of the seas—which was of great significance during the era. Admiralty issues were often volatile because they involved one of the sharpest constitutional conflicts of the day, the power of Congress to regulate interstate commerce relative to state POLICE POWERS. The cases heard by the Court during Wayne's tenure involved taxation, licensing, and slavery, and

PORTRAIT BY JOHN MAIER, COLLECTION OF THE SUPREME COURT OF THE UNITED STATES

James Moore Wayne

"A CORPORATION . . . SEEMS TO US TO BE A PERSON, THOUGH AN ARTIFICIAL ONE, INHABITING AND BELONGING TO THAT STATE [OF INCORPORATION], AND THEREFORE ENTITLED, FOR THE PURPOSE OF SUING AND BEING SUED, TO BE DEEMED A CITIZEN OF THAT STATE."

the Court was often divided due to its inability to agree upon the extent of power vested in the Constitution's COMMERCE CLAUSE. Wayne generally voted in favor of the federal government's interests. In the so-called *Passenger Cases* of 1849, when the Court invalidated New York and Massachusetts laws that imposed taxes on incoming ship passengers, Wayne wrote in his concurring opinion that Congress had exclusive control over interstate commerce.

Politically, the dividing point in Wayne's federalism was the very issue that split the nation into Civil War—slavery. As a slave owner, he struggled to find justification for preserving the institution even as the federal government opposed it. He believed that Congress had no power to interfere with slavery under the Due Process Clause of the FIFTH AMENDMENT, and thus concurred in Chief Justice ROGER BROOKE TANEY's opinion in *Dred Scott v. Sandford*, 60 U.S. 393, 19 How. 393, 15 L. Ed. 691 (1857), which upheld the legality of slavery. The decision fueled animosities which led to the Civil War.

Southerners detested Wayne's decision to remain on the Court during the war. Yet even as he was denounced as a traitor and his property in Georgia was seized, he supported the cause of union. He remained on the bench until his death on July 7, 1867.

WEAPONS   A comprehensive term for all instruments of offensive or defensive combat, including items used in injuring a person.

The term *weapons* includes numerous items that can cause death or injury, including firearms, EXPLOSIVES, chemicals, and nuclear material. Because weapons pose a danger to the safety and well-being of individuals and communities, federal, state, and local statutes regulate the possession and use of weapons.

A dangerous or deadly weapon is one that is likely to cause death or great bodily harm. A handgun, a hand grenade, or a long knife are examples of deadly weapons. A weapon capable of causing death is, however, not necessarily a weapon likely to produce death. For example, an ordinary penknife is capable of causing

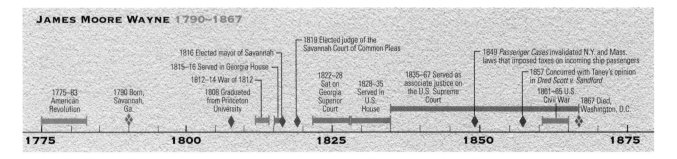

JAMES MOORE WAYNE 1790–1867

1775–83 American Revolution

1790 Born, Savannah, Ga.

1808 Graduated from Princeton University

1812–14 War of 1812

1815–16 Served in Georgia House

1816 Elected mayor of Savannah

1819 Elected judge of the Savannah Court of Common Pleas

1822–28 Sat on Georgia Superior Court

1828–35 Served in U.S. House

1835–67 Served as associate justice on the U.S. Supreme Court

1849 *Passenger Cases* invalidated N.Y. and Mass. laws that imposed taxes on incoming ship passengers

1857 Concurred with Taney's opinion in *Dred Scott v. Sandford*

1861–65 U.S. Civil War

1867 Died, Washington, D.C.

1775   1800   1825   1850   1875

death, but it is not considered a deadly weapon.

The regulation of firearms in the United States has proved controversial. Opponents of GUN CONTROL argue that the SECOND AMENDMENT to the U.S. Constitution makes the right to bear arms an inherent and inalienable right. Nevertheless, federal and state laws regulate who may own firearms and impose other conditions on their use. The passage in 1993 of the Brady Handgun Violence Prevention Act (18 U.S.C.A. § 921 et seq.) was the first major federal gun control law. The Brady Act bars felons and selected others from buying handguns, establishes a five-day waiting period for purchase, requires the local police to run background checks on handgun buyers, and mandates the development of a federal computer database for instant background checks.

The 1994 federal crime bill addressed deadly weapons used by criminals. The law (108 Stat. 1796) banned nineteen assault-type firearms and other firearms with similar characteristics. It limited the magazine capacity of guns and rifles to ten rounds, but exempted firearms, guns, and magazines that were legally owned when the law went into effect.

The deadliness of chemical explosives was demonstrated by the April 1995 bombing of the federal courthouse in Oklahoma City, Oklahoma. In response, Congress passed the 1996 Anti-Terrorism and Effective Death Penalty Act. (P.L. 104-132). The act increases the penalties for conspiracies involving explosives and for the possession of nuclear materials, criminalizes the use of chemical weapons, and requires plastic explosives to contain "tagging" elements in the explosive materials for detection and identification purposes.

Unless proscribed by statute, possessing or carrying a weapon is not a crime, nor does it constitute a BREACH OF THE PEACE. However, most states make it a crime to carry a prohibited or concealed weapon. The term *concealed* means hidden, screened, or covered. The usual test for determining whether a weapon is concealed is whether the weapon is hidden from the general view of individuals who are in full view of the accused and close enough to see the weapon if it were not hidden. If the surface of a weapon is covered, the fact that its outline is distinguishable and recognizable as a weapon does not prevent it from being illegally concealed. In addition, most states have enacted laws mandating longer prison terms if a firearm was used in the commission of the crime.

Law enforcement officers who must carry weapons in order to perform their official duties ordinarily are exempted from statutes governing weapons. Private citizens may apply to the local police department for a permit to carry a firearm. Permits are generally granted if the person carries large sums of money or valuables in his or her business, or can demonstrate a particular need for personal protection.

See also DEADLY FORCE; SELF-DEFENSE.

WEBER, MAX Max Weber was a German sociologist and political economist who is best known for his theory of the development of Western capitalism that is based on the "Protestant Ethic." In addition, Weber wrote widely on law and religion, including groundbreaking work on the importance of BUREAUCRACY in modern society. He also worked to establish the discipline of sociology based on an objective scholarship.

Weber was born on April 21, 1864, in Erfurt, Germany, into a wealthy manufacturing family. He studied at the Universities of Heidelberg and Berlin and joined the faculty at Heidelberg in 1896. A prolific writer and scholar, Weber resigned his professorship in 1907 after coming into an inheritance that made him financially independent, allowing him to devote all his energies to scholarship.

Weber's most famous work, *The Protestant Ethic and the Spirit of Capitalism* (1904–1905), introduced the concept of the "Protestant Ethic." Weber theorized that certain Protestant religious beliefs promoted the growth of capitalism. He claimed a relationship existed between success in capitalist ventures and Protestant (in particular, Calvinist and Puritan sects) theology. The Calvinist doctrine of predestination posited that individuals could never know

BIOGRAPHY

THE GRANGER COLLECTION, NEW YORK

Max Weber

"[THE] MODERN JUDGE IS A VENDING MACHINE INTO WHICH THE PLEADINGS ARE INSERTED TOGETHER WITH THE FEE AND WHICH THEN DISGORGES THE JUDGMENT TOGETHER WITH THE REASONS MECHANICALLY DERIVED FROM THE CODE."

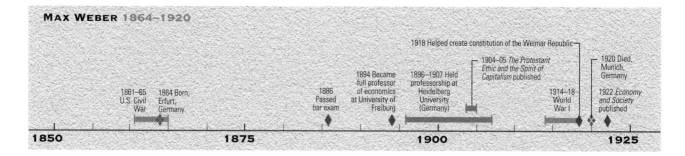

MAX WEBER 1864–1920

1861–65 U.S. Civil War

1864 Born, Erfurt, Germany

1886 Passed bar exam

1894 Became full professor of economics at University of Freiburg

1896–1907 Held professorship at Heidelberg University (Germany)

1904–05 *The Protestant Ethic and the Spirit of Capitalism* published

1918 Helped create constitution of the Weimar Republic

1914–18 World War I

1920 Died, Munich, Germany

1922 *Economy and Society* published

1850   1875   1900   1925

if they were to receive God's salvation. This doctrine bred psychological insecurity in John Calvin's followers, who eventually looked for signs that might indicate they were in God's grace. From this search for signs developed the Protestant Ethic, which called for unceasing commitment to work and ascetic abstinence from any enjoyment of the profit realized from such labors. The result, Weber argued, was the rapid accumulation of capital that fueled the rise of Western capitalism.

Weber also analyzed how politics, government, and law have developed in Western and non-Western cultures. He proposed the idea of the charismatic leader, who exhibited both religious and political authority. Weber was more interested, however, in the development of modern government and the growth of bureaucracy. Bureaucracy is a method of organization based on specialization of duties, action according to rules, and a stable order of authority. For Weber, bureaucracy was an expression of "rationality," which in his terminology meant the use of rules and procedures to determine outcomes rather than sentiment, tradition, or rules of thumb.

Weber's sociological theories had a great impact on twentieth century sociology. He developed the notion of "ideal types," which were examples of situations in history that could be used as reference points to compare and contrast different societies. This approach analyzes the basic elements of social institutions and examines how these elements relate to one another.

Weber died on June 14, 1920, in Munich, Germany.

WEBSTER, DANIEL Daniel Webster was a nineteenth-century lawyer, representative, senator, secretary of state, and one of the great orators in U.S. history. A man of prodigious talent and great political ambition, Webster reversed himself on issues involving the economy and SLAVERY in hopes of becoming president. As the greatest constitutional lawyer of his day, he helped shape the nationalist jurisprudence favored by Chief Justice JOHN MARSHALL.

Webster was born on January 18, 1782, in Salisbury, New Hampshire. He entered Dartmouth College when he was fifteen and graduated in 1801. He then studied law with an attorney in Boston before becoming a member of the New Hampshire bar in 1805. Webster moved to Portsmouth, New Hampshire in 1807 and quickly developed a legal association with the shipowners and merchants of the city. Webster became the spokesperson for the Portsmouth business community, who opposed the

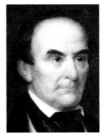

Daniel Webster

Jefferson administration's trade restrictions with Great Britain and France. His vehement denunciations of the trade EMBARGO and the War of 1812 against Great Britain led to his election to the U.S. House of Representatives in 1812. He aligned himself with the pro-British Federalist party and endorsed a strong national government.

Webster left Congress in 1817 and relocated to Boston where he emerged as an eminent attorney, specializing in constitutional law. His reputation increased when he became involved in three landmark cases. In the first, *Trustees of Dartmouth College v. Woodward*, 17 U.S. (4 Wheat.) 518, 4 L. Ed. 629 (1819), Webster successfully defended his former college against the state of New Hampshire's attempt to disregard the corporate CHARTER of the school and make it a public institution. The Court, with Chief Justice Marshall writing the opinion, ruled that a corporate charter was a CONTRACT that could not be impaired.

In that same year, Webster argued for the validity of the BANK OF THE UNITED STATES and against the right of a state to tax a federal institution in *McCulloch v. Maryland*, 17 U.S. (4 Wheat.) 316, 4 L. Ed. 579. Again, Chief Justice Marshall agreed with Webster's nationalist philosophy, finding that the Necessary and Proper Clause provided the basis for Congress's creation of a national bank and that "the government of the Union, though limited in its power, is supreme within its sphere of action."

Five years later, in *Gibbons v. Ogden*, 22 U.S. (9 Wheat.) 1, 6 L. Ed. 23 (1824), Webster argued against navigation monopolies granted by the state of New York to private individuals. Chief Justice Marshall and the Court sided with Webster, holding that the Constitution's COMMERCE CLAUSE empowered Congress to regulate interstate commerce, establishing a precedent that had far-reaching effects in the economic expansion of the nineteenth century.

With these accomplishments to his credit, Webster returned to the U.S. House of Representatives in 1822, where he represented Massachusetts for the next five years. In the House he chaired the Judiciary Committee and opposed the 1824 TARIFF, believing that it would injure the merchant class. Following his election to the U.S. Senate in 1826, however, Webster made one of his famous reversals and embraced the need for a tariff. He endorsed the tariff of 1828.

Webster's skills as an orator were renowned. Oral arguments before the Supreme Court could last several days, requiring attorneys to have both mental and physical stamina. Webster excelled in oral argument but he was also

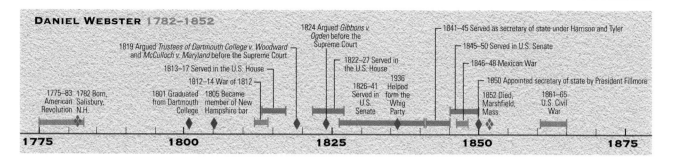

famous for his public addresses. In 1826 he delivered addresses on the deaths of JOHN ADAMS and THOMAS JEFFERSON. In 1830 he debated Senator Robert Y. Hayne of South Carolina, who favored a coalition between Western and Southern states to benefit both areas in tariffs and land prices. Webster opposed this sectionalism and denounced the doctrine of nullification, which upheld the right of a state to declare a federal law invalid within its boundaries. Webster's phrase "Liberty and Union, now and forever, one and inseparable!," came from the Hayne debate and helped cement his popularity in the North.

In 1836 Webster abandoned the Federalist party and helped form the Whig Party, made up of groups opposed to President ANDREW JACKSON and the Democrats. He was considered for the Whig presidential nomination in 1836 but was defeated. In 1841 President WILLIAM HENRY HARRISON appointed Webster secretary of state. When Harrison died shortly after taking office, President JOHN TYLER asked Webster to remain at his post.

The Tyler administration was a troubled one, largely because Tyler was a Democrat with a cabinet of Whigs. His decision to reject a Whig measure establishing a new national bank caused a revolt in his cabinet, with most members resigning in protest. Webster alone remained to aid Tyler, motivated by the possibility of becoming his vice-presidential running mate in 1844. However, Tyler was not renominated. As secretary of state, Webster did negotiate the Webster-Ashburton Treaty, which established the boundary line for Maine.

Webster returned to the Senate in 1845, with his salary supplemented by a fund raised by Boston and New York businessmen. Critics charged that he had surrendered his political independence to manufacturing interests. As a senator he opposed the Mexican War and the acquisition of Texas. He opposed slavery but feared civil war. Because of this fear Webster supported the COMPROMISE OF 1850. This act admitted California into the Union as a free state, gave the Utah and New Mexico territories the right to determine the slavery issue for

"GOD GRANT LIBERTY ONLY TO THOSE WHO LOVE IT, AND ARE ALWAYS READY TO GUARD AND DEFEND IT."

themselves at the time of their admission to the Union, outlawed the slave trade in the District of Columbia, and gave the federal government the right to return fugitive slaves under the FUGITIVE SLAVE ACT (9 Stat. 462).

In 1850 President MILLARD FILLMORE appointed Webster secretary of state. He used his influence to enforce the Compromise of 1850, especially the Fugitive Slave Act. Though the act was unpopular in the North, Webster sought to demonstrate to Southern politicians his determination to uphold the law. Aside from promoting national unity, Webster dreamed of a "Union" party that would help make him president in 1852. However, Webster died on October 24, 1852, at his farm in Marshfield, Massachusetts.

CROSS-REFERENCES

Gibbons v. Ogden; McCulloch v. Maryland; Trustees of Dartmouth College v. Woodward.

WEBSTER v. REPRODUCTIVE HEALTH SERVICES

In *Webster v. Reproductive Health Services*, 492 U.S. 490, 109 S. Ct. 3040, 106 L. Ed. 2d 410 (1989), the United States Supreme Court reviewed the constitutionality of several Missouri statutes restricting access to ABORTION services and counseling. *Webster* is significant because it narrowed the Supreme Court's holding in the landmark case *Roe v. Wade*, 410 U.S. 113, 93 S. Ct. 705, 35 L. Ed. 2d 147 (1973), by modifying the trimester analysis under which the constitutionality of abortion regulations had been evaluated during the intervening sixteen years.

The case arose in 1986 when seven Missouri statutes regulating abortion were challenged in a CLASS ACTION filed in the United States District Court for the Western District of Missouri. The class action was brought on behalf of all health care professionals who were providing abortion services in the state of Missouri, and on behalf of all pregnant women who were seeking access to those services. The federal district court declared all seven statutes unconstitutional, and the United States Court of Appeals for the Eighth Circuit affirmed the district court's decision. The Missouri attorney general appealed the case to the United States Supreme Court.

Webster splintered the nine justices sitting on the Supreme Court. Chief Justice WILLIAM REHNQUIST wrote the Court's plurality opinion, joined by Justices BYRON WHITE and ANTHONY KENNEDY. Justices SANDRA DAY O'CONNOR and ANTONIN SCALIA wrote separate concurring opinions. Justices HARRY BLACKMUN and JOHN PAUL STEVENS wrote separate dissenting opinions, with Justices WILLIAM BRENNAN and THURGOOD MARSHALL joining Blackmun's dissent.

The plurality opinion was separated into three parts. First, the Court upheld the constitutionality of Missouri Revised Statutes section 1.205.1, which provided that the "life of each human being begins at conception," and that all "unborn children have protectable interests in life, health, and well-being." The plaintiffs had argued that this provision was inconsistent with previous cases in which the Court had prohibited states from adopting a single theory of when life begins. The Supreme Court disagreed with this argument, concluding that this statutory language had no operative legal effect because it was contained in a legislative preamble. Thus, this particular Missouri statute raised no constitutional issue for the Court to decide.

Second, the Court upheld the constitutionality of Missouri Revised Statutes section 188.20, which prohibited abortions at public hospitals or on other property owned by the state. The plaintiffs had asserted that the Constitution guarantees every woman access to public facilities for the purpose of obtaining an abortion. The Court took exception with this argument, observing that "[n]othing in the Constitution requires states to enter or remain in the business of performing abortions." Instead, the Court said, states may take affirmative steps to encourage childbirth over abortion, which is exactly what the state of Missouri did in this case. Although the statute in question prevented women from seeking abortion services at public facilities, the Court noted that pregnant women in Missouri could still obtain abortion services from private health care providers.

Third, the Court upheld the constitutionality of Missouri Revised Statutes section 188.029, which required physicians to perform certain medical tests when there was reason to believe a fetus had reached at least twenty weeks of gestational age. These tests, which included assessments of fetal weight and lung maturity, were designed to determine the viability of an unborn child. Because this statute created a PRESUMPTION of viability at twenty

weeks, the plaintiffs contended that it violated the trimester framework established by *Roe v. Wade*, 410 U.S. 113, 93 S. Ct. 705, 35 L. Ed. 2d 147 (1973).

In *Roe* the Supreme Court ruled that states have no legitimate interest in regulating abortion during the first trimester of pregnancy, and that the decision to terminate a pregnancy during this period rests solely with the pregnant woman and her attending physician. During the second trimester, the Court said in *Roe*, states may pass abortion regulations that are reasonably related to preserving the mother's health. During the third trimester, *Roe* held that states may ban abortion altogether, unless requiring childbirth would endanger the life of the mother. The *Roe* decision was based on the premise that states have a compelling interest in protecting fetal life that is triggered by the onset of the third trimester, at which point fetuses typically become viable outside the womb.

In *Webster* the Supreme Court acknowledged that the Missouri statute clashed with the *Roe* trimester analysis by compelling doctors to perform viability examinations during the second trimester of pregnancy, even though such tests were intended to protect the life of a fetus and were unrelated to preserving maternal health. However, the rigid trimester formula created by *Roe*, the Court pointed out, failed to take into account that some fetuses reach viability before the twenty-fifth week of pregnancy. The Court also queried why a state's interest in protecting fetal life should be cognizable only after the second trimester. States have an important interest in protecting fetal life throughout pregnancy, the Court posited.

The Court then held that the Missouri statute requiring viability examinations during the second trimester was reasonably related to this important governmental interest. The Court emphasized that its holding in *Webster* would leave undisturbed the fundamental holding of *Roe*. The Court reiterated that pregnant women still enjoy a legal right to abortion that is protected by the Due Process Clause of the Fifth and Fourteenth Amendments to the United States Constitution. At the same time, the Court said that its decision in *Webster* had modified the *Roe* trimester analysis by permitting states to regulate abortions prior to the twenty-fifth week of pregnancy.

In his concurring opinion, Justice Scalia expressed regret that the Court had not taken this opportunity to completely overrule *Roe*. The legality of abortion, Scalia argued, is a political issue that should be decided by state legislatures, whose members are democratically elected to office, and not by federal courts, whose members are appointed to the bench for life. In her concurring opinion, Justice O'Connor urged a more moderate approach. Prior to the point in which a fetus reaches viability, O'Connor advocated, states should be allowed to pass any abortion regulations that do not "unduly burden" a women's right to terminate her pregnancy. According to O'Connor, the severity of a particular regulatory burden would be evaluated on a case-by-case basis. This "undue burden" analysis was eventually adopted by the Supreme Court in *Planned Parenthood v. Casey*, 505 U.S. 833, 112 S. Ct. 2791, 120 L. Ed. 2d 674 (1992).

Of the two dissenting opinions, Blackmun's was the more vigorous. As the author of the *Roe* opinion, Blackmun chastised the Court for permitting Missouri to regulate abortion during the second trimester of pregnancy in contravention of established PRECEDENT, and characterized the Court's opinion as an invitation to enact draconian abortion regulations. The plurality opinion conceded that the Court's holding in *Webster* would enable states to regulate abortion earlier in a pregnancy, but reminded the dissenting justices that the decision of how early would partially rest with the American people and their elected representatives.

CROSS-REFERENCES

Fetal Rights; Fourteenth Amendment; Privacy; *Roe v. Wade*; Substantive Due Process.

WEDDINGTON, SARAH RAGLE

Sarah Ragle Weddington is Texas lawyer, teacher, author, and public speaker who is best known as the lawyer who took the case on ABORTION rights, *Roe v. Wade*, 410 U.S. 113, 93 S. Ct. 705, 35 L. Ed. 2d 147 (1973), to the Supreme Court and prevailed. Since *Roe*, Weddington has been a vigorous defender of the decision. During the administration of President JIMMY CARTER, Weddington served in a series of key posts that involved WOMEN'S RIGHTS.

Weddington was born on February 5, 1945 in Abilene, Texas. She earned a bachelors degree from McMurray College in 1965 and a law degree from the University of Texas at Austin in 1967. She was admitted to the Texas bar in 1967.

"LIFE IS AN ONGOING PROCESS. IT IS ALMOST IMPOSSIBLE TO DEFINE A POINT AT WHICH LIFE BEGINS OR PERHAPS EVEN AT WHICH LIFE ENDS."

BIOGRAPHY

Sarah Ragle Weddington

Following her admission to the bar, Weddington opened a law practice in Austin. Soon after she was approached by a group of women who needed free legal research concerning their inability to secure legal abortions in Texas. Weddington began a CLASS ACTION lawsuit and named as her plaintiff "Jane Roe," a fictitious name for a woman who was pregnant and wished to terminate her pregnancy.

The case eventually reached the U.S. Supreme Court, where, at age twenty-seven, Weddington presented her oral argument that a woman's right to choose was based on the constitutional right to PRIVACY. In a controversial opinion written by HARRY A. BLACKMUN, the Court agreed with Weddington, striking down state laws that made abortions illegal. *Roe* was a landmark case and made Weddington a national figure. The decision, however, also galvanized opposition to abortion, setting off a contentious national debate that continued into the 1990s.

Weddington served in the Texas House of Representatives from 1972 to 1977. She also continued to practice law in Texas until 1977, when she was appointed general counsel to the U.S. Department of Agriculture in Washington, D.C. In 1979 President Carter made Weddington a special presidential assistant. In this post, she chaired an intergovernmental task force of fifteen agencies and made economic issues and the EQUAL RIGHTS AMENDMENT her priorities. In 1980 Weddington was a U.S. delegate to the second World Conference of Women in Copenhagen, Denmark.

Weddington teaches prelaw at the University of Texas and is a popular speaker at colleges and civic organizations. She is an ardent defender of abortion rights and often debates those who seek to overturn *Roe*. In 1992 she published *A Question of Choice*, which articulates her position on abortion rights and other gender issues.

See also ROE V. WADE.

WEIGHT OF EVIDENCE

Measure of credible PROOF on one side of a dispute as compared with the credible proof on the other, particularly the PROBATIVE evidence considered by a JUDGE or JURY during a TRIAL.

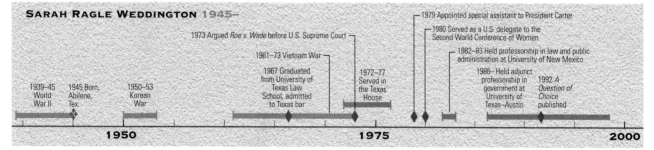

SARAH RAGLE WEDDINGTON 1945–

1939–45 World War II

1945 Born, Abilene, Tex.

1950–53 Korean War

1961–73 Vietnam War

1967 Graduated from University of Texas Law School; admitted to Texas bar

1973 Argued *Roe v. Wade* before U.S. Supreme Court

1972–77 Served in the Texas House

1979 Appointed special assistant to President Carter

1980 Served as a U.S. delegate to the Second World Conference of Women

1982–83 Held professorship in law and public administration at University of New Mexico

1986– Held adjunct professorship in government at University of Texas–Austin

1992 *A Question of Choice* published

1950   1975   2000

JOHN BARR/THE GAMMA LIAISON NETWORK

Jurors had a tough time weighing the voluminous evidence presented in the O. J. Simpson murder trial. Here, criminalist Dennis Fung examines photographs of blood stains.

The trier of fact in a civil or criminal trial, whether a judge or a jury, must review the EVIDENCE presented, evaluate it, and determine if it meets the standard of proof. If it meets this standard, the trier of fact must return a VERDICT in favor of the plaintiff in a civil suit and must convict a defendant in a criminal trial. If the evidence does not meet the standard of proof, the trier of fact must find for the defendant in a civil or criminal case. These decisions are based on the concept of the "weight of evidence."

The weight of evidence is based on the believability or persuasiveness of evidence. The probative value (tending to convince a person of the truth of some proposition) of evidence does not necessarily turn on the number of WITNESSES called, but rather the persuasiveness of their TESTIMONY. For example, a witness may give uncorroborated but apparently honest and sincere testimony that commands belief, even though several witnesses of apparent respectability may contradict her. The question for the jury is not which side has more witnesses, but what testimony they believe.

Particular evidence has different weight in inducing belief with respect to the facts and circumstances to be proved. Evidence that is indefinite, vague, or improbable will be given less weight than evidence that is direct and unrefuted. For example, a criminal defendant's testimony that he had never been at the scene of a crime would be given little weight if his FINGERPRINTS were found at the crime scene and witnesses TESTIFY they saw him at the scene. Similarly, evidence given by a witness who testifies from personal observation is of greater weight than evidence offered by a witness who is testifying from general knowledge alone.

In a civil trial, the plaintiff's burden of proof is the preponderance of the evidence standard, which means that the plaintiff must convince the trier of fact that the evidence in support of his case outweighs the evidence offered by the defendant to oppose it. In contrast, criminal trials require that the weight of evidence proving a defendant's guilt must be BEYOND A REASONABLE DOUBT.

In a number of JURISDICTIONS, judges are prohibited from instructing juries on the weight to be given to evidence. In other states, the judge is permitted to give a balanced and fair assessment of the weight she believes should be ascribed to the evidence. All jurisdictions prohibit the judge from instructing the jury on what weight is to be given to the testimony of any witness or class of witnesses. The judge may not state that any particular piece of admissible evidence is or is not entitled to receive weight or consideration from the jury. The judge is also forbidden either to aid a jury or to infringe upon its role in weighing the evidence or in deciding upon the facts. In addition, the judge, in giving her INSTRUCTIONS to the jury, has no right to prescribe the order and manner in which the evidence should be examined and weighed by the jury, or to tell the jurors how they shall consider any evidence that has been received by the court.

See also PREPONDERANCE OF EVIDENCE.

WEIGHTS AND MEASURES 📖 A comprehensive legal term for uniform standards ascribed to the quantity, capacity, volume, or dimensions of anything. 📖

The regulation of weights and measures is necessary for science, industry, and commerce. The importance of establishing uniform national standards was demonstrated by the drafters of the U.S. Constitution, who gave Congress in Article 1, Section 8, the power to "fix the Standard of Weights and Measures." During the nineteenth century, the Office of Standard Weights and Measures regulated measurements. In 1901 it became the National Bureau of Standards, and in 1988 it was renamed the National Institute of Standards and Technology.

The states may also regulate weights and measures, provided their regulations are not in opposition to any act of Congress. Legislation that adopts and mandates the use of uniform system of weights and measures is a valid exercise of the POLICE POWER, and such laws are constitutional. In the early twentieth century the National Bureau of Standards coordinated standards among states and held annual conferences at which a model state law of weights and measures was updated. This effort has resulted in almost complete uniformity of state laws.

Though U.S. currency was settled in a decimal form, Congress has retained the English weights and measures systems. France adopted the metric system in the 1790s, starting an international movement to make the system a universal standard, replacing national and regional variants that made scientific and commercial communication difficult.

THOMAS JEFFERSON was an early advocate of the metric system and in an 1821 report to Congress, Secretary of State JOHN QUINCY ADAMS urged its acceptance. However, Congress steadfastly refused.

Despite hostility to making the metric system the official U.S. system of weights and measures, its use was authorized in 1866. The U.S. also became a signatory to the Metric Convention of 1875, and received copies of the International Prototype Meter and the International Prototype Kilogram in 1890. In 1893 the Office of Weights and Measures announced that the prototype meter and kilogram would be recognized as fundamental standards from which customary units, the yard and the pound, would be derived.

The metric system has been adopted by many segments of U.S. commerce and industry, as well as by virtually all of the medical and scientific professions. The international acceptance of the metric system led Congress in 1968 to authorize a study to determine whether the U.S. should convert. Though the resulting 1971 report recommended shifting to the metric system over a ten-year period, Congress declined to pass appropriate legislation.

WEINSTEIN, JACK B. For more than a quarter of a century, Jack B. Weinstein has championed the fight for an independent judiciary. As a federal district judge (and later chief judge) for the Eastern District of New York, he has written, lectured, and testified about the importance of fostering strong, free-thinking jurists in the U.S. courts. As a young judge, he exerted his independence by eschewing the traditional black robe in the courtroom (except for ceremonial occasions), and as a senior judge he continued to go his own way by refusing to hear drug cases because he disagreed with federal SENTENCING guidelines.

Weinstein's independence has also manifested itself in his innovative approach to the organization and disposition of mass TORT cases (large-scale PERSONAL INJURY litigation); he has been a central figure in mass tort litigation related to subjects such as the chemical known as Agent Orange and silicon breast implants. Weinstein has written that judges must not isolate themselves from society if they are to make informed decisions. His commitment to that philosophy has been reinforced by the variety of his own life experiences.

Weinstein was born on August 10, 1921, in Wichita, Kansas. Though born in Kansas, Weinstein was raised in the Williamsburg and Bensonhurst communities near Brooklyn, New York. His father, Harry Louis Weinstein, was a salesman; his mother, the former Bessie Helen Brodach, was an amateur actress. As a toddler, Weinstein accompanied his mother to auditions, and by age eight, he too was performing on stage. During the Depression, he brought home twenty-five dollars a week to supplement the family income. He carried an Actor's Equity card for years. After high school, Weinstein put himself through Brooklyn College by working on the docks in New York Harbor. He received his bachelor of arts degree in 1943, but not before his college education had been interrupted by service in World War II. Weinstein, who later described himself as a "submariner," was a lieutenant in the U.S. Navy and Navy Reserve from 1942 to 1946.

On October 10, 1946, Weinstein married Evelyn Horowitz. When he entered the law school at Columbia University the following year, the first of his three sons had already been born. His wife worked nights as a social worker to support the family, while Weinstein took care of the new baby and attended classes. He received his bachelor of laws degree from Columbia Law School in 1948 and was admitted to the New York bar in 1949.

After graduation, he clerked for New York Court of Appeals Judge Stanley H. Fuld. Two years later, in 1950, he partnered with William Rosenfeld to open a New York City law firm. His specialty was litigation. The partnership

BIOGRAPHY

UPI/CORBIS-BETTMANN

Jack B. Weinstein

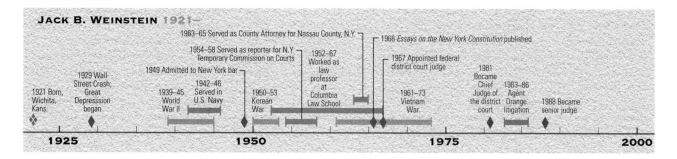

JACK B. WEINSTEIN 1921–

1921 Born, Wichita, Kans.

1929 Wall Street Crash; Great Depresssion began

1939–45 World War II

1942–46 Served in U.S. Navy

1949 Admitted to New York bar

1950–53 Korean War

1954–58 Served as reporter for N.Y. Temporary Commission on Courts

1952–67 Worked as law professor at Columbia Law School

1963–65 Served as County Attorney for Nassau County, N.Y.

1966 *Essays on the New York Constitution* published

1961–73 Vietnam War

1967 Appointed federal district court judge

1981 Became Chief Judge of the district court

1983–86 Agent Orange litigation

1988 Became senior judge

1925   1950   1975   2000

ended in 1952 when Weinstein returned to Columbia Law School as an associate professor of law.

For the next fifteen years, Weinstein forged multiple and overlapping careers as a teacher, lawyer, and public servant. From 1952 to 1954, he was special counsel for the New York Joint Legislative Committee on Motor Vehicle Problems; counsel to New York State Senator Seymour Halpern; research assistant at the New York State Senate, and a volunteer at the Legal Aid Society of New York.

Beginning in 1954, Weinstein spent four years as a consultant to, and reporter for, the New York Temporary Commission on Courts. He made a name for himself by heading a panel that rewrote the rules governing how civil cases are practiced in New York courts; he was soon recognized as a leading U.S. authority on the rules of CIVIL PROCEDURE. In large part due to his work in this area, he was made a full professor of law at Columbia in 1956.

The demand for Weinstein's expertise grew along with his reputation. While maintaining a full schedule of classes at Columbia, he served as advisor to, or member of, numerous academic, civil, judicial, legal, legislative, and government groups from 1957 to 1962.

He also became more active in political circles. From 1963 to 1965, Weinstein served as county attorney for Nassau County, New York. He also served as counsel to a number of New York state legislative committees. In 1966 he was named commissioner of the Temporary New York State Commission on Reform and Simplification of the Constitution, and he was an advisor to the New York State Constitutional Convention the following year.

Weinstein began writing and publishing in the late 1950s. Some of his early works include *Cases and Materials on Evidence* (with Morgan and Maguire, 1957); *Elements of Civil Procedure* (with Rosenberg, 1962); *Essays on the New York Constitution* (1966); *A New York Constitution Meeting Today's Needs and Tomorrow's Challenges* (1967); and *Manual of New York Civil Procedure* (with Korn and Miller, 1967).

When a federal district court vacancy occurred in early 1967, Weinstein's national prominence as an educator, author, and public servant made him a logical choice for the position. He was appointed U.S. district judge for the Eastern District of New York on April 15, 1967, by President LYNDON B. JOHNSON. He entered duty on May 1, 1967.

From the beginning, he was an independent and innovative jurist. He wore a business suit to court rather than the traditional black robe, and

"WIDESPREAD ACCESS TO THE COURTS FOR PEOPLE AS WELL AS IDEAS IS DESIRABLE. GENERALLY, ALL THOSE WHO MAY BE AFFECTED BY JUDICIAL DECISIONS WHICH ARE QUASI-LEGISLATIVE IN CHARACTER SHOULD HAVE SOME CHANNEL OF COMMUNICATION WITH THE COURT."

he could often be found sitting at a courtroom conference table *with* the parties in a dispute, rather than presiding from the bench. He believed that judicial trappings only served to distance and separate the public from a system that should be accessible to everyone.

His style and his determination to make the system open and flexible enough to address the real problems of real people sometimes left him open to attack—and reversal. Sheila L. Birnbaum, an attorney who frequently appeared in his court, said, "He often reached what he believed to be the right result and then reached to expand the law to get there." This tendency earned him the nickname "Reversible Jack."

As a judge, he maintained his ties to academia. He was an adjunct professor of law at Columbia from the time of his appointment to the bench in 1967 until 1995. He served in a similar capacity at Brooklyn Law School. Over the years, he has been a visiting professor of law at George Washington University, Georgetown University, Harvard University, New York University, the University of Colorado, and the University of Texas. He has also been a frequent lecturer on other legal campuses around the United States and the world. Similarly, Weinstein continued to publish in his field of expertise while on the bench. His seven-volume *Weinstein's Evidence*, and *Weinstein's Evidence Manual*, both written with Professor Margaret Berger, were first published in 1975.

In 1981 Weinstein became chief judge of the district court, and he began to make his mark in the area of complex mass tort litigation. From 1983 to 1986, Weinstein worked with chemical manufacturers and Vietnam War veterans to settle the thousands of Agent Orange cases clogging the courts. Within months of taking over the five-year-old dispute, Weinstein pressured chemical manufacturers and plaintiffs' lawyers to establish a $180 million fund for veterans taking part in the CLASS ACTION.

As chief judge, Weinstein continued to be a watchdog for those in society most vulnerable to exploitation. In 1984 he ordered the federal government to rewrite MEDICARE forms, making them more understandable to average senior citizens.

Weinstein took senior (or semiretired) status in 1988. Exercising his right as a senior judge to choose the cases he would hear, he decided that he would concentrate on complex cases and would not hear routine matters—including drug cases. Weinstein does not agree with federal sentencing guidelines for drug offenses. He has written that the strict sentences imposed in drug cases often do not fit the crime, impose exceptional hardship on families and dependent children, and have not proven to be an appropriate or effective deterrent.

In one of his first cases as a senior judge, Weinstein overturned a jury verdict against the Long Island Lighting Company (LILCO), allowing the utility to settle a long and nasty dispute with customers over the construction of a nuclear power plant. Weinstein's ruling led to an agreement between LILCO and its customers—and a cut in utility rates.

In 1990 Weinstein was asked to tackle the backlog of asbestos-injury cases in the nation's courts. Weinstein and nine other judges developed a plan to consolidate the cases into three groups (or classes) for trial. Though initially rejected by the U.S. Court of Appeals for the Sixth Circuit, a judicial panel on multidistrict litigation finally agreed, in 1991, to consolidate all pending asbestos cases in the Eastern District of Pennsylvania (*In re Asbestos Products Liability Litigation*, 771 F. Supp. 415). The following year Weinstein helped to consolidate cases involving the anti-miscarriage drug DES. And later in 1992, he recommended the consolidation of more than forty suits involving repetitive-stress injury.

Through his work, Weinstein developed a philosophy for handling mass tort cases: obtain scientific and medical information as early in the process as possible, consolidate cases for ease of administration, and cooperate with the state courts. Although consolidation of mass tort cases provides for convenience and economy of effort, Weinstein admits that the system is not perfect and that reform is necessary. In September 1992 he told the *Wall Street Journal* that many people caught up in mass tort cases feel "alienated and dehumanized" and that the present system does not always meet their individual needs.

Weinstein continues to serve as senior judge in the Eastern District of New York. He also continues to serve the people and the profession by his active involvement in many legal service organizations, including the American Academy of Arts and Sciences, American Judicature Society, American Law Institute, American Association of University Professors, American Bar Association, Institute for Judicial Administration, International Association of Jewish Lawyers and Jurists, National Legal Aid and Defender Association, Society of American Law Teachers, and International Society of Public Teachers of Law.

WEIS, JOSEPH FRANCIS, JR. In March 1989, senior federal appeals court judge Joseph Francis Weis, Jr., was handed the awesome task of chairing a congressional committee to examine issues and problems facing U.S. courts and to develop a long-range plan for the future of the federal JUDICIARY. Though segments of the U.S. court system had been examined and fine-tuned throughout U.S. history, the formation of the Federal Courts Study Committee in 1989 marked the first time in almost one hundred years that any entity was granted such broad and sweeping authority to review the system and propose changes to it. Professor Daniel J. Meador, of the University of Virginia School of Law, called the mandate a "once-in-a-century undertaking." The only analogous review of the FEDERAL COURTS took place in the 1890s and resulted in the creation of the federal courts of appeals.

Under Weis's leadership, the Federal Courts Study Committee took just fifteen months to produce a monumental report containing one hundred specific recommendations for U.S. court reform. Many of the committee's recommendations were adopted immediately, and others were expected to influence court reform well into the twenty-first century.

Congress chose the right person to chair the historic committee. Weis's natural abilities as a leader and a consensus builder have been evident throughout his life. Born March 12, 1923, in Pittsburgh, Weis was the first of four sons in the family of Joseph Francis Weis and Mary Flaherty Weis. He graduated from local schools and set out to follow a path inspired by his father, a prominent trial attorney.

Weis entered Duquesne University in 1941 with the intention of attending law school immediately after graduation. His plans were interrupted by World War II. In 1943 he left college to enlist. He fought in France with the Third Army's Fourth Armored Division, and he was wounded twice during his tour of duty. Weis returned home with a Bronze Star and a Purple Heart—and he continued to serve in the Army Reserve long after he returned to college. He retired with the rank of captain in 1948.

Weis received a bachelor of arts degree from Duquesne University in 1947 and a doctor of jurisprudence degree from the University of Pittsburgh Law School in 1950. While in law school, he developed an interest in scholarly writing as editor of the law review.

Admitted to the Pennsylvania bar in 1950, Weis joined three former classmates to establish the law firm of Sheriff, Lindsay, Weis, and McGinnis. Two years later he realized a lifelong dream when he partnered with his father in the firm of Weis and Weis. Weis's three younger brothers joined the firm as they completed their studies, creating a thriving family enterprise.

BIOGRAPHY

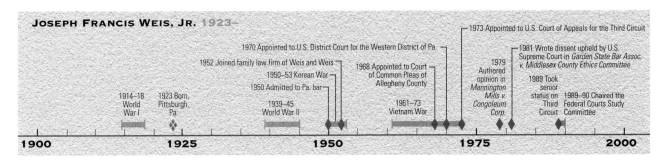

JOSEPH FRANCIS WEIS, JR. 1923–

1914–18 World War I

1923 Born, Pittsburgh, Pa.

1939–45 World War II

1950 Admitted to Pa. bar

1950–53 Korean War

1952 Joined family law firm of Weis and Weis

1961–73 Vietnam War

1968 Appointed to Court of Common Pleas of Allegheny County

1970 Appointed to U.S. District Court for the Western District of Pa.

1973 Appointed to U.S. Court of Appeals for the Third Circuit

1979 Authored opinion in *Mannington Mills v. Congoleum Corp.*

1981 Wrote dissent upheld by U.S. Supreme Court in *Garden State Bar Assoc. v. Middlesex County Ethics Committee*

1989 Took senior status on Third Circuit

1989–90 Chaired the Federal Courts Study Committee

1900   1925   1950   1975   2000

A skillful trial attorney like his father, Weis was active in the Academy of Trial Lawyers of Allegheny County from 1960 to 1968, serving as president from 1966 to 1967. He became a recognized expert on trial procedures and was a frequent lecturer on the subject.

His expertise led to an appointment as judge of the Court of Common Pleas of Allegheny County in 1968. In May 1970 Weis was appointed to the U.S. District Court for the Western District of Pennsylvania. In February 1973 President RICHARD M. NIXON appointed him to the U.S. Court of Appeals for the Third Circuit.

Early in his career on the federal bench, Weis showcased his expertise on INTERNATIONAL LAW when he authored the opinion in *Mannington Mills v. Congoleum Corp.*, 595 F.2d 1287 (3d Cir. 1979). This oft-cited opinion made him a sought-after member of many international legal forums.

Weis also authored a number of important opinions in the field of legal and judicial ETHICS. One of these was the dissenting opinion in *Garden State Bar Ass'n v. Middlesex County Ethics Committee*, 651 F.2d 154 (3d Cir. 1981), which was later reversed by the U.S. Supreme Court (*Middlesex County Ethics Committee v. Garden State Bar Ass'n*, 457 U.S. 423, 102 S. Ct. 2515, 73 L. Ed. 2d 116 [1982]). Another was the majority opinion in *Stretton v. Disciplinary Board*, 944 F.2d 137 (3d Cir. 1991), which reversed a lower court's ruling that struck down a Pennsylvania judicial ethics rule barring judicial candidates from telling voters about their legal and political views.

It was, however, in the areas of technology, courtroom design, structure, rules, and administration that Weis truly distinguished himself. In the Third Circuit he chaired committees experimenting with videoconference arguments and videotape trial proceedings. For the JUDICIAL CONFERENCE OF THE UNITED STATES, Weis was chairman of the Standing Committee on Rules of Practice and Procedure, member of the Committee on Administration of the Bankruptcy System, member of the Subcommittee

"SENTENCES ARE INEVITABLY ONLY APPROXIMATIONS AND [LEGISLATIVE] EFFORTS TO MAKE THEM SCIENTIFICALLY PRECISE ARE DOOMED TO FAILURE."

on Judicial Improvements, and chairman of the Supreme Court Advisory Committee on Civil Rules. For the AMERICAN BAR ASSOCIATION, he served on the Committee on Technology and the Courts and the Committee on Design of Court Rooms and Court Facilities.

In 1989, after sixteen years on the federal bench and hundreds of hours of committee service, Weis announced that he would take senior (or semiretired) status and begin winding down his judicial career. His timing could not have been worse. At the time of his announcement, he did not know that Chief Justice WILLIAM H. REHNQUIST was about to tap him for the most demanding and significant task of his judicial career.

For years Congress had considered various bills to study mounting procedural and workload problems in the U.S. courts. In the fall of 1988 Congress finally created the Federal Courts Study Committee (Pub. L. No. 100-702, 102 Stat. 4644 [1988] [codified at 28 U.S.C.A. § 331]). Unlike previous committees that were conceived to examine parts of the court system, the Federal Courts Study Committee was charged with examining issues and problems facing the entire court system in the United States—and with developing the first ever long-range plan for addressing the issues and correcting the problems. Chief Justice Rehnquist appointed fifteen committee members, including federal and state judges, members of Congress, private attorneys, a state public defender, and a Department of Justice official. He named Weis to chair the committee.

Weis assumed the leadership role with his characteristic sense of duty. For the first three months following his appointment, Weis and his committee conducted a thorough survey of the federal judiciary to help focus the issues and problems. They also solicited input from citizens' groups, bar associations, research groups, law school deans and other academics, chief probation officers, pretrial services chiefs, and federal public defenders.

By December 1989, they had drafted a preliminary report that clearly focused on the overriding problem and made a number of recommendations for addressing it. Workload was cited as the biggest barrier to efficiency and equal justice. Between 1958 and 1988, the number of cases filed in the district courts had tripled, and the number of appeals filed in the circuits had increased more than tenfold. Public hearings on the preliminary report were held in nine U.S. cities beginning in January 1990.

The final report was presented to the president, the chief justice of the U.S. Supreme Court, Congress, the Conference of State Chief Justices, and the State Justice Institute in the spring of 1990. It outlined one hundred substantive changes in the areas of court administration and operation, designed to reduce the workload and enhance the quality of U.S. justice. Among the recommendations: redirect narcotics cases to STATE COURTS, narrow the JURISDICTION of federal courts, create a tier of specialized courts (a disability claims court and special bankruptcy appeals panels), and encourage ALTERNATIVE DISPUTE RESOLUTION in civil cases. Sixteen procedural and noncontroversial recommendations were introduced and passed during the following congressional session.

On April 26, 1993, Weis was awarded the Devitt Distinguished Service to Justice Award, which is administered by the American Judicature Society. This award is named for Edward J. Devitt, a former chief U.S. district judge for Minnesota. It acknowledges the dedication and contributions to justice made by all federal judges, by recognizing the specific achievements of one judge who has contributed significantly to the profession. He was honored for his work on the Federal Courts Study Committee and a lifetime achievement in the area of court reform.

Weis continues to hear cases as a senior judge. He writes and speaks frequently about court issues and the committee work that capped off his long career as a courtroom innovator and reformer.

WELCH, JOSEPH NYE Joseph Nye Welch represented the U.S. Army in the Army-McCarthy hearings held in the U.S. Senate in April through June 1954.

Welch was born in Primghar, Iowa, on October 22, 1890, the youngest of seven children born in a poor farm family. Welch's mother encouraged him to succeed in school. He was intrigued by the law even as a boy and enjoyed watching trials whenever he could. After clerking for two years in a real estate office, he entered Grinnell College in Iowa and graduated Phi Beta Kappa in 1914. Welch then entered Harvard Law School with a $600 scholarship and earned his bachelor of laws degree in 1917.

Welch attended Army Officer Candidate School when the U.S. entered World War I, but the war ended before he received his commission as a second lieutenant. He served briefly in the legal division of the U.S. Shipping Board. Welch joined the Boston law firm of Hale and Dorr in 1919 and became a partner in 1923 and a senior partner in 1936. He practiced civil law, particularly in the areas of antitrust, libel, estates, wills, and tax litigation, and he oversaw the firm's trial department.

Welch is known for serving as special counsel to the Department of the Army in Senate hearings involving Wisconsin Senator JOSEPH R. McCARTHY. Welch served without compensation for the job. The hearings were held before the Senate's Special Subcommittee on Investigations of the Government Operations Committee, chaired by McCarthy. Televised to millions of Americans, the hearings showed political theater of a kind never seen before.

The issues in the hearings were a mass of attacks, innuendo, and counterattacks involving Senator McCarthy and Secretary of the Army Robert T. Stevens. McCarthy, widely known for his forceful attempts to ferret out suspected or imagined subversives in the government, had made repeated demands in late 1953 for access to confidential Army files on loyalty and security because he alleged that the Army had employed subversives. In addition, McCarthy was agitated over the case of an Army dentist, Irving Peress. Peress, a member of the left-wing American Labor party, had been promoted to major in late 1953 according to provisions automatically applicable to drafted doctors. Soon thereafter, he was ordered discharged when the military learned that he had declined to answer questions regarding his political beliefs. McCarthy learned about the case before the discharge and summoned Peress to speak before the subcommittee. Peress invoked the FIFTH AMENDMENT when asked about his political views, and McCarthy demanded that he be court-martialed.

While McCarthy was pressuring the Army, the press uncovered a story regarding an unpaid, sometime consultant to the subcommittee, G. David Schine. Schine, a friend of the subcommittee's chief counsel ROY COHN, had been called by the draft board in July 1953. Cohn and McCarthy purportedly tried unsuccessfully to arrange a commission for Schine in the Army, Navy, or Air Force. McCarthy and Cohn were also charged with improperly pressuring the Army to promote Schine. In response,

"UNTIL THIS MOMENT, SENATOR [McCARTHY], I THINK I NEVER REALLY GAUGED YOUR CRUELTY OR YOUR RECKLESSNESS . . . HAVE YOU NO SENSE OF DECENCY, SIR, AT LONG LAST? HAVE YOU LEFT NO SENSE OF DECENCY?"

BIOGRAPHY

Joseph Nye Welch

APWIDE WORLD PHOTOS

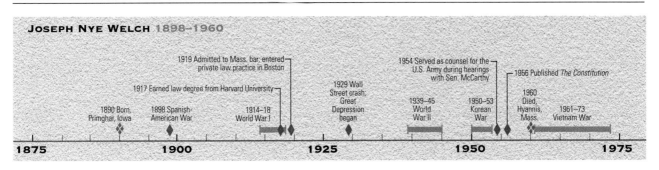

JOSEPH NYE WELCH 1898–1960

1890 Born, Primghar, Iowa
1898 Spanish-American War
1914–18 World War I
1917 Earned law degree from Harvard University
1919 Admitted to Mass. bar; entered private law practice in Boston
1929 Wall Street crash; Great Depression began
1939–45 World War II
1950–53 Korean War
1954 Served as counsel for the U.S. Army during hearings with Sen. McCarthy
1956 Published *The Constitution*
1960 Died, Hyannis, Mass.
1961–73 Vietnam War

1875   1900   1925   1950   1975

McCarthy claimed that the Army was holding Schine "hostage" to blackmail McCarthy into stopping his investigation.

In stark contrast to the domineering, goading, and downright bullying demeanor of McCarthy, Welch appeared calm, genteel, and well prepared in the hearing room. He managed to inject a bit of humor into the proceedings on more than one occasion. When Welch questioned a witness about how he had come into possession of a photograph, he asked the witness if he thought it came from a pixie. Senator McCarthy interrupted to ask for the definition of a pixie. Welch replied, "I should say, Mr. Senator, that a pixie is a close relative of a fairy. Shall I proceed, sir? Have I enlightened you?"

The thirty-six days of hearings resolved little, and legal issues remained muddled. The dramatic climax came on June 9, 1954, when McCarthy attacked Frederick G. Fisher, Jr., a member of Welch's Boston firm, for supposed Communist leanings. During law school at Harvard, Fisher had belonged to the National Lawyer's Guild, an organization with purported Communist ties. At the time of the hearings, Fisher was a Republican (as was McCarthy) and a respected lawyer. Welch responded, "Little did I dream you could be so reckless and so cruel as to do an injury to that lad. . . . I like to think that I am a gentleman, but your forgiveness will have to come from someone other than me." When McCarthy persisted in his diatribe, Welch cut him off, exhorting him to exhibit a sense of decency. Welch then left the hearing room, as the spectators broke into loud applause.

Though the outcome of the investigation was inconclusive, McCarthy's conduct during the widely publicized hearings eventually cost him support from moderates who had long tolerated him. Later that year, the Senate took a rare step and voted to censure McCarthy for his unbecoming conduct.

Welch was a family man who preferred a quiet life, but he did not return to obscurity after the hearings. His courtroom persona captured the nation's interest, and in 1956 he became the narrator of a highly praised television series on the constitutional history of the United States. He also wrote a book, *The Constitution*, to accompany the series. He took on other roles, culminating in his portrayal of a judge in the 1959 movie *Anatomy of a Murder.* Reviews of the film praised his performance.

Welch was married in 1917 and had two sons. His wife died in 1956, and he remarried the next year. He died on October 6, 1960, in Hyannis, Massachusetts.

See also COMMUNISM.

WELFARE Government benefits distributed to impoverished persons to enable them to maintain a minimum standard of well-being.

Providing welfare benefits to poor people has been controversial throughout U.S. history. Since the colonial period, government welfare policy has reflected the belief that the indigent are responsible for their poverty, leading to the principle that governmental benefits are a PRIVILEGE and not a RIGHT. Until the Great Depression of the 1930s, state and local governments bore some responsibility for providing assistance to the poor. Generally, such assistance was minimal at best, with church and volunteer agencies providing the bulk of any aid.

The NEW DEAL policies of President FRANKLIN D. ROOSEVELT included new federal initiatives to help those in poverty. With millions of people unemployed during the 1930s economic depression, welfare assistance was beyond the financial resources of the states. Therefore, the federal government provided funds either directly to recipients or to the states for maintaining a minimum standard of living.

Between 1935 and 1996, federal programs were established that provided additional welfare benefits, including medical care (MEDICAID), public housing, food stamps, and Supplemental Security Income (SSI). By the 1960s, however, criticism began to grow that these programs had created a "culture of dependency," which discouraged people from leaving the welfare rolls and finding employment. Defenders of public welfare benefits acknowledged that the system was imperfect, noting the financial disincentives associated with taking a low-paying job and losing the array of benefits, especially medical care. However, defenders of the system pointed out that millions of children are the prime beneficiaries of welfare assistance, and that removing adults from welfare affects these children.

During the 1980s and 1990s, the criticism of public welfare escalated dramatically. Some states began to experiment with programs that required welfare recipients to find work within a specified period of time, after which welfare benefits would cease. Job training and CHILD CARE are important components of such programs and proponents of such "workfare" programs acknowledged that this approach saves little money in the short term. They contended, however, that workfare would reduce welfare costs and move people away from government dependency over the long term.

These state efforts paved the way for radical changes in federal welfare law. On August 22, 1996, President BILL CLINTON, a Democrat, signed the Personal Responsibility and Work Opportunity Reconciliation Act of 1996 (popularly known as the Welfare Reform Act), a bill passed by the Republican-controlled Congress. The act eliminated welfare programs, placed permanent ceilings on the amount of federal funding for welfare, and gave each state a block grant of money to help run its welfare programs. The law also directs each state legislature to come up with a new welfare plan that meets new federal criteria. Under the 1996 law, federal funds can be used only to provide a total of five years of aid in a lifetime to a family. These and other provisions radically transformed welfare law and welfare programs.

Federal Social Security Programs
Until the 1996 Welfare Reform Act, the federal government financed the three major welfare programs in the country through the SOCIAL SECURITY ACT OF 1935 (42 U.S.C.A. § 301 et seq.): Supplemental Security Income (SSI), Medicaid, and Aid to Families with Dependent Children (AFDC). The 1996 law abolished the AFDC program. These programs are in addition to the benefits available to the aged, disabled, and unemployed workers and their dependents. Unlike the benefits based on the employment record of a worker, welfare benefits are distributed to people who demonstrate eligibility by establishing financial need.

Supplemental Security Income Indigent persons who are aged or disabled receive monthly checks through the SSI program to help provide them with a minimum standard of living. In 1974 SSI assumed the responsibility

Number of Welfare Recipients and Percent of U.S. Population, 1960 to June 1997

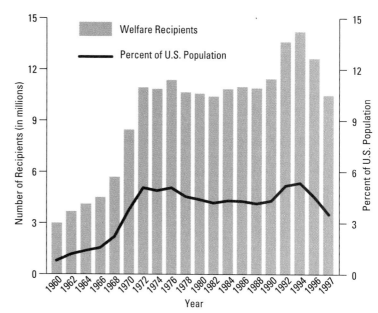

Source: U.S. Department of Health and Human Services, Administration for Children and Families, August 1997.

for three separate plans previously administered by the states for these recipients. Funds are taken from the U.S. Treasury to provide monthly benefits at a standard rate nationwide. Where state funds already supply such benefits, they supplement the amount provided by the federal government.

The creation of the SSI program meant that applicants had to meet the same standards of eligibility in every state. Applicants must prove they are residents and citizens of the United States. The 1996 Welfare Reform Act cut billions of dollars of aid for legal ALIENS, and completely excluded legal aliens from receiving SSI benefits. No new noncitizens could be added to the program after the date of enactment, and all legal aliens who were receiving SSI benefits will eventually be removed from the rolls, unless they met one of the law's exceptions. A recipient will not receive benefits for any full month that he is not living within the fifty states or the District of Columbia. Inmates in a public institution cannot collect SSI unless they reside in a community-run group home with a maximum of sixteen residents.

The passage of the Contract with America Advancement Act of 1996 (P.L. 104-221), made a significant change in the basic philosophy of the SSI program. Beginning on the date of enactment (March 29, 1996), new applicants for SSI disability benefits are not eligible for ben-

A BRIEF HISTORY OF WELFARE REFORM

The Personal Responsibility and Work Opportunity Reconciliation Act of 1996, 110 Stat. 2105, popularly known as the Welfare Reform Act, is the most significant piece of welfare legislation since the New Deal administration of Franklin D. Roosevelt. The 1996 act was the culmination of a thirty-year debate over the effectiveness of government welfare programs and the proper role of government assistance. The act's goals of moving people off the welfare rolls, limiting the amount of time on public assistance, and mandating that welfare recipients work were based on the idea of personal responsibility. For conservatives, the law delivered a blow to the modern liberal welfare state. For liberals, the act raised as many questions as it answered. It was unclear how states would provide training to welfare recipients that would allow them to find employment paying a living wage. More ominously, what would happen to children when families lost their welfare benefits permanently?

The history of welfare reform reveals that the question of personal responsibility versus assistance to those in need has been a constant in the debate over welfare. Dissatisfaction with welfare began during the 1950s. Critics began to assert that the federal Aid to Families with Dependent Children (AFDC) program had made welfare a way of life, rather than simply short-term assistance, for many in the program. With this perception, a backlash set in.

In the 1950s and early 1960s, welfare reform was limited to various states' attempts to impose residency requirements on welfare applicants and remove illegitimate children from the welfare rolls. Many states also passed so-called man in the house rules, which cut off benefits when a man lived in the home. By the late 1960s, such laws had been struck down on the ground that the Equal Protection Clause of the Fourteenth Amendment requires the government to treat all persons in similar situations equally.

During the 1960s President Lyndon B. Johnson's administration declared an ostensible "war on poverty" with its Great Society programs: Head Start, the Job Corps, Food Stamps, and Medicaid funded education, job training, direct food assistance, and direct medical assistance, respectively. Although the poverty rate declined in the 1960s, more than 4 million new recipients signed up for welfare.

IN FOCUS

With the election of President Richard M. Nixon in 1968, the conservative backlash against liberal policies began to take hold. Nixon was the first president since Roosevelt to offer major national welfare legislation. His 1969 Family Assistance Plan, however, pleased neither liberals nor conservatives. Nixon proposed giving needy families with children $1,600 annually; as a work incentive, they would be allowed to keep any earned income up to approximately $4,000. More importantly, all welfare recipients except mothers with children under the age of three would be required to work. Liberals rejected the plan because they believed that the support levels were too low and that the work requirement was punitive. Conservatives were unimpressed by Nixon's goal of reducing the welfare bureaucracy through a program that appeared to expand public assistance. The program died in Congress in 1972.

Instead of reform, welfare programs underwent major expansions during the Nixon administration. States were required to provide food stamps, and Supplemental Security Income (SSI) consolidated aid for aged, blind, and disabled persons. The Earned Income Credit provided the working poor with direct cash assistance in the form of tax credits. As spending grew, so did the welfare rolls.

During the 1970s advocates of welfare reform promoted the theory of "workfare." The idea initially referred to working off welfare payments through public service jobs, but it developed into the concept of using training and education to help recipients gain independence. By the 1980s workfare had emerged as the future of welfare reform.

President Ronald Reagan came into office in 1981 as a harsh critic of welfare. During his first term, he helped secure deep cuts in AFDC spending, including the reduction of benefits to working recipients of public assistance. In addition, the states were given the option of requiring the majority of recipients to participate in workfare programs.

During the 1980s the welfare system was subjected to many critical attacks, most notably in sociologist Charles Murray's book *Losing Ground: American Social Policy, 1950–1980* (1984). Murray argued that welfare hurt the poor by making them less well off and discouraging them from working. The system effectively trapped single-parent families in a cycle of welfare dependency, creating more, rather than less, poverty. Murray proposed abolishing federal welfare and replacing it with short-term local programs. Though many criticized Murray's data and conclusions, most agreed that welfare produced disincentives to work.

During the 1980s forty states set up so-called welfare-to-work programs that provided education and training. The federal Family Support Act of 1988 (23 U.S.C.A. § 125) adopted this approach, directing all states to phase in comprehensive welfare-to-work programs by 1990. Each state was to implement education, job training, and job placement programs for welfare recipients. Nevertheless, the initiative proved unsuccessful because the states lacked the money needed for federal matching funds. By 1993 only one in five eligible recipients was enrolled in a training program.

Thus, the stage was set for the 1996 welfare reform legislation. It did much of what Murray had advocated: it made personal responsibility and work central to the welfare agenda, and it shifted welfare to the states. State governments were given fixed blocks of money, which they could use as they saw fit, as long as they imposed work requirements and limited a family's stay on welfare to five years. By placing ceilings on the amount of money states receive for welfare, the 1996 act announced that public welfare programs would shrink rather than grow over time.

efits if drug addiction or alcoholism is a material factor in their disability. Unless they can qualify on some other medical basis, they cannot receive disability benefits. Previously, if a person had a medical condition that prevented them from working, he was disabled for SSI purposes, regardless of the cause of the disability.

All persons who are otherwise qualified must show that their incomes are below the levels prescribed by federal law and that they have no ASSETS that can be used for their support. Various rules regulate the calculation of an applicant's income. A person need not be totally devoid of assets in order to receive benefits. A home, for example, does not count as an asset, and the government does not impose LIENS (charges against property to secure the payment of a debt) against the homes of recipients of SSI benefits.

Medicaid The largest government welfare program that provides benefits other than money for indigent persons is Medicaid. Medicaid was enacted in 1965 as an amendment to the Social Security Act of 1935, (Title XIX, 42 U.S.C.A. 1396). A state receives federal money if it furnishes additional financing and administers a medical program for the poor that satisfies federal standards. A state can supplement federal benefits with its own funds. Medicaid is designed to make private medical care available to impoverished people. As long as their procedures are REASONABLE, states can establish their own methods of determining a Medicaid applicant's income and resources and whether the applicant qualifies for aid.

Prior to the abolition of the AFDC program in the 1996 reform law, children and parents who received AFDC automatically qualified for Medicaid. The 1996 law provides Medicaid coverage to all families that meet their state's July 1996 AFDC income and asset standards. When a family becomes ineligible for Medicaid coverage due to increased earnings or CHILD SUPPORT income, it becomes eligible for transitional Medicaid, regardless of whether the family received assistance under the block grant program that has replaced AFDC.

As with SSI and other programs, however, the 1996 law denies Medicaid eligibility to most legal immigrants. Except for REFUGEES, those who have claimed political asylum, and a few other categories, immigrants entering the United States are ineligible for Medicaid for five years, with states having the option of extending this ban for a longer period. Immigrants who had been receiving Medicaid as a result of receiving SSI are not eligible for Medicaid once their SSI benefits are cut off.

Medicaid furnishes at least five general categories of treatment, including inpatient hospital service, outpatient hospital services, laboratory and x-ray services, skilled nursing home services, and physicians' services. Generally each of these services is available to treat conditions that cause acute suffering, endanger life, result in illness or infirmity, interfere with the capacity for normal activity, or present a significant handicap. In addition, all states provide eye and dental care and prescription drugs. Almost all states provide physical therapy, hospice care, and rehabilitative services.

Medicaid is a "vendor" plan because payment is made directly to the vendor (the person or entity which provides the services) rather than to the patient. Only approved nursing homes, physicians, and other providers of medical care are entitled to receive Medicaid payments for their services. Since the early 1970s, rising medical costs have placed financial pressures on the Medicaid program. Consequently, health care providers are not fully reimbursed for the services they provide to Medicaid patients. When Medicaid began, persons who were eligible had the right to select their own doctors, hospitals, or other medical facilities. Because of skyrocketing medical expenditures, almost all states have received waivers from the federal government concerning the choice of physician.

Aid to Families with Dependent Children Prior to 1996, the most controversial component of the welfare system was the AFDC program. AFDC was established by Congress to ensure the welfare and protection of needy dependent children by providing them and a custodial relative with basic necessities within the framework of the family relationship. It was abolished in the 1996 welfare reform act, replaced by block grants to the states to fund welfare under new sets of rules and requirements. The block grant, which is entitled the Temporary Assistance to Needy Families (TANF) block grant, converts AFDC to fixed funding. Under TANF, states receive a fixed level of resources for income support and work programs based on what they spent on these programs in 1994, without regard to subsequent changes in the level of need in a state.

Every state was required to establish an AFDC system within broad federal guidelines, with the federal government providing funds for the state programs. The state plan had to be applied uniformly throughout the state, with the state providing some funding itself and designating one state agency to administer the program. Even though the 1996 law eliminated AFDC, many of the general categories and definitions contained in state-AFDC statutes and regulations will likely remain relevant in new state welfare program laws for determining eligibility.

A child is classified "dependent" if he has no parental support or care because of the death of a parent, the abandonment by a parent, or the physical or mental incapacity of a parent to fulfill the responsibilities to a child. Once a child qualifies as dependent under these standards, the state agency will decide whether the child is "needy." Each state establishes a minimum income level of subsistence. If the income of a child and the members of his family are below this level, these individuals are deemed needy. All sources of income actually received by the family are considered, as well as the value of all the family's assets.

Under the old AFDC system, each state fashioned exemptions depending upon the circumstances of the case. For example, a state might allow a portion of Social Security benefits received because of the death of a parent to be saved for the child's future education.

Once the state agency determines the income of members of a family and decides whether their assets are sufficient to meet their needs, it compares their income to the standard of need applied in that state. The standard of need is based on the number of family members, sometimes up to a specific maximum. Under the old law, if the family's income was inadequate to provide what the state considered a minimum amount for the family's needs, AFDC benefits were issued. Under the 1996 law, there is no explicit requirement that the families get cash aid, making it possible for the states to provide VOUCHERS or services rather than cash help. The law specifically eliminates the promise of help and eliminates individual entitlement to aid under federal law. In addition, if a state runs out of block grant funds for the year, and does not provide state funds, it can place new applicants on waiting lists. Under the old law, states received federal funds on an open-ended, entitlement basis.

The 1996 law placed a yearly limit of $16.4 billion nationally on federal welfare spending that replaced AFDC and several other programs, with no provision to raise the limit in the future. Within this financial framework, the states have greater autonomy in determining how to spend the funds on welfare. However, the 1996 law imposed several important changes in national welfare policy.

The 1996 law directs the states to increase the number of persons on welfare who work. By 2002, a minimum of half the families receiving public assistance must have an adult working a minimum of thirty hours per week. If states do not meet these requirements, they can be penalized by losing a percentage of their TANF block grants. Adults cannot be penalized for failure to meet work requirements if their failure is based on the inability to find or afford child care for a child under the age of six. Otherwise, if an adult recipient refuses to participate in a work program, states must reduce the family's assistance by a pro rata amount. States, however, have the option of increasing this penalty, including the termination of assistance to the entire family. Adults can also lose Medicaid as well as cash aid.

One of the criticisms of the AFDC program was that it allowed teenage mothers to set up independent living arrangements and receive AFDC. The 1996 law directs that minor parents can only receive TANF block grant funds if they are living at home or in another adult-supervised setting. They must attend high school or an alternative educational or training program as soon as their child is at least twelve weeks old.

The most radical change in abolishing AFDC and moving to the TANF block grants was the limitation on families receiving TANF funds. Federal funds can only be used to provide a total of five years of aid in a lifetime to a family. The law provides that states may give hardship exemptions of up to twenty percent of their average monthly caseload. However, the law also permits states to set limits shorter than five years.

A state welfare assistance plan must set forth objective criteria for the delivery of benefits and for fair and equitable treatment, as well as how the state will provide opportunities for recipients to appeal decisions against them. While the law and regulations governing AFDC were explicit regarding appeal rights, the 1996 law is more general in this area, leaving each state to devise DUE PROCESS protections in state law.

Food and Food Stamps The federal government provides food to poor people through several types of programs, including nutrition programs, and, most importantly, the Food Stamp program.

The federal government sponsors special nutrition plans to promote child welfare. Such programs, including the Child and Adult Care Food Program (CACFP), provide federal grants of money and food to nonprofit elementary and secondary schools and to child-care institutions so that they can serve milk, well-balanced meals, and snacks to the children. Additional money is provided so that free or reduced-price food and milk can be given to children of needy families. These programs provide lunch and breakfast to children in public and private non-profit schools. Pregnant and nursing mothers and their children up to age four who live in areas that have large numbers of people who are considered nutritional risks are eligible for a special program that supplies food supplements.

The Food Stamp program, as provided by the Federal Food Stamp Act of 1964, is the most significant food plan in the United States. Needy individuals or households obtain food stamps (or official coupons) that can be exchanged like money at authorized stores. Some states create electronic banking accounts for welfare benefits, including food stamps, that allow a person to purchase food using an electronic bank card. The person's account is debited the amount of the cash value of the stamps when he purchases food at a store.

The federal government pays for the amount of the benefit received, and the states pay the costs of determining eligibility and distributing the stamps. The value of the food stamp allotment that state agencies are authorized to issue is based on the "thrifty food plan," a low-cost food budget, reduced by an amount equal to thirty per cent of the household income. Prior to 1996, poor families with children that spent more than fifty per cent of their income for housing would have had their excess shelter costs included in calculating the amount of food stamps received. The 1996 law placed a maximum amount for the food stamp deduction for shelter costs.

Public Housing Since the late 1930s, the federal government has provided funds to build public housing for the poor. Almost all programs rely on local public housing agencies created by state law or by a local government unit authorized by the state. Contracts between the Department of Housing and Urban Development and the local agency provide the means for the transfer of the federal funds.

Applicants for public housing must meet income requirements. So as not to penalize people for improving their financial condition, TENANTS usually can continue to live in public housing after they surpass the income level that admitted them to the project. As the tenant's

income increases, she might be charged a higher rent so that the rent can be kept lower for other tenants with greater need. Federal law limits the percentage of a tenant's income that can be charged for rent in low-income housing projects.

Welfare Rights With the development of the welfare system, the courts have been called on to resolve disputes involving welfare recipients and government agencies. The most important case concerning the scope of welfare rights is *Dandridge v. Williams*, 397 U.S. 471, 90 S. Ct. 1153, 25 L. Ed. 2d 491 (1970). In *Dandridge*, a California law set an upper limit on the amount of welfare benefits that a family could receive, preventing larger families from receiving the same amount per person as smaller families. The Court found that states might reasonably theorize that large families can take advantage of economies unavailable to smaller households. The EQUAL PROTECTION Clause of the FOURTEENTH AMENDMENT does not require a state to choose between resolving every aspect of a problem and not resolving the problem at all, as long as the state's action is reasonably related to the goal of the legislation and free of invidious discrimination.

CROSS-REFERENCES

Health Care Law; Health Insurance; Homeless Person; Old Age, Survivors, and Disability Insurance; Social Security.

BIOGRAPHY

WELLS-BARNETT, IDA BELL Ida Bell Wells-Barnett was a prominent and often controversial African American reformer who spoke out against racial oppression in the United States at the turn of the twentieth century. The daughter of slaves, Wells-Barnett conducted a self-described crusade for justice to protest the savage lynchings of hundreds of African Americans in the South. Her impassioned antilynching lectures and publications had an enormous effect on public opinion in the United States and Great Britain. Outspoken and self-confident, Wells-Barnett was viewed with hostility by many whites and rebuffed by several African American leaders who resented her frequent criticism of their efforts. Yet, even her detractors conceded that Wells-Barnett's

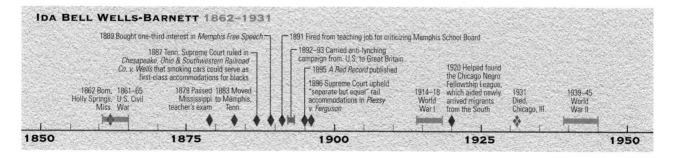

IDA BELL WELLS-BARNETT 1862–1931

1889 Bought one-third interest in *Memphis Free Speech*

1891 Fired from teaching job for criticizing Memphis School Board

1887 Tenn. Supreme Court ruled in *Chesapeake, Ohio & Southwestern Railroad Co. v. Wells* that smoking cars could serve as first-class accommodations for blacks

1892–93 Carried anti-lynching campaign from U.S. to Great Britain

1895 *A Red Record* published

1896 Supreme Court upheld "separate but equal" rail accommodations in *Plessy v. Ferguson*

1920 Helped found the Chicago Negro Fellowship League, which aided newly arrived migrants from the South

1862 Born, Holly Springs, Miss.

1861–65 U.S. Civil War

1879 Passed Mississippi teacher's exam

1883 Moved to Memphis, Tenn.

1914–18 World War I

1931 Died, Chicago, Ill.

1939–45 World War II

1850   1875   1900   1925   1950

unshakable commitment to the social, political, and economic advancement of African Americans propelled the struggle for CIVIL RIGHTS.

Born July 16, 1862, in Holly Springs, Mississippi, Wells-Barnett was the oldest of eight children of James Wells and Elizabeth Warrenton Wells. After the Civil War, her father was a carpenter and a leader in local Reconstruction activities. Wells-Barnett attended Shaw University (later renamed Rust College), an African American school for all grade levels established in Holly Springs in 1866 by Freedmen's Aid, a church-sponsored effort to educate former slaves. The northern Methodist missionaries who taught at the school considered Wells-Barnett an exemplary student.

When Wells-Barnett was sixteen years old, her parents and youngest brother died in a yellow fever epidemic. Wells-Barnett insisted on raising her surviving siblings while teaching school in a rural district. By 1883, her brothers were old enough to begin work as carpenters, so Wells-Barnett and her sisters moved to Memphis, to live with an aunt. Wells-Barnett attended classes at Fisk University and taught school in Memphis until 1891, when she was fired from her job for criticizing the segregationist policies of the Memphis School Board. Angry articles by Wells-Barnett in the small newspaper *Free Speech and Headlight* denounced the limited educational opportunities for African Americans in "SEPARATE-BUT-EQUAL" Memphis schools. Writing under the pen name Iola, Wells-Barnett discovered her talent for journalism and her calling as a social activist.

Wells-Barnett became co-owner and editor of *Free Speech* and a vocal opponent of JIM CROW LAWS in the South. In one *Free Speech* article, she described her own frustrating 1884 lawsuit against the Chesapeake, Ohio, & Southwestern Railroad. The dispute began when Wells-Barnett boarded a train in Memphis en route to Woodstock, Tennessee. After taking her usual seat in the "ladies car," which was a first-class coach, she and the other African American women in that car were told by the conductor to move to the smoking car, which was not first-class. By Tennessee law, African Americans were to be assigned separate and equal accommodations on public transportation.

When Wells-Barnett refused to sit in the smoking car, she was forced off the train. Later, she sued the railroad and won $500 in damages from a lower state court. Her triumph was short-lived, however, because the award was overturned in 1887 by the Supreme Court of Tennessee, which determined that a smoking car could indeed serve as a first-class accommodation for African Americans (*Chesapeake, Ohio,*

"ETERNAL VIGILANCE IS THE PRICE OF LIBERTY, AND IT DOES SEEM THAT NOTWITHSTANDING ALL THOSE SOCIAL AGENCIES AND ACTIVITIES THERE IS NOT VIGILANCE, WHICH SHOULD BE EXERCISED IN THE PRESERVATION OF OUR RIGHTS."

& Southwestern Railroad Co. v. Wells, 85 Tenn. (1 Pickle) 613, 4 S.W. 5 [1887]). The Tennessee high court suggested that Wells-Barnett's real motive in refusing to sit in the smoking car was to harass the railroad and to lay the groundwork for a profitable lawsuit. The court chastised Wells-Barnett for failing to try in GOOD FAITH to secure a comfortable seat. The stark injustice of the court's reversal fueled Wells-Barnett's determination to speak out against the mistreatment of African Americans.

For Wells-Barnett, the pivotal event in her activist career was the lynching in 1892 of her friends Calvin McDowell, Thomas Moss, and Henry Stewart, three African American merchants from Memphis. The men owned the People's Grocery, a thriving operation that had cut into the profits of its white competitors. When a mob of white men was deputized to arrest the three merchants on trumped-up criminal charges, violence erupted, and the innocent African Americans were hanged.

Wells-Barnett was outraged. She wrote a scathing editorial in *Free Speech*, denouncing not only the murder of her friends but also the offensive, widely accepted rationale for most lynchings. Wells-Barnett observed that contrary to southern myth, lynchings were rarely if ever spontaneous group acts in retaliation for sexual misconduct by African American men. A lynch mob was actually a barbaric mechanism for maintaining power among whites and for denying African Americans their civil rights. Protecting the reputation of southern white women was a smoke screen. Wells-Barnett also asserted that any sexual liaisons between African American men and white women were consensual, an observation that enraged much of the conservative white population.

After the editorial was published, an angry throng of white men stormed the *Free Speech* office and destroyed Wells-Barnett's printing press. Wells-Barnett was in Philadelphia at the time.

These episodes of mob rule, so contrary to the democratic ideal, led Wells-Barnett to launch an antilynching campaign. Wells-Barnett relied not only on righteous indignation but on shocking national statistics to make her case against lynching. In articles and speeches, she quoted a grim fact: in 1894, 132 legal executions were carried out in the United States, and 197 lynchings occurred. African Americans were receiving the death penalty from self-appointed white citizens without the benefit of criminal investigations, formal charges, legal representation, or trials. Wells-Barnett's findings were published in 1895 in a detailed book entitled *A Red Record: Tabulated*

Statistics and Alleged Causes of Lynchings in the United States, 1892–1893–1894.

In 1893, Wells-Barnett carried her anti-lynching campaign to Great Britain in the hope of exerting international pressure on U.S. legislators to enact antilynching laws. She was well received in Great Britain and spoke to large crowds. While in Europe, she was a guest at several women's civic clubs and was impressed with their worthwhile, community-minded activities. Wells-Barnett exported the idea to the United States, where African American women's clubs flourished.

In 1895, Wells-Barnett married Ferdinand L. Barnett, the first African American state's attorney in Illinois. After the marriage, Wells-Barnett curtailed her international speaking but continued to write in national publications. The couple lived in Chicago and had four children. Wells-Barnett worked hard to improve conditions for African Americans in Chicago by serving as a social worker and community organizer.

Wells-Barnett was well-known throughout the United States, yet the political power she craved eluded her. Although she was involved in the formation of the NATIONAL ASSOCIATION FOR THE ADVANCEMENT OF COLORED PEOPLE, she alienated many of her African American colleagues with her sharp tongue and unbending manner. Also, she was an unreserved critic of the accommodationist position favored by Booker T. Washington, the founder of Tuskegee Institute and the most influential African American leader at the time. Wells-Barnett favored a militant approach to achieving racial equality and was not welcome in the Washington camp. Other women such as Mary McLeod Bethune eventually eclipsed Wells-Barnett in influence. A combination of politics and personal animosity prevented Wells-Barnett from achieving the level of African American leadership she sought.

Although Wells-Barnett felt stymied near the end of her career, she earned an honored and lasting place in history as one of the first African American civil rights activists. Daughter Alfreda M. Barnett Duster wrote that Wells-Barnett "fought a lonely and almost single-handed fight, with the single-mindedness of a crusader, long before men or women of any race entered the arena" (Wells 1970, xxxii).

Wells-Barnett died in Chicago on March 25, 1931, at the age of sixty-eight. In 1950 the city of Chicago named her one of the twenty-five most outstanding women in its history.

WELSH v. UNITED STATES   A 1970 U.S. Supreme Court decision, *Welsh v. United States*, 398 U.S. 333, 90 S. Ct. 1792, 26 L. Ed. 2d 308, held that a person could be exempted from compulsory military service based solely on moral or ethical beliefs against war.

The VIETNAM WAR was an unpopular conflict that depended on the military draft to maintain adequate numbers of persons in the ARMED SERVICES. A man who was selected for compulsory military service could be excused if he signed a statement in the Selective Service form that provided: "I am, by reason of my religious training and belief, conscientiously opposed to participation in war of any form." In *Welsh*, the Supreme Court ruled that a person did not have to profess a religious belief to qualify for CONSCIENTIOUS OBJECTOR status. Under *Welsh*, a person's strongly held moral or ethical beliefs can provide an adequate basis for exemption from military service.

In 1966 Elliot A. Welsh II was convicted for refusing to submit to induction into the armed forces in violation of federal law, and was sentenced to imprisonment for three years. Welsh had signed the conscientious objection statement after crossing out "my religious training and." He believed that killing in war is unethical and immoral, and the sincerity of his beliefs was not questioned. However, his conscientious-objector claim was denied because it was not predicated upon a belief in a "Supreme Being," which was a statutory requirement for an exemption at that time.

Welsh appealed his conviction to the U.S. Supreme Court. The Court ruled that a draft registrant's conscientious objection to all war must be derived from his moral, ethical, or religious convictions about what is right and wrong and that it had to be maintained with the intensity of more conventional religious beliefs. If a draft registrant's beliefs represent an analogue to worship of God—if they serve as a religion in the person's life—then the draft registrant is entitled to a religious conscientious objector exemption, just as someone whose conscientious opposition to war stems from orthodox religious beliefs.

The government argued that Welsh's convictions were predominantly philosophical, sociological, or personal in nature and therefore were within the statutory exclusion for conscientious objector status. The Court rejected this argument, ruling that this provision should not be construed to exclude those who are opinionated about domestic and international affairs or those whose conscientious objection to participation in all wars is based upon PUBLIC POLICY considerations. It concluded that only those persons whose beliefs are not fervently held or whose objections to war are based on considerations of expediency or pragmatism could be excluded from conscientious objector status.

In this case, the Court held that Welsh's beliefs met its test and therefore he was entitled to conscientious objector status and a reversal of his conviction.

WESLEY, CARTER WALKER

BIOGRAPHY

Carter Walker Wesley was a prominent African American attorney and newspaper publisher who fought a long legal battle with the state of Texas and the Texas Democratic party to end the racially discriminatory WHITE PRIMARY. Wesley, a member of the NATIONAL ASSOCIATION FOR THE ADVANCEMENT OF COLORED PEOPLE (NAACP), also sought to unite African American newspaper owners through the National Negro Publishers Association.

Wesley was born in 1892 in Houston, Texas. He received a bachelor's degree from Fisk University in Nashville, Tennessee, in 1917 and a law degree from Northwestern University in 1922. He practiced law in Muskogee, Oklahoma, with John Atkins, but the pair moved to Houston in 1927 to engage in additional business opportunities, including a real estate firm, an insurance company, and a newspaper, the *Houston Informer*. James M. Nabrit, Jr., also a Northwestern Law School graduate, joined them to form the law firm of Nabrit, Atkins, and Wesley.

Wesley usually concentrated on his business ventures and let Nabrit handle most of the legal work. However, because Wesley was committed to ending racial discrimination, he personally handled important cases involving the CIVIL RIGHTS of African Americans. He and Nabrit took the case of Dr. A. L. Nixon of El Paso, Texas, who had been prevented from VOTING in the Democratic primary election because he was black. Nixon had earlier challenged a state law that permitted the Democratic party to exclude African Americans from the primary. In *Nixon v. Herndon*, 273 U.S. 536, 47 S. Ct. 446, 71 L. Ed. 759 (1927), the U.S. Supreme Court ruled that the state could not formally endorse the white primary.

Texas responded, however, by basing the white primary solely on a resolution adopted by the state Democratic party. Texas claimed that it had no role in the primary and therefore the FOURTEENTH AMENDMENT's Equal Protection Clause did not apply. Wesley and Nabrit challenged this theory, but in *Grovey v. Townsend*, 295 U.S. 45, 55 S. Ct. 622, 792 L. Ed. 1292 (1932), the Court upheld the Texas white primary. Undaunted, Wesley continued to press for an end to the white primary. Finally, in *Smith v. Allwright*, 321 U.S. 649, 64 S. Ct. 757, 88 L. Ed. 987 (1944), the Court overruled the *Grovey* decision and struck down the Texas white primary as a violation of the FIFTEENTH AMENDMENT's prohibition against voting discrimination based on race.

Wesley remained a staunch supporter of the NAACP and civil rights but shifted his emphasis to publishing. He formed the National Negro Publishers Association (now called the National Newspaper Publishers Association) in 1941, which became a means of communication for African American publishers throughout the United States. Wesley eventually became publisher and editor of a chain of affiliated newspapers in Texas, Louisiana, Alabama, and California.

Wesley died in Houston in 1969.

WEST COAST HOTEL CO. v. PARRISH

The Supreme Court's decision in *West Coast Hotel Co. v. Parrish*, 300 U.S. 379, 57 S. Ct. 578, 81 L. Ed. 703 (1937), marked the end of an era in U.S. constitutional jurisprudence. The Court in *Parrish* repudiated SUBSTANTIVE DUE PROCESS and the "freedom of contract" doctrine that prior courts had used to invalidate state laws that regulated business and labor. By reversing PRECEDENT, the Court sent a signal to Congress and state legislatures that it would exercise judicial restraint and not stand in the way of legislation that had a legitimate government purpose.

In the case the West Coast Hotel Company challenged the constitutionality of the state of Washington's MINIMUM WAGE law for women. Elsie Parrish, a hotel chambermaid, had filed a lawsuit seeking to recover the difference between the wages paid her and the minimum wage prescribed by law. The hotel company

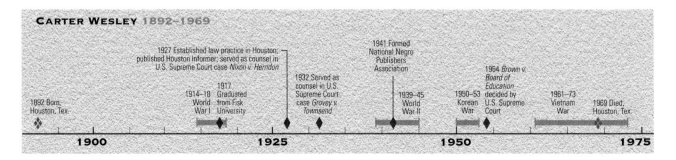

CARTER WESLEY 1892–1969

1892 Born, Houston, Tex.

1914–18 World War I

1917 Graduated from Fisk University

1927 Established law practice in Houston; published Houston Informer; served as counsel in U.S. Supreme Court case *Nixon v. Herndon*

1932 Served as counsel in U.S. Supreme Court case *Grovey v. Townsend*

1939–45 World War II

1941 Formed National Negro Publishers Association

1950–53 Korean War

1954 *Brown v. Board of Education* decided by U.S. Supreme Court

1961–73 Vietnam War

1969 Died, Houston, Tex.

1900   1925   1950   1975

argued that the wage law violated the Due Process Clause of the FOURTEENTH AMENDMENT. The Washington Supreme Court upheld the law, and the company appealed to the U.S. Supreme Court.

Many observers believed that the Court would strike down the law because of its decision in *Adkins v. Children's Hospital*, 261 U.S. 525, 43 S. Ct. 394, 67 L. Ed. 785 (1923), which invalidated a minimum wage law for women and children. The Court in *Adkins* had reiterated that the Due Process Clause of the Fourteenth Amendment barred states from interfering with the freedom of employees to negotiate the terms of their employment with their employers. This doctrine of substantive due process was used to limit the substance of government regulations and other activities that affected "life, liberty, and property." Substantive due process was the basis for the freedom of contract doctrine that the Court had used to strike down state laws that regulated hours and work conditions, as well as wages.

However, in *Parrish* the Court, on a 5–4 vote, rejected the freedom of contract doctrine. Chief Justice CHARLES EVANS HUGHES noted that the Constitution does not refer to freedom of contract. Rather, it proscribes deprivation of liberty without DUE PROCESS OF LAW. Hughes pointed out that freedom is not absolute. Moreover, "the liberty safeguarded is liberty in a social organization which requires the protection of law against the evils which menace the health, safety, morals, and welfare of the people." Thus, constitutional LIBERTY is "necessarily subject to restraints of due process" as long as government regulation is reasonable and furthers the interests of the community. He branded the *Adkins* decision as "a departure from the true application of the principles governing the regulation by the state of the relation of employer and employed."

The decision was made at the height of the Great Depression. Hughes took JUDICIAL NOTICE of "the unparalleled demands for relief" arising out of the economic hard times. He concluded that the state of Washington was free to correct the abusive practices of "unconscionable employers" who disregard the public interest.

Parrish marked the end of an era in U.S. constitutional law. Substantive due process as a limitation on government power in the field of economic regulation became a dead letter.

See also NEW DEAL.

WESTLAW WESTLAW® is an interactive COMPUTER-ASSISTED LEGAL RESEARCH service that is provided to subscribers by West Group, a subsidiary of Thomson Legal Publishing. WEST-LAW provides access to a vast amount of legal information at both the state and federal levels, including the full text of legislation, administrative materials, executive decrees, and judicial decisions, as well as summaries of jury VERDICTS and SETTLEMENTS. WESTLAW also offers access to an array of nonlegal materials, including daily newspapers from each of the fifty states, telephone and address directories, death records, credit bureau listings, secretary of state filings, STOCK prices, ANNUAL REPORTS of public companies, profit and loss statements of private companies, and personal asset holdings.

WESTLAW subscribers purchase a SOFT-WARE package that allows them to dial through their personal computers over a telephone line into a central mainframe located in Eagan, Minnesota. The mainframe stores information in more than 10,000 databases that can be searched individually or in combination. For example, a tax attorney may choose to limit a search to an individual database containing only federal judicial decisions, or he may choose to expand his search to a combination database that contains treasury regulations, revenue rulings, technical advice memorandum, and federal judicial decisions.

WESTLAW has more than forty specialized databases that group legal materials by area of practice, including international law, immigration, health and medicine, environmental law, securities, bankruptcy, banking, civil rights, insurance, energy, entertainment, labor, education, and intellectual property. Secondary legal materials, such as LAW REVIEWS, scholarly commentaries, and academic TREATISES, are also available on WESTLAW. All materials accessed on WESTLAW can be printed offline, downloaded to a floppy disc, or transmitted to a fax or electronic mail destination.

There are two principal methods of searching individual and combination databases, Natural Language and Terms and Connectors. Natural Language, known to WESTLAW subscribers as WIN® (Westlaw is Natural™), allows users to search WESTLAW with sentences written in plain English. Terms and Connectors, also known as Boolean logic, is a search method that permits users to specify which terms will appear in retrieved documents, and their proximity to each other. Suppose an attorney is asked to research whether her client committed the intentional tort of ASSAULT, even though there was no physical contact between the plaintiff and defendant. An effective Natural Language search might be as simple as the following: "Does the intentional tort of assault require physical contact between the plaintiff and defendant?" On the other hand, an effective Terms and Connectors search would require greater specificity such as the following: "intentional tort" /p physical /3 contact /s assault.

Words in quotation marks are treated as phrases in Terms and Connectors searching, and must appear in the retrieved documents exactly as they appear in quotation marks. Terms on each side of a /p must appear in the same paragraph; terms on each side of a /s must appear in the same sentence; and terms on each side of a numeric connector such as /3 must appear a designated number of terms apart. The sample Terms and Connectors search tells WESTLAW to retrieve documents in which the phrase "intentional tort" appears in the same paragraph as the term "physical," which itself must appear within three terms of "contact," which, in turn, must appear in the same sentence as "assault." The sample Natural Language search tells WESTLAW to perform a statistical analysis of the search terms for the purpose of retrieving documents in which the least common terms appear the greatest number of times.

Introduced in 1975, WESTLAW was designed to supplement traditional methods of manual legal research. In this regard, WESTLAW, along with its chief competitor, LEXIS-NEXIS, has made legal research easier, faster, more accurate, and more up-to-date. Although WESTLAW continues to add hundreds of new databases each year, traditional legal research has not been entirely replaced. Many legal materials remain accessible only at law libraries. Comprehensive coverage of other legal materials is not always provided online. For example, WESTLAW coverage of the *United States Code Annotated*® begins in 1989, though the print version of the U.S.C.A. was first published in 1927. WESTLAW subscription packages can also be expensive, and as a result, not all lawyers subscribe. Nonetheless, for those legal materials falling within the coverage of WESTLAW, this online service provides subscribers with one of the most efficient ways of accessing them.

See also LEGAL PUBLISHING; LEXIS.

WESTMINSTER, FIRST STATUTE OF 📖 A law enacted in 1275 to enforce some of the provisions of MAGNA CHARTA and to liberalize the law of England. 📖

The First Statute of Westminster was enacted by a parliament meeting at Westminster, England, during the reign of King Edward I. The statute was more like a code, containing fifty-one chapters that dealt with many facets of English civil and criminal law.

The statute was the first effort by Edward I

Edward I was king of England when parliament passed the First Statute of Westminster in 1275.

to consolidate and reform English law and procedure. Among its many provisions, the act extended protection of church property from acts of violence and spoliation by the king and nobility and provided for freedom of popular elections for the offices of SHERIFF, CORONER, and CONSERVATOR OF THE PEACE.

The statute also contained a declaration to enforce the enactment of Magna Charta, the charter granted by King John to the barons at Runnymede on June 15, 1215. Magna Charta regulated the administration of justice, defined the jurisdictions of church and state, limited taxation, and secured the personal liberty of the subjects and their rights of property. The statute prohibited excessive fines, which might operate as perpetual imprisonment. It also regulated the levying of tolls, which were imposed arbitrarily by the barons and by cities and boroughs, and restrained the powers of the officers of the king.

The statute amended the criminal law by making RAPE a serious crime, but not a capital one. The law also defined *peine forte et dure*, a "strong and hard punishment" that was inflicted upon those who were accused of a FELONY and stood silent, refusing to plead either guilty or not guilty. The statute permitted a person to be imprisoned and starved until submission. An individual who chose to stand mute under the threat of *peine forte et dure* often did so to ensure that his family would inherit his goods and estates. If he entered a plea and was later tried and convicted, his goods would pass to the crown.

The statute also introduced simpler and more expeditious procedures for civil and criminal matters.

WESTMINSTER, SECOND STATUTE OF

An English law enacted in 1285 that converted ESTATES in FEE SIMPLE conditional into estates in FEE ENTAIL and rendered them INALIENABLE, thereby strengthening the power of the nobility.

In 1285 King Edward I summoned the great lords and councillors of England to a parliament in Westminster to consider changes in how land could be conveyed. The result was the enactment of the Second Statute of Westminster, which is sometimes referred to as the Statute de Donis Conditionalibus (Latin for "concerning conditional gifts").

Under FEUDALISM in England, the crown and nobility controlled all of the land. The nobility sought to restrain the transfer of real PROPERTY and to ensure that property would stay within family lines.

The Second Statute of Westminster addressed this issue by changing property law. At COMMON LAW, an estate in fee simple conditional was a TITLE to land limited to some particular heirs, exclusive of others. Under fee simple conditional, relatives other than a person's children could inherit the person's estate. The statute changed this by converting such an estate into a fee entail, which restricted ownership of land to a particular family line. Thus, an estate in land descended to a person's children and through them to the person's grandchildren in a direct line. However, upon the death of the first owner of the estate who did not have living children, the land would revert to the original grantor's line, which meant that the land would revert to the local lord or to the crown.

See also FEE TAIL.

WESTMINSTER HALL

A building connected to the houses of Parliament in London, England, that formerly housed the superior courts.

Westminster Hall was the home of English superior courts until they were moved to the Strand in the early 1880s. Construction of the hall began in 1097; the hall is 240 feet long, 67½ feet wide, and 90 feet high. In addition to holding regular court sessions, the hall was the focal point of medieval political life.

Many famous trials were held in the hall. Sir Thomas More (1478–1535), lord CHANCELLOR for Henry VIII (1491–1547), was sentenced to death for refusing to recognize royal supremacy over the church. Charles I (1600–49) was sentenced to death for treason, and Warren Hastings (1732–1818) was impeached for his handling of the East India Company.

Westminster Hall contained the KING'S BENCH, the Court of CHANCERY, and the Court of COMMON PLEAS. Until the eighteenth century, it had no partitions or screens to divide the courts from the open hall.

The hall was part of Westminster Palace, which, except for the hall and St. Stephen's Chapel, was destroyed by fire in 1834. The houses of Parliament were constructed next to the hall between 1840 and 1860.

WEST SAXON LAGE

The laws of the West Saxons, who lived in the southern and western counties of England, from Kent to Devonshire, during the Anglo-Saxon period.

Before the Norman Conquest in 1066, the Anglo-Saxon rulers of England employed a set of laws to govern their kingdom. The collection of laws, called the West Saxon lage, helped support the structure of early English society.

Ine, the Anglo-Saxon king of the West Saxons, or Wessex, ruled from 688 to 726. He was a powerful ruler and the first West Saxon king to issue a code of laws. Alfred the Great, king of Wessex from 871 to 899, promulgated a code of laws based on Ine's work as well as the Book of Exodus and the codes of Aethelberht of Kent (560–616) and Offa of Mercia (757–96). Ine's code, which concerned itself with judicial procedures and the listing of punishments to be inflicted for various offenses, was preserved by Alfred as an appendix to his code. Though Alfred's laws avoided unnecessary changes in custom, his code limited the practice of the BLOOD FEUD and imposed heavy penalties for breach of oath or pledge.

The West Saxon lage is believed to have evolved from Ine's and Alfred's codes. The legal scholar SIR WILLIAM BLACKSTONE (1723–80) concluded that the lage was the municipal law for much of England before the Norman Conquest.

WEST'S LEGAL DIRECTORY

West's Legal Directory™ (WLD) is a searchable online directory of law firms, judges, and attorneys in the United States, Puerto Rico, the Virgin Islands, Canada and Europe. WLD is available on WESTLAW®, West CD-ROM Libraries™, the INTERNET (www.wld.com), and a host of other electronic media outlets, such as CompuServe, Prodigy, and America Online. However, WLD is not available in print. WLD contains information regarding private, government, and corporate offices and attorneys, as well as profiles of courts, judges, and law school professors. Law student resumés are accessible to potential employers, but not to other law students or professors.

First introduced in 1989, WLD provides access to a vast amount of information. More than 1 million profiles are contained in WLD, including profiles of hundreds of thousands of attorneys. Every attorney is offered a free basic listing that includes attorney name, firm name and address, telephone and fax numbers, areas of practice, bar admissions, and law school. For a monthly fee, attorneys can obtain an expanded listing that includes career accomplishments, such as educational achievements, published works, and service awards. Law firm profiles include the information contained in a basic listing along with names of representative clients, business references and pro bono activities. Judicial profiles include educational background, past positions, memberships and affiliations, published works, classes taught, honors received, and significant cases decided.

WLD updates its profiles daily on WEST-LAW, monthly on the Internet, and quarterly on CD-ROM. WLD information may be searched in the WLD database, or in component databases. Component databases, such as WLD-MN, WLD-TAX, and WLD-JUDGE, allow users to narrow their search to legal directories designed for particular geographic locations, practice areas, or professional titles. WLD may be searched using the Terms and Connectors search method or fill-in-the-blank templates.

See also COMPUTER-ASSISTED LEGAL RESEARCH; WESTLAW.

WEST VIRGINIA STATE BOARD OF EDUCATION v. BARNETTE

In *West Virginia State Board of Education v. Barnette*, 319 U.S. 624, 63 S. Ct. 1178, 87 L. Ed. 1628 (1943), the United States Supreme Court was asked to review the constitutionality of a West Virginia law compelling public school children to salute the American FLAG and recite the Pledge of Allegiance. In striking down the law as an unconstitutional deprivation of FREEDOM OF SPEECH and freedom of RELIGION, the Supreme Court overruled its earlier decision in *Minersville School District v. Gobitis*, 310 U.S. 586, 60 S. Ct. 1010, 84 L. Ed. 1375 (1940), which upheld the constitutionality of a similar Pennsylvania regulation despite FIRST AMENDMENT objections.

Barnette arose in 1942 when the West Virginia State Board of Education adopted a resolution requiring all public school children to salute the American flag and recite the Pledge of Allegiance as part of the official activities carried out by teachers of kindergarten through twelfth grade. Students who failed to salute the flag or recite the Pledge of Allegiance at appropriate times were subject to discipline, including expulsion from school and detention at state institutions for juvenile delinquents. Parents were subject to prosecution for the noncon-

forming behavior of their children.

A lawsuit was filed on behalf of the Jehovah's Witnesses, a religious group whose members believe that it is blasphemous to worship, serve, or pledge allegiance to any secular image because such idolatry interferes with their undivided loyalty to God. Several children of this faith had been disciplined in West Virginia schools for refusing to salute the flag or recite the Pledge of Allegiance, and a number of parents had been prosecuted for allowing their children to engage in such unpatriotic demonstrations. Upon hearing the lawsuit, the United States District Court for the Southern District of West Virginia issued an INJUNCTION restraining the state from continuing to enforce the school board resolution. *Barnette v. West Virginia State Board of Education*, 47 F.Supp. 251 (1942). The school board then appealed the case directly to the United States Supreme Court.

In a 6-3 decision the Supreme Court struck down the resolution because it contravened the First Amendment to the United States Constitution. The Court said that the resolution violated the students' freedom of speech and freedom of religion. "The very purpose of a Bill of Rights," the Court explained, is "to withdraw certain subjects from the vicissitudes of political controversy, to place them beyond the reach of majorities. . . ." The Court emphasized that under the BILL OF RIGHTS neither freedom of speech nor freedom of worship may be curtailed by the popular vote of a legislative assembly, unless it is through the amendment process set forth in Article V of the federal Constitution, and then only with the approval of three-fourths of the states.

The Court observed that the Founding Fathers "set up government by consent of the governed, and the Bill of Rights denies those in power any legal opportunity to coerce that consent." Saluting the American flag and reciting the Pledge of Allegiance are forms of symbolic expression, the Court ruled. Refusing to salute the flag or recite the Pledge of Allegiance may be a form of political protest, the Court pointed out, or it may reflect a conscientious decision made by a person of devout religious belief. In either case, the Court concluded, such symbolic expression is protected by the First Amendment. "If there is any fixed star in our constitutional constellation," the Court wrote, "it is that no official, high or petty, can prescribe what shall be orthodox in politics, nationalism, religion, or other matters of opinion or force citizens to confess by word or act their faith therein."

In overruling *Gobitis*, the Supreme Court questioned the premise upon which that case rested. In *Gobitis* the Court said that national security is contingent upon national unity, and that government may choose any reasonably necessary means to foster cohesion among its citizens, including compulsory flag salute regulations. After *Gobitis*, the Court took heed of the dissension caused by its decision. Citing a number of civic organizations who compared the mandatory flag salute regulations in the United States to similar laws that had been promulgated in Nazi Germany, the Court in *Barnette* stated that national security is hardly vindicated by permitting the government to expel a handful of children from school.

The government may instruct children on the value of patriotism, and it may acquaint students with the historical importance of the American flag, but the Court cautioned that government must not become a partisan of any religion, class, or faction in doing so. When states are fulfilling their crucial mission of educating impressionable children, the Court stressed, public schools must not "strangle the free mind at its source, and teach youth to discount important principles of government as mere platitudes."

See also SYMBOLIC SPEECH.

WHALING 📖 The hunting of whales for food, oil, or both. 📖

The hunting of whales by Eskimos and Native Americans began around 100 A.D. in North America. In Europe the systematic hunting of whales began during the Middle Ages and greatly expanded in the seventeenth century. Whaling was driven by the desire to procure whale oil and sperm oil. Whale oil comes from baleen whales and is an edible product that was used in the making of margarine and cooking oil. Sperm oil, which comes from sperm whales, was used for illuminating lamps, as an industrial lubricant, and as a component of soaps, cosmetics, and perfumes.

During the nineteenth century, the U.S. whaling fleet dominated the world industry. Most of the seven hundred U.S. ships sailed out of New Bedford and Nantucket, Massachusetts. However, the industry went into a steep decline with the discovery and exploitation of petroleum during the late nineteenth century. Though new uses for sperm oil were developed, the U.S. fleet gradually disappeared.

In the early twentieth century, concerns were raised about the dwindling whale population. An international movement to regulate the hunting of whales met resistance from Scandinavian countries and Japan, but in 1931 the League of Nations Convention for the Regulation of Whaling was convened. The convention proved unsuccessful because several important whaling states refused to participate.

Annual international whaling conferences led to the International Convention for the Regulation of Whaling in 1946, which established the International Whaling Commission (IWC). The IWC was charged with the conservation of whale stocks. It limited the annual Antarctic kill and created closed areas and hunting seasons throughout the world. Despite these initiatives and others over the years, the whale population edged closer to extinction, and the IWC agreed in 1982 to prohibit commercial whaling beginning in 1986. Commercial whaling has continued, however, often under the fiction of capturing specimens for scientific research.

In 1990 a scientific study was begun to determine if the whaling moratorium should be lifted. Though the study indicated that whale populations were growing, in 1993 the United States refused to agree to a resumption of commercial whaling, and the IWC agreed. The United States warned that if a country (primarily Japan, Norway, or Iceland) ignored the IWC conservation program and resumed commercial whaling without IWC approval, that country's actions would be reviewed, and sanctions would be considered where appropriate.

See also ENVIRONMENTAL LAW; FISH AND FISHING.

WHARVES 📖 Structures erected on the margin of NAVIGABLE WATERS where vessels can stop to load and unload cargo. 📖

Cities located on lakes, rivers, and oceans usually have at least one wharf, where ships can deliver and pick up passengers and load and unload various types of goods. The law regarding wharves deals with access to wharves, rates that may be charged, and LIABILITY issues surrounding the use of these facilities.

There are public and private wharves. Public wharves, which can be used with or without paying a fee, ordinarily belong to a government organization, such as a city or town. Private wharves are owned or leased by individuals for their own private use. Such a wharf may be opened to the public in exchange for a one-time payment or a rental fee. If the public is allowed to use the private wharf, it becomes a quasi-public facility that is open to all who are able to pay the charges. Whether a particular wharf is public or private depends mainly on its use, rather than on its ownership.

There are several terms peculiar to wharves. *Wharfage* in its most general sense refers to the use of a wharf in the usual course of navigation for such practices as loading and unloading goods and passengers. In a more restricted sense, the term *wharfage* refers to a charge or rent for the use of the wharf. A *wharfinger* is an individual who maintains a wharf for the purposes of receiving goods for hire. The term *dock* refers to an enclosure for the reception of vessels as well as a place where ships are built and repaired. It can include bulkheads, piers, slips, a waterway, wharves, and the space between wharves.

Government Regulation Though the federal government has reserved the right to control and regulate the use of wharves, the JURISDICTION and control of these facilities is generally in the hands of the states where the wharves are located. Government supervision is ordinarily exercised through statutes that give stipulated powers to local boards and commissions. Such powers include the power to supervise and regulate wharf construction, use, and maintenance, the depth of waters surrounding wharves, and their lighting and policing.

Wharfage Rates Local laws may govern wharfage rates for the use of public wharves. The rates may be fixed to benefit and increase commerce in the port, but the rates must be reasonable.

A user will be subject to a charge, even for limited periods of time. Such charges may be graduated on the basis of the gross tonnage of the vessel using the wharf. When the costs for the use of private wharves are not regulated, the parties may freely bargain for compensation, and there is no requirement of reasonableness.

Liability The proprietors of wharves have the legal obligation to provide a safe berth and must use reasonable care to keep the dock in a reasonably safe condition for use by vessels invited to enter it. The owner of the dock must exercise reasonable diligence to discover the existence of defects, obstructions, and other hazards that would make the wharf unsafe to vessels. The owner is liable for harm incurred by a vessel that results from the owner's failure to meet this duty. Wharf proprietors have been found liable for injuries to vessels resulting from an uneven ocean bottom or from submerged obstructions, such as rock, cinders, or a sunken ship.

A vessel must be furnished with ordinary mooring devices. The wharf owner owes a duty of reasonable care in maintaining the fastenings for a vessel, including the duty of inspecting the line securing the vessel. NEGLIGENCE by the wharf owner in failing to properly moor the vessel will result in liability for injuries to the vessel and its crew. However, if an employee of the ship supervises the mooring, the responsibility shifts to the owners of the ship.

Injuries to Wharves The proprietor of a wharf has a right to use and enjoy the property undisturbed by the negligent conduct of others. A wharf proprietor can recover DAMAGES for injury to the wharf that results from the negligent operation of a vessel.

See also SHIPPING LAW.

BIOGRAPHY

Henry Wheaton

HARVARD LAW ART COLLECTION

WHEATON, HENRY Henry Wheaton served as the REPORTER of decisions for the U.S. Supreme Court and later became a diplomat and a scholar of INTERNATIONAL LAW. Wheaton is recognized for establishing a high level of accuracy, timeliness, and scholarship for Supreme Court reporters. A dispute with his successor, however, lead to a landmark case that had a profound effect on U.S. COPYRIGHT law and public information.

Wheaton was born on November 27, 1785, in Providence, Rhode Island. He graduated from Rhode Island College (today known as Brown University) and then studied law in France in 1802. Upon his return that year he established a law practice in Providence.

Wheaton became a friend and colleague of U.S. Supreme Court Justice JOSEPH STORY, who shared Wheaton's passion for legal scholarship. In 1816 Story persuaded Wheaton to move to Washington, D.C., and take the position of reporter of decisions for the Court. Wheaton agreed, becoming the first paid reporter recognized by law.

Wheaton attended court sessions, accurately reported oral arguments and the written deci-

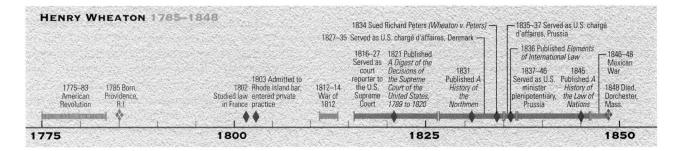

HENRY WHEATON 1785–1848

1834 Sued Richard Peters *(Wheaton v. Peters)*
1827–35 Served as U.S. chargé d'affaires, Denmark
1835–37 Served as U.S. chargé d'affaires, Prussia

1816–27 Served as court reporter to the U.S. Supreme Court
1821 Published *A Digest of the Decisions of the Supreme Court of the United States, 1789 to 1820*
1831 Published *A History of the Northmen*
1836 Published *Elements of International Law*
1837–46 Served as U.S. minister plenipotentiary, Prussia
1845 Published *A History of the Law of Nations*
1846–48 Mexican War

1775–83 American Revolution
1785 Born, Providence, R.I.
1802 Studied law in France
1803 Admitted to Rhode Island bar; entered private practice
1812–14 War of 1812
1848 Died, Dorchester, Mass.

1775   1800   1825   1850

sions of the Court, collected the decisions, and then published them within one year. Wheaton became the first reporter to supply ANNOTATIONS with the Court's decisions, sometimes anonymously assisted by Story. In 1820 Wheaton consolidated prior Court decisions into *A Digest of the Decisions of the Supreme Court of the United States, 1789 to 1820.*

In 1827 Wheaton left the reporter position and entered the U.S. foreign service. He served as chargé d'affaires (a diplomatic representative below ambassador) in Denmark from 1827 to 1835. He became adept at treaty negotiations and was made chargé d'affaires to the Prussian court in 1835. In 1837 he was appointed minister plenipotentiary and served in that position until 1846.

Wheaton was a noted writer and legal scholar. He published *A History of the Northmen* in 1831, in which he argued that Scandinavian explorers had landed on the North American continent several centuries before the expedition of Christopher Columbus. Wheaton also published *Elements of International Law* (1836) and *A History of the Law of Nations* (1845).

Wheaton became embroiled in a legal dispute with Richard Peters, Jr., his successor as Supreme Court reporter, over Peters's use of Wheaton's published case decisions. Wheaton lost the right to control the copyright of decisions that he had reported, in the process giving the Supreme Court the opportunity to clarify the boundaries between COMMON LAW and statutory copyright.

Wheaton died on March 11, 1848, in Dorchester, Massachusetts.

WHEATON v. PETERS The 1834 decision by the U.S. Supreme Court, *Wheaton v. Peters*, 33 U.S. (8 Pet.) 591, 8 L. Ed. 1055, delineated the differences between rights in a COPYRIGHT at COMMON LAW and in federal statutory law.

Wheaton v. Peters was the first significant copyright decision by the Supreme Court. A copyright grants the creator of an artistic or creative work a limited MONOPOLY in its use, based on the PUBLIC POLICY that such a monopoly encourages creativity and invention. In *Wheaton*, the Court established the basic foundation of U.S. copyright law, holding that the statutory requirements for securing a copyright must be strictly followed and that copyright exists primarily for the benefit of society and not the creator.

The case centered on whether Supreme Court decisions, which were public documents, could be copyrighted. HENRY WHEATON, the official REPORTER of decisions for the Court between 1816 and 1827, sued Richard Peters, Jr.,

his successor, for violating the copyright Wheaton obtained for his twelve volumes of Supreme Court decisions, entitled *Wheaton's Reports*. Peters had published and sold a book called *Condensed Reports of Cases in the Supreme Court of the United States*, which contained every Court decision from its inception to 1827, when *Peters's Report* began publication. Wheaton charged that the *Condensed Reports* contained all the reports of cases in the first volume of *Wheaton's Reports* without any significant abbreviation or alteration and that the publication and sale of this work infringed on his copyright. Wheaton sought an INJUNCTION to stop the sale of the work.

Peters denied that the publication infringed any copyright Wheaton claimed to possess. In addition, Peters asserted that Wheaton did not have a valid copyright because he failed to satisfy all the federal statutory requirements that were essential for the creation of copyright. The trial court agreed with Peters and dismissed the lawsuit. Wheaton then appealed to the Supreme Court.

The Court affirmed the lower court decision and made three rulings that defined copyright law in the United States. First, the Court rejected Wheaton's contention that he possessed a perpetual copyright in his *Reports* under the common law of Pennsylvania. Though Wheaton may have complied with Pennsylvania procedures on securing a copyright, the Court held that the common law of Pennsylvania did not address the issue of copyrights and therefore the state could not grant any protection to LITERARY PROPERTY.

The Court also rejected Wheaton's argument that he had complied with the applicable provisions of the federal copyright law and therefore was entitled to copyright protection. The 1802 copyright law required a series of steps to secure a copyright: a book was to be deposited with the clerk of the appropriate district court, the record made by the clerk was to be inserted in the first or second page, public NOTICE was to be given in the newspapers, and within six months after publication a copy of the book was to be deposited in the Department of State.

During the trial, there was uncertainty about whether Wheaton gave public notice and deposited the book in the Department of State. Wheaton asserted that he had completed the first two acts, which were sufficient to perfect his copyright. The Supreme Court, however, disagreed. It stated that the significance and wisdom of a law is a matter for the legislature, and not the Court, to determine. Therefore, all four steps were required to perfect TITLE.

Finally, the Court held that no reporter could have any copyright in the written opinions issued by the Court and that the Court could not grant such a right to any reporter. This holding was essential to the free flow of public information, for if Wheaton could control through copyright the distribution of court decisions, then other private actors could copyright and publish other public information, such as congressional debates or statutes, and restrict its dissemination.

WHEREAS 📖 On the contrary, although, when in fact. An introductory statement of a formal document. 📖

The term *whereas* is used two ways in the law. It is derived from Middle English and can mean "on the contrary," as in the sentence, The orange juice can label said "fresh squeezed," whereas the contents were made from orange juice concentrate.

In the law the term *whereas* also is used as the introductory word to a recital in a formal document. A recital contains words of introduction to a CONTRACT, STATUTE, PROCLAMATION, or other writing. In a contract a whereas clause is an introductory statement that means "considering that" or "that being the case." The clause explains the reasons for the execution of the contract and, in some cases, describes its purpose. The whereas clause may properly be used in interpreting the contract. However, it is not an essential component for its operative provisions.

Court orders typically use whereas clauses before the clause or clauses containing the directions of the court. For example, a court might declare that "whereas the plaintiff made a motion to compel the production of certain documents, and whereas the court has held a hearing on the motion and is fully advised on the matter, now therefore it is hereby ordered that the motion to compel the production of the documents requested is hereby denied."

When *whereas* is placed at the beginning of a legislative BILL, it means "because" and is followed by an explanation for the enactment of the legislation.

Finally, *whereas* is often used in official proclamations to project the solemnity of the occasion.

The term has been criticized as an overused legal formalism that clutters contracts and other legal documents. Legal formalism means the special usages of the language of law, many of which are archaic and which are flourishes of a style long dead.

WHEREBY 📖 By or through which; by the help of which; in accordance with which. 📖

For example, in the PROMISSORY NOTE clause "whereby he promised and agreed for value received to pay," the term *whereby* is equivalent to the phrase *and by it.*

WHEREFORE 📖 For which reason. 📖

The term *wherefore* is frequently used in an AVERMENT (a positive statement of fact set out in the PLEADINGS that must be filed with a court by the parties to a legal action)—for example, "wherefore the defendant says that such contract was and is void."

WHISKEY REBELLION In 1794 thousands of farmers in western Pennsylvania took up arms in opposition to the enforcement of a federal law calling for the imposition of an excise tax on distilled spirits. Known as the "Whiskey Rebellion," this INSURRECTION represented the largest organized resistance against federal authority between the American Revolution and the Civil War. A number of the whiskey rebels were prosecuted for TREASON in what were the first such legal proceedings in the United States.

Congress established the excise tax in 1791 to help reduce the $54 million national debt. The tax was loathed across the country. For a small group of farmers west of the Allegheny Mountains, the federal excise tax was singularly detestable. Bartering was the chief means of exchange in this frontier economy, and distilled spirits were the most commonly traded commodity. Cash was a disfavored currency in western Pennsylvania during the late eighteenth century, but whiskey, especially Monongahela Rye, was as valuable as gold. Whiskey was considered an all-purpose liquor, with locals using it for cooking and medicine, and drinking it at social occasions, among other uses.

By modern standards the excise tax of 1791 does not seem oppressive. Distillers were taxed based on the size of their stills. Stills with the capacity to annually produce at least 400 gallons of whiskey were taxed between 7 and 18 cents a gallon, depending on the proof of the liquor. Distillers who made stronger whiskey paid a higher tax. Smaller stills were taxed at a rate of 10 cents for every month a still was in operation, or 7 cents for every gallon produced, whichever was lower. Based on these rates, the average distiller was required to pay only a few dollars in liquor tax each year. But even an annual tax of $5 would have consumed a large percentage of the disposable income earned by farmers in the barter-based economy of western Pennsylvania.

The rebellion began in Pittsburgh during October of 1791 when a group of disguised farmers snatched a federal tax collector from his

A government inspector was tarred and feathered during the Whiskey Rebellion in western Pennsylvania in 1794. The rebels believed that by the Revolutionary War, along with independence from Great Britain, they had won the right to be free from all government taxation.

bed, and marched him five miles to a blacksmith shop where they stripped him of his clothes, and burned him with a poker. Over the next three years dozens of tax collectors were beaten, shot at, tarred and feathered, and otherwise terrorized, intimidated, and humiliated. The home and plantation of John Neville, the chief tax collector for southwestern Pennsylvania, were burned to the ground.

By 1794 the excise tax lay largely uncollected in western Pennsylvania. The national debt was rising, and respect for federal authority was waning. Rebel forces had swelled to 5,000. In October President GEORGE WASHINGTON dispatched 15,000 troops to quell the resistance. Led by ALEXANDER HAMILTON, Washington's secretary of state, the federal troops met little opposition. Within a month, most of the rebels had dispersed, disavowed their cause, or left the state. Keeping a few soldiers in western Pennsylvania to maintain order, the federal army departed for Philadelphia, having arrested more than 150 people suspected of criminal activity.

In May of 1795 the Circuit Court for the Federal District of Pennsylvania indicted thirty-five defendants for an assortment of crimes associated with the Whiskey Rebellion. One of the defendants died before trial began, one defendant was released because of mistaken identity, and nine others were charged with minor federal offenses. Twenty-four rebels were charged with serious federal offenses, including high treason. Two men, John Mitchell and Philip Vigol, were found guilty of treason, and sentenced to hang. Seventeen defendants were convicted of lesser crimes, and sentenced to prison terms of various lengths. Upon learning that none of the convicted rebels were principally responsible for instigating the armed resistance, Washington pardoned each of them.

By extinguishing the Whiskey Rebellion, the U.S. government withstood a formidable chal-

lenge to its sovereignty. Preceded by SHAYS'S REBELLION in 1786, and followed by FRIES'S REBELLION in 1799, the Whiskey Rebellion is distinguished by its size. While all three rebellions were motivated by their opposition to burdensome taxes, neither Daniel Shays nor John Fries ever gathered more than a few hundred supporters at any one time. On at least one occasion, as many as 15,000 men and women marched on Pittsburgh in armed opposition to the federal excise tax on whiskey.

The Whiskey Rebellion also occupies a distinguished place in American jurisprudence. Serving as the backdrop to the first treason trials in the United States, the Whiskey Rebellion helped delineate the parameters of this constitutional crime. Article III, Section 3 of the U.S. Constitution defines treason as "levying War" against the United States. During the trials of the two men convicted of treason, Circuit Court Judge WILLIAM PATERSON instructed the jury that "levying war" includes armed opposition to the enforcement of a federal law. This interpretation of the Treason Clause was later applied during the trial of John Fries, and remains valid today.

WHISTLEBLOWING ◖ The disclosure by a person, usually an employee, in a government agency or private enterprise; to the public or to those in authority, of mismanagement, corruption, illegality, or some other wrongdoing. ◖

Since the 1960s, the public value of *whistleblowing* has been increasingly recognized. Federal and state statutes and regulations have been enacted to protect *whistleblowers* from various forms of retaliation. Even without a statute, numerous decisions encourage and protect whistleblowing on grounds of PUBLIC POLICY. In addition, the federal False Claims Act (31 U.S.C.A. § 3729) will reward a whistleblower who brings a lawsuit against a company that makes a false CLAIM or commits FRAUD against the government.

APWIDE WORLD PHOTOS

IRS agent Jennifer Long blew the whistle on the agency after IRS inspectors harassed her during a grievance she had with a supervisor.

Persons who act as whistleblowers are often the subject of retaliation by their employers. Typically the employer will discharge the whistleblower, who is often an at-will employee. An at-will employee is a person without a specific term of employment. The employee may quit at any time and the employer has the right to fire the employee without having to cite a reason. However, courts and legislatures have created exceptions for whistleblowers who are at-will employees.

Whistleblowing statutes protect from discharge or discrimination an employee who has initiated an investigation of an employer's activities or who has otherwise cooperated with a regulatory agency in carrying out an inquiry or the enforcement of regulations. Federal whistleblower legislation includes a statute protecting all government employees. 5 U.S.C.A. §§ 2302(b)(8), 2302(b)(9). In the federal CIVIL SERVICE, the government is prohibited from taking, failing to take, or threatening to take any personnel action against an employee because the employee disclosed information that she reasonably believed showed a violation of law, gross mismanagement, gross waste of funds, abuse of authority, or a substantial and specific danger to public safety or health. In order to prevail on a claim, a federal employee must show that a protected disclosure was made, that the accused official knew of the disclosure, that retaliation resulted, and that there was a genu-

ine connection between the retaliation and the employee's action. If a federal statute does provide a remedy for retaliatory discharge, the discharged employee may not rely on a state's public policy exception to the employment-at-will doctrine.

Many states have enacted whistleblower statutes, but these statutes vary widely in coverage. Some statutes apply only to public employees, some apply to both public and private employees, and others apply to public employees and employees of public contractors.

Some statutes cover a broad array of circumstances, such as those that prohibit employers from dismissing workers in reprisal for disclosing information about, or seeking a remedy for, a violation of law, gross mismanagement, gross waste of funds, abuse of authority, or a specific danger to public safety and health. Other statutes are narrow in scope, such as one that limits the protection of public and private employees to retaliation for reporting possible violations of local, state, or federal environmental statutes. A whistleblower statute may limit protection to discussions of agency operations with members of the legislature or to disclosure of information to legislative committees or courts.

In whistleblower cases, states follow their general rules for determining whether a public policy CAUSE OF ACTION exists in favor of the employee. Therefore, in states in which WRONGFUL DISCHARGE actions must have a statutory basis, the case will be dismissed if the plaintiff was not exercising a statutory right or performing a statutory duty, or if the employer did not violate a statutorily enacted public policy. In many cases, the courts have refused to recognize a whistleblower's claim because no clearly mandated statutory policy has been identified. In a state that only recognizes a public policy cause of action if the employee is fired for refusing to violate public policy, that rule may preclude causes of action by whistleblowers.

Employees who blow the whistle on matters that affect only private interests will generally be unsuccessful in maintaining a cause of action for discharge in violation of public policy. As a general rule, employees claiming that they were discharged for disclosing internal corporate improprieties have been unsuccessful in establishing public policy exceptions to the at-will rule. Complaints about internal company policy also do not involve public policy supporting unjust dismissal suits.

Under the federal False Claims Act, any person with knowledge of false claims or fraud against the government may bring a lawsuit in his own name and in the name of the United States. As long as the information is not publicly disclosed and the government has not already sued the defendant for the fraud, the whistleblower, who is called a RELATOR in this action, may bring a False Claims Act case.

The relator files the case in FEDERAL COURT under SEAL (in secret), and gives a copy to the government. The government then has sixty days to review the case and decide whether it has merit. If the government decides to join the case, the case is unsealed, a copy is served on the defendant, and the government and the relator work together in the case as co-plaintiffs. If the government declines to join the suit, the relator may proceed alone. In a successful False Claims Act case the relator will receive at least fifteen percent but not more than twenty-five percent of the proceeds of the action or settlement of the claim, depending upon the extent to which the person substantially contributed to the prosecution of the action.

See also EMPLOYMENT AT WILL; EMPLOYMENT LAW.

WHITE, BYRON RAYMOND As an associate justice, Byron Raymond White sat on the U.S. Supreme Court from 1962 to 1993. White had an eclectic career. He was a college and pro football star during the 1930s and 1940s and an assistant attorney general under ROBERT F. KENNEDY from 1960 until 1962, the year his friend President JOHN F. KENNEDY appointed him to the Supreme Court. As a justice, White charted a pragmatic and low-key course on the bench: he enunciated no single judicial philosophy, although judicial restraint sometimes appeared as a feature of his reasoning. For part of his career, he was seen as a moderate. Toward the end, however, he voted conservatively on social issues such as ABORTION, AFFIRMATIVE ACTION, and homosexual rights.

Born on June 8, 1917, in Fort Collins, Colorado, White was the son of working class parents. As a youth, he picked beets in the poor community, but he excelled in athletics and scholastics. He attended the University of Colorado on an academic scholarship and in 1937, became the premier running back in college football. So accomplished was "Whizzer"

PHOTOGRAPHER: JOSEPH H. BAILEY COLLECTION OF THE SUPREME COURT OF THE UNITED STATES.

Byron Raymond White

White on the gridiron that when he threatened not to play in the Cotton Bowl—because it would interfere with his studying—the state's governor intervened in order to convince him to play. He graduated in 1938 as class valedictorian.

White's journey to the bench was not direct. In 1939 he accepted a Rhodes Scholarship to study at Oxford University in England, where he became a lifelong friend of John F. Kennedy. He subsequently played in the National Football League and led the league in rushing while also studying law at Yale University, where he graduated with high honors in 1946. During World War II White joined the Navy and served in the Pacific. After the war, he clerked for Chief Justice FRED M. VINSON from 1946 to 1947. For the next thirteen years, White practiced law in Denver, Colorado. His organizational support for the presidential candidacy of John F. Kennedy led to his being appointed second in charge of the Justice Department in 1960. After two years of selecting judges and helping steer the department's support of the CIVIL RIGHTS MOVEMENT, White was nominated to the Supreme Court to fill the vacancy created by the resignation of Justice CHARLES WHITTAKER.

White's tenure on the Court was marked by judicial pragmatism and unpredictability. Defying expectations that he would be a centrist, White swayed between liberal and conservative positions. He consistently supported the constitutionality of CIVIL RIGHTS reforms during the mid-1960s in cases dealing with VOTING rights. Thirty years later, he continued to take a firm stance on the issue of SCHOOL DESEGREGATION: in 1992 he wrote the majority opinion in *U.S. v. Fordice*, 505 U.S. 717, 112 S. Ct. 2727, 120 L. Ed. 2d 575 (1992) which ordered Mississippi to take additional steps to desegregate its state colleges. White's tendency to vote conservatively also became apparent early in his tenure on the Court. In 1966 he dissented from the Court's decision in *Miranda v. Arizona*, 384 U.S. 436, 86 S. Ct. 1602, 16 L. Ed. 2d 694 (1966), which established the so-called Miranda Rule requiring police officers to read arrested persons their constitutional rights. Believing

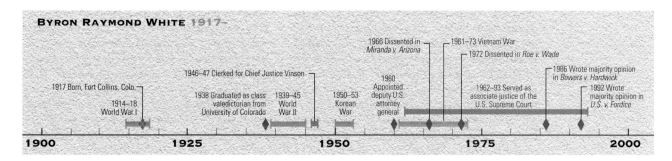

BYRON RAYMOND WHITE 1917–

1917 Born, Fort Collins, Colo.
1914–18 World War I
1938 Graduated as class valedictorian from University of Colorado
1946–47 Clerked for Chief Justice Vinson
1939–45 World War II
1950–53 Korean War
1960 Appointed deputy U.S. attorney general
1966 Dissented in *Miranda v. Arizona*
1961–73 Vietnam War
1962–93 Served as associate justice of the U.S. Supreme Court
1972 Dissented in *Roe v. Wade*
1986 Wrote majority opinion in *Bowers v. Hardwick*
1992 Wrote majority opinion in *U.S. v. Fordice*

1900   1925   1950   1975   2000

that it would only weaken the ability of the police to do their job, White called the decision "a deliberate calculus to prevent interrogations, to reduce the incidence of confessions and pleas of guilty and to increase the number of trials."

This conservatism was grounded in pragmatism. In 1972 White was one of two justices dissenting from the majority decision that established a woman's right to abortion (*Roe v. Wade*, 410 U.S. 113, 93 S. Ct. 705, 35 L. Ed. 2d 147 [1973]). His four-page dissent avoided the moral issues involved and attacked the majority's reading of the constitution: they had exceeded the Court's power. He could find no constitutional basis for "valu[ing] the convenience of the pregnant mother more than the continued existence and development of the life or potential life that she carries." Similarly, his 1986 majority opinion in *Bowers v. Hardwick*, 478 U.S. 186, 106 S. Ct. 2841, 92 L. Ed. 2d 140 (1986) dispassionately held that a Georgia statute criminalizing SODOMY—oral and anal sex— did not violate the constitutional rights of homosexuals. He simply found no "fundamental right to engage in homosexual sodomy" and refused to find a new right in the constitution's Due Process Clause—doing so, he wrote, would make the Court vulnerable to criticisms of judicial activism.

In the 1980s and 1990s White's liberal tendencies were all but exhausted. He frequently sided with the conservative voting bloc on the Court. In case after case, he joined the conservative majority in opposing abortion rights, curtailing affirmative action programs, restricting federal civil rights laws, and allowing the use of illegally-acquired police evidence in court. As was his wont, he uniquely refused to read his opinions from the bench and, instead, merely indicated whether the Court upheld or reversed the decisions of lower courts. He retired in 1993.

See also GAY AND LESBIAN RIGHTS.

WHITE, EDWARD DOUGLASS

In his three decades as a lawmaker and justice, Edward Douglass White left a powerful and sometimes controversial mark on American law. White's career spanned from the end of the nineteenth century to the early years of the twentieth. From 1891 to 1894, he served as a U.S. Senator from his home state of Louisiana, distinguishing himself by almost single-minded devotion to the state's farming interests. His appointment to the U.S. Supreme Court came in 1894, but White delayed joining the Court until finishing political battles in the Senate. In 1910 he became the first associate justice to be

"THE COURT IS MOST VULNERABLE AND COMES NEAREST TO ILLEGITIMACY WHEN IT DEALS WITH JUDGE-MADE CONSTITUTIONAL LAW HAVING LITTLE OR NO COGNIZABLE ROOTS IN THE LANGUAGE OR DESIGN OF THE CONSTITUTION."

BIOGRAPHY

Edward Douglass White

made chief justice, a position he held until his death in 1921. White's legacy includes his contribution to antitrust jurisprudence, which long shaped how the Court viewed the area of law concerned with unfair business competition.

Born on November 3, 1845, in Lafourche Parish, Louisiana, White was the son of wealthy sugar farmers. Educated in Jesuit schools during his youth, he later attended Georgetown College. From 1861 to 1863 he fought in the Civil War on the side of the Confederacy and was captured and imprisoned by Union forces. Private legal study followed the war, and after being admitted to the Louisiana bar in 1868, he established a private practice.

The origin of White's political and judicial careers reflected the spoils systems of late nineteenth century politics. In the 1870s White served as a lieutenant to Louisiana Governor Francis T. Nicholls. Nicholls appointed him to the state supreme court in 1878, a post which lasted only until the governor's electoral defeat in 1880. But after the governor battled back into office in 1888, he appointed White to a newly vacant seat in the U.S. Senate. Serving in office from 1891 to 1894, Senator White understood how to serve the system that had created him: he used the position almost entirely to advance the interests of his state's sugar growers.

In 1894 President GROVER CLEVELAND nominated White to the U.S. Supreme Court. For several weeks White, who still had the state's sugar interests on his mind, could not be persuaded to leave the Senate. He remained there to ensure passage of the Wilson-Gorman Tariff Act, a protectionist bill that served the interests of domestic sugar producers. A year later, White eagerly voted to uphold his favorite provisions of the Wilson-Gorman Tariff Act, but a majority of justices struck down those provisions in *Pollock v. Farmer's Loan and Trust Co.*, 157 U.S. 429, 15 S. Ct. 673, 39 L. Ed. 759 (1895).

White's major contribution came in the area of ANTITRUST law. In the late nineteenth century, the issue of regulating business competition was a paramount issue before lawmakers and the courts. Congress passed the SHERMAN ANTI-TRUST ACT in 1890 (15 U.S.C.A. § 1 et seq.) in order to combat the unfair constraint of trade that was rampant in the nation's biggest markets. Section 1 of the Sherman Act prohibits every contract, combination, or conspiracy to restrain trade. White found this provision contrary to his probusiness sentiments. He argued for reading the act objectively: constraints upon trade should be declared illegal only when they are unreasonable.

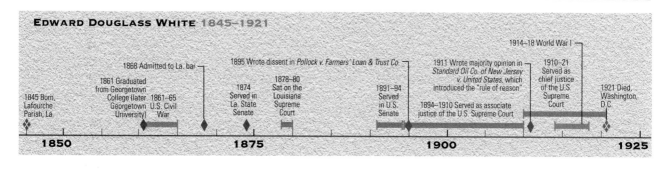

EDWARD DOUGLASS WHITE 1845–1921

1845 Born, Lafourche Parish, La.

1861 Graduated from Georgetown College (later Georgetown University)

1861–65 U.S. Civil War

1868 Admitted to La. bar

1874 Served in La. State Senate

1878–80 Sat on the Louisiana Supreme Court

1895 Wrote dissent in *Pollock v. Farmers' Loan & Trust Co.*

1891–94 Served in U.S. Senate

1894–1910 Served as associate justice of the U.S. Supreme Court

1911 Wrote majority opinion in *Standard Oil Co. of New Jersey v. United States*, which introduced the "rule of reason"

1910–21 Served as chief justice of the U.S. Supreme Court

1914–18 World War I

1921 Died, Washington, D.C.

1850 1875 1900 1925

In 1911, a year after his elevation to chief justice, White persuaded a majority of the Court to accept his view. It was contained in his most important opinion as a justice, *Standard Oil Co. of New Jersey v. United States*, 221 U.S. 1, 31 S. Ct. 502, 55 L. Ed. 619 (1911). This landmark decision affected the course of antitrust jurisprudence by introducing the so-called rule of reason. According to White, the Sherman Act only prohibits unreasonable RESTRAINTS OF TRADE that hurt the "public interest."

White's application of the rule of reason gave the Supreme Court more power to interpret the Sherman Act, and the approach dominated its decisions for the next two decades. Much like the earlier phases of his career, White's tenure as chief justice was marked by his changing constitutional views, and his strong belief in judicial power. He died on May 19, 1921 in Washington, D.C.

WHITEACRE 🕮 A fictitious designation used by legal writers to describe a parcel of land. 🕮

Whiteacre is frequently used with BLACK-ACRE, another fictitious designation, in order to distinguish one piece of land from another.

WHITEMAN, MARJORIE MILLACE Marjorie Millace Whiteman was a scholar and expert in INTERNATIONAL LAW who served in the U.S. State Department from 1929 to 1970. She participated in the drafting of the UNITED NATIONS Charter and the 1948 UNIVERSAL DECLARATION OF HUMAN RIGHTS, and as a scholar published a fifteen-volume *Digest of International Law* between 1963 and 1972.

Whiteman was born on November 30, 1898 in Liberty Center, Ohio. She graduated from

"THE ONLY PURPOSE WHICH AN ELABORATE DISSENT CAN ACCOMPLISH, IF ANY, IS TO WEAKEN THE EFFECT OF THE OPINION OF THE MAJORITY, AND THUS ENGENDER WANT OF CONFIDENCE IN THE CONCLUSIONS OF COURTS OF LAST RESORT."

BIOGRAPHY

Marjorie Millace Whiteman

Ohio Wesleyan University in 1920 and received LL.B. and J.S.D. degrees from Yale Law School in 1927 and 1928, respectively. At Yale, Whiteman studied with Edwin M. Borchard, a leading international law scholar. After law school, Whiteman served as a research associate with the Columbia University Research Commission on Latin America. She joined the State Department in 1929 as special assistant to the department's legal advisor Green H. Hackworth, a position she held until Hackworth's election to the INTERNATIONAL COURT OF JUSTICE in 1946.

In the State Department Whiteman became a specialist in international organizations. In 1945 she helped draft the United Nations Charter and the 1948 Universal Declaration of Human Rights. She served as legal counsel to ELEANOR ROOSEVELT when Roosevelt represented the United States on the United Nations Commission on Human Rights.

Whiteman had a strong interest in, and knowledge of, inter-American affairs. She played a major role in many Pan-American conferences and proposed the idea of consultation for the inter-American system. In 1948 she took part in the conference at Bogotá, Columbia which drafted the Charter of the Organization of American States.

When the State Department was reorganized in 1949, Whiteman was named the first assistant legal advisor for American republic affairs, which involved relationships with Central and South America. In 1965 Whiteman became the first counselor for international law in the Office of Legal Advisor (an office in the Department of State that advises the secretary

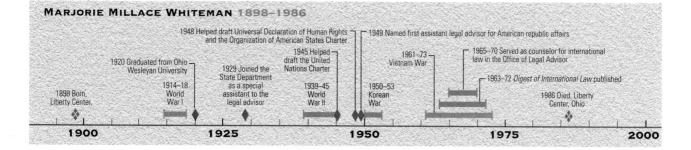

MARJORIE MILLACE WHITEMAN 1898–1986

1898 Born, Liberty Center,

1914–18 World War I

1920 Graduated from Ohio Wesleyan University

1929 Joined the State Department as a special assistant to the legal advisor

1939–45 World War II

1945 Helped draft the United Nations Charter

1948 Helped draft Universal Declaration of Human Rights and the Organization of American States Charter

1949 Named first assistant legal advisor for American republic affairs

1950–53 Korean War

1961–73 Vietnam War

1965–70 Served as counselor for international law in the Office of Legal Advisor

1963–72 *Digest of International Law* published

1986 Died, Liberty Center, Ohio

1900 1925 1950 1975 2000

of state on all matters of international law arising in the conduct of U.S. foreign relations), a position she held until her retirement in 1970.

Despite her activities in the State Department, Whiteman found time for scholarly work in international law. She was a major contributor to Hackworth's eight-volume *Digest of International Law* (1937–1943), and established herself as a world expert with the publication of her *Digest of International Law.*

Whiteman died on July 6, 1986, in Liberty Center, Ohio.

WHITE PRIMARY 📖 A legal device once employed by some Southern states to prevent African Americans from exercising their right to vote in a meaningful way. 📖

In the 1920s Southern states began using the *white primary* as a way of limiting the ability of African Americans to play a part in the political process. The white primary was an effective device because of the virtual one-party political system in the South that existed until the late 1960s. In all but a few areas nomination by the DEMOCRATIC PARTY was tantamount to election, with Republicans often not bothering to run in the general elections.

In order to keep African Americans out of the political process, the Democratic party in many states adopted a rule excluding them from party membership. The state legislatures worked in concert with the party, closing the primaries to everyone except party members. The Supreme Court had ruled in 1921, in *Newberry v. United States*, 256 U.S. 232, 41 S. Ct. 469, 65 L. Ed. 913, that political parties were private organizations and not part of the government election apparatus. Therefore, by means of the white primary device, African Americans were disenfranchised without official STATE ACTION that would have triggered JUDICIAL REVIEW under the FOURTEENTH AMENDMENT's Equal Protection Clause.

Beginning in the late 1920s the Supreme Court reviewed a series of cases involving the white primary. In *Nixon v. Herndon*, 273 U.S. 536, 47 S. Ct. 446, 71 L. Ed. 759 (1927), the Court ruled that the state could not formally endorse the white primary, but in *Grovey v. Townsend*, 295 U.S. 45, 55 S. Ct. 622, 79 L. Ed. 1292 (1935), it upheld a Texas white primary that was based solely on a resolution adopted by the state Democratic party.

In *United States v. Classic*, 313 U.S. 299, 61 S. Ct. 1031, 85 L. Ed. 1368 (1941), the Court ruled that the federal government could regulate party primaries to prevent voter FRAUD. In recognizing that primaries were part of a state's electoral scheme, it overruled the *Newberry* precedent and weakened the *Grovey v. Townsend*

holding. Finally, in *Smith v. Allwright*, 321 U.S. 649, 64 S. Ct. 757, 88 L. Ed. 987 (1944), the Court overruled the *Grovey* decision and struck down the white primary as a violation of the FIFTEENTH AMENDMENT's prohibition against voting discrimination based on race.

Following *Smith v. Allwright*, Texas Democrats established a private association from which African Americans were excluded. The members of the association held "preprimary" elections to select candidates for the Democratic primaries. The Supreme Court declared in *Terry v. Adams*, 345 U.S. 461, 73 S. Ct. 809, 97 L. Ed. 1152 (1953), that the preprimary device was unconstitutional, as it made the primary and general elections "perfunctory ratifiers" of the decisions made during the preprimary process.

CROSS-REFERENCES

Civil Rights; Civil Rights Movement; Elections; Voting.

WHITE SUPREMACY GROUPS 📖 Organizations that believe the Caucasian race is superior to all races and therefore seek to either separate the races in the United States or to remove all non-Caucasians from the nation. 📖

White supremacy is an umbrella label applied to the beliefs of a number of groups of activists in the United States. Although the beliefs of the various groups differ in some particulars, they share a desire to preserve what they call the "genetic purity" of the Caucasian race. Among the better known white supremacist organizations are the KU KLUX KLAN, the Aryan Nations and its offshoot the Order, the White Patriot Party, and the White American Resistance movement. These groups also are anti-Semitic, as they classify Jews as non-Caucasian. Some members of white supremacy groups have committed violent acts against nonwhites and those whites who are opposed to their beliefs.

The Ku Klux Klan has been the most enduring white supremacy group. It was established after the Civil War and became a white underground resistance group to Reconstruction in the South. Klan members used violence and intimidation against newly enfranchised African Americans as a way of restoring white supremacy in the states of the former confederacy. Dressed in white robes and sheets to disguise themselves, Klan members burned property, whipped, beat and sometimes killed African Americans and their white supporters in nighttime raids. These violent acts led Congress to pass the Force Act in 1870 and the KU KLUX KLAN ACT in 1871, measures that authorized the president to suspend the WRIT of HABEAS CORPUS, suppress disturbances by force, and impose heavy penalties upon terrorist organizations. By

the end of the 1870s, the Klan had virtually disappeared.

The Klan reemerged in 1915, adding new enemies to its list. The revitalized organization drew upon anti-immigrant, anti-Catholic, anti-Semitic, and anti-Communist prejudices, believing that the ethnic character of U.S. society was changing and that white Protestants were losing their dominant position. The reinvigorated Klan extended its reach outside the South and into the Midwest, drawing most of its members from small towns. By the late 1920s, Klan membership exceeded four million nationally. Klan members participated in marches, parades, and nighttime cross burnings. Klan membership dropped dramatically during the Great Depression of the 1930s and the national organization was virtually disbanded in 1944.

The CIVIL RIGHTS MOVEMENT of the 1960s reignited interest in the Klan in the South. Klan members terrorized civil rights workers, with many instances of bombings, beatings, and shootings. The Klan was ultimately unsuccessful in preventing the expansion of CIVIL RIGHTS for African Americans and membership declined again. However, there was a resurgence of Klan activity in the late 1970s and early 1980s, with most groups located in southern towns and cities. Since 1981, the Southern Poverty Law Center, located in Montgomery, Alabama, has monitored Klan activity through an effort called "Klanwatch." It issues a quarterly report that identifies Klan leaders, locations, and activities.

Neo-Nazi groups, which base their beliefs on ADOLF HITLER's Nazi ideology, have been active since the 1960s. The American Nazi Party conducted many demonstrations during the 1960s and 1970s. In the 1980s and 1990s other groups have arisen that espouse similar racist and anti-Semitic beliefs, most promi-

White supremacists use the freedom of speech to criticize nonwhites and Jews. This group is demonstrating in favor of white power and against Martin Luther King Day.

nently the group Aryan Nations, also known as the Church of Jesus Christ Christian. The "religion" of the Aryan Nations is the "Christian Kingdom Identity Movement," whose adherents believe that white Europeans are the chosen people of the Bible, that Jews are the offspring of Satan, and that all others are fit only for slavery.

The rise of VANDALISM and violent crimes by persons associated with white supremacy groups led states to enact "HATE CRIME" statutes. These laws provide additional penalties if a jury finds a defendant intentionally selected a victim based on race, religion, color, national origin, or sexual orientation. In addition, federal civil rights statutes that derive from the original 1870s anti-Klan laws have been used to prosecute members of white supremacy groups for their ideologically-based criminal acts.

In the 1990s white supremacy groups have been linked to right-wing MILITIA organizations. These militia groups, while espousing anti-government violence, often share a belief in white supremacy.

CROSS-REFERENCES

Jim Crow Laws; Second Amendment *In Focus:* Private Militias; Terrorism.

WHITEWATER Whitewater is the name given to the scandal involving President BILL CLINTON, First Lady HILLARY RODHAM CLINTON, members of the Clinton administration, and private individuals and public officials in Arkansas. Though the alleged wrongdoing took place before Clinton was elected president in 1992, investigations by an independent counsel continued into Clinton's second term of office. As with President RICHARD M. NIXON's WATERGATE scandal, the focus of the independent counsel's investigation shifted from the underlying event to the question of whether the president and members of his administration participated in a cover up. The role of Hillary Clinton in all of these events also became a target of investigators. As in Watergate, the Whitewater scandal quickly became politicized. Democrats accused Republicans in Congress as well as the Republican independent counsel of conducting a political witch hunt.

Whitewater is the name of a failed resort development on the White River in the Ozark Mountain region of Arkansas. In 1978 Bill Clinton, then Arkansas attorney general, and Hillary Clinton joined a partnership with James and Susan McDougal to form Whitewater Development Corporation, a real estate development firm that built vacation homes near the White River. When Clinton was elected governor that year, he appointed James McDougal his top aide.

In 1980 Clinton lost his re-election race. McDougal bought the Madison Bank and Trust in 1980 and in 1982 purchased a small savings and loan company and renamed it Madison Guaranty. In 1982 Clinton was again elected governor.

By 1984 Madison Guaranty Savings and Loan was in financial trouble, with federal regulators questioning its lending practices and its financial stability. Under Arkansas law, the state's securities commission could have closed Madison Guaranty. However, in January 1985, Clinton appointed Beverly B. Schaffer to head the commission. She approved two STOCK sale plans to raise money to keep Madison Guaranty solvent. Madison had retained the Rose Law Firm of Little Rock to help it secure approval of its stock sale applications. Hillary Clinton, the wife of the governor, worked as an attorney at Rose and was also a partner of McDougal in the Whitewater development. In addition, McDougal held a fund-raising event for governor Clinton in 1985 to help pay off a Clinton campaign debt. Investigators later determined some of the money was improperly withdrawn from depositor funds.

Despite the stock sales, the bank failed to raise enough capital, and by 1986, the Resolution Trust Corporation (RTC), the federal agency responsible for handling savings and loan failures, took over the bankrupt thrift. McDougal was charged with bank FRAUD. Four years later, McDougal was acquitted of the charge, based on an INSANITY DEFENSE. Meanwhile, the Whitewater development proved a financial disappointment, providing the Clintons with losses rather than profits. The Clintons sold their interest in the Whitewater corporation before Bill Clinton was sworn in as president in 1993.

The Whitewater scandal is grounded in these events of the 1970s and 1980s. It appeared that McDougal had been helped by his business partner Hillary Clinton, the wife of the governor. She had appointed the securities commissioner who allowed the failing thrift institution to stay open. By the time Bill Clinton was running for president in 1992, the national news media was investigating whether favors had been granted and CONFLICTS OF INTEREST had been overlooked in apparent disregard for Arkansas state law.

The news media and members of Congress pursued Whitewater during the first months of Clinton's presidency. The July 1993 suicide of Deputy White House Counsel Vincent Foster heightened interest in Whitewater, as Foster had several links to it. Foster had worked at the Rose Law Firm with Hillary Clinton, had handled the sale of the Clintons' interest in Whitewater, and had talked to an attorney who had previously prepared a report for the Clintons on the investment just hours before his suicide. Finally, after Foster's death, White House staff removed Whitewater files from Foster's office. Critics suspected that the removal of files was part of a White House cover up, while others speculated that Foster had been murdered to prevent the disclosure of damaging information.

In October 1993, the RTC asked the Department of Justice to investigate whether Madison's funds had been illegally siphoned into the Whitewater corporation and whether Madison illegally gave money in 1985 to pay off Clinton's campaign debt. Though President Clinton steadfastly denied any wrongdoing by himself or the first lady, Attorney General JANET RENO came under intense pressure to appoint an INDEPENDENT COUNSEL. She at first refused, noting that the independent counsel law had expired in 1992 (5 U.S.C.A. § 1211). Any counsel appointed by her would appear to be politically tainted.

Nevertheless, in January 1994, Reno appointed Robert B. Fiske, Jr., a former U.S. attorney and Wall Street lawyer, SPECIAL PROSECUTOR to investigate the Clintons' involvement in Whitewater and any potential links between Foster's suicide and his intimate knowledge of the Whitewater scandal.

Fiske surprised the Clinton Administration in March 1994 by serving SUBPOENAS on White House and Treasury Department officials. The investigation had shifted from one solely concerned with past deeds in Arkansas, to one that included current official behavior. Fiske discovered that senior Treasury Department officials, who oversee the work of the RTC, had discussed the Madison Guaranty probe with White House Counsel Bernard Nussbaum and other aides. This appeared improper, as it is highly unusual for regulatory agencies to discuss their probes with the parties they are investigating. As a result, the Treasury Department officials resigned.

Despite this embarrassment, the Clinton administration was pleased with Fiske's first report, issued in June 1994. He concluded that Foster's suicide had nothing to do with Whitewater and that the Treasury Department and White House meetings were not illegal. Fiske's report recommended that no criminal charges be filed and generally supported the administration's position on Whitewater.

During the summer of 1995, Senate and House committees held hearings on Whitewater. The hearings were mostly concerned with the propriety of the Treasury-White House meetings. The committee reports that followed cleared administration officials of any wrong-doing.

The course of the special counsel's investigation changed dramatically in August 1994. In July Congress had enacted the Independent Counsel Act (28 U.S.C.A. §§ 591-599), which meant that a three-judge panel of the U.S. court of appeals had to appoint an independent counsel for Whitewater. Attorney General Reno sought to have Fiske appointed, but the three-judge panel refused, citing a possible conflict of interest because he had been appointed by Reno, a member of the Clinton Administration. Instead, the panel appointed Kenneth W. Starr, a Bush administration solicitor general, a former federal appeals court judge, and a conservative Republican. Starr reopened all aspects of the investigation and reissued a subpoena for the Rose law firm billing records of Hillary Clinton. The first lady informed Starr that the records could not be located. In April 1995, Starr interviewed the Clintons privately.

In January 1996 Hillary Clinton's billing records were found on a table in the White House residence book room after two years of searching. An aide claimed she had found them in August 1995 but did not realize their significance until coming across them again. The discovery of the records was met with skepticism, with Starr subpoenaing Hillary Clinton in a criminal probe to determine if the records were intentionally withheld. The first lady testified before a GRAND JURY about the billing records.

Meanwhile, a Senate Special Whitewater Committee, chaired by New York Senator Alfonse D'Amato, conducted hearings in the last half of 1995, examining Whitewater and Foster's suicide, and the actions of White House staff. In June 1996, the committee divided along party lines in making its final report. Republican senators concluded that White House officials abused their power by trying to monitor and derail investigations of the Clintons, and that Hillary Clinton may have obstructed justice by concealing the Rose law firm billing records. Democratic senators dissented, finding no evidence to support the Republican allegations.

In 1996 President Clinton testified on videotape in two Arkansas criminal trials brought by Starr's prosecution team that concerned bank fraud. In the first trial James and Susan McDougal and Arkansas Governor Jim Guy Tucker were convicted of fraud and CONSPIRACY in connection with questionable loans made through Madison Guaranty. In the second case bankers Herby Branscom, Jr., and Robert Hill were acquitted of illegally using bank funds to reimburse themselves for political contributions, including contributions to Clinton's gubernatorial and presidential campaigns.

Starr continued to investigate Hillary Clinton's role in the Rose law firm's work for Madison Guaranty and the missing billing records. She had stated several times she had done little work on Madison, but at least one associate in the firm disputed her accounts. In 1997 Starr subpoenaed the notes of government attorneys who had met with the first lady prior to her grand jury testimony. The White House refused to comply with the subpoena, arguing that disclosure would violate the confidentiality of the attorney-client relationship. Starr took the matter to court and won court approval to enforce the subpoena from the Eighth Circuit Court of Appeals. *In re Grand Jury Subpoenas Duces Tecum*, 78 F.3d 1307 (1996). The appeals court agreed with Starr, ruling that the government attorneys were not the first lady's private counsel, but rather administration officials. Therefore, there was no attorney-client relationship and the notes were ordered surrendered. When the Supreme Court refused to hear an appeal from the Clinton Administration on this issue, the notes were given to Starr.

In 1997 Democrats and the Clinton administration escalated their criticisms of Starr and his investigation, arguing that Starr's conservative Republican affiliation had tainted the objectivity of the probe. Starr's credibility was hurt by his announcement in February 1997 that he would leave his position to become dean of the Pepperdine College law school and the head of a new public policy school. The new school was funded by a conservative Republican with ties to persons who had asserted a White House conspiracy concerning the death of Foster and subsequent events. Starr, who was criticized for leaving an unfinished investigation, reversed his decision, announcing he would not take the Pepperdine positions until the probe was concluded. Even Senator D'Amato was critical of this reversal, concluding that Starr's indecision about staying hurt his credibility.

WHITTAKER, CHARLES EVANS

Charles Evans Whittaker served as an associate justice on the U.S. Supreme Court from 1957 to 1962. The Missouri-born Whittaker practiced law for thirty years before being appointed to the federal bench in 1954. He served on the U.S. District Court in Missouri until 1957, when President DWIGHT D. EISENHOWER nominated him for a position on the Supreme Court. His appointment and service have been the subjects of caustic commentary, for Whittaker was not

BIOGRAPHY

Charles Evans Whittaker

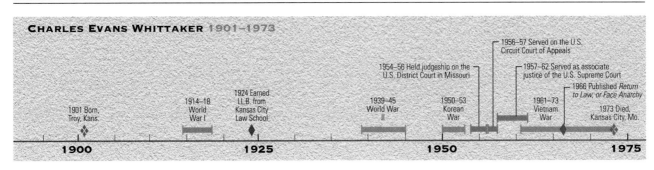

1956–57 Served on the U.S. Circuit Court of Appeals

1954–56 Held judgeship on the U.S. District Court in Missouri

1957–62 Served as associate justice of the U.S. Supreme Court

1966 Published *Return to Law, or Face Anarchy*

1901 Born, Troy, Kans.

1914–18 World War I

1924 Earned LL.B. from Kansas City Law School

1939–45 World War II

1950–53 Korean War

1961–73 Vietnam War

1973 Died, Kansas City, Mo.

1900   1925   1950   1975

cut out for the duties of the higher court: he served only five years before retiring in a state of physical exhaustion.

Born on February 22, 1901, in Troy, Kansas, Whittaker was the son of farmers. As a teenager, he knew that he wanted to be a lawyer: the ambitious high school student enrolled in law school during his senior year. Graduating in 1923 from the University of Kansas City Law School, where he was recognized for his talents as an orator, he passed the state bar and immediately began practicing for the law firm of Watson, Gage, & Ess. He litigated cases for the same Missouri firm for three decades.

Unlike countless other lawyers who used political careers to gain entry to the judiciary, Whittaker was plucked from relative obscurity. In fact, he generally avoided politics. He had a modest reputation in his home state for his work in corporate law and on the state bar, and this reputation attracted the attention of U.S. Attorney General Herbert Brownell, who selected him for the U.S. District Court in Missouri. Whittaker presided as a judge on the court from 1954 to 1956.

During this period, Whittaker displayed a lack of appreciation for certain constitutional rights. In 1955 he heard *Davis v. University of Kansas City*, 129 F. Supp. 716 (W.D. Mo. 1955), a lawsuit brought by a professor claiming he had been unfairly dismissed from the University of Kansas City for refusing to tell a Senate subcommittee whether or not he was a Communist. Such cases were typical in the COLD WAR era, as was Whittaker's dismissal of the claim. But the judge's outburst from the bench was not: he announced that the public should not tolerate teachers who belong to a "declared conspiracy by a godless group to overthrow our government." Although ostensibly recognizing the professor's FIFTH AMENDMENT right not to incriminate himself, Whittaker, in effect, believed that he was bound to answer.

In 1957 President Eisenhower appointed Whittaker to the Supreme Court to replace the outgoing Justice STANLEY REED. Whittaker became the first judge from the Western District

"PRIVATE-PROPERTY RIGHTS ARE THE SOIL IN WHICH OUR CONCEPT OF HUMAN RIGHTS GROWS AND MATURES. AS LONG AS PRIVATE-PROPERTY RIGHTS ARE SECURE, HUMAN RIGHTS WILL BE RESPECTED AND WILL ENDURE AND EVOLVE."

BIOGRAPHY

George Woodward Wickersham

to be elevated to the Court. Generally, he voted conservatively. He wrote no significant opinions, and, indeed, had little discernible judicial philosophy. In 1959 his appointment came under attack from the attorney (and eventual Chief Justice) WILLIAM REHNQUIST who wrote a scathing article attacking the U.S. Senate for not adequately considering Whittaker's nomination. In the *Harvard Law Review* Rehnquist noted dryly that the Senate hearings had revealed detailed information about the young Whittaker's life and education, but discussed nothing about his views on due process and equal protection.

In any event, Whittaker's views quickly did not matter. He found the work of the Supreme Court overly taxing, and, by 1962, suffering from exhaustion, he accepted his physician's advice that he retire. Some distinction was made as to his *retiring* rather than *resigning* and, as a result, he was allowed to continue to take part in Supreme Court ceremonies. No invalid, however, he later returned to legal practice, a move that set him apart from other modern justices. He died on November 26, 1973, in Kansas City, Missouri.

WICKERSHAM, GEORGE WOODWARD

As U.S. attorney general from 1909 to 1913, George Woodward Wickersham was an aggressive enforcer of federal ANTITRUST LAWS. Late in his career, he headed a commission that conducted the first comprehensive national investigation of the U.S. criminal justice system.

Wickersham was born on September 19, 1858, in Pittsburgh, Pennsylvania. He attended Lehigh University from 1873 to 1875 and received a bachelor of laws degree from the University of Pennsylvania in 1880. Before he graduated, he was admitted to the Pennsylvania bar. He practiced for two years in Philadelphia before moving to New York City where he joined the established law firm of Strong and Cadwalader. Wickersham became a partner in the firm four years later.

President WILLIAM HOWARD TAFT appointed Wickersham attorney general in March 1909. Wickersham helped draft the SIXTEENTH AMEND-

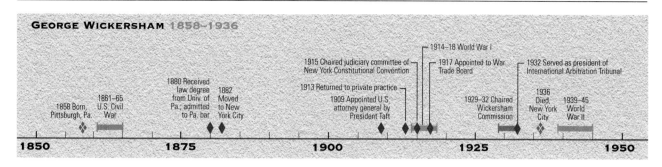

GEORGE WICKERSHAM 1858–1936

1858 Born, Pittsburgh, Pa.

1861–65 U.S. Civil War

1880 Received law degree from Univ. of Pa.; admitted to Pa. bar

1882 Moved to New York City

1909 Appointed U.S. attorney general by President Taft

1913 Returned to private practice

1914–18 World War I

1915 Chaired judiciary committee of New York Constitutional Convention

1917 Appointed to War Trade Board

1929–32 Chaired Wickersham Commission

1932 Served as president of International Arbitration Tribunal

1936 Died, New York City

1939–45 World War II

1850   1875   1900   1925   1950

MENT to the U.S. Constitution, adopted in 1913, that authorized Congress to levy an IN-COME TAX. He concentrated his efforts on prosecuting monopolistic corporations for antitrust violations under the Sherman Act (15 U.S.C.A. § 1 et seq. [1890]). In *Standard Oil Co. of New Jersey v. United States*, 221 U.S. 1, 31 S. Ct. 502, 55 L. Ed. 619 (1911), and other important antitrust cases, he participated in the oral arguments before the U.S. Supreme Court.

Wickersham also became the first attorney general to use consent decrees, which allow defendants to agree to negotiated SETTLEMENTS, without resort to court trials. Nineteen of forty-seven suits begun by Wickersham ended in such decrees.

After leaving office in 1913, Wickersham returned to his law practice. In 1915 he attended the New York Constitutional Convention and chaired its Judiciary Committee. After the U.S. entry into World War I, President WOODROW WILSON appointed Wickersham to the War Trade Board.

Wickersham is best remembered, however, for heading the National Commission of Law Observance and Law Enforcement, which came to be known as the WICKERSHAM COMMIS-SION. President HERBERT HOOVER named the commission to investigate the rise in crime and to determine whether, given the level of gangland violence, repeal of PROHIBITION was needed.

The commission, which included ROSCOE POUND, the noted legal scholar and court reformer, could not agree on the Prohibition issue, but its fourteen-volume report revealed disturbing features in the U.S. criminal justice system. It brought to public attention the use of "third-degree" interrogation methods against criminal suspects and the need for more professional police forces. In addition, it condemned the existing prison system and advocated the use of PROBATION and PAROLE as humane solutions to crime.

Wickersham completed his public service in 1932 as president of the International Arbitration Tribunal under the Young Plan, which in

"WE EXPECT LEGISLATION TO CONFORM TO PUBLIC OPINION, NOT PUBLIC OPINION TO YIELD TO LEGISLATION."

1929 had negotiated the REPARATIONS to be paid by Germany for World War I.

Wickersham died on January 25, 1936, in New York City.

WICKERSHAM COMMISSION

The Wickersham Commission is the popular name for the National Commission on Law Observance and Enforcement, which was appointed by President HERBERT HOOVER in 1929. The commission, which derived its name from its chairperson, former attorney general GEORGE W. WICKERSHAM, conducted the first comprehensive national study of crime and law enforcement in U.S. history. Its findings, which were published in fourteen volumes in 1931 and 1932, covered every aspect of the criminal justice system, including the causes of crime, police and prosecutorial procedures, and the importance of PROBATION and PAROLE.

Hoover established the commission to address several important issues. With the passage of the EIGHTEENTH AMENDMENT, PROHIBITION had begun in 1920, making the manufacture or sale of alcoholic beverages illegal. By 1929 illegal sale of ALCOHOL by ORGANIZED CRIME had become a national problem. In addition, gangland murders in Chicago in the late 1920s raised concerns about crime. Hoover appointed the commission to address the issue of crime in general, but he also sought a way to resolve the debate over continuing Prohibition.

The commission included many distinguished national leaders and academics, including Harvard law professor ROSCOE POUND. The commissioners hired a research staff to interview police, prosecutors, defense attorneys, judges, social workers, probation officers, prison administrators, and others involved in the criminal justice system. The commission's wide-ranging investigation was influenced by the comprehensive crime surveys conducted by the states of Missouri and Illinois in the 1920s. Some members of the commission had participated in those studies.

The publication of the commission's findings in 1931 and 1932 was obscured by the hard times brought on by the Great Depression.

Nevertheless, the volume entitled *Lawlessness in Law Enforcement* shocked the nation. This volume constituted an indictment of the police misconduct the commission had found throughout the country. The report described the widespread use of the "third degree"—the willful infliction of pain and suffering on criminal suspects—and other types of police brutality. In addition, it revealed corruption in many cities' criminal justice systems and documented instances of BRIBERY, ENTRAPMENT, COERCION of WITNESSES, fabrication of EVIDENCE, and illegal WIRETAPPING.

The report on *Lawlessness in Law Enforcement* led to police reform efforts in many municipalities. These efforts were reinforced by volume fourteen, *The Police*, which called for professional police departments, staffed by more highly qualified police officers and insulated from political pressures.

Other reports included *Prosecution*, which described the rise of PLEA BARGAINING and the decline of the JURY trial, *Criminal Statistics, Crime and the Foreign Born, The Cost of Crime, Penal Institutions, Probation and Parole*, and *The Causes of Crime*. The latter volume concluded that sociological factors had a direct effect on criminal activity.

The commission's report on *The Enforcement of the Prohibition Laws of the United States* was a forthright examination of the failure by federal, state, and local police to enforce Prohibition. The report documented the inadequacy of federal law enforcement and described the political, economic, geographical, and human difficulties in preventing the manufacture and sale of intoxicating liquor. Despite evidence of police corruption and the rise of organized crime, the commission recommended that the Eighteenth Amendment not be repealed. Instead, it urged all levels of government to spend more money and effort on enforcing the Prohibition laws. The commission's recommendations on Prohibition were ignored. In 1933 Congress passed an amendment repealing Prohibition, and state ratification conventions quickly endorsed the amendment. Ratification of the

LIBRARY OF CONGRESS

John Henry Wigmore

"SOME DAY, IT MAY BE HOPED, THE METHOD OF RATIONALIZATION WILL BE RECOGNIZED IN SYSTEMATIC TREATMENT OF ALL LEGAL IDEAS, AND NOT MERELY OF THE FUNDAMENTAL INSTITUTIONS."

TWENTY-FIRST AMENDMENT, bringing Prohibition's demise, came on December 5, 1933.

WIGMORE, JOHN HENRY John Henry Wigmore ranks as one of the most important legal scholars in U.S. history. A law professor and later dean of Northwestern University Law School from 1901 to 1929, Wigmore was a prolific writer in many areas of the law. He is renowned for his ten-volume *Treatise on the Anglo-American System of Evidence in Trials at Common Law,* (1904–05), which is usually referred to as *Wigmore on Evidence*. Legal scholars consider this TREATISE one of the greatest books on law ever written.

Wigmore was born on March 4, 1863, in San Francisco, California. He graduated from Harvard University in 1883 and entered Harvard Law School in 1884. While attending law school he helped found the *Harvard Law Review*, which was to become the preeminent legal journal. After graduating in 1887, Wigmore was admitted to the Massachusetts bar and entered private practice in Boston. He supplemented his income by doing research and writing for Chief Justice Charles Doe of the New Hampshire Supreme Court.

In 1889 Wigmore moved to Tokyo, Japan, to accept the post of chief professor of Anglo-American law at Keio University. In addition to his teaching duties, Wigmore wrote extensively and researched Japanese legal history. Extremely adept at languages, he became fascinated by the field of comparative law and pursued this interest throughout his life.

Wigmore returned to the United States in 1892 and accepted a teaching position with Northwestern University Law School in 1893. He taught a variety of courses, including evidence, torts, and international law. In 1901 he accepted the position of dean, a post he held until his mandatory retirement in 1929. As dean, Wigmore raised money to build the Albert Gary Library, one of the finest university law libraries in the United States, as well as a new law school building. He recruited some of the leading legal scholars of his day and made Northwestern one of the most prominent U.S. law schools.

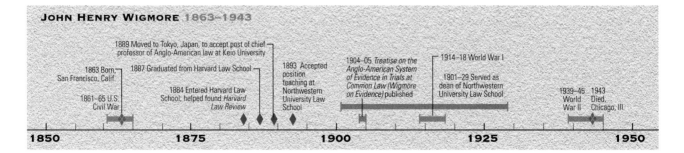

JOHN HENRY WIGMORE 1863–1943

1889 Moved to Tokyo, Japan, to accept post of chief professor of Anglo-American law at Keio University

1863 Born, San Francisco, Calif.

1887 Graduated from Harvard Law School

1884 Entered Harvard Law School; helped found *Harvard Law Review*

1861–65 U.S. Civil War

1893 Accepted position teaching at Northwestern University Law School

1904–05 *Treatise on the Anglo-American System of Evidence in Trials at Common Law (Wigmore on Evidence)* published

1914–18 World War I

1901–29 Served as dean of Northwestern University Law School

1939–45 World War II

1943 Died, Chicago, Ill.

1850   1875   1900   1925   1950

Wigmore's output as a writer was astounding. He produced forty-six original volumes of legal scholarship, thirty-eight edited volumes, and over eight hundred articles, pamphlets, and reviews. Much of Wigmore's writing was not of timeless quality, but his treatise on EVIDENCE is recognized as a classic because of the scope of its coverage and the insightful explanations of doctrine drawn from the most advanced U.S. jurisprudence.

Wigmore died April 20, 1943, in Chicago.

WILDCAT STRIKE 📖 An employee work stoppage that is not authorized by the LABOR UNION to which the employees belong. 📖

When employees join a union, they give the union the right to collectively bargain with their employers concerning the terms and conditions of work. Since the passage in 1932 of the NORRIS-LAGUARDIA ACT (29 U.S.C.A. § 101 et seq.), employees have had the right to STRIKE for the purpose of demanding concessions from their employers. However, when employees go on strike without union authorization, their action is called a *wildcat strike*. Federal courts have held that wildcat strikes are illegal under the NATIONAL LABOR RELATIONS ACT (NLRA) of 1935 (29 U.S.C.A. § 151 et seq.), and employees may be discharged by their employers for participating in wildcat strikes.

A wildcat strike brings into conflict sections 7 and 9(a) of the NLRA. Section 7 protects employees who bargain collectively and engage in other concerted activities for the purpose of COLLECTIVE BARGAINING. Section 9(a) states that representatives chosen for the purpose of collective bargaining shall be the exclusive representatives of all the employees in that bargaining unit. Because wildcat strikers engage in concerted activity without the authorization of their union, they appear to be both protected because of section 7 and unprotected because of section 9(a). The critical issue is whether the wildcat strikers should be protected to the same extent as strikers authorized by the union, or whether their activity is unprotected because of the exclusivity principle behind section 9(a).

The Supreme Court ruled in *Emporium Cap-* *well Co. v. Western Addition Community Organization,* 420 U.S. 50, 95 S. Ct. 977, 43 L. Ed. 2d 12 (1975) that when wildcat strikers bargain separately, they are not protected by the NLRA. Most lower courts have applied *Emporium Capwell* broadly, holding that all wildcat strikers are unprotected. Therefore, even when wildcat strikers have not attempted to bargain separately, the majority rule is that the strike is unprotected activity.

Ordinarily a wildcat strike constitutes a violation of an existing collective bargaining contract, so the strikes are not protected unless the whole union joins them and ratifies the protest. The union may, however, discipline its members for participating in a wildcat strike and impose fines.

See also LABOR LAW; WAGNER ACT.

WILDE, OSCAR Oscar Wilde was a nineteenth century Irish poet, novelist, and playwright who mocked social conventions and outraged English society with his unconventional ideas and behavior. Wilde's relevance to the law is based on his 1895 criminal trial, in which he was convicted of committing homosexual acts and sentenced to two years imprisonment. Historians of law and sexuality regard the trial as a pivotal event, as it demonstrated that the legal system could be used to punish gays and lesbians.

Wilde was born on October 16, 1854, in Dublin, Ireland. He was a talented writer who achieved prominence with his first effort, *Poems,* in 1881. Many of his subsequent works are considered classics, including the novel, *The Picture of Dorian Gray* (1891), and the plays *Lady Windermere's Fan* (1892) and *The Importance of Being Earnest* (1895).

Outwardly Wilde appeared to lead an ordinary life. He married Constance Lloyd in 1884 and fathered two sons. In 1895, however, rumors of Wilde's homosexual activities began to circulate, culminating in a scandalous LIBEL trial.

The Marquess of Queensberry, whose name is associated with the accepted standards of boxing regulations, started the controversy by publicizing Wilde's sexual preferences. The

BIOGRAPHY

LIBRARY OF CONGRESS

Oscar Wilde

"ALL AUTHORITY IS QUITE DEGRADING."

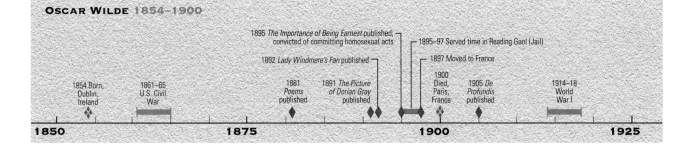

OSCAR WILDE 1854–1900

1850 — 1854 Born, Dublin, Ireland — 1861–65 U.S. Civil War — 1875 — 1881 *Poems* published — 1891 *The Picture of Dorian Gray* published — 1892 *Lady Windmere's Fan* published — 1895 *The Importance of Being Earnest* published; convicted of committing homosexual acts — 1895–97 Served time in Reading Gaol (Jail) — 1897 Moved to France — 1900 Died, Paris, France — 1905 *De Profundis* published — 1914–18 World War I — 1900 — 1925

marquess had discovered that his son, Alfred Douglas, had a homosexual relationship with Wilde, and he was determined to sever the ties. In February 1895, the marquess publicly accused Wilde of being homosexual. English law made homosexual relations a criminal offense.

Wilde professed innocence and took the marquess to court for criminal libel. At trial, the marquess's lawyer produced letters written by Wilde to Alfred Douglas, and their affectionate terminology was damaging to Wilde's case. As witnesses revealed his affiliations with male prostitutes and other men, Wilde considered retracting his accusation. The jury found the marquess not guilty, thus lending some credibility to his accusation against Wilde.

Soon after the conclusion of the trial, Wilde was arrested with a young man, accused of homosexual activities, and put on trial. At the trial, more information about his sexual activities emerged. The prosecution also introduced a poem by Alfred Douglas and questioned Wilde about several loving references to him.

Wilde's lawyers denounced the witnesses as characters of ill repute and pointed out conflicting facts in their testimonies. The trial ended in a HUNG JURY, but Wilde was retried in May 1895. This time Wilde was found guilty and sentenced to two years in prison. He was released from Reading Gaol in May 1897 and moved to France. He wrote a long letter to Douglas filled with recriminations against the younger man, which was published posthumously in edited form as *De Profundis* in 1905. Wilde died on November 30, 1900, in Paris.

See also GAY AND LESBIAN RIGHTS.

WILKINS, ROY Roy Wilkins was a prominent U.S. CIVIL RIGHTS leader, serving as the executive secretary of the NATIONAL ASSOCIATION FOR THE ADVANCEMENT OF COLORED PEOPLE (NAACP) from 1955 to 1977. Wilkins guided the NAACP during a time when momentous changes improved the civil rights of African Americans and other racial minorities. Criticized as too conservative and unwilling to shift the NAACP's focus from legal challenges and political lobbying to the nonviolent direct-

action tactics of Dr. MARTIN LUTHER KING, JR., and black power groups, Wilkins worked with Congress and Presidents JOHN F. KENNEDY and LYNDON B. JOHNSON to secure legislation that changed the status quo on racial inequality.

Wilkins was born in 1901 in St. Louis, Missouri. He was abandoned by his father shortly after his mother died and was taken in by an uncle who lived in Duluth, Minnesota. Wilkins later moved to St. Paul and graduated from the University of Minnesota. In 1923 he went to work as a journalist for the *Kansas City Call*, a newspaper published by and for the African American community in Kansas City, Missouri. He soon became managing editor of the paper.

In 1931 he was appointed assistant executive secretary of the NAACP, the largest civil rights organization in the United States. His first major campaign was a telegram and letter-writing protest against comedian Will Rogers, who used the word "nigger" four times in his premier broadcast over the NBC radio network. As a result, Rogers switched to the more acceptable term "darky."

From 1934 to 1949, Wilkins edited *The Crisis*, the official magazine of the NAACP. During this period Wilkins was a trusted adviser and protégé of executive secretary Walter White. The NAACP's strategy for improved civil rights for African Americans began in the 1920s with a series of lawsuits that contested both the SEPARATE-BUT-EQUAL doctrine of racial segregation and the denial of VOTING rights based on race. Led by gifted attorneys that included future U.S. Supreme Court Justice THURGOOD MARSHALL, the NAACP made steady progress in the 1930s and 1940s. The campaign to end school segregation reached its climax in 1954 with the landmark case of *Brown v. Board of Education of Topeka, Kansas*, 347 U.S. 483, 74 S. Ct. 686, 98 L. Ed. 873. Wilkins played a major role in preparing the case for trial and appeal. The decision itself did not eliminate racially segregated schools, but it did remove the legal justification for the discriminatory practice.

BIOGRAPHY

NATIONAL ARCHIVES

Roy Wilkins

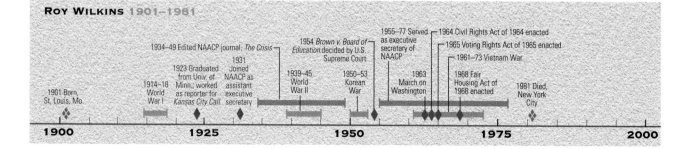

ROY WILKINS 1901–1981

1901 Born, St. Louis, Mo.

1914–18 World War I

1923 Graduated from Univ. of Minn.; worked as reporter for *Kansas City Call*

1931 Joined NAACP as assistant executive secretary

1934–49 Edited NAACP journal, *The Crisis*

1939–45 World War II

1950–53 Korean War

1954 *Brown v. Board of Education* decided by U.S. Supreme Court

1955–77 Served as executive secretary of NAACP

1963 March on Washington

1961–73 Vietnam War

1964 Civil Rights Act of 1964 enacted

1965 Voting Rights Act of 1965 enacted

1968 Fair Housing Act of 1968 enacted

1981 Died, New York City

1900   1925   1950   1975   2000

Wilkins was named executive secretary of the NAACP in 1955, following the death of White. The association proceeded to extend the gains of *Brown* through more lawsuits, both in the South and, in the 1960s and 1970s, in the North. Until the late 1950s, the NAACP was regarded as a militant organization, uncompromising in its commitment to racial equality. With the birth of the modern CIVIL RIGHTS MOVEMENT, led by Martin Luther King, Jr., the NAACP appeared more conservative. Where Wilkins and the NAACP leadership believed in using the legislative and judicial process to achieve racial equality, King and his followers favored civil disobedience and other forms of nonviolent direct action.

Though Wilkins and the NAACP leadership were uncomfortable with this approach, Wilkins sought to make alliances with the new leaders. He helped organize the March on Washington in 1963, which catapulted King to national attention. The NAACP supported many of the sit-ins and marches of the period, but it rarely initiated them. Wilkins preferred to concentrate on the political process.

He played a major role in the passage of the CIVIL RIGHTS ACT of 1964 (42 U.S.C.A. § 2000a et seq.), the VOTING RIGHTS ACT OF 1965 (42 U.S.C.A. § 1973 et seq.), and the Fair Housing Act of 1968 (42 U.S.C.A. § 3601 et seq.). Wilkins worked with President Johnson and key senators and representatives on these measures.

Militant leaders of the rising black power movement in the late 1960s charged that Wilkins and the NAACP were not radical enough. Wilkins rejected black separatism, seeking instead an integrated, color-blind society. With a plainspoken and laconic demeanor, Wilkins refused to indulge in emotional rhetoric, concentrating instead on making reasoned arguments for racial equality.

In 1977 Wilkins ended his service as executive secretary of the NAACP and was succeeded by BENJAMIN L. HOOKS. Wilkins died September 8, 1981.

WILL A document in which a person specifies the method to be applied in the management and distribution of his ESTATE after his death.

A will is the legal instrument that permits a person, the TESTATOR, to make decisions on how his estate will be managed and distributed after his death. At COMMON LAW, an instrument disposing of PERSONAL PROPERTY was called a "testament," whereas a will disposed of REAL PROPERTY. Over time the distinction has disappeared so that a will, sometimes called a "last will and

"AT FIRST COLOR DOESN'T MEAN VERY MUCH TO LITTLE CHILDREN, BLACK OR WHITE. ONLY AS THEY GROW OLDER AND ABSORB POISONS FROM ADULTS DOES COLOR BEGIN TO BLIND THEM."

testament," disposes of both real and personal property. If a person does not leave a will, or the will is declared invalid, the person will have died INTESTATE, resulting in the distribution of the estate according to the laws of descent and distribution of the state in which the person resided. Because of the importance of a will, the law requires it to have certain elements to be valid. Apart from these elements, a will may be ruled invalid if the testator made the will as the result of undue influence, fraud, or mistake.

A will serves a variety of important purposes. It enables a person to select her HEIRS rather than allowing the state laws of DESCENT AND DISTRIBUTION to choose the heirs, who, although blood relatives, might be people the testator dislikes or with whom she is unacquainted. A will allows a person to decide which individual could best serve as the executor of her estate, distributing the property fairly to the beneficiaries while protecting their interests, rather than allowing a court to appoint a stranger to serve as administrator. A will safeguards a person's right to select an individual to serve as GUARDIAN to raise her young children in the event of her death.

The failure to execute a will might ultimately reduce the financial worth of the estate because additional legal fees and time delays usually ensue when a court must appoint an administrator or guardian or deal with a matter that could have been settled easily by a will.

The right to dispose of property by a will is controlled completely by statute. Since the 1970s, many states have adopted all or parts of the Uniform Probate Code, which attempts to simplify the laws concerning wills and estates. When a person dies, the law of her domicile (permanent RESIDENCE) will control the method of distribution of her personal property, such as money, STOCK, or automobiles. The real property, such as farm or vacant land, will pass to the intended heirs according to the law of the state in which the property is located. Though a testator may exercise much control over the distribution of property, state laws protect spouses and children by providing ways of guaranteeing that a spouse will receive a minimum amount of property, regardless of the provisions of the will.

Requirements of a Will A valid will cannot exist unless three essential elements are present. First, there must be a COMPETENT testator. Second, the document purporting to be a will must meet the execution requirements of statutes, often called the Statute of Wills, designed to ensure that the document is not a fraud but is the honest expression of the testa-

Howard Hughes, seen here with actress Ava Gardner, did not write a will and so his property was divided according to the law.

tor's intention. Third, it must be clear that the testator intended the document to have the legal effect of a will.

If a will does not satisfy these requirements, any person who would have a financial interest in the estate under the laws of descent and distribution can start an ACTION in the PROBATE court to challenge the validity of the will. The persons who inherit under the will are proponents of the will and defend it against such an attack. This proceeding is known as a will contest. If the people who oppose the admission of the will to probate are successful, the testator's estate will be distributed according to the laws of descent and distribution or the provisions of an earlier will, depending on the facts of the case.

Competent Testator A competent testator is a person who is of sound mind and requisite age at the time that he makes the will, not at the date of his death when it takes effect. Anyone over a minimum age, usually eighteen, is legally capable of making a will as long as he is competent. A person under the minimum age dies intestate (regardless of efforts to make a will), and his property will be distributed according to the laws of descent and distribution.

An individual has TESTAMENTARY capacity (sound mind) if he is able to understand the nature and extent of his property, the natural objects of his bounty (to whom he would like to leave the estate), and the nature of the testamentary act (the distribution of his property when he dies). He must also understand how these elements are related so that he can express the method of disposition of property.

A testator is considered mentally incompetent (incapable of making a will) if she has a recognized type of mental deficiency, such as mental retardation or severe mental illness. Mere eccentricities, such as the refusal to bathe, are not considered insane delusions, nor are mistaken beliefs or prejudices about family members. A person who uses drugs or ALCOHOL can validly execute a will as long as she is not under the influence of drugs or intoxicated at the time she makes the will. Illiteracy, old age, or severe physical illness do not automatically deprive a person of a testamentary capacity, but they are factors to be considered along with the particular facts of the case.

Execution of Wills Every state has statutes prescribing the formalities to be observed in making a valid will. The requirements relate to the writing, signing, witnessing, or attestation of the will in addition to its publication. These legislative safeguards prevent tentative, doubtful, or coerced expressions of desire from controlling the manner in which a person's estate is distributed.

Writing Wills usually must be in writing but can be in any language and inscribed with any material or device on any substance that results in a permanent record. Generally, most wills are printed on paper to satisfy this requirement. Many states do not recognize as valid a will that is handwritten and signed by the testator. In states that do accept such a will, called a holographic will, it usually must observe the formalities of execution unless exempted by statute. Some JURISDICTIONS also require that such wills be dated by the testator's hand.

Signature A will must be signed by the testator. Any mark, such as an *X*, a zero, a check mark, or a name intended by a competent testator to be her SIGNATURE to authenticate the will, is a valid signing. Some states permit another person to sign a will for a testator at the testator's direction or request or with her consent.

Many state statutes require that the testator's signature be at the end of the will. If it is not, the entire will may be invalidated in those states, and the testator's property will pass according to the laws of descent and distribution. The testator should sign the will before the witnesses sign, but the reverse order is usually permissible if all sign as part of a single transaction.

Witnesses Statutes require a certain number of witnesses to a will. Most require two, although others mandate three. The witnesses sign the will and must be able to ATTEST (certify) that the testator was competent at the time she made the will.

Though there are no formal qualifications for a WITNESS, it is important that a witness not have a financial interest in the will. If a witness has an interest, his TESTIMONY about the circumstances will be suspect because he will profit by its admission to probate. In most states such witnesses must either "PURGE" their interest under the will (FORFEIT their rights under the will) or be barred from testifying, thereby defeating the testator's testamentary plan. If, however, the witness also would inherit under the laws of descent and distribution should the will be invalidated, he will forfeit only the interest in excess of the amount he would receive if the will were voided.

Acknowledgment A testator is usually required to PUBLISH the will—that is, to declare to the witnesses that the instrument is his will. This declaration is called an ACKNOWLEDGMENT. No state requires, however, that the witnesses know the contents of the will.

Although some states require a testator to sign the will in the presence of witnesses, the majority require only an acknowledgment of the signature. If a testator shows the signature on a will that he has already signed to a witness and acknowledges that it is his signature, the will is thereby acknowledged.

Attestation An ATTESTATION clause is a CERTIFICATE signed by the witnesses to a will reciting performance of the formalities of execution that the witnesses observed. It usually is not required for a will to be valid, but in some states it is evidence that the statements made in the attestation are true.

Testator's Intent For a will to be admitted to probate, it must be clear that the testator acted freely in expressing her testamentary intention. A will executed as a result of undue influence, fraud, or mistake can be declared completely or partially void in a probate proceeding.

Undue Influence UNDUE INFLUENCE is pressure that takes away a person's free will to make decisions, substituting the will of the influencer. A court will find undue influence if the testator was capable of being influenced, improper influence was exerted on the testator, and the testamentary provisions reflect the effect of such influence. Mere advice, persuasion, affection, or kindness does not alone constitute undue influence.

Questions of undue influence typically arise when a will deals unjustly with persons believed to be the natural objects of the testator's bounty. However, undue influence is not established by inequality of the provisions of the will, because this would interfere with the testator's ability to dispose of the property as she pleases. Examples of undue influence include threats of violence or criminal prosecution of the testator, or the threat to abandon a sick testator.

Fraud FRAUD differs from undue influence in that the former involves MISREPRESENTATION of essential facts to another to persuade her to make and sign a will that will benefit the person who misrepresents the facts. The testator still acts freely in making and signing the will.

The two types of fraud are fraud in the execution and fraud in the INDUCEMENT. When a person is deceived by another as to the character or contents of the document she is signing, she is the victim of fraud in the execution. Fraud in the execution includes a situation where the contents of the will are knowingly misrepresented to the testator by someone who will benefit from the misrepresentation.

Fraud in the inducement occurs when a person knowingly makes a will but its terms are based on material misrepresentations of facts made to the testator by someone who will benefit from the testator's beliefs in such lies.

Persons deprived of benefiting under a will because of fraud or undue influence can obtain relief only by contesting the will. If a court finds fraud or undue influence, it may prevent the wrongdoer from receiving any benefit from the will and may distribute the property to those who contested the will.

Mistake When a testator intended to execute his will but by MISTAKE signed the wrong document, that document will not be enforced. Such mistakes often occur when a husband and wife draft mutual wills. The document that bears the testator's signature does not represent his testamentary intent, and therefore his property cannot be distributed according to its terms.

Special Types of Wills Some states have statutes that recognize certain kinds of wills that are executed with less formality than ordinary wills when the wills are made under circumstances that reduce the possibility of fraud.

Holographic Wills A holographic will is completely written and signed in the handwrit-

Howard Hughes and the Mormon Will

When billionaire recluse Howard Hughes died in 1976, it appeared that he had not left a will. Attorneys and executives of Hughes's corporations began an intensive search to find a will, while speculation grew that Hughes might have left a holographic (handwritten) will. One attorney publicly stated that Hughes had asked him about the legality of a holographic will.

Soon after the attorney made the statement, a holographic will allegedly written by Hughes appeared on a desk in the Salt Lake City headquarters of the Church of Jesus Christ of Latter-day Saints, more commonly known as the Mormon Church. After a preliminary review, a document examiner concluded that the will might have been written by Hughes. The Mormon Church then filed the will in the county court in Las Vegas, Nevada, where Hughes's estate was being settled.

The will, which became known as the Mormon Will, drew national attention for a provision that gave one-sixteenth of the estate, valued at $156 million, to Melvin Dummar, the owner of a small gas station in Willard, Utah. Dummar told reporters that in 1975 he had picked up a man who claimed to be Howard Hughes and had dropped him off in Las Vegas.

Though Dummar first said he had no prior knowledge of the will or how it appeared at the church headquarters, he later claimed that a man drove to his service station and gave him the will with instructions to deliver it to Salt Lake City. Dummar said he had destroyed the instructions.

Investigators discovered that Dummar had checked out a library copy of a book called *Hoax*, which recounted the story of Clifford Irving's forgery of an "autobiography" of Hughes. The book contained examples of Hughes's handwriting. Document examiners demonstrated that Hughes's handwriting had changed before the time the Mormon Will supposedly was written. In addition, the examiners concluded that the will was a crude forgery. Nevertheless, it took a seven-month trial and millions of dollars from the Hughes estate to prove that the will was a fake. In the end, the court ruled that the will was a forgery.

No valid will was ever found. Dummar's story later became the subject of the 1980 motion picture *Melvin and Howard*.

---

ing of the testator, such as a letter that specifically discusses his intended distribution of the estate after his death. Many states do not recognize the validity of holographic wills, and those that do require that the formalities of execution be followed.

Nuncupative Wills A NUNCUPATIVE WILL is an oral will. Most states do not recognize the validity of such wills because of the greater likelihood of fraud, but those that do impose certain requirements. The will must be made during the testator's last sickness or in expectation of IMMINENT death. The testator must indicate to the witnesses that he wants them to witness his oral will. Such a will can dispose of only personal, not real, property.

Soldiers' and Sailors' Wills Several states have laws that relax the execution requirements for wills made by soldiers and sailors while on active military duty or at sea. In these situations a testator's oral or handwritten will is capable of passing personal property. Where such wills are recognized, statutes often stipulate that they are valid for only a certain period of time after the testator has left the service. In other instances, however, the will remains valid.

Revocation of a Will A will is AMBULATORY, which means that a competent testator may change or REVOKE it at any time before his death. REVOCATION of a will occurs when a person who has made a will takes some action to indicate that he no longer wants its provisions to be binding and the law abides by his decision.

For revocation to be effective, the INTENT of the testator, whether EXPRESS or IMPLIED, must be clear, and an act of revocation consistent with this intent must occur. Persons who wish to revoke a will may use a CODICIL, which is a document that changes, revokes, or amends part or all of a validly executed will. When a person executes a codicil that revokes some provisions of a previous will, the courts will recognize this as a valid revocation. Likewise, a new will that completely revokes an earlier will indicates the testator's intent to revoke the will.

Statements made by a person at or near the time that he intentionally destroys his will by burning, mutilating, or tearing it clearly demonstrate his intent to revoke.

Sometimes revocation occurs by operation of law, as in the case of a MARRIAGE, DIVORCE, birth of a child, or the sale of property devised in the will, which automatically changes the legal duties of the testator. Many states provide that when a testator and spouse have been divorced but the testator's will has not been revised since the change in marital status, any disposition to the former spouse is revoked.

Protection of the Family The desire of society to protect the spouse and children of a decedent is a major reason both for allowing testamentary disposition of property and for placing limitations upon the freedom of testators.

Surviving Spouse Three statutory approaches have developed to protect the surviving spouse against disinheritance: dower or curtesy, the elective share, and community property.

Dower or curtesy At common law, a wife was entitled to DOWER, a life interest in one-third of the land owned by her husband during the marriage. CURTESY was the right of a husband to a life interest in all of his wife's lands. Most states have abolished common-law dower and curtesy and have enacted laws that treat husband and wife identically. Some statutes subject dower and curtesy to payment of DEBTS, and others extend rights to personal property as well as land. Some states allow dower or curtesy in addition to testamentary provisions, though in other states dower and curtesy are in lieu of testamentary provisions.

Elective share Although a testator can dispose of her property as she wishes, the law recognizes that the surviving spouse, who has usually contributed to the accumulation of property during the marriage, is entitled to a share in the property. Otherwise, that spouse might ultimately become dependent on the state. For this reason, the ELECTIVE SHARE was created by statute in states that do not have community property.

Most states have statutes allowing a surviving spouse to elect either a statutory share (usually one-third of the estate if children survive, one-half otherwise), which is the share that the spouse would have received if the decedent had died intestate, or the provision made in the spouse's will. As a general rule, surviving spouses are prohibited from taking their elective share if they unjustly engaged in DESERTION or committed BIGAMY.

A spouse can usually waive, release, or contract away her statutory rights to an elective share or to dower or curtesy by either an antenuptial (also called prenuptial) or postnuptial agreement, if it is fair and made with knowledge of all relevant facts. Such agreements must be in writing.

Community property A COMMUNITY PROPERTY system generally treats the husband and wife as co-owners of property acquired by either of them during the marriage. On the death of one, the survivor is entitled to one-half the property, and the remainder passes according to the will of the decedent.

Children Generally parents can completely DISINHERIT their children. A court will uphold such provisions if the testator specifically mentions in the will that he is intentionally disinheriting certain named children. Many states, however, have PRETERMITTED HEIR provisions, which give children born or adopted after the execution of the will and not mentioned in it an intestate share, unless the omission appears to be intentional.

Other Limitations on Will Provisions The law has made other exceptions to the general rule that a testator has the unqualified right to dispose of his estate in any way that he sees fit.

Charitable Gifts Many state statutes protect a testator's family from disinheritance by limiting the testator's power to make charitable gifts. Such limitations are usually operative only where close relatives, such as children, grandchildren, parents, and spouse, survive.

Charitable gifts are limited in certain ways. For example, the amount of the gift can be limited to a certain proportion of the estate, usually 50 percent. Some states prohibit deathbed gifts to CHARITY by invalidating gifts that a testator makes within a specified period before death.

Ademption and Abatement ADEMPTION is where a person makes a declaration in his will to leave some property to another and then reneges on the declaration, either by changing the property or removing it from the estate. ABATEMENT is the process of determining the order in which property in the estate will be applied to the payment of debts, taxes, and expenses.

The gifts that a person is to receive under a will are usually classified according to their nature for purposes of ademption and abatement. A specific BEQUEST is a GIFT of a particular identifiable item of personal property, such as an antique violin, whereas a specific DEVISE is an identifiable gift of real property, such as a specifically designated farm.

A demonstrative bequest is a gift of a certain amount of property—$2,000, for example—out of a certain fund or identifiable source of property, such as a savings account at a particular bank.

A sample will

I, _____ , a resident of and domiciled in the City of _____ , County of _____ and State of _____ , do hereby make, publish and declare this as and for my Last Will and Testament.

1. **Gift of Specific Articles of Personal Property.** I give and bequeath the following articles of personal property to the following persons:

(a) The ivory chess set that belonged to father, to my brother, _____ .

(b) The Haviland china set that belonged to mother, to my sister, _____ .

(c) The Dresden mantel clock, to my niece, _____ .

2. **Gift of Rest of Tangible Personal Property.** I give and bequeath all the rest of the tangible personal property which I shall own at my death to my wife, _____ , if she shall survive me. I hope, but do not require, that she will distribute certain articles out of this property to my children, children-in-law, and grandchildren in accordance with a memorandum which I shall leave addressed to her.

3. **Gifts of Money.** I give and bequeath the following amounts of money to the following persons or organizations:

(a) One Thousand Dollars ($1,000) to each of my grandchildren who shall survive me.

(b) Five Thousand Dollars ($5,000) to my son, _____ , if he shall survive me.

(c) Five Thousand Dollars ($5,000) to my daughter, _____ , if she shall survive me.

(d) Five Thousand Dollars ($5,000) to the Church of _____ , _____ .

If the total of gifts in this Article shall exceed fifteen per cent (15%) of the amount available for distribution by my executor, then all gifts in this Article shall be ratably reduced so that the total of such gifts does not exceed such fifteen per cent (15%). In making this determination the decision of my executor as to the value of assets available for distribution shall be conclusive.

4. **Gift of Residue.** All the rest, residue and remainder of my estate, real, personal and mixed, of whatsoever nature and wheresoever situate, of which I shall die seized or possessed, or to which I shall be in anywise entitled at the time of my death, including any legacies which may lapse or be invalid or for any reason fail to take effect, and including all property over which I shall have at the time of my death any power of appointment or disposal, which I shall not have otherwise exercised or released, I give, devise, bequeath and appoint to my wife, _____ , or, if she shall not survive me, in equal shares to any children of mine who may survive me, but if any child of mine shall predecease me leaving issue who shall survive me, such issue shall take *per stirpes* the share which such deceased child would have taken had he or she survived me.

5. **Shares of Minors.** If any of the persons who take under this Will is under the age of twenty-one (21) years at the time title vests in him or her, I authorize my executor in his discretions to retain his or her share, to manage, invest and reinvest the same and apply the net income therefrom or such portion thereof and such portion of the principal as my executor may deem necessary for the proper education, support and general welfare of such minor until he or she attains the age of twenty-one (21) years, at which time I direct my executor to transfer or pay to such minor the accumulated income, if any, and the balance of the principal. My executor is authorized to retain any part of such income not so used and to reinvest the same.

In lieu of making application of the net income and principal, if any, for the benefit of any such minor, I authorize my executor to make payment thereof to a parent of the minor or to any other person having the care of the minor or directly to the minor, without obligation to look to the proper application thereof by the person receiving it.

6. **Powers of Executor.** I confer upon my executor, with respect to the management and administration of any property, real or personal, including property held under a power in trust, the following discretionary powers, without limitation by reason of specification:

(a) To retain any such property for such period of time as he may deem advisable without liability for depreciation or loss; to deposit any moneys at any time constituting a part of my estate in one or more banks, savings or commercial, in such form of account, whether or not interest-bearing, and without limitation as to the amount of any such account, or in the discretion of my executor, to hold any such moneys uninvested.

(b) To lease real property for such period, with or without an option to purchase, and upon such terms as he may deem advisable.

A sample will
(continued)

(c) To borrow money for any purpose whatsoever and to mortgage real property and pledge personal property as security for such loans.

(d) To sell, exchange or otherwise dispose of any or all of my property, real or personal, at public or private sale, at any time and from time to time, for such consideration and upon such terms, including terms of credit, as he shall deem advisable.

(e) In his discretion to vote, in person or by proxy, or consent for any purpose, in respect of any stocks or other securities constituting assets of my estate; to exercise or sell any rights of subscription or other rights in respect thereof.

(f) In making distribution of any property to persons entitled thereto hereunder, to convey, transfer, or pay over the same in kind or in money, or partly in kind and partly in money, and for such purposes to transfer and assign undivided interests in any such property.

7.   **Common Disaster Clause.** In the event that any beneficiary under this Will and I shall die in a common accident or disaster or under such circumstances that it is difficult or impracticable to determine who survived the other, then I direct that for the purpose of this Will such beneficiary shall be deemed to have predeceased me.

8.   **Payment of Taxes.** I direct that there shall be no apportionment among the persons beneficially interested of any estate, transfer, succession or other inheritance taxes or any interest thereon imposed by the United States or any state thereof or any foreign country in so far as such taxes and interest are imposed with respect to any property or interests passing under this Will, any insurance on my life, any trusts, gifts or other transfers created or made by me or any property or accounts owned jointly by me and any other person or persons. All such taxes shall be paid by my executor and treated as an expense of administering my estate.

9.   **Appointment of Executor.** (a) I hereby nominate and appoint my friend and lawyer, _____ , as my executor hereunder. In the event that he shall fail for any reason to qualify or, having qualified, shall cease for any reason to act, then I nominate and appoint the _____ Bank of _____ , to act as executor in the place and stead of _____ .

(b) Any corporation into which the _____ Bank may be merged or with which it may consolidate, or any corporation resulting from any merger, consolidation or reorganization to which the _____ Bank shall be a party, or any corporation which shall succeed to all or substantially all of the business or assets of the _____ Bank, shall be substituted hereunder for the _____ Bank.

(c) I direct that no bond or other security shall be required of any executor acting hereunder for the faithful performance of his or its duties, any law of any state or jurisdiction to the contrary notwithstanding.

10.   **Afterborn Children.** In making this Will I have considered the possibility that there may be children born to me hereafter and I intend to make no provision for any such children other than those made hereinabove by this Will.

11.   **Revocation Clause.** I hereby revoke all wills and codicils heretofore made by me.

In Witness Whereof, I, _____ , have hereunto set my hand and seal and have signed my initials on each of the _____ preceding pages this _____ day of _____ , 19____ .

_____ [L.S.]

The foregoing instrument was signed, sealed, published and declared by _____ the above-named testator, as and for his last Will and Testament in our presence, all being present at the same time, and thereupon we, at his request and in his presence and in the presence of each other, have initialed each of the previous pages and have hereunto subscribed our names as witnesses this _____ day of _____ , 19____ , at the City of _____ and State of _____ .

_____   residing at   _____
                                             _____

_____   residing at   _____
                                             _____

_____   residing at   _____
                                             _____

A general bequest is a gift of property payable from the general ASSETS of the testator's estate, such as a gift of $5,000.

A residuary gift is a gift of the remaining portion of the estate after the satisfaction of other dispositions.

When specific devises and bequests are no longer in the estate or have been substantially changed in character at the time of the testator's death, this is called ademption by extinction, and it occurs irrespective of the testator's intent. If a testator specifically provides in his will that the beneficiary will receive his gold watch, but the watch is stolen prior to his death, the gift adeems and the beneficiary is not entitled to anything, including any insurance payments made to the estate as reimbursement for the loss of the watch.

Ademption by SATISFACTION occurs when the testator, during her lifetime, gives to her intended beneficiary all or part of a gift that she had intended to give the beneficiary in her will. The intention of the testator is an essential element. Ademption by satisfaction applies to general as well as specific legacies. If the subject matter of a gift made during the lifetime of a testator is the same as that specified in a testamentary provision, it is presumed that the gift is in lieu of the testamentary gift where there is a parent-child or grandparent-parent relationship.

In the abatement process, the intention of the testator, if expressed in the will, governs the order in which property will abate to pay taxes, debts, and expenses. Where the will is silent, the following order is usually applied: residuary gifts, general bequests, demonstrative bequests, and specific bequests and devises.

CROSS-REFERENCES

Decedent; Demonstrative Legacy; Estate and Gift Taxes; Executors and Administrators; General Legacy; Holograph; Husband and Wife; Illegitimacy; Intestate Succession; Legacy; Living Will; Parent and Child; Postmarital Agreement; Premarital Agreement; Residuary Clause; Specific Legacy; Trust.

WILL, HUBERT LOUIS Hubert Louis Will was appointed U.S. district judge for the Northern District of Illinois on October 27, 1961, by President JOHN F. KENNEDY. Like Kennedy, Will has been called an idealist and a pragmatist. His challenge to other federal judges is famous: produce the highest quality justice in the shortest time, and at the lowest cost, consistent with that quality. To meet his own challenge, Will has developed innovative case-management techniques over the years— and he has willingly shared them, through judicial seminars, with many of the nation's leading jurists.

BIOGRAPHY

Will was among the first to use pretrial scheduling conferences, pretrial orders, and standardized pretrial order forms to organize and supervise the course of a trial from the outset. His aversion to lengthy and costly trials has caused him to be, at times, an outspoken critic of the United States' trial lawyers. He is a longtime crusader for higher professional standards and better practice skills within the trial bar. Lawyers seldom take issue with Will's position on the issue. He was a respected trial lawyer for almost twenty years before coming to the federal bench.

Will was born April 23, 1914, in Milwaukee. As a law student at the University of Chicago he was among a select group of students chosen to meet with Attorney CLARENCE DARROW for informal Sunday afternoon discussions on legal topics. One of Darrow's favorites was VOIR DIRE, which is the preliminary examination of prospective jurors or witnesses to inquire into their competence. As a judge, Will continues to enjoy the dynamics of the jury selection process.

In 1937 Will earned a doctor of jurisprudence degree from the University of Chicago. In 1938 he accepted a position with the general counsel's staff of the U.S. SECURITIES AND EXCHANGE COMMISSION. Several months later, he went to work as special secretary to U.S. senator ROBERT F. WAGNER, of New York. During his tenure as special secretary, he also served as clerk of the Senate Committee on Banking and Currency. In 1940 Will joined the Tax Division of the Department of Justice as a special assistant to the U.S. attorney general. It was in the Tax Division that Will got his first real courtroom experience. There, he briefed and argued cases in the U.S. Court of Claims and various district courts. He also tried cases in all the circuit courts of appeals and the U.S. Supreme Court.

In the years immediately preceding World War II, Will served as general counsel for the Office of Price Administration and as tax counsel to the U.S. alien property custodian. By 1943, he was active in the military as a member of the Office of Strategic Services. He later served as acting chief of the Counter Espionage Branch in the European theater of operations. Before the war ended, he earned a promotion to captain and a citation for bravery. He remains active in veterans' affairs.

At the close of the war, Will and his family (his wife and four children) returned to Chicago, where he joined the law firm of Pope and Ballard. A year later, he became a partner in the firm of Nelson, Boodell, and Will. From 1949 to 1961, Will made his name as a tough—and

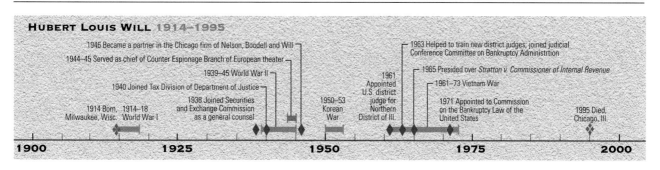

HUBERT LOUIS WILL 1914–1995

1914 Born, 1914–18 Milwaukee, Wisc. World War I

1938 Joined Securities and Exchange Commission as a general counsel

1940 Joined Tax Division of Department of Justice

1939–45 World War II

1944–45 Served as chief of Counter Espionage Branch of European theater

1946 Became a partner in the Chicago firm of Nelson, Boodell and Will

1950–53 Korean War

1961 Appointed U.S. district judge for Northern District of Ill.

1961–73 Vietnam War

1963 Helped to train new district judges; joined Judicial Conference Committee on Bankruptcy Administration

1965 Presided over *Stratton v. Commissioner of Internal Revenue*

1971 Appointed to Commission on the Bankruptcy Law of the United States

1995 Died, Chicago, Ill.

1900   1925   1950   1975   2000

winning—trial attorney. As a consequence of his work and reputation, Will was well-known in Chicago circles of the Democratic party. His name was soon added to a short list of possible appointees to the federal bench. In October 1961, President Kennedy named Will U.S. district judge for the Northern District of Illinois. In 1965 Will called on his tax litigation background when he presided over the trial and acquittal of former Illinois governor William G. Stratton on charges of tax evasion (*Stratton v. Commissioner of Internal Revenue*, 54 T.C. 255 [T.C. 1970]).

As a new judge, Will faced a staggering number of cases, and he was often frustrated when valuable courtroom time was devoted to issues he would not have bothered to handle as an attorney. Recognizing the need to better manage the volume and disposition of his cases, Will turned to colleagues for advice and assistance. Seasoned federal judges had practical suggestions for the newest among them, but no forum for sharing that expertise. To address this problem, Will was asked to join senior judges on a planning committee charged with developing training seminars for new district judges. His input and insight proved valuable. By 1963, Will was part of a permanent faculty responsible for training new judges. He remained on the faculty for the next twenty-five years.

Throughout the 1960s, Will experimented with methods to improve court procedures. The first standard forms for prisoners' HABEAS CORPUS petitions and CIVIL RIGHTS complaints were drafted in his chambers. Will acknowledged that the forms were a simple solution, but saw them as essential to sorting valid prisoner pleas from those that were "recreation for people with time on their hands."

In the area of civil litigation, Will was a vocal advocate of BIFURCATED TRIALS, or trials in which certain issues are considered separately, for example, guilt and punishment, liability and damages. He was among the first to use pretrial scheduling conferences, pretrial orders, and standardized pretrial order forms to control the course of a trial from the outset. An amendment

"JUDGES FOR CENTURIES HAVE THOUGHT THAT THEY WERE JUST SUPPOSED TO BE SKILLED REFEREES WHO WOULD STEP INTO THE RING WHEN THE LAWYER COMBATANTS SAID THEY WERE READY TO FIGHT."

to rule 16 of the Federal Rules of Civil Procedure covering pretrial scheduling conferences is often called the Will rule. He is also known for the twenty questions rule, which limits the number of INTERROGATORIES without court approval, and the straight face test, cautioning attorneys against taking a "position on any issue in any case that he or she cannot take with a straight face."

Throughout the 1960s, Will traveled to other districts to demonstrate case management techniques. His most famous bit of grandstanding took place when he set out to prove that the use of individual calendaring systems could improve judicial efficiency and clear courtroom backlogs. While carrying a full caseload in the Northern District of Illinois, Will served for just three days a month on the district court in Philadelphia, where he disposed of more than one hundred cases in under ten months.

In addition to experimenting with general courtroom efficiency, Will gave special attention to the administration of BANKRUPTCY cases in the federal system. He joined the Judicial Conference Committee on Bankruptcy Administration in 1963. In the decade that followed, he developed criteria for adding bankruptcy judgeships, proposed limits on bankruptcy administration costs, and revised bankruptcy rules in his own jurisdiction. In recognition of his expertise, Will was appointed to the Commission on the Bankruptcy Law of the United States in 1971 by Chief Justice WARREN E. BURGER. Many of the commission's recommendations are now the law of the land.

Since the mid-1970s, Will has served the Courts of Appeals for the Second, Fifth, Seventh, District of Columbia, and Federal Circuits. He has also continued to take temporary assignments in the district courts of Milwaukee and Madison, Wisconsin; South Bend, Indiana; Phoenix, Arizona; and Springfield, Illinois.

WILLFUL 📖 Intentional; not accidental; voluntary; designed. 📖

There is no precise definition of the term *willful* because its meaning largely depends on the context in which it appears. It generally signifies a sense of the intentional as opposed to the inadvertent, the deliberate as opposed to the unplanned, and the voluntary as opposed to the compelled. After centuries of court cases, it has no single meaning, whether as an adjective (*willful*) or an adverb (*willfully*).

Statutes and case law have adapted the term *willful* to the particular circumstances of action and inaction peculiar to specific areas of the law, including tort law, criminal law, workers' compensation, and unemployment compensation. A willful violation, for example, may mean a deliberate INTENT to violate the law, an intent to perform an act that the law forbids, an intent to refrain from performing an act that the law requires, an indifference to whether or not action or inaction violates the law, or some other variant.

In criminal-law statutes, *willfully* ordinarily means with a bad purpose or criminal intent, particularly if the proscribed act is MALA IN SE (an evil in itself, intrinsically wrong) or involves MORAL TURPITUDE. For example, willful MURDER is the unlawful killing of another individual without any excuse or MITIGATING CIRCUMSTANCES. If the forbidden act is not wrong in itself, such as driving over the speed limit, *willfully* is used to mean intentionally, purposefully, or knowingly.

Under WORKERS' COMPENSATION acts, willful misconduct by an employee means that he intentionally performed an act with the knowledge that it was likely to result in serious injuries or with reckless disregard of its probable consequences. A finding of "willful misconduct" prevents the employee from being awarded compensation for his injuries.

Under UNEMPLOYMENT COMPENSATION laws, an employee who is fired on willful misconduct grounds is not entitled to recover unemployment compensation benefits. Common examples of such willful misconduct include excessive absenteeism, habitual lateness, deliberate violations of an employer's rules and regulations, reporting for work in an intoxicated condition, and drinking alcoholic beverages while on the job.

Franklin H. Williams

"THE MASS MEDIA CONSTANTLY TAUNT THE GHETTO WITH THE AFFLUENCE OF MODERN SOCIETY."

WILLIAMS, FRANKLIN H. Franklin H. Williams was a lawyer, government administrator, and ambassador who played an important role in the modern CIVIL RIGHTS MOVEMENT. As an attorney with the NATIONAL ASSOCIATION FOR THE ADVANCEMENT OF COLORED PEOPLE (NAACP), Williams worked to desegregate public schools, public housing, and employment.

Williams was born on October 22, 1917, in Flushing, New York. He graduated from Lincoln University in Pennsylvania in 1941 and served in a racially-segregated unit of the U.S. Army in World War II. He graduated from Fordham University Law School in 1945.

After receiving his law degree, Williams accepted a position with the NAACP. From 1945 to 1950, Williams was an assistant special counsel for the NAACP's Legal Defense and Educational Fund and a special assistant to THURGOOD MARSHALL, the head of the fund who later became an associate justice of the U.S. Supreme Court. Williams worked with Marshall during the NAACP's efforts to desegregate public education, which were significantly aided by the 1954 Supreme Court decision in *Brown v. Board of Education of Topeka, Kansas*, 347 U.S. 483, 74 S. Ct. 686, 98 L. Ed. 873. *Brown* overruled the 1896 decision of *Plessy v. Ferguson*, 163 U.S. 537, 16 S. Ct. 1138, 41 L. Ed. 256, which had allowed racially-segregated facilities on trains and by implication in public schools.

In 1950 Williams became the NAACP's regional director of the western states. Under his leadership, the office pushed for legislation on minority employment, open housing, and other civil rights issues. In 1959 Williams left the organization to become an assistant attorney general of California, where he was instrumental in setting up the state's constitutional rights section.

In 1961 Williams became special assistant to Sargent Shriver, who helped establish the Peace Corps. In 1963 Williams served as director of the African regional division. In the same year, Williams became the first African American to serve as U.S. representative to the United Nations Economic and Social Council.

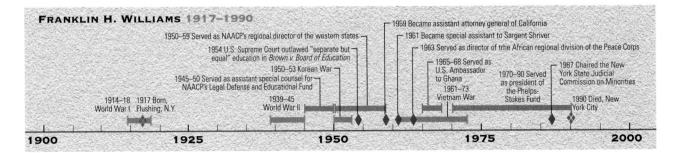

FRANKLIN H. WILLIAMS 1917–1990

1959 Became assistant attorney general of California
1950–59 Served as NAACP's regional director of the western states
1954 U.S. Supreme Court outlawed "separate but equal" education in *Brown v. Board of Education*
1961 Became special assistant to Sargent Shriver
1963 Served as director of the African regional division of the Peace Corps
1950–53 Korean War
1965–68 Served as U.S. Ambassador to Ghana
1987 Chaired the New York State Judicial Commission on Minorities
1945–50 Served as assistant special counsel for NAACP's Legal Defense and Educational Fund
1970–90 Served as president of the Phelps-Stokes Fund
1914–18 World War I
1917 Born, Flushing, N.Y.
1939–45 World War II
1961–73 Vietnam War
1990 Died, New York City

1900   1925   1950   1975   2000

In 1965 President LYNDON B. JOHNSON appointed Williams as the U.S. ambassador to Ghana. He held the post until 1968 and is credited with improving what had been strained relations between the U.S. and Ghana.

Williams returned to New York City after leaving his diplomatic post. He headed the Urban Center at Columbia University and served as vice chairperson of the New York Board of Higher Education. In 1987 Williams chaired the New York State Judicial Commission on Minorities, which examined the treatment of minorities in the state's courts.

Williams also served as president of the Phelps-Stokes Fund from 1970 to 1990. This foundation was established in 1911 to improve educational opportunities for African Americans, Native Americans, and Africans. One of Williams's first moves as president was to persuade the foundation's board to divest itself of holdings in corporations doing business with South Africa, which at that time was governed by a white minority employing the racially-segregated practices of apartheid. Williams's divestiture action was later adopted by other foundations and institutions.

Williams died on May 20, 1990, in New York City.

WILLIAMS, GEORGE HENRY George Henry Williams served as U.S. attorney general from 1871 to 1875. A state and territorial judge, as well as a U.S. senator, Williams was nominated to be chief justice of the United States by President ULYSSES S. GRANT in 1873 but he was never confirmed.

Williams was born on March 23, 1823 in New Lebanon, New York. He received an academic education, studied law, and was admitted to the New York bar in 1844. Williams moved to Ft. Madison, Iowa and established a law practice, but in 1847 he was elected a state district judge. In 1853 he moved west again, becoming chief justice of the Oregon territory, remaining on the bench until 1857.

In 1865 he was elected to represent Oregon in the U.S. Senate. He aligned himself with the Radical Republicans, who opposed President

"I BELIEVE I HAVE LIVED LONGER AND HAPPIER THAN IF I HAD BEEN RAISED TO [THE] EXALTED OFFICE [OF CHIEF JUSTICE]."

BIOGRAPHY

LIBRARY OF CONGRESS

George Henry Williams

ANDREW JOHNSON's programs for the South during Reconstruction. The animosity between Congress and Johnson led to ARTICLES OF IMPEACHMENT against Johnson. Williams supported the IMPEACHMENT of Johnson but the Senate attempt to convict Johnson failed by one vote.

After Williams lost his Senate seat, President Grant appointed Williams attorney general in 1871. His term as attorney general was unremarkable but his reputation was damaged by the events surrounding his failed nomination as chief justice in 1873. There were allegations that Williams had participated in FRAUDULENT activities involving voting in Oregon, but the organized bar on the East Coast also feared that as a frontier lawyer from Oregon, Williams was ill-prepared to preside over a Court that decided many complex commercial cases. A man of little formal education, he appeared too undistinguished to serve on the Court. It is likely, however, that the many political scandals involving corruption in the Grant administration unfairly tarnished Williams' nomination.

When it became clear that his nomination was doomed, Williams asked President Grant to withdraw his name from consideration. He continued as attorney general for two more years, resigning in 1875.

Williams abandoned national politics after his resignation and returned to Oregon, where he practiced law for many years in Portland. His last public position was as mayor of Portland from 1902 to 1905. He died on April 4, 1910, in Portland, Oregon.

WILLIAMS ACT A 1968 federal law that amended the Securities and Exchange Act of 1934 (15 U.S.C.A. § 78a et seq.) to require mandatory disclosure of information regarding cash tender offers.

When an individual, group, or CORPORATION seeks to acquire control of another corporation, it may make a TENDER OFFER. A tender offer is a proposal to buy shares of STOCK from the stockholders for cash or some type of corporate security of the acquiring company. Since the mid-1960s, cash tender offers for corporate takeovers have become favored over the tradi-

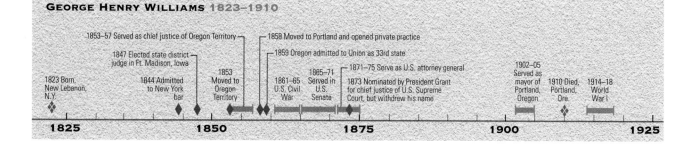

GEORGE HENRY WILLIAMS 1823–1910

1853–57 Served as chief justice of Oregon Territory

1847 Elected state district judge in Ft. Madison, Iowa

1858 Moved to Portland and opened private practice

1859 Oregon admitted to Union as 33rd state

1823 Born, New Lebanon, N.Y.

1844 Admitted to New York bar

1853 Moved to Oregon Territory

1861–65 U.S. Civil War

1865–71 Served in U.S. Senate

1871–75 Serve as U.S. attorney general

1873 Nominated by President Grant for chief justice of U.S. Supreme Court, but withdrew his name

1902–05 Served as mayor of Portland, Oregon

1910 Died, Portland, Ore.

1914–18 World War I

1825   1850   1875   1900   1925

tional alternative, the PROXY campaign. A proxy campaign is an attempt to obtain the votes of enough shareholders to gain control of the corporation's BOARD OF DIRECTORS.

Because of abuses with cash tender offers, Congress passed the Williams Act in 1968, whose purpose is to require full and fair disclosure for the benefit of stockholders, while at the same time providing the offeror and management equal opportunity to fairly present their cases.

The act requires any person who makes a cash tender offer (which is usually 15 to 20 percent in excess of the current market price) for a corporation that is required to be registered under federal law to disclose to the federal SECURITIES AND EXCHANGE COMMISSION (SEC) the source of the funds used in the offer, the purpose for which the offer is made, the plans the purchaser might have if successful, and any CONTRACTS or understandings concerning the target corporation.

Filing and public disclosures with the SEC are also required of anyone who acquires more than 5 percent of the outstanding shares of any class of a corporation subject to federal registration requirements. Copies of these disclosure statements must also be sent to each national securities exchange where the SECURITIES are traded, making the information available to shareholders and investors.

The law also imposes miscellaneous substantive restrictions on the mechanics of a cash tender offer, and it imposes a broad prohibition against the use of false, misleading, or incomplete statements in connection with a tender offer. The Williams Act gives the SEC the authority to institute enforcement lawsuits.

See also MERGERS AND ACQUISITIONS.

WILLISTON, SAMUEL Samuel Williston was a noted law professor and the primary authority on CONTRACT law in the United States during the early twentieth century. A professor of law at Harvard Law School from 1890 to 1938, his books *The Law of Sales* (1906) and *The Law on Contracts* are recognized as leading TREATISES.

Williston was born on September 24, 1861, in Cambridge, Massachusetts. He earned a bachelors degree from Harvard University in

"THE MODERN LAW RIGHTLY CONSTRUES BOTH ACTS AND WORDS AS HAVING THE MEANING WHICH A RESONABLE PERSON PRESENT WOULD PUT UPON THEM IN VIEW OF THE SURROUNDING CIRCUMSTANCES."

BIOGRAPHY

Samuel Williston

1882 and then worked for three years to earn the money needed to attend Harvard Law School. In 1888 Williston graduated from law school and established successful law practices in Boston and Cambridge.

In 1890 Williston accepted a professorship at Harvard Law School. As an assistant professor, Williston turned down many promising career opportunities, including offers of deanships at three other law schools and a position as reporter to the Massachusetts Supreme Court, which might have led to a judicial appointment on the high court.

During his career at Harvard, Williston aligned himself with legal formalism, which in the early twentieth century dominated legal thought in the United States. Legal formalism views the law as a body of scientific rules from which legal decisions may be readily deduced. Existing rules are elevated into the category of self-evident truths. In practice this meant that the law was unconcerned with social and economic forces. For Williston and other legal formalists, law was essentially conservative.

The desire for form and structure permeates Williston's writings. He believed that the law must be stated as simply as possible and that it must be certain. If the law is simple and certain, it can be used by parties to resolve their disputes without litigation, which Williston thought was the hallmark of a sound legal system. Therefore, he argued that the best course for the law was the construction of broad general rules.

Williston was able to apply his legal philosophy to the American Law Institute's *Restatement of Contracts*. The purpose of the *Restatement* was to set forth the basic principles of contract law by means of a coherent series of "black letter" principles, drafted with precision, that were consistent with the best traditions of the COMMON LAW, rooted in PRECEDENT, yet flexible enough to accommodate growth and development in the law. Williston explained each principle with commentary and concrete examples of its application.

Williston died on February 18, 1963, in Cambridge, Massachusetts.

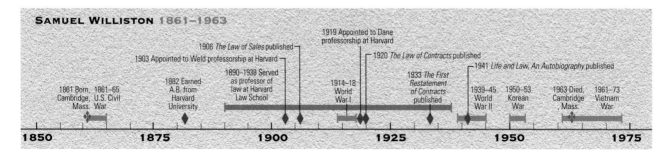

SAMUEL WILLISTON 1861–1963

1906 *The Law of Sales* published

1903 Appointed to Weld professorship at Harvard

1919 Appointed to Dane professorship at Harvard

1890–1938 Served as professor of law at Harvard Law School

1920 *The Law of Contracts* published

1933 *The First Restatement of Contracts* published

1941 *Life and Law, An Autobiography* published

1861 Born, Cambridge, Mass.

1861–65 U.S. Civil War

1882 Earned A.B. from Harvard University

1914–18 World War I

1939–45 World War II

1950–53 Korean War

1963 Died, Cambridge, Mass.

1961–73 Vietnam War

1850   1875   1900   1925   1950   1975

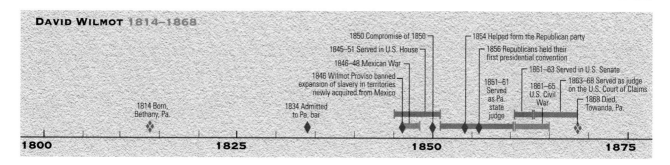

DAVID WILMOT 1814–1868

1850 Compromise of 1850
1845–51 Served in U.S. House
1846–48 Mexican War
1846 Wilmot Proviso banned expansion of slavery in territories newly acquired from Mexico
1854 Helped form the Republican party
1856 Republicans held their first presidential convention
1861–63 Served in U.S. Senate
1851–61 Served as Pa. state judge
1861–65 U.S. Civil War
1863–68 Served as judge on the U.S. Court of Claims
1868 Died, Towanda, Pa.
1814 Born, Bethany, Pa.
1834 Admitted to Pa. bar

1800   1825   1850   1875

WILMOT, DAVID David Wilmot was a lawyer, judge, U.S. senator and member of the U.S. House of Representatives. From 1845 to 1851 the Pennsylvania Democrat served in the House and it was there that he drew national attention for his 1846 proposal called the WILMOT PROVISO. The proviso banned the expansion of SLAVERY into the territories newly acquired from Mexico. Wilmot's disenchantment with slavery and the Democratic party's support of it eventually led him to help form the Republican party.

Wilmot was born on January 20, 1814, in Bethany, Pennsylvania. He studied the law with an attorney and became a member of the Pennsylvania bar in 1834. He established a law practice in Towanda and was soon recognized as an able lawyer.

However, politics drew Wilmot's interest. He became active in the Democratic party and in 1845 he was elected to the U.S. House of Representatives. Wilmot strongly supported President JAMES POLK and the Mexican War that began in 1845. When President Polk requested a congressional appropriation of $2 million to purchase land from Mexico, however, Wilmot vehemently objected to suggestions that slavery could be established in the newly acquired areas. He introduced the Wilmot Proviso to ban the spread of slavery but could not secure passage by both houses of Congress.

Wilmot left Congress in 1851, disenchanted with the COMPROMISE OF 1850, which admitted California into the Union as a free state but gave the Utah and New Mexico territories the right to determine the slavery issue for themselves at the time of their admission to the Union. Most disturbing to Wilmot were the new powers given to the federal government to enforce the FUGITIVE SLAVE ACT (9 Stat. 462).

Wilmot served as a Pennsylvania state judge from 1851 to 1861. In 1854 he, along with disaffected members of the Democratic and Whig parties, helped form the Republican party. The Republican party was antislavery and adopted the Wilmot Proviso language as part of its platform. Wilmot became a prominent member of the party and was elected to the U.S. Senate in 1861.

BIOGRAPHY

David Wilmot

"DEMOCRACY IS A PRINCIPLE OF ETERNAL JUSTICE."

A strong defender of the Union, Wilmot supported President ABRAHAM LINCOLN in the early years of the Civil War. Lincoln appointed Wilmot a judge of the U.S. Court of Claims in 1863, a post in which he served until 1868.

Wilmot died on March 16, 1868 in Towanda, Pennsylvania.

WILMOT PROVISO 📖 An unsuccessful 1846 congressional amendment that sought to ban SLAVERY in territories newly acquired from Mexico. 📖

The 1846 Wilmot Proviso was a bold attempt by opponents of slavery to prevent its introduction in the territories purchased from Mexico following the Mexican War. Named after its sponsor, Democratic representative DAVID WILMOT of Pennsylvania, the proviso never passed both houses of Congress, but it did ignite an intense national debate over slavery that led to the creation of the antislavery Republican party in 1854.

The Mexican War of 1845–1846 was fueled, in part, by the desire of the United States to annex Texas. President JAMES POLK asked Congress in August 1846 for $2 million to help him negotiate peace and settle the boundary with Mexico. Polk sought the acquisition of Texas and other Mexican territories. Wilmot quickly offered his proposal, known as the Wilmot Proviso, which he attached to President Polk's funding measure. The proviso would have prohibited slavery in the new territories acquired from Mexico, including California.

The proviso injected the controversial slavery issue into the funding debate, but the House approved the bill and sent it to the Senate for action. The Senate, however, adjourned before discussing the issue.

When the next Congress convened, a new appropriations bill for $3 million was presented, but the Wilmot Proviso was again attached to the measure. The House passed the bill and the Senate was forced to consider the proposal. Under the leadership of Senator JOHN C. CALHOUN of South Carolina and other proslavery senators, the Senate refused to accept the Wilmot amendment, approving the funds for negotiations without the proviso.

For several years, the Wilmot Proviso was offered as an amendment to many bills, but it was never approved by the Senate. However, the repeated introduction of the proviso kept the issue of slavery before the Congress and the nation. The COMPROMISE OF 1850, which admitted California as a free state but left the issue of slavery up to the citizens of New Mexico and Utah, created dissension within the Democratic and Whig parties. The strengthening of federal enforcement of the FUGITIVE SLAVE ACT (9 Stat. 462) angered many northerners and led to growing sectional conflict.

The creation of the Republican party in 1854 was based on an antislavery platform that endorsed the Wilmot Proviso. The prohibition of slavery in any new territories became a party tenet, with Wilmot himself emerging as Republican party leader. The Wilmot Proviso, while unsuccessful as a congressional amendment, proved to be a battle cry for opponents of slavery.

WILSON, JAMES Lawyer, author, theorist and justice, James Wilson helped write the U.S. Constitution and served as one of the first justices of the U.S. Supreme Court. Wilson emigrated from Scotland in the mid 1760s, studied law, and quickly gained prominence and success in Philadelphia. As a Federalist, Wilson believed in strong central government. This theme pervaded the pamphlets he wrote in the 1770s and 1780s. These highly influential tracts won him a national reputation. In 1787, he was a leading participant at the Constitutional Convention where the U.S. Constitution was written. Wilson served on the Supreme Court from 1789 to 1798, but the latter years of his life ended in disgrace.

Born on September 14, 1742, near St. Andrews, Scotland, Wilson came from a rural working class background. His quick intelligence took him far from his roots, however. He attended the University of St. Andrews from 1757 to 1759, the University of Glasgow from 1759 to 1763, and the University of Edinburgh from 1763 to 1765. At the age of twenty-three, he set out to make his fortune by emigrating to the American colonies, where he promptly be-

BIOGRAPHY

James Wilson

"LAWS MAY BE UNJUST . . . MAY BE DANGEROUS, MAY BE DESTRUCTIVE; AND YET NOT BE UNCONSTITUTIONAL."

gan studying law under one of America's best lawyers, JOHN DICKINSON. Two years later, in 1767, he was admitted to the Pennsylvania bar.

Over the next two decades, Wilson wrote political pamphlets that brought him national attention and launched his public career. In 1774 he argued that the American colonies should be free from the rule of British lawmakers in his widely read *Considerations on the Nature and Extent of the Legislative Authority of the British Parliament.* His writing soon led to involvement in the planning for American independence. He represented Pennsylvania at the CONTINENTAL CONGRESS from 1775 to 1776, and 1782 to 1783, and signed the DECLARATION OF INDEPENDENCE in 1776.

Wilson's most important role came at the Constitutional Convention in 1787, where he argued on behalf of key features of the Constitution such as the SEPARATION OF POWERS, which divided federal government into three parts, and the sovereignty of the people. A year later he helped persuade Pennsylvania to adopt the Constitution.

In 1789 President GEORGE WASHINGTON considered Wilson for the position of chief justice of the U.S. Supreme Court, a post Wilson desired but never attained. He became an associate justice, and, in the same year, was made the first law professor of the University of Pennsylvania. The few short opinions he wrote for the Court embodied his strong FEDERALISM. His most famous opinion was *Chisholm v. Georgia,* 2 U.S. (2 Dall.) 419, 1 L. Ed. 440 (1793), which upheld the right of citizens of one state to sue a different state.

But despite the accomplishments of his early life, Wilson remained a minor figure on the Court. As a result of bad investments he became heavily in debt in the 1790s, and he was jailed twice before fleeing his creditors. He died on August 21, 1798, in North Carolina, a pauper and a fugitive from justice.

WILSON, WOODROW Educator, political reformer, and the twenty-eighth president of the United States, Woodrow Wilson significantly affected domestic and international affairs during his two terms in office. Wilson

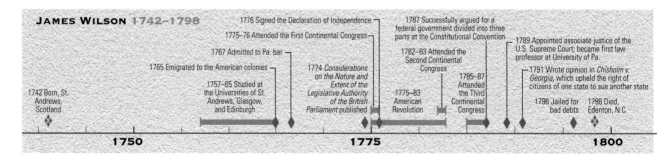

JAMES WILSON 1742–1798

1742 Born, St. Andrews, Scotland

1757–65 Studied at the Universities of St. Andrews, Glasgow, and Edinburgh

1765 Emigrated to the American colonies

1767 Admitted to Pa. bar

1774 *Considerations on the Nature and Extent of the Legislative Authority of the British Parliament* published

1775–76 Attended the First Continental Congress

1776 Signed the Declaration of Independence

1775–83 American Revolution

1782–83 Attended the Second Continental Congress

1785–87 Attended the Third Continental Congress

1787 Successfully argued for a federal government divided into three parts at the Constitutional Convention

1789 Appointed associate justice of the U.S. Supreme Court; became first law professor at University of Pa.

1791 Wrote opinion in *Chisholm v. Georgia,* which upheld the right of citizens of one state to sue another state

1796 Jailed for bad debts

1798 Died, Edenton, N.C.

1750   1775   1800

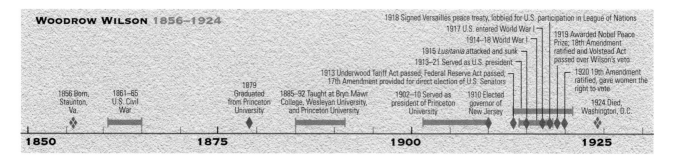

WOODROW WILSON 1856–1924

1918 Signed Versailles peace treaty, lobbied for U.S. participation in League of Nations
1917 U.S. entered World War I
1914–18 World War I
1919 Awarded Nobel Peace Prize; 18th Amendment ratified and Volstead Act passed over Wilson's veto
1915 *Lusitania* attacked and sunk
1913–21 Served as U.S. president
1913 Underwood Tariff Act passed; Federal Reserve Act passed; 17th Amendment provided for direct election of U.S. Senators
1920 19th Amendment ratified, gave women the right to vote

1856 Born, Staunton, Va.
1861–65 U.S. Civil War
1879 Graduated from Princeton University
1885–92 Taught at Bryn Mawr College, Wesleyan University, and Princeton University
1902–10 Served as president of Princeton University
1910 Elected governor of New Jersey
1924 Died, Washington, D.C.

1850   1875   1900   1925

made advances in education while he was the president of Princeton University in the early 1900s, before entering politics as the governor of New Jersey in 1910. He was elected president first in 1912 and again in 1916. He emerged from the tragedy of WORLD WAR I as an international leader who campaigned widely for the creation of the LEAGUE OF NATIONS—the post-war international organization that was the forerunner of the UNITED NATIONS. But political battles with a reluctant Congress ultimately dashed his hopes of U.S. participation in the League.

Born on December 28, 1856, in Staunton, Virginia, Wilson was the third of four children of devout religious parents, Janet Woodrow Wilson and Joseph Ruggles Wilson. The Civil War prevented him from beginning school until the age of nine, but the intellectual atmosphere fostered largely by his father, a Presbyterian minister, helped him excel. After graduation from Princeton University in 1879, he studied law at the University of Virginia and became a member of the bar in 1882. He established a law practice in Atlanta, Georgia, but later returned to school to study political science at Johns Hopkins University, earning his doctorate in 1886.

Professionally, Wilson worked in the area of education before entering politics. Between 1885 and 1892, he taught history and political economy first at Bryn Mawr College, then at Wesleyan University, and finally at Princeton. As president of Princeton from 1902 to 1910, he became known as an educational reformer. His improvements to teaching were welcomed until he set out on a bold plan to reform the social structure of the school by eliminating class distinctions, an effort that was severely criticized. Elected governor of New Jersey in 1910, he pursued reform policies that won greater approval: he improved WORKER'S COMPENSATION and the school system while also providing for better control of PUBLIC UTILITIES.

In 1912 the strength of Wilson's accomplishments at Princeton and as governor helped take him into the White House. Running as a Democrat, he also benefited from a rift in the

LIBRARY OF CONGRESS

Woodrow Wilson

"AMERICA WAS SET UP AND OPENED HER DOORS, IN ORDER THAT ALL MANKIND MIGHT COME AND FIND WHAT IT WAS TO RELEASE THEIR ENERGIES IN A WAY THAT WOULD BRING THEM COMFORT AND HAPPINESS AND PEACE OF MIND."

Republican party that split votes between THEODORE ROOSEVELT and WILLIAM HOWARD TAFT.

Wilson called his domestic program the New Freedom. It consisted of far-ranging economic and labor reforms. In a dramatic return to an old tradition, he addressed Congress personally, asking for passage of the legislation, and it largely complied. In 1913 the Underwood Tariff Act instituted the INCOME TAX but decreased the TARIFF on certain imports. The Federal Reserve Act of 1913 (38 Stat. 251), which reorganized the national banking system, is regarded as the most important banking reform in history. It gave the federal government control over the FEDERAL RESERVE BOARD while also providing agricultural credits to farmers.

The extent of Wilson's idealism can be seen in other significant reforms. In 1914 the Federal Trade Commission was established to discourage business corruption, and the Clayton Antitrust Act (15 U.S.C.A. § 12 et seq.) was passed in order to restrict businesses from monopolizing—unfairly dominating—individual markets. Three constitutional amendments were ratified during the Wilson administration: the provision for the direct election of U.S. senators in 1913 (SEVENTEENTH AMENDMENT); the prohibition of the manufacture, sale, and transportation of liquor in 1917 (EIGHTEENTH AMENDMENT); and the granting of the right to vote to women in 1920 (NINETEENTH AMENDMENT).

Wilson's foreign affairs policies encountered serious difficulties. In Mexico, which was in the throes of upheaval, the arrest of U.S. military personnel precipitated a U.S. invasion. U.S. troops also retaliated when Mexican revolutionary Francisco "Pancho" Villa invaded New Mexico. Wilson ordered troops to pursue him into Mexico. Relations between the two nations remained a problem throughout the Wilson administration.

World War I and its aftermath tested Wilson. The United States was neutral at the onset of war in 1914. Despite the entreaties of allies, it did not enter the war until nearly two years after Germany began attacking ships with submarines and sank the English ship *Lusitania* on May 7, 1915, killing more than one hundred

U.S. passengers. More German attacks on ships carrying U.S. passengers forced Wilson's hand. In 1917 his war speech included the celebrated phrase, "the world must be made safe for democracy." As the defeat of Germany became imminent in 1918, he put forth his Fourteen Points, a postwar program that he hoped would establish a lasting peace.

Besides economic, political, and geographic proposals, Wilson's plan proposed the creation of an international peacekeeping body to be called the League of Nations. Traveling to Europe in 1918 for the signing of a peace treaty at Versailles, France, Wilson was praised. This praise was not heard at home, where domestic criticism of his proposed League of Nations forced him to make concessions. He traveled widely across the nation campaigning on behalf of his plan. Ultimately, however, opposition in the U.S. Senate, based on the conviction that the United States should stay out of European affairs, scuttled plans for U.S. participation in the League. Wilson also suffered personally at this time. A stroke in 1919 made him an invalid for the rest of his life.

History has sometimes judged Wilson to be too much of an idealist, particularly in foreign affairs. The disastrous Versailles Treaty, in particular, sowed the seeds of a second World War. Yet his leadership during the war was inspirational, and his plan for international participation after the war was largely achieved in later decades under the aegis of the United Nations. For these accomplishments, he was awarded the 1919 Nobel Peace Prize. He died on February 3, 1924, in Washington, D.C.

See also TREATY OF VERSAILLES.

WIND UP 📖 The last phase in the DISSOLUTION of a PARTNERSHIP or CORPORATION, in which accounts are settled and ASSETS are liquidated so that they may be distributed and the business may be terminated. 📖

The dissolution of a corporation or a partnership culminates in the wind up of all legal and financial affairs of the business. State statutes govern the dissolution process for both types of business organizations, based on the need to insure that CREDITORS, stockholders, and other interested parties receive a fair ACCOUNTING of the LIQUIDATION and distribution of the business assets.

When a corporation announces that it will dissolve and end its legal existence, it is only the beginning of the end. Dissolution marks the end of business as usual, but corporate existence continues for the limited purpose of paying, settling, and collecting DEBTS. Once this is done, the corporation may wind up and distribute the remaining assets.

Winding up a business involves selling off all of the business's assets. Going out of business sales typically involve steep discounts to move merchandise quickly.

A general partnership will dissolve when a change occurs in the relation of the partners caused by any partner ceasing to be associated in the carrying on of the business. In the absence of a contrary agreement by the partners, a dissolution involves reducing the partnership assets to cash, paying creditors, and distributing to partners the value of their respective interests, as well as the performance of existing CONTRACTS. Once this phase is completed, the partnership may wind up by distributing assets. Once the wind up has occurred, the termination of the partnership is complete.

A partnership contract that is silent as to the procedures for wind up and liquidation must defer to the provisions of the Uniform Partnership Act (UPA), which has been adopted by virtually all of the states. The same rules of winding up and liquidation apply to all partnerships, regardless of their nature or business. Section 37 of the UPA provides that unless otherwise agreed, the partners who have not wrongfully dissolved the partnership or the legal representative of the last surviving solvent partner have the right to wind up the partnership affairs, provided, however, that any partner, his legal representative, or his assignee may obtain, for good cause, winding up by a court.

IN RE WINSHIP In the case *In re Winship*, 397 U.S. 358, 90 S. Ct. 1068, 25 L. Ed. 2d 368 (1970), the U.S. Supreme Court ruled that the Due Process Clause of the FOURTEENTH AMENDMENT to the U.S. Constitution requires proof BEYOND A REASONABLE DOUBT before a juvenile may be adjudicated delinquent for an act that would constitute a CRIME were the child an adult. *Winship* expanded the constitutional protections afforded by *In re Gault*, 387 U.S. 1, 87 S. Ct. 1428, 18 L. Ed. 2d 527 (1967), in which the Supreme Court ruled that MINORS accused of delinquent acts must receive NOTICE of any charges pending against them, and be given a reasonable opportunity to defend themselves during a fair HEARING in which they enjoy the RIGHT TO COUNSEL, the right not to incriminate themselves, and the right to confront and cross-examine adverse WITNESSES.

Twelve-year-old Samuel Winship was charged under the New York Family Court Act (NYFCA) with stealing $112 from a woman's pocketbook, an act that would have constituted the crime of LARCENY if Winship had been an adult. At the conclusion of the proceedings against Winship, the family court judge made a finding of delinquency by a preponderance of the evidence, the standard of PROOF set forth in section 744(b) of the NYFCA. The judge acknowledged on the record that the state had not proven its case beyond a reasonable doubt. As a consequence for his transgression, Winship was placed in a juvenile training facility for a minimum period of eighteen months.

Winship appealed the adjudication of delinquency to the New York Supreme Court (an intermediate court of appeals in New York), where he challenged the constitutionality of the NYFCA. Winship claimed that he was denied due process because the NYFCA required the family court to apply a quantum of proof less stringent than beyond a reasonable doubt. After the court rejected this challenge, Winship appealed the case to the New York Court of Appeals (the highest court in the state of New York), which affirmed the decisions of both lower courts. *In the Matter of Samuel W. v. Family Court*, 24 N.Y.2d 196, 247 N.E.2d 253, 299 N.Y.S.2d 414 (1969).

The court of appeals relied on the traditional distinction between juvenile and criminal proceedings in explaining its decision to affirm the lower court. State intervention in delinquency matters is traditionally justified under the doctrine of PARENS PATRIAE, a paternalistic theory of juvenile justice in which the government seeks to protect the welfare of minors by providing wayward youth with medical help, counseling, discipline, and other assistance deemed necessary by a court or by social services.

In contrast to the remedial and rehabilitative nature of many juvenile dispositions, criminal sanctions are intended to serve four different purposes: punishment, retribution, deterrence, and confinement. While most criminal proceedings are open to the public, nearly all juvenile proceedings are conducted in private under strict orders of confidentiality. Because adult criminal defendants generally have more at stake than minors accused of delinquency, criminal proceedings involving adults are designed to be more adversarial in nature. Con-versely, juvenile proceedings are administered with greater flexibility to meet the needs of each delinquent child.

Based on these distinctions, the court of appeals concluded that the remedial goals of juvenile justice are better served when the guilt or innocence of a minor is determined by a preponderance of the evidence. Application of the reasonable doubt standard in delinquency proceedings, the court of appeals reasoned, would result in a greater number of acquittals. More troubled children would return home without aid from juvenile justice programs, the court surmised, and delinquency problems would exacerbate.

In reversing the New York Court of Appeals, the U.S. Supreme Court emphasized two points. First, the Court underscored the importance of the reasonable doubt standard. Proof beyond a reasonable doubt, the Court said, is a standard deeply rooted in the nation's history, and forms an integral part of the fundamental freedoms protected by the Due Process Clause. The Court noted that since colonial times every person accused of wrongdoing in America has been entitled to a PRESUMPTION OF INNOCENCE until proven guilty beyond a reasonable doubt by the government.

Second, the Court indicated that this standard of proof is not necessarily limited to criminal cases, but may apply in other proceedings in which an accused faces a potential deprivation of life, liberty, or property. Winship faced confinement in a juvenile training facility for a period of up to six years because his detention order was subject to annual extension by the family court until his eighteenth birthday. Ordinarily, the Supreme Court observed, the law reserves such lengthy periods of confinement for adult FELONY offenders. But when juvenile defendants are exposed to adult-like penal sanctions, the Court held, they must be protected by the same procedural safeguards as adult criminal defendants, including the right to be presumed innocent until proven guilty beyond a reasonable doubt.

Despite the sweeping language of *In re Winship* and *In re Gault*, juveniles are not always afforded the same protections as adults under the Due Process Clause. For example, in *McKeiver v. Pennsylvania*, 403 U.S. 528, 91 S. Ct. 1976, 29 L. Ed. 2d 647 (1971), the Supreme Court ruled that there is no constitutional right to JURY trial in juvenile proceedings. So long as the judge presiding over a juvenile matter is fair and impartial, the Supreme Court said, due process has been provided.

CROSS-REFERENCES

Due Process of Law; *In re Gault*; Juvenile Law; Preponderance of Evidence.

WIRETAPPING 📖 A form of electronic eavesdropping accomplished by seizing or overhearing communications by means of a concealed recording or listening device connected to the transmission line. 📖

The introduction of the telegraph and the telephone in the nineteenth century made electronic eavesdropping possible and raised fundamental issues concerning personal PRIVACY. Wiretapping is a particular form of ELECTRONIC SURVEILLANCE that monitors telephonic and telegraphic communication. Since the late 1960s, law enforcement officials have been required to obtain a SEARCH WARRANT before placing a wiretap on a criminal suspect.

Police departments began tapping phone lines in the 1890s. The placing of a wiretap is relatively easy. A suspect's telephone line is identified at the phone company's switching station and a line, or "tap," is run off the line to a listening device. The telephone conversations may also be recorded.

The U.S. Supreme Court, in the 1928 case of *Olmstead v. United States*, 277 U.S. 438, 48 S. Ct. 564, 72 L. Ed. 944, held that the tapping of a telephone line did not violate the FOURTH AMENDMENT'S prohibition against unlawful searches and seizures, so long as the police had not trespassed on the property of the person whose line was tapped. Justice LOUIS D. BRANDEIS argued in a dissenting opinion that the Court had employed an outdated mechanical and spatial approach to the Fourth Amendment and failed to consider the interests in privacy that the amendment was designed to protect.

For almost forty years the Supreme Court maintained that wiretapping was permissible in the absence of a TRESPASS. When police did trespass in federal investigations, the EVIDENCE was excluded in federal court. Under the Federal Communications Act of 1934 (47 U.S.C.A. 151 et seq.), private citizens are prohibited from intercepting any communication and divulging its contents.

The Supreme Court reversed course in 1967, with its decision in *Katz v. United States*, 389 U.S. 347, 88 S. Ct. 507, 19 L. Ed. 2d 576. The Court abandoned the *Olmstead* approach of territorial trespass and adopted one based on the REASONABLE expectation of privacy of the victim of the wiretapping. Where an individual has an expectation of privacy, the government is required to obtain a warrant for wiretapping.

Congress responded by enacting provisions in the Omnibus Crime Control and Safe Streets Act of 1968 (18 U.S.C.A. § 2510 et seq.) that established procedures for wiretapping. All wiretaps were banned except those approved by a court. Wiretaps were legally permissible for a

Authorized Intercepts of Communication in 1993

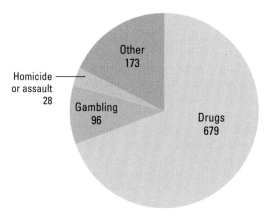

Data for jurisdictions with statutes authorizing or approving interception of wire or oral communication.

Source: Administrative Office of the U.S. Courts, *Report on Applications for Orders Authorizing or Approving the Interception of Wire, Oral or Electronic Communications (Wiretap Report)*, annual.

designated list of offenses, if a court approved. A wiretap may last a maximum of thirty days and notice must be provided to the subject of the search within ninety days of any application or a successful interception.

In 1986 Congress extended wiretapping protection to electronic mail in the Electronic Communications Privacy Act (ECPA), (8 U.S.C.A. § 2701 et seq.). The law, also known as the "Wiretap Act," makes it illegal to read private E-mail.

CROSS-REFERENCES

E-mail; *Olmstead v. United States;* Pen Register; Search and Seizure; Telecommunications.

WIRT, WILLIAM William Wirt served as U.S. attorney general from 1817 to 1829, the longest tenure in U.S. history. Wirt is recognized as one of the most important holders of that office, as he increased its prestige, established administrative record keeping, and defined the functions and authority of the attorney general that have remained unchanged.

Wirt was born on November 8, 1772, in Blaidensburg, Maryland. He was educated at private schools and for a time worked as a private tutor. Wirt studied law and became a member of the Virginia bar in 1792. Though he established a private practice and showed remarkable talent as a lawyer, he was drawn into Virginia politics. He served as clerk of the Virginia House of Delegates in 1800 and in 1802 was chancellor of the eastern district of Virginia. Wirt's political involvement led to friendships with several prominent Virginians, including THOMAS JEFFERSON, JAMES MADISON, and JAMES MONROE.

In 1807 President Jefferson appointed Wirt prosecuting attorney in the TREASON trial of

BIOGRAPHY

William Wirt

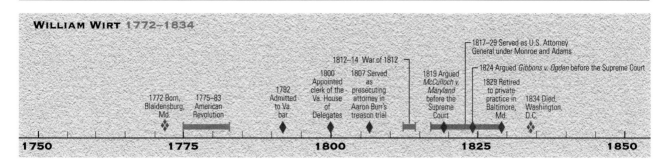

WILLIAM WIRT 1772–1834

1772 Born, Blaidensburg, Md.

1775–83 American Revolution

1792 Admitted to Va. bar

1800 Appointed clerk of the Va. House of Delegates

1807 Served as prosecuting attorney in Aaron Burr's treason trial

1812–14 War of 1812

1819 Argued *McCulloch v. Maryland* before the Supreme Court

1817–29 Served as U.S. Attorney General under Monroe and Adams

1824 Argued *Gibbons v. Ogden* before the Supreme Court

1829 Retired to private practice in Baltimore, Md.

1834 Died, Washington, D.C.

1750 · 1775 · 1800 · 1825 · 1850

AARON BURR. Though Burr was acquitted of all charges, Wirt had entered the national political arena. He continued to practice law, but he was also a Latin scholar and an author. In 1817 he published *Sketches of the Life and Character of Patrick Henry*.

In that same year President Monroe appointed Wirt attorney general. When Wirt entered his office for the first time he discovered that none of his eleven predecessors had left any books or records to document what they had done. Appalled at this lack of institutional memory, Wirt announced that he would keep a regular record of every official opinion he rendered for the use of his successors. This collection became known as the *Official Opinions of the Attorney General*, which has been maintained by every succeeding attorney general.

Wirt's most important contribution as attorney general was to define what activities his office could lawfully engage in and what advice it could give. Until Wirt's administration, the attorney general had routinely advised Congress and had advised EXECUTIVE BRANCH department heads in matters of policy. After reviewing the JUDICIARY ACT OF 1789, Wirt noted that the attorney general had no authority to advise Congress, and that the advice the attorney general could give to the president and department heads must be confined to MATTERS OF LAW. Therefore, Wirt ceased issuing opinions to Congress and only gave legal advice, policies that his successors have, with few deviations, honored.

During his long service, Wirt argued numerous cases before the U.S. Supreme Court, including the landmark cases of *McCulloch v.*

Maryland, 17 U.S. (4 Wheat.) 316, 4 L. Ed. 579 (1819) and *Gibbons v. Ogden*, 22 U.S. (9 Wheat.) 1, 6 L. Ed. 23 (1824). In *McCulloch* the Court affirmed the power of Congress to charter a national bank and denied states the right to tax a federal instrumentality. In *Gibbons* the court upheld the right of the federal government to control matters of interstate commerce. The case involved the authority of a state to grant private individuals monopolies to operate steamboats in navigable waters over which the federal government had authority. The Court held that the U.S. Constitution's COMMERCE CLAUSE empowered Congress to regulate interstate commerce, establishing a PRECEDENT that had far-reaching effects in the economic expansion of the nineteenth century.

Wirt served in both Monroe administrations and in the administration of President JOHN QUINCY ADAMS. He left office in 1829 and moved to Baltimore, where he practiced law. He died on February 18, 1834, in Washington, D.C.

See also GIBBONS V. OGDEN; MCCULLOCH V. MARYLAND.

WISDOM, JOHN MINOR John Minor Wisdom, a judge of the U.S. Court of Appeals for the Fifth Circuit, was one of the most influential jurists of the CIVIL RIGHTS era. He was prominent among southern judges who endured political pressures and physical threats for enforcing *Brown v. Board of Education* and for making other rulings that advanced the fight for equality under the law. (*Brown v. Board of Education of Topeka, Kansas*, 347 U.S. 483, 74 S. Ct. 686, 98 L. Ed. 873 [1954], was the landmark U.S. Supreme Court case that held racial segregation in public education to be against the law.)

BIOGRAPHY

HALSTEAD/GAMMA LIAISON

John Minor Wisdom

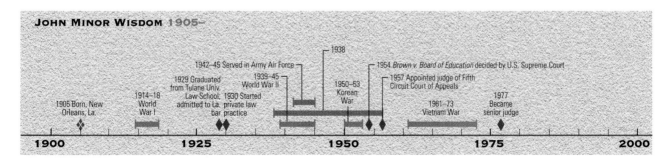

JOHN MINOR WISDOM 1905–

1905 Born, New Orleans, La.

1914–18 World War I

1929 Graduated from Tulane Univ. Law School; 1930 Started admitted to La. private law bar practice

1942–45 Served in Army Air Force

1939–45 World War II

1938

1950–53 Korean War

1954 *Brown v. Board of Education* decided by U.S. Supreme Court

1957 Appointed judge of Fifth Circuit Court of Appeals

1961–73 Vietnam War

1977 Became senior judge

1900 · 1925 · 1950 · 1975 · 2000

Wisdom and his prominent colleagues on the Fifth Circuit court (Judges John R. Brown of Houston, Texas, Richard T. Rives of Montgomery, Alabama, and Elbert Parr Tuttle of Atlanta, Georgia) were known derisively as "The Four" by those who disapproved of their work. Under their gavels, JIM CROW LAWS were declared unconstitutional, African Americans were granted voting rights, racial discrimination in jury selection was curbed, and state colleges and universities were desegregated. Though proud of his work, Wisdom was quick to point out that he was just one of many judges responsible for advancing the fight for civil rights in the old South. And in many ways, he was an unlikely individual to figure so prominently in the cause.

Born in New Orleans, Louisiana, on May 17, 1905, Wisdom was a product of the old South, and he grew up accustomed to the privileges and prejudices of the white aristocracy. His father, Mortimer Norton Wisdom, had been a pallbearer for General Robert E. Lee. His mother, Adelaide Labatt Wisdom, limited her son's youthful associations to people of his own social class and standing. It was not until Wisdom enrolled at Virginia's Washington and Lee University in 1921 that he was exposed to a more diverse cross section of the population and began to develop a broader view of the world. He received his bachelor of arts degree in 1925.

Wisdom entered the law school at Tulane University in 1925. He completed his studies in the spring of 1929 and was admitted to the Louisiana bar the same year. After law school, he joined several classmates to establish a New Orleans law practice. The firm of Wisdom, Stone, Pigman, and Benjamin endured in one variation or another for thirty years.

Wisdom established another enduring union on October 24, 1931, when he married Bonnie Stewart Mathews. They had three children.

By the late 1930s, Wisdom was combining careers in law and education. He was named adjunct professor of law at Tulane University law school in 1938 (a position he held until 1957). It was during this period that Wisdom began to see the importance of providing equal educational opportunities to all members of society.

His views were affirmed during the World War II years when he worked closely, for the first time, with poor and undereducated southern whites and blacks. Wisdom served in the Army Air Force from 1942 to 1946. Before the war's end, he had attained the rank of lieutenant colonel and been awarded the Legion of Merit.

After World War II, Wisdom returned to Louisiana and the practice of law. He also entered the political arena. By 1952 he was a member of the Republican National Committee for Louisiana and is sometimes called the man who made DWIGHT D. EISENHOWER president of the United States. At the 1952 Republican National Convention in Chicago, Wisdom led a fight to have Louisiana's Eisenhower delegates seated in place of those committed to Ohio Senator Robert A. Taft. Wisdom's success was the turning point in Eisenhower's bid for the nomination.

In 1954 Eisenhower named Wisdom to the President's Commission on Anti-Discrimination in Government Contracts. His work on the commission earned him national respect, and in 1957 he was appointed, again by Eisenhower, to the U.S. Court of Appeals for the Fifth Circuit.

He served the court and the nation for more than thirty years, as a judge from 1957 to 1977 and then as a senior judge. (Wisdom assumed senior, or semi-retired, status on January 15, 1977.)

In his years on the bench Wisdom participated in deciding almost five thousand cases, signed one thousand published majority opinions, and wrote nearly as many unnumbered PER CURIAMS and unpublished opinions. Colleagues say his place in history is assured by his unique ability to clearly express the court's opinions. Many of Wisdom's opinions defined civil rights law in the United States. In *Meredith v. Fair,* 298 F.2d 696 (1962), Wisdom desegregated the University of Mississippi. In *United States v. Louisiana,* 225 F. Supp. 353 (E.D. La. 1963), he affirmed the duty of federal courts to protect federally guaranteed rights and eloquently discussed the disfranchisement of African Americans in Louisiana. And, in *Dombrowski v. Pfister,* 227 F. Supp. 556 (E.D. La. 1964), *rev'd,* 380 U.S. 479 85 S. Ct. 1116, 14 L. Ed. 2d 22 (1965), the U.S. Supreme Court upheld his powerful dissent and enjoined the state of Louisiana from using legislative and judicial processes to harass civil rights leaders with unwarranted prosecution.

History and the law have accorded landmark status to at least two of Wisdom's cases. In *United States v. Jefferson County Board of Education,* 372 F.2d 836; 380 F.2d 385 (en banc); *cert. denied,* 389 U.S. 840 (1967), he used AFFIRMATIVE ACTION to desegregate schools "lock, stock, and barrel." And, in *Local 189, United Papermakers and Paperworkers v. United States,* 416 F.2d 980 (1969), *cert. denied,* 397 U.S. 919 (1976), he used a "rightful place" theory to prohibit the awarding of jobs based on a racially discriminatory seniority system.

Wisdom's expertise went beyond civil rights. He also wrote landmark opinions in the fields of admiralty, antitrust, evidence, and labor law. He wrote the majority opinion in the first appellate case to hold a manufacturer of insulation material liable for failing to warn workers of the dangers associated with asbestos (*Borel v. Fibreboard Products Corp.*, 493 F.2d 1076 [1973], *cert. denied*, 439 U.S. 1129).

Now in his nineties, Wisdom has reduced his workload but continues to hear cases for the U.S. Court of Appeals in New Orleans, Louisiana, and at other locations around the country.

WITAN An Anglo-Saxon term that meant wise men, persons learned in the law; in particular, the king's advisers or members of his council.

In England, between the sixth and tenth centuries, a person who advised an Anglo-Saxon king was called a *witan*, or wise man. A witan's basic duty was to respond when the king asked for advice on specific issues. A witan gave his advice in the Witenagemote, or assembly of wise men. This assembly was the forerunner of the English Parliament.

The Witenagemote was the great council of the Anglo-Saxons in England, comprising the aristocrats of the kingdom, along with bishops and other high ecclesiastical leaders. This council advised and aided the king in the general administration of government. The Witenagemote attested to the king's grants of land to churches or laypersons and consented to his proclamation of new laws or new statements of ancient customs. The council also assisted the king in dealing with rebels and persons suspected of disloyalty. The king determined both the composition of the council and its meeting times.

The Witenagemote generally met in the open air in or near some city or town. Members were notified by public notice or particular summons issued by the king's select council. When the throne was vacant, the body also met without notice to elect a new king.

After the Norman Conquest in 1066, the council was called the *commune concillium*, or common council of the realm. This was transformed into the Curia Regis, or King's Council, and by the late thirteenth century, it was called Parliament. The character of the institution also changed during this period. It became a court of last resort, especially for determining disputes between the king and his nobles and, ultimately, from all inferior tribunals.

WITHERSPOON v. ILLINOIS   In the 1960s and 1970s, the U.S. Supreme Court reviewed many issues surrounding the constitutionality of CAPITAL PUNISHMENT. In *Witherspoon v. Illinois*, 391 U.S. 510, 88 S. Ct. 1770, 20 L. Ed. 776 (1968), the Court examined the practice of authorizing PROSECUTORS in death penalty cases to exclude from the JURY persons who were opposed to capital punishment. The Court held that states could not exclude persons who had "conscientious scruples" or who were generally against capital punishment.

In 1960 an Illinois jury convicted William C. Witherspoon of murder and sentenced him to death. Witherspoon challenged the constitutionality of both his conviction and his death sentence. His APPEAL was based on an Illinois statute that provided that in murder trials a prospective juror could be challenged for cause and removed from the jury panel if, upon examination, the prospective juror declared that she was opposed to, or had conscientious scruples against, capital punishment. Using this statute, the prosecution in Witherspoon's case removed almost half the prospective jurors during jury selection.

Witherspoon argued that the law unfairly deprived him of his right to a fair trial under the Sixth and Fourteenth Amendments because the state had allowed to be seated only jurors who were in favor of capital punishment. After the Illinois courts rejected his appeals, the U.S. Supreme Court agreed to decide whether a state could constitutionally inflict the death penalty pursuant to the VERDICT of a jury composed in this manner.

The Court reversed the state courts and agreed that the Illinois statute was unconstitutional. Justice POTTER STEWART, in his majority opinion, held that it cannot be assumed that a juror who describes himself as having conscientious principles against imposition of the death penalty or against its imposition in an appropriate case thereby states that he would never vote in favor of the death penalty or would not consider doing so in the case at hand. Unless the juror asserts unequivocally that he would automatically vote against the death penalty, irrespective of what the trial might reveal, it cannot be assumed that this is the juror's position.

Stewart said that the determination of whether to sentence a defendant to life imprisonment or capital punishment cannot be made by a panel intentionally structured to inflict the death penalty. In such a situation, the state crosses the boundary of neutrality. The Court declared that the maximum that can be required of jurors in a capital case is that they be amenable to considering all penalties provided by state law and not be irrevocably committed

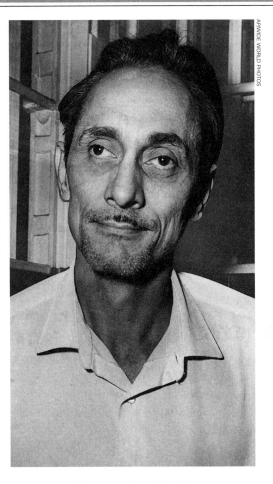

AP/WIDE WORLD PHOTOS

In Witherspoon v. Illinois, *the death sentence of William Witherspoon was reversed although his conviction stood. The Court ruled that the death sentence cannot be imposed by a jury from which people with conscientious scruples against capital punishment were excluded.*

before trial to voting against the death penalty irrespective of the facts and circumstances that the proceeding might disclose.

The *Witherspoon* decision forced states to rewrite their laws concerning jury selection in capital punishment cases. A general opposition to capital punishment is an insufficient ground for challenging a prospective juror. The prosecutor must probe to determine whether the person's beliefs would deter her from reaching an impartial verdict as to the defendant's guilt, or whether the person would never vote to impose the death penalty. If a person's views on capital punishment would affect her determination of the case, the person may properly be removed from the jury.

WITHHOLDING TAX The amount legally deducted from an employee's wages or salary by the employer, who uses it to prepay the charges imposed by the government on the employee's yearly earnings.

The federal INCOME TAX system is a "pay-as-you-go" system that requires wage earners to pay federal tax as they earn income. The federal government enforces this system through a withholding tax on wages and salary income. A taxpayer who does not have enough tax with-

held may be subject to penalties for underpayment.

In 1942 the federal government instituted a one-time withholding tax as a revenue-raising device during World War II. Withholding taxes are now a permanent method of collecting income taxes at the state and federal levels. Each pay period an employer is required to withhold tax from each employee's gross salary and send it to the INTERNAL REVENUE SERVICE (IRS) and to the state revenue collection agency, if the state has an income tax.

When a person is hired for a salaried job, the new employee must complete a federal W-4 form, which authorizes the employer to retain a certain amount of the employee's earnings to be forwarded to the government to satisfy the employee's federal income tax liability. The W-4 consists of a certificate showing the withholding allowances claimed by the employee and a worksheet in the form of an abbreviated tax return. The employee estimates her income, deductions, credits, and exemptions to determine how many withholding allowances to claim. The more allowances claimed, the less tax is taken out each pay period. The goal is to have the withheld taxes equal the yearly tax liability.

Taxpayers who underestimate the withholding tax needed to satisfy their tax liability may have to pay a penalty for underpayment. The IRS encourages taxpayers to review their financial situation periodically and file amended W-4 forms.

Backup withholding is a way of assuring that tax is paid on DIVIDEND and interest income. If a taxpayer does not provide his Social Security number to the payer of dividend or interest income, such as a bank, the institution must withhold a "backup" of 31 percent of each payment until the taxpayer provides the number.

WITHIN THE STATUTE Encompassed by, or included under, the provisions and scope of a particular law.

In the U.S. legal system, a person who is charged with violating a STATUTE must have committed actions that are specifically addressed in the law. When a person's actions comport with the language of the law, the actions are said to be "within the statute."

Troublesome questions arise, however, when a statute is too general or not specific enough in providing information on the proscribed acts. For example, VAGRANCY laws were used to arrest and detain persons the police believed had or were about to commit crimes. A person could be arrested for having no permanent address or for moving "aimlessly" through the streets. In *Papachristou v. Jacksonville*, 405 U.S. 156, 92 S. Ct. 839, 31 L. Ed. 2d 110 (1972), however, the U.S. Supreme Court ruled that a Florida vagrancy statute was unconstitutional because it was too VAGUE to be understood. The Court emphasized that a person cannot avoid engaging in criminal conduct, if prior to engaging in it, he cannot determine that the conduct is forbidden by law. See also VOID FOR VAGUENESS.

In criminal law, the courts apply the rule of lenity to deal with ambiguities in criminal statutes. The general rule is that an ambiguity in a criminal statute should be resolved in favor of the defendant. Therefore, a court will choose the more lenient interpretation in determining the punishment.

WITHOUT DAY

A term used to describe a final ending or ADJOURNMENT of a session of a legislature or a court; the English translation of the Latin phrase *sine die*.

When a state legislature or Congress makes a final adjournment of a legislative session, the presiding officer typically ends the session by announcing to the body that "the house (or senate) stands adjourned, sine die." The use of the phrase SINE DIE, or its English equivalent, without day, is more than a legal formality carried over from the COMMON LAW. The use of *without day* signifies finality and triggers constitutional requirements that the governor or president must meet if he wishes to sign legislation that has been passed in the last days of a legislative session.

For example, the president of the United States has ten days to sign or VETO a bill. If Congress adjourns without day before the ten days have expired, however, and the president has not signed the bill, it is said to have been subjected to a *pocket veto*. A pocket veto deprives Congress of the chance to override a formal veto. State governors have similar pocket veto powers.

In addition, once a legislature makes a final adjournment, it generally cannot call itself back into special session. In this situation the governor or president is authorized to call a special session of the legislature. The legislature, however, retains the right to adjourn the special session. If a legislature merely recesses for a holiday or vacation break, it may reconvene at its discretion.

In the modern legal system, without day has little importance as a legal formality. At one time it meant the final dismissal of a case. The Latin phrase *Quod eat sine die* ("that he go without day") was the old form of a JUDGMENT for the defendant; it had the effect of discharging the defendant from any further appearances in court.

WITHOUT PREJUDICE

Without any loss or WAIVER of rights or privileges.

When a lawsuit is dismissed, the court may enter a JUDGMENT against the plaintiff with or without prejudice. When a lawsuit is dismissed *without prejudice*, it signifies that none of the rights or privileges of the individual involved are considered to be lost or waived. The same holds true when an ADMISSION is made or when a MOTION is denied without prejudice.

The inclusion of the term *without prejudice* in a judgment of dismissal ordinarily indicates the absence of a decision on the MERITS and leaves the parties free to litigate the matter in a subsequent ACTION, as though the dismissed action had not been started. Therefore, a dismissal without prejudice makes it unnecessary for the court in which the subsequent action is brought to determine whether that action is based on the same cause as the original action, or whether the identical parties are involved in the two actions.

The purpose and effect of the words *without prejudice* in a judgment, ORDER, or DECREE dismissing a suit are to prohibit the defendant from using the doctrine of RES JUDICATA in any later action by the same plaintiff on the subject matter. The doctrine of res judicata (from the Latin, "a thing decided") is based on the importance of finality in the law. If a court decides a case, the subject of that case is firmly and finally decided between the persons involved in the suit, so no new lawsuit on the same subject may be brought by the persons involved. Therefore, the words *without prejudice* protect the plaintiff from a defendant's res judicata defense.

A court may also enter judgment *with prejudice*, however. This signifies that the court has made an ADJUDICATION on the merits of the case and a final disposition, barring the plaintiff from bringing a new lawsuit based on the same subject. If a new lawsuit is brought, a defendant can properly invoke res judicata as a defense, because a court will not relitigate a matter that has been fully heard before. Often a court will enter a judgment with prejudice if the plaintiff has shown BAD FAITH, misled the court, or persisted in filing FRIVOLOUS lawsuits.

WITHOUT RECOURSE

A phrase used by an endorser (a signer other than the original maker) of a NEGOTIABLE INSTRUMENT (for example, a CHECK or PROMISSORY NOTE) to mean that if payment of the instrument is refused, the endorser will not be responsible.

An individual who endorses a check or promissory note using the phrase *without re-*

course specifically declines to accept any responsibility for payment. By using this phrase, the endorser does not assume any responsibility by virtue of the endorsement alone and, in effect, becomes merely the assignor of the TITLE to the paper.

A without recourse endorsement is governed by the laws of COMMERCIAL PAPER, which have been codified in Article 3 of the UNIFORM COMMERCIAL CODE (UCC). The UCC has been adopted wholly or in part by every state, establishing uniform rights of endorsers under UCC § 3-414(1).

A without recourse endorsement is a qualified endorsement and will be honored by the courts if certain requirements are met. Any words other than "without recourse" should clearly be of similar meaning. Because the payee's name is on the back of the note, he is presumed to be an unqualified endorser unless there are words that express a different intention. The denial of recourse against a prior endorser must be found in express words. An implied qualification, based on the circumstances surrounding the endorsement to a third party, will not be recognized by the courts. An ASSIGNMENT of a note is generally regarded as constituting an endorsement, and the mere fact that an instrument is assigned by express statement on the back does not make the signer a qualified endorser.

The qualification without recourse, or its equivalent, is limited to the immediate endorsement to which it applies. It may precede or follow the name of the endorser, but its proximity to the name should be such as to give a subsequent purchaser reasonable NOTICE of the endorsement to which it applies.

A person might agree to accept a check without recourse if the person believes she could collect the money in question. Often the purchaser of such a note will acquire it at a substantial discount from the FACE VALUE of the note, in recognition that the purchaser can only seek to collect the money from the original maker of note.

An example of a without recourse note is a personal check written by A, the maker, to B, the payee. B, in turn pays off a debt to C by endorsing the check and adding the without recourse phrase. If A's bank refuses to pay C the check amount because A has insufficient funds in his checking account, C cannot demand payment from B. C will have to attempt to collect the money from A.

WITNESSES Individuals who provide EVIDENCE in legal proceedings before a tribunal. Persons who have sufficient knowledge of a fact or occurrence to TESTIFY about it and who give TESTIMONY under OATH in court, concerning what they have seen, heard, or otherwise observed.

Legal proceedings, especially TRIALS, depend on witnesses to present the factual evidence to the fact finder, which may be a JUDGE or a JURY. Witnesses who have knowledge about the facts of the case and who are legally COMPETENT are required to appear in court and testify. Typically each side has its own set of witnesses, who will provide evidence favorable to one side. However, the witness must submit to CROSS-EXAMINATION by the other side.

Attendance Individuals who are called as witnesses have a public obligation to attend the court or legislative tribunal to which they are summoned and to give testimony. Constitutional and statutory provisions provide that the parties to a civil lawsuit have a right to compel essential witnesses to appear. This is done through the service of legal process called a SUBPOENA, which is issued by the court. The state is also entitled to COMPULSORY PROCESS in any proceeding in which it has an interest, either civil or criminal. An individual accused of a crime has the right to compulsory process in order to obtain witnesses on his behalf. However, the right to compel witnesses does not ensure the actual attendance of the witnesses.

In a criminal trial, a witness whose testimony is crucial to either the defense or prosecution is called a MATERIAL witness. In most states, a material witness may be required to post a BOND guaranteeing her appearance. In cases where a bond cannot be issued, a material witness may be confined by the police until she testifies.

Courts have INHERENT power to compel the attendance of necessary witnesses but this power is also generally granted by statute. State constitutions and statutes grant legislative and administrative bodies the right to compel the attendance of a witness to provide testimony concerning the issue under investigation.

An individual who receives a subpoena is bound to obey it and appear in court. Once a witness appears in court, he may be forced to attend court until dismissed by the court or by the party who summoned him. A witness must remain after the day named in the subpoena, without being served with a new subpoena, if he is wanted. Likewise, when a party or third person is present in court, the person can be called and compelled to testify without a subpoena.

A person who fails to appear and testify subject to a subpoena can be punished for CONTEMPT. In addition, the failure to appear may result in the potential witness being liable to the individual who summoned her for any DAMAGES that result from her nonappearance. Damages that result from a postponement of the trial because of the failure of a witness to attend can also be assessed. However, when the facts can be proved without the testimony of the defaulting witness, the individual who summoned the witness has no right to recover damages from her.

A witness who is not able to appear at trial may give testimony beforehand and have it recorded on videotape. The witness is examined and cross-examined by the parties and the tape is then shown at trial.

Right to Compensation Compensation for witnesses is governed by statute and is not designed to reward them for testifying. Its purpose is merely to pay their expenses while they are away from home or work.

A witness must be in attendance in the court to be entitled to compensation, even in cases where he is not called upon to testify or proves to be incompetent to serve as a witness. Witnesses who are subpoenaed are entitled to travel expenses. Compensation for voluntary attendance depends upon state law. Some statutes provide that a witness who attends voluntarily without being subpoenaed is entitled to a daily allowance and mileage, while other state laws provide only a daily allowance, or no compensation at all.

Competency The general rule is that a person is competent to testify if she is able to perceive, remember, and communicate, and believes that she is morally obligated to tell the truth. Legislatures have the authority to set a standard of competency for witnesses in all cases. In the case of young children, the court must assess whether the child is competent to testify.

Expert Witnesses An expert witness is a person who, by reason of education or specialized experience is allowed to testify at a trial not just about the facts of the case but also about the professional conclusions he draws from the facts. Medical, scientific, and technical experts are commonly used, but other types of experts can be used, depending upon the facts of the case. For example, in an employment discrimination case, an economist might serve as an expert witness, providing professional testimony about discriminatory wage patterns in the affected industry. Experts witnesses generally charge a fee for their services.

Relationship to a Party Generally a witness is not disqualified merely because she is related to one of the parties by blood or marriage. Such a relationship only affects the CREDIBILITY, not the competency, of the witness.

GLASHEN GRAPHICS/THE PICTURE CUBE

At COMMON LAW, husbands and wives were considered to be incompetent as witnesses for or against each other in civil or criminal proceedings. This consideration was based on the legal presumption that the testifying spouse was too strongly interested in the outcome of the proceedings to testify truthfully. Most states have modified the common law rule so that either spouse can testify for or against the other in civil cases. In criminal cases, one spouse can ordinarily offer testimony in favor of the other. A spouse can voluntarily testify against the other in federal prosecutions. In addition, a spouse who is a victim of the other spouse's criminal act may testify.

Privileged Communications As a matter of public policy, certain relationships are held to be confidential and certain communications are privileged against disclosure by a witness. A witness cannot refuse to testify about a matter disclosed in a private conversation in confidence and in reliance upon the witness's promise of secrecy unless the law recognizes it as a CONFIDENTIAL COMMUNICATION. Certain communications arising between an attorney and client, a husband and wife, priest and penintent, and a physician and patient are privileged against disclosure by a witness.

An individual who refuses to either provide testimony or to answer proper questions when examined before a court is liable for contempt. A mere evasive or noncommittal answer does not, however, constitute a refusal to answer that is punishable by contempt, at least when the court does not direct the witness to be more specific in his answers. A witness cannot be penalized for refusing to answer questions when the answers would violate his privilege against SELF-INCRIMINATION under the FIFTH AMENDMENT to the U.S. Constitution.

Eyewitness testimony, where available, is typically the most powerful evidence in a lawsuit. Police at the scene of this motorcycle accident will be looking for witnesses to explain how the accident occurred.

Credibility Courts and juries may accept all of a witness's testimony, reject all of it, or accept part of it. A credible witness is an individual whose statements are reasonable and believable. A witness's statements are generally accepted as true unless her testimony has been discredited. Courts are reluctant to impute PER-JURY (lying under oath) to an apparently credible witness because a witness is, in general, presumed to speak the truth.

Anything that may shed light on the accuracy, truthfulness, and sincerity of a witness can be brought out by the parties. The fact finder must decide the amount of credit to be given the person's testimony. Either party can prove facts that tend to show the weight that should be given to testimony on either side.

A party has the right in either a civil or criminal case to introduce evidence attacking the credibility of a witness for his adversary. The term *to impeach a witness* means to question the individual's truthfulness by offering evidence that tends to show that the witness should not be believed. A party has the right under the SIXTH AMENDMENT to confront witnesses and to cross-examine witnesses who testify on behalf of the prosecution in a criminal case.

CROSS-REFERENCES

Attorney-Client Privilege; Cameras in Court; Hearsay; Husband and Wife; Marital Communications Privilege; Physician-Patient Privilege; Privileged Communication; Scientific Evidence; Sexual Abuse *In Focus:* Child Testimony in Day Care Center Sexual Abuse Cases; Shield Laws.

WOLCOTT, ALEXANDER

BIOGRAPHY

President JAMES MADISON's appointment of Alexander Wolcott to the U.S. Supreme Court was a tribute to Wolcott's political loyalty, not his legal acumen. Nominated by Madison on February 4, 1811, Wolcott was a well-connected Republican regarded by Federalists and most historians as unqualified for the High Court. Unable to win support even among fellow Republicans, Wolcott saw his confirmation rejected by the U.S. Senate, 24–9.

Wolcott was born in Windsor, Connecticut, on September 15, 1758, to Dr. Alexander Wolcott and Mary Richards Wolcott. After attending Yale College, he studied law and eventually practiced in Massachusetts and Connecticut. Wolcott married Frances Burbank in 1785 and settled in Middletown, Connecticut, where he became a port customs collector and an influential Republican.

Wolcott was appointed to the Supreme Court in 1811 to fill a vacancy left by the death of Associate Justice WILLIAM CUSHING. He was not Madison's first choice for the bench. Before Wolcott, Madison nominated former U.S. attorney general LEVI LINCOLN. Lincoln refused the honor, even after winning confirmation by the U.S. Senate. Madison then turned to Wolcott, primarily for political reasons. Although Wolcott was a recognized leader among Republicans, few people believed he had the professional ability to serve on the Supreme Court. Lincoln supported Wolcott, but Federalists condemned his appointment, calling Wolcott depraved and his nomination abominable.

Opposition to the Connecticut customs official was unusually strong because of his public support of the Embargo Act of 1807. The act, signed by President THOMAS JEFFERSON, prevented exports from England, France, and other countries from entering U.S. ports. The law was extremely unpopular with U.S. merchants and farmers whose profits were diminished by the reduced trade. Wolcott's endorsement of the EMBARGO, as well as his undeniable lack of judicial talent, doomed his nomination.

After Wolcott's rejection by the U.S. Senate, Madison appointed JOHN QUINCY ADAMS to serve on the Court. Adams, later the nation's sixth president, also turned down the seat, despite a unanimous Senate confirmation. The position eventually went to JOSEPH STORY, of Massachusetts, who at age thirty-two became the youngest person in U.S. history to sit on the Supreme Court.

After the confirmation defeat, Wolcott continued his political career, participating in the Connecticut state constitutional convention of 1818. At the convention, Wolcott sparked debate by supporting the expulsion of any judge who declared a legislative act unconstitutional.

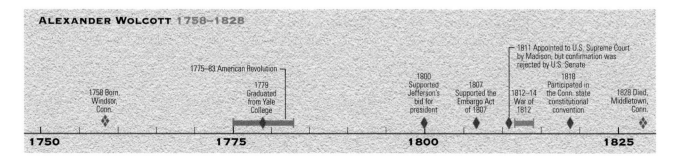

ALEXANDER WOLCOTT 1758–1828

1758 Born, Windsor, Conn.

1775–83 American Revolution

1779 Graduated from Yale College

1800 Supported Jefferson's bid for president

1807 Supported the Embargo Act of 1807

1811 Appointed to U.S. Supreme Court by Madison, but confirmation was rejected by U.S. Senate

1812–14 War of 1812

1818 Participated in the Conn. state constitutional convention

1828 Died, Middletown, Conn.

1750   1775   1800   1825

He also favored limitations on JUDICIAL REVIEW, the Supreme Court's power to interpret laws.

Wolcott died in Middleton on June 26, 1828, at age sixty-nine.

WOMEN'S RIGHTS 📖 The effort to secure equal rights for women and to remove gender discrimination from laws, institutions, and behavioral patterns. 📖

The women's rights movement began in the nineteenth century with the demand by some women reformers for the right to vote, known as SUFFRAGE, and for the same legal rights as men. Though the vote was secured for women by the NINETEENTH AMENDMENT to the U.S. Constitution in 1920, most of the gains women have made in achieving legal equality and ending gender discrimination have come since the 1960s. CIVIL RIGHTS legislation of that era was primarily focused on ensuring that African Americans and other racial minorities secured EQUAL PROTECTION of the laws. However, the inclusion of sex as a protected category under the CIVIL RIGHTS ACT of 1964 (42 U.S.C.A. § 2000e et seq.) gave women a powerful legal tool to end SEX DISCRIMINATION and to erase cultural stereotypes about females.

The modern women's rights movement began in the 1960s and gained momentum with the development of the scholarly field of FEMINIST JURISPRUDENCE in the 1970s. The quest for women's rights has led to legal challenges in the areas of employment, domestic relations, reproductive rights, education, and criminal law. Although the women's rights movement failed to secure ratification of the EQUAL RIGHTS AMENDMENT (ERA), the courts have generally been receptive to claims that demand recognition of rights under the Equal Protection Clause of the FOURTEENTH AMENDMENT.

Nineteenth Century Women's Rights Movement The effort to secure women's rights began at a convention in Seneca Falls, New York, in 1848. A group of women and men drafted and approved the "Declaration of Sentiments," an impassioned demand for equal rights for women, including the right to vote. The declaration was modeled after the language and structure of the DECLARATION OF INDEPENDENCE of 1776. Many of those gathered at Seneca Falls, including early women's rights leaders SUSAN B. ANTHONY and ELIZABETH CADY STANTON, had been active in the abolitionist movement, seeking an end to SLAVERY. However, these women realized that they were second-class citizens, unable to vote and possessing few legal rights, especially if they were married. Some leaders, like LUCY STONE, saw parallels between women and slaves: both were expected to be passive, cooperative, and obedient. In addition, the legal status of both slaves and women was unequal to that of white men.

After the Civil War ended in 1865, many of these reformers fully committed their energies to gaining women's suffrage. Stanton and Anthony established the National Woman Suffrage Association (NWSA), that sought an amendment to the U.S. Constitution similar to the FIFTEENTH AMENDMENT, which gave nonwhite men the right to vote. In 1872 Anthony was prosecuted for attempting to vote in the presidential election. Stone, on the other hand, helped form the American Woman Suffrage Association (AWSA). AWSA worked for women's suffrage on a state by state basis, seeking amendments to state constitutions.

The U.S. Supreme Court was hostile to women's suffrage. In *Minor v. Happersett*, 88 U.S. 162, 22 L. Ed. 627 (1875), the Court rejected an attempt by a woman to cast a ballot in a Missouri election. The Court stated that the "Constitution of the United States does not confer the right of suffrage upon any one." In addition, the Court said, "Women were excluded from suffrage in nearly all the States by the express provision of their constitutions and laws." In essence, the Court relied on past exclusions to justify current exclusions, concluding that because women had never been allowed to vote, they could continue to be excluded.

The attitude of the Court in *Minor* was foreshadowed three years earlier in the concurring opinion of Justice JOSEPH P. BRADLEY in *Bradwell v. Illinois*, 83 U.S. 130, 21 L. Ed. 442 (1872). Bradley supported the Illinois Supreme Court's denial of MYRA BRADWELL's application to practice law in the state. Bradley articulated the widely held view that the "natural and proper timidity and delicacy which belongs to the female sex evidently unfits it for many of the occupations of civil life." He further concluded that the "paramount destiny and mission of woman are to fulfill the noble and benign offices of wife and mother. This is the law of the Creator."

By the late nineteenth century, lobbying of state legislatures by AWSA and other suffrage supporters began to bear fruit. A few states changed their statutes to permit female suffrage. By 1912 nine states had extended the franchise to include women. In 1918 President WOODROW WILSON endorsed women's suffrage, and Congress soon adopted a constitutional amendment granting women the right to vote and submitting the amendment to the states for ratification. In 1920 the Nineteenth Amendment was added to the Constitution, immediately doubling the potential electorate.

Domestic Relations in the Nineteenth Century The legal inequality that Lucy Stone and other women's rights leaders argued against was evident in the relationship of HUSBAND AND WIFE. Under English COMMON LAW, which was adopted by the states after independence, the identity of the wife was merged into that of the husband; he was a legal person but she was not. Upon MARRIAGE, he received all her PERSONAL PROPERTY, and managed all property owned by her. In return, the husband was obliged to support his wife and children. A married woman, therefore, could not sign a CONTRACT without the signature of her husband.

In a society that had no government welfare system, a wife's property could be squandered by a profligate or drunken husband, leaving her without financial means if the husband died or abandoned her. By the 1850s, women's rights supporters convinced many state legislatures to pass Married Women's Separate Property Acts. These acts gave women the legal right to retain ownership and control of property they brought to the marriage.

Women also secured the right to have custody of their children after a DIVORCE. Traditionally, fathers retained custody of their children. This tradition weakened in the nineteenth century, as judges fashioned two doctrines governing CHILD CUSTODY. The "best-interest-of-the-child" doctrine balanced the new right of the mother to have custody of the child against the assessment of the needs of the child. The "TENDER YEARS" doctrine arose after the Civil War, giving mothers a presumptive right to their young children.

Reproductive Rights in the Nineteenth Century The fertility rate of white women declined steadily during the nineteenth century. In part this was the result of using BIRTH CONTROL and ABORTION to control family size. By the 1870s, a woman's right to make decisions about reproduction was restricted by federal and state laws. The most famous was the federal Comstock Law of 1873, which criminalized the transmission and receipt of "obscene," "lewd," or "lascivious" publications through the U.S. mail. The law specified that materials designed, adapted, or intended "for preventing conception or producing abortion" were included in the list of banned items. Some states passed laws banning the use of contraceptives.

A woman's opportunity to have an abortion was outlawed by the states during the latter part of the nineteenth century. Abortions, which increased markedly in the 1850s and 1860s, especially among middle-class white women, had been legal until the fetus "quickened," or moved inside the uterus. The American Medical Association and religious groups led the successful move to have state legislatures impose criminal penalties on persons performing abortions. In some states, the women who had abortions could also be held criminally liable.

The Modern Women's Rights Movement For many decades of the twentieth century, supporters of women's rights had little success in legislatures or in the courts. Gender inequality meant that women could legally be discriminated against in employment, education, and other important areas of everyday life. The CIVIL RIGHTS MOVEMENT of the 1960s drew the support of many college-educated women, much like the women who supported the abolitionist cause a little more than a hundred years before. Like their predecessors, these civil rights workers realized that discrimination based on race existed side by side with discrimination based on gender. The result was the birth of the modern feminist movement and the quest for women's rights.

Legislation Title VII of the Civil Rights Act of 1964 was a major step forward for women's rights. Title VII prohibited employment discrimination based on sex, giving women the ability to challenge the actions of employers or potential employers. The Pregnancy Discrimination Act of 1978 (PDA), 42 U.S.C.A. § 2000e(k), prohibits discrimination against employees on the basis of pregnancy and childbirth with respect to employment and benefits. The Equal Credit Opportunity Act, 15 U.S.C.A. § 1691, prohibits discrimination in the extension of CREDIT on the basis of sex or marital status. Title IX of the Education Amendments of 1972, 20 U.S.C.A. §§ 1681–1686, prohibits sex discrimination in educational institutions receiving federal financial assistance, and covers exclusion on the basis of sex from noncontact team sports. Title IX revolutionized women's collegiate athletics, forcing COLLEGES AND UNIVERSITIES to fund women's athletics at a level comparable to men's athletics.

The Equal Rights Amendment The Equal Rights Amendment was the central goal of the women's rights movement in the 1970s. Congress passed the ERA and sent it to the states for ratification on March 22, 1972. The operative language of the ERA stated, "Equality of rights under the law shall not be denied or abridged by the United States or by any State on account of sex." The effect of the amendment would have been limited to the actions of any government or government official, acting in his official capacity. In addition to its symbolic effect, the ERA would have shifted the burden of proof in litigation alleging discrimination from the person making the complaint to the public officials who were denying that the discrimination had occurred. Such an effect would have been significant, because the party with the responsibility for carrying the burden of proof must do so successfully or else lose the litigation.

Congress initially required the ERA to be ratified by three-fourths of the states (thirty-eight states) seven years from the time Congress sent the amendment to the states. By 1978 thirty-five of the thirty-eight states had ratified the amendment. Proponents of the ERA secured an extension of the ratification deadline to June 30, 1982. A determined effort by conservative groups opposed to the ERA prevented any additional states from ratifying the amendment by the 1982 deadline. However, some states have amended their constitutions to include an equal rights amendment.

Intermediate Judicial Scrutiny Without the Equal Rights Amendment, women's rights supporters faced a more difficult task in convincing the courts to set aside state laws and policies that perpetuated inequality and sex discrimination. The main constitutional tool for litigating women's rights cases has been the Equal Protection Clause of the Fourteenth Amendment. A key issue in equal protection analysis by the courts is what standard of judicial scrutiny to apply to the challenged legislation. Since the 1970s, the Supreme Court has applied "heightened" or "intermediate" judicial scrutiny to cases involving matters of discrimination based on sex.

In 1971 the Supreme Court, in *Reed v. Reed*, 404 U.S. 71, 92 S. Ct. 251, 30 L. Ed. 2d 225, extended the application of the Equal Protection Clause of the Fourteenth Amendment to gender-based discrimination. Women's rights supporters sought to have the Court include sex as a "suspect classification." The SUSPECT CLASSIFICATION doctrine holds that laws classifying people according to race, ethnicity, and religion are inherently suspect and are subject to the "strict scrutiny" test of JUDICIAL REVIEW. STRICT SCRUTINY forces the state to provide a COMPELLING STATE INTEREST for the challenged law and demonstrate that the law has been narrowly tailored to achieve its purpose. If a suspect classification is not involved, the Court will apply the "rational basis" test, which requires the state to provide any REASONABLE ground for the legislation. Under strict scrutiny, the government has a difficult burden to meet, while under rational basis, most laws will be upheld.

The Supreme Court has refused to make sex a suspect classification, but it did not impose the RATIONAL BASIS TEST on matters involving sex discrimination. Instead, the Court developed the intermediate or heightened scrutiny test. As articulated in *Craig v. Boren*, 429 U.S. 190, 97 S. Ct. 451, 50 L. Ed. 2d 397 (1976), "classifications by gender must serve *important* governmental objectives and must *be substantially related* to achievement of those objectives." Thus, intermediate scrutiny lies between strict scrutiny and rational basis.

The Supreme Court has sustained numerous challenges to gender-based discrimination, thereby mandating equal rights under the law. It has established the right of equality in laws dealing with survivors' benefits (*Weinberger v. Wiesenfeld*, 420 U.S. 636, 95 S. Ct. 1225, 43 L. Ed. 2d 514 [1975]), ALIMONY (*Orr v. Orr*, 440 U.S. 268, 99 S. Ct. 1102, 59 L. Ed. 2d 306 [1979]), sex-based mortality tables (*City of Los Angeles Department of Water and Power v. Manhart*, 435 U.S. 702, 98 S. Ct. 1370, 55 L. Ed. 2d 267 [1978]), and PENSIONS (*Arizona Governing Committee v. Norris*, 463 U.S. 1073, 103 S. Ct. 3492, 77 L. Ed. 2d 1236 [1983]).

Nevertheless, the Court has upheld laws that apply sex-based distinctions. In *Michael M. v. Superior Court*, 450 U.S. 464, 101 S. Ct. 1200, 67 L. Ed. 2d 437 (1981), the Court upheld a STATUTORY RAPE law that set different ages of consent for females and males. The Court also upheld, in *Rostker v. Goldberg*, 453 U.S. 57, 101 S. Ct. 2646, 69 L. Ed. 2d 478 (1981), the Military Selective Service Act (50 U.S.C.A. App. § 451 et seq.), passed by Congress in 1980, though only men are required to register.

The Court has granted women equal rights to attend publicly funded colleges and universities that have traditionally enrolled only men. In *United States v. Virginia*, __U.S.__, 116 S. Ct. 2264, 135 L. Ed. 2d 735 (1996), the Court ruled that the Virginia Military Institute (VMI), a publicly funded military college, must end its all-male enrollment policy and admit women. According to the Court, the all-male policy violated the Equal Protection Clause of the Fourteenth Amendment.

Reproductive Rights The reproductive rights of women were recognized by the Supreme Court in the 1960s and 1970s, overturning one hundred years of legislation that restricted birth control and banned legal abortions. In the 1980s and 1990s, however, the Court retreated, allowing states to place restrictions on abortion.

In *Griswold v. State of Connecticut*, 381 U.S. 479, 85 S. Ct. 1678, 14 L. Ed. 2d 510 (1965),

The Campaign to Defeat the ERA

After a fifty-year struggle, in March 1972 Congress approved the Equal Rights Amendment (ERA), a move that appeared to pave the way for the quick and easy adoption of the amendment by the states. Under the Constitution, thirty-eight states are required for ratification, and within a year of congressional approval, thirty states had ratified the amendment. At this point, however, a concerted opposition campaign stopped the momentum for the ERA dead in its tracks.

The most intense opposition to the ERA came from conservative religious and political organizations, including the right-wing John Birch Society and STOP ERA, a group led by conservative firebrand Phyllis S. Schlafly. Supporters of the ERA had cast it as mainly a tool to improve the economic position of women. Opponents, however, saw the amendment as a means of undermining traditional cultural values, especially those concerned with the family and the role of women in U.S. society. The U.S. Supreme Court's decision legalizing abortion,

Roe v. Wade, 410 U.S. 113, 93 S. Ct. 705, 35 L. Ed. 2d 147 (1973), also affected the ratification struggle, as the emerging right-to-life movement saw the ERA as an additional legal basis for a woman's right to an abortion.

During the 1970s and early 1980s, fierce lobbying took place in state legislatures that were considering the ERA. Opponents pointed out that during the U.S. Senate debate on the ERA, a host of amendments that would have restricted the reach of the amendment were defeated. These included prohibitions against drafting women into the military and allowing women to serve in combat. The defeat of other amendments to the ERA led opponents to claim that women would lose the right to child support and certain special privileges and exemptions based in state and federal law. Opponents also warned that the passage of the ERA would lead to unisex public toilet facilities and the abolition of traditionally gender-based segregated facilities. Finally, many opponents saw the ERA as a means to remove criminal laws dealing with homosexual acts.

Although the deadline for ratification was extended for thirty months, ERA supporters were never able to gain the additional states needed for ratification.

---

the Court struck down a Connecticut law that made the sale and possession of birth control devices to married couples a MISDEMEANOR. The law also prohibited anyone from assisting, abetting, or counseling another in the use of birth control devices. In *Griswold*, the Court announced that the Constitution contained a general, independent right of PRIVACY.

Seven years later, in *Eisenstadt v. Baird*, 405 U.S. 438, 92 S. Ct. 1029, 31 L. Ed. 2d 349 (1972), the Court struck down a Massachusetts law that banned the distribution of birth control devices. In this case, the Court established that the right of privacy is an individual right, not a right enjoyed only by married couples.

These two cases paved the way for *Roe v. Wade*, 410 U.S. 113, 93 S. Ct. 705, 35 L. Ed. 2d 147 (1973), which struck down a Texas law that banned abortions. Writing for the majority, Justice HARRY A. BLACKMUN concluded that the right to privacy "is broad enough to encompass a woman's decision whether or not to terminate her pregnancy." More importantly, he stated that the right of privacy is a fundamental right. This meant that the state of Texas had to meet the strict scrutiny test of constitutional review. The Court held that Texas' interest in preventing abortion did not become compelling until

that point in pregnancy when the fetus becomes "viable" (capable of "meaningful life outside the mother's womb"). Beyond the point of viability, the Court held that the state may prohibit abortion, except in cases where it is necessary to preserve the life or health of the mother.

The *Roe* decision provided women with the right to continue or terminate a pregnancy, at least up to the point of viability. However, by the 1980s, a more conservative Supreme Court began upholding state laws that placed restrictions on this right. In *Webster v. Reproductive Health Services*, 492 U.S. 490, 109 S. Ct. 3040, 106 L. Ed. 2d 410 (1989), the Court upheld a Missouri law that forbids state employees from performing or assisting in abortions, or counseling women to have abortions. It also prohibited the use of state facilities for these purposes and required all doctors who would perform abortions to conduct viability tests on fetuses at or beyond twenty weeks' gestation. Though it appeared that the Court might overturn *Roe* in *Planned Parenthood v. Casey*, 505 U.S. 833, 112 S. Ct. 2791, 120 L. Ed. 2d 674 (1992), it reaffirmed the essential holding of *Roe* that the constitutional right of privacy is broad enough to include a woman's decision to terminate her pregnancy.

Domestic Violence The right of women to be free from DOMESTIC VIOLENCE has drawn increasing concern and support since the 1970s. The issue of spousal abuse, in which most of the victims are women, has led to changes in state and federal law. Many states have repealed laws that prevented a wife from filing a marital RAPE charge against her husband. State laws have been toughened against domestic violence and many court systems have attempted to be more consistent in enforcing and prosecuting these laws. A spouse who has been attacked or harassed by a marital partner may obtain an order for protection, which prohibits the aggressor from contacting the victim. The federal Violence Against Women Act, passed in 1994 (108 Stat. 1796, 1902), seeks to ensure that orders for protection are given full faith and credit in every state, not just in the state where the order was made. Persons who commit domestic abuse are banned from possessing a firearm and anyone facing a RESTRAINING ORDER for domestic abuse is prohibited from possessing a firearm. In addition, the law established a federal CAUSE OF ACTION for gender-motivated violence. Victims of a FELONY crime of violence may bring a civil suit for damages or equitable relief in federal or state court.

CROSS-REFERENCES

Dworkin, Andrea; Family Law; Fetal Rights; Friedan, Betty; *Griswold v. Connecticut*; Ireland, Patricia; MacKinnon, Catharine; Millett, Katherine; National Organization for Women; Pornography; *Roe v. Wade*; Sexual Harassment; Steinem, Gloria; *United States v. Virginia*.

WOODBURY, LEVI

Levi Woodbury served on the U.S. Supreme Court as an associate justice from 1845 to 1851. Woodbury's career encompassed a range of positions in state and federal government. By the time of his nomination by President JAMES K. POLK, he had served as a state judge, governor, U.S. senator, and as secretary of both the U.S. Navy and Treasury. A lifelong advocate of STATES' RIGHTS, this position guided him throughout his brief tenure on the Court. He rarely stood out except in the occasional instance when he dissented. A proponent of SLAVERY, he worried about the Court's poten-

"I CARRY WITH ME, AS A CONTROLLING PRINCIPLE, THE PROPOSITION THAT STATE POWERS, STATE RIGHTS, AND STATE DECISIONS ARE TO BE UPHELD WHEN THE OBJECTION TO THEM IS NOT CLEAR."

BIOGRAPHY

ARTIST UNKNOWN, COLLECTION OF THE SUPREME COURT OF THE UNITED STATES.

Levi Woodbury

tial for exacerbating national tensions over the volatile issue.

Woodbury was born on December 22, 1789, in Francestown, New Hampshire. He graduated from Dartmouth College in 1809 and then studied at the LITCHFIELD LAW SCHOOL. After his admission to the New Hampshire bar in 1812, he began practicing law while gradually preparing himself for politics. In 1816 he served as clerk of the state senate, and in 1817 entered the judiciary as associate justice of the New Hampshire Superior Court.

Woodbury was passionate about states' rights, the cause of the Jeffersonian Republicans. His marriage in 1819 to Elizabeth Clapp, the daughter of a wealthy merchant, helped advance his aspirations, and in 1823 he won election as governor of New Hampshire. In 1825 he became speaker of the state House of Representatives, and then served two terms as a U.S. senator, from 1825 to 1831 and from 1841 to 1845. During the interim, he served twice in the cabinet of President ANDREW JACKSON: first as U.S. secretary of the Navy (1831-1834) and then as U.S. secretary of the Treasury (1834-1841), a position he held for the first four years of MARTIN VAN BUREN's administration also.

In 1845 Polk chose Woodbury to fill the vacancy left by the death of Justice JOSEPH STORY. The Court was led by Chief Justice ROGER BROOKE TANEY, whom Woodbury often joined in decisions. Notably, he generally agreed with the majority on the Taney Court in its reading of the U.S. Constitution's Contract Clause. The Contract Clause was an important subject of constitutional interpretation during the era, and the Court invoked it in order to limit the power of states to regulate business and economic matters.

Woodbury left no landmark opinions. However, he occasionally dissented when he thought the Court was trampling the rights of states: he dissented from the Court's decisions to extend the boundaries of federal jurisdiction over national waters and, in the so-called *Passenger Cases* of 1849, to strike down state laws that provided for taxing immigrants upon their arrival.

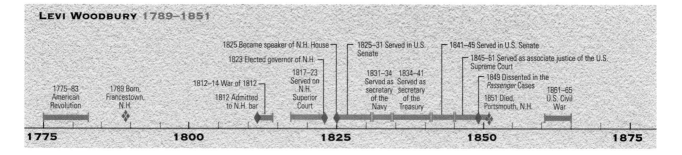

LEVI WOODBURY 1789-1851

1775-83 American Revolution

1789 Born, Francestown, N.H.

1812-14 War of 1812

1812 Admitted to N.H. bar

1817-23 Served on N.H. Superior Court

1823 Elected governor of N.H.

1825 Became speaker of N.H. House

1825-31 Served in U.S. Senate

1831-34 Served as secretary of the Navy

1834-41 Served as secretary of the Treasury

1841-45 Served in U.S. Senate

1845-51 Served as associate justice of the U.S. Supreme Court

1849 Dissented in the *Passenger* Cases

1851 Died, Portsmouth, N.H.

1861-65 U.S. Civil War

1775   1800   1825   1850   1875

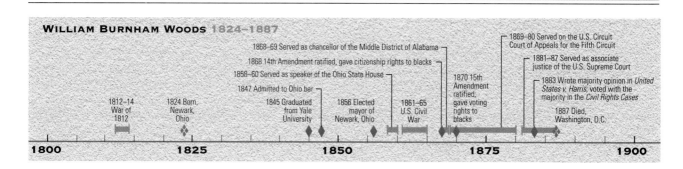

WILLIAM BURNHAM WOODS 1824–1887

- 1869–80 Served on the U.S. Circuit Court of Appeals for the Fifth Circuit
- 1868–69 Served as chancellor of the Middle District of Alabama
- 1868 14th Amendment ratified, gave citizenship rights to blacks
- 1858–60 Served as speaker of the Ohio State House
- 1847 Admitted to Ohio bar
- 1881–87 Served as associate justice of the U.S. Supreme Court
- 1883 Wrote majority opinion in *United States v. Harris;* voted with the majority in the *Civil Rights Cases*
- 1812–14 War of 1812
- 1824 Born, Newark, Ohio
- 1845 Graduated from Yale University
- 1856 Elected mayor of Newark, Ohio
- 1861–65 U.S. Civil War
- 1870 15th Amendment ratified; gave voting rights to blacks
- 1887 Died, Washington, D.C.

1800   1825   1850   1875   1900

WOODS, WILLIAM BURNHAM William Burnham Woods served on the U.S. Supreme Court as an associate justice from 1881 to 1887. Woods's legal career led him into politics in his native Ohio, where he was a mayor and a member of the Ohio General Assembly before the Civil War. In the war, he fought on the side of the Union as a commander, and afterward he moved to Alabama where he began a judicial career in the late 1860s. President RUTHERFORD B. HAYES appointed Woods to the U.S. Supreme Court, where his conservative philosophy generally favored states' rights over federal power.

Born on August 3, 1824, in Newark, Ohio, Woods was the son of a farmer. He attended Western Reserve College, graduated from Yale University in 1845, and was admitted to the Ohio bar in 1847. Over the next fourteen years, he practiced law while involving himself in the state's Democratic party. He mounted a successful campaign for the mayoralty of Newark in 1856, and twice won election to the Ohio General Assembly where he served from 1857 to 1861.

When the Civil War began, Woods volunteered for an Ohio regiment. He fought for the Union in several battles, including Shiloh and Vicksburg, and gradually rose through the ranks. By the time the war was drawing to a close, he was a commander under General William T. Sherman. Woods led Sherman's troops in the brutal march to the sea in Georgia that destroyed all the cities and towns between Atlanta and Savannah.

After the war, Woods changed his life. He left Ohio and moved to Alabama, became a Republican, and commenced a judicial career. In 1868 he served as chancellor of the state's Middle Chancery Division of Alabama, which made him the presiding judge of the state's EQUITY courts, the now-antiquated system of justice that dealt with common claims. He held the position until 1880, when his reputation prompted President ULYSSES S. GRANT to appoint him a U.S. district judge in the Fifth Circuit. Woods's judicial conservatism began to

William Burnham Woods

"THE RIGHTS . . . ENUMERATED IN THE FIRST EIGHT . . . AMENDMENT[S] OF THE CONSTITUTION OF THE UNITED STATES ARE [IPSO FACTO] FUNDAMENTAL PRIVILEGES OF THE CITIZENS OF THE UNITED STATES . . . AND THE STATES ARE INHIBITED FROM IMPAIRING OR ABRIDGING THEM."

develop during this period; however, he still took a somewhat tolerant view of federal power, especially with regard to the government's power to protect CIVIL RIGHTS.

In 1881 President Hayes nominated Woods to the U.S. Supreme Court. Once in the Court's conservative majority, his judicial priorities changed. Following the Civil War, Congress had enacted new civil rights laws aimed at ending racial discrimination; equally important to this end was the ratification of the FOURTEENTH AMENDMENT to the U.S. Constitution in 1868. But the Supreme Court soon undermined these efforts. In 1883 it struck down provisions of the Civil Rights Act of 1875; Woods joined in the 8 to 1 majority in the so-called CIVIL RIGHTS CASES, 109 U.S. 3, 3 S. Ct. 18, 27 L. Ed. 835.

Woods's intolerance for federal reform efforts marked his last years on the Court. Like the majority of the justices, he took a narrow view of the Fourteenth Amendment. He wrote the majority opinion in *United States v. Harris*, 106 U.S. 629, 1 S. Ct. 601, 16 Otto 629, 27 L. Ed. 290 (1883), which held unconstitutional a federal law protecting African Americans from the terrorist KU KLUX KLAN organization. Woods stated that such powers properly belonged to states rather than the federal government. He died on May 14, 1887, in Washington D.C.

WOODS AND FORESTS 📖 A comprehensive term for a large collection of trees in their natural setting and the property on which they stand. 📖

State and federal laws govern the harvesting, reforestation, and other uses of woods and forests. The federal government maintains a system of national forests under the direction of the Forest Service, and most states also have forested land set aside as reserves.

State Regulation A state may properly compel and encourage private owners to participate in programs for the reforestation of land. It can mandate that private property owners who are engaged in commercial lumbering operations provide for reforesting by leaving a certain number of trees for reseeding purposes, or by restocking the area with seedlings. The property owner's LOGGING permit can be granted with the condition that he participate in the reforestation program.

A state can also give its forestry department the authority to arrange for the planting of roadside trees and to regulate the cutting and trimming of trees along the highways. In addition, various state statutes have been enacted to provide for the nurture and protection of shade and ornamental trees on public streets and highways. These statutes are based on a state's POLICE POWER, which is to be used to promote the GENERAL WELFARE of its citizens.

State laws require precautions to be taken against forest fires. The state can prevent property owners from setting fires during the summer without permission, or it can authorize a state forester to determine whether an owner of forest land has provided sufficient protection against fire. During drought periods, when the fire danger is increased, the public may be prohibited from entering forests and woodlands.

National and State Forests Since the early twentieth century it has been federal policy to reserve federally owned wooded areas as national forests. The goal is to improve and protect these areas so they can provide timber to be used by the public. Congress has the authority to provide for the development and maintenance of national forests and to acquire land for such purposes. Federal laws and regulations concerning national forests and their protection are paramount and preempt conflicting state laws. The Forest Service, which is a branch of the Department of Agriculture, manages and regulates national forests and grasslands.

When a national forest is created, the reserved land is no longer subject to use for private purposes, except according to applicable statutes and regulations. The Forest Service can, therefore, issue permits for the occupancy of and the cutting of timber within national forests.

The granting of logging rights to private companies has proved controversial since the mid-1960s, when the practice of clearcutting was introduced. Clearcutting is a method of harvesting and regenerating timber in which all trees are cleared from a site and a new, even-aged stand of timber is grown. Many conservation and citizen groups object to clearcutting in the national forests, citing soil and water degradation, unsightly landscapes, over-harvesting, destruction of diversity of plants and animals,

National Forest System, 1970 to 1993

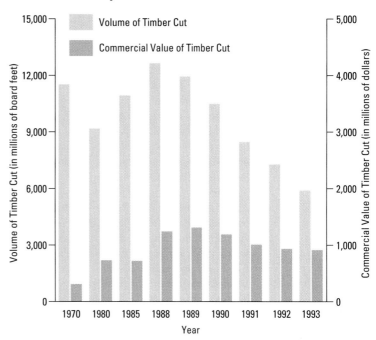

For fiscal years ending in year shown. Volume is in million board feet. Commercial value is in millions of dollars.

Source: U.S. Forest Service, Agriculture Statistics, annual; and unpublished data.

and other damages and abuses. Clearcutting accounted for sixty-three percent of the national forest area harvested between 1984 and 1994. Beginning in 1992, however, the Forest Service modified its policies to reduce clearcutting.

A portion of the proceeds from the use of national forests is given to the state in which the forest is located. The funds are to be spent for the benefit of public schools and roads in the counties that encompass the forest.

Generally a state can create forest reserves when they are reasonably necessary to promote the public welfare. A state can also levy taxes for the support of such forests.

See also ENVIRONMENTAL LAW.

WORCESTER v. GEORGIA The settling of North America by white persons involved the displacement of Native Americans, who lived in tribal societies throughout the continent. During the colonial period, many wars took place between settlers and Native Americans. The colonists ultimately prevailed in these conflicts and negotiated treaties that required the tribes to give up much of their territory. After the formation of the United States, state and federal government leaders agreed that the nation needed to establish a national policy toward Native Americans. By the 1820s the solution to the "Indian problem" had become their removal and resettlement in the "Great American

Desert" to the west. In 1830 Congress passed the Indian Removal Act (4 Stat. 411) and appropriated $500,000 for that purpose.

In the 1830s the Cherokee Indians used the U.S. legal system to assert their TREATY rights and seek protection from the encroachment of the Georgia state government. In *Cherokee Nation v. Georgia*, 30 U.S. (5 Pet.) 1, 8 L. Ed. 25 (1831), and *Worcester v. Georgia*, 31 U.S. (6 Pet.) 515, 8 L. Ed. 483 (1832), the U.S. Supreme Court wrestled with the issue of Indian tribal sovereignty. Were Indian tribes independent nations akin to foreign states such as Great Britain and France?

In *Cherokee Nation*, the Cherokee contended that they were a foreign state and therefore could sue the state of Georgia in federal court under diversity JURISDICTION. Chief Justice JOHN MARSHALL ruled that FEDERAL COURTS had no jurisdiction over such a case because Indian tribes were merely "domestic dependent nations" existing "in a state of pupilage. Their relation to the United States resembles that of a ward to his guardian." The decision established the premise that Indian nations do not possess all of the attributes of SOVEREIGNTY that the word *nation* normally implies.

In *Worcester*, while not overruling *Cherokee Nation*, Marshall issued the opinion of the Court that the Cherokee were a nation with the right to retain independent political communities. Georgia had passed legislation making it a crime for white persons to live in Cherokee country without first obtaining a LICENSE from the state. The Cherokee challenged this license requirement. The Supreme Court agreed with the Cherokee and held that the Georgia laws were unconstitutional because they violated treaties, the Contract and Commerce Clauses of the Constitution, and the sovereign authority of the Cherokee nation.

The case arose when Georgia indicted Samuel A. Worcester, a missionary of the American Board of Commissioners for Foreign Missions, and six other white persons for the offense of "residing within the limits of the Cherokee nation without a license." All seven defendants were convicted and sentenced to four years in prison.

Worcester and the other defendants appealed to the Supreme Court, arguing that Georgia had no jurisdiction over Cherokee sovereign territory. Under the Constitution, Congress has the power to regulate commerce with the Indian tribes. The Indian Commerce Clause (Article I, Section 8, Clause 3) is the main source of federal power over Indian tribes. Worcester contended that this clause demonstrated that the federal government had exclusive jurisdiction over the establishment and regulation of intercourse with the Indians. In addition, Worcester pointed to treaties between the United States and the Cherokee nation. No state could interfere with these agreements, which were the supreme law of the land.

Chief Justice Marshall, writing for the majority, agreed with Worcester's legal position and found that the relationship between the existing treaties and the constitutionality of the state law was the paramount issue. Marshall reviewed the colonizing of the continent and noted that the colonists' legal basis for claiming the land as their own was questionable:

> It is difficult to comprehend the proposition, that the inhabitants of either quarter of the globe could have rightful original claims of dominion over the inhabitants of the other, or over the lands they occupied; or that the discovery of either by the other should give the discoverer rights in the country discovered, which annulled the pre-existing rights of its ancient possessors.

Marshall analyzed two treaties negotiated between the United States and the Cherokee. He found that these agreements recognized the national character of the Cherokee and their right of self-government. In addition, the treaties guaranteed their lands, and the federal government assumed the duty of protecting the integrity of the agreement.

Marshall then pointed out that from the beginning of the Republic, Congress had enacted a series of laws to regulate trade and intercourse with Indian tribes. These laws treated the tribes as nations, respected their rights, and sought to give the tribes the protection that the treaties stipulated. He concluded that "Indian nations are distinct political communities, having territorial boundaries, within which their authority is exclusive, and having a right to all the lands within those boundaries, which is not only acknowledged, but guaranteed by the United States."

In light of *Cherokee Nation*, a key question was whether a treaty negotiated with Indians should be treated differently than one negotiated with a foreign nation. Marshall concluded that it should not.

> The words "treaty" and "nation" are words of our own language, selected in our diplomatic and legislative proceedings, by ourselves, having each a definite and well understood meaning. We have applied them to Indians, as we have applied them to the other nations of the earth. They are applied to all in the same sense.

Therefore, Marshall ruled that the Cherokee nation was a "distinct community occupying its own territory," where the laws of Georgia had no force. The Cherokee were vested with the power to determine whether the citizens of Georgia could enter their territory, subject to treaty provisions and acts of Congress. He concluded that "the whole intercourse between the United States and this nation, is, by our constitution and laws, vested in the government of the United States."

The decisions involving the Cherokee nation established the basic principles of Indian sovereignty. Indian tribes, by occupying North America, possessed some elements of preexisting sovereignty. This sovereignty could be diminished or eliminated by the United States, but not by the individual states. Finally, because the tribes had limited sovereignty and were dependent on the United States for protection, the United States had a TRUST responsibility. This meant that the U.S. government was a trustee with the duty of looking after the best interests of Native Americans, who were wards of the government.

The legal victory proved of little benefit to the Cherokee nation, however. The demand for land in Georgia grew more intense after gold was discovered on Cherokee land. More ominously, President ANDREW JACKSON, who favored the removal of the Cherokee nation and other Indian tribes, refused to enforce the Court's decision. His refusal illustrated the problem that occurs when one branch of government refuses to honor the decision of another branch. During Jackson's term of office (1829–1837), ninety-four removal treaties were negotiated, demonstrating his resolve to move the Indian tribes westward.

In December 1835 the Treaty of New Echota, signed by a small minority of the Cherokee, ceded to the United States all their land east of the Mississippi River for $5 million. Though the tribe sought to repudiate the treaty, they were unsuccessful. Under the Indian Removal Act, the Cherokee were forced to leave Georgia beginning in 1838. Nearly a quarter of the 15,000 Cherokee died during the relocation. The Cherokee called the western trek to Oklahoma and Indian Territory the "Trail of Tears."

See also NATIVE AMERICAN RIGHTS.

WORDS AND PHRASES® 📖 A multivolume set of law books published by West Group containing thousands of judicial definitions of words and phrases, arranged alphabetically, from 1658 to the present. 📖

Words and Phrases is a legal research and reference work that is aimed primarily at law-

yers. It was first published in 1940 and has been continuously updated since then. It contains words and phrases that have taken on special meaning in the law.

The interpretation or meaning attributed to a word or phrase in a statute, court rule, administrative regulation, business document, or agreement often determines rights, duties, obligations, and liabilities of the parties. Many court decisions are based on the meaning attributed by an APPELLATE COURT to a single word or phrase. *Words and Phrases* allows a person to hone in on pertinent cases by selecting key words or phrases contained in a document.

Prior to the introduction of online and CD-ROM legal research tools, a work such as *Words and Phrases* played a key role in legal research by leading the researcher to a PRIMARY AUTHORITY, such as a case, statute, or constitutional provision. In 1996 WESTLAW introduced *Words and Phrases* as part of its online service. Whenever possible, *Words and Phrases* entries are written in the exact language the court employed.

WORDS OF ART 📖 The vocabulary or terminology of a particular art, science, or profession, particularly those expressions that are peculiar to it. 📖

Though a society may share a common language, there are many specialized uses of words based on human activities. An examination of any profession, for example, will yield many expressions that are idiomatic or peculiar to it. For the person working within the profession, these become words of art, which usually convey a meaning much different from the normal use of these words, or which may be completely baffling to an outsider.

Because the law is based on the expression of language, it contains thousands of words of art. Many persons working outside the legal profession would recognize that "taking the Fifth" means that a person is asserting his or her protection against self-incrimination under the Fifth Amendment to the U.S. Constitution. However, very few persons would understand that an *appellant* is the party bringing an appeal, while a *respondent* is the party against whom the appeal is taken. *Appellant* and *respondent* are words of art.

See also TERMS OF ART.

WORDS OF LIMITATION 📖 The words in a DEED or WILL that indicate what type of ESTATE or rights the person being given land receives. 📖

Words of limitation are used to indicate the duration or terms of the CONVEYANCE of REAL PROPERTY. There are many types of limitations that can be expressed in a deed or a will. For example, a GRANTOR might make a deed that conveys a parcel of land "to A until B marries." A's estate is restricted by these words of limitation, since A is given the land for only a specified length of time (the time before B marries).

A grantor may also place restrictions on who may receive property by employing words of limitation. For example, a grantor might convey property "to A and the heirs of her body." The words *heirs of her body* limit the persons who can inherit the property and are, therefore, recognized as words of limitation.

WORDS OF PURCHASE 📖 Language used in connection with a TRANSFER of REAL PROPERTY that identifies the grantees or designees who take the interest being conveyed by DEED or WILL. 📖

The term *words of purchase* is a technical conveyancing expression, a TERM OF ART in real property law that has nothing to do with the ordinary meanings of the word *purchase.*

The word *purchase* in the expression means that real property is being transferred by deed or will, not inherited through the laws of DESCENT AND DISTRIBUTION. Whether the property is bought or given away, if the transfer is by deed or will, it is a purchase in this usage.

The act or process of acquiring real property by deed or will is called taking by purchase, even though it was a GIFT. The person who acquires real property by deed or will is called a purchaser, even though this person may have paid nothing.

Words of purchase are the words in a deed or will that tell who takes an interest in real property. The expression is contrasted with words of limitation, which are words in a deed or will that tell how long that interest will last. For example, in a deed to Whiteacre "To A for life," *To A* are words of purchase, *for life* are words of limitation.

WORKERS' COMPENSATION 📖 A system whereby an employer must pay, or provide INSURANCE to pay, the lost wages and medical expenses of an employee who is injured on the job. 📖

Workers' compensation law is governed by statutes in every state. Specific laws vary with each JURISDICTION, but key features are consistent. An employee is automatically entitled to receive certain benefits when she suffers an occupational disease or accidental PERSONAL INJURY arising out of and in the COURSE OF EMPLOYMENT. Such benefits may include cash or wage-loss benefits, medical and career rehabilitation benefits, and in the case of accidental death of an employee, benefits to dependents. The NEGLIGENCE and FAULT of either the employer or the

employee usually are IMMATERIAL. INDEPENDENT CONTRACTORS are not entitled to workers' compensation benefits, and in some states domestic workers and agricultural workers are excluded or only partially covered.

It is the goal of workers' compensation to return the injured employee quickly and economically to the status of productive worker without unduly harming the employer's business. A worker whose INJURY is covered by the workers' compensation statute loses the COMMON-LAW right to sue the employer for that injury, but injured workers may still sue third parties whose negligence contributed to the work injury. For example, a truck driver injured in a rear-end collision by an unemployed third party would be entitled to collect workers' compensation and also to sue the third party for negligence. In such cases a plaintiff who recovers money from a third-party lawsuit must first repay the employer or INSURER that paid workers' compensation benefits. The plaintiff may keep any remaining money. Many jurisdictions permit the employer or its insurer to sue negligent third parties on the employee's behalf to recover funds paid as workers' compensation benefits.

In most states parties to workers' compensation disputes resolve them in an administrative, rather than judicial, tribunal. Courts usually relax the standard rules of procedure, EVIDENCE, and conflict of laws to allow for expediency and simplicity in keeping with the goal of getting an injured worker the benefits necessary to return to work.

Health Expenditures for Workers' Compensation Injuries, 1960–1993

Includes medical benefits paid under public law by private insurance carriers and self-insurers.

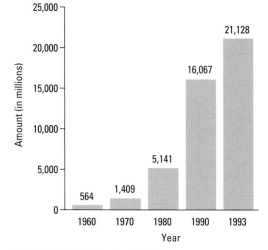

Source: U.S. Health Care Financing Administration

Workers' compensation statutes require most employers to purchase private or state-funded insurance, or to self-insure, to make certain that injured workers receive proper benefits. The cost of insurance is reflected in the cost of goods or services produced by the employer; thus the cost of workers' compensation LIABILITY is passed ultimately to consumers.

Workers' compensation law is somewhat unique in that negligent acts of either the employer or the injured employee generally are irrelevant to the determination of compensability. Victims of injuries not related to work in most cases must prove the negligence of another party before recovering money in a lawsuit. Conversely, a defendant in a personal injury lawsuit may avoid or mitigate liability to a plaintiff whose own negligence caused or contributed to the personal injury. Yet workers' compensation is a no-fault law, and an employee's negligence or an employer's lack of negligence is usually not a factor.

The underlying social philosophy of this no-fault system is evident when one considers what would happen without workers' compensation. For example, assume a responsible employer encourages a safe workplace and implements a rule requiring workers to obtain the assistance of a coworker before climbing a tall ladder to a storage area. One employee, hurrying to get her work done for the day, ignores this rule and climbs the ladder without assistance. When she reaches the top of the ladder, it shifts and she falls, injuring her spine and paralyzing her legs.

Society could choose to treat this injured worker in one of three basic ways. It could refuse to render any aid, instead forcing the injured worker to seek help from friends or family. If the worker was without ties to persons both willing and able to assist, this plan would leave her destitute. A second option would be to give her government aid, or WELFARE, such as MEDICAID or food stamps. This alternative would be less speculative but still not ideal because it would force local taxpayers to pay for the worker's benefits regardless of whether they had any connection to the injury.

The third solution is the workers' compensation system. This system preserves the injured worker's dignity and well-being by providing an income and medical care and keeping her off welfare. The system passes the cost of compensating injured workers to consumers of products that, through their manufacture, cause the workers to get injured. Thus the social philosophy underlying workers' compensation is the efficient and dignified provision of financial and medical benefits to those injured on the job and the allocation of the expense to an appropriate source: the consumer.

Workers' compensation is also distinguishable from other personal injury laws where negligence is a factor because although the employer is liable for paying injured workers' benefits, the purpose of workers' compensation is not to punish or hurt the employer. For this reason, an integral component of workers' compensation is the requirement that employers purchase workers' compensation insurance, or provide a self-insured fund, to pay the benefits. This way, the employer can pass along the cost of insurance to the purchasers of the employer's product.

History Workers' compensation laws in the United States developed during the early 1900s as a result of the industrial age and growing numbers of industrial injuries. Before these laws were developed, workers injured on the job often found themselves without remedy against their employer or their fellow workers.

The law of VICARIOUS LIABILITY developed in England in approximately 1700 to make the master, or employer, liable for the acts of the servant, or employee. Yet the 1837 English case *Priestly v. Fowler*, 3 M. & W. 1, 150 Reprint 1030, created the fellow servant exception to the general rule of a master's vicarious liability; no longer would the master be held liable for an employee's negligence in causing injury to a coworker.

After *Priestly*, courts in the 1800s continued to develop employer defenses to liability for injured workers. One such defense, ASSUMPTION OF THE RISK, allowed employers to escape liability with the questionable logic that employees could avoid or decline dangerous work duties. Another defense, contributory negligence, allowed employers to escape liability, notwithstanding the employer's negligence, where the employee was also negligent. Therefore, during a century of burgeoning industry and its inherent risk of work-related accidents, workers faced nonexistent or inadequate remedies for their injuries.

At the end of the nineteenth century, state lawmakers recognized the problem and began studying the compensation system developed in Germany in 1884. Rooted largely in its socialistic tradition, Germany's compensation system mandated that employers and employees share in the cost of paying benefits to workers disabled by sickness, accident, or old age. Britain followed suit in 1897 with the British Compensation Act, which later became the model for many state workers' compensation laws in the

United States. In 1910 representatives of various state commissions met at a conference in Chicago and drafted the Uniform Workmen's Compensation Law. Although not overwhelmingly adopted, this uniform law became the blueprint for state workers' compensation statutes. All but eight states had adopted a workers' compensation law by 1920, and in 1963 Hawaii became the last state to do so.

Accident and Injury Workers' compensation benefits are most commonly provided to workers who are injured by a specific accident on the job, such as the worker who trips and falls down the employer's staircase, or the worker who gets a hand caught in factory machinery. But a compensable accidental injury might also include an OCCUPATIONAL DISEASE, such as an employee's lung disease that resulted from his exposure to asbestos in the workplace. Cumulative trauma associated with work duties, such as carpal tunnel syndrome caused by repetitive keyboard work, also can be compensable.

Jurisdictions differ as to whether work-related mental illness is compensable. In the majority of states, mental illness caused by work, such as stress, anxiety, or depression, is not compensable. A common exception to this rule exists when a specific accident or injury at work leads to mental illness. For example, an employee who suffers from panic attacks upon hearing the phone ring at work generally will not be entitled to workers' compensation benefits. But an employee who witnesses a vicious ASSAULT AND BATTERY at work, and who then develops anxiety and panic attacks as a result, would be entitled to compensation in most jurisdictions.

Requirements for Benefits An injured worker is entitled to workers' compensation benefits only if the injury arose out of and in the course of employment. The first part of this requirement, "arising out of employment," ensures that there is a causal connection between the work and the injury. Usually the employee has the burden of proving that the injury was caused by exposure to an increased RISK from employment.

In determining whether an injury is compensable, it is helpful to categorize the risk causing the injury in one of three ways. First, there is the risk that is associated distinctly with the employment. An example would be a house painter injured in a fall from a scaffold; the house painter would not have been on the scaffold but for his employment. This type of injury is always compensable as arising out of employment.

The second category of risk is risk that is personal to the claimant. An example is a worker who develops lung cancer due to years of smoking. Assuming this cancer was not caused by carcinogens in the workplace and would have developed notwithstanding employment, the disease would be considered personal and not arising out of employment. Injuries from purely personal risks are never compensable.

The third category of risk, neutral risk, is the most problematic in determining the compensability of a work injury. Neutral risks are neither distinct to the employment nor distinctly personal. Examples would include a teacher shot in a drive-by shooting while standing in his classroom; an auto mechanic bitten by a stray dog while dumping oil into an outdoor receptacle; and an executive struck by lightning when walking to his car after a meeting.

Whether an injury resulting from a neutral risk is compensable is difficult to predict and often depends on the jurisdiction of the tribunal, the nature of the injury, and the precise facts surrounding the accident. For example, injuries caused by lightning are usually compensable if the claimant can show that the work conditions increased the risk of being struck. An employee struck while working atop a metal electric pole likely would receive workers' compensation benefits for a lightning injury or death, whereas an employee struck walking to her car after her work shift would have a more difficult time collecting benefits. In *Reich v. A. Reich & Sons Gardens, Inc.*, 485 S.W. 2d 133 (Mo. Ct. App. 1972), the employee was killed by lightning while standing next to several vehicles in a wheat field. The court deemed the death compensable, citing TESTIMONY that the employee's risk of being hit by lightning was greater than that of other people in the vicinity, who were sheltered in cars and buildings and were not standing in an open field.

Using the same logic, injuries from sunstroke, freezing, and other effects of heat and cold exposure arise out of the course of employment if the employee can show that such exposure was greater than that to which the general public was exposed. Workers who contract contagious diseases at work will receive benefits upon a showing that the workplace offered an increased risk of exposure.

Another type of neutral-risk injury is an ASSAULT. Most courts will deem an assault as arising out of the course of employment if the nature or setting of the work increased the risk of assault or if a quarrel that led to the assault originated at work. In *Bryan v. Best Western/*

Coachman's Inn, 885 S.W.2d 28 (Ark. 1994), the claimant worked as a security guard at a motel. The claimant and the motel night clerk were involved in a personal dispute, which led to a fight between the claimant and the night clerk's boyfriend, injuring the claimant. The court held that even though the dispute was personal and not related to work, the claimant, because of his job, faced an increased risk of assault. His injuries therefore were compensable.

Even idiopathic injuries, or injuries resulting from risks personal to the employee as opposed to risks associated with the job, may be compensable if the job contributes to the risk or aggravates the injury. An employee who misses breakfast and suffers a fainting spell ordinarily will not be entitled to workers' compensation, because the fainting spell does not arise out of employment. But if the same worker faints and in so doing hits her head on her desk and fractures her skull, her injury will be compensable. In *Silverman v. Roth*, 9 A.D.2d 591, 189 N.Y.S.2d 311 (1959), the employee died of heart failure after suffering a heart attack and falling from a ladder. The precise sequence of events was impossible to determine. Nevertheless, the court awarded benefits, citing evidence that even if the heart attack occurred before the fall from the ladder, the heart condition would have been aggravated by the shock of the fall, and thus the fall from the ladder was a contributing factor in the employee's death.

In addition to the requirement that an injury arise out of employment, the employee seeking workers' compensation also must show that the injury arose "in the course of employment." To arise in the course of employment, the injury must take place within the employment period, in a location where it is reasonable for the employee to be, and while the employee is fulfilling work duties. This does not mean that the employee must actually be doing his job, or doing it within the precise work hours, when the injury occurs for it to be compensable. Distinguishing between injuries that do or do not arise out of the course of employment is often a difficult and confusing task.

One common issue arises when an employee is injured going to or from work. Clearly, employment necessitates that an employee travel to work and home again. Yet it is not the purpose of workers' compensation to protect the employee from the risk of travel. Courts have, through the years, reached a compromise: an employee with fixed hours and work locale going to or coming from work generally is covered by workers' compensation if the injury occurs on the employer's premises.

This rule can lead to rather harsh results, as in *Heim v. Longview Fibre Co.*, 41 Wash. App. 745, 707 P.2d 689 (1985). There, the claimant was driving his motorcycle through the usual exit from his employer's premises when a co-worker turning into the premises hit the claimant, killing him. The precise location of the crash was fewer than five feet from the employer's property, on a public access road to the plant used by company personnel. Nevertheless, the court held that the injury did not arise in the course of employment and denied death benefits. Employees injured off work premises may still recover damages in tort against any persons whose negligence caused them harm.

Some courts, recognizing the harshness of the premises rule, have attempted to extend the premises rule to include injuries that occur within a reasonable distance of the employer's premises. And most courts recognize the compensability of an injury that occurs off the employer's premises when an employee is going to or coming from work, where the trip itself is a substantial part of the employee's service to the employer. In *Urban v. Industrial Commission*, 34 Ill. 2d 159, 214 N.E.2d 737 (Ill. App. Ct. 1966), the employee, a traveling salesperson, was killed in a car accident while driving in the direction of his home, although the evidence was not clear that he was actually returning home. The court ruled the death to be compensable.

Benefits Workers' compensation provides two general categories of benefits to injured workers: INDEMNITY benefits and medical benefits. Indemnity benefits compensate for the worker's loss of income or earning capacity resulting from the work-related injury. Depending on the employee's medical status and ability to work following the injury, she may be

Construction work can be very dangerous, requiring workers to perform tasks high above the ground. Worker's compensation benefits were designed to provide income for workers who become injured on the job.

entitled to different types of indemnity benefits. A worker whose injury is only temporary and does not preclude her ability to work her normal job duties and hours typically will not receive indemnity benefits because her injury has no effect on her ability to earn a living. A worker whose injury temporarily causes him to miss time from work will be entitled to payment of all or a portion of his lost wages, known as temporary partial disability benefits. A worker whose injury temporarily renders him unable to work at all may receive temporary total DISABIL-ITY, which is usually a portion of the worker's average wage. A worker who is able to work at least part time but who has a work-related permanent disability may be entitled to permanent partial disability benefits. The formula for permanent partial disability benefits varies from jurisdiction to jurisdiction but usually considers the employee's average weekly wage combined with the degree of permanent disability. Finally, a worker who is permanently disabled from working at all may be entitled to permanent total disability benefits.

A frequently disputed issue between an employer and an injured employee is the degree that the employee's injury restricts her from returning to suitable employment, mitigating the need for indemnity benefits. Some state statutes permit or require the employer to provide an injured employee with vocational rehabilitation, job search assistance, or job retraining if the injury would otherwise prevent the employee from returning to gainful work.

In the case of a compensable work-related death, the DECEDENT's spouse, dependent children, or both spouse and children may be entitled to dependency benefits. Most jurisdictions pay death benefits to a spouse until the spouse dies or remarries, and to children until they reach age eighteen. Other jurisdictions place limits on benefit amount or duration.

Employees injured on the job also may receive reasonable and necessary medical benefits that are related to the work injury. Such benefits are compensable if they serve to cure the injury, or, if the injury is incurable, relieve its effects. These benefits may include medical treatments such as sutures, casts, or surgery; psychiatric or psychological treatments; hospital, nursing, and physical therapy treatments; chiropractic or podiatric treatments; prescription medications; supplies such as wheelchairs or wrist braces; orthopedic mattresses; or attendant care services. Most workers' compensation statutes also provide for the reimbursement of the employee's travel expenses incurred in obtaining medical services.

The System Today Workers' compensation has been criticized as an expensive component of doing business and a system made more expensive by undetected FRAUD. What was intended to provide the employer and the injured worker with an amicable and humane resolution of a work injury often results in contentious disputes and costly litigation. Some employees feign injury to receive wage-loss benefits, and some employers balk at providing benefits to legitimately injured workers for fear that insurance PREMIUMS will rise. But the system has been effective in keeping injured employees employed and promoting the importance of a safe workplace.

CROSS-REFERENCES
Employment Law; Labor Law; Master and Servant.

WORK PRODUCT RULE 📖 A legal doctrine that provides that certain materials prepared by an ATTORNEY who is acting on behalf of his or her CLIENT during preparation for litigation are privileged from DISCOVERY by the attorney for the opposition party. 📖

Under rules of civil and criminal procedure, as well as some statutes, parties to a civil lawsuit or a criminal prosecution must provide each other with information about the pending litigation. If a party will not disclose information during the discovery process, a court may issue an ORDER compelling the production of EVIDENCE.

The work product rule is an exception to the concept of sharing information. This rule is based on the attorney-client relationship, which includes maintaining the confidentiality of information given by the client. The general rule is that legal research, records, correspondence, reports, or memoranda are attorney work product to the extent that they contain the opinions, theories, strategies, mental impressions, or conclusions of the client, the attorney, or persons participating in the case with the attorney, such as a jury consultant.

The U.S. Supreme Court, in *Hickman v. Taylor*, 329 U.S. 495, 67 S. Ct. 385, 91 L. Ed. 451 (1947), upheld the legitimacy of the work product rule contained in the Federal Rules of Civil Procedure. Since the *Hickman* decision, there have been numerous cases in federal and state courts involving disputes over what constitutes non-discoverable work product.

For example, in *Bondy v. Brophy*, 124 F.R.D. 517 (D. Mass. 1989), the federal district court ruled that the work product rule applied to information obtained by an investigator hired by the attorney for Edna Bondy, the ADMINISTRA-TOR of a PROBATE estate, to look into DECEDENT

John Harrington's property TRANSFERS. Bondy sued Carolyn Brophy regarding one of the transfers, and Brophy sought to obtain information from the investigator, including identities of persons investigated, identities of persons contacted, and copies of any and all written reports. She argued that the work product rule only applied to information gathered for a trial or litigation and that at the time of the investigation, no litigation was contemplated. The court rejected her argument, finding that the information collected was not in the ordinary course of business, nor was it typical for the administrator of an estate to hire an investigator to look into property transfers of a decedent. The only reasonable inference is that the investigator was hired because Bondy had questions about these transfers and was considering appropriate legal action if the inquiry turned up evidence of questionable conduct. Moreover, the investigator was hired by Bondy's lawyer. Under these circumstances, the investigator's report and the names of persons he contacted enjoyed qualified protection under the work product rule.

See also ATTORNEY-CLIENT PRIVILEGE.

WORLD BANK The International Bank for Reconstruction and Development, commonly referred to as the World Bank, is an international financial institution whose purposes include assisting the development of its member nations' territories, promoting and supplementing private foreign investment, and promoting long-range balanced growth in international trade.

The World Bank was established in July 1944 at the UNITED NATIONS Monetary and Financial Conference in Bretton Woods, New Hampshire. It opened for business in June 1946 and helped in the reconstruction of nations devastated by World War II. Since the 1960s the World Bank has shifted its focus from the advanced industrialized nations to developing third-world countries.

The World Bank is comprised of a number of separate institutions. The three major institutions are the International Bank for Reconstruction and Development (IBRD), the International Development Association (IDA), and the International Finance Corporation (IFC). The IBRD, the bank's most important component, lends funds directly, guarantees loans made by others, or participates in these loans. The IDA, which was established in 1960, lends to low-income countries on more favorable terms, charging a small service fee but no interest. It gets its funds from more affluent member countries. The IFC, established in

1956, provides loans to private business in developing countries.

Twenty-nine nations joined the World Bank in 1945. By 1996 the bank had 180 members. The bank is governed by an executive board and a managing director. Voting in the bank is weighted according to the initial contributions to the bank's capital, which historically has given the U.S. government a dominant voice in the bank's affairs.

In 1996 almost one-third of the bank's loans went to the world's poorest countries. The bank has moved away from financing large-scale infrastructure projects, such as roads, railways, and power facilities. Since the 1970s the bank has provided an increasing number of loans to developing countries for agricultural, educational, and population programs. The goals of these loan programs have been to raise the standard of living and to increase self-sufficiency.

The World Bank also offers advisory services to countries seeking to reform their banking and finance systems. It has also launched InfoDev, an initiative to secure resources from corporations, foundations, and governments to promote reform and investment in the developing world through improved access to information technology.

WORLD COURT The World Court, which is officially called the INTERNATIONAL COURT OF JUSTICE (ICJ), is the principal judicial organ of the UNITED NATIONS. The court is virtually the same institution as its predecessor, the Permanent Court of International Justice, which was established at the direction of the LEAGUE OF NATIONS and functioned from 1922 to 1946. The court is located at The Hague, Netherlands.

The court consists of fifteen judges, no two of the same nationality, selected for nine-year terms by the U.N. General Assembly and Security Council, voting separately. Five are chosen every three years. As a group, the judges are supposed to represent the principal forms of civilization and the major legal systems of the world. Decisions of the court are by a simple majority of those voting, with nine constituting a quorum, although smaller panels of judges may be formed in special cases. In practice, the full court usually hears most of its cases. The official languages of the court are English and French.

The Statute of the Court, which sets forth its organization, competence, and procedure, was adopted in 1945 as an annex to the U.N. Charter. Therefore, all members of the U.N. are automatically parties to the statute. Other states may become parties upon conditions de-

World Court Decisions

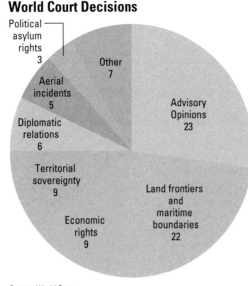

Source: World Court.

termined by the U.N. General Assembly and Security Council. Switzerland, San Marino, and Liechtenstein have become parties to the statute.

The function of the World Court is to resolve disputes between sovereign states. Disputes may be placed before the court by parties upon conditions prescribed by the U.N. Security Council. No state, however, may be subject to the JURISDICTION of the court without the state's consent.

Consent may be given by express agreement at the time the dispute is presented to the court, by prior agreement to accept the jurisdiction of the court in particular categories of cases, or by treaty provisions with respect to disputes arising from matters covered by the treaty.

Under article 36 of the court's statute, a state may declare in advance its acceptance of the jurisdiction of the court. The declaration may be unconditional or on condition that other parties to the dispute also accept the same obligation. States may make reservations that limit the extent or effect of their declarations of acceptance of jurisdiction. The United States, for example, has severely limited its own acceptance by a reservation that excepts all matters that the United States chooses to regard as within its domestic jurisdiction.

Once the court has acquired jurisdiction of a case, its decision is legally binding upon the parties. There is no provision for APPEAL. Once states have accepted jurisdiction of the court and permitted a case to go to JUDGMENT, they have usually complied with the decision. Under article 94 of the U.N. Charter, if a party does not comply with the obligations imposed on it

by the court, the prevailing party may seek recourse from the Security Council. In 1984, in *Nicaragua v. United States*, the United States temporarily withdrew its prior acceptance of compulsory jurisdiction in disputes relating to Central America. Despite the withdrawal, the court proceeded with the case and decided on a 12–3 vote that the United States had breached INTERNATIONAL LAW by seeking the overthrow of the Marxist Nicaraguan regime through the funding of counterrevolutionary groups. The court ruled that the United States should pay Nicaragua REPARATIONS, but the United States blocked Nicaragua's attempt to appeal to the U.N. Security Council for satisfaction of the judgment.

The court may render advisory opinions on legal questions when requested to do so by the General Assembly, the Security Council, or other U.N. organs or agencies. For example, the World Health Organization and the General Assembly requested advisory opinions on the legality of nuclear weapons under international law. The World Court held hearings, in which forty-five nations testified. It issued an advisory opinion in July 1996, which held that it was illegal for a nation to threaten nuclear war.

The court is used infrequently, which suggests that most states prefer to handle their disputes by political means or by recourse to tribunals where the outcome may be more predictable or better controlled by the parties.

The first international war crime trial in fifty years was convened by a three-judge panel of the World Court in 1996. The panel heard evidence of WAR CRIMES committed by Dusan Tadic, a Bosnian Serb accused of taking part in a systematic reign of terror in which he committed crimes against humanity in connection with systematic attacks against the non-Serb population of Bosnia. In May 1997 Tadic was convicted of the war crimes. However, the Bosnian Serb leaders who orchestrated the war crimes remained free and therefore beyond the jurisdiction of the court.

WORLD WAR I World War I was an international conflict primarily involving European nations that was fought between 1914 and 1918. The United States did not enter the conflict until April 1917, but its entry was the decisive event of the war, enabling the Allies (Great Britain, France, Italy, and Russia) to defeat the Central Powers (Germany, Austria-Hungary, Turkey, and Bulgaria). The leadership of President WOODROW WILSON led to both the conclusion of hostilities and the creation of the LEAGUE OF NATIONS, an international organization dedicated to resolving disputes without war.

The war began on July 28, 1914, when Austria-Hungary declared war on Serbia. During the late nineteenth century, European nations had negotiated military alliances with each other that called for mutual protection. The Austria-Hungary declaration of war triggered these alliance commitments, leading to the widening of the war between the Allies and Central Powers.

During the next four years, the war was fought primarily on three fronts and on the Atlantic Ocean. The western front was in France, where Germany was opposed by France, Great Britain, and eventually the United States. The eastern front was in Russia, where Germany and Austria-Hungary opposed Russia. The southern front was in Serbia and involved Austria-Hungary and Serbia.

In August 1914 Germany invaded Belgium and then moved into France. German forces were unable to achieve a decisive victory, however, and the war soon became a conflict of fixed battle lines. French, British, and German soldiers lived and fought in trenches, periodically making assaults on the enemy by entering the "no man's land" between the two sets of trenches. The use of machine guns, tanks, gas warfare, and artillery in these confined battlefields generated unprecedented human carnage on the western front.

Though Germany had more success on the eastern front, neither side had sufficient economic and military strength to achieve victory. In 1916 and early 1917, Wilson sought to bring about negotiations between the Allies and Central Powers that would lead, in his words, to "peace without victory." Wilson's efforts at first appeared promising, but German military successes convinced the Central Powers that they could win the war.

Germany's use of submarine warfare proved to be the key element in provoking the United States' entry into the war. In 1915 a German submarine had torpedoed without warning the British passenger steamship *Lusitania* off the southern coast of Ireland. Nearly 1,200 persons died, including 128 U.S. citizens. Popular feeling in the United States against Germany was intense, leading to calls for declaring war on Germany. Wilson, however, sought a diplomatic solution. Though Germany rebuked his call for assuming responsibility for the tragedy, it did not sink any more passenger liners without warning.

Wilson abandoned his peacemaking efforts when Germany announced that unrestricted submarine warfare would begin on February 1, 1917. This meant that U.S. merchant ships

were in peril, despite the fact that the United States was a neutral in the war. Wilson broke diplomatic relations with Germany on February 3 and asked Congress later that month for authority to arm merchant ships and take other protective measures. In mid-March German submarines sank three U.S. merchant ships, with heavy loss of life. Wilson called a special session of Congress for April 2 and asked for a declaration of war on Germany. Congress obliged, and on April 6, 1917, Wilson signed the declaration.

The United States immediately moved to raise a large military force by instituting a military draft. It took months, however, to raise, train, and dispatch troops to Europe. The first eighty-five thousand members of the American Expeditionary Force (AEF), under the command of General John J. Pershing, arrived in France in June 1917. By the end of the war in November 1918, there were two million soldiers in the AEF.

Germany realized that U.S. war production and financial strength reduced Germany's chances of victory. In March 1918 Germany launched its last great offensive on the western front. U.S. troops saw their first extended action in the Battle of the Marne, halting the German advance on June 4. During the second Battle of the Marne, U.S. and French troops again stopped the German advance and successfully counterattacked. The Allies began pushing back the German army all along the western front, signaling the beginning of the end of German resistance.

Wilson renewed his peace efforts by proposing a framework for negotiations. On January 8, 1918, he delivered an address to Congress that named Fourteen Points to be used as the guide

American soldiers fire at a German position along the Western Front in France. The entry of the United States into World War I in 1917 tipped the scales in favor of the Allied Powers and they soon won the war against the Axis Powers.

for a peace settlement. The fourteenth point called for a general association of nations that would guarantee political independence and territorial integrity for all countries. In October 1918 Germany asked Wilson to arrange a general armistice based on the Fourteen Points and the immediate start of peace negotiations. Germany finally capitulated and signed an armistice on November 11, 1918.

The 1919 TREATY OF VERSAILLES ended World War I and imposed disarmament, REPARATIONS, and territorial changes on Germany. The treaty also established the League of Nations, an international organization dedicated to resolving world conflicts peacefully. Wilson, however, was unable to convince the U.S. Senate to ratify the treaty, because it was opposed to U.S. membership in the League of Nations.

World War I also saw the 1917 Bolshevik REVOLUTION in Russia. The specter of a worldwide Communist movement generated fears in the United States that socialists, anarchists, and Communists were undermining democratic institutions. During the war, socialist opponents of the war were convicted of SEDITION and imprisoned. In 1920 the federal government rounded up six thousand ALIENS who it considered to be politically subversive. These "Palmer Raids," named after Attorney General A. MITCHELL PALMER, violated basic civil liberties. Agents entered and searched homes without WARRANTS, held persons without specific charges for long periods of time, and denied them legal counsel. Hundreds of aliens were deported.

See also COMMUNISM; SOCIALISM.

WORLD WAR II World War II began in 1939 as a conflict between Germany and the combined forces of France and Great Britain, and eventually included most of the nations of the world before it ended in August 1945. It caused the greatest loss of life and material destruction of any war in history, killing twenty-five million military personnel and thirty million civilians. By the end of the war, the United States had become the most powerful nation in the world, the possessor of atomic weapons. The war also increased the power of the Soviet Union, which gained control of Eastern Europe and part of Germany.

World War II was caused in large part by the rise of totalitarian regimes in Germany and Italy and by the domination of the military in Japan. In Germany, ADOLF HITLER, head of the National Socialist or Nazi party, became chancellor in 1933. Within a short time, he had assumed dictatorial rule. Hitler broke the Versailles Treaty, which had ended World War I and disarmed Germany, and proceeded with a massive buildup of the German armed forces. Hitler believed that the German people were a master race that needed more territory. His first aim was to reunite all Germans living under foreign governments. In 1936 he reclaimed the Rhineland from French control and in 1938 annexed Austria to Germany. That same year he took over the German areas of Czechoslovakia and in 1939 annexed all of that country.

Though France and Great Britain had acquiesced to Germany's actions, they soon realized that Hitler had greater ambitions. When Germany invaded Poland on September 1, 1939, Great Britain and France declared war on Germany. With the invasion of Poland, World War II had begun. Poland was quickly defeated, and for a period of time a "phony war" ensued, with neither side making any military moves. This changed in the spring of 1940, when Germany invaded Holland, Belgium, and France. Again, German military forces overwhelmed their opponents, leaving Great Britain the only outpost against Germany.

During the 1930s the United States government had avoided involvement in European affairs. This traditional policy of "isolationism" became more problematic after the war began in 1939. President FRANKLIN D. ROOSEVELT moved away from an isolationist foreign policy and sought to assist Great Britain and France, while keeping the United States a neutral party to the conflict. This led to the repeal of the arms embargo in the Neutrality Act of 1939 (22 U.S.C.A. § 441), allowing the sale of military equipment to Great Britain and France.

After the fall of France to Germany in 1940, Roosevelt became even more determined to assist Great Britain. He persuaded Congress to pass the LEND-LEASE ACT of 1941 (55 Stat. 31). Lend-Lease provided munitions, food, machinery, and services to Great Britain and other Allies without immediate cost.

U.S. interests in the Pacific were threatened by the rise of Japanese militarism in the 1930s. The Japanese invasion of Manchuria in 1931 signaled a new direction for Japan. Its military leaders, who dominated the government, sought to conquer large parts of Asia. In 1936 and 1937 Japan signed treaties with Germany and Italy (headed by dictator BENITO MUSSOLINI), creating what was called the Axis powers.

In 1937 Japan began an undeclared war against China. When Japan occupied Indochina in 1940, the United States stopped exporting gasoline, iron, steel, and rubber to Japan and froze all Japanese assets in the United States. In the fall of 1941, the extremist Japanese general Hideki Tōjō became leader of the cabinet. His cabinet began planning a war with the United States, as Japan realized it could not attain its imperial goals without defeating the United States.

The devastating Japanese attack on the U.S. naval base at Pearl Harbor, Hawaii, on December 7, 1941, resulted in a U.S. declaration of war on Japan the following day. Germany and Italy, as part of the Axis powers alliance, then declared war on the United States.

The attack on the United States led to severe consequences for Japanese Americans. On February 19, 1942, President Roosevelt issued Executive Order No. 9,066, directing the forced relocation of all 112,000 Japanese Americans living on the West Coast (70,000 of them U.S. citizens) to detention camps in such places as Jerome, Arkansas, and Heart Lake, Wyoming. Roosevelt issued the order after military leaders, worried about a Japanese invasion, argued that national security required such drastic action.

The U.S. Supreme Court upheld the forced relocation in *Korematsu v. United States*, 323 U.S. 214, 65 S. Ct. 193, 89 L. Ed. 194 (1944). Justice Hugo L. Black noted that curtailing the rights of a single racial group is constitutionally suspect but that in this case military necessity justified the exclusion of Japanese Americans from the West Coast. In retrospect, historians have characterized the removal and detention as the most drastic invasion of individual CIVIL RIGHTS by the government in U.S. history.

The United States joined Great Britain and the Soviet Union in an alliance against Germany, Italy, and Japan. The Allies determined that priority would be given to defeating Germany and Italy. The Soviet Union, under the leadership of Joseph Stalin, had signed a non-aggression pact with Germany in 1939, just days before Germany's invasion of Poland. In June 1941 Hitler renounced the agreement and invaded the Soviet Union. The Russian front would prove to be the bloodiest of the war, killing millions of civilians as well as millions of soldiers.

The Allies stemmed Axis advances in 1942. On the Russian front, the Soviet troops won a decisive victory at the Battle of Stalingrad. Following this battle, Soviet forces began the slow process of pushing the German army back toward its border. The U.S. Army achieved success in routing German forces from North Africa in 1942, paving the way for the invasion of Sicily and Italy in 1943.

On June 6, 1944 ("D-Day"), the Allies mounted an amphibious landing on France's Normandy coast. The D-Day invasion surprised the German military commanders, who did not

Trenches were dug in the hopfields near Kent, England, during World War II for the pickers and their families to take refuge during the Battle of Britain. These children watch the skies during the battle.

expect an invasion at this location. In a short time, U.S. and British forces were able to break out of the coastal areas and move into France. U.S. forces liberated Paris on August 25.

Germany could not succeed in fighting a two-front war. By early 1945 it was clear that an Allied victory was inevitable. On April 30, 1945, with the Russian army entering Berlin, Hitler committed suicide. On May 7 Germany unconditionally surrendered.

The war in the Pacific was primarily a conflict between Japanese and U.S. forces. The U.S. Navy inflicted substantial damage to the Japanese fleet at the Battle of Midway in June 1942. Following Midway, the U.S. forces began invading Japanese-held islands in the South Pacific. This was a slow and costly process because Japanese soldiers were taught to fight to the death. However, the process proved successful. From 1942 to 1945, U.S. forces invaded numerous islands, the last being Okinawa, which is close to the Japanese mainland. Despite fierce resistance, the U.S. forces prevailed.

In 1945 the U.S. military prepared for the invasion of Japan. Though a Japanese defeat appeared inevitable, an invasion would result in heavy U.S. casualties. President Harry S. Truman, who had become president in April 1945 after the death of President Roosevelt, approved the dropping of atomic bombs on Japan. On August 6 the city of Hiroshima was bombed, and three days later Nagasaki was devastated by another nuclear attack. Japan opened peace negotiations on August 10 and surrendered on September 2.

Wartime conferences among Roosevelt, Stalin, and British prime minister Winston Churchill led to the creation of the United Nations in 1945. At the Yalta Conference in 1945, the leaders agreed to divide Germany, as well as the city of Berlin, into four zones of occupation, controlled by forces from the three countries and France. Germany was to have its industrial base rebuilt, but its armaments industries were to be abolished or confiscated. The leaders also approved the creation of an international court to try German leaders as war criminals, setting the stage for the NUREMBERG TRIALS. The Soviet army's occupation of Eastern Europe soon gave way to the creation of Communist governments under the influence of the Soviet Union.

CROSS-REFERENCES

Communism; Hirohito; Japanese American Evacuation Cases; *Korematsu v. United States;* Tokyo Trial; United Nations; War Crimes; Yalta Agreement.

WORTHIER TITLE DOCTRINE 📖 A COM-

MON LAW rule that provides that a CONVEYANCE of REAL PROPERTY by a GRANTOR to another person for life with a limitation to the grantor's HEIRS creates a REVERSION in the grantor by which his or her heirs acquire the property only upon the death of the grantor, not upon the death of the person who has been granted the property for life. 📖

The worthier title doctrine comes from English feudal real property law and is based on the presumption that a TITLE by descent (land inherited by an heir) is worthier (better) than a title by conveyance (purchase.) If a grantor or a TESTATOR attempts to convey a future interest in land to the grantor's heirs, the heirs would be getting by conveyance what they would otherwise take by descent, making the conveyance void.

For example, A deeds Blackacre to B for life, and then to the heirs of A. The effect of the doctrine is that A has a reversion (a future interest remaining with A in the property), while B has a LIFE ESTATE. The words *to the heirs of A* are WORDS OF LIMITATION, which are required under the worthier title doctrine. If the heirs acquire the property at all, it is only after the death of the owner. If the heirs had a REMAINDER interest in the property, they would acquire it after the death of B, the GRANTEE with the life estate, regardless of whether A, the grantor, was alive or dead. The deed or will would have to contain language such as "to B for life and to C, D, E, (the heirs) in fee."

The worthier title doctrine has been abolished in many states by the UNIFORM PROBATE CODE, § 2-710. Where the doctrine has been abolished, language in a governing instrument describing the beneficiaries of a disposition as the transferor's *heirs, heirs at law, next of kin, distributees, relatives,* or *family,* or language of similar import, does not create a reversionary interest in the transferor. In effect, the reversion interest is eliminated and the heirs receive their unrestricted remainder interest in the property.

James Skelly Wright

WRIGHT, JAMES SKELLY James Skelly

Wright served as a federal district judge in Louisiana from 1949 to 1962 and a federal court of appeals judge in Washington, D.C., from 1962 to 1987. Wright distinguished himself as a district judge in the 1950s when he forced the desegregation of the New Orleans, Louisiana, public schools and the city's public transportation system. Wright continued this course on the federal appeals court, when he ordered sweeping changes in the discriminatory policies of the District of Columbia's school system.

Wright was born on January 14, 1911, in New Orleans. He graduated from Loyola University in New Orleans in 1931 and earned a law degree from Loyola Law School in 1934. Unable to find legal work in the Great Depression, Wright taught high school and lectured in history at Loyola until 1937, when he became an assistant U.S. attorney in New Orleans. During World War II he served in the U.S. Coast Guard as the legal aide to an admiral at the U.S. Embassy in London.

After the war, Wright briefly practiced law in Washington, D.C., before moving back to New Orleans. In 1948 President HARRY S. TRUMAN named him U.S. attorney in New Orleans, and a year later, appointed him a judge on the federal district court in New Orleans.

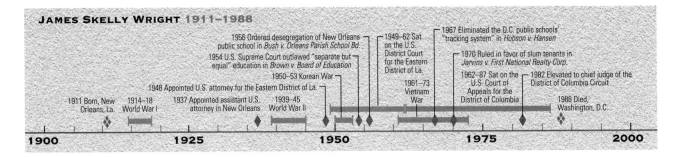

JAMES SKELLY WRIGHT 1911–1988

1956 Ordered desegregation of New Orleans public school in *Bush v. Orleans Parish School Bd.*

1954 U.S. Supreme Court outlawed "separate but equal" education in *Brown v. Board of Education*

1950–53 Korean War

1948 Appointed U.S. attorney for the Eastern District of La.

1911 Born, New Orleans, La.

1914–18 World War I

1937 Appointed assistant U.S. attorney in New Orleans

1939–45 World War II

1949–62 Sat on the U.S. District Court for the Eastern District of La.

1961–73 Vietnam War

1967 Eliminated the D.C. public schools' "tracking system" in *Hobson v. Hansen*

1970 Ruled in favor of slum tenants in *Jarvins v. First National Realty Corp.*

1962–87 Sat on the U.S. Court of Appeals for the District of Columbia

1982 Elevated to chief judge of the District of Columbia Circuit

1988 Died, Washington, D.C.

1900   1925   1950   1975   2000

Wright's thirteen years on the district bench were controversial. In the wake of the Supreme Court's decision in *Brown v. Board of Education of Topeka, Kansas*, 347 U.S. 483, 74 S. Ct. 686, 98 L. Ed. 873 (1954), which outlawed state-sponsored racial segregation of public schools, Wright granted the NAACP's request to desegregate the New Orleans public schools. His decision in *Bush v. Orleans Parish School Bd.*, 138 F.Supp. 337 (1956), was met with resistance by virtually every public official in Louisiana. By the time Wright assumed the appellate bench in 1962, he had issued forty-one rulings and had INJUNCTIONS in force against the governor, the attorney general, the superintendent of education, the state police, the national guard, all district attorneys, all sheriffs, all mayors, all police chiefs, and the state legislature.

In 1962 President JOHN F. KENNEDY wished to appoint Wright to the U.S. Court of Appeals for the Fifth Circuit, which is based in New Orleans. Vehement opposition from Southern senators dissuaded Kennedy from going forward with the nomination. Instead, he appointed Wright to the U.S. Court of Appeals for the District of Columbia.

As an appellate judge, Wright continued his career of judicial activism. He took major steps toward eliminating discrimination against poor African Americans in the district's public schools. To this end, he ordered sweeping changes in the schools. In *Hobson v. Hansen*, 269 F. Supp. 401 (D.D.C. 1967), he eliminated the "tracking" system, which attempted to place schoolchildren according to mental ability in hopes of stimulating smart children and helping slower ones. However, this system often resulted in placement along racial lines, with most African Americans being placed in lower tracks, and whites being placed in upper tracks. In other cases Wright broadened the concept of illegal discrimination to include "de facto" discrimination (where segregation exists mainly because of social and economic patterns).

Wright also issued rulings that advanced CONSUMER PROTECTION. He ruled in favor of the rights of slum tenants to withhold rent for dilapidated and rat-infested dwellings (*Javins v. First National Realty Corp.*, 428 F.2d 1071 [D.C. Cir. 1970]), and provided remedies for poor consumers who had signed "UNCONSCIONABLE" contracts, which contained excessive rates of interest and threatened them with repossession of goods if they failed to make payments. (*Williams v. Walker-Thomas Furniture Co.*, 350 F.2d 445 [D.C. Cir. 1965]).

Throughout his years on the bench, Wright espoused what he once described as a jurisprudence of "goodness," which he said was inspired

"THERE ARE SOCIAL AND POLITICAL PROBLEMS WHICH AT TIMES SEEM TO DEFY RESOLUTION [IN THE POLITICAL ARENA]. IN SUCH SITUATIONS . . . THE JUDICIARY MUST BEAR A HAND AND ACCEPT ITS RESPONSIBILITY TO ASSIST IN THE SOLUTION WHERE CONSTITUTIONAL RIGHTS HANG IN THE BALANCE."

by the work of Supreme Court Chief Justice EARL WARREN. In this jurisprudence, what was "fair" was often more important than what had been held in previous cases.

Wright retired in 1987. He died on August 6, 1988, in Washington, D.C.

See also SCHOOL DESEGREGATION.

WRIT 📖 An ORDER issued by a court requiring that something be done or giving authority to do a specified act. 📖

The development of English COMMON LAW relied on the courts to issue writs that allowed persons to proceed with a legal action. Over time the courts also used writs to direct other courts, SHERIFFS, and attorneys to perform certain actions. In modern law, courts primarily use writs to grant extraordinary relief, to grant the right of APPEAL, or to grant the sheriff authority to seize property. Most other common-law writs were discarded in U.S. law, as the courts moved to simpler and more general methods of starting CIVIL ACTIONS.

U.S. courts commonly use several extraordinary writs, which are issued only when the courts believe that usual remedies have failed. The writ of HABEAS CORPUS, sometimes called the "great writ," is probably the best-known example of a writ. A writ of habeas corpus is a legal document ordering anyone who is officially holding the petitioner (the person requesting the writ) to bring him into court to determine whether the detention is unlawful. A FEDERAL COURT can hear an application for a writ of habeas corpus by a state prisoner who is being held in CUSTODY, allegedly in violation of the U.S. Constitution or the laws of the United States.

The writ of MANDAMUS is an extraordinary writ that directs a public official or government department to take an action. It may be sent to the EXECUTIVE BRANCH, the legislative branch, or a lower court. The famous case of *Marbury v. Madison*, 5 U.S. (1 Cranch) 137, 2 L. Ed. 60 (1803), which established the right of JUDICIAL REVIEW of congressional statutes, was an action for a writ of mandamus. William Marbury asked the court to issue the writ to Secretary of State JAMES MADISON, commanding him to deliver his judicial commission. The Court, however, refused to issue the writ of mandamus.

The writ of prohibition is another extraordinary writ and is the opposite of a writ of mandamus, because it commands a government official *not* to take a specified action. The most common use of the writ is by an APPELLATE COURT to a lower court, commanding the lower court to refrain from a proposed action. For example, a trial court might grant a request by the news media to release information from a court file.

A defendant who objects to the release could petition for a writ of prohibition from the court of appeals. If the appellate court issues the writ, the trial court may not release the information. See also PROHIBITION, WRIT OF.

The writ of CERTIORARI is an extraordinary writ issued by an appellate court that is used by that court when it has discretion on whether to hear an appeal from a lower court. If the writ is denied, the lower court decision remains unchanged. The U.S. Supreme Court has used the PETITION and writ of certiorari to control its caseload since 1925.

The extraordinary writ of QUO WARRANTO starts a proceeding in which the state challenges the legality of the use of an office, FRANCHISE, CHARTER, or other right that can be held or used under authority of the state. For example, a writ of quo warranto would be used to remove a person who illegally holds public office, or to nullify an illegal amendment to a municipal charter.

A writ of ATTACHMENT is a court order used to force obedience to another order or a JUDGMENT of the court. It was originally used to order a sheriff or law enforcement officer to take a disobedient party into custody and to bring her before the court to answer for the CONTEMPT. In modern law, a writ of attachment orders seizure of the defendant's property rather than the defendant's person to secure the satisfaction of a judgment that has not yet been secured. Modern law limits the scope and effect of attachment procedures to safeguard the defendant's rights to LIBERTY and DUE PROCESS OF LAW.

A writ of EXECUTION may be issued after a plaintiff wins a judgment in a civil case and is awarded DAMAGES. The writ directs the sheriff to take the property of the defendant in satisfaction of the court-imposed debt.

A writ of ENTRY is an instrument used in an ACTION brought to recover land wrongfully withheld from the true owner or TENANT entitled to POSSESSION and use of the land. It establishes who is entitled to possession of a parcel of land but does not settle the issue of who is the true owner. The central inquiry is which of the two individuals has the superior right of possession and use of the land at the time of the action.

To determine the priority of the rights of the parties fighting over land, the court must consider how and when each individual acquired ownership or possession. In general, modern laws permit the recovery of monetary damages for rent or abuse of property, as well as recovery of possession of the land. The individual who has been in possession of the land may be compensated for any improvements he has made in the property.

The writ of entry is used in only a few states to recover the possession of land. It has been replaced by the action to recover possession of REAL PROPERTY.

A writ of ERROR is an order issued from an appellate court directed to the judge of a lower court, mandating the judge to release the trial record of an action in which the judge has entered a final judgment. The appellate court issues the writ so that it may review the case and either reverse, correct, or affirm the lower-court decision. Most states have replaced the writ of error with a simpler appellate document, usually called the notice of appeal.

WRITS OF ASSISTANCE CASE

The *Writs of Assistance* case involved a legal dispute during 1761 in which sixty-three Boston merchants petitioned the Massachusetts Superior Court to challenge the legality of a particular type of SEARCH WARRANT called a writ of assistance. Also known as *Paxton's Case*, the *Writs of Assistance* case contributed to the Founding Fathers' original understanding of SEARCH AND SEIZURE law, planted the seeds of JUDICIAL REVIEW in the United States, and helped shape the U.S. concept of NATURAL LAW.

Parliament created the writ of assistance during the seventeenth century. Once issued, the writ authorized government officials to look for CONTRABAND in private homes and businesses. Normally, the writ placed no limitations on the time, place, or manner of a given search. In the eighteenth century, customs officials in America used the writ to investigate colonial merchants who were suspected of SMUGGLING goods into the country. The writ generally commanded all CONSTABLES, PEACE OFFICERS, and nearby subjects to help customs officials carry out a search.

The *Writs of Assistance* case arose when James Paxton, a Massachusetts customs official, applied to the superior court for a writ of assistance. JAMES OTIS, JR., advocate general for the colony of Massachusetts, resigned his post to represent the merchants who opposed the writ. Appearing before Chief Justice Thomas Hutchinson, Otis and his cocounsel, Oxenbridge Thacher, made four arguments against the legality of the writ.

First, Thacher challenged the authority of the Massachusetts Superior Court to issue the writ. Thacher conceded that Parliament had passed a law in 1662 granting the English Court of Exchequer the power to issue the writ in Great Britain and passed a second law in 1696 enabling customs officials to apply for the writ in America. However, Thacher argued that neither law specified which courts in America could issue the writ. Thus, Thacher said that the Massachusetts Superior Court was never expressly delegated authority to issue the writ.

Second, Otis challenged the procedure by which the writs were issued. Otis argued that bare suspicion should not be enough to support an application for the writ. Otis maintained that no writ should be issued unless the official making the application is first placed under OATH and made to disclose the EVIDENCE on which the application is based. Otis also suggested that every writ application should be carefully reviewed by an impartial third party, and not the judges who had been appointed to the Massachusetts Superior Court. Those judges, Otis charged, were predisposed in favor of granting the writ.

Third, Otis challenged the writ applications for lack of specificity. A lawful writ application, Otis asserted, must identify the person, place, or thing to be searched. Under English law, customs officials were authorized to search for contraband in any house, shop, cellar, warehouse, room, or other place where uncustomed goods might be hidden. If colonial residents resisted, customs officials were authorized to break open doors, chests, trunks, and other packages that might lead to incriminating evidence. Because the duration of the writ was perpetual and could be executed at any time of the day or night, Otis said, the law failed to respect the sanctity of a person's home and private life.

Fourth, Otis challenged Parliament's autocratic authority. Parliament has no power to pass legislation, Otis claimed, that is against fundamental principles of law. When Parliament enacts legislation that contravenes fundamental principles of reason and EQUITY, such legislation must be struck down by the courts. Otis contended that Parliament was not above the law and that any parliamentary act against the constitution was void.

In response to these arguments, lawyers for the government asserted that the Massachusetts Superior Court possessed no discretion to deny Paxton's application for the writ. Parliament had granted the English Court of Exchequer the power to issue the writ in Great Britain and authorized customs officials to apply for the writ in America. Parliament also gave the Massachusetts Superior Court the same powers as the English Court of Exchequer. Because the Court of Exchequer had been lawfully issuing the writ for years in Great Britain, lawyers for the government argued, the Massachusetts Superior Court enjoyed the same legal authority.

Chief Justice Hutchinson and his colleagues agreed with the lawyers for the government.

THE GRANGER COLLECTION, NEW YORK

James Otis, Jr., resigned his post as advocate general of the colony of Massachusetts to represent the merchants who challenged the writs of assistance, a kind of search warrant that allowed officials to search homes or businesses at any time.

They unanimously voted to grant Paxton's application in this particular case and affirmed the legality of the writ across Massachusetts. Although Otis, Thacher, and their clients lost the case, they transformed the writ into a rallying cry of the American Revolution. Colonial opposition to the writ quickly evolved from civil disobedience to armed resistance. By 1769 many colonial courts had grown reluctant to issue the writ. This series of events prompted JOHN ADAMS to exclaim that the *Writs of Assistance* case gave birth to the "Child Independence!"

In addition to fueling the revolutionary spirit in the colonies, the *Writs of Assistance* case presented the first formidable challenge to general search warrants in the colonies. Otis thought that more restrictions should be placed on the government's authority to intrude upon places ordinarily kept private by homeowners and business proprietors. In America, Otis argued, the law should require that all searches be conducted pursuant to a lawful warrant that is obtained by an official who is placed under oath before a neutral third party and compelled to disclose the precise nature of any incriminating evidence. Any warrant that might be issued should fully describe the person or premises to be searched. The FOURTH AMENDMENT to the U.S. Constitution established these principles as a permanent part of U.S. criminal procedure.

The *Writs of Assistance* case also planted the seeds of judicial review in the United States. Judicial review is the power of the judiciary to invalidate legislative acts that violate a constitutional provision or principle. The English system of government did not recognize judicial review during the eighteenth century. Neither a COMMON-LAW COURT nor the crown possessed the power to overturn a law duly enacted by Parliament. In the United States, Otis suggested in the *Writs of Assistance* case that legislative acts that contravene the Constitution must be struck down by courts of law.

Finally, the *Writs of Assistance* case helped shape the contours of natural law in the United States. Some people believe in natural law, a body of unwritten principles derived from religion, morality, and secular philosophy. In certain instances natural law is said to transcend the written rules and regulations that are enacted by government. During the *Writs of Assistance* case, Otis argued that the written laws of Parliament are limited by unwritten principles of reason and equity. The "constitution" to which Otis referred was itself an unwritten body of English COMMON-LAW principles. (The United States Constitution was not ratified until 1787.)

WRONG 📖 A violation, by one individual, of another individual's legal rights. 📖

The idea of rights suggests the opposite idea of wrongs, for every RIGHT is capable of being violated. For example, a right to receive payment for goods sold implies a wrong on the part of the person who owes, but does not make payment. In the most general point of view, the law is intended to establish and maintain rights, yet in its everyday application, the law must deal with rights and wrongs. The law first fixes the character and definition of rights, and then seeks to secure these rights by defining wrongs and devising the means to prevent these wrongs or provide for their redress.

The CRIMINAL LAW is charged with preventing and punishing public wrongs. Public wrongs are violations of public rights and duties that affect the whole community.

A private wrong, also called a civil wrong, is a violation of public or private rights that injures an individual and consequently is subject to civil redress or compensation. A civil wrong that is not based on breach of CONTRACT is a TORT. Torts include ASSAULT, BATTERY, LIBEL, SLANDER, intentional infliction of mental distress, and damage to property. The same act or omission that makes a tort may also be a breach of contract, but it is the NEGLIGENCE, not the breaking of the contract, that is the tort. For example, if a lawyer is negligent in representing his client, the lawyer may be sued both for MALPRACTICE, which is a tort, and for breach of the lawyer-client contract.

The word *wrongful* is attached to numerous types of injurious conduct. For example, *wrongful death* is a type of lawsuit brought on behalf of a deceased person's beneficiaries that alleges that the death was attributable to the willful or negligent conduct of another. However, even in these special contexts, the words *wrong, wrongful*, and *wrongfully* do not sharply delineate the exact nature of the wrongness. Their presence merely signifies that something bad has occurred.

WRONGFUL BIRTH 📖 A MEDICAL MALPRACTICE claim brought by the parents of a child born with birth defects, alleging that negligent treatment or advice deprived them of the opportunity to avoid conception or terminate the pregnancy. 📖

A wrongful birth action is conceptually similar to a wrongful life action. In a wrongful birth action, parents seek DAMAGES for a child born with birth defects. The claim for damages is based on the cost to parents of raising an unexpectedly defective child. In a WRONGFUL LIFE action, the child seeks damages for being born with a birth defect rather than not being born.

A wrongful birth action was first recognized in *Jacobs v. Theimer*, 519 S.W.2d 846 (Tex. 1975). The case involved an ACTION by the parents of a child born with defects caused by the mother contracting rubella in her first month of pregnancy. The claim was that the defendant was negligent in failing to diagnose the rubella in the mother. The Texas Supreme Court allowed damages, but only for expenses reasonably necessary for the care and treatment of the child's impairment. The parents were not awarded any noneconomic damages such as damages for pain and suffering.

Most wrongful birth suits had little chance of succeeding before the decriminalization of ABORTION by the U.S. Supreme Court in *Roe v. Wade*, 410 U.S. 113, 93 S. Ct. 705, 35 L. Ed. 2d 147 (1973), since the parents of a child with birth defects could not argue that they would have had an abortion had they known of the defect. In addition, some courts were reluctant to award damages, ruling that it was impossible to weigh the economic and emotional costs of raising an impaired child against the intangible joys of parenthood.

Since the mid-1970s, however, more than twenty states have recognized wrongful birth actions that enable parents to collect some or all of their child care expenses if they can prove NEGLIGENCE. With improved genetic testing, medical providers can routinely determine early in pregnancy the presence of certain birth defects in the fetus. This imposes on medical providers the duty to order the correct tests and to properly diagnose the results.

See also TORT LAW; WRONGFUL PREGNANCY.

WRONGFUL DEATH

WRONGFUL DEATH ▣ The taking of the life of an individual resulting from the willful or negligent act of another person or persons. ▣

If a person is killed because of the wrongful conduct of a person or persons, the decedent's HEIRS and other BENEFICIARIES may file a wrongful death action against those responsible for the DECEDENT's death. This area of TORT LAW is governed by statute. Wrongful death statutes vary from state to state, but in general they define who may sue for wrongful death and what, if any, limits may be applied to an award of DAMAGES.

Originally, wrongful death statutes were created to provide financial support for widows and orphans and to motivate people to exercise care to prevent injuries. A wrongful death action is separate and apart from criminal charges, and neither proceeding affects nor controls the other. This means that a defendant acquitted of murder may be sued in a CIVIL ACTION by the victim's family for wrongful death.

An action for wrongful death may be brought for either an intentional or unintentional act that causes an INJURY that results in death. A blow to the head during an altercation that later results in death is an injury that is intentionally caused. The driver of an automobile who unintentionally causes the death of another in an accident may be held liable for her NEGLIGENCE. An individual who, in violation of local law, neglects to enclose a swimming pool in his yard can be held liable for the omission or failure to act if a child is attracted to the pool and subsequently drowns.

Wrongful death statutes do not apply to an unborn fetus, as an individual does not have a distinct legal status until she is born alive. If an infant is born alive and later dies as a result of an injury that occurred prior to birth, an action may be brought for wrongful death.

Who May Sue The individuals entitled to sue for wrongful death are enumerated in each state statute. Many statutes provide for recovery by a surviving spouse, next of kin, or children. Some states permit a surviving spouse to bring an action even in the event of a separation, but not if the surviving spouse was guilty of desertion or failure to provide support.

Ordinarily, children may bring suit for the wrongful death of their parents, and parents may sue for the wrongful death of their children. In some states, only MINOR children are allowed to sue for the death of a parent. Similarly, some state statutes preclude a parent from recovery for the death of an adult child who is financially independent or married.

Immunity from Suit In the absence of a legal exception, the surviving beneficiaries may

A woman demonstrated in support of a Florida wrongful death bill in honor of her deceased mother.

sue any person who caused the injuries that precipitated the death.

A traditional exception to this rule has been applied to family members. This doctrine is known as *family immunity* and means that an individual is protected from suit by any member of his family. This rule was intended to promote family harmony and to prevent family members from conspiring to DEFRAUD an INSURANCE company. However, its strict application prevented children from legitimately collecting insurance money. Therefore, many states have discarded the strict rule of family IMMUNITY. Some limitations have been retained, such as allowing an adult child to sue a parent but not allowing a minor child to do so.

Wrongful death actions filed against state or local government will be allowed to go forward only if the state has waived its sovereign immunity, a doctrine that bars lawsuits against the government. Since the 1960s a majority of states have relinquished the right to claim SOVEREIGN IMMUNITY in many instances. Therefore, if a child drowns in a municipal swimming pool, the parents may be able to sue the city for wrongful death based on negligence.

In states that allow wrongful death actions to be brought against government, there is generally a strict NOTICE requirement. The plaintiff must promptly notify the government that a lawsuit is contemplated in order to give the government an opportunity to estimate the potential losses to its budget. The time period for filing a notice may be as short as thirty, sixty, or ninety days. Failure to file a notice of claim precludes the possibility of a lawsuit.

The Defendant's Responsibility In order to sue for wrongful death, it must be proven that the acts or omissions of the defendant were the PROXIMATE CAUSE of the decedent's injuries and death. This means that the defendant's wrongful conduct must have created a natural, direct series of events that led to the injury.

An employer may be held responsible for injuries caused by an employee during the course of her employment.

Damages The law of each state governs the amount of damages recoverable by statutory beneficiaries. COMPENSATORY DAMAGES, which are intended to make RESTITUTION for the amount of money lost, are the most common damages awarded in wrongful death actions. Plaintiffs who prevail in a wrongful death lawsuit may recover medical and funeral expenses in addition to the amount of economic support they could have received if the decedent had lived and, in some instances, a sum of money to compensate for grief or loss of services or companionship.

Determining the amount of damages in a wrongful death action requires taking into account many variables. To compute compensation, the salary that the decedent could have earned can be multiplied by the number of years he most likely would have lived and can be adjusted for various factors, including inflation. Standard actuarial tables serve as guides for the life expectancy of particular groups identified by age or gender. The decedent's mental and physical health, along with the nature of his work, can be taken into consideration by a jury.

Damages cannot always be calculated on the basis of potential earnings because not everyone is employed. Courts have set minimum yearly dollar amounts for the worth of an individual's housekeeping and for child care services. Moreover, an additional recovery might be justified on the basis of grief and loss of companionship.

PUNITIVE DAMAGES may be awarded in a wrongful death case if the defendant's actions were particularly reckless or heinous. Punitive damages are a means of punishing the defendant for her action and are awarded at the discretion of the jury.

Any damages recovered are distributed among the survivors subject to the statutes of each state. Courts frequently divide an award based on the extent of each beneficiary's loss.

Limitations on Recovery of Damages Some states limit the amount of money that can be recovered in a wrongful death action. For example, many state and local governments that waive sovereign immunity set a maximum amount of damages that can be recovered for a wrongful death. However, a number of states do not limit the amount of damages for wrongful death.

International treaties limit the amount recoverable for the death of passengers on international airlines. WORKERS' COMPENSATION laws, which exist in some form in every state, place limits upon an employer's LIABILITY. Employers must carry insurance for their employees that compensates workers based on a legal schedule for each type of injury or for death. In return for carrying such insurance, employers are immune from negligence suits. The result is that the amount workers can recover is limited, but recovery is guaranteed for injury or death sustained in the course of employment.

WRONGFUL DISCHARGE 📖 An at-will employee's CAUSE OF ACTION against his former employer, alleging that his discharge was in violation of state or federal antidiscrimination statutes, PUBLIC POLICY, an implied contract, or an implied covenant of GOOD FAITH and fair dealing. 📖

At COMMON LAW, an employment CONTRACT of indefinite duration can be terminated by either party at any time for any reason. The United States is the only major industrial power that maintains a general EMPLOYMENT-AT-WILL rule. Since the 1950s, however, many courts have allowed discharged at-will employees to bring suits alleging wrongful discharge from employment.

An at-will employee may allege that her discharge is based on illegal discrimination. The CIVIL RIGHTS ACT of 1964, 42 U.S.C.A. § 2000e et seq., contains broad prohibitions against discrimination in employment based on race, color, religion, national origin, or sex. Discrimination against persons forty years old and over is banned by the Age Discrimination in Employment Act, 29 U.S.C.A. § 621 et seq. (1967). In addition, an at-will employee may use state antidiscrimination statutes to contest a discharge.

A majority of states allow an at-will employee to proceed with a wrongful discharge action that is based on public policy. This means that an employer cannot legally discharge an employee if the employee refused the employer's request to violate a specific federal or state statute, or a professional code of ETHICS. In addition, it is against public policy to discharge an employee who exercises a statutory right, such as the right to apply for WORKER'S COMPENSATION benefits for an on-the-job injury. An employee is also protected if his "whistle-blowing" activity or other conduct exposing the employer's wrongdoing resulted in a retaliatory discharge.

Employees may sue for wrongful discharge in almost half of the states on the basis of an EXPRESS or IMPLIED promise by the employer, which constitutes a UNILATERAL CONTRACT. In a unilateral contract, one party makes a PROMISE and receives PERFORMANCE from the other party. Typically, this type of wrongful discharge action will be based on a statement by the employer that expressly or implicitly promises employees a degree of job security. Ordinarily, such statements are found in employee handbooks or in policy statements given to employees when they are hired.

Some courts have interpreted such statements as unilateral contracts in which the employer promises not to discharge the employees except for just cause and in accordance with certain procedures. The difficulty with suits based on the employer's promise from the employee's perspective is that the employer may eliminate the possibility of a suit by issuing a policy statement that expressly disclaims any right to continuing employment.

Some at-will employees have based their suits on an implied COVENANT (promise) of good faith and fair dealing. The discharged employee typically contends that the employer has indicated in various ways that the employee has job security and will be treated fairly. For example, long-time employees who have consistently received favorable evaluations might claim that their length of service and positive performance reviews were signs that their jobs would be secure as long as they performed satisfactorily. However, few JURISDICTIONS have recognized any good-faith-and-fair-dealing exceptions to the employment at-will practice.

See also EMPLOYMENT LAW.

WRONGFUL LIFE 📖 A type of MEDICAL MALPRACTICE claim brought on behalf of a child born with birth defects, alleging that the child would not have been born but for negligent advice to, or treatment of, the parents. 📖

Since the early 1970s, TORT actions for wrongful life have been filed in U.S. courts. In a typical wrongful life ACTION, the parents of a child born with birth defects sue on behalf of the child. Generally, the parents sue their doctor or a medical testing company for NEGLIGENCE, claiming that the failure to diagnose an illness in the mother—for example, rubella in the early stages of pregnancy—prevented the opportunity for the mother to have an ABORTION. As a result, the child is born with impaired health.

Essentially, the child alleges that because of the defect, he would have been better off not being born at all. To bring a wrongful life action, the defect must be one that could only have been averted by preventing the birth of the child; otherwise the child would bring an ordinary negligence action. Other types of defects that can be diagnosed early in pregnancy include Tay-Sachs disease, sickle cell anemia, neurofibromatosis, and Down's syndrome.

Only a small number of states permit wrongful life actions. The many courts that have rejected wrongful life claims have cited two general reasons. First, the courts are reluctant to hold that a plaintiff can recover DAMAGES for being alive when the law and civilization in general have placed a high value on the presence of human life, not on its absence. Second, the basic rule of tort compensation is that the plaintiff is to be put in the position that she would have been in if the defendant had not been negligent. This is impossible in wrongful life actions because the contention is not that in the absence of negligence by the defendant, the plaintiff would have had a healthy, unimpaired life, but rather that if the defendant had not been negligent, the plaintiff would not have been born.

The computation of damages in a wrongful life action is based on the claim that the value of the life of the disabled child is less than the value of never having been born. The California Supreme Court, in *Turpin v. Sortini*, 31 Cal.3d 220, 182 Cal. Rptr. 337, 643 P.2d 954 (1982), stated that the wrongful life action is another form of a medical malpractice action, and that recovery should not be allowed for pain and suffering and other general damages, but rather only for those extraordinary medical and other expenses incurred during the child's lifetime.

See also WRONGFUL BIRTH; WRONGFUL PREGNANCY.

WRONGFUL PREGNANCY 📖 A claim by parents for DAMAGES arising from the negligent performance of a sterilization procedure or ABORTION, and the subsequent birth of a child. 📖

In wrongful pregnancy cases (also known as wrongful conception), parents file a NEGLIGENCE action against the medical provider for failing to perform a sterilization or abortion correctly, which results in the birth of a healthy but unwanted child. Wrongful pregnancy cases are different from *wrongful birth* cases. In WRONGFUL BIRTH actions, the provider is charged with negligence in failing to diagnose a birth defect, which would have allowed the mother to have an abortion instead of giving birth to a child with birth defects.

Parents in wrongful pregnancy ACTIONS may be able to sue for damages on the basis of the cost of the unsuccessful procedure and any pain or suffering associated with the sterilization or abortion. The parents may also recover damages for the medical expenses, pain, and suffering attributable to the pregnancy, the mother's lost wages due to the pregnancy, the husband's LOSS OF CONSORTIUM during the pregnancy, and the economic and emotional costs of rearing the child to maturity. Of these, the claims for the costs of rearing the child have presented the most difficulty for the courts.

Some courts have taken the position that the costs of raising a child are not recoverable damages. Another objection that has been raised is that allowing damages for the cost of rearing a healthy child requires the parents to deny the worth of the child, which may cause considerable emotional harm to the child when he eventually learns of the lawsuit. However, the plaintiffs may still be able to recover damages for the costs of the pregnancy and the birth if they can prove negligence.

Other courts have allowed recovery for the expenses of rearing the child, but insist that they be offset by the benefits of having a normal, healthy child.

See also TORT LAW; WRONGFUL LIFE.

WYATT, WALTER   Walter Wyatt served as REPORTER of decisions of the U.S. Supreme Court from 1946 to 1963. Prior to becoming reporter, Wyatt spent almost thirty years working for the FEDERAL RESERVE BOARD as an attorney. Wyatt's tenure was marked by a series of important decisions, including *Brown v. Board of Education*, 347 U.S. 483, 74 S. Ct. 686, 98 L. Ed. 873 (1954), which struck down state-sponsored, racially segregated schools.

Wyatt was born on July 20, 1893, in Savannah, Georgia. He attended the University of Virginia Law School and served as editor in chief of the *Virginia Law Review*, graduating in 1917. During World War I, he was a member of the Legal Advisory Board of the Selective Service.

In 1922 Wyatt took a position as law clerk with the Federal Reserve Board in Washington, D.C. He rose from assistant to counsel to

BIOGRAPHY

general counsel of the Board of Governors of the Federal Reserve System. From 1936 to 1946, Wyatt also served as general counsel to the federal Open Market Commission.

The Supreme Court appointed Wyatt its reporter in 1946. Because the position had been vacant for more than two years, Wyatt edited volumes 322 to 325 of the *United States Reports*, which had been previously published without editorial review. During his seventeen years as reporter, Wyatt edited or coedited 123 volumes of decisions, writing a SYLLABUS for each opinion that highlights the important points of each case.

Wyatt also published numerous works on banking law throughout his career.

Wyatt retired from his position in 1963. He died in Washington, D.C., on February 26, 1978.

WYGANT v. JACKSON BOARD OF EDUCATION   The U.S. Supreme Court has held that an employer can grant preferential treatment to racial minorities under a private, voluntary affirmative action program. Affirmative action is a concerted effort by an employer to rectify past discrimination against specific classes of individuals by giving temporary preferential treatment to the hiring and promoting of individuals from these classes until such time as true equal opportunity is achieved. The use of affirmative action is based on Title VII of the CIVIL RIGHTS ACT of 1964 (42 U.S.C.A. § 2000e et seq.). It has proved controversial, with many white persons claiming affirmative action is in fact "reverse discrimination."

The case of *Wygant v. Jackson Board of Education*, 476 U.S. 267, 106 S. Ct. 1842, 90 L. Ed. 2d 260 (1986), involved minority preferences in teacher layoffs. In the face of a budget crisis, the Jackson, Mississippi, Board of Education was forced to cut teaching positions. Under the terms of the CONTRACT with the teachers' union, the board laid off more senior white teachers in order to retain less senior minority teachers. The white teachers who were laid off fought the decision, arguing that the minority preference plan unfairly discriminated against them on the

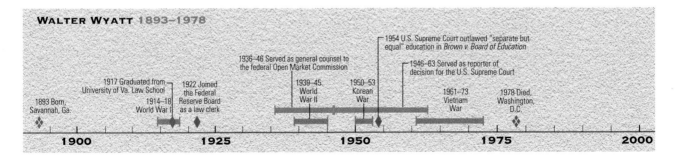

WALTER WYATT 1893–1978

1893 Born, Savannah, Ga.

1914–18 World War I

1917 Graduated from University of Va. Law School

1922 Joined the Federal Reserve Board as a law clerk

1936–46 Served as general counsel to the federal Open Market Commission

1939–45 World War II

1950–53 Korean War

1954 U.S. Supreme Court outlawed "separate but equal" education in *Brown v. Board of Education*

1946–63 Served as reporter of decision for the U.S. Supreme Court

1961–73 Vietnam War

1978 Died, Washington, D.C.

1900   1925   1950   1975   2000

basis of race, thus violating Title VII and the Equal Protection Clause of the FOURTEENTH AMENDMENT to the U.S. Constitution.

Though there was no majority opinion, the Supreme Court agreed that the school board had violated the Constitution. Writing for a plurality, Justice LEWIS F. POWELL found that race-based preferences must be subjected to the strict scrutiny standard of EQUAL PROTECTION review. Strict scrutiny reverses the ordinary presumption of constitutionality, with the government carrying the burden of proof that its challenged policy is constitutional. To withstand strict scrutiny, the government must show that its policy is necessary to achieve a COMPELLING STATE INTEREST. If this is proved, the state must then demonstrate that the legislation is narrowly tailored to achieve the intended result. Strict scrutiny is far more stringent than the traditional RATIONAL BASIS TEST, which only requires the government to offer a reasonable ground for the legislation.

Applying strict scrutiny, the plurality concluded that the school board had no compelling interest in remedying "societal discrimination" and suggested that prior institutional discrimination supplied the only permissible justification for "race-based remedies." However, even if the school board had discriminated in the past, "the burden that a preferential-layoffs scheme imposes on innocent parties" would be too great to be constitutionally acceptable. Powell noted that while minority hiring goals "impose a diffuse burden, often foreclosing only one of several opportunities, layoffs impose the entire burden of achieving racial equality on particular individuals, often resulting in serious disruption of their lives." That burden was too intrusive and therefore failed the strict scrutiny requirement that a race-based remedy be narrowly tailored to achieve its ends.

The *Wygant* decision imposed a higher burden on government to justify affirmative action programs, especially when white employees are laid off in order to retain minority employees. The Court left open, however, the possibility that it would find other governmental interests

to be sufficiently important or compelling to sustain the use of affirmative action policies.

CROSS-REFERENCES

Civil Rights; Employment Law; Equal Employment Opportunity Commission; *United Steelworkers v. Weber.*

BIOGRAPHY

George Wythe

"THERE IS NO COUNTRY IN THE WORLD . . . SUCH AS THE UNITED STATES ITSELF—IN WHICH CAPITAL, MANAGEMENT, LABOR AND RESOURCES MAY BE JOINED TOGETHER FOR MORE PRODUCTION, TO THE MUTUAL ADVANTAGE OF ALL CONCERNED."

WYTHE, GEORGE George Wythe was an attorney, judge, signer of the DECLARATION OF INDEPENDENCE, and first professor of law in the United States. A mentor to THOMAS JEFFERSON, Wythe educated a number of men who went on to achieve prominence in law and politics.

Wythe was born in 1726 in Elizabeth City, Virginia. After his admission to the Virginia bar in 1746, Wythe settled in Williamsburg, then the seat of government in the colony. He became active in politics, serving as a member of the House of Burgesses from 1754 to 1755 and from 1758 to 1768. He later served as clerk of the house from 1769 to 1775. An ardent supporter of independence, Wythe drafted a fiery motion opposing the STAMP ACT of 1764. However, the house was compelled to rewrite the motion and adopt a softer tone. Wythe attended the CONTINENTAL CONGRESS in 1775 and 1776 and signed the Declaration of Independence.

During these years of politics and revolution, Wythe maintained a successful law practice. Many students sought his counsel, including Jefferson, who studied law with Wythe in the 1760s and viewed him as his mentor. As Jefferson rose in stature and power, Wythe became part of his circle. In 1776 Wythe, Jefferson, GEORGE MASON, and Edmund Pendleton revised the Virginia Code.

Jefferson used his influence to have Wythe appointed the first law professor in the United States. Wythe taught at the College of William and Mary from 1779 to 1789. One of his first students was JOHN MARSHALL, later chief justice of the United States. While teaching, Wythe also pursued a judicial career and presided as a judge in the Virginia Chancery Court from 1778 to 1788. In 1789 he was appointed chancellor of Virginia, which required him to move to Richmond. Wythe established a private law

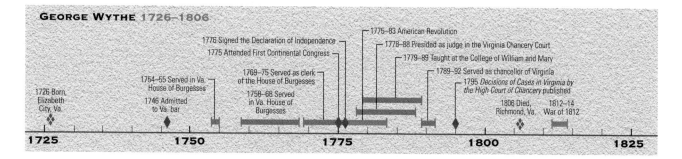

GEORGE WYTHE 1726–1806

1726 Born, Elizabeth City, Va.

1746 Admitted to Va. bar

1754–55 Served in Va. House of Burgesses

1758–68 Served in Va. House of Burgesses

1769–75 Served as clerk of the House of Burgesses

1775 Attended First Continental Congress

1776 Signed the Declaration of Independence

1775–83 American Revolution

1778–88 Presided as judge in the Virginia Chancery Court

1779–89 Taught at the College of William and Mary

1789–92 Served as chancellor of Virginia

1795 *Decisions of Cases in Virginia by the High Court of Chancery* published

1806 Died, Richmond, Va.

1812–14 War of 1812

1725   1750   1775   1800   1825

school there and had as one of his pupils the future U.S. senator from Kentucky, HENRY CLAY. Wythe resigned as chancellor in 1792. He published a selection of his court decisions in *Decisions of Cases in Virginia by the High Court of Chancery* in 1795.

Wythe died on June 8, 1806, in Richmond, Virginia, of poisoning. His grandnephew and heir, George Wythe Sweeney, was acquitted of the murder. At trial the only witness was an African American, who was disqualified from testifying under the laws of Virginia.

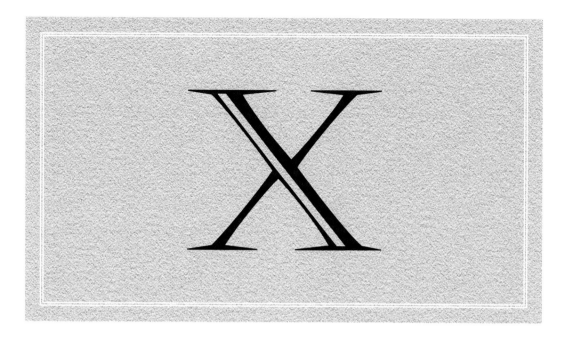

"X" AS A SIGNATURE

"X" as a SIGNATURE refers to a cross that is printed in lieu of an individual's signature. A signature is required to authenticate WILLS, DEEDS, and certain commercial instruments. Typically, individuals sign their full names when executing legal documents. Sometimes, however, individuals use only their initials or other identifying mark. For illiterate, incompetent, or disabled people, this mark is often the letter X. Documents signed with an X sometimes raise questions as to their validity and enforceability.

For example, wills must be signed by the TESTATOR in order to be valid and enforceable. A testator's signature may take the form of his full name, nickname, initials, or other identifying mark, including a thumbprint or blood splotch. In many JURISDICTIONS testators may authenticate their last will and testament with the letter X. Before an X may be treated as a binding signature during a proceeding to contest a will, courts commonly require the TESTIMONY of two people who witnessed the signature. The WITNESSES may also be questioned by the court to determine if the testator declared her intention of completing the will by signing it in this fashion. In other states the law requires courts to invalidate wills that are signed with an X unless the testator was physically or mentally incapable of signing her full name. Similar rules are applied by courts when evaluating the enforceability of REAL ESTATE deeds that are signed with an X.

Signatures also form the legal basis of NEGOTIABLE INSTRUMENTS. Section 3-401(2) of the UNIFORM COMMERCIAL CODE (UCC) provides that "[n]o person is liable on an instrument unless his signature appears thereon." The UCC defines the term *signature* as any name, trade name, assumed name, word, or other identifying mark used in lieu of a signature (§ 3-401(2)). The term *signed* is defined by the UCC as any symbol executed or adopted by a party with the "present intention of authenticating a writing" (§ 1-201(39)). Thus, commercial instruments, such as CHECKS and PROMISSORY NOTES, may be signed by affixing any symbol that an individual intends to represent his signature. Consequently, courts will enforce commercial CONTRACTS signed with an X without regard to an individual's mental or physical ability to sign her full name, though mental or physical incapacity may be relevant if a particular contract is alleged to be the product of OVERREACHING, UNDUE INFLUENCE, or COERCION.

X RATING

A classification devised by the Motion Picture Association of America (MPAA) and the National Association of Theater Owners (NATO) in 1968 to designate certain films containing excessive violence or explicit sexuality. It was replaced in 1990 by the NC-17 rating (no one 17 and under admitted).

Since the 1920s the U.S. movie industry has practiced self-regulation to forestall government CENSORSHIP. In 1968 MPAA and NATO adopted a MOVIE RATING system that is based on age classification. Any film produced or distributed by members of MPAA must receive a rating from a Ratings Board, which is part of its Classification and Rating Administration. There are five rating classifications: G (suitable for all ages), PG (parental guidance suggested), PG-13

Movies may be advertised as rated XXX in order to attract customers, but this is not a rating from the Motion Picture Association of America, which rates movies produced by its members.

(may not be suitable for children under age 13), R (restricted, children younger than age 17 must be accompanied by a parent or guardian), and, until 1990, X (no one under age 17 admitted.) In 1990 the X rating was changed to NC-17.

The distinction between the R and the X rating was based on the overall sexual or violent content of a movie. A movie was given an R rating if it contained adult themes, nudity, sex, and profanity. A movie given an X rating contained an accumulation of brutal or sexually connotative language or explicit sex, or excessive and sadistic violence.

Over time very few MPAA-produced movies were given an X rating. If an X rating was awarded, a producer would usually reedit the film to qualify for an R rating. This reediting was done because theater owners generally refused to book X-rated movies, thereby reducing the size of the potential audience. In the 1970s the X rating concept was used by the producers and exhibitors of pornographic movies as a promotional device. Though these films were not MPAA productions and the producers could not submit their films for review, the X rating was not trademarked by MPAA. This meant that pornographic films could be advertised as X-rated or XXX-rated, which suggested that MPAA's X rating was a code for hardcore PORNOGRAPHY.

Because of this problem, the X rating was changed in 1990 to NC-17. MPAA sought to reaffirm the original intent of the 1968 ratings design, in which the "adults-only" category

explicitly describes a movie that most parents would not want their children to see. Despite the attempt to remove the taint of pornography from the adults-only category, the NC-17 rating, like the X rating before it, is avoided by motion picture companies. Theater owners remain opposed to exhibiting films that substantially restrict the size of the potential audience, many of whom are seventeen years old or younger.

See also ENTERTAINMENT LAW; THEATERS AND SHOWS.

XYY CHROMOSOMAL ABNORMALITY DEFENSE A legal theory that holds that a defendant's XYY chromosomal abnormality is a condition that should relieve him or her of legal responsibility for his or her criminal act.

Criminologists have examined many theories as to why a person becomes a criminal. Since the nineteenth century, biological theories have been proposed that seek to link criminal behavior with innate characteristics, yet these theories have been strongly challenged by the scientific community. With the development of modern genetics, scientists have noted abnormalities in the chromosomal structure of some people.

A chromosome is the threadlike part of the cell that carries hereditary information in the form of genes. The normal human genetic complement consists of 23 pairs of chromosomes. One of these pairs determines sex. Women have two X chromosomes and men usually have an X and a Y chromosome. However, in 1 in 500 to 1,000 live male births, an individual has an extra Y chromosome. This XYY abnormality is often characterized by tallness and severe acne and sometimes by skeletal malformations and mental deficiency.

With the discovery of the XYY abnormality in 1961, some social scientists proposed a link between the abnormality and aggressive and impulsive behavior. This "supermale" syndrome seemed confirmed when studies of prison populations showed the presence of the abnormality to be significantly higher than in the general population.

Armed with these studies, defense attorneys sought to use the XYY chromosomal abnormality as a criminal DEFENSE theory. However, the defense has never been successfully used in the United States. Though the abnormality can be easily diagnosed using a blood test, the courts have rejected the defense because of the lack of conclusiveness of SCIENTIFIC EVIDENCE regarding the theory of criminality.

The legal community's misgivings have been confirmed by subsequent studies of the general population, especially those in which affected individuals were observed from early childhood over a long period of time. These studies have cast serious doubt on the validity of linking the chromosomal anomaly directly to behavioral abnormalities. Numerous XYY individuals live normal lives as law-abiding citizens.

XYZ AFFAIR 📖 A diplomatic scandal involving France and the United States in 1797–1798. 📖

The XYZ Affair was a diplomatic incident that almost led to war between the United States and France. The scandal inflamed U.S. public opinion and led to the passage of the Alien and Sedition Acts of 1798 (1 Stat. 570, 596). Though the affair caused an unofficial naval war, the two countries were able to negotiate their differences and end their conflict in 1800.

The affair took place during one of the Napoleonic wars between France and Great Britain. The French regarded the United States as a hostile nation, particularly after the signing of Jay's Treaty in 1794. This treaty settled some of the problems that continued to cause friction between the United States and Great Britain after the peace treaty of 1783 that granted the colonies independence. Consequently, President JOHN ADAMS appointed Charles Pinckney minister to France in 1796 in an attempt to ease French-U.S. relations.

After Charles Talleyrand, the French foreign minister, refused to recognize Pinckney, Adams appointed a commission to France, consisting of Pinckney, JOHN MARSHALL, and Elbridge Gerry. Before official negotiations on a treaty to establish peaceful relations and normalize trade could occur, Talleyrand sent three French agents to meet with the commission members. The agents suggested that Talleyrand would agree to the treaty if he received from the United States a $250,000 bribe and France received a $10 million loan. The commission refused, with Pinckney quoted as saying, "No! No! Not a sixpence!"

Outraged, the commission sent a report to Adams, who inserted the letters X, Y and Z in place of the agents' names and forwarded the report to Congress. Congress and the public were angered at the attempted blackmail. An undeclared naval war took place between the two nations between 1798 and 1800. Anticipating a declared war with France, Congress enacted the Alien and Sedition Acts. These internal security laws were aimed at French and Irish immigrants, who were thought to be supportive of France. The acts lengthened the period of naturalization for ALIENS, authorized the president to expel any alien considered dangerous, permitted the detention of subjects of an enemy nation, and limited FREEDOM OF THE PRESS.

Talleyrand, unwilling to risk a declared war with the United States, sought an end to the dispute. The next U.S. delegation sent to France was treated with appropriate respect, and the Treaty of Morfontaine, which restored normal relations between France and the United States, was signed in 1800.

See also VIRGINIA AND KENTUCKY RESOLVES.

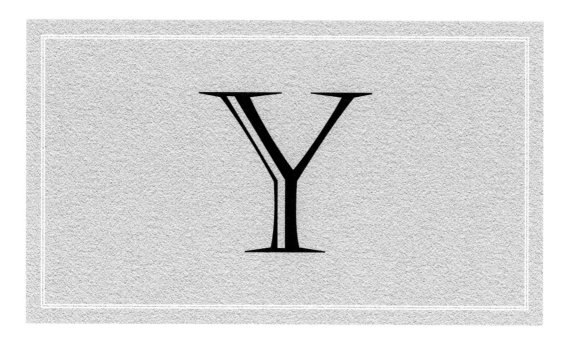

YALTA AGREEMENT

YALTA AGREEMENT 📖 A WORLD WAR II accord made in 1945 between Great Britain, the United States, and the Soviet Union. 📖

British prime minister Winston Churchill, U.S. president FRANKLIN D. ROOSEVELT, and Soviet premier JOSEPH STALIN met from February 4 to 11, 1945, at Yalta, in the Crimea. The conference, the last attended by all three of these leaders, produced an agreement concerning the prosecution of the war against Japan, the occupation of Germany, the structure of the UNITED NATIONS, and the postwar fate of Poland, Czechoslovakia, Hungary, Romania, and Bulgaria. The Yalta agreement proved to be controversial, as many in the United States criticized Roosevelt for abandoning Eastern Europe to the Communists.

Roosevelt came to Yalta seeking early Soviet participation in the war against Japan. Fearing that Japan would not surrender easily, Roosevelt promised Stalin the return of territories lost following the Russo-Japanese War of 1905. Stalin agreed to declare war on Japan, but only ninety days after the surrender of Germany. With the surrender of Japan in August 1945, which followed the dropping of nuclear bombs by the United States on the cities of Hiroshima and Nagasaki, the Soviet Union obtained the promised territories after expending minimal military effort.

Roosevelt also sought Stalin's approval of the U.N. Charter, which had already been drafted. Stalin had previously insisted that each of the sixteen Soviet republics be represented and that the permanent members of the Security Council retain a permanent veto on all issues, not just those involving sanctions or threats to peace. Roosevelt and Churchill objected to this proposal, and at Yalta, Stalin agreed to three seats for the Soviet Union in the General Assembly and a limited veto.

The postwar status of Germany was also settled at Yalta. Germany was to be divided into four zones of occupation by the three countries and France, as was the city of Berlin. Germany was to have its industrial base rebuilt but its armaments industries were to be abolished or confiscated. The leaders also approved the creation of an international court to try German leaders as war criminals, setting the stage for the NUREMBERG TRIALS.

The most troublesome issue was the fate of the Eastern European countries that Germany had conquered during the war. The Soviet army occupied most of the territory, making it difficult for Churchill and Roosevelt to bargain with Stalin on this point. It was agreed that interim governments in these countries would give way to democratically elected regimes as soon as practicable. On Poland, Churchill and Roosevelt abandoned the London-based Polish government-in-exile, agreeing that members of this group must work with the Soviet-dominated group with headquarters in Lublin, Poland.

In the aftermath of World War II the results envisioned in the Yalta agreement on Eastern Europe proved illusory. Communist regimes were established by the Soviet Union, accompanied by the destruction of democratic political groups. The legacy of Yalta continued until the collapse of COMMUNISM and the emergence of democracy in the late 1980s and early 1990s.

YEAR BOOKS 📖 Books of legal cases, or reporters, published annually in England from the thirteenth to the sixteenth century. 📖

The development of English COMMON LAW was based on the law of the case. Lawyers and courts relied on previous court decisions that involved similar issues of law and fact. The law of the case could not take hold, however, until cases were recorded, reported, and eventually published. The English Year Books, which were created in about 1290, are the first example of a reporting system. Though they were informal and often contained running commentary about the judges' personalities and the lawyers' quips, the Year Books were referred to increasingly by judges and lawyers.

During the reign of King Edward I (1272-1307) legal materials began to be collected into separate books for each year. During this early period the Year Books were extremely informal. They contained accounts by anonymous scribes and law students of courtroom proceedings and arguments that helped explain the judicial decision. The quality of the reports varied according to the abilities of the note takers. Despite these shortcomings, the reports conveyed basic procedural information to lawyers and students, but they stated few rules of law.

English legal publishing began in 1481 with the printing of the Year Book. Until that time Year Books had been prepared and circulated in handwritten copies. It was during this period that the Year Books became more professional and uniform. They were published at the expense of the Crown, but they were not official reports of cases. The printed versions were arranged by year, but it sometimes took two or three years after a case had been decided for it to be reported.

The compilation of Year Books ceased in 1535 during the reign of King Henry VIII, for reasons that remain unclear. Thereafter court reports were issued in a different form by named reporters.

Since the late nineteenth century, modern critical editions of the Year Books have been prepared by the SELDEN SOCIETY. Legal historians have found the Year Books a rich source of information about law and life in medieval England.

YELLOW DOG CONTRACT 📖 An employment agreement whereby a worker promises not to join a LABOR UNION or promises to resign from a union if he or she is already a member. 📖

Until the 1930s, employers were able to use a variety of measures to prevent employees from joining labor unions. One of the most effective was the yellow dog contract, which frequently forced employees to either sign an agreement not to join a union or be fired. Courts upheld the legality of yellow dog contracts and frequently struck down state laws that sought to outlaw them. The enactment of the WAGNER ACT in 1935 (29 U.S.C.A. § 151 et seq.) finally put an end to these types of agreements.

The U.S. Supreme Court's hostility to efforts by government to outlaw the yellow dog contract was rooted in the concept of "liberty of contract." Near the end of the nineteenth century, the Court used the due process provisions of the Fifth and Fourteenth Amendments to the U.S. Constitution to strike down federal and state laws regulating business. These amendments provide that no government was to "deprive any person of life, liberty, or property, without due process of law." The Court interpreted this prohibition to include the negotiating of terms of employment between an employer and an employee.

Therefore, in *Adair v. United States*, 208 U.S. 161, 28 S. Ct. 277, 52 L. Ed. 436 (1908), the Court struck down a federal law that protected union members by prohibiting yellow dog contracts and the discharge or blacklisting of employees for union activities. In his majority opinion Justice JOHN HARLAN presumed that there was equal bargaining power between an employer and an employee, and that the law was an unreasonable intrusion on personal LIBERTY and PROPERTY RIGHTS, as guaranteed by the FIFTH AMENDMENT.

When Kansas enacted a law prohibiting yellow dog contracts, the Court declared the law unconstitutional under the FOURTEENTH AMENDMENT as an infringement of freedom of contract. *Coppage v. Kansas*, 236 U.S. 1, 35 S. Ct. 240, 59 L. Ed. 441 (1915).

The Wagner Act of 1935 gave employees the right to join unions and to bargain collectively with their employers. Congress outlawed the yellow dog contract and other UNFAIR LABOR PRACTICES on the part of employers, finding that these practices were contrary to public policy. Existing yellow dog contracts were declared unenforceable by the courts. The Supreme Court's upholding of the constitutionality of the Wagner Act in *NLRB v. Jones & Laughlin Steel Corp.*, 301 U.S. 1, 57 S. Ct. 615, 81 L. Ed. 893 (1937), meant the end of the yellow dog contract.

See also LABOR LAW; SUBSTANTIVE DUE PROCESS.

YICK WO v. HOPKINS An 1896 U.S. Supreme Court decision, *Yick Wo v. Hopkins*, 118 U.S. 356, 6 S. Ct. 1064, 30 L. Ed. 220 (1886), held that the unequal application of a law violates the Equal Protection Clause of the FOURTEENTH AMENDMENT to the U.S. Constitution.

A law that is racially neutral on its FACE may be deliberately administered in a discriminatory way, or it may have been enacted in order to disadvantage a racial minority. In *Yick Wo v. Hopkins*, the Supreme Court stated for the first time that a state or municipal law that appears to be fair on its face will be declared unconstitutional under the Fourteenth Amendment because of its discriminatory purpose.

Yick Wo, a native and subject of China, was convicted and imprisoned for violating an ORDINANCE of the city of San Francisco, California, which made it unlawful to maintain a laundry "without having first obtained the consent of the board of supervisors, except the same be located in a building constructed either of brick or stone." The 1880 ordinance was neutral on its face, but its purpose and its administration appeared suspect to Yick Wo and other Chinese. Most laundries in San Francisco were owned by Chinese and were constructed out of wood. The few laundries owned by whites were located in brick buildings. At the time the ordinance was passed, Chinese immigration had brought around 75,000 Chinese to California, half of whom lived in San Francisco. The white population became increasingly anti-Chinese and sought ways to control the Chinese population.

In 1885 the San Francisco Board of Supervisors denied Yick Wo and two hundred other Chinese laundry owners their LICENSES, even though their establishments had previously passed city inspections. After he was denied his license, Yick Wo continued to operate his business. He was eventually arrested and jailed for ten days for violating the ordinance. More than one hundred and fifty other Chinese laundry owners were also arrested for violating the ordinance.

On appeal to the U.S. Supreme Court, Yick Wo argued that the ordinance violated the Fourteenth Amendment, as the law denied him EQUAL PROTECTION of the laws. He pointed out that only one-quarter of the laundries could operate under the ordinance, with 73 owned by non-Chinese and only one owned by a Chinese. San Francisco contended the ordinance was a valid exercise of the police powers granted by the U.S. Constitution to cities and states.

Justice STANLEY MATTHEWS, writing for a unanimous court, struck down the ordinance. Matthews looked past the neutral language to strike down the ordinance as a violation of the Fourteenth Amendment's Equal Protection

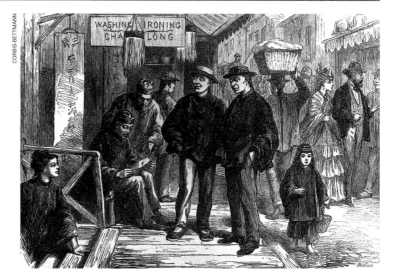

Clause. He found that the division between wood and brick buildings was an "arbitrary line." Moreover, whatever the intent of the law may have been, the administration of the ordinance was carried out "with a mind so unequal and oppressive as to amount to a practical denial by the state" of equal protection of the laws.

Matthews held that:

Though the law itself be fair on its face, and impartial in appliance, yet, if it is applied and administered by public authority with an evil eye and an unequal hand, so as practically to make unjust and illegal discriminations between persons in similar circumstances, material to their rights, the denial of equal justice is still within the prohibition of the constitution.

Because the unequal application of the ordinance furthered "unjust and illegal discrimination," the Court ruled that the ordinance was unconstitutional under the Fourteenth Amendment.

Yick Wo has become a central part of CIVIL RIGHTS jurisprudence. If a law has a discriminatory purpose or is administered unequally, courts will apply the Fourteenth Amendment and strike down the law. *Yick Wo* is also the source of modern civil rights disparate-impact cases, in which discrimination is established by statistical inequality rather than through proof of intentional discrimination.

YIELD 📖 Current return from an investment or expenditure as a percentage of the price of investment or expenditure. 📖

The term *yield* is the proportionate rate that income from an investment bears to the total cost of the investment. For example, a ten dollar profit on a one hundred dollar invest-

In Yick Wo v. Hopkins, *the Supreme Court ruled that a law that is fair on its face but has a discriminatory purpose is unconstitutional. An 1880 San Francisco city ordinance made it illegal to run a laundry in a building not constructed with stone or brick. The ordinance was directed at Chinese and Chinese Americans, many of whom ran laundries in wooden buildings.*

ment represents a 10 percent yield. Thus, a yield for STOCK dividends or BOND interest paid will be expressed as a percentage of the current price. A yield can also refer to the bond COUPON or stock DIVIDEND rate divided by the purchase price.

There are several specific types of yields. On bonds, a current yield is the annual interest paid divided by the current market price of the bond. As interest rates fall, the market price of the bond rises; as they rise, bond prices fall. The current yield reflects the actual rate of return on a bond. For example, a 9.5 percent bond with a FACE VALUE of $1,000 yields $95 per year. If this bond is purchased in the secondary bond market for $1,100, the interest will still be $95 a year, but the current yield will be reduced to 8.6 percent because the new owner paid more for the bond.

A nominal yield is the annual income received from a fixed-income security divided by the face value of the security. It is stated as a percentage figure. For example, if a security with a face value of $5,000 generated $500 in income, the nominal yield would be 10 percent.

On bonds, a yield to maturity is a complex calculation that reflects the overall rate of return an investor would receive from a bond if the bond is held to maturity and the interest payments are reinvested at the same rate. It takes into account the purchase price, the coupon yield, the time to maturity, and the time between interest payments.

A net yield is the rate of return on an investment after deducting all costs, losses, and charges for investment. A dividend yield is the current annual dividend divided by the market price per share of stock. A yield spread refers to differences in yields between various issues of SECURITIES.

YORK-ANTWERP RULES 📖 A group of directives relating to uniform BILLS OF LADING and governing the settlement of maritime losses among the several interests, including ship and cargo owners. 📖

Maritime law includes international agreements, national laws on shipping, and private agreements voluntarily adhered to by the parties involved in shipping contracts. The York-Antwerp Rules of General Average are the best known example of such private agreements, as they establish the rights and obligations of the parties when cargo must be jettisoned from a ship.

Under the law of general average, if cargo is jettisoned in a successful effort to refloat a grounded vessel, the owners of the vessel and the cargo saved are required to absorb a pro-

portionate share of the loss, in order to compensate the owner of the cargo that has been singled out for sacrifice. All participants in the maritime venture contribute to offset the losses incurred. The law of general average became an early form of marine insurance.

The York-Antwerp Rules were first promulgated in 1890 and have been amended several times, most recently in 1994. They are the result of conferences of representatives of mercantile interests from many countries. The rules provide uniform guidelines on the law of general average that are included in private shipping agreements and depend upon their voluntary acceptance by the maritime community. These international rules ensure uniformity and determine the rights and obligations of the parties.

The rules are incorporated by reference into most bills of lading (documents given by a shipping company that list the goods accepted for transport and sometimes list the terms of the shipping agreement), CONTRACTS of affreightment (a contract with a ship owner to hire the ship, or part of it, for the carriage of goods), and marine insurance policies.

The York-Antwerp Rules attempt to cover many types of expenses associated with an imperiled ship. For example, the rules provide for recovery by the ship owner of the costs of repair, loading and unloading cargo, and maintaining the crew, if these expenses are necessary for the safe completion of the voyage. Claims are generally made against the insurer of the cargo and the ship owner's insurance underwriters.

See also ADMIRALTY AND MARITIME LAW; SHIPPING LAW.

BIOGRAPHY

Owen D. Young

YOUNG, OWEN D. Owen D. Young was a prominent corporate lawyer and businessperson who played a major part in negotiating German REPARATIONS following World War I. His 1929 proposal to restructure reparations, called the Young Plan, was an attempt to relieve financial pressure on Germany and end active oversight of its economy by the United States, Great Britain, and France.

Young was born on October 27, 1874, in Van Hornesville, New York. He graduated from St. Lawrence University in 1894 and earned a law degree from Boston University in 1896. He later completed a doctorate in Hebrew literature in 1923 from St. Lawrence.

Young practiced law in Boston from 1896 until 1913, when he moved to New York City where he served as general counsel for the General Electric Company. He was chairperson of the board of directors from 1922 to 1939,

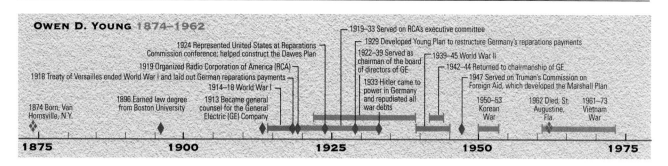

and again from 1942 to 1944. Young also organized Radio Corporation of America (RCA) in 1919 and was its honorary chairperson from its inception until 1929.

In 1924 Young and Charles G. Dawes represented the United States at the post–World War I reparations conference. The TREATY OF VERSAILLES had mandated that a Reparations Commission be formed to determine how much Germany was to pay the Allies for war destruction and to set the terms of payment. The German government complained that the payment schedule was unrealistic. In response, the U.S. representatives helped formulate the Dawes Plan under which Germany was to make billions of dollars of reparations stretching over a period of years.

The German economy prospered from 1924 to 1929 but it still could not make its annual reparations payment. The Reparations Commission, seeking to resolve the issue, appointed Young in 1929 to head a committee to develop a workable reparations plan. Young played a major role in creating the proposal, which reduced German reparations to approximately $26 billion, one-third the amount originally assessed in 1921. Payments were spread out over fifty-eight years, ending in 1988, and were to be made to the new Bank for International Settlements. The Young plan also called for the dissolution of the Reparations Commission and an end to Allied occupation of the Rhineland. The German government quickly agreed to these terms.

Despite the more favorable terms, rightwing German opposition leaders campaigned against the Young Plan, seeing it as another attempt to humiliate Germany. ADOLF HITLER and his Nazi party demanded the government repudiate the war debt and the war-guilt clause of Versailles upon which the debt was based. Nevertheless, the plan was approved by the German Reichstag. When Hitler came to power in 1933, however, he refused to recognize the plan and repudiated all war debts, making the Young Plan a dead letter.

Young died on July 11, 1962, in St. Augustine, Florida.

"MANAGERS [ARE] NO LONGER ATTORNEYS FOR STOCKHOLDERS, THEY [ARE] BECOMING TRUSTEES OF AN INSTITUTION."

YOUNGSTOWN SHEET & TUBE CO. v. SAWYER

In *Youngstown Sheet & Tube Co. v. Sawyer*, 343 U.S. 579, 72 S. Ct. 863, 96 L. Ed. 1153 (1952), the Supreme Court reviewed the constitutionality of an EXECUTIVE ORDER directing the secretary of commerce to seize possession of the nation's steel mills during a labor dispute, and keep them operating while hostilities continued in the KOREAN WAR. Also known as the Steel Seizure Case, *Youngstown Sheet & Tube* stands for the proposition that the EXECUTIVE BRANCH has no constitutional authority to seize possession of private property, even if it is for public use during times of national emergency, because such authority is vested in the lawmaking powers of Congress.

The case arose from a labor dispute between American steel companies and their employees over the terms of a COLLECTIVE BARGAINING AGREEMENT that was under negotiation in 1951. Employees wanted higher wages, but management protested that such increases could only be met through drastic price hikes. President HARRY S. TRUMAN opposed further price hikes because the economy was already suffering from inflation. On the other hand, Truman feared that any disruption in domestic steel production would impede the American war effort in Korea, which was entering its second year, and imperil the safety of U.S. military troops.

When negotiations between labor and management reached an impasse, the employees' representative, United Steelworkers of America, C.I.O., announced its intention to commence a nationwide STRIKE on April 12, 1952, at 12:01 a.m. A few hours before the strike was to begin, Truman issued Executive Order 10340, which commanded the secretary of commerce, Charles Sawyer, to seize most of the nation's steel mills, and keep them running.

In carrying out this order, the secretary directed the presidents of the seized steel companies to serve as operating managers for the U.S. government. Until directed otherwise, each president was to operate his plant in accordance with the rules and regulations prescribed by the secretary. While obeying these orders under protest, the steel companies filed a lawsuit in U.S. District Court for the District of Columbia, seeking declaratory relief to invalidate the executive order and injunctive relief to restrain its enforcement.

On April 30, 1952, the district court issued a PRELIMINARY INJUNCTION immediately restraining the secretary of commerce from continuing the seizure and possession of the steel mills. On that same day, the U.S. Court of Appeals for the District of Columbia stayed the district court's order on the grounds that resolution of such an issue is more appropriate for the U.S. Supreme Court. Granting CERTIORARI three days later, the Supreme Court decided the case on June 12, 1952.

In a 6-3 decision, the Supreme Court invalidated the executive order, and affirmed the district court's judgment. Justice HUGO BLACK delivered the opinion of the Court. Truman's power to issue the order, the Court said, derives, if at all, from an act of Congress, or from the U.S. Constitution. There are no other sources for PRESIDENTIAL POWER, the Court wrote.

The Court found that Truman had not acted pursuant to congressional authority. Prior to issuing the order, Truman had given Congress formal notice of the impending seizure. However, neither house responded. The Court also observed that Congress had considered amending the Labor Management Relations Act of 1947, 61 Stat. 136, popularly known as the TAFT-HARTLEY ACT, to include a provision authorizing the seizure of steel mills in times of national crisis. Yet Congress rejected the idea. Nor was there any other federal statutory authority, the Court stressed, from which presidential power to seize a private business could be fairly IMPLIED.

The Court next turned to the president's constitutional powers. Article II of the Constitution delegates certain enumerated powers to the executive branch. Unlike Article I, which gives Congress a broad grant of authority to make all laws that are "necessary and proper" in exercising its legislative function, Article II limits the authority of the executive branch to narrowly specified powers.

Consistent with Article II, the Court said, a president may recommend the enactment of a particular bill, VETO objectionable legislation, and "faithfully execute" laws that have been passed by both houses of Congress. As commander in chief, the president of the United States is vested with ultimate responsibility for the nation's armed forces. However, the Court

emphasized, the office of the president has no constitutional authority outside the language contained within the FOUR CORNERS of the Constitution.

Lawyers for the executive branch had argued that the presidency carries with it certain INHERENT powers that may be reasonably inferred from the express provisions of the Constitution. During times of national emergency, the government's lawyers argued, the president may exercise these inherent powers without violating the Constitution. Since wartime is traditionally considered a time of national emergency, the president's seizure of the steel mills represented a legitimate exercise of his inherent powers.

The Supreme Court disagreed with these arguments. Conceding that a strike could threaten national security by curtailing the production of armaments, the Court said that the commander in chief's authority to prosecute a foreign war does not empower him to seize private property in an effort to resolve a domestic labor dispute. "This is a job for the Nation's lawmakers," Justice Black wrote, "not for its military authorities." Black reminded the executive branch that only Congress can authorize the taking of private property for public use under the EMINENT DOMAIN CLAUSE of the FIFTH AMENDMENT to the U.S. Constitution.

Justices FELIX FRANKFURTER, WILLIAM O. DOUGLAS, HAROLD BURTON, TOM CLARK, and ROBERT JACKSON each wrote a concurring opinion. Frankfurter suggested that the powers expressly enumerated in Article II may be supplemented by long-standing executive practice, though he said there was no historical precedent for Truman's action in this case. With the exception of Jackson, the other concurring justices elaborated on points made by Justice Black in the Court's opinion.

Jackson's concurring opinion has garnered much attention from constitutional scholars, and is the most frequently cited opinion in *Youngstown Sheet & Tube*. Jackson articulated an overarching theory of federal executive power in the United States. According to Jackson, there are three tiers of presidential authority. When a president acts in conjunction with Congress, Jackson wrote, executive power is at its zenith because the president may rely on his own authority plus that of the legislative branch. When a president acts contrary to congressional will, executive power is at its nadir because the president must rely solely on his expressly delegated authority minus that of the legislative branch. And when a president acts in an area where Congress has been silent, executive power is uncertain, and may fluctuate depending on the circumstances.

Justice FRED VINSON dissented, joined by Justices STANLEY REED and SHERMAN MINTON. The dissent underscored the importance of steel production to the military effort in Korea. During the two years of hostilities in Southeast Asia, the dissent noted, Congress directed the president to secure the nation's defenses, sometimes doing so in a very general and open-ended manner. Thus, the dissent argued, Truman had received some authority from Congress to take action in the name of national defense and the PUBLIC INTEREST.

The dissent also relied on history, pointing out that JAMES MADISON advocated instilling the executive branch with initiative and vigor. President ABRAHAM LINCOLN, the dissent continued, showed initiative during the Civil War by ordering the seizure of all rail and telegraph lines leading to Washington, D.C., even though he lacked congressional approval. In this light, the dissent concluded, Truman's seizure of the steel mills was supported by historical precedent.

Youngstown Sheet & Tube is considered a seminal case regarding the SEPARATION OF POWERS among the coordinate branches of the federal government. The U.S. Constitution separates the powers of the federal government among the executive, legislative, and judicial branches. The constitutional authority of each branch is limited by the express language of the Constitution, and by the powers delegated to the coordinate branches.

Article I gives Congress the power to make the law. Article II gives the president the power to execute or implement the law, while Article III gives the federal judiciary the power to interpret and apply the law. The popular notion of "checks and balances" rests upon this conception of the separation of powers.

Despite the clear separation of constitutional powers, presidents, members of Congress, judges, and laypeople have debated whether the executive branch is vested with additional inherent or implied powers. On one side of the debate are those who believe the presidency enjoys a residue of autocratic power. According to these individuals, such power may be exercised by the president in times of national emergency, and is limited only by the president's good judgment. On the other side of the debate are those who believe the executive branch may not exercise any power that is not explicitly granted by the federal Constitution or federal statute.

Youngstown Sheet & Tube went a long way toward settling this debate. Occasionally presidents still assert claims of EXECUTIVE PRIVILEGE and executive IMMUNITY. In some instances FEDERAL COURTS recognize such claims, but oftentimes they do not. President RICHARD M. NIXON's unsuccessful attempt to insulate tape recordings made at the White House during the WATERGATE political scandal from a federal investigation is one notable example of a failed assertion of executive immunity (*United States v. Nixon*, 418 U.S. 683, 94 S. Ct. 3090, 41 L. Ed. 2d 1039 [1974]). In many such cases, *Youngstown Sheet & Tube* has provided the backdrop for judicial analysis of executive authority under constitutional law.

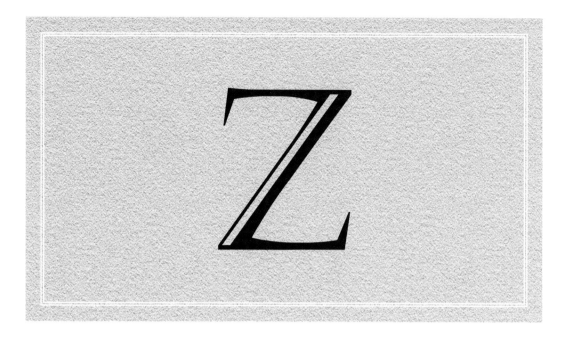

ZENGER, JOHN PETER

ZENGER, JOHN PETER In August of 1735 John Peter Zenger, a printer for the *New York Weekly Journal*, was prosecuted for seditious libel. Although Zenger may have been technically guilty of the crime as it was then defined by English law, a jury made up of twelve Americans acquitted the defendant in one of the earliest acts of colonial resistance to British authority during the eighteenth century.

Zenger printed the allegedly seditious articles following a legal dispute between two public officials, William Cosby and Rip Van Dam. Cosby was appointed governor of New York in 1731, but did not officially take office until 1732. During the interim, Van Dam, the current governor, continued to discharge his official responsibilities, and collect a salary. Cosby, believing that he was entitled to the salary collected by Van Dam during this period, sued the lame duck governor for restitution. When the New York Supreme Court decided in favor of Van Dam, Cosby removed Chief Justice Lewis Morris and replaced him with James DeLancey, a judge who was friendlier to the new governor.

On November 1, 1733, the first issue of the *New York Weekly Journal* appeared. The *Journal* was financially supported by Morris, edited by Van Dam's attorney, and printed by Zenger, a German immigrant with little education. In a series of articles, the *Journal* accused Cosby of conspiring to persecute the inhabitants of New York and tainting their judicial system. Since Cosby had altered the composition of the state supreme court by replacing a political adversary with a political ally, the articles printed in the *Journal* possessed a kernel of truth.

In January of 1734 Cosby attempted to imprison Zenger for seditious libel, but DeLancey failed to convince a GRAND JURY to indict him. Ten months later a second grand jury declined to indict Zenger, prompting the governor's council to command the destruction of all offensive *Journal* articles. When a third grand jury refused to issue an INDICTMENT against Zenger, Cosby ordered his attorney general to charge Zenger with seditious libel by "information," an alternative legal procedure by which criminal proceedings may be instituted against a defendant.

The INFORMATION accused Zenger of having printed several false, scandalous, and defamatory articles that tended to bring the governor into disrepute. The case was tried before the New York Supreme Court and Chief Justice DeLancey. Zenger's lawyers, Alexander and William Smith, challenged the JURISDICTION of the court to hear the dispute, and questioned DeLancey's impartiality. In response, DeLancey disbarred both attorneys. Subsequently, Andrew Hamilton, one of the most noted advocates in the colonies, agreed to represent Zenger for the trial's duration.

The nub of Hamilton's defense rested upon the veracity of the articles printed in the *Journal*. Acknowledging that truth was not a defense to seditious libel under the COMMON LAW of England, Hamilton suggested that Americans enjoyed greater freedom than citizens of Great Britain, including the right to print truthful criticisms of the government and its officials. A published allegation of official misconduct,

Hamilton argued, does not amount to libel unless proven false by the government.

DeLancey instructed the jurors to consider only the factual question of whether Zenger had printed or published the articles in issue. The court said it would decide the legal question of whether they were libelous. However, Hamilton had earlier intimated that the jurors enjoyed the prerogative to ignore the judge's instructions, and render a VERDICT according to their collective conscience and the interests of justice. Contemporary observers reported that the jurors took only a "small time" before returning a verdict of "not guilty."

Zenger's trial served as a fountainhead for two different principles of American law. First, the Zenger trial represents the first case in America in which truth was asserted as a defense to an action for libel. Although Americans were denied this defense under the common law of many jurisdictions during the two centuries that followed the Zenger trial, truth is now a constitutionally protected defense under the First Amendment. In *New York Times Co. v. Sullivan*, 376 U.S. 254, 84 S. Ct. 710, 11 L. Ed. 2d 686 (1964), the U.S. Supreme Court cited the Zenger trial as one of the building blocks in this area of libel law.

Second, the Zenger trial represents one of the first cases in which jury nullification was exercised in America. During the 1990s state and federal courts continue to recognize the right of juries to disregard the law and acquit certain defendants in order to prevent oppression by the government or to otherwise promote the interests of justice. This prerogative, which stems from the jury's role as the conscience of the community, is not formally acknowledged in a number of jurisdictions. However, in those jurisdictions that do recognize it, at least one court has pointed out that "[t]he roots of jury nullification in this country reach back to 1735 and the prosecution of Peter Zenger for seditious libel" *U.S. v. Datcher*, 830 F.Supp. 411 (M.D. Tenn. 1993).

CROSS-REFERENCES

Libel and Slander; *New York Times v. Sullivan*; Sedition.

ZERO BRACKET AMOUNT ◫ A lump-sum allowance of income that a taxpayer could receive without imposition of any federal INCOME TAX because it was considered equivalent to the standard amount of deductions usually taken by an average taxpayer. It was replaced by the STANDARD DEDUCTION in the TAX REFORM ACT OF 1986. 100 Stat. 2085, 26 U.S.C.A. §§ 47, 1042. ◫

The zero-bracket amount was so named because a zero rate of taxation was applied to it.

Its financial value was determined by the filing status of the taxpayer. If a taxpayer had more deductions that qualified as ITEMIZED DEDUCTIONS than the zero-bracket amount, she could itemize deductions, but the itemized deductions were reduced by the zero bracket amount. That figure was subtracted from the taxpayer's ADJUSTED GROSS INCOME to find her TAXABLE INCOME, upon which the income tax liability was computed.

Congress eliminated the zero-bracket amount in the Tax Reform Act of 1986, replacing it with the standard deduction. The standard deduction is a specific dollar amount that can be deducted from income by those taxpayers who do not itemize their deductions because their deductions do not exceed the standard deduction assigned to them. The base amount of the standard deduction depends on the taxpayer's filing status (single, married filing jointly, married filing separately, head of household, or qualifying widow or widower).

ZONING ◫ The separation or division of a municipality into districts, the regulation of buildings and structures in such districts in accordance with their construction and the nature and extent of their use, and the dedication of such districts to particular uses designed to serve the GENERAL WELFARE. ◫

Zoning, the regulation of the use of REAL PROPERTY by local government, restricts a particular territory to residential, commercial, industrial, or other uses. The local governing body considers the character of the property as well as its fitness for particular uses. It must enact the regulations in accordance with a well-considered and comprehensive plan intended to avoid arbitrary exercise of government power. A comprehensive plan is a general design to control the use of properties in the entire municipality, or at least in a large portion of it. Individual pieces of property should not be singled out for special treatment. For example, one or two lots may not be placed in a separate zone and subjected to restrictions that do not apply to similar adjoining lands.

Zoning ordinances divide a TOWN, city, village, or COUNTY into separate residential, commercial, and industrial districts, thereby preserving the desirable characteristics of each type of setting. These laws generally limit dimensions in each zone. Many regulations require certain building features and limit the number and location of parking and loading areas and the use of signs. Other regulations provide space for schools, parks, or other public facilities.

Zoning helps city planners bring about orderly growth and change. It controls population density and helps create attractive, healthful residential areas. In addition, zoning helps assure property owners and residents that the characteristics of nearby areas will remain stable.

In some states a municipality has the right to be heard on proposed zoning in an adjoining community. Courts have upheld this so-called extraterritorial zoning as an exercise of the POLICE POWER of the state, with the goal of serving the general welfare of both communities and creating harmony among the uses of a given area, without regard to political boundaries.

Following the lead of New York City, which passed the first major zoning ORDINANCE in 1916, most urban communities throughout the country have enacted zoning regulations.

Zoning is not merely the division of a city into districts and the regulation of the structural and architectural designs of buildings within each district. It also requires consideration of future growth and development, adequacy of drainage and storm sewers, public streets, pedestrian walkways, density of population, and many other factors that are within legislative competence.

Building codes, which govern the safety and structure of buildings, do not contradict zoning ordinances, but exist side by side with them. Both rest on the police power: zoning stabilizes the use of property, and building codes ensure the safety and structure of buildings. Zoning is intended to have a relative permanency, whereas building codes are much more flexible because they must keep abreast of new materials and other technological advances.

Municipalities have power to zone property only if a state grants it by statute or it is derived from constitutional provisions. Zoning ordinances must be REASONABLE because by their nature they restrain the use of property that the owners could otherwise use as they chose. The landowner cannot complain as long as the power to zone is used in the PUBLIC INTEREST and for the general welfare of the community impartially and without compensation.

The regulations must meet the demands of the constitutional prohibition against taking private property for public use without JUST COMPENSATION as mandated by the Fifth and Fourteenth Amendments to the U.S. Constitution as well as by the constitutions of the states. The U.S. Supreme Court decided three cases that have had considerable impact in this area: *Lucas v. South Carolina Coastal Council*, 505 U.S. 1003, 112 S. Ct. 2886, 120 L. Ed. 2d 798 (1992), *Lujan v. National Wildlife Federation*, 497

Through zoning, communities identify particular locations for residential, commercial, and industrial uses of land. The lot in this picture is zoned R–1, meaning it is a one acre property for residential use.

U.S. 871, 110 S. Ct. 3177, 111 L. Ed. 2d 695 (1990), and *Dolan v. City of Tigard*, 512 U.S. 374, 114 S. Ct. 2309, 129 L. Ed. 2d 304 (1994). The decisions made it more difficult for municipalities to require that land developers give up part of their property for public purposes, such as access to lake shores, sidewalks, access roads, and parks. If the government needs the land, it must compensate the owner by exercising its power of EMINENT DOMAIN and condemning the property.

Courts have held that a zoning regulation is legal or valid if it is reasonable and not arbitrary and bears a reasonable and substantial relation to the public health, safety, comfort, morals, and general welfare and if the means employed are reasonably necessary for the accomplishment of its purpose. An ordinance is invalid if its enforcement will preclude use of the property for any purpose to which it is reasonably adapted. In determining whether a regulation is reasonable, no single factor is controlling. Those factors normally considered are need for the adoption, the purpose, location, size, and physical characteristics of the land, and the character of the neighborhood. Also considered are the effect on the value of property, the amount by which property values are decreased, the notion of the general welfare (that is, what is best for the community at large), and the density, population, and aesthetics of the area.

Traffic, use of nearby land, and length of time the property has been vacant are also relevant.

An ordinance that is reasonable when enacted may prove to be unreasonable, and hence may be set aside by a court, if circumstances have changed. Zoning regulations must promote the good of all the people in the community rather than further the desires of a particular group, and the power cannot be invoked to further private interests that conflict with the rights of the public. Restrictions based solely on race or OCCUPANCY of property within certain districts are invalid. A classification that discriminates against a racial or religious group can only be upheld if the state demonstrates an overwhelming interest that can be served no other way. The regulation must be clear and specific. It must describe districts with certainty, and if maps are necessary, it should include references to them. The standards governing conduct of the administrator must be clear. The fact that regulations have not been enforced does not prevent their enforcement. Only persons whose rights are injured by regulations may attack them. An invalid enactment is without effect and confers no rights and imposes no duties.

Regulations must be in accordance with a comprehensive plan, which may be separate or part of the zoning regulation. SPOT ZONING of individual parcels of property in a manner different from that of surrounding property, primarily for the private interests of the owner of the property so zoned, may be improper but not illegal in all cases. Spot zoning disregards the requirement that zoning be in accordance with a comprehensive plan. It may be valid if there is a reasonable basis for distinguishing the parcel from surrounding parcels.

Zoning regulations may validly prescribe a type of building, location of utility lines, restrictions on accessory buildings or structures, and preservation of historical areas and buildings. General rules of construction apply to restrictions affecting architectural and structural design of buildings and open spaces. Such rules apply to building setbacks from the streets and other boundaries, size and height of buildings, number of rooms, floor space or area and cubic feet, and minimum cost of buildings. They also apply to frontage of lots, minimum lot area, front, rear, and side yards, off-street parking, the number of buildings on a lot, and the number of dwelling units in a certain area. Regulations may restrict areas to single-family homes or to multifamily dwellings or townhouses. An ordinance may permit the construction of a building intended for nonresidential use, such as a school, church, hospital, or charitable institution, in a residential district.

Municipalities have gained some flexibility in their regulations by authorizing special use permits in certain districts. This gives them the power to impose restrictions and requirements that might not otherwise be possible under the strict classification of the district.

It is also possible to create a unit development in an entire district or a large part of one, with plans and restrictions governing the entire project. This arrangement may mix some commercial and residential uses and "clustering" of certain properties, leaving room for green spaces and parkways.

A municipality may use broad discretion to fix the location and boundaries of business, commercial, and industrial districts and has the power to review and periodically update zoning regulations. This should be done whenever growth and progress require. Failure or refusal to make a change in regulations when they are clearly appropriate in view of development may be regarded as unreasonable, arbitrary conduct. Only the legislative body empowered to enact zoning regulations has the power to amend them. This must be done with the same formality, including required NOTICES and HEARINGS, as the original enactment. Neither the courts nor boards of zoning appeals should undertake such AMENDMENT, regardless of how archaic the regulations may be.

Zoning ordinances may permit or prohibit certain uses and may create whole districts devoted only to residence, commerce, or industry. When a structure's use does not conform to a zoning ordinance but the structure existed before the adoption or amendment of the ordinance, the structure has NONCONFORMING USE status, sometimes called legal nonconforming use. A vested legal nonconforming use is safeguarded by the Constitution unless it is abandoned or terminated. It is a PROPERTY RIGHT that cannot be taken away without just compensation. However, the nonconforming use structure may not be expanded, its use may not be changed, and, under many laws, if it is destroyed by fire or other cause, it may not be rebuilt.

Zoning regulations are subject to interpretation by the courts where their meaning is unclear. Because such laws are in DEROGATION of the COMMON LAW, they are to be construed strictly, but they should receive a reasonable and fair construction in the light of the public good they propose to serve.

Boards of zoning appeals are created by statutes. They are QUASI-JUDICIAL bodies because they conduct hearings with sworn TESTIMONY by WITNESSES and a TRANSCRIPT is made, which courts may review. Municipalities generally require permits for building or remodeling and certificates of occupancy after inspection discloses conformity with applicable codes. An owner without legal training who contests a zoning requirement would be ill-advised to try to argue his case alone because the members of the board, the municipal attorney, and the planning official have long experience, knowledge of the law, and a built-in tendency to favor their interpretations of the ordinances.

Where full compliance with the strict letter of the ordinance works a hardship on the owner, the board of appeals or governing body may grant a VARIANCE, which is toleration of a slight violation of the ordinance. The owner, however, may not create her own hardship by willfully violating the law.

Zoning regulations may be enforced by MANDAMUS, an action that results in a JUDGMENT of a court compelling the appropriate public officers to carry out their duty; by INJUNCTION, which results in a court ORDER forbidding the use or structure that is in violation; and by civil FORFEITURE actions or criminal prosecutions. Adjoining owners or citizens at large may have standing to enforce the ordinances where the municipal officers fail to do so. Some ordinances provide for a certain sum to be paid to the municipality for each day of violation. Some courts enforce these penalties strictly, whereas others are more lenient, as long as compliance with the ordinances is achieved in a reasonable time.

CROSS-REFERENCES

Adjoining Landowners; Condemnation; Fifth Amendment; Landmark; Land-Use Control; Municipal Corporation; Theaters and Shows.

ABBREVIATIONS

A.	Atlantic Reporter
A. 2d	Atlantic Reporter, Second Series
AAA	American Arbitration Association; Agricultural Adjustment Act of 1933
AAPRP	All African People's Revolutionary Party
ABA	American Bar Association; Architectural Barriers Act, 1968
ABM Treaty	Anti-Ballistic Missile Treaty of 1972; antiballistic missile
ABVP	Anti-Biased Violence Project
A/C	Account
A.C.	Appeal Cases
ACAA	Air Carrier Access Act
ACF	Administration for Children and Families
ACLU	American Civil Liberties Union
ACS	Agricultural Cooperative Service
Act'g Legal Adv.	Acting Legal Advisor
ACUS	Administrative Conference of the United States
ACYF	Administration on Children, Youth, and Families
A.D. 2d	Appellate Division, Second Series, N.Y.
ADA	Americans with Disabilities Act of 1990
ADAMHA	Alcohol, Drug Abuse, and Mental Health Administration
ADC	Aid to Dependent Children
ADD	Administration on Developmental Disabilities
ADEA	Age Discrimination in Employment Act of 1967
ADR	alternative dispute resolution
AEC	Atomic Energy Commission
AECB	Arms Export Control Board
A.E.R.	All England Law Reports
AFDC	Aid to Families with Dependent Children
aff'd per cur.	affirmed by the court
AFIS	automated fingerprint identification system
AFL	American Federation of Labor
AFL-CIO	American Federation of Labor and Congress of Industrial Organizations
AFRes	Air Force Reserve
AFSCME	American Federation of State, County, and Municipal Employees
AGRICOLA	Agricultural Online Access
AIA	Association of Insurance Attorneys
AID	artificial insemination using a third-party donor's sperm; Agency for International Development

AIDS	acquired immune deficiency syndrome
AIH	artificial insemination using the husband's sperm
AIM	American Indian Movement
AIUSA	Amnesty International, U.S.A. Affiliate
AJS	American Judicature Society
ALEC	American Legislative Exchange Council
ALF	Animal Liberation Front
ALI	American Law Institute
ALJ	administrative law judge
All E.R.	All England Law Reports
ALO	Agency Liaison
A.L.R.	American Law Reports
AMA	American Medical Association
Am. Dec.	American Decisions
amdt.	amendment
Amer. St. Papers, For. Rels.	American State Papers, Legislative and Executive Documents of the Congress of the U.S., Class I, Foreign Relations, 1832–1859
AMVETS	American Veterans (of World War II)
ANA	Administration for Native Americans
Ann. Dig.	Annual Digest of Public International Law Cases
ANZUS	Australia–New Zealand–United States Security Treaty Organization
AOA	Administration on Aging
APA	Administrative Procedure Act of 1946
APHIS	Animal and Plant Health Inspection Service
App. Div.	Appellate Division Reports, N.Y. Supreme Court
Arb. Trib., U.S.-British Convention of 1853	Arbitration Tribunal, Claim Convention of 1853, United States and Great Britain
ARS	Advanced Record System
Art.	article
ASCS	Agriculture Stabilization and Conservation Service
ASM	available seatmile
ASPCA	American Society for the Prevention of Cruelty to Animals
Asst. Att. Gen.	Assistant Attorney General
AT&T	American Telephone and Telegraph
ATFD	Alcohol, Tobacco and Firearms Division
ATLA	Association of Trial Lawyers of America
ATTD	Alcohol and Tobacco Tax Division
ATU	Alcohol Tax Unit
AZT	azidothymidine
BALSA	Black-American Law Student Association
BATF	Bureau of Alcohol, Tobacco and Firearms
BCCI	Bank of Credit and Commerce International
BEA	Bureau of Economic Analysis
Bell's Cr. C.	Bell's English Crown Cases
Bevans	United States Treaties, etc. *Treaties and Other International Agreements of the United States of America, 1776–1949* (compiled under the direction of Charles I. Bevans) (1968–76)
BFOQ	bona fide occupational qualification
BI	Bureau of Investigation
BIA	Bureau of Indian Affairs; Board of Immigration Appeals
BJS	Bureau of Justice Statistics
Black.	Black's United States Supreme Court Reports
Blatchf.	Blatchford's United States Circuit Court Reports
BLM	Bureau of Land Management
BLS	Bureau of Labor Statistics
BMD	ballistic missile defense
BOCA	Building Officials and Code Administrators International
BPP	Black Panther Party for Self-Defense

Brit. and For.	British and Foreign State Papers
Burr.	James Burrows, *Report of Cases Argued and Determined in the Court of King's Bench during the Time of Lord Mansfield* (1766–1780)
BVA	Board of Veterans Appeals
c.	Chapter
C³I	Command, Control, Communications, and Intelligence
C.A.	Court of Appeals
CAA	Clean Air Act
CAB	Civil Aeronautics Board
CAFE	corporate average fuel economy
Cal. 2d	California Reports, Second Series
Cal. 3d	California Reports, Third Series
CALR	computer-assisted legal research
Cal. Rptr.	California Reporter
CAP	Common Agricultural Policy
CATV	community antenna television
CBO	Congressional Budget Office
CCC	Commodity Credit Corporation
CCDBG	Child Care and Development Block Grant of 1990
C.C.D. Pa.	Circuit Court Decisions, Pennsylvania
C.C.D. Va.	Circuit Court Decisions, Virginia
CCEA	Cabinet Council on Economic Affairs
CCR	Center for Constitutional Rights
C.C.R.I.	Circuit Court, Rhode Island
CD	certificate of deposit
CDA	Communications Decency Act
CDBG	Community Development Block Grant Program
CDC	Centers for Disease Control and Prevention; Community Development Corporation
CDF	Children's Defense Fund
CDL	Citizens for Decency through Law
CD-ROM	compact disc read-only memory
CDS	Community Dispute Services
CDW	collision damage waiver
CENTO	Central Treaty Organization
CEQ	Council on Environmental Quality
CERCLA	Comprehensive Environmental Response, Compensation, and Liability Act of 1980
cert.	*certiorari*
CETA	Comprehensive Employment and Training Act
C & F	cost and freight
CFC	chlorofluorocarbon
CFE Treaty	Conventional Forces in Europe Treaty of 1990
C.F. & I.	Cost, freight, and insurance
CFNP	Community Food and Nutrition Program
C.F.R.	Code of Federal Regulations
CFTC	Commodity Futures Trading Commission
Ch.	Chancery Division, English Law Reports
CHAMPVA	Civilian Health and Medical Program at the Veterans Administration
CHEP	Cuban/Haitian Entrant Program
CHINS	children in need of supervision
CHIPS	child in need of protective services
Ch.N.Y.	Chancery Reports, New York
Chr. Rob.	Christopher Robinson, *Reports of Cases Argued and Determined in the High Court of Admiralty* (1801–1808)
CIA	Central Intelligence Agency
CID	Commercial Item Descriptions
C.I.F.	Cost, insurance, and freight
CINCNORAD	Commander in Chief, North American Air Defense Command
C.I.O.	Congress of Industrial Organizations

C.J.	chief justice
CJIS	Criminal Justice Information Services
C.J.S.	Corpus Juris Secundum
Claims Arb. under Spec. Conv., Nielsen's Rept.	Frederick Kenelm Nielsen, *American and British Claims Arbitration under the Special Agreement Concluded between the United States and Great Britain, August 18, 1910* (1926)
CLE	Center for Law and Education
CLEO	Council on Legal Education Opportunity
CLP	Communist Labor Party of America
CLS	Christian Legal Society; critical legal studies (movement), Critical Legal Studies (membership organization)
C.M.A.	Court of Military Appeals
CMEA	Council for Mutual Economic Assistance
CMHS	Center for Mental Health Services
C.M.R.	Court of Military Review
CNN	Cable News Network
CNO	Chief of Naval Operations
C.O.D.	cash on delivery
COGP	Commission on Government Procurement
COINTELPRO	Counterintelligence Program
Coke Rep.	Coke's English King's Bench Reports
COLA	cost-of-living adjustment
COMCEN	Federal Communications Center
Comp.	Compilation
Conn.	Connecticut Reports
CONTU	National Commission on New Technological Uses of Copyrighted Works
Conv.	Convention
Corbin	Arthur L. Corbin, *Corbin on Contracts: A Comprehensive Treatise on the Rules of Contract Law* (1950)
CORE	Congress of Racial Equality
Cox's Crim. Cases	Cox's Criminal Cases (England)
CPA	certified public accountant
CPB	Corporation for Public Broadcasting, the
CPI	Consumer Price Index
CPSC	Consumer Product Safety Commission
Cranch	Cranch's United States Supreme Court Reports
CRF	Constitutional Rights Foundation
CRS	Congressional Research Service; Community Relations Service
CRT	critical race theory
CSA	Community Services Administration
CSAP	Center for Substance Abuse Prevention
CSAT	Center for Substance Abuse Treatment
CSC	Civil Service Commission
CSCE	Conference on Security and Cooperation in Europe
CSG	Council of State Governments
CSO	Community Service Organization
CSP	Center for the Study of the Presidency
C-SPAN	Cable-Satellite Public Affairs Network
CSRS	Cooperative State Research Service
CSWPL	Center on Social Welfare Policy and Law
CTA	*cum testamento annexo* (with the will attached)
Ct. Ap. D.C.	Court of Appeals, District of Columbia
Ct. App. No. Ireland	Court of Appeals, Northern Ireland
Ct. Cl.	Court of Claims, United States
Ct. Crim. Apps.	Court of Criminal Appeals (England)
Ct. of Sess., Scot.	Court of Sessions, Scotland
CU	credit union

CUNY	City University of New York
Cush.	Cushing's Massachusetts Reports
CWA	Civil Works Administration; Clean Water Act
Dall.	Dallas' Pennsylvania and United States Reports
DAR	Daughter of the American Revolution
DARPA	Defense Advanced Research Projects Agency
DAVA	Defense Audiovisual Agency
D.C.	United States District Court
D.C. Del.	United States District Court, Delaware
D.C. Mass.	United States District Court, Massachusetts
D.C. Md.	United States District Court, Maryland
D.C.N.D.Cal.	United States District Court, Northern District, California
D.C.N.Y.	United States District Court, New York
D.C.Pa.	United States District Court, Pennsylvania
DCS	Deputy Chiefs of Staff
DCZ	District of the Canal Zone
DDT	dichlorodiphenyltricloroethane
DEA	Drug Enforcement Administration
Decl. Lond.	Declaration of London, February 26, 1909
Dev. & B.	Devereux & Battle's North Carolina Reports
Dig. U.S. Practice in Intl. Law	Digest of U.S. Practice in International Law
Dist. Ct. D.C.	United States District Court, District of Columbia
D.L.R.	Dominion Law Reports (Canada)
DNA	deoxyribonucleic acid
DNase	deoxyribonuclease
DNC	Democratic National Committee
DOC	Department of Commerce
DOD	Department of Defense
Dodson	Dodson's Reports, English Admiralty Courts
DOE	Department of Energy
DOER	Department of Employee Relations
DOJ	Department of Justice
DOS	disk operating system
DOT	Department of Transportation
DPT	diphtheria, pertussis, and tetanus
DRI	Defense Research Institute
DSAA	Defense Security Assistance Agency
DUI	driving under the influence; driving under intoxication
DWI	driving while intoxicated
EAHCA	Education for All Handicapped Children Act of 1975
EBT	examination before trial
ECPA	Electronic Communications Privacy Act of 1986
ECSC	Treaty of the European Coal and Steel Community
EDA	Economic Development Administration
EDF	Environmental Defense Fund
E.D.N.Y.	Eastern District, New York
EDP	electronic data processing
E.D. Pa.	Eastern District, Pennsylvania
EDSC	Eastern District, South Carolina
E.D. Va.	Eastern District, Virginia
EEC	European Economic Community; European Economic Community Treaty
EEOC	Equal Employment Opportunity Commission
EFF	Electronic Frontier Foundation
EFT	electronic funds transfer
Eliz.	Queen Elizabeth (Great Britain)
Em. App.	Temporary Emergency Court of Appeals

ENE	early neutral evaluation
Eng. Rep.	English Reports
EOP	Executive Office of the President
EPA	Environmental Protection Agency; Equal Pay Act of 1963
ERA	Equal Rights Amendment
ERISA	Employee Retirement Income Security Act of 1974
ERS	Economic Research Service
ESF	emergency support function; Economic Support Fund
ESRD	End-Stage Renal Disease Program
ETA	Employment and Training Administration
ETS	environmental tobacco smoke
et seq.	*et sequentes* or *et sequentia;* "and the following"
EU	European Union
Euratom	European Atomic Energy Community
Eur. Ct. H.R.	European Court of Human Rights
Ex.	English Exchequer Reports, Welsby, Hurlstone & Gordon
Exch.	Exchequer Reports (Welsby, Hurlstone & Gordon)
Eximbank	Export-Import Bank of the United States
F.	Federal Reporter
F. 2d	Federal Reporter, Second Series
FAA	Federal Aviation Administration; Federal Arbitration Act
FAAA	Federal Alcohol Administration Act
FACE	Freedom of Access to Clinic Entrances Act of 1994
FACT	Feminist Anti-Censorship Task Force
FAO	Food and Agriculture Organization of the United Nations
FAR	Federal Acquisition Regulations
FAS	Foreign Agricultural Service
FBA	Federal Bar Association
FBI	Federal Bureau of Investigation
FCA	Farm Credit Administration
F. Cas.	Federal Cases
FCC	Federal Communications Commission
FCIA	Foreign Credit Insurance Association
FCIC	Federal Crop Insurance Corporation
FCRA	Fair Credit Reporting Act
FCU	Federal credit unions
FDA	Food and Drug Administration
FDIC	Federal Deposit Insurance Corporation
FDPC	Federal Data Processing Center
FEC	Federal Election Commission
Fed. Cas.	Federal Cases
FEMA	Federal Emergency Management Agency
FFB	Federal Financing Bank
FGIS	Federal Grain Inspection Service
FHA	Federal Housing Authority
FHWA	Federal Highway Administration
FIA	Federal Insurance Administration
FIC	Federal Information Centers; Federation of Insurance Counsel
FICA	Federal Insurance Contributions Act
FIFRA	Federal Insecticide, Fungicide, and Rodenticide Act
FIP	Forestry Incentives Program
FIRREA	Financial Institutions Reform, Recovery, and Enforcement Act
FISA	Foreign Intelligence Surveillance Act of 1978
FMCS	Federal Mediation and Conciliation Service
FmHA	Farmers Home Administration
FMLA	Family and Medical Leave Act of 1993
FNMA	Federal National Mortgage Association, "Fannie Mae"
F.O.B.	free on board

FOIA	Freedom of Information Act
FPC	Federal Power Commission
FPMR	Federal Property Management Regulations
FPRS	Federal Property Resources Service
FR	Federal Register
FRA	Federal Railroad Administration
FRB	Federal Reserve Board
FRC	Federal Radio Commission
F.R.D.	Federal Rules Decisions
FSA	Family Support Act
FSLIC	Federal Savings and Loan Insurance Corporation
FSQS	Food Safety and Quality Service
FSS	Federal Supply Service
F. Supp.	Federal Supplement
FTA	U.S.-Canada Free Trade Agreement, 1988
FTC	Federal Trade Commission
FTS	Federal Telecommunications System
FUTA	Federal Unemployment Tax Act
FWPCA	Federal Water Pollution Control Act of 1948
GAO	General Accounting Office; Governmental Affairs Office
GAOR	General Assembly Official Records, United Nations
GA Res.	General Assembly Resolution (United Nations)
GATT	General Agreement on Tariffs and Trade
Gen. Cls. Comm.	General Claims Commission, United States and Panama; General Claims Commission, United States and Mexico
Geo. II	King George II (Great Britain)
Geo. III	King George III (Great Britain)
GM	General Motors
GNMA	Government National Mortgage Association, "Ginnie Mae"
GNP	gross national product
GOP	Grand Old Party (Republican)
GOPAC	Grand Old Party Action Committee
GPA	Office of Governmental and Public Affairs
GPO	Government Printing Office
GRAS	generally recognized as safe
Gr. Br., Crim. Ct. App.	Great Britain, Court of Criminal Appeals
GRNL	Gay Rights National Lobby
GSA	General Services Administration
Hackworth	Green Haywood Hackworth, *Digest of International Law* (1940–44)
Hay and Marriott	Great Britain. High Court of Admiralty, *Decisions in the High Court of Admiralty during the Time of Sir George Hay and of Sir James Marriott, Late Judges of That Court* (1801)
HBO	Home Box Office
HCFA	Health Care Financing Administration
H.Ct.	High Court
HDS	Office of Human Development Services
Hen. & M.	Hening & Munford's Virginia Reports
HEW	Department of Health, Education, and Welfare
HHS	Department of Health and Human Services
Hill	Hill's New York Reports
HIRE	Help through Industry Retraining and Employment
HIV	human immunodeficiency virus
H.L.	House of Lords Cases (England)
H. Lords	House of Lords (England)
HNIS	Human Nutrition Information Service
Hong Kong L.R.	Hong Kong Law Reports
How.	Howard's United States Supreme Court Reports
How. St. Trials	Howell's English State Trials
HUAC	House Un-American Activities Committee

HUD	Department of Housing and Urban Development
Hudson, Internatl. Legis.	Manley O. Hudson, ed., *International Legislation: A Collection of the Texts of Multipartite International Instruments of General Interest Beginning with the Covenant of the League of Nations* (1931)
Hudson, World Court Reps.	Manley Ottmer Hudson, ed., *World Court Reports* (1934–)
Hun	Hun's New York Supreme Court Reports
Hunt's Rept.	Bert L. Hunt, *Report of the American and Panamanian General Claims Arbitration* (1934)
IAEA	International Atomic Energy Agency
IALL	International Association of Law Libraries
IBA	International Bar Association
IBM	International Business Machines
ICBM	intercontinental ballistic missile
ICC	Interstate Commerce Commission
ICJ	International Court of Justice
IDEA	Individuals with Disabilities Education Act, 1975
IEP	individualized educational program
IFC	International Finance Corporation
IGRA	Indian Gaming Regulatory Act, 1988
IJA	Institute of Judicial Administration
IJC	International Joint Commission
ILC	International Law Commission
ILD	International Labor Defense
Ill. Dec.	Illinois Decisions
ILO	International Labor Organization
IMF	International Monetary Fund
INA	Immigration and Nationality Act
IND	investigational new drug
INF Treaty	Intermediate-Range Nuclear Forces Treaty of 1987
INS	Immigration and Naturalization Service
INTELSAT	International Telecommunications Satellite Organization
Interpol	International Criminal Police Organization
Int'l. Law Reps.	International Law Reports
Intl. Legal Mats.	International Legal Materials
IPDC	International Program for the Development of Communication
IPO	Intellectual Property Owners
IPP	independent power producer
IQ	intelligence quotient
I.R.	Irish Reports
IRA	individual retirement account; Irish Republican Army
IRCA	Immigration Reform and Control Act of 1986
IRS	Internal Revenue Service
ISO	independent service organization
ISSN	International Standard Serial Numbers
ITA	International Trade Administration
ITI	Information Technology Integration
ITO	International Trade Organization
ITS	Information Technology Service
ITU	International Telecommunication Union
IUD	intrauterine device
IWC	International Whaling Commission
IWW	Industrial Workers of the World
JCS	Joint Chiefs of Staff
JDL	Jewish Defense League
JOBS	Jobs Opportunity and Basic Skills
John. Ch.	Johnson's New York Chancery Reports
Johns.	Johnson's Reports (New York)
JP	justice of the peace

K.B.	King's Bench Reports (England)
KGB	Komitet Gosudarstvennoi Bezopasnosti (the State Security Committee for countries in the former Soviet Union)
KKK	Ku Klux Klan
KMT	Kuomintang
LAPD	Los Angeles Police Department
LC	Library of Congress
LD50	lethal dose 50
LDEF	Legal Defense and Education Fund (NOW)
LDF	Legal Defense Fund, Legal Defense and Educational Fund of the NAACP
LEAA	Law Enforcement Assistance Administration
L.Ed.	Lawyers' Edition Supreme Court Reports
LMSA	Labor-Management Services Administration
LNTS	League of Nations Treaty Series
Lofft's Rep.	Lofft's English King's Bench Reports
L.R.	Law Reports (English)
LSAS	Law School Admission Service
LSAT	Law School Aptitude Test
LSC	Legal Services Corporation; Legal Services for Children
LSD	lysergic acid diethylamide
LSDAS	Law School Data Assembly Service
LTBT	Limited Test Ban Treaty
LTC	Long Term Care
MAD	mutual assured destruction
MADD	Mothers against Drunk Driving
MALDEF	Mexican American Legal Defense and Educational Fund
Malloy	William M. Malloy, ed., *Treaties, Conventions, International Acts, Protocols, and Agreements between the United States of America and Other Powers* (1910–38)
Martens	Georg Friedrich von Martens, ed., *Noveau recueil général de traités et autres act es relatifs aux rapports de droit international* (Series I, 20 vols. [1843–75]; Series II, 35 vols. [1876–1908]; Series III [1909–])
Mass.	Massachusetts Reports
MCH	Maternal and Child Health Bureau
Md. App.	Maryland, Appeal Cases
M.D. Ga.	Middle District, Georgia
Mercy	Movement Ensuring the Right to Choose for Yourself
Metc.	Metcalf's Massachusetts Reports
MFDP	Mississippi Freedom Democratic party
MGT	Management
MHSS	Military Health Services System
Miller	David Hunter Miller, ed., *Treaties and Other International Acts of the United States of America* (1931–1948)
Minn.	Minnesota Reports
MINS	minors in need of supervision
MIRV	multiple independently targetable reentry vehicle
Misc.	Miscellaneous Reports, New York
Mixed Claims Comm., Report of Decs.	Mixed Claims Commission, United States and Germany, Report of Decisions
M.J.	Military Justice Reporter
MLAP	Migrant Legal Action Program
MLB	major league baseball
MLDP	Mississippi Loyalist Democratic party
Mo.	Missouri Reports
Mod.	Modern Reports, English King's Bench, etc.
Moore, Dig. Intl. Law	John Bassett Moore, *A Digest of International Law*, 8 vols. (1906)
Moore, Intl. Arbs.	John Bassett Moore, *History and Digest of the International Arbitrations to Which the United States Has Been a Party*, 6 vols. (1898)

Morison	William Maxwell Morison, *The Scots Revised Report: Morison's Dictionary of Decisions* (1908–09)
M.P.	member of Parliament
MPAA	Motion Picture Association of America
mpg	miles per gallon
MPRSA	Marine Protection, Research, and Sanctuaries Act of 1972
M.R.	Master of the Rolls
MS-DOS	Microsoft Disk Operating System
MSHA	Mine Safety and Health Administration
NAACP	National Association for the Advancement of Colored People
NAAQS	National Ambient Air Quality Standards
NABSW	National Association of Black Social Workers
NAFTA	North American Free Trade Agreement, 1993
NARAL	National Abortion Rights Action League
NARF	Native American Rights Fund
NARS	National Archives and Record Service
NASA	National Aeronautics and Space Administration
NASD	National Association of Securities Dealers
NATO	North Atlantic Treaty Organization
NAVINFO	Navy Information Offices
NAWSA	National American Woman's Suffrage Association
NBA	National Bar Association
NBC	National Broadcasting Company
NBLSA	National Black Law Student Association
NBS	National Bureau of Standards
NCA	Noise Control Act; National Command Authorities
NCAA	National Collegiate Athletic Association
NCAC	National Coalition against Censorship
NCCB	National Consumer Cooperative Bank
NCE	Northwest Community Exchange
NCJA	National Criminal Justice Association
NCLB	National Civil Liberties Bureau
NCP	national contingency plan
NCSC	National Center for State Courts
NCUA	National Credit Union Administration
NDA	new drug application
N.D. Ill.	Northern District, Illinois
NDU	National Defense University
N.D. Wash.	Northern District, Washington
N.E.	North Eastern Reporter
N.E. 2d	North Eastern Reporter, Second Series
NEA	National Endowment for the Arts
NEH	National Endowment for the Humanities
NEPA	National Environmental Protection Act; National Endowment Policy Act
NFIP	National Flood Insurance Program
NGTF	National Gay Task Force
NHRA	Nursing Home Reform Act, 1987
NHTSA	National Highway Traffic Safety Administration
Nielsen's Rept.	Frederick Kenelm Nielsen, *American and British Claims Arbitration under the Special Agreement Concluded between the United States and Great Britain, August 18, 1910* (1926)
NIEO	New International Economic Order
NIH	National Institutes of Health, the NIH
NIJ	National Institute of Justice
NIRA	National Industrial Recovery Act; National Industrial Recovery Administration
NIST	National Institute of Standards and Technology, the NIST
NITA	National Telecommunications and Information Administration
N.J.	New Jersey Reports

N.J. Super.	New Jersey Superior Court Reports
NLRA	National Labor Relations Act
NLRB	National Labor Relations Board
No.	Number
NOAA	National Oceanic and Atmospheric Administration
NOW	National Organization for Women
NOW LDEF	National Organization for Women Legal Defense and Education Fund
NOW/PAC	National Organization for Women Political Action Committee
NPDES	National Pollutant Discharge Elimination System
NPL	national priorities list
NPR	National Public Radio
NPT	Non-Proliferation Treaty
NRA	National Rifle Association; National Recovery Act
NRC	Nuclear Regulatory Commission
NSC	National Security Council
NSCLC	National Senior Citizens Law Center
NSF	National Science Foundation
NSFNET	National Science Foundation Network
NTIA	National Telecommunications and Information Administration
NTID	National Technical Institute for the Deaf
NTIS	National Technical Information Service
NTS	Naval Telecommunications System
NTSB	National Transportation Safety Board
N.W.	North Western Reporter
N.W. 2d	North Western Reporter, Second Series
NWSA	National Woman Suffrage Association
N.Y.	New York Court of Appeals Reports
N.Y. 2d	New York Court of Appeals Reports, Second Series
N.Y.S.	New York Supplement Reporter
N.Y.S. 2d	New York Supplement Reporter, Second Series
NYSE	New York Stock Exchange
N.Y. Sup.	New York Supreme Court Reports
NYU	New York University
OAAU	Organization of Afro American Unity
OAP	Office of Administrative Procedure
OAS	Organization of American States
OASDI	Old-age, Survivors, and Disability Insurance Benefits
OASHDS	Office of the Assistant Secretary for Human Development Services
OCED	Office of Comprehensive Employment Development
OCHAMPUS	Office of Civilian Health and Medical Program of the Uniformed Services
OCSE	Office of Child Support Enforcement
OEA	Organización de los Estados Americanos
OFCCP	Office of Federal Contract Compliance Programs
OFPP	Office of Federal Procurement Policy
OICD	Office of International Cooperation and Development
OIG	Office of the Inspector General
OJARS	Office of Justice Assistance, Research, and Statistics
OMB	Office of Management and Budget
OMPC	Office of Management, Planning, and Communications
ONP	Office of National Programs
OPD	Office of Policy Development
OPEC	Organization of Petroleum Exporting Countries
OPIC	Overseas Private Investment Corporation
Ops. Atts. Gen.	Opinions of the Attorneys-General of the United States
Ops. Comms.	Opinions of the Commissioners
OPSP	Office of Product Standards Policy
O.R.	Ontario Reports
OR	Official Records

OSHA	Occupational Safety and Health Administration
OSHRC	Occupational Safety and Health Review Commission
OSM	Office of Surface Mining
OSS	Office of Strategic Services
OST	Office of the Secretary
OT	Office of Transportation
OTA	Office of Technology Assessment
OTC	over-the-counter
OUI	operating under the influence
OWBPA	Older Workers Benefit Protection Act
OWRT	Office of Water Research and Technology
P.	Pacific Reporter
P. 2d	Pacific Reporter, Second Series
PAC	political action committee
Pa. Oyer and Terminer	Pennsylvania Oyer and Terminer Reports
PATCO	Professional Air Traffic Controllers Organization
PBGC	Pension Benefit Guaranty Corporation
PBS	Public Broadcasting Service; Public Buildings Service
P.C.	Privy Council (English Law Reports); personal computer
PCIJ	Permanent Court of International Justice
	Series A—Judgments and Orders (1922–30)
	Series B—Advisory Opinions (1922–30)
	Series A/B—Judgments, Orders, and Advisory Opinions (1931–40)
	Series C—Pleadings, Oral Statements, and Documents relating to Judgments and Advisory Opinions (1923–42)
	Series D—Acts and Documents concerning the Organization of the World Court (1922–47)
	Series E—Annual Reports (1925–45)
PCP	phencyclidine (no need to spell out)
P.D.	Probate Division, English Law Reports (1876–1890)
PDA	Pregnancy Discrimination Act of 1978
PD & R	Policy Development and Research
Perm. Ct. of Arb.	Permanent Court of Arbitration
Pet.	Peters' United States Supreme Court Reports
PETA	People for the Ethical Treatment of Animals
PGM	Program
PHA	Public Housing Agency
Phila. Ct. of Oyer and Terminer	Philadelphia Court of Oyer and Terminer
PHS	Public Health Service
PIC	Private Industry Council
Pick.	Pickering's Massachusetts Reports
PIK	Payment in Kind
PINS	persons in need of supervision
PIRG	Public Interest Research Group
P.L.	Public Laws
PLAN	Pro-Life Action Network
PLI	Practicing Law Institute
PLO	Palestine Liberation Organization
PNET	Peaceful Nuclear Explosions Treaty
POW-MIA	prisoner of war–missing in action
Pratt	Frederic Thomas Pratt, *Law of Contraband of War, with a Selection of Cases from the Papers of the Right Honourable Sir George Lee* (1856)
Proc.	Proceedings
PRP	potentially responsible party
PSRO	Professional Standards Review Organization
PTO	Patents and Trademark Office
PURPA	Public Utilities Regulatory Policies Act

PUSH	People United to Serve Humanity
PWA	Public Works Administration
PWSA	Ports and Waterways Safety Act of 1972
Q.B.	Queen's Bench (England)
Ralston's Rept.	Jackson Harvey Ralston, ed., *Venezuelan Arbitrations of 1903* (1904)
RC	Regional Commissioner
RCRA	Resource Conservation and Recovery Act
RCWP	Rural Clean Water Program
RDA	Rural Development Administration
REA	Rural Electrification Administration
Rec. des Decs. des Trib. Arb. Mixtes	G. Gidel, ed., *Recueil des décisions des tribunaux arbitraux mixtes, institués par les traités de paix* (1922–30)
Redmond	Vol. 3 of Charles I. Bevans, *Treaties and Other International Agreements of the United States of America, 1776–1949* (compiled by C. F. Redmond) (1969)
RESPA	Real Estate Settlement Procedure Act of 1974
RFRA	Religious Freedom Restoration Act
RICO	Racketeer Influenced and Corrupt Organizations
RNC	Republican National Committee
Roscoe	Edward Stanley Roscoe, ed., *Reports of Prize Cases Determined in the High Court of Admiralty before the Lords Commissioners of Appeals in Prize Causes and before the Judicial Committee of the Privy Council from 1745 to 1859* (1905)
ROTC	Reserve Officers' Training Corps
RPP	Representative Payee Program
R.S.	Revised Statutes
RTC	Resolution Trust Company
Ryan White CARE Act	Ryan White Comprehensive AIDS Research Emergency Act of 1990
SAC	Strategic Air Command
SACB	Subversive Activities Control Board
SADD	Students against Drunk Driving
SAF	Student Activities Fund
SAIF	Savings Association Insurance Fund
SALT I	Strategic Arms Limitation Talks of 1969–72
SAMHSA	Substance Abuse and Mental Health Services Administration
Sandf.	Sandford's New York Superior Court Reports
S and L	savings and loan
SARA	Superfund Amendment and Reauthorization Act
Sawy.	Sawyer's United States Circuit Court Reports
SBA	Small Business Administration
SCLC	Southern Christian Leadership Conference
Scott's Repts.	James Brown Scott, ed., *The Hague Court Reports*, 2 vols. (1916–32)
SCS	Soil Conservation Service
SCSEP	Senior Community Service Employment Program
S.Ct.	Supreme Court Reporter
S.D. Cal.	Southern District, California
S.D. Fla.	Southern District, Florida
S.D. Ga.	Southern District, Georgia
SDI	Strategic Defense Initiative
S.D. Me.	Southern District, Maine
S.D.N.Y.	Southern District, New York
SDS	Students for a Democratic Society
S.E.	South Eastern Reporter
S.E. 2d	South Eastern Reporter, Second Series
SEA	Science and Education Administration
SEATO	Southeast Asia Treaty Organization
SEC	Securities and Exchange Commission
Sec.	Section
SEEK	Search for Elevation, Education and Knowledge
SEOO	State Economic Opportunity Office

SEP	simplified employee pension plan
Ser.	Series
Sess.	Session
SGLI	Servicemen's Group Life Insurance
SIP	state implementation plan
SLA	Symbionese Liberation Army
SLBM	submarine-launched ballistic missile
SNCC	Student Nonviolent Coordinating Committee
So.	Southern Reporter
So. 2d	Southern Reporter, Second Series
SPA	Software Publisher's Association
Spec. Sess.	Special Session
SRA	Sentencing Reform Act of 1984
SS	Schutzstaffel (German for Protection Echelon)
SSA	Social Security Administration
SSI	Supplemental Security Income
START I	Strategic Arms Reduction Treaty of 1991
START II	Strategic Arms Reduction Treaty of 1993
Stat.	United States Statutes at Large
STS	Space Transportation Systems
St. Tr.	State Trials, English
STURAA	Surface Transportation and Uniform Relocation Assistance Act of 1987
Sup. Ct. of Justice, Mexico	Supreme Court of Justice, Mexico
Supp.	Supplement
S.W.	South Western Reporter
S.W. 2d	South Western Reporter, Second Series
SWAPO	South-West Africa People's Organization
SWAT	Special Weapons and Tactics
SWP	Socialist Workers party
TDP	Trade and Development Program
Tex. Sup.	Texas Supreme Court Reports
THAAD	Theater High-Altitude Area Defense System
TIA	Trust Indenture Act of 1939
TIAS	Treaties and Other International Acts Series (United States)
TNT	trinitrotoluene
TOP	Targeted Outreach Program
TPUS	Transportation and Public Utilities Service
Tripartite Claims Comm., Decs. and Ops.	Tripartite Claims Commission (United States, Austria, and Hungary), Decisions and Opinions
TRI-TAC	Joint Tactical Communications
TRO	temporary restraining order
TS	Treaty Series, United States
TSCA	Toxic Substance Control Act
TSDs	transporters, storers, and disposers
TTBT	Threshold Test Ban Treaty
TVA	Tennessee Valley Authority
UAW	United Auto Workers; United Automobile, Aerospace, and Agricultural Implements Workers of America
U.C.C.	Uniform Commercial Code; Universal Copyright Convention
U.C.C.C.	Uniform Consumer Credit Code
UCCJA	Uniform Child Custody Jurisdiction Act
UCMJ	Uniform Code of Military Justice
UCPP	Urban Crime Prevention Program
UCS	United Counseling Service
UDC	United Daughters of the Confederacy
UFW	United Farm Workers
UHF	ultrahigh frequency
UIFSA	Uniform Interstate Family Support Act

UIS	Unemployment Insurance Service
UMDA	Uniform Marriage and Divorce Act
UMTA	Urban Mass Transportation Administration
UNCITRAL	United Nations Commission on International Trade Law
UNCTAD	United Nations Conference on Trade and Development
UN Doc.	United Nations Documents
UNDP	United Nations Development Program
UNEF	United Nations Emergency Force
UNESCO	United Nations Educational, Scientific, and Cultural Organization
UNICEF	United Nations Children's Fund
UNIDO	United Nations Industrial and Development Organization
Unif. L. Ann.	Uniform Laws Annotated
UN Repts. Intl. Arb. Awards	United Nations Reports of International Arbitral Awards
UNTS	United Nations Treaty Series
UPI	United Press International
URESA	Uniform Reciprocal Enforcement of Support Act
U.S.	United States Reports
USAF	United States Air Force
U.S. App. D.C.	United States Court of Appeals for the District of Columbia
U.S.C.	United States Code
U.S.C.A.	United States Code Annotated
U.S.C.C.A.N.	United States Code Congressional and Administrative News
USCMA	United States Court of Military Appeals
USDA	U.S. Department of Agriculture
USES	United States Employment Service
USFA	United States Fire Administration
USICA	International Communication Agency, United States
USSC	U.S. Sentencing Commission
U.S.S.R.	Union of Soviet Socialist Republics
UST	United States Treaties
USTS	United States Travel Service
v.	*versus*
VA	Veterans Administration, the VA
VGLI	Veterans Group Life Insurance
Vict.	Queen Victoria (Great Britain)
VIN	vehicle identification number
VISTA	Volunteers in Service to America
VJRA	Veterans Judicial Review Act of 1988
V.L.A.	Volunteer Lawyers for the Arts
VMI	Virginia Military Institute
VMLI	Veterans Mortgage Life Insurance
VOCAL	Victims of Child Abuse Laws
WAC	Women's Army Corps
Wall.	Wallace's United States Supreme Court Reports
Wash. 2d	Washington Reports, Second Series
WAVES	Women Accepted for Volunteer Service
WCTU	Women's Christian Temperance Union
W.D. Wash.	Western District, Washington
W.D. Wis.	Western District, Wisconsin
WEAL	West's Encyclopedia of American Law, Women's Equity Action League
Wend.	Wendell's New York Reports
WFSE	Washington Federation of State Employees
Wheat.	Wheaton's United States Supreme Court Reports
Wheel. Cr. Cases	Wheeler's New York Criminal Cases
Whiteman	Marjorie Millace Whiteman, *Digest of International Law*, 15 vols. (1963–73)
WHO	World Health Organization
WIC	Women, Infants, and Children program
Will. and Mar.	King William and Queen Mary (Great Britain)

WIN	WESTLAW Is Natural; Whip Inflation Now; Work Incentive Program
WIU	Workers' Industrial Union
W.L.R.	Weekly Law Reports, England
WPA	Works Progress Administration
WPPDA	Welfare and Pension Plans Disclosure Act
WWI	World War I
WWII	World War II
Yates Sel. Cas.	Yates' New York Select Cases

BIBLIOGRAPHY

SUBSTANTIVE DUE PROCESS
Riggs, Robert E. 1990. "Substantive Due Process in 1791." *Wisconsin Law Review* 1990.

SUICIDE
Vital Statistics of the United States. 1994. Washington, D.C.: U.S. Government Printing Office.

SUNDAY CLOSING LAWS
"The First Amendment Religion Clauses and Labor and Employment Law in the Supreme Court, 1984." 1986. *New York Law School Law Review* 31 (winter).
Raucher, Alan. 1994. "Sunday Business and the Decline of Sunday Closing Laws: A Historical Overview." *Journal of Church and State* 36 (winter).

SUPREMACY CLAUSE
Stephens, Otis H., Jr., and John M. Scheb II. 1993. *American Constitutional Law.* St. Paul: West.

SUPREME COURT
Stephens, Otis H., Jr., and John M. Scheb II. 1993. *American Constitutional Law.* St. Paul: West.

SUPREME COURT OF THE UNITED STATES
Stephens, Otis H., Jr., and John M. Scheb II. 1993. *American Constitutional Law.* St. Paul: West.

SURGEON GENERAL
Kluger, Richard. 1996. *Ashes to Ashes.* New York: Knopf.
Office of Surgeon General site. 1997. World Wide Web (April 12).
United States Government Manual, 1996–1997. Washington, D.C.: U.S. Government Printing Office.

SURROGATE MOTHERHOOD
Andrews, Lori B. 1995. "Beyond Doctrinal Boundaries: A Legal Framework for Surrogate Motherhood." From the symposium New Directions in Family Law. *Virginia Law Review* 81 (November). 2343.

Birck, Mary Lynne. 1994. "Modern Reproductive Technology and Motherhood: The Search for Common Ground and the Recognition of Difference." *University of Cincinnati Law Review* 62 (spring).
Hall, Mark A., and Ira Mark Ellman. 1990. *Health Care Law and Ethics.* St. Paul: West.
Macklin, Ruth. 1994. *Surrogates and Other Mothers: The Debates over Assisted Reproduction.* Temple Univ. Press.
Rae, Scott B. 1994. *The Ethics of Commercial Surrogate Motherhood: Brave New Families?* Westport, Conn.: Praeger.

SUSPECT CLASSIFICATIONS
Stephens, Otis H., Jr., and John M. Scheb II. 1993. *American Constitutional Law.* St. Paul: West.

SUSPENDED SENTENCE
Ferdico, John N. 1992. *Ferdico's Criminal Law and Justice Dictionary.* St. Paul: West.

SUTHERLAND, GEORGE
Hall, Kermit L. 1989. *The Magic Mirror: Law in American History.* New York: Oxford Univ. Press.
Stephens, Otis H., Jr., and John M. Scheb II. 1993. *American Constitutional Law.* St. Paul: West.

SWAYNE, NOAH HAYNES
Stephens, Otis H., Jr., and John M. Scheb II. 1993. *American Constitutional Law.* St. Paul: West.

SWIFT V. TYSON
Stephens, Otis H., Jr., and John M. Scheb II. 1993. *American Constitutional Law.* St. Paul: West.

SYMBOLIC SPEECH
American Civil Liberties Union site. 1997. World Wide Web (July 4).
Citizens Flag Alliance site. 1997. World Wide Web (July 4).
Stephens, Otis H., Jr., and John M. Scheb II. 1993. *American Constitutional Law.* St. Paul: West.

TAFT, ALPHONSO

Brown, Gloria. 1992. "The Tafts: The Cleveland Branch of Ohio's Famous Political Family." *Cleveland Plain Dealer* (April 12).

Pollak, Louis H. 1989. " 'Original Intention' and the Crucible of Litigation." *University of Cincinnati Law Review.*

Rhodes, Irwin S. 1972. "The Founding of the Cincinnati Bar Association." *Cincinnati Historical Society Bulletin* 30.

Wecker, David. 1993. "Retiree Will Miss This Musty Library." *Cincinnati Post* (November 25).

Wilson, James Grant, and John Fiske, eds. 1888–1889. *Appleton's Cyclopaedia of American Biography.* New York: Appleton.

TAFT, WILLIAM HOWARD

Stephens, Otis H., Jr., and John M. Scheb II. 1993. *American Constitutional Law.* St. Paul: West.

TAMM, EDWARD A.

Burger, Warren E. 1986. "Tribute to Edward Allen Tamm." *Georgetown Law Journal* 74 (August).

Washington Post. 1985. Obituary, September 23.

TANEY, ROGER BROOKE

Justice Department. 1985. *Attorneys General of the United States, 1789–1985.* Washington, D.C.: U.S. Government Printing Office.

Stephens, Otis H., Jr. and John M. Scheb II. 1993. *American Constitutional Law.* St. Paul: West.

TAX COURT

United States Government Manual, 1996–1997. Washington, D.C.: U.S. Government Printing Office.

TAX EVASION

Mertens, Jacob, Jr. 1996. *Mertens Law of Federal Income Taxation.* Rochester, N.Y.: Clark Boardman Callaghan.

TELECOMMUNICATIONS

Sapranov, Walt, and Anne E. Franklin. 1997. "Summary of the Telecommunications Act of 1996." Gerry, Friend, and Sapranov law firm site. World Wide Web (March 5).

TEMPERANCE MOVEMENT

Lash, Kurt T. 1995. "The Second Adoption of the Establishment Clause: The Rise of the Nonestablishment Principle." *Arizona State Law Journal* 27 (winter).

Walker, Vaughn R. 1995. "Comment: Federalizing Organized Crime." *Hastings Law Journal* 46 (April).

TEMPORARY RESTRAINING ORDER

Shoben, Elaine W., and William Murray Tabb. 1989. *Remedies: Cases and Problems.* Westbury, N.Y.: Foundation Press.

TENANCY BY THE ENTIRETY

Kurtz, Sheldon F., and Herbert Hovenkamp. 1987. *Cases and Materials on American Property Law.* St. Paul: West.

"Real Property." 1994. *SMH Bar Review.*

TENANCY IN COMMON

Kurtz, Sheldon F., and Herbert Hovenkamp. 1987. *Cases and Materials on American Property Law.* St. Paul: West.

TENDER YEARS DOCTRINE

Bookspan, Phyllis T. 1993. "From a Tender Years Presumption to a Primary Parent Presumption: Has Anything Really Changed? . . . Should It?" *Brigham Young University Journal of Public Law* 8 (January).

Katz, Sanford N. 1992. " 'That They May Thrive' Goal of Child Custody: Reflections on the Apparent Erosion of the Tender Years Presumption and the Emergence of the Primary Caretaker Presumption." *Journal of Contemporary Health Law and Policy, Catholic University* 8 (spring).

Radke, Lynn E. 1993. "Michigan's New Hearsay Exception: The 'Reinstatement' of the Common Law Tender Years Rule." *University of Detroit Mercy Law Review* 70 (winter).

TERRELL, MARY ELIZA CHURCH

Stephens, Otis H., Jr., and John M. Scheb II. 1993. *American Constitutional Law.* St. Paul: West.

TERRITORIES OF THE UNITED STATES

Van Dyke, Jon M. 1992. "The Evolving Legal Relationships between the United States and Its Affiliated U.S.-Flag Islands." *University of Hawaii Law Review* 14 (fall).

TERRITORY

Cohen, Samuel J. 1992. "The Extension of U.S. Tax Treaties to U.S. Territories, as Illustrated by the Example of Guam." *UCLA Pacific Basin Law Journal* 11 (fall).

TERRORISM

Backgrounder: Terrorism. 1997. Federal Emergency Management Agency site, World Wide Web (April 30).

Close Up Foundation Domestic Terrorism Page. 1997. Close Up Foundation site, World Wide Web (April 30).

TERRY V. OHIO

Lafave, Wayne R., and Jerold H. Israel. 1985. *Criminal Procedure: Hornbook Series,* student edition. St. Paul: West.

TEST CASE

Johnson, David Ole Nathan; Milavetz, Gallop, and Milavetz, P.A., Edina, MN. 1997. Telephone interview, August 1.

TESTIFY

Ferdico, John N. 1992. *Ferdico's Criminal Law and Justice Dictionary.* St. Paul: West.

Mellinkoff, David. 1992. *Mellinkoff's Dictionary of American Legal Usage.* St. Paul: West.

TEXAS V. WHITE

Stephens, Otis H., Jr., and John M. Scheb II. 1993. *American Constitutional Law.* St. Paul: West.

THIRD AMENDMENT
Fields, William S. 1989. *The Third Amendment: Constitutional Protection from the Involuntary Quartering of Soldiers. Military Law Review* 124.

THIRTEENTH AMENDMENT
Glasser, Ira. 1991. *Visions of Liberty.* New York: Arcade.

Smolla, Rodney A. 1997. *Federal Civil Rights Acts.* 3d ed. Vol. 1. New York: Clark Boardman Callaghan.

Witt, Elder, ed. 1979. *The Supreme Court and Individual Rights.* Washington, D.C.: Congressional Quarterly.

THOMAS, CLARENCE
Contemporary Black Biography. 1992. Vol. 2. Detroit: Gale Research.

THOREAU, HENRY DAVID
Moss, Joyce, and George Wilson. 1995. *Profiles in American History.* Vol. 4. Detroit: Gale Research.

THORNBURGH, RICHARD LEWIS
Christian Science Monitor site. 1997. World Wide Web (March 16).

THURMOND, JAMES STROM
Butterfield, Fox. 1995. *All God's Children.* New York: Knopf.

Clemson University and State of South Carolina sites. 1996. World Wide Web (October 14).

TIMESHARE
Mellinkoff, David. 1992. *Mellinkoff's Dictionary of American Legal Usage.* St. Paul: West.

TOBACCO
Barnes, Deborah E., and Lisa A. Bero. 1996. "Industry-funded Research and Conflict of Interest: An Analysis of Research Sponsored by the Tobacco Industry through the Center for Indoor Air Research." *Journal of Health Politics, Policy and Law* 21 (fall).

Boyd, Margaret A. 1996. "Butt Out!! Why the FDA Lacks Jurisdiction to Curb Smoking of Adolescents and Children." *Journal of Contemporary Health Law and Policy* 13.

Correia, Edward O. 1997. "State and Local Regulation of Cigarette Advertising." *Journal of Legislation* 23.

"Costs Due to Tobacco Use," published December 1995 by Missouri ASSIST (American Stop Smoking Intervention Study). 1997. Missouri State Health site. World Wide Web.

"D.C. Circuit Refuses to Compel OSHA to Comply with Self-Imposed Deadlines for Initiating Workplace Smoking Ban." 1996. *West's Legal News* (December 2).

Fleming, Joseph Z. 1997. *Analysis of Relevant Labor, Employment Discrimination and Humanitarian Relief Laws Affecting Sports, Arts, and Entertainment Industries.* SB34 ALI-ABA 461.

Hatfield, Christine. 1996. "The Privilege Doctrines— Are They Just Another Discovery Tool Utilized by the Tobacco Industry to Conceal Damaging Information?" *Pace Law Review* 16 (summer).

Hymes, Christine. 1995. "Clean Indoor Air: Who Has It and How To Get It—A Functional Approach to Environmental Tobacco Smoke." *Missouri Environmental Law and Policy Review* 2 (June).

Jeruchimowitz, Howard K. 1997. "Tobacco Advertisements and Commercial Speech Balancing: A Potential Cancer to Truthful, Nonmisleading Advertisements of Lawful Products." *Cornell Law Review* 82 (January).

Kelder, Graham E., Jr., and Richard A. Daynard. 1997. "The Role of Litigation in the Effective Control of the Sale and Use of Tobacco." *Stanford Law and Policy Review* 8 (winter).

Kuhlengel, Kimberly K. 1995. "A Failure to Preempt an Unfair Advertising Claim May Result in Undue Restrictions on Cigarette Manufacturers." *Southern Illinois University Law Journal* 19 (winter).

Krulwich, Andrew S. 1996. "The FDA's Attempt to Regulate Cigarettes Exceeds Its Authority." *Food and Drug Law Journal* 51.

Lars, Noah. 1996. "Statutory 'Smoke' and Mirrors." *Food and Drug Law Journal* 51.

Lee, Theodora R. 1997. "Privacy Issues in the Workplace." *Practising Law Institute/Literature* 558.

Ludwikowski, Mark R. 1996. "Proposed Government Regulation of Tobacco Advertising Uses Teens to Disguise First Amendment Violations." *CommLaw Conspectus* 4.

Morris, Frank C., Jr. 1997. *Privacy and Defamation in Employment.* SB42 ALI-ABA 201.

National Smokers Alliance. 1996. "Study Challenges EPA Report on ETS." Congressional Research Service site. World Wide Web.

"Restaurant and Bar Managers Fear Federal Workplace Smoking Ban Would Mean Business Drop." 1996. *West's Legal News* (November 26).

Richards, Jef I. 1996. "Politicizing Cigarette Advertising." *Catholic University Law Review* 45 (summer).

Rimer, Darren S. 1995. "Secondhand Smoke Damages: Extending a Cause of Action for Battery against a Tobacco Manufacturer." *Southwestern University Law Review* 24.

Sablone, Kathleen. 1996. "A Spark in the Battle between Smokers and Nonsmokers: *Johannesen v. New York City Department of Housing Preservation and Development.*" *Boston College Law Review* 36 (April).

Scharf, Irene. 1995. "Breathe Deeply: The Tort of Smokers' Battery." *Houston Law Review* 32 (fall).

Sculco, Thomas W. 1992. "Smokers' Rights Legislation: Should the State 'Butt Out' of the Workplace?" *Boston College Law Review* 22 (July).

"Smokers Need Not Apply as Companies Try to Clear the Air." 1997. *West's Legal News* (January 7).

Vallone, Melissa A. 1996. "Employer Liability for Workplace Environmental Tobacco Smoke: Get Out of the Fog." *Valparaiso University Law Review* 30 (spring).

Venverich, Sally L. 1994. "The Harkin Amendment: The Constitutionality of Limiting Deductions for Tobacco Advertising." *Saint Louis University Public Law Review* 13.

Whatley, Michael. 1996. "The FDA v. Joe Camel: An Analysis of the FDA's Attempt to Regulate Tobacco and Tobacco Products under the Federal Food, Drug and Cosmetic Act." *Journal of Legislation* 22.

"Worksites and Businesses Fact Sheet," published December 1995 by Missouri ASSIST (American Stop Smoking Intervention Study). 1997. Missouri State Health site. World Wide Web.

TOKYO TRIAL

Christenson, Ron. 1991. *Political Trials in History: From Antiquity to Present.* New Brunswick, N.J.: Transaction Press.

Liddell Hart, B. H. 1970. *History of the Second World War.* New York: Putnam.

Manchester, William R. 1973. *The Glory and the Dream: A Narrative History of America, 1932–1972.* New York: Bantam.

———. 1978. *American Caesar: Douglas MacArthur 1880–1964.* Boston: Little, Brown.

Pritchard, R. John. 1995. "The International Military Tribunal for the Far East and Its Contemporary Resonances." *Military Law Review* 149.

TONKIN GULF RESOLUTION

Moss, Joyce, and George Wilson. 1995. *Profiles in American History.* Vol. 8. Detroit: Gale Research.

TOUCEY, ISAAC

Justice Department. 1985. *Attorneys General of the United States, 1789–1985.* Washington, D.C.: U.S. Government Printing Office.

TRADE DRESS

American Law Institute. 1995. *Restatement (Third) of Unfair Competition.* New York: American Law Institute.

Practising Law Institute (PLI). 1995. *Recent Trends in the Law of Trade Dress,* by Stephen F. Mohr. Corporate Law and Practice Course Handbook series.

TRADEMARK LAW

Kane, Siegrun D. 1987. *Trademark Law, A Practitioner's Guide.* New York: Practising Law Institute.

Wincor, Richard, and Irving Mandel. 1980. *Copyrights, Patents, and Trademarks: The Protection of Intellectual and Industrial Property.* London: Oceana.

TRADE NAME

American Law Institute. 1995. *Restatement (Third) of Unfair Competition.* New York: American Law Institute.

TRADE SECRET

American Law Institute. 1995. *Restatement (Third) of Unfair Competition.* New York: American Law Institute.

TRANSPORTATION DEPARTMENT

U.S. Government Manual, 1996–1997. Washington, D.C.: U.S. Government Printing Office.

TRASK, MILILANI

Trask, Mililani. 1991. "Historical and Contemporary Hawaiian Self-Determination: A Native Hawaiian Perspective." *Arizona Journal of International and Comparative Law* 8.

Zehr, Mary Ann. 1993. "Look Deeper into Indian Country." *Foundation News* 34 (September–October).

TRAYNOR, ROGER J.

Kragen, Adrian A., 1983. "A Legacy of Accomplishment." *California Law Review* 71 (July).

McCall, James R., 1984. "In Memoriam: Roger J. Traynor." *Hastings Law Journal* 35 (May).

White, G. Edward. 1983. "Tribute: Roger Traynor." *Virginia Law Review* 69 (November).

TREASON

Stier, Max. 1992. "Corruption of the Blood and Equal Protection: Why the Sins of the Parents Should Not Matter." *Stanford Law Review* 44.

TREASURY DEPARTMENT

U.S. Government Manual, 1996–1997. Washington, D.C.: U.S. Government Printing Office.

TREATY

Stephens, Otis H., Jr., and John M. Scheb II. 1993. *American Constitutional Law.* St. Paul: West.

TRIAL

Mauet, Thomas A. 1992. *Fundamentals of Trial Techniques.* Boston: Little, Brown.

Singleton, John V. "Jury Trial: History and Preservation." *Trial Lawyers Guide.*

TRUMAN, HARRY S.

Stephens, Otis H., Jr., and John M. Scheb II. 1993. *American Constitutional Law.* St. Paul: West.

TRUSTEES OF DARTMOUTH COLLEGE V. WOODWARD

Mark, Gregory A. 1987. "The Personification of the Business Corporation in American Law." 1987. *University of Chicago Law Review* 54 (fall).

Stites, Francis N. 1972. *Private Interest and Public Gain: The Dartmouth College Case, 1819.* Amherst: Univ. of Massachusetts Press.

TUTTLE, ELBERT PARR

"Excerpts from the Elbert Tuttle Portrait Ceremony and Eleventh Circuit Historical Society Ceremony." 1983. *Cornell Law Review* (January 24).

Tuttle, Elbert P. "In Memorium. To My Dear Friend, John R. Brown." 1993. *Texas Law Review* (April).

TWELFTH AMENDMENT

Stephens, Otis H., Jr., and John M. Scheb II. 1993. *American Constitutional Law.* St. Paul: West.

TWENTIETH AMENDMENT

Stephens, Otis H., Jr., and John M. Scheb II. 1993. *American Constitutional Law.* St. Paul: West.

TWENTY-FIFTH AMENDMENT

Stephens, Otis H., Jr., and John M. Scheb II. 1993. *American Constitutional Law.* St. Paul: West.

TWENTY-FIRST AMENDMENT

Stephens, Otis H., Jr., and John M. Scheb II. 1993. *American Constitutional Law.* St. Paul: West.

TWENTY-FOURTH AMENDMENT

Stephens, Otis H., Jr., and John M. Scheb II. 1993. *American Constitutional Law.* St. Paul: West.

TWENTY-SECOND AMENDMENT

Stephens, Otis H., Jr., and John M. Scheb II. 1993. *American Constitutional Law.* St. Paul: West.

TWENTY-SEVENTH AMENDMENT

Bernstein, Richard B. 1992. "The Sleeper Wakes: The History of the Twenty-seventh Amendment." *Fordham Law Review* 61 (December).

Dalzell, Stewart, and Eric J. Beste. 1994. "Is the Twenty-seventh Amendment 200 Years Too Late?" *George Washington Law Review* 62 (April).

Paulsen, Michael Stokes. 1993. "A General Theory of Article V: The Constitutional Lessons of the Twenty-seventh Amendment." *Yale Law Journal* 103 (December).

TWENTY-SIXTH AMENDMENT

Stephens, Otis H., Jr., and John M. Scheb II. 1993. *American Constitutional Law.* St. Paul: West.

TWENTY-THIRD AMENDMENT

Stephens, Otis H., Jr., and John M. Scheb II. 1993. *American Constitutional Law.* St. Paul: West.

TYING ARRANGEMENT

Klarfeld, Peter J. *Tying Arrangements and Exclusive Dealing.* 1994. New York: Practising Law Institute.

TYLER, JOHN

Stephens, Otis H., Jr., and John M. Scheb II. 1993. *American Constitutional Law.* St. Paul: West.

ULTIMATE FACTS

Hall, Kermit L. 1989. *The Magic Mirror: Law in American History.* New York: Oxford Univ. Press.

Wright, Charles Alan, and Arthur J. Miller. 1990. *Federal Practice and Procedure: Federal Rules of Civil Procedure.* St. Paul: West.

ULTRA VIRES

Practising Law Institute (PLI). 1995. *Dealing with Governmental Entities,* by Frank R. Snodgrass. Corporate Law and Practice Course Handbook series, PLI order no. 1114.

UNCONSCIONABLE

Mellinkoff, David. 1992. *Mellinkoff's Dictionary of American Legal Usage.* St. Paul: West.

Stephens, Otis H., Jr., and John M. Scheb II. 1993. *American Constitutional Law.* St. Paul: West.

UNDUE INFLUENCE

Calamari, John D., and Joseph M. Perillo. 1977. *The Law Contracts.* 2d ed. St. Paul: West.

UNENUMERATED RIGHTS

Dworkin, Ronald M. 1992. "Unenumerated Rights: Whether and How *Roe* Should Be Overruled." *University of Chicago Law Review* 59.

Posner, Richard A. 1992. "Legal Reasoning from the Top Down and from the Bottom Up: The Question of Unenumerated Constitutional Rights." *University of Chicago Law Review* 59.

UNFAIR COMPETITION

American Law Institute. 1995. *Restatement (Third) of Unfair Competition.* New York: American Law Institute.

UNIFORM COMMERCIAL CODE

Benfield, Marion W., Jr., and William D. Hawkland. 1992. *Sales: Cases and Materials.* 3d ed. Westbury, N.Y.: Foundation Press.

UNIFORM CONSUMER CREDIT CODE

Letsou, Peter V. 1995. "The Political Economy of Consumer Credit Regulation." *Emory University Law Journal* 44.

Mellinkoff, David. 1992. *Mellinkoff's Dictionary of American Legal Usage.* St. Paul: West.

UNIFORM PROBATE CODE

Averill, Lawrence H., Jr. 1992. "An Eclectic History and Analysis of the 1990 Uniform Probate Code." *Albany Law Review* 55.

UNITED NATIONS

Holtje, James. 1995. *Divided It Stands: Can the United Nations Work?* Atlanta: Turner Publishing.

U.N. Department of Public Information. 1996. Overview/Organs site. World Wide Web (July).

_____. 1997. Overview/Finance site. World Wide Web (March).

_____. 1997. Overview/News site. World Wide Web (March).

United Nations. 1986. *Everyone's United Nations.* 10th ed. New York: United Nations.

_____. 1989. *Basic Facts about the United Nations.* New York: United Nations.

UNITED STATES V. NIXON

Stephens, Otis H., Jr., and John M. Scheb II. 1993. *American Constitutional Law.* St. Paul: West.

UNITED STEELWORKERS V. WEBER

Stephens, Otis H., Jr., and John M. Scheb II. 1993. *American Constitutional Law.* St. Paul: West.

UNITRUST

Smith, Michael. 1997. "Charitable Remainder Trusts."

Reinhart, Boerner, Van Deuren, Norris, and Rieselbach (law firm in Milwaukee, Wisconsin) site. World Wide Web (April 30).

UNJUST ENRICHMENT

Calamari, John D., and Joseph M. Perillo. 1977. *The Law Contracts.* 2d ed. St. Paul: West.

UNLAWFUL ASSEMBLY

Stephens, Otis H., Jr., and John M. Scheb II. 1993. *American Constitutional Law.* St. Paul: West.

UNLAWFUL COMMUNICATIONS

Justice Department. 1996. *Domestic Violence, Stalking, and Antistalking Legislation: Annual Report to Congress, March 1996.* Washington, D.C.: Justice Department, Office of Justice Programs, National Institute of Justice.

UNLAWFUL DETAINER

Office of Minnesota Attorney General. 1997. "Landlords and Tenants: Rights and Responsibilities." St. Paul: Office of Minnesota Attorney General.

U.S. CIVIL WAR

Stephens, Otis H., Jr., and John M. Scheb II. 1993. *American Constitutional Law.* St. Paul: West.

U.S. COURT OF VETERANS APPEALS

Carraway, J. Christopher. 1994. "Color as a Trademark under the Landham Act: Confusion in the Circuits and the Need for Uniformity." *Law and Contemporary Problems* 57 (fall).

Cragin, Charles L. 1994. "The Impact of Judicial Review on the Department of Veterans Affairs' Claims Adjudication Process: The Changing Role of the Board of Veterans' Appeals." *Maine Law Review* 46.

Farley, John J. III. 1991. "The New Kid on the Block of Veteran's Law: The United States Court of Veterans Appeals." *Federal Bar News and Journal* 38 (November–December).

Federal Circuit Bar Association. 1993. "Cases and Recent Developments." *Federal Circuit Bar Journal* 3 (fall).

Federal Court site. 1997. World Wide Web.

Fischer, Mathew J. 1994. "The Equal Access to Justice Act: Are the Bankruptcy Courts Less Equal Than Others?" *Michigan Law Review* 92.

Helfer, Laurence R. 1992. "The Politics of Judicial Structure: Creating the United States Court of Veterans Appeals." *Connecticut Law Review* 25 (fall).

Jennings, Raymond J., Jr. 1994. "*Friedman v. United States*, the First Competent Board Rule and the Demise of the Statute of Limitations in Military Physical Disability Cases." *Army Lawyer* (June).

Nebeker, Frank Q. 1994. "Jurisdiction of the United States Court of Veterans Appeals: Searching Out the Limits." *Maine Law Review* 46.

Parker, Robert M., and Leslie J. Hagin. 1994. "Federal Courts at the Crossroads: Adapt or Lose!" *Mississippi College Law Review* 211 (spring).

Sisk, Gregory C. 1994. "The Essentials of the Equal Access to Justice Act." *Louisiana Law Review* 55.

Tegfeldt, Jennifer A. 1993. "A Few Practical Considerations in Appeals before the Federal Circuit." *Federal Circuit Bar Journal* 3 (fall).

West Publishing Company. 1993. "The Eleventh Annual Judicial Conference of the United States Court of Appeals for the Federal Circuit." *Federal Rules Decisions* 153.

West Publishing Company. 1993. "Report of the National Commission on Judicial Discipline and Removal." *Federal Rules Decisions* 152.

Zillman, Donald N. 1994. "Veterans Law Symposium: Introduction." *Maine Law Review* 46.

U.S. COURTS OF APPEALS

United States Government Manual, 1996–1997. Washington, D.C.: U.S. Government Printing Office.

U.S. INFORMATION AGENCY

Gormly, Charles F. 1995. "The United States Information Agency Domestic Dissemination Ban: Arguments for Repeal." *Administrative Law Journal of American University* 9.

U.S. MARSHALS SERVICE

U.S. Government Manual, 1996–1997. Washington, D.C.: U.S. Government Printing Office.

U.S. POSTAL SERVICE

U.S. Government Manual, 1996–1997. Washington, D.C.: U.S. Government Printing Office.

U.S. Postal Service site. 1997. World Wide Web (April 30).

U.S. TRADE REPRESENTATIVE, OFFICE OF

Office of the U.S. Trade Representative site. 1997. World Wide Web (May 1).

U.S. Government Manual, 1996–1997. Washington, D.C.: U.S. Government Printing Office.

USURY

Association of Progressive Rental Organizations (APRO) site. 1997. World Wide Web (July 26).

Letsou, Peter V. 1995. "The Political Economy of Consumer Credit Regulation." *Emory University Law Journal* 44.

Pimentel, Eligio. 1995. "Renting-to-own: Exploitation or Market Efficiency?" *Law and Inequality Journal* 13.

UTILITARIANISM

Bentham, Jeremy. 1990. *A Fragment on Government.* Edited by H. L. A. Hart and J. H. Burns. Cambridge: Univ. of Cambridge Press.

Honderich, Ted, ed. 1995. *Oxford Companion to Philosophy.* Oxford: Univ. of Oxford Press.

Posner, Richard A. 1992. *Economic Analysis of Law.* 4th ed. Boston: Little, Brown.

VAGRANCY

Stephens, Otis H., Jr., and John M. Scheb II. 1993. *American Constitutional Law.* St. Paul: West.

VANDALISM

Ferdico, John N. 1992. *Ferdico's Criminal Law and Justice Dictionary.* St. Paul: West.

Mellinkoff, David. 1992. *Mellinkoff's Dictionary of American Legal Usage.* St. Paul: West.

VAN DEVANTER, WILLIS

Friedman, Leon, and Fred L. Israel, eds. 1995. *The Justices of the United States Supreme Court, 1789–1969: Their Lives and Major Opinions.* New York: Chelsea House.

VARIANCE

Ferdico, John N. 1992. *Ferdico's Criminal Law and Justice Dictionary.* St. Paul: West.

Mellinkoff, David. 1992. *Mellinkoff's Dictionary of American Legal Usage.* St. Paul: West.

VAUGHN, GEORGE L.

Kluger, Richard. 1974. *Simple Justice.* New York: Knopf.

Low, W. Augustus, and Virgil A. Clift, eds. 1984. *Encyclopedia of Black America.* New York: Da Capo Press.

Stephens, Otis H., Jr., and John M. Scheb II. 1993. *American Constitutional Law.* St. Paul: West.

VENUE

Court TV site. 1997. Order of Judge Richard P. Matsch. World Wide Web (July 19).

Stephens, Otis H., Jr., and John M. Scheb II. 1993. *American Constitutional Law.* St. Paul: West.

VERDICT

Mellinkoff, David. 1992. *Mellinkoff's Dictionary of American Legal Usage.* St. Paul: West.

VERIFY

Ferdico, John N. 1992. *Ferdico's Criminal Law and Justice Dictionary.* St. Paul: West.

Mellinkoff, David. 1992. *Mellinkoff's Dictionary of American Legal Usage*. St. Paul: West.

VETERANS AFFAIRS DEPARTMENT

U.S. Government Manual, 1996–1997. Washington, D.C.: U.S. Government Printing Office.

VETO

"Line Item Veto." 1997. Congressional Institute site. World Wide Web (July 18).

Stephens, Otis H., Jr., and John M. Scheb II. 1993. *American Constitutional Law*. St. Paul: West.

VEXATIOUS LITIGATION

Ferdico, John N. 1992. *Ferdico's Criminal Law and Justice Dictionary*. St. Paul: West.

Mellinkoff, David. 1992. *Mellinkoff's Dictionary of American Legal Usage*. St. Paul: West.

VICE PRESIDENT

Stephens, Otis H., Jr., and John M. Scheb II. 1993. *American Constitutional Law*. St. Paul: West.

VICTIMS OF CRIME

Stephens, Otis H., Jr., and John M. Scheb II. 1993. *American Constitutional Law*. St. Paul: West.

VIETNAM WAR

Stephens, Otis H., Jr., and John M. Scheb II. 1993. *American Constitutional Law*. St. Paul: West.

VIRGINIA AND KENTUCKY RESOLVES

Stephens, Otis H., Jr., and John M. Scheb II. 1993. *American Constitutional Law*. St. Paul: West.

VIRGINIA DECLARATION OF RIGHTS

Stephens, Otis H., Jr., and John M. Scheb II. 1993. *American Constitutional Law*. St. Paul: West.

VOID FOR VAGUENESS

Lafave, Wayne R., and Austin W. Scott. 1986. *Criminal Law*. 2d ed. St. Paul: West.

VOLSTEAD, ANDREW

A History of Yellow Medicine County, Minnesota, 1872–1972. Granite Falls, MN: Yellow Medicine County Historical Society, and Carl and Amy Narvestad.

Rose, Arthur P., ed. *An Illustrated History of Yellow Medicine County*.

Volstead Papers. St. Paul: Minnesota Historical Society. *Men of Minnesota*. 1915.

VOLUNTARY ACT

LaFave, Wayne R., and Austin W. Scott, Jr. 1995. *Criminal Law*. St. Paul: West.

VOTING

National Association of the Deaf site. 1997. "What Is Motor Voter?" World Wide Web (July 23).

Stephens, Otis H., Jr., and John M. Scheb II. 1993. *American Constitutional Law*. St. Paul: West.

VOTING RIGHTS ACT OF 1965

Stephens, Otis H., Jr., and John M. Scheb II. 1993. *American Constitutional Law*. St. Paul: West.

WAGE ASSIGNMENT

Ferdico, John N. 1992. *Ferdico's Criminal Law and Justice Dictionary*. St. Paul: West.

Mellinkoff, David. 1992. *Mellinkoff's Dictionary of American Legal Usage*. St. Paul: West.

WAGE EARNER'S PLAN

Mellinkoff, David. 1992. *Mellinkoff's Dictionary of American Legal Usage*. St. Paul: West.

Oran, David. 1991. *Oran's Dictionary of the Law*. 2d ed. St. Paul: West.

WAGNER, ROBERT FERDINAND

Stephens, Otis H., Jr., and John M. Scheb II. 1993. *American Constitutional Law*. St. Paul: West.

WAGNER ACT

Stephens, Otis H., Jr., and John M. Scheb II. 1993. *American Constitutional Law*. St. Paul: West.

WAITE, MORRISON REMICK

Aynes, Richard L. 1993. "On Misreading John Bingham and the Fourteenth Amendment." *Yale Law Journal* 103 (October).

WAIVER

Ferdico, John N. 1992. *Ferdico's Criminal Law and Justice Dictionary*. St. Paul: West.

Mellinkoff, David. 1992. *Mellinkoff's Dictionary of American Legal Usage*. St. Paul: West.

Oran, Daniel. 1991. *Oran's Dictionary of the Law*. 2d ed. St. Paul: West.

WALLACE, GEORGE

Charlotte Observer. 1987 (January 18).

Charlotte Observer. 1994 (February 13).

Charlotte Observer. 1986 (August 11).

Frady, Marshall. 1968. *Wallace*. New York: New American Library.

Lesher, Stephan. 1994. *George Wallace*. Reading, Mass.: Addison-Wesley.

Mailer, Norman. 1972. *St. George and the Godfather*. New York: New American Library.

Wallace, George, Jr., and James Gregory. 1975. *The Wallaces of Alabama*. Chicago: Follet Publishing.

WALLACE, JOHN WILLIAM

Stephens, Otis H., Jr., and John M. Scheb II. 1993. *American Constitutional Law*. St. Paul: West.

WAR

Stephens, Otis H., Jr., and John M. Scheb II. 1993. *American Constitutional Law*. St. Paul: West.

WAR CRIMES

Christenson, Ron. 1991. *Political Trials in History: From Antiquity to Present*. New Brunswick, N.J.: Transaction Press.

Podgers, James. 1996. *The World Cries for Justice: The International Criminal Tribunals for the Former Yugoslavia and Rwanda Hold the Key to the Next Advance in International Law*. American Bar Association Journal (April).

WARD, NATHANIEL

Cahn, Mark D. 1989. "Punishment, Discretion, and the Codification of Prescribed Penalties in Colonial Massachusetts." *American Journal of Legal History* 33.

Hall, Kermit L. 1989. *The Magic Mirror: Law in American History*. New York: Oxford Univ. Press.

WARRANT

Ferdico, John N. 1992. *Ferdico's Criminal Law and Justice Dictionary*. St. Paul: West.
Stephens, Otis H., Jr., and John M. Scheb II. 1993. *American Constitutional Law*. St. Paul: West.

WARRANTY

Benfield, Marion W., Jr., and William D. Hawkland. 1992. *Sales: Cases and Materials*. Westbury, N.Y.: Foundation Press.

WARRANTY DEED

Mellinkoff, David. 1992. *Mellinkoff's Dictionary of American Legal Usage*. St. Paul: West.

WARREN, EARL

Hall, Kermit L. 1989. *The Magic Mirror: Law in American History*. New York: Oxford Univ. Press.
Stephens, Otis H., Jr., and John M. Scheb II. 1993. *American Constitutional Law*. St. Paul: West.

WARREN COMMISSION

O'Neill, William L. 1971. *Coming Apart: An Informal History of America in the 1960s*. New York: Quadrangle Books.

WARREN COURT

Hall, Kermit L. 1989. *The Magic Mirror: Law in American History*. New York: Oxford Univ. Press.
Stephens, Otis H., Jr., and John M. Scheb II. 1993. *American Constitutional Law*. St. Paul: West.

WASHINGTON, BUSHROD

Friedman, Leon, and Fred L. Israel, eds. 1969. *The Justices of the United States Supreme Court, 1789– 1969: Their Lives and Major Opinions*. New York: Chelsea House.

WASHINGTON, GEORGE

Hall, Kermit L. 1989. *The Magic Mirror: Law in American History*. New York: Oxford Univ. Press.
Stephens, Otis H., Jr., and John M. Scheb II. 1993. *American Constitutional Law*. St. Paul: West.

WASHINGTON V. GLUCKSBERG

"Health Care—Right to Die: Supreme Court Unanimously Upholds State Laws against Criminally Assisted Suicide." 1997. *United States Law Week* (July 1).

WATERGATE

Stephens, Otis H., Jr., and John M. Scheb II. 1993. *American Constitutional Law*. St. Paul: West.

WATER POLLUTION

Rogers, William H., Jr. 1977. *Environmental Law Hornbook* St. Paul: West.
_____. 1986. *Environmental Law: Air and Water Pollution*. St. Paul: West.

WATER RIGHTS

Cunningham, Roger, William Stoebuck, and Dale Whitman. 1993. *The Law of Property*. St. Paul: West.
Freyfogle, Eric. 1996. *Water Rights and the Common Wealth. Environmental Law* 26.

Scott, Anthony and Georgina Coustalin. 1995. *The Evolution of Water Rights. Natural Resources Journal* 35.

WATTLETON, FAYE

Igus, Toyomi, ed. 1991. *Book of Black Heroes: Great Women in the Struggle*. New York: Scholastic.

WEBSTER, DANIEL

Stephens, Otis H., Jr., and John M. Scheb II. 1993. *American Constitutional Law*. St. Paul: West.

WEIGHT OF EVIDENCE

Ferdico, John N. 1992. *Ferdico's Criminal Law and Justice Dictionary*. St. Paul: West.
Mellinkoff, David. 1992. *Mellinkoff's Dictionary of American Legal Usage*. St. Paul: West.
Oran, Daniel. 1991. *Oran's Dictionary of the Law*. 2d ed. St. Paul: West.

WEINSTEIN, JACK B.

"Jack Weinstein: A Jurist Who's Willing to Lead." 1993. *National Law Journal* (December 27).
"The Man Who's Cutting Through the Asbestos Mess." 1991. *Business Week* (January 28).
"Newsmaker: Jack B. Weinstein." 1992. *National Law Journal* (January 6).
Weinstein, Jack B. 1994. "Learning, Speaking, and Acting: What Are the Limits for Judges?" *Judicature*. (May–June).

WEIS, JOSEPH F., JR.

American Judicature Society. 1990. "Future of Our Federal Courts." *Judicature* 74 (June–July).
American Judicature Society. 1990. "The Judicial Improvements Act of 1990: Editor's Introduction." *Judicature* (August–September).
Carmody, Cris. 1990. "Federal Courts Study Committee Issues Final Report." *Judicature* 74 (June–July).
Lavelle, Marianne, Fred Strasser, and Marcia Coyle. "Court Changes." 1990. *National Law Journal* (April 16).
Robinson, T. Sumner. 1989. "Time to Study the Courts." *National Law Journal* (March 22).
Strasser, Fred, and Marcia Coyle. "Court Study." 1989. *National Law Journal* (December 18).
Weis, Joseph F., Jr. 1989. "The Federal Courts Study Committee Begins Its Work." *St. Mary's Law Journal* 21.
_____. 1989. "The Federal Rules and the Hague Conventions: Concerns of Conformity." *University of Pittsburgh Law Review* 50 (spring).
_____. 1992. "The Federal Sentencing Guidelines—It's Time for a Reappraisal." *American Criminal Law Review* (spring).

WELCH, JOSEPH NYE

Griffith, Robert. 1987. *The Politics of Fear: Joseph R. McCarthy and the Senate*. 2d ed. Amherst, Mass.: Univ. of Massachusetts Press.
The New York Times Film Reviews, 1959–1968. 1990. New York: Times Books and Garland.
Variety Film Reviews, 1959–1963. 1983. New York and London: Garland.

WELFARE

Stephens, Otis H., Jr., and John M. Scheb II. 1993. *American Constitutional Law*. St. Paul: West.

Super, David A., Susan Steinmetz, and Cindy Mann. 1996. "The New Welfare Law." Washington: Center on Budget and Policy Priorities site. World Wide Web (August 13).

WELLS-BARNETT, IDA B.

Franklin, John Hope, and August Meier, ed. 1982. *Black Leaders of the Twentieth Century*. Urbana, Ill.: Univ. of Illinois Press.

Igus, Toyomi, ed. 1991. *Book of Black Heroes. Vol. 2: Great Women in the Struggle*. New York: Scholastic, 1991.

Wells, Ida B. 1970. *Crusade for Justice: The Autobiography of Ida B. Wells*. Chicago: Univ. of Chicago Press.

WESLEY, CARTER WALKER

Kluger, Richard. 1974. *Simple Justice*. New York: Knopf.

Low, W. Augustus, and Virgil A. Clift, eds. 1984. *Encyclopedia of Black America*. New York: Da Capo Press.

Stephens, Otis H. Jr., and John M. Scheb II. 1993. *American Constitutional Law*. St. Paul: West.

WEST COAST HOTEL CO. V. PARRISH

Stephens, Otis H., Jr., and John M. Scheb II. 1993. *American Constitutional Law*. St. Paul: West.

WESTLAW

Olstad, Anne L., and Gary E. Peter. 1994. *Discovering WESTLAW: The Essential Guide*. St. Paul: West.

WHISKEY REBELLION

Christenson, Ron. 1991. *Political Trials in History: From Antiquity to Present*. New Brunswick, N.J.: Transaction Press.

Hall, Kermit L. 1989. *The Magic Mirror: Law in American History*. New York: Oxford Univ. Press.

WHITEMAN, MARJORIE MILLACE

Leich, Marian Nash. 1986. "Marjorie M. Whiteman (1898–1986)." *American Journal of International Law* 80.

WHITE PRIMARY

Stephens, Otis H., Jr., and John M. Scheb II. 1993. *American Constitutional Law*. St. Paul: West.

WHITE SUPREMACY GROUPS

Hall, Kermit L. 1989. *The Magic Mirror: Law in American History*. New York: Oxford Univ. Press.

Southern Poverty Law Center (Montgomery, Ala.) site. 1997. World Wide Web (June 24).

WHITEWATER

Washington Post site: Whitewater archive. 1997. World Wide Web.

WHITTAKER, CHARLES

Atkinson, David N., and Lawrence H. Larsen. 1995. "A Case Study in Federal Justice: Leading Bill of Rights Proceedings in the Western District of Missouri." *Creighton Law Review* 28 (April).

Downs, Robert C. 1996. "The First 100 Years UMKC School of Law: An Abridged History." *UMKC Law Review* 64 (summer).

Wasby, Stephen L. 1988. "Justice Harry A. Blackmun in the Burger Court." *Hamline Law Review* 11 (summer).

WICKERSHAM COMMISSION

Hall, Kermit L. 1989. *The Magic Mirror: Law in American History*. New York: Oxford Univ. Press.

Walker, Samuel. 1980. *Popular Justice: A History of American Criminal Justice*. New York: Oxford Univ. Press.

WICKERSHAM, GEORGE WOODWARD

Hall, Kermit L. 1989. *The Magic Mirror: Law in American History*. New York: Oxford Univ. Press.

Justice Department. 1985. *Attorneys General of the United States, 1789–1985*. Washington, D.C.: U.S. Government Printing Office.

WILDCAT STRIKE

Hall, Kermit L. 1989. *The Magic Mirror: Law in American History*. New York: Oxford Univ. Press, 1989.

WILKINS, ROY

Branch, Taylor. 1988. *Parting the Waters: America in the King Years, 1954–63*. New York: Simon & Schuster.

Kluger, Richard. 1976. *Simple Justice*. New York: Knopf.

O'Neill, William L. 1971. *Coming Apart: An Informal History of America in the 1960s*. New York: Quadrangle Books.

WILL, HUBERT L.

Cole, Jeffrey N., and Robert E. Shapiro. 1993. "Interview with Judge Herbert L. Will." *Litigation* 20, no. 1.

WILLIAMS ACT

Tyson, William C., and Andrew A. August. 1983. "The Williams Act after Rico: Has the Balance Tipped in Favor of Incumbent Management?" *Hastings Law Journal* 35.

WILLIAMS, GEORGE HENRY

Justice Department. 1985. *Attorneys General of the United States, 1789–1985*. Washington, D.C.: U.S. Government Printing Office.

WILLISTON, SAMUEL

Boyer, Allen D. 1994. "Samuel Williston's Struggle with Depression." *Buffalo Law Review* 42.

WILMOT, DAVID

Hall, Kermit L. 1989. *The Magic Mirror:* Law in American History. New York: Oxford Univ. Press.

WILMOT PROVISO

Hall, Kermit L. 1989. *The Magic Mirror: Law in American History*. New York: Oxford Univ. Press.

WIND UP

Mellinkoff, David. 1992. *Mellinkoff's Dictionary of American Legal Usage*. St. Paul: West.

Oran, Daniel. 1991. *Oran's Dictionary of the Law*. 2d ed. St. Paul: West.

WIRETAPPING

Stephens, Otis H., Jr., and John M. Scheb II. 1993. *American Constitutional Law*. St. Paul: West.

WIRT, WILLIAM

Justice Department. *Attorneys General of the United States, 1789–1985*. Washington, D.C.: U.S. Government Printing Office.

WITHERSPOON V. ILLINOIS

Stephens, Otis H., Jr., and John M. Scheb II. 1993. *American Constitutional Law.* St. Paul: West.

WITHIN THE STATUTE

Ferdico, John N. 1992. *Ferdico's Criminal Law and Justice Dictionary.* St. Paul: West.

Mellinkoff, David. 1992. *Mellinkoff's Dictionary of American Legal Usage.* St. Paul: West.

Oran, Daniel. 1991. *Oran's Dictionary of the Law.* 2d ed. St. Paul: West.

WITHOUT DAY

Oran, Daniel. 1991. *Oran's Dictionary of the Law.* 2d ed. St. Paul: West.

WITHOUT PREJUDICE

Ferdico, John N. 1992. *Ferdico's Criminal Law and Justice Dictionary.* St. Paul: West.

Mellinkoff, David. 1992. *Mellinkoff's Dictionary of American Legal Usage.* St. Paul: West.

Oran, Daniel. 1991. *Oran's Dictionary of the Law.* 2d ed. St. Paul: West.

WITHOUT RECOURSE

Mellinkoff, David. 1992. *Mellinkoff's Dictionary of American Legal Usage.* St. Paul: West.

Oran, Daniel. 1991. *Oran's Dictionary of the Law.* 2d ed. St. Paul: West.

WITNESSES

Oran, Daniel. 1991. *Oran's Dictionary of the Law.* 2d ed. St. Paul: West.

Stephens, Otis H., Jr., and John Scheb II. 1993. *American Constitutional Law.* St. Paul: West.

WOLCOTT, ALEXANDER

Brant, Irving. 1970. *The Fourth President: A Life of James Madison.* Indianapolis: Bobbs-Merrill Co.

Witt, Elder, ed. 1990. *Guide to the U.S. Supreme Court.* 2d ed. Washington, D.C.: Congressional Quarterly.

WOMEN'S RIGHTS

Hall, Kermit L. 1989. *The Magic Mirror: Law in American History.* New York: Oxford Univ. Press, 1989.

National Organization of Women site. 1997. World Wide Web (July 11).

Stephens, Otis H., Jr., and John M. Scheb II. 1993. *American Constitutional Law.* St. Paul: West.

WORDS OF ART

Ferdico, John N. 1992. *Ferdico's Criminal Law and Justice Dictionary.* St. Paul: West.

Oran, Daniel. 1991. *Oran's Dictionary of the Law.* 2d ed. St. Paul: West.

WORDS OF LIMITATION

Mellinkoff, David. 1992. *Mellinkoff's Dictionary of American Legal Usage.* St. Paul: West.

Oran, Daniel. 1991. *Oran's Dictionary of the Law.* 2d ed. St. Paul: West.

WORKERS' COMPENSATION

Larson, Lex K., and Arthur Larson. 1996. *The Law of Workmen's Compensation.* New York: Bender.

WORLD BANK

"The 1996 World Bank Annual Report." 1997. World Bank site. World Wide Web (June 1).

WORLD COURT

Pioneer Planet site. 1997. World Wide Web (June 2).

WORLD WAR I

Stephens, Otis H., Jr., and John M. Scheb II. 1993. *American Constitutional Law.* St. Paul: West.

WORLD WAR II

Stephens, Otis H., Jr., and John M. Scheb II. 1993. *American Constitutional Law.* St. Paul: West.

WORTHIER TITLE DOCTRINE

Mellinkoff, David. 1992. *Mellinkoff's Dictionary of American Legal Usage.* St. Paul: West.

Oran, Daniel. 1991. *Oran's Dictionary of the Law.* 2d ed. St. Paul: West.

WRIGHT, JAMES SKELLY

Monroe, Bill. 1988. "In Memoriam: J. Skelly Wright." 1988. *Harvard Law Review* 102.

WRIT

Mellinkoff, David. 1992. *Mellinkoff's Dictionary of American Legal Usage.* St. Paul: West.

Oran, Daniel. 1991. *Oran's Dictionary of the Law.* 2d ed. St. Paul: West.

WRITS OF ASSISTANCE CASE

Bailyn, Bernard. 1992. *The Ideological Origins of the American Revolution.* Cambridge: Harvard Univ. Press.

Hall, Kermit, Paul Finkelman, and William Wiecek. 1991. *American Legal History: Cases and Materials.* New York: Oxford Univ. Press.

Levy, Leonard. 1988. *Original Intent and the Framers' Constitution.* New York: Macmillan.

Stoner, James. 1992. *Common Law and Liberal Theory: Coke, Hobbes, and the Origins of American Constitutionalism.* Lawrence, Kan.: Univ. Press of Kansas.

Wood, Gordon. 1969. *The Creation of the American Republic 1776–1787.* New York: Norton.

WRONG

Ferdico, John N. 1992. *Ferdico's Criminal Law and Justice Dictionary.* St. Paul: West.

Mellinkoff, David. 1992. *Mellinkoff's Dictionary of American Legal Usage.* St. Paul: West.

Oran, Daniel. 1991. *Oran's Dictionary of the Law.* 2d ed. St. Paul: West.

WYATT, WALTER

Stephens, Otis H., Jr., and John M. Scheb II. 1993. *American Constitutional Law.* St. Paul: West.

WYGANT V. JACKSON BOARD OF EDUCATION

Stephens, Otis H., Jr., and John M. Scheb II. 1993. *American Constitutional Law.* St. Paul: West.

"X" AS A SIGNATURE

Clarkson, Kenneth W., Roger L. Miller, and Gaylord A. Jentz. 1986: *West's Business Law: Text and Cases.* St. Paul: West.

McGovern, William M., Sheldon F. Kurtz, and Jan E. Rein. 1988. *Wills, Trusts, and Estates: The Hornbook Series.* St. Paul: West.

X RATING
Valenti, Jack. 1997. "The Voluntary Movie Rating System." Motion Picture Association of America site. World Wide Web (May 31).

YELLOW DOG CONTRACT
Hall, Kermit L. 1989. *The Magic Mirror: Law in American History.* New York: Oxford Univ. Press.
Stephens, Otis H., Jr., and John M. Scheb II. 1993. *American Constitutional Law.* St. Paul: West.

YICK WO V. HOPKINS
Stephens, Otis H., Jr., and John M. Scheb II. 1993. *American Constitutional Law.* St. Paul: West.

YIELD
Oran, Daniel. 1991. *Oran's Dictionary of the Law.* 2d ed. St. Paul: West.

YORK-ANTWERP RULES
Oran, Daniel. 1991. *Oran's Dictionary of the Law.* 2d ed. St. Paul: West.

ZENGER, JOHN PETER
Christenson, Ron. 1991. *Political Trials in History: From Antiquity to Present.* New Brunswick, N.J.: Transaction Press.

ZERO BRACKET AMOUNT
Oran, Daniel. 1991. *Oran's Dictionary of the Law.* 2d ed. St. Paul: West.